Writing Today

RICHARD JOHNSON-SHEEHAN
Purdue University

CHARLES PAINE
University of New Mexico

Longman

Boston Columbus Indianapolis New York San Francisco Upper Saddle River
Amsterdam Cape Town Dubai London Madrid Milan Munich Paris Montreal Toronto
Delhi Mexico City São Paulo Sydney Hong Kong Seoul Singapore Taipei Tokyo

Publisher: Joseph Opiela
Acquisitions Editor: Lauren A. Finn
Senior Development Editor: Meg Botteon
Senior Supplements Editor: Donna Campion
Senior Media Producer: Stefanie Liebman
Senior Marketing Manager: Sandra McGuire
Production Manager: Jacqueline A. Martin
Project Coordination, Text Design, and Electronic Page Makeup: Nesbitt Graphics, Inc.
Cover Designer/Manager: Wendy Ann Fredericks
Cover Art: Wendy Ann Fredericks; icons, istockphoto.com
Photo Researcher: Julie Tesser
Senior Manufacturing Buyer: Alfred C. Dorsey
Printer and Binder: Courier Corporation/Kendallville
Cover Printer: Phoenix Color Corporation

For permission to use copyrighted material, grateful acknowledgment is made to the copyright holders on pp. 846–847, which are hereby made part of this copyright page.

4 5 6 7 8 9 10—CRK—12 11 10

Longman
is an imprint of

www.pearsonhighered.com

ISBN-13: 978-0-205-61744-9
ISBN-10: 0-205-61744-1

Contents

PART 1
Getting Started   xxiv

PART 2
Using Genres to Express Ideas   34

PART 3
Developing a Writing Process   326

PART 4
Strategies for Shaping Ideas   390

PART 5
Doing Research   448

PART 6

Getting Your Ideas Out There   540

PART 7
Anthology of Readings 586

PART 8
Handbook 798

Thematic Contents

Preface

Writing Today began with a few basic assumptions. First, we believe that students want to learn writing skills that will help them succeed in college and in their careers. Second, students need a writing guide that presents information clearly, simply, and in a way that is easy to reference. Third, writing instructors prefer a teaching tool that is both practical and flexible, allowing them to adapt its content to their own pedagogical approaches and teaching styles.

To help students with the kinds of writing they do in their college courses and in their lives outside of the classroom, *Writing Today* provides tools they can use to respond effectively to many different writing situations. This book teaches *genres* of writing (memoirs, analyses, reports, proposals, etc.) and *strategies* for writing (narration, comparison, argumentation, etc.) as well as *processes* for writing (planning, drafting, revising, etc.).

Writing Today is an easy-to-use book that fits the way today's students read, learn, and process information. We believe they respond best to the interactive writing style we use in *Writing Today:* the instruction is brief and to the point; key concepts are immediately defined and reinforced; sections and paragraphs are short; important points are clearly labeled and supported by instructional visuals. This straightforward presentation of complex information creates a genuinely interactive reading experience in which students access information *when they are ready for it*.

We know from our own experiences as teachers and writing program administrators that pedagogical approaches and teaching styles vary—and that the best writing guides support a range of instructors. The variety of writing purposes (expressive, informative, persuasive, etc.) and writing projects in *Writing Today* support a broad range of curricular goals. Writing instructors can choose the order in which they teach these chapters and combine them into units that fit their course designs.

We have found that writing instructors want to help students understand that genres are not rigid templates but are rather a set of versatile tools that guide every aspect of the writing process. In other words, instructors want students to develop *genre awareness* and *genre know-how*. We emphasize paying attention to how communities get things done with words and images. We also believe that people learn best by doing; therefore, we emphasize inquiry, practice, production, and active research. Students need to become versatile writers who can respond effectively to a changing world.

The approach we take in the book is informed by our personal observations and by much of the best research done in the field of writing studies over the last twenty years. The approach is also supported by findings that are emerging from our research with the Consortium for the Study of Writing in College (a collaboration between the National Survey of Student Engagement and the Council of Writing Program Administrators). Surveys conducted in 2008 and 2009 by the CSWC of more than 65,000 students at 157 schools found that when faculty assigned challenging and diverse writing assignments, students reported deeper learning, increased practical competence, and greater personal and social gains.

How This Book Is Organized

Writing Today features brief chapters and plainly labeled sections, creating obvious access points that help students find what they need when they need it.

PART 1

Getting Started

Purposefully brief, the first three chapters are designed to get students up and running right away. They introduce the five elements of rhetorical situations (topic, angle, purpose, readers, and context) and explain why and how using genres will help students to write successfully.

PART 2

Using Genres to Express Ideas

These chapters help students master ten commonly assigned kinds of writing that form the foundation of an adaptable portfolio of skills. Students explore expressive, informative, analytical, and persuasive genres that help them respond effectively to a majority of academic and workplace writing situations.

PART 3

Developing a Writing Process

Stand-alone chapters on planning, organization, style, design, and revision offer strategies students can apply to any writing situation. Instructors can assign them alongside the genre chapters.

PART 4

Strategies for Shaping Ideas

Straightforward chapters on drafting introductions and conclusions, developing paragraphs and sections, and incorporating rhetorical strategies (such as narration, classification, and comparison and contrast) provide resources for writing those sections of papers where students often find themselves stuck. A chapter on argument explores appeals and fallacies, and a chapter on collaboration helps students work effectively in groups.

PART 5

Doing Research

The ability to research effectively is critical to students' success in college and in their careers. Students learn to engage in inquiry-driven research, evaluate sources, and work with sources by paraphrasing, quoting, and synthesizing. Up-to-date coverage of MLA and APA styles includes citation examples and model papers.

PART 6

Getting Your Ideas Out There

Today's students have more opportunities to present their work publicly than ever before. Students learn how to use social networking and other Web applications for rhetorical purposes. Students learn best practices for creating a professional portfolio of their work. Basics such as succeeding on essay exams and giving presentations are covered indepth as well.

PART 7

Anthology of Readings

The anthology showcases the ten genres of writing explored in Part 2. These additional readings serve as models, suggest situations in which specific genres are particularly effective, offer material for response, and help students discover their own research topics.

PART 8

Handbook

Designed to be as accessible and usable as possible, the handbook gives students a quick resource for issues of grammar, usage, and punctuation.

Ways to Fit This Book to Your Teaching Approach

Flexibility is a chief strength of *Writing Today*. The first three chapters form a foundation, but remaining chapters can be taught in any order or combination to suit individual teaching approaches and objectives.

A Process Approach. Students want to learn a writing process that suits their own working habits and writing styles. The chapters in Part 2 tailor the writing process with strategies specific to different genres. Part 3, "Developing a Writing Process," provides additional chapters on prewriting, drafting, designing, revising, and editing that can be assigned with any project.

A Genre-Based Approach. Genres aren't templates into which writers simply pour words: they are tools writers can use to help them invent ideas and plan, research and draft, design and edit. *Writing Today* covers real-world writing—such as analyses, evaluations, reports, and proposals—that help students solve real problems and achieve specific goals.

A Purposes or Aims-Based Approach. Instructors who teach an aims approach to writing encourage students to be aware of their audience and purpose as they write to express, inform, analyze, or persuade. This approach works hand-in-hand with a genre-based approach: knowing the genre helps writers better understand a text's purpose, readers, and context.

A Strategies or Patterns-Based Approach. Instructors who teach rhetorical patterns (narrative, description, comparison and contrast, cause and effect, etc.), will find them embedded in this book. Part 4, "Strategies for Shaping Ideas," shows how strategies work with and within genres to help students organize and shape their ideas. *Writing Today* applies the strengths of a patterns-based approach to more complex kinds of documents.

An Academic Approach. Students learn the kinds of writing common in the General Education curriculum, such as narratives, rhetorical analyses, literary analyses, reviews, and argument essays. They also learn the foundations of the kinds of writing common in advanced academic classes, such as profiles, commentaries, reports, and proposals. Strategies for writing from sources—including paraphrasing, quoting, citing, and documenting sources—are covered in Part 5.

An Argument-Based Approach. *Writing Today* presents a rhetorical approach to writing. Several genres in Part 2, such as rhetorical analyses, commentaries, position papers, and proposals are purposefully designed to be argument-based; this content is labeled with ARGUMENT in the table of contents. Chapter 22 helps students determine what is arguable and anticipate opposing points of view while also explaining the four stases, the classical appeals, and logical fallacies.

An Integrated, Multimodal Approach. Instructors teaching multimodal composition courses know there are few writing guides that teach critical twenty-first century composing skills and even fewer that offer multimodal assignments. *Writing Today* assumes that students compose electronically and research online, and it offers strategies for writers to plan and collaborate online, include visuals in print texts, create visual texts, create media projects, and post compositions to the Web.

Distance Learning and Online Teaching. *Writing Today* was designed to be easily adaptable to online and hybrid learning environments. The book's comprehensiveness and flexibility provide strong scaffolding on which distance learning, online, and hybrid courses can be developed. Its highly accessible design allows students to quickly find the information they need while learning on their own and composing at their computers. The Pearson eText can be used alone or embedded in a suite of online writing, research, and grammar resources delivered in MyCompLab.

Features of This Book

Interactive writing style. Instruction is brief and to the point. Key concepts are immediately defined and reinforced. Paragraphs are short and introduced by heads that preview content. This interactive style helps students skim, ask questions, and access information when they are ready for it—putting them in control of their learning.

At-A-Glance. Each Part 2 chapter opens with a diagram that shows one or two common ways to organize a genre's key elements, giving an immediate and visual orientation to the genre. Students learn to adapt this organization to suit their rhetorical situation as they read the chapter.

End-of-chapter activities. Exercises conclude every chapter in the book to help students understand and practice concepts and strategies.

- **Talk About This** questions prompt classroom discussion.
- **Try This Out** exercises suggest informal writing activities students can complete in class or as homework.
- **Write This** prompts facilitate longer, formal writing assignments.

One Student's Work. A student-written example in each writing project chapter shows the kinds of issues students might explore in a specific genre of writing as well as the angles they might take. Annotations highlight the writer's key rhetorical decisions so the reading can be used either for discussion or as a model.

Quick Start Guide. This practical review includes action steps and appears in each chapter to get students writing quickly. Students spend less time reading about writing and more time working on their own compositions. They can also use the Quick Start Guide as a quick way to gain familiarity with a genre before reading the chapter.

Microgenre. A microgenre applies features of major genres to narrow rhetorical situations. For example, in Chapter 5, students apply features of a profile to a résumé; in Chapter 12, those of a proposal to a pitch. Each Microgenre in Part 2 includes a description, an example, and a writing activity, encouraging students to experiment and play by stretching genre conventions.

Readings and Prompts. Six readings—two in each project chapter and four in the anthology—offer models of each genre. Question sets after each reading encourage critical engagement.

- **A Closer Look** questions facilitate analytical reading.
- **Ideas for Writing** questions prompt responses, analyses, and different genres of writing.
- **A Few Ideas for Composing** activities (in the anthology) encourage writing that further explores each genre's possibilities.

A Multimodal Approach. Today's writers compose electronic texts, work with visual and audio tools, insert graphics, and collaborate with others online. Each chapter includes strategies for working in a multimodal environment. Multimodal assignments appear in "Write This" and in "A Few Ideas for Composing." Chapters in Part 6 offer guidance on creating and posting compositions in online environments.

Correlation to the WPA Outcomes Statement

Writing Today helps teachers and students address learning outcomes for first-year composition courses identified by the Council of Writing Program Administrators: rhetorical knowledge; critical thinking, reading, and writing; processes; knowledge of conventions; and composing in electronic environments. Both of us have been leaders in this organization, and we believe strongly that these outcomes reflect the kinds of abilities that students should master in these courses. Specific connections between the text's chapters and the WPA Outcomes appear in the Instructor's Manual; a brief overview appears on the inside back cover of this book.

Supplements

The Instructor's Manual. The Instructor's Manual opens with an introduction to genre theory and a discussion of how genre theory can be applied to the first-year writing curriculum. Subsequent chapters discuss classroom management, syllabus-building, and teacher-student communication in both traditional and hybrid or online learning spaces. The second section is a collection of syllabi for teachers using rhetorical strategies/patterns approaches or purposes/aims-based approaches, as well as syllabi for different term lengths. The third section offers teaching strategies and support for *every* chapter in the book, as well as discussion of how each chapter aligns with the WPA Outcomes Statement. Finally, the last section of the Manual provides additional support for teaching the readings and using the activities and writing prompts in the Anthology.

PEARSON
mycomplab The only online application to integrate a writing environment with proven resources for grammar, writing, and research, MyCompLab gives students help at their fingertips as they draft and revise. Instructors have access to a variety of assessment tools including commenting capabilities, diagnostics and study plans, and an e-portfolio. Created after years of extensive research and in partnership with faculty and students across the country, MyCompLab offers a seamless and flexible teaching and learning environment built specifically for writers.

Interactive Pearson eText. An e-book version of *Writing Today* is also available in MyCompLab. This dynamic, online version of the text is integrated throughout MyCompLab to create an enriched, interactive learning experience for writing students.

CourseSmart. Students can subscribe to *Writing Today* as a CourseSmart eText (at CourseSmart.com). The site includes all of the book's content in a format that enables students to search the text, bookmark passages, save their own notes, and print reading assignments that incorporate lecture notes.

Acknowledgments

Of course, a book like this one is never the work of one or two people, even though our names appear on the cover. We would like to thank our editors, Lauren Finn, Meg Botteon, and Joe Opiela for their great ideas and persistence. We would also like to thank our colleagues, Scott Sanders, Susan Romano, Wanda Martin, Michelle Kells, Karen Olson, David Blakesley, Irwin Weiser, and Shirley Rose, for their feedback on our ideas. We also want to thank our students, especially our graduate students, for trying out some of these materials in their classes and helping us refine the ideas and approaches in this book. Mark Pepper, Danielle Cordaro, Leigh Johnson, and Katie Denton were very helpful with choosing readings and finding student texts to include as examples. We are appreciative of our thoughtful and enthusiastic reviewers, whose feedback over years of writing helped us articulate, shape, and sharpen our vision:

Ryan Allen, *University of Louisville;* Katherine Baker, *College of Southern Nevada;* John Barrett, *Richland College;* Lisa Bickmore, *Salt Lake Community College;* Jacqueline A. Blackwell, *Thomas Nelson Community College;* Patricia Webb Boyd, *Arizona State University;* Ron Christiansen, *Salt Lake Community College;*

T. Allen Culpepper, *Tulsa Community College, Southeast Campus;* Tamera Davis, *Northern Oklahoma College;* Dominic Delli Carpini, *York College of Pennsylvania;* Paul Dombrowski, *University of Central Florida;* Carlton Downey, *Houston Community College;* Chitralekha Duttagupta, *Arizona State University;* Jeremiah Dyehouse, *The University of Rhode Island;* William FitzGerald, *Rutgers University–Camden;* Susanmarie Harrington, *The University of Vermont;* Matthew Hartman, *Ball State University;* Dave Higginbotham, *University of Nevada, Reno;* Krista Jackman, *The University of New Hampshire;* Jay Jordan, *The University of Utah;* Margaret Konkol, *University at Buffalo, The State University of New York;* Andrew J. Kunka, *University of South Carolina Sumter;* Betty LaFace, *Bainbridge College;* Karen Laing, *College of Southern Nevada;* William B. Lalicker, *West Chester University of Pennsylvania;* Steve Lazenby, *University of North Carolina at Charlotte;* Robert Lively, *Truckee Meadows Community College;* Joleen Malcolm, *University of West Florida;* Rachel Maverick, *Richland College;* Shellie Michael, *Volunteer State Community College;* Susan Miller, *The University of Utah;* Rhonda Morris, *Santa Fe College;* Mary Ellen Muesing, *University of North Carolina at Charlotte;* Lori Mumpower, *University of Alaska Anchorage;* Michael Pennell, *The University of Rhode Island;* Jason Pickavance, *Salt Lake Community College;* Jennifer Pooler-Courtney, *University of North Carolina at Charlotte;* Sarah A. Quirk, *Waubonsee Community College;* Timothy D. Ray, *West Chester University of Pennsylvania;* Peggy L. Richards, *The University of Akron;* Mauricio Rodriguez, *El Paso Community College;* Dan Royer, *Grand Valley State University;* Stephen Ruffus, *Salt Lake Community College;* Andrew Scott, *Ball State University;* Brittany Stephenson, *Salt Lake Community College;* Stacey Tartar-Esch, West Chester *University of Pennsylvania;* Bradley A. Waltman, *College of Southern Nevada;* Elizabeth Wardle, *University of Central Florida;* Leah Williams, *The University of New Hampshire;* John Ziebell, *College of Southern Nevada*

And finally, we would like to thank our families for their patience and support while we worked on this project. Thank you, Susan, Kellen, Dana, Tracey, Emily, and Collin.

About the Authors

Richard Johnson-Sheehan is a Professor of Rhetoric and Composition at Purdue University. At Purdue, he has directed the Introductory Composition program, and he has mentored new teachers of composition for many years. He teaches a variety of courses in composition and professional writing, as well as classical rhetoric and the rhetoric of science. He has published widely in these areas. His prior books on writing include *Technical Communication Today,* now in its third edition, and *Writing Proposals,* now in its second edition. Professor Johnson-Sheehan was awarded 2008 Fellow of the Association of Teachers of Technical Writing and has been an officer in the Council for Writing Program Administrators.

Charles Paine is an Associate Professor of English at the University of New Mexico, where he teaches undergraduate courses in first-year, intermediate, and professional writing as well as graduate courses in writing pedagogy, the history of rhetoric and composition, and other areas. At UNM, he directed the Rhetoric and Writing Program and the First-Year Writing Program. He is an active member of the Council of Writing Program Administrators and currently serves on its Executive Board. He cofounded and coordinates the Consortium for the Study of Writing in College, a joint effort of the National Survey of Student Engagement and the Council of Writing Program Administrators. The Consortium conducts general research into the ways that undergraduate writing can lead to enhanced learning, engagement, and other gains related to student successs.

PART 1 Getting Started

PART OUTLINE

Sometimes the hardest part about writing is **GETTING STARTED**. *In these chapters, you will learn strategies for discovering a topic, identifying your purpose, profiling your readers, and adapting to your context.*

Writing and Genres

Writing gives you the power to get things done with words and images. It allows you to respond successfully to the events and people around you, whether you are trying to improve your community, pitch a new idea at work, or just text with your friends.

The emergence of new writing situations—new places for writing, new readers, and new media—means writing today involves more than just getting words and images onto a page or screen. Writers need to handle a wide variety of situations with diverse groups of people and multiple technologies. Learning to navigate among these complex situations is the real challenge of writing in today's world.

What Are Genres?

In this book, you will learn how to use writing *genres* to interpret these complex situations and respond to them successfully. Defining the word *genre* is difficult. Mistakenly, genres are sometimes defined by their structure alone (e.g., "A report has five parts: introduction, methods, results, discussion, and conclusion"). But this understanding of genre is a bit misleading. Genres are not fixed or rigid patterns to be followed mechanically. They are not forms into which we insert sentences and paragraphs.

Genres are ways of writing and speaking that help people interact and work together. In other words, genres reflect the things people do, and they are always evolving because human activities change over time to suit new social situations and new challenges. Genres *do* offer somewhat stable patterns for responding to typical situations. More importantly, though, they reflect how people act, react, and interact in these situations. Genres are meeting places—and *meaning* places.

Up until now, your writing courses have probably taught you how to master one genre—the academic essay—and write for one kind of reader—your teachers. In college, you will need to master and write in a variety of genres that help you to achieve different kinds of goals. This book will help you develop this "genre know-how," which you can use to strengthen your writing in college courses and in your career. You will also master a useful "genre set" that will allow you to respond successfully to a variety of important situations.

With this book, you will learn how to recognize and adapt genres for your own needs. You will become a more agile writer with a greater awareness of the differences among readers and contexts. You will become more proficient at analyzing specific writing situations and at adapting your writing to them.

Using Genres to Write Successfully

For writers, genres offer flexible approaches to writing that reflect how people in communities interact with each other. They provide strategies for analyzing and interpreting what is happening around you. Once you understand your current situation, you can then use genres to focus your creativity, generate new ideas, and present those ideas to others. You can use words and images to mold reality to your advantage.

Readers use genres, too. They use them as guideposts to orient themselves to a text, helping them to anticipate what they are likely to find in the document and how they can use the information in it. Readers are never passive spectators. They bring specific expectations with them and they respond to your writing, in part, according to those expectations. As a writer, when you understand what your readers expect to find, you can make strategic choices about what information you will include and how you will present your ideas (Figure 1.1). Knowing what your readers expect of a particular genre gives you insight about how to compose your text. It gives you power.

Writing with Genres

As a writer, you can use a genre to help you make sense of a complex situation, invent your ideas, and write a text that achieves your purpose and meets the expectations of your readers. Here are the most important things to remember about genres:

Genres Are Flexible. Genres are as flexible and changeable as the human activities they represent. It is helpful to

FIGURE 1.1 College Writing Requires Genre Know-How

Writing matters because it is one way people get things done. College writing will teach you "genre know-how," the ability to size up writing situations and respond to them appropriately.

identify the common features of each genre, so you can use it to help you interpret and write, but keep in mind that genres reflect human activities. As a result, genres should be viewed as flexible and adaptable to the evolving reality around you.

Genres Adjust to Fit Various Situations. When the audience or context changes, a genre needs to be adjusted to suit the new situation. An argument that worked previously with some readers or in a particular context might not work with different readers or in another context.

Genres Evolve to Suit Various Fields. Each discipline adapts common genres to its own needs and purposes. A report written by a biologist, for example, will share many characteristics with a report written by a manager at a corporation, but there will also be notable differences in the content, organization, style, and design of the text.

Genres Shape Situations and Readers. When you choose a particular genre, you are deciding what kinds of issues will be highlighted and what role your readers will play. For instance, readers know that when they encounter a memoir (a type of literary genre), they should read thoroughly and follow the story line. Quite differently, when readers encounter a report (a workplace genre), they assume they can "raid" the text for the specific information they need, that is, they can skip and skim.

Genres Can Be Played With. You can be creative and play with the conventions of genres. Can you use a memoir to review a book? Can you use a rhetorical analysis to study a painting? Sure you can. Genres are stretchy. But if you are going to go against your readers' expectations of the genre, you need to do so consciously and for a specific purpose.

Genres in Movies

You are already very familiar with the concept of genres in media and entertainment. To illustrate how genres work, let's take a look at how they function in the movie industry. Movies can be sorted by the genres that were used to make them (Figure 1.2). Movie genres include romantic comedies, action flicks, documentaries, murder mysteries, musicals, science fiction and fantasy, horror, thrillers, and others. These genres aren't formulas that the writers and directors must follow. Instead, they are familiar patterns that audiences will recognize and understand.

Once the audience recognizes the genre of the movie, they form specific expectations about what kinds of things they will—and will not—experience. For example, a romantic comedy usually explores the amusing awkwardness and pratfalls of a new relationship. Two people meet and feel an attraction to each other. But then, events beyond their control keep them apart and cause humorous misunderstandings. Eventually, the two star-crossed lovers realize they truly do love each other and find a way at the end of the movie to be together.

Directors of successful romantic comedies use the boundaries and conventions of this genre to help them work creatively and produce something that is both recognizable

FIGURE 1.2 Movie Genres

Usually, moviegoers recognize the genre of a movie even before they step into the theatre. Movie studios use posters and previews to help audiences know what to expect and how to interpret the movie.

and new. Genres aid the director's creativity by providing guidelines about how the movie should be structured, scripted, visually designed, musically scored, and even edited. Genres also constrain movies by helping directors determine what is "in bounds" and what is "out of bounds." Good directors work creatively within a genre to create something original.

Movies that flop often don't follow a recognizable genre or—even worse—formulaically follow a common genre in a trite way. A movie that strictly uses a genre formulaically feels painfully predictable and shallow. The people in the audience get bored and tune out when they realize that the movie is mechanically following a genre in a predictable way.

Like successful movie directors, effective writers need to fully understand the genres they are using. Genres help writers figure out where to start and how to proceed. They allow writers to create something fresh and new, while also helping them to organize and control their message in a way that readers will recognize and comprehend. In this sense, good writers (like good movie directors) are always balancing the old, familiar, and stable with the new, creative, and dynamic.

Genre and the Writing Process

So, how can genres help you write better? Think of something you already do well. Perhaps you are a good swimmer or a solid basketball player. Maybe you are a great video game player. Do you play the guitar, or do you like to make pottery? Have you learned a martial art? Do you like to do yoga?

To do something well, you first needed to learn the *process* for doing it. Someone else, perhaps a teacher, coach, parent, or friend, showed you the process and helped you get better at it (Figure 1.3, page 6). Then, once you knew that process, you worked on improving and refining your skills. You gained confidence. Before long, you developed the "know-how" for that activity—not just the skill to do it, but also an ability to

FIGURE 1.3 Learning to Do Something Involves Learning a Process

In order to do something you enjoy, you first had to learn a step-by-step process for doing it. Once you mastered the process and it became second nature, you could make it yours by refining and adapting it.

be innovative and original. When you reached this point, you could then start being creative and trying out new ideas.

Writing is similar to the other things you enjoy doing. To write well, you first need to develop your own writing process. Strong writers aren't born with a special gift, and they aren't necessarily smarter than anyone else. Strong writers have simply learned and mastered a reliable writing process that allows them to generate new ideas and shape those ideas into something readers will find interesting and useful.

Using a Writing Process

A writing process is a series of steps that leads you from your basic idea to a finished document. Over time, you will develop your own unique writing process, but the following six steps work well as a starting place:

Analyze the rhetorical situation. Identify the genre you are being asked to use or the genre that fits the needs of your project. Then define your topic, state your purpose, and analyze your readers and the contexts in which your text will be read or used.

Invent your ideas. Use inquiry and research to generate your own ideas and discover what others already know about your topic.

Organize and draft your paper. Arrange and compose your ideas into familiar patterns that your readers will recognize and find useful.

Choose an appropriate style. Use techniques of plain and persuasive style to clarify your writing and make it more compelling.

Design your document. Develop an appropriate page layout and use visuals to make your ideas more accessible and attractive to readers.

Revise and edit your work. Improve your writing by rewriting, reorganizing, editing, and proofreading your work.

Experienced writers tend to handle each of these steps separately, but a writing process shouldn't be followed mechanically from one step to the next. Instead, experienced writers tend to move around among these steps as needed (Figure 1.4). For instance, while drafting your paper, you may find you need to invent more content. Or, while revising, you may decide that you need to rethink the style of the text.

Why bother with a writing process at all? Can't you just write the paper? Truth is, as projects grow more complex and important, you need to give yourself time to generate and refine your ideas. A reliable writing process helps you do things one step at a time. In the long run, following a writing process will save you time and will help you to write something that is more creative and interesting to your readers.

Using Genre as a Guiding Concept

The genre you are using should influence each stage of your writing process, as shown in Figure 1.4. The genre will help you make decisions about the content of your paper, how your paper should be organized, what style would be appropriate, and what kind of design would work best. Then, as you revise and edit your paper, you can use the genre to guide any changes to the text. So as you write, keep the genre you are following in mind. Use the genre as a source for creativity.

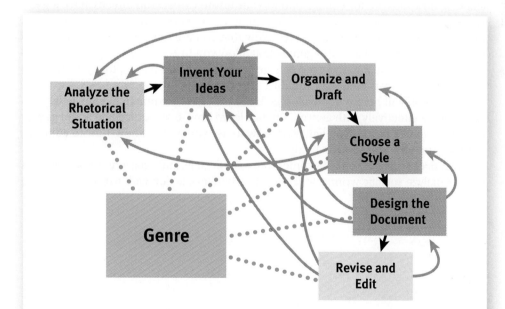

FIGURE 1.4 A Writing Process

Good writers tend to work through steps as they develop their work. They move among these steps in ways that fit their own work habits and personalities.

For example, if you are writing a movie review, the "review genre" (discussed in Chapter 6, "Reviews") will help you make decisions about what kinds of information your readers will expect. Should you tell them the plot of the movie? Should you describe the characters? Should you give away the ending? The genre will provide you with a model organization, so you can arrange your ideas in a pattern that your readers will expect. The genre also helps you to make informed decisions about what kind of style and design would work.

The purpose of a genre is to help you figure out how people tend to act, react, and interact in the situation in which you are writing. So if you tell your readers you are giving them a "movie review," they will have some expectations about the content, organization, style, and design of that text. If you meet those expectations, they will probably find the review useful and easy to read. If you bend those expectations, they might find your review creative or unique. However, if you completely violate their expectations for a movie review, your readers will likely be confused or frustrated with your work.

Using Genres in College and in Your Career

This genre-based approach to writing might be new to you. It's the next step toward learning how to write for college and in your future career. You already have a good sense about how the "essay genre" is used, and you know what your professors, as readers, expect from academic essays. Now that you are in college, you will need to master and write in a variety of genres that allow you to achieve new goals. You need to learn how to write for advanced college courses and workplace situations in which the academic essay is no longer suitable.

This book will help you develop genre know-how, the practical knowledge and skill to write effectively with genres. You will learn how to recognize and adapt genres for your own needs, and you will learn how to use your genre know-how to adjust to unique situations and specific readers.

This book will help you to become a versatile, flexible, and agile writer. You will learn how to analyze specific writing situations and then take action with words and images.

At the end of each chapter in this book, you will find something called the "Quick Start Guide." The purpose of the Quick Start Guides is to help you get up and running as soon as possible. You can use these guides for review or to preview the essential information in the chapter. Here is the essential information in this chapter.

KNOW What a Genre Is

Genres are ways of writing and speaking that help people communicate and work together in specific situations. Genres offer relatively stable patterns for writing, but more importantly, they reflect how humans act, react, and interact in everyday situations. Genres are meeting places—and *meaning* places.

GET Some "Genre Know-How"

Genre know-how is the ability to use genres to analyze and interpret what is happening around you. When you have genre know-how, you can use genres to focus your creativity, generate new ideas, and present those ideas to others.

KEEP in Mind That Genres Are Flexible

Genres are as flexible and changeable as the human activities they represent. They need to be adjusted to suit evolving situations. They can be stretched and messed around with, to a degree.

DEVELOP Your Writing Process

A writing process is a series of steps that leads you from your basic idea to a finished document. Developing and refining your writing process will save you time and effort in the long run.

USE Genres in College and in Your Career

A genre-based approach to writing helps you master a "genre set" that can be used in advanced college courses and in the workplace. The genre set taught in this book will cover most of the texts you will write in college and in your career.

1. In a group, first ask each person to talk briefly about his or her favorite movie genre; then, as a group, choose one of those genres to discuss. Describe the genre and its characteristics: What do all or most movies in this genre include? What kinds of characters do they have? What happens in them? Then talk about some of the best and worst movies that fit the genre. What do the best movies do well? Why do the worst movies fail?

2. In your group, brainstorm and list all the television shows you can think of. Then divide these shows into genres. What characteristics did you use to sort these shows into categories? What elements made you choose to put a show in one genre instead of another? Are there any shows that seem to stretch or bend genres, or that straddle more than one genre? If so, how do the producers of these shows bend the genres to come up with something new?

3. With your group, brainstorm and list all the restaurant genres you can think of. Then choose one restaurant genre to explore further. (For instance, one restaurant genre might be the coffee shop, which might include Starbucks, Caribou Coffee, and a variety of local coffee shops.) Describe the characteristics that all or most of the restaurants in the genre share. What guideposts signal to customers what kind of restaurant they are in? How are restaurant customers expected to behave, and how do the restaurants' characteristics encourage or require such behaviors?

1. On the Internet, find a Web page or Web site that conforms to a familiar Web site genre. For your professor (who may not know about this genre), write a one-page document that describes the Web site and explains the genre and how it works (how people use Web sites like this one, the genre's general features, how and why writers create texts in that genre, how and why readers come to such texts). You should also explain whether you think the Web site uses the genre properly and highlight any places where you think it could be improved by using the genre better.

2. When a movie uses the well-known features of a genre to make fun of that genre, it's called a parody. For instance, the *Scary Movie* movies are parodies of horror flicks. *Get Smart* is a parody of spy movies. Think of other parodies that use a genre in order to poke fun at it. For your professor or your group, write a one-page description of a movie that parodies a particular genre, the genre it makes fun of, and the features of genre that are specifically targeted by the parody.

3. For five minutes, freewrite about your favorite movie or television show. Freewriting means just putting your pen on the paper (or your fingers on the keyboard) and writing anything that comes to mind. Don't stop until the five minutes are up. Don't correct any errors or change anything. After five minutes of writing, read through your freewrite and underline any of your comments that relate to the genre of the movie. Then, in your group, discuss the parts you underlined.

4. Consider a kind of writing activity that you do frequently and are good at. It might be texting your friends, e-mailing people, working on a social networking profile, writing college application essays, or the five-paragraph essay. Write informally about the features of this writing and how those features affect the people who use this kind of writing (both writers and readers). Describe the setting of such writing (where it occurs and in what medium). Finally, describe the writing itself: What kind of content is typical, how is that content organized, what kind of language is used? In what ways does the genre determine who the participants can and cannot be?

5. Imagine that you have been asked to direct a movie that crosses two very different genres. For example, you might be asked to tell a horror story as a romantic comedy, or you might be asked to convert a historical documentary into an action flick. In a one-page paper written for your professor, explain how this merging of genres might offer some creative opportunities. What kinds of problems would it cause? Do you know any movies that do this kind of genre bending or genre merging? Are these movies successful, and do you find them entertaining?

Write This

1. **Describe a genre.** Find a longer nonfiction document that seems to be using a specific genre. Write a three-page analysis in which you describe the document's content, organization, style, and design. Then explain how its genre highlights certain kinds of information and ignores other kinds of information. Show how the style and design of the document is well suited (or ill suited) for the intended readers.

2. **Review a movie for a Web site or blog.** Write a three-page review of a movie you saw recently for a blog or movie review Web site. In your review, identify the genre of the movie and the common characteristics of that genre. Then show your readers how the movie exhibited those characteristics. Toward the end of your review, tell your readers whether you thought the movie was good or not by discussing how well it worked within its genre. Compare it to other successful movies in that genre.

PEARSON
mycomplab

For additional reading, writing, and research resources, go to **www.mycomplab.com.**

2

Topic, Angle, Purpose

Imagine that one of your professors has given you a new writing assignment. What should you do first? Of course, you should read the assignment closely. Take a deep breath. Then ask yourself a few specific questions about what you are being asked to do:

What am I being asked to write about? (Topic)

What is new or has changed recently about this topic? (Angle)

What exactly is the assignment asking me to do or accomplish? (Purpose)

Who will read this document and what do they expect? (Readers)

Where and when will they be reading this document? (Context)

These kinds of questions are also helpful in the workplace. When you are writing something for a client or your supervisor, you can use these five questions to help you figure out what you need to accomplish.

These questions are the basic elements of what we will be calling the "rhetorical situation" throughout this book (Figure 2.1). Before you start writing any text, you should first gain an understanding of your rhetorical situation: topic, angle, purpose, readers, and context. In this chapter, we will discuss the first three of these elements. Then, in Chapter 3, "Readers, Contexts, and Rhetorical Situations," we will discuss techniques and strategies for profiling your readers and anticipating the contexts in which they will experience your document.

Gaining a clear understanding of your topic, angle, and purpose will help you decide which genre is most appropriate for your writing project.

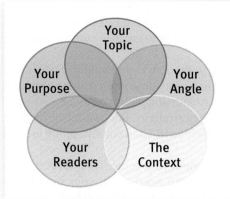

FIGURE 2.1 Five Elements of the Rhetorical Situation

Before you start writing, consider these five elements of the rhetorical situation, which will help you get started on your work.

Topic: What Am I Writing About?

In college, either the topics for your papers will be assigned or you will be asked to come up with your own topics to write about. When your professor supplies the topic, he or she might say something like this:

> For this paper, I want you to write about the Civil Rights movement in the 1960s.

> Shakespeare's *King Lear* is often held up as a masterpiece of Renaissance tragedy. We will explore why this play is still popular today.

> Our next subject will be "mating and dating" in college, and we will be using our own campus for field research.

If your professor does not supply a topic, you will need to decide for yourself what you are writing about. In these cases, you should pick a topic that intrigues you and one about which you have something interesting to say.

In the workplace, the topics of your documents will be different than the ones you wrote about in college, but you should still begin by identifying clearly what you are writing about. A client or your supervisor may request a written document from you in the following way:

> Our organization is interested in receiving a proposal that shows how we can lower our energy costs with sustainable energy sources, especially wind and solar.

> Please write a report that explains the sociological causes behind the sudden rise in violence in our city's south side neighborhoods.

> Evaluate these three road surfaces to determine which one would be best for repaving 2nd Street in the downtown area.

Once you have clearly identified your topic, you should explore its boundaries or scope, trying to figure out what is "inside" your topic and what is "outside" the topic. A good way to determine the boundaries of your topic is to create a concept map like the one shown in Figure 2.2.

To make a concept map, start out by writing your topic in the middle of your computer screen or a sheet of paper. Circle it, and then write down everything connected with it that comes to mind. For example, let's say your sociology professor wants you to write about the romantic relationships of college students. Put "dating and mating in college" in the middle of a sheet of paper and circle it. Then start mapping around that topic, as shown in Figure 2.2.

Write down all the things you already know about your topic. Then, as you begin to run out of ideas, go online and enter some of the words from your map into a search engine like *Google, Yahoo!,* or *Ask.com.* The search engine will bring up links to numerous other ideas and sources of information about your topic. Read through these sources and add more ideas to your concept map.

As your map fills out, you might ask yourself whether the topic is too large for the amount of time you have available. If so, pick the most interesting ideas from your map and create a second concept map around them alone. This second map will often help you narrow your topic to something you can handle.

FIGURE 2.2 Creating a Concept Map About Your Topic
A concept map is a helpful way to get your ideas onto the screen or a piece of paper.

Angle: What Is New About the Topic?

Completely new topics are rare. On just about every issue, someone has said something about it already. That's fine. You don't need to discover a completely new topic for your writing project. Instead, you need to come up with a new *angle* on a topic. Your angle is your unique perspective or view on the issue.

One way to come up with your angle is to ask yourself, "What has changed recently about this topic that makes it especially interesting right now?" For example, let's say you are searching the Internet for articles about college dating trends. You find a 2001 report from the Institute for American Values called "Hooking Up, Hanging Out, and Hoping for Mr. Right: College Women on Dating and Mating Today" (Figure 2.3). The report is getting a little out of date, but you mostly agree with the sociologists who wrote it, especially the part about college students wanting marriage but shying away from commitment.

Your experiences as a college student, however, give you some additional insights or "angles" into this topic. Plus, times have changed a little since the report came out. You believe that the hooking-up culture has been replaced by a culture of "serial monogamy" in which many college students now go through a series of short-term emotional and physical relationships while they are in college. These so-called monogamous relationships may last a few months or perhaps a year, but most people don't expect them to lead to marriage. That's your angle.

You decide to do a little freewriting to see if your angle works. Freewriting involves opening a new page in your word processor and writing anything that comes to mind for about five minutes (Figure 2.4, page 16). When freewriting, don't stop to correct or revise. Just keep writing anything that comes into your head.

Dating and mating in college is a very large topic—too large for a five- to ten-page paper. But if you write a paper that explores a specific angle (e.g., the shift from a hooking-up culture to a culture of serial monogamous relationships) you can say something really interesting about how people date and mate in college.

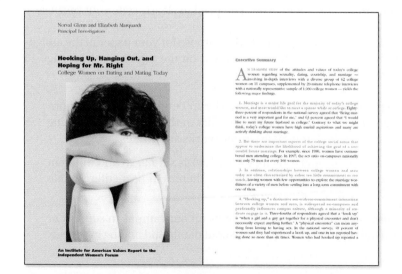

FIGURE 2.3 A Report on Your Topic

This report, published in 2001, looks like a great source for information on your topic, but it's growing a little dated. Your own experiences as a college student today may give you some new ways to see the topic.

FIGURE 2.4
Freewriting to Find Your Angle

Freewriting about your topic helps you test your new angle. Just write freely for five to ten minutes without making revisions or corrections.

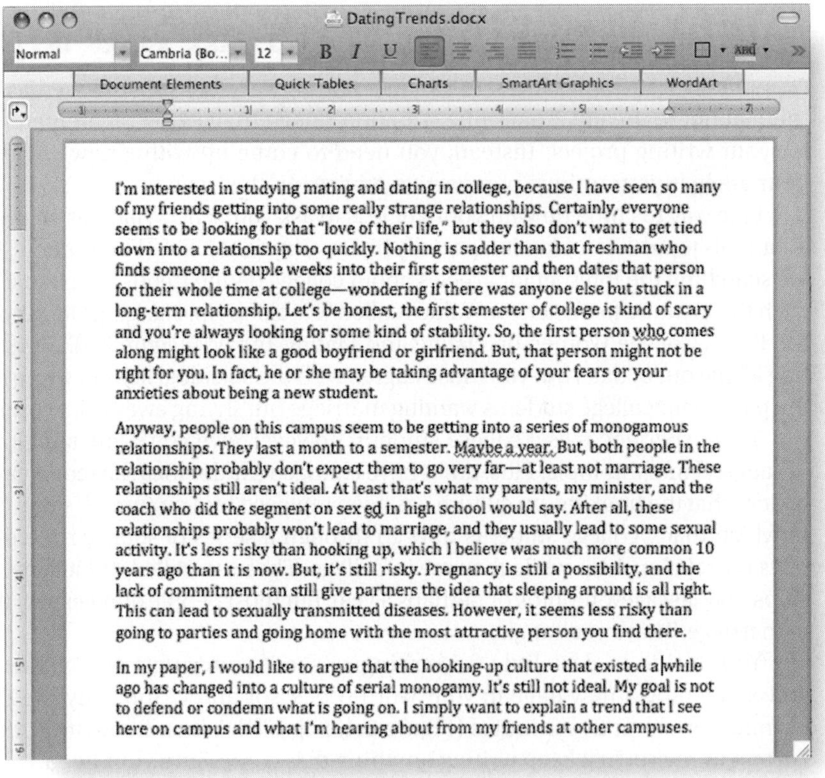

I'm interested in studying mating and dating in college, because I have seen so many of my friends getting into some really strange relationships. Certainly, everyone seems to be looking for that "love of their life," but they also don't want to get tied down into a relationship too quickly. Nothing is sadder than that freshman who finds someone a couple weeks into their first semester and then dates that person for their whole time at college—wondering if there was anyone else but stuck in a long-term relationship. Let's be honest, the first semester of college is kind of scary and you're always looking for some kind of stability. So, the first person who comes along might look like a good boyfriend or girlfriend. But, that person might not be right for you. In fact, he or she may be taking advantage of your fears or your anxieties about being a new student.

Anyway, people on this campus seem to be getting into a series of monogamous relationships. They last a month to a semester. Maybe a year. But, both people in the relationship probably don't expect them to go very far—at least not marriage. These relationships still aren't ideal. At least that's what my parents, my minister, and the coach who did the segment on sex ed in high school would say. After all, these relationships probably won't lead to marriage, and they usually lead to some sexual activity. It's less risky than hooking up, which I believe was much more common 10 years ago than it is now. But, it's still risky. Pregnancy is still a possibility, and the lack of commitment can still give partners the idea that sleeping around is all right. This can lead to sexually transmitted diseases. However, it seems less risky than going to parties and going home with the most attractive person you find there.

In my paper, I would like to argue that the hooking-up culture that existed a while ago has changed into a culture of serial monogamy. It's still not ideal. My goal is not to defend or condemn what is going on. I simply want to explain a trend that I see here on campus and what I'm hearing about from my friends at other campuses.

Purpose: What Should I Accomplish?

Your purpose is what you want to accomplish—that is, what you want to explain or prove to your readers. To this point, figuring out your topic and angle has helped you determine *what* you are writing about. Now, you need to clearly state your purpose—*why* you are writing.

Your professor may have already identified a purpose for your paper in the assignment sheet, so check there first. Assignments based on the topics given on page 13 might look like this:

Your objective in this paper is to show how Martin Luther King's use of nonviolence changed the dynamics of racial conflict in the 1960s, undermining the presumption of white dominance among blacks and whites.

In your paper, show how Shakespeare's *King Lear* is similar to and different from his other tragedies. Then discuss why the themes in *Lear* still resonate with today's audiences.

I want you to use close observation of students on our campus to support or debunk some of the common assumptions about dating and mating in college.

If you need to come up with your own purpose for the paper, ask yourself what you believe and what you would like to prove about your topic. For example, at the end of the freewrite in Figure 2.4, a purpose statement is starting to form:

> In my paper, I would like to argue that the hooking-up culture that existed a decade ago has changed into a culture of serial monogamy. It's still not ideal. My goal is not to defend or condemn what is going on. I simply want to explain a trend that I see here on campus and what I'm hearing about from my friends at other campuses.

This statement is still a bit rough and it lacks a clear focus, but the purpose of the project is starting to take shape.

In some situations, your purpose statement could also be called your "thesis statement." In this book, we use the term "purpose statement," because we want you to remember that this statement ultimately expresses what you believe or what you are trying to prove. Your purpose statement also defines what genre you are likely to follow. For example, the word "argue" in the rough purpose statement above signals that the author will likely be writing a position paper, a commentary, or a research report. It helps to remember that documents in college and in the workplace tend to be written for two primary reasons: to *inform* and to *persuade*. So your purpose statement will usually be built around some of the verbs shown in Figure 2.5.

You can consult this list of verbs if you are having trouble coming up with your purpose statement. Start by determining whether you are trying to *inform* your readers or trying to *persuade* them. Then pick the key word that best describes what you are trying to accomplish.

Informative Papers	Persuasive Papers
to inform	to persuade
to describe	to convince
to define	to influence
to review	to argue
to notify	to recommend
to instruct	to change
to advise	to advocate
to announce	to urge
to explain	to defend
to demonstrate	to justify
to illustrate	to support

FIGURE 2.5
Common Verbs Used in Purpose Statements

Choosing the Appropriate Genre

Once you have sketched out your topic, angle, and purpose, you can choose which genre would be appropriate for your project. The appropriate genre depends on what you are trying to do and who you are writing for. Perhaps your professor has already identified the genre by asking you to write a "report," a "literary analysis," or a "proposal." If so, you can turn to that chapter in this book to learn about the expectations for that genre (Chapters 4–13).

If you are allowed to choose your own genre, or if you are writing something on your own, the best way to figure out which genre would work best is to look closely at your purpose statement. Keep in mind, though, that genres are not formulas or recipes to be followed mechanically. Instead, each one reflects how people in various communities and cultures do things with words and images. They are places where people make meaning together. Figure 2.6 shows how your purpose statement can help you figure out which genre is most appropriate for your writing situation.

The genre that fits your purpose statement will help you make strategic decisions about how you are going to invent the content of your document, organize it, develop an appropriate style, and design it for your readers.

FIGURE 2.6
Identifying the Appropriate Genre

My Purpose	The Appropriate Genre
"I want to write about the meaning of something I experienced in my life."	Memoir (Chapter 4)
"I want to describe someone else."	Profile (Chapter 5)
"I need to critique something I saw, experienced, or read."	Review (Chapter 6)
"I want to show why someone or something does or does not demonstrate high quality."	Evaluation (Chapter 7)
"I need to explain and interpret a work of literature or art."	Literary Analysis (Chapter 8)
"I need to explain why a text or speech was effective or persuasive, or not."	Rhetorical Analysis (Chapter 9)
"I want to express my opinion about the people and events around me."	Commentary (Chapter 10)
"I want to argue for my beliefs or opinions."	Position Paper (Chapter 11)
"I want to propose a solution to a problem."	Proposal (Chapter 12)
"I need to explain an issue by doing research about it."	Report (Chapter 13)

Ready to start right now? Here are some techniques and strategies for identifying your topic, angle, and purpose.

IDENTIFY Your Topic

Your topic will be assigned by your professor or you will need to come up with it yourself. Either way, figure out what interests you about the topic. Then use a concept map to determine what issues are related to your topic.

NARROW Your Topic

Ask yourself whether the topic is too large for the amount of time you have available. If it might be too large, pick the most interesting ideas from your map and create a second concept map around them. This second map should help you narrow your topic to something you can handle.

DEVELOP Your Angle

Your angle is your unique perspective on the topic. A good way to develop an angle is to ask yourself, "What has changed recently about this topic that makes it especially interesting right now?" You might also ask what unique perspective you could offer on this issue.

WRITE Down Your Purpose

Your purpose is what you want to accomplish—that is, what you want to explain or prove to your readers. Decide whether you are *informing* your readers or *persuading* them. Then write a purpose statement that says exactly what you are going to do. The verbs shown in Figure 2.5 might help.

CHOOSE the Appropriate Genre

The best way to figure out which genre would work best for your project is to look closely at your purpose statement. The chart in Figure 2.6 will help you decide which genre would work for the document you want to write. In some cases, your professor will tell you which genre to use.

1. With a small group, list some topics that people often discuss and argue about. For example, what do people talk about on television or the radio? What do they argue about at local gathering places like cafés, restaurants, or bars? What are some things people discuss with their friends or families? With your group, come up with ten things that you yourselves have discussed or argued about over the last few days.

2. Take a look at today's news on Web sites like *CNN.com, FoxNews.com,* or *MSNBC.com.* What are some of the topics in the news today? You will notice that totally new topics aren't all that common. However, there are new angles developing all the time. With your group, discuss the new angles you notice on these topics. How do the reporters come up with these new angles? What has changed recently to create some of these new angles?

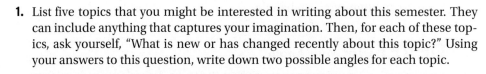

1. List five topics that you might be interested in writing about this semester. They can include anything that captures your imagination. Then, for each of these topics, ask yourself, "What is new or has changed recently about this topic?" Using your answers to this question, write down two possible angles for each topic.

2. Think of a topic that catches your interest. For five minutes, create a concept map that includes everything you can think of about this topic. Now, look at your concept map and find a part of this topic that you would like to explore further. Then freewrite on that part for five more minutes and see what kinds of ideas begin to emerge. Would this "narrower" topic be easier to write about than the topic you started with?

3. Pick a topic and angle that interests you and develop a purpose statement for a paper about that topic. Your purpose statement doesn't need to be perfect right now, but try to describe what you want to achieve in your paper. Do you want to inform your readers about your topic or do you want to persuade them? Now, build your purpose statement around one of the words shown in the chart in Figure 2.5.

4. Using the topic and purpose statement from the exercise above, identify which genre would be most appropriate for writing about this topic. Figure 2.6 provides a chart that shows how to use your purpose statement to figure out which genre you should use. Once you've determined which genre to use, flip to that chapter in Part 2, "Using Genres to Express Ideas," to see what that genre usually involves.

1. **Identify a topic, angle, and purpose.** Choose a writing assignment from one of your professors. Using the steps and concepts discussed in this chapter, determine the topic you are being asked to write about and come up with a unique angle on it. Then draft a purpose statement for your assignment. Write an e-mail to your professor in which you identify the topic, angle, and purpose of the paper you will be writing. Then discuss which genre would be appropriate for this assignment and why.

2. **E-mail your professor about a new angle on a topic.** Pick any topic that interests you and find a new angle on that topic. Use concept mapping to explore and narrow your topic. Then write a rough purpose statement that shows what you want to achieve in your paper.

   Using the chart in Figure 2.6, choose a genre that would help you to say something meaningful and interesting about this issue. Turn to the chapter in Part 2 that discusses the genre you chose. Using the diagram that appears early in the chapter, sketch a brief outline on this topic.

   Finally, write an e-mail to your professor in which you explain how you would go about writing an argument on this topic. Explain your topic, angle, purpose, readers, and the genre you would use. Tell your professor why you think your approach to the topic would be effective for your readers.

Readers, Contexts, and Rhetorical Situations

In your college courses and in your career, you will need to write to real people who will read and use your documents in specific times and places. Your writing needs to inform them, persuade them, achieve your purpose, and get something done.

In the previous chapter, you learned how to identify your topic, angle, and purpose. In this chapter, you will learn how to achieve your purpose by developing *reader profiles* and sizing up the *contexts* in which people will read your work. Together, this information makes up the *rhetorical situation*—that is, the topic, angle, purpose, readers, and context. Each rhetorical situation is unique, because every new situation puts into play a specific writer with a purpose, writing for specific readers who are encountering the work at a unique time and place.

When you have sized up the rhetorical situation, you can use genres more successfully to accomplish what you want to achieve. Identifying your topic, angle, and purpose allows you to figure out which genre would work best. Understanding your readers and the contexts in which they will experience your text will help you adjust the genre to fit their expectations.

Profiling Readers

In college and in the workplace, you will usually be writing for other people, not your-self. So before writing, you need to develop a reader profile that helps you adapt your ideas to their expectations and the situations in which they will use your document.

A profile is an overview of your readers' traits and characteristics. At a minimum, you should develop a *brief reader profile* that gives you a working understanding of the people who will be reading your text. If time allows, you should create an *extended reader profile* that will give you a more in-depth view of their expectations, values, and attitudes.

A Brief Reader Profile

To create a brief reader profile, you can use the Five-W and How questions to help you describe the kinds of people who will be reading your text (Figure 3.1).

Who Are My Readers? What are their personal characteristics? How old are they? What cultures do they come from? Do they have much in common with you? Are they familiar with your topic already or are they completely new to it?

What Are Their Expectations? What do they need from you and your docu-ment? What do they want, exactly? What ideas excite them, and what things bore them? What information do they need to help them accomplish their personal and professional goals?

Where Will They Be Reading? In what locations might they read your document? Will your readers be sitting at their desks, in a meeting, or on an airplane? Will they be reading from a printed page, a computer screen, or a small-screen reading device like a smartphone?

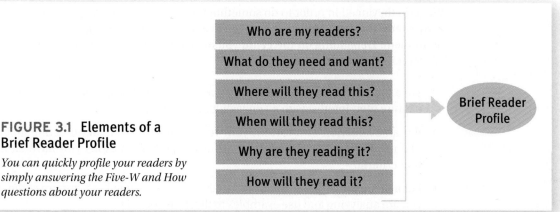

FIGURE 3.1 Elements of a Brief Reader Profile

You can quickly profile your readers by simply answering the Five-W and How questions about your readers.

Who are my readers?

What do they need and want?

Where will they read this?

When will they read this?

Why are they reading it?

How will they read it?

Brief Reader Profile

When Will They Be Reading? Does the time of day affect how they will read your document? Will they be reading it when the issues are hot and under discussion? Will they be reading it at a time when they can think about your ideas slowly and carefully?

Why Will They Be Reading? Why will they pick your document up? Do their reasons for reading the document match your purpose in writing it? Do they want to be informed, or do they need to be persuaded?

How Will They Be Reading? Will they read slowly and carefully? Will they skip and skim? Will they read some parts carefully and some parts quickly or not at all?

Your answers to the Five-W and How questions will give you a brief reader profile to help you start writing. For simple documents, a brief profile like this one might be enough. For larger, more complex documents, you will need to dig a little deeper to develop a more thorough understanding of your readers.

An Extended Reader Profile

You should always remember that your readers probably understand issues differently than you do. Their expectations, values, and attitudes will be unique, and sometimes even contradictory to yours. Meanwhile, complex genres, like the ones discussed in this book, usually require a more thorough understanding of the people who will be reading the text.

To write successfully in these complex rhetorical situations, you might find it helpful to create an *extended reader profile* that goes beyond answering the Who, What, Where, When, Why, and How questions. An extended reader profile will help you to better anticipate what your readers expect, what they value, and what their attitudes are toward you and your topic.

What Are Their Expectations? Your readers probably picked up your document because they *expect* or *need* something. Do they need to know something specific? What do they need in order to do something or achieve a goal? Make a list of the two to five items that your readers expect you to address in your document for it to be useful to them. Depending on the genre you are using, your readers will be looking for various kinds of information:

- For a memoir or profile, your readers will expect you to use descriptive detail and capture their interest with an engaging narrative.

- For an evaluation or a review, your readers may expect you to define and explain the evaluation criteria you are using and the reasons you have chosen that criteria.

- For a literary analysis or rhetorical analysis, you may need to summarize the text you are analyzing and use examples to illustrate its style.

- For a position paper or commentary, they will expect you to back up your claims with facts, examples, and solid reasoning.

- For a report or a proposal, your readers will expect you to provide background information to allow them to understand the current situation. They will also be looking for specific plans and recommendations to help them solve problems.

If you can figure out your readers' expectations, you are well on your way to knowing what to include in your document and how to present it.

What Are Their Values? *Values* involve personal beliefs, social conventions, and cultural expectations. Your readers' values have been formed through their personal experiences, family or religious upbringing, and social/cultural influences.

Personal values. Your readers' personal beliefs can be hard to predict, but you can take a few educated guesses. Think about your readers' upbringings and experiences. What are their core beliefs? What makes your readers different or unique? How are your readers similar to you and what personal values do you and your readers likely hold in common?

Social values. Your readers' values are also shaped by the conventions, practices, and customs of their society. How do people do things in their social circles? What expectations does their society place on them? What traditions or codes govern their behavior?

Cultural values. Your readers' culture may influence their behavior in ways even they don't fully understand. What do people in your readers' culture value? How are these cultural values similar to or different from your cultural values?

Mistakenly, writers sometimes assume that their readers hold the same values they do. Even people very similar to you in background and upbringing may hold values that are different from yours. Meanwhile, people whose cultures and upbringings are different from yours may have distinctly different ways of seeing the world.

What Is Their Attitude Toward You and the Issue? Your readers will also have a particular *attitude* about your topic and, perhaps, about you. Are they excited, or are they bored? Are they concerned or apathetic, happy or upset about your topic? Do they already accept your ideas, or are they deeply skeptical? Are they feeling positive toward you or negative? Will they welcome your views or be hostile to them? Are they joyful or angry, optimistic or pessimistic?

If your readers are positive and welcoming toward your views, you will want to take advantage of their goodwill by giving them persuasive reasons to agree with you. If they are negative or resistant, you will want to use solid reasoning, ample examples, and good style to counter their resistance and win them over.

Anticipating all of your readers' expectations, values, and attitudes can be especially difficult if you try to do it all in your head. That's why professional writers often

Types of Readers	Expectations	Values	Attitudes
Most Important Readers:			
Second Most Important Readers:			
Third Most Important Readers:			

FIGURE 3.2 A Reader Analysis Worksheet

A Reader Analysis Worksheet is a helpful tool for understanding your readers and making good decisions about the content, organization, style, and design of your document.

like to use a Reader Analysis Worksheet like the one shown in Figure 3.2 to help them create an extended profile of their readers.

Using the Reader Analysis Worksheet is easy. On the left, list the types of readers who are likely to read your document, ranking them by importance. Then fill in what you know about their expectations, values, and attitudes. If you don't know enough to fill in a few of the squares on the worksheet, just put question marks (?) there. Question marks signal places where you may need to do some additional research on your readers.

An extended reader profile blends your answers to the Five-W and How questions with the information you added to the Reader Analysis Worksheet. These two reader analysis tools should give you a strong understanding of your readers and how they will interpret your document.

Analyzing the Context

The *context* of your document involves the external influences that will shape how your readers interpret and react to your writing. It is important to remember that readers react to a text moment by moment. So the happenings around them can influence their understanding of your document.

Your readers will be influenced by three kinds of contexts: place, medium, and social and political issues.

Place

Earlier, when you developed a brief profile of your readers, you answered the Where and When questions to figure out the locations and times in which your readers would use your document. Now go a little deeper to put yourself in your readers' place.

What are the physical features of this place?

What is visible around the readers, and what can they hear?

What is moving or changing in this place?

Who else is in this place, and what do they want from my readers?

What is the history and culture of this place, and how does it shape how people view things?

A place is never static. Places are always changing. So figure out how this changing, evolving place influences your readers and their interpretation of your text (Figure 3.3).

The genre of your document may help you to imagine the places where people are likely to read your document. Proposals and reports tend to be read in office settings, and they are often discussed in meetings. Memoirs, profiles, reviews, and commentaries tend to be read in less formal settings—at home, on the bus, or in a café. Once you know the genre of your document, you can make decisions about how it should be designed and what would make it more readable in a specific place.

FIGURE 3.3 The Influence of Place

The place where your readers encounter your writing will strongly influence their interpretation of your ideas.

Medium

The medium is the technology that your readers will use to experience your document. Each medium (e.g., paper, Web site, public presentation, video, podcast) will shape how they interpret your words and react to your ideas:

Paper documents. Paper documents are often read more closely than on-screen documents. With paper, your readers may be more patient with longer documents and longer paragraphs. Document design, which is discussed in Chapter 17, "Designing," makes the text more attractive and helps your readers read more efficiently. People appreciate graphics and photographs that enhance and reinforce the words on the page, but visuals aren't mandatory. Paper documents, however, are often less accessible than on-screen documents, because they are harder to store and keep track of.

Electronic documents. When people read text on a screen, like a Web site or a blog, they usually scan it, reading selectively for the information they need. In other words, your on-screen readers will be "raiding" the text to locate specific facts and information. They are not going to be patient with a long document, and they will tend to avoid reading large paragraphs. They will appreciate any visuals, like graphs, charts, and photographs, that you can add to enhance their understanding. You can turn to Chapter 29, "Using the Internet," for more ideas about how to write for the screen.

Public presentations. Presentations tend to be much more visual than on-screen and print documents. A presentation made with *PowerPoint* or *Keynote* usually boils an original text down to bullet points that highlight major issues and important facts. Your readers will focus on the items you choose to highlight, and they will rely on you to connect these items and expand on them. Turn to Chapter 32, "Presenting Your Work," for more ideas about how to make great presentations.

Podcasts or videos. A podcast or video needs to be concise and focused. Hearing or seeing a text can be very powerful in this multimedia age; however, amateurs are easy to spot. So your readers will expect a polished, tight presentation that is carefully produced. Your work should get to the point and not waste their time, or they will turn to something else. You can turn to Chapter 29, "Using the Internet," to learn how to make podcasts and videos and upload them to the Internet.

Paper is no longer the only medium for writing. So you should always keep in mind that your texts will likely appear in electronic media. These various media shape how readers will experience your text and interpret your ideas.

Social and Political Influences

Now, think about how current trends and events will influence how your readers interpret what you are telling them. Always keep in mind that your readers will encounter your writing in specific and real contexts that are always undergoing change. The change can be quick and dramatic, or it can be slow and almost imperceptible.

Social trends. Pay attention to the social trends that are influencing you, your topic, and your readers. You originally decided to write about this topic because you believe it is important right now. What are the larger social trends that will influence how people in the near and distant future understand this topic? What is changing in your society that makes this issue so important? Most importantly, how do these trends directly or indirectly affect your readers?

Economic trends. For many issues, it all comes down to money. What economic factors will influence your readers? How does their economic status shape how they will interpret your arguments? What larger economic trends are influencing you and your readers?

Political trends. Also, keep any political trends in mind as you analyze the context for your document. On a micropolitical level, how will your ideas affect your readers'

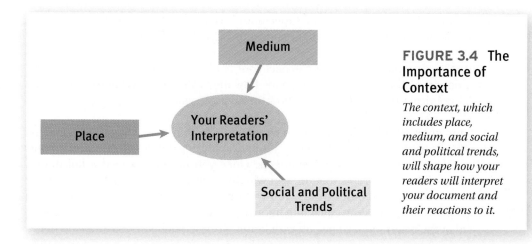

FIGURE 3.4 The Importance of Context

The context, which includes place, medium, and social and political trends, will shape how your readers will interpret your document and their reactions to it.

relationships with you, their families, their colleagues, or their supervisors? On a macropolitical level, how will political trends at the local, state, federal, and international levels shape how your readers interpret your ideas?

Readers, naturally, respond to the immediate context in which they live (Figure 3.4). If you understand how place, medium, and social and political trends influence your readers, you can better adapt your work to their specific expectations, values, and attitudes.

Genres and the Rhetorical Situation

We threw quite a bit of material at you in this chapter and in the previous one. Here's the point and a brief overview. Genres are used to respond to specific types of rhetorical situations. So when choosing the appropriate genre, you first need to completely understand the situation to which you are responding:

Topic. What is the exact topic your document is going to discuss? What information is "inside" the topic's boundaries and what is "outside" those boundaries? Have you sharpened your topic enough to allow you to handle it in the time and space you have available?

Angle. What is new or different about your approach to this topic? What has happened recently that makes your topic especially interesting to you and your readers right now? What makes your ideas about this topic different than the ideas of others?

Purpose. What exactly do you want to achieve in this document? What do you want your readers to believe or do after they are finished reading it? What are your goals in writing this text?

Readers. What are your readers' expectations, values, and attitudes? How do these characteristics shape the content, organization, style, and design of your document?

Contexts. In what places do you expect your readers to encounter your document? How does the medium of your text shape how they will read it? What economic and social-political trends will influence how they react to what you are saying?

It might seem like a lot of work to figure all these things out, especially when the deadline is not that far away. In reality, though, analyzing the rhetorical situation only takes a few minutes for most documents. Once you have developed a full understanding of the rhetorical situation, you will find that writing the document is faster and more efficient. In other words, you will save time, because you won't go down dead ends and spend time collecting information you don't need. A few minutes invested at the beginning will pay off with better writing that takes less time and effort.

Need to quickly analyze your readers and the context for your document? Here are some steps to help you get started.

CREATE a Brief Profile of Your Readers

Using the Five-W and How questions, figure out *who* your readers are, *what* they need, *where* and *when* they will be reading the document, *why* they are reading it, and *how* they will be reading it. A sentence or two for each question should be enough to develop a brief profile.

KNOW Your Readers' Expectations

On a basic level, what are the two to five pieces of information your readers *expect* or *need* you to tell them for your document to be useful?

FIGURE OUT Your Readers' Values

Write down your readers' personal, social, and cultural values, and try to anticipate how these values will shape your document.

ANTICIPATE Your Readers' Attitudes About You and Your Topic

Try to figure what your readers' mind-set will be. Will they be excited or bored, concerned or apathetic, happy or upset? Are they already convinced or deeply skeptical? Are they feeling positive toward you or negative? Will they welcome your views or be hostile to them? Are they glad or angry, optimistic or pessimistic?

THINK About How Place and Medium Affect Your Readers

The physical place where they are reading may affect how closely they are reading and dictate what they need you to highlight for them. The medium of your document (e.g., paper, screen, presentation, podcast) will also shape how they interpret your ideas.

CONSIDER Social and Political Trends

Identify any current trends or events that might color your readers' understanding of your writing. What social trends affect your topic? How does money influence the situation? How does your project touch on micropolitical and macropolitical trends?

1. Choose an advertisement from a magazine or a newspaper. In a group, figure out the advertisement's purpose, target readers, and the contexts in which it was used. Be as specific and thorough as you can as you define the following:

   - *Purpose:* What is the advertisement trying to do? Use key words like *persuade, inform, entertain,* and others to describe its objectives.
   - *Readers:* What are the expectations, values, and attitudes of the target readers? How does the advertisement try to use those expectations, values, and attitudes to its advantage?
   - *Context:* Describe the place and medium of the advertisement as well as the social, economic, and political trends that might influence how it is interpreted. How do these contextual factors influence how readers respond to this ad?

   Finally, do you think the ad is effective in persuading or influencing its intended readers? For which readers would it be most effective, and for which ones would it not?

2. Think of a time when you did not communicate effectively. With your group, discuss why the communication failed. What happened? Describe how you misread the situation, and why the audience or readers reacted as they did. How could you have better handled the situation if you had known the expectations, values, and attitudes of the audience or readers? If you had better understood the social and political issues, how might you have been more successful?

3. With your group, make a list of ten things that motivate people to agree with others or to take action. Discuss how these motives influence the ways people make decisions in real life. What are some ways you could use these motivations in your written work to persuade or influence people?

1. Imagine that you are an advertising specialist who has been asked to develop an advertising campaign to sell digital audio players (MP3, iPod, or other audio device) to people over 60 years old. Figure out these customers' expectations, values, and attitudes toward the product. Then figure out how place and social and political factors shape their decisions about buying this kind of product. In a one-page memo to your professor, explain how you might use this knowledge to create an advertising campaign for this new market.

2. You have probably seen those electronic billboards that use light-emitting diodes (LEDs) to display content. These billboards offer more flexibility than traditional billboard media, because different advertisements can be displayed at different times of the day.

   Imagine that you are creating ads for these kinds of billboards. First, choose a product you want to advertise. Now create two thumbnail sketches (with images and words) for the billboard for two different contexts:

   - *Context A:* rush hour, when drivers are stopped at traffic lights in front of the billboard for as long as 90 seconds.
   - *Context B:* normal drive time, when drivers may not stop at all, but drive by and have as little as two seconds to glance at the billboard.

Write a one-page memo explaining how the two versions differ in response to the differing contexts. Explain why each version's design and content is right for the context.

3. For your next project in this class, do a brief reader analysis in which you answer the Five-W and How questions about your readers. Then do an expanded reader analysis in which you explore their expectations, values, and attitudes. In a one-page memo to your professor, explain the differences between your brief analysis and the extended analysis. What does the extended analysis reveal that the brief analysis didn't reveal? Would the brief analysis be enough for this project? Why? Or do you think the extended analysis would help you write a more effective document?

Write This

1. **Evaluate an argument.** Find an opinion article about an issue that interests you and write a two-page evaluation in which you discuss how well the writer has adapted his or her article for its context. You can find a variety of opinion articles in your local or school newspapers (in the "opinion" section) or on the Internet (blogs, personal pages, online newspaper opinion sections and the responses to them). Mark up the text, paying attention to how the writer addresses the following contextual issues:

   - *Place:* First, note how the place in which the article was published and where it will likely be read influences the way readers interact with it.
   - *Medium:* How does the medium shape the way people read the text and what they will focus on?
   - *Social and Political Trends:* What have people been saying about the issue? If it's a hot topic, what makes it hot? What larger trends have motivated the writer to write this argument?

   In your evaluation, explain how the author of this opinion article adjusted his or her argument to the context in which it appears. Discuss whether you felt the opinion article succeeded. How might it be improved?

2. **Rewrite an online text for a different reader.** Find a brief document on the Internet that is aimed toward a specific kind of reader. Then rewrite the document for a completely different type of reader. For example, if it was originally aimed at a young reader, rewrite it for an older reader.

   To complete this assignment, you will need to do a brief and extended reader analysis of your new readers.

   When you are finished rewriting the document, write a brief e-mail to your professor in which you explain how the change in readers changed the content, organization, style, and design of your rewrite. Attach your new version of the text to your e-mail.

For additional reading, writing, and research resources, go to **www.mycomplab.com**.

2 Using Genres to Express Ideas

PART OUTLINE

Writing well means responding effectively to diverse situations. In these chapters, you will learn how to use ten **GENRES** and ten "**MICROGENRES**" that will help you write about yourself, be critical, take a stand, pitch your ideas, and argue with others.

4

Memoirs

The words *memoir* and *memory* come from the same root word, but memoirs involve more than an author sharing his or her memories. While telling an autobiographical story, good memoirs explore and reflect on a central theme or question. They rarely provide explicit answers to those questions. Instead, they invite readers to explore and reflect with the narrator to try to unravel the deeper significance of the recounted events.

Writers create memoirs when they have true personal stories that they hope will inspire others to reflect on or understand interesting questions or social issues. Readers come to memoirs expecting to engage with authors and their stories. They expect to encounter new perspectives and insights that are fresh and meaningful.

Today, memoirs are more popular than ever. They are common on best-seller lists of books. Some recent memoirs, such as Jeanette Walls' *Glass Castles* about growing up in a dysfunctional family and Frank McCourt's *Angela's Ashes* about his childhood in Ireland, sold millions of copies. Meanwhile, blogs and social networking sites give ordinary people opportunities to post their reflections on their lives.

In college, professors will sometimes ask you to write about your life to explore where you came from and how you came to hold certain beliefs. In these assignments, the goal is not just to recount events but to unravel their significance and arrive at insights that help you explore and engage more deeply with the issues discussed in the class.

Memoirs

This diagram shows a basic organization for a memoir, but other arrangements of these sections will work, too. You should alter this organization to fit the features of your topic, angle, purpose, readers, and context.

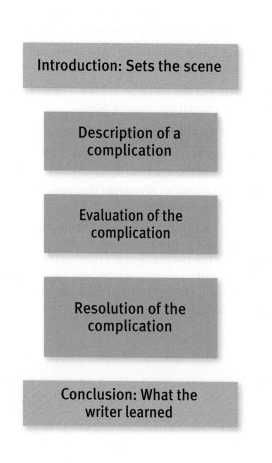

Introduction: Sets the scene

Description of a complication

Evaluation of the complication

Resolution of the complication

Conclusion: What the writer learned

Overview

Using rich detail, memoirs tell a personal story in which an event or series of events leads the writer to new insights about life. They tend to have these main features:

- **An engaging title** that hints at the memoir's overall meaning or "theme."
- **An introduction with a "lead"** that captures the reader's interest or sets a scene.
- **A complication,** a tension or conflict that must be resolved in some way by the end of the story. This tension or conflict can be between people's values, beliefs, desires, or needs. It could be a conflict within the author as he or she moves from one life stage to another or discovers something previously unknown. Or it could be something new, challenging, discomforting, or frightening.
- **A plot** that draws the reader forward as the memoir moves through a series of scenes or stages.
- **Intimacy between the narrator and the reader,** allowing the writer to speak with readers in a personal one-on-one way.
- **Rich and vivid details** that give the story greater imagery, texture, and impact.
- **A central theme or question** that is rarely announced or answered explicitly, but that the narrator explores and reflects on with the reader.
- **A new understanding or revelation** that presents a moment of growth, transformation, or clarity in the writer.

Memoirs tend to include these features and follow a pattern like the one shown on page 37. Later in this chapter, we will go over each of these features in more depth. Keep in mind that the memoir genre organization, as with all genres, should not be followed mechanically. Instead, you should adjust the content, organization, style, and design to fit your topic, purpose, and readers, and the context in which your memoir will be read.

ONE STUDENT'S WORK
Memoirs

Engaging title that hints at the memoir's overall theme.

Surprising lead introduces the conflict.

Binky and Toodles: A Frontier Saga

Alisa Harris

This spring break, my family *finally* murdered Binky and Toodles.
Binky and Toodles are my New Mexico farming family's once-cherished buffalo. My father christened the buffalo Binky and Toodles when they came

to live with us in August of 2005. Binky and Toodles were shaggy and large. They had long matted hair and big angry faces. Later in this post, find a picture of Binky (or perhaps it is Toodles) eating our grass.

My father and mother bought Binky and Toodles to develop our character. To my parents, developing character means shoveling things out of buffalo pens. Shoveling things makes you morally strong, so we shoveled things for Binky and Toodles. We picked hay bales up out of our field and stacked them high in our barn and took them out every day and fed them to Binky and Toodles and then shoveled everything Binky and Toodles produced, and we grew into men and women of strong moral fiber.

> Sets the scene and narrates the background using rich and vivid details.

We learned responsibility and stick-to-it-iveness. We learned courage in the face of great danger, especially when our neighbor declared that he never entered a buffalo pen without arming himself to the teeth—to put himself out of his misery in case the wild animal charged. Indeed, Toodles (or it could have been Binky) made two attempts at escape, but we found an inner strength in the face of this fearful disaster.

> The narrator establishes and maintains a steady tone.

Two years went by, and having by now quite grown up into men and women of strong moral fiber, we questioned the continued utility of housing, feeding, and shoveling for Binky and Toodles. We began to secretly wonder if our father and mother had formed a sort of attachment to the great beasts, perhaps to console themselves as we one by one left their small farm for the big city of Hillsdale. My parents denied any untoward fondness for Binky and Toodles, but

> Tension and conflict are introduced.

still the bovids remained, hale and hearty and chomping down hay and producing large piles to shovel.

Then my little sister Lizzy pitifully requested the demise of the buffalo for a Christmas present. My father hesitated and hedged . . . until he calculated the hay bill for Binky and Toodles. Then he made a short call to the butcher's, loaded Binky and Toodles into the trailer, and bid them a tender goodbye.

Our freezer is now full of Binky and Toodles, all resting in peace and chopped up into hamburger. (We considered using every hair, hoof, and horn of the beasts, as the thrifty Native Americans did in pioneer days, but we found that coats made of buffalo hair are not still in style.)

We hear that buffalo meat is considered exotic in the big city. We at least find it costly—not just in the tears, sweat, and blood of a true frontier family, but also in hay bales. My parents, in fact, are beginning to wonder if there is an easier way to grow men and women of strong moral fiber. (Raising chickens, perhaps?) I close the saga of Binky and Toodles with the fervent prayer that their spirits are now loping free in the Happy Hunting Grounds of the Great Spirit of Strong Moral Fiber, in the Big Western Sky.

> Conclusion recounts what was learned.

Inventing Your Memoir's Content

Your goal in a memoir is to uncover the meaning of your past for your readers *and* for yourself. When starting out, you shouldn't be too concerned about what your point will be. Instead, begin with an interesting event or series of events from your life that you want to explore.

Inquiring: Finding an Interesting Topic

With your whole life as potential subject matter, deciding what to write about and narrowing your topic can be a challenge. Think about the times in your life when you did something challenging, scary, or fun. Think about the times when you felt pain or great happiness. Think about the times when something important happened to you, helping you make a discovery about yourself or someone else.

Now, on your screen or a piece of paper, make a brainstorming list of as many of these events as you can remember (Figure 4.1). Don't think too much about what you are writing down. These events don't need to be earthshaking. Just list the stories you like to tell others about yourself.

Inquiring: Finding Out What You Already Know

Memoirs are about memories—of course—but they are also about your reflections on those memories. You need to do some personal inquiry to pull up those memories and then reflect on them to figure out what they meant at the time and what they mean to you now. Pick an event from your brainstorming list and use some of the following techniques for reflecting on that event.

Make a Map of the Scene. In your mind's eye, imagine the place where the event happened. Then draw a map of that place (Figure 4.2). Add in as many details as you can remember—names, buildings, people, events, landmarks. You can use this map to help you tell your story.

Storyboard the Event. In comic strip form, draw out the major scenes in the event. It's fine to use stick figures, because these drawings are only for you. They will help you remember and sort out the story you are trying to tell.

Record Your Story as a Podcast or Video. Tell your story into your computer's audio recorder or into a camcorder. Then you may want to transcribe it to the written page. Sometimes it's easier to tell the story verbally and then turn it into written text.

> **Possible Topics for a Memoir**
> Breaking my leg skiing
> Winning the clothing design competition
> Failing that geometry class
> The trip to Mexico
> Death of Fred Sanders
> Leaving home to go to college
> Meeting Senator Wilkins
> Discovering Uncle Jim is gay
> When Bridgeport's downtown flooded
> When the car broke down in Oklahoma
> Going to the state volleyball finals
> Not making the cheerleading team

FIGURE 4.1 Brainstorming to Find Topics

Brainstorming is a good way to list possible topics for your memoir. Try to think of moments when something important happened that changed your life.

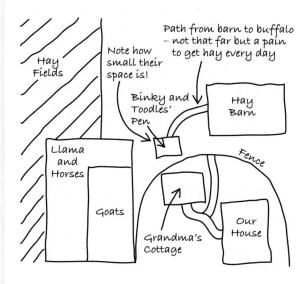

FIGURE 4.2 Making a Map of the Scene

Sometimes drawing a map of the scene where an event happened can help you reconstruct it and remember important details. Here is a map of the farm described in Alisa Harris's memoir.

Do Some Role Playing. Use your imagination to put yourself into the life of a family member or someone close to you. Try to work through events as that person might have experienced them, even events that you were part of. Then compare and contrast that person's experiences with your own, giving special consideration to any tensions or conflicts.

Researching: Finding Out What Others Know

Research can help you better understand the event or times you are writing about. For instance, a writer describing her father's return from the Persian Gulf War (1990–1991) might want to find out more about the history of this war. She could find out about soldiers' experiences by reading personal stories about the Gulf War at *The Memory Archive* (memoryarchive.org). When researching your topic, you should try to find information from the following three types of sources:

Online Sources. Use Internet search engines to find information that might help you understand the people or situations in your memoir. This information can be especially helpful if you are recounting an experience from a time when you were very young and had little or no awareness of what was happening in the world. Understanding the historical context better might help you to frame your memoir. Or maybe you could find information on psychology Web sites that could help explain your behavior or the behavior you witnessed.

Print Sources. At your campus or public library, look for newspapers or magazines that might have reported something about the event you are describing. Or you can find historical information in magazines from the period or a history textbook. These resources can help you explain the conditions that shaped how people behaved.

Empirical Sources. Research doesn't only happen on the Internet and in the library. Interview people who were involved with the events you are describing in your memoir. If possible, revisit the place you are writing about. Write down any observations, describe things as they are now, and look for details that you might have forgotten or missed.

Organizing and Drafting Your Memoir

To create a good memoir, you will need to go through a series of drafts in order to discover what your theme is, how you want to recount the events, what tone will work best, and so forth. So don't worry about doing it "correctly" as you write your first, or even your second, draft. Just try to write out your story. When you revise, you can work on making it all hold together.

Setting the Scene in Rich Detail

Start out by telling the whole story without worrying too much about the structure you will use. At first, you might just describe what happened. Then, once you have the basic series of events written down, start adding in as much detail as you can. Write as much as you can. Be sure to give rich descriptions of people, places, and things.

The People. What did your characters do that hints at who they are? What did they say? How did they behave? What were their blind spots? What did they care about, and what were they ambivalent about?

The Scenes. What did each scene look like? How did it feel or smell? What did you taste or hear? What is the history of this place—both its public history and your personal history?

Dialogue. What was said before and after the event? Who said what to whom? How did they say it? Were they angry? excited? thrilled? scared?

These kinds of details are some of the most important features of your memoir. Your memoir will be more realistic if you give the readers enough detail to reconstruct the scene, people, and events for themselves.

Describing the Complication

The *complication* in your memoir is the problem or challenge that you or others needed to resolve. So pay special attention to figuring out how this complication came about and why people reacted to it in a particular way.

The Event. What exactly happened? Who did it and what did they do? Was the event sudden or did it take a long time to develop?

The Complication. What was really at stake here? What was the essential conflict or complication that caused this story to be something more than an everyday event? How did you or the other people in the story feel about that tension?

The Immediate Reaction. How did people react to the event? What were their emotions? What did their reaction look like? Did they do anything that they later regretted?

Evaluating and Resolving the Complication

After the initial reaction, you should show how you and others evaluated and resolved the complication. The complication isn't necessarily a problem that needs to be fixed. Instead, you should show how the people involved tried to make sense of the complication, reacted to the change, and moved forward.

The Evaluation. What did you and other people think was happening? Were there any misunderstandings? Did you talk about the appropriate ways to respond? Did you or others come up with a plan?

The Resolution. What did you decide to do? Were you successful in resolving the complication, or partially successful? If so, how did you handle it? If you weren't successful, how did you make changes to adjust to the new situation? How did other people make adjustments?

Concluding with a Point

Your conclusion describes, directly or indirectly, not only what you learned but also what your reader should have learned from your experiences. You should avoid writing a "and the moral of the story is . . ." or a "they lived happily ever after" ending, but you should strive for something that feels like the events or people reached some kind of closure.

Your conclusion is where you are going to make your point. For example, you might state it directly, as in Wang Ping's "Book War" at the end of this chapter:

> When I saw stars rising from their eyes, I knew I hadn't lost the battle. The books had been burnt, but the story went on.

If, however, you think your point is obvious to readers, you can leave it unstated. In these situations, you can give readers a glimpse into the future. Or you can provide a final sentence or passage that hints at your memoir's meaning, as Joe Mackall does in his memoir, "Words of My Youth," which appears at the end of this chapter:

> An excellent question. I honestly do not know. I have no idea. The slur just seems to have been out there, there and somehow not there, like incense, like the way a Wiffle ball whips and dips, the way adults laugh at things kids don't understand, the way background noise from a baseball game leaks out of

transistor radios, the way bits of gravel bounce out of pickup truck beds, the way factory fires flirt with the night sky, the way sonic booms burst the lie of silence.

Whether your main point is stated directly or unstated, your readers should come away from your memoir with a clear sense of what you wanted them to learn from your experience.

Choosing an Appropriate Style

A memoir's style and tone depends on how you want to portray yourself as the narrator of the story. Choose a style that works for you, your story, and your reader. If you want your narrator (you) to have a casual attitude, that's the style and tone you want to strive for. If the narrator's relationship to the story is more formal, then the style will be more formal.

Evoking an Appropriate Tone

Tone refers to the attitude, or stance, that is taken toward the subject matter and the reader. That is, a certain "tone of voice" arises from the words on a page. For instance, in the story about Binky and Toodles, Alisa Harris uses an ironic tone (a sort of fake reverence or piety) to draw the reader in on a private joke at the expense of her parents and their concerns about "strong moral fiber." Wang Ping's tone in the memoir at the end of this chapter is serious and sincerely reverent, which mirrors the author's attitude about books, stories, and their power.

At times, whether you're writing the first draft or polishing your final draft, you may want to strategically establish a certain tone. Here's how to do it with concept mapping. First think of a key word that describes the tone you want to set. Then, put that word in the middle of your screen or a piece of paper and circle it (Figure 4.3). Now create a concept map around that key word. Write down any words that you tend to associate with this tone. Then, as you put words on the screen or paper, try to come up with more words that are associated with these new words. Eventually, you will fill the screen or sheet.

In the draft of your memoir, look for places where you can use these words. If you use them strategically throughout the memoir, your readers will sense the tone, or attitude. This will help you develop your central "theme," the idea or question that the entire memoir explores. You only need to use these words sparingly to achieve the effect you want. If you use too many of these words, your readers will sense that you are overdoing it, because your tone will be too strong.

Using Dialogue

Allow the characters in your memoir to reveal key details about themselves through dialogue rather than your narration. Use dialogue occasionally to reveal themes and ideas that are *key* to understanding your memoir. Here are some guidelines for using dialogue effectively:

Use Dialogue to Further the Story. Anytime you use dialogue, the story should move forward. Dialogues between characters are key moments that should change the flow of the story in an important way.

Write the Way Your Characters Speak. People often don't speak in proper English, grammatical sentences, or full thoughts. When using dialogue, take advantage of opportunities to show how people really talk.

Trim the Extra Words. In real dialogue, people often say more than they need to say. You can trim out the unnecessary details, most of the "ums" and "ahs," and the repetitions. Your dialogue should be as crisp and tight as possible.

Identify Who Is Talking. The readers should know who is talking, so make sure you use dialogue tags (e.g., *he said, she said, he growled, she yelled*). Not every statement needs a dialogue tag; however, if you leave off the tag, make sure it's obvious who said the line.

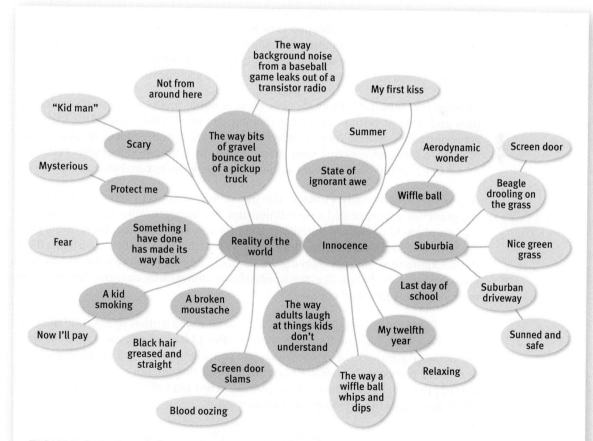

FIGURE 4.3 Creating a Tone with a Concept Map

A concept map is a good tool for helping you set a tone in your memoir. Simply choose the words or phrases that best describe the tone you are looking for and create a concept map around them. Here, a concept map around the ideas of "innocence" and "reality of the world" are in the center, with other word and phrase clusters surrounding them.

Create Unique Voices for Characters. Each of your characters should sound different. You can vary their tone, cadence, dialects, or style to give them each a unique voice.

Be careful not to overuse dialogue in your memoir. The most compelling way to use dialogue is when you want characters to reveal something about themselves but you don't want to come out and say, "This is what this person thought."

What if you cannot remember what people actually said? Is it ethical to present your best but imperfect memories of that dialogue? Clearly, all memories are filtered and do not exactly capture what really happened. So, as long as you remain true to what you remember, you can invent some of the details and still write ethically.

Designing Your Memoir

Memoirs, like almost all genres today, can use visual design to reinforce the written text. You can augment and deepen your words with images or sound. For instance, if you are writing about something that happened to you in the third grade, you might include an image of yourself and a third-grade friend, or you might include images and sound from national events that were occurring at that time.

Choose the Medium. To guide your choices about media, strategically weigh the pros and cons of various media for helping you reach your intended readers and achieving your purpose. Your intended readers might be more moved by an audio file of you reading and enacting your memoir than by a written document. Perhaps a movie or a multimedia document would better allow you to convey your ideas.

Add Visuals, Especially Photos. Use one or more photos to make or emphasize a key point, set a tone, or add a new dimension. For instance, Alisa Harris chose to include a photo of one of her buffalo. This photo only reinforces the ironic tone: Does the farm look like it's on the frontier? Does the buffalo (with the llama—a llama?!—in the background seemingly dancing on its back) appear to be ranging on the wild open prairie? The photo, like the words Harris strategically employs, increases the memoir's ironic tone and message.

Find a Place to Publish. You might want to go a step further to get your story out there. Web sites, like the *Memory Archive,* offer places where you can share your memories (Figure 4.4). Otherwise, you might consider putting your memoirs on a blog or on your *Facebook* or *MySpace* page. Remember, though, not to reveal information publicly that might embarrass you or put you at any kind of risk. Save your most personal information and photographs for yourself.

Revising and Editing Your Memoir

A good memoir is lean, with little or no fat. After drafting and gathering feedback from your classmates, professor, and/or friends and family, work toward a final draft that is as polished as possible. Cut out anything that does not advance the story or help you develop your characters or message.

FIGURE 4.4 The Memory Archive

The Memory Archive is a great place to publish your memoir or read others' memoirs. Go to www.memoryarchive.org.

Make Your Title Enticing. Keep trying out new titles. Work toward a title that both sounds interesting to a reader who knows nothing about your memoir and captures something essential about your story. Try reading through your memoir to find an arresting image or statement that you can turn into a title.

Craft the Perfect Lead. Look at your lead, the beginning sentence or short paragraph that is supposed to capture the readers' interest. A compelling lead casts your readers into the drama of your memoir and makes them lean forward with questions they hope your memoir will answer. Does it introduce some idea or question that is important to the memoir's point? Does it focus down to an important image, idea, or point? Does it set the right tone for the rest of the memoir? You can turn to Chapter 19, "Drafting Introductions and Conclusions," for more ideas about crafting your lead.

Reevaluate the Details and Cut the Fat. Look at every aspect of the memoir—the narrative, the dialogue, the setting—and take out what is not absolutely necessary. Long stories are simply boring. When it comes to storytelling, less is often more. Provide your readers with just enough detail and character development to make them want to keep reading.

The revision and editing phase is where you are going to take your story from interesting to compelling. So leave plenty of time to rework your ideas and words. In some cases, you might need to "re-vision" your whole memoir because you figure out something important as you are writing. If so, have the courage to make those changes. The effort will be worth it.

The Literacy Narrative

The literacy narrative is a kind of memoir that focuses on how the author learned to read and write or on some formative experience that involved writing and speaking. Literacy narratives usually have all the elements of other memoirs. They don't just recount a series of events, but carefully work those events into a plot with a complication. Quite often, the author describes overcoming some obstacle, perhaps the quest for literacy itself or the need to overcome some barrier to learning. Literacy narratives describe a transformation or take readers through a narrative that ends with a new understanding, insight, or question to ponder.

Literacy narratives are distinguished from other memoirs by a single feature: they focus on the author's experiences with reading and writing. Keep in mind that "literacy" encompasses more than learning to read and form letters on the traditional printed page. New writing situations are emerging due to new contexts, readers, purposes, and media. Learning to negotiate among these readers and situations is the real challenge of becoming literate in today's world. What literacy *is* constantly changes. New situations, technologies, and other changes require each of us to constantly acquire new literacy skills. All of these challenges are fair game for a literacy narrative.

Literacy narratives should have all the features described in this chapter's Overview on page 38. Be sure to pay attention to the conflict or tension: What challenge did you face and how did you resolve it—or fail to resolve it? Also, how did the experience change you? What new understanding (positive or negative) did you come away with? And finally, think about the larger theme: What significance does your story have, and what does it tell readers about literacy or what questions does it encourage your readers to reflect on?

WRITE **your own literacy narrative.** Remember that "literacy" includes a broad range of activities, skills, knowledge, and situations. Choose a significant incident or set of related incidents in your life that involved coming to terms with literacy. Write your literacy narrative as a memoir, paying attention to the memoir's features. Possible subjects include:

- encountering a new kind of literacy, and the people involved
- working with or helping others with literacy issues
- encountering a new communication technology
- a situation where your literacy skills were tested
- a particular book, work of literature, or other communication that changed your outlook

From *Narrative of the Life of Frederick Douglass*

Frederick Douglass

In the following excerpt from one of the best-known literacy narratives ever written, Douglass describes his determination as a young slave in America to become literate, even though the effort put him in grave personal danger.

I lived in Master Hugh's family about seven years. During this time, I succeeded in learning to read and write. In accomplishing this, I was compelled to resort to various stratagems. I had no regular teacher. My mistress, who had kindly commenced to instruct me, had, in compliance with the advice and direction of her husband, not only ceased to instruct, but had set her face against my being instructed by any one else. . . . The plan which I adopted, and the one by which I was most successful, was that of making friends of all the little white boys whom I met in the street. As many of these as I could, I converted into teachers. With their kindly aid, obtained at different times and in different places, I finally succeeded in learning to read. When I was sent of errands, I always took my book with me, and by going one part of my errand quickly, I found time to get a lesson before my return. I used also to carry bread with me, enough of which was always in the house, and to which I was always welcome; for I was much better off in this regard than many of the poor white children in our neighborhood. This bread I used to bestow upon the hungry little urchins, who, in return, would give me that more valuable bread of knowledge. I am strongly tempted to give the names of two or three of those little boys, as a testimonial of the gratitude and affection I bear them; but prudence forbids;—not that it would injure me, but it might embarrass them; for it is almost an unpardonable offence to teach slaves to read in this Christian country. It is enough to say of the dear little fellows, that they lived on Philpot Street, very near Durgin and Bailey's ship-yard. I used to talk this matter of slavery over with them. I would sometimes say to them, I wished I could be as free as they would be when they got to be men. "You will be free as soon as you are twenty-one, *but I am a slave for life!* Have not I as good a right to be free as you have?" These words used to trouble them; they would express for me the liveliest sympathy, and console me with the hope that something would occur by which I might be free.

Douglass introduces the complication.

The scene is set, while background information is provided up front.

Vivid descriptions of people and places.

Douglass shows how he resolved the conflict.

The conclusion reveals the larger point of the narrative: the injustice of slavery.

Here's one basic approach for creating an engaging memoir that makes a point.

CHOOSE the Event or Series of Events You Want to Write About

Use the brainstorming exercises to come up with a list of events and choose the one that could become an effective memoir.

QUESTION Your Memory About the Event(s)

Figure out what you know and what can you imagine about the event. What can you find out about the place, the objects in that place, and the people and what they did?

DO Some Research

If you want to find out more about the time, the place, or a person in your memoir, do some background research to find out what things were really like.

DRAFT the Story

Write the story, including all the events that relate to it. Describe people, their actions, and places with rich and vivid detail.

FIND the Message or Theme

Reflect on what you've written and decide what "theme" you want this story to evoke for your readers. "Pets and people" is a topic not a theme; "To what degree can pets replace people in our lives?" is a theme.

DEVELOP an Appropriate Tone or Voice

Develop your narrator's voice and use dialogue to add different voices to your story.

EDIT the Story to Its Essentials

When you ask yourself, *What is essential to the theme of my memoir?* you'll probably end up cutting a lot out of your original draft. Good memoirs are to the point; they should include only what is essential.

Book War

WANG PING

In this memoir, author Wang Ping writes about learning to read and growing up during the Cultural Revolution, a tumultuous time in Chinese history. As you read, pay attention to how she uses even simple events to draw out meaning and relevance.

I discovered "The Little Mermaid" in 1968. That morning, when I opened the door to light the stove to make breakfast, I found my neighbor reading under a streetlight. The red plastic wrap indicated it was Mao's collected work. She must have been there all night long, for her hair and shoulders were covered with frost, and her body shivered from cold. She was sobbing quietly. I got curious. What kind of person would weep from reading Mao's words? I walked over and peeked over her shoulders. What I saw made me shiver. The book in her hands had nothing to do with Mao; it was Hans Christian Andersen's fairy tales, and she was reading "The Little Mermaid," the story that had lit my passion for books since my kindergarten. I had started school a year earlier so that I could learn how to read the fairy tales by myself. By the end of my first grade, however, the Cultural Revolution began. Schools were closed, libraries sealed. Books, condemned as "poisonous weeds," were burnt on streets. And I had never been able to get hold of "The Little Mermaid."

My clever neighbor had disguised Andersen's "poisonous weed" with the scarlet cover of Mao's work. Engrossed in the story, she didn't realize my presence behind her until I started weeping. She jumped up, fairy tales clutched to her budding chest. Her panic-stricken face said she was ready to fight me to death if I dared to report her. We stared at each other for an eternity. Suddenly she started laughing, pointing at my tear-stained face. She knew then that her secret was safe with me.

She gave me 24 hours to read the fairy tales, and I loaned her *The Arabian Nights,* which was missing the first fifteen pages and the last story. But the girl squealed and started dancing in the twilight. When we finished each other's books, we started an underground book group with strict rules for safety, and we had books to read almost every day, all "poisonous" classics.

Soon I excavated a box of books my mother had buried beneath the chicken coop. I pried it open with a screwdriver, and pulled out one treasure after another: *The Dream of the Red Chamber, The Book of Songs, Grimm's Fairy Tales, The Tempest, The Hunchback of Notre Dame, Huckleberry Finn, American Dream,* each wrapped with waxed paper to keep out moisture.

I devoured them all, in rice paddies and 5 wheat fields, on my way home from school and errands. I tried to be careful. If I got caught, the consequence would be catastrophic, not only for myself, but also for my entire family. But my mother finally discovered I had unearthed her treasure box, and set out to destroy these "time bombs"—if I was caught reading these books, the whole family would be destroyed. She combed every possible place in the house: in the deep of drawers, under the mattress and floor boards. It was a hopeless battle: my mother knew every little trick of mine. Whenever she found a book, she'd order me to tear the pages and place them in the stove, and she'd sit nearby watching, tears in her eyes. And my heart, our hearts, turned into cinder.

When the last book went, I sat with my chickens. Hens and roosters surrounded me, pecking at my closed fists for food. As tears flowed, the Little Mermaid became alive from inside. She stepped onto the sand, her feet bled terribly, and she could not speak, yet how her eyes sang with triumph. Burning with a fever similar to the Little Mermaid's, I started telling stories to my siblings, friends, and neighbors—stories I'd read from those forbidden treasures, stories I made up for myself and my audience. We gathered on summer nights, during winter darkness. When I saw stars rising from their eyes, I knew I hadn't lost the battle.

The books had been burnt, but the story went on.

A CLOSER LOOK AT
Book War

1. What happens to the reader in the first paragraph? Pretend you are reading in slow motion and pinpoint the moment at which some detail draws you in to surprise you. Is it effective?

2. Make a list of the events that occur. What happens in each scene? What changes in each scene? How do these events work together to form a plot?

3. What is the complication in "Book War"? What is at stake in this memoir, and whose values does the narrator struggle with? In the resolution of the story, whose values win out in the end, and how clear is that resolution?

IDEAS FOR
Writing

1. Which of your family's stories do you remember most? Freewrite for five minutes, telling this story. Be sure to note details about the setting and characters. What happened? What did it mean to you then, and what does it mean to you now?

2. Memoirs like "Book War" are sometimes called "literacy narratives." They tell the story of learning to read or write, or they tell the story of coming to grips with some new aspect of literacy—for example, the power of stories to make change, the promise of literacy and education for achieving one's dreams, and so on. What is your literacy narrative? Write a brief memoir in which you tell a story about how you learned to read and/or write.

Words of My Youth

JOE MACKALL

Joe Mackall is an author of books about culture and his own life. In this memoir, he talks about growing up in the suburbs. Notice how his voice seems to emerge from the text as he tells his story.

I stand at the edge of my suburban driveway on Fairlawn Drive, sunned and safe. My friend Mick and I play Wiffle ball. Each swing of the bat sends the ball flying into the mystery grip of physics and aerodynamic wonder. The ball appears headed straight up before some hidden hand of wind and speed and serrated plastic jerks it over to the lawn of the widow next door. Mrs. Worth's boxer drools the day away, watching from the backyard in its own state of ignorant awe.

We take turns "smacking the shit" out of the plastic ball. I don't notice, not right away, an older kid—a man really—walking down the other side of the street, his eyes straight ahead. Not from around here. As the kid-man gets closer, I focus more intently on the game, as if this focus will protect me from what's about to happen. I chase the ball as if catching it matters more than anything, more than my first kiss or my last day of school. I make careful throws, keeping my eye on the ball, trying to anticipate the direction of its flight and fall.

I fear—as I so often fear—that something I have done has found its way back to me. And now I'll pay. Five or six houses away now, the kid-man crosses the street. He's not from around here, but I recognize him from somewhere. There's something in the way the kid-man never looks around, as if his entire world centers on a horizon only he can see. He's smoking. Not a good sign. I pick the ball up off the boxer's drool-wet lawn, wipe the drool on my jeans, and toss it a few feet in the air. When I look up I see the kid-man—black hair

greased and straight, a broken mustache, patches of dirt and beard—punch Mick in the nose. Mick bends over and covers his nose with cupped hands in one motion. Blood oozes through his summer-stained fingers and drips onto the hot cement. Although the kid-man—eighteen, nineteen, probably—has just punched Mick in the face, I'm stunned stupid when the kid-man walks over to me and slams me in the nose. We run to the porch.

"My girlfriend's not a dyke," the kid-man says, as he lights a new cigarette from the old and walks off.

It's true. We have called the man's girlfriend a dyke. Often and repeatedly. But still, standing behind the harsh-sounding, cool-sounding word with blood dripping from my nose, I who only a minute ago was playing Wiffle ball on a summer afternoon, realize I cannot define nor do I understand the word we all so love to use.

II

Again on the Wiffle ball driveway, also summer, also my twelfth year, I call one of my Gentile friends a dumb Jew. Soon all of us revel in the discovery of this new slur. This new way of degrading each other catches on quickly. Not one of the Catholic boys schooled in the Judeo-Christian tradition is sure why calling somebody a dumb Jew is derogatory. But we celebrate this new slur anyway. But wait. Wasn't Jesus a Jew? Isn't Bill Rosenberg a Jew? We all love Bill. This must be something else. It sounds different. It sounds like it shouldn't be said. So we say it and love saying it, we boys without weapons.

The screen door slams. My mother has caught the sound of the slur. She motions for me to come inside. "Tell your friends to go home," she says. I do not have to. They're gone. This is 1971, and the suburbs. Somebody's parent is everybody's parent. Parents stick together. They know who the real enemy is.

She grabs my hair and pulls me into the house. Inside my head I'm screaming.

I do not say a word.

"What did you say out there? What were 10 you saying?"

I understand that my mother knows the answer to her questions. I realize I had better not repeat what I said outside, not even in answer to her questions. I know she never wants to hear that again. Not ever. Not from me. Not from anybody.

"Where did you ever hear a thing like that? That kind of talk?" she asks.

An excellent question. I honestly do not know. I have no idea. The slur just seems to have been out there, there and somehow not there, like incense, like the way a Wiffle ball whips and dips, the way adults laugh at things kids don't understand, the way background noise from a baseball game leaks out of transistor radios, the way bits of gravel bounce out of pickup truck beds, the way factory fires flirt with the night sky, the way sonic booms burst the lie of silence.

A CLOSER LOOK AT
Words of My Youth

1. A memoir doesn't just recount events but selects and arranges those events into a "plot" that helps the reader infer causation, or a sense of what causes what. There seem to be two stories here, but is there a single plot? What single question or theme is evoked from this plot? Outline the two stories and show how they follow a single plot.

2. In this memoir, the Wiffle ball is more than an object that the narrator and his friends throw and smack. The Wiffle ball itself—the actual object and the way it behaves when it is thrown—serves as a symbol of some other idea or problem. How is the Wiffle ball used to illustrate other concepts in this memoir? Examine the memoir's final sentence closely.

3. Compare the ending of "Words of My Youth" with the ending of "Book War" or the ending of "Binky and Toodles: A Frontier Saga." How do the endings differ and how do they help the memoirs achieve their purposes?

IDEAS FOR
Writing

1. Explain the purpose of "Words of My Youth." What theme or question is Mackall encouraging readers to explore with him? Try to articulate that question or theme in a single sentence. Write a one-page response in which you identify that question and explain what Mackall wants readers to take away from his memoir.

2. Mackall chooses to use strong and perhaps offensive language, and to describe violent events and offensive behavior. In a one-page response to this memoir, discuss whether you feel the language and events were warranted, considering what you believe is the central theme/question of the story.

1. Ask each member of your group to tell a funny story about himself or herself (something PG-13, please). After each person tells his or her story, compare the organization of the story to the typical organization of a memoir. What are some of the similarities and differences between these funny stories and memoirs?

2. With a group of people in your class, talk about the physical space where you did a lot of your learning in elementary school. Is there a classroom or other space prominent in your memories? Describe sensory details: how the furniture was arranged, who sat or stood where, the background noises, perhaps even the smells of that place.

3. Do some people who don't really know you have a false idea about who you are? Perhaps it's an impression or image that you yourself have adopted, encouraged, or just never bothered to correct. Describe this mistaken or alternative impression of yourself that some people hold to your group. Tell a story that illustrates the "you" others see, and how that image or impression just doesn't capture the real you.

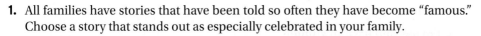

1. All families have stories that have been told so often they have become "famous." Choose a story that stands out as especially celebrated in your family.

   a. Briefly relate that story. If you're writing the story, make it less than 300 words; if you're telling it in a small group, make it less than three minutes.

   b. Now explain (in writing or orally) *why* that story is a favorite. What does it *mean* to those who tell it? Does it mean the same thing for everyone involved? *When* is it told? What purpose does it serve? What *point* does it make about your family—what is its significance? Do different people draw different meanings from the story? What general *theme* does it evoke, and why is that theme important for your family?

2. Find a memoir in a book or magazine, or on the Internet. Think about how changing the intended audience and/or the medium might help the memoir reach a different set of readers. What other medium would you choose, and how would you alter the original memoir to adapt it to this medium?

3. Authors write memoirs because they have a point they want to get across to their readers. If you wanted to "repurpose" your memoir to, say, a profile, a proposal, or a research report, how might you do it? How would its angle and purpose change? When you change genres, the nature of the text changes. The readers themselves may change and their expectations change significantly; tone needs to change, as does style and many other factors. List specifically what would change if you used a different genre to handle the subject of your memoir.

1. **Write a memoir.** Write a five-page memoir in which you explore your relationship with another member of your family. Choose an event or series of events that could illustrate that relationship and explore its tensions. Identify a complication or a struggle of values. Then show how you and this other family member evaluated the complication and resolved it. End your memoir by telling your readers what you learned from this experience.

2. **Create a map or a storyboard.** Create a map or a storyboard and write a three-page memoir about a specific event in your life. Develop your memoir by paying special attention to the scene, the people, and the events (actions, dialogue, thoughts) that make up the plot. Be sure that your memoir evokes some significant message or theme that you want your reader to understand.

3. **Write a "six-word memoir."** A six-word memoir tries to tell a story in just six words. For instance, when the famous writer Ernest Hemingway was challenged to tell a story in just six words, he responded: "For sale: baby shoes, never worn." *Smith Magazine* challenged famous and unknown writers to contribute and received over 11,000 responses, some of which were collected in *Not Quite What I Was Planning: Six-Word Memoirs by Writers Famous and Obscure*. Here are a few of them:

   - I'm ten, and have an attitude.
   - Anything's possible with an extension cord.
   - Revenge is living well, without you.
   - My reach always exceeds my grasp.
   - Never should have bought that ring.
   - Found true love after nine months.

mycomplab

For additional reading, writing, and research resources, go to **www.mycomplab.com.**

Profiles

Profiles are used to describe interesting people, their significance, and their contributions. They are not full-blown life stories. Instead, profiles try to create a snapshot of a person by taking a specific, focused angle that allows the writer to capture something essential—an insight, idea, theme, or social cause. Some of the best profiles focus on people who seem ordinary but are representative of a larger issue.

When writing a profile, you should strive to reveal a fundamental quality of your subject. Keep this question in mind: "What larger idea about this person do I want to emerge from the profile?" For instance, if you are writing a profile of someone from your hometown (e.g., the mayor, a coach, or a family member), you would want to show what makes this person unique or special in some way. You want to make him or her representative of something greater.

Profiles appear in a variety of print and online publications. They are common in magazines like *People, Rolling Stone,* and *Time.* Web sites like *Slate.com, National Review Online,* and *Politico* regularly feature profiles. They are also mainstays on cable channels like ESPN, the History Channel, and the Biography Channel.

In college and in your career, you will likely need to write profiles about others and yourself for corporate Web sites, brochures, reports, and proposals. Profiles are sometimes called backgrounders, biographies, or bios, and they appear under titles like "About Us" or "Our Team." And, finally, you might want to write your own profile for social networking sites like *Facebook, MySpace,* or *LinkedIn.*

Profiles

Here are two possible organizational patterns for writing a profile. The pattern on the left is good for describing your subject. The pattern on the right is best for telling a story about your subject. Other arrangements of these sections will work, too. You should organize your profile to fit your topic, angle, purpose, readers, and context.

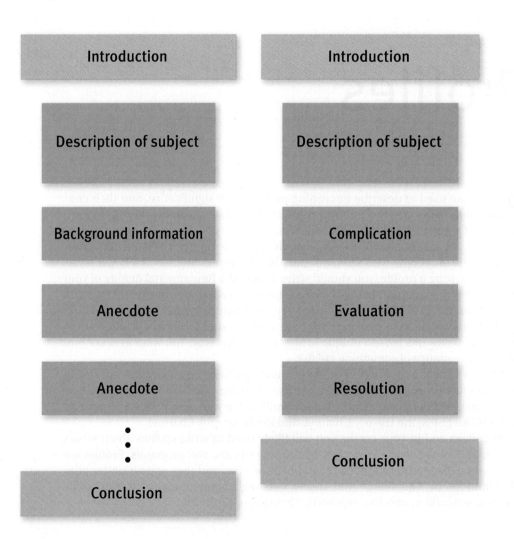

Introduction

Description of subject

Background information

Anecdote

Anecdote

⋮

Conclusion

Introduction

Description of subject

Complication

Evaluation

Resolution

Conclusion

Overview

Profiles paint a portrait or tell a story. That portrait or story can stick to the basic facts (as in a biographical sketch) or provide an intimate depiction of the subject. Profiles have some or all of these features:

- **A person** whose experiences allow you to explore a topic, issue, idea, or theme that is interesting to you and your readers.

- **An interesting angle** that captures a single dominant impression about the subject.

- **A description of the person** that allows readers to visualize and imagine him or her.

- **Background information** that describes the setting or broader social context in which the subject lives and works.

- **Anecdotes** that reveal this person's character through actions and dialogue.

- **A theme,** or larger central issue about the subject and his or her world that goes beyond the surface and factual details to larger questions. Most profiles examine not only the actual person but also what the person stands for or typifies. Sometimes this theme involves some sort of tension or an important question, which the profile provokes readers into pondering.

ONE STUDENT'S WORK
Profiles

Brother, Life Coach, Friend

Katie Koch

On a spring morning at a Boston high school, Wyatt Posig, a caseworker in the Massachusetts Department of Youth Services, has some good news for Chris, an affable seventeen-year-old with a sleepy smile and an armed robbery conviction. Posig thinks he may have found Chris an office job for the summer.

There's only one problem—the internship calls for business attire. Posig has been trying to get clothing vouchers for Chris, whose wardrobe runs to the type of oversized checked shirts and baggy pants he's wearing today. "I might have some ties for you," Posig says. Chris shrugs indifferently at the dilemma. (Some names and details have been changed.)

> The profile starts by setting a scene showing subject at work, what he *does*.

continued

It wasn't too long ago that Posig was an intern himself. Now, just a year out of college, he is one of a handful of caseworkers assigned to a pilot program designed to give Boston's juvenile offenders some much-needed support as they leave detention centers and reenter their communities. In search of a better way to cut recidivism, the state introduced the program last year, tweaking a model

Photo by Kathleen Dooher.

developed by the National Center on Addiction and Substance Abuse at Columbia University. Each of Boston's neighborhood community centers now has a dedicated caseworker to act as a consistent presence in these troubled kids' lives: an amalgam of older brother, life coach, negotiator, and friend. For Dorchester's teens, that person is Posig.

He started prepping for the role years ago, studying sociology at BU and coordinating the Big Siblings program. He worked summer internships at the Department for Children and Families in his hometown of Burlington, Vermont. "I've always known I wanted to work with young people in this situation," Posig says. "I really thrive on being able to help them out. And for whatever reason, I've been able to connect with kids really easily my entire life."

It helps that he could almost pass for a teenager. Tall and lanky, with a smattering of freckles and a dark red beard, he sticks to a uniform of loose shirts and jeans. He spends most of his day checking up on his clients, taking them to dental appointments, or letting the kids vent to him in his office. For the ten boys in his caseload, none of whom have fathers living at home, Posig is a role model, but not in the traditional sense.

"The other caseworkers are the parent figures," he says. "I'm more of a brother. The difficult part is that you want to be the kids' friend, but you also want to get that respect"—a hard thing to earn as the youngest guy in the office. But Posig brings a youthful energy to the Dorchester Community Reentry Center: he leads the daily staff meeting, chats up his coworkers, and—perhaps a first for world-weary social workers—does it all without caffeine. (He's never had a cup of coffee, he says.)

"I turned twenty-three yesterday," Posig says. "But none of the kids knows that."

Curtis, one of the center's charges, just celebrated a birthday as well. There were no parties, as Posig and coworker Sheila Cooper learn when they visit him that afternoon at Casa Isla, a lockup in Quincy for twenty boys ages

eleven to seventeen. Curtis arrives in the visitors' room, and Cooper and Posig quickly assume their roles: Cooper, the tough-love veteran caseworker, and Posig, the tentative, encouraging upstart. "It's good to see you," Posig says. "It's not good to see you locked up, but it's good to see you."

Cooper starts to grill him: why did he call them down for a meeting? "I miss y'all," Curtis finally confesses. Just seven days away from his release, the fifteen-year-old is tense. "Don't tell the other kids you're waiting to get out," Posig advises, "or they'll test you." He later explains that it's not uncommon for an offender to slip up near the end of a sentence, back for a new crime just weeks after being let out. When Curtis is released, Posig's task will be to help him navigate the everyday challenges of school, family, and work that can make life on the inside seem relatively easy—even desirable.

Still, Posig is optimistic about Curtis's chances, perhaps more so than Curtis himself. In the year he's been on the job, he's witnessed success stories: one of his kids has never missed a day of work, and another recently made the honor roll. His attitude, he hopes, is contagious.

Inventing Your Profile's Content

Begin by choosing a person who is fascinating to you and who would be interesting to your readers. Although it's tempting to try to write about a celebrity, it is hard to get beyond the hype to the reality of his or her life. Instead, look for someone who is unique but not famous. Here are some possible places where you can find your subject:

- People who have influenced you

- Historical figures

- People you have met at work or while volunteering

- People you know through social and cultural groups

- People who are doing things that you would like to be doing one day

- People whose lifestyles are different or unusual

- People who have done something wrong

- A group of people rather than an individual

For a profile assignment in college, it is usually best to pick someone to whom you have access or someone about whom much information is already available. The key is finding a person who is interesting to *you,* because if you aren't interested in this person, you will find it very difficult to make him or her interesting to others.

Inquiring: Finding Out What You Already Know

Once you find your subject, take some time to think about what makes this person unique or interesting. Your aim is to find an angle that will depict your subject in a way that makes your profile interesting and meaningful. Use one or more of the following methods to generate ideas for your profile.

Answer the Five-W and How Questions.   Journalists often use the Five-W and How questions (who, what, where, when, why, how) to start generating ideas for a profile. Who is your subject? Who has been influenced by this person? Who is involved with this person regularly? What has your subject done that is especially interesting to you and your readers? Where did your subject come from? When and where did your subject do the things that interest you and your readers? Why does he or she think, look, or behave in unique ways? How does he or she react to other people and events? How does he or she move or talk? How did this person's origins shape his or her outlook on life?

Freewrite.   Darken your computer screen or take out a blank sheet of paper. Then, for about five minutes, write down everything you know about your subject without stopping. Write about what makes him or her interesting. Just write.

Use Cubing.   Cubing involves using writing to explore your subject from six different viewpoints or perspectives (Figure 5.1). *Describe* this person by paying attention to your senses. *Compare* him or her to someone or something else. *Associate* this person with related issues or things you already know about. *Analyze* this person, looking for any patterns, hidden questions, or unique characteristics. *Apply* your subject as a character by describing him or her in action. *Argue* for or against this person: Do you believe he or she is right or wrong, a saint or a scoundrel?

Try a few different prewriting and invention methods to draw out what you already know about this person. Chapter 14, "Inventing Ideas and Prewriting," describes some other methods you might try.

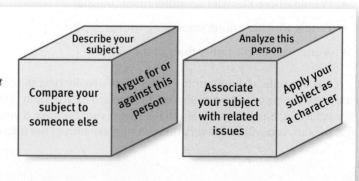

FIGURE 5.1 Using Cubing to Inquire About Your Subject

Cubing is a good way to study your subject from different viewpoints or perspectives. Each side of the cube urges you to see the person you are profiling somewhat differently, generating new ideas and insights.

Researching: Finding Out What Others Know

Good research is essential to writing an interesting profile. When you start researching your subject, you should begin by identifying a variety of online, print, and empirical sources.

Online Sources. Use an Internet search engine to gather biographical or historical information on this person. Then gather background information on the time period and place in which this person lives (or lived).

Print Sources. Consult newspapers, magazines, and books to find out about the time period and place in which this person lives (or lived). These print sources are probably available at your campus library or a local library.

Empirical Sources. Interview your subject and/or talk to people who know or knew this person. You might also ask your subject whether you can observe or even shadow him or her.

Interviewing. An interview is often the best way to gather information for a profile. If you want to do an interview, keep in mind that phone calls or e-mails are often good ways to ask people questions about themselves or others.

Remember to script your questions before your interview. Be sure to *listen and respond*—asking follow-up questions that engage with what the interviewee has told you. Some open-ended questions you might ask include:

- "What do you think is most interesting/important about what you do?"

- "In all, what did this experience mean for you, and what do you think it should mean for others?"

- "What's the most important idea you want people to understand about your story/work?"

Shadowing. If you decide to "shadow" your subject (with the person's permission, of course), you will learn more about your subject's world, the people in it, and how your subject interacts with them. Keep your notebook, a camera, and perhaps a digital recorder handy to capture anything that might translate into an interesting angle or a revealing quotation.

In Chapter 25, "Finding Sources and Collecting Information," you can learn more about interviewing and other empirical forms of research.

As you collect information, make sure you are using reliable sources. There is a great amount of gossip and misinformation out there, especially on the Internet. So anything you find should be confirmed by at least a few different sources. If something sounds too good (or too far-fetched) to be true, it probably is.

Organizing and Drafting Your Profile

The organization of a profile should help you draw readers in and keep their attention. As you organize your ideas and write your first draft, you should keep a couple of key questions in mind:

What do you find most interesting, surprising, or important? As you researched your subject, what did you discover that you weren't expecting? How can you make this discovery interesting for your readers?

What important conflicts does your subject face? People are most interesting when they are facing important challenges. What is the principal conflict for your subject? What is he or she trying to overcome?

Keep in mind that the profile is one of the most flexible genres. Don't feel as though the information needs to appear in any specific order. You can arrange the information you collected in a variety of ways to suit your topic, purpose, and readers and the contexts in which they will read the profile.

The Introduction

Get a quick, strong start with a lead that hints at or captures the theme of the profile. For instance, in her profile of Prudencia Martin Gomez at the end of this chapter, Jody Ipsen begins with a rich description of the Guatemalan jungle. Then she moves quickly toward the drama—the conflict—in which her subject is caught.

Your introduction should identify your subject, directly or indirectly reveal your purpose, and stress the importance of the subject. In some types of profiles, you might want to state a main point in the introduction and offer some immediate background on your subject.

Description of the Subject

Your readers should be able to visualize the person you are describing and perhaps sense that person in other ways. Use plenty of details to describe how this person looks, moves, and sounds. In some situations, you might describe how this person smells or would feel if touched.

Background on the Subject

As you describe your subject, you might also place him or her in a setting or tell your readers something about the time periods and places in which he or she lives or lived.

Anecdotes

Tell one or more stories that reveal your subject's character and beliefs. Your stories should also illustrate the theme or point of your profile.

Dialogue or Quotes

Keep your ears open for dialogue and quotable statements from your subject and from others, especially quotes that capture important ideas. Try to find dialogue or quotes that reflect your overall theme or your dominant impression of this person. However, don't overdo the use of dialogue or quotes. Because quotes receive special attention from readers, reserve them for ideas that are especially important.

The Conclusion

Profiles shouldn't just end; they should leave an impression. Because endings, like beginnings, get special notice from readers, your conclusion should include information, ideas, or images that you want to be prominent. You can end in almost any way so long as you leave your readers with an impression that will stay with them.

Choosing an Appropriate Style

If possible, the style of your profile should reflect your subject's personality and voice. For instance, if the person you are profiling is energetic and restless, you should use words that express that energy (e.g., dynamic, on the go, lively, brisk, vibrant), while using abruptly short sentences and phrases to quicken the readers' pace. But if you want your readers to perceive your subject's calm thoughtfulness, you might choose words that imply calm, while using longer sentences to slow down the pace.

For instance, in the student example above, Katie Koch's word choices and sentences echo her subject's "youthful energy."

> But Posig brings a youthful energy to the Dorchester Community Reentry Center: he leads the daily staff meeting, chats up his coworkers, and—perhaps a first for world-weary social workers—does it all without caffeine. (He's never had a cup of coffee, he says.)

Similarly, in the profile of Prudencia Martin Gomez at the end of this chapter, Jody Ipsen uses words that connote outrage and emotion to reflect the victims' feelings about the Guatemalan civil war. To punctuate these emotions, Ipsen uses brief clauses separated by semicolons; she repeats the word "they" again and again to build the pace. And she ends with a metaphor that merges the victims' grief with the Guatemalan jungle.

> At night the hills of Guatemala heave with grief. Slain victims of the dirty little war weep for their dead children; they cry of starvation and disease; they howl for the pregnant mothers whose babies were cut out of their bellies; they wail when the bullets were shot out of U.S. helicopters; they bawl as they bleed to death from their severed limbs by the cold blooded killers. In the morning the trees drip with tears where their families were hanged.

Quite differently, when she describes Prudencia, Ipsen's sentences are measured and matter of fact.

> Prudencia and Ismael were going to marry once he saved enough money to build them a home in Guatemala. Prudencia, with a petite frame and long black hair that flowed past her hips, had simple pleasures, like gazing at the stars and thinking of the promise of joining Ismael someday. In May of 2007, at the age of 19, she left Todos Santos to surprise her boyfriend, who was living somewhere in California. Like most migrants, she traveled with a coyote (guide), through the veins of Mexico's underground, avoiding immigration police and bandits who rob Central Americans. She then walked approximately fifty miles from the border of Sasabe, Mexico to the outskirts of Tucson, Arizona. With only a gallon of water and the clothes in her backpack, Prudencia trudged through the desert under the scorching summer sun for approximately four to five days. Coyotes often abandon the sick or injured migrants in order to get the remainder of their group across. She was later found dead by humanitarians who were notified by her boyfriend that she was left behind by the group.

This style allows the readers to meet Prudencia at a calmer, less intense pace.

You might find that the best way to develop a voice or tone in your profile is to imagine your subject's personality and feelings. Then put yourself into that character (develop a persona) and write from that perspective. Chapter 16, "Choosing a Style," offers some other strategies for developing a specific tone or voice in your writing.

Designing Your Profile

Profiles usually take on the design of the medium (e.g., magazine, newspaper, Web site, television documentary) in which they will appear. A profile written for a magazine or newspaper will look different than a profile written for a report or proposal. So as you think about the appropriate design for your profile, think about what would work with the kind of medium in which it will appear.

Using Photography.   When writing for any medium, consider using photographs of your subject, especially ones that reflect the theme of your profile. For example, the photograph of Wyatt Posig in Katie Koch's profile of him effectively portrays his personality and the place where he works. Posig looks serious but confident. He is pictured with the young men he works with, one of whom is diligently working on a math problem, while the others stare out the window.

Captions are helpful for explaining the picture and reinforcing the profile's theme. Captions can simply state the subject's name, describe a detail, or summarize. Captions might also include a direct quotation from your subject that you want your readers to notice.

Adding Pull Quotes or Breakouts.   Readers often skim profiles to see if the subject interests them. You want to stop them from skimming by giving them an access point into the text. One way to catch their attention is to use a pull quote or breakout that quotes something from the text. Pull quotes appear in a large font and are usually placed in the margins or a gap in the text. These kinds of quotes will grab the readers' attention and encourage them to start reading. You can turn to Chapter 17, "Designing," to learn more about using pull quotes and other page design features.

Revising and Editing Your Profile

Since your profile is talking about someone else's life, or perhaps your own, you want it to be as polished as possible. More than likely, your first draft will be a bit plain and static. Usually, it takes two or three drafts to bring forward the theme you want and the appropriate style.

Trim the Details That Do Not Advance Your Theme. Remember that this is a profile, not a life story. While details are important, make sure that you carefully choose only those details that advance the theme you want your readers to carry away. Unnecessary details will only distract your readers and blur your meaning.

Rethink the Organization. If your first drafts follow a strictly chronological sequence (e.g., "Babe Ruth was born on February 6, 1895 in . . ."), you might look for another organization that allows you to better highlight important facts about your subject. For instance, you might begin by building a setting before you introduce the person you are profiling. Maybe you want to tell an anecdote that helps you grab the readers.

Refine Your Voice. Your voice and tone are not going to emerge fully in your first draft. Professional writers know that, so they wait until the revision phase to sharpen these elements of their text. Try reading your profile out loud to yourself, or have someone read it to you. Mark places where your style seems flat. Then use better choices of words to enhance the voice and tone you are seeking.

Enhance and Amplify the Theme. Ultimately, the theme is what your readers will take a way from your profile. So trace the theme through your profile to make sure it plays a role in each part of your profile. In most cases, the theme will be most apparent in the conclusion, so make sure it is properly amplified at this point. You can use quotes to bring out this theme in the conclusion, or perhaps you might just come out and tell the readers what this person means to you.

Proofread. Don't let the person you are profiling down by leaving in a bunch of typos, spelling errors, and grammatical mistakes. Proofread your profile at least a few times to find those flaws that undermine the quality of your work.

The Résumé

At this point in your college career, it probably doesn't seem like you need a résumé—at least not for a few more years. Résumés, after all, are job-finding tools used to describe someone's background, experience, and qualifications to potential employers. Increasingly, though, résumés are being used for college-related purposes, like scholarships, applications, internships, and co-ops.

A résumé is a profile of yourself that usually fits on one page. Like a profile, your résumé offers some basic facts about your life. It should tell a story about your education, work experience, awards, and activities. Your résumé needs to make a good impression, because it is the first item your readers, including employers, will see.

For a college student or recent college graduate, the *archival résumé* is usually the most familiar and appropriate. It includes the following features:

Career objective. A career objective is a sentence or phrase that describes the career you are seeking.

Educational background. Your educational background should list your current college degree and any other degrees in reverse chronological order—most recent to least recent. List your major and minors. Sometimes career-related coursework is listed here.

Work experience. Any jobs, internships, or co-ops that you have held should be listed, starting with the most recent and working to the least recent.

Skills. Résumés often include a section that lists career-related skills, such as leadership training, computers, languages, bookkeeping, public speaking, and so on.

Awards and activities. List any awards you have earned and any organized activities in which you have participated. Scholarships can appear here.

References. Your references are the people who will vouch for you, including professors, current and former supervisors, and other professionals. In most résumés, the line "References available upon request" appears at the bottom of the page.

A résumé of a graduating college student is shown on page 69. She has a great amount to show, because she steadily worked on filling out her résumé while she was in college.

WRITE **your future résumé.** Write the résumé you would like to have when you graduate from college. Put down your degree, major, and the year you will graduate. List jobs, internships, and co-ops you would like to do before graduating. Identify the skills you want to develop while you are at college. List the activities you want to participate in while at college. Your résumé should fit on one page.

Anne Simmons Franklin

834 County Line Rd.
Hollings Point, Illinois 62905

Home: 618-555-2993
Mobile: 618-555-9167
E-mail: afranklin@unsb5.net

Name and
contact
information
placed up front.

CAREER OBJECTIVE

A position as a naturalist, specializing in agronomy, working for a distribution company that specializes in organic foods.

Career objective
describes
position sought.

EDUCATIONAL BACKGROUND

Bachelor of Science, Southern Illinois University, expected May 2010.
Major: Plant and Soil Science
Minor: Entomology
GPA: 3.2/4.0

WORK EXPERIENCE

Intern Agronomist, December 2009–August 2010
Brighter Days Organic Cooperative, Simmerton, Illinois

Work experience
is supported
with details.

- Consulted with growers on organic pest control methods. Primary duty was sale of organic crop protection products, crop nutrients, seed, and consulting services.
- Prepared organic agronomic farm plans for growers.
- Provided crop-scouting services to identify weed and insect problems.

Field Technician, August 2009–December 2009
Entomology Department, Southern Illinois University

- Collected and identified insects.
- Developed insect management plans.
- Tested organic and nonorganic pesticides for effectiveness and residuals.

SKILLS

Computer Experience: Access, Excel, Outlook, PowerPoint, and Word.
Global Positioning Systems (GPS). Database Management.
Machinery: Field Tractors, Combines, Straight Trucks, and Bobcats.
Communication Skills: Proposal Writing and Review, Public Presentations, Negotiating, Training, Writing Agronomic and Financial Farm Plans.

Skills are listed
separately for
emphasis.

AWARDS AND ACTIVITIES

Awarded "Best Young Innovator" by the Organic Food Society of America
Member of Entomological Society of America
Vice-President, Entomology Club, Southern Illinois University, 2008–present

Awards and
activities are
listed later in
the résumé.

REFERENCES AVAILABLE UPON REQUEST

Need to get going with your profile? Here are some ideas to help you start.

CHOOSE Someone Interesting to Write About

Find someone who is fascinating to you and would be interesting to your readers. The best subjects are people who are unique in some way or symbolic of something important.

FIGURE OUT What You Already Know About This Person

Use invention tools like the Five-W and How questions, freewriting, and cubing to study your subject from a variety of perspectives.

RESEARCH Your Subject

Find information about your subject on the Internet or in print sources. Also, if possible, interview your subject or people who know this person well.

DRAFT Your Profile

Start out strong by grabbing the readers in your introduction. Then, in the body of the profile, use ample detail to paint a portrait of this person. Avoid writing this person's complete life story. Instead, pick an event or series of anecdotes that capture your subject.

DEVELOP an Appropriate Style

The appropriate style for your profile usually reflects the personality or feelings of the person you are profiling. You can use word choice and sentence length to portray a specific voice or tone.

LOCATE Some Photographs, If Available

Look for photographs that illustrate the person and the theme at the heart of your profile.

STRESS the Theme

You want your profile to do more than simply describe someone. Use this person's life as a symbol of something larger or more significant. That's your theme.

REVISE and Edit

Always remember that this profile is about someone else's life. So do your best to clarify the content, straighten out the organization, and refine your writing style.

Prudencia

JODY L. IPSEN

*Jody Ipsen is a humanitarian worker for immigrant rights and a freelance writer. A
version of this piece appeared in a newspaper, the* Tucson Citizen, *titled "Immigration:
Why Prudencia Died." Ipsen is collecting her profiles and other work into a book,*
When the Women Wept: Cries from the Migrant Trail. *She has adapted one of her
book's chapters into this brief profile.*

The tropical jungle, dense with massive tree canopies, palm fronds, mango trees, red coffee berries, tangled vines and creeping ferns against the morning sun explodes like a massive jade from the land. The early morning fog casts the gem in a gauzy film, like an ephemeral phantom that flees when the Maya sun rises. Through the winding roads of the tropics to the highlands of Guatemala, shepherds, dressed in their red and blue trajes (clothing specific to their region) tend their sheep. Small fires coil in vertical rings and roosters rouse the sleep. It is hard to imagine that in 1982, plus or minus a few years, Todos Santos, a village in the clouds, was torched to the ground by U.S.-trained paramilitary, who also massacred thousands of indigenous men, women and children. The civil war that spilt the blood and cut the heads off of thousands continues to haunt the living.

At night the hills of Guatemala heave with grief. Slain victims of the dirty little war weep for their dead children; they cry of starvation and disease; they howl for the pregnant mothers whose babies were cut out of their bellies; they wail when the bullets were shot out of U.S. helicopters; they bawl as they bleed to death from their severed limbs by the cold blooded killers. In the morning the trees drip with tears where their families were hanged.

Unfortunately many men and women flee Guatemala despite the peace accord that was signed in 1996. Under the Freedom of Information Act, the CIA released documents of its covert operations during the Cold War. According to the CIA report titled *Sterilizing a "Red Infection,"* David M. Barret readily admits the United States' clandestine complicity in the civil war resulting in hundreds of thousands of deaths. During the Cold War, the CIA and the U.S. government gained tremendous currency by selling fear that Guatemala was a rising communist country.

Both John Dulles, former Secretary of State, and Allen Dulles, former Director of the CIA, played pivotal roles in the overthrow of the Guatemalan government. Allen Dulles was a shareholder in The United Fruit Company. His investments were threatened by the possible expropriation of land that President Jacobo Árbenz Guzmán wanted returned to peasant farmers.

In December of 1958, John Foster Dulles 5 said, "The United States of America does not have friends; it has interests." The interests of the United Fruit Company were of foremost importance despite an unforeseen turn of heinous events.

CIA documents reported that "Washington used the CIA and U.S. Ambassador John Peurifoy to support and direct certain Guatemalan military leaders in overthrowing Árbenz's government. It was also psychological warfare—cleverly deceptive efforts to persuade Guatemala's citizens and political/military leaders that a major invasion force was steadily moving toward the nation's capital. . . ."

Some eleven years later and thousands of miles away in the Sonoran desert, thirty-three concerned humanitarians caravanned along a dusty road to a remote region approximately twenty miles west of Tucson, Arizona. Discarded backpacks, filthy jeans, brittle water bottles and worn shoes spread across miles of greasewood, mesquite trees, and devil's claws. In the bed of a truck, Father Bob Carney covered his mouth and nose with a bandana to avoid choking on the fine dust that creates the stunning sunsets in Arizona. It was over 100 degrees at 5:30 PM and the heat burned our skin.

Prudencia Martin Gomez was from Todos Santos, Guatemala, a small Maya village in the Cuchumatanes Mountains. At nineteen, Prudencia was migrating to California to join her boyfriend, Ismael. She was abandoned by her group when she fell ill from dehydration and heat exposure. She died on June 15, 2007, in the Tucson Sector of the Sonoran desert. The recorded temperature that day was 115 degrees.

Her boyfriend, Ismael, a young man, had already migrated to the United States when he couldn't find work as a teacher in Todos Santos. Although he was raised by his grandparents near the western coast of Guatemala and was formally educated, he was shunned by his community when he returned, due in large part to his father's grizzly involvement in the civil war.

Prudencia wasn't a casualty of the war, 10 but instead a victim of the devastating consequences that sprouted from the bloody aftermath. Families remain divided, communities are in chaos, and lack of trust for one another creates divisive animosity among the Mayas, especially those families who had ties to the war.

During the 1980's, Todos Santos was scorched to the ground. Crops were burned, homes were seared, Mayas were chopped to pieces. Other families fled to remote regions of the mountains, hiding from the military while subsisting on tree roots and vegetation. Many died from starvation, disease and blight.

Under the auspice of the United States' secret directives during the 1980's, Ismael's father was forced to join the ranks of the military or be murdered, and fought against his own ilk, which had deleterious effects on Ismael's professional opportunities.

Prudencia had heard the gruesome stories juxtaposed to the stories of wealth and of what dreams may come while weighing them against the few jobs available to Maya women, due to the lack of civil rights for women and because of racial tensions that exist between indigenous and non-indigenous peoples of Guatemala. Prudencia was convinced that her future existed inside the United States of America.

Prudencia and Ismael were going to marry once he saved enough money to build them a home in Guatemala. Prudencia, with a petite frame and long black hair that flowed past her hips, had simple pleasures, like gazing at the stars and thinking of the promise of joining Ismael someday. In May of 2007, at the age of 19, she left Todos Santos to surprise her boyfriend, who was living somewhere in California. Like most migrants, she traveled with a coyote (guide), through the veins of Mexico's underground, avoiding immigration police and bandits who rob Central Americans. She then walked approximately fifty miles from the border of Sasabe, Mexico to the outskirts of Tucson, Arizona. With only a gallon of water and the clothes in her backpack, Prudencia trudged through the desert under the scorching summer sun for approximately four to five days. Coyotes often abandon the sick or injured migrants in order to get the remainder of their group across. She was later found dead by humanitarians who were notified by her boyfriend that she was left behind by the group.

By the end of the civil war in 1996, it is esti- 15 mated that over 200,000 people were murdered. In 2007, three thousand women were murdered in Guatemala. Many believe the murderers are the formerly U.S.-trained Guatemalan military and police. In an attempt to bring back the conservative mano dura party (iron fist), the military instills fear through mutilations in order to persuade the country only the fist can stop the violence. So many of the disappeared women are later found mutilated and remain forever unidentified.

Ostensibly, many of the migrants leaving Guatemala find themselves without work or in Ismael's situation, without a community. The fallout of the civil war continues despite the ongoing efforts of Amnesty International. The legacy of death and destruction due in large part to U.S. covert operations thwarts any mechanisms to restore Guatemalan life to prewar conditions.

According to Intelligence scholar, Christopher Andrew, "The Guatemala affair [was] a disreputable moment—Eisenhower was 'directly responsible' for 'death and destruction, yet showed no signs of embarrassment then or later over his 'bullying of a banana republic.'"

In July of 2008, a shrine was erected at the site where Prudencia died.

A CLOSER LOOK AT
Prudencia

1. Ipsen chooses not to begin with a description of her subject, Prudencia, and does not even mention her until the second paragraph of the second section. How does this delay affect your understanding of Prudencia?

2. Examine the overall structure. Ipsen moves back and forth from the Guatemalan civil war and the United States' role in that war to the story of Prudencia Martin Gomez. In what ways does this complex organization enhance your understanding of her subject?

3. Ipsen chooses not to come out and tell the reader what she believes is the message or theme of this profile. That is, she uses an "open form" that leaves such conclusions to the reader. How would the impact of this piece have changed had she chosen to directly state her theme?

4. Ipsen has chosen to give this profile a one-word title, not "Prudencia Martin Gomez" or "The Tragedy of Prudencia Martin Gomez," but just "Prudencia." While "Prudencia" refers literally to the person profiled, prudencia is Spanish for "prudence," which can mean "discretion, carefulness, and the foresight to avoid danger and mishap"; it can also mean "the habit of mind of discerning what is good and moral." How does this ironic double sense of Prudencia enhance the meaning of the profile? What larger questions does it raise? Who has acted prudently and who has not?

IDEAS FOR
Writing

1. Write a brief commentary responding to this profile. Do some research on the Guatemalan civil war and the United States' role in it. Do you believe the United States was justified in taking part in this civil war? When should the United States be involved in these kinds of situations, and when should it stand aside?

2. Ipsen has spent years as a humanitarian helping immigrants who risk their lives migrating to the United States. Obviously, she feels passionately about this social and political cause, and the individuals who are caught up in these issues. Write a letter to the editor in which you express your own views about immigration and the plight of people like Prudencia. When should the United States allow people like Prudencia to enter the country legally? What lines would you draw to keep illegal immigrants out?

The Near-Fame Experience

JENNIFER SENIOR

Project Runway is one of the many reality shows that came out in the last decade. These shows often take otherwise ordinary people and give them the opportunity to pursue their dreams. In this profile, which appeared in New York Magazine *in August 2007, Jennifer Senior follows up with one of the winners. Pay attention to the contrast between what people think happens to these celebrities and what sometimes really happens.*

McCarroll, baby-faced and hoodie-clad, works in the sort of space you'd expect from a fellow who dreams in fabric. It's outfitted with four sewing machines and oceans of material arranged in brilliant spectral sequence; his spring 2007 collection hangs on a rack in the corner, anchored by a quilt skirt so audaciously outsized it could easily double as a bedspread. But bedding itself is missing from this studio, as is a kitchen and a shower, which matters more in this case than it ordinarily would: Though he's the first-season winner of *Project Runway*, Jay, 32, is still homeless in New York.

"I haven't been living anywhere for two years," he says. "I sleep at other people's houses. I sleep here if I'm drunk."

Jay was one of the Bravo network's first guinea pigs in the competition reality genre, a brightly imaginative new form that mixes the more mundane conceits of *The Real World* and *Survivor* with contests involving genuine skill. In exchange for a few weeks of reality-style exploitation, contestants have a chance to show the world what they can do— with a sewing machine, with a pair of scissors, in a kitchen, in an undecorated room— and in the aftermath find their careers in full bloom. But the shows, it turns out, are the easy part. "I have a fucking gazillion e-mails from all over the world from people asking,

Why isn't your stuff out there?" says Jay. "Yet financially, I have no way to get them a product because I got pushed out of a boat and into the ocean, as if, *Oh, you can survive now.*"

This isn't what one would assume, of course. One would assume he'd be a money magnet after his star turn. Certainly Jay assumed as much. "You don't think I took the fucking bus to New York the day after I won the show, thinking someone was going to come up to me on the street and say, *You're awesome, here's money?*" he asks. "I thought that for two years. But I've given up on that."

Had Bravo not invented *Project Runway*, 5 Jay would probably still be back in Lehman, Pennsylvania, where he ran a vintage-clothing store (before that, he was producing online porn). But because of the show, Bravo and Bravo watchers expected quite a bit more from him. *Project Runway* wasn't some competition gimmick like *Fear Factor* or *The Amazing Race*, where the contestants' skills only served the needs of the show. Jay's talents were practical and real, and Bravo gave him a platform to showcase them. If he couldn't succeed in the aftermath, why were we watching? Of what use was the show?

That's pretty much how Jay saw it, too. He'd worked for five straight months, with zero pay and little sleep, to appear on *Project*

Runway and create a collection for Bryant Park. Audiences adored him. The show owed much of its success, let's face it, to him. So what did Jay get out of it?

The trouble is, celebrity came easily to Jay. Business did not. On the show, Jay was wicked and entertaining and cheerfully provocative, but he hardly had the means, savvy, or professional temperament to navigate the New York fashion world. (His first voice-mail message to me, ever: *Hey Jen, this is Jay McCarroll . . . Um, I am free tonight and all day tomorrow to do this bullshit. Fucking call me, would you?*) "A week after I won the show, I met with two ladies from Banana Republic at the top of the Soho House, which is like, big time," he says. "And they were like, 'Oh, we can give you numbers for factories to get your clothes produced.' But that was to-tally not anything like what I needed. What I needed was someone to sit down with me and say, *Here's how you start a fashion label.*"

Before long, the blogs started to howl that Jay's work was nowhere to be seen, and Tim Gunn, the kindly host and soul of *Project Runway,* was wondering aloud to the press why Jay hadn't gained more momentum; he also castigated him for being a diva.

"My hands have been creatively crippled for two years—all those fucking eyes on me, reading that I'm a waste on blogs," he says. He looks genuinely unhappy now, and younger than his 32 years—a reminder that there's an *enfant* in *enfant terrible,* a person one feels just as apt to protect as to throttle. "I was just an artist before this happened," he adds. "Now I'm an artist with a fucking clock ticking."

A CLOSER LOOK AT
The Near-Fame Experience

1. One of the themes in this profile is that Jay is sometimes his own worst enemy. How does the writer of the profile demonstrate that characteristic without coming out and directly saying it?

2. This profile uses a narrative structure to tell its story. Find the typical elements of a narrative (i.e., setting, complication, evaluation, resolution, conclusion). How is this profile similar to a typical narrative, and how is it different?

3. How does the writer use dialogue to give insight into Jay's thoughts and character? Why do you think dialogue rather than description is sometimes the best way to give insight into who a person really is? What advantages does dialogue have over description? What are some potential disadvantages to using dialogue?

IDEAS FOR
Writing

1. Freewrite for five minutes about how you feel about Jay after reading this profile. Do you feel sympathetic? Do you think he has wasted his time and talents? If you were in Jay's place, how might you have handled things differently?

2. Play the *believing/doubting game* with this profile. Write a brief response in which you believe Jay and understand his troubles. What is the root of his problems? Why has he struggled to get a start, despite his talent and his success on *Project Runway*? Then write a response in which you doubt Jay's sincerity and abilities. Why do you think he has caused some of his own struggles? What is it about creative people (or perhaps humans in general) that causes them to self-destruct in this way?

1. Pair off with a partner. Interview your partner about his or her life at college. Ask about his or her daily routine. Ask about what this person does that's unique or different from a typical college student. Ask about what this person believes about life and the college experience. If you were writing a profile about this person, what angle would you take? What would the theme of that profile be?

2. With your group, study and discuss the theme of the portrait below, taken by Charles C. Ebbets (1905–1978) of workmen perched on a steel beam on the 69th floor of the Rockefeller Center in 1932. How are these workers portrayed? What word or phrase captures their attitude? Considering the historical context of this picture—the Great Depression—what message is conveyed about America at the time and its people? What larger theme do these eleven men represent?

© Charles C. Ebbets/Ebbets Photo Graphics.

3. With your group, come up with five national issues that you all seem to care about. They don't have to be enormous issues. For each of these issues, pick a person or type of person who is symbolic of that problem or its solution. Then talk about how a profile of these people could be used to help readers understand the issue you linked with them.

1. Choose one of the profiles included in this chapter and analyze it using the features listed in this chapter's Overview. Does the profile adhere exactly to these features? List three ways the profile matches this description of the genre. Then list three ways the profile does not match the description. Hand in your list to your professor.

2. On the Internet, find a profile of someone who interests you. Present this profile to your writing group, identifying its strengths and weaknesses. Did the profile catch your attention in the introduction? If so, how did it do this? Then identify the theme of the profile and show your group how the author uses the profile to make a larger point.

3. Look at the obituary section of your local newspaper. How are these obituaries similar to profiles? How are they different? With your group, list five characteristics that distinguish obituaries from typical profiles. Hand in your list to your professor.

1. **Profile someone you know.** Write a profile of someone you know well and like—for example, a roommate, friend, acquaintance, coworker, or relative. Think about why you find this person interesting: they're quirky, hard working, funny, unusual, and so on. Talk to others about this person to collect a variety of viewpoints and possibly gain new insights. Paint a verbal portrait of this person that views him or her from a specific angle and that captures something essential about him or her—an idea, social cause, insight, or theme.

2. **Create a profile with graphics or audio/video elements.** Write a profile about a historical figure who comes from your state or country. Using the Internet and print sources, find out as much as you can. Then interview an expert who has studied this person in depth. Paint a verbal portrait of this person that views him or her from a specific angle and that captures something essential—an idea, social cause, insight, or theme. Add pictures taken from the Internet or elsewhere. Or turn your profile into a podcast or video.

3. **Write a profile of someone who is supposed to represent your generation.** Choose as your subject a person who is used as a cultural icon to explain young people in general and your generation in particular. What common experiences do you and your friends share with this person? What is it about this person's unique experiences or persona that has made him or her an icon (for better or worse) for your generation? In what ways does this person best represent (or not) what you think your generation stands for?

PEARSON
mycomplab

For additional reading, writing, and research resources, go to **www.mycomplab.com**.

6

Reviews

While in college and during your career, you will be asked to write reviews in which you discuss whether something was successful or not. Reviews offer critical discussions of movies, books, software, music, products, services, performances, and many other items, helping readers to understand the subject's strengths and limitations.

In essence, a review expresses the reviewer's informed opinion about the subject and explains why the reviewer came to that opinion. Reviewers need to do more than simply state whether they liked or didn't like something. Instead, they need to base their opinions on some *common expectations* that they share with their readers. When writing a review, your opinion is important, but it needs to be based on your shared assumptions with readers about what makes something successful or not.

Reviews tend to be found in magazines and newspapers and on the Internet. You probably check out the reviews before deciding to see a movie, buy a book, go to a performance, or download some music. Reviews help you determine whether you would enjoy something before you buy it. Sometimes, people also like to read reviews after they experience something to see if others agree with their opinion about it.

In college courses, professors will use reviews to give you a chance to express your opinion about the arts, architecture, books, politics, education, fashion, and other issues. When assigning a review, professors are typically looking for your ability to support your opinions by discussing something in a knowledgeable way. Reviews give you a chance to demonstrate your understanding of a subject, while also allowing you to express your opinion in an informed way.

Reviews

These diagrams show two possible organizations for a review, but other arrangements of these sections will work, too. You should alter these organizations to fit your topic, angle, purpose, readers, and context.

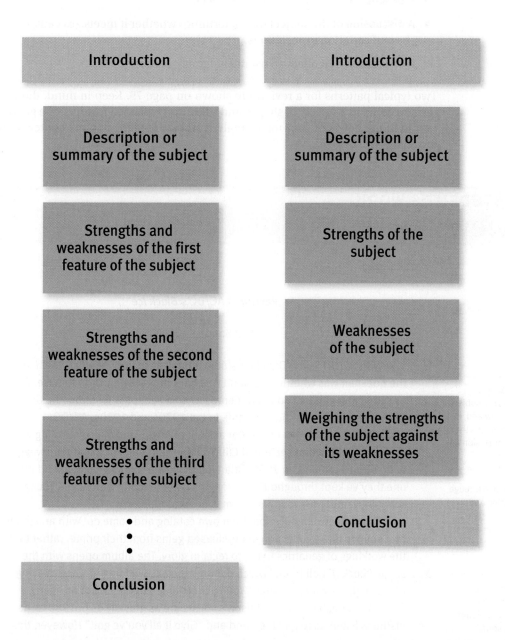

Overview

A review typically has the following features:

- **An introduction** that identifies the subject being reviewed or evaluated.

- **A description** or summary of the subject.

- **A discussion** of the subject that determines whether it meets, exceeds, or falls short of common expectations.

- **A conclusion** that offers an overall judgment of the subject.

Two typical patterns for a review are shown on page 79. Keep in mind, though, that reviews come in a variety of shapes and sizes. You will need to adjust the genre's pattern to fit the needs of your topic, angle, purpose, readers, and the context in which the review will be read.

ONE STUDENT'S WORK
Reviews

Review of AC/DC's *Black Ice*

Kim Sanders, UCLA

Immediately identifies the subject of the review and, in this case, states the overall conclusion up front.

With *Black Ice*, AC/DC's first studio album since 2000's *Stiff Upper Lip*, the question was whether the band was back in black or just on thin ice. But as screaming guitars and a thunderous rhythm section attest from the first track, these guys still shoot to thrill. In the 1970s and 1980s, AC/DC combined the rhythmic, two-guitar assault of Angus and Malcolm Young with the deafening rhythm section of Cliff Williams and Phil Rudd and the swagger of first Bon Scott and, in 1980, Brian Johnson. The formula worked, and it's one they've kept throughout their lengthy career—along with Angus Young's schoolboy uniform—and this album is no exception.

Sets the tone through an engaging and entertaining style with plays on words.

They borrow liberally from their own catalog and come out with an album that sounds like a collection of unreleased gems from their prime, rather than the workings of geriatrics trying to reclaim glory. The album opens with the single "Rock N' Roll Train," which features the axe-wielding brothers playing riffs as tight as ever and Angus Young launching into the first of his many frenzied, squealing solos. Johnson's vocals are as gravelly as in 1980 as he instructs listeners to join the band and "Give it all you've got." However, this

Proceeds chronologically through the album song by song.

song reveals the album's one great tragedy. The ganglike backing vocals that became the band's calling card, inspiring shout-along choruses such as those heard on "T.N.T." and "Jailbreak," are absent. Instead, there are sing-along echoes that sound like they belong on a Bon Jovi record.

"Anything Goes" is a relatively melodic track, with Johnson sounding like a hard-rock John Cougar Mellencamp—if Mellencamp smoked a pack a day and strained his vocal cords. He's backed by a harmonic riff reminiscent of "Thunderstruck."

> Discusses strengths and then weaknesses.

The band quickly gets back into more familiar territory with the throbbing bass and feverish lead licks of "War Machine," whose backing chorus vocals pay a snarling homage to Judas Priest's "Breaking the Law."

Perhaps the only filler on the album, "Smash N' Grab," is immediately followed by "Spoilin' For a Fight," a revisited "Hard as a Rock" that induces just as much fist-raising and head-banging as the original.

> Writes critically throughout the review, stating her reactions and explaining why she reacted as she did.

"Decibel" channels the main riff and vocal tone of ZZ Top's "Waitin' for the Bus" before the sustained power chords and raw vocals kick in, and Angus Young launches into another shredding solo.

Building a steady accretion of instruments, "Stormy May Day"—a play on the T. Bone Walker classic "Stormy Monday"—amplifies the band's blues influences, from the eerie guitar tonality to the main riff and dark, ominous imagery.

However, the band returns to its trademark themes of fast women, screaming guitars, and rock 'n' roll on "She Likes Rock N' Roll," with its funk drum beat and descending licks that recall "Back in Black."

> Qualifies generally positive review with criticism of one aspect. Signals that qualification with the transition "however."

The classic rhythmic emphasis can be heard in the steady riff, repeating chorus, and pounding drums of "Money Made"; the appreciated chords of "Hells Bells" can be heard on "Rock N' Roll Dream."

The album closes with the title track, with its powerful guitars, heavy bass, and intense vocals. Angus Young plays another maniac solo that sounds as though he is skidding on black ice, while the steady beat and vocals drive the song forward relentlessly.

Black Ice isn't a new generation's *Back in Black*. It may not be a "runaway train running off the track"—but it's a solid album that could be slipped into a mix of classic AC/DC, and no one would notice the difference. Put simply, it rocks, and with the tragedies that occur when most bands try to recapture their mojo, that's quite an accomplishment. Especially when you're wearing a schoolboy uniform. And for that, AC/DC, we salute.

> A strong conclusion repeats the overall judgment from the first paragraph but also adds something new and interesting.

Inventing Your Review's Content

Of course, in order to write a review of something, you need to spend some time experiencing it. If you're reviewing a movie, you need to go see it. If you're reviewing a book, you need to read it. If you're reviewing a product or service, you need to use it. That's the fun part.

But wait. Before you see the movie, read the book, or use the product, you should do a little inquiry and background research to help you view your subject from a critical perspective. Inquiry will help you determine what you and your readers expect of your subject. Background research will help you develop a fuller understanding of your subject's history and context.

Inquiring: Finding Common Expectations

The foundation of a good review is the set of common expectations that you and your readers share about what makes something successful or not. Those expectations are not usually stated directly in the review itself. Instead, the reviewer assumes his or her readers share some assumptions about the thing being reviewed.

For example, let's say you want to write a review of an action movie that just arrived in the theaters. Your first challenge is to decide what features make an action movie successful. In other words, you need to figure out what moviegoers, namely you and your readers, expect from a movie like the one you are going to review.

So use an invention strategy like brainstorming to help you list all the things most people would expect from the kind of movie you are reviewing. As fast as you can, write out a list like the one shown in Figure 6.1. Then put a star or asterisk next to the three to six items that are most important to you.

More than likely, if you asked a group of people to make their own lists of expectations for an action movie, they would produce lists similar to yours. They might use different words and they might put stars next to a few other items, but most people would agree on what makes a good action film. That's what we mean by "common expectations." They are expectations that you and your readers already share.

Once you have identified the features you believe are most important, sort the unstarred items on your list under the starred ones. For example, the list shown in Figure 6.1 could be sorted into six major categories:

- Noble But Flawed Hero

- Complex and Sinister Villain

- A Romantic Relationship

- Fast-Paced Plot

- Stunts and Chase Scenes

- Music That Enhances Scenes

Having created your list of common expectations, you will have a better idea about what you and your readers will be looking for in this kind of movie.

Features of a Good Action Movie

*Great hero
Memorable lines
Love interest that doesn't sidetrack movie
Real or potential victims of villain
Character evolution, especially hero
Suspense
Interesting setting
Something unexpected
Chase scenes
Use of weapons
*Complex and sinister villain
*Fast-paced plot
Fighting scenes
Some irony, but not too much
Hero needs to be flawed in some way
Mystery to be solved
*Amazing stunts

Cool special effects
Unexpected humor
Intense music soundtrack
Strong set of values
Villain is brilliant
*Music that sets the moods for scenes
Hero's desire for revenge
Opening scene that grabs audience
Social pressures on hero to give up
Good friends for hero
Low expectations for hero
Recognizable actors
Dark lighting
Somewhat realistic, even if fantasy
Characters worth caring about
Rivalry between hero and villain
Violence that has purpose and meaning

FIGURE 6.1
Using Brainstorming to List Common Expectations

Brainstorming is a good way to come up with a list of elements that you and your readers would expect the subject of your review to have.

Researching: Gathering Background Information

The best reviewers do some background research before they experience their subject to help them understand its finer points.

Answer the Five-W and How Questions. Using the Internet or print sources like magazines and newspapers, find out as much about your subject as possible. When collecting information to write a review, you might start out with an Internet search, typing your subject's name or title into the search line. Look for answers to the Five-W and How questions:

- Who were its creators or original developers?

- What exactly are you reviewing?

- When and where was it created?

- Why was it created—for what purpose?

- How was it made?

Then follow up with print sources, which are available at your campus library. In magazines, newspapers, and academic journals, look for more background information on your subject and the people who participated in it.

Locate Other Reviews of Your Subject. You might also use an Internet search engine or your library's indexes and databases to help you find other reviews on your subject. What have others said about the movie, album, performance, restaurant, or product that you are reviewing? Other reviewers might bring up issues that you hadn't thought about.

Be very careful not to use the words or ideas of another reviewer without citing them. In academic settings, borrowing ideas without citation is plagiarism. In professional settings, it could violate copyright laws. Of course, it is not uncommon for reviews to arrive at similar conclusions and even to refer to each other, but your review needs to be original in wording and presentation.

Interview or Survey Others. Depending on your subject, you might find an expert you could interview. On almost any college campus, someone is an expert about your subject. This person might help you understand what to look for when you experience your subject. You could also survey others who have already seen the movie, eaten at the restaurant, listened to the music, and so on. What did they think of your subject? How did they react to it? What did they like and dislike about it?

Prepare to Do Field Observations. Grab your laptop or notebook and get ready to do some field observations of your subject. In a field observation, you would watch your subject closely *and* pay attention to how others react to it. For example, while watching an action movie, take notes about how the audience reacted to particular scenes. Did they laugh? Did they groan? Did they seem to enjoy themselves, or were they dismissive of the film?

Researching: Go Experience It

This might sound obvious, but part of your research involves experiencing your subject. Go see the movie. Go eat at the restaurant. Read the book. Your inquiry and background research should help you experience your subject from an informed and critical perspective.

Being critical means being aware of your own reactions to your subject. For example, when you are reviewing a movie, allow yourself to experience the movie as a regular moviegoer. But also step back and experience the movie critically as a reviewer. If something in the movie is funny, go ahead and laugh, but then ask yourself *why* you laughed. If you thought the food at a restaurant was bland, ask yourself *why* you had that reaction.

It helps if you can take down some notes as you are experiencing your subject. Your inquiry and research should have given you some things to keep in mind as you experience your subject. During the experience, keep notes about whether your subject measures up to common expectations. Also keep notes about why you came to these conclusions.

After you experience your subject, you might also spend some time playing the Believing and Doubting Game to draw out some ideas for your review.

Believing. First, imagine that you are going to write an overly positive review. What did you like? What were your subject's strengths? What stood out as superior? How did your subject exceed your expectations?

Doubting. Now imagine that you are going to write a very negative review. What didn't you like? What didn't work? What were the weakest aspects of your subject? What annoyed or irritated you? What didn't fit your expectations or the genre?

Synthesizing to Find Common Ground. Now examine the two sides of the game to consider which features are most important to you and your readers. Where do they agree, and where do they strongly disagree? Which side do you think is right?

While synthesizing, try to figure out how you really feel about your subject. Where do you stand among the people who would totally dislike your subject or would totally love it?

Organizing and Drafting Your Review

The organization of a review tends to be rather straightforward, so drafting these kinds of documents is often easier than drafting other documents.

The Introduction

In your introduction, you should identify your topic (the subject of your review) and offer enough background information to familiarize your readers with it. You should also identify your purpose directly or indirectly. You don't need to say something like "My purpose is to review . . ." but it should be clear to your readers that you are writing a review.

> Reviewing a classic action movie like *The Bourne Identity* is always challenging, because these kinds of movies develop a cult following of fans who are no longer able to watch from a critical perspective.

> When I decided to dine at Bistro 312, I was determined to begin with an open mind and leave behind my usual biases against French food.

Later in the introduction, you may want to tell your readers your overall assessment of your subject (your main point). In some reviews, though, you may not want to tell your readers your verdict up front. Reviewers of movies, music, and performances, for instance, will often wait until the conclusion before they finally give their overall judgment.

Description or Summary of the Subject

Now you need to familiarize your readers with the subject of your review. Begin by assuming that your readers have not seen the movie, read the book, eaten at the restaurant, or gone to the performance, so you will need to give them a brief description or summary of your subject. You have a couple of options:

Chronological Description or Summary. Describe or summarize your subject by leading your readers through the major scenes of the movie, book, or performance. At this point in your review, you should offer an objective description without making any evaluative comments. Your goal is to describe or summarize your subject well enough that your readers do not need to actually see your subject or read it to understand your review.

Feature-by-Feature Description. If you are reviewing something that is stationary, like a building or a piece of artwork, your best approach would be to describe your subject feature by feature. Divide your subject into two to five major parts and then describe each part separately. Make sure you use your senses to include plenty of detail. What does it look like? How does it sound, taste, smell, and feel?

In most reviews, this description or summary tends to be one substantial paragraph. This part of the review rarely goes over three paragraphs unless the review or evaluation is particularly long.

Discussion of Strengths and Shortcomings

Earlier, you generated a list of three to six common expectations that you and your readers have about your subject. Point out its strengths—how the subject met these expectations—and any shortcomings—how the subject failed to meet these expectations—and explore why.

> The primary strength of the *The Bourne Identity* is the characters of Jason Bourne and his reluctant partner, Marie. Both Jason and Marie have typical desires and fears that make them very human. Jason seems like a regular guy, even though he discovers that he has unexplainable fighting abilities and expertise with weaponry. The audience wants Jason and Marie to survive and escape. . . .
>
> On the downside, the absence of a great villain means *The Bourne Identity* lacks some of the intensity of a typical action movie. The forces of evil in this movie are mostly faceless bureaucrats who send one-dimensional assassins to kill Jason Bourne. The audience has trouble focusing its anger on one person or a few people, because there is no single evil-doer in the movie. Instead . . .

Early in each paragraph, make a direct claim about a strength or shortcoming of your subject. Then, in the rest of the paragraph, support that claim with reasoning, examples, quotes, facts, and any other evidence you need to prove your point.

In this part of the review, go ahead and express your opinion. That's what readers expect from you. They want you to tell them exactly how you felt about the movie, the book, the restaurant, or the performance.

Conclusion

The conclusion of your review will usually be brief, perhaps a few sentences. In your conclusion, you should state or restate your overall assessment of the subject. Then you might offer a look to the future.

Overall, I found *The Bourne Identity* to be a thoroughly entertaining film, despite its few weaknesses. Matt Damon carries the film with one of his best performances. The film also leaves plenty of loose ends to be explored in its two equally entertaining sequels, *The Bourne Supremacy* and *The Bourne Ultimatum*. This movie certainly deserves to be listed among the classics of action movies.

Avoid introducing any new information in the conclusion. Your conclusion should bring your readers around to your main point.

Choosing an Appropriate Style

The style of your review depends on your readers and the places where they will encounter your review. Most readers will expect your review to be entertaining as well as factually correct. A review written for a mainstream newspaper, magazine, or Web site should use a lively style that matches your reaction to the movie, book, or performance.

Use Plenty of Detail

Reviews need detail. Whether you are reviewing a movie or a restaurant, you need to provide lots of descriptive detail to help your readers envision what you are discussing. For example, when you are summarizing a movie, you want to describe the characters and the action in vivid detail. You want the readers to be able to imagine what the movie actually looked like and sounded like. Similarly, if you are reviewing a new restaurant, you want your readers to imagine the taste of the food, while hearing the same sounds you heard and smelling the same smells.

One way to add detail to your review or evaluation is to concentrate on your senses:

Sight: What colors did you see? How were people dressed and how did they behave? What objects did you notice as you were observing? What were the reactions of other people around you?

Hearing: What sounds did you hear? How did people talk? What sounds did you enjoy and which noises irritated you? Were people laughing? If you closed your eyes, what did you hear?

Taste: If you had a chance to sample some food or drink, what did it taste like? Did you enjoy the taste? If so, what made it pleasurable? Did something taste awful? Use specific details to tell your readers why you felt that way.

Touch: How did things feel? Did you brush your hands over any surfaces? What did that feel like? Were surfaces rough or smooth, cold or hot, hard or soft?

Smell: What scents did your nose pick up? Did you enjoy the smells, or did they turn you off? What smells came through the strongest and which ones were not immediately obvious?

Of course, you don't need to use something from all five senses in your review. Movie reviews are about what you saw and heard, not what you smelled or touched.

Restaurant reviews are mostly about what you saw, tasted, and smelled. Keep all your senses open and take notes on what you detected. You never know what kinds of details might be useful as you draft and revise your review.

Set the Appropriate Tone

The tone of your review should reflect your reaction to the subject, and your voice should be entertaining to your readers. If you were really excited by the movie you saw, the tone of your review should reflect your excitement. If you thought a particular restaurant was disgusting, your readers should sense that disgust in the tone of your writing. A concept map can help you set a specific tone in your writing.

If you occasionally slip words from your concept map into your writing, your readers will sense the tone you are trying to set. So if you thought a movie like *The Bourne Identity* was intense, using words associated with intensity will give your readers that feeling, too. If you thought the restaurant was disgusting, using words from a cluster around the word "disgusting" will signal that tone to your readers.

Changing the Pace

You might also pay added attention to pace in your review. Typically, shorter sentences will make the pace of your writing feel faster, because they increase the heartbeat of the text. So if you are describing action scenes in a movie, you might try using shorter sentences to increase the intensity of your writing. If you want to describe a hectic day at a restaurant, shorter sentences can help to create a feeling of frantic chaos. Longer sentences slow the pace down. So if you are describing a calm, peaceful restaurant or a slow scene in a movie, use longer sentences to slow down the pace of your writing.

FIGURE 6.2
Adding a Still or Clip from a Movie

In your review, you might add a still from a movie or even a link to the trailer.

Designing Your Review

Typically, the format and design of reviews depend on where they will appear or be used. A review written to appear in a newspaper, magazine, or on a blog should be designed to fit that setting.

Choose the Appropriate Medium. Paper is fine, but you should consider other media, like a Web site, a blog, or even a podcast, for making your review available to the public. Today, the vast majority of movie, book, and product reviews appear on the Internet.

Add Photographs, Audio, or Video Clips. Depending on what you are reviewing, you might consider adding a photograph of the item, such as a book cover, a still from the movie, or a picture of the product (Figure 6.2). In some cases, such as a movie, you might be able to add in a link to a trailer or a clip from a scene. If you plan to publish your review or post it on a Web site, though, make sure you ask permission to use any photos or screenshots.

Revising and Editing Your Review

When you are finished drafting and designing your review, leave yourself an hour or more to revise and edit your work. Revising and editing will help you sharpen your claims and develop better support for your opinions.

Determine Whether Your Opinion Has Evolved. Sometimes while you are reviewing something, your opinion will evolve or change. Watching a movie closely or a reading a book carefully, for example, might cause you to gain more respect for it, or you might see some flaws that you did not notice before. If your opinion has evolved, you will need to rewrite and revise the review to fit your new opinion.

Review Your Expectations. Now that you are finished reviewing your subject, look at your list of common expectations again. Did you cover all these expectations in your review? Did any new expectations creep into your draft?

Improve Your Tone. The tone of a review is important, because readers expect to be entertained while reading. Look for places where your voice seems a little flat and revise those parts of the review to add interest for readers.

Edit and Proofread. As always, carefully check your work for grammar mistakes, typos, and misspellings. Your credibility with readers will be harmed if they notice mistakes in your writing. Errors make you look careless at best, and uninformed and unintelligent at worst.

While you are finishing up your review or evaluation, put yourself in your readers' place. What kinds of information and details would help you make a decision about whether to see a movie, eat at a restaurant, or read a book? Keep in mind that your readers have not seen or experienced your subject. Your job is to let them experience it through you, so they can make a decision about whether they want to see it, read it, or buy it.

The Rave

Did you ever really like something? Did you really, really, really like it? Have you ever been completely blown away by a movie, song, play, novel, meal, or concert?

You should write a rave about it. A rave is an over-the-top review that is more about feelings and reactions than reason. In a rave, the reviewer suspends his or her ability to think rationally about the subject of the review. Instead, he or she shares that out-of-control feeling with the readers.

But how do you write a rave review without looking like you've lost it, you've gone off the deep end, drank the Kool-Aid? Here are some strategies:

Figure out what you liked best about it. There were probably one or two qualities that made this one "the best ever." What were those qualities and why did they make the experience so incredible?

Summarize it briefly. Summarize or describe your subject briefly, but use only positive terms and graphic details to illustrate your points.

Compare it favorably to the classics. Tell readers that your subject belongs with the classics and name those classics. Don't say it's better than the classics, because your readers will be skeptical. Instead, tell the readers it's just as good.

Use metaphors and similes to describe your experience. Metaphors and similes that use food and fighting work well: "It left us hungry for more." "The crowd was drooling with anticipation." "It was delicious." "We were stunned." "It knocked me for a loop." "I felt like I had been elbowed in the head."

Tell the readers they *must* experience it. You're not just recommending they experience it, you're telling them they *must* do it.

Amplify and exaggerate. Liberally use words like "awesome," "incredible," "unbelievable," "fantastic," "amazing," and "astounding." Use the word "very" a little too often. Tell the readers it's one of the most important things ever written, filmed, created, cooked, played. Call it an instant classic.

Don't let up. In a rave review, there is no going halfway. This was the best thing that has happened to you in your life, this year, this month, this week, or at least today (pick one).

Have fun. Raves are about expressing your raw emotions about the things you love. You want readers to feel what you felt. They know you're being irrational. That's the best part about a rave.

WRITE **your own rave.** Think of a movie, television show, book, restaurant, or place that you really, really enjoyed. Then write a three-page rave review in which you share your enthusiasm with your readers. Let yourself go a little.

Review: *Star Trek* Is Exhilarating

Tom Charity

Did somebody just reach through the space-time continuum and pull out a white rabbit?

Even diehard Trekkers might agree that Capt. James Tiberius Kirk's best days are behind him, but by going boldly back into the past for Star *Trek*—a "reboot" of the famed series—director J.J. Abrams and crew have done more than prove the point. They've presented him with a whole *new* future.

This exhilarating blockbuster gets under way at warp speed with a prologue that climaxes with Jim's birth—under fire from angry Romulans—and the heroic self-sacrifice of his father, who goes down with his Starfleet command. Life, death and special effects!

The widow Kirk doesn't get much of a look. Next thing we know, James T. is an angry teenager hot-rodding in a vintage convertible and nearly throwing himself off a cliff in the process. A few years later, he's still the impetuous hothead, getting into a barroom brawl with a company of space cadets and then reporting to the Academy himself the next morning.

A Cold War hero who doves could dig, Kirk has always been a projection of American "soft power," a gunboat commander on an intergalactic peacekeeping mission. He's not perfect, but his flaws are human—and in the Cold War context, *American* flaws: he's stubborn (or determined), irrational (independent) and above all, emotional (feeling). He never met an alien of the opposite sex he didn't like or a problem too complex for his gut.

These traits have a youthful, Kennedy-esque character, so it makes sense that they're accentuated in Chris Pine's portrait of the captain as a raw Starfleet recruit, bucking the system. No offense to William Shatner, but it's been a long, long time since Kirk was this sexy.

Spock traditionally mitigates Kirk's hot-blooded excess with a dose of cold, hard logic. In the classic Gene Roddenberry scheme of things, the *Enterprise* runs most smoothly with both men side by side on the bridge.

In this new, young, sometimes angry *Star Trek*—written by Abrams cohorts Roberto Orci and Alex Kurtzman (*Alias*)—most of the running time they're banging heads, rubbing each other the wrong way. In the development most likely to dismay "Trek" traditionalists, they even have eyes for the same girl (Zoe Saldana as a prickly Uhura).

Despite the tension between them, Zachary Quinto's young Spock is considerably less aloof than Leonard Nimoy's; Quinto stresses confusion and earnest self-doubt where Nimoy mined cool irony. The performance

Compares movie favorably to the classics.	
The author uses words that amplify and even exaggerate.	
Movie is summarized briefly.	
Similes are used to amplify and explain.	

continued

Review (continued)

makes sense, in context, but the balance of the story doesn't allow the younger actor to step out the of older Vulcan's shadow in the same way.

This is definitively Kirk's—and Chris Pine's—movie: brash, confident and affectionate.

It's cleverly cast across the board, from Winona Ryder, quietly effective as Spock's earthling mom, to Eric Bana, a tattooed and wrathful Romulan. Karl Urban ("Bones" McCoy), John Cho (Sulu), Anton Yelchin (Chekov) and Simon Pegg (Scotty) are physically close enough to evoke their counterparts from the original show, but they're not the finished article, which is where a lot of humor comes in. Orci and Kurtzmann have crafted brisk, snappy scenes for each of them, playfully bouncing off our shared sense of these men's future (our past).

You'll notice I haven't explained the plot, and I don't propose to try. Whether it will stand the test of time—or even a second viewing—I don't know. But I do know I watched this movie with a big smile on my face; it's a film with a near-permanent twinkle in its eye.

The new *Enterprise* is a joy to behold. The movie positively gleams with big-budget production design and deep-space special effects. If the studios are smart, they'll be lining up to get J.J. Abrams to rejuvenate every other washed-up franchise in town. May his work live long and prosper.

The reviewer doesn't let up with his positive review.

Need to write a review? Here's what you need to get going.

FIND Something You Want to Review

Your professor may tell you what you should review. If not, choose something that you can analyze critically, not something you absolutely adore or detest. You want to pick something you can assess fairly.

FIGURE OUT Your and Your Readers' Common Expectations

List two to seven qualities that you and your readers would expect something like your subject to have.

GATHER Background Information on Your Subject

Using online and print sources, collect background information on your subject and read other reviews. You might interview an expert.

GO Experience It

As you are experiencing your subject, pay attention to your own reactions as a regular participant and as a critical observer.

DRAFT Your Review

Introduce your subject and describe it. Then describe its strengths and weaknesses. Finish with a conclusion that offers your overall judgment.

DEVELOP an Appropriate Writing Style

The style of your review depends on where it will appear and who will read it. Most reviews use a lively tone that is entertaining to readers.

ADD Graphics to Support Your Written Text

A few graphics, like photographs and movie stills, will help you to visually illustrate what you are talking about.

REVISE and Edit

Keep in mind that your opinion of the subject may have changed while you were reviewing it. If so, you may need to revise the whole argument to fit your current opinion.

Long Overdue: A Review of the Movie *Juno*

CARINA CHOCANO

The movie Juno *went on to be one of the big hits of 2008. But when it first came out, reviewers weren't quite sure what to make of it.* Juno *was quirky, even for an independent film, and it played on the boundaries between conservative and liberal values. In this review, which was one of the first reviews of* Juno, *Carina Chocano, writing for the* Los Angeles Times, *explores the quirks and playfulness of this unique movie.*

In *Juno*, a spunky teenage girl (Ellen Page) named after the Roman goddess of women and childbirth gets herself accidentally knocked-up and decides to carry the pregnancy to term and then give "the thing" (as she fondly refers to her unborn progeny) up for adoption to a picture-perfect couple she finds advertised in the local *PennySaver*.

If the premise sounds like just the thing to raise a few eyebrows at some conservative media watchdog groups, wait until they see how it turns out. Of course, any forthcoming blasts of righteous condemnation will probably only add to the overall experience of the movie, which is already about as entertaining as it gets. Directed by Jason Reitman (*Thank You for Smoking*) from a screenplay by hot newcomer and media darling Diablo Cody, whose memoir *Candy Girl* recounted her year as an "unlikely stripper" in Minnesota, *Juno* is hilarious and sweet-tempered, perceptive and surprisingly grounded. It's also a gust of fresh air, perspective-wise, in that it follows the gestational misadventures of a girl, whose hotness is not actually her most salient characteristic, from the girl's point of view.

At first, it seems as if the script is going to stay glib and superficial and that Juno will communicate via rimshot zingers exclusively, even in moments of crisis. Page first appears on-screen walking to the drugstore, chugging Sunny Delight from a gallon jug on her way to buy yet another home pregnancy test. Pint-sized and intense, Juno has a sardonic nonchalance that masks whatever emotional turmoil she's going through. But her deadpan stance occasionally falls away to reveal what she is—a young kid in a tough spot, which only makes her earlier bravado feel all the more authentic. Although some of her one-liners feel forced, others capture the sardonic lack of affect that cool adolescent girls—and we haven't seen them on-screen, it seems, since *Ghost World* came out in 2001—find so comforting. "I'm going to call Women Now," she tells her best friend, Leah (Olivia Thirlby), after breaking the news of her pregnancy, "because they help women now."

It also helps that the sublime Michael Cera has been cast as Bleeker, Juno's buddy and secret admirer and the unlikely father of her baby. A track geek whose milky, short-clad thighs, intense (possibly myopic) gaze and terry cloth headbands make him more intriguing than he knows, Bleeker belongs to the same genus as the characters Cera played in *Superbad* and *Arrested Development*—smart, awkward, sincere, serious, weirdly irresistible. A gruff-but-lovable J.K. Simmons and a saucy Allison Janney are equally adorable as Juno's dad and stepmom, Mac and Brenda MacGuff, whom Cody and Reitman treat with a degree of affection and respect rarely afforded to parents in teen comedies. ("You're not going to be a Pop-Pop," Brenda tells Mac at one point. "Someone else is going to find a blessing from Jesus in this garbage dump of a situation.")

But the movie doesn't truly blossom until 5 Juno meets and starts to get to know Mark and Vanessa Loring (Jennifer Garner and Jason Bateman), a beautiful couple in their mid-30s who live in lovingly sterilized McMansion in a gated community. A serious, soft-spoken executive who is desperate for a baby but has been unable to conceive, Vanessa comes across at first like a type-A control freak. Juno identifies more easily with Mark, a former musician who writes commercial jingles and yearns for his lost youth.

Despite having opted for a "closed" adoption, which means she'll have no involvement in the baby's life as it grows up, Juno finds herself nonetheless drawn to the Lorings' house as she feels the need to share the experience with someone who cares and feels more and more alienated from her classmates.

Mark, who works from home alone, is always glad to see her, though for him, Juno's visits are a chance to regress, haul out the comic books and swap music mixes. As much as Juno enjoys their camaraderie, it's tinged with a sense that they're communicating from parallel dimensions—she's hanging out with his inner high-schooler while her grown-up self finds his immaturity appalling.

Meanwhile, the more she gets to know Vanessa, the more she understands what her choice means. In one of the movie's most beautiful scenes—Garner is touchingly awkward in it—Juno encourages Vanessa to talk to the baby in her belly, and Vanessa delivers what is perhaps the movie's least clever, most heartbreaking line, a shy "I can't wait to meet you" so intimate you forget she's talking to the baby through another person, at a mall. Funny as *Juno* is, it's scenes like these that ultimately make it so satisfying. Deceptively superficial at the outset, the movie deepens into something poignant and unexpected.

A CLOSER LOOK AT
Long Overdue: A Review of the Movie *Juno*

1. The writer of the review, Chocano, summarizes the plot of the movie early in the article. What features of the movie does she decide to share with the readers? How much does she reveal, and what did she decide to leave out of the summary? If you haven't seen the movie, *Juno*, did she offer you enough information to give you an overall sense of it?

2. What are some common expectations the reviewer assumes that her readers share with her about a movie like *Juno*? List three to five of these common expectations. How does this particular movie bend or play with those common expectations to come up with something original or new?

3. Does the review give away the ending of the movie? Where would the ending of the movie appear if the reviewer decided to "spoil" it for the readers? How close does the reviewer get to giving it away, and how much did she reveal about the ending?

1. *Juno* received mostly positive but mixed reviews. In 2008, there were few major movies, so critics had reservations about putting this movie on their nomination lists for awards. Find three other reviews on the Internet that show a mixture of responses to this movie. Then write a brief position paper in which you show both sides of the argument and express your opinion about whether the movie was award-winning caliber or not. You will need to see the movie to answer this question.

2. One of the interesting aspects of the movie *Juno* was the inability of critics to pin down its politics, especially regarding the abortion issue. On one hand, the character Juno is doing exactly what conservatives would recommend for a teenager who cannot raise the child herself, that is, putting her baby up for adoption. But, Juno's and others' cavalier attitudes about sex and relationships took away some of the idealism of the adoption process. On the other hand, for progressives, Juno seems to be an odd messenger for pro-choice positions or a liberal understanding of sexuality. Write a three-page commentary in which you discuss the political complexities of this film. Discuss whether you feel these complexities were helpful or harmful toward understanding the political issues around teen pregnancy and adoption.

Violent Media Is Good for Kids

GERARD JONES

In this article from Mother Jones *magazine, Gerard Jones, a well-known comic book author, uses the review genre to make a broader argument: that children should be exposed to violence through the media.*

At 13 I was alone and afraid. Taught by my well-meaning, progressive, English-teacher parents that violence was wrong, that rage was something to be overcome and cooperation was always better than conflict, I suffocated my deepest fears and desires under a nice-boy persona. Placed in a small, experimental school that was wrong for me, afraid to join my peers in their bumptious rush into adolescent boyhood, I withdrew into passivity and loneliness. My parents, not trusting the violent world of the late 1960s, built a wall between me and the crudest elements of American pop culture.

Then the Incredible Hulk smashed through it.

One of my mother's students convinced her that Marvel Comics, despite their apparent juvenility and violence, were in fact devoted to lofty messages of pacifism and tolerance. My mother borrowed some, thinking they'd be good for me. And so they were.

But not because they preached lofty messages of benevolence. They were good for me because they were juvenile. And violent.

The character who caught me, and freed me, was the Hulk: overgendered and undersocialized, half-naked and half-witted, raging against a frightened world that misunderstood and persecuted him. Suddenly I had a fantasy self to carry my stifled rage and buried desire for power. I had a fantasy self who was a self: unafraid of his desires and the world's disapproval, unhesitating and effective in action. "Puny boy follow Hulk!" roared my fantasy self, and I followed.

I followed him to new friends—other sensitive geeks chasing their own inner brutes—and I followed him to the arrogant, self-exposing, self-assertive, superheroic decision to become a writer. Eventually, I left him behind, followed more sophisticated heroes, and finally my own lead along a twisting path to a career and an identity. In my 30s, I found myself writing action movies and comic books. I wrote some Hulk stories, and met the geek-geniuses who created him. I saw my own creations turned into action figures, cartoons, and computer games. I talked to the kids who read my stories. Across generations, genders, and ethnicities I kept seeing the same story: people pulling themselves out of emotional traps by immersing themselves in violent stories. People integrating the scariest, most fervently denied fragments of their psyches into fuller senses of selfhood through fantasies of superhuman combat and destruction.

I have watched my son living the same story—transforming himself into a bloodthirsty dinosaur to embolden himself for the plunge into preschool, a Power Ranger to muscle through a social competition in kindergarten. In the first grade, his friends started climbing a tree at school. But he was afraid: of falling, of the centipedes crawling on the trunk, of sharp branches, of his friends' derision. I took my cue from his own fantasies and read him old Tarzan comics, rich in combat and bright with flashing knives. For two weeks he lived in them. Then he put them aside. And he climbed the tree.

But all the while, especially in the wake of the recent burst of school shootings, I heard pop psychologists insisting that violent stories are harmful to kids, heard teachers begging parents to keep their kids away from "junk culture," heard a guilt-stricken friend with a son who loved Pokémon lament, "I've turned into the bad mom who lets her kid eat sugary cereal and watch cartoons!"

That's when I started the research.

"Fear, greed, power-hunger, rage: these are aspects of our selves that we try not to experience in our lives but often want, even need, to experience vicariously through stories of others," writes Melanie Moore, Ph.D., a psychologist who works with urban teens. "Children need violent entertainment in order to explore the inescapable feelings that they've been taught to deny, and to reintegrate those feelings into a more whole, more complex, more resilient selfhood."

Moore consults to public schools and local governments, and is also raising a daughter. For the past three years she and I have been studying the ways in which children use violent stories to meet their emotional and developmental needs—and the ways in which adults can help them use those stories healthily. With her help I developed Power Play, a program for helping young people improve their self-knowledge and sense of potency through heroic, combative storytelling.

We've found that every aspect of even the trashiest pop-culture story can have its own developmental function. Pretending to have superhuman powers helps children conquer the feelings of powerlessness that inevitably come with being so young and small. The dual-identity concept at the heart of many superhero stories helps kids negotiate the conflicts between the inner self and the public self as they work through the early stages of socialization. Identification with a rebellious, even destructive, hero helps children learn to push back against a modern culture that cultivates fear and teaches dependency.

At its most fundamental level, what we call "creative violence"—head-bonking cartoons, bloody videogames, playground karate, toy guns—gives children a tool to master their rage. Children will feel rage. Even the sweetest and most civilized of them, even those whose parents read the better class of literary magazines, will feel rage. The world is uncontrollable and incomprehensible; mastering it is a terrifying, enraging task. Rage can be an energizing emotion, a shot of courage to push us to resist greater threats, take more control than we ever thought we could. But rage is also the emotion our culture distrusts the most. Most of us are taught early on to fear our own. Through immersion in imaginary combat and identification with a violent protagonist, children engage the rage they've stifled, come to fear it less, and become more capable of utilizing it against life's challenges.

I knew one little girl who went around exploding with fantasies so violent that other moms would draw her mother aside to whisper, "I think you should know something about Emily. . . ." Her parents were separating, and she was small, an only child, a tomboy at an age when her classmates were dividing sharply along gender lines. On the playground she acted out "Sailor Moon" fights, and in the classroom she wrote stories about people being stabbed with knives. The more adults tried to control her stories, the more she acted out the roles of her angry heroes: breaking rules, testing limits, roaring threats.

Then her mother and I started helping her tell her stories. She wrote them, performed them, drew them like comics: sometimes bloody, sometimes tender, always blending the images of pop culture with her own most private fantasies. She came out of it just as fiery and strong, but more self-controlled and socially competent: a leader among her peers, the one student in her class who could truly pull boys and girls together.

I worked with an older girl, a middle-class "nice girl," who held herself together through a chaotic family situation and a tumultuous adolescence with gangsta rap. In the mythologized street violence of Ice T, the rage and strutting of his music and lyrics, she found a theater of the mind in which she could be powerful, ruthless, invulnerable. She avoided the heavy drug use that sank many of her peers, and flowered in college as a writer and political activist.

I'm not going to argue that violent entertainment is harmless. I think it has helped inspire some people to real-life violence. I am going to argue that it's helped hundreds of people for every one it's hurt, and that it can help far more if we learn to use it well. I am going to argue that our fear of "youth violence" isn't well-founded on reality, and that the fear can do more harm than the reality. We act as though our highest priority is to prevent our children from growing up into murderous thugs—but modern kids are far more likely to grow up too passive, too distrustful of themselves, too easily manipulated.

We send the message to our children in a hundred ways that their craving for imaginary gun battles and symbolic killings is wrong, or at least dangerous. Even when we don't call for censorship or forbid "Mortal Kombat," we moan to other parents within our kids' earshot about the "awful violence" in the entertainment they love. We tell our kids that it isn't nice to play-fight, or we steer them from some monstrous action figure to a pro-social doll. Even in the most progressive households, where we make such a point of letting children feel what they feel, we rush to substitute an enlightened discussion for the raw material of rageful fantasy. In the process, we risk confusing them about their natural aggression in the same way the Victorians confused their children about their sexuality. When we try to protect our children from their own feelings and fantasies, we shelter them not against violence but against power and selfhood.

A CLOSER LOOK AT
Violent Media Is Good for Kids

1. In this review, Gerard Jones argues that violent media prepares kids for a violent world while letting them work out their aggression in a constructive way. His review mostly talks about how comic books can do this. Should parents use violent media to help children conquer their fears and channel their aggressive feelings? If you agree with Jones, are there limits to the amount of violent media that children can consume? If you disagree with him, do you think it is best to shield children from all forms of violence?

2. Jones uses a clear voice, or tone, in this review. How would you describe his voice or tone? What words in the review signal that tone for you? How does the length of his sentences speed up or slow down the pace of the reading? How does his use of emotion draw readers in, so they can empathize with his position?

3. This review is not typical, because it reviews several forms of violent media. What is Jones using as his common expectations for deciding whether a form of violent media is good or bad for a child? Locate the places in his review where he directly or indirectly identifies these common expectations.

IDEAS FOR
Writing

1. Write a rebuttal of Jones's argument in this review (see Chapter 11, "Position Papers," to learn about rebuttal). Evidence shows that children are negatively affected by violent media and that it might cause them to be more aggressive. How can you use this evidence to argue against Jones's persuasive argument? Where are the weaknesses in his argument? Is he relying on faulty assumptions or drawing unsound conclusions? Do you think he is altogether wrong, or is he generally correct? How might you modify his argument to make it more in line with your own experiences?

2. Television seems to be increasingly violent, especially as networks compete with cable channels for viewers. Pick a show that you have never seen before that includes some violence. Write a review of the television show, paying special attention to whether the violence is being used to propel the story or just to keep the attention of the audience. What are your common expectations for acceptable violence in a television show? Does the episode you watched meet or exceed your expectations? Do you think more violence would have made the show better? Could the show still be good without the violence?

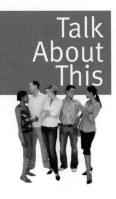
1. With a group in your class, discuss a movie that you all have seen. What did you like about the movie, and what were some of its limitations? As you discuss the movie, take note of the issues that seem to be part of the discussion. What are some expectations that your group members seem to have in common? Are there any issues that some members seem to care about but others don't? When people disagree, what do they disagree about?

2. In class, talk about what you want a reviewer to discuss in a typical music or movie review. How much do you want the reviewer to reveal about the movie? What kinds of reviews do you find most helpful when you are considering whether to buy music? Do you like reviewers whose work reveals their personalities or do you prefer objective reviewers who seem to stick to the facts? Are there any movie, music, or book reviewers that you seem to trust more than others? Why?

3. Examine and critique the following passage, which is taken from a review of a Greek restaurant. Describe which aspects of the review work well. Explain how it could be improved so that it meets the expectations readers have for reviews.

> Among the appetizers, everybody in the group agreed that the spanakopita was by far the best but that the hummus was not up to par. There was some disagreement about the entrees. Personally, I liked the chicken souvlaki and dolmades plate, but two members of the group preferred the "Greek Combo," which includes dolman, spanakopita, souvlaki, broiled scampi, and mousaka.

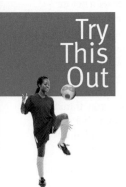
1. On the Internet, find a video advertisement that you can review. Most companies put their most recent advertisements on their Web sites, or you can find them on video-sharing Web sites like *YouTube* or *Hulu*. Write a review of the advertisement in which you critique its effectiveness. Tell your readers why you thought it worked, failed, or just irritated you. Your review should run about two pages.

2. Choose a movie and write two one-page reviews for it. Your first review should be positive. Focus on your and your readers' common expectations and say mostly positive things about the movie. The second review should be negative. Focus on elements that would cast the movie in a negative light. Then, in a memo to your professor, explore how your decisions about what to consider changed your review and what you had to say about the movie. Could you reconcile these two reviews into one that is balanced?

3. Find a review on the Internet. The review can be about music, movies, television, or just about anything. In a one-page response to your professor, explain how the review works. Discuss its content, organization, style, and design. Did you find the review effective? What were its strengths and how could it be improved?

1. **Write a review for your campus newspaper.** Imagine that you are a reviewer for your campus newspaper or another local newspaper. You can review music, books, poetry, movies, video games, television, sports teams, or just about anything that you enjoy doing. Write a three- to four-page review of a subject you choose. Be sure to summarize your subject for your readers, who probably haven't seen, heard, or experienced it. Then discuss your subject based on expectations that you and your readers share. Explain to your readers why you are giving your subject a positive or negative review.

2. **Write an opposing review.** Find a review on the Internet that you disagree with. Then in a brief response to the Web site, write an opposing review. Your review should be written as a response to the original review, showing why you felt differently about the subject. Next, write a one-page cover memo to your professor in which you explain your strategy for rebutting the original review. Also, discuss why you believe someone might find your review of the subject stronger than the original review.

3. **Write a rave about something you *despise*.** Here's an opportunity to really challenge yourself. Think of something you have experienced recently that you absolutely loathed. You should choose something that other people would be able to experience for themselves—a book, a class, a sport, a restaurant, a vacation spot. First, as a brainstorming exercise, write down exactly what you hated about the experience, just to get it out of your system. Then put yourself in the position of someone who would have actually enjoyed the same thing. Write your rave from that imagined point of view, using as many details from your original brainstorming as possible. (However tempted you may be, don't get carried away by sarcasm or irony.)

PEARSON
mycomplab

For additional reading, writing, and research resources, go to **www.mycomplab.com.**

7

Evaluations

Evaluations are similar to reviews in several ways, but they are also significantly different. In a review, a writer expresses his or her opinion, which is based on common expectations about what makes something appealing or effective. In an evaluation, the writer uses a *specific set of criteria* to determine the quality and effectiveness of a product, service, or person. In consumer magazines, like *Consumer Reports*, evaluations are used to assess the quality of products like cars, televisions, and mobile phones. In the workplace, personnel evaluations are used to determine how well an employee is doing his or her job.

The main difference between writing a *review* of something and writing an *evaluation* is simple. An evaluation uses a set of clearly defined criteria to objectively measure the quality of the subject. A review relies on the unstated "common expectations," which are shared between the writer and reader, to support an opinion.

In your advanced college courses, you will write evaluations that assess the quality of projects and products related to your field of study. In the workplace, evaluations are critical, because they help people understand the merits and shortcomings of products, services, and employees. In fact, when you start your first professional job, chances are good that your supervisor will need to write an evaluation of you in the first six months of your employment.

Evaluations

Here are two basic organizations for an evaluation, but other arrangements of these sections will work, too. You should alter these organizational patterns to fit your topic, angle, purpose, readers, and context.

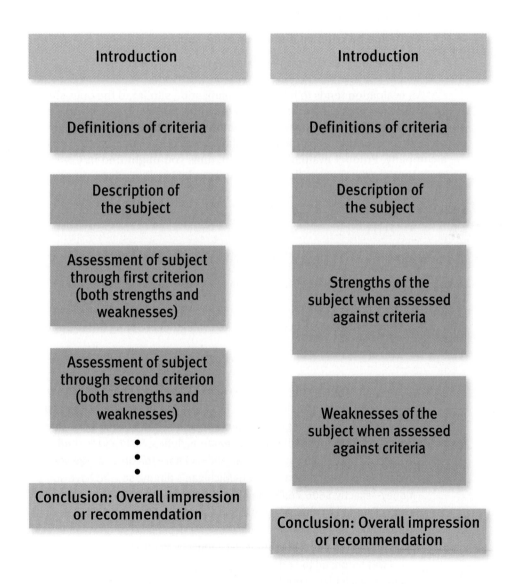

Introduction	Introduction
Definitions of criteria	Definitions of criteria
Description of the subject	Description of the subject
Assessment of subject through first criterion (both strengths and weaknesses)	Strengths of the subject when assessed against criteria
Assessment of subject through second criterion (both strengths and weaknesses)	Weaknesses of the subject when assessed against criteria
Conclusion: Overall impression or recommendation	Conclusion: Overall impression or recommendation

Overview

An evaluation typically has the following features:

- **An introduction** that identifies the subject being evaluated.

- **A set of defined criteria** that can be used to measure the quality or effectiveness of the subject.

- **A description** of the subject.

- **A criterion-by-criterion discussion** of the subject.

- **A conclusion** that offers an overall assessment of the subject.

An evaluation tends to follow an organization similar to the ones shown on page 103. These patterns can be altered to fit the topic, purpose, reader, and context of your evaluation. In some cases, the organization for an evaluation will be rigid. Personnel reviews, for example, are almost formulaic, because they need to be consistent within a company. Product evaluations, like the ones you might find in *Consumer Reports* magazine, are much more flexible, so they can be used to judge a range of items.

ONE STUDENT'S WORK
Evaluations

How We Ended Up in Louisville: An Evaluation of Spring Break Options

Danielle Cordaro

Writer provides background information.

My junior year in high school, I went to Cancun for spring break. My senior year I went to Miami, Florida. Of course, my parents paid for everything. But now that I'm in college, my parents are off the hook. They figure that paying for my tuition fulfills all their parental duties. So last year I had to figure out how to go on spring break and still have fun on a college student's budget. I work part time at Western Michigan's library, so I did have some money—exactly $606.76. Some of our friends were planning on going to exotic places like Jamaica or the Virgin Islands, but the remaining five of us were in the same boat in terms of funds. We decided to sit down and decide what we wanted out of our spring vacation.

I was surprised to find out that our priorities and preferences had changed since high school. Most of us weren't really looking for a big party;

we just wanted to get away from school and relax. We decided on a few key criteria. First, we wanted to go somewhere that provided a good mix of activity and relaxation time for five days and six nights. Second, lodging and food could not cost us more than $60 per person per night. Finally, we agreed to use no more than one tank of gas each way to get to and from our destination. That meant that, in our most fuel-efficient car, we could go a maximum of 360 miles from Kalamazoo, Michigan.

The criteria are identified and defined.

Weighing Our Options

Looking at a map, I came up with three possible places to go, which included South Haven, Michigan, Chicago, and Louisville. Then I used my criteria to weigh the pros and cons of each one.

Option 1: Cabining in South Haven, Michigan

Pros: South Haven is only about an hour's drive from Kalamazoo. Right on Lake Michigan, it's a hopping place for college students during the summer months. In the spring, before the water is warm enough to swim in, it's a bit more subdued. The upside about visiting in spring is there are not too many tourists around, which makes activities out in nature more peaceful. South Haven has miles of hiking trails along the shores of Lake Michigan, as well as canoeing, fishing, and horseback riding. There's shopping in the downtown area and a few inexpensive good restaurants. Other plusses include the accommodations. One nice thing about vacationing in Michigan in the middle of April is that it is considered the "off-season." For $200 I found a luxury cabin with accommodations for five people. The cabin included a hot tub outside, a whirlpool bath inside, a large flat-screen HDTV.

The criteria are used to discuss pros and cons of each option.

Cons: There isn't much to do in town, and not many other college students would be around. A few restaurants and bars would be open during the off-season, but they aren't too exciting. Going to South Haven would mean having to make our own fun. So we might find ourselves hanging out in our "luxury cabin" bored out of our minds. You can only hang out in the hot tub and watch that flat-screen HDTV so much before wanting to get out and see some people.

Option 2: Living Large in Chicago

Pros: Chicago is an exciting city with a lot to do. The shopping on Michigan Avenue is legendary. Inexpensive, more educational activities include the Museum of Contemporary Art, the Shedd Aquarium, and the Field Museum. If we wanted to pamper ourselves, we could go to a day spa. One great thing about Chicago is the inexpensive public transportation. If we planned things right, we could avoid cabs and take the elevated train

continued

pretty much everywhere, including to the surrounding suburbs for a few dollars. The restaurants in Chicago are also fantastic, as well as the nightlife. There was no way we could get bored in Chicago—as long as our money held out.

Cons: Chicago is expensive. Parking alone can cost up to twenty dollars a day, even at your own hotel. Good food and adequate lodging are also expensive with meals and hotel running about $80 per person per day. Even at that price, the accommodations wouldn't be luxurious. I was able to find a room in our budget, but one of us would have to sleep on a rollaway cot.

Option 3: Living Ritzy and Spelunking in Kentucky

Pros: Louisville is farther from Kalamazoo than South Haven or Chicago, but offers some of the appeal of both. Downtown Louisville has a lot of character and cute shops, though it's not as ritzy as Chicago. Another nice thing is that there are a lot of interesting things to do that don't involve expensive activities like shopping. Just outside the city are historic landmarks from the pre–Civil War era, as well as hiking and other outside activities. There are even some underground caves you can hike through in Mammoth Park. Best of all, Louisville is a lot less expensive than Chicago. I was able to find two much nicer rooms in Louisville for the price of one in Chicago. Louisville also has some great restaurants that, again, were about half the price of those in Chicago. Food and hotel would be about $50 a day per person, which was well within our budget.

Cons: All right, telling your friends you're going to Louisville for Spring Break is not going to get many oohs and aahs. One of my Cancun-bound friends asked me, "Are you visiting your grandma or something?" We would also need to spend more on gas to make this trip happen. We would need to top off the tank on the way to and from Louisville. Driving down to Mammoth Cave would add more cost.

Drum Roll Please: Our Decision

After a lot of consideration, we decided to go to Louisville. All of us had been to both Chicago and South Haven, but none of us had ever been to Louisville. The trip was great. We spent three days in Louisville just hanging out downtown and enjoying the great shopping and restaurants. The hotel was excellent, too. We had a pool, a hot tub, and a workout room. The last two days we spent in the Mammoth cave area. We stayed at a nice inexpensive bed and breakfast and explored during the day. It wasn't the kind of vacation my friends had in Jamaica on their parents' dime, but it was nice to find out we could put together a trip on a budget, stick to it, and have a pretty good time in the process.

The author considers the needs and values of her readers.

The author's lively style and humor appeals to her target audience.

Here, the author tells readers her decision.

Inventing Your Evaluation's Content

The primary goal of an evaluation is to offer an objective assessment of the subject. So what exactly does it mean to be "objective"? It means observing something in a way that minimizes personal bias and feelings. Being objective means using a set of criteria developed in advance to make an impartial and independent assessment of a product, service, or person.

Philosophers might argue that there is no such thing as objectivity because opinions and feelings unavoidably influence how we view the world. Nevertheless, you can identify and minimize those biases, while gaining a critical perspective on your subject. The secret is to develop your set of criteria up front. If your readers agree with your criteria, they will likely agree with your assessment of the product, service, or person you are evaluating.

Inquiring: Developing a Set of Criteria

Your first task is to decide what you want to evaluate. Your professor may assign you something to evaluate, like a specific car model, your dorm's food service, or a mobile phone service. If you are allowed to choose your own subject, pick something that you can evaluate objectively. If you absolutely adore or bitterly detest something, that subject might not be the best one for your review. You want to pick something you can be unbiased about.

Now, using brainstorming, make a list of the qualities you would expect your subject to have. For example, let's say you want to evaluate this year's Mini Cooper Clubman (Figure 7.1). What are the qualities you would expect this kind of car to have?

You probably want a sporty car like this one to be quick and responsive. You want it to get good gas mileage without sacrificing fun. And, let's be honest, you want a car that looks good and seems different from the other cars on the road. Your brainstorming list might include some or all of the items shown in Figure 7.2.

This list is a good one, but it's a little too long to work as a set of criteria. After all, if you wrote individually about each of these qualities, your evaluation would become tiresome for readers. So turn this long brainstorming list into a shorter list of five to seven criteria, and sort all these qualities into a handful of major categories:

FIGURE 7.1 How Would You Evaluate This Car?

An evaluation of a product, like a car, needs to rely on more than an opinion or how someone feels about it. An evaluation should be based on a defined list of criteria.

- **External Appearance:** cool look, smooth lines, attractive colors, available accessories, distinctive appearance

- **Performance:** good acceleration, handles turns well, stops quickly, reliable, traction control, stability system

- **Interior Comfort:** minimal engine noise, easy-to-use controls, readable dials, legroom, headroom, space for passengers, comfortable seats

FIGURE 7.2
Brainstorming
for Qualities

*Brainstorming is a
good way to start
figuring out your
criteria for an
evaluation. List all
the qualities you
would expect your
subject to have.*

Things I would expect in a car

Cool appearance	Available options
Suitable engine	Good gas mileage
Reliability	Available accessories
Ability to sustain a crash	Low maintenance costs
Visibility on the road	Ability to carry passengers
Smooth lines	Ability to carry stuff
Stop quickly	Safety
Minimal engine noise	Airbags
Low repair costs	Side crash support
Reasonable price	Crumple zones
Good performance	Stability systems
Good acceleration	Traction control
Comfortable interior	

- **Expenses:** affordable list price, good gas mileage, low maintenance costs, affordable accessories, low repair costs, warranty

- **Safety:** safety features, airbags, crumple zones, good crash test results, performance at high-speeds, visibility on road

Your criteria should include qualities that both you and your readers will agree on. In other words, at this point, you're setting down some rules for doing the evaluation. If you and your readers agree on these "rules," then chances are good they will accept your conclusions about your subject. If, however, they disagree with your criteria, then it's unlikely they will agree with your evaluation.

Also, keep in mind that different kinds of readers will have different expectations. Sports car enthusiasts will have different expectations for the new Mini Cooper Clubman than construction workers who need to haul around equipment. Choose your criteria with your readers' needs and expectations in mind.

Researching: Defining Your Set of Criteria

You're off to a good start so far, but now you need to *define* what you mean by these specific criteria. That way, readers will know what you mean by words like "performance" or "interior comfort."

You're going to need to do some research to figure out what experts consider acceptable and unacceptable when evaluating something like your subject. For example, to evaluate a car, you should do some Internet research through sources like the Insurance Institute for Highway Safety (IIHS) or the National Highway Traffic Safety Administration (NHTSA). Car magazines would also be helpful to determine what a buyer should expect for costs, visual appeal, and comfort.

As you do your research, look for both "quantitative" and "qualitative" information to help assess your subject. Quantitative information involves elements for which you can compare numbers, such as sticker price, gas mileage, and years of warranty coverage. Qualitative issues involve aspects that cannot be measured, such as the car's physical attractiveness or its interior comfort. Your research should give you a good idea about what kinds of measurable and nonmeasurable qualities would be expected in the product, service, or person you are evaluating.

Researching: Gathering Information on Your Subject

With your criteria identified and defined, you can now collect information on the subject of your evaluation. Your criteria should help you pinpoint the kinds of information you need to fully assess the product, service, or person you are writing about.

The strongest evaluations are ones that "triangulate" their facts through a combination of online, print, and empirical sources.

Search the Internet. If you are evaluating a product or service, you might start out by using Internet search engines to see what others have written about your subject. On the Internet, you should be able to locate many of the facts you need to determine whether your subject measures up against your criteria. You might also find some other evaluations written by experts. It's fine to read those evaluations and even to use them as sources, but don't let them bias your own evaluation. Instead, use other evaluations to understand the differing assessments of your subject.

Observe Your Subject in Action. Keeping your criteria in mind, examine and interact with your subject. If you are evaluating a car, for example, go out and take a test drive. If you are evaluating a service, try it out and keep notes about how well that service worked. Make sure you keep detailed notes. Also, pay attention to your reaction and the reactions of others when you are observing or interacting with your subject.

Experiment on Your Subject. Organizations like the Consumers Union and Underwriters Laboratories actually do experiments on products. They test drive cars, drop toasters, and crank up the volume on stereos. These experiments help them generate data to measure the quality and usefulness of a product. For some kinds of products, you might be able to set up experiments that determine which products are better than others.

Interview or Survey Others. Depending on your subject, you might find an expert you could interview. On almost any college campus, someone is probably an expert who knows about your subject. This person might be able to give you some useful information or provide you with some helpful quotes that you could include in your evaluation. You could also survey people about their opinions. What do they think of your subject? How did they react to it? What do they like and dislike about it?

Find Print Information. Most products and services will be discussed in popular and trade magazines that are available at your library. Popular magazines that specialize in your subject's area, such as *Bicycling* for bicycles or *Outside* for camping equipment, can be especially helpful. Trade magazines, which cover a specific industry, are typically more technical than popular magazines, but they do a good job of covering what is happening behind the scenes with specific products and services.

Organizing and Drafting Your Evaluation

The organizational patterns of evaluations are typically straightforward, as shown on page 103.

Introduction

Your evaluation's introduction should identify your topic (the subject of your evaluation) and purpose (your intention to evaluate it). Typically, the introduction will include a brief description of the subject as well as some background information.

In your introduction, you may or may not want to state your overall assessment of your subject (your main point). In most workplace situations, you should state this assessment up front, so your readers can immediately find your main point and then observe how you came to your decision as they read the body of your evaluation. In nonworkplace documents, like magazine articles, you might decide to wait until the conclusion of the evaluation to give your overall assessment of your subject. That way, your readers will feel as though you led them to your final decision.

Defining Your Criteria

Defining your criteria means creating some guidelines that will help you and your readers determine if your subject is measuring up to objective standards. For example, here are some possible criteria one student developed for evaluating whether a Mini Cooper Clubman would be a good car for a recent college graduate:

External Appearance: Let's be honest. A recent college graduate expects his or her car to look cool and turn some heads. It needs to stand out. The days of minivans and other grocery-getters will come soon enough, but a person in his or her twenties should purchase a car that looks unique and distinctive. Its body should have smooth lines and interesting curves. The choices of colors should be bold: reds, dark blue, bright yellow. And the buyer should be able to accessorize the car with sport kits, alloy wheels, spoilers, and other personalizing features.

Performance: Again, it's too early in life to settle for a car that just gets from Point A to Point B. A new graduate's car needs to have some zip. It needs to accelerate to 60 mph in less than 10 seconds. It needs to be able to handle that commuter traffic, with good stability, reliable traction, and controlled stops that avoid skidding.

Interior Comfort: Most young people are willing to give up some comfort for an attractive interior. But, they shouldn't have to sacrifice easy-to-use controls and readable dials. Any car, even a sporty one, should have ample headroom and legroom for the driver and his or her friends. Road trips are always a possibility, so the car needs to be able to hold at least three passengers with stuff. The cabin should also be quiet enough to allow easy conversation. The engine noise should not drown out someone talking.

Expenses: Money will be tight with student loans to pay off and lots of other stuff to buy. So the car can't be a cash sinkhole. A first car needs to cost something in the low $20,000 range. It's going to need to have high gas mileage (upper 20 to low 30 mpg) and the maintenance costs will need to be less than a few hundred per year. The warranty is especially important for a young car buyer. It needs to give at least three years of full coverage, so any breakdowns will be covered. Any car should be reliable, meaning minimal repairs, for at least six years.

Safety: In the excitement of car shopping, safety might be forgotten. New college graduates have a lot to live for, so the car needs to be safe. These days, airbags and antilock brakes are mostly standard. The car should receive at least a "Good" rating in front and side crash protection from the Insurance Institute for Highway Safety (IIHS). The car should be visible enough to be seen from a distance and from another car's side and rear windows.

Criteria usually mix measurable and nonmeasurable qualities to describe what is considered good or bad by the evaluator. For example, in the criteria above, the person doing the evaluation is rather specific about quantities like the price of the car and its gas mileage. Actual ranges of performance are given for these kinds of measurable features. However, qualitative issues involving appearance, such as choices of paint color, are described for readers but not in a measurable way.

Description of the Subject

Now that you have defined your criteria for the readers, it is time to offer a full description of your subject. First provide an overall description of how it looks. Then divide your subject into its major parts and describe each of these parts separately. Depending on the length of your evaluation, your description might be a paragraph to a few paragraphs long.

Your description should be as objective as possible. Save any evaluative comments or opinions for later.

The Mini Cooper Clubman looks like the popular standard Minis, but it is somewhat larger in size. It still has that sporty, retro, all-too-British look with round headlamps, a snub nose, and wheels that seem a little too big for its body. The body itself is a sleekly rounded box, with a chrome grill and an additional set of lights in the front that makes it look ready for a road rally. The Clubman is 3.2 inches wider in stance than the standard Mini, and it is about 10 inches longer. The extra room and the double rear doors, called "split rear barn doors," make it seem like a miniature station wagon. The Clubman also has a side "club door" that allows easier access to the rear seats.

According to the Mini Cooper Web site, The Clubman has a 1.6L 16-valve engine that gives it 118 horsepower (a 172 horsepower engine is also available). The car gets 37 mpg on the highway and 28 mpg in town. It can reach 60 mph in 8.9 seconds, and it has a top speed of 125 mph.

The Clubman comes with many of the safety features that are becoming standard on cars today. It has antilock brakes and dynamic stability control. The car has a six-airbag system with front and side airbags for the driver and passengers. Its 4 foot, 8.1 inch height makes it more visible than most comparable sports cars its size.

The Clubman's suggested retail price is $20,850, and it comes with a four-year/50,000 mile limited warranty with full maintenance for three years or 36,000 miles. Because the Clubman is still somewhat new on the market, reliability ratings are not available. However, the standard Mini Cooper has been known to have minor reliability problems, and *Consumer Reports* gives it an average reliability rating.

In this description, the car has been divided into four major areas: exterior, engine, safety features, and costs. Each of these features is then described in some depth.

Assessment of the Subject

Now that you have defined your criteria and described your subject, you are ready to make some judgments about it. Evaluations tend to follow one of two paths at this point:

Criterion-by-criterion pattern: You can address each criterion separately, discussing the subject's strengths and weaknesses. (See the diagram on the left on page 103.)

Strengths-and-weaknesses pattern: You can discuss all of the subject's strengths according to your criteria. Then you can discuss the subject's weaknesses, again addressing all the criteria at once. (See the diagram on the right on page 103.)

Which one is better? Both patterns work fine in just about any situation. The criterion-by-criterion evaluation is probably better for longer evaluations, because it will allow you to balance your positive comments with your criticisms. The strengths-and-weaknesses pattern works well for smaller evaluations. Here is an example of a strengths-and-weaknesses discussion of the Mini Cooper Clubman, addressing the criterion "external appearance."

External Appearance

The appearance of the Mini Cooper Clubman still turns heads, though the larger body takes away some of the sporty look of the original Minis. The Clubman still has that boxy but nicely rounded look that stands out from other cars. Its colors are playfully bright, and the chrome in front really makes it look retro. There are many accessories available, like sport packages, striping, grill ornaments, and British flag mirrors and roof, to make it even more distinctive. Let's be honest— the car looks fun to drive. It's the kind of car that your friends will beg you to take to the store. It's the kind of car that gets looks from people you might want to meet.

The downside of the larger Clubman is that it appears less agile than the original. Having become familiar with the standard Minis over the last few years, people immediately sense the larger size of the Clubman. It's kind of like seeing one of your old friends who has recently gained a little weight. The car still looks good, but it doesn't appear as nimble and quick as in the past.

In this sample text, both the strengths and weaknesses are discussed. Notice how these comments are based on the defined criterion offered earlier.

This section of the evaluation is the place to express your opinion about the subject. Your opinions, however, should be based on the criteria that you defined earlier in the evaluation. This direct connection between criteria and your comments in this section will make your evaluation sound objective to the readers.

Conclusion

Your readers will expect the conclusion to wrap up with an overall assessment of the subject. You may have already stated your overall assessment in the introduction. If so, you should state it again here, with more emphasis. If you didn't state your overall assessment in the introduction, you need to state it very clearly here.

The Mini Cooper Clubman is a great car, and we recommend it for any new college graduate who has found a decent job. For such a cool car with good performance, it is reasonably priced. It also has the additional space needed for the college grad who occasionally needs to cram friends or a pile of stuff into a car. Your minivan days may be ahead of you, so you should buy a car like this one now.

A good conclusion briefly states the main point of the evaluation. Then it stresses the importance of the subject and offers readers a "look to the future." The conclusion should be as short and concise as possible. No new information should be introduced at this point in the evaluation.

Choosing an Appropriate Style

Evaluations typically use a "plain style" because they are supposed to sound objective. Plain style doesn't mean a flat, boring tone. It means the sentences tend to be simple and straightforward and the paragraphs make direct claims and provide support for those claims.

Keep Sentences Simple and Active

Badly written evaluations can sound stuffy and convoluted because their authors want to share too much technical information with readers, or they rely too heavily on the passive voice. These authors want to sound like experts, but they really just confuse and lose readers. For example,

> It is widely recognized that the Mini Cooper is an automobile that is beloved among a segment of trendy, youthful individuals who desire a sporty car that is exceptional and attains above average fuel economy.

This sentence is overly complex, using passive voice and complicated wording. Using the plain style techniques discussed in Chapter 16, "Choosing a Style," you can simplify this kind of sentence.

> Young people love the Mini Cooper because it is a unique, sporty car that gets good gas mileage.

This simpler sentence puts a doer (young people) in the subject slot and uses an active verb (love). The sentence also simplifies the wording for readers: "beloved among a segment of trendy, youthful individuals" becomes "Young people love," and "attains above average fuel economy" becomes "gets good gas mileage." The meaning is the same, but the revised sentence is much easier to read (and much less stuffy).

Here's some text that sounds too technical:

> The 1.6L 16-valve alloy engine with a 6-speed Gertrag transmission employs a transverse engine design with fully variable valve lift and timing to improve responsiveness and capacity in variable driving conditions.

This sentence is just too complicated for most people. Phrases like "transverse engine design" and "variable valve lift and timing" are engineering gobbledygook to most readers. So unless your readers are automotive engineers, you can simplify the sentence by removing some of the technical jargon.

> The engineers who designed the Mini Cooper Clubman decided to use a powerful 1.6L 16-valve engine that quickly responds to the driver's wishes.

This simpler sentence still tells the readers what they want to know without all the technical information that they don't need.

Avoid Clichés

Evaluations occasionally devolve into strings of clichés because the author wants to sound like an insider who knows the lingo of the field.

> The Clubman has the ponies to gitty up and go, and its brakes allow you to stop on a dime. Get ready for whistles from people on the street, because this little spitfire is ready to turn heads and leave the competition in the dust.

The occasional cliché is fine, but strings of clichés like the ones in this example sentence become tiresome and irritating to readers. In reality, these tired phrases signal laziness and a lack of creativity from the author. After all, clichés really just show that the author does not want to make an effort to speak plainly or come up with original ways to express ideas. Here's a revision of the sentence:

> The Clubman's engine and brakes work together well, giving the car excellent acceleration and the ability to stop quickly if needed. The Clubman is a car that people will notice on the street, and it has the power and agility to leave other cars behind.

This rewritten sentence sounds more objective and professional, because it uses original phrasings to express some important points.

Designing Your Evaluation

In an evaluation, it's important to show as well as tell. If you are evaluating a product, your readers want to see that product. If you are evaluating a service, it would be helpful if your readers could visualize that service.

That said, evaluations typically are not designed to be flashy. They tend to take on the design of the place in which they are published. Evaluations of cars, for example, tend to show up in car magazines or on Web sites, which have their own established designs. Evaluations of people, like those used in the workplace, often follow prescribed formats to ensure consistency.

Use Photographs and Graphics. It is not difficult to find a photograph of your subject on the Internet or shoot one of your own. A photograph will help your readers gain familiarity with the item or service you are evaluating (Figure 7.3). The photograph should clearly illustrate some of the features you are discussing in your evaluation.

Tables and graphs are also widely used in evaluations. *Cars.com*, a Web site that offers evaluations of cars, uses tables like the one shown in Figure 7.3 to give readers a quick overview of the strengths and weaknesses of each vehicle.

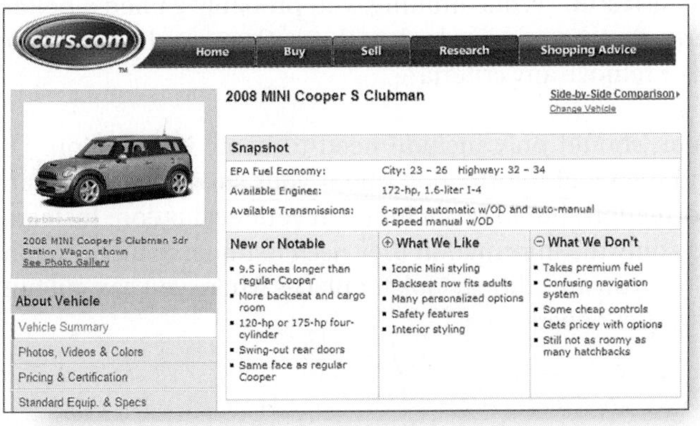

FIGURE 7.3 Using a Table to Highlight Strengths and Weaknesses

This table from the Cars.com *Web site gives readers a quick overview of the features, strengths, and weaknesses of the Mini Cooper S Clubman.*

Add Headings. Evaluations tend to be informative and somewhat technical, so headings are especially helpful for your readers. By scanning the headings, your readers should be able to figure out the organization of your evaluation at a glance. That way, they can scan some parts of the evaluation and read closely the parts that concern them most.

Good headings are "access points" at which readers enter the text. Section headings forecast the section's ideas and main points. Make sure your headings are lively and descriptive, not boring and flat. Headings should draw readers into the text, tempting them to delve into each section.

Boring, Flat Headings	Lively, Descriptive Headings
Description	Looking Over the Mini Cooper
Criteria	The Benchmarks for Success
External Appearance	A Pleasure to See
Interior Comfort	Snug but Comfortable
Expenses	Affordable and Reliable
Safety	Surprisingly Safe
Conclusion	A Real Winner

Your headings can even offer a quick snapshot of your assessment. The "lively" headings shown here, for example, give a sense of how the evaluator felt about the Mini Cooper.

Revising and Editing Your Evaluation

Revising and editing your evaluation is a crucial final step. If your evaluation is weak in content, badly organized, and contains grammatical and spelling errors, your readers are going to question your judgment as an evaluator. On the other hand, a polished, professional evaluation will build readers' confidence in what you say.

Take Another Look at Your Criteria. While drafting, you probably gained a better understanding of your criteria. So take another look at them. Can you sharpen their definitions? Should you add or remove any criteria?

Cut the Fat. Your evaluation should only include need-to-know information. Of course, you are going to find plenty of information about your subject—more than you need. Not all of that information should be included in your evaluation. Instead, you want to give your readers only the information they *need* to understand how you came to your conclusions. So as you are editing, look for places where you can cut out extra information that readers don't need.

Tighten Up the Organization. Evaluations tend to have rather tight, crisp organizations. The introduction should tell readers your subject, purpose, and main point, while offering just enough background information to familiarize them with the subject. In the body of the evaluation, major claims should come up front in paragraphs, so readers can find them easily.

As mentioned earlier, readers should be able to quickly figure out the organization of the evaluation by glancing at the headings or scanning the first lines of the paragraphs. The organization of the evaluation should make the information easy to access, even for readers who are not reading closely.

Find and Eliminate Errors. Factual errors, grammatical problems, and misspellings will undermine the credibility of your evaluation. Proofread carefully and double-check your facts for accuracy.

Don't hesitate to ask a friend or a roommate to look over your evaluation and mark any potential errors. In college, it's always better to let your friends find your errors than your professors.

Even more importantly, in the workplace, factual errors and a lack of proofreading will eventually harm your reputation and your career. It's that important. So save some time at the end of your writing process to carefully proofread your work.

The Slam

In the past, you have probably bought something, seen something, or tasted something that was the "worst ever." Want to get even? Write a slam about it.

A slam is a no-holds-barred knock-down evaluation in which you go beyond objectivity and express your anger and frustration. Slams usually appear on the Internet on consumer Web sites, where evaluators are less inhibited about expressing themselves. Here's how to write a slam:

Develop criteria for evaluating it. Start out by defining your criteria, just like a normal evaluation. Your criteria should be fair and objective, even though you are going to say some nasty things about your subject.

Figure out what you detested most about it. You probably have a list of things you didn't like about it, but what was the quality you despised the most? This quality will likely be the centerpiece of your slam.

Talk about your high expectations when you bought it. The more optimistic you were, the better. You want to show that this product or service didn't just come up short—it undermined your trust or faith in a way that cannot be forgiven.

Use similes to describe your experience. Similes are a great way to illustrate your frustration and express your dismay. "My steak tasted like a shingle seared in the sun for a few hours." "The flight attendant treated us like galley slaves chained to oars."

Amplify and exaggerate. Make sure you use words that express how you really feel, such as "horrible," "unbelievably bad," "putrid," or "I wanted to gnaw off my arm to get out of there." Use words and phrases that are unusual and uncommon, if possible.

Don't use profanity. It's tempting to toss a few verbal grenades. Your slam will actually be stronger without those kinds of words. Profanity isn't shocking anymore, and it shows a lack of imagination. Instead, find clever, creative ways to express yourself.

Don't apologize. When slamming something, writers might feel the urge to apologize for being so angry, vindictive, or upset. Don't. It's not *your* fault they messed up. Express your anger. Let it out.

WRITE your own slam. Think of a product or service that failed miserably. Then write a three-page slam that vents your anger. If possible, download a picture of the product or service, so your readers can see what you are talking about.

The Worst Car I Ever Owned

Mark Vaughn

Truth be told, I didn't even own the worst car I ever owned. I sort of inherited it and curated it for a while, then passed it on to the next grieving relative.

It was a horrible, deathly red Ford Pinto (we called it the Pinto Bean) that had been in my family for maybe a decade, belching blue smoke the whole time. It belched the blue smoke on deceleration, though, meaning that the valves were bad but the rings were still good. That was reassuring. Bad rings would have meant the whole thing was going to blow at any minute. But if all you had was bad valves, well, then there was hope that you'd make it to somewhere with a pay phone.

The criteria are stated in a humorous way.

The Pinto was merely a symptom of my overall economic wretchedness at the time. I was living like a rodent in a one-room apartment seven blocks north of the USC campus, shared variously with a few other graduate students, law students and medical students and a large number of Brazilians who came and went as immigration enforcement in Los Angeles ebbed and flowed. I never got the full story on the Brazilians, except that long ago, somebody from Brazil had played on the USC volleyball team. Word got out down around São Paulo, and the Brazilians began to filter in and out for years after that. No one asked any questions, the bills were paid in cash of small denominations, and I never learned any Portuguese.

Registration on the car was handled much like the gas, electric, and water bills at the time: It was still in the name of some poor sap from many years ago who probably had no idea his credit was being dangled over the pit by a Brazilian guava vine. I kept mailing in the $27 each year, and the

Uncommon words add some zing.

DMV kept mailing yet another sticker. Some years, I didn't even have the $27, so I waited until some bored law enforcement presence wrote me up for it.

At the time, I was also a reporter for a wire service in Los Angeles called City News Service, so I drove the wretched Pinto to the finest hotels in the city, where I spoke to civic, political, and entertainment figures, then drove the smoking Bean back to the City News offices in the Bradbury Building at 4th and Broadway to write my copy.

continued

The Worst Car I Ever Owned (continued)

The car left choking blue smoke in Southern California's finest valet parking spots.

The Bean wouldn't start if it was too hot. Normally, I just waited for a while, as one did with Fords, and tried again. It always eventually fired up. But one time, I had just interviewed either California governor George "Duke" Deukmejian or Senator Pete Wilson at a Republican fundraiser at the fabulous Century Plaza Hotel. I was out back near the Plaza's trash bins (my usual free parking place), trying to get the Pinto started, when some guy in a suit who had a wire in his ear said I had to "start it and get it out of here." Apparently, either I or the Pinto was seen as a security threat. Maybe Wilson was running for president at the time; I don't remember.

"I'd love to start it," was all I could think to say.

An hour or so later, it started, and I drove off. Wilson never became president. Coincidence? I think not.

Shortly after that, I moved up to the luxury of a 1964 Volkswagen van with a cracked block. Once I got a new block in the VW, the Bean was passed on without ceremony to the next relative in the line of succession. I heard years later that it finally died in an unusually large (even for it) cloud of blue smoke, on the 91 freeway headed east, perhaps trying to will itself back to the Detroit of its birth to die with dignity among the rusting carcasses of East Dearborn. It never made it, instead being bought on the spot for $35 by a surly junk man with a smoking tow truck. He paid cash in small denominations.

Exaggeration amplifies the message.

Here are some steps and strategies to help you get started on your evaluation.

FIND Something to Evaluate

If your professor allows you to choose your own subject, find something that interests you and that you can evaluate objectively.

DEFINE Your Criteria

Develop a list of three to seven criteria that reflect what you and your readers care about. Revisit these criteria as you write to make sure they still match your purpose and your readers' interests.

DO Some Background Research

Using online and print sources, find information about your subject that allows you to address your criteria. You might also interview experts on your subject.

EXPERIENCE It, Test It

With your criteria in mind, go out and experience your product or service. Put it to the test. Consult your criteria to help you focus on certain characteristics. Take field notes.

DRAFT Your Evaluation

While drafting, define your criteria as clearly as possible. Then, after describing your subject, follow one of two basic patterns: a criterion-by-criterion pattern or a strengths-and-weaknesses pattern. Conclude with an overall evaluation.

MAINTAIN an Objective Style

Stick to the criteria you've defined and strike a balanced tone. This doesn't mean that your tone will be boring, only that it should make you appear to be a fair judge.

DESIGN with Pictures, Tables, and Headings

Add visuals that reinforce your text. Help readers scan your evaluation by adding tables that summarize features and headings.

REVISE and Edit

As you revise, make sure your criteria match your readers' values and attitudes. Also, proofread to correct errors that will damage your credibility.

2008 Mini Cooper S Clubman—Road Test

TONY SWAN

This evaluation from Car and Driver *offered one of the first looks at the new Mini Cooper S Clubman, a larger version of the popular Mini Cooper S. In this evaluation, pay attention to how the writer, Tony Swan, sets up his criteria and uses them to evaluate a car that doesn't fit the typical mold.*

We have here a philosophical issue rooted in semantics. *Webster's New World* tells us that "mini" refers to "something that is very small in size . . . especially as compared to others of the same kind." The Clubman is the largest car ever to wear Mini logos, and it raises questions, such as: When does a Mini cease to be a Mini and become something else—a Midi, maybe? And what limits, if any, does a brand name impose on its products?

Mini faithful might argue that "compared to others of the same kind" is not possible because Minis are a breed apart, and in any case, the Clubman still ranks near the bottom of the dimension charts of cars for sale in the U.S.—only the Smart Fortwo is distinctly smaller. Still, there are many excellent subcompact hatchbacks that are similar in size and offer more room, some with a surprisingly high fun-to-drive index, all with much lower price tags (the Honda Fit, for one).

To this, the faithful might respond, "Yeah, but the Clubman will blow their doors off." No argument there. At 2856 pounds, the Clubman S is 234 pounds heavier than the last Cooper S we tested ["Power Toys," May 2007], but it's still capable of scooting to 60 mph in 6.8 seconds. That's 0.6 second slower than the standard Cooper S, but a Honda Fit requires almost nine seconds to achieve mile-a-minute velocity. We anticipate that the naturally aspirated Cooper Clubman would deliver similar results: not quite as quick as the three-door Cooper, but quicker than the Fit or other subcompacts.

So, it's about quickness, with added cargo or people capacity. As well as agility. But if the idea is expanded interior volume with a respectable power punch and the moves of a world-class welterweight, there are rides that will get those extra passengers and/or cargo from A to B with more room, and in more haste, for about the same money. The price $22,975, 0 to 60 in 5.4 seconds, max cargo of 43 cubic feet comes to mind.

What the Mazdaspeed 3 and others— Subaru WRX, VW GTI, for example—lack, though, is cuteness. Make that cuteness with attitude. It's the character trait that made the original British Mini—particularly the Cooper and Cooper S—a hit back in the go-go Sixties, and it's also at the core of BMW's successful Mini resurrection. The question is: Just how big can something get before cuteness fades? (If you know the answer to this question, Macaulay Culkin would like to hear from you.)

This expansion—call it the elastic Mini phenomenon—is not without precedent. In the heyday of the original, there were several variants: the Austin Mini Seven Countryman, the Morris Mini Traveller, and the Jeep-like

Mini Moke. In 1961, a quarter-ton pickup joined the lineup, followed a year later by a Mini Van, a panel van with Morris badges.

And, of course, there was a Clubman, from 1969 to 1980—you didn't really think that name sprang from the brow of someone named Wolfgang, right?—and a Clubman Estate. Its maker, BMC, sought to elevate the Estate above the other variants with the option of genuine wood trim on the exterior, though the execution left a bit to be desired as the wood was simply glued to the body panels.

What almost all those variations had in common was the brilliant front-drive architecture of the original 1959 Mini, on a wheelbase stretched by about four inches and with a body shell lengthened by about 10 inches. In the spirit of repetitive history, these are very similar to the increases that went into the creation of the modern Mini Clubman. So, with that precedent, you may wonder why we're skeptical about this latter-day stretch job.

Just this: Even with an extra 10 inches of sheetmetal, a first-generation Mini Clubman was only some 130 inches long, which still seems to be within *Webster's* definition of mini. But the new one is something else.

Dimensions. Creating this "unique shoot- 10 ing brake," as it's called in the company literature, entailed lengthening the wheelbase 3.2 inches, to 100.3, and a 155.8-inch wagon body, 10.2 inches longer than the standard Mini, according to the manufacturer, and at 56.4 inches, the Cooper S Clubman is also an inch taller than its three-door counterpart.

From the front bumper to the B-pillar, the Clubman's sheetmetal is the same as the standard Mini's. The new bodywork was added from that point aft, culminating in a squared-off stern. You don't need a tape measure to perceive the benefits of the expansion, in part because the design team thoughtfully installed a rear-hinged demi-door, officially, the "Clubdoor"—replete with a seatbelt, on the right side of the car (re-

member the old Saturn coupe?)—the better to eyeball the rear-seat space and, if so inclined, climb right in there.

There is a proviso to climbing in, though. The rear seat is in fact useful as a rear seat—Mini lists a legroom increase of 2.4 inches—but with 32.3 inches total, it's not a limo; getting two adults settled back there requires cooperation from those up front.

But there's no asterisk to the increase in cargo volume. Like all hatchbacks, the standard Mini provides far more cargo usefulness than a three-box car with a formal trunk. And the Clubman delivers more—33 cubic feet with the rear seatback folded down, versus 24 for the standard Mini.

Dynamically, the Clubman S suffers little from its stretching on the corporate rack. The 172-hp, 1.6-liter turbo needs a bit more time to hustle the extra mass to 60, true enough, but the disparity probably won't be apparent to an owner in daily driving. (For those who want a little more pace, Mini has a new 208-hp John Cooper Works package for the Cooper S and Clubman S: from $29,200 for the former, $31,450 for the latter.)

Beyond the minor sacrifice in accelera- 15 tion, the Clubman delivers the same eager, let's-play feel as its smaller stablemate—the kind of go-get-'em persona that has distinguished the Mini since its 2002 resurrection. In fact, the Clubman's longer wheelbase and better weight distribution—58.1 percent front/41.9 percent rear versus 62.7/37.3—may be an advantage in quick transitions, though this is hard to quantify owing to the irritating vigilance of the stability control, which asserts itself at the first hint of oversteer. Make that the first hint of *impending* oversteer.

Grip, provided by a set of optional Dunlop SP Sport 01 DSST run-flat tires (205/45R-17), is plentiful, at 0.88 g, which also enhances braking (159 feet from 70 mph). The rack-and-pinion steering combines surgical precision with knife-fighter responses, and the strut front suspension and multilink rear—augmented in this test car by the stiffer Sport package ($1500)—all but eliminate body roll, which is why Mini reviewers keep referring to go-kart handling.

We were impressed with the prompt throttle response of the Mini's new turbo motor in its comparison-test debut last year, and that's still true when it's towing this bigger package. Fuel economy can also be impressive—the feds rate the Clubman S with a six-speed manual transmission at 26 mpg city/34 highway, although, as they say, your actual mileage will vary depending on how often you dip into full boost. We averaged 26 mpg over the course of our test.

The Getrag manual gearbox was another strong point, with one demerit: Although the engagements were exceptionally positive, it was a little too easy to select reverse when the intent was first gear, a problem we also noted in our Clubman preview [December 2007]. The alternative to the manual is an Aisin six-speed automatic with paddle shifters. We prefer the manual.

And at the end of the day, we prefer the standard Mini to the Clubman. Here's why.

One. Those side-hinged doors at the rear 20 may have retro roots and nifty hinges that allow for a wide opening, but their functionality doesn't measure up to a hatchback, particularly if it's raining, and when they're closed, the junction of their framing creates an irritating blind spot in the middle of the driver's rear view. Doors like these have disappeared from everything but big vans for a reason.

Two. A longer load floor with a relatively low roofline can make for an awkward reach to get at stuff stowed toward the front.

Three. As noted, the rear seat may be habitable, which can't be said for the standard Mini, but comfort isn't included.

Four. To our eye, the Clubman's proportions look awkward from certain angles. Cuteness, pursued with such determination by the Mini design teams, is diminished.

Five. The ride quality that goes with the Sport package and its Dunlop run-flat tires is just this side of unendurable on choppy pavement, though to be fair, the same criticism applies to regular Minis so equipped.

We decided to appeal to an outside 25 authority—the owner of a 2003 Mini Cooper S with the Works. Make that the happy owner, someone who really loves her Mini. Here's her take on the stretch version: "The Clubman is a compromise that undermines what's unique about the Mini Cooper."

Hey, *she* said it, not us.

2008 Mini Cooper S Clubman—Road Test

1. Find and list the criteria the writer is using to evaluate the Mini Cooper S Clubman. Where do these criteria appear in the evaluation, and how does he define them? Do you know exactly what the writer means by each of these criteria?

2. Evaluations are supposed to be as objective as possible, but evaluations in a car magazine like *Car and Driver* also need to be interesting (and fun) to read. How does the writer balance his objective analysis of the Mini Cooper S Clubman with the sense of fun and excitement that would keep readers interested in the article?

3. This evaluation includes quite a few technical details and data. How does the evaluator present this technical information without overwhelming readers with numbers and specifics? Do you think the writer could have included less technical information, or do you think more was needed?

1. On the Internet or in the archives at your campus library, find the original evaluation of a car you drive or a car that you have ridden in. Do you think the evaluator accurately described the car? Are there some things about the evaluation that you would like to correct? Write a one-page letter to the editor to the original magazine in which you share your experiences driving or riding in the car. Your letter should praise the evaluation for its accuracies or criticize it for inaccuracies.

2. Using the criteria discussed in Swan's evaluation, write a 200-word evaluation of a completely different kind of vehicle (e.g., a pickup truck, a dump truck, a bus, a bike). What does the evaluation criteria reveal about this very different vehicle? What does it neglect to identify? Try writing the review in a humorous way, comparing and contrasting the vehicle you chose with a sportscar like the Mini Cooper S Clubman.

There's Something About Breckenridge

JEFF HEMMEL

In this article from an online skiing magazine, Jeff Hemmel uses the evaluation genre to describe why he and his friends have fallen in love with Breckenridge, a Colorado ski resort. Hemmel's criteria are not defined in a straightforward way, but you will notice that he indirectly defines the characteristics that make a great ski resort. Then he uses those criteria to show why Breckenridge is his favorite winter escape.

I was wearing shorts, looking out my home office window at palm trees, when I made the call. "Breckenridge, last weekend of the season," was all I had to say. I could already picture the scene at the opposite end of the phone line—a guy in business casual, sitting at a desk, the annoying hum of responsibility hanging in the air. "Let me think about it," he said, and was gone.

Right then and there, I started packing my bags.

You see, we live in Florida . . . on neighboring islands . . . surrounded by the Gulf of Mexico. On this day in mid-April, the temperature hovered in the 80s, and throngs of Spring Break co-eds had just left our beaches. Heck, my 6-year-old was already well into t-ball season. Yet on my calendar was a note that I simply could not avoid. And on the other end of that conversation was my good friend Marty Kullman, a guy who had just learned to ride while visiting my family during what we call our "bail on Florida and live in Utah" portion of the winter.

Within the hour, the phone was ringing. "I just found a flight to Denver that leaves at 7," was all he had to say. "And I'm pulling the trigger." Less than 24 hours later we're sitting on the Colorado Super Chair, ascending Breck's legendary Peak 8.

Other mountains offer steeper terrain. 5 Other mountains have far less crowds. Other mountains may have even had better snow conditions the third weekend in April 2007. But when the opportunity comes to end the season with one last, fun weekend of riding in a season that you thought was history, for me, one resort comes to mind.

There's just something about Breckenridge . . .

Changes in latitude

Truth be told, there was something about Breckenridge at the beginning of the season, too. That's when my wife and I pulled a similar last-minute escape, enjoying three days of Breck's legendary slopes, all in the midst of the Chevrolet Grand Prix snowboard series. We thought the comp would make it a zoo. Instead, it was fun, carving up the mountain one minute, stopping at the pipe and watching the pros carve up the U-tube the next. In a way, it's like paying homage to Breck's legendary history. This was one of the first resorts to allow snowboarding. Today, its Freeway terrain park, with its oversized hits and 22-foot, Zaugg-cut Superpipe, is considered one of the best freestyle spots in the nation for boarders and two-plankers alike, home to everyone from legendary shredder Todd Richards to current X-Games defending pipe jock, Steve Fisher.

It's one amazing playground, albeit one that, into my 40s and with three knee surgeries under my belt, we opt to take in only as spectators. On this bluebird April day, we roll up to the park like everyone else, and then join the crowd on the perimeter taking in the jaw-dropping action. My challenge is at the bottom, a kiddie—make that old-guy friendly—park known as Trygve's. Here, I jump right to the front of the hesitant throngs eyeing the various hits, slide my low-level rails with authority, and claim at least a good 12 inches of air off a jump before throwing in a few steezy slashes on the lip of the pipe. Looking back at Marty as he ponders his first-ever rail, I almost want to thump my chest. That's when

the 7-year-old I probably just cut off frontside boardslides the flat box, spins a 180 on the rainbow rail, and pulls an effortless 360 off the jump where I just busted out my telephone-book size air. I tell him to enjoy his anterior cruciate ligaments while he's young, he looks at me like I'm ancient, and we're off.

While the park area at Peak 8 may be legendary, Breckenridge obviously thinks it can get better. This season, the resort has instituted a "park-progression system" on the mountain that will retain the beginner park and pipe (I'm there dude!), add an intermediate park, and still showcase the expert-level park and pipe on Freeway. Aspiring riders will be able to comfortably feel out terrain park riding at Trygve's, progress to the new intermediate area on Park Lane, and still be up close and personal to the pro-level action in Freeway. To facilitate the intermediate area, the resort has invested in a new snowmaking system that will be dedicated to the Park Lane run.

Peak 8, however, is not all rippers and 10 shredders. It's also a great all-around area as well, with a wonderful mix of greens and blues to skier's right off the Colorado Super Chair. Head skier's left and you'll find a number of fun, if short, blacks. You can also access these directly from the Rocky Mountain Super Chair. In fact, on our first visit to Breckenridge, my wife and I rarely left this side of the mountain. It offers a mix of lengthy, playful runs that are almost always impeccably groomed. Heavily trafficked areas like Peak 8 can get quickly tracked out at most resorts; at Breckenridge, my last run was often almost as fun as the first.

Changes in attitude

While Peak 8 may have been a playground to get the trip started, by afternoon we've made our way to Peak 9, where Marty is quickly learning to enjoy the wide expanse of blues. No less than four lifts unload close to the top of the mountain. But despite the area's reputation as hosting Breck's biggest crowds, we find lift lines surprisingly short. We lap the high-speed Beaver Run and Mercury Super Chairs most often, enjoying the lengthy Cashier, Bonanza, and Columbia runs, before moving over to the blue/black American and Peerless. As expected, the increased steepness is helping Marty's riding truly begin to flow. As for me, the spring conditions are good for both my ego and knee, and in a year that offered precious few powder days, I'm having a banner weekend in the slop. The only hiccup comes when I lead us mistakenly down the aptly named Four O'Clock, attempting to work our way back over to Peak 8. By the time I realize the mistake, we're a small neighborhood and forest away from the action. We sweat off a few pounds making our way back to the top of Trygve's park.

For the uninitiated, Breckenridge consists of primarily four peaks, numbered 7–10, with two distinct base areas at Peaks 8 and 9. Each offers the basic slopeside amenities, but only Peak 9 currently offers hotel-style lodging. On the drive up Ski Hill Road to Peak 8, you'll find a more quaint collection of houses and condos. Where's the pseudo-Alpine village that seems to be the cornerstone of every major ski area nowadays? It's not there, at least not yet. Instead, Breckenridge offers a real-life town below, complete with an actual Main Street and lots of Colorado charm. Like many western towns, it was born out of the Gold Rush. Today, it's the largest historic district in Colorado, and features nearly 80 restaurants and bars, nearly 200 shops, and a multitude of hotels, inns, condos, and bed and breakfasts. I know, my wife led us through most of it in December. With Marty, our treks into town have a little more purpose.

The lack of any significant base area, however, poses a logistical challenge in crowded Summit County. As a result, Breckenridge underwent some big changes heading into the 2006/2007 season. Most significant is the new BreckConnect gondola that runs from the base of Peak 8 to the town below. (A Peak 7 station will be coming online in 2008/2009.) In the past, resort-run buses carried the vast hordes of visitors to the mountain. Today, the

sleek new gondola whisks visitors from central parking areas just outside Main Street to the resort above in about seven minutes. In a year that has become almost a rallying call to acknowledge global warming, it's estimated the gondola saved nearly 20,400 gallons of fuel.

We, too, do our part. Thanks to Breck's amiable Communications honcho Nicky DeFord, we're situated in The Great Divide Lodge, and enjoy the short walk to the high-speed Beaver Run quad. Life is good.

Rocky mountain high

Or at least, was good. At nearly 10,000 feet at its base, Breckenridge is high. And by Day 3, Marty is feeling the effects. He starts mumbling about not seeing too clearly before breakfast. By the time we're ready to gear up, he's on the phone with his ophthalmologist. I express concern, offer a few well-chosen words of condolence when he says he doesn't think he'll be able to ride this morning, then leave him in time for first chair once I figure he's not dying. Hey, a guy's gotta have his priorities straight.

Solo, I take advantage of the opportunity to hit Peak 10, and its fun variety of blacks. It has actually snowed overnight, and the opportunity to get fresh powder, no matter how thin, can't be ignored. Things are very quiet on this side of the mountain, which leaves areas like the Burn, which drops to skier's left off the Falcon Super Chair, relatively untouched. Breckenridge's true steeps, however, are reserved for the summit of Peak 8, 400 acres of expert and intermediate terrain once solely reserved for hikers, but now reached by the new Imperial Express Super Chair. At 12,840 feet, this is the highest lift in North America, accessing the highest lift-served terrain. From the 12,998-foot summit, you can pick out Baldy Mountain, Quandary Peak, Ten Mile Range, Lake Dillon, and nearby Keystone. You can also drop into numerous bowls, one of which, Imperial Bowl, even provides plenty of mellow runs for intermediates who rarely get the chance to ski or ride an above-the-treeline bowl. *USA Today* has called the Imperial

Express a "must-ski experience." I call it the answer to all those who complain Breckenridge is just too mellow to be challenging.

Coming back down from the clouds I get a call from Marty, who's feeling a lot better and doesn't want to miss out on the last official day in both Breck's—and our—season. We meet back up at the base of Peak 9, then spend the next several hours riding our favorite trails, dividing our time between the cruisers of Peak 9 and the park-heavy slopes of Peak 8. The Peak 8 Super Connect lift makes it possible, spanning the distance between the two areas in a timely manner.

For the sake of the story, we even venture over to Peak 7, which we find quiet and welcome. Unfortunately, we also find its collection of blues far too mild, and grow bored after only several runs. A great place to escape Breck's crowds with the little ones, but on this final day of the season, not the place we want to waste precious time. We hone our rail skills during a few more runs on Peak 8, then make our way back across to Peak 9, where we close out this rapidly warming day in the sticky, wet snow, literally pond-skimming in the lift lines, and just generally doing what one does best in spring conditions—having fun.

Something anything

So just what is it about Breckenridge? It's everything. The variety of terrain spread out over 2200-plus acres; the impeccable grooming on intermediate and beginner runs; the thrilling bowls located above the treeline; the elite parks and skiers and riders who call it home.

Or maybe it's just that Breckenridge is real. 20 No one manufactured the town's character. It's been fine tuned through the years. It's as much a part of the ski resort as the ski resort is part of the town. Beginning on Main Street, rising through the legendary parks and fun-filled cruisers, and topped with dramatic peaks and bowls, Breckenridge is the real thing.

Especially when you've got three final, unexpected days to play in the snow.

A CLOSER LOOK AT
There's Something About Breckenridge

1. Hemmel does not directly state his criteria up front. Instead, he defines his criteria as he describes various aspects of Breckenridge. Look through the article and identify a few of the criteria that he is using to evaluate Breckenridge. How does he define each of these criteria?

2. This evaluation uses a great amount of detail to add visuality and energy. Find three different places where Hemmel uses detail. How does his use of detail help you visualize this ski resort?

3. Hemmel uses a great amount of ski terminology and slang in this evaluation. Do you think this kind of phrasing is appropriate for his readers? Did you understand what he was saying? What happened in places where you didn't understand a ski term or a phrase?

IDEAS FOR
Writing

1. Write a profile of a place where you like to go to relax and have fun. In your profile, treat this place as though it were a person. Describe its characteristics. Tell your readers what makes this place interesting and what makes it alive. Your profile should try to capture the soul of this place.

2. Write a proposal in which you persuade your friends to join you on a trip during spring break. Your proposal should explain why your friends need to get away and lay out a step-by-step plan. Don't forget to consider issues of time and money. Conclude by discussing the costs and benefits of your plan.

1. With a group in class, list ten products that you might be interested in evaluating. What kinds of products did your group list? Did these items share any common characteristics? Discuss why you would be interested in writing or reading an evaluation of these specific products. Why might you seek an evaluation of these products before purchasing them?

2. Working in a group or by yourself, choose a specific product or service and develop two different sets of criteria, each set appropriate for a certain audience. After choosing the product or service:

   a. Define your first set of readers clearly (use the ideas in Chapter 3, "Readers, Contexts, and Rhetorical Situations," to help you), including their expectations, values, and attitudes. You might even choose a specific publication in which your evaluation will appear.

   b. Now brainstorm to generate a list of criteria for that audience.

   c. Repeat Steps a and b for the second audience. Have some fun with this. Choose an audience with completely different expectations, values, and attitudes.

   How did the switch to a different audience change your set of criteria? What does this tell you about the importance of understanding your audience early on in the drafting process?

3. Imagine that your university is tossing out its grading system. It now wants to evaluate students the way companies evaluate employees. This kind of evaluation, the administration argues, will give better feedback to students and provide potential employers and graduate schools with a better sense of each student's strengths and abilities. What criteria could be used in this new kind of evaluation system for students? Would you prefer a system like this one? What are its strengths and what are its limitations?

1. Look for an evaluation on the Internet for a product or service that interests you. Write a one- to two-page review of that evaluation. What are its strengths and weaknesses? Were the criteria defined? Did the evaluation include enough facts to show how the author came up with his or her overall conclusion? What kinds of information were not included in the evaluation that you might have found useful?

2. Find two evaluations about the same product on the Internet. Write a one- to two-page memo in which you compare and contrast the differences between the evaluations. Did they use different criteria? Did one evaluation stress a particular feature of the subject more than the other evaluation? What did the two evaluations reveal about the evaluators themselves? What were their biases? Why did the reviewers come to different (or perhaps similar) conclusions about the subject?

3. With a group, devise a set of criteria for evaluating your next writing assignment in this class. What are some common qualities that you could use to assess your next assignment? Do you think some criteria, such as organization or style, are more important than others? Should these criteria receive more weight in the evaluation process? Create a list of criteria with definitions and hand them in to your professor.

1. **Write an evaluation of a car.** Write a three- to four-page evaluation of a car, besides the Mini Cooper, that interests you. You can use the criteria developed for the Mini Cooper in this chapter, but make sure you define the criteria in your own way. Then write an evaluation in which you explain why the car exceeds, meets, or fails to meet expectations.

2. **Post a rebuttal of an evaluation on the Internet.** Choose a product or service to evaluate and develop a set of criteria for evaluating it. Then write a three- to four-page evaluation in which you discuss its strengths and weaknesses. Turn this evaluation into a text that would be appropriate for a Web site or blog about this kind of product or service. Include images or video, and provide helpful links to additional information.

3. **Evaluate a product or service.** Write an evaluation for a household product you own (e.g., a blender, toaster, stereo, popcorn popper). Define a set of specific criteria, then evaluate your subject according to expectations that you and your readers share. Explain to your readers why you are giving your subject a positive or negative evaluation.

PEARSON
mycomplab

For additional reading, writing, and research resources, go to **www.mycomplab.com**.

Literary Analyses

A literary analysis poses an *interpretive question* about a literary text and then uses that question to explain the text, its author, or the historical context in which it was written. Your aim in a literary analysis is to provide your readers with new and interesting insights into the work by examining it closely.

Literary analyses explain the meaning of a text, analyze its structure and features, and examine it through the lenses of historical, cultural, social, biographical, and other contexts. An effective literary analysis helps readers understand what makes a literary work thought-provoking, revealing, or enjoyable. Literary analyses also contribute to the larger scholarly conversation about the meaning and purpose of literature.

When writing a literary analysis, you shouldn't feel like you need to prove that you have the "correct" or "right" interpretation. Instead, your literary analysis should invite your readers to consider the work from new and interesting angles, while showing them how a particular angle can lead to fresh insights.

The literary analysis genre overlaps in many ways with the rhetorical analysis genre, which is discussed in Chapter 9. Both genres study texts closely to understand why they have particular effects on readers. Rhetorical analyses, however, tend to study all forms of texts, while literary analyses usually examine fictional or poetic texts, often using them as ways to understand humanity and culture.

Literary analyses are used in a variety of courses, not just English courses. For example, a history class studying the Progressive Era in America might read Upton Sinclair's novel *The Jungle*. A class examining the sociology of poverty might read a short story by Edwidge Danticat (one of which is included in this chapter). Professors across the disciplines assign literary works that provide insights into the subjects they want to explore with their students.

Literary Analyses

These diagrams show two possible basic organizations for a literary analysis, but other arrangements will work, too. You should adjust these organizational patterns to fit your topic, angle, purpose, readers, and context.

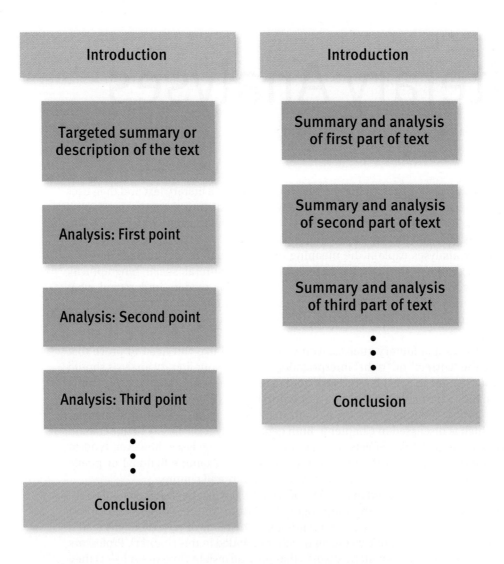

Overview

Literary analyses have these features:

- **An introduction** that identifies the literary work you are analyzing and its background. The introduction should also identify an interpretive question that will drive the analysis and provide an angle you will follow as you interpret the story for your readers.

- **Targeted summaries or descriptions of the text** that focus *only* on the events or features that play a key role in your interpretation. These summaries and descriptions are usually brief.

- **Quoted material** taken directly from the text that helps to move your interpretation forward and illustrate your points.

- **Support for your interpretation** that uses solid reasoning to show how your interpretation makes sense and offers insights into the interpretive question. Evidence is taken from the work itself (and sometimes other places) to support your interpretation.

- **A conclusion** that helps readers understand the big picture by describing the significance of the interpretation or by pointing out the additional questions that need to be addressed.

Literary analyses are written in a variety of ways. The diagram on page 132 shows a couple of useful organizations that you can alter to fit the needs of your topic, angle, purpose, readers, and context.

ONE STUDENT'S WORK
Literary Analyses

(Turn to page 148 to read "A Wall of Fire Rising.")

Doing the Right Thing in Edwidge Danticat's "A Wall of Fire Rising"

Nick Baca

Edwidge Danticat's "A Wall of Fire Rising" is on the surface a fairly simple story, but it concludes mysteriously as a powerful and disturbing meditation about love, memory, and doing what's right. The story includes just three main characters. Guy and Lili are the dreadfully poor but happy, loving, and responsible parents of Little Guy. The parents' greatest hope is to protect

The writer begins with a single-sentence statement that introduces the literary work under consideration.

A targeted summary/
description focuses
only on aspects that
are crucial to
understanding the
interpretive question.

Little Guy from the meanness of their world and to provide him with the possibility of a bright future. The action is also quite simple, most of it occurring among just the three of them. However, in the final climactic scene, both the characters and action become complex, strange, and very disturbing. In fact, Guy's actions—stealing the factory owner's balloon and jumping to his death as his family looks on—seem completely out of character. He is clearly a loving and responsible father and husband, but his final deed seems perverse, selfish, and horribly irresponsible.

Prominently states
the interpretive
question.

The main claim
answers the
interpretive question.

Why does Guy do this crazy, horrible final deed, depriving his family of a father and husband, just for a few self-indulgent moments on a joy ride? Strangely enough, seen from the perspective of Haitian poverty and Guy's desire to leave something important for his son, Guy's final deed, perhaps, makes terribly perfect sense. It could be that Little Guy's memorized speeches bring Guy to a new understanding about his desires for the "true freedom" of Boukman's speeches. Guy wants more for his son than food and shelter; he wants Little Guy to have a lasting memory of Guy that provides him with the courage to pursue true freedom. Guy also wants to pursue true freedom for the sake of his own father's memory, breaking the intergenerational chain of oppression and poverty. Guy's final deed is described best, perhaps, by one of the market women's shouts—"Beautiful."

An alternative
interpretation is
described in this
paragraph and argued
against in the next.

Guy's final deed could be interpreted as merely a cowardly escape from a hopeless life of crushing poverty and meanness, but that interpretation does not match up with what we learn about Guy and about his relationship to Lili and Little Guy. It's true that hunger and despair are always close at hand. For instance, the narrator spends several paragraphs describing Lili's methods for "kill[ing] the vermin in the stomach that made poor children hungry" (58). We learn also that Lili spends much of her effort each day to trying "to scrape together that night's meal" (70). Their home is small and dark; Guy has never even seen his wife unclothed "in broad daylight" (69). The outside world is described always as menacing. For instance, the sounds outside their shack are described this way: "Lilly could hear the whispers of the market women, their hisses and swearing as their sandals dug into the sharp-edged rocks on the road" (69). It's true, such a world might drive a person to despair and suicide.

However, while Guy's life is certainly full of despair, it is also full of love and hope. That hope is energized powerfully by his son's memorized speeches from the Haitian revolutionary, Boukman. The Boukman of Little Guy's speeches, like Guy, looks forward to creating a better world, and not for himself but for those living now and those from the past: "*Not only those people whose dark hollow faces I see daily in the fields, but all those souls who have gone ahead to haunt my dreams.*" Boukman, like Guy, struggles not just for himself but also for the memories of "*a loving father, a valiant love, a beloved friend*" (79). Similarly, Guy is no self-centered father, as all his actions show. For instance, his son "never goes to bed hungry" (74), and Guy does "not want to set a bad example for his son by indulging in very small pleasures" (70). Furthermore, Guy has a soul mate in Lili. Although they have their disagreements, Lili understands Guy's deepest longings, and Guy knows that very well, as he explains the night before he steals the balloon:

> "Sometimes I know you want to believe in me," he said. "I know you're wishing things for me. You want me to work at the mill. You want me to get a pretty house for us. I know you want these things too, but mostly you want me to feel like a man. That's why you're not one to worry about, Lili, I know you can take things as they come." (73)

Although Guy's life is difficult, he is neither selfish nor irresponsible. On the contrary, the meaning of his life seems to come from his hopes for his Lili and especially for Little Guy.

The final scene of this short story is horrible and sad, but it could also be seen, strangely, as beautiful and even uplifting. Actually, both sets of emotions are present, and the tension between them is what gives the conclusion so much power. It seems pretty clear that Guy waits until Lili and Little Guy have arrived at the market before "climbing over the side of the basket" and then, apparently, letting go, "hurtling down towards the crowd" so that he "crash[es] not far from where Lili and the boy were standing, his blood immediately soaking the landing spot" (77). How strange and awful. What kind of person commits suicide in front of his loved ones? Isn't that the deed of the "disgruntled" family member who wants to take the ultimate revenge on his family? But that is not the case here, and both Little Guy and Lili seem to understand that immediately. Lili claims him, proudly it seems: "'He is mine,' she said to young Assad. 'He is my family. He belongs to me'" (78). Over his corpse, Little Guy once again recites his lines from Boukman, this time not in the character of Boukman but perhaps in the character of his own father, this time not as a boy in a play but with "his voice rising to a man's grieving roar" (79). Lili too seems to understand perfectly. When the foreman asks her "Do you want to close the eyes?" she responds with a knowing "No, leave them open. . . . My husband, he likes to look at the sky" (80).

Margin notes:

Interpretation is supported with quotations from story (some quotations are complete sentences, others are phrases).

Long quotations (more than three lines) are in block quotes.

Interpretation goes beyond the surface by showing how a deeper and more careful reading leads to interesting insights.

Quotation omits some words from the original text, indicated with an ellipsis.

> The conclusion does not merely summarize or repeat the analysis but addresses new and larger questions.

Danticat's story is so disturbing because it just doesn't make sense that Guy's suicide could result merely from despair and self-indulgence, as both Lili and Little Guy seem to understand immediately. And yet Guy's horrible final deed, his horrible suicide carried out in the sight of his family, actually makes a kind of perfect sense in the context of Guy's world. It is still hard to accept that suicide is ever "doing the right thing," but there is much more to Guy's action, at least in his mind and perhaps in actuality. Stealing the balloon is a symbolic gesture *toward* freedom, not an actual attempt to *gain* freedom. (If Guy had wanted to actually pursue freedom, he would have remained in the balloon to try and land in a place where freedom is possible.) Little Guy's Boukman says, "*I call on everyone and anyone so that we shall all let out one piercing cry that we may either live freely or we should die*" (71). Perhaps Guy has answered Boukman's call with his own "piercing cry" to "live freely or die." His cry looks both to the future, to inspire his own son, and to the past, as a son in memory of his "loving father." In this way, this horrible, mysterious, and tragic tale is actually uplifting and beautiful.

Works Cited

Danticat, Edwidge. "A Wall of Fire Rising." *Krik? Krak?* New York: Random House, 1996. 51–80. Print.

Inventing Your Literary Analysis's Content

The first challenge in writing a literary analysis is finding an interesting *interpretive question* about the work you are studying. As you read and research the text, look for signs and evidence that might offer insights that go beyond the obvious.

Read, Reread, Explore

If the literary work is a short story or novel, read it at least twice. If it is a poem, read it again and again, silently and aloud, to get a feel for how the language works and how the poem makes you feel. As you read the text, mark or underline anything that intrigues or puzzles you. Write observations and questions in the margins.

Inquiring: What's Interesting Here?

As you are reading and exploring the text, try to come up with an interesting question that focuses on the work's genre, plot, characters, or use of language. The goal here is to find your interpretive question, which will serve as your angle into the text.

Explore the Genre. In your literature classes, your professors will use the term *genre* somewhat differently than it is used in this book. Literary works fall into four major genres: fiction, poetry, drama, and literary nonfiction.

Literary Genre	Subgenres
Fiction	short stories, novellas, novels, detective novels, science fiction, romance, mysteries, horror, fantasy, historical fiction
Poetry	limericks, sonnets, ballads, epic poems, haikus, ballads, villanelle, odes, sestinas, open verse
Drama	plays, closet dramas, comedies, tragedies, romances, musicals, operas
Literary nonfiction (or nonfiction prose)	memoirs, profiles (of people, places, events), biographies, histories, essays, nature writing, religion, politics

While examining the text, ask yourself why the author chose this genre or subgenre of literature and not another one. Why a poem rather than a story? Why a short story rather than a novel?

Also, look for places where the author follows the genre or strays from it. How does the genre constrain what the author can do? How does the author bend the genre to fit the story that he or she wants to tell? How does the author use this genre in a unique or interesting way?

Explore the Plot. Plot refers not just to the sequence of events but also to how the events arise from the main conflict in the story. How do the events in the story unfold? Which events are surprising or puzzling? What is the complication or conflict on which the narrative is based? How do the characters react to it? And how is this conflict resolved?

Keep in mind that conflict often arises from characters' values and beliefs and from the setting in which the characters reside. What conflicts do you sense in the story as your read? Are there conflicts between characters, between characters and their surroundings, between characters' aspirations, or between competing values and beliefs?

Finally, pay special attention to the critical moment in the story, called the *climax*. What happens and why is this moment so crucial? How is the conflict resolved, for better or worse?

Explore the Characters. The characters are the people who inhabit the story or poem. Who are they? What kinds of people are they? Why do they act as they do? What are their values, beliefs, and desires? How do they interact with each other, or with their environment and setting? You might explore the psychology or motives of the characters, trying to figure out the meaning behind their decisions and actions.

Explore the Setting. What is the time and place of the story? What is the broader setting—culture, social sphere, historic period? What is the narrow setting—the details about the particular time and place? How does the setting constrain the characters by establishing their beliefs, values, and actions? How does the setting become a symbol that colors the way readers interpret the work? Is the setting realistic, fantastical, ironic, or magical?

Explore the Language and Tone. How does the author's tone or choices of words color your attitude toward the characters, setting, or theme? What feeling or mood does the work's tone evoke, and how does that tone evolve as the story or poem moves forward?

Also, pay attention to the author's use of metaphors, similes, and analogies. How does the author use these devices to deepen the meaning of the text or bring new ideas to light? What images are used to describe the characters, events, objects, or setting? Do those images become metaphors or symbols that color the way readers understand the work, or the way the characters see their world?

Literary works usually cannot be broken down into simple tidy messages or lessons, but authors want their work to affect readers in some way. They want their words to influence the way readers view the world and what they believe. So as you are exploring the text from different angles, try to figure out what message or theme the author is trying to convey.

Researching: What Background Do You Need?

While most literary analyses focus primarily on the literary text itself, you should also research the historical background of a work or author. Depending on the assignment and where you want to take it, you can use Internet or print sources to find resources that provide insights into the work, its impact, and the author's intentions.

Research the Author. Learning about the author can often lead to interpretive insights. The author's life experiences may help you understand his or her intentions. You might study the events that were happening in the author's time, because the work itself might directly or indirectly respond to them.

Research the Historical Setting. You could also do research about the text's historical setting. If the story takes place in a real setting, you can read about the historical, cultural, social, and political forces that were in play at that time and in that place.

Research the Science. Human and physical sciences can often give insights into human behavior, social interactions, or natural phenomena. Sometimes additional research into psychology, sociology, biology, and other sciences can give you interesting insights into characters and events.

Organizing and Drafting Your Literary Analysis

So far, you have read the literary work carefully, taken notes, done some research, and perhaps written some informal responses. Now, how should you dive in and begin drafting? Here are some ideas for getting your ideas down on the page.

The Introduction

Introductions in literary analyses usually include a few common features:

Include Background Information That Leads to Your Interpretive Question. Draw your reader into your analysis by starting with a question or information that your reader is already familiar with, and then move steadily toward your interpretive question and your claim. Show your reader why this is an interesting question that will lead to new insights about the work or other broader concerns.

State Your Interpretive Question Prominently and Clearly. Make sure your reader understands the question that your analysis will investigate. If necessary, make it obvious by saying something like, "This analysis will explore why. . . ." That way, your readers will clearly understand your purpose.

State Your Claim at or Near the End of the Introduction. State your main claim about the literary work. Your main claim should answer your interpretive question. Figure 8.1 on page 140 shows how a few interpretive questions might be answered by some possible claims.

The Body of Your Analysis

In the body paragraphs, you should take your reader point by point through your analysis, showing them that your interpretation makes sense and leads to interesting new insights.

Summarize and Describe Key Aspects of the Work. You can assume that your readers will be familiar with the literary work, so you don't need to provide a complete summary or fully explain who characters are. But there may be aspects of the work that are crucial to your analysis and that need to be brought to your readers' attention. You may wish to focus on a particular scene, or on certain features, such as a character, interactions between characters, language, symbols, plot features, and so forth. Discuss *only* those aspects of the work that are crucial to understanding your analysis.

Build Your Case, Step by Step. Keep in mind that the goal of a literary analysis is not to prove that your interpretation is correct but to show that it is plausible and leads to interesting insights into the text and related matters. Take your readers through your analysis point by point. Back up each key point with reasoning and evidence, and make connections to your main claim.

FIGURE 8.1
Interpretive
Questions and
Interpretive
Claims

Interpretive Questions	Interpretive Claims
Why does Guy (who seems to be a loving and responsible parent and husband) steal the balloon and jump to his death?	Guy has been deeply affected by Boukman's words, believing that the ultimate gift he can give to his family is to follow Boukman's rallying words that "we shall all let out one piercing cry that we may either live freely or we should die." Stealing the balloon is such a "piercing cry." Little Guy's recitation of Boukman's great speeches about living freely inspires Guy to break the cycle of despair that has devastated his father's life and his own life, and that will likely devastate Little Guy's life. It is the ultimate gift both for his father (justifying his struggles) and for his son (inspiring him to live freely). The psychic damage of pervasive poverty is so strong that even a loving and responsible father and husband like Guy can be driven to horrible deeds.
What does the balloon represent for Guy?	Representing the possibility of escape and freedom, the balloon provides Guy with the opportunity to prove himself as a capable man (not just a man whose only worth is as a latrine cleaner), one who deserves to pursue his freedom.
How and why does the narrator contrast the home setting with the public settings of the Haitian shantytown?	By moving back and forth between Guy's and Lili's loving shanty and the inhospitable shantytown, the story paints a stark contrast between the two worlds and shows how love and responsibility are perhaps impossible in a world of such dreadful poverty.
How does the setting drive the character and plot?	The environment in which Guy lives is all-important, as it drives his character toward feeling deep sadness about the past and keen anxiety about the future. Hence, the setting drives the characters, and the characters drive the plot. By showing the reader how powerful such an environment can be, Danticat creates a story that makes an emotional and very effective argument against poverty.

Cite and Quote the Text to Back Up and Illustrate Your Points. The evidence for your interpretation should come mostly from the text itself. Show your readers what the text says by quoting and citing it.

Include Outside Support, Where Appropriate. Although you can bring in concepts and ideas from outside the text, make sure your ideas are anchored by what is actually written in the text you are studying. Don't just use the text as a springboard to dive off into some other topic. Stay focused on what happens in the literary work.

The Conclusion

Your conclusion should bring your readers around to the main point that you expressed in the introduction. Your conclusion should also point the reader in new directions. Up to this point in the literary analysis, your readers will expect you to closely follow the text. In the conclusion, though, they will allow more leeway. In a sense, you've earned the right to speculate and consider other ideas.

So, if you want, take on the larger issues that were dealt with in this literary work. What conclusions or questions does your analysis suggest? What challenges does the author believe we face? What is the author really trying to say about people, events, and the world we live in?

Choosing an Appropriate Style

Literary analyses invite readers into a conversation about a literary work. Therefore, the style should be straightforward but also inviting and encouraging.

Use the "Literary Present" Tense

The literary present tense involves talking about the work and the characters as though they live in the present day. For example, you might say,

> Little Guy is excited about his role in the play, and while his mother is happy for Little Guy, his father's reactions suggest he is troubled by the speech.

> Many of Langston Hughes's poems recount the struggles of African Americans but are often tinged with definite optimism and hope.

When discussing the author historically, however, use the past tense.

> Langston Hughes was well-known in his time as a Harlem Renaissance poet. He often touched on themes of equality and expressed a guarded optimism about equality of treatment for all races.

Integrate Quoted Text

Weave words and ideas from the literary text into your words and ideas, and avoid quotations that are detached from your ideas. For example, you can include a quotation at the end of your own sentence:

> The outside world is described always as menacing. For instance, the sounds outside their shack are described this way: "Lilly could hear the whispers of the market women, their hisses and swearing as their sandals dug into the sharp-edged rocks on the road" (69).

You could also take the same sentence from the story and weave a "tissue" of quotations into your words:

> The world outside their home is described as menacing. Even "the whispers of the market women" are just "hisses and swearing," and even the road, with its sharp-edged rocks" seems hostile (69).

Make sure any sentences that include quotations remain grammatically correct. When you omit words from your quotation, use ellipses.

When You Quote, Tell Readers What You Want Them to Notice. Whenever you take a quote from the text, explain how the quotation supports your point and your overall claim. Don't leave your readers hanging with a quotation and no commentary. Tell them what the quote means.

Move Beyond Personal Response

Literary analyses are always partly personal, but they are not merely personal. While your professor may encourage you to delve into your personal reactions in your response papers, in your literary analysis you will need to move beyond that personal response to a discussion of the literary work itself. In other words, describe what the text does, not just what it does to you.

Cast Interpretations as Speculative. Literary analyses are interpretive, not absolute and final. When you want your readers to understand that you are interpreting, use words and phrases such as "perhaps," "it could be," "may," "it seems clear that," "seems," and "probably."

> Little Guy and Lili *seem* to immediately understand that Guy has been motivated by something more noble than just a joy ride in a balloon. For instance, Lili *expresses* no sense of shame about her husband's actions, as she claims his body proudly: "'He is mine,' she said to young Assad. 'He is my family. He belongs to me'" (78).

Designing Your Literary Analysis

Typically, literary analyses use a simple and traditional design, following the MLA format for manuscripts: double-spaced, easy-to-read font, one-inch margins, MLA documentation style (see Chapter 27). Always consult with your professor about which format he or she wants you to use.

Headings and graphics are becoming more common in literary analyses. If you want to use headings or graphics, ask your professor if they are allowed. Headings will help you organize your analysis and make transitions between larger sections. In some cases, you may want to add graphics, especially if the literary work you are analyzing uses illustrations or if you have a graphic that would illustrate or help explain a key element in your analysis.

Design features like headers and page numbers are usually welcome, because they help professors and your classmates keep the pages in order. Also, if you discuss your work in class, page numbers help your readers easily find what is being discussed.

Revising and Editing Your Literary Analysis

Once you have drafted your literary analysis, take the time to make sure that you have created a piece that will engage readers and lead them to new and interesting insights about the literary work you are analyzing. Here are some issues to consider as you revise and edit your draft:

Make Sure the Interpretive Question and Its Importance Are Clearly Stated. If your readers are to engage with you in a conversation about the literary work, they first need to understand your interpretive question and the angle you are exploring. They also need to understand why your interpretive question is important or interesting and how it will lead to insights about the work that go beyond a surface reading.

Check Your Main Claim, or What Your Interpretation Reveals About the Work. Your reader will also want to completely understand what your interpretation reveals about the work. State your main claim clearly, prominently, and completely near the end of your introduction. You may have already written a main claim (working thesis) early in the drafting process, but as you fill out your analysis, you will get a better and better sense of exactly what your interpretation is about and why it is interesting and important. Return to your claim again and again to adjust and refine it.

Check Whether Your Analysis Remains Focused on Your Interpretive Question and Main Claim. Every paragraph should further develop your interpretation. Examine your topic sentences and make sure each paragraph moves your interpretation further along. If you find yourself going off on a tangent, revise or eliminate that part of the analysis.

Make Sure You Cite, Quote, and Explain Specific Parts of the Literary Text. Use the text as evidence to support your claims. Although you may wish to bring in ideas and sources from outside the text, make sure your reader understands exactly how the material in the literary text itself leads you to your interpretation.

Verify That You Have Cited the Text Appropriately. When you quote the text or describe a specific part of it, your readers will want to know exactly where in the text they can find that material. So use MLA documentation style to cite any quotes or sources. Also, include a "Works Cited" page that identifies the edition of your literary text and any other sources you consulted.

Make sure you spend ample time revising and editing your work. The real reader of your literary analysis is probably a professor, perhaps an English professor. That kind of reader is more sensitive than most to good (and bad) organization and style. So the extra time spent revising and editing will greatly improve his or her impression of your work.

The Reading Response

Here's something that happens more and more in courses in every college discipline. Your professor assigns a reading response as "informal writing." A literature professor might ask you to write about your first reaction to a poem to help you explore its meaning. An anthropology professor might ask you to describe your reactions to the rituals of a different culture. In the workplace, trainers and consultants often use informal writing exercises to help teams of employees explore ideas together—a kind of brainstorming.

Your professors may assign a wide variety of reading response assignments, but no matter what the specific assignment, make sure you do the following:

Read the prompt carefully.   Make sure you understand exactly what your professor wants you to do. Pay attention to the verbs. Are you supposed to summarize, explore, speculate, analyze, identify, explain, define, evaluate, apply, or something else?

Try out new ideas and approaches.   Informal writing can be your chance to speculate, explore, and be creative. Be sure you understand what your professor expects, but reading responses can allow you to stretch your thinking into new areas.

Show that you have read, understand, and can work with the material.
Ground your response in the material you are being asked about. When writing about a story or poem, come back to the text with quotes, summaries, and descriptions. If the reading involves a concept, make sure your response shows that you understand or can use the concept to address the prompt.

Branch out and make connections (if appropriate).   Look for the broader implications and for connections with other issues from the course. With informal writing like reading responses, you're usually allowed to or even encouraged to take risks and speculate. If you're not sure whether your professor wants you to do this, ask.

WRITE **your own reading response.**   Ground your response in the text itself by describing or summarizing aspects of the text or by quoting it. Then move to generating new ideas and insights, making connections between the text and something else (something you know about from personal experience). Because this is an informal response, speculate and take risks. Have fun exploring the text while you write your response.

Reading response assignment

Here is an example of the kind of response prompt you might be assigned in a literature class. This prompt is about a poem by the African American writer Langston Hughes (1902–1967). The professor's prompt follows the poem; the student's response is on the next page.

I, Too

I, too, sing America.

I am the darker brother.
They send me to eat in the kitchen
When company comes,
But I laugh,   5
And eat well,
And grow strong.

Tomorrow,
I'll be at the table
When company comes.   10
Nobody'll dare
Say to me,
"Eat in the kitchen,"
Then.

Besides,   15
They'll see how beautiful I am
And be ashamed—

I, too, am America.

Reading response prompt for "I, Too"

Write a response paper that is at least three pages long and that incorporates at least two quotations from the poem. Langston Hughes's poem renders a general social issue concrete and tangible with his central metaphor of being sent to the kitchen. Examine this metaphor closely. Explain how it works in the poem and why you think Hughes chose *this* metaphor? That is, how does it add to the impact or meaning of the poem in terms of tone, theme, or overall message?

Specifies use of at least two quotes.

Be sure to discuss concept of kitchen as metaphor.

The two key verbs are *examine* and *explain*.

continued

A Student's Reading Response

Informal reading response uses personal pronouns *I* and *me*.

Satisfies the prompt by quoting the poem, and discussing the metaphor.

Directly addresses the prompt (why Hughes "chose *this* metaphor").

Connects poem and its context.

Makes further connections to the present day.

On my first reading of Hughes's "I, Too," what jumped out at me is optimism and patience. This feeling comes from the narrator's saying "[t]omorrow, / I'll be at the table / When company comes." He seems full of confidence and hope. But then I read the prompt and started really thinking hard about the kitchen and that happy picture changed in my mind. Reading it, I would see in my mind's eye a clear picture of a "darker brother / They send . . . to eat in the kitchen / When company comes." I get an almost perfect picture of a kitchen with an old-fashioned table and a big old white stove. I think Hughes chose the metaphor of the kitchen because it suggests a home and a family—like America really is one family. The word *family* isn't in the poem, but the kitchen and his calling himself a "darker *brother*" implies family.

And this "family" is pretty messed up, making the "darker brother" hide away. So I also think Hughes wanted to show how crazy and unnatural it was for the American family to be divided between lighter and darker. It's interesting that the narrator is confident that the family will be restored to healthiness and naturalness. But now, that optimism that seemed so rosy at first seems like injustice.

I guess he uses the kitchen metaphor because it's harder to visualize a "family." And then all this leads to an idea that's *really* hard to visualize—injustice. Maybe that's the central idea, even though nothing like this word ever appears. I wonder if that's the message for the audience in 1932. Maybe in 1932, there was reason to believe our American "family" would soon work things out, but actually it has not worked things out. I think that while the whole poem is a metaphor for the political and social situation of America in 1932, it could actually be replayed again and again across the 1900s. In American history, we learned that African Americans were confident about equality after World War II (which didn't happen) and after the Civil Rights Movement (which didn't happen). So the poem in retrospect is really sad. It even reminds me of when Obama was elected U.S. President. People were saying, "Now things will be different." I hope it's not just the "I, Too" poem playing out one more time. No wonder he says at the end, "They'll see how beautiful I am / And be ashamed."

Here are some quick steps to get you going on your literary analysis.

READ the Literary Work at Least Twice and Narrow Your Topic

Make sure you're very familiar with the work you'll be analyzing so you can examine the text closely. If you have response papers or other notes, look at them closely, too.

STATE Your Interpretive Question

In one sentence, try to write down the question that you want to answer in your analysis. This will probably change as you draft your analysis and continue delving deeply into the text, so don't worry about making it perfect. This is just to get you started; you'll refine this later.

DO Some Inquiry and Research

Using your reading notes, decide what intrigues you most about the work. Then do some outside research on the text, its author, and the historical period in which it was written.

IDENTIFY Your Main Claim

Come up with a main claim that answers your interpretive question. Your main claim will probably change and evolve, so just write down your best guess at this point.

DRAFT Your Analysis

Take your reader step by step through the analysis. Use targeted summaries and quotes to direct readers' attention to specific aspects of the text (not the whole text).

REVISIT Your Introduction and Conclusion

After drafting, go back to your introduction and refine your interpretive question and interpretive claim. After reading through your analysis once more, go to your conclusion and make sure that it brings readers back to your main claim and then branches out in new directions.

DESIGN, Revise, and Edit

The design of a literary analysis is typically simple and straightforward. However, make sure you format the document the way your professor requests. Then revise by sharpening your topic sentences and making sure each paragraph stays focused on answering your interpretive question. Make sure you use the literary present tense and cite the text properly.

A Wall of Fire Rising

EDWIDGE DANTICAT

Edwidge Danticat was born in the city of Port-au-Prince, Haiti, in 1969 and immigrated to the United States with her parents (a cab driver and textile worker) at the age of twelve. She is the author of three plays and seven novels. She has edited books and published a memoir, Brother, I'm Dying, *in 2007. In 1995, she published,* Krik?Krak!, *her only collection of short stories, which includes "A Wall of Fire Rising" and was a finalist for the National Book Award. More information about Danticat's literary themes and personal background can be found in the literary analysis, "An Interview with Edwidge Danticat" on page 158.*

"Listen to what happened today," Guy said as he barged through the rattling door of his tiny shack.

His wife, Lili, was squatting in the middle of their one-room home, spreading cornmeal mush on banana leaves for their supper.

"Listen to what happened *to me* today!" Guy's seven-year-old son—Little Guy—dashed from a corner and grabbed his father's hand. The boy dropped his composition notebook as he leaped to his father, nearly stepping into the corn mush and herring that his mother had set out in a trio of half gourds on the clay floor.

"Our boy is in a play." Lili quickly robbed Little Guy of the honor of telling his father the news.

"A play?" Guy affectionately stroked the 5 boy's hair.

The boy had such tiny corkscrew curls that no amount of brushing could ever make them all look like a single entity. The other boys at the Lycée Jean-Jacques called him "pepper head" because each separate kinky strand was coiled into a tight tiny ball that looked like small peppercorns.

"When is this play?" Guy asked both the boy and his wife. "Are we going to have to buy new clothes for this?"

Lili got up from the floor and inclined her face towards her husband's in order to receive her nightly peck on the cheek.

"What role do you have in the play?" Guy asked, slowly rubbing the tip of his nails across the boy's scalp. His fingers made a soft grating noise with each invisible circle drawn around the perimeters of the boy's head. Guy's fingers finally landed inside the boy's ears, forcing the boy to giggle until he almost gave himself the hiccups.

"Tell me, what is your part in the play?" 10 Guy asked again, pulling his fingers away from his son's ear.

"I am Boukman," the boy huffed out, as though there was some laughter caught in his throat.

"Show Papy your lines," Lili told the boy as she arranged the three open gourds on a piece of plywood raised like a table on two bricks, in the middle of the room. "My love, Boukman is the hero of the play."

The boy went back to the corner where he had been studying and pulled out a thick book carefully covered in brown paper.

"You're going to spend a lifetime learning those." Guy took the book from the boy's hand and flipped through the pages quickly. He had to strain his eyes to see the words by the light of an old kerosene lamp, which that night—like all others—flickered as though it was burning its very last wick.

"All these words seem so long and heavy," Guy said. "You think you can do this, son?" 15

"He has one very good speech," Lili said. "Page forty, remember, son?"

The boy took back the book from his father. His face was crimped in an of-course-I-remember look as he searched for page forty.

"Bouk-man," Guy struggled with the letters of the slave revolutionary's name as he looked over his son's shoulders. "I see some very hard words here, son."

"He already knows his speech," Lili told her husband.

"Does he now?" asked Guy. 20

"We've been at it all afternoon," Lili said. "Why don't you go on and recite that speech for your father?"

The boy tipped his head towards the rusting tin on the roof as he prepared to recite his lines.

Lili wiped her hands on an old apron tied around her waist and stopped to listen.

"Remember what you are," Lili said, "a great rebel leader. Remember, it is the revolution."

"Do we want him to be all of that?" Guy asked. 25

"He is Boukman," Lili said. "What is the only thing on your mind now, Boukman?"

"Supper," Guy whispered, enviously eyeing the food cooling off in the middle of the room. He and the boy looked at each other and began to snicker.

"Tell us the other thing that is on your mind," Lili said, joining in their laughter.

"Freedom!" shouted the boy, as he quickly slipped into his role.

"Louder!" urged Lili. 30

"Freedom is on my mind!" yelled the boy.

"Why don't you start, son?" said Guy. "If you don't, we'll never get to that other thing that we have on our minds."

The boy closed his eyes and took a deep breath. At first, his lips parted but nothing came out. Lili pushed her head forward as though she were holding her breath. Then like the last burst of lightning out of clearing sky, the boy began.

"A wall of fire is rising and in the ashes, I see the bones of my people. Not only those people whose dark hollow faces I see daily in the fields, but all those souls who have gone ahead to haunt my dreams. At night I relive once more the last caresses from the hand of a loving father, a valiant love, a beloved friend."

It was obvious that this was a speech written by a European man, who gave to the slave revolutionary Boukman the kind of European phrasing that might have sent the real Boukman turning in his grave. However, the speech made Lili and Guy stand on the tips of their toes from great pride. As their applause thundered in the small space of their shack that night, they felt as though for a moment they had been given the rare pleasure of hearing the voice of one of the forefathers of Haitian independence in the forced baritone of their only child. The experience left them both with a strange feeling that they could not explain. It left the hair on the back of their necks standing on end. It left them feeling much more love than they ever knew that they could add to their feeling for their son. 35

"Bravo," Lili cheered, pressing her son into the folds of her apron. "Long live Boukman and long live my boy."

"Long live our supper," Guy said, quickly batting his eyelashes to keep tears from rolling down his face.

• • •

The boy kept his eyes on his book as they ate their supper that night. Usually Guy and Lili would not have allowed that, but this was a special occasion. They watched proudly as the boy muttered his lines between swallows of cornmeal.

The boy was still mumbling the same words as the three of them used the last of the rainwater trapped in old gasoline containers and sugarcane pulp from the nearby sugarcane mill to scrub the gourds that they had eaten from.

When things were really bad for the fam- 40 ily, they boiled clean sugarcane pulp to make what Lili called her special sweet water tea. It was supposed to suppress gas and kill the vermin in the stomach that made poor children hungry. That and a pinch of salt under the tongue could usually quench hunger until Guy found a day's work or Lili could manage to buy spices on credit and then peddle them for a profit at the marketplace.

That night, anyway, things were good. Everyone had eaten enough to put all their hunger vermin to sleep.

The boy was sitting in front of the shack on an old plastic bucket turned upside down, straining his eyes to find the words on the page. Sometimes when there was no kerosene for the lamp, the boy would have to go sit by the side of the road and study under the street lamps with the rest of the neighborhood children. Tonight, at least, they had a bit of their own light.

Guy bent down by a small clump of old mushrooms near the boy's feet, trying to get a better look at the plant. He emptied the last drops of rainwater from a gasoline container on the mushroom, wetting the bulging toes sticking out of his sons' sandals, which were already coming apart around his endlessly growing feet.

Guy tried to pluck some of the mushrooms, which were being pushed into the dust as though they wanted to grow beneath the ground as roots. He took one of the mushrooms in his hand, running his smallest finger over the round bulb. He clipped the stem and buried the top in a thick strand of his wife's hair.

The mushroom looked like a dried insect 45 in Lili's hair.

"It sure makes you look special," Guy said, teasing her.

"Thank you so much," Lili said, tapping her husband's arm. "It's nice to know that I deserve these much more than roses."

Taking his wife's hand, Guy said, "Let's go to the sugar mill."

"Can I study my lines there?" the boy asked.

"You know them well enough already," 50 Guy said.

"I need many repetitions," the boy said.

． ． ．

Their feet sounded as though they were playing a wet wind instrument as they slipped in and out of the puddles between the shacks in the shantytown. Near the sugar mill was a large television screen in a iron grill cage that the government had installed so that the shantytown dwellers could watch the state-sponsored news at eight o'clock every night. After the news, a gendarme would come and turn off the television set, taking home the key. On most nights, the people stayed at the site long after this gendarme had gone and told stories to one another beneath the big blank screen. They made bonfires with dried sticks, corn husks, and paper, cursing the authorities under their breath.

There was a crowd already gathering for the nightly news event. The sugar mill workers sat in the front row in chairs or on old buckets.

Lili and Guy passed the group, clinging to their son so that in his childhood naïveté he wouldn't accidentally glance at the wrong person and be called an insolent child. They didn't like the ambiance of the nightly news watch. They spared themselves trouble by going instead to the sugar mill, where in the past year they had discovered their own wonder.

Everyone knew that the family who 55 owned the sugar mill were eccentric "Arabs," Haitians of Lebanese or Palestinian descent whose family had been in the country for generations. The Assad family had a son who, it seems, was into all manner of odd things, the most recent of which was a hot-air balloon, which he had brought to Haiti from

America and occasionally flew over the shan-tytown skies.

As they approached the fence surround-ing the field where the large wicker basket and deflated balloon rested on the ground, Guy let go of the hands of both his wife and the boy.

Lili walked on slowly with her son. For the last few weeks, she had been feeling as though Guy was lost to her each time he reached this point, twelve feet away from the balloon. As Guy pushed his hand through the barbed wire, she could tell from the look on his face that he was thinking of sitting inside the square basket while the smooth rainbow surface of the balloon itself floated above his head. During the day, when the field was open, Guy would walk up to the basket, star-ing at it with the same kind of longing that most men display when they admire very pretty girls.

Lili and the boy stood watching from a distance as Guy tried to push his hand deeper, beyond the chain link fence that sep-arated him from the balloon. He reached into his pants pocket and pulled out a small pock-etknife, sharpening the edges on the metal surface of the fence. When his wife and child moved closer, he put the knife back in his pocket, letting his fingers slide across his son's tightly coiled curls.

"I wager you I can make this thing fly," Guy said.

"Why do you think you can do that?" Lili 60 asked.

"I know it," Guy replied.

He followed her as she circled the sugar mill, leading to their favorite spot under a watch light. Little Guy lagged faithfully be-hind them. From this distance, the hot-air balloon looked like an odd spaceship.

Lili stretched her body out in the knee-high grass in the field. Guy reached over and tried to touch her between her legs.

"You're not one to worry, Lili," he said. "You're not afraid of the frogs, lizards, or snakes that could be hiding in this grass?"

"I am here with my husband," she said. 65 "You are here to protect me if anything hap-pens."

Guy reached into his shirt pocket and pulled out a lighter and a crumpled piece of paper. He lit the paper until it burned to an ashy film. The burning paper floated in the night breeze for a while, landing in fragments on the grass.

"Did you see that, Lili?" Guy asked with a flame in his eyes brighter than the lighter's. "Did you see how the paper floated when it was burned? This is how that balloon flies."

"What did you mean by saying that you could make it fly?" Lili asked.

"You already know all my secrets," Guy said as the boy came charging towards them.

"Papa, could you play *Lago* with me?" 70 the boy asked.

Lili lay peacefully on the grass as her son and husband played hide-and-seek. Guy kept hiding and his son kept finding him as each time Guy made it easier for the boy.

"We rest now." Guy was becoming breath-less.

The stars were circling the peaks of the mountains, dipping into the cane fields be-longing to the sugar mill. As Guy caught his breath, the boy raced around the fence, run-ning as fast as he could to purposely make himself dizzy.

"Listen to what happened today," Guy whispered softly in Lili's ear.

"I heard you say that when you walked in 75 the house tonight," Lili said. "With the boy's play, I forgot to ask you."

The boy sneaked up behind them, his face lit up, though his brain was spinning. He wrapped his arms around both their necks.

"We will go back home soon," Lili said.

"Can I recite my lines?" asked the boy.

"We have heard them," Guy said. "Don't tire your lips."

The boy mumbled something under his 80 breath. Guy grabbed his ear and twirled it un-til it was a tiny ball in his hand. The boy's face contorted with agony as Guy made him kneel in the deep grass in punishment.

Lili looked tortured as she watched the boy squirming in the grass, obviously terrified of the crickets, lizards, and small snakes that might be there.

"Perhaps we should take him home to bed," she said.

"He will never learn," Guy said, "if I say one thing and you say another."

Guy got up and angrily started walking home. Lili walked over, took her son's hand, and raised him from his knees.

"You know you must not mumble," she said. 85

"I was saying my lines," the boy said.

"Next time say them loud," Lili said, "so he knows what is coming out of your mouth."

That night Lili could hear her son muttering his lines as he tucked himself in his corner of the room and drifted off to sleep. The boy still had the book with his monologue in it clasped under his arm as he slept.

• • •

Guy stayed outside in front of the shack as Lili undressed for bed. She loosened the ribbon that held the old light blue cotton skirt around her waist and let it drop past her knees. She grabbed half a lemon that she kept in the corner by the folded mat that she and Guy unrolled to sleep on every night. Lili let her blouse drop to the floor as she smoothed the lemon over her ashen legs.

Guy came in just at that moment and 90 saw her bare chest by the light of the smaller castor oil lamp that they used for the later hours of the night. Her skin had coarsened a bit over the years, he thought. Her breasts now drooped from having nursed their son for two years after he was born. It was now easier for him to imagine their son's lips around those breasts than to imagine his anywhere near them.

He turned his face away as she fumbled for her nightgown. He helped her open the mat, tucking the blanket edges underneath.

Fully clothed, Guy dropped onto the mat next to her. He laid his head on her chest, rubbing the spiky edges of his hair against her nipples.

"What was it that happened today?" Lili asked, running her fingers along Guy's hairline, an angular hairline, almost like a triangle, in the middle of his forehead. She nearly didn't marry him because it was said that people with angular hairlines often have very troubled lives.

"I got a few hours' work for tomorrow at the sugar mill," Guy said. "That's what happened today."

"It was such a long time coming," Lili said. 95

It was almost six months since the last time Guy had gotten work there. The jobs at the sugar mill were few and far between. The people who had them never left, or when they did they would pass the job on to another family member who was already waiting on line.

Guy did not seem overjoyed about the one day's work.

"I wish I had paid more attention when you came in with the news," Lili said. "I was just so happy about the boy."

"I was born in the shadow of that sugar mill," Guy said. "Probably the first thing my mother gave me to drink as a baby was some sweet water tea from the pulp of the sugarcane. If anyone deserves to work there, I should."

"What will you be doing for your day's 100 work?"

"Would you really like to know?"

"There is never any shame in honest work," she said.

"They want me to scrub the latrines."

"It's honest work," Lili said, trying to console him.

"I am still number seventy-eight on the 105 permanent hire list," he said. "I was thinking of putting the boy on the list now, so maybe by the time he becomes a man he can be up for a job."

Lili's body jerked forward, rising straight up in the air. Guy's head dropped with a loud thump onto the mat.

"I don't want him on that list," she said. "For a young boy to be on any list like that might influence his destiny. I don't want him on the list."

"Look at me," Guy said. "If my father had worked there, if he had me on the list, don't you think I would be working?"

"If you have any regard for me," she said, "you will not put him on the list."

She groped for her husband's chest in the dark and laid her head on it. She could hear his heart beating loudly as though it were pumping double, triple its normal rate.

"You won't put the boy on any lists, will you?" she implored.

"Please, Lili, no more about the boy. He will not go on the list."

"Thank you."

"Tonight I was looking at that balloon in the yard behind the sugar mill," he said. "I have been watching it real close."

"I know."

"I have seen the man who owns it," he said. "I've seen him get in it and put it in the sky and go up there like it was some kind of kite and he was the kite master. I see the men who run after it trying to figure out where it will land. Once I was there and I was one of those men who were running and I actually guessed correctly. I picked a spot in the sugarcane fields. I picked the spot from a distance and it actually landed there."

"Let me say something to you, Guy—"

"Pretend that this is the time of miracles and we believed in them. I watched the owner for a long time, and I think I can fly that balloon. The first time I saw him do it, it looked like a miracle, but the more and more I saw it, the more ordinary it became."

"You're probably intelligent enough to do it," she said.

"I am intelligent enough to do it. You're right to say that I can."

"Don't you think about hurting yourself?"

"Think like this. Can't you see yourself up there? Up in the clouds somewhere like some kind of bird?"

"If God wanted people to fly, he would have given us wings on our backs."

"You're right, Lili, you're right. But look what he gave us instead. He gave us reasons to want to fly. He gave us the air, the birds, our son."

"I don't understand you," she said.

"Our son, your son, you do not want him cleaning latrines."

"He can do other things."

"Me too. I can do other things too."

A loud scream came from the corner where the boy was sleeping. Lili and Guy rushed to him and tried to wake him. The boy was trembling when he opened his eyes.

"What is the matter?" Guy asked.

"I cannot remember my lines," the boy said.

Lili tried to string together what she could remember of her son's lines. The words slowly came back to the boy. By the time he fell back to sleep, it was almost dawn.

• • •

The light was slowly coming up behind the trees. Lili could hear the whispers of the market women, their hisses and swearing as their sandals dug into the sharp-edged rocks on the road.

She turned her back to her husband as she slipped out of her nightgown, quickly putting on her day clothes.

"Imagine this," Guy said from the mat on the floor. "I have never really seen your entire body in broad daylight."

Lili shut the door behind her, making her way out to the yard. The empty gasoline containers rested easily on her head as she walked a few miles to the public water fountains. It was harder to keep them steady when the containers were full. The water splashed all over her blouse and rippled down her back.

The sky was blue as it was most mornings, a dark indigo-shaded turquoise that would get lighter when the sun was fully risen.

Guy and the boy were standing in the yard waiting for her when she got back.

"You did not get much sleep, my handsome boy," she said, running her wet fingers over the boy's face.

"He'll be late for school if we do not go 140 right now," Guy said. "I want to drop him off before I start work."

"Do we remember our lines this morning?" Lili asked, tucking the boy's shirt down deep into his short pants.

"We just recited them," Guy said. "Even I know them now."

Lili watched them walk down the footpath, her eyes following them until they disappeared.

As soon as they were out of sight, she poured the water she had fetched into a large calabash, letting it stand beside the house.

She went back into the room and slipped 145 into a dry blouse. It was never too early to start looking around, to scrape together that night's meal.

• • •

"Listen to what happened again today," Lili said when Guy walked through the door that afternoon.

Guy blotted his face with a dust rag as he prepared to hear the news. After the day he'd had at the factory, he wanted to sit under a tree and have a leisurely smoke, but he did not want to set a bad example for his son by indulging his very small pleasures.

"You tell him, son," Lili urged the boy, who was quietly sitting in a corner, reading.

"I've got more lines," the boy announced, springing up to his feet. "Papy, do you want to hear them?"

"They are giving him more things to say 150 in the play," Lili explained, "because he did such a good job memorizing so fast."

"My compliments, son. Do you have your new lines memorized too?" Guy asked.

"Why don't you recite your new lines for your father?" Lili said.

The boy walked to the middle of the room and prepared to recite. He cleared his throat, raising his eyes towards the ceiling.

"There is so much sadness in the faces of my people. I have called on their gods, now I call on our gods. I call on our young. I call on our old. I call on our mighty and the weak. I call on everyone and anyone so that we shall all let out one piercing cry that we may either live freely or we should die."

"I see your new lines have as much 155 drama as the old ones," Guy said. He wiped a tear away, walked over to the chair, and took the boy in his arms. He pressed the boy's body against his chest before lowering him to the ground.

"Your new lines are wonderful, son. They're every bit as affecting as the old." He tapped the boy's shoulder and walked out of the house.

"What's the matter with Papy?" the boy asked as the door slammed shut behind Guy.

"His heart hurts," Lili said.

• • •

After supper, Lili took her son to the field where she knew her husband would be. While the boy ran around, she found her husband sitting in his favorite spot behind the sugar mill.

"Nothing, Lili," he said. "Ask me nothing 160 about this day that I have had."

She sat down on the grass next to him, for once feeling the sharp edges of the grass blades against her ankles.

"You're really good with that boy," he said, drawing circles with his smallest finger on her elbow. "You will make a performer of him. I know you will. You can see the best in that whole situation. It's because you have those stars in your eyes. That's the first thing I noticed about you when I met you. It was your eyes, Lili, so dark and deep. They drew me like danger draws a fool."

He turned over on the grass so that he was staring directly at the moon up in the sky.

She could tell that he was also watching the hot-air balloon behind the sugar mill fence out of the corner of his eye.

"Sometimes I know you want to believe in me," he said. "I know you're wishing things for me. You want me to work at the mill. You want me to get a pretty house for us. I know you want these things too, but mostly you want me to feel like a man. That's why you're not one to worry about, Lili. I know you can take things as they come."

"I don't like it when you talk this way," she said. 165

"Listen to this, Lili. I want to tell you a secret. Sometimes, I just want to take that big balloon and ride it up in the air. I'd like to sail off somewhere and keep floating until I got to a really nice place with a nice plot of land where I could be something new. I'd build my own house, keep my own garden. Just *be* something new."

"I want you to stay away from there."

"I know you don't think I should take it. That can't keep me from wanting."

"You could be injured. Do you ever think about that?"

"Don't you ever want to be something new?" 170

"I don't like it," she said.

"Please don't get angry with me," he said, his voice straining almost like the boy's.

"If you were to take that balloon and fly away, would you take me and the boy?"

"First you don't want me to take it and now you want to go?"

"I just want to know that when you dream, 175 me and the boy, we're always in your dreams."

He leaned his head on her shoulders and drifted off to sleep. Her back ached as she sat there with his face pressed against her collar bone. He drooled and the saliva dripped down to her breasts, soaking her frayed polyester bra. She listened to the crickets while watching her son play, muttering his lines to himself as he went in a circle around the field. The moon was glowing above their heads. Winking at them, as Guy liked to say, on its way to brighter shores.

Opening his eyes, Guy asked her, "How do you think a man is judged after he's gone?"

How did he expect her to answer something like that?

"People don't eat riches," she said. "They eat what it can buy."

"What does that mean, Lili? Don't talk to 180 me in parables. Talk to me honestly."

"A man is judged by his deeds," she said. "The boy never goes to bed hungry. For as long as he's been with us, he's always been fed."

Just as if he had heard himself mentioned, the boy came dashing from the other side of the field, crashing in a heap on top of his parents.

"My new lines," he said. "I have forgotten my new lines."

"Is this how you will be the day of this play, son?" Guy asked. "When people give you big responsibilities, you have to try to live up to them."

The boy had relearned his new lines by 185 the time they went to bed.

That night, Guy watched his wife very closely as she undressed for bed.

"I would like to be the one to rub that piece of lemon on your knees tonight," he said.

She handed him the half lemon, then raised her skirt above her knees.

Her body began to tremble as he rubbed his fingers over her skin.

"You know that question I asked you be- 190 fore," he said, "how a man is remembered after he's gone? I know the answer now. I know because I remember my father, who was a very poor struggling man all his life. I remember him as a man that I would never want to be."

• • •

Lili got up with the break of dawn the next day. The light came up quickly above the trees. Lili greeted some of the market women as they walked together to the public water fountain.

On her way back, the sun had already melted a few gray clouds. She found the boy standing alone in the yard with a terrified expression on his face, the old withered mushrooms uprooted at his feet. He ran up to meet her, nearly knocking her off balance.

"What happened?" she asked. "Have you forgotten your lines?"

The boy was breathing so heavily that his lips could not form a single word.

"What is it?" Lili asked, almost shaking 195 him with anxiety.

"It's Papa," he said finally, raising a stiff finger in the air.

The boy covered his face as his mother looked up at the sky. A rainbow-colored balloon was floating aimlessly above their heads.

"It's Papa," the boy said. "He is in it."

She wanted to look down at her son and tell him that it wasn't his father, but she immediately recognized the spindly arms, in a bright flowered shirt that she had made, gripping the cables.

• • •

From the field behind the sugar mill a group 200 of workers were watching the balloon floating in the air. Many were clapping and cheering, calling out Guy's name. A few of the women were waving their head rags at the sky, shouting, "Go! Beautiful, go!"

Lili edged her way to the front of the crowd. Everyone was waiting, watching the balloon drift higher up into the clouds.

"He seems to be right over our heads," said the factory foreman, a short slender mulatto with large buckteeth.

Just then, Lili noticed young Assad, his thick black hair sticking to the beads of sweat on his forehead. His face had the crumpled expression of disrupted sleep.

"He's further away than he seems," said young Assad. "I still don't understand. How did he get up there? You need a whole crew to fly these things."

"I don't know," the foreman said. "One of 205 my workers just came in saying there was a man flying above the factory."

"But how the hell did he start it?" Young Assad was perplexed.

"He just did it," the foreman said.

"Look, he's trying to get out!" someone hollered.

A chorus of screams broke out among the workers.

The boy was looking up, trying to see if his 210 father was really trying to jump out of the balloon. Guy was climbing over the side of the basket. Lili pressed her son's face into her skirt.

Within seconds, Guy was in the air hurtling down towards the crowd. Lili held her breath as she watched him fall. He crashed not far from where Lili and the boy were standing, his blood immediately soaking the landing spot.

The balloon kept floating free, drifting on its way to brighter shores. Young Assad rushed towards the body. He dropped to his knees and checked the wrist for a pulse, then dropped the arm back to the ground.

"It's over!" The foreman ordered the workers back to work.

Lili tried to keep her son's head pressed against her skirt as she moved closer to the body. The boy yanked himself away and raced to the edge of the field where his father's body was lying on the grass. He reached the body as young Assad still knelt examining the corpse. Lili rushed after him.

"He is mine," she said to young Assad. 215 "He is my family. He belongs to me."

Young Assad got up and raised his head to search the sky for his aimless balloon, trying to guess where it would land. He took one last glance at Guy's bloody corpse, then raced to his car and sped away.

The foreman and another worker carried a cot and blanket from the factory.

Little Guy was breathing quickly as he looked at his father's body on the ground. While the foreman draped a sheet over Guy's corpse, his son began to recite the lines from his play.

"A wall of fire is rising and in the ashes, I see the bones of my people. Not only those people whose dark hollow faces I see daily in the fields, but all those souls who have gone ahead to haunt my dreams. At night I relive once more the last caresses from the hand of a loving father, a valiant love, a beloved friend."

"Let me look at him one last time," Lili 220 said, pulling back the sheet.

She leaned in very close to get a better look at Guy's face. There was little left of that countenance that she had loved so much. Those lips that curled when he was teasing her. That large flat nose that felt like a feather when rubbed against hers. And those eyes, those night-colored eyes. Though clouded with blood, Guy's eyes were still bulging open. Lili was searching for some kind of sign—a blink, a smile, a wink—something that would remind her of the man that she had married.

"His eyes aren't closed," the foreman said to Lili. "Do you want to close them, or should I?"

The boy continued reciting his lines, his voice rising to a man's grieving roar. He kept his eyes closed, his fists balled at his side as he continued with his newest lines.

"There is so much sadness in the faces of my people. I have called on their gods, now I call on our gods. I call on our young. I call on our old. I call on our mighty and the weak. I call on everyone and anyone so that we shall all let out one piercing cry that we may either live freely or we should die."

"Do you want to close the eyes?" the 225 foreman repeated impatiently.

"No, leave them open," Lili said. "My husband, he likes to look at the sky."

A CLOSER LOOK AT
A Wall of Fire Rising

1. Make a list of specific words and phrases that characterize or describe the story's settings, characters, and interpersonal relationships: the family's home; the shantytown and other areas outside the home; Guy's personality and character; Lili's personality and character; the relationships among family members; the relationship between Guy and Lili. (If you form groups, each group can take one or two of these topics and present their lists to the class.) Now, write a paragraph that describes that setting, character, or relationship. It should have a strong topic sentence and should include quoted words, phrases, sentences, and possibly passages. Use the strategies in "Choosing an Appropriate Style" to help you integrate the story's words with your own (and be sure to use the literary present tense when appropriate).

2. The setting for this story is a Haitian shantytown. Do some research on Haitian shantytowns to find out what they're like and what it's like to live in one. Try to find pictures depicting them and life there. What role does the setting itself play in the story? Our environment affects us in ways that are both profound and subtle. How does this setting affect the reader's view of the story and its characters, and how does the setting affect the characters' views of themselves?

3. If you were going to produce a movie based on this short story, how would you do it? Which actors would you choose to play the roles of each character? How would you try to capture the mood of the story with visual effects: lighting, camera angles, and so on? If you wanted to be as true to the story as possible (not just the events, but its mood and tone), what would this movie look like? Write a one-minute "pitch" for your movie and present it to the class. (The pitch is a microgenre similar to proposals; see Chapter 12).

1. After reading Renée H. Shea's "An Interview with Edwidge Danticat," write a reading response that addresses how learning about the author has colored or even changed your interpretation of "A Wall of Fire Rising." What is it about Danticat's background, values, beliefs, or motivations that made you see things differently? What do you understand about the story that you didn't understand before? What do you see in the story that you didn't see before? In general, does knowing an author's background help you to understand and appreciate a literary work?

2. Develop your own interpretive question about "A Wall of Fire Rising" and write a literary analysis about the short story. Use the strategies described in "Inventing Your Literary Analysis's Content" to help you develop your question. Focus your analysis on the text.

An Interview with Edwidge Danticat

RENÉE H. SHEA

In the following interview, Danticat discusses the stories included in Krik? Krak! *with interviewer Renée H. Shea, who provides background and commentary on the stories and quotes directly from the interview. Danticat reveals a great deal about her background, about her feelings toward Haiti and the people who live and die there, and about what she wants to accomplish with her literary work. Renée H. Shea is a professor of English at Bowie State University, one of the oldest Historically Black Colleges, where she has directed the first-year writing program. She publishes on the subject of Caribbean women writers, including Danticat.*

Krik? Krak! Somewhere by the seacoast I feel a breath of warm sea air and hear the laughter of children. An old granny smokes her pipe, surrounded by the village children. . . . "We tell stories so that the young ones will know what came before them. They ask Krik? We say Krak! Our stories are kept in our hearts."

This epigraph sets the stage and tone for the nine stories of the heart by Haitian-born

Edwidge Danticat in her recent collection entitled *Krik? Krak!* In these tales of the politics and people of Haiti, past and present, on their island home and in newly formed immigrant communities, she lures us not simply to read but to participate in the tradition of Krik? Krak! that she remembers from childhood:

"Krik? Krak!" is call-response but also it's this feeling that you're not merely an observer—you're part of the story. Someone says, "Krik?" and as loud as you can you say, "Krak!" You urge the person to tell the story by your enthusiasm to hear it.

So compelling are these stories, filled with the myth and poetry of Haiti, that as one ends, it is hard not to call out a resounding, "Krak!" to keep the momentum of Danticat's storytelling going.

Taken individually, several stories are stunning in the power of both the tale and language. "Children of the Sea" is told as a dialogue between two young lovers—one on a boat bound for Miami, the other reporting from Haiti on the horrors wrought by the TonTon Macoutes. The young man reports the desperate life of himself and the "thirty-six other deserting souls on this little boat" and the story-within-the-story of Celianne. Pregnant after a gang rape by the TonTon Macoutes, Celianne fled her accusing family, and when she gives birth aboard the boat to a stillborn child, she refuses to give it up. Finally forced to throw the baby overboard, she follows by jumping into the sea. The young woman's story of her family's struggle in Haiti, the increasing violence, and the lengths her father finally goes to protect her are counterpoint. The nightmarish reality of the TonTon Macoutes is challenged by the fierce love of the two young people; the unnamed he wonders, "Maybe the sea is endless. Like my love for you," and she exclaims, "I love you until my hair shivers at the thought of anything happening to you." The vividness of their "letters" belies the reality that only we can hear both voices. Will he survive? Will she? Will their written records?

What will survive is memory, a collective spirit that the young man speculates may be "life eternal, among the children of the deep blue sea, those who have escaped the chains of slavery to form a world beneath the heavens and the blood-drenched earth where you live." Danticat changed the original title of this story, "From the Ocean Floor," to "Children of the Sea" to emphasize the link to the Middle Passage:

> It's a very powerful image—from the ocean floor. No one knows how many people were lost on The Middle Passage. There are no records or graves—and the ocean floor is where our fossils are. That journey from Haiti in the 1980s is like a new middle passage. Not to romanticize it, but the comforting thing about death is that somehow all these people will meet. I often think that if my ancestors are at the bottom of the sea, then I too am part of that. So we are all children of the sea. There are no museums, no graves, really no place to visit—there's a timelessness about it.

. . .

The passion of the two young people in "Children of the Sea" reappears, though in a horrific form, in "Between the Pool and the Gardenias," a sublimely written story of a maid in Port-au-Prince whose childlessness drives her finally to claim a dead baby she finds "on the dusty curb, wrapped in a small pink blanket, a few inches away from a sewer." Naming the baby Rose, the woman nurtures her, gives into "a sudden desire to explain to her my life," and keeps Rose in her room until the baby "began to smell like the intestines after they hadn't sold for a few days." Before the woman can bury her beloved Rose in order to free her spirit, her lover, assuming she has killed the child with some voodoo-related purpose, calls the authorities. This stark story combines a plot of almost Gothic horror and a lyrical simplicity that is chilling, perhaps never more so than during a public reading of this story when a baby in the audience cried and cried—"an eerie coincidence," muses Danticat, who describes the story's origin:

> The woman in this story is so many different women. It began as a story about someone who wants something so badly that she'll go to any length, but then I started thinking, "what if?" and "what if . . ."—taking it further and further. In some ways, it's the story of a woman who wants a child very badly and then finds one. That should be a happy ending, but then you ask, "What if it is a child that she doesn't have in mind?" It pushes reality further and forces you to realize the depths of the person's wanting to have a child. As long as it's possible to overlook the reality, she can have the child briefly. But then she ends up paying a very high price.

Krik? Krak! is populated with stories of mothers and daughters, several of them about searches for connections between generations that grew up in different countries. In "New York Day Women," a daughter watches in surprise as her mother makes her way from her home in Brooklyn to Madison Avenue, where in Central Park she cares for a young child while his Yuppie mother does her hour-long jog. The imagined dialogue between mother and daughter underscores the different worlds they inhabit, though the tone is playful: The mother sews lace collars on her daughter's company softball T-shirts because she wants her to "look like a lady playing softball." In "Caroline's Wedding," the twin occasion of one daughter's new American citizenship and her older sister's wedding prompt the sisters and their mother to forge new relationships while preserving ways and means of the old. In "The Missing Peace," Lamort, so named because her mother died giving birth to her, helps an American who has come to Haiti in search of her journalist mother, an "old regime journalist. For a newspaper called *Liberté* in Port-au-Prince." The connection between the two grows as the older recognizes the futility of her search, and the younger claims her mother's legacy by taking her name, Mary Magdalene.

Mothers and daughters are familiar terrain to Danticat, whose first novel, *Breath, Eyes, Memory*, centered on Martine and her daughter, Sophie. That novel, however, extended the central ties to a sustaining web of women that includes grandmothers, aunts, cousins, and other members of the female community. Danticat dedicates *Krik? Krak!* to her aunts Josephine and Marie Rose—"And to Paule Marshall, the greatest kitchen poet of all."

> It's so important for people to read things that somehow mirror their own experience. I remember when I was in junior high school and read Paule Marshall. *Brown Girl, Brownstones* was the first book that was similar to what we were going through. My father always had a desire to own property. He wanted to buy a house. We had to have something concrete, a piece of the country, a piece of the land—like the people in this novel: they wanted to have a brownstone. I had three brothers, and I'm the only girl. In most of my adolescence, that was okay, but I had to be in the kitchen with my mother, learning how to cook. Marshall's essay on "kitchen poets" describes something very similar to when my mother's sisters would come over—their talking, the way they said things, their faces. It was so beautiful! I used to resent being in the kitchen with them because I wanted

to be with the boys, but then I read Marshall's essay. She talks about doing her homework on the kitchen table while the women were talking about home, what was happening there, what they're doing—and just sort of soaking it in. She called it "kitchen poetry." After reading that, I didn't resent so much being in the kitchen. I felt like part of a sisterhood, and I remember feeling then that I didn't necessarily have to rebel.

• • •

To read Danticat is to learn about Haiti—the folklore and myth, the traditions, and the history. Two of the stories in *Krik? Krak!* involve actual historical events, one of these, "Wall of Fire Rising," indirectly. Two very poor parents proudly listen to their young son recite his part in the school play of Boukman, the legendary runaway slave who in 1791 organized a revolt in Haiti. Guy, the father, trapped in a janitor's job at the sugar mill, dreams of piloting the hot air balloon owned by the mill's owner. Lili, the mother, dreams of her son. The tension between the parents' views of their child's future is symbolized in their view of the balloon: When Lili points out, "If God wanted people to fly, he would have given us wings on our backs," Guy replies, "But look what he gave us instead. He gave us reasons to fly. He gave us the air, the birds, our son."

In this story, which Danticat began as an undergraduate, language both reflects and defies the history of imperialism. As the young boy's speech opens, "A wall of fire is rising and in the ashes, I see the bones of my people," and the parents "felt as though for a moment they had been given the rare pleasure of hearing the voice of one of the forefathers of Haitian independence in the forced baritone of their only child." The narrator

comments, however, that "It was obvious that this was a speech written by a European man, who gave to the slave revolutionary Boukman the kind of European phrasing that might have sent the real Boukman turning in his grave." Such subtle evidence of the profound impact of Haiti's colonial past is characteristic of Danticat, who explains:

> You can see the Creole texts of what Boukman was saying, but I've read it in books where it sounds like Shakespeare. In plays, it's "frenchized"—kind of washed of the anger. [The young character] and his family are living it. They're bringing the revolutionary sense back.

The revolutionary spirit returns, too, in "1937," a story centering on the Dominican Republic's dictator Rafael Leonard Trujillo Molina's massacre of Haitians at the river separating Haiti from the Dominican Republic. Written as a kind of history told through magical realism, "1937" opens: "My Madonna cried. A miniature teardrop traveled down her white porcelain face, like dew on the tip of early morning grass. When I saw the tear, I thought, surely that my mother had died." The narrator of this story visits her mother, imprisoned like many others on suspicion of being a "lougarou" or witch: "They were said to have been seen at night rising from the ground like birds on fire." Learning of her mother's death from a prescient old woman, the daughter returns to the prison where she asks, "What would be the use" of watching when the body is burned. The old woman replies that the prison officials "will make these women watch, and we can keep them company." As the narrator agrees, she "remembers" the story of 1937 and her mother flying: "Weighted down by my body inside hers, she leaped from Dominican soil into the water, and out again on the Haitian side of the river. She glowed red when she came out, blood clinging to her skin, which at that moment looked as though it were in flames." She understands her connections and her place in time and history, both through the bonds of women.

This story previews Danticat's next novel, which centers on the massacre of 1937:

> Right now, I'm talking about it more than working on it. It's going to stay in the 1930s, and it's one woman's survival story. I've been researching this for a very long time, but the narrative way of telling the story didn't present itself until very recently. I was thinking about the ending: I write first and last chapters to give myself perimeters. At the end, there is an old woman telling the story, like a woman who is still alive today looking back at the '30s on the massacre and how she survived. I'll do more research by going to that place in Haiti, but first, I wanted to have the character.
>
> When I mentioned in one reading that I was working on a novel about the 1937 massacre, people called me with information, books, articles. I often think I'm in a communal endeavor. People are investing in what I'm doing. I've gotten tons of books about the massacre. Writers often feel as though they're writing alone, but I feel a sense of solidarity. I have a lot of collaborators! This is a part of history that's not in the history books; it's not something we talk about. But it's about survivors, and we're children of survivors.

Taken together, the stories in *Krik? Krak!* have a continuity derived from recurrent themes and motifs, yet they are more profoundly bound by a spiritual vision where "the warm sea air" and "the laughter of children"

coexist with the painful history of slavery and more recent violence:

> My idea was to have a progression. The first story would be "1937" and the last, historically, "Caroline's Wedding." We also go from Haiti to the New York stories. My editor and I chose them with that idea in mind. Just naturally from writing the stories over several years, some of the characters recurred, so that came together too. But we ended up with a different order because my editor thought that "Children of the Sea" is a story that's easy to get into; also, it has "krik? krak!" in it, which introduces the idea of why to write the stories. The book was put together with the idea of the stories flowing together and complementing one another.

• • •

Such interconnections, resonances, echoes, and blending are best described by Danticat's own image of braids in the final selection, "Epilogue: Women Like Us," a poetic coda to the nine stories: "When you write, it's like braiding your hair. Taking a handful of coarse unruly strands and attempting to bring them unity. Your fingers have still not perfected the task. Some of the braids are long, others are short. Some are thick, others are thin. Some are heavy. Others are light. Like the diverse women in your family. Those whose fables and metaphors, whose similes and soliloquies, whose diction and *je ne sais quoi* daily slip into your survival soup, by way of their fingers."

Recurring characters are one connection: the main character of "Between the Pool and the Gardenias" is the goddaughter of Lili from "A Wall of Fire Rising" and the granddaughter of Defile, the alleged lougarou in "1937." When asked if not knowing Haitian myths and folklore makes it difficult to appreciate her work, Danticat calls on yet another connection in response:

> I think more of the depths of emotion. The stories deal with humanity and what we all go through. Different people will walk away learning different things; there'll be differences even among people from Haiti.

Generations of women strengthen these 15 connections. Even death cannot break the line, as she writes in the Epilogue: "The women in your family have never lost touch with one another. Death is a path we all take to meet on the other side. What goddesses have joined, let no one cast asunder. With every step you take, there is an army of women watching over you. We are never any farther than the sweat on your brows or the dust on your toes."

· · ·

An image that recurs throughout Danticat's work is the butterfly as symbol of both continuing life and transformation. In "Dream of the Butterflies," a poetic vignette published in *The Caribbean Writer* in 1991, violence is juxtaposed with tenderness, danger with safety, and, finally, sheer hatred with pure love. She sees the redemptive butterfly as suggesting that hope triumphs even in the face of terrible loss:

> There aren't that many legends in Haiti about butterflies, but I'm fascinated by the idea of transformation. I think in some ways we all think we could go from a caterpillar to a butterfly—that whole metamorphosis is a metaphor for life, especially a life of poverty or struggle because you hope that this is temporary and that one way or another, you'll get wings. It's the Christian ideal we grew up with that people are willing to suffer very much if that means one day they'll get their wings and fly. Haiti has such beautiful butterflies in all different colors.

The most uncanny connections seem to assert themselves in the life of this author who bears witness:

> The year I wrote "Children of the Sea" there were so many boating accidents; whole families would be wiped out. One woman I had read about was Marie Micheline, whose mother and daughter were on the boat with her. They all died.

Danticat dedicated the original publication of this story as follows: "In ancestral kinship, I offer this piece to Marie Micheline Marole, her daughters, and her granddaughters—three generations of women lost at sea." Coincidentally—or maybe not—another Marie Micheline played a key role in Danticat's life:

> My cousin Marie Micheline taught me to read. I started school when I was three, and she would read to me when I came home. In 1987, when I was in France, there was a shooting outside her house—where her children were. She had a seizure and died. Since I was away from her, my parents didn't tell me right away. They were afraid I might have a reaction. But around that same time, I was having nightmares; somehow I knew. Marie Micheline was very dear to me. When I read about this woman who drowned, I was so struck that they had the same name.

In *Krik? Krak!*, Danticat serves a "survival soup" of characters struggling to find a place of peace, a sliver of happiness, a glimmer of a brighter future amid terrorism and political chaos. Ultimately, it is in these stories that they find a moment of grace, stories that Danticat believes give people "a sense of the things that I have inherited." It's a rich inheritance—and one, we can be thankful, she generously shares.

A CLOSER LOOK AT
An Interview with Edwidge Danticat

1. Although the structure of Shea's article does not match the literary analysis genre as described in this chapter, it uses many of the same strategies and accomplishes many of the same purposes as a literary analysis. Read through this article again and note where Shea addresses these issues: literary genre, language, and tone; plot; characters; image, metaphor, and symbol; overall structure; setting; and theme and significance. What does Shea's article accomplish that a literary analysis usually cannot?

2. What *genre* is this? Clearly it's an "interview," but it is a subgenre of the traditional interview genre in that it does not follow the usual "Q&A" format. For instance, the interviewer doesn't *just* ask questions, and readers don't get the sense that they're reading a transcript of the interview in the sequence it originally occurred.

    a. First, describe the features of this genre that distinguish it from the traditional interview, addressing not just the structure but also the style.

    b. Second, explain how this interview genre differs in the effect it has on readers: What does it help them understand or feel that a traditional interview cannot?

    c. Finally, make up a descriptive name for this interview subgenre that distinguishes it from the traditional interview.

3. In the epilogue to *Krik? Krak!*, Danticat says, "When you write, it's like braiding your hair," and then goes on to explain the analogy. Danticat's analogy may or may not match your experience with the writing process. How would you extend her analogy to better describe your own writing process, or what analogy better describes the writing process you follow?

IDEAS FOR
Writing

1. Practice summarizing and quoting. Choose one of the extended passages in this literary analysis that most interested you. Write a brief summary of that passage in which you use your own words to capture the message. If you quote, do not quote entire sentences, but limit yourself to quotes that are one to six words long and incorporate them into your own sentences. (For help with summarizing and quoting, consult "Choosing an Appropriate Style" from this chapter and Chapter 26, "Quoting, Paraphrasing, and Citing Sources.")

2. Conduct an interview with someone about their work (whatever that is) and create a three-page interview written in a style and structure that is inspired by or is similar to Shea's. Like Shea, you should try to capture something essential and interesting about your interviewee's work. You can interview a friend, classmate, family member, acquaintance, or stranger. It doesn't have to be someone famous, or someone whose work is fascinating, but try to get at some feature of the work that is remarkable.

3. Write a five-page literary analysis of "A Wall of Fire Rising" that incorporates information from Shea's interview to provide insight or support for your analysis. Incorporate the words written by Shea, spoken by Danticat, or both. Be sure to provide context for your quotations or summaries, so that your reader understands where the quoted words come from.

1. In a group, consider how you could analyze a movie in the same way that you analyze a literary work. Start out by selecting a movie that most of you have seen or are familiar with. Then generate an "interpretive question" about the movie. Ask yourself, "What do I/we want to understand by going beneath the surface of the movie?" In a single sentence, write down your interpretive question, and in another single sentence, write down your interpretive claim.

2. Ask each member of your group to bring in a short poem. Discuss the poem as a literary work by paying attention to its genre, plot, characters, setting, and use of language and tone. What intrigues you about each poem? What makes them interesting and worth talking about?

3. Find a literary analysis on the Internet. Point to specific places in the analysis where the author makes the following moves:

    a. Identifies an interpretive question

    b. Makes an interpretive claim that addresses that question

    c. Examines the text itself to support the interpretation

    d. Goes outside the text (with information about the author, the social or historical setting, etc.) to develop the interpretation

    e. Provides insights that go beyond the obvious

Talk About This

1. Read Langston Hughes's "I, Too" (page 145). Generate an "interpretive question" about the poem. Ask yourself, "What do I want to understand by going beneath the surface of the poem?" Focus on just one question and delve deeply into it.

    a. Address your interpretive question by discussing the specifics of the poem. Focus at first on the poem itself rather than what you might know about the author or the time it was written. Finally, come up with one aspect of the poem that makes a plausible case about its message, what makes it effective, thought provoking, revealing, or enjoyable.

    b. In a single sentence, write down your interpretive question. In another single sentence, write down your main claim.

2. Practice summarizing, describing, and quoting by choosing a scene or feature (character, plot, setting, etc.) from "A Wall of Fire Rising" that you find interesting. First, summarize that scene or feature as clearly and efficiently as possible in two or three sentences. Second, rework what you've written to weave in quoted words and phrases that are particularly important to the summary. Be sure to use quotation marks and parenthetical citations to show which words are quoted and where they came from.

3. Search the Internet to find literary definitions of the word "genre." Cut and paste those definitions into a single file. Now, look back at the definition of genre in Chapter 1, "Writing and Genres." How are the literary definitions of genre different than the one used in this book? Are there any similarities? In a response to your professor, try to reconcile these two definitions of genre in a way that makes both useful.

Try This Out

1. **Analyze a short story or poem.** Write a four- to five-page literary analysis of a short story or poem that poses an interesting interpretive question and offers an interpretive claim that explains the work's message or significance or that analyzes its structure and features (character, symbol, setting, etc.). Be sure that you focus on the text itself for your interpretation.

   Alternative: Rather than write about a short story or a poem, write a literary analysis of a work that may not be considered exactly "literary," such as a movie, a song, or a television show.

2. **Create a multimedia literary analysis of a song or poem.** Drawing on a variety of media (images, sound, or text), create an electronic multimedia presentation of a song or poem. Choose whatever medium you are comfortable with (or that you want to learn), such as a podcast, Web page, or *PowerPoint* slide presentation. Combine these media to provide your audience with an experience that goes beyond the text and presents them with something new—a new insight, analysis, or interesting juxtaposition.

3. **Turn a review into a literary analysis.** Write an informal two-page review of a movie, a TV show, or a work in some other medium. Then transform the review into a more formal three- to four-page literary analysis using the strategies described in this chapter. Pose an interpretive question and make a claim that answers the question. Quote and describe the text. Then explain the message or significance of the work you are analyzing. Your literary analysis should use an academic tone, so make changes to the style where appropriate.

PEARSON
mycomplab

For additional reading, writing, and research resources, go to **www.mycomplab.com**.

Rhetorical
Analyses

The purpose of a rhetorical analysis is to determine how and why texts are influential, or not. Advertisers, marketing analysts, and public relations agents use rhetorical analyses to understand how well their messages are influencing target audiences and the general public. Political scientists and consultants use rhetorical analyses to determine which ideas and strategies will be most persuasive to voters and consumers. Meanwhile, historians and rhetoricians use rhetorical analyses to study historic speeches and documents to understand how and why they were influential in their day and perhaps still influential today.

Ultimately, the objective of a rhetorical analysis is to show why a text was *effective* or *persuasive*. By studying texts closely, we can learn how writers and speakers sway others and how we can be more persuasive ourselves.

In your college courses, you may be asked to write rhetorical analyses that explore historical and present-day documents, advertisements, and speeches. These assignments are not always called "rhetorical analyses" but any time you are being asked to analyze a nonfiction text, you are probably being asked to write a rhetorical analysis. Also, depending on your career after college, your supervisors may ask you to closely analyze your organization's marketing materials and messages to determine their effectiveness. These critiques are rhetorical analyses, too.

Rhetorical Analyses

Here are two possible organizations for a rhetorical analysis, but other arrangements of these sections will work, too. You should adjust these organizational patterns to fit your topic, angle, purpose, readers, and context.

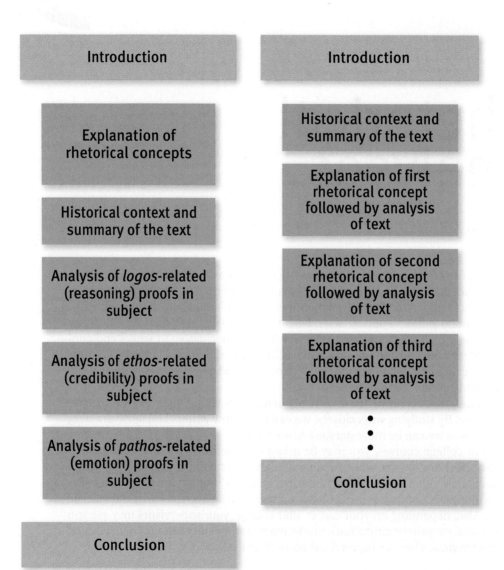

Introduction

Explanation of rhetorical concepts

Historical context and summary of the text

Analysis of *logos*-related (reasoning) proofs in subject

Analysis of *ethos*-related (credibility) proofs in subject

Analysis of *pathos*-related (emotion) proofs in subject

Conclusion

Introduction

Historical context and summary of the text

Explanation of first rhetorical concept followed by analysis of text

Explanation of second rhetorical concept followed by analysis of text

Explanation of third rhetorical concept followed by analysis of text

•
•
•

Conclusion

Overview

Rhetorical analyses can be written a variety of ways. Nevertheless, they tend to have some common features:

- **An introduction** that identifies the subject of your analysis, states your purpose and main point, offers background information on the subject, and stresses its importance.
- **An explanation of the rhetorical concepts** that you will use to analyze the subject.
- **A description or summary of your subject** that sets it in a historical context.
- **An analysis of the subject** through the chosen rhetorical concepts.
- **A conclusion** that states or restates your main point and looks to the future.

Rhetorical analyses come in many forms and sizes. For the sake of simplicity, the diagram on page 168 shows two common patterns used for rhetorical analyses. The pattern on the left examines the uses of reasoning (*logos*), credibility (*ethos*), and emotion (*pathos*) in a text. This is one of the most common types of rhetorical analysis; however, other kinds of rhetorical concepts can be used as the basis of a rhetorical analysis, including metaphor, narrative, genre, style, and others.

ONE STUDENT'S WORK
Rhetorical Analyses

Rhetorical Analysis of the *Keep America Beautiful* Public Service Announcement (1971)

Wes Rodenburg

The original *Keep America Beautiful* public service announcement (PSA) aired for the first time on Earth Day in 1971, and it is widely credited for inspiring environmental consciousness and changing minds about pollution. The commercial features Chief Iron Eyes Cody (Fig. 1), a movie actor who has since become an icon of the environmental movement. At the beginning of the PSA, Chief Iron Eyes paddles his birch bark canoe down an American river. The river is natural and beautiful at the beginning, but as the chief paddles

> Background information helps the readers to understand the text.

continued

downstream it is transformed into an industrial and mechanical world of black oil, soot, coal, and garbage. Chief Iron Eyes makes his way to shore with his canoe. After he pulls his canoe from the water, he has a bag of garbage thrown at his feet from a car on an interstate. A stern-voiced narrator then intones, "Some people have a natural abiding respect for the beauty that was once this country, and some people don't. People start pollution, and people can stop it." Chief Iron Eyes turns to the camera with a tear in his eye. The PSA ends as a symbol for *Keep America Beautiful* fills the screen. This PSA is one of the best examples of how environmental groups can appeal to broader audiences with emotion (*pathos*), authority (*ethos*), and reasoning (*logos*).

Fig. 1. Chief Iron Eyes Cody.

> Here is the author's main point.

> The advertisement is summarized here.

Using Emotions to Draw a Contrast Between the Ideal and Real

This PSA's appeals to emotion are its strongest arguments. As the commercial starts, we can see Chief Iron Eyes Cody in what we could consider to be his native land. He sits proud and tall as he paddles downstream. We can see his eyes and his face, and he looks as though he has heard some troubling news. The shot pans out and we see his silhouette against a gold-splashed river, pristine as can be. Then, the beauty of this natural scene comes to a crashing halt as a crumpled newspaper page floats by the canoe. The music shifts from a native-sounding melody to a mechanical booming sound. The silhouette of the chief and his canoe—the only reminder we have of what nature is intended to look like—is then shadowed as we reach an apex of filth: garbage-ridden water, smoggy air, oil, and a massive steel barge. This scene dwarfs his canoe, and the music begins to sound desperate as it reaches its peak. The chief is turned transparent, a ghost of what respect human kind had for the earth, and he is juxtaposed against what is now: smoke stacks and pollution. Quietly overwhelmed, the chief pulls his canoe ashore where still more waste permeates the surroundings. The trash thrown at the chief's feet feels like a final insult that punctuates the scene.

> The use of *pathos* is discussed.

We now know who is responsible for this tragedy: it is us. Our sense of emotional shame is triggered by the contrasts we have just seen. The floating newspaper, the smog, sludge, smoke, muck, oil, grease, fumes, and garbage. Pollution is everywhere, and we now know that we are the cause. It is our fault—humanity's fault. The appeal to *pathos* then reaches its pinnacle as the chief sheds a tear for what we have done to this land. We see a great contrast between the environment as he knew it and the way it is now.

Using a Symbolic Figure to Create a Sense of Authority

Dressed in classic Native American clothing, Chief Iron Eyes Cody is a symbol of our fading past that appeals to our sense of *ethos*. When most people think of Native Americans, they think of how they taught the original settlers to live off of the land. They think about the respect that American natives had for the land and nature. When the narrator says, "some people have a deep abiding respect for this country, and some people don't," the contrast between Chief Iron Eyes and his polluted surroundings feels sharp. In this way, the symbolic *ethos* of the chief demonstrates that the ruination around him is our doing, not his. He takes us on a journey that slowly opens our eyes to what we are responsible for— ruining nature. One might even suggest that the chief may be analogous to the earth itself. As the pollution thickens, the image of the chief fades from a vibrantly dressed native chief to a silhouette until he becomes a ghost of the past. The chief does nothing to change the pollution, nor does he attempt to change it. Instead he observes it and feels it with pain, remorse, and despair. That's the only thing that he and the earth can do.

> Credibility proofs (*ethos*) are discussed here.

> Analysis explains the meaning of the advertisement.

Using Reasoning to Drive Home the Point

Finally, the PSA uses *logos* to drive home its point: "People start pollution, people can stop it." After this logical statement, we are given a five-second display of the *Keep America Beautiful* symbol, suggesting an answer. In the Web version, a Web site address is given where people can access information on how they can do something about pollution. The logic is inescapable: If you really care about the environment, stop doing more damage and start getting active in cleaning up the mess. The viewer's next logical question is almost inescapably "how can I do something?"

> The PSA's use of an appeal to reason is analyzed here.

The *Keep America Beautiful* PSA has been a model for reaching out to the public about environmental issues. Its use of emotion, authority, and reasoning brings us face-to-face with our transgressions against nature. This PSA woke many people up and urged them to change their ways. Of course, the pollution problem has not been solved, but we seem to have turned the corner. Chief Iron Eyes is watching to see if we succeed.

Inventing Your Rhetorical Analysis's Content

When preparing to write a rhetorical analysis, the first thing you need to do is closely read the text you are analyzing. Read through it at least a couple of times, taking special note of any places where the author seems to make important points or perhaps misses an opportunity to do so.

Inquiring: Highlight Uses of Proofs

Now, do some analysis. When looking closely at the text, you will notice that authors tend to use three kinds of *proofs* to persuade you:

Reasoning (*logos*): appealing to readers' common sense, beliefs, or values

Credibility (*ethos*): using the reputation, experience, and values of the author or an expert to support claims

Emotion (*pathos*): using feelings, desires, or fears to influence readers

Rhetoricians often use the ancient Greek terms, *logos, ethos,* and *pathos,* to discuss these three kinds of proofs, so we have used them here. Let's look at these concepts more closely.

Highlighting Uses of Reasoning (*Logos*). The word *logos* in ancient Greek means "reasoning" in English. This word is the basis for the English word, "logic," but *logos* involves more than using logic to prove a point. *Logos* also involves appealing to someone else's common sense and using examples to demonstrate a point. Here are some common ways people use reasoning to influence the beliefs and opinions of others:

If . . . then: "If you believe X, then you should believe Y also."

Either . . . or: "Either you believe X, or you believe Y."

Cause and effect: "X is the reason Y happens."

Costs and benefits: "The benefits of doing X are worth/not worth the cost of Y."

Better and worse: "X is better/worse than Y because . . ."

Examples: "For example, X and Y demonstrate that Z happens."

Facts and data: "These facts/data support my argument that X is true or Y is false."

Anecdotes: "X happened to these people, thus demonstrating Y."

As you analyze the text, highlight these uses of reasoning so you can figure out how the writer uses *logos* to influence people.

Highlighting Uses of Credibility (*Ethos*). The Greek word *ethos* means "credibility," "authority," or "character" in English. It's also the basis for the English word, "ethics." *Ethos* could mean the author's credibility or the use of someone else's credibility to support an argument.

Highlight places in the text where the author is using his or her authority or credibility to prove a point:

Personal experience: "I have experienced X, so I know it's true and Y is not."

Personal credentials: "I have a degree in Z" or "I am the director of Y." "So I know about the subject of X."

Good moral character: "I have always done the right thing for the right reasons, so you should believe me when I say that X is the best path to follow."

Appeal to experts: "According to Z, who is an expert on this topic, X is true and Y is not true."

Identification with the readers: "You and I come from similar backgrounds and we have similar values; therefore, you would likely agree with me that X is true and Y is not."

Admission of limitations: "I may not know much about Z, but I do know that X is true and Y is not."

Expression of good will: "I want what is best for you, so I am recommending X as the best path to follow."

Use of "insider" language: Using special terminology or referring to information that only insiders would understand.

When you are looking for *ethos*-related proofs, look carefully for places where the author is trying to use his or her character or experience to sway readers' opinions.

Highlighting Uses of Emotion (*Pathos*). Finally, look for places where the author is trying to use *pathos,* or emotions, to influence readers. The psychologist Robert Plutchik suggests there are eight basic emotions: joy, acceptance, fear, surprise, sadness, disgust, anger, and anticipation. As you analyze the text, highlight places where the author is using these basic emotions to persuade readers.

Promise of gain: "By agreeing with us, you will gain trust, time, money, love, advancement, reputation, comfort, popularity, health, beauty, or convenience."

Promise of enjoyment: "If you do things our way, you will experience joy, anticipation, fun, surprises, enjoyment, pleasure, leisure, or freedom."

FIGURE 9.1 Advertising and Emotions

Advertising relies heavily on pathos *arguments, because there isn't much time available to persuade a customer to buy something.*

Fear of loss: "If you don't do things this way, you risk losing time, money, love, security, freedom, reputation, popularity, health, or beauty."

Fear of pain: "If you don't do things this way, you may feel pain, sadness, grief, frustration, humiliation, embarrassment, loneliness, regret, shame, vulnerability, or worry."

Expressions of anger or disgust: "You should be angry or disgusted because X is unfair to you, me, or someone else."

Some other common emotions that you might find are annoyance, awe, calmness, confidence, courage, disappointment, delight, embarrassment, envy, frustration, gladness, grief, hate, happiness, hope, horror, humility, impatience, inspiration, joy, jealousy, loneliness, love, lust, nervousness, nostalgia, paranoia, peace, pity, pride, rage, regret, resentment, shame, sorrow, shock, suffering, thrill, vulnerability, worry, and yearning.

Frequently, writers will not state emotions directly. Instead, they will inject feelings by using emotional stories about others or by incorporating images that illustrate the feelings they are trying to invoke. Advertisements, for example, rely heavily on using emotions to sell products (Figure 9.1).

Researching: Finding Background Information

Once you have highlighted the proofs (i.e., *logos, ethos, pathos*) in the text, it's time to do some background research on the author, the text, and the context in which the work was written and used.

Online Sources. Using Internet search engines and electronic databases, find out as much as you can about the person or company who wrote the text and any issues that he, she, or they were responding to. What historical events led up to the writing of the text? What happened after the text was released to the public? What have other people said about it?

Print Sources. Using your library's catalog and article databases, dig deeper to understand the historical context of the text you are studying. How did historical events or pressures influence the author and the text? Did the author need to adjust the text in a special way to fit the audience? Was the author or organization that published the text trying to achieve particular goals or make a statement of some kind?

Empirical Sources. In person or through e-mail, you might interview an expert who knows something about this text, its author, or the context of the text you are analyzing. An expert can help you gain a deeper understanding of the issues and people involved in the text. You might also show the text to others and note their reactions to it. You can use surveys or informal focus groups to see how people respond to the text.

As always, keep track of your sources. You will need to cite them in your text and list them in the works-cited list at the end of your rhetorical analysis.

Organizing and Drafting Your Rhetorical Analysis

At this point, you should be ready to start drafting your rhetorical analysis. As mentioned earlier, rhetorical analyses can follow a variety of organizational patterns, but those shown on page 168 are good models to follow. You can modify these where necessary as you draft your ideas.

Keep in mind that you don't actually need to use rhetorical terms, such as *logos, ethos,* and *pathos,* in your rhetorical analysis, especially if your readers don't know what these terms mean. Instead, you can use words like "reasoning," "credibility," and "emotion," which will be more familiar to your readers.

The Introduction

Usually, the introduction to a rhetorical analysis is somewhat brief. In this part of your analysis, you want to include up to five items:

- Identify the subject of your analysis (the text you are analyzing).

- State the purpose of your analysis (e.g., to explain why this text was effective or persuasive, or not).

- State your main point about the text (e.g., "This text was persuasive because . . .").

- Provide some background information on the text, its author, and the historical context in which it was produced and received.

- Stress the importance of the text, telling readers why its rhetorical strategies are significant.

These items can be arranged in just about any order in your introduction, so write them down and then figure out what order best suits your rhetorical analysis and your readers.

Explanation of Rhetorical Concepts

After the introduction, you should define and explain the rhetorical concepts you are using to analyze the text. So if you are using *logos, ethos,* and *pathos,* you would need to explain how these concepts are defined. For example, here is how a student defined *pathos* in her rhetorical analysis:

> *Pathos,* which involves using emotion to influence someone else, is a commonly used rhetorical tactic in advertisements aimed at teenage girls. Emotional scenes and images are used to grab the teen's attention and often make her feel

something negative, like less confident, insecure, undesirable, unattractive, anxious, or dependent (Holt et al. 84).

Of course, the product being pushed by the advertiser is then put forward as a solution to that supposed inadequacy in the teen's life. For example, as psychologist Tina Hanson points out, teenage girls don't really need a cabinet full of haircare products (73). The typical teenage girl's hair is already healthy, shiny, full, and rich in color. Yet, television and magazine advertisements from haircare companies, which make shampoo, conditioner, and dye, routinely show frustrated teens unsatisfied with their hair. Usually the message being sent to a teen is "You don't even know you need this product, but everyone else knows you do, especially guys." The images show a discouraged girl who risks losing friends or being embarrassed because her hair isn't perfect.

In your rhetorical analysis, you don't need to cover all three of the rhetorical proofs mentioned in this chapter. Instead, you might decide to concentrate on just one of them, like *pathos*, so you can develop a fuller definition of that concept for your readers.

Also as mentioned earlier, keep in mind that other rhetorical concepts besides *logos, ethos,* and *pathos* are available. For instance, you could choose to study the metaphors used in a text, or perhaps its genre, style, or use of narrative. If you choose one of these other rhetorical concepts, you will need to define and explain that concept to your readers.

Provide Historical Context and Summary

To give your readers an overall understanding of the text you are analyzing, give them some historical background on it. Then summarize the text for them.

Historical Context: Tell your readers the history of the text. Who wrote it or presented it? Who was the target reader or audience? Where and when did the text appear? Why was the text produced or written?

Summary: Spend anywhere from one to five paragraphs summarizing the content of the text. Most summaries follow the organization of the text itself, highlighting the main points and stressing the most important features. Your summary of the text should be completely in your own words, with select quotes taken from the text. When summarizing, do not express your own opinions about the text or its message. Instead, just give the readers an objective overview of the content of the text.

The aim of this historical context section is to give your readers enough background to understand the text you are analyzing. For example, here is the historical context and a summary of an advertisement for Red Bull:

Advertisements for energy drinks rely heavily on emotion to make sales to college students. These unique soft drinks, which usually contain high amounts of caffeine and calories, began to grow in popularity in the late 1990s.

Red Bull, one of the most popular brands, actually was invented in the 1970s in Thailand, and it was first exported to the United States in 1997 (FundingUniverse). From the beginning, Red Bull's advertising has been squarely aimed at college students, telling them that they need to have extra energy to get through their hectic days. One of its recent advertising campaigns, which is called "Red Bull Gives You Wings," began in 2005 with simple hand-drawn movies like the one shown in Figure 1.

In this advertisement, a bird relieves himself on a man who looks a lot like a professor. The man then drinks a can of Red Bull and sprouts wings. He flies above the bird, pulls down his pants, and proceeds to return the favor (off-screen, thankfully). The viewer hears the bird screech in horror as an image of a can of Red Bull fills the screen, but we can all imagine what happened.

Fig. 1. "Red Bull Gives You Wings."

During the span of the 30-second advertisement, the man transforms from being a seemingly helpless victim to a superheroic figure who can take vengeance on the bird. Drinking Red Bull is shown to be the way he gains this new power.

The length of your summary depends on your readers. If they are already familiar with the text you are analyzing, your summary should be brief. You don't want to bore your readers by telling them something they already know. If, however, they are not familiar with the text, your summary should be longer and more detailed.

Analysis of the Text

Now it is time to analyze the text for your readers. Essentially, you are going to interpret the text for them, using the rhetorical concepts you defined earlier in the rhetorical analysis.

There are two main ways to organize this section:

* You can follow the organization of the text you are analyzing, starting from the beginning and working to the end of the text. Apply the rhetorical concepts to each major section of the text you are analyzing.

* You can discuss the text through each rhetorical concept separately. For instance, if you are analyzing the uses of *logos*, *ethos*, and *pathos* in a text, you would separately discuss the text's use of each kind of proof.

For example, here is a discussion of *pathos* in the Red Bull advertisement:

Using Emotion to Sell Red Bull

Like much advertising aimed at young people, the Red Bull advertisement uses emotions to bring home its argument. In this advertisement, the use of humor is what gives the message its emotional punch.

Many young people feel like the professor in this advertisement, because they perceive that they are ultimately powerless in society. So when someone else treats them badly, young people usually assume they need to just take it. In this case, the Red Bull advertisement shows the bird relieving itself on the professor-like character. In most situations, the man would simply need to suffer that humiliation. But, he has a secret weapon, Red Bull. He drinks a can, sprouts wings, and humorously takes revenge on the bird.

The story itself is an emotional parable that reflects the life of most young people. The bird represents all the things in young peoples' lives that humiliate and embarrass them but that they cannot fix. The professor-like man, though not young, is a figure that students can relate to, because he is still in the educational system and seems powerless in his own ways. So when he is able to actually use a product like Red Bull to take revenge, young people not only laugh but also feel an emotional release of their own frustration. The emotional message to young people is, "Drink Red Bull, and you can get back at all those people who crap on you."

The humor, coupled with the revenge theme, makes the advertisement's use of emotion very effective. According to Mark Jefferson, a professor at Penn State who studies advertisements, the use of revenge is very effective for college students. "Students often feel powerless in a world that tells them they are adults but refuses to give them power. Advertisements that tap into that frustration in a humorous way are very powerful" (23).

In this discussion of emotion, the writer is applying her definition of *pathos* to the advertisement. This allows her to explain the use of emotion to sell Red Bull. She can now go on to discuss the use of *logos* and *ethos* in the ad. Or, if she has more to say about *pathos*, she might make her rhetorical analysis about the use of *pathos* alone.

The Conclusion

When you have finished your analysis, it's time to wrap up your argument. Keep this part of your rhetorical analysis brief. A paragraph or two should be enough. You should answer one or more of the following questions:

- Ultimately, what does your rhetorical analysis reveal about the text you studied?

- What does your analysis tell your readers about the rhetorical concept(s) you used to analyze the text?

- Why is your explanation of the text or the rhetorical concept(s) important to your readers?

- What should your readers look for in the future with this kind of text or this persuasion strategy?

Minimally, the key to a good conclusion is to restate your main point about the text you analyzed.

Choosing an Appropriate Style

The style of a rhetorical analysis depends on your readers and where your analysis might appear. If you are writing your analysis for an online magazine like *Slate* or *Salon*, readers would expect you to write something colorful and witty. If you are writing the argument for an academic journal, your tone would need to be more formal. Here are some ideas for using an appropriate style in your rhetorical analysis:

Use Lots of Detail to Describe the Text. In as much detail as possible, tell readers the *who, what, where, when, how,* and *why* of the text you are analyzing. Also, use details to describe what the text looks like, sounds like, and feels like. Above all, you want readers to experience the text, even if they haven't seen or read it themselves.

Minimize the Jargon and Difficult Words. When analyzing something, you might be tempted to puff up your language with lots of specialized terminology and complex words. These kinds of complex words will unnecessarily make your text harder to read.

Improve the Flow of Your Sentences. Rhetorical analyses are designed to explain a text as clearly as possible, so you want your writing to flow easily from one sentence to the next. The best way to create this kind of flow is to use the "given-new" strategies that are discussed in Chapter 20, "Developing Paragraphs and Sections." Given-new involves making sure each new sentence takes something like a word, phrase, or idea from the previous sentence.

Pay Attention to Sentence Length. If you are writing a lively or witty analysis, you will want to use shorter sentences to make your argument feel more active and fast-paced. If you are writing for an academic audience, longer sentences will make your analysis sound more formal and proper. Keep in mind that your sentences should be "breathing length."

As mentioned earlier in this chapter, rhetorical terms like *logos, ethos,* and *pathos* do not need to appear in your rhetorical analysis. If you are writing for readers who probably don't know what these terms mean, you are better off using words like "reasoning," "credibility," or "emotion." If you want to use the actual rhetorical terms, make sure you define them for readers.

Designing Your Rhetorical Analysis

Computers make it possible to use visuals in a rhetorical analysis. You can download pictures from the Internet, use a scanner to insert an image of the text, or take a picture with a digital camera. You could even include a video or audio podcast, so your readers can experience the text you are analyzing. Here are some things you might try out:

"Red Bull Gives You Wings"

Energy drinks are a product that relies heavily on emotion for sales to high school and college students. These soft drinks, which usually contain high amounts of caffeine and calories, began to grow in popularity in the late 1990's. Red Bull, one of the most popular brands, actually was invented in the 1970s in Thailand, and it was first exposed to the United States in 1997 (*Fundinel University*). From the beginning, its advertising has been squarely aimed at college students, telling them that they need to have extra energy to get through their hectic days. It's current version of the "Red Bull Gives You Wings" slogan began in 2005 with simple hand-drawn movies like the one shown in Figure 1.

Fig. 1. Red Bull Gi ves You Wings."

In this advertisement, a bird relieves himself on a man who looks a lot like a professor. The man then drinks a Red Bull and sprouts wings. He flies above the bird, undoes his pants, and proceeds to return the favor *offscreen*. The viewer hears the bird screech in horror as a can of Red Bull fills the screen, but we can all imagine what happened.

During the span of 30-second advertisement, the man transforms from being a seemingly weak victim to a *superheroic* figure that can take vengeance on the bird. The experience of drinking of Red Bull is shown to be the moment that gives him this new power.

FIGURE 9.2 Adding a Screen Shot to Your Analysis

A screen shot is an easy way to put an image into your rhetorical analysis.

Download Images from the Internet. If you are reviewing a book or a historical document, you could download an image of its cover and include that image in your rhetorical analysis. That way, readers can actually see what you are talking about.

Add a Screen Shot. If you are writing about an advertisement from the Internet, you can take a picture of your screen (i.e., a screen shot). Then include that screen shot in your analysis (Figure 9.2). On a PC, you can push the Print Screen button to capture a screen shot. Then you can use the cropping tool to remove the parts of the image you don't want. On a Mac, just type Command-Shift-3 for a shot of the whole screen or Command-Shift-4 for a cursor that allows you to take a picture of part of the screen.

Include a Link to a Podcast. If you are analyzing a video or audio text (perhaps something you found on *YouTube*), you can put a link to that text in your analysis. Or you can include the Web address so readers can find the text themselves. If your analysis will appear online, you can use a link to insert the podcast right into your document.

Make a Web Site. Your rhetorical analysis could be made into a Web site. The home page could be the introduction, and you could provide links to the rest of your analysis. You could add images and links to other sites, which will allow readers to better experience the text you are analyzing.

Why not be creative? Look for ways to use technology to let your readers access the text you are analyzing.

Revising and Editing Your Rhetorical Analysis

Rhetorical analyses tend to be medium-sized documents, so they are easy to revise and edit. One of the challenges of editing a rhetorical analysis is keeping your definitions of key terms consistent throughout the argument. If you aren't careful, your definitions of rhetorical concepts will evolve as you analyze a text. So you want to make sure you are using your terms consistently.

Recheck Definitions of the Rhetorical Concepts. Early in the analysis, you defined one or more rhetorical concepts you used to analyze the text. Now that you have finished drafting your analysis, make sure you actually used those definitions, as you described them. You might find that you need to revise or refine your definitions, or you might need to rewrite parts of your analysis to fit those original definitions.

Expand Your Analysis. Did you cover all the angles? Could you say more? Look for gaps in your analysis of the text. For example, if you were talking about the use of emotion in a Red Bull ad, are there some additional emotional elements you didn't talk about or could expand on?

Copyedit for Clarity. Take a closer look at your paragraphs and sentences. Can you make them plainer? Can you put better claims at the beginnings of paragraphs? Can you work on improving the flow of the sentences?

Read Your Work Out Loud. Your ears are more sensitive to phrasing problems than your eyes. So read your rhetorical analysis out loud to yourself, or have someone read it to you. Mark any places where something sounds odd or makes you stumble. Then edit those marked places.

As always, a solid effort at proofreading will only improve your work (and your professor's response to it). Some people find it helpful to print out the document, so they can proofread on paper. Errors are often easier to find on paper than they are on the screen.

The Ad
Critique

An ad critique evaluates an advertisement to show why it was or was not effective. If the ad is persuasive, show the readers why it works. An ad critique can also help you explain why you like or dislike a particular type of advertisement. You should aim your critique at people like you who are consumers of mass media and products.

Today, ad critiques are becoming common on the Internet, especially on blogs. They give people a way to express their reactions to the kinds of advertisements being thrown at them. Here are some strategies for writing an ad critique:

Summarize the ad. If the ad appeared on television or the Internet, describe it objectively in one paragraph. Tell your readers the *Who, What, Where,* and *When* of the ad. If the ad appeared in a magazine or other print medium, you can scan it or download the image from the sponsor's Web site and insert the image into your document.

Highlight the unique quality that makes the advertisement stand out. There must be something remarkable about the ad that caught your attention. What is it? What made it stand out from all the other ads that are similar to it?

Describe the typical features of ads like this one. Identify the three to five common features that are usually found in this type of advertisement. You can use examples of other ads to explain how a typical ad would look or sound.

Show how this ad is different from the others. Compare the features of the ad to similar advertisements. Demonstrate why this ad is better or worse than its competitors.

Use ample amounts of detail. Throughout your critique, use plenty of detail to help your readers visualize or hear the ad. You want to replicate the experience of seeing or hearing it.

WRITE **your own ad critique.** While watching television or reading a magazine, find an ad that seems different. Then write a two-page critique in which you explain why it was effective or not. Don't forget to scan, download, or take a picture of the ad so you can include it in your critique.

Salesjerk

Seth Stevenson

The Spot: *A man demonstrates an absorbent towel called the "Shamwow." It cleans up spills, polishes cars, washes dishes, and so forth. "Eight Shamwows for $19.95," goes the salesman's closing argument. "Comes with a 10-year warranty. Here's how to order."*

The ad is summarized.

There's something captivating about Vince, the Shamwow pitchman. I always perk up when I hear those initial, outer-borough syllables: "Hi, it's Vince wit Shamwow. Dis is fuh da house, da car." A friend of mine—a guy who's never succumbed to an infomercial come-on—says he finds himself strangely tempted to order a Shamwow each time he watches Vince's spiel.

There are zillions of ads like this on late-night TV. A pitchman (or -woman) demonstrates a household product, then issues an aggressive "call to action" (as the marketing lingo goes). You're urged to "act now" and given a phone number or Web site through which you can order the product. Often, there's a time limit ("call in the next 20 minutes"), and you're promised free bonus items for beating the deadline. Ads of this ilk generally wash right over me. What makes the Shamwow ad different?

In part, it's the astonishing capabilities of the product. (Holds 20 times its weight in liquid! Instantly extracts cola spills from your carpet! Lasts for 10 years! I'm certain all of this is 100 percent true!) But lots of products make impressive claims. The real star here is Vince, who demonstrates an impressive and subtle mastery of the pitchman's art.

The who, what, where, when is described.

The first thing I notice is the physical grace. Vince puts the Shamwow through its paces with the fluid dexterity of a three-card monte dealer. Cleaning up spills appears not just effortless, but *fun*.

There's a genius, too, in his hectoring tone. He makes us feel like idiots for even entertaining the notion of not buying a Shamwow. "You're gonna spend $20 every month on paper towels, anyway," he says, palms up and head tilted back. He seems truly dumbfounded that anyone might fail to see the wisdom of dropping 28 bucks (including shipping) on a set of rags.

Here are the unique qualities that make the ad stand out.

Vince also conveys a street-smart persona—with his headset microphone, rat-a-tat phrasing and fuhgeddaboudit confidence—that's intended to get the viewer thinking, "Hey, this guy's sharp. He knows a good deal." (It may also get us thinking, "Hey, this guy's a douche. He needs a better haircut." But that's a secondary issue.)

I've made several attempts to get in touch with Vince, hoping to quiz him about the finer points of his delivery. As of this writing, my phone

continued

Salesjerk (continued)

calls have not been returned. But Internet sleuthing suggests (and a Shamwow spokesman confirms) that Vince is a man named Vince Offer.

Offer's history includes lawsuits waged against the Farrelly brothers, Anna Nicole Smith, and the Church of Scientology. He also wrote and directed the 1999 film *The Underground Comedy Movie*. The *New York Post* review gave the film zero stars, said it "may be the least amusing comedy ever made," and asked, "How can the War Crimes Tribunal indict Slobodan Milosevic but let Vince Offer still walk the streets?"

Lots of detail helps readers visualize the ad.

Harsh! But hey, Vince is certainly not boring, and therein lies a significant component of his effectiveness. The guy's jerky, aggrieved attitude jumps off the screen—particularly when he berates his own crew, snapping, "You followin' me, camera guy?" Vince manages, in the course of a minute spent swiping counters and dabbing at carpets, to make us wonder, "Whoa, what's the deal with this freak?" That makes the ad an attention-grabber, and it helps the Shamwow stand out from a crowded field of useless doohickeys.

The reviewer shows how this ad is different from the others.

Vince's abrasive manner might also mark a unique, new strategy in the annals of pitchdom. TV salespeople tend to be warmly enthusiastic, not confrontational. Watch the crew of hosts on the Home Shopping Network. Their role is to serve as easily wowed surrogates for the viewer. They'll run their fingers along the jeweled necklines of a knit separates collection, rapturously whispering, "Look. At. That." The constant ruse is that the hosts covet these products for themselves.

Billy Mays—likely the most famous pitchman of the last decade—also traffics in friendly excitement. A black-bearded fellow who shills for OxiClean, Hercules Hooks, Ding King, and other as-seen-on-TV dreck, Mays' celebrity no doubt stems from his signature, high-decibel style. (He locks into his upper vocal register and stays there for minutes-long, breathless monologues. Check out the *YouTube* clip of Mays doing multiple takes as he seeks the perfect way to yell, "You don't need a cabinet full of cleaners!") But through all the screaming, Mays is always an upbeat pal of the viewer—never a sneering bully.

Can Vince become the next Billy Mays—a ubiquitous, mercenary pitchman hawking products up and down the TV dial? I don't see why not. If anything, the current moment's more suited to Vince's smooth-talking condescension than to Mays' earnest fervor. Jaded consumers expect to get snowed and almost distrust the very pretense of trustworthiness. As my friend who's been tempted by the Shamwow puts it: "What I think I like about Vince is that he is up front and seemingly comfortable with his schtick. He appears to be saying, 'I am a carnie huckster, you know it and I know it, but that's OK because this product is that good.'"

Need to write a rhetorical analysis? Here are some steps to get you going.

FIND a Text You Want to Analyze

Pick something you find intriguing. The best texts are ones that seem curiously persuasive to you (or not persuasive at all). You might also look for texts that are historically important.

HIGHLIGHT the Uses of *Logos*, *Ethos*, and *Pathos*

Read through the text, marking places in the text where the author uses reasoning (*logos*), credibility (*ethos*), or emotion (*pathos*).

RESEARCH the Context

Use a variety of sources to do background research on the text you are analyzing. Find out as much as you can about the author and the historical context in which he or she created the text. Use interviews or surveys to measure how others react to the text you are studying. Interview experts who know about this kind of text.

DRAFT Your Rhetorical Analysis

A rhetorical analysis typically has the following sections: Introduction, Definitions of Rhetorical Concepts, Historical Context and Summary, Analysis, and Conclusion. Draft each section separately.

CHOOSE an Appropriate Style

Your style depends on your readers, the place where your analysis will appear, and the text you are analyzing. Use ample details and good pacing to match your analysis's style to the place where it could be published.

DESIGN Your Rhetorical Analysis

Some graphics, especially screen shots, would make the text you are analyzing easier for readers to understand. If you want to do something more advanced, you might try creating a Web site or an audio or video podcast to an on-screen text.

REVISE and Edit

You have gone this far. Now, finish the job. Do some revising and editing to make your rhetorical analysis shine. Look for any inconsistencies. Fill out places where more information might be helpful.

How Obama Does That Thing He Does

JACK SHAFER

When President Barack Obama was emerging as a viable candidate in the 2008 presidential primaries, commentators began to take notice of the power of his oratory. People in the crowd were literally swooning at his words, and he had an amazing ability to tap into their emotions. In this rhetorical analysis, Jack Shafer uses rhetorical concepts to explain how Obama does it.

Barack Obama bringeth rapture to his audience. They swoon and wobble, regardless of race, gender, or political affiliation, although few understand exactly why he has this effect on them.

No less an intellect than *The New Yorker*'s George Packer confesses that moments after a 25-minute campaign speech by Obama in New Hampshire concluded, he couldn't remember exactly what the candidate said. Yet "the speech dissolved into pure feeling, which stayed with me for days," he writes.

Given that many of his speeches are criminally short on specifics, as Leon Wieseltier writes, how does Obama do that thing he does? A 2005 paper by University of Oregon professor of rhetoric David A. Frank unpeels Obama's momentous 2004 Democratic National Convention keynote address for clues to his method. Obama's spellbinding oration earned near-universal raves, including one from establishment conservative Rich Lowry, editor of *National Review*, and its echoes can be heard in every speech he's given as a candidate for president.

Obama relies, Frank writes, on a "rhetorical strategy of consilience, where understanding results through translation, mediation, and an embrace of different languages, values, and traditions." He credits the *New Republic*'s Noam Scheiber with translating Obama's cross-cultural signals in a 2004 campaign profile that documents the candidate's leap from the Illinois senate to the U.S. Senate. Scheiber observes:

> Whereas many working-class voters are wary of African American candidates, whom they think will promote black interests at the expense of their own, they simply don't see Obama in these terms. This allows him to appeal to white voters on traditional Democratic issues like jobs, health care, and education—just like a white candidate would.

Bill Clinton disarmed race for blacks by inviting them to talk about it. Obama disarms race for white people by largely avoiding the topic. When he does talk about race, he makes sure to juxtapose the traumas experienced by nonblacks with those experienced by African Americans, but without ever equating the two. His rhetoric is designed to bridge the space between whites and blacks so they can occupy a place where common principles reside and the "transcendent value of justice," as Frank writes, can be shared.

For instance, in a 2005 speech honoring civil rights hero John Lewis, Obama talks about campaigning for the Senate in Cairo, Ill., a town synonymous with overt racism. Obama is accompanied by Sen. Dick Durbin, to whom he directly compares himself. Obama calls himself "a black guy born in Hawaii with a father from Kenya and a mother from Kansas" and Durbin "the son of Lithuania immigrants born into very modest means in east St. Louis." They're both improbable success stories, and had the pair visited Cairo together 30 years previous, who knows what would have happened?

Obama's worries about what sort of reception he and Durbin will receive turn out to be baseless: It's an enthusiastic, mixed crowd, a living demonstration of the racial progress we've made, thanks to the courage of John Lewis and people like him.

In his 2004 convention speech, Obama concedes that we Americans have our differences. While race, geography, politics, and sexual orientation may separate individuals, he insists "there is not a liberal America and a conservative America—there is the United States of America. There is not a black America and a White America and Latino America and Asian America—there's the United States of America." The same words issued by George W. Bush's mouth would move nobody, but a boundary walker like Obama has a way of making them sound genuine. The bonus point for Obama is that by calling for unity, he can also subtly reject the identity politics that have crippled the Democratic Party.

As the candidate who prides himself on disagreeing without being disagreeable, Obama takes on a Christlike quality for lots of people, especially white people. If a white American doesn't feel guilty about race, you can be almost certain that he feels anxious about it. Believe me, if these people had a street address where they could go and get absolution, they'd take the next taxi. Obama has a talent for extending forgiveness to the guilty and the anxious without requiring an apology from them first. Go forth and sin no more, he almost says, and never mind the reparations. No wonder they call him the brother from another planet.

He also knows how to comfort voters with a national narrative of his own invention. As Frank writes, the Song of Obama usually begins with references to Thomas Jefferson, a self-contradicting political thinker whose stock—for good reason—has not always been high in African American circles. Next, he ropes in Abraham Lincoln, whom he describes as less than a perfect emancipator in a 2005 speech. And yet Obama, a tall, gangly, lawyer whose political career was made in Springfield, Ill., slyly compared himself to Lincoln when he declared for the presidency. Lincoln, Obama said, was "a tall, gangly, self-made Springfield lawyer" who "tells us that there is power in words" and "tells us there is power in conviction." 10

Obama's national narrative notes both Roosevelts before calling on Martin Luther King Jr. and, as everybody knows, Ronald Reagan. The implication, of course, is that the Obama candidacy stands as the fulfillment of the American ideal, and by casting their ballot for him, voters can participate in that transcendent moment. It's a dizzying notion. No wonder George Packer's mind went vacant after he heard Obama speak.

In his speeches, Obama pretends to be a hero out of Joseph Campbell. He talks about being on a journey that is about more than just *hope* and *change*. If you want to walk together down his American road, he wants you to be prepared for hard work. It's never going to be easy. He warns his listeners to beware of the cynics and the they-say and they-said naysayers who believe the quest is hopeless.

Obama speeches aren't all nonstop inspiration, mind you. Just as John McCain is stuck on addressing "my friends" in his speeches, Obama can't resist starting a sentence with "now, I know" and loves to do battle with the nefarious "some who will." But his genuine good humor, his bassoon-and-gravel voice, and a trust quotient that equals that of Walter Cronkite help him over those humps.

In a response to Frank's paper (published in tandem with it), Mark Lawrence McPhail of Miami University warns of the downside of the Obama vision, which he regards as, in the 1994 words of Stephen L. Carter, one that "almost nobody really believes in but almost everybody desperately wants to."

McPhail rails against "Obama's 'audacious 15 hope,'" which he considers "at best naïve, and at worst opportunistic." Skipping the much-needed national conversation about race in favor of Obamaism in the sky won't bring peace, and it won't bring justice, McPhail believes.

Obama's grand rhetoric did, however, win him 90 percent of the black vote and 52 percent of the white vote in the Virginia primary this week. Voters might not know what he said, but they have a good idea of what he means.

A CLOSER LOOK AT
How Obama Does That Thing He Does

1. In this review, Shafer does not actually use the words *logos, pathos,* and *ethos.* However, locate the places in the article where he talks about how Obama uses reasoning, authority, and emotion to persuade his audiences.

2. How does Shafer compare Obama's use of rhetoric to that of other great orators, like Franklin Delano Roosevelt, Martin Luther King, and Ronald

Reagan? What are some similarities among these great speakers, and how is Obama different from them?

3. According to Shafer, how did Obama treat race differently in the 2008 campaign than others have in the past? What effect did this different approach to race have on his own life story and his political career?

IDEAS FOR
Writing

1. Since winning the 2008 election, do you think Obama's rhetoric has changed? Write a two-page response to Shafer's article in which you compare and contrast the Obama he describes in this article with the Obama you know as president. Toward the end of the article, Shafer expresses some doubts about whether Obama's oratorical skills will be the basis for effective leadership of the nation. Knowing what you know about Obama as president, do you think Shafer was right?

2. Write a three-page profile of another person who has strong rhetorical skills in speech or writing. The person you choose could be a historical figure or someone contemporary. You could also pick someone you know personally (e.g., a professor, family member, clergymember, etc.). Your profile should introduce this person and explain why he or she has such strong communication skills. Use the concepts of *logos, ethos*, and *pathos* to support your profile.

What's a Girl to Read?

LIZA FEATHERSTONE

In this article, Liza Featherstone discusses the current magazines available to teenage girls. Traditionally, these kinds of magazines have been about image, fashion, and relationships. Featherstone detects a shift, with some magazines changing for the better and others repackaging the same old themes. In this rhetorical analysis, pay attention to how she criticizes and applauds the ways some magazines use emotion and credibility to attract young women.

Trying to seduce as many underage girls as possible, corporate publishing has adopted the buzzword "real" as its come-on of the moment. Rightly sensing that there is a vacuum in the teen magazine market—the fastest-growing segment of the population has, like, nothing to read—publishers have dreamed up *Jump, Teen People, Twist* and *Glossy. Teen People*, which hit the newsstands this month, promises "real teens, real style." *Jump*'s slogan is "For girls who dare to be real." It makes sense that realness should become a market niche—existing teen magazines like *Seventeen* and *YM* being so decidedly unreal.

But how much realer is this new crop? "Reality" is a place where bodies come in all shapes and sizes, and girls have a political, intellectual and creative life of their own. Despite their pretenses, commercial teen magazines' reality bureaus are still pretty short-staffed.

Time Inc.'s Joe Camel, *Teen People*, deserves some credit for putting out a model-free magazine. Only a third of *Teen People* is devoted to fashion and beauty, and it has refreshingly little advice about how to find a boyfriend. *Teen People* also nods to the not-so-girly girls with profiles of girl sport-climbers and in-line streetskaters. But it's a sad commentary on the state of the glossies that these achievements are even worth mentioning, since *Teen People* is clearly nothing more than a way to hook future *People* readers on celebrity worship—and on a made-in-Hollywood world view (movies are praised for making you "believe in love"). Worse, *Teen People* trivializes girls' achievements; a profile of *Party of Five*'s Jennifer Love Hewitt is almost entirely dedicated to her clothes and her love life. But *Teen People*'s most heinous crime is unskeptically quoting—just five pages away from a full-page *Dawson's Creek* ad, but who's noting such minutia—one of the cast members of *Dawson's Creek* as claiming, "We're a mouthpiece for real teens." Did *Teen People* even "watch" that show? Talk to the hand.

Jump, just a few issues old, from the fitness-oriented Weider Publishing, is a refreshing paean to the active girl—"stylin' snowboarders" and girl hockey players fill its pages; nail polishes recommended are quick-drying (which assumes you have something better to do than sit around and fan your nails). *Jump* clearly has feminist intentions; a first-person story by a girl who suffered from chronic acne offers a powerful indictment of how girls are made to suffer over any physical flaw. But at points *Jump* reads like a 90s *Cosmo:* Pressure to be skinny is replaced by pressure to be "buff," and a plea to girls not to worry about being model-perfect is written by a boy.

The message is clear: It's OK that boys and magazines still have the last word on what makes you sexy.

Twist, a bimonthly launched this month 5 by Bauer Publishing, fails at realness even more dismally. It does try to boost girls' body images; "Do our bellies really need busting?" is an eloquent plea for self-acceptance, and the magazine commendably names "Anti-Waifs" as a "Trend We Love . . . Finally! Hollywood is recognizing that you don't have to be scary skinny to shine." But check out their wussy examples—Jewel, Jennifer Aniston, Neve Campbell—no Janeane Garofalo or, hello, Kate Winslet, who was the romantic lead in the blockbuster of the year? Is it too utopian to hope that actresses with real meat on their bones could be presented as sexy icons in a commercial teen magazine? *Twist* shows some models of color, and recently ran a short item on how Janet Jackson gets her "rad red highlights," but these half-hearted hi-fives to multiculturalism are dwarfed by a full-page feature on "How can I get smooth silky hair"—in which the strived-after tresses shown are, you guessed it, blonde.

Aggravating as these body problems are, *Twist*'s assault on girls' minds is even worse. We know only one thing for certain about a girl who picks up a magazine: She doesn't spend every single minute of her life watching TV. So what else does *Twist* recommend she read? Books that might as well be TV shows because they are: the *Party of Five*, *Buffy the Vampire Slayer*, *Moesha* and *X-Files* book series. *Twist* also plugs supermodel autobiography *Veronica Webb Sight*. Whatever. *Twist* manages to have even less respect for readers' intelligence than its older sister glossies; while *Seventeen*, to its credit, has always featured fiction-writing contests, *Twist*'s idea of reader participation is—no joke—a "love quiz" contest.

Then there's *Glossy*, a Web magazine newly launched in print, which doesn't remotely aspire to realness. It makes *YM* look like the Seneca Falls Declaration.

OK, OK. My catty sniping is all very well, but ultimately, what's a girl to read? Luckily there are a number of alternatives to these mind-numbing infomercials: independently published magazines written by and for teenage girls. These magazines are not only more feminist than their glossy counterparts, they're far smarter, more racially diverse, and yes, more real.

Rochester, N.Y.-based *Blue Jean*, an ad-free bimonthly, offers, to use its own words, an "alternative to the fashion and beauty magazines targetting young women." Ani "I-refuse-to-sell-out-to-the-McMusic-industry" diFranco graces the cover of the January/February "Women We Love" issue with gritty style—not your father's *Esquire*'s "Women We Love": in addition to Ani, *Blue Jean* loves Third Wave activist Rebecca Walker, soccer star Mia Hamm, tennis pro Venus Williams (and "the sassy swing of her beaded hair"), author Veronica Chambers, teen novelist Jean Crowell and Hard Candy nail polish entrepreneur Dineh Mohajer, and features interviews with both Missy "Misdemeanor" Elliott and Rosa Parks.

Teen Voices, a national quarterly run out 10 of Boston that roughly estimates its readership at 45,000, focuses on urban girls—taking on issues from teen pregnancy and body mutilation to "Snowboarding on the Cheap!" Articles ask: Was the court decision in the Boston Latin affirmative action case fair? Are cartoons sexist? Do animals have rights? How do you get over shyness? Should you get a tattoo? *Teen Voices* has a fine mix of politics, personal stuff, book and record reviews, fiction and poetry.

Hues, a feisty, multi-cultural quarterly, has a high-quality, attractive, innovative layout—on shiny paper (none of this hard-to-read, self-marginalizing newsprint). Its current issue features "Get On the Bus!" an account of Philadelphia's little-covered Million Woman March; "Making It Big," a profile of a successful and gorgeous 190-pound model who's outspoken in her criticism of the fashion industry; advice on looking for a good job "before you give up and accept a lifetime position at Minimun-Wages-R-Us"; an undercover look at phone sex; and a cultural dialogue between two young Indian women about arranged marriage. They've also run pieces on "Ghetto Feminism" and a "Swimsuit Issue" featuring women of all colors, shapes and sizes. *Hues* was recently acquired by New Moon publishing, the creator of the younger girls' magazine *New Moon*; it will go bimonthly next year.

Reluctant Hero is a Canadian quarterly with some serious feminist analysis—"Birds do it, Bees do it, Boys sure do. Why is it so taboo for girls to have a libido?"—asking why boys on TV shows don't listen to girls' desires (they pursue girls who aren't interested, harass them endlessly, and end up winning them over in the end). *Reluctant*

Hero also explores cliques, sexual harassment and peer mediation, and asks that timeless question that you will probably never see in a commercial teen magazine—"Why Are Girls So Mean?" Other features cheer girls' creativity and ambitions: "Be a Mega Zine Queen," "Does Science Have a Gender?" and "Getting a Record Deal."

These magazines are so good that re-reading them actually made me dislike *Jump, Teen People* and *Twist* even more. Though these commercial ventures are, considering the territory, a step in the right direction, girls themselves can do so much better. It's too soon to say for sure how many readers the mainstream newcomers have attracted, but *Teen People* is reportedly selling like the Titanic. The independents don't attract Gap ads, and, at least in *Blue Jean*'s case, wouldn't even if they could; they need support. Subscribe, request them at your bookstore or library, make a contribution, show them to your favorite teenager—or millionaire investor. Let's hope the talent behind this girls' alternative press gets the encouragement it deserves to keep on keeping it real.

A CLOSER LOOK AT
What's a Girl to Read?

1. In her article, Featherstone says this about these new magazines: "The message is clear: It's OK that boys and magazines still have the last word on what makes you sexy." What does Featherstone believe is the alternative to this common theme in magazines aimed at teenage girls? How do the magazines she supports change this dynamic?

2. How does image, especially images of the body, become an issue of credibility (*ethos*) in teen

magazines? How do these magazines use or misuse images of celebrities and models to promote a specific ideal of what teenage girls should aspire to?

3. According to Featherstone, how do these kinds of magazines play on the emotions of teenage girls? Does she suggest that there are good ways to use emotional arguments aimed at girls? What are some of the inappropriate ways that emotions are used in these magazines and their advertisements?

IDEAS FOR
Writing

1. At your campus library or local library, find a magazine that is aimed toward women. Write a two-page review in which you use the concepts of *logos, ethos,* and *pathos* to discuss how this magazine and its advertisers try to persuade its readers. Your review should be aimed at the target audience for the magazine. Tell them whether the magazine is effective or not.

2. Write a proposal in which you pitch an idea for a new kind of magazine aimed at college-age women or men. Pick a specific angle or niche that sets your magazine apart from the magazines that are already aimed at these markets. Your proposal should first discuss the absence of magazines like yours. Then describe the magazine and its market.

1. With a group in your class, discuss the ways people try to persuade you. How do family members try to persuade you? How do your friends try to persuade you? In what ways do their persuasive strategies differ from the ways advertisers try to persuade people?

2. List some ways people try to use their credibility (*ethos*) or emotion (*pathos*) to persuade others. Supposedly, using reason (*logos*) is the most reliable way to persuade someone, and yet we use credibility and emotion all the time to get our points across. Why? When are arguments from credibility and emotion even more persuasive than arguments that rely on reason?

3. With a group, make a list of your favorite five commercials on television and a list of five commercials you cannot stand. Why do people in your group find some of these commercials interesting and worth watching? Why are some commercials so irritating that you want to turn the television off? As a group, create a list of ten do's and don'ts of advertising to college students.

1. Find an advertisement in a magazine that you think is persuasive (or not). Then write a one-page analysis of the advertisement in which you discuss why you think it is effective (or not). Look closely at its uses of reasoning, credibility, and emotion. What kinds of support does the advertiser rely on most? What do these rhetorical strategies say about the people the advertiser is targeting?

2. Imagine that a political candidate has hired you to explain how to persuade college students to vote for him or her. The candidate sees college students as very important, but is frustrated by some students' ability to see through the political spin. In a one- to two-page brief, explain what college students find persuasive these days and what kinds of message would get them to go to the polls.

3. Find a rhetorical analysis on the Internet that you can study. These documents are rarely called "rhetorical analyses." Instead, they tend to be critiques of advertisements, speeches, or documents. You can find good examples on Web sites like *Slate.com* or the *New York Times* Web site (nytimes.com). Write a one-page discussion in which you study the organization, style, and design of the rhetorical analysis. How does it work? What kinds of rhetorical elements does the reviewer pay attention to? Do you agree with the reviewer's analysis?

Write This

1. **Analyze a text.** Choose a historical, nonfiction text you find interesting and write a five-page rhetorical analysis of it. Your analysis should define the rhetorical concepts you will use to study the document. It should summarize the text and offer some historical background on it. Then offer a close analysis of the text, explaining why it is effective or not.

2. **Analyze something else as a rhetorical text.** Find something other than a written text for your rhetorical analysis. You could study the architecture of a building, the design of a sculpture, the way someone dresses, or perhaps how someone acts. Using the rhetorical concepts of *logos*, *ethos*, and *pathos*, discuss how designs or people can be persuasive in nonverbal ways. Write a five-page paper or create a Web site in which you explain the ways in which reason, credibility, and emotion can be conveyed in without using words.

3. **Critique an advertisement or advertising campaign.** Choose an advertisement or a series of advertisements that you enjoy or detest. Then write a five-page rhetorical analysis in which you explain why the ad or series is effective or ineffective. You should embed a visual, like a screen shot, scan, or video, somewhere in your analysis so your readers can see what you are analyzing.

10

Commentaries

Do you like to express your opinions about what's happening around you? Writing commentaries will give you a chance to get your ideas out there. Commentaries are used to express opinions on current issues and events, offering new and interesting perspectives that help readers understand the world in which they live.

When writing a commentary, you are contributing something new to an ongoing public conversation. Your goal is to convince readers to agree with you and, perhaps, to change their minds. Meanwhile, readers of commentaries want to grasp the issue under discussion and understand the author's angle quickly and easily. They want to learn something new and figure out how someone else views an important issue. To catch their attention, a commentary needs to snap, making its point quickly and memorably.

Many college writing assignments are forms of commentary. Your professors will ask you to write your opinions about current events or describe your reactions to a reading. They will ask you to take a stand on an issue or consider opposing sides of a controversy. In upper-level courses, professors often ask students to write opinion pieces to demonstrate that they have a firm grasp on a subject and to express what they believe.

You will likely find plenty of opportunities to write commentaries in your career. In this age of around-the-clock news coverage, the Internet and television are overflowing with commentaries. Editorials, op-ed essays, and letters to the editor are regular features of news Web sites, newspapers, and magazines. Meanwhile, blogs and social networking sites, like *Facebook* and *MySpace*, allow people to write commentaries on current events and the world around them.

Commentaries

This diagram shows a basic organization for a commentary. When writing a commentary, you should explain the current event or issue. Then offer support for your opinion. Other arrangements of these sections can be used, so you should alter this organization to fit your topic, angle, purpose, readers, and context.

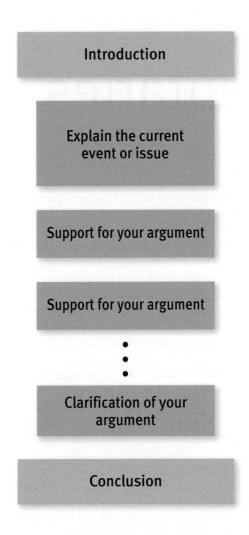

Introduction

Explain the current event or issue

Support for your argument

Support for your argument

•
•
•

Clarification of your argument

Conclusion

Overview

Commentaries take a new angle on a timely topic and back up their claims with good reasoning and solid evidence. They include some or all of these features:

- **A topic** based on current events or current issues.

- **An introduction** that immediately engages the reader by clearly announcing the *issue* under examination, the writer's main claim, and the angle he or she will take on this topic.

- **An explanation of the current event or issue** that reviews what happened and the ongoing conversation about it.

- **An argument for a specific position** that includes reasoning, evidence, examples, and observations.

- **A clarification** that qualifies the argument, avoiding the tendency to overgeneralize or oversimplify the topic.

- **A conclusion** that offers an overall assessment of the issue, highlights its importance to readers, and looks to the future.

The diagram on page 196 shows a typical structure for a commentary. Always keep in mind that the commentary genre is very flexible. You don't need to include every feature shown here or to arrange them in this order. Instead, the content, organization, style, and design of your commentary should be appropriate to your topic, purpose, readers, and the context in which it will be read.

ONE STUDENT'S WORK
Commentaries

Why My Generation Doesn't Care About Performance Enhancement

David Meany

Steroids in sports might come as a big shock to most of America, but not to my generation. Here's why. When it comes to sports stars, Hollywood celebrities, and political leaders, my generation (I'm 18 years old) has very low expectations. It's not that we're cynical or completely jaded; it's just that we don't hold these people up as role models. We don't really care if their morals are pure. We would say that we're simply realistic, that we see

Identifies the topic, purpose, and main point.

continued

the world as it is. These celebrities—politicians, movie and TV stars, and, yes, sports figures—do whatever it takes to get ahead. The rest of us are different.

Let me back up just a little. I'm a huge baseball fan and always have been. I love baseball's history, in fact, all of sports history. Way back in grade school, when it was time to do a book report, I'd find a sports biography: Babe Ruth, Cal Ripkin, Babe Didrikson, Roy Campanella, Joe Namath, Julius "Dr. J" Erving. Even nonhuman sports stars, like Sea Biscuit and Dan Patch, made great reads and reports. I grew up obsessed with Cal Ripken and his quest to break Lou Gehrig's record for consecutive games played. When I was younger and had more time, I could tell you the starting lineup and batting order for every Major League baseball team. So, yes, I was a total baseball nerd.

Explains the current issue and reviews the ongoing conversation.

So now Barry Bonds and Roger Clemens have been caught shooting up, or creaming up, or doing whatever athletes do nowadays to get those steroids into their systems and building muscle, giving them strength and stamina that no steroid-free human could ever hope for. Talking heads on ESPN express outrage (Bryant and Quinn). Sports radio personalities howl in disgust. Even eggheads like commentator George Will moan about a "stain on baseball" (A31). Meanwhile, the Mitchell Report, a tell-all treatise written for the Commissioner of Baseball, says that investigations are "critical to effectively identifying and disciplining players who continue to violate Major League Baseball's rules and policies" (286).

And you know what, I don't care, and most of my generation doesn't care because we're more realistic than older generations. Some might say we're more cynical, but it's a question of expectations. We expect our celebrities and leaders to have low ethical standards.

Uses reasoning and examples to support his argument.

Having low ethical standards, doing whatever it takes, that's how people get to be prominent figures in the first place. A person still has to work hard, but a person has to be willing to succeed "at any cost" if they want to really make it big. Look at our recent presidents and members of Congress. You can't stay out of the gutter and make it through an election successfully. Barack Obama and John McCain tried, but they ended up slinging the mud. Look at our Hollywood celebrities, like Paris Hilton, Justin Timberlake, and Lindsay Lohan. Sure, they have talent, but lots of people have talent, maybe even more talent than the stars who "make it." But not everyone has the will to succeed at any cost. That's how people get to be really successful. They're not normal people. Look what happens to celebrities between films or concerts: they're exposed as drug-using, law-breaking creeps. A little sunshine reveals some very dark corners.

I don't know if it's always been that way, or if scandals are just more out in the open these days. The Internet and other never-ending news shows have made it easier to uncover celebrity secrets, and harder to maintain the myth that those who have made it got there fair and square. We know better. I think we're just a little more realistic than people were a generation back.

Americans of my generation just don't expect their sports figures, Hollywood celebrities, and political leaders to be pure and free from the taint of scandal and unfair play. We know that these people probably abide by the credo that "If you're not cheatin', you're not trying." These people are not our heroes and don't deserve to be. They know it, and we know it.

I'm not saying we are a cynical generation, just that we are cynical about one thing in particular: celebrities of all kinds. When it comes to how we expect ourselves to behave, our standards are as high as any generation's. We expect ourselves, for the most part, to abide by common decency and commonsense values. My friends and I (and most of my generation) believe in fair play and honesty, and we expect the same from the people we have to deal with. For example, we play by the rules (most of us) when it comes to academics, too. Most of us don't cheat; most of us look down on people who do.

Clarifies and qualifies his position.

I'm talking about the people who really make it big. I don't trust them. I don't look up to them to help me figure out how to live my life. They're not my heroes, and that's just fine with me. It's just the way America works right now. We look elsewhere to find out how to live. We're pretty smart that way. I think we're a little more savvy about these things than previous celebrity-worshipping generations of Americans.

Concludes by restating the main point.

Works Cited

Mitchell, George. *Report to the Commissioner of Baseball of an Independent Investigation into the Illegal Use of Steroids and Other Performance Enhancing Substances by Players in Major League Baseball.* New York: Office of the Commissioner of Baseball, 2007. Print.

Bryant, Howard, and T.J. Quinn. "Has MLB Changed Since the Mitchell Report?" *ESPN.com.* ESPN, 12 Dec. 2008. Web. 4 Mar. 2009.

Will, George. "A Stain on Baseball." *Washington Post* 8 Dec. 2004: A31. Print.

Inventing Your Commentary's Content

When writing a commentary about a current event or issue, you should begin by listening. After all, if you want to join a conversation, you first need to understand it. Nobody wants to hear from someone who dives right into a debate but hasn't taken the time to figure out what people have said so far. Also, listen carefully for the important things people are *not* saying, for the insightful angle they are *not* pursuing. In other words, attend to the gaps in the conversation that you can fill in.

To start, you need a good topic. Commentaries are usually written in response to events that are happening right now. So watch the news, read news Web sites, or search newspapers and magazines to find an event or issue that people are talking about. Your topic should be something you personally care about and something about which you could say something interesting.

Inquiring: Finding Out What You Already Know

Once you have a topic, find out what you already know about it. A great way to get your ideas out there is to play the Believing and Doubting Game. Playing this game with your topic can help you see different sides of an issue while coming up with an angle that is uniquely your own. There are three steps in the game—believing, doubting, and synthesizing:

Believing. Begin by studying one side of your topic from the perspective of a true believer. Assume that this side is completely correct and that all assertions—even if they are contradictory—are valid. Then freewrite or brainstorm for five minutes to figure out the arguments a true believer might come up with. What evidence might support this side of the argument? From what vantage point would the believer's side make the most sense? Even if you initially disagree with this side of the argument, try to imagine yourself in agreement and come up with reasons that support the position or idea.

Doubting. Now, imagine that you are a staunch critic, a complete skeptic. Do another five-minute freewrite or brainstorm in which you look for errors in the believer's side of the argument. What logical weaknesses can you find in the believer's argument? How could you undermine that argument and get others to doubt it too? If you take everything the believer says literally, what problems will arise? What are your greatest fears about the consequences of the believer's argument? How would you show others that the believer's side of the argument cannot be true?

Synthesizing. Finally, put the true believer and the true doubter at the two ends of a spectrum and figure out where you personally would stand on this issue. If you did a good job of playing the Believing and Doubting Game, you should better understand both sides of the issue. You should also be able to figure out your angle on this topic— that is, your personal point of view. What are the major issues that separate the two

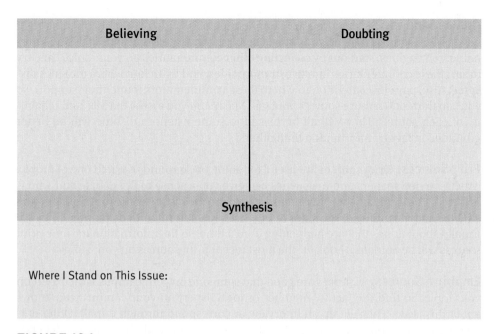

FIGURE 10.1
A Worksheet for Playing the Believing and Doubting Game

Try using this worksheet when playing the Believing and Doubting Game. On the left, list everything a true believer might say. On the right, list everything a true skeptic might say. Then try to find common ground in the "Synthesis" area between the two positions. Also, identify where you stand on this issue.

sides? What are some of the assumptions and key terms that each side uses and how do they use them differently? Where might the two sides actually find common ground?

Figure 10.1 shows a worksheet that you might find helpful when playing the Believing and Doubting Game. In the two top columns, list everything you can think of to support these opposing positions. Then, in the "Synthesis" area, write down the issues that the two sides hold in common and find out where you fit between the two positions. Concisely state your position in the section "Where I Stand on This Issue."

Researching: Finding Out What Others Know

A successful commentary needs to be built on a foundation of solid research. However, commentaries are different from other texts because they usually respond to issues that are in the news right now. As a writer, you are commenting about events that are still unfolding and about which all the facts are not known. So your goal is to figure out what others are saying and where their support comes from. That way, you can find information that will let you add something meaningful to the conversation.

Online Sources. Because you are commenting on events that are happening right now, online sources may be your most useful resources for information. Using Internet search engines, start out by collecting other commentaries on your topic. Then try to sort these commentaries into two or more sides, and figure out where the sides disagree. Also, pay close attention to where these commentators found their support, so you can track down those sources yourself. Make sure you assess the bias and reliability of each source. They will all be biased to some extent, but some will be better grounded in factual information than others.

Print Sources. Print sources are useful for doing background research on your topic. Articles in newspapers and magazines can give you a sense of the debate and who is involved. Books, meanwhile, may help you explore the history of the topic and develop a better understanding of the sides of the issue. Keep in mind that commentaries are usually about issues that are happening in real time, so the information in some print sources will be outdated. Look for the most recent print sources on your subject.

Empirical Sources. Chances are good that someone on your campus is an expert on your topic. So find the faculty member or local expert on your campus who knows about this issue. Then set up an interview or correspond through e-mail. Other empirical methods you could use might include surveys or field observations, depending on your topic.

As always, you should triangulate your sources. For most commentary topics, it is common to collect mostly online sources, with print sources a distant second. Triangulating your sources should help you confirm facts and better understand all sides of the issue. For more on triangulation, see Chapter 25, "Finding Sources and Collecting Information."

Organizing and Drafting Your Commentary

Commentaries succeed when they grab the readers' attention and then lead them through a series of arguments that support a specific position. So as you organize and draft your commentary, think about what kinds of information would be most persuasive to your readers. You won't have time to explain everything to them, so figure out what kinds of information they need to know and what would help you make the strongest case.

The Introduction

While drafting your introduction, always remember that your readers will be interested in what you have to say only if you offer them something new and interesting that they had not considered before.

Readers want to know—quickly—what topic you are addressing, what your purpose is, and what new angle you are bringing to the conversation. For example:

> With the recent release of the Mitchell report, the subject of steroids and other performance-enhancing drugs in baseball has once again come to the forefront. But considering that this topic has been widely discussed for many years now, isn't it about time people moved beyond the emotional, self-righteous moralizing and finally started looking at the issue in a more informed, rational way? (Todd Boyd, "A More Sophisticated Look at Steroids in Baseball")

In this introduction, the author identifies his topic and reveals his angle on the issue.

Your introduction should also be clear about what you want to prove (your main point). Sometimes it is helpful to just come right out and tell your readers your position:

> My argument is this: . . .

> But here's the point I want to make: . . .

> In all, I argue that . . .

This kind of statement gives your readers a good sense of where you are going with your commentary.

Explain the Current Event or Issue

Depending on your readers' familiarity with the topic, you should explain what has happened already and summarize the ongoing conversation about that event. If your readers are already familiar with the topic, you can keep this section of the commentary brief. Just give them enough background to remember the event or the origins of the debate.

If the topic is not familiar to your readers, you should provide enough background information to help them understand the event or issue. Start out by explaining what happened, who was involved, where and when it happened, how it happened, and why. As much as possible, you should show them both sides (or all sides) of the issue. Summarize what others have said about this topic.

The objective of this section is to show your readers that you understand the conversation and that you are able to see more than one side. You will have more credibility if people believe you are considering all sides seriously and giving everyone a fair hearing.

Support Your Position

After explaining the current event or issue, it is time to present support for your side of the argument. Look at your notes and identify the strongest two to five major reasons why you believe you are right about this issue. You don't need to include all of your evidence—your readers would find all that information tiresome and tedious. Instead, pick out your best reasons and devote your time to explaining them.

In a brief commentary, each of these major reasons will likely receive a paragraph or two of coverage. State a claim (topic sentence) early in the paragraph and then use examples, details, reasoning, facts, data, quotations, anecdotes, and anything else you can think of to support that claim:

Topic sentence.

Major reason and support for it.

Further, I have never been convinced that the use of performance enhancers alone automatically translates into superior athletic performance. The Mitchell report proves this point. For every Roger Clemens and Barry Bonds mentioned, there's a relatively nameless scrub who popped up on the list as well. If steroids were the all-encompassing elixir that so many people assume they are, then wouldn't every player who indulged in them be able to put up the kinds of numbers that Clemens and Bonds did over their long careers? The point is, though Clemens and Bonds both have been accused of using steroids—and both have denied those allegations—there had to be an immense amount of talent there in the first place in order for them to be so much more successful than their peers. (Todd Boyd, "A More Sophisticated Look at Steroids in Baseball")

Each major reason for your argument should support the main point you stated in the introduction. Your support needs to steadily build up your argument for your side of the issue.

Clarification of Your Position

Before concluding your commentary, you might want to show readers that you are aware of the complexities of the issue. So you should clarify your argument by pointing out that new information or events might alter your ideas and approaches to the topic. Also, you can qualify your argument by conceding that the issue is not simple and the problem is not easy to solve. Writers often signal such clarifications with phrases like these:

I'm not arguing here for a complete . . . , but only . . .

I understand, of course, that . . .

I'm only suggesting that . . .

I recognize that the people on the other side want to do the right thing, too.

Typically a clarification will only need a paragraph, depending on the length of your commentary.

Without this clarification, your readers might accuse you of "painting with too broad a brush"—that is, generalizing too far or failing to consider the fine but important points of an issue. Your clarification will help deflect or prevent those kinds of criticisms.

The Conclusion

Your final words should leave readers with a clear statement of your position and a sense of your commitment to it. Restate your main point, preferably in stronger terms than you used in the introduction. You might also reemphasize the importance of the topic and offer a look to the future. Then finish the conclusion with a memorable anecdote, figure of speech, turn of phrase, or arresting image that will give readers something to think about. For example:

> However flawed the Mitchell report might be, it is a golden opportunity to begin addressing this issue in a more forthright manner. Otherwise the church of baseball is no more than a Kool-Aid-drinking cult. (Todd Boyd, "A More Sophisticated Look at Steroids in Baseball")

In this brief two-sentence conclusion, the writer states his main point, stresses the importance of the topic, looks to the future, and provides a clever turn of phrase that gives the readers something to think about.

Choosing an Appropriate Style

The commentary genre tends to use a spirited style, which often sets it apart from other argumentative genres, such as position papers or proposals. To catch your readers' attention, you need to develop a strong sense of your persona with your commentary's style. Start out by thinking about how you want to sound to your readers. How do you want them to imagine you? How do you want them to react to your voice? What tone should they hear as they read? Here are a few ways to develop your style.

Get into Character

As you draft and revise your commentary, try to imagine yourself playing a role like an actor. If you want to sound angry, imagine you are angry as you write. If you want to sound upbeat, imagine you are in an upbeat mood. You need to get into character before you start drafting or revising.

Getting into character works because it allows you to write with less inhibition. You're playing a role, so you can freely let those emotions and that tone spill onto the screen or page. As you draft, use your writing to explore the specific emotion or tone you are trying to project to your readers.

Imitate a Well-Known Writer

Try imitating the style of a well-known critic or commentator whose work you like to read. Then find a few articles written by this person that use a style similar to the one you want to use in your commentary. Look closely at how this person achieves that particular style or tone. Does he or she use details or words in a particular way? Are the sentences long or short? Does he or she use analogies, metaphors, or similes to express complex thoughts? How does this writer convey excitement, anger, or other emotions you are seeking to express?

It's best if you *avoid* imitating the style of an article on the topic you are writing about. That way, while imitating the style of an article, you won't mistakenly plagiarize the writer's ideas or words.

Match Your Tone to Your Reader's Expectations

It's important to know the context for your document—that is, *where* your commentary will appear and *who* your potential readers are. If your potential readers expect an informal, colloquial commentary, then you should adopt that informal style. For instance, if you're writing for an online discussion and the writers all speak in casual terms, you should probably do the same. On the other hand, if you're writing to a local newspaper or magazine with a more formal tone, then you should match that level of formality.

Use Analogies, Similes, and Metaphors

Since commentaries typically handle complex topics that can be difficult to understand, writers often turn to analogies, similes, and metaphors to make the unfamiliar seem more familiar. For example, here is how commentator Todd Boyd uses an analogy to explain why professional athletes should be allowed to use performance-enhancing drugs:

> Metaphor suggesting baseball is a business.

> The analogy draws parallels to other kinds of workplaces.

In a society driven by capital, productivity is the objective. Baseball players need to be productive in order to increase their own salaries. But, more importantly, their play needs to bolster the profits of their owners. This comes into play in a major way as it pertains to human growth hormone. Players use HGH to recover from injuries faster, so they can come back and help their team. You cannot be productive if you're hurt. You cannot help your team if you cannot play. The pressure to return from injury is ingrained in us from the earliest possible age. When you factor in the intense public scrutiny that accompanies player salaries these days, the pressure on the individual is greatly heightened. So, in the interest of being more productive and more accountable, players feel forced to do whatever they can to get healthy as fast as possible. It is hypocritical to criticize players for "doggin' it" and exaggerating their injuries, and then turn around and lambaste them for using HGH when attempting to accelerate their recovery. (Todd Boyd, "A More Sophisticated Look at Steroids in Baseball")

Essentially, Boyd is drawing an analogy between the world of manufacturing (capital, productivity, profits) and sports to explain why performance-enhancing drugs should be allowed in a business like professional baseball.

Analogies, similes, and metaphors also have the benefit of adding a visual element to an argument. In the paragraph above, for example, it is easy to visualize baseball players as laborers who are creating a profitable product for the owners. Boyd is using this analogy to counter the usual image of professional baseball players as grown men who are merely playing a game.

Designing Your Commentary

As you design your document, pay attention to its medium and what's possible in that medium. For example, if your commentary will appear on a Web site or blog, adding design features like photos and other graphics is much easier than in, say, an opinion article written for a newspaper or magazine.

Commentaries rarely appear in a stand-alone format. Instead, they appear within larger documents, like Web sites, newsletters, newspapers, and magazines. So as you are thinking about what design would be appropriate, pay attention to the place where your commentary is likely to appear.

Include Photography. Because commentaries address current events and issues, you may want to snap a few pictures or download photographs from the Internet to show what you are talking about. If you are taking your own photographs with a digital camera or a mobile phone, you can download them to your computer and then insert them into your document. Most word processors have an Insert function in their top menu that will put the picture wherever you set your cursor on the page.

You can also insert pictures that you have downloaded from the Internet. When using a PC, you can use the right button on your mouse to download a picture you want. Click on the picture. A menu will appear that allows you to download the image to your hard drive. Then use the Insert function to put the photograph into your document.

If you are using the picture for a strictly academic purpose (e.g., a paper for class), you don't need to ask permission to use it. However, if you are using the picture in a public way (e.g., on a Web site or blog, in a publication, on a poster, etc.) you will need to ask permission from the person who owns it. An e-mail to the owner of the Web site where you found the photo is usually the best way to ask permission. If you don't get permission to use it, you will be in violation of copyright law. Don't do that.

Add Pull Quotes to Emphasize Important Points. You have probably seen pull quotes in print and online magazines. Pull quotes draw attention to a key sentence or short passage from the text that captures some essential point, question, or idea (Figure 10.2). Sometimes the pull quote functions as a subtitle, or an alternative title.

When readers are deciding whether they want to read a particular commentary, they usually skim the page or screen for the following elements: the title, a pull quote, and the first and maybe the second paragraph. A pull quote that grabs their attention and tells them the angle and tone of your commentary will help readers decide whether they should read your commentary. But don't overdo it. Reserve pull quotes

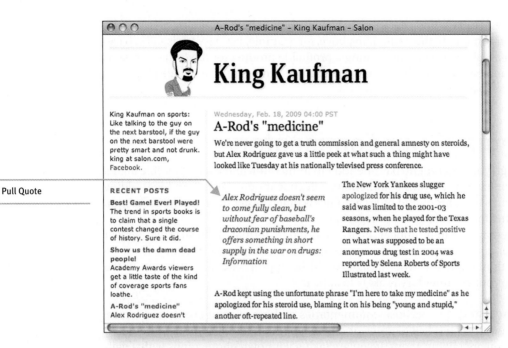

Pull Quote

FIGURE 10.2   A Pull Quote

A pull quote captures an essential point, question, or idea from the text. They are helpful for drawing the readers' attention to the text.

for the really big, attention-grabbing ideas. As a rule of thumb, use only one or two pull quotes per written page, and no more than one per screen.

Revising and Editing Your Commentary

As you revise, keep in mind that you want your commentary to be noticed, to stand out among all the other commentaries your readers have available. But you also want to seem reasonable so that readers will listen, take your ideas seriously, and consider your ideas as they think about the issue and carry the conversation forward.

Strengthen the Sense That You're Listening to All Sides.   Refer to what others have said and done. Incorporate the ideas of others with brief summaries, paraphrases, and quotations. When appropriate, recognize the value of others' viewpoints and the importance of listening to all sides. Make sure that you come across not as a naysayer or cynic, but as someone who listens carefully and considers all reasonable sides of an issue.

Set Your Ideas Apart from Those of Others. Make sure your readers understand how and why your views are different from those of others. Tell the readers what sets your views apart, but be careful not to sound condescending or dismissive about people who disagree with you.

Refine Your Persona. As you finish your final draft, look back at what you have written and make sure that you are projecting the intended persona. Do you want to be seen as a reasonable peacemaker who strives to bring people together and manage conflict so that the conversation is productive? Or do you want to be viewed as someone who is raising tough issues and telling uncomfortable truths?

Proofread (and Proofread Again). Fair or not, if there are grammatical errors, misspellings, and typos littering your argument, the ideas in your commentary will be judged negatively. So spend plenty of time going through your commentary to fix these kinds of errors. Your readers are more likely to trust your reasoning if your text is error-free.

Before you hand in your commentary, let it sit for at least a few hours. Then read it through one last time, looking for problems in content, organization, style, and design. A little distance will help you polish it.

Letter to
the Editor

A letter to the editor is a brief commentary that is written for the opinions section of a newspaper, magazine, and news Web site. Though addressed "to the editor," they are written for the larger readership. Letters to the editor usually respond directly to a specific news item or an opinion piece in the publication.

Letters to the editor often force you to distill your argument to 250 words or less. Here's how to write a great one:

Address and summarize a specific issue, story, or opinion piece. Editors tend to publish only letters that respond directly to an issue or current event that was written about or reported in their publication.

State your purpose precisely. If you are challenging what was said previously, express concisely what you believe was inaccurate, misstated, or misunderstood. If you are agreeing with the original text, explain why you agree with it.

Support your argument with personal experiences. Letters to the editor often use personal experiences to challenge or validate a story or opinion piece.

Support your argument with factual evidence. Back up your argument or challenge the text to which you are responding with carefully researched data, historical facts, quotations, and other details.

Recognize logical fallacies. Target logical fallacies in the text to which you are responding, and be careful not to use them yourself. See Chapter 22, "Using Argumentative Strategies."

Avoid condescension. When you disagree with a news story or opinion piece, it's tempting to be sarcastic or insulting. But if you keep your tone professional, readers will be more receptive to your views and your letter will have a better chance at publication.

Keep revising until you have expressed your views as concisely as possible.

WRITE your own letter to the editor. Find an article on a news Web site, in a magazine, or from a newspaper that is no more than a week old. Then write a letter to the editor that reacts in a positive or critical way. Give your professor contact information (address, e-mail address) for the editors to whom you could send your letter.

Why I'm Against the Statewide Smoking Ban

Michael Spatz

It could be easily argued that when it comes to statewide smoking bans, typical 18- to 22-year-old college students are the ones most affected. Smoking is a habit often picked up during a person's college years. And while Lawrence's smoking ban has already been law for half a decade, I do not think a statewide smoking ban is what the state of Kansas needs right now.

Identifies specific issue being addressed.

Main point.

The economic effects of a statewide smoking ban are obvious. Bars and taverns lose the business of smokers, which, in some cases, is enough to close down the establishment. According to the Department of Labor, the unemployment rate in Kansas for March 2009 was 6.5 percent, the highest in 26 years. A statewide smoking ban would only further handcuff bars and taverns across the state in their fight to stay above water during this recession.

Supports argument with factual evidence.

More important than the economic effects are the health effects. The effects that smoking has on a smoker are proven. The effects of secondhand smoke, however, are extremely debatable. According to the Health News Digest, "The results do not support a causal relation between environmental tobacco smoke and tobacco-related mortality, although they do not rule out a small effect."

Factual evidence.

One last defense against a smoking ban deals with a core American value: freedom. If a bar owner wants to cater to smokers in his or her privately owned establishment, what gives a state government the right to deny that bar owner? Smoking is legal.

On a personal note, I am a social smoker. On average, I smoke probably twice a month, I won't ever be picking up the habit of being a regular smoker. My solution is simple. If a bar owner chooses to accommodate smokers, that's his or her right. If a bar owner chooses to keep his establishment a nonsmoking place, that is equally his or her right.

Supports his argument with personal experiences.

A few months ago, I saw an anti-smoking poster on campus. One of the ways it stated to avoid picking up the habit was to not associate with smokers. This disgusted me. It gave the impression that smokers are less than human and need to be completely isolated from non-smokers. Smoking bans have already hit my home state and my college town. I can only hope for significant resistance in the 29 states, Kansas included for now, that they haven't reached.

Restates his main point in a memorable way.

Are you ready to start writing your commentary? Here are some ideas to help you do it.

FIND a Current Event or Current Issue That Interests You

Pay attention to the news or the events happening around you. Commentaries are typically written about things that are currently happening.

FIND OUT What You Already Know and Believe About Your Topic

Use invention techniques like freewriting, brainstorming, or the Believing and Doubting Game to find out what you already know or believe about your topic.

DO Research on the Event or Issue

Online sources are especially helpful when writing about current events or issues. Print and empirical sources are helpful for collecting background information on the topic.

DRAFT Your Commentary

Your introduction needs to grab the readers' attention. Then explain the current event or issue. Support your side of the argument and clarify your position. Use a brief conclusion to restate your main point, and try to end with a clever turn of phrase that gives the readers something to think about.

LIVEN UP Your Style

Commentaries are known for their lively and engaging style. People enjoy reading them for the content and the colorful way the ideas are expressed. So get into character and let your emotions get onto the page.

CONSIDER the Design

Because they often appear in larger documents, commentaries tend to follow the design of the Web site, newspaper, or magazine in which they appear. Nevertheless, you should look for photography that will support or illustrate your argument. Pull quotes will allow you to highlight important ideas and quotes.

REVISE and Edit

Spend some time working and reworking your ideas. While revising and editing, pay special attention to your voice and tone. You want to polish your writing so that it stands out from the other commentaries available on the topic.

Brain Enhancement Is Wrong, Right?

BENEDICT CAREY

In this commentary, Benedict Carey, a New York Times *columnist who writes about science-related issues, looks at the use of drugs to enhance mental abilities. Pay attention to how Carey gradually builds his argument with solid reasoning and factual information.*

So far no one is demanding that asterisks be attached to Nobels, Pulitzers or Lasker awards. Government agents have not been raiding anthropology departments, riffling book bags, testing professors' urine. And if there are illicit trainers on campuses, shady tutors with wraparound sunglasses and ties to basement labs in Italy, no one has exposed them.

Yet an era of doping may be looming in academia, and it has ignited a debate about policy and ethics that in some ways echoes the national controversy over performance enhancement accusations against elite athletes like Barry Bonds and Roger Clemens.

In a recent commentary in the journal *Nature,* two Cambridge University researchers reported that about a dozen of their colleagues had admitted to regular use of prescription drugs like Adderall, a stimulant, and Provigil, which promotes wakefulness, to improve their academic performance. The former is approved to treat attention deficit disorder, the latter narcolepsy, and both are considered more effective, and more widely available, than the drugs circulating in dorms a generation ago.

Letters flooded the journal, and an online debate immediately bubbled up. The journal has been conducting its own, more rigorous survey, and so far at least 20 respondents have said that they used the drugs for nonmedical purposes, according to Philip Campbell, the journal's editor in chief. The debate has also caught fire on the Web site of the *Chronicle of Higher Education*, where academics and students are sniping at one another.

But is prescription tweaking to perform 5 on exams, or prepare presentations and grants, really the same as injecting hormones to chase down a home run record, or win the Tour de France?

Some argue that such use could be worse, given the potentially deep impact on society. And the behavior of academics in particular, as intellectual leaders, could serve as an example to others.

In his book, *Our Posthuman Future: Consequences of the Biotechnology Revolution*, Francis Fukuyama raises the broader issue of performance enhancement: "The original purpose of medicine is to heal the sick, not turn healthy people into gods." He and others point out that increased use of such drugs could raise the standard of what is considered "normal" performance and widen the gap between those who have access to the medications and those who don't—and even erode the relationship between struggle and the building of character.

"Even though stimulants and other cognitive enhancers are intended for legitimate clinical use, history predicts that greater availability will lead to an increase in diversion, misuse and abuse," wrote Dr. Nora Volkow, director of the National Institute on Drug Abuse, and James Swanson of the University of California at Irvine, in a letter to *Nature*. "Among high school students, abuse of prescription medications is second only to cannabis use."

But others insist that the ethics are not so clear, and that academic performance is different in important ways from baseball, or cycling.

"I think the analogy with sports doping is 10 really misleading, because in sports it's all about competition, only about who's the best runner or home run hitter," said Martha Farah, director of the Center for Cognitive Neuroscience at the University of Pennsylvania. "In academics, whether you're a student or a researcher, there is an element of competition, but it's secondary. The main purpose is to try to learn things, to get experience, to write papers, to do experiments. So in that case if you can do it better because you've got some drug on board, that would on the face of things seem like a plus."

She and other midcareer scientists interviewed said that, as far as they knew, very few of their colleagues used brain-boosting drugs regularly. Many have used Provigil for jet lag, or even to stay vertical for late events. But most agreed that the next generation of scientists, now in graduate school and college, were more likely to use the drugs as study aids and bring along those habits as they moved up the ladder.

Surveys of college students have found that from 4 percent to 16 percent say they have used stimulants or other prescription drugs to improve their academic performance—usually getting the pills from other students.

"Suppose you're preparing for the SAT, or going for a job interview—in those situations where you have to perform on that day, these drugs will be very attractive," said Dr. Barbara Sahakian of Cambridge, a co-author with Sharon Morein-Zamir of the recent essay in *Nature*. "The desire for cognitive enhancement is very strong, maybe stronger than for beauty, or athletic ability."

Jeffrey White, a graduate student in cell biology who has attended several institutions, said that those numbers sounded about right. "You can usually tell who's using them because they can be angry, testy, hyperfocused, they don't want to be bothered," he said.

Mr. White said he did not use the drugs 15 himself, considering them an artificial shortcut that could set people up for problems later on. "What happens if you're in a fast-paced surgical situation and they're not available?" he asked. "Will you be able to function at the same level?"

Yet such objections—and philosophical concerns—can vaporize when students and junior faculty members face other questions: What happens if I don't make the cut? What if I'm derailed by a bad test score, or a mangled chemistry course?

One person who posted anonymously on the *Chronicle of Higher Education* Web site said that a daily regimen of three 20-milligram doses of Adderall transformed his career: "I'm not talking about being able to work longer hours without sleep (although that helps)," the posting said. "I'm talking about being able to take on twice the responsibility, work twice as fast, write more effectively, manage better, be more attentive, devise better and more creative strategies."

Dr. Anjan Chatterjee, an associate professor of neurology at the University of Pennsylvania who foresaw this debate in a 2004 paper, argues that the history of cosmetic surgery—scorned initially as vain and unnatural but now mainstream as a form of self-improvement—is a guide to predicting the trajectory of cosmetic neurology, as he calls it.

"We worship at the altar of progress, and to the demigod of choice," Dr. Chatterjee said. "Both are very strong undercurrents in the culture and the way this is likely to be framed is: 'Look, we want smart people to be as productive as possible to make everybody's lives better. We want people performing at the max, and if that means using these medicines, then great, then we should be free to choose what we want as long as we're not harming someone.' I'm not taking that position, but we have this winner-take-all culture and that is the way it is likely to go."

People already use legal performance enhancers, he said, from high-octane cafe Americanos to the beta-blockers taken by musicians to ease stage fright, to antidepressants to improve mood. "So the question with all of these things is, Is this enhancement, or a matter of removing the cloud over our better selves?" he said.

20

The public backlash against brain-enhancement, if it comes, may hit home only after the practice becomes mainstream, Dr. Chatterjee suggested. "You can imagine a scenario in the future, when you're applying for a job, and the employer says, 'Sure, you've got the talent for this, but we require you to take Adderall.' Now, maybe you do start to care about the ethical implications."

A CLOSER LOOK AT
Brain Enhancement Is Wrong, Right?

1. List five ways that this argument by Carey meets the typical expectations of a commentary. Pay special attention to its content, organization, and style.

2. Identify the writer's main point in this article. What do you think Carey is arguing for in this article? What is he arguing against?

3. Carey tries to identify and explain both sides of this issue. Look closely at the article to identify where he is talking about one side of the issue and then where he talks about the other side.

IDEAS FOR
Writing

1. Write two one-page responses to Carey's article. In your first response, argue for the use of brain-enhancing drugs. What are the main reasons that would support using drugs to do better at school or work? In your second response, argue against the use of these drugs at school and the workplace. What are some of the potential problems? Is this kind of drug use a form of cheating? What are some of the additional costs of using these kinds of drugs?

2. Using the Internet and print sources, do some research on the two drugs, Adderall and Provigil, mentioned in this article. Then write a three-page brief (see the Microgenre in Chapter 13, "Reports")

in which you share your research with your readers. Your report should be analytical, not opinionated. You want to offer an objective discussion of this issue, using the information you collected.

3. Write a four-page proposal in which you suggest a way to handle this looming problem of brain-enhancement drug use on your campus. If you consider these drugs a form of cheating, how should the college control their use so that some students don't have an unfair advantage over others? If you think they are all right, how should the university or others make them available so that everyone can benefit from their help?

Oops! I'll Do It Again. And Again. And Again . . .

JAMES BOWMAN

In this article, conservative commentator James Bowman comments on the practice of allowing people to keep doing things over and over until they succeed. He argues that young people should be allowed to fail—for their own good. In this article, look at how he uses examples to illustrate his major points.

Beginning next month, the College Board will allow high-school students who have taken the SATs multiple times to submit only their highest score to the colleges to which they are applying. Called "Score Choice," this policy brings the SAT into line with the ACT, the rival college-entrance examination, and it is supposedly designed to reduce the stress that this examination places on students worried about their futures.

Of course, Score Choice will also give what many would see as an unfair advantage to those who can afford the time and the money to take the test more than once—and the more they can take it, the greater the advantage. For colleges, it must make the job of assessing their applicants' abilities more difficult and may thus contribute to the trend toward downgrading or eliminating standardized testing in college admissions.

But Score Choice is also a manifestation of the do-over mentality whose insidious creep into the larger culture has been made apparent over the past several months by the queue of failed businessmen and financiers who have come to Washington with their hands out, asking to be rescued from the consequences of their own poor answers to life's examination questions.

Friedrich Hayek once wrote, in "The Constitution of Liberty," that a free society depends on the willingness of its people to take respon-sibility for their actions. Not to do so is not merely to create what we have all lately learned to call "moral hazard," but to jeopardize the very foundation of our free institutions.

If we had to point to a cause of today's 5 all-but-universal sentiment in favor of re-warding the improvident, we might want to look first to the self-esteem movement in education. Many of the financial hotshots now wielding begging bowls must have been schoolchildren in the 1980s, when this curious philosophy took hold of our educators.

Back then, in Maryland's Montgomery County, near Washington, the school district banned placing students in alphabetical order for fear that the self-esteem of those whose names began with the later letters of the alphabet would suffer.

In 1986, California was the first state to introduce self-esteem education as such. It was based on the assumption that constant praise for even the feeblest effort would encourage schoolchildren to do better. In fact, it simply removed the incentive for them to work hard. The de-emphasis on competition in school sports and the grade inflation that has become so unfortunate a feature of the academy since then have had similar effects.

Studies have shown that, while American students perform poorly compared with many foreigners of the same age, they are top of the charts when it comes to how well they think they have performed. Artificially pumping up their self-esteem produces only self-deception in the first instance and frustration and anger when—or if—the truth must be faced.

Maybe it is our instinctive recognition of this fact which has made "American Idol" the most popular show on television. There, people are forced to face unwelcome truths about their abilities—most of them from the British judge, Simon Cowell, whose unconcern about treading on people's vanities makes him sound deliciously naughty in a world based on self-esteem. The loud resentment felt by many of those whose illusions have been punctured is another manifestation of this culture-wide sense of entitlement.

A friend of mine not long ago listened to 10 her 8-year-old granddaughter play a piece on the piano and suggested to her that she needed to practice some more. The child burst into tears. "Grandma," she wailed. "You're not proud of me!"

We do children no favors by teaching them that they have a right to a favorable outcome in all that they do. It used to be the case that education was thought of not just as the acquisition of knowledge—still less as the acquisition of credentials—but as a form of character building. And one of the ways to build character is to submit students to the same sorts of stresses and failures that adult life does, in order to teach them how to cope with such things.

There are some signs that the worst may be over. Last summer, after the British Olympic team did better than expected in Beijing, the Labour prime minister, Gordon Brown, gave a speech saying that competition was a good thing after all.

But much of our popular culture is still wedded to the assumptions behind the self-esteem movement. On her most recent album, the popular chanteuse Joni Mitchell rewrote Rudyard Kipling's famous poem, "If . . . ," changing his words,

If you can fill the unforgiving minute
With sixty seconds' worth of distance run . . .

to her own,

If you can fill the journey of a minute
With sixty seconds worth of wonder
and delight.

Of course, there are no more unforgiving minutes in the wonder and delight of Ms. Mitchell's imaginary land of endless do-overs—which gives the lie to her subsequent promise: "Then the Earth is yours and everything that's in it, / But more than that I know you'll be all right."

No you won't. If you fail, sooner or later 15 that failure will have to be recognized, confronted and put to rights. Not to do so in a timely fashion is only to spread the consequences of failure much more widely—to the whole educational system in the case of the SATs and the ordinary taxpayer in the case of the bailouts. Both deserve better.

A CLOSER LOOK AT
Oops! I'll Do It Again. And Again. And Again . . .

1. According to Bowman, failure is an important component of life that many of today's young people don't experience. What are a few of his arguments in favor of failing?

2. Exactly what or whom does Bowman blame for this trend in our culture? Why does he believe people are no longer expected or allowed to fail?

3. The lyrics from Joni Mitchell's song are a curious addition to this commentary. They don't seem to obviously support Bowman's argument. Look up Joni Mitchell on the Internet. Could Bowman have other reasons for wanting to include Mitchell and her lyrics in his commentary?

IDEAS FOR
Writing

1. Write a one-page letter to the editor in which you respond to Newman's commentary. You might rebut his argument by pointing out the benefits of giving people second chances. You might challenge his examples as extraordinary and not the norm. Or you might agree with his argument, offering further evidence that the fear of failure is corrupting American culture.

2. Write a four-page position paper in which you argue for or against allowing more failure in college courses. Your position paper should be aimed at your university's Dean of Students or another ad-

ministrator who is responsible for maintaining academic integrity on your campus. Do you believe students are given too many second chances? Or, do you believe students learn best by being allowed to do assignments and retake tests until they succeed?

3. Bowman's writing style is different than that of many of the authors collected in this book. Write a two-page rhetorical analysis in which you explain why you think his commentary is or is not an effective argument. As you invent and draft your rhetorical analysis, pay close attention to how he uses content, organization, and style to make his argument.

1. Ask each member of your group to describe a conversation he or she had with friends or family about a controversial current event or issue. What was the content and style of that discussion? How did you try to get your ideas across to the others? Did any participant in the discussion become upset or stop listening? If so, what went wrong? Why couldn't your friends or family get along well enough to discuss ideas in depth?

2. With your group, list seven issues or events being covered in the news right now. Pick two of these issues and discuss the different sides of the debate. Then go around the group and talk about how each member would approach writing a commentary about these two topics. What would your angle be? What could you add to the conversation about each topic?

3. Do you know someone whose participation in a discussion almost always results in discomfort, negative feelings, or anger? Do you enjoy conversing with this person, or do you avoid it? What does this person do that prompts such negative consequences? With your group, list five things that some people do to undermine discussions of important issues.

1. Listen to at least two news and opinion shows from different television or radio networks. Be attentive to how the pundits represent and exchange their differing viewpoints and (supposedly) try to influence each other as they influence the audience. What do you notice about the "conversation" and its characteristics? Is there a reasonable exchange of ideas? Do the people in the discussion seem to want to persuade the other participants to adopt their viewpoints, or simply to dominate the others? Do they ever seem to listen to each other?

2. Find an interesting opinion piece from a print or online magazine and bring it to class. With your group, talk about the written and visual features that make this piece effective. Then discuss the features that were not used that *could have* made it more effective. For instance, what is the writer's angle? What is he or she trying to achieve (purpose)? What is his or her main point? What does the commentary do to grab readers' attention and help them decide quickly whether it's worth reading?

3. Find a commentary in a newspaper or magazine, or on a news Web site. In a one-page analysis written to your professor, describe the commentary's content, organization, style, and design. What kinds of information does the writer use to support his or her points? Does the organization reflect the commentary organization described in this chapter? How would you describe the style, and how does the writer achieve this style? Finally, what design features are used to support the written text and make it more visually attractive?

Write This

1. **Express your opinion.** Imagine that you've been invited to begin writing a weekly opinion piece (editorial) for your local community newspaper, campus newspaper, or some other regularly published venue that regularly carries commentaries. Pick an issue or current event that is in the news right now. Write a four-page commentary in which you express your own view on this issue. While inventing your argument, first figure out what you already know by using invention techniques, such as the Believing and Doubting Game. Then draft your argument, paying special attention to how you organize and support your ideas.

2. **Post your views on a Web site.** Most news Web sites allow readers to comment on the articles. Find one of these commentary areas and read the twenty most recent comments posted. What are some of the points of contention? Can you detect two or more sides to the debate? Write a two-page contribution to the discussion. Be sure to respond to the original article as well as to what others have written. Hand in your commentary to your professor along with a one-page reflection in which you discuss the original article, the comments others had written, and the approach you took with your commentary.

3. **Start your own blog.** Blogs are popular places for writers to publish their commentaries on current events. Imagine that you would like to start your own blog. What topics would you write about? What angles would you take on them? Write a half-page description of your blog for your professor. Then write three 250-word entries, which you would publish on your blog. If you want, you could use this assignment to start your own blog on a free blogging service like *Blogger*, *Blogspot*, or *WordPress*.

PEARSON
mycomplab

For additional reading, writing, and research resources, go to **www.mycomplab.com.**

Position Papers

If you like to engage with the ideas of others, you will enjoy writing position papers. The purpose of a position paper is to explain both sides of a controversy and then argue for one side over the other. This two-sided approach is what makes position papers and argument essays different from commentaries (Chapter 10). A commentary usually only expresses the author's personal opinion about a current issue or event. A position paper explains both sides and discusses why one is stronger or better than the other.

Your goal is to fairly explain your side and your opponents' side of the issue, while highlighting the differences between these opposing views. You need to use solid reasoning and factual evidence to persuade your readers that your view is more valid or advantageous than your opponents' view.

In college, your professors will ask you to write position papers that analyze and evaluate both (or all) sides of an issue and then argue for one side or another. In the workplace, corporate position papers are used to argue for or against business strategies or alternatives. The ability to argue effectively is a useful skill that will help you throughout your life.

Position Papers

This diagram shows two basic organizations for a position paper, but other arrangements of these sections will work, too. In the pattern on the left, the opponents' position is described up front with its limitations; then your own position is explained with its strengths. In the pattern on the right, you make a point-by-point comparison, explaining why your position is better than your opponents'. You should alter this organization to fit your topic, angle, purpose, readers, and context.

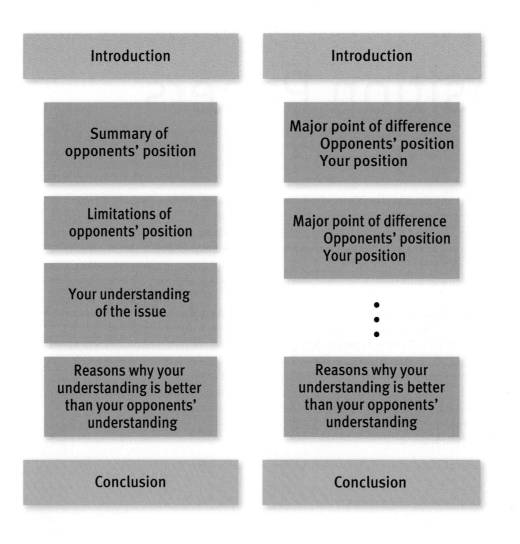

Introduction	Introduction
Summary of opponents' position	Major point of difference Opponents' position Your position
Limitations of opponents' position	Major point of difference Opponents' position Your position
Your understanding of the issue	• • •
Reasons why your understanding is better than your opponents' understanding	Reasons why your understanding is better than your opponents' understanding
Conclusion	Conclusion

Overview

Arguing can be fun, but you need to argue fairly and reasonably if you want to win over your readers. The strongest position papers and argument essays present both sides of an issue as objectively as possible and then persuade readers that one side is superior to the other. They tend to have the following features:

- **An introduction** that states the issue being debated, identifies the issue's two or more sides, and usually makes an explicit claim (thesis) that the position paper will support.

- **An objective summary** of your opponents' understanding of the issue.

- **A point-by-point discussion** of the limitations of your opponents' understanding.

- **A summary** of your side's understanding of the issue.

- **A point-by-point discussion** of why your side's understanding is superior to your opponents' understanding.

- **A conclusion** that drives home your main point and looks to the future.

This genre tends to be organized two ways, as shown on page 222. With some topics, you may need to show that there are more than two sides to the argument. In these cases, the pattern on the left can be expanded to include discussions of these other positions. It is best, though, to try to boil the issue down to two major sides. Otherwise, your readers will find it difficult to keep the sides of the argument straight.

ONE STUDENT'S WORK
Position Papers

Allowing Guns on Campus Will Prevent Shootings, Rape

Tyler Ohmann

A graduate student leaving an evening class walks along the poorly lit sidewalk to the parking lot—it is a long, cold walk in the pitch-black night, and the student grows wary as shadows begin lurking in the distance. Suddenly, someone jumps out in front of the student, immediately threatening her with force. Before the student can react, she is raped and robbed. This is a very

The writer sets the scene to grab readers.

continued

scary scenario, and one that happens on the SCSU campus every year. It seems like every week we get an e-mail citing another attack on students somewhere on or near campus. However, all of these attacks could be prevented if we allow students to carry guns as a means of self-defense.

Here is his main point.

Although safety is my biggest concern, there are other arguments that point to this solution as well.

Point-by-point comparison of two positions.

First, it is our Second Amendment right to bear arms. Although debates have gone on about how it should be interpreted, I believe it means that if law abiding, trained and eligible citizens would like to carry a gun with them in self-defense, they should be able to. Right now, that does not include campus. "The law, as it stands now, does not prohibit carry on campus," said Terence McCloskey, SCSU campus leader for Students for Concealed Carry on Campus (SCCC). "It allows universities to establish rules restricting carry on campus by students and staff." According to the March 2007 Safety and Security bulletin in section 2.1, "Alcoholic beverages, non-regulated drugs, explosives, guns and ammunition are not permitted on SCSU property." This rule, I believe, is a violation of my Second Amendment rights.

Opponents' views are presented fairly.

The second reason guns should be allowed is because it will give students, such as the one in the scenario, a sense of security and comfort when they are in a normally uncomfortable situation or area. The opposition would say that although the person with the gun is comfortable, it makes others around that person uncomfortable or afraid to speak up in class. Well, let me ask you this: How often do you feel uncomfortable or scared about someone near you having a gun when you go to a movie theater? Probably not too often. However, McCloskey said that 1 percent of Minnesotans have a permit to carry guns. "That means that every time they go to a movie theater with around 200 people inside, they are sitting with two people that are carrying a gun," McCloskey said. There are people all around us that have guns, and it seems to be handled just fine. After all, the 1 percent that do carry guns have to meet certain requirements—guns are not handed out to just anyone.

Opponents' views are presented fairly.

Minnesota law requires everyone to have a permit in order to own a handgun, and to obtain one you must be 21 years of age, be a U.S. citizen, have training in the safe use of a pistol, not be a felon, not have a domestic violence offense in the last 10 years, not be a person convicted of stalking, as well as many other restrictions. You can find these laws on the State of Minnesota Web site.

The final reason that guns should be allowed to be carried by students who obtain a permit is that it could prevent a tragic shooting like the one at Virginia Tech a couple of years ago. "Our best and our brightest are in an unprotected environment and are essentially being led to the slaughter," said Keith Moum in an article in the *Missourian*. "It's not as graphic as that, but it clearly shows that there is an element out there that has targeted college students, and campus policy has left them with no way to defend themselves." If guns had been allowed on that campus, that tragedy may have been either averted or at least minimized.

So in order to make the SCSU campus and other campuses nationwide a safe, comfortable environment for everyone, we need to allow the ability to carry a gun on campus. Not only will it make a student carrying a gun feel safe, it can prevent a tragic shooting, a robbery, or a rape. It is our right. Let us exercise it.

> The main point is driven home.

Inventing Your Position Paper's Content

When writing a position paper, you should try to summarize both sides of the issue as fairly as possible. If readers sense that you are distorting your opponents' view, they might doubt whether your views are trustworthy. So let your facts and reasoning do the talking for you. If your position is truly stronger, you should be able to explain both sides fairly and then demonstrate to readers why your side is the stronger one.

Inquiring: Identifying Points of Contention

To begin generating content for your position paper, first identify the major points on which you and your opponents disagree. A brainstorming list like the one shown in Figure 11.1 on page 226 is often the best way to identify these major points.

Use two columns. In the left column, write "My position" and list all the arguments you can think of to support your case. In the right column, write "My opponents' position" and list your opponents' best arguments for their side of the case. When listing your opponents' ideas, you should do so from their perspective. What are their strongest arguments? What would they likely say to defend their position?

When you have filled out your brainstorming lists, put checkmarks next to the two to five most important points on which you and your opponents seem to disagree. These are called "points of contention" between your side and your opponents' side of the argument.

Researching: Finding Out What Others Know

Now it is time to do some research. You can use your two-column brainstorming list as a guide to doing research on your topic. Collect sources that support both sides of the argument. You should look for a variety of online, print, and empirical sources.

My position: Concealed weapons on campus are a greater risk than no handguns on campus.

Students, faculty, and staff will feel less safe on campus if guns are allowed.

Alcohol could cause a lapse in judgment.

Campus police don't want guns on campus.

Universities may be liable if an accident happens.

In a shooting incident, police cannot tell the criminals from the people defending themselves with guns.

Bullets from a defender's gun may strike innocent people in a classroom.

Students are less mature and may use their guns to threaten others or play games.

Some students will carry guns without a concealed-carry permit.

Guns on campus will cause parents to fear sending their students to our university.

Guns locked in cars won't be any use in a shooting.

Less stable students are the ones most interested in carrying guns.

We can strengthen security if campus is thought to be unsafe.

Accidents do happen, and the university will be liable.

My opponents' position: Students, faculty, and staff should be able to carry concealed handguns on campus.

More shootings on college campuses have happened recently.

Gun-free campuses disarm citizens who could end campus shootings.

Violent people would think twice about shooting at a campus.

More mentally ill students are going to college these days.

Universities would not be such easy targets for shooters.

A shooting could be ended quickly.

It may take minutes for security to arrive at the scene of a shooting.

Gun accidents are very rare.

Gun ownership is a constitutional right.

People with guns would need to be licensed and weapons concealed.

People will carry guns anyway, so it's best to have it regulated.

Only way to stop someone with a gun is to use a gun.

Guns on campus could be left in car.

People will feel more confident and less scared on campus.

People will be able to be on campus at night.

FIGURE 11.1 Brainstorming to Identify Major Points of Contention

When brainstorming about your topic, just write down anything about your topic that comes to mind.

Again, put yourself in your opponents' place as you research their side of the issue. If you were your opponent, how would you build your argument? What would be your best points? What kinds of sources would you use to support your points? After all, if you only look for sources that support your side of the argument, there is a good chance you will miss your opponents' best reasons for holding their opinion. Then it would be easy for your opponents to undermine your argument by showing that you have not considered one or more important ideas.

Online Sources. The Internet can be helpful for generating content, but you need to be especially careful about your sources when you are preparing to write a position paper. Countless people will offer their opinions on blogs and Web sites, but these sources are often heavily biased and may provide little support to back up their opinions. When researching, you should look for factual sources on the Internet and avoid sources that are too biased. Also, keep an eye out for credible television documentaries and radio broadcasts on your subject, because they will often address both sides of the issue in a journalistic way.

Print Sources. Print documents will likely be your most reliable sources of factual information. Look for magazines, academic journals, and books, because these sources tend to be more careful about their facts and have less bias. Through your library's Web site, try using the *Readers' Guide* to find magazine articles and *periodical indexes* to find academic articles. Your library's *online catalog* is a good place to search for books.

Empirical Sources. Facts you generate yourself will be very useful for backing up your claims about your topic. Set up an interview with an expert on your topic, or create a survey that will generate some data. Do some field observations. If you really want to dig up some interesting information, interview an expert who holds an opposing view to your own. This kind of interview will help you understand both sides of the issue much better.

Remember, you are looking for information that is credible and not too biased. It is fine to use sources that make a strong argument for one side or the other, but you need to make sure these sources are backed up with facts, data, and solid sources.

Organizing and Drafting Your Position Paper

The key to organizing a position paper is to remember that you need to tell both sides of the story. As you are drafting your argument, it might help to imagine yourself in a debate with another person (Figure 11.2, page 228). If you were in a public debate, how would you express your best points and win over the audience? Meanwhile, try to anticipate your opponents' best arguments for their position.

The Introduction

Identify your topic and offer some background information to help your readers understand what you are writing about. State your purpose clearly by telling readers that you are going to explain both sides of the issue and then demonstrate why yours is stronger. You might offer your main point (thesis) here in the introduction, or you can save it for the conclusion, especially if you think readers might resist your argument. Look for a good grabber to catch readers' attention at the beginning of your introduction.

FIGURE 11.2 Imagining a Debate with Your Opponents

When drafting a position paper or argument essay, sometimes it helps to imagine yourself debating an opponent. How would you win over the audience? What might your opponent say, and how would you counter?

Summary and Limitations of Your Opponents' Position

Here is the tough part. Try to explain your opponents' side of the issue in a straightforward way. You do not need to argue for their side, but you should explain their side in a way that your readers would consider fair and reasonable. Where possible, use quotes from your opponents' arguments to explain their side of the issue. Paraphrasing or summarizing their argument is fine too, as long as you do it fairly.

As straightforwardly as possible, explain the limitations of your opponents' position. What exactly are they missing? What have they neglected to consider? What are they ignoring in their argument? Again, you want to highlight these limitations as objectively as possible. This is not the place to be sarcastic or dismissive. You want to fairly point out the weaknesses in your opponents' argument.

Your Understanding of the Issue

Then it's your turn. Explain your side of the argument by taking your readers through the two to five points of contention, showing them why your side of the argument is stronger. Here is where you need to use your sources to back up your argument. You need to use good reasoning, examples, facts, and data to show readers why your opinion is more credible.

Reasons Why Your Understanding Is Stronger

Before moving to your conclusion, you might spend a little time comparing and contrasting your opponents' views with your own. Briefly, go head to head with your opponents, showing readers why your view is stronger. At this point, it is all right to concede some points to your opponents. Your goal is to show readers that your view is stronger *on balance.* In other words, both sides probably have their strengths and weaknesses. You want to show that your side has more strengths and fewer weaknesses than your opponents' side.

Conclusion

Bring your argument to a close by stating or restating your thesis and looking to the future. Here is where you want to drive your main point (thesis) home by telling your readers exactly what you believe. Then show how your position leads to a better future than your opponents' position. Overall, your conclusion should be brief (a paragraph in most position papers).

The diagram on page 222 shows two possible patterns for organizing your position paper, but as you draft, you may come up with another pattern that fits your topic better. The key is to present both sides of the issue as fairly as possible.

Choosing an Appropriate Style

The style of your position paper will help you distinguish your side from your opponents' side. Even though your goal is to be *factually* fair to your opponents, there is nothing wrong with using style to make your side sound more appealing and exciting.

Use Plain Style to Describe Your Opponents' Position

You should not be sarcastic or dismissive of your opponents' side of the argument. Instead, describe the other side's argument as plainly as possible. In Chapter 16, "Choosing a Style," you will find helpful strategies for writing plainly, like putting the subjects of your sentences up front and using active verbs. You will also find techniques for writing better paragraphs that use clear topic sentences. If you use these plain style techniques to describe your opponents' side of the argument, it will sound like you are fairly and objectively summarizing their views.

Use Similes, Metaphors, and Analogies When Describing Your Position

When you are describing your side of the argument, you want to present your case as visually as possible. Similes, metaphors, and analogies are a great way to help your readers visualize your argument.

A simile compares something unfamiliar to something familiar:

Simile (X Is Like Y)

A college campus in which students carry guns would be like a tense Old West frontier town.

Sharing music is like lending a good book to a friend, not pirating a ship on the high seas.

Metaphor (X Is Y)

If a shooting incident did occur, the classroom would turn into a deadly crossfire zone, with armed students and police firing away at anyone with a gun in his or her hand. No one would be able to tell the difference between the original shooter and students with their weapons drawn.

The purpose of the music industry's lawsuits is to throw a few unfortunate college students to the lions. That way, they can hold up a few bloody carcasses to scare the rest of us.

Analogy (X Is to Y Like A Is to B)

For some people, a gun has the same comforting effect as a safety blanket to a baby. Neither a gun nor a blanket will protect you from those imaginary monsters, but both can give you a make-believe feeling of security.

The music industry's lawsuits are like your old Aunt Martha defending her tin of chocolate chip cookies at the church potluck. The industry offers a plate of delicious songs, but only the "right people" are allowed to enjoy them. College students aren't the right people because we don't have enough money.

Try some of these "persuasive style" techniques to enhance the power of your argument. Similes, metaphors, and analogies will make your writing more visual and colorful, and they will also help you come up with new ways to think and talk about your topic. You can learn more about persuasive style in Chapter 16, "Choosing a Style."

Use Top-Down Paragraphs

Your argument needs to sound confident, and your readers should be able to find your major points easily. So, in your paragraphs, put each major point in the first or second sentence. Don't put your major points in the middle of your paragraphs or at the end because your readers won't find them easily. A top-down style will make you sound more confident, because you are stating your major claims and then proving them.

Define Unfamiliar Terms

Your readers may or may not be familiar with the topic of your argument. So if you use any specialized or technical terms, you should provide quick parenthetical or sentence definitions to explain them.

Sentence Definition

A conceal-carry permit is the legal authorization that allows private citizens to carry a handgun or other weapon on their person or in a secure place nearby.

Peer-to-peer file sharing involves using a network of computers to store and share files without charge.

Parenthetical Definitions

Colleges have traditionally invoked an "opt-out" statute, a law that allows the ban of weapons where posted, to keep concealed handguns off their campuses.

Music sharing should become illegal when a person *burns* the songs (i.e., puts them on a CD) and sells them to someone else.

Designing Your Position Paper

More and more, you will find that your professors appreciate the addition of helpful visuals and the use of good page design. If your work looks professional, they will likely have a more favorable impression of it.

Use Descriptive Headings. Each of the major sections in your position paper should start with a clear heading that identifies what the section is about. For example, you could use headings like these:

The Case for Allowing Concealed Guns on Campus

The Limitations of Allowing Guns on Campus

Why Concealed Guns on Campus Are Dangerous

Conclusion: Why the Risks of Concealed Weapons Aren't Worth It

You might use bold type to help your headings stand out, and you might use a larger font size where appropriate. Make sure your headings are formatted consistently.

Add Photographs and Illustrations. If you are writing about a local issue or an issue with a local angle, you might grab a digital camera and take a few pictures to use in your paper. The Internet might also be a good place to download a few pictures and illustrations to add a visual element to your text.

In your document, make sure you label your visuals with a number and title, and include a caption to explain them. If you download a photograph or other illustration from the Internet, you will need to cite your source in the caption and in your bibliography. If you want to put your position paper on the Internet, you will need to ask permission from the owners of the photograph to use it on your Web site.

Include Helpful Graphs, Diagrams, and Charts. Position papers often discuss trends in our society, so you might look for ways to use graphs that illustrate those trends. If you collected data or found data on the Internet, you might create a graph or chart to present that data visually. Or, if you found a helpful graph on the Internet, you could use it in your own document, as long as you cite it properly. Graphs and charts should have a title, and you should use figure numbers in your written text to refer readers to the visual (e.g., "In Figure 2, the graph shows . . .").

Design the Page to Make It More Readable and Attractive. Let's be honest. A double-spaced, 1-inch margin essay just looks boring. Your professors might appreciate your efforts to design a document that is more readable and more attractive (Figure 11.3, page 232). A header or footer would be nice. Maybe you could use two columns instead of one. Your headings could be bolder and more colorful. Of course, if your professor asks for something specific like "Your essay must use 12-point Times, be double-spaced, and use 1-inch margins," then you will need to format it that way. But if there are no guidelines, you might ask whether designing the document is acceptable.

Number the Pages. Page numbers might seem like a simple thing, but they are helpful when discussing a position paper with other students or with your professor. Your word processor can add them automatically to the top or bottom of each page.

Campus Violence

In 1999, the American College Health Association (ACHA) Executive Committee adopted a position statement for the Association that addresses acts of violence, bias, and other violations of human rights that have been occurring all too often within or adjacent to college communities:

> The American College Health Association is deeply saddened by the many acts of violence, hate crimes and loss of life over this past year. We, the members of the Association, believe that for a campus community to be truly healthy, it must be guided by the values of multicultural inclusion, respect, and equality. Intolerance has no place at an institution of higher learning. The Association supports all individuals regardless of sexual orientation, race, national origin, age, religion, or disability. We encourage all campus health professionals to be actively engaged in the struggle to end oppression, to prevent bias-related violence in our campus communities, and to take action to eradicate injustice. (ACHA, 1999)

Since this timely position statement was developed, acts of violence have continued to force U.S. colleges and universities to address the dangerous and alarming violent events that send shockwaves throughout many campuses and compromise students' and employees' health and safety. Campus shootings, murder-suicides, homicides, hate crimes based on gender, race, ethnicity, or sexual orientation, suicides, assaults, hazing, and arson require us to conduct fresh analyses and create new paradigms for preventing and decreasing all campus violence.

This paper will adopt the World Health Organization definition of violence as:

> The intentional use of physical force or power, threatened or actual, against oneself, another person, or against a group or community, that either results in or has a high likelihood of resulting

in injury, death, psychological harm, maldevelopment or deprivation. (Krug, Dahlberg, Mercy, Zwi, & Lozano, p. 4)

ACHA's *Healthy Campus 2010* establishes national health objectives and serves as a basis for developing plans to create college health programs and improve student health (ACHA, 2002). Healthy Campus identifies Injury and Violence Prevention as a key leading health indicator. The goal is to "reduce disabilities, injuries and deaths due to injury and violence" (p. 51). Specifically, ACHA seeks to reduce homicides, physical assaults, intimate partner violence, emotional abuse, sexual abuse, rape and attempted rape, physical fighting, and weapon carrying. In addition, a goal is to increase the annual rate of reporting of rape and attempted rape to the police and via surveys.

The purpose of this ACHA White Paper is to confront this serious college health issue through analyzing campus violence patterns, types of violence, methodological problems with collecting campus crime data, underlying issues related to campus violence, and promising practices to prevent and address campus violence.

Scope of the Problem

There are approximately 16 million students enrolled in 4,200 colleges and universities (U.S. Department of Education, 2002). The Violence Against Women Act (1994) mandated the study of campus victimization. The National Crime Victimization Survey (NCVS) gathers data on crimes reported to the police from a nationally representative sample of U.S. households. Beginning in 1995, the Bureau of Justice Statistics added new items to the survey regarding student victims of crime.

According to the Violent Victimization of College Students report (Baum & Klaus, 2005), between 1995 and 2002, college students ages 18-24 were victims of approximately 479,000 crimes annually: rape/sexual assault, robbery, aggravated assault, and simple assault. Overall, the violent crime rate declined 54%. These data include both part-time and full-time students attending private or public

---

10 / ACHA Campus Violence White Paper

Campus Sexual Assault Victims' Bill of Rights (1992). This law requires that all colleges and universities, both public and private, that participate in federal student aid programs afford sexual assault survivors certain basic rights. The accuser and accused must have the same opportunity to have others present at judicial hearings. Both parties shall be informed of the outcome of any disciplinary proceeding. Survivors shall be informed of their options to notify law enforcement. Survivors shall be notified of counseling services and of options for changing academic and living situations.

Campus Sex Crimes Prevention Act (2000). This act provides for the collection and disclosure of information about convicted, registered sex offenders either enrolled in or employed at institutions of higher education.

University duty to warn

Courts have held that policy and federal law permit notification of family or others (usually by the dean of students) but do not create a duty to notify (Jain v. State of Iowa, 2000). The Family Educational Rights and Privacy Act (FERPA) permits notification as a health or safety issue. Psychologists and psychiatrists have a duty to warn if specific threats are made against specific people by their clients. Privacy obligations of administrators may provide greater flexibility than confidentiality obligations of professional counseling or medical staff. Courts have ruled that colleges have a duty to provide "reasonable supervision of students" and "take reasonable steps to protect students" (Jain v. State of Iowa).

Recommendations

These recommendations are based on the ACHA 2003 Annual Meeting Legal Symposium on High-Risk Students, an invited address by Nancy Tribbensee (2003) (see also Lake & Tribbensee, 2002).

- Make necessary a consultative approach across departments and administrative lines to manage high-risk student behavior.

- Educate faculty and graduate assistants, staff, and other students about the importance of early referral for distressed students.

- Address environmental issues such as drugs and alcohol.

- Develop an early warning system, such as a Student Assistance Coordinating Committee,

---

where troubled students are discussed and prevention plans are developed.

The following recommendations are taken from Epstein (2002):

- Legal council should undertake a legal review of the campus violence prevention plan.

- Institute a policy to identify types of prohibited speech as disruptive to the educational environment.

- Establish a campus ban on firearms.

- Expand campus mental health services.

- Encourage students/staff to report verbal and written threats, weapons, and bizarre behaviors.

- Have protocols in place for conveying information regarding dangerous situations and threats.

Epstein (2002) recommends development of a protocol that addresses bystander reports for each college or university campus. While recognizing conflicting issues of unjust accusations vs. not reporting potential risks that become actual hazards, the policy should ensure due process, confidentiality of the bystander whenever possible, rights of the suspected student, and constitutional validity of the policy itself. College administration must be aware of the risks associated with bystander disclosure and protect that person's rights and safety.

It is extremely important to have protocols in place for conveying information regarding dangerous situations and threats and search and seizure, as well as checking the reliability of third-party tips. A strong emphasis must be placed on increasing staff and student awareness of policies and procedures so that untrained personnel minimize risk. With regard to concerns for violation of privacy issues, Epstein (2002) suggested that one way to involve students is to ask incoming students to sign a release that will allow administrators to take action if their behavior warrants concern and becomes erratic.

Resources: Innovative Programs and Suggested Readings

Promising and innovative sexual violence prevention programs have been developed that are intended for college males only, females only, mixed-gendered audiences, athletes, fraternity members, and

---

FIGURE 11.3
Designing a Position Paper

Your position paper doesn't need to look boring and hard to read. The designers of this paper on campus violence use headings, bullets, indentation, and columns to make the text more accessible.

Revising and Editing Your Position Paper

As you draft your position paper, your ideas will evolve. Some shift in your opinion is natural because writing about something gives you the opportunity to think about it in greater depth and consider other viewpoints. Drafting your argument will also force you to back up your claims, which may cause you to rethink your position a little.

Now that you are finished drafting, you need to spend time revising and "re-visioning" your argument to make sure the whole paper holds together. In other words, you don't want to argue one thing at the beginning of the position paper and then argue something a little different at the end. The whole argument needs to work together to prove your main point or thesis.

Remove Any Digressions. When arguing, you might find yourself temporarily drifting off topic. These moments are called *digressions*, and you should remove them from the final version of your paper. Check each paragraph to make sure you are discussing your topic and not going off in a direction that expands or sidetracks your argument.

Back-Check the Evidence for Your Claims. Make sure your claims are backed up with solid support. If you make a claim about your position or your opponents' position, that statement should be followed up with facts, data, examples, reasoning, or quotations. Short paragraphs are usually a signal that you are not backing up your claims, because such paragraphs typically include only a claim with minimal support.

Improve the Flow of Your Sentences. Try reading your draft out loud to yourself or someone else. Mark any places where you stumble or hear something that doesn't sound right. Then use the "plain style" methods discussed in Chapter 16, "Choosing a Style," to make your sentences flow better.

Make Your Writing More Visual. Look for places where you can use more detail and color to bring your writing to life. Describe things and people. Look for places where you can use similes and metaphors to add a visual component to your writing.

Ask a friend or roommate to read through your position paper to highlight places where you could revise. Also, your university may have a Writing Lab where you can get help with locating places in your essay that need revision.

Revising and editing are critical to developing solid position papers and argument essays because your readers (i.e., your professors or supervisors) place a high value on clear, thoughtful writing. If they sense that you did not revise and edit your work, they will rate your work lower.

The Rebuttal

A rebuttal counters or refutes an argument. Rebuttals often appear as letters to the editor. They are also used in the workplace to argue against potentially damaging reviews, evaluations, position papers, and reports. Knowing how to write a rebuttal is an important part of defending your beliefs, projects, and research.

The main difference between a rebuttal and a position paper is that a rebuttal responds directly to the points made in the original argument. After responding to your opponent's argument point by point, you then offer a better counterargument. Here are some strategies for writing a successful rebuttal:

Review your opponent's argument briefly. Objectively summarize the original argument's main point and its major claims.

Challenge any hidden assumptions behind your opponent's claims. Look for unstated assumptions in each major claim of your opponent's argument. These are weak points that you can challenge.

Challenge the facts. If the author cites any facts, locate the original source to see if any data or details are outdated, inaccurate, exaggerated, or taken out of context. If the author has no supporting facts, then you can point that out in your rebuttal.

Challenge the authority of the sources. If possible, question whether the author's sources are truly authoritative on the issue. Unless a source is rock solid, you can question the reliability of the information taken from it.

Examine whether emotion is overcoming reason or evidence. If the author is allowing his or her feelings to fuel the argument, you can suggest that these emotions are clouding his or her judgment on the issue.

Look for logical fallacies. Logical fallacies are forms of weak reasoning that you can use to challenge your opponents' ideas. You can learn more about logical fallacies in Chapter 22, "Using Argumentative Strategies."

Offer a solid counterargument. Offer a different understanding of the issue supported by authoritative research.

WRITE **your own rebuttal.** Find a position paper in a newspaper or on a Web site that you disagree with. Write a two-page rebuttal in which you refute the original argument and offer a counterargument. Your goal is to win readers over to your side.

Letter to the Editor on Climate Story

Russ Walker and David Roberts

Politico did a disservice to its readers in publishing the Nov. 25 story, "Scientists urge caution on global warming." It reports that "climate change skeptics"—the too-charitable name given those who deny the existence of climate change in the face of overwhelming evidence and the testimony of every reputable scientific organization—are watching "a growing accumulation of global cooling science and other findings that could signal that the science behind global warming may still be too shaky to warrant cap-and-trade legislation."

> Opponent's position is reviewed.

While reasonable people may debate the value of cap-and-trade legislation, and it is certainly worth reporting on how its congressional opponents are strategizing to block it, it is simply false to point to a "growing accumulation" of evidence rendering basic climate science "shaky." There is no such accumulation; there is no such science. If there were, perhaps the author would have cited some of it—it is telling that she did not.

Instead, she relies on the work of Joseph D'Aleo, a meteorologist (meteorology is the study of weather, not climate). D'Aleo's lack of qualifications in climate science would be less relevant if he had published his work on "global cooling" in peer-reviewed scientific journals. Instead, it appears in the *Farmers' Almanac*.

> Challenges authority of sources.

Incidentally, D'Aleo's professional association, the American Meteorological Association, is one of dozens of leading national and international scientific groups to endorse the broad consensus on anthropogenic climate change. For some reason, the author did not reference or quote a single one of the hundreds if not thousands of scientists who might have vouchsafed that consensus (inexplicably, the one countervailing quote is given to Al Gore's spokeswoman). If she had spoken with mainstream climate scientists, she would have discovered that they are not "urging caution" on global warming—they are running around, to paraphrase ex-CIA chief George Tenet, with their hair on fire, increasingly radicalized by the ignorance and delay of the world's governments in the face of the crisis.

> Points out that the original article missed key sources of information.

Also glossed over is the fact that the organizations backing D'Aleo's work—National Consumer Coalition, Americans for Tax Reform, the National Center for Policy Analysis and Citizens for a Sound Economy—are (for better or worse) conservative interest groups, not science

continued

organizations. Similarly, the "Global Warming Petition Project" the author cites is one of the oldest, most discredited hoaxes in the "skeptic" handbook. It first emerged in 1998, when it was promptly disavowed and disowned by the Academy of Sciences. The petition is deceptive: Only a handful of signatories come from relevant scientific disciplines, it is open to signature by anyone willing to fill out an online form and there is no clear way to document the scientific credentials of those who have signed. (One clever blogger signed up his dog.) The petition is rereleased every few years and debunked all over again, inevitably after snookering a few journalists.

Meanwhile, respected and nonpolitical scientific bodies are firmly united when it comes to climate change—humanity's reliance on carbon-based fuels is pumping dangerous amounts of CO_2 into the atmosphere, leading to a steady rise in average global temperature and attendant ill effects including droughts, the spread of infectious diseases, and sea level rise. This basic consensus is as well-established in mainstream science as any finding in biology or chemistry, endorsed with a greater than 90 percent degree of confidence by the reports of the Intergovernmental Panel on Climate Change.

> Offers a counter-argument.

Journalists working on climate issues will recognize the bogus evidence and outlier scientists featured in *Politico*'s piece; they are regularly highlighted by the office of Sen. James Inhofe. Though Inhofe's long campaign of disinformation on climate science is eagerly consumed and propagated by political allies dead set on opposing any government action on global warming, mainstream science and climate journalists have long since learned to disregard it. There's a reason Inhofe's campaign is waged via press conferences and online petitions rather than peer-reviewed science.

> Here is the main point with an ending that snaps.

Climate change is an incredibly complex topic; the policy prescriptions for addressing it are wide open for debate; the maneuverings of various industries and interest groups are well worth documenting. But the basic science is quite clear, and *Politico* should take the subject seriously enough not to equate the views of a small group of ideological deniers with a consensus reached over decades of intense data collection, study, and peer review.

Here are some quick steps for writing a position paper.

IDENTIFY a Debatable Topic

A debatable topic has at least two sides. Choose the side that you agree with. Then narrow your topic to something suitable for a position paper. Think about what is new or has changed about your topic recently.

IDENTIFY the Points Separating Your Views from Opponents' Views

Using brainstorming or another prewriting tool, put down everything you know about your topic. Then write down everything your opponents believe about this issue. When you are finished, put stars or checkmarks next to the issues on which you and your opponents disagree.

RESEARCH Both Sides of the Topic

Collect materials that support both sides of the issue, because you want to discover your opponents' best reasons for supporting their side. You can authoritatively counter their position as you support your own.

ORGANIZE Your Materials and Draft Your Argument

Position papers are organized to explain both sides of the issue. Be sure you give fair and adequate space to explaining as well as refuting your opponents' argument.

CHOOSE Your Style

When explaining your opponents' position, use a "plain style" with simple sentences and paragraphs. When you explain your own position, add energy to your argument by using similes, metaphors, and analogies.

DESIGN the Document

Position papers tend to be rather plain in design. However, you might look for opportunities to add visuals to support your argument. Consider using columns, headings, and other elements to make the document more attractive.

REVISE and Edit

As you draft your argument, your position may evolve. Give yourself time to modify your argument and refine your points. Proofreading is critical because readers will see errors as evidence that your argument has not been fully thought through.

In Defense of Torture

SAM HARRIS

This position paper, written by Sam Harris, who is best known for his book The End of Faith, *makes an argument that "torture may be an ethical necessity." Harris uses a combination of emotional and logical appeals to persuade his readers. Notice how he concedes points to his opponents in strategic ways, which allows him to bring forward his own arguments for torture.*

Imagine that a known terrorist has planted a bomb in the heart of a nearby city. He now sits in your custody. Rather than conceal his guilt, he gloats about the forthcoming explosion and the magnitude of human suffering it will cause. Given this state of affairs—in particular, given that there is still time to prevent an imminent atrocity—it seems that subjecting this unpleasant fellow to torture may be justifiable. For those who make it their business to debate the ethics of torture this is known as the "ticking-bomb" case.

While the most realistic version of the ticking bomb case may not persuade everyone that torture is ethically acceptable, adding further embellishments seems to awaken the Grand Inquisitor in most of us. If a conventional explosion doesn't move you, consider a nuclear bomb hidden in midtown Manhattan. If bombs seem too impersonal an evil, picture your seven-year-old daughter being slowly asphyxiated in a warehouse just five minutes away, while the man in your custody holds the keys to her release. If your daughter won't tip the scales, then add the daughters of every couple for a thousand miles—millions of little girls have, by some perverse negligence on the part of our government, come under the control of an evil genius who now sits before you in shackles. Clearly, the consequences of one person's uncooperativeness can be made so grave, and his malevolence and culpability so trans-

parent, as to stir even a self-hating moral relativist from his dogmatic slumbers.

I am one of the few people I know of who has argued in print that torture may be an ethical necessity in our war on terror. In the aftermath of Abu Ghraib, this is not a comfortable position to have publicly adopted. There is no question that Abu Ghraib was a travesty, and there is no question that it has done our country lasting harm. Indeed, the Abu Ghraib scandal may be one of the costliest foreign policy blunders to occur in the last century, given the degree to which it simultaneously inflamed the Muslim world and eroded the sympathies of our democratic allies. While we hold the moral high ground in our war on terror, we appear to hold it less and less. Our casual abuse of ordinary prisoners is largely responsible for this. Documented abuses at Abu Ghraib, Guantanamo Bay, and elsewhere have now inspired legislation prohibiting "cruel, inhuman or degrading" treatment of military prisoners. And yet, these developments do not shed much light on the ethics of torturing people like Osama bin Laden when we get them in custody.

I will now present an argument for the use of torture in rare circumstances. While many people have objected, on emotional grounds, to my defense of torture, no one has pointed out a flaw in my argument. I hope my case for torture is wrong, as I would be much happier standing side by side with all the good people who oppose torture categorically. I invite any reader who discovers a problem with my argument to point it out to me in the comment section of this blog. I would be sincerely grateful to have my mind changed on this subject.

Most readers will undoubtedly feel at this 5 point that torture is evil and that we are wise not to practice it. Even if we can't quite muster a retort to the ticking bomb case, most of us take refuge in the fact that the paradigmatic case will almost never arise. It seems, however, that this position is impossible to square with our willingness to wage modern war in the first place.

In modern warfare, "collateral damage"—the maiming and killing of innocent noncombatants—is unavoidable. And it will remain unavoidable for the foreseeable future. Collateral damage would be a problem even if our bombs were far "smarter" than they are now. It would also be a problem even if we resolved to fight only defensive wars. There is no escaping the fact that whenever we drop bombs, we drop them with the knowledge that some number of children will be blinded, disemboweled, paralyzed, orphaned, and killed by them.

The only way to rule out collateral damage would be to refuse to fight wars under any circumstances. As a foreign policy, this would leave us with something like the absolute pacifism of Gandhi. While pacifism in this form can constitute a direct confrontation with injustice (and requires considerable bravery), it is only applicable to a limited range of human conflicts. Where it is not applicable, it seems flagrantly immoral. We would do well to reflect on Gandhi's remedy for the Holocaust: he believed that the Jews should have committed mass suicide, because this "would have aroused the world and the people of Germany to Hitler's violence." We might wonder what a world full of pacifists would have done once it had grown "aroused"—commit suicide as well? There seems no question that if all the good people in the world adopted Gandhi's ethics, the thugs would inherit the earth.

So we can now ask, if we are willing to act in a way that guarantees the misery and death of some considerable number of innocent children, why spare the rod with known terrorists? I find it genuinely bizarre that while the torture of Osama bin Laden himself could be expected to provoke convulsions of conscience among our leaders, the perfectly foreseeable (and therefore accepted) slaughter of children does not. What is the difference between pursuing a course of action where we run the risk of inadvertently subjecting some innocent men to torture, and pursuing one in which we will inadvertently kill far greater numbers of innocent men, women, and children? Rather, it seems obvious that the misapplication of torture should be far *less* troubling to us than collateral damage: there are, after all, no *infants* interned at Guantanamo Bay. Torture need not even impose a significant risk of death or permanent injury on its victims; while the collaterally damaged are, almost by definition, crippled or killed. The ethical divide that seems to be opening up here suggests that those who are willing to drop bombs might want to abduct the nearest and dearest of suspected terrorists—their wives, mothers, and daughters—and torture *them* as well, assuming anything profitable to our side might come of it. Admittedly, this would be a ghastly result to have reached by logical argument, and we will want to find some way of escaping it. But there seems no question that accidentally torturing an innocent man is better than accidentally blowing him and his children to bits.

In this context, we should note that many variables influence our feelings about an act of physical violence. The philosopher Jonathan Glover points out that "in modern war, what is most shocking is a poor guide to what is most harmful." To learn that one's grandfather flew a bombing mission over Dresden in the Second World War is one thing; to hear that he killed five little girls and their mother with a shovel is another. We can be sure that he would have killed many more women and girls by dropping bombs from pristine heights, and they are likely to have died equally horrible deaths, but his culpability would not appear the same. There is much to be said about the disparity here, but the relevance to the ethics of torture should be obvious. If you think that the equivalence between torture and collateral damage does not hold, because torture is up close and personal while stray bombs aren't, you stand convicted of a failure of imagination on at least two counts: first, a moment's reflection on the horrors that must have been visited upon innocent Afghanis and Iraqis by our bombs will reveal that they are on par with those of any dungeon. If our intuition about the wrongness of torture is born of an aversion to how people generally behave while being tortured, we should note that this particular infelicity could be circumvented pharmacologically, because paralytic drugs make it unnecessary for screaming ever to be heard or writhing seen. We could easily devise methods of torture that would render a torturer as blind to the plight of his victims as a bomber pilot is at thirty thousand feet. Consequently, our natural aversion to the sights and sounds of the dungeon provide no foothold for those who would argue against the use of torture.

To demonstrate just how abstract the [10] torments of the tortured can be made to seem, we need only imagine an ideal "torture pill"—a drug that would deliver both the instruments of torture and the instrument of their concealment. The action of the pill would be to produce transitory paralysis and transitory misery of a kind that no human being would willingly submit to a second time. Imagine how we torturers would feel if, after giving this pill to captive terrorists, each lay down for what appeared to be an hour's nap only to arise and immediately confess everything he knows about the workings of his organization. Might we not be tempted to call it a "truth pill" in the end? No, there is no ethical difference to be found in how the suffering of the tortured or the collaterally damaged appears.

Opponents of torture will be quick to argue that confessions elicited by torture are notoriously unreliable. Given the foregoing, however, this objection seems to lack its usual force. Make these confessions as unreliable as you like—the chance that our interests will be advanced in any instance of torture need only equal the chance of such occasioned by the dropping of a single bomb. What was the chance that the dropping of bomb number 117 on Kandahar would effect the demise of Al Qaeda? It had to be pretty slim. Enter Khalid Sheikh Mohammed: our most valuable capture in our war on terror. Here is a character who actually seems to have stepped out of a philosopher's thought experiment. U.S. officials now believe that his was the hand that decapitated the *Wall Street Journal* reporter Daniel Pearl. Whether or not this is true, his membership in Al Qaeda more or less rules out his "innocence" in any important sense, and his rank in the organization suggests that his knowledge of planned atrocities must be extensive. The bomb has been ticking ever since September 11th, 2001. Given the damage we were willing to cause to the bodies and minds of innocent children in Afghanistan and Iraq, our disavowal of torture in the case of Khalid Sheikh Mohammed seems perverse. If there is even one chance in a million that he will tell us something under torture that will lead to the further dismantling of Al Qaeda, it seems that we should use every means at our disposal to get him talking. (In fact, the *New York Times* has reported that Khalid Sheikh Mohammed was tortured in a procedure known as "water-boarding," despite our official disavowal of this practice.)

Which way should the balance swing? Assuming that we want to maintain a coherent ethical position on these matters, this appears to be a circumstance of forced choice: if we are willing to drop bombs, or even risk that rifle rounds might go astray, we should be willing to torture a certain class of criminal suspects and military prisoners; if we are unwilling to torture, we should be unwilling to wage modern war.

In Defense of Torture

1. Harris uses several hypothetical situations to argue that torture may be needed in some special cases. What are these hypothetical situations, and do you find them persuasive in convincing you to accept torture as an option?

2. Find two places where Harris concedes a point to his opponents about torture. How does he make a concession without undermining his own argument? Do these concessions make his argument stronger or weaker?

3. Harris's final sentence says, "if we are unwilling to torture, we should be unwilling to wage modern war." He comes to this conclusion by comparing the deaths of innocent people (i.e., collateral damage) with the treatment of terrorists. Do you find his comparison between innocent people and terrorists effective or not?

Writing

1. This position paper was published in 2005. Now we know much more about the Bush administration's use of torture before and during the Iraq war. Write a briefing in which you objectively describe how torture was used during the Iraq war.

2. Write a rebuttal to Harris's argument. Where are the weak points in his argument? Can you see any ways to use his own arguments against him? What does he seem to be missing and what kinds of questionable claims does he make?

Friends with Benefits: Do *Facebook* Friends Provide the Same Support as Those in Real Life?

KATE DAILEY

Social networking sites like Facebook *and* MySpace *have challenged our ideas about what it means to be a "friend." Today, people can keep in touch with others who might otherwise have faded into the past. Also, we can be "friends" with people we barely know who share common interests or backgrounds. In this position paper, pay attention to how Dailey builds her argument and notice where she summarizes the other side of the debate.*

I have a friend named Sue. Actually, "Sue" isn't her real name, and she isn't really a friend: she's something akin to a lost sorority sister— we went to the same college, participated in the same activities and had a lot of mutual respect and admiration for one another. But since graduation, we've fallen out of touch, and the only way I know about Sue, her life and her family is through her *Facebook* updates. That's why I felt almost like a voyeur when Sue announced, via *Facebook*, the death of her young son. I was surprised she had chosen to share something so personal online— and then ashamed, because since when did I become the arbiter of what's appropriate for that kind of grief?

The more I thought about it, the more I realized *Facebook* might be the perfect venue for tragic news: it's the fastest way to disseminate important information to the group without having to deal with painful phone calls; it allowed well-meaning friends and acquaintances to instantly pass on condolences, which the family could read at their leisure, and it eliminated the possibility that were I to run into Sue in the supermarket, I'd ask unknowingly about her son and force her to replay the story over again.

Numerous studies have shown that a strong network of friends can be crucial to getting through a crisis, and can help you be healthier in general. But could virtual friends, like the group of online buddies that reached out to Sue, be just as helpful as the flesh-and-blood versions? In other words, do *Facebook* friends—and the support we get from them— count? These questions are all the more intriguing as the number of online social-network users increases. *Facebook* attracted 67.5 million visitors in the U.S. in April (according to ComScore Inc.), and the fastest-growing demographic is people over 35. It's clear that connecting to friends, both close and distant, via the computer will become more the norm than novelty.

Researchers have yet to significantly study the social implications of *Facebook*, so what we do know is gleaned from general studies about friendship, and some of the emerging studies about online networking. First, a definition of "friend": In research circles, experts define a friend as a close, equal, voluntary partnership—though Rebecca G. Adams, a professor of sociology at the University of North Carolina, Greensboro, says that in reality, "friendships don't have to be equal or close, and we know from research that friendships aren't as voluntary as they seem," because they're often constricted by education, age and background. Friends on *Facebook* seem to mimic, if not replicate, this trend—there are people online that you are more likely to chat with every day, while others only make an appearance once or twice a year, content to spend the rest of the time residing silently in your friend queue. (Though the *Facebook* friends with whom you have frequent social interaction might not be people you interact with often in "real life.")

In life, having 700 people in your circle of friends could get overwhelming, but that's less of an issue online. "Research suggests that people are only intermittently in touch with many of their online 'friends' but correspond regularly with only a few good friends," says Shelley E. Taylor, professor of psychology at The University of California, Los Angeles. "That said, creating networks to ease the transition to new places can be hugely helpful to people, offsetting loneliness until new friends are made."

In other words, *Facebook* may not replace the full benefits of real friendship, but it definitely beats the alternative. I conducted a very informal poll via my *Facebook* status update, asking if *Facebook* makes us better friends. A high-school pal, with whom I haven't spoken in about 10 years, confessed that since she had her baby, corresponding via *Facebook* has been a lifeline—and even if she wasn't actively commenting, it was nice to know what people were up to. "Any electronic communication where you don't have to be in the same physical space is going to decrease feelings of isolation," says Dr. Adams.

Several people in my online network admit that *Facebook* doesn't make them a better friend, but a better acquaintance, more likely to dash off a quick happy birthday e-mail, or to comment on the photo of a new puppy. But that's not a bad thing. Having a large group of "friends" eager to comment on your daily life could be good for your self-esteem. When you get a new job, a celebratory lunch with your best friends will make you feel good and make for a fantastic memory. But the boost you get from the 15 *Facebook* friends who left encouraging comments can also make you happy.

"The way to think of this is before the Internet, we wouldn't see our acquaintances very often: every once in a while, we might show up at a wedding and suddenly have 100 of our closest friends around," says James Fowler, associate professor of political science at the University of California, San Diego. "With *Facebook*, it's like every day is a wedding." And just like leaving a wedding may leave you feeling energized and inspired by reconnecting to old pals, so can spending time on *Facebook*, says Fowler.

While Fowler's research also shows that bad habits like smoking and weight gain can be contagious among close friends, emotions like happiness and sadness are easily transferable through acquaintances. The good news? "Because happiness spreads more easily then unhappiness, getting positive comments from your *Facebook* friends is more likely to make you happy than sad," he says.

Shy people who may not always be able 10 to engage friends in the real world are finding solace in the structure of *Facebook*. Though people who identify as shy have a smaller circle of *Facebook* friends than those who don't, they are better able to engage with the online friends they do have. "Because people don't have to interact face-to-face, that's why we're seeing them having relationships: they can think more about what they have to say and how they want to say it," says Craig Ross, a graduate student in psychology at the University of Windsor who studies online social networks.

And what of my "friend" "Sue"? Can the support she received from *Facebook* friends upon learning about the death of her son replicate the support that would come from friends stopping by the house? It's impossible to replace the warm feelings—or brain-boosting endorphins—that come from human-on-human contact, and you can't send someone a casserole through *Facebook*. But grieving online can have powerful and productive benefits. Diana Nash, professor of psychology at Marymount Manhattan College, who has studied how college students use *MySpace* to deal with grief, notes that, "One of the primary desires that we all have is for someone to really listen to us in a deep kind of way. They want to be listened to," she says. Her research shows that by sharing their grief on *MySpace*, her subjects felt more listened to and more visible, and doing so helped them heal.

Posting personal experiences, no matter how painful, also allows acquaintances who have lived through similar experiences to reach out, either with information about support groups or just an empathetic ear. "The idea of sharing a commonality helps make it a little more bearable. You're not alone, and there are others going through what you went through," says Nash. "It doesn't take away the pain, but it can lessen the pain and make you feel not so alone."

The majority of times we reach out on *Facebook*, however, it's not about a tragedy, but a smaller problem for which we need advice: good movers in the San Francisco area, a copy of yesterday's newspaper, answers to a question about taxes. This is another place where the large *Facebook* networks come in handy. In real life, people tend to befriend people who think thoughts and live very similar lives to their own, but because on *Facebook* people often "friend" classmates, people met at parties, and friends-of-friends, the networks include individuals who wouldn't make the "real friend" cut. Having that diversity of opinion and experience available online increases the diversity of responses received when posting a question, which allows you to make a better-informed decision.

Still, there are experts who worry that too much time online keeps us from living satisfying lives in the real world. "It's great to have a lot of *Facebook* friends, but how many of those will friends will show when you're really in trouble?" asks Michael J. Bugeja, a professor of communications at Iowa State University of Science and Technology and author of *Interpersonal Divide: The Search for Community in a Technological Age*. He notes the

world of difference between someone typing a frowny emoticon upon hearing that you've been in a car crash and showing up to help you get home. He also says that *Facebook*, with its focus on existing relationships—and its ability to codify and categorize those relationships—in some ways belies the promise of the Internet. "Rather than opening us up to a global community, it is putting us into groups," he says.

That's why *Facebook* works best as an 15 amplification of a "real life" social life, not a replacement—even as time and technology progress and the lines between online interactions and real-world experiences continue to blur.

A CLOSER LOOK AT
Friends with Benefits

1. In this position paper, the definition of the word "friend" seems open for debate. Dailey offers a couple of different definitions of a friend, a traditional definition and a social-networking site definition. How are these two types of friends similar, and how are they different?

2. This position paper talks about how habits can be contagious among friends, like smoking and weight gain. Bailey, however, sees this kind of con-

tagiousness as a good thing because of *Facebook*. Why?

3. A good position paper fairly describes the other side of the debate, usually early in the argument. However, in this position paper, Dailey waits until the end to clearly state her oppositions' argument. What do these people find wrong with calling people on *Facebook* "friends"?

IDEAS FOR
Writing

1. Write a three-page commentary in which you discuss the future of friendships in an electronically networked world. Do you think people will lose touch with each other, because they are mostly interacting through texting, social networking sites, or e-mail? Or do you think electronic networking is actually making relationships stronger? What are some of the benefits of friendships through electronic networking? What are some of the downsides?

2. Find one of your childhood friends on *Facebook, MySpace,* or another social networking site. Write a two-page profile of your friend using only evidence drawn from his or her page. On his or her page, your friend has tried to project a particular image. What is that image? How is that image similar to or different from the person you know or knew personally?

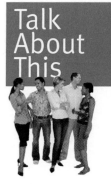
1. With a small group, make a list of some challenging issues facing our society to-day. Pick an issue and explore both sides. What are the two to five major points of contention between the two sides of the issue? What are the strengths of each side? What are the limitations of each side?

2. With your class, list ten effective and ineffective ways to argue. What is the best way to get your point across to someone else? What are your most effective strate-gies? Then list some of the worst ways to argue. What are some of the annoying ways in which other people have tried to persuade you? How did you react to some of these less effective methods?

3. Think about arguments you have had with friends, family members, and other people you care about. With a small group, discuss why these arguments are sometimes more difficult than arguments with people who are not so close to you. Do you have any strategies for arguing effectively with people you care strongly about? Do you avoid these kinds of arguments? If so, why?

1. Look at the opinions section of your local newspaper. Pick one of the issues that is being discussed in the editorials, commentaries, or letters to the editor. On your screen or a piece of paper, list the positions and the kinds of support offered by one of the writers. Then list the points the opponents might make to counter these positions and support their own opinions. In a memo to your professor, explain both sides of the argument as fairly as possible. Then show why you think one side or the other has the stronger argument.

2. Find a position paper or argument essay on the Internet. You might look for these arguments in the online versions of newspapers or magazines. In a two-page memo to your professor, analyze the argument and explain whether you think the author is arguing effectively or not. Did the author fairly represent both sides of the issue? Is the author too biased, or does he or she neglect any strengths of the opponents' position or the limitations of his or her own position?

3. Pick a topic that you feel strongly about. Create a two-column brainstorming list that explores the issues involved with this topic. Then identify the two to five main points of contention that separate you from someone who disagrees with you about this topic. In a one-page memo to your professor, discuss the strengths and limitations of your side of the issue and your opponents'. Explain what kinds of in-formation you would need to collect to support your best arguments and high-light the limitations of your opponents' views.

1. **Write a position paper on a local issue.** Write a five-page position paper in which you explore both sides of a contentious local issue. Pick an issue that affects you directly and try to fairly represent both sides of the issue. Explain your opponents' side of the issue as clearly and fairly as possible. Then point out the limitations of their side. Explain your side of the issue and concede any limitations of your side. Then persuade your readers that your understanding of the issue is stronger and more reasonable than your opponents' understanding.

2. **Create a multimedia presentation.** Illegal downloading of music has been an important issue on college campuses recently. Some students are being sued by the music industry, and they are being forced to pay thousands of dollars in damages and fines. Create a ten-slide presentation in which you state your opinion about downloading music "illegally" off the Internet. Explain your opponents' understanding of the issue. Then explain your side and show why you think your understanding is stronger than your opponents'. Your presentation could be made with *PowerPoint*, *Keynote*, or any other presentation software. Try adding photographs, charts, video, and audio, where appropriate.

3. **Argue that something bad for people is really good for them.** In a five-page position paper, argue that something people traditionally assume is "bad" (e.g., playing video games, being overweight, seeing violence in movies, watching television, cramming for an exam) is actually good. Summarize the conventional assumptions about why something is bad. Then use research to show that it is actually good for people.

12

Proposals

People write proposals to explore problems and offer plans for solving those problems. In your advanced college courses, your professors will ask you to write proposals that explain how to improve your community or that describe research projects you want to do. In the workplace, proposals are used to develop new strategies, take advantage of new opportunities, and pitch new projects and products.

The aim of a proposal is to help readers understand the *causes* and *effects* of a problem and to persuade them that your step-by-step plan offers the best solution for that problem. Your readers will expect your proposal to be clearly written and persuasive. They expect you to try to win them over with strong reasoning, good examples, and appropriate appeals to authority and emotion.

In today's workplace, the proposal is one of the most common genres. Any time someone wants to solve a problem or present new ideas, he or she will be asked to "write the proposal." In college, proposals are growing more popular as a genre, because advanced courses are becoming more team-oriented and project-centered. Your professors will put you into teams and ask you to write proposals that describe the projects you want to pursue. This chapter will show you how to use proposals to invent your ideas and explain them clearly and persuasively to your readers.

Proposals

This diagram shows a basic organization for a proposal, but other arrangements of these sections will work, too. You should alter this organization to fit your topic, angle, purpose, readers, and context.

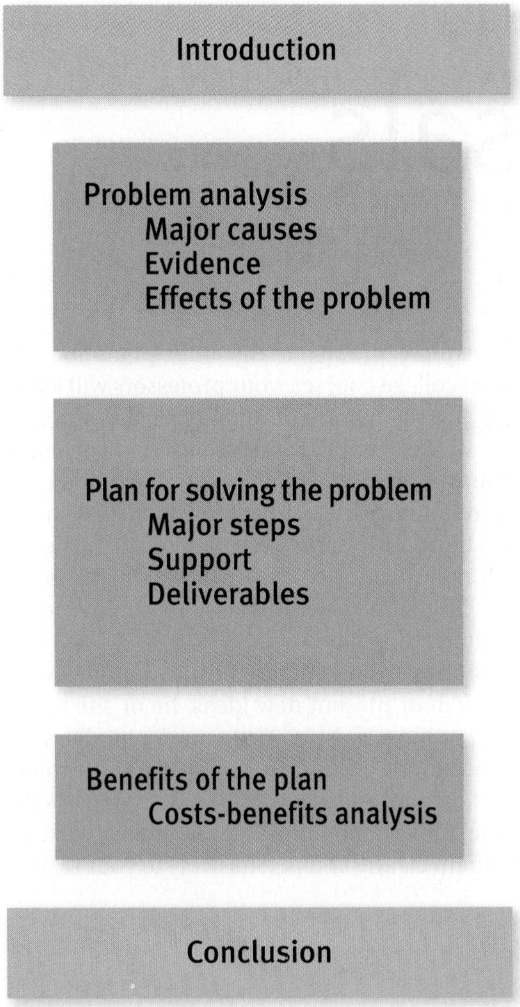

Introduction

Problem analysis
    Major causes
    Evidence
    Effects of the problem

Plan for solving the problem
    Major steps
    Support
    Deliverables

Benefits of the plan
    Costs-benefits analysis

Conclusion

Overview

A proposal is one of the more complicated genres you will be asked to write. Here are a proposal's typical features:

- **An introduction** that defines a problem and stresses its importance.

- **An analysis** of the problem, discussing its causes, and its effects.

- **A detailed plan** that shows step by step how to solve the problem.

- **A costs-benefits analysis** that measures the benefits of the plan against its costs.

- **A conclusion** that looks to the future and stresses the importance of taking action.

Proposals tend to follow an organization like the one shown on page 248, but this pattern can be changed to suit your topic, angle, purpose, readers, and context. For each unique situation, sections can be merged or moved around to address the needs of the specific readers and the situations in which the proposal will be used.

There are several kinds of proposals used in the workplace. A *solicited proposal* is written when someone requests it. For example, a client may use a "Request for Proposals," also called an RFP, to request proposals from companies that can provide a specific service. *Unsolicited proposals* are not requested by the readers. They are often used to pitch new ideas or to sell a company's services.

Proposals are also used "internally" and "externally." *Internal proposals* are written to people within a company or organization. They might pitch a new idea or product to a supervisor or to management. *External proposals* are written to people outside the company or organization.

Another type of proposal is the grant proposal, which researchers and nonprofit organizations use to obtain funding for their projects.

ONE STUDENT GROUP'S WORK
Proposals

This is the executive summary of a proposal written by students at the University of California–Santa Barbara in May 2006. It describes a plan for transforming their campus into a carbon-neutral site. An executive summary, which often accompanies very long reports, is written for the convenience of decision-makers and includes all of the structural features of the full proposal.

Descriptive title tells readers what the proposal is about.

CHANGING THE CAMPUS CLIMATE:
Strategies to Reduce Greenhouse Gas Emissions at The University of California, Santa Barbara

Fahmida Ahmed I Jeff Brown I David Felix I Todd Haurin I Betty Seto

May 2006

A Bren School of Environmental Science and Management Master's Project

Color and images attract readers' attention.

Sponsored by
National Association of Environmental Law Societies

EXECUTIVE SUMMARY

Background & Significance

Anthropogenic climate change is arguably the most significant problem of our generation. Unfortunately, its drivers – greenhouse gas (GHG) emissions from energy use and land use changes – are among the most integral inputs to the current economic system. Furthermore, the range of possible effects of climate change – from rising sea levels to increases in extreme weather events – makes addressing the consequences of climate change especially challenging and important.

Recognizing this, much of the world (and almost all "developed" countries) is starting to act to reduce GHG emissions, with both the Kyoto Protocol coming into force and the European Union (EU) implementing its Emissions Trading Scheme recently. Unfortunately, the United States has no equivalent national GHG emissions reduction regulation. Given this lack of leadership at the federal level, action at the state and local level is all the more important, and a number of initiatives are underway (e.g., Northeastern State's Regional Greenhouse Gas Initiative, U.S. Mayors Climate Protection Agreement) that will help reduce GHG emissions and demonstrate that doing so need not be detrimental to local and state economies.

Indeed, California is already leading the way with a number of policies enacted (e.g., Assembly Bill 1493 (Pavley), Renewable Portfolio Standard) or in the development stages that directly or indirectly address global warming. With the Governor's new executive order (S-3-05) committing California to eighty percent reductions below 1990 levels by 2050, California is likely to continue to be a leader into the future.

Set against this background is the University of California (UC), an institution that educates tomorrow's business, political, and intellectual leaders. As the main higher education institution within California, the UC system is well positioned to play a pivotal role in California's climate strategy. UCSB, with its history of environmental stewardship, can serve as a model to public universities and other UC schools to show that greenhouse gas emissions mitigation is the right thing to do. Furthermore, universities can reap the following benefits from prioritizing the reduction of greenhouse gas emissions:

- Reduce campus energy costs;
- Hedge against future climate regulations and energy price volatility;
- Transform markets for low-cost climate mitigation technologies through their large purchasing power; and,
- Improve the reputation of the University.

Ultimately, UCSB, and the wider UC system, has the responsibility of producing tomorrow's leaders and citizens who will significantly influence California's and the U.S.'s response to global warming. Therefore, commitments to reduce greenhouse gas emissions from campuses are of great importance.

Introduction defines the topic and links it to the larger, global issue.

The problem and its causes are described.

The purpose of the proposal is stated here.

The benefits of implementing the plan are described up front.

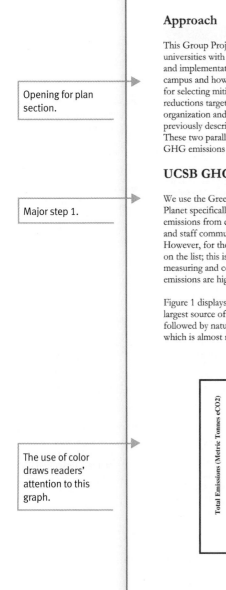

Approach

This Group Project encourages UCSB to be a leader, and to provide lessons learned to other universities with a similar vision. Our efforts can be divided into two inter-related tracks — analysis and implementation. In the analysis phase, we characterize the main sources of GHG emissions on campus and how they are likely to change in the future, identify mitigation strategies, develop criteria for selecting mitigation strategies, and analyze the feasibility of several prominent emissions reductions targets. In the implementation phase, we seek to understand UCSB as a complex organization and to both identify institutional obstacles that constrain the implementation of the previously described mitigation strategies and opportunities to maneuver around the obstacles. These two parallel and complementary tracks are aimed at inducing UCSB to actually reduce its net GHG emissions over time and to receive the associated benefits previously discussed.

UCSB GHG Emissions Inventory

We use the Greenhouse Gas Inventory Calculator (volume 4.0), developed by Clean Air – Cool Planet specifically for universities, to create a GHG inventory for UCSB. The inventory includes emissions from electricity consumption, natural gas consumption, the UCSB fleet, student, faculty and staff commuting, faculty and staff air travel, fugitive emissions of coolants, and solid waste. However, for the purposes of our primary analysis, we only consider the first *three* emissions sources on the list; this is because these are the emissions sources for which the University is committed to measuring and certifying with the California Climate Action Registry (CCAR), and the other emissions are highly uncertain because of poor data quality.

Figure 1 displays UCSB's GHG emissions by source over the past 15 years. Electricity is the single largest source of GHG emission at UCSB, representing roughly two thirds of total emissions, followed by natural gas, representing roughly one third of total emissions, and the campus fleet, which is almost negligible.

Figure 1: UCSB GHG Emissions by Source

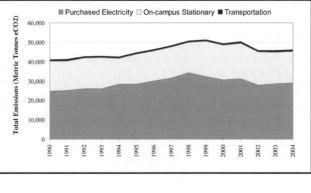

6

Opening for plan section.

Major step 1.

The use of color draws readers' attention to this graph.

In 2004, the most recent year for which we have complete data, total GHG emissions were approximately 46,000 metric tons of carbon dioxide equivalent (MTCO$_2$e). Interestingly, total emissions peak in 1999 and shrink by approximately two percent per year through 2004. This emissions reduction was not caused by a reduction in enrollment or building square footage; rather it was largely due to significant new investments in energy efficiency on campus precipitated by the California energy crisis. This is a promising finding and suggests that UCSB has the potential to reduce its climate footprint without reducing enrollment or campus size.

Emissions Targets Applied to UCSB

Determining an appropriate reduction target for GHG emissions is a critical first step towards long term emissions reductions. We analyze what three separate emissions targets would look like as applied to UCSB through 2020 – the U.S. targets from the first commitment period of the Kyoto Protocol (7% below 1990 levels by 2010), the first two California state targets (2000 levels by 2010, 1990 levels by 2020), and Climate Neutrality (net zero GHG emissions by 2020).

Major step 2.

First, we project UCSB's GHG emissions through 2020 given current emissions levels and assumptions about campus growth. Given historical emissions levels of roughly 2.25 MTCO$_2$e per student and anticipated growth of approximately 300 students per year through 2020, we project total emissions through 2020 (see solid red line in Figure 2). Second, we apply the three potential targets to UCSB in order to understand the scale of emissions reductions that would be required to meet the specific targets (displayed in Figure 2 as the vertical distance between the projected emissions line and any particular target line).

Figure 2: Projected Emissions and Potential Targets

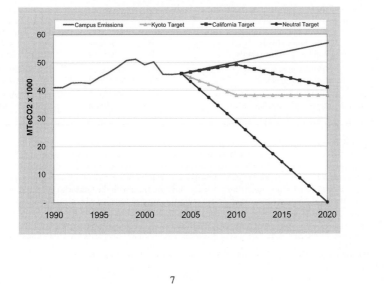

Line graph tells a simple story that readers can understand at a glance.

Major step 3.

Mitigation Strategies

We profile a range of mitigation strategies available to UCSB, including energy efficiency and conservation projects, on campus renewable energy projects, alternative fuel vehicles, and external mitigation options (e.g., carbon offsets, renewable energy credits).[1] For each mitigation mechanism we provide the capital cost, associated savings (e.g., energy), annual GHG reduction potential, net cost per unit of GHG reduced[2], and payback period.

Feasibility Analysis of Meeting Specific Targets

Major step 4.

We identify the specific combination of mitigation mechanisms that would enable UCSB to meet the previously discussed emissions targets. We assume a consistent mechanism choice logic that reflects UCSB priorities – we first select projects with no capital costs that yield savings, then we select projects that yield the highest savings over time (best in terms of $/ MTCO$_2$e), and finally, once all mechanisms with costs below the price of external offsets (an estimated average of $11/MTCO$_2$e) have been exhausted, the University meets all additional emissions reductions through the purchase of carbon offsets (see Figure 3).

Figure 3: Mitigation Mechanism Schedule for CA Targets

Table presents complex data in an accessible way.

Year Stage	Mechanisms	Potential MT/year	Capital Cost	NPV/MT	Annual Saving
ASAP Stage A	**Energy star computer settings**	310	$0	196	$94,000
	Fleet smaller vehicles	33	$0	215	$9,545
	Fleet ethanol	1	$0		$0
2011 Stage B	**HVAC Upgrade – Air Handlers 1**	573	$200,000	245	$112,000
	HVAC Commissioning	340	$120,000	241	$71,159
	HVAC Upgrade – Filters	607	$372,323	196	$184,053
	EE – Fume Hoods	55	$80,000	156	$14,298
	Building baseline awards	14	$15,000	127	$4385
2012 Stage C	**HVAC Upgrade – Fans**	914	$1,574,464	125	$277,048
	Lighting Upgrades	835	$1,797,762	97	$252,919
2013 Stage D	**HVAC Upgrade – Air Handlers 2**	174	$550,000	42	$45,328
	Reduce fleet driving – bikes	1	$2500	11	$27
	Begin purchasing offsets	763	$8,091	-11	$0

Figure 4 illustrates the specific four stage emissions reduction path that UCSB could take to meet the first two California targets – the 2010 and 2020 standards (see dashed line in Figure 4). The solid trend line shows how UCSB can reduce its GHG emissions through time with the implementation of on-campus projects with costs lower than the external offset price; these on campus emissions reduction opportunities keep UCSB on track with the California goals through 2012. After that point, the most inexpensive mitigation mechanisms have been exhausted, and

---

[1] The mitigation mechanisms profiled in this section represent examples of the types of projects UCSB could implement to reduce its emissions, rather than an exhaustive or fully comprehensive survey of the University's mitigation options.

[2] This includes the upfront capital cost and the discounted savings over the lifetime of the project.

purchasing offsets becomes the next cheapest alternative. Therefore, we assume that UCSB purchases external offsets to make up the difference in subsequent years.

Figure 4: Four Stage Emissions Reduction Path

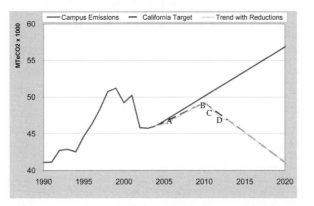

Graphs show trends.

This combination of mechanisms has a net present value (NPV) of $2.6 million, including the cost of offsets through 2020, suggesting that the University could meet the California targets through 2020 according to the previously described emissions path and save a significant amount of money in the process. This emissions trajectory does require some significant capital investments after 2010 (when the emissions target increases in stringency); but, as the cash flow analysis below illustrates, these capital investments are recouped quickly through energy savings (see Figure 5).

Figure 5: Cash Flow for CA Targets

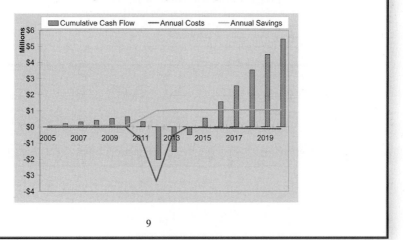

According to our analysis, meeting the California targets not only appears feasible through 2020 despite significant campus growth, it also appears to be justified solely on the economics. We performed similar analyses for two additional targets – the Kyoto Protocol and Climate Neutrality – and observe similar findings. These targets imply more aggressive emissions reductions, both in timing and the absolute level of emissions reductions. In terms of NPV, this turns out to increase the savings associated with the mitigation strategies – because they are implemented earlier, which captures more years of energy savings – and to increase the number of offsets purchased. We find the NPV of the savings to be $5.8 million for the Kyoto targets and $4.3 million for Climate Neutrality. Finally, as a sensitivity analysis, we perform the same calculations using an offset price of $30/MTCO$_2$e, which is similar to the current price of carbon in the EU market; we find a NPV of savings equaling $4.3 million, $2.1 million, and -$0.2 million for the Kyoto, California, and Climate Neutrality targets, respectively.

Implementation

Given the previous analysis, it would seem that UCSB should already be implementing GHG mitigation strategies. To some extent it is – through the energy efficiency projects implemented by the Facilities Management team, the efforts to green UCSB buildings by a virtual Office of Sustainability, and efforts to reduce the use of single occupancy vehicles through the Transportation Alternative Program, among others – and the results of these efforts can be seen in the declining aggregate GHG emission trend over the past 5 years (see Figure 1). Although, UCSB has typically done so with energy savings or reduced traffic congestion in mind, not GHG emissions. We argue that reduction in GHG emissions is another important reason for UCSB to consider – one that points towards increasing the overall scale and the immediacy of their current efforts.

Notwithstanding their significant previous efforts, there are a number of institutional obstacles that constrain UCSB from implementing more GHG mitigation projects, and from doing so more immediately. These include:

- The state funding allocation system, which allots separate funds for capital projects and for operations and prevents borrowing from the operations budget to fund capital projects;
- Lack of funding in general and restrictions on UCSB's access to capital;
- Lack of an information management system for GHG emissions, which hinders efforts to understand emissions sources and trends; and,
- Institutional inertia and risk averseness.

Addressing these barriers is integral to the implementation of any significant GHG reduction policy.

Our Group's Direct Contribution to GHG mitigation:

- Facilitation of UCSB membership with California Climate Action Registry.

- Design of The Green Initiative Fund (a student fee based revolving fund for environmental projects on campus), which passed on April 24, 2006.

- Participation in the development of the Campus Sustainability Plan

---

> Authors look ahead to the next phase of the project.

Final Recommendations and Conclusion

Based on our mitigation and institutional analyses, and from our experience engaging with the relevant decision makers at UCSB over the past year, we identify a main recommendation and five supporting recommendations that would put UCSB on track to be a leader in responding to climate change.

Key Recommendation

With consideration to the financial findings of our research and evaluation of institutional barriers, **UCSB should make a firm commitment to meet the California GHG reduction targets**.

In order to accomplish this, UCSB should:
1. Use aggregate GHG emissions targets as a metric in long-term campus planning documents.
2. Turn the "Sustainability Working Team" of the Campus Planning Committee's Sub-Committee on Sustainability into a real Office of Sustainability.
3. Implement zero cost emissions reduction projects first, followed by the most cost effective (i.e., highest $/ MTCO$_2$e) projects.
4. Focus on identifying additional cost-effective GHG mitigation opportunities on campus, such as energy efficiency.
5. Work with administrators at other UC schools to press UCOP and the state legislature for capital budget funding reform as one of the top priorities.

These recommendations should allow UCSB to reap the multiple benefits previously discussed, including significant dollar savings, improved environmental performance, and positive public relations opportunities. Furthermore, UCSB's leadership on addressing climate change has the potential to have significant impacts beyond the UCSB campus, including:

- Mobilizing other public universities, in the UC system and beyond, to address climate change;
- Demonstrating the feasibility – indeed benefits – of meeting the first two commitments of the California targets; and,
- Educating the students of UCSB, as future consumers, investors, professionals, and leaders.

Ultimately, it is these longer term and broader scale implications of UCSB's actions today that make climate mitigation so important. As David Orr (2000), a professor of Environmental Studies at Oberlin College puts it: *"Education is done in many ways, the most powerful of which is by example."* It is time for UCSB to educate – its students, other universities, and California businesses – by example.

 Using this Group Project as a model, NAELS is working to implement a nationwide campaign to develop bottom-up climate leadership through its Campus Climate Neutral (CCN) program – an ambitious and unprecedented grassroots effort to mobilize graduate students around the United States to lead the way to aggressive, long-term climate solutions.

Conclusion wraps up by stating the argument concisely.

Summarizes main point(s).

Discussion of benefits.

A look to the future.

11

Inventing Your Proposal's Content

When writing a proposal, your first challenge is to fully understand the problem you are trying to solve. Then you can come up with a plan for solving it.

Inquiring: Defining the Problem

You should start out by figuring out the boundaries of your topic and what you want to achieve with your proposal.

State Your Proposal's Purpose. A good first step is to state the purpose of your proposal in one sentence. A clear statement of your purpose will help you focus your research and save you time.

> The purpose of this proposal is to show how college students can help fight global climate change.

Narrow Your Topic and Purpose. Make sure you aren't trying to solve a problem that is too big. Look at your purpose statement again. Can you narrow the topic to something more manageable? Specifically, can you take a local approach to your subject by discussing how the problem affects people where you live or in your state? Can you talk about your topic in terms of recent events?

> The purpose of this proposal is to show how our campus can significantly reduce its greenhouse gas emissions, which are partly responsible for global climate change.

Find Your Angle. Figure out what might be unique or different about how you would approach the problem. What is your new angle?

> We believe attempts to conserve energy offer a good start toward cutting greenhouse emissions, but these effects will only take us part of the way. The only way to fully eliminate greenhouse gas emissions here on campus is to develop new sources of clean, renewable energy.

Inquiring: Analyzing the Problem

Now you need to identify and analyze the major causes of the problem, so you can explain them to your readers.

Identify the Major and Minor Causes of the Problem. A good way to analyze a problem is to use a concept map to determine what you already know about the causes of the problem. To create a concept map, put the problem you are analyzing in the middle of your screen or a sheet of paper. Then write the two to five major causes of that problem around it (Figure 12.1).

Keep Asking "What Changed?" As you explore the problem's major causes, keep asking yourself, "What has changed to create this problem?" If you pay attention to

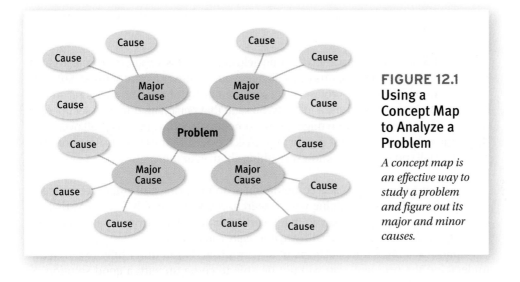

**FIGURE 12.1
Using a
Concept Map
to Analyze a
Problem**

*A concept map is
an effective way to
study a problem
and figure out its
major and minor
causes.*

the things that are changing about your topic, you will find it easier to identify what is causing the problem itself.

Analyze the Major and Minor Causes. Once you have identified two to five major causes, find the "minor causes" that are causing them. Ask yourself, "What are the two to five minor causes of each major cause? What has changed recently that created each of the major causes or made them worse?" Figure 12.1 shows how a concept map can illustrate both major and minor causes, allowing you to develop a comprehensive analysis of the problem.

Researching: Gathering Information and Sources

Your concept map will give you a good start, but you are going to need to do some solid research on your topic. When doing research, you need to collect information from a variety of sources. You should "triangulate" your research by drawing material from online, print, and empirical sources.

Online Sources. Choose some keywords from your concept map, and use Internet search engines to gather background information on your topic. Pay special attention to Web sites that identify the causes of the problem you are exploring. Also, look for documentaries, podcasts, or broadcasts on your subject. You might find some good sources on *YouTube, Hulu,* or the Web sites of television networks.

Print Sources. Your best print sources will usually be newspapers and magazine articles, because most proposals are written about current or local problems. You can run keyword searches in newspaper and magazine archives on the Internet, or you can use the *Readers' Guide* at your library to locate magazine sources. On your library's Web site, you might also use research indexes to find articles in academic journals. These articles tend to offer more empirically grounded discussions of issues in our society.

Empirical Sources. Set up interviews, do field observations, or survey people to gather empirical evidence that supports or challenges your online and print sources. Someone on your campus, perhaps a professor or a staff member, probably knows a great amount about the topic you have chosen to study. So send that person an e-mail to set up an interview. If you aren't sure who might know something about your topic, call over to the department that seems closest to your topic. Ask the person who answers the phone if he or she can tell you who might know something about your topic.

As always, you should use a combination of online, print, and empirical sources to gather information. While doing your research, you will probably find ideas that you can add to the concept maps you made earlier, or you will discover that some of the causes you originally came up with are not really causes at all.

Solid research is the backbone of any proposal. If you don't fully research and understand the problem, you will not be able to come up with a good solution. So give yourself plenty of time to gather and triangulate your sources.

Inquiring: Planning to Solve the Problem

With your preliminary research finished, you are now ready to start developing a plan to solve the problem. A plan is a step-by-step strategy for getting something done. Essentially, when writing a plan, you are telling your readers, "If we take these steps, we will solve the problem I just described to you."

Map Out Your Plan. Again, a concept map is a useful tool for figuring out your plan. Start out by putting your best solution in the middle of your screen or a piece of paper. Then ask yourself, "What are the two to five major steps we need to take to achieve this goal?" Write those major steps around your solution and connect them to it with lines (Figure 12.2).

Explore Each Major Step. Now, consider each of the major steps one at a time. Ask yourself, "What are the two to five steps we need to take to achieve each of these major steps?" For example, if one of your major steps is "develop alternative sources of energy," what steps would your university need to take to do that?

1. The university might look for grants or donations to help it do research on converting its campus to renewable energy sources like wind power or solar energy.

2. The university might explore ways to replace the inefficient heating systems in campus buildings with geothermal heating and cooling systems.

3. The university might convert its current fleet of buses and service vehicles to biodiesel or plug-in hybrids.

Each major step can be broken down further into minor steps that offer more detail.

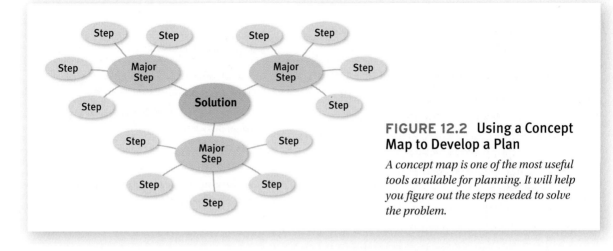

FIGURE 12.2 Using a Concept Map to Develop a Plan

A concept map is one of the most useful tools available for planning. It will help you figure out the steps needed to solve the problem.

Figure Out the Costs and Benefits of Your Plan. With your plan mapped out, you should now identify its costs and benefits. Essentially, your goal is to determine whether the benefits of your plan outweigh the costs. After all, nothing is free. So someone, probably your readers, will need to give up something (like money) to put your plan into action. You want to prove to your readers that the benefits are worth the costs. When figuring out the costs and benefits, brainstorming is an especially helpful tool. You can use it to list all the costs of your plan and then use it to list all the benefits (Figure 12.3, page 262).

Researching: Find Similar Projects

Now that you have developed your plan, do some more research. Again, you should gather information from online, print, and empirical sources. This time, though, look for projects similar to the one you are proposing. There is a good chance that someone else has already been trying to solve this problem.

Of course, you don't want to copy their solution—their plan probably won't work for your situation anyway—but you might learn what others have tried before, what has worked, and what hasn't worked.

As you do your research, also try to find sources that will help you fill out and support your plan. More than likely, your research is going to uncover new strategies and complications that you would not have thought of yourself. Incorporate those strategies into your own plan, and try to come up with ways to work around the complications. Always make sure you keep track of your sources, so you can cite them in your proposal.

Be prepared to alter your plan as you come across new strategies and new information. Research will almost always bring new ideas to your attention that you might want to use in your proposal.

Benefits of My Plan to Make Our Campus Carbon Neutral	Costs of My Plan
Help save humanity from apocalyptic end (!)	Transformation costs will be high, perhaps even $100 million
Reduce this university's dependence on foreign oil	University will need to invest in energy research and training
Help clean up local air, water, and soil	
Widely distributed power sources, which will make us less vulnerable to energy system failures	Need to retrain current power plant employees
Not contribute to ecological destruction involved with mining coal and drilling for oil	University will need to stress energy conservation as system evolves
Help create more local jobs for a "green economy"	
Millions of dollars in energy savings, starting in 10 years	
Be ahead of energy policy changes that are coming anyway	
Make our campus modern and forward thinking, which is attractive to top students	

FIGURE 12.3 Costs and Benefits of Your Plan

Brainstorming can help you list the costs and benefits of your plan. Your goal is to show your readers that the benefits of your plan outweigh the costs.

Organizing and Drafting Your Proposal

Organizing and drafting a large document like a proposal can be challenging, but here is where your hard work doing inquiry and research will finally pay off. The best way to draft a proposal is to write each of its major sections separately. Draft each major section as though it is a small argument on its own.

The Introduction

An introduction to a proposal will typically make up to five moves, which can be made in just about any order:

State the topic. Tell your readers what the proposal is about.

State the purpose. State the purpose of your proposal in one or two sentences.

State the main point. Briefly, tell readers your solution.

Provide background information. Give readers just enough historical information to understand your topic.

Stress the importance of the topic to the readers. Tell readers why they should care about this topic.

In the introduction to a proposal, you should almost always state your topic, purpose, and main point. The other two moves are optional, but they become more important and necessary in larger proposals.

Description of the Problem, Its Causes, and Its Effects

You should now describe and analyze the problem for your readers, showing them its causes and effects. Look at your concept map and your research notes to identify the two to five major causes of the problem. Then draft this section of the proposal around those causes (Figure 12.4).

Opening Paragraph. Use the opening paragraph to clearly describe the problem and perhaps stress its importance.

> The problem we face is that our campus is overly dependent on energy from the Anderson Power Facility, a 20-megawatt coal-fire plant on the east side of campus that belches out many tons of carbon dioxide each year. At this point, we have no alternative energy source, and our backup source of energy is the Bentonville Power Plant, another coal-fire plant 50 miles away. This dependence on the Anderson Plant causes our campus's carbon footprint to be large, and it leaves us vulnerable to power shortages and rising energy costs.

Body Paragraphs. Explain the causes of the problem, providing plenty of support for your claims. Here is an example discussion of one cause among a few others that the writers want to include.

> The primary reason the campus is so reliant on coal-fire energy is the era when the campus was built. Our campus is like many others in the United States. The basic infrastructure and many of the buildings were built in the early twentieth century when coal was the cheapest source of energy and no one could have anticipated problems like global warming. A coal-fire plant, like the one on the east side of campus, seemed like the logical choice. As our campus has grown, our energy needs have increased exponentially. Now, on any given day, the campus needs anywhere from 12 to 22 megawatts to keep running (Campus Energy Report, 22).

Closing Paragraph. You might consider closing this section with a discussion or summary of the effects of the problem if no action is taken. In most cases, problems grow worse over time, so you want to show readers what will happen if they choose not to do anything.

> Our dependence on fossil fuels for energy on this campus will begin to cost us more and more as the United States and the global community are forced to address global climate change. More than likely, coal-fire plants like ours will need to be

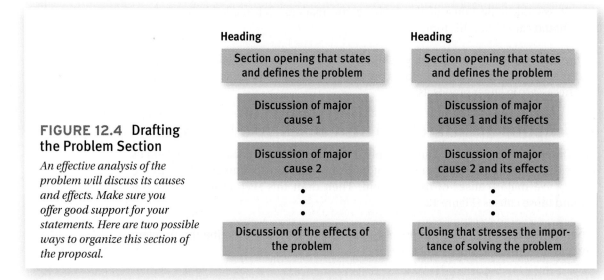

FIGURE 12.4 Drafting the Problem Section

An effective analysis of the problem will discuss its causes and effects. Make sure you offer good support for your statements. Here are two possible ways to organize this section of the proposal.

completely replaced or refitted with expensive carbon capture equipment (Gathers, 12). Also, federal and state governments will likely begin putting a "carbon tax" on emitters of carbon dioxide to encourage conservation and conversion to alternative energy. These costs could run our university many millions of dollars. Moreover, the costs to our health cannot be overlooked. Coal-fire plants, like ours, put particulates, mercury, and sulfur dioxide into the air that we breath (Vonn, 65). The costs of our current coal-fire plant may seem hidden now, but they will eventually bleed our campus of funds and continue to harm our health.

Figure 12.4 shows two of the more common patterns for the Problem section, but other patterns will work, too. You can use whichever pattern helps you best explain the causes and effects of the problem to your readers.

Description of Your Plan

Draft the Plan section next. In this section, you want to describe step by step how the problem can be solved (Figure 12.5). The key to success in this section is to tell your readers *how* you would solve the problem and *why* you would do it this way.

Opening Paragraph. The opening paragraph of this section should be brief. Tell the readers your solution and give them a good reason why it is the best approach to the problem. Give your plan a name. For example:

The best way to make meaningful cuts in greenhouse gas emissions on our campus would be to replace our current coal-fire power plant with a 12-turbine wind farm and install solar panels on all campus buildings. The "Cool Campus Project" would cut greenhouse gas emissions by half within ten years, and we could eliminate all greenhouse emissions within twenty years.

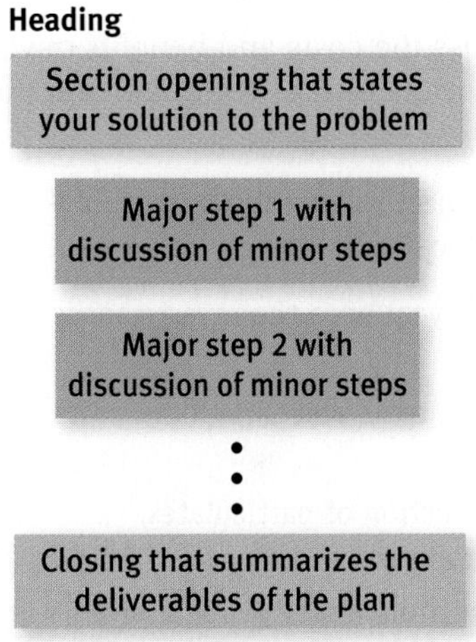

Heading

> Section opening that states your solution to the problem
>
> Major step 1 with discussion of minor steps
>
> Major step 2 with discussion of minor steps
>
> •
> •
> •
>
> Closing that summarizes the deliverables of the plan

FIGURE 12.5 Drafting the Plan Section

Your Plan section should walk readers through your solution step by step. After you state each major step, discuss the minor steps and explain why they are needed.

Body Paragraphs. The body paragraphs for this section should then tell the readers step by step how you would carry out your plan. Usually, each paragraph will start out by stating a major step.

Step Three: Install a 12-Turbine Wind Farm at the Experimental Farm

The majority of the university's electricity needs would be met by installing a 12-turbine wind farm that would generate 18 megawatts of energy per day. The best place for this wind farm would be at the university's Experimental Farm, which is two miles west of campus. The university already owns this property and the area is known for its constant wind. An added advantage to placing a wind farm at this location is that the Agriculture Department could continue to use the land as an experimental farm. The turbines would be operating above the farm, and the land would still be available for planting crops.

Closing Paragraph. In the closing paragraph of this section, you should summarize the *deliverables* of the plan. Deliverables are the things you will deliver to the readers when the project is completed:

When the Cool Campus Project is completed, the university will be powered by a 12-turbine wind farm and an array of solar panels mounted on campus buildings. This combination of wind and solar energy will generate the 20 megawatts needed by campus on regular days, and it should be able to satisfy the 25 megawatts needed on peak usage days.

Don't get locked into the pattern shown in Figure 12.5. You might find other, more effective patterns for describing your plan, depending on the solution you are proposing.

Discussing the Costs and Benefits of Your Plan

A good way to round out your argument is to discuss the costs and benefits of your plan. You want to show readers the two to five major benefits of your plan and then argue that these benefits outweigh the costs.

> In the long run, the benefits of the Cool Campus Project will greatly outweigh the costs. The major benefits of converting to wind and solar energy include—
>
> - A savings of $1.2 million in energy costs each year once the investment is paid off.
> - The avoidance of millions of dollars in refitting costs and carbon tax costs associated with our current coal-fire plant.
> - The improvement of our health due to the reduction of particulates, mercury, and sulfur dioxide in our local environment.
> - A great way to show that this university is environmentally progressive, thus attracting students and faculty who care about the environment.
>
> We estimate the costs of the Cool Campus Project will be approximately $20 million, much of which can be offset with government grants. Keep in mind, though, that our coal-fired plant will need to be refitted or replaced soon anyway, which would cost millions. So the costs of the Cool Campus Project would likely be recouped within a decade.

Costs do not always involve money, or money alone. Sometimes, the costs of the plan will be measured in effort or time. Be sure to mention any nonmonetary costs, so they are not a surprise to your readers.

The Conclusion

Your proposal's conclusion should be brief and to the point. By now, you have told the readers everything they need to know, so you just need to wrap up and leave your readers in a position to say yes to your plan. Here are a few moves you might consider making in your conclusion:

Restate your main claim. Again, tell the readers what you wanted to prove in your proposal. Your main claim first appeared in the introduction. Now bring the readers back around to it, showing that you proved your argument.

Restress the importance of the topic. Briefly, tell the readers why this topic is important. You want to leave them with the sense that this issue needs to be addressed as soon as possible.

Look to the future. Proposal writers often like to leave readers with a description of a better future. A "look to the future" should only run a few sentences or a brief paragraph.

Offer contact information. Tell readers who to contact and how to contact that person if they have questions, want more information, or are interested in discussing the proposal.

Your conclusion should not be more than a couple of brief paragraphs, even in a large proposal. The goal of your conclusion is to wrap up quickly.

Choosing an Appropriate Style

Proposals are persuasive documents by nature, so your style should be convincing to match your proposal's content. In Chapter 16, "Choosing a Style," you can learn about how to use persuasive style techniques. For now, here are some easy strategies that will make your proposal sound more convincing:

Create an Authoritative Tone.   Pick a tone that expresses a sense of authority. Then create a concept map around it (Figure 12.6). You should weave these terms from your concept map into your proposal, creating a theme that sets the desired tone.

Use Metaphors and Similes.   Metaphors and similes allow you to compare new ideas to things that are familiar to your readers. For example, calling a coal-fire plant a "smoke-belching tailpipe" will make it sound especially unattractive to your readers, making them more inclined to agree with you. Or, you might use a metaphor to discuss your wind turbines in terms of "farming" (e.g., harvesting the wind, planting wind turbines in a field, reaping the savings) because that will sound good to most people.

Pay Attention to Sentence Length.   Proposals should generate excitement, especially at the moments when you are describing your plan and its benefits. To raise the heartbeat of your writing, shorten the sentences at these key places in your proposal. Elsewhere in the proposal, keep the sentences regular length (breathing length). See Chapter 16, "Choosing a Style," for more on sentence length and style.

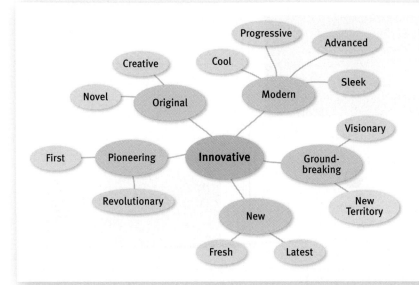

FIGURE 12.6
Mapping an Authoritative Tone

Put a word that describes the tone you want in the center of your screen or a piece of paper. Then map out all the words and phrases you can think of associated with that tone. You can then use these terms in your proposal to create the appropriate tone.

Minimize the Jargon. Proposals can get somewhat technical, depending on the topic. So look for any jargon words that could be replaced with simpler words or phrases. If a jargon word is needed, make sure you define it for readers.

Designing Your Proposal

Your proposal needs to be attractive and easy to use, so leave yourself some time to design the document and include graphics. Good design will help your proposal stand out, while making it easy to read. Your readers will also appreciate graphics that enhance and support your message.

Create a Look. Figure out what image your proposal should project to the readers. Do you want your proposal to appear progressive or conservative? Do you want it to look exciting or traditional? Then make choices about fonts, columns, and photographs that reflect that design (Figure 12.7).

Use Meaningful Headings. When they first pick up your proposal, your readers will likely scan it before reading. So your headings need to be meaningful and action-oriented. Don't just use headings like "Problem" or "Plan." Instead, use headings like "Our Campus's Global Warming Problem" or "Introducing The Cool Campus Initiative."

Include Relevant, Accurate Graphics. Proposals often talk about trends, so you should look for places where you can use charts or graphs to illustrate those trends. Where possible, put data into tables. Use photographs to help you explain the problem or show examples of your solution.

FIGURE 12.7
Setting a Proposal's Tone with Design

Your proposal shouldn't look boring. Instead, use design to create a tone for your proposal and make it easier to read. The photographs, bulleted lists, graphic icons, and color used in this proposal set a professional tone that gives the authors credibility and engages the readers.

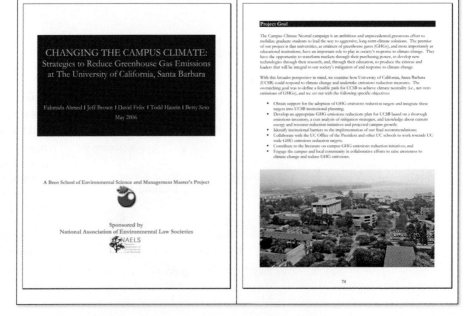

Use Lists to Highlight Important Points. Look for places in your proposal where you list key ideas or other items. Then, where appropriate, put those ideas into bulleted lists that are more scannable for readers.

Create White Space. You might want to expand your margins to add some white space. Readers often like to take notes in the margins of proposals, so a little extra white space is useful. Also, extra white space makes the proposal seem more welcoming and easier to understand.

Revising and Editing Your Proposal

Proposals are often large, complex documents, so make sure you save time for revising and editing. Since proposals are designed to persuade others, you need to make sure that your proposal is well written and nearly flawless. Solid revision and careful editing will help you raise the quality of your document to a higher level.

Let Someone Else Edit Your Work. Your professor may set up a "peer editing" session in which you can let someone else look over your work. Ask your editor to pay special attention to the content, organization, style, and design of your proposal. If peer editing is not available in class, ask a friend or a roommate to look over your work. Tell him or her to be critical and challenge your ideas.

Look for Inconsistencies in Content. As you drafted your proposal, your ideas about the topic probably evolved and changed as you learned more about it. So make sure your analysis of the problem matches up with your plan for solving it. In your Costs and Benefits section, make sure you have summarized the most important benefits mentioned in your plan and listed out the costs. Finally, your introduction and conclusion should be consistent with each other in both content and style.

Get Rid of the Extra Stuff. Look for places where you have included material that goes beyond the readers' need to know. It is always tempting to tell the readers everything you know about your topic, but they only need information that will help them make a decision. So cut out any extra information they probably don't need or want.

Tweak the Design. When the whole proposal is put together, look for places where the design is inconsistent or looks odd. Then make adjustments to get rid of those problems. Check the headings to make sure they are consistent. Look over the graphics to ensure that they are properly placed and easy to read.

Don't Forget to Proofread! Proofreading is always important, but it is essential for proposals. If your readers see misspellings and grammatical errors, they are going to doubt the soundness of your ideas. Even small problems like typos will sabotage your entire proposal. So read it through carefully, and have others look it over as well.

As you are editing your proposal, keep in mind that you are trying to persuade readers to trust you and your ideas. A professional, polished proposal will build their confidence in you and your ideas. Inconsistencies and small errors will undermine your whole argument.

The Pitch

Pitches are brief proposals made to people who can offer their support (usually money) for your ideas. Pitches tend to be about one minute long, which means you need to be focused, concise, and confident. You're promoting yourself as much as you are selling your idea.

Here are some good strategies for making a persuasive one-minute pitch:

Introduce yourself and establish your credibility. Remember that people invest in other *people,* not in projects. So tell them *who* you are and *what* you do.

Grab them with a good story. You need to capture your listeners' attention right away, so ask them, "What if _____?" or explain, "Recently, _____ happened and we knew there must be a better way."

Present your big idea in one sentence. Don't make them wait. Hit them with your best idea up front in one sentence.

Give them your best two or three reasons for doing it. The secret is to sell your idea, not explain it. List your best two or three reasons with minimal explanation.

Mention something that distinguishes you and your idea from the others. What is unique about your idea? How does your idea uniquely fit your listener's prior investments?

Offer a brief cost-benefits analysis. Show them very briefly that your idea is worth their investment of time, energy, or money.

Make sure they remember you. End your pitch by telling them something memorable about you or your organization. Make sure you put your contact information in their hand (e.g., a business card or résumé). If they allow it, leave them a written version of your pitch.

The pitch shown here was written by a team of students at Brigham Young University for an elevator pitch competition. It won the competition.

WRITE your own pitch. Think of an original product, company, or service that you can offer (please keep it PG-13). Then write a one-minute pitch that sells your idea to someone who can say yes and give you the resources to make it a reality.

One Page Genealogy

Adam Abraham and Kolby Oswald

My name is Adam and I am with One Page Genealogy. One Page Genealogy is a not-for-profit organization dedicated to researching using technology to improve genealogy research. Now, to give you an understanding of our opportunity:

The introduction identifies the speaker and the product.

My father, Mike, is a genealogical enthusiast. He spends hours of his time in front of a computer entering in data about his family—when they were born, when they died, and so on. Mike has a notebook over five inches thick with printouts of his genealogy information. He can never find the information he needs between all of the footnotes, complex history charts, and such. I certainly get lost when I look at his notebook, and frankly, I would not even want to start to dig through his information.

Here is a good story that readers can identify with.

My dad's family is important to him, as are all of our families. We want him, and the millions of other genealogists in the world, to be able to use the research they spend so much time on.

One Page Genealogy takes all of the information stored on these hundreds or thousands of individual printouts and combines them into one succinct and attractive printout that families will be proud to frame on their wall, or use in their genealogy research.

The big idea is presented in one sentence.

Now, 99 percent of you are thinking: "I am not a genealogist; I don't even think my information exists out there." Honestly, I am not either, but for 90 percent of you, we could log on right now and generate a print-out for your family within minutes because chances are it is already done for you.

Aside from pornography, genealogy is the number one most researched topic on the Internet. I mean honestly, I am sure everyone here today has seen or received a pop-up or banner ad for ancestry.com. The market is huge and the potential is even greater. Our target market is individuals between the ages of 35–60. But, you know, the beautiful thing is that the market is global! It doesn't matter if you are Japanese, Chinese, Italian, North American, or South American. As long as you have a pulse, and you care about where you came from . . . YOU WILL BUY IT!

These qualities distinguish the ideas from similar ideas.

Let's take a look at the cost structure and profit analysis. The major expense incurred with software development is by Research and Development. BYU Computer Science department has produced all of the software for OPG for FREE! Revenue per page: $50. Cost per page: $5–8. The margins are great!

The pitch ends with a memorable cost-benefit analysis.

Here are some quick steps to get you working on your proposal.

IDENTIFY the Problem You Want to Solve

In one sentence, write down the topic and purpose of your proposal. Then narrow the topic to something you can manage.

ANALYZE the Problem's Causes and Effects

Use a concept map to analyze the problem's two to five major causes. Then use another concept map to explore the effects of the problem if nothing is done about it.

DO Your Research

Search the Internet and your library to collect sources. Then use empirical methods like interviews or surveys to help you support or challenge the facts you find.

DEVELOP Your Plan for Solving the Problem

Using a concept map, figure out the two to five major steps needed to solve the problem. Then figure out what minor steps will be needed to achieve each of these major steps.

FIGURE OUT the Costs and Benefits of Your Plan

Look at your Plan section closely. Identify any costs of your plan. Then list all the benefits of solving the problem your way. You want to make sure the benefits of your solution outweigh the costs.

DRAFT the Proposal

Try drafting each major section separately, treating each one like a small document on its own.

DESIGN Your Proposal

Your proposal needs to look professional and easy to read. Make choices about fonts, graphics, and document design that best suit the materials you are presenting to your readers.

REVISE and Edit

Proposals are complicated documents, so you should leave plenty of time to revise and edit your work.

The Wild Bunch

ROBERT SULLIVAN

In this proposal, environmental writer Robert Sullivan tries to strike a balance between the needs of bicyclists and drivers in New York City. He uses the proposal genre as a way to organize his argument and make his case. First, he identifies a problem, its causes and effects. Then he lays out a step-by-step way for bicyclists, motorists, and pedestrians to share the city streets. His argument is primarily aimed at bicyclists, but watch how he also speaks to nonbicyclists as he tries to prove his points.

Sometimes, when I am biking, I remember the '80s, and I shudder. I remember, in other words, when biking was an extreme sport, when, if you were a biker, you had a lot of locks and a lot more nerve.

Just the other day, when I was enjoying the bike lane down Clinton Street in my neighborhood, Cobble Hill, Brooklyn, I stopped at a red light. And after the crossing guard smiled and chatted with me, after the cars pulled up alongside me and did not honk, I experienced a flashback from 1987: my regular trip from West 113th Street to Central Park, navigating honks and taunts, the mayhem that was then on Cathedral Parkway.

In those days, when I got into the park, I thought I had really achieved something, in terms not of stamina or increased heart rate, but of survival. Riding a bike in New York was like spelunking or white-water rafting, and in those days, bikers traveled best at night, when traffic was light. In the absence of bike lanes, we looked for parks to move through; we stayed on the side streets, and most New Yorkers then did not believe bikers should be anywhere in the city, much less on the streets. This was what I was remembering the other day when, as the light changed, I began to pedal and a biker went racing by and nearly killed me.

Well, not literally. Literally, he only scared the bejesus out of me and brushed my arm, no big deal. The crossing guard shook her head. "Jerk," she said.

When I got to Atlantic Avenue, a street I 5 would be nervous about crossing if I were in an armored vehicle, I stopped to wait for the light as a helmetless man, riding with his child on a seat, weaved wobbly between me, the taxi and the pedestrians trying to cross, uttering not even an "on your right." He pulled silently out into traffic, stopping halfway across the intersection to let a tractor-trailer wail by before he finished crossing against the light, the toddler in back thinking heaven knows what.

Meanwhile, another biker was about to pass him, and pedestrians in the intersection now scattered like deer. And I was thinking, "No wonder they hate us."

Because they do hate us, they being nonbikers and us being bikers.

Stimulus bills with federal money for transportation come and go, but we bikers appear to be staying. For once in our biking lives, New York is really listening to us, helping our numbers grow, with new bike racks, bike shelters, biking incentives (a proposal for an indoor parking requirement for new buildings, for instance) and, of course, bike lanes.

* * *

To be clear, cars are more likely to kill nonbikers; we still live in a world ruled by the ruthless car. But as someone who has been knocked off his bike by an S.U.V. making an illegal right on red (pretty hard, but I just got bruises and a busted front wheel), who has been hit by a cab veering into a bike lane (not that hard) and who has been knocked down as a pedestrian in a crosswalk by a Ford Econovan (really hard, as in broken knee, lots of stitches in the head and weeks of crutches and physical therapy), I admit that my knees feel wobbly when I see a guy ride against the light in a busy intersection with a child in the seat behind him.

As someone who has been honked and 10 screamed at by drivers when I am proceeding carefully along a wide, bike-friendly street, I acknowledge that my blood boils, just from a public relations standpoint, when I see a guy do that. Because again, they hate us.

The nature of the hate has changed. Once, they hated us because we were a rarity, like a rat in the kitchen, a pest. Now, they hate us because we are ubiquitous.

In a 12-hour survey one day last summer, the city counted 12,583 bikers on the Staten Island Ferry, the East River bridges and the Hudson River bike path—up 35 percent from the year before in what Janette Sadik-Khan, the city's transportation commissioner, called an "unprecedented increase." Transportation Alternatives, an advocacy group, estimates that 131,000 bikers in the city commute to work daily.

· · ·

There was a time when bikers couldn't imagine the city giving to us, even when it tried. In a previous earth-friendly period, Mayor John Lindsay chickened out on bike lanes after Fifth Avenue businesses complained. In 1980, before "sustainable" was everybody's middle name, Mayor Ed Koch put in bike lanes separated by concrete and asphalt barriers on Fifth Avenue and Avenue of the Americas, and then ripped them out after not seeing any bikers in them.

Today, the Transportation Department has gotten serious about biking, and in just three years, the agency has painted bike lanes (good), constructed bike lanes separated by parked cars (great) and bike lanes separated by medians or barriers (the best) and installed bike signals, bike signs and many bike symbols painted on the street. Some of these symbols are clear, although I'm not sure I understand others. What do the biker and double arrows mean when painted on a busy street without a bike lane? Good luck?

Though bikers are hated, pedestrian 15 deaths and injuries on Ninth Avenue in Chelsea immediately declined in the area of the physically separated bike lane, as reported on streetsblog.org, news blog of the Livable Streets Initiative, which advocates creating sustainable cities. In December, Community Board 4 voted in favor of creating a bike lane on Eighth Avenue between 14th and 23rd Streets.

There are still detractors; Fox News aired a report a few months ago blaming the new bike lane on Grand Street for not only clogging up car traffic in Lower Manhattan but—potentially!—putting pedestrians' lives in danger. Less reported was the story of the biker who was—actually!—killed by a truck driver in a hit-and-run in October. But despite such criticism, people are gradually losing the car-centric view of Manhattan and are sensing that the streets are for more than automobiles.

We bikers, in other words, have been on the receiving end. Now, as much as we would perhaps prefer not to, we must stop to look at ourselves and realize that we have a little giving to do. I am talking about perceptions, about the things we should do outside the letter of the law, like the way we try not to kill the person in front of us in the revolving doors.

• • •

The Brooklyn Bridge is an important front in the bike publicity war; it is a place where bikes are losing. The essential conflict can be grossly caricatured like this: Guys dressed as if they are in the Pyrenees stage of the Tour de France try to set speed records as Italian tourists linger in the middle of the bridge to get a photo of their cousin, Paolo, backed by the Empire State Building.

Bikers won't stop, fearing they will lose a few tenths of a second off their times; and tourists from former Soviet republics confuse the phrase "Get out of the bike lane, you jerk" with "Enjoy your stay."

Confusion ensues, slowing down the furious bikers and dragging into the mix City Hall–area office workers who are just trying to get in a little lunch break walk-a-cise but are now risking loss of limb. [20]

Next comes another species of biker, which I call the Really Cool Biker, because they are really cool—usually younger than the Lance Armstrong types, wearing skinny jeans and a windbreaker imprinted with, say, the name of a bar or a bowling alley, and riding a sleek, fixed-gear frame bike that I myself am too uncool to even adequately describe.

Now, as the Tour de France vs. the tourist melee is exploding, the Really Cool Bikers attempt to skirt the scrum of tourists, using the moment of chaos as an obstacle course, causing tourists to break like pheasants after a bad shot. The Really Cool Bikers speed silently around terrified bystanders, leaving a trail of bike-induced horror. Even bike commuters complain about bikers on the Brooklyn Bridge.

Once, cars were the natural enemy of bikers, and vice versa. But as the Brooklyn Bridge biking shows, now that the city has made some progress in holding back the cars, bikers have begun to treat people the same way the cars they used to battle do—in other words, like the enemy.

Likewise, for pedestrians seeking to complain, bikes are easier to attack than cars, a fact that plays on the strength of the bike. It is driven by a human being you can see and communicate with more readily than you can with a guy in a car whose windows are shut and whose stereo is blasting.

• • •

Despite the presence of bike lanes, we [25] see many bikes on the sidewalk, and bikers riding the wrong way down streets, alarming cabdrivers at the light. For biking to make it to the next level, for bikes to be completely accepted as the viable form of city transportation that they are, bikers must switch sides. They must act like people and stop acting like cars.

This means doing things that we, the bikers of New York, would have laughed at just a few years ago. It means getting a little personal, though not that personal. Acting like people means that we have to do things that we frankly don't want to do and things that we want cars to do, like slow down.

As far as bikers go, I've become a kind of laughingstock because I wait at traffic lights. Recently, as I waited in a bike lane at Atlantic Avenue for a light to change, a woman in her 70s, walking hunched with a cane, approached the crosswalk smiling—until she spotted me. Then she began shouting as I waited behind the crosswalk, "Well, are you going to stop?" I assured her I was waiting. She grimaced. "How do I know you're not going to go?" she asked.

A good point. But I stood my ground, smiled and tried to win the point by not doing anything. Just as she finished crossing, two Lance Armstrong types whipped through the crosswalk and pulled past the red light, waiting to slip through the crossing traffic. The woman who had crossed looked back at me and started shouting again. "See?" she said, proclaiming herself the winner. "You're going to run me over!"

Which brings me to four sure-to-be-scoffed-at suggestions for better bike P.R.:

NO. 1: How about we stop at major [30] intersections? Especially where there are school crossing guards, or disabled people crossing, or a lot of people during the morning or evening rush. (I have the law with me on this one.) At minor intersections, on far-from-traffic intersections, let's at least stop and go.

NO. 2: How about we ride with traffic as opposed to the wrong way on a one-way street? I know the idea of being told which way to go drives many bikers bonkers. That stuff is for cars, they say. I consider one-way streets anathema—they make for faster car traffic and more difficult crossings. But whenever I see something bad happen to a biker, it's when the biker is riding the wrong way on a one-way street.

There will be caveats. Perhaps your wife is about to go into labor and you take her to the hospital on your bike; then, yes, sure, go the wrong way in the one-way bike lane. We can handle caveats. We are bikers.

NO. 3: How about we stay off the sidewalks? Why are bikers so incensed when the police hand out tickets for this? I'm only guessing, but each sidewalk biker must believe that he or she, out of all New York bikers, is the exception, the one careful biker, which is a very car way of thinking.

NO. 4: How about we signal? Again, I hear the laughter, but the bike gods gave us hands to ring bells and to signal turns. Think of the possible complications: Many of the bikers behind you are wearing headphones,

and the family in the minivan has a Disney DVD playing so loudly that it's rattling your 30-pound Kryptonite chain. Let them know what you are thinking so that you can go on breathing as well as thinking.

• • •

Maybe I have been hit too hard by cars [35] while biking, but I foresee a time when my street will be filled with bicycles, when streets will have car lanes and when bike lanes will be transformed into bike-only streets, which is essentially the same as a physically separated bike lane like the one on Ninth Avenue. This bike-centered city life even happened over the summer, when cars were kept off Park Avenue between the Brooklyn Bridge and Central Park and the city did not shut down, nor did bikers kill people.

Bikes don't kill people; cars kill people. I know this, I feel this (big scar on head), and when I think of my bike heroes and bike role models, when I imagine the tone of the new bike culture, I think of civility. I think of Murray Kempton, the great baroque sentence maker who wrote for the *New York Post* and the *New York Review of Books* and biked on what I remember as a three-speed, pedaling to his word processor, wearing an early Walkman.

I think of Alayne Patrick, the owner of the Brooklyn boutique Layla, cruising through Cobble Hill wearing something Indian that was made even more fashionable by the fact that she is on an extremely cool Scandinavian bike. I think of my father, Brooklyn-born, Queens-raised and biking up on a beaten-up 10-speed when we were kids to tell us to head home. "Why drive?" he used to say. "It costs money, and a bike's more fun."

A CLOSER LOOK AT
The Wild Bunch

1. Sullivan argues that bicycling has changed in New York since the 1980s. How is bicycling different now, according to him, and how have the changes in bicycling brought about the problems that he is trying to solve in this proposal?

2. This proposal includes several anecdotes that support Sullivan's argument. How does he use these brief stories to bring the problem to life and make his solution sound more persuasive?

3. Find Sullivan's plan in this proposal. What exactly is he proposing and what are the steps in his plan? What are the benefits for bicyclists (and others) if they accept his proposal?

IDEAS FOR
Writing

1. Do bicyclists on your campus frustrate you? Write a commentary in which you describe the behavior of bicyclists on your campus. Use the arguments in Sullivan's proposal to help you come up with your own ways to make your campus safer.

2. Write a report in which you study the use of bicycles on your campus. Is bicycling on the rise at your university? If so, what should be done to accommodate this increase in bicyclists? What changes should be put into place to keep everyone safe? At the end of your report, make a few recommendations for improving bicycling and bicycle safety on and near campus.

From Degrading to De-Grading

ALFIE KOHN

In this proposal, which was published in High School *magazine, Alfie Kohn first explains the problems with using grades to motivate students in high school. Then he describes how high schools could evaluate students in other ways. Kohn, an education reformer, has published numerous books, has been featured in a variety of magazines and newspapers, and has appeared on the* Oprah Winfrey Show.

You can tell a lot about a teacher's values and personality just by asking how he or she feels about giving grades. Some defend the practice, claiming that grades are necessary to "motivate" students. Many of these teachers actually seem to enjoy keeping intricate records of

Alfie Kohn, "From Degrading to De-Grading." Copyright 1999 by Alfie Kohn. Abridged from an article in *High School* magazine with the author's permission. For the complete text, as well as other resources, please see www.alfiekohn.org.

students' marks. Such teachers periodically warn students that they're "going to have to know this for the test" as a way of compelling them to pay attention or do the assigned readings—and they may even use surprise quizzes for that purpose, keeping their grade books at the ready.

Frankly, we ought to be worried for these teachers' students. In my experience, the most impressive teachers are those who despise the whole process of giving grades. Their aversion, as it turns out, is supported by solid evidence that raises questions about the very idea of traditional grading.

Three main effects of grading

Researchers have found three consistent effects of using—and especially, emphasizing the importance of—letter or number grades:

1. *Grades tend to reduce students' interest in the learning itself.* One of the most well-researched findings in the field of motivational psychology is that the more people are rewarded for doing something, the more they tend to lose interest in whatever they had to do to get the reward (Kohn, 1993). Thus, it shouldn't be surprising that when students are told they'll need to know something for a test—or, more generally, that something they're about to do will count for a grade—they are likely to come to view that task (or book or idea) as a chore.

While it's not impossible for a student to be concerned about getting high marks and also to like what he or she is doing, the practical reality is that these two ways of thinking generally pull in opposite directions. Some research has explicitly demonstrated that a "grade orientation" and a "learning orientation" are inversely related (Beck et al., 1991; Milton et al., 1986). More strikingly, study after study has found that students—from elementary school to graduate school, and across cultures—demonstrate less interest in learning as a result of being graded (Benware and Deci, 1984; Butler, 1987; Butler and Nisan, 1986;

Grolnick and Ryan, 1987; Harter and Guzman, 1986; Hughes et al., 1985; Kage, 1991; Salili et al., 1976). Thus, anyone who wants to see students get hooked on words and numbers and ideas already has reason to look for other ways of assessing and describing their achievement.

2. *Grades tend to reduce students' preference for challenging tasks.* Students of all ages who have been led to concentrate on getting a good grade are likely to pick the easiest possible assignment if given a choice (Harter, 1978; Harter and Guzman, 1986; Kage, 1991; Milton et al., 1986). The more pressure to get an A, the less inclination to truly challenge oneself. Thus, students who cut corners may not be lazy so much as rational; they are adapting to an environment where good grades, not intellectual exploration, are what count. They might well say to us, "Hey, you told me the point here is to bring up my GPA, to get on the honor roll. Well, I'm not stupid: the easier the assignment, the more likely that I can give you what you want. So don't blame me when I try to find the easiest thing to do and end up not learning anything."

3. *Grades tend to reduce the quality of students' thinking.* Given that students may lose interest in what they're learning as a result of grades, it makes sense that they're also apt to think less deeply. One series of studies, for example, found that students given numerical grades were significantly less creative than those who received qualitative feedback but no grades. The more the task required creative thinking, in fact, the worse the performance of students who knew they were going to be graded. Providing students with comments in addition to a grade didn't help: the highest achievement occurred only when comments were given instead of numerical scores (Butler, 1987; Butler, 1988; Butler and Nisan, 1986).

In another experiment, students told they would be graded on how well they learned a social studies lesson had more trouble understanding the main point of the text than did students who were told that no

5

grades would be involved. Even on a measure of rote recall, the graded group remembered fewer facts a week later (Grolnick and Ryan, 1987). A brand-new study discovered that students who tended to think about current events in terms of what they'd need to know for a grade were less knowledgeable than their peers, even after taking other variables into account (Anderman and Johnston, 1998). . . .

The practical difficulties of abolishing letter grades are real. But the key question is whether those difficulties are seen as problems to be solved or as excuses for perpetuating the status quo. The logical response to the arguments and data summarized here is to say: "Good Heavens! If even half of this is true, then it's imperative we do whatever we can, as soon as we can, to phase out traditional grading." Yet many people begin and end with the problems of implementation, responding to all this evidence by saying, in effect, "Yeah, yeah, yeah, but we'll never get rid of grades because . . ."

It is also striking how many educators 10 never get beyond relatively insignificant questions, such as how many tests to give, or how often to send home grade reports, or what grade should be given for a specified level of achievement (e.g., what constitutes "B" work), or what number corresponds to what letter. Some even reserve their outrage for the possibility that too many students are ending up with good grades, a reaction that suggests stinginess with A's is being confused with intellectual rigor. The evidence indicates that the real problem isn't grade inflation; it's grades. The proper occasion for outrage is not that too many students are getting A's, but that too many students have accepted that getting A's is the point of going to school.

Common objections

Let's consider the most frequently heard responses to the above arguments—which is to say, the most common objections to getting rid of grades.

First, it is said that students expect to receive grades and even seem addicted to them. This is often true; personally, I've taught high school students who reacted to the absence of grades with what I can only describe as existential vertigo. (Who am I, if not a B+?) But as more elementary and even some middle schools move to replace grades with more informative (and less destructive) systems of assessment, the damage doesn't begin until students get to high school. Moreover, elementary and middle schools that haven't changed their practices often cite the local high school as the reason they must get students used to getting grades regardless of their damaging effects—just as high schools point the finger at colleges.

Even when students arrive in high school already accustomed to grades, already primed to ask teachers, "Do we have to know this?" or "What do I have to do to get an A?", this is a sign that something is very wrong. It's more an indictment of what has happened to them in the past than an argument to keep doing it in the future.

Perhaps because of this training, grades can succeed in getting students to show up on time, hand in their work, and otherwise do what they're told. Many teachers are loath to give up what is essentially an instrument of control. But even to the extent this instrument works (which is not always), we are obliged to reflect on whether mindless compliance is really our goal. The teacher who exclaims, "These kids would blow off my course in a minute if they weren't getting a grade for it!" may be issuing a powerful indictment of his or her course. Who would be more reluctant to give up grades than a teacher who spends the period slapping transparencies on the overhead projector and lecturing endlessly at students about Romantic poets or genetic codes? Without bribes (A's) and threats (F's), students would have no reason to do such assignments. To maintain that this proves something is wrong with the kids—or that grades are simply "necessary"—suggests a willful refusal to examine one's classroom practices and assumptions about teaching and learning.

"If I can't give a child a better reason for studying than a grade on a report card, I ought to lock my desk and go home and stay there." So wrote Dorothy De Zouche, a Missouri teacher, in an article published in February . . . of 1945. But teachers who can give a child a better reason for studying don't need grades. Research substantiates this: when the curriculum is engaging—for example, when it involves hands-on, interactive learning activities—students who aren't graded at all perform just as well as those who are graded (Moeller and Reschke, 1993).

Another objection: it is sometimes argued that students must be given grades because colleges demand them. One might reply that "high schools have no responsibility to serve colleges by performing the sorting function for them"—particularly if that process undermines learning (Krumboltz and Yeh, 1996, p. 325). But in any case the premise of this argument is erroneous: traditional grades are not mandatory for admission to colleges and universities.

Making change

A friend of mine likes to say that people don't resist change—they resist being changed. Even terrific ideas (like moving a school from a grade orientation to a learning orientation) are guaranteed to self-destruct if they are simply forced down people's throats. The first step for an administrator, therefore, is to open up a conversation—to spend perhaps a full year just encouraging people to think and talk about the effects of (and alternatives to) traditional grades. This can happen in individual classes, as teachers facilitate discussions about how students regard grades, as well as in evening meetings with parents, or on a website—all with the help of relevant books, articles, speakers, videos, and visits to neighboring schools that are farther along in this journey.

The actual process of "de-grading" can be done in stages. For example, a high school might start by freeing ninth-grade classes from grades before doing the same for upperclassmen. (Even a school that never gets beyond the first stage will have done a considerable service, giving students one full year where they can think about what they're learning instead of their GPAs.)

Another route to gradual change is to begin by eliminating only the most pernicious practices, such as grading on a curve or ranking students. Although grades, per se, may continue for a while, at least the message will be sent from the beginning that all students can do well, and that the point is to succeed rather than to beat others.

Anyone who has heard the term "authentic assessment" knows that abolishing grades doesn't mean eliminating the process of gathering information about student performance—and communicating that information to students and parents. Rather, abolishing grades opens up possibilities that are far more meaningful and constructive. These include narratives (written comments), portfolios (carefully chosen collections of students' writings and projects that demonstrate their interests, achievement, and improvement over time), student-led parent-teacher conferences, exhibitions and other opportunities for students to show what they can do.

Of course, it's harder for a teacher to do these kinds of assessments if he or she has 150 or more students and sees each of them for 45–55 minutes a day. But that's not an argument for continuing to use traditional grades; it's an argument for challenging these archaic remnants of a factory-oriented approach to instruction, structural aspects of high schools that are bad news for reasons that go well beyond the issue of assessment. It's an argument for looking into block scheduling, team teaching, interdisciplinary courses—and learning more about schools that have arranged things so each teacher can spend more time with fewer students (e.g., Meier, 1995).

Administrators should be prepared to respond to parental concerns, some of them completely reasonable, about the prospect of edging away from grades. "Don't you value excellence?" You bet—and here's the evidence that traditional grading undermines excellence. "Are you just trying to spare the self-esteem of students who do poorly?" We are concerned that grades may be making things worse for such students, yes, but the problem isn't just that some kids won't get A's and will have their feelings hurt. The real problem is that almost all kids (including yours) will come to focus on grades and, as a result, their learning will be hurt.

If parents worry that grades are the only window they have into the school, we need to assure them that alternative assessments provide a far better view. But if parents don't seem to care about getting the most useful information or helping their children become more excited learners—if they demand grades for the purpose of documenting how much better their kids are than everyone else's, then we need to engage them in a discussion about whether this is a legitimate goal, and whether schools exist for the purpose of competitive credentialing or for the purpose of helping everyone to learn (Kohn, 1998; Labaree, 1997).

Above all, we need to make sure that objections and concerns about the details don't obscure the main message, which is the demonstrated harm of traditional grading on the quality of students' learning and their interest in exploring ideas.

High school administrators can do a world of good in their districts by actively supporting efforts to eliminate conventional grading in elementary and middle schools. Working with their colleagues in these schools can help pave the way for making such changes at the secondary school level.

In the meantime

Finally, there is the question of what classroom teachers can do while grades continue to be required. The short answer is that they should do everything within their power to make grades as invisible as possible for as long as possible. Helping students forget about grades is the single best piece of advice for creating a learning-oriented classroom.

When I was teaching high school, I did a lot of things I now regret. But one policy that still seems sensible to me was saying to students on the first day of class that, while I was compelled to give them a grade at the end of the term, I could not in good conscience ever put a letter or number on anything they did during the term—and I would not do so. I would, however, write a comment—or, better, sit down and talk with them—as often as possible to give them feedback.

At this particular school I frequently faced students who had been prepared for admission to Harvard since their early childhood—a process I have come to call "Preparation H." I knew that my refusal to rate their learning might only cause some students to worry about their marks all the more, or to create suspense about what would appear on their final grade reports, which of course would defeat the whole purpose. So I said that anyone who absolutely had to know what grade a given paper would get could come see me and we would figure it out together. An amazing thing happened: as the days went by, fewer and fewer students felt the need to ask me about grades. They began to be more involved with what we were learning because I had taken responsibility as a teacher to stop pushing grades into their faces, so to speak, whenever they completed an assignment.

What I didn't do very well, however, was to get students involved in devising the criteria for excellence (what makes a math solution elegant, an experiment well-designed, an essay persuasive, a story compelling) as well as deciding how well their projects met those criteria. I'm afraid I unilaterally set the criteria and evaluated the students' efforts. But I have seen teachers who were more willing to give up control, more committed to helping students participate in assessment and turn that into part of the learning. Teachers who work with their students to design powerful alternatives to letter grades have a replacement ready to go when the school finally abandons traditional grading—and are able to minimize the harm of such grading in the meantime.

References

Anderman, E. M., and J. Johnston. "Television News in the Classroom: What Are Adolescents Learning?" *Journal of Adolescent Research* 13 (1998): 73–100.

Beck, H. P., S. Rorrer-Woody, and L. G. Pierce. "The Relations of Learning and Grade Orientations to Academic Performance." *Teaching of Psychology* 18 (1991): 35–37.

Benware, C. A., and E. L. Deci. "Quality of Learning With an Active Versus Passive Motivational Set." *American Educational Research Journal* 21 (1984): 755–65.

Butler, R. "Task-Involving and Ego-Involving Properties of Evaluation: Effects of Different Feedback Conditions on Motivational Perceptions, Interest, and Performance." *Journal of Educational Psychology* 79 (1987): 474–82.

Butler, R. "Enhancing and Undermining Intrinsic Motivation: The Effects of Task-Involving and Ego-Involving Evaluation on Interest and Performance." *British Journal of Educational Psychology* 58 (1988): 1–14.

Butler, R., and M. Nisan. "Effects of No Feedback, Task-Related Comments, and Grades on Intrinsic Motivation and Performance." *Journal of Educational Psychology* 78 (1986): 210–16.

De Zouche, D. "'The Wound Is Mortal': Marks, Honors, Unsound Activities." *The Clearing House* 19 (1945): 339–44.

Grolnick, W. S., and R. M. Ryan. "Autonomy in Children's Learning: An Experimental and Individual Difference Investigation." *Journal of Personality and Social Psychology* 52 (1987): 890–98.

Harter, S. "Pleasure Derived from Challenge and the Effects of Receiving Grades on Children's Difficulty Level Choices." *Child Development* 49 (1978): 788–99.

Harter, S. and Guzman, M. E. "The Effect of Perceived Cognitive Competence and Anxiety on Children's Problem-Solving Performance, Difficulty Level Choices, and Preference for Challenge." Unpublished manuscript, University of Denver. 1986.

Hughes, B., H. J. Sullivan, and M. L. Mosley. "External Evaluation, Task Difficulty, and Continuing Motivation." *Journal of Educational Research* 78 (1985): 210–15.

Kage, M. "The Effects of Evaluation on Intrinsic Motivation." Paper presented at the meeting of the Japan Association of Educational Psychology, Joetsu, Japan, 1991.

Kohn, A. *Punished by Rewards: The Trouble with Gold Stars, Incentive Plans, A's, Praise, and Other Bribes.* Boston: Houghton Mifflin, 1993.

Kohn, A. "Only for My Kid: How Privileged Parents Undermine School Reform." *Phi Delta Kappan,* April 1998: 569–77.

Krumboltz, J. D., and C. J. Yeh. "Competitive Grading Sabotages Good Teaching." *Phi Delta Kappan,* December 1996: 324–26.

Labaree, D. F. *How to Succeed in School Without Really Learning: The Credentials Race in American Education.* New Haven, Conn.: Yale University Press, 1997.

Meier, D. *The Power of Their Ideas: Lessons for America from a Small School in Harlem.* Boston: Beacon, 1995.

Milton, O., H. R. Pollio, and J. A. Eison. *Making Sense of College Grades.* San Francisco: Jossey-Bass, 1986.

Moeller, A. J., and C. Reschke. "A Second Look at Grading and Classroom Performance: Report of a Research Study." *Modern Language Journal* 77 (1993): 163–69.

Salili, F., M. L. Maehr, R. L. Sorensen, and L. J. Fyans, Jr. "A Further Consideration of the Effects of Evaluation on Motivation." *American Educational Research Journal* 13 (1976): 85–102.

A CLOSER LOOK AT
From Degrading to De-Grading

1. This article follows the organization of a traditional proposal. Look through the article and identify the places where Kohn describes (a) the problem, its causes, and its effects, (b) a solution to the problem, including any major and minor steps, and (c) the benefits of accepting his plan.

2. Some of Kohn's major points are supported with empirical evidence and some aren't. Do you think the use of empirical evidence in this proposal makes parts of his argument more credible? Why or why not? In places where he has not backed up his argument with empirical sources, do you find his arguments reasonable and solid? Why or why not?

3. In your opinion, what are Kohn's three strongest arguments against grading and what are his two weakest arguments? What are his three best ideas for alternative ways to evaluate and motivate students? What are the two ideas in his plan that you are most skeptical about?

IDEAS FOR
Writing

1. Write a letter to the editor of *High School* magazine in which you agree or disagree with Kohn's argument. If you agree with his argument, how do your experiences as someone who graduated from (survived) high school match up with Kohn's descriptions? What parts of his plan do you think would work? If you disagree with him, where do his criticisms and ideas for reform fall short? Do you think he is wrong, or do you have a better way to reform the system of grades that is used in high school (and college)?

2. Write a position paper in which you argue for or against the use of grading in college. Many of Kohn's criticisms against grading might be applicable to college, too. But what are some important differences between grading in college and high school? If you are arguing for keeping grades, can you think of a way to improve the system? If you are against grades in college, can you offer a solution that would still keep students motivated and allow professors to gauge whether students had learned the materials?

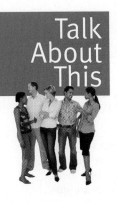

1. What are some of the problems on your college's campus? With a group in your class, list them and pick one that seems especially troublesome. What do you think are the causes of this problem? What has changed recently to bring this problem about or make it worse? Discuss this problem with a group of other people in your class.

2. Now try to figure out a way to solve this campus problem. What would be a good solution to this problem? Can you think of a few other solutions? With a small group, discuss the costs and benefits of solving the problem in different ways.

3. With a group in class, find a proposal on the Internet that you can discuss. Look closely at the proposal's content, organization, style, and design. Do you think the proposal is effective? What are its strengths? What are its weaknesses? If you were going to revise this proposal, what are some of the things you would change?

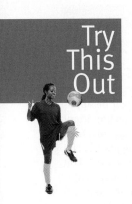

1. Find a proposal on the Internet by entering keywords like "Proposal and (Topic)" into a search engine. Write a one-page analysis of the proposal, describing how it explains the problem and offers a plan for solving it. In your analysis, tell your readers whether you think the proposal is or is not effective. Explain why you think so, and offer suggestions about how the proposal could be improved.

2. List five problems that are facing our society right now. Pick one that interests you and then try to narrow the topic down to something you can manage in a small proposal. Use a concept map to explore what you already know about the problem, its causes, and its effects. Then do research on the subject by collecting online and print sources on it. Draft a one- or two-page analysis of the problem that explores its causes and effects.

3. Find a proposal on the Internet that is badly designed. Do a makeover of the design to improve the look and usability of the proposal. What would make it more appealing to readers? How could design techniques be used to make it easier to scan or easier to understand? You should create two sample pages that illustrate your design.

1. **Propose your own solution.** Write a proposal that solves a problem in our society or in your life. Explore the causes of the problem and then come up with a plan that solves it. Then identify all the benefits that would come about if the problem were solved according to your plan. The best topics for proposals are ones that affect your life in some way. Pick a problem that you feel strongly about or something that affects your everyday life. Your proposal should run about seven to ten pages. Include graphics and make sure the document is well designed.

2. **Remake a proposal into a multimedia presentation.** Using a search engine, find a proposal available on the Internet. Transform the proposal into a presentation that incorporates multimedia features. You can use presentation software, overhead projector slides, flipcharts, or posters. Then write a one-page rhetorical analysis for your professor that introduces the proposal and describes how you altered the original proposal's content, organization, style, and design to make it work as a multimedia presentation.

3. **Propose something absurd.** One of the most famous "proposals" is Jonathan Swift's "A Modest Proposal" in which he suggests consuming Irish children as a way to solve a famine. Swift's intent was to draw attention to the desperation of the Irish, while shaming absent English landlords. Write an ironic five-page proposal like Swift's that proposes an absurd solution for an important problem. Remember that the key to irony is to bring about a positive change by shaming the people who are at fault.

PEARSON
mycomplab

For additional reading, writing, and research resources, go to **www.mycomplab.com.**

13

Reports

R eports are used to describe research findings, analyze those findings, and make recommendations. When writing a report, you need to do more than present the facts. You also need to interpret your results and help your readers understand the information you've collected.

The report genre has many versions, including *research reports, recommendation reports, completion reports, feasibility reports,* and *scientific reports.* No matter what career you choose, from business to engineering to fashion design to science, writing reports will be an important part of your professional life. You will need to write reports regularly to explain issues and offer recommendations to supervisors, clients, and customers.

In college, your professors will ask you to write reports about important issues and projects. As you take more advanced courses, your projects will grow more complex, creative, and collaborative. Professors in your advanced courses will ask you to use reports to analyze specific issues and present your findings.

Learning to write reports is an important skill that you should master right now. Reports tend to be complex documents, but once you know how they work, you can write these kinds of documents more effectively and efficiently.

Reports

To help you remember this structure, you might memorize the acronym, IMRaD, which is widely used by professional researchers. IMRaD stands for Introduction, Methods, Results, and Discussion.

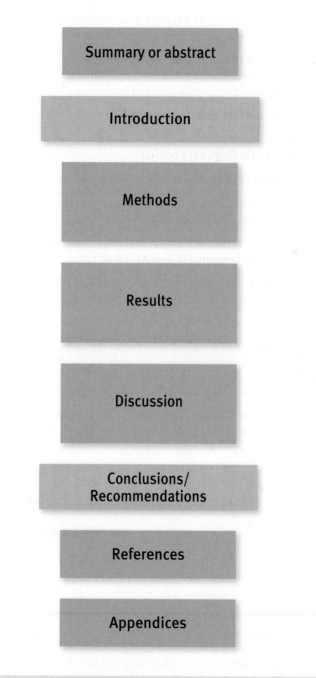

Summary or abstract

Introduction

Methods

Results

Discussion

Conclusions/
Recommendations

References

Appendices

Overview

The report genre is flexible, allowing it to be used in a variety of ways. A typical report, however, tends to have the following features:

- **Executive summary or abstract** that summarizes the major sections of the report. Small reports (less than four pages) may not have this feature.

- **Introduction** that defines a research question or problem and explains why it is important to the reader. The introduction clearly states the purpose and main point of the report, while offering background information on the topic.

- **Methods section** that describes how the research was carried out and how the data and other evidence were collected.

- **Results or Findings section** that presents the results of the research objectively.

- **Discussion section** that analyzes the results and explains what they mean.

- **Conclusion/Recommendations** that restates the main point of the report and offers specific recommendations.

- **References** that provides a list of references or works cited in a standardized citation style (usually MLA or APA style).

- **Appendices** that offer additional sources and other materials related to the report's topic that readers might find useful. Reports don't always include this feature.

ONE STUDENT'S WORK
Reports

This report was written for a class that assigned research reports on "gender identity," our sense of self in terms of being male or female, and how this identity is shaped by both cultural and biological factors.

Gender Stereotypes and Toys: Is It Nature or Nurture?

Scott Walker, University of New Mexico

Abstract

In order to better understand the roles that nature vs. nurture play in the formation of gender identity, I performed a field research study at a large-chain toy store. There I recorded information about how toys were marketed to young children in terms of images, gender stereotypes, and other factors. I found that

A brief abstract summarizes the entire report, section by section.

almost all toys were marked by gender, with the exception of learning materials and some products associated with movies, music, or television. Older children's toys were only slightly more gender distinctive than infants' toys. Finally, I speculate about the repercussions of such marketing on gender identity and how parents might help children resist such stereotyping.

Introduction

Scientists and cultural theorists have long argued about whether nature or nurture (biology or culture) is responsible for gender differences between men and women. Both sides, however, agree that gender differences can be seen even in very young children. Researchers who argue that gender differences are due to "nature" usually emphasize the role played by evolution (Lippa, 2002). They suggest that the differences in behavior between boys and girls exist because human evolution has manipulated genes and hormones over time to increase behavioral differences (Choi, 2001). They even argue that girls and boys respond differently to specific colors, especially pink, for biological reasons (Alexander, 2003).

Those who argue that gender differences are due to "nurture" usually focus on the differences between boys' and girls' socialization in their culture. They maintain that children are taught by their culture, through rewards and modeling, to engage in certain gender behaviors and hold specific attitudes (Lippa, 2002; Paige, 2008). The nurture side of the debate says that as an individual grows up, he or she begins to become aware of how males and females are expected to behave (Ball, 2006). These gender roles, they argue, are taught almost from the moment we are born: boys are expected to be strong, tough, independent, and unemotional, while girls are expected to be nurturing, sensitive, dependent, and expressive. According to the nurture side of the debate, these behaviors are drilled so deeply into our heads from the moment we are born that they seem natural and inborn.

The toys that boys and girls play with offer a good way to study gender differences, because toys are some of the earliest and strongest shapers of gender identity (Blakemore, LaRue, & Olejnik, 1979). Through reinforcement and modeling, boys and girls are taught to play with toys that are considered appropriate for their gender. Infant boys get fire trucks and infant girls get baby dolls. Then the adults around them continue to reinforce gender stereotypes consciously and unconsciously by buying specific kinds of

Report follows the IMRaD organization, each section marked by headings.

Introduction begins by establishing the question that the field research will address.

Sources are used to show the two sides of an argument about gender development.

continued

toys for their children and others' children (Pollitt, 1995; Clark, 2000). The stereotyping is less for infants, according to Campenni (1999), and it grows greater for older children.

In this research study, my aim was to explore how toys affect gender socialization. My research will not, of course, settle the nature vs. nurture debate once and for all. However, by conducting field research at a large toy store, my goal was to gain some insights into how toys shape boys' and girls' sense of gender. My hypothesis is that gender differences in toys help establish gender identity from the beginning of life and that these differences become more apparent as children grow older. As I will show, I discovered definite differences between toys marketed to girls and boys, and these gender differences are more marked for older children than for very young children. But, I also learned that these differences are established earlier than I originally expected

Methodology: Visiting a Toy Store

To test my hypothesis, my methodology included collecting sources at the university library and running searches for sources on the Internet. My Internet and library sources helped me prepare for the empirical part of my study, which was a visit to a well-known chain toy store, where I observed the marketing of toys and how children interacted with them. Chain toy stores are arranged by children's ages because people shop with a particular child of a particular age in mind. So I began my observations in the infant and toddlers' (ages 0–3) section. Then I moved to the young children's (ages 4–6) section and finished in the preteens' (ages 7–12) section.

In each section, I spent a half hour taking careful field notes about the characteristics of toys and how they were marketed, noting (a) the name of the toy, (b) its stated or unstated purpose, and (c) any visual features such as choice of colors, decals, images of boys or girls, and other visual cues that signaled gender. In the left column of a two-column notebook, I described the features of the toys, their packaging, and the ways in which they were displayed.

Then I returned to each section of the store for an hour each to observe how children in the store interacted with the toys. In the right column of my two-column notebook, I recorded how they reacted similarly or differently to various types of toys.

When possible, I also described situations in which adults, usually parents, seemed to be encouraging or discouraging children from playing with specific kinds of toys. I listened carefully for clues from parents directing children in gendered terms (e.g., "Caleb, those ponies are for girls" or "Brittany, did you see the dolls over there?").

The purpose of the study and the hypotheses are stated near the end of the introduction.

A brief methods section is sufficient to describe how he conducted the research.

Admittedly, my methods are influenced my own cultural biases. I, too, have been raised by my culture to view some toys, colors, and images as associated with one gender or the other. For example, while observing, I assumed that the pink toys are aimed at girls, and the camouflage toys are aimed at boys. As I wrote my field notes, though, I tried to set those cultural biases aside and pay attention to children's voluntary reactions to specific toys and their displays.

> Author concedes his own potential biases, which may affect his research.

Results: Three Types of Areas in Each Section

As I entered each area of the store, it was immediately obvious which toys were directed at boys and which were directed at girls. Even from a distance, the toys were made distinct by color: the pink and purple areas were the girls' sections, while the red, black, and blue areas were the boys' sections.

> Results describe his most important findings.

Infant and Toddler (0 to 3 Years Old) Area

In the Infant and Toddler area, the boys' and girls' areas were clearly marked with signs that said "Boys" and "Girls."

In the boys' area, there were toys like construction trucks and equipment, fire engines, trains, and racecars. They were usually painted with bold and bright colors (red, blue, yellow, and orange). Human figures in this area were always male (construction workers, repairmen, firemen, police officers, etc.). Sports were a common theme, with lots of toddler-sized equipment for baseball, golf, soccer, and basketball.

In the girls' area, the products were surprisingly "mommy" or "princess" oriented—more than I expected. There were rolling "activity walkers," which looked suspiciously like baby strollers. Dolls, especially babies, were common. Animals seemed to be a common theme, especially puppies and kittens. The colors in this section were pink, purple, light blue, and yellow. These colors were generally much softer than the ones in the boys' section. All the characters were female, and most of them were wearing makeup. Pictures of princesses were common, and there was a wide assortment of cuddly, soft, and polka-dot patterned toys. There was no sports equipment in this area.

> Details in this section are used to describe what was observed.

Young Children (4 to 6 Years) Area

In the Young Children area, there were clear differences between the male and female parts of the aisle, although the learning materials were, once again, directed at both genders.

The boys' area consisted of a wide assortment of male action figures, as well as toy lions, gorillas, sharks, tigers, and aliens. I noted a wide variety of

> Author maintains an objective tone in the results section.

continued

construction and sports toys, including toolboxes and balls. There were huge, intricate play sets with cars, soldiers, pirates, and male workers (they often had tool belts or fire hats). Nearly everything was colored blue, black, orange, and other dark and bold colors. Flames were a common design on the toys for this age.

Then, as I entered the female section, I had to stop to let my eyes adjust to the change in color. Almost every toy was pink with white or purple accents. The dolls were all female and nearly always had makeup on (even the baby dolls). One toy set typified the girls' toys in this area: the "Little Mommy" toy set that comes with dolls (wearing lipstick and blush), strollers, and cribs.

Preteen (7 to 12 Years) Area

The Preteen area continued many of the patterns I noticed in the earlier areas.

The boys' area was, again, dominated by reds, blues, and blacks. Nearly everything had a "cool" or aggressive design on it, like flames or fangs. The boys' bikes had names like "Hummer," "Rhino," and "Corruption." There was a lot of sports equipment here.

The girls' area, on the other hand, consisted almost entirely of pink and purple toys covered in flowers and bubbles. The most common sight in this area was a variety of Hannah Montana toys. There were many Barbie-doll sets, one with "Up to 2000 combinations!" of clothes and shoes. There were at least 25 different cooking sets. There were bikes here as well, but they were clearly painted pink or purple for girls with flower decals, and they had names like "Belly," "Twirl," "Malibu," and "Hannah Montana." Any sports equipment in this area had pink or purple splashed on it.

Adult Redirection

I only observed a few instances in which adults seemed to be redirecting their children toward toys designed for their gender. In the Infant and Toddler area, a boy was attracted to some stuffed animals that were in the girls' section. His father asked him if he wanted to "check out" the sports equipment. In a few cases, parents entered the aisle and pointed out where their girl or boy could find the toys for them. A mother directed her young boy to a display with pirates. For the most part, though, even the youngest children seemed to go immediately to the toys that were marked for their gender. In a couple situations, young boys seemed especially eager to get out of the girls section to go over to the boys part of the aisle. I didn't notice girls feeling equally uncomfortable in the boys part of the aisle.

Discussion: Divided from the Start

Overall, I found that the differences between toys marketed to boys and girls were very distinct with few exceptions. These gender distinctions were clear even in the Infant and Toddler toys area, which I did not expect. My findings show that gender stereotypes are reinforced early and consistently in the marketing of toys.

As might have been predicted, the dolls and action figures for boys and girls were very different and clearly reinforced gender stereotypes. Baby dolls and supplies were aimed at girls, even in the toddler years. The Barbie-doll sets for preteen girls seemed to suggest that shopping and spending money on clothing, makeup, and accessories is a good thing. The dolls themselves reinforced the "skinny, blonde, big-breasted, and most often white" stereotype. Almost always, the preteen dolls and even the dolls for young children were outfitted with revealing clothes. The female characters for young children and preteens were mostly princesses and fashion dolls. The dolls (excuse me, "action figures") that represented males were all construction workers, soldiers, policemen, superheroes, firefighters, and so forth. There were no chefs, fathers, or fashion models in the boys' toys sections.

Interestingly, color seemed to be an important way to distinguish one gender's toys from the other. Pinks and purples, as expected, were used to mark products for girls. The packaging for girls' toys usually had muted, soft colors, like pastels and other homey tones. But there wasn't an equivalent exclusive color scheme for boys, except perhaps black. Red, blue, and green tended to be in the boys' area, but most girls would not have a problem with using with a blue soccer ball or wearing a red bike helmet. Black was a color that seemed exclusive to boys, but not in the same way pink marked a product for girls. This seems in line with Campenni's conclusion that feminine toys are "stereotyped more than masculine toys" (121).

Originally, when I started my research, I assumed that toys would start out mostly gender neutral and differ as children grew older. That's actually not true. Even toddler toys were clearly marked as appropriate for boys and girls. I cannot imagine that it matters to an infant boy if he plays with a pink kitten or to a toddler girl if she plays with a flame-streaked fire truck. In the marketing world of toys, however, these kinds of gendered distinctions are obviously important and parents go along with it.

I also expected to see more parental prompting about which toys were appropriate for their boys and girls. In the end, I didn't see much of that kind

> The discussion analyzes the findings and explains what they mean.

> Author discusses his main conclusions about what he observed.

continued

of behavior. The girls, even toddlers, seemed to know immediately which toys were designed for them. The boys didn't hesitate to run over to their toys either. As I mentioned before, I did notice that the boys were more distressed when they were being held up in the girls' area. It seems like they were aware that the toys in the girls' area were not for them.

Conclusions: Nurture Is Important

So, what insights can we gain into the how the differences in toys affect children's sense of gender? I don't think I resolved the nature vs. nurture debate, but I am convinced that nurture is a powerful force in determining how children figure out what a culture expects for their gender.

The main point of the report is expressed clearly.

All in all, toys reinforce gender expectations for children, probably more than most people realize. They tell little boys that they should grow up to be tough workers or sports stars, that they should love cars, trucks, sports, and anything ferocious, and that they should be aggressive and adventurous. Little girls should grow up to be clean, neat mothers, shoppers, performers, and fashion models.

However, gender is not destiny. There is somehow still room for individuality that breaks free of the stereotypes. As long as parents participate actively in the raising of their children, they can overcome the gender expectations and stereotypes of today's world.

References

List of references gives bibliographic information for everything cited in the text.

Alexander, G. M. (2003). An evolutionary perspective on sex-typed toy preferences: Pink, blue, and the brain. *Archives of Sexual Behavior, 32,* 7–14.

Ball, R. (2006). Dreaming of a pink Christmas. *The F Word: Contemporary UK Feminism.* Retrieved from http://www.thefword.org.uk/features/2006/12/pink_christmas

Blakemore, J. E., LaRue, A. A., & Olejnik, A. B. (1979). Sex-appropriate toy preference and the ability to conceptualize toys as sex-role related. *Developmental Psychology, 15,* 339–340.

Campenni, C. E. (1999). Gender stereotyping of children's toys: A comparison of parents and non-parents. *Sex Roles, 40,* 121–138.

Choi, P. (2001). Genes and gender roles: Why is the nature argument so appealing? *Sexualities, Evolution, and Gender, 3,* 279–285.

Clark, B. (2000). *Girls, boys, books, toys: Gender in children's literature and culture.* Baltimore, MD: Johns Hopkins University Press.

Lippa, R. A. (2002). *Gender, nature, and nurture.* Mahwah, NJ: Lawrence Erlbaum Associates, Inc.

Paige, J. (2008). Why action figures and dolls are bad gifts for gender
     stereotyping. Retrieved from http://www.helium.com/items/700248
     -reflections-why-action-figures-and-dolls-are-bad-gifts-for-gender
     -stereotyping
Pollitt, K. (1995, October 8). HERS: Why boys don't play with dolls. *The New
     York Times*. Retrieved from http://www.nytimes.com

Inventing Your Report's Content

When starting a research project, you first need to figure out your topic, your research question, and your hypothesis. Then you need to discover what you already know about your topic and come up with a systematic way to find out what others know. And finally, you need to use your research skills to generate findings, analyze those findings, and develop your conclusions or recommendations. In other words, much needs to happen before you sit down to draft your report.

Inquiring: Developing Your Research Question and Hypothesis

Start out by identifying your topic, angle, research question, and hypothesis.

Topic. Define your topic and then narrow it down to something you can handle in the time you have available. Reports tend to be large compared to other documents, so you may be tempted to pick a topic that is very large (e.g., violence, eating disorders, alternative energy, etc.), but these topics are way too broad. Instead, you need to choose a much narrower topic within a larger topic (e.g., recent incidents of violence on campus, how first-year college students with eating disorders adapt to dorm food, using wind energy to power your dormitory). A narrower topic will allow you to focus your research and come up with more useful results and recommendations.

Angle. The best way to narrow down your topic is to find the *angle* you want to pursue. Completely new topics are rare, but there are always new angles you can explore on existing topics. To help you find your angle, ask yourself: What has changed about this topic recently? How does this topic affect us locally?

Research Question. Now, it's time to develop your *research question*. Your research question should state your topic and identify an issue that your research will address.

As discussed in Chapter 24, "Starting Research," your research question also needs to be as focused as possible.

> **Too Broad:** Why do people eat so much fast food?
>
> **Focused Research Question:** Why do college students turn to fast food as a way to help them handle stressful situations?
>
> **Too Broad:** Why do crows behave the way they do?
>
> **Focused Research Question:** Why do crows tend to live here on campus in the winter and how can we encourage them to go somewhere else?
>
> **Too Broad:** Are children becoming more violent?
>
> **Focused Research Question:** Do violent video games cause children to act out more violently in their everyday lives?

Hypothesis. Once you have figured out your research question, you should turn it into a *hypothesis* that will guide your research. Your hypothesis is your best guess—for the moment—about how your research question will be answered.

> My hypothesis is that fast food contains ingredients like salt, protein, carbohydrates, and fat that give our bodies short-term fuel for overcoming threatening moments. This craving is due to evolution. Our minds, when anxious or stressed, start thinking about the needs of short-term survival, not long-term health.
>
> My hunch is that crows congregate on our campus in the winter because there is ample food available and sources of warmth. Also, they are intelligent birds and have strong social bonds, so campus provides a consistent safe place for them to live together through the winter.
>
> My hypothesis is that today's children may fantasize more about violence due to video games, but these games actually make children less violent because they can work through their aggression in a virtual environment.

Your hypothesis is your best guess for now, and it will probably change as you move forward with your research. You're not committed to proving it. Instead, you are going to find evidence that confirms or contradicts your hypothesis. Then you will need to revise it to fit your findings. You can turn to Chapter 24, "Starting Research," for help with creating a good hypothesis.

Inquiring: Finding Out What You Already Know

There is a good chance you already know quite a bit about your topic. That's why you or your professor chose it in the first place. So first discover what is already stored away in your gray matter about your topic.

Why Fast Food When We're Stressed?

Tastes good, so it comforts us.

Fast food has salt, protein, fat, and carbs, which we do need.

Our bodies can't tell the difference between threats that are physical and psychological, so it reacts to stress the same way by seeking fuel.

Bodies need quick fuel to handle stressful situations.

Survival now, deal with consequences later.

Survival requires more short-term fuel, so the body expects to burn it off.

Your body is telling you to eat!

It's in your head. Your body isn't hungry. It's just getting ready for "fight or flight." It's anticipating that you're going to need to move quickly.

Constant stress causes obesity, which can lead to diabetes (?).

Refined foods, like sugar and white flour, are like rocket fuel. They are easier to process, and our bodies are very efficient at using and storing them.

Lack of sleep puts stress on the body, causing us to crave junk food.

High-stress situations, like exams, cause us to look for "comfort food." Mentally, an exam is treated as a threat, much like a fight with another person or getting away from a dangerous animal.

Ironically, the fast food leads to higher stress, because the temporary high turns into a crash. That's fine in the wild, where threats tend to be brief. ("Oh good, you survived. Now rest for a moment.")

But, in the modern world, stress can continue for a long time, so more junk food is needed to satisfy the craving and avoid the crash.

We need to plan our eating for stressful situations.

What kinds of healthy foods will help us cope without also adding to our waists?

Exercise might be a way to satisfy that "fight or flight" urge and overcome stressful moments.

Issue 1: Craving these ingredients is a natural response.

Issue 2: Body treats stressful situations as physical threat.

Issue 3: Desire to "fight or flight" causes cravings.

Issue 4: Planning eating will help avoid coping with junk food.

Issue 5: Exercise helps cope with fight or flight feeling.

FIGURE 13.1 Brainstorming on Your Topic

A brainstorming list is a great way to put your ideas on the screen or a piece of paper. It will also help you identify the two to five major issues you will probably explore as you do research for your report.

Begin by brainstorming about your topic (Figure 13.1). Put your topic at the top of a piece of paper. Then list everything you know about that topic. Do this for five minutes or more. When you are finished brainstorming, identify two to five major *issues* on your list that you could explore further in your research. Circle these issues or make a special mark next to them. At this point, you could do some freewriting or Internet research to see which issue might make a good topic for your report.

Researching: Creating a Research Plan

When you are finished writing down what you already know, you should have a good idea about where your research project is going. Now it's time to figure out how you are going to do your research (i.e., your research methods).

You will need to develop a step-by-step plan for finding information. A concept map is an especially helpful tool for developing your research methods. It will help you figure out the steps you need to take when you are doing your research (Figure 13.2). You can map out your research methods like this:

1. In the middle of the screen or page, write down your research question.

2. Write down the two to five *major steps* you will need to take to answer that research question. Circle them.

3. For each major step, write down two to five *minor steps* that you would need to take to achieve that major step. Circle them and draw lines to connect them to the major steps.

The key question you should keep asking yourself is, "How?" "*How* am I going to answer that question? *How* am I going to find that information? *How* am I going to generate that data?" To help you answer these questions, you might turn to Chapter 24, "Starting Research," for ideas about doing your research.

You can then turn your concept map into an outline, as shown in Figure 13.3. Your methodology should include all three kinds of sources (i.e., online, print, and empirical) so you can "triangulate" the facts you discover while doing your research. Triangulation, as discussed in Chapter 25, "Finding Sources and Collecting

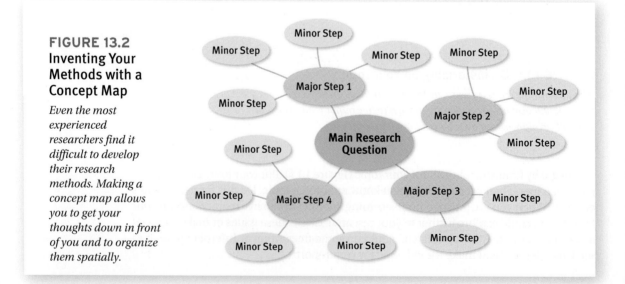

**FIGURE 13.2
Inventing Your
Methods with a
Concept Map**

*Even the most
experienced
researchers find it
difficult to develop
their research
methods. Making a
concept map allows
you to get your
thoughts down in front
of you and to organize
them spatially.*

Research Question: Why Do Stressed Out People Eat So Much Fast Food?

Major Step 1: Search for Online Sources

- Review hospital Web sites for information about fast food
- Look on *WebMD* and other medical Web sites
- Find documentaries about fast food at library or through Netflix
- Search fast food companies' Web sites for nutrition information

Major Step 2: Find Print Sources

- Visit the Student Health Center to collect pamphlets on stress and diet
- Use *Readers' Guide* to find articles in health magazines
- Find articles in medical journals at library
- Check out nutrition and health textbooks in library
- Go to bookstore to browse books that discuss stress and food

Major Step 3: Do Empirical Research

- Interview nutritionist here on campus
- Create survey for college students
- Observe stressed people at the Student Union
- Interview spokesperson for McDonalds, Taco Bell, or Arby's

FIGURE 13.3
Outlining a Methodology

A concept map can easily be turned into an outline like the one shown here. List your major steps and then arrange the minor steps beneath them.

Information," is a way to cross-reference your sources to determine the strength and the usefulness of the information they offer.

Researching: Gathering Sources and Revisiting Your Hypothesis

Your research will inevitably turn up new ideas and concepts that you didn't know about when you started the project. That's good. When doing research for a report, your objective is *not* to simply find sources that prove what you believed at the start of the project. Instead, your objective is to do open-ended inquiry into your topic, letting the facts *lead* you to answers.

As you do research for your report, you will probably find information and facts that challenge your hypothesis. That's not a bad thing. Your original hypothesis was only your best guess when you began your research. Now that you know more about your topic, you should be willing to modify or even completely change your hypothesis to fit the information you've collected.

Good research is a cyclical process (Figure 13.4, page 300). You should keep returning to your hypothesis to see if you have changed your mind about how you will answer your research question. Your ideas will evolve as you figure things out. Eventually, as you finish doing your research, your hypothesis will solidify and become the main point (or thesis) of your report. At that point, you can start drafting your report with confidence.

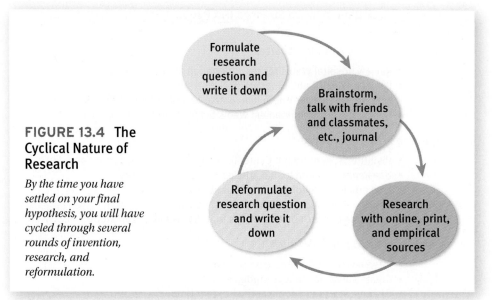

FIGURE 13.4 The Cyclical Nature of Research

By the time you have settled on your final hypothesis, you will have cycled through several rounds of invention, research, and reformulation.

Organizing and Drafting Your Report

The best way to draft a report is to write each major section separately. If you draft each section one at a time, you will avoid feeling overwhelmed by the size of the document.

Executive Summary or Abstract

Executive summaries usually devote a small paragraph to each major section of the report. Abstracts tend to be only one paragraph, devoting a sentence or two to each section of the report. The executive summary or abstract should be written after you have finished drafting the rest of the report.

Introduction

An introduction in a report will typically make up to five moves.

State the topic. Tell your readers what the report is about.

State the purpose. In one or two sentences, explain what the report is going to do or achieve.

State the main point. State the overall conclusion of your report (i.e., what you discovered in your research).

Provide background information. Briefly, give readers enough historical information about your topic to help them understand it.

Explain why the topic is important to readers. Tell readers why they should care about this topic.

These moves can be made in just about any order, and they are not all necessary. Minimally, your introduction should tell your readers the report's topic, purpose, and main point.

Methods Section

Explain your research methods step by step in a way that would allow your readers to replicate your research. Each major step will usually receive at least one paragraph of coverage (Figure 13.5). Explain *how* you did each step and *why* you did it that way.

Findings or Results Section

Choose the two to five most important findings or results from your research. In larger reports, each major finding should at least receive its own paragraph. Your job in this section is to describe what you found. Where possible, use graphics, such as charts, graphs, and tables, to present the data you've collected.

Discussion Section

Discuss your results and what they mean. Show how your results answer your research question. Researchers often boil their results down to two to five "conclusions." In most reports, each conclusion will need a paragraph to discuss how it supports the hypothesis and its implications. As shown in Figure 13.6 on page 302, the

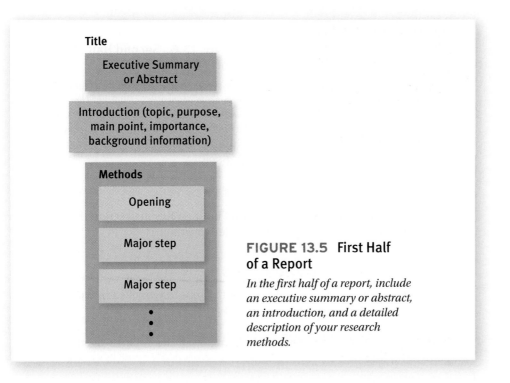

FIGURE 13.5 First Half of a Report

In the first half of a report, include an executive summary or abstract, an introduction, and a detailed description of your research methods.

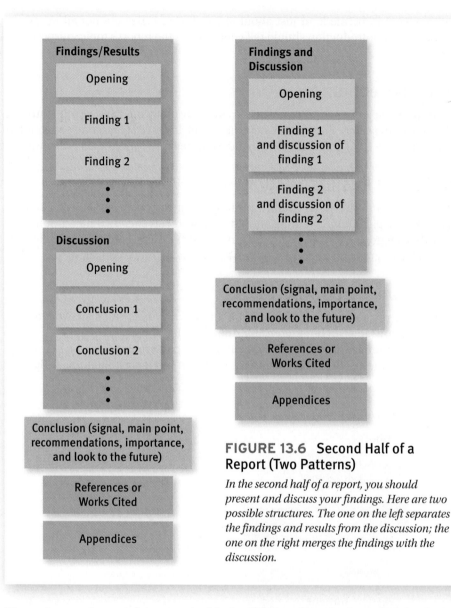

FIGURE 13.6   Second Half of a Report (Two Patterns)

In the second half of a report, you should present and discuss your findings. Here are two possible structures. The one on the left separates the findings and results from the discussion; the one on the right merges the findings with the discussion.

Discussion section can be merged with the Findings/Results section if the findings and discussion of those findings can be handled together.

Conclusion/Recommendations

The conclusion of your report should be brief. A report's conclusion typically makes all or some of the following moves.

Restate your main point. One more time, state the report's overall main point or finding.

Make two to five recommendations. Using the results of your research, make some recommendations about what should be done about this issue. Reports often present these recommendations in a list.

Reemphasize the importance of the topic. Explain briefly why your readers should care about this topic and take action.

Look to the future. Reports often end with a small paragraph that describes what will happen in the near and distant future.

Your conclusion should be brief, perhaps only two or three paragraphs. Your goal is to leave your readers with a clear sense of what you discovered and what should be done about it.

References or Works Cited

Provide bibliographic information for any sources you have cited. For APA style, they should be listed under the title "References." For MLA style, call them "Works Cited." Turn to Chapters 27 and 28 for help with your references.

Appendices

In the appendices, put any other materials you collected or created such as surveys and questionnaires. Appendices might also contain data charts, graphs, previous reports, or other documents that your readers might find useful.

When drafting, it may help to draft larger sections in the report as separate documents, each with their own opening paragraph and a few body paragraphs. Figure 13.6 shows a couple of different patterns that will help you organize the more complicated sections of your report.

Choosing an Appropriate Style

Reports usually sound neutral and objective. Your readers expect you to give them information in a straightforward way. As a result, reports are usually written in a plain style. Here are some plain style techniques that work particularly well with the report genre.

Strike an Objective, Down-to-Business Tone. Write efficiently and authoritatively and focus on presenting information to your readers as clearly as possible. You should let the information be the main attraction of the report, not you. Occasionally, you might use the first person point of view (e.g., "I distributed the questionnaire to 35 students" or "We ran the experiment again") but don't make yourself the center of the report. Try to stay in the background as much as possible by minimizing your use of the first person point of view.

Use Top-Down Paragraphs. Consistently put each paragraph's main claim or statement in the first or second sentence of the paragraph (i.e, the topic sentence). Then use the remainder of the paragraph to prove or support that claim or statement. Putting topic sentences at the top of each paragraph will help your readers locate the most important information. Moreover, if your readers only have limited time to skim your report, they can get an overall understanding by reading only the topic sentences.

Use Plain Sentences. Your sentences should be simple and straightforward. In each sentence, move your subject (i.e., what the sentence is about) to an early position, and use active verbs where possible. Look for ways to minimize your use of excessive prepositional phrases. Make sure sentences are "breathing length"—not too long to be said out loud in one breath.

Minimize Passive Voice as Much as Possible. Passive voice is common in reports (e.g., "These field observations were reinforced by our survey."), especially in scientific reports. However, active voice is often stronger and easier to read, so you should look for places where you can turn passive sentences into active sentences. Active voice will help your readers understand who or what did the action (e.g., "The survey results confirm these field observations.").

Get Rid of Nominalizations. Because reports are usually technical, they sometimes overuse nominalizations, which can cloud the meaning of sentences. A nominalization happens when the action in the sentence appears as a noun rather than a verb. *Hint:* Look for words that end in "-tion."

> **Nominalization:** This report offers a presentation of our findings on the consumption of fast food by Clemson students.
>
> **Revised:** This report presents our findings on the amount of fast food consumed by Clemson students.

> **Nominalization:** We make a recommendation that stressed-out students get exercise instead of turning to junk foods that harm their health.
>
> **Revised:** We recommend that stressed-out students get exercise instead of turning to junk foods that harm their health.

Nominalizations make your writing less clear because they hide the action in a sentence. If you move the action into the sentence's verb, your meaning will be much clearer to your readers.

Define Jargon and Other Technical Terms. In research reports, jargon words and technical terms are common and often unavoidable. When you use a jargon word or a technical term for the first time, give your readers a sentence definition or parenthetical definition to clarify its meaning.

Sentence Definition: Low-density lipoprotein cholesterol (LDL) is a waxy substance that causes fat to build up in the walls of larger arteries.

Parenthetical Definition: The extreme amount of salt in most fast food can cause hypertension, a condition in which a person's blood pressure rises to an abnormally high level and potentially does damage to the heart.

In moderation, jargon and technical terms are fine. Just define these words so your readers understand what you are talking about.

In Chapter 16, "Choosing a Style," you can find additional helpful advice about how to write clearly and plainly. Plain style will make your report sound authoritative and objective.

Designing Your Report

Reports usually aren't flashy documents, but that doesn't mean they should look unattractive and difficult to read. Your report's page design and graphics will often determine whether your readers actually read your report and whether they can quickly find the information they are looking for.

Design a "Raidable" Page Layout. People rarely read reports from front to back. Instead, they "raid" reports for the information they need. So use clear headings to highlight key sections and important information. Put critical pieces of information in lists, tables, or graphics to make them easy to find. Figure 13.7 shows

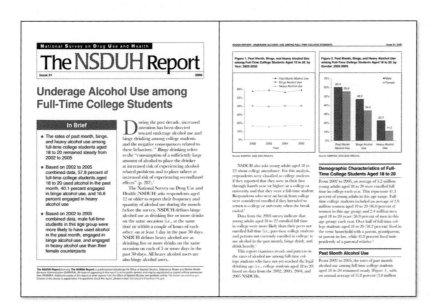

FIGURE 13.7
A Raidable Page Layout

The design of a report needs to be attractive and accessible to readers. In this report, the authors use headings, graphics, color, and boxes to highlight important information.

a report that uses an attractive, raidable page layout. The headings are easy to locate, and the graphics support the written text. The use of color attracts the reader to the text. In other words, there are plenty of *access points* to begin reading this document.

Use Meaningful Headings. Your report's headings should give readers a clear idea about what is in each section of the report. You don't need to use *Methods, Results, Discussion,* and *Conclusion* as headings. Instead, you can give readers a sense of what they will find in each section with descriptive and interesting headings:

> Our Research Methods: Going Undercover in the World of Fast Food
>
> Our Findings: Stress Drives People to Fast Food
>
> Our Recommendations: Battling the Expanding Waistline with Good Information

Use Tables, Graphs, and Charts to Reinforce Written Text. Where possible, find ways to put your data and other facts into tables, graphs, and charts. Your graphics should reinforce the written text, not replace it. Also, make sure you refer to the graphics by number (e.g., "See Figure 2"), so readers know when to look for them.

Use Photographs to Illustrate or Emphasize Key Points. With the availability of digital cameras, photographs are now common in research reports. If you find something difficult to describe, perhaps you can take a picture of it and add it to your report. Make sure you refer to the photograph in the text and include a title and caption.

Insert a Table of Contents. If your report is over six pages long, insert a table of contents to help readers see the big picture and locate specific information easily. Most word-processing programs will automatically generate a table of contents if you use the Styles feature.

Whatever you do, keep your paragraphs brief and to the point and use headings and graphics to give your readers access points into the text. Otherwise, they just won't read your report. Designing a report does not take long, and your readers will appreciate a document that is attractive and easy to use.

Revising and Editing Your Report

Because research reports tend to be large documents, the revising and editing phase is critical to improving your report's quality. Here are some guidelines that will help you revise and edit your document:

Clarify the Purpose of the Report. In your introduction, make sure your purpose is stated clearly and prominently. Does this statement clearly tell your readers what the report will do? Now that you are finished drafting, would it be possible to state your purpose in an even clearer, more direct way? Did your purpose evolve while you were drafting your report? If so, rewrite your purpose to reflect what your report actually achieves.

Look for Gaps in Content. Search out places where you are making any unsupported statements or claims. Each major point needs to be backed up with some evidence that you have drawn from online, print, or empirical sources. If you find a gap in your support, look in your notes for evidence to fill that gap. If you don't have any evidence, you need to do more research or you will have to remove that statement or claim.

Find Nonessential Information That Can Be Cut. Include only need-to-know information and locate any places where your report goes off topic. Keep in mind that you probably found more information than you need. Not all of that material needs to go into your report. So slash any information that does not help you support or prove your major points in the report.

Pay Special Attention to Your Report's Paragraphs. Strong paragraphs are essential in a report because they help people scan and read quickly (reports are rarely read for enjoyment). Spend some extra time making sure you use good topic sentences early in your paragraphs. Then improve the readability of your paragraphs by weaving their sentences together better.

Review Your Recommendations. Your recommendations are key to the success of your report. So make sure your recommendations follow logically from your findings and discussion. In other words, don't recommend something unless your report gives clear evidence to support that action.

Proofread Carefully. Reports are typically large, complex documents, so there are plenty of opportunities for typos, garbled sentences, spelling mistakes, and grammatical errors. Proofread carefully. Read your report out loud to help you find errors and weak sentences. Ask your friends to read your report carefully. Proofreading is especially important because errors in your report will signal shoddy research to your readers. If they find errors, they will be less likely to trust your findings.

Yes, time is short when you reach the revision and editing phase. The deadline is here. But don't skimp on revising and editing your report. Your hard work doing research, drafting, and designing will be undermined if your report isn't thoroughly revised.

The Brief

A brief is a short report used to inform an organization's management or clients about an important issue. The ability to write *briefs* and present *briefings* is a valuable skill in the workplace, and it's becoming increasingly important in college as well.

Briefs are becoming more popular in advanced college courses and on the Internet. Professors in management and engineering courses are asking for briefs from student teams working on projects. News Web sites publish briefs that offer factual information on important stories. For example, *Slate.com* calls its brief the "Explainer." Think tanks, like the Pew Foundation and the Brookings Institution, publish briefs on their Web sites that are designed to influence public policy.

Here is how to write a brief:

Introduce your topic and state your purpose. Your brief's introduction should identify the topic of the brief and tell readers that you are explaining the topic or giving an update on it.

State the facts. As objectively as possible, state the facts that you have collected. You should cite any sources you have collected, but you don't need to explain fully how you collected the facts you are providing.

Add a graphic. If possible, put your data into a graph, chart, or table. Add a photograph if it would help illustrate your point.

Discuss why these facts are important. Relate the facts to current trends and events. Discuss the facts in measurable terms by describing potential costs and benefits.

Forecast the importance of the issue. Conclude your brief by describing the future of this issue for readers. If these trends continue, what will happen in the near and distant future? How will the situation change?

WRITE your own brief. Choose an issue on your campus that interests you. Write a two-page brief in which you objectively explore this issue. Keep your opinions to a minimum.

Twitter and Status Updating
Amanda Lenhart and Susannah Fox

In the past three years, developments in social networking and internet applications have begun providing internet users with more opportunities for sharing short updates about themselves, their lives, and their whereabouts online. Users may post messages about their status, their moods, their location and other tidbits on social networks and blogging sites, or on applications for sending out short messages to networks of friends like Twitter, Yammer and others.

Introduction states topic and offers background information.

As of December 2008, 11% of online American adults said they used a service like Twitter or another service that allowed them to share updates about themselves or to see the updates of others.

Results of study are stated objectively.

Twitter and similar services have been most avidly embraced by young adults. Nearly one in five (19%) online adults ages 18 and 24 have ever used Twitter and its ilk, as have 20% of online adults 25 to 34. Use of these services drops off steadily after age 35 with 10% of 35 to 44 year olds and 5% of 45 to 54 year olds using Twitter. The decline is even more stark among older internet users; 4% of 55 to 64 year olds and 2% of those 65 and older use Twitter.

The use of Twitter is highly intertwined with the use of other social media; both blogging and social network use increase the likelihood that an individual also uses Twitter. Twitter users and status updaters are also a mobile bunch; as a group they are much more likely to be using wireless technologies—laptops, handhelds and cell phones—for internet access, or cell phones for text messaging.

Overall, Twitter users engage with news and own technology at the same rates as other internet users, but the ways in which they use the technology—to communicate, gather and share information—reveals their affinity for mobile, untethered and social opportunities for interaction. Moreover, Twitter as an application allows for and enhances these opportunities, so it is not so surprising that users would engage in these kinds of activities and also be drawn to an online application that expands those opportunities.

Conclusion states why facts are important.

Here are some quick strategies to get you going on that report.

DEVELOP Your Research Question and Hypothesis

Write down an interesting research question about your topic—a question you would like to answer with some research. Then turn that question into a hypothesis (your best guess about how that research question will be answered).

FIND Out What You Already Know

Use prewriting tools to get your ideas out on the screen or a piece of paper. Star or highlight your best ideas. Then share your ideas with your friends and classmates.

FIND Out What Others Know

Develop a research plan that uses a combination of online, print, and empirical sources to find information. Interview experts on campus to find out more.

REVISIT Your Hypothesis

After you have done a good amount of research, look at your hypothesis again. Does it need to be modified or refined?

ORGANIZE and Draft Your Report

Organize your draft into sections and write one section at a time. The most common organization for a report is this: Executive Summary/Abstract, Introduction, Methods, Findings/Results, Discussion, Conclusion/Recommendations, References, and Appendices.

CHOOSE an Appropriate Style

Reports are almost always written in plain style, because this style sounds objective and authoritative. Use plain sentences and top-down paragraphs with solid topic sentences. The best style is one that sounds neutral and objective.

DESIGN the Document

Create an attractive and accessible page layout. Use active headings to help readers locate important information. Put your data and facts into tables, graphs, and charts, so your readers can see how they support the written text.

REVISE and Edit

Revise headings so they clearly state the points you want to make. Edit your paragraphs to make them easy to scan.

My Own Private B.O.

DAVE JOHNS

In this research report, Dave Johns uses science to test whether it is possible to use an "odorprint" to identify people, especially criminals and terrorists. Johns uses himself as a test subject, taking his and other family members' body odor to a scientist for testing. Pay attention to how Johns uses and bends the report genre to answer his research question.

This month the Department of Homeland Security announced plans to study the potential of body odor as a means of identifying criminals and figuring out when they're lying. The work will expand on basic research into the chemistry of the so-called human "odorprint," which scientists say is as distinct as DNA. At first whiff, the notion that individual B.O. is as special as a snowflake sounds like a rotten joke. But body odor has proved its value as a biometric for seven centuries, ever since man first started hunting bad guys with the original B.O. detector: the bloodhound.

While dogs certainly deserve a long scratch behind the ears for clueing us in to the odorprint, their days as our elite odor gumshoes may be numbered. (Canines are not as reliable as we once thought: Although the best can match scents with 85 percent accuracy, poorly trained or feeble-nosed dogs may do no better than chance.) Now scientists are figuring out their own, more accurate ways to scrutinize an odorprint. Research on electronic noses may also reveal secrets about how humans recognize each other by B.O. We know, for example, that mothers can pick out their babies by smell, and babies their mothers. Scientists call this the "armpit effect" and suspect that many other animals recognize kin by comparing body odors. This got me wondering: Could the techniques of modern B.O. analysis be used like DNA testing to reconstruct family relationships from drops of sweat? Could this analysis work on my own family? I asked one of the top researchers in the field of criminal odorprinting to help me find out.

Florida International University chemist Kenneth Furton studies the smells that might be of greatest use in a crime investigation. These, he says, are the ones that come from the hands. (Murderers rarely wield weapons in their underarms.) For the last five years, Furton has been cataloging the many chemicals that compose hand scent, including odoriferous acids, alcohols, aldehydes, hydrocarbons, esters, ketones, and nitrogen-containing compounds.

It's a rich brew, but hardly the rankest in the human odor-sphere. Hands don't contain apocrine glands, the funky B.O. factories that reside in the armpit and groin and broadcast sexual status updates. But they do have tons of eccrine sweat glands, used for thermoregulation, and oil-producing sebaceous glands, which generate their own odor signatures. These aromas mix with volatiles from our dead skin cells and exhaled breath before wafting in a plume of body heat.

I challenged Furton to construct my family tree based only on data from our sweaty hands. He had never attempted such an analysis before and made no claim that it would be possible. Yet he agreed to give it a shot. I dragooned my mother, father, Uncle Merritt, and identical-twin first cousins Ricky and Johnny into the experiment. 5

Odor collection proceeded according to protocol in a pair of secure, television-equipped locations. In Virginia, my mother, father, and I meticulously washed our hands without soap and then waved them around until dry. Next, we rubbed our hands to lather them up with sweat and then clasped them around a piece of gauze. For 10 minutes, we held our hands before us, as if in prayer, while our B.O. impregnated the cloth and we watched *Rachel Maddow*. I am told that during odor collection in California, my uncle and cousins took in a crappy Golden State Warriors game. Three scent samples were obtained from each person and then shipped to Furton's grad student Davia Hudson in Florida, who ran them through a gas chromatograph and mass spectrometer.

The results were intriguing, though hardly Nobel-worthy. Hudson said our odor profiles were "very similar" but that there was "low reproducibility" among the samples collected from each individual, likely due to contamination. So she discarded one outlier from each subject. Even still, one of the "good" samples collected from my mother came up 94 percent similar to one from her nephew Johnny, which didn't make much sense. The two of them were closer in scent than Johnny and his identical-twin brother Ricky. (Twins should smell alike.)

Still, to my eyes the family odor tree that emerged smelled like home. According to the data, I shared my dad's aroma, with similar ratios of citrus and tallow that surely reflected our shared heritage chomping pork-rib sandwiches. The clones, Ricky and Johnny, were quite alike but for a burnt note that lingered around Ricky, perhaps a side effect of his weakness for Caramel Frappuccinos. In general, the males had similar odor profiles, with the exception of my uncle, who seemed to come from another B.O. planet. He excreted the rudest bouquet—subtly oily, pungent, and sweet—which jibed with behavioral data from

the dinner table. The only person who showed a hint of similarity with him—in one sample—was his sister, my mother, who is, after all, more like him than she'd like to admit.

The B.O. wheel

They say you are what you eat, and when it comes to B.O., it's true. Body odor can be heavily colored by diet and also by the fragrant beauty products that we use. For this reason, one of the biggest challenges faced by odorprint researchers is to ferret out which chemicals constitute the "primary odor"—the root B.O. bouillon that can't be altered by diet and perfume. When I ran the results of my family experiment past George Preti, a smell researcher whose odorprint work has been funded by the Defense Advanced Research Projects Agency, his main criticism was that several of the odorants used to build my family tree were probably environmental. For example, my cousin Ricky and my uncle both had linalool on their hands, a ubiquitous fragrance compound used in soaps, shampoos, and detergents. But Preti conceded that the notion that I might smell more like my dad than my mom was not outlandish. Unlike genetics, he said, odor inheritance is "not a 50-50 mix."

It may not be surprising to learn that [10] B.O. does indeed vary by gender—a recent study claimed that men smell like cheese while women smell of grapefruit or onions. It also reflects age: Preti's lab has found several odorants that increase with advancing years, such as the aldehyde nonanal. (This is not the molecule others have implicated in "old person smell.") There may even be racial differences in primary odors: Asians, for example, have fewer apocrine sweat glands than blacks or whites. In a new book about scent called *Headspace*, Amber Marks reports that in the 1990s a British electronic-nose company was approached by South African police and asked for the "odor signature" of black people. The company refused, but an employee told Marks that they could have derived such an ethnic odor-type if they'd tried.

If the prospect of a racial B.O. taxonomy gives you the willies, the history of smell discrimination offers no comfort. In the 19th century, Finns, Eskimos, Jews, and others were judged by vigilant European doctors to possess a characteristic unpleasant smell. (Asian docs thought Europeans were the foul ones.) Blacks were thought to be at greater risk of shark attack due to their "ammoniacal" odor. Blondes were said to smell "musky." The old, like "dry leaves." Lunatics, "fetid and penetrating." In 1829, a French scientist proposed a new smell-based forensic identification method but ran into problems discriminating dark-haired women from fair-haired men. Today we know these odor classes are absurd; humans can't even smell the difference between their own B.O. and that of a chimpanzee. But there are some broad patterns to B.O. flavor.

In any event, a new era of odor profiling may soon be upon us. Furton foresees a day when crime scene odor evidence might help cops establish a dossier: fiftysomething Irish-American male, wears Axe body spray, loves garlic. If cops had a suspect, they could trail him and covertly collect an odor sample using a scent capture contraption without touching him or asking permission.

While for centuries our B.O. obsession has focused on preventing its unwelcome trespass, today's worry may be in protecting our right to "odor privacy." For one thing, a body smell may convey private medical information: Both Preti and Furton are seeking the smell signatures of cancer and diabetes, and Furton is studying the odor differences between depressed and nondepressed individuals. Unlike DNA-rich blood or saliva, scent cannot be withheld from authorities because—alas—there is no "off button" for B.O. And, indeed, scent surveillance is already in use. In 2007, *Der Spiegel* reported that German authorities had collected scent samples from activists in advance of the G8 summit.

Privacy hurdles aside, the odor chemists' greatest challenge may be in overcoming our mistrust of smell. Odors can linger, sometimes for days, and they are invisible, so it can be hard to pin down their origins. An old grade-school maxim—"he who smelt it dealt it"—illustrates the risks in making accusations based on olfactory evidence. At this point, it's not clear that odor science has the tools to move past this folk wisdom.

A CLOSER LOOK AT
My Own Private B.O.

1. Where exactly does Johns identify his research question in this report? Locate the exact sentence where he states this question.

2. The Methods section in this report is rather informal. Nevertheless, Johns does describe the methods he and a scientist used to answer the basic research question. What are the steps in Johns's research methodology and where does he explain them?

3. How does Johns inject humor into this report? Find five places where he says something that is meant to be funny. Why are these comments or observations funny? What sets them apart from the other sentences in this report?

IDEAS FOR
Writing

1. How do you feel about using body odor as a way to identify people? Each day, it seems like scientists are coming up with new ways to find more out about you, to the point of perhaps invading your privacy. Write a position paper in which you argue for or against using this kind of technology to gather information on people and to identify them.

2. Write a brief profile of a place, using senses other than sight. What does this place smell like? What are some sounds you associate with this place? What kinds of textures or even tastes are unique? Your profile should treat this place almost as a person, using all your senses except sight to describe it to someone else.

Report of the APA Task Force on the Sexualization of Girls: Executive Summary

EILEEN L. ZUBRIGGEN, REBECCA L. COLLINS, SHARON LAMB, TONI-ANN ROBERTS, DEBORAH L. TOLMAN, L. MONIQUE WARD, AND JEANNE BLAKE

This report was published by the American Psychological Association (APA). It offers a broad review of research done on portrayals of girls in the media. The report's methodology describes how the researchers analyzed a variety of articles on this important and complex topic. We have included only the executive summary here. Pay attention to how it follows the report genre pattern and uses an objective style.

Report of the Task Force on the Sexualization of Girls

Executive Summary

Journalists, child advocacy organizations, parents, and psychologists have argued that the sexualization of girls is a broad and increasing problem and is harmful to girls. The APA Task Force on the Sexualization of Girls was formed in response to these expressions of public concern.

APA has long been involved in issues related to the impact of media content on children. In 1994, APA adopted a policy resolution on Violence in Mass Media, which updated and expanded an earlier resolution on televised violence. In 2004, the APA Task Force on Advertising and Children produced a report examining broad issues related to advertising to children. That report provided recommendations to restrict advertising that is primarily directed at young children and to include developmentally appropriate disclaimers in advertising, as well as recommendations regarding research, applied psychology, industry practices, media literacy, advertising, and schools. In 2005, APA adopted the policy resolution on Violence in Video Games and Interactive Media, which documented the negative impact of exposure to violent interactive media on children and youth and called for the reduction of violence in these media. These resolutions and reports addressed how violent media and advertising affect children and youth, but they did not address sexualization.

The APA Task Force on the Sexualization of Girls was tasked with examining the psychological theory, research, and clinical experience addressing the sexualization of girls via media and other cultural messages, including the prevalence of these messages and their impact on girls and the role and impact of race/ethnicity and socioeconomic status. The task force was charged with producing a report, including recommendations for research, practice, education and training, policy, and public awareness.

This report examines and summarizes psychological theory, research, and clinical experience addressing the sexualization of girls. The report (a) defines sexualization; (b) examines the prevalence and provides examples of sexualization in society and in cultural institutions, as well as interpersonally and intrapsychically; (c) evaluates the evidence suggesting that sexualization has negative consequences for girls and for the rest of society; and (d) describes positive alternatives that may help counteract the influence of sexualization.

There are several components to sexualization, and these set it apart from healthy sexuality. Sexualization occurs when

- a person's value comes only from his or her sexual appeal or behavior, to the exclusion of other characteristics;
- a person is held to a standard that equates physical attractiveness (narrowly defined) with being sexy;
- a person is sexually objectified—that is, made into a thing for others' sexual use, rather than seen as a person with the capacity for independent action and decision making; and/or
- sexuality is inappropriately imposed upon a person.

All four conditions need not be present; any one is an indication of sexualization. The fourth condition (the inappropriate imposition of sexuality) is especially relevant to children. Anyone (girls, boys, men, women) can be sexualized. But when children are imbued with adult sexuality, it is often imposed upon them rather than chosen by them. Self-motivated sexual exploration, on the other hand, is not sexualization by our definition, nor is age-appropriate exposure to information about sexuality.

Evidence for the Sexualization of Girls

Virtually every media form studied provides ample evidence of the sexualization of women, including television, music videos, music lyrics, movies, magazines, sports media, video games, the Internet, and advertising (e.g., Gow, 1996; Grauerholz & King, 1997; Krassas, Blauwkamp, & Wesselink, 2001, 2003; Lin, 1997; Plous & Neptune, 1997; Vincent, 1989; Ward, 1995). Some studies have examined forms of media that are especially popular with children and adolescents, such as video games and teen-focused magazines.

1

In study after study, findings have indicated that women more often than men are portrayed in a sexual manner (e.g., dressed in revealing clothing, with bodily postures or facial expressions that imply sexual readiness) and are objectified (e.g., used as a decorative object, or as body parts rather than a whole person). In addition, a narrow (and unrealistic) standard of physical beauty is heavily emphasized. These are the models of femininity presented for young girls to study and emulate.

In some studies, the focus was on the sexualization of female characters across all ages, but most focused specifically on young adult women. Although few studies examined the prevalence of sexualized portrayals of girls in particular, those that have been conducted found that such sexualization does occur and may be increasingly common. For example, O'Donohue, Gold, and McKay (1997) coded advertisements over a 40-year period in five magazines targeted to men, women, or a general adult readership. Although relatively few (1.5%) of the ads portrayed children in a sexualized manner, of those that did, 85% sexualized girls rather than boys. Furthermore, the percentage of sexualizing ads increased over time.

Although extensive analyses documenting the sexualization of girls, in particular, have yet to be conducted, individual examples can easily be found. These include advertisements (e.g., the Skechers "naughty and nice" ad that featured Christina Aguilera dressed as a schoolgirl in pigtails, with her shirt unbuttoned, licking a lollipop), dolls (e.g., Bratz dolls dressed in sexualized clothing such as miniskirts, fishnet stockings, and feather boas), clothing (thongs sized for 7- to 10-year-olds, some printed with slogans such as "wink wink"), and television programs (e.g., a televised fashion show in which adult models in lingerie were presented as young girls). Research documenting the pervasiveness and influence of such products and portrayals is sorely needed.

Societal messages that contribute to the sexualization of girls come not only from media and merchandise but also through girls' interpersonal relationships (e.g., with parents, teachers, and peers; Brown & Gilligan, 1992). Parents may contribute to sexualization in a number of ways. For example, parents may convey the message that maintaining an attractive physical appearance is the most important goal for

girls. Some may allow or encourage plastic surgery to help girls meet that goal. Research shows that teachers sometimes encourage girls to play at being sexualized adult women (Martin, 1988) or hold beliefs that girls of color are "hypersexual" and thus unlikely to achieve academic success (Rolón-Dow, 2004). Both male and female peers have been found to contribute to the sexualization of girls—girls by policing each other to ensure conformance with standards of thinness and sexiness (Eder, 1995; Nichter, 2000) and boys by sexually objectifying and harassing girls. Finally, at the extreme end, parents, teachers, and peers, as well as others (e.g., other family members, coaches, or strangers) sometimes sexually abuse, assault, prostitute, or traffic girls, a most destructive form of sexualization.

If girls purchase (or ask their parents to purchase) products and clothes designed to make them look physically appealing and sexy, and if they style their identities after the sexy celebrities who populate their cultural landscape, they are, in effect, sexualizing themselves. Girls also sexualize themselves when they think of themselves in objectified terms. Psychological researchers have identified *self-objectification* as a key process whereby girls learn to think of and treat their own bodies as objects of others' desires (Frederickson & Roberts, 1997; McKinley & Hyde, 1996). In self-objectification, girls internalize an observer's perspective on their physical selves and learn to treat themselves as objects to be looked at and evaluated for their appearance. Numerous studies have documented the presence of self-objectification in women more than in men. Several studies have also documented this phenomenon in adolescent and preadolescent girls (McConnell, 2001; Slater & Tiggemann, 2002).

Consequences of the Sexualization of Girls

Psychology offers several theories to explain how the sexualization of girls and women could influence girls' well-being. Ample evidence testing these theories indicates that sexualization has negative effects in a variety of domains, including cognitive functioning, physical and mental health, sexuality, and attitudes and beliefs.

Although most of these studies have been conducted on women in late adolescence (i.e., college age), findings are likely to generalize to younger adolescents and to girls, who may be even more strongly affected because their sense of self is still being formed.

Cognitive and Emotional Consequences

Cognitively, self-objectification has been repeatedly shown to detract from the ability to concentrate and focus one's attention, thus leading to impaired performance on mental activities such as mathematical computations or logical reasoning (Frederickson, Roberts, Noll, Quinn, & Twenge, 1998; Gapinski, Brownell, & LaFrance, 2003; Hebl, King, & Lin, 2004). One study demonstrated this fragmenting quite vividly (Fredrickson et al., 1998). While alone in a dressing room, college students were asked to try on and evaluate either a swimsuit or a sweater. While they waited for 10 minutes wearing the garment, they completed a math test. The results revealed that young women in swimsuits performed significantly worse on the math problems than did those wearing sweaters. No differences were found for young men. In other words, thinking about the body and comparing it to sexualized cultural ideals disrupted mental capacity. In the emotional domain, sexualization and objectification undermine confidence in and comfort with one's own body, leading to a host of negative emotional consequences, such as shame, anxiety, and even self-disgust. The association between self-objectification and anxiety about appearance and feelings of shame has been found in adolescent girls (12–13-year-olds) (Slater & Tiggemann, 2002) as well as in adult women.

Mental and Physical Health

Research links sexualization with three of the most common mental health problems of girls and women: eating disorders, low self-esteem, and depression or depressed mood (Abramson & Valene, 1991; Durkin & Paxton, 2002; Harrison, 2000; Hofschire & Greenberg, 2001; Mills, Polivy, Herman, & Tiggemann, 2002; Stice, Schupak-Neuberg, Shaw, & Stein, 1994; Thomsen, Weber, & Brown, 2002; Ward, 2004). Several studies (on both teenage and adult women) have found associations between exposure to nar-

row representations of female beauty (e.g., the "thin ideal") and disordered eating attitudes and symptoms. Research also links exposure to sexualized female ideals with lower self-esteem, negative mood, and depressive symptoms among adolescent girls and women. In addition to mental health consequences of sexualization, research suggests that girls' and women's physical health may also be negatively affected, albeit indirectly.

Sexuality

Sexual well-being is an important part of healthy development and overall well-being, yet evidence suggests that the sexualization of girls has negative consequences in terms of girls' ability to develop healthy sexuality. Self-objectification has been linked directly with diminished sexual health among adolescent girls (e.g., as measured by decreased condom use and diminished sexual assertiveness; Impett, Schooler, & Tolman, 2006). Frequent exposure to narrow ideals of attractiveness is associated with unrealistic and/or negative expectations concerning sexuality. Negative effects (e.g., shame) that emerge during adolescence may lead to sexual problems in adulthood (Brotto, Heiman, & Tolman, in press).

Attitudes and Beliefs

Frequent exposure to media images that sexualize girls and women affects how girls conceptualize femininity and sexuality. Girls and young women who more frequently consume or engage with mainstream media content offer stronger endorsement of sexual stereotypes that depict women as sexual objects (Ward, 2002; Ward & Rivadeneyra, 1999; Zurbriggen & Morgan, 2006). They also place appearance and physical attractiveness at the center of women's value.

Impact on Others and on Society

The sexualization of girls can also have a negative impact on other groups (i.e., boys, men, and adult women) and on society more broadly. Exposure to narrow ideals of female sexual attractiveness may make it difficult for some men to find an "acceptable" partner or to fully enjoy intimacy with a female partner (e.g., Schooler & Ward, 2006).

Adult women may suffer by trying to conform to a younger and younger standard of ideal female beauty. More general societal effects may include an increase in sexism; fewer girls pursuing careers in science, technology, engineering, and mathematics (STEM); increased rates of sexual harassment and sexual violence; and an increased demand for child pornography.

Positive Alternatives to the Sexualization of Girls

Some girls and their supporters, now and in the past, have resisted mainstream characterizations of girls as sexual objects. A variety of promising approaches exist to reduce the amount of sexualization that occurs and to ameliorate its effects.

Because the media are important sources of sexualizing images, the development and implementation of school-based media literacy training programs could be key in combating the influence of sexualization. There is an urgent need to teach critical skills in viewing and consuming media, focusing specifically on the sexualization of women and girls. Other school-based approaches include increased access to athletic and other extracurricular programs for girls and the development and presentation of comprehensive sexuality education programs.

Strategies for parents and other caregivers include learning about the impact of sexualization on girls and co-viewing media with their children in order to influence the way in which media messages are interpreted. Action by parents and families has been effective in confronting sources of sexualized images of girls. Organized religious and other ethical instruction can offer girls important practical and psychological alternatives to the values conveyed by popular culture.

Girls and girls' groups can also work toward change. Alternative media such as "zines" (Web-based magazines), "blogs" (Web logs), and feminist magazines, books, and Web sites encourage girls to become activists who speak out and develop their own alternatives. Girl empowerment groups also support girls in a variety of ways and provide important counterexamples to sexualization.

Recommendations

I. Research

A solid research base has explored the effects of having an objectified body image or viewing objectified body images in the media. Much previous work, however, has focused on women. Future studies focusing on girls are needed. In addition, more culturally competent, focused work is required to document the phenomenon of the sexualization of girls; to explore the short- and long-term harm of viewing, listening to, and buying into a sexualized pathway to power; and to test alternative presentations of girlhood, sexuality, and power. We recommend that psychologists conduct research to:

1. Document the frequency of sexualization, specifically of girls, and examine whether sexualization is increasing.

2. Examine and inform our understanding of the circumstances under which the sexualization of girls occurs and identify factors involving the media and products that either contribute to or buffer against the sexualization of girls.

3. Examine the presence or absence of the sexualization of girls and women in all media but especially in movies, music videos, music lyrics, video games, books, blogs, and Internet sites. In particular, research is needed to examine the extent to which girls are portrayed in sexualized and objectified ways and whether this has increased over time. In addition, it is important that these studies focus specifically on sexualization rather than on sexuality more broadly or on other constructs such as gender-role stereotyping.

4. Describe the influence and/or impact of sexualization on girls. This includes both short- and long-term effects of viewing or buying into a sexualizing objectifying image, how these effects influence girls' development, self-esteem, friendships, and intimate relationships, ideas about femininity, body image, physical, mental, and sexual health, sexual satisfaction, desire for plastic surgery, risk factors for early pregnancy, abortion, and sexually transmitted infections, attitudes toward women, other girls, boys, and men, as well as educational aspirations and future career success.

4

5. Explore issues of age compression ("adultification" of young girls and "youthification" of adult women), including prevalence, impact on the emotional well-being of girls and women, and influences on behavior.

6. Explore differences in presentation of sexualized images and effects of these images on girls of color; lesbian, bisexual, questioning, and transgendered girls; girls of different cultures and ethnicities; girls of different religions; girls with disabilities; and girls from all socioeconomic groups.

7. Identify media (including advertising) and marketing alternatives to sexualized images of girls, such as positive depictions of sexuality.

8. Identify effective, culturally competent protective factors (e.g., helping adolescent girls develop a nonobjectified model of normal, healthy sexual development and expression through school or other programs).

9. Evaluate the effectiveness of programs and interventions that promote positive alternatives and approaches to the sexualization of girls. Particular attention should be given to programs and interventions at the individual, family, school, and/or community level.

10. Explore the relationship between the sexualization of girls and societal issues such as sexual abuse, child pornography, child prostitution, and the trafficking of girls. Research on the potential associations between the sexualization of girls and the sexual exploitation of girls is virtually nonexistent, and the need for this line of inquiry is pressing.

11. Investigate the relationships between international issues such as immigration and globalization and the sexualization of girls worldwide. Document the global prevalence of the sexualization of girls and the types of sexualization that occur in different countries or regions and any regional differences in the effects of sexualization. Assess the effects of sexualization on immigrant girls and determine whether these effects are moderated by country of origin, age at immigration, and level of acculturation.

12. Conduct controlled studies on the efficacy of working directly with girls and girls' groups that address these issues, as well as other prevention/intervention programs.

13. Researchers who are conducting studies on related topics (e.g., physical attractiveness, body awareness, or acceptance of the thin ideal) should consider the impact of sexualization as they develop their findings.

II. Practice

As practitioners, psychologists can perform a valuable service by raising awareness of the negative impact of the sexualization of girls—on girls, as well as on boys, women, and men. As individuals and in collaboration with others, practitioners are encouraged to address the sexualization of girls. We recommend:

1. That APA make the Report of the Task Force on the Sexualization of Girls available to practitioners working with children and adolescents in order to familiarize them with information and resources relevant to the sexualization of girls and objectifying behavior on the part of girls.

2. That APA make the Report of the Task Force on the Sexualization of Girls available to practitioners as a source of information on assisting girls in developing the skills necessary to advocate for themselves and counter these adverse messages, taking into account the impact and influence of family and other relationships.

III. Education and Training

Education and training focusing on the prevalence and impact of the sexualization of girls are needed at all levels of psychology to raise awareness within the discipline of psychology and among psychologists about these important issues. We recommend:

1. That APA disseminate information about the Report of the Task Force on the Sexualization of Girls to instructors at the middle-school, high-school, and undergraduate levels and to chairs of graduate departments of psychology.

2. That information from the Report of the Task Force on the Sexualization of Girls be considered for inclusion in future revisions of the *National Standards for High School Psychology Curricula* and *Guidelines on the Undergraduate Psychology Major* by the groups charged with revising these documents.

3. That chairs of graduate departments of psychology and of graduate departments in other areas in which psychologists work be encouraged to consider information from the Report of the Task Force on the Sexualization of Girls as curricula are developed within their programs and to aid in the dissemination of the report.

4. That information from the Report of the Task Force on the Sexualization of Girls be considered for development as continuing education and online academy programming, in partnership with APA's Continuing Education in Psychology Office.

5. That the Ethics Committee and APA Ethics Office consider and use this report in developing ethics educational and training materials for psychologists and make this report available to the group responsible for the next revision of the APA "Ethical Principles of Psychologists and Code of Conduct."

IV. Public Policy

APA, in collaboration with other organizations and through its advocacy efforts, is encouraged to advocate for and better support understanding of the nature and impact of the sexualization of girls, as well as identification and broad implementation of strategies to combat this serious societal problem. We recommend:

1. That APA advocate for funding to support needed research in the areas outlined above.

2. That APA advocate for funding to support the development and implementation by public agencies and private organizations of media literacy programs, including interactive media, in schools that combat sexualization and objectification.

3. That APA advocate for the inclusion of information about sexualization and objectification in health and other related programs, including comprehensive sex education and other sexuality education programs.

4. That APA encourage federal agencies to support the development of programming that may counteract damaging images of girlhood and test the effects of such pro-

grams, for example, Web "zines" (i.e., Web magazines), extracurricular activities (such as athletics), and programs that help girls feel powerful in ways other than through a sexy appearance.

5. That APA work with Congress and relevant federal agencies and industry to reduce the use of sexualized images of girls in all forms of media and products.

V. Public Awareness

The task force offers the following recommendations with the goal of raising public awareness about this important issue. Achieving this goal will require a comprehensive, grassroots, communitywide effort. Participants and stakeholders will include parents and other caregivers, educators, young people, community-based organizations, religious communities, the media, advertisers, marketing professionals, and manufacturers. Overarching strategies will be needed to build linkages and partnerships among the community members. If the goal of raising public awareness is left unmet, the mission of this work will be significantly curtailed. We recommend:

1. That APA seek outside funding to support the development and implementation of an initiative to address the issues raised in this report and identify outside partners to collaborate on these goals. The long-term goals of this initiative, to be pursued in collaboration with these outside partners, should include the following:

• Develop age-appropriate multimedia education resources representing ethnically and culturally diverse young people (boys and girls) for parents, educators, health care providers, and community-based organizations, available in English and other languages, to help facilitate effective conversations about the sexualization of girls and its impact on girls, as well as on boys, women, and men.

• Convene forums that will bring together members of the media and a panel of leading experts in the field to examine and discuss (a) the sexualization of girls in the United States, (b) the findings of this task force report, and (c) strategies to increase awareness about this issue and reduce negative images of girls in the media.

- Develop media awards for positive portrayals of girls as strong, competent, and nonsexualized (e.g., the best television portrayal of girls or the best toy).

- Convene forums with industry partners, including the media, advertisers, marketing professionals, and manufacturers, to discuss the presentation of sexualized images and the potential negative impact on girls and to develop relationships with the goal of providing guidance on appropriate material for varying developmental ages and on storylines and programming that reflect the positive portrayals of girls.

2. That school personnel, parents and other caregivers, community-based youth and parenting organizations, and local business and service organizations encourage positive extracurricular activities that help youth build nurturing connections with peers and enhance self-esteem based on young people's abilities and character rather than on their appearance.

References

Abramson, E., & Valene, P. (1991). Media use, dietary restraint, bulimia, and attitudes toward obesity: A preliminary study. *British Review of Bulimia and Anorexia Nervosa, 5,* 73-76.

Brotto, L., Heiman, J., & Tolman, D. (in press). Towards conceptualizing women's desires: A mixed methods study. *Journal of Sex Research.*

Brown, L. M., & Gilligan, C. (1992). *Meeting at the crossroads: Women's psychology and girls' development.* Cambridge, MA: Harvard University Press.

Durkin, S. J., & Paxton, S. J. (2002). Predictors of vulnerability to reduced body image satisfaction and psychological well-being in response to exposure to idealized female media images in adolescent girls. *Journal of Psychosomatic Research, 53,* 995-1005.

Eder, D. (with Evans, C. C., & Parker, S). (1995). *School talk: Gender and adolescent culture.* New Brunswick, NJ: Rutgers University Press.

Fredrickson, B. L., & Roberts, T-A. (1997). Objectification theory: Toward understanding women's lived experience and mental health risks. *Psychology of Women Quarterly, 21,* 173-206.

Fredrickson, B. L., Roberts, T., Noll, S. M., Quinn, D. M., & Twenge, J. M. (1998). That swimsuit becomes you: Sex differences in self-objectification, restrained eating, and math performance. *Journal of Personality and Social Psychology, 75,* 269-284.

Gapinski, K. D., Brownell, K. D., & LaFrance, M. (2003). Body objectification and "fat talk": Effects on emotion, motivation, and cognitive performance. *Sex Roles, 48,* 377-388.

Gow, J. (1996). Reconsidering gender roles on MTV: Depictions in the most popular music videos of the early 1990s. *Communication Reports, 9,* 151-161.

Grauerholz, E., & King, A. (1997). Primetime sexual harassment. *Violence Against Women, 3,* 129-148.

7

Harrison, K. (2000). The body electric: Thin-ideal media and eating disorders in adolescents. *Journal of Communication, 50,* 119-143.

Hebl, M. R., King, E. G., & Lin, J. (2004). The swimsuit becomes us all: Ethnicity, gender, and vulnerability to self-objectification. *Personality and Social Psychology Bulletin, 30,* 1322-1331.

Hofschire, L. J., & Greenberg, B. S. (2001). Media's impact on adolescents' body dissatisfaction. In J. D. Brown & J. R. Steele (Eds.), *Sexual teens, sexual media* (pp. 125-149). Mahwah, NJ: Erlbaum.

Impett, E. A., Schooler, D., & Tolman, D. L. (2006). To be seen and not heard: Femininity ideology and adolescent girls' sexual health. *Archives of Sexual Behavior, 21,* 628-646.

Krassas, N., Blauwkamp, J. M., & Wesselink, P. (2001). Boxing Helena and corseting Eunice: Sexual rhetoric in *Cosmopolitan* and *Playboy* magazines. *Sex Roles, 44,* 751-771.

Krassas, N. R., Blauwkamp, J. M., & Wesselink, P. (2003). "Master your Johnson": Sexual rhetoric in *Maxim* and *Stuff* magazines. *Sexuality & Culture, 7,* 98-119.

Lin, C. (1997). Beefcake versus cheesecake in the 1990s: Sexist portrayals of both genders in television commercials. *Howard Journal of Communications, 8,* 237-249.

Martin, K. A. (1998). Becoming a gendered body: Practices in preschools. *American Sociological Review, 63,* 494-511.

McConnell, C. (2001). An object to herself: The relationship between girls and their bodies. *Dissertation Abstracts International, 61*(8B), p. 4416.

McKinley, N. M., & Hyde, J. S. (1996). The Objectified Body Consciousness Scale. *Psychology of Women Quarterly, 20,* 181-215.

Mills, J., Polivy, J., Herman, C. P., & Tiggemann, M. (2002). Effects of exposure to thin media images: Evidence of self-enhancement among restrained eaters. *Personality and Social Psychology Bulletin, 28,* 1687-1699.

Nichter, M. (2000). *Fat talk: What girls and their parents say about dieting.* Cambridge, MA: Harvard University Press.

O'Donohue, W., Gold, S. R., & McKay, J. S. (1997). Children as sexual objects: Historical and gender trends in magazines. *Sexual Abuse: Journal of Research & Treatment, 9,* 291-301.

Plous, S., & Neptune, D. (1997). Racial and gender biases in magazine advertising: A content analytic study. *Psychology of Women Quarterly, 21,* 627-644.

Rolón-Dow, R. (2004). Seduced by images: Identity and schooling in the lives of Puerto Rican girls. *Anthropology and Education Quarterly, 35,* 8-29.

Schooler, D., & Ward, L. M. (2006). Average joes: Men's relationships with media, real bodies, and sexuality. *Psychology of Men and Masculinity, 7,* 27-41.

Slater, A., & Tiggemann, M. (2002). A test of objectification theory in adolescent girls. *Sex Roles, 46,* 343-349.

Stice, E., Schupak-Neuberg, E., Shaw, H., & Stein, R. (1994). Relation of media exposure to eating disorder symptomatology: An examination of mediating mechanisms. *Journal of Abnormal Psychology, 103,* 836-840.

Thomsen, S. R., Weber, M. M., & Brown, L. B. (2002). The relationship between reading beauty and fashion magazines and the use of pathogenic dieting methods among adolescent females. *Adolescence, 37,* 1-18.

Vincent, R. C. (1989). Clio's consciousness raised? Portrayal of women in rock videos, re-examined. *Journalism Quarterly, 66,* 155-160.

Ward, L. M. (1995). Talking about sex: Common themes about sexuality in the prime-time television programs children and adolescents view most. *Journal of Youth & Adolescence, 24,* 595-615.

Ward, L. M. (2002). Does television exposure affect emerging adults' attitudes and assumptions about sexual relationships? Correlational and experimental confirmation. *Journal of Youth and Adolescence, 31,* 1-15.

Ward, L. M. (2004). Wading through the stereotypes: Positive and negative associations between media use and Black adolescents' conceptions of self. *Developmental Psychology, 40*, 284-294.

Ward, L. M., & Rivadeneyra, R. (1999). Contributions of entertainment television to adolescents' sexual attitudes and expectations: The role of viewing amount versus viewer involvement. *Journal of Sex Research, 36*, 237-249.

Zurbriggen, E. L., & Morgan, E. M. (2006). Who wants to marry a millionaire? Reality dating television programs, attitudes toward sex, and sexual behaviors. *Sex Roles, 54*, 1-17.

9

A CLOSER LOOK AT
Report of the APA Task Force on the Sexualization of Girls

1. The report concludes that girls are victimized by oversexualization in American culture. Look closely at this report, and identify three to five *causes* of the sexualization of girls. Then identify three to five *effects* of this sexualization on girls, women, and American culture.

2. Where and how does the report define "sexualization"? Based on your own experiences, do you agree with these definitions? Have you experienced these kinds of conditions in your own life?

3. Look over the recommendations of the report. Which of these recommendations would make the most significant changes in American culture? Which of these recommendations could actually change how girls and women perceive themselves and how they are portrayed in the American media?

IDEAS FOR
Writing

1. Write a three-page memoir describing an event in which you, or someone else, were sexualized as described in this report. First, set the scene and describe the event as a complication that disrupts that scene. Then describe how the event was evaluated and resolved. End your memoir by discussing what was learned. Keep in mind that sexualization is not the same as sexual assault.

2. Write a two-page response to this report in which you react to its findings and recommendations. What parts of the report do you agree with? What parts do you disagree with? Would you expand or narrow the report's definitions of sexualization? How might you expand or alter the study?

1. With your group, brainstorm all of the different "reports" that you can think of—lab reports, research reports, recommendation reports, police reports, credit reports, and other report types that you might have come across. Come up with five characteristics that all these reports have in common. Then list one thing about each report that makes it unique.

2. Find and download a report from the Internet. To find a report, put "Report" and a topic that interests you into an Internet search engine like *Google, Yahoo!,* or *Ask.* (You might include ".pdf" or ".doc" in the search line to narrow the search.) A list of reports should pop up. With your group, discuss the following questions:

   a. Does this report clearly state its topic and purpose?

   b. Does it clearly state what issue the research will address? That is, does it state its "research question" in a direct way?

   c. Is it written in a way that allows you to understand the report's gist and its structure quickly, without having to read every word? What strategies does it use to make scanning possible?

3. After reading the student example in this chapter, discuss with your group how this report does or does not match the genre of the research report. Separately, consider its content, organization, style, and design. What are the strengths of this report? What could be improved?

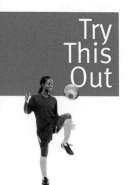
1. Make a list of five topics on which you might want to do research. Then pick three of these topics, choose an angle, and narrow them down to something that you could handle in a report. When choosing an angle, try to figure out why this issue is interesting right now. Share your topic ideas with your group to see which one they like best.

2. Devise a research question that interests you. Then turn it into a hypothesis. Using a prewriting tool, such as brainstorming or a concept map, sketch out a research methodology that would allow you to answer this question and prove or disprove your hypothesis. Turn your methodology into an outline. Then write a one-page memo to your professor that reviews your outline and discusses why you would pursue this research question this way.

3. Use an Internet search engine to find a report on the issue you are or will be investigating. Write a one-page analysis of the report. Does the report have all the elements described in this chapter? Were there gaps in the report? Was the report organized well? Is the style appropriate for the topic? Could the report be designed in a way that makes it more attractive and accessible?

1. **Turn a print report into a multimedia presentation.** On the Internet, find a report and transform it into a multimedia presentation that has ten to fifteen slides. Use presentation software like *PowerPoint* or *Keynote* to help you organize the information and make it attractive to an audience. Don't add any new content to the report, and remove any content that goes beyond the audience's need to know. Where possible, add graphs, charts, photographs, and other visuals that will help explain the topic. When you are finished making the presentation, write a two-page memo to your professor in which you introduce the report and explain how changing the medium of the report altered how people will experience it.

2. **Write a field research report.** A field research report gives you a chance to collect data about local issues in your community or on campus. To write one, you need to pose a research question, devise a method for answering it, do the research, and interpret your findings. Working on your own or in a small group, do these activities:

   a. Make a list of interesting or urgent issues or questions that your community or campus faces. What are some of the more annoying problems on your college's campus that you know about or that are in the news?

   b. Choose one that seems especially annoying. What has changed recently to bring this problem to a head?

   c. Discuss this problem with a group of other people in your class.

   d. Choose one angle of that issue and turn it into a research question that could be answered by doing field research (interviews, surveys, observations). State that research question briefly but clearly and thoroughly.

   e. Turn your research question into a hypothesis.

   Show your research question and hypothesis to your professor. If he or she approves it, begin your research. Devise your methodology and do your research. Write an eight-page report on your topic.

3. **Answer an eccentric question in an experimental report.** Pose an odd question that you would like to answer (e.g., "How big are the splatters from eggs dropped from different heights?" "How do people react when they see a strangely worded sign?"). Then devise a research methodology and come up with some results. Write a brief report that presents your findings. Include pictures or other graphics. Have some fun with your experiments.

PEARSON
mycomplab

For additional reading, writing, and research resources, go to **www.mycomplab.com**.

Developing a Writing Process

PART OUTLINE

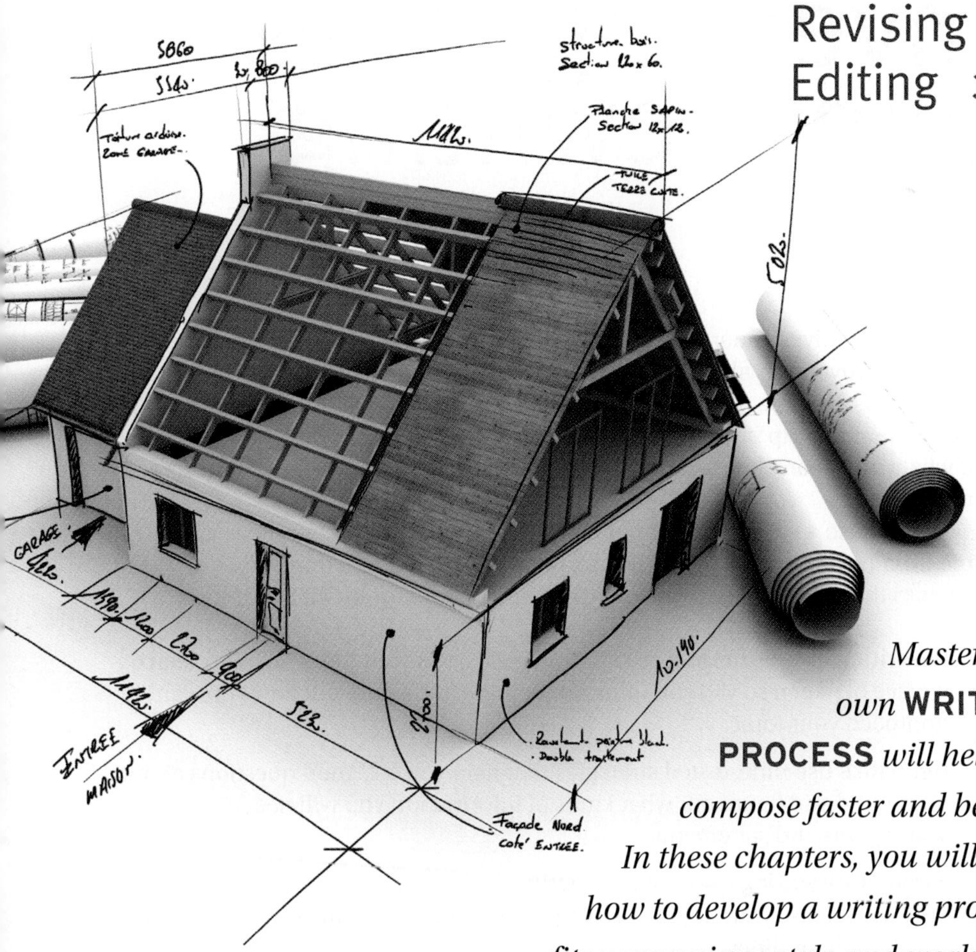

*Mastering your
own* **WRITING
PROCESS** *will help you
compose faster and better.
In these chapters, you will learn
how to develop a writing process that
fits your unique style and work habits.*

CHAPTER

14

Inventing Ideas
and Prewriting

Invention involves generating new ideas and inquiring into topics that you find interesting. Invention also helps you discover and create the content of your document. In this chapter, you will learn some simple but powerful invention strategies that will help you tap into your natural creativity. These strategies will help you figure out what you already know about your topic and get those ideas onto your screen or a piece of paper.

Writers use a variety of techniques to help them invent their ideas and see their topic from new perspectives. In this chapter, we will discuss three types of invention strategies that you can use to generate new ideas and inquire into your topic:

Prewriting uses visual and verbal strategies to put your ideas on the screen or a piece of paper, so you can think about them and figure out how you want to approach your topic.

Heuristics use time-tested strategies that help you ask good questions about your topic and figure out what kinds of information you will need to support your claims and statements.

Exploratory writing uses reflective writing to help you better understand how you feel about your topic and turn those thoughts into sentences, paragraphs, and outlines.

Some of these invention strategies will work better for you than others. So try them all to see which ones help you best tap into your creativity.

Prewriting

Prewriting helps you put your ideas on your screen or a piece of paper, though usually not in an organized way. Your goal while prewriting is to figure out what you already know about your topic and to start coming up with new ideas that go beyond what you already know.

Concept Mapping

One of the most common prewriting tools is *concept mapping*. To create a concept map, write your topic in the middle of your screen or a piece of paper (Figure 14.1). Put a circle around it. Then write down as many other ideas as you can about your topic. Circle those ideas and draw lines that connect them with your original topic and with each other.

The magic of concept mapping is that it allows you to start throwing your ideas onto the screen or a blank page without worrying whether they make sense at the moment. Each new idea in your map will help you come up with other new ideas. Just keep going. Then, when you run out of new ideas, you can work on connecting ideas together into larger clusters.

For example, Figure 14.1 shows a concept map about the pitfalls of male fashion on a college campus. A student made this concept map for a position paper. She

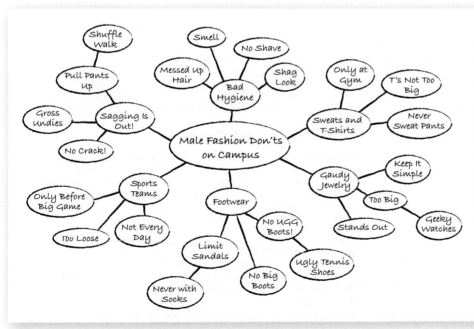

FIGURE 14.1
Using a Concept Map

A concept map will help you get your ideas out onto the screen or a piece of paper. Put your ideas down and then draw lines to connect larger clusters of ideas.

started out by writing "Male Fashion Don'ts on Campus" in the middle of a sheet of paper. Then she began jotting down anything that came to mind about that topic. Eventually, the whole sheet was filled out. She then linked ideas together into larger clusters.

With her ideas in front of her, she can now figure out what she wants to write about. The larger clusters might become major topics in her argument paper (e.g., sweats and T-shirts, jewelry, footwear, hygiene, saggy pants, and sports uniforms). Or she could pick one of those clusters (e.g., footwear) and write her paper about that narrower topic.

If you like concept mapping, you might try one of the free mapping software packages available online, including *Compendium, Free Mind, VUE,* and *XMIND.*

Freewriting

To freewrite, all you need to do is open a page on your computer or pull out a piece of notebook paper. Then write as much as you can for five to ten minutes, putting down anything that comes into your mind. Don't worry about making real sentences or paragraphs. If you find yourself running out of words, try finishing phrases like "What I mean is . . ." or "Here's my point. . . ."

When using a computer, some people like to turn off the monitor or close their eyes as they freewrite. That way, the words they have already written won't keep them from writing down new ideas. Plus, a dark screen will help you avoid the temptation to go back and fix those typos and garbled sentences.

Figure 14.2 shows an example freewrite. The text has typos and some of the sentences make no sense. That's fine.

FIGURE 14.2 Freewriting

When you are freewriting, just let the ideas flow and see where they lead you. In this sample, the writer didn't stop to correct typos. She just moved from one topic to the next. The result is a little chaotic, but now she has several new ideas to work with.

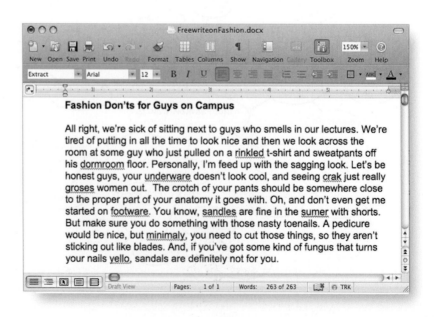

When you are finished freewriting, go through your text, highlighting or under-lining your best ideas. Some people find it helpful to do a second, follow-up freewrite in which they concentrate on those best ideas alone.

Brainstorming or Listing

Another kind of prewriting is *brainstorming*, which is also called *listing*. To brain-storm about your topic, open a new page on your screen or pull out a piece of paper. Then list everything that comes to mind about your topic. As in freewriting, you should just keep listing ideas for about five to ten minutes without stopping.

Next, pick your best idea from your list and create a second brainstorming list in a second column. Again, list everything that comes to mind about this best idea. Making two lists will help you narrow your topic and deepen your thoughts about it.

Storyboarding

Movie scriptwriters and advertising designers use a technique called storyboarding to help them sketch out their ideas. *Storyboarding* involves drawing a set of pictures that show the progression of your ideas. Storyboards are especially useful when you are working with genres like memoirs, reports, or proposals, because they show how something happens or happened step by step. They are useful for helping you visual-ize the "story."

The easiest way to storyboard about your topic is to fold a regular piece of paper into four or eight panels. Then, in each of the panels, draw a scene or a major idea in-volving your topic. Stick figures are fine. Don't worry about making your drawings look good. We can't all be artists.

Storyboarding is similar to turning your ideas into a comic strip. You add panels to your storyboards and cross them out as your ideas evolve. You can also add dia-logue into the scenes and put captions underneath each panel to show what is hap-pening. Storyboarding often works best for people who like to think in drawings or pictures rather than in words and sentences.

Using Heuristics

You already use heuristics, but the term is probably not familiar to you. A *heuristic* is a discovery tool that helps you ask insightful questions or follow a specific pat-tern of thinking. Writers often memorize the heuristics that they find especially useful. Here, we will review some of the most popular heuristics, but many others are available.

Asking the Journalist's Questions

The most common heuristic is a tool called the *journalist's questions*, which we like to call the "Five-W and How questions." Writers for newspapers, magazines, and televi-sion use these questions to help them sort out the details of a story.

Who was involved?

What happened?

Where did the event happen?

When did it happen?

Why did it happen?

How did it happen?

Write each of these questions separately on your screen or a piece of paper. Then answer each question in as much detail as you can. Make sure your facts are accurate, so you can reconstruct the story from your notes. If you don't know the answer to one of these questions, put down a question mark. A question mark signals a place where you might need to do some more research.

When using the Five-W and How questions, you might also find it helpful to ask, "What has changed recently about my topic?" If you pay attention to what has changed or is changing about your topic, you will likely discover what makes this topic most interesting to your readers. Paying attention to change will also help you determine your "angle" on the topic (i.e., your unique perspective or view).

Using the Five Senses

Writers also like to use their five senses as a heuristic to explore a topic and invent their ideas, especially when they are following descriptive genres, such as memoirs, profiles, reviews, or reports. When trying to describe something to your readers, concentrate on each of your senses one by one:

Sight What can you see? What does it look like? What colors or shapes do you see?

Hearing What sounds can you hear? What do people or objects sound like?

Smell What can you smell? Does anything have a distinctive scent?

Touch What do things feel like? Are they rough or smooth? Are they cold or hot?

Taste Are there any tastes involved? If so, are they sweet, salty, sour, stale, delicious?

Some senses will be more important to your writing project than others. Using all five senses will help you experience your topic from a variety of standpoints. These vivid descriptions will give your readers a richer understanding of your subject with added detail.

Investigating *Logos, Ethos, Pathos*

Aristotle, a philosopher and rhetorician, realized that arguments tend to draw on three kinds of proof: reasoning (*logos*), authority (*ethos*), and emotion (*pathos*). Today, writers still use these Greek terms as a heuristic to remind themselves to gather evidence from all three kinds of proof. This three-part heuristic works especially well for argumentative papers, such as commentaries, position papers, proposals, and reports.

Logos. *Logos* includes any reasoning and examples that will support your claims. You can use logical statements to prove your points, or you can use real or realistic examples to back up your claims. Here are some basic strategies that you can use to support your ideas with *logos:*

If . . . then: "If you believe X, then you should believe Y also."

Either . . . or: "Either you believe X, or you believe Y."

Cause and effect: "X is the reason Y happens."

Costs and benefits: "The benefits of doing X are worth/not worth the cost Y."

Better and worse: "X is better/worse than Y because . . ."

Examples: "For example, X and Y demonstrate that Z happens."

Facts and data: "These facts/data support my argument that X is true (or Y is false)."

Anecdotes: "X happened to these people, thus demonstrating Y."

Ethos. *Ethos* involves information that will help you build your authority and reputation with readers. If you are an expert on a particular topic, you can use your own experiences to support your argument. For example, a person majoring in fashion design has more *ethos* about the topic of clothing than others. If you are not an expert on your topic, then you can draw from sources written by experts to add *ethos* to your writing. Here are a few ways to use *ethos* in your writing:

Personal experience: "I have experienced X, so I know it's true and Y is not."

Personal credentials: "I have a degree in Z" or "I am the director of Y." "So I know a lot about the subject of X."

Good moral character: "I have always done the right thing for the right reasons, so you should believe me when I say that X is the best path to follow."

Appeal to experts: "According to Z, who is an expert on this topic, X is true and Y is not true."

Identification with the readers: "You and I come from similar backgrounds and we have similar values; therefore, you would likely agree with me that X is true and Y is not."

Admission of limitations: "I may not know much about Z, but I do know that X is true and Y is not."

Expression of goodwill: "I want what is best for you, so I am recommending X as the best path to follow.

Use of "insider" language: Using jargon words or referring to information that only insiders would understand.

Pathos. *Pathos* relates to emotional support for your argument. To use emotion in your writing, think about the aspects of your topic that make people happy, mad, sad, anxious, concerned, surprised, disgusted, joyful, or fearful. You can appeal to these emotions to persuade people to see things your way. Here are some strategies for using emotion:

Promise of gain: "By agreeing with us, you will gain trust, time, money, love, advancement, reputation, comfort, popularity, health, beauty, or convenience."

Promise of enjoyment: "If you do things our way, you will experience joy, anticipation, fun, surprises, enjoyment, pleasure, leisure, or freedom."

Fear of loss: "If you don't do things this way, you risk losing time, money, love, security, freedom, reputation, popularity, health, or beauty."

Fear of pain: "If you don't do things this way, you may feel pain, sadness, grief, frustration, humiliation, embarrassment, loneliness, regret, shame, vulnerability, or worry."

Expressions of anger or disgust: "You should be angry or disgusted because X is unfair to you, me, or others."

Emotion alone usually won't create the strongest arguments. Instead, you should use emotion to support your *logos*-based or *ethos*-based arguments. Emotion will add power and feeling to your argument, while heightening the intensity for your readers. Figure 14.3 shows the introduction to a first draft in which the author uses emotion to support her *logos* and *ethos* arguments.

Cubing

A cube has six sides, and cubing asks you to explore your topic through six "sides" or angles.

1. **Describe it.** What does your topic look like? What are its color and shape? How big or small is it? What is it made of?

2. **Compare it.** What is like? What is it *not* like? In what ways is it similar to or different from things that are more familiar to your readers?

3. **Associate it.** What does it remind you of? What other topics is it related to that you know something about?

4. **Analyze it.** What patterns run through your topic? What are its hidden questions or meanings? Who created it? What has changed that makes it important?

5. **Apply it.** How could you or someone else use it? Who would use it? What good would it do them? What harm might it do?

6. **Argue for or against it.** What arguments could you or someone else make for or against your topic?

As a fashion design major (and a woman), let me offer you guys a little helpful advice about attracting women on campus. College women view campus differently than most men. Guys see campus as a place to go to class and study, perhaps throw a frisbee. So, showing up in a faded t-shirt, sweatpants, and flipflops might seem all right. Quite differently, women see campus as a place to socialize and meet friends, in addition to doing class-related stuff. For women, campus is a place to see people and be seen. Consequently, women don't like to be seen with guys who look like they were just shot out of a wrinkle gun. But, if you guys make a few simple wardrobe changes, women are going to notice you.

Pathos	
Logos	
Pathos	
Ethos	
Logos	

FIGURE 14.3   A First Draft That Uses *Logos*, *Pathos*, and *Ethos* for Support

In this first draft of an essay's introduction, the author uses a combination of reasoning, authoritative, and emotional appeals to persuade her readers.

Exploratory Writing

Exploratory writing helps you to reflect on your ideas about a topic and to put down your thoughts for further consideration. Essentially, exploratory writing is "writing about writing" that allows you to think about your writing projects with a little more distance.

Journaling, Blogging, or Microblogging

Some writers find it helpful to keep a regular journal or blog to reflect on their experiences and generate new ideas. You can write down your thoughts and think about your life without the pressure of drafting the full argument.

Journaling.   This kind of exploratory writing can be done in a notebook or on your computer. The key to writing a journal is to add something new every day. In your journal, you can talk about the things that happen to you and what is going on in your world.

Blogging.   Blogging is very similar to journaling but blogs are public texts (Figure 14.4, page 336). You can sign up for a blog at several blogging Web sites, often for free. You may not want everyone to read your innermost ideas—but then, of course, you might! Some personal blogs develop their own cult followings. For more on blogging, see Chapter 29 "Using the Internet."

FIGURE 14.4 A Blog

Journals or blogs can be helpful for coming up with new ideas and reflections. This blog was found on Blogger.com, a free blogging Web site.

Microblogging. You can use a microblog like *Twitter*, *Plurk*, or *Jaiku* to describe what is happening to you. Besides keeping your friends informed about where you are and what you are doing, your microblog can track your thoughts and experiences.

Before writing a new entry into your journal or blog, go back and read what you wrote previously. That way, you can build from your previous thoughts or use them as a springboard for coming up with new ideas. If you are writing a blog, you can check out what others have written in response to your posts.

Writing an Exploratory Draft

Sometimes it is helpful to write an "exploratory draft" before you begin trying to write a rough draft. In an exploratory draft, write about how you feel about the topic and what you already know about it. Write down some of the main points you want to make in your paper and what kinds of information or examples you will need to support your points. Your exploratory draft is also a good place to express your concerns about the project and come up with some strategies for handling them.

In this position paper, I want to make an argument that guys should dress nicer on campus. But I don't want to come off as some kind of fashion snob or diva.

I also don't want to give the impression that I think everyone has enough money to buy designer clothes. I strongly believe that looking good is not a matter of money or being physically attractive. It's about making good choices and taking a few minutes to think about what looks good to others. I guess my main goal in this paper is to give guys good reasons to dress nicer on campus. Yeah, I'll need to tweak them a little to get their attention. My writing style will probably need to be funny or even teasing. If they get a little angry, maybe they'll think a little more about how they look. It would be nice if I could find some pictures that demonstrate good fashion choices. Nothing GQ. Just normal guys on campus making good choices about clothing. Maybe I need a digital camera to get some of those kinds of pictures. That would help me show my readers what I mean.

The purpose of an exploratory draft is not to write the paper itself but to use writing to help you explore your topic and sort out your ideas.

Exploring with Presentation Software

Presentation software, such as Microsoft's *PowerPoint,* OpenOffice's *Impress,* or Apple's *KeyNote,* can be a powerful tool for doing exploratory writing about your subject. The software can help you create slides, making a bulleted list of your major subjects and key points. Then you can fill out the slides with details, pictures, and graphs. Presentation software is a fast and easy way to explore your topic and organize your ideas. Try this:

1. Create a new page in your favorite presentation software.

2. On the title slide, type a title for your paper that identifies your topic. In the subtitle area, type in your angle on that topic.

3. Think of two to five major topics that will be discussed in your argument. Create separate slides for each of those major topics.

4. On the slide for each major topic, list two to five issues that you might need to talk about in your paper.

5. As you fill in each slide, look for opportunities to add visuals, such as photographs, charts, and graphs.

If you don't know something about one of your major topics, just leave that slide blank for now. These gaps in slides signal places where you need to do more exploration or research.

When you are finished filling in the slides as best you can, your might find it helpful to change your screen to Slide Sorting View, so you can see an overview of your whole text (Figure 14.5, page 338). This view will allow you to move slides around to figure out how to best organize your ideas.

When you are finished exploring your topic with the presentation software, you will have a good outline for writing your paper. Plus, you will have collected the photographs, charts, and other visuals you need to design the document.

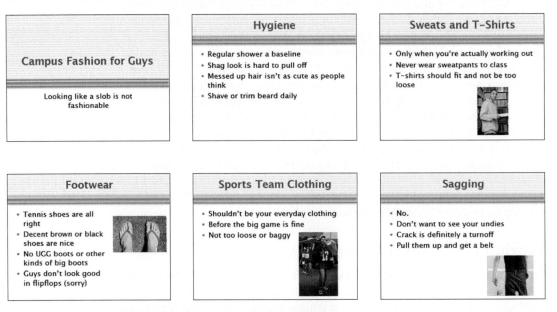

FIGURE 14.5 Outlining with Presentation Software

Presentation software can help you make a quick outline of your argument and insert graphics.

Taking Time to Invent and Prewrite

When writing a paper, it is very tempting to jump straight to the drafting stage of the writing process. After all, time spent prewriting, using heuristics, and doing exploratory writing might seem like time away from your real task—getting that assignment finished. In the end, the secret to invention is to give yourself the time and space to explore your ideas.

Above all, think of "invention" as a separate stage in your writing process. Set aside some time to discover and form your ideas before you start trying to draft your paper. You will be more creative. Plus, you will actually save time, because you won't just sit at your computer staring into the screen.

Start developing the content of your document. Here are some techniques for prewriting, using heuristics, and doing some exploratory writing.

DO Some Prewriting to Get the Ideas Flowing

Prewriting uses visual and verbal strategies to help you figure out what you already know about your topic and how you want to approach it. Try making a concept map, freewriting, doing some brainstorming, or making a storyboard on your topic.

USE Heuristics to Draw Out Your Ideas

A heuristic is a discovery tool that helps you ask insightful questions or follow a specific pattern of thinking. Some of the common heuristics are the Five-W and How questions, the five human senses, *logos/ethos/pathos*, and cubing.

REFLECT on Your Topic with Exploratory Writing

Exploratory writing is "writing about writing" that allows you to think about your writing projects with a little more distance. You can do some journaling or blogging. Or you can write an exploratory draft that lets you talk about what you want to write about. Presentation software can be a useful tool for putting your ideas on the screen in an organized way.

GIVE Yourself Time to Invent Your Ideas

It's tempting to jump right to the drafting stage. That deadline is looming. But you will find that you write more efficiently and better if you give yourself time to sort through your ideas first.

1. List three times in your life when you have been especially inventive or innovative. Why did you decide to take the more creative path rather than the ordinary path? Tell your group about these creative moments and how they came about.

2. With your group, list five celebrities who you think are especially original and innovative. What unique characteristics make each of them creative? Can you find any common characteristics that they all share?

3. What kinds of invention strategies have you learned previously, and what has worked for you in the past? With your group, talk about methods you have used in the past to come up with new ideas for projects.

1. Create a concept map about a topic that interests you. What are the one or two most interesting issues in your concept map? Put one of those issues in the middle of your screen or a piece of paper and create a second concept map on this narrower version of the topic. Ask yourself, "What has changed to make this topic interesting right now?" Doing so will help you find a new angle on your topic.

2. For about five minutes, freewrite about a topic for your next paper in this class. When you are finished, pick your best idea and freewrite for another five minutes. This second freewrite will help you develop a solid understanding of the topic, purpose, and angle for your paper.

3. Check into some of the free blogging services available online. What are some of the pros and cons of each blogging site? If you don't have a blog of your own, what kind of blog might you enjoy keeping?

1. **Invent with presentation software.** For your next project in this class, start out by creating a version of your document with presentation software. Begin with a title slide that includes your title and main point. Then create slides for the major points in your paper. Add a slide for the conclusion. Then go back and fill in the bullet points for each of your major points. Find any graphics you can and add them to the slides. When you have finished creating your "presentation," use the slide sorter feature to move slides around. When you are finished, talk through your presentation with your group.

2. **Start keeping a journal or blog.** For the next two weeks, keep a journal or a blog. Spend a little time each day writing something about the topic of your next paper. Then, as you draft, design, and edit your paper, write about your successes and challenges while developing the document. Hand in your journal or your blog's URL with the final draft of your paper.

For additional reading, writing, and research resources, go to **www.mycomplab.com.**

Organizing and
Drafting

I n the previous chapter, you learned how to "invent" the content of your paper by using prewriting, heuristics, and exploratory writing to be creative and gather information. In this chapter, you will learn about the second stage in the writing process: how to use genres to organize your ideas and write a draft of your paper.

The genre you choose will help you determine where your ideas and the information you gathered should appear in the text. The genre helps you organize your ideas into a shape that is familiar to you and your readers. Remember, genres are not formulas to be followed mechanically. Instead, genres follow flexible patterns that reflect how people act, react, and interact in the real world. The organization of a genre, in other words, reflects how people get things done.

Using Genres to Organize Your Ideas

As your documents grow longer and more complex, genres will help you dramatically improve your writing. Genres follow organizational patterns that reflect the activities you will do in your college classes and in the workplace. For example, the report genre, (discussed in Chapter 13) reflects the steps that you should follow when doing research on a topic:

1. Define a research question and hypothesis

2. Develop a method for answering that research question

3. Gather results

4. Discuss those results

5. Draw conclusions and/or recommendations

It's no coincidence, then, that the report genre calls for five sections that reflect this research process: *introduction, methods, results, discussion*, and *recommendations*. Once you know that a report tends to be organized into these five sections, you can arrange the information you have gathered to fit what your readers expect.

Should you mechanically follow a genre as a fixed pattern? Absolutely not. A genre's organization can be adjusted to suit your purpose and the unique characteristics of the rhetorical situation. Genres are flexible and "stretchy," allowing writers to move, combine, and divide sections as needed.

Drafting Introductions, Bodies, and Conclusions

Genres commonly used in college and in the workplace have some organizational features that you can commit to memory. Specifically, genres for college and the workplace almost always include an introduction, body, and conclusion:

Introduction. The purpose of the introduction is to set a "context" for the body of the document. The introduction usually tells readers your topic, purpose, and main point. It might also offer background information on your topic and stress its importance to readers. Introductions can range in size from a small paragraph to several paragraphs.

Body. The body presents the "content" of the document. Essentially, the body provides the facts, reasoning, examples, quotations, data, and anything else needed to support or prove your document's main point and achieve its purpose.

Conclusion. At the end of the document, the conclusion reestablishes the context for the document by restating your main point (usually with more emphasis), restating why your topic is important to your readers, and offering a look to the future. Your conclusion should be as brief as possible, from a small paragraph to at most a few paragraphs.

To help you remember this three-part pattern, sometimes it helps to keep the time-tested speechwriter's pattern in mind: "Tell them what you're going to tell them. Tell them. Then tell them what you told them."

In Chapter 19, "Drafting Introductions and Conclusions," you will learn more about how to write strong beginnings and endings for your documents. You can turn there now if you are looking for immediate advice on writing introductions and conclusions.

Sketching an Outline

An outline can be an important tool for organizing your ideas, especially as the documents you write grow larger and more complex. In the workplace, most people sketch out a rough outline to help them sort out their ideas. Your outline doesn't need to be formal, but it should list the major parts of your document. Your outline is a map you will follow when drafting your document.

Creating a Basic Outline

When creating a basic outline, you first need to decide which genre you are following and turn to that chapter in Part 2 of this book. At the beginning of each genre chapter, you will see a diagram illustrating one or two organizational patterns that the genre tends to follow. These patterns should give you an overall idea about which sections should appear in your outline.

Here's the easy part. Type or write "I. Introduction" on your screen or a piece of paper. Then type or write "X. Conclusion" at the bottom. After all, you already know your document will need an introduction and a conclusion. For now, use an "X" with the conclusion, because you aren't sure how many sections will be needed for the body of your text.

Filling Out Your Outline

Here's the hard part. Start listing the major sections that will appear in your document. Give each one an uppercase roman numeral (e.g., II, III, IV, V, VI, VII, etc.). The genre you are following should give you a good idea about how many sections you will need (Figure 15.1). *Hint:* If your roman numerals are nearing X (that's ten sections), you probably have too many sections. If that's the case, some of your sections should be combined or removed.

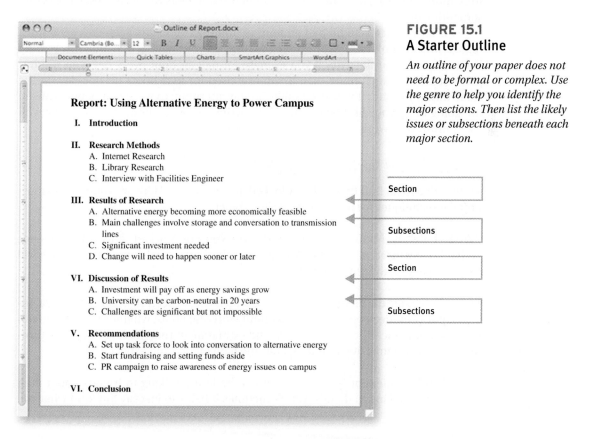

FIGURE 15.1
A Starter Outline

An outline of your paper does not need to be formal or complex. Use the genre to help you identify the major sections. Then list the likely issues or subsections beneath each major section.

When you have finished listing the major sections, list the issues or subsections that will appear in each of these major sections. Each major section should include about two to five issues or subsections.

How will you know what to include in each section? That's where the invention strategies you learned about in the previous chapter will help you. Look at the ideas and keywords you came up with during the invention phase, and put them into your outline.

Drafting Through Writer's Block

Writer's block happens to everyone, even the most experienced writers. Here are some strategies for keeping the words flowing, and for working through those moments of writer's block.

Drafting (Almost) Every Day

The worst thing you can do is start drafting the night before your paper is due. You will often hear people say things like, "I write best under pressure" or "I need to figure out what I'm going to say before I start writing." These kinds of statements are warning signals that a writer is procrastinating. After all, people don't really write well under pressure, and the best way to figure out what you have to say is to write something down.

Our best advice is to do half an hour of drafting every day. Each day, set aside a regular time in the morning or evening to work on your writing assignments. Writing is like exercising at the gym. If you exercise for half an hour every day, you will improve steadily—much more than if you exercised for four hours on one day. In the same way, if you say, "I'm setting aside Sunday afternoon to write that paper," you are not going to do your best work. But, if you write for half an hour every day, you will easily finish your work—and you will write better.

Overcoming Writer's Block

Almost all writers find themselves blocked at some point. Here are some of the most popular techniques for overcoming writer's block:

"What I Really Mean Is. . . ." Whenever you are blocked, finish the sentence "What I really mean is. . . ." You will discover that simply finishing this sentence will help you get past the temporary block.

Lower Your Standards While Drafting. Stop trying to get it right on the first try. Instead, put your ideas on the screen without worrying about whether they are intelligent or grammatically correct. Then spend extra time during the revision phase turning those ideas into a document that has the high quality you expect.

Talk It Out. Professional writers can often be found talking to friends about their work or even talking to themselves. Sometimes it helps to just say out loud what you want to write. Then, after you have rehearsed the text a few times, you should find your ideas easier to write it down.

Change How and Where You Write. If you normally draft on a computer, try switching over to pen and paper for a little while. If you normally write in your dorm room, try a change of scenery by going over to the library or out on central campus. Sometimes the change in medium or location will help you loosen up.

Use Both Sides of Your Brain. The right side of your brain is more visual than your left. So use invention techniques like concept mapping, freewriting, and cubing to tap into that visual creativity. These techniques will help you put your ideas on the screen. Then the left side of your brain can organize them into sentences and paragraphs.

Write an E-mail. Start writing your document as an e-mail to a friend. E-mail is often a more familiar writing environment, allowing you to relax as you write.

Talk to Your Professor. Your professors probably have some helpful ideas about how to draft your papers. Visit your professors during office hours. They are there to help you.

Go to the Writing Center. If your campus has a writing center, you should drop by for some help. You can talk your ideas over with an experienced writer who can offer you some advice and strategies.

Stop Procrastinating. Procrastination is the usual culprit behind writer's block. The pressure of a deadline can cause your brain to freeze. So start each project early, and write a little every day. Your writer's block will evaporate.

Your first year of college is the best time to develop good writing habits. Don't wait until your advanced courses or your first job to form these habits, because it will be too late.

Organization is the key to presenting your ideas in a meaningful, orderly way. It also allows you to highlight the important information that your readers need.

USE Genres to Organize Your Ideas

Genres are not formulas, but they do offer helpful patterns for organizing the content of your document. Chapters 4–13 will give you a good idea of how each genre is typically organized.

DIVIDE Your Document into an Introduction, Body, and Conclusion

Almost all nonfiction genres include an introduction, body, and conclusion. The introduction "tells them what you're going to tell them." The body "tells them." And the conclusion "tells them what you told them."

SKETCH an Outline

Outlines may seem a bit old-fashioned, but an informal outline is often a good way to sort your ideas into sections of a document. Don't worry about all those roman numerals. Just list the subjects you want to cover in your document.

DRAFT Your Document

Drafting is about putting your rear end in the seat and keeping your hands on the keyboard. Try drafting for half an hour almost every day.

OVERCOME Writer's Block

It happens to everyone. The techniques discussed in this chapter should help you get over those moments.

1. With a group, discuss how you were taught to outline papers in high school. Do you think outlining works well for you? In which situations do outlines seem to work best?

2. Have you ever waited until the last moment to write a paper for one of your classes? If you got a good grade, why do you think you did well despite procrastinating? If you didn't do well, what do you think you should have done differently to avoid waiting until the last moment?

3. When does writer's block happen most frequently to you? Can you think of ways to avoid writer's block in the first place? When writer's block happens, which strategies have you used to get writing again?

Talk About This

1. As you draft your next paper, keep a log of how much time you spend drafting. When you hand your paper in, look at your log. Where have you devoted more or less time to the project? How can you spread your time out better on the project to strengthen your writing?

2. Do some research on the writing habits of one of your favorite contemporary authors. How often do they write, and how much time do they devote to it each day? Do they offer any wisdom about how to overcome writer's block? Write an e-mail to your professor about this author's writing habits.

Try This Out

1. **Analyze your writing process.** In a brief report, describe how you currently draft your documents. How much time do you usually devote to drafting? Which strategies or routines help you draft a paper? Next, offer some ideas for improving how you draft documents. Which techniques for overcoming writer's block in this chapter would be most helpful for you?

2. **Interview a professional through e-mail.** Set up an e-mail interview with a professional in your desired career or a professor in your major. Ask that person about his or her writing process and pay special attention to what he or she says about organizing ideas and drafting documents. Ask how documents are organized in his or her field. Ask how he or she learned how to write those kinds of documents. In a brief profile, describe how your subject uses writing in his or her personal life.

Write This

For additional reading, writing, and research resources, go to **www.mycomplab.com**.

16

Choosing
a Style

Style is not something you have or you don't have. Instead, style is a way of expressing your attitude and feelings about a topic. It is a way of establishing your character and a sense of authority with your readers. In a word, style is about the quality of your writing.

Style is *not* flowery language or ornamentation. It's *not* about sprinkling in a few adjectives to make dull sentences more interesting or colorful. Sometimes inexperienced writers will talk about "my style," as though each writer possesses one unique voice or way of writing. In reality, the best style for your document depends on your topic, the rhetorical situation, and the genre that you are using.

There is no correct style for a particular genre; however, certain genres are associated with specific styles. For example, scientific reports tend to be written in a plain, objective style. Movie reviews are often colorful and upbeat. In some circumstances, though, a scientific report could use an upbeat style and a movie review could be serious. Ultimately, the style you choose depends on the rhetorical situation for your document.

In this chapter, you will learn strategies to strengthen your style and improve the power of your writing.

Writing in Plain Style

Plain style is the basis of all other writing styles. The usual advice to writers is to "write clearly" or "write in concrete language" as though making up your mind to do so is all it takes. Actually, using plain style is a skill that requires some practice. Once you learn a few basic guidelines, writing plainly will become a natural strength.

Guideline 1: Clarify What or Who the Sentence Is About

Often, difficult sentences simply lack a clear subject. For example, consider the following sentence:

Original:

Seven months after our Spring Break trip to Vail in which a bunch of us travelled around the front range of the Rockies, my roommates' fond memories of the trip were enough to ignore the nagging reality that the trip itself had yet to be fully paid for.

What is this sentence about? The word "memories" is currently in the subject position, but the sentence might also be about "months," "vacation," "bunch of us," "my roommates," or "trip." A sentence like this one is hard to understand because readers cannot easily locate the subject of the sentence.

To clarify this sentence, you first need to decide what the sentence is about. Then you can move that subject into the subject position of the sentence. For example, when this sentence is reconstructed around "my roommates and I" it is much easier to understand.

Revised:

Seven months after our Spring Break trip to Vail, my roommates and I still have fond memories of travelling around the front range of the Rockies, which helps us ignore the nagging reality that we haven't paid for the trip yet.

This sentence is still difficult to read, but it is clearer now because the noun in the subject position (i.e., "my roommates and I") is what the sentence is about.

Guideline 2: Make the "Doer" the Subject of the Sentence

Readers tend to focus on who or what is doing something in a sentence, so whenever possible, try to move the "doer" into the subject position. For example, which of the following sentences is clearer?

On Monday morning, the report was completed just in time by Sheila.

On Monday morning, Sheila completed the report just in time.

Most readers would point to the second sentence, because Sheila, the subject of this sentence, is doing something. Meanwhile, the subject of the first sentence, the report, is just sitting still, not doing anything.

Guideline 3: Put the Subject Early in the Sentence

Subconsciously, your readers start every sentence looking for the subject. The subject is the anchor of the sentence, so the longer you make them wait for it, the harder the sentence will be to read.

Original:

If the Sandia Mountains ecosystem experiences another drought like the one observed from 2000–2009, black bears will suffer severely from a lack of available food and water.

Revised:

Black bears will suffer severly from lack of available food and water if the Sandia Mountains ecosystem experiences another drought like the one from 2000–2009.

The second sentence is easier to read, because the subject arrives early in the sentence. When readers find that anchor, they immediately know how to read the rest of the sentence.

Guideline 4: State the Action in the Verb

In each sentence, ask yourself what the doer is doing. Then move that action into the verb position and put the verb as close to the subject as possible.

Original:

The detective is the person who conducted an investigation into the homicide that happened last night on 4th Avenue.

Revised:

The detective investigated last night's homicide on 4th Avenue.

The original sentence is harder to understand because the action (investigation) is not a verb, and it's buried later in the sentence. The revised sentence is easier to understand because the action (investigate) is in the verb position, and it's close to the subject.

Guideline 5: Eliminate Nominalizations

Nominalizations are perfectly good verbs and adjectives that have been turned into awkward nouns:

Original:

Students have an expectation that all professors will be rigorous and fair in the assignment of grades.

Revised:

Students expect all professors to be rigorous and fair when assigning grades.

Original:

Our discussion about the matter allowed us to make a decision to go to Florida for spring break this year.

Revised:

We discussed our spring break options and decided to go to Florida this year.

By turning nominalizations into verbs, you can simplify and shorten a sentence. You also make the sentence more active because the action is being expressed in the verb.

Guideline 6: Boil Down the Prepositional Phrases

Prepositional phrases follow prepositions, like *in, of, by, about, over,* and *under.* These phrases are necessary in writing, but they can be overused.

Original:

This year's increase *in* the success *of* the basketball team *called* the Hokies *of* Virginia Tech **offered a demonstration** *of* the importance *of* a coach *with* a national reputation *for* the purposes *of* recruiting.

Revised:

This year's successful Virginia Tech Hokies basketball team demonstrated the importance *of* a nationally known coach *for* recruiting.

In the examples above, the prepositions have been italicized and the prepositional phrases are blue. Notice how prepositional phrases can create "chains" of phrases that make the sentence harder to read.

To eliminate prepositional phrases, try turning some of them into adjectives. For example, "in the success of the basketball team called the Hokies of Virginia Tech" was boiled down to "successful Virginia Tech basketball team." You don't need to eliminate all prepositional phrases, but you can simplify a sentence by eliminating some of them.

Guideline 7: Eliminate Redundancies

To stress an important idea, some writers mistakenly turn to redundant phrasing. For example, they might say "unruly mob" as though some mobs are not unruly. Or, they might talk about "active participants" as though people can participate without doing anything. In some cases, they are tempted to use two or more synonyms that mean the same thing to modify a noun.

Original:

We are demanding important, significant changes to university policies.

Revised:

We are demanding significant changes to university policies.

Original:

The London plague of 1665 was especially deadly and lethal for the poor, who could not escape to the countryside.

Revised:

The London plague of 1665 was especially deadly for the poor, who could not escape to the countryside.

Redundancies should be eliminated because they use two or more words to do the work of one. As a result, readers need to do twice the work to understand one basic idea.

Guideline 8: Use Sentences That Are Breathing Length

You should be able to read a sentence out loud in one comfortable breath. If a sentence runs on and on—even if it is grammatically correct—it makes readers feel like they are mentally holding their breath. By the end of an especially long sentence, readers are more concerned about when the sentence will end than what the sentence is saying.

On the other hand, if you only use short sentences, your readers will feel like they are breathing too quickly. Each period at the end of a sentence signals, "Take a breath." So many short sentences together will make readers feel like they are hurrying.

Here are two ways to make your sentences breathing length:

- Sentences that cannot be said out loud comfortably in one breath should be shortened or cut into two sentences. (Don't asphyxiate your readers!)

- Sentences that are too short should be combined with other short sentences around them. (Don't make them hyperventilate, either!)

Plain style takes some practice, but writing clearly is not that hard to master. These eight guidelines will help you transform your writing into something that is easy to read. This is the essence of plain style.

Establishing Your Voice

When reading, all of us, including your readers, hear a voice that sounds out the words. The best way to create a specific voice in a text is to decide what *tone* you want your readers to hear as they read your writing.

In other words, think about how you want your voice to sound: excited, angry, joyful, sad, professional, disgusted, objective, happy, compassionate, surprised, optimistic, aggressive, regretful, anxious, tense, affectionate, or sympathetic.

After you choose a specific tone, you can create your voice by getting into character or imitating other writers.

Get into Character

While drafting, one easy way to establish your voice is to imagine yourself playing a role, as in a movie or a play. You need to get into character before you start drafting your paper. This is common advice given to creative writers, but role playing works for writing nonfiction, too.

For instance, you may need to write about a topic that is serious or tragic, but you happen to be in a good mood that day. Or perhaps you are writing about something that should be exciting, but you just aren't feeling thrilled.

The best way to handle these situations is to pretend that you are feeling "serious" or "excited" while you are working on the first draft of your document. You might even imagine that you are someone else who is serious or excited about your topic. Get into character, and then let that character compose from his own point of view.

Imitate Other Writers

Imitation was once a common way for people to learn how to improve their voice and tone. Teachers of speech and writing would regularly ask their students to imitate the style of well-known speakers and writers to practice new stylistic techniques.

Imitation is not widely used to teach writing today, but you can still use it to improve your own style. Choose an author whose work you enjoy. Pay close attention to his or her style. How does the choice of words shape what the writer says? How do the writer's sentences convey his or her meaning? As you are drafting or revising your next paper, use some of those word choices and sentence strategies to convey your own ideas. When imitating someone else, you will usually end up blending elements of his or her writing style with elements of yours.

Of course, be careful not to use the exact words or ideas of the writer or text you are imitating. That's plagiarism. To avoid any chance of plagiarism, try imitating the style of a text that was written on a completely different topic than the one you are writing about.

Writing Descriptively with Tropes

Tropes, which are usually referred to as "figurative language," are good devices for helping you write visually. They include analogies, similes, metaphors, and onomatopoeia, which use language in ways that invite readers to see an issue from new and different perspectives. Trope, in the ancient Greek, means "turn."

Use Similes and Analogies

A *simile* is a figure of speech in which one thing is compared to something that has similar features but is also very different.

> My car is like an old boyfriend. I still love it and we've had some great times together, but it's becoming unreliable and a little clunky. For now, I'm hanging on to it until something sleeker and sportier comes along.

> Up ahead, two dozen white pelicans were creating a spiral staircase as they flew. It looked like a feathered DNA molecule. Their wings reflected the sun. The light shifted, and they disappeared. (Terry Tempest Williams, *Refuge*)

A simile makes a comparison, "X is like Y," or "X is as Y," asking the readers to make visual connections between two different things. Comparing a car to an old boyfriend, for instance, calls up all kinds of interesting visual relationships.

Analogies are similes that work at two levels. When using an analogy, you are saying, "X is like Y, as A is like B."

> Like police keeping order in a city, white blood cells patrol your body's bloodstream controlling viruses and bacteria that want to do you harm.

> In the 17th century, England's reliance on imported salt was similar to the United States' dependence on foreign oil today. England's Queen Elizabeth I was especially anxious about her nation's reliance on salt from France, her nation's old enemy (Kurlansky, *Salt*, 195). So, she pushed hard for increased domestic production and sought to open other, more dependable sources of foreign salt. Indeed, England's build-up of its navy in the 17th century was prompted in part by its need to protect the importation of salt.

Analogies are used to highlight and explain complex relationships. A good analogy allows readers to visualize similar features between two things.

Use Metaphors

Metaphors are much more powerful than similes and analogies, and they tend to work at a deeper level. There are two types of metaphors that you can use to add power and depth to your writing: simple metaphors and cultural metaphors.

A *simple metaphor* states that one thing is something else, "X is Y."

> Mr. Lewis's face is an aged parchment, creased and wrinkled from his years of sailing.

> Vince, our boss, threw one grenade after another in our meeting.

> My bike is now my car—because I can't afford gas anymore!

On the surface, these metaphors say something patently false (i.e., a face is a parchment, the boss threw grenades in the meeting, a bike is a car), which urges readers to figure out an alternative meaning that fits the situation. The meaning they come up with will be much more visual than a standard description.

A simple metaphor can be extended:

> Mr. Lewis's face is an aged parchment, creased and wrinkled from his years of sailing. In his bronze skin, you can see months spent sailing in the

Caribbean. The wrinkles around his eyes reveal many years of squinting into the wind. His bent nose and a scar on his chin bear witness to the storms that have thrown him to the deck. His bright eyes peer out from beneath his white brow, hinting at a lifetime of memories that nonsailors like me will never have.

In this example, you can see the power of a fertile metaphor. You can use it to create a perspective or a unique way of "seeing" something.

There are also larger *cultural* metaphors that shape the way people think about issues. For example, here are some common metaphors that we almost take for granted:

Time is money (e.g., spend time, waste time, saved time, lost time)

Thought is light (e.g., he is bright, she was in the dark, they enlightened me)

Argument is war (e.g., she defended her argument, she attacked my claims)

Cultural metaphors like the "war on cancer" or the "war on drugs" have become so standard that we do not challenge them. And yet, the "war on X" metaphor urges us to think of a subject in a certain way.

Use Onomatopoeia

Onomatopoeia is a big word that stands for a rather simple idea. It means using words that sound like the things you are describing.

The fire *crackled* in the fireplace.   She *screeched*, "I hate this class!"

He *shuffled* down the hallway.   The trees *fluttered* in the wind.

Using onomatopoeia isn't difficult. As you draft or revise, think about the sounds that are associated with your subject. Then look for some words that actually capture those sounds.

Improving Your Writing Style

With a little practice, you can dramatically improve the power and intensity of your writing by simply paying attention to its style. You can help your readers "see" and "hear" what you are writing about. You can speed up their reading pace or slow it down—and they won't even realize you're doing it.

But good style takes time and practice. As you draft and revise, look for places to use detail, similes, analogies, metaphors, and onomatopoeia to add intensity to your writing.

If you practice these techniques, they will become a natural part of your writing skills. Then you will be able to use them without even trying.

Remember that style is a choice that you can and should make. Style is a way to express your attitude and feelings about a topic, while establishing your character and a sense of authority.

USE Plain Style

Plain style is the basis of all other writing styles. By choosing an appropriate subject for each sentence and moving it to an early place, you can clarify your writing for readers. Put the action of the sentence in the verb. Then eliminate nominalizations, boil down prepositional phrases, and eliminate redundancies.

ESTABLISH Your Voice

Think of a voice or tone that would be appropriate for your text. Then put that voice into your writing by getting into character or imitating other writers. Practice using other writers' styles and adapt their strategies to your own context and purpose.

USE Similes, Analogies, and Metaphors

Similies, analogies, and metaphors highlight relationships among different things and ideas. They allow readers to see your topic in new and interesting ways.

EXPLORE and Challenge Cultural Metaphors

Pay attention to the cultural metaphors that shape how we think. You can use those cultural metaphors or challenge them.

EVOKE Atmosphere with Sound

You can also describe something by using sound. An onomatopoeia is a word that sounds like the thing it is describing (e.g., crackling fire, shuffling walk, screeching voice). You can also use shorter and longer sentences to speed up or slow down the pace of the text.

1. With a group of people from your class, make a list of ten people who you consider stylish. What about them signals that they have good style?

2. With your group, talk about the ways people adopt a particular style or voice. Are there situations in your life when you need to adopt a different style or voice then you normally would?

3. Find three texts on the Internet that demonstrate three different styles. Have each member of your group explain why he or she likes or dislikes the style of each document. How does the style of each document fit or not fit the needs of its readers and contexts?

Talk About This

1. Find a text or author that you would like to imitate. Then, with that text on your desk or screen, try to write about a different topic but use the style of that text. Try to match its use of tone, metaphors, similes, detail, and sentence length.

2. Searching the Internet, explore the different uses of a common cultural metaphor. What does this cultural metaphor say about how we think about these subjects in our culture?

3. Come up with your own simile or metaphor—perhaps something absurd. Pick any metaphor that comes to mind. Try freewriting for three minutes with your simile or metaphor in front of you. Does the simile or metaphor give you any new insights? At what point does the simile or metaphor become far-fetched or absurd?

Try This Out

1. **Analyze a cultural metaphor.** Find a common cultural metaphor and write an analysis in which you discuss its strengths and weaknesses. Where does the metaphor fail to capture the full meaning of its subject?

2. **Review the style of an online document.** Choose a document on the Internet that exhibits good style and write a review of the document's use of any figurative language, rich descriptions, or other stylistic strategies.

Write This

PEARSON
mycomplab

For additional reading, writing, and research resources, go to **www.mycomplab.com.**

17

Designing

Imagine your own reaction to a large document with no pictures, no headings, no graphics, and no lists. Each page throws big blocks of paragraphs at you, page after page. Every page looks like a brick wall of words. If you're like most people, you wouldn't even want to start reading.

Good design makes the information in a document more accessible, and it makes reading that document more pleasurable. A well-designed text helps readers quickly locate the information they need. If your document looks accessible and attractive, readers are going to want to spend more time reading it. If it looks difficult and unattractive, they might not read it at all.

In this chapter, you will learn some basic strategies for designing your documents and creating graphics. These strategies work with any genre, depending on the kinds of information you want to share with your readers.

Before You Begin Designing

After drafting, spend some time thinking about what kind of design features would work best in this kind of text.

Genre. What design features and graphics are typical for the genre of this document? You might search for examples of the genre on the Internet to gain a sense of how they tend to look. The comments about design in Part 2 of this book will also give you some good ideas about how a specific genre uses design and graphics.

Purpose. How can you use design and graphics to achieve your purpose? Think about how your document's page layout (e.g., headings, columns, margin notes, color) could be used to highlight important information and make it more accessible to readers. Also, look for places where graphics can be used to support the written part of your text.

Readers. What kinds of design features and graphics will your readers expect or prefer? For some genres, like reports, readers are "raiders," so they expect the design to help them locate the information they need. Other genres, like memoirs, are designed to be read in a more leisurely way, so that text doesn't need to be "raidable."

Context. In what situations will readers use the document, and how do these situations shape how it should look? Think about the places where readers will use it and how they will use it.

Now you're ready to design your text. To get you started, we will begin with some basic principles of design.

Five Basic Principles of Design

Good design creates a sense of order and gives your readers *access points* to help them locate the information they need. Here are five basic principles of design that will help you make your documents accessible and attractive:

1. **Balance.** Your text should look balanced from left to right and top to bottom.

2. **Alignment.** Related words and images should be aligned vertically on the page to reveal the text's structure and its hierarchy of information.

3. **Grouping.** Related images and ideas should be put near each other on the page, so readers see them as groups.

4. **Consistency.** Design features should be used consistently and predictably, helping readers quickly interpret the layout of each page and locate the information they need.

5. **Contrast.** Items on the page that are different should *look* different, creating a feeling of boldness and confidence.

These five principles are based on the Gestalt theory of design, which is used by many graphic designers, clothing designers, architects, and artists. Once you learn these principles, you should find it easy—and perhaps even fun—to design your texts.

Design Principle 1: Balance

To balance a text, imagine that a page from your document has been placed on a point, like a pencil point. Everything you add to the left side of the page needs to be balanced with something on the right. If you add a picture to the left side, you will need to add text or perhaps another picture on the right.

For example, look at the page from a report shown in Figure 17.1 (page 360). On this page, the drawing of a hawk on the left has what graphic designers call "weight."

FIGURE 17.1
A Balanced Design

Balance creates a sense of order in documents. This page is balanced both left to right and top to bottom.

The drawing of the hawk is balanced with the written text on the right.

The header and footer balance the page on the top and bottom

This drawing strongly attracts the readers' eyes to it. So to offset this drawing, the designers decided to put a large block of two-column text on the right. Meanwhile, the heavy green borders at the top and bottom of the sheet balance with each other, making the page feel stable and steady from top to bottom.

Balance is not a matter of making the page look symmetric (the same on the left and right). The items on the left and right of the page should balance, but they don't need to mirror each other.

Balancing a Page

When graphic designers talk about how much the items on the page "weigh," they are talking about how strongly elements will attract the readers' eyes to them. For example, on a Web page, animated images weigh more than images that don't move. (That's why advertisers often use dancing people in their Internet ads.)

Here are some guidelines for balancing the features on a page:

- Pictures weigh more than written text.

- Color items weigh more than black and white items.

- Big items weigh more than small ones.

- Strange shapes weigh more than standard shapes.

- Things on the right side of the page weigh more than things on the left.

- Things on the top of the page weigh more than things on the bottom.

- Moving features, like Web page animations, weigh more than static ones.

You can use these guidelines to help you balance just about any page. As you design your document, don't be afraid to move items around on the page to see how they look.

Using Columns

You might also try using columns to create a balanced document design. The page shown in Figure 17.1, for example, uses a three-column layout to structure the page and create a sense of balance. The designers of this page decided to devote the left column to graphics, and they saved the right two columns for written text.

Design Principle 2: Alignment

Your readers will subconsciously search for visual relationships among items on the page. If two items line up on the page, they will assume that those two items are related in some way. If a picture, for example, is vertically aligned with a caption, list, or block of text on a page, readers will naturally assume that they go together.

For example, in Figure 17.2, the absence of alignment means the page on the left gives no hint about the levels of information, making it difficult for readers to find what they are looking for in the text. The page on the right, on the other hand, uses vertical alignment to highlight the levels in the text. Most readers would find the text on the right easier to read, because they immediately understand how the information is structured.

To create vertical alignment in your page design:

- Use margins and indentation consistently to highlight the hierarchy of the information.

- Use bulleted lists or numbered lists whenever possible to set off related information from the main text.

- Adjust the placement of any photographs or graphics to align vertically with the text around them, so readers see them as belonging together.

To check alignment on a page, use a straightedge, like a ruler or the edge of a piece of paper, to determine if items on the page line up.

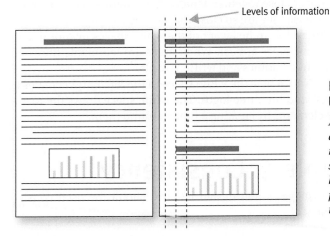

FIGURE 17.2
Using Vertical Alignment

Aligning text vertically allows you to show different levels of information in the text, making the document easier to read and scan. The page on the left is harder to read because it has minimal alignment. The page on the right uses alignment to signal the levels of information in the text.

FIGURE 17.3
Using Grouping

Grouping is a good way to help readers put items together on the page. In this page, for example, you can see four distinct blocks of information that are grouped together, making the text easier to read.

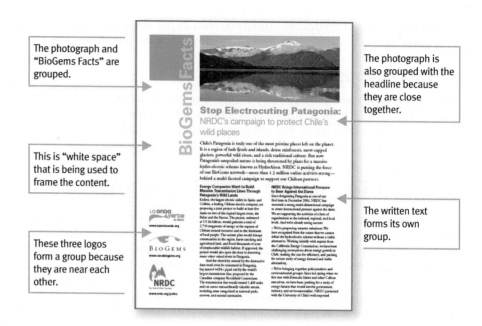

The photograph and "BioGems Facts" are grouped.

This is "white space" that is being used to frame the content.

These three logos form a group because they are near each other.

The photograph is also grouped with the headline because they are close together.

The written text forms its own group.

Design Principle 3: Grouping

The design principle "grouping" takes advantage of your readers' tendency to see any items on a page that are close together as belonging to a group. If a photograph appears near a block of text, your readers will naturally assume that the image and text are related. Similarly, if a heading appears near a block of written text, the readers will see the heading as belonging with the written text.

Figure 17.3 shows a page design that uses grouping well. The "BioGems Facts" on the top left of the page is put close to the picture of mountains on the top right, creating a group. The three logos in the bottom left are grouped together, forming a unit. Also, the picture and the green headline, "Stop Electrocuting Patagonia," can be seen as one group because they appear close together. Finally, the columns of text are naturally seen as a group, too, because they are so close together on the page.

One key to using grouping well is to be aware of the white spaces in your document's design where no text or images appear. When areas are left blank, they become eye-catching frames around graphics and written words.

Look again at Figure 17.3. Notice how the white space in the left margin creates a frame for the "BioGems Facts" and the three logos. The white space draws the readers' attention to these visual elements by creating a frame around them.

Design Principle 4: Consistency

The principle of consistency suggests that design features should be used consistently throughout the document:

- Headings should be used in a predictable and repeatable way.

- Pages should follow a predictable design pattern.

- Lists should use consistent bullets or numbering schemes.

- Headers, footers, and page numbers should be used to help make each page look similar to the others.

Consistency creates a sense of order in your document's design, so your readers know what to expect. If the page design or features like headings or images are used consistently, your readers will find it easier to understand how your document is structured.

Choosing Typefaces

A good first step toward consistency is to choose appropriate typefaces. A typeface is the design of the letters in your written text (e.g., Times Roman, Arial, Bookman, Helvetica). As a basic guideline, you should only choose one or two typefaces for your document. Many graphic designers like to choose one typeface for the headings and a different typeface for the main text.

There are two basic types of typeface: serif and sans serif. A serif typeface, like Times Roman, New York, or Bookman, has small tips (serifs) at the ends of the main strokes in each letter (Figure 17.4). Sans serif typefaces like Arial and Helvetica do not have these small tips. ("Sans serif" means "without serifs" in French.)

Serif fonts are considered more formal and traditional. They are useful for the main text and parts of a document where readability is important. Most people think sans serif fonts, like Helvetica and Arial, look more modern. They are especially useful for titles, headings, footers, captions, and parts of a document where you want to catch readers' eyes.

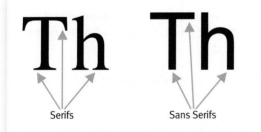

Serifs Sans Serifs

FIGURE 17.4 Serif vs. Sans Serif Typefaces

Serif fonts, like Times Roman on the left, have serifs, while sans serif fonts, like Arial on the right, do not have them.

Using Headings Consistently

Headings are very useful visual elements in any kind of document, but you need to use them consistently (Figure 17.5, page 364). Make some choices up front about the levels of headings you will use.

FIGURE 17.5 Levels of Headings

The headings you choose for your document should be clearly distinguishable from the body text and from each other. That way, your readers can see the hierarchy of your text clearly.

> ## Document Title: The Best College Paper Ever Written
>
> ### First-Level Headings
>
> These "A heads" divide a document into its major sections. They are usually significantly larger and bolder and use a different font than the body text.
>
> *Second-Level Headings*
>
> These "B heads" divide sections into smaller subsections. While these use the same font as the first-level headings, they should differ significantly in size or style (such as italics).
>
> **Third-Level Headings.** These "C heads" might be the same font and size as the body text (and appear on the same line), but use bold or italics to distinguish them.

Title. The title of the document should be sized significantly larger than other headings in the text. You might consider using color to set off the title, or you could center it.

First-Level Headings ("A Heads"). These are the most common headings. They divide your text into its major sections. First-level headings are often bold and slightly larger than the text used in the body of the document.

Second-Level Headings ("B Heads"). These are used when you need to divide a large section in your document into even smaller parts. These headings tend to use italics and can be the same size as the body text.

Third-Level Headings ("C Heads"). These are usually the smallest level of headings. They are often italicized or boldfaced and placed on the same line as the body text.

Headings help readers in a few important ways. First, they offer access points into the text, giving readers obvious places to locate the information they need. Second, they highlight the structure of the text, breaking down the larger document into smaller blocks of information. Third, they give readers places to take breaks from reading sentence after sentence, paragraph after paragraph.

Headings are also beneficial to you as the writer, because they help you make transitions between large sections of the document. Instead of a clumsy, "And now, let me move on to the next issue" kind of statement, you can use a heading to quickly and cleanly signal the transition to a new subject. Headings also allow you, as the writer, to easily see the overall structure of your text so you can check the logic and sequence.

Design Principle 5: Contrast

The fifth and final design principle is *contrast*. Using contrast means making different items on the page look significantly different. Your headings, for example, should look significantly different than the main text. Your title should also be clearly distinguishable from your headings.

There are a variety of ways to create contrast in your document's design. You can change the size of the font, add color, use shading, and use highlighting features like boldface, italics, or underlining. The sample report shown in Figure 17.6 uses contrast in several important ways:

- The blue banner across the top, "Geothermal Technologies Program, Colorado," clearly contrasts with the rest of the items on the page because it uses big lettering and a bold color.

- Below the banner, the italicized text contrasts sharply with the body text, helping it stand out on the page.

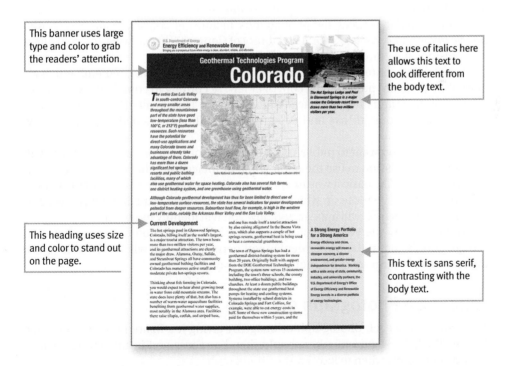

This banner uses large type and color to grab the readers' attention.

The use of italics here allows this text to look different from the body text.

This heading uses size and color to stand out on the page.

This text is sans serif, contrasting with the body text.

FIGURE 17.6 Using Contrast

Contrast makes a page look more readable and attractive. This page uses several kinds of contrast to capture the readers' attention.

- The blue heading "Current Development" is clearly distinguishable from the body text because it is larger and uses color.

- In the blue screened box on the right of the page, the use of a sans serif font helps to distinguish this text from the body text just to its left.

The secret to using contrast is experimenting with the page design to see how things look. So be daring and explore how items on the page look when you add contrast. Try making visual features larger, bolder, more colorful, or different.

Using Photography and Images

With the design capabilities of today's computers, you should always look for ways to add photography and other images to your document. To add a picture, you can use a digital camera or a mobile phone to snap the picture, or you can download a picture from the Internet.

Downloading Photographs and Images from the Internet

If you find a photograph or image on the Internet that you want to use, save the image to your hard drive, and insert it into your document.

Some popular sources for photographs include *Flickr.com, Photobucket.com, Google Images,* and *Zooomr.com*. The Library of Congress (http://www.loc.gov) offers many historical pictures that you can use for free.

When using photographs and images taken from the Internet, remember that almost all of them are protected by copyright law. According to copyright law, you can use photographs and images for academic purposes. This is called "fair use." You can find out more about fair use and copyright law at the U.S. Copyright Office (www.copyright.gov).

However, if you want to publish your document or put it on the Internet, you will need to ask permission to use the photograph or image from the person or organization that owns it. The easiest way to ask permission is to send an e-mail to the person who manages the Web site on which you found the image. Explain how you want to use the image, where it will appear, and how you will identify its source.

In most cases, the Web site owner will give you permission or explain how you can get permission. If the owner denies you permission, you will not be able to use the photograph or image in any nonacademic way.

Labeling a Photograph or Image

You should label each photograph or image by giving it a figure number and a title (Figure 17.7). The figure number should then be mentioned in the written text, so your readers know when to look for the photograph.

Captions are not mandatory, but they can help your readers understand how the image relates to the written text.

FIGURE 17.7 Labeling a Photograph

Proper labeling will help readers understand how the graphic supports the written text.

Figure number and title.

Fig. 1: A Tiktaalik

The Tiktaalik was a prehistoric fish that had four legs. Paleontologists think this creature fills the fossil gap between fish and early limbed animals.

Caption and source information.

Source: Natl. Sci. Found., Oct. 2008; Web; 19 Mar. 2009.

Using Graphs and Charts

Graphs and charts can also be helpful additions to your documents, especially if you are presenting data to your readers. Genres like reports and proposals routinely use graphs and charts to illustrate data. These graphics can also be useful in evaluations and position papers to provide support for claims in the written text.

Creating a Graph or Chart

If you need to make your own graph or chart, your best option might be to use the spreadsheet program, such as *Excel* or *Quattro Pro,* that came bundled with your word-processing software (Figure 17.8). Simpler graphs can be made in presentation software, like *PowerPoint* or *Keynote.*

These spreadsheet and presentation software packages can help you create quick graphs and charts from a data set. Then you can insert the graphic right into your document. (Your word processor will probably have a Chart feature that will take you to the spreadsheet program.) Once you have created the graph, you should add a title and label the horizontal x-axis and vertical y-axis (Figure 17.8, page 368). These axes need to be clearly labeled, so readers know exactly what they measure.

After you have inserted your graph into your document, make sure you have labeled it properly and provided a citation for the source of the data. To label the graph, give it a number or letter and a title. For example, the graph in Figure 17.8 is called "Figure 5: Average Rainfall, SW Counties by Decade." After you have labeled

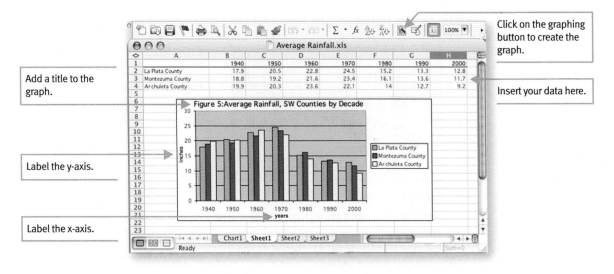

FIGURE 17.8   Using Spreadsheet Software to Make a Graph

A spreadsheet is a helpful tool for creating a graph. Enter your data and then click the graphing button to create a graph. Then you can insert the graph into your document.

the graph, include your source below the graph using a common citation style (e.g., MLA, APA).

In the written part of your document, refer to the graphic by its number, so readers know when to refer to it. When you want the readers to consider the graph, write something like, "As shown in Figure 5, the annual rainfall. . . ." Or, you can simply put "(Figure 5)" at the end of the sentence where you refer to the graph.

Choosing the Appropriate Graph or Chart

You can use various kinds of graphs and charts to display your data. Each graph or chart allows you to tell a different story to your readers.

Line Graph.   A line graph is a good way to show measurements or trends over time. In a line graph, the vertical axis (y-axis) displays a measured quantity, such as temperature, sales, growth, and so on. The horizontal axis (x-axis) is usually divided into time increments such as years, months, days, or hours. See Figure 17.9.

Bar Chart.   Bar charts are used to show quantities, allowing readers to make visual comparisons among different amounts. Like line graphs, bar charts can be used to show fluctuations in quantities over time. See Figure 17.10.

Pie Charts.   Pie charts are useful for showing how a whole quantity is divided into parts. These charts are a quick way to add a visual element into your document, but they should be used sparingly. They take up a great amount of space in a document while usually presenting only a small amount of data. See Figure 17.11.

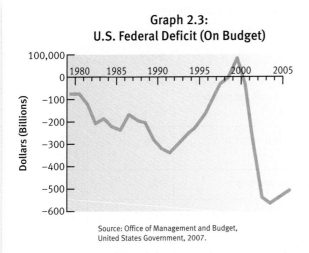

Graph 2.3:
U.S. Federal Deficit (On Budget)

Source: Office of Management and Budget,
United States Government, 2007.

FIGURE 17.9
Line Graph

A line graph is a good way to show a trend over time. In this graph, the line reveals a trend that would not be apparent from the data alone.

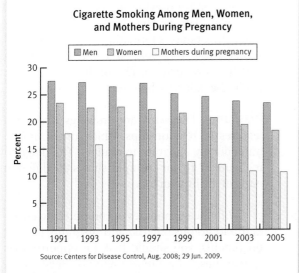

Cigarette Smoking Among Men, Women, and Mothers During Pregnancy

Source: Centers for Disease Control, Aug. 2008; 29 Jun. 2009.

FIGURE 17.10 Bar Chart

A bar chart allows you to show quantities, especially quantities changing over time.

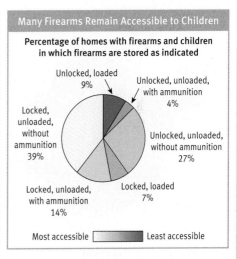

Many Firearms Remain Accessible to Children

Percentage of homes with firearms and children in which firearms are stored as indicated

Source: Schuster et al., 2000.

FIGURE 17.11 Pie Chart

A pie chart is a good way to show how a whole is divided into parts. When using a pie chart, you should label the slices of the pie and add the numerical information that was used to create the chart.

FIGURE 17.12
Table

A table offers a great way to show data efficiently. This table combines words and data to illustrate differences between boys' and girls' malicious uses of the Internet.

Online Rumors Tend to Target Girls *Have you, personally, ever experienced any of the following things online?*		
	Boys	**Girls**
Someone taking a private e-mail, IM, or text message you sent them and forwarding it to someone else or posting it where others could see it	13%	17%
Someone sending you a threatening or aggressive e-mail, IM, or text message	10%	15%
Someone spreading a rumor about you online	9%	16%
Someone posting an embarrassing picture of you online without your permission	5%	7%
At least one of the forms of cyberbullying listed above	23%	36%

Source: *Few Internet and American Life Project Parents and Teens Survey,* 2006.

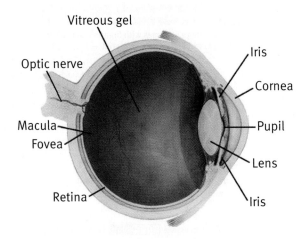

Labels: Vitreous gel, Optic nerve, Macula, Fovea, Retina, Iris, Cornea, Pupil, Lens, Iris

FIGURE 17.13   A Diagram

A diagram is only partially realistic. It shows only the most important features and concentrates on relationships instead of showing exactly what the subject looks like.

Tables. Tables provide the most efficient way to display data or facts in a small amount of space. In a table, information is placed in horizontal rows and vertical columns, allowing readers to quickly locate specific numbers or words that address their interests (Figure 17.12).

Diagrams. Diagrams are drawings that show features or relationships, which might not be immediately apparent to readers. The diagram in Figure 17.13, for example, shows the different parts of the human eye.

With the capabilities of computers to create and add graphs, charts, and diagrams to your documents, you should look for opportunities to use these illustration methods. Readers expect these kinds of visuals, especially in reports and proposals, to reinforce and clarify your main points.

Now it's time to make your document look better. Here are some basic strategies for designing your document.

REVIEW Your Genre, Purpose, Readers, and Context

Your document's design should reflect and reinforce the genre and the overall purpose of your text. Design features should also be appropriate for your readers and the contexts in which your document will be used.

BALANCE the Text

Use design features to balance elements on the left and right as well as on the top and bottom of the page.

ALIGN Items Vertically on the Page

Look for opportunities to vertically align items on the page. Indenting text and aligning graphics with text will help create a sense of hierarchy and structure in your document.

GROUP Related Items Together

Put items near each other that are meant to be seen together. Photos should be near any text they reinforce. Headings should be close to the paragraphs they lead off. Use white space to frame items you want to be seen as a group.

CHECK the Document for Consistency

Your headings and other design features should be used consistently throughout the document. Make sure you use lists consistently.

ADD Some Contrast

Items on the page that are different should look significantly different. Use color and font size to make written text stand out.

INCLUDE Photographs, Graphs, and Charts

Add your own photographs or images downloaded from the Internet to your document. Create graphs or charts to illustrate data and complex ideas. Number, title, and caption these visuals so readers understand how the images connect to your text.

Talk About This

1. Ask each member in your group to bring a favorite magazine. Discuss the magazine's full-page advertisements and their use of design features. Pay special attention to the use of balance, alignment, grouping, consistency, and contrast.

2. Discuss the design of your favorite Web sites. What kinds of design features make it a favorite? What design features help you access information more easily?

3. On campus or in the community, find a flyer or brochure that you think is a failure in design. With your group, discuss how the document could be redesigned to make it more accessible and attractive.

Try This Out

1. Find a document on the Internet, on campus, or at your workplace that shows minimal attention to design. Then do a "design makeover" to make the document more accessible and attractive to readers.

2. Write a brief critique of the visual elements of a document you found on campus or at your workplace. Show how each of these five design principles makes its design effective or ineffective.

3. Practice downloading photographs and images and inserting them into a document. Add figure numbers and titles to the images. Include captions that explain the images and their relevance to your document.

Write This

1. **Evaluate the design of a document.** Write an evaluation in which you discuss the visual design of a document of your choice. Your analysis should consider whether the design is appropriate for the document's topic, purpose, readers, and context.

2. **Redesign a document on a computer.** Choose a document you wrote earlier in the semester. Redesign the document with your computer, using some of the concepts and principles discussed in this chapter. Then write a brief evaluation in which you discuss your design decisions.

18

Revising and Editing

N ow it's time to take your text from "good" to "excellent" by revising and editing it. This chapter shows you how to revise and edit your work at four different levels. Each level asks you to concentrate on different aspects of your text, moving from global issues to small details.

Level 1: Global Revision reexamines and adjusts the document's overall approach, using genre to sharpen its topic, angle, purpose, and appropriateness for the readers and context.

Level 2: Substantive Editing pays attention to the document's content, organization, and design.

Level 3: Copyediting focuses on revising the style for clarity, persuasion, and consistency, paying close attention to paragraphs and sentences.

Level 4: Proofreading examines and revises surface features, such as grammatical correctness, spelling, and usage.

As shown in Figure 18.1 on page 374, you should work from the "global level" (global editing) to the "local level" (proofreading). That way, you can start out making large-scale changes to your document. Then, as the paper gets closer to finished, you can focus exclusively on style and correctness.

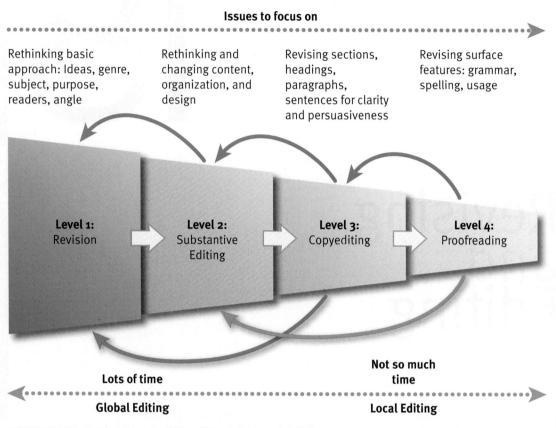

Issues to focus on

Rethinking basic approach: Ideas, genre, subject, purpose, readers, angle

Rethinking and changing content, organization, and design

Revising sections, headings, paragraphs, sentences for clarity and persuasiveness

Revising surface features: grammar, spelling, usage

Level 1: Revision

Level 2: Substantive Editing

Level 3: Copyediting

Level 4: Proofreading

Lots of time

Not so much time

Global Editing

Local Editing

FIGURE 18.1 The Four Levels of Revising and Editing

Whether you are revising and editing your own work or helping someone else revise and edit their work, the process can be broken down into four levels. The idea is to progress toward a final, polished draft efficiently, taking care of the big issues first (purpose, audience) and then moving toward final editing and polishing.

Level 1: Global Revision

All right. You finished your first draft. Now it's time to reexamine and reconsider your project's topic, angle, and purpose, and your understanding of the readers and the context.

Figure 18.2 shows an excerpt of a student's proposal when it was a first draft. Figure 18.3 (on page 377) shows how Brad's original notes helped him challenge his ideas and rethink how he could persuade his readers to agree with him.

America Is Addicted to Oil

When I hear all the whining about gas prices, it makes me really mad. After all, it's not like we haven't been warned. Economists and environmentalists have been telling the American people for years that this day of reckoning would come. Now it's here, and everyone is acting like they have been completely caught off guard. They don't have solutions. They just want another hit of their drug.

This crisis reminds me of people trying to quit smoking. I started smoking when I was 16 and I smoked for three years until I started college. Why did I stop? Well, I knew it was bad for me, but mostly I couldn't afford it anymore. That's kind of where America is right now. We know our addiction to oil is bad for us, but as long as it doesn't cost too much, we keep using. We'll deal with the effects later. So, why can't we break our addiction to oil like a smoker breaks the nicotine addiction?

How do we stop being addicted to oil? One of my friends gave me a book that helped me stop smoking. It is called *Seven Tools to Beat Addiction*, and it's by a social/clinical psychologist who has helped many people beat their addictions to smoking, sex, pornography, drugs, gambling, etc. The seven tools he describes would work well to help American get off its oil habit, like when I stopped smoking:

1. *Values:* Build a foundation of values—We need to rethink what it means to be a nation again. Americans need to stop being so greedy and selfish.

2. *Motivation:* Activate our desire to quit—It's not going to happen until we admit we have a problem and want to break our addiction.

> Brad notices that his topic is mostly about gasoline prices, not about other oil-related issues (see his notes in Figure 18.3).

> Brad figures out that his best angle is the "Our addiction to oil is like an addiction to nicotine." He decides to stress that angle in the next draft.

continued

FIGURE 18.2 Rough Draft

With global revision, you need to look at the big picture and rethink your basic approach. Here is an excerpt from student writer Brad's rough draft of a proposal. Figure 18.3 shows part of his global revision.

FIGURE 18.2
Rough Draft
(continued)

3. *Reward:* Weigh the costs and benefits of addiction—Imagine all the money we'll save if it's not all going over to Saudi Arabia and Russia! Plus, pollution will go down and we'll be more healthy.

4. *Resources:* Identify strengths and weaknesses—We have lots of possible sources of alternative energy. Plus, we already have lots of highly educated people who can figure this stuff out.

> Brad realizes that this list is messy and long. So he decides to trim it down, while expanding on some of the more important concepts.

5. *Support:* Get help from those nearest to us—Right now, other nations are a little upset with us. But, if they see us on the right track, they will probably start working with us, not against us.

6. *A Mature Identity:* Grow into self-respect and responsibility—For the last decade, our nation has been acting like an immature brat on the world stage. It's time to start acting like a mature country again.

7. *Higher Goals:* Pursue and accomplish things of value—Maybe we can strive for a better, cleaner world instead of just trying figure out how we can keep the cheap gas flowing.

> He sees that he needs to expand on the argument in this paragraph. Right now it's mostly broad statements with minimal concrete support.

Getting over an addiction is tough. I still feel those cravings for nicotine. Getting ourselves off oil is going to be hard and even a little painful. We are going to be tested, and our pushers will be waiting for us to fail. But the benefits of ending our oil addiction has so many benefits. We will save money, our health, and improve our national security. We've taken the first step. We admitted we have a problem. Now, let's get to work.

Notes on First Draft (Global Revision)

I'm writing a proposal to fix our dependence on oil as an energy source.

Topic: My topic is how to solve the oil crisis that we are facing right now. I need to concentrate mostly on consumer's need for gasoline to drive. Also, I want to bring in some of the environmental benefits of transitioning to alternative fuels. I want to show how seeing oil as an addiction can be a path to solving the problem.

Angle: My angle is the metaphor "America is addicted to oil." What happens if we took that metaphor seriously and treat oil as a drug that America is addicted to? As someone who was addicted to nicotine, I think I have some insight into how it feels to fight an addiction and what it takes to win.

Purpose: I don't think my purpose is clearly stated in this draft. So, here it is in one sentence: The purpose of my paper is to argue that America needs to treat oil as a drug and we need to recognize that we are addicted to that drug; so, we need to use drug rehab steps to end our addiction. (That's messy).

Readers: Mostly, I thought I was writing to everyone, but now I realize that I am writing mostly to younger people who can't afford these gas prices and really want to do something to change the world.

> *Expectations*— First my readers need to understand the real problem. Then they need a clear strategy for solving that problem. The media keeps acting as though this problem is really about gas prices. That's just a symptom of the deeper problem underneath. My readers need to see that the prices are not the real problem.

> *Values*—My values are similar to my readers' values. They care about the environment, but they also like the freedom of driving and traveling. They're also realistic about this problem. They want to do the right thing, but they know an easy solution isn't out there.

> *Attitudes*—They are probably frustrated with the gas prices like most people. I would like to tap into their frustration, turn it into anger, and then get my readers to consider my solution. Get angry at that drug! It's the best way to fight it!

Here are Brad's notes to help him with the global revision process.

Brad realizes that he needs to narrow his topic.

He points out that his purpose is not fully stated in this first draft.

Brad analyzes his readers to figure out how he can use their expectations, values, and attitudes to persuade them.

FIGURE 18.3 Global Revision

Brad's professor asked him to reflect on his first draft. In these notes, Brad is examining what he hopes to accomplish with a global revision of his proposal draft.

Challenge Your Draft's Topic, Angle, and Purpose

You need to challenge your first draft to make sure it's doing what you intended. Reread your draft, paying special attention to the following global issues:

Topic. How has your topic evolved since you started? Do you now have a better understanding of the boundaries of your topic? Can you sharpen the topic, or does it need to be broadened a little? Can you find any places where your paper strays from the topic? Can you find any gaps in your coverage where you don't address a key issue about your topic?

Angle. Have you shown what is new about your topic or what has changed recently? Have you connected your paper to any recent events or changes in our culture? Have you uncovered any unexpected or surprising issues that complicate or challenge your own views?

Purpose. Is your purpose clear in the introduction of your paper, and have you achieved that purpose by the conclusion? Does your purpose need to be more focused?

Chapter 2 discusses these issues in depth if you would like more strategies for shaping your topic, angle, and purpose.

Think About Your Readers (Again) and the Context

As you drafted your paper, chances are good that you gained a better understanding of your readers' expectations, values, and attitudes. Now try to put yourself in your readers' place to imagine how they will react to your ideas and the way you have expressed them.

Expectations. Have you given readers all the information they need to make a decision? What additional information do they need if they are going to agree with you? Are there any places in your paper where you can cut out information that goes beyond what the readers need to know?

Values. Are your readers' values different from yours? If so, have you anticipated their values and how their values might cause them to react differently to your ideas than you would? Can you add anything that would appeal to their sense of values or help build trust between you and them?

Attitudes. Have you adjusted the text to fit your primary readers' attitude about your topic? If they have a positive attitude about your topic, have you reinforced that attitude? If they have a negative attitude, have you given them good reasons to think differently about your topic?

Now look at the context for your document. Again, it's likely that you have developed a stronger understanding of the place, medium, and social-political issues that will influence how your readers receive and interpret your ideas.

Place. How will the physical place in which readers experience your document shape how they read it? What will they see, hear, and feel? What is moving in this place, and who will be there? How will the history and culture of this place shape how readers will interpret what you are saying?

Medium. How does the technology you used to present the information shape how people read it? Paper documents are received differently than on-screen documents. Information provided as presentations, videos, and podcasts will also be understood in unique ways.

Social and Political Influences. What current social, economic, and political trends are in play with your topic and readers? How will your ideas affect your readers' relationships with others or their economic and political concerns?

If you need more help profiling your readers and understanding the contexts in which they will use your document, turn to Chapter 3, "Readers, Contexts, and Rhetorical Situations."

Level 2: Substantive Editing

When doing "substantive editing," you should look closely at the content, organization, and design of your document. Read through your paper again, paying attention to the following issues:

Determine Whether You Have Enough Information (or Too Much)

Your paper needs to have enough information to support its claims and explain your ideas to readers, but you don't want to include more content than you need.

- ❑ Does your purpose statement and main claim (usually in the introduction and/or the conclusion) describe what you're achieving in this paper?

- ❑ Are your claims in the body of the paper expressed completely and accurately? Could you express them in a more prominent, precise, or compelling way?

- ❑ Can you find any places where your ideas need more support or where your claims need more evidence drawn from sources?

- ❑ Are there any digressions? Can you trim the text down?

If you need more information or sources to back up your ideas, turn to Chapter 25, "Finding Sources and Collecting Information."

Reorganize Your Work to Highlight Major Ideas

Your readers will expect your document to conform to the genre's typical organizational pattern. This does not mean mechanically following a formula, but it does mean that your document should reflect the features your readers will expect in this genre.

- ❑ Does your paper have each of the sections that are usually included in this genre? If not, are you making a conscious choice to leave out a section or merge it with something else?

❏ Does your introduction do its job according to the conventions of the genre? Does it draw your readers in, introduce them to the topic, state the purpose and main claim, and stress the importance of the subject?

❏ Are your main ideas prominent enough? If not, can you move these main ideas to places where your readers are more likely to see them?

❏ Does the conclusion do its job according to the conventions of the genre? Does it restate the main point of the whole paper, reemphasize the importance of the topic, and offer a look to the future?

❏ Do the introduction and conclusion echo each other? If not, can you adjust your introduction and conclusion so they are clearly talking about the same topic, angle, and purpose?

Chapter 19 discusses introductions and conclusions, and Chapter 20 discusses paragraphing and sections.

Look for Ways to Improve the Design

Review how your document looks, focusing on whether the design is a good fit for your readers. The design should make your text easier to read and more attractive.

❏ Does the design of the document match your readers' expectations for the genre? Is the visual "tone" of the design appropriate for this genre?

❏ From a distance, does the text look inviting, interesting, and easy to read? Can you use page design, images, or color to make it more attractive and inviting to your readers?

❏ Have you used the design principles of balance, alignment, grouping, consistency, and contrast to organize and structure the page layout?

❏ Have you used graphics and charts to reinforce and clarify the written text while adding a visual element to the document?

Chapter 17, "Designing," offers some helpful strategies for improving the design of your document.

Ask Someone Else to Read Your Work

Substantive editing is a good time to ask others to review your work. Ask a friend or someone from your class to read through your text. Tell him or her to concentrate on content, organization, and design. For now, your editor can ignore any typos or grammatical errors, because right now you need feedback on higher-level features and problems in the text.

For example, Figure 18.4 shows some helpful substantive editing comments from Rachel, a person in Brad's class, on his second draft. Brad has made significant improvements to his first draft (shown in Figure 18.2). Rachel's thorough comments will help him improve it even more, because they highlight the proposal's weaknesses in content, organization, and design.

America Is Addicted to Oil

When gasoline prices rose dramatically in the summer of 2008, American citizens whined and complained. They called for more oil to be pumped from the arctic, from the shores of California and Florida, from shale oil deposits in Colorado. They yelled at gas station attendants and wrote angry letters to newspapers and members of Congress.

But it's not as though we didn't see this coming. For years, economists, conservationists, and political leaders have been telling the American public that the cheap ride on foreign oil would be coming to an end. The demand for oil was continually going up, especially with emerging economies like those in China, India, and Brazil demanding more oil. Yet, people kept buying big cars and commuting longer and longer distances. It's not as though we weren't warned.

Back up these claims with cites from sources.

America is a junkie, and oil is our heroin. In this proposal, I would like to show how treating oil as an addiction can help us get out of this terrible situation and perhaps even save the planet.

Your purpose statement is clear, but it could be less blunt.

How do we stop being addicted to oil? As someone who stopped smoking, I know just how difficult it can be to break an addiction. After smoking for almost three years, I decided that I wanted to quit. One of my friends gave me a book written by psychologist Stanton Peele called *Seven Tools to Beat Addiction,* which I will discuss below.

I noticed that you don't really have a section that discusses the problem. Instead, you just go straight to the solution. Maybe you should spend a little more time talking about the causes and effects of the problem.

Values: Build a foundation of values—We need to have a national conversation about what we value as Americans. Right now, our society is running on consumerism, greed, and selfishness. We need to build or rebuild a sense of common values in which the community's needs balance with the desires of the individual.

continued

FIGURE 18.4 Substantive Editing

Brad revised his first draft for a peer review session the next day. Here is the second draft and substantive editing comments from Rachel in his writing group.

This is cool, but some outside support would make it stronger.

A picture, chart, or graph would support what you are saying here.

This list could be designed better to make it more readable.

Some quotes from sources would make this part much stronger.

Motivation: Activate our desire to quit—Both major political parties need to reach consensus on this issue and then work together to solve it. We cannot kick the habit if one party or the other is telling us we don't really have a problem.

Reward: Weigh the costs and benefits of addiction—Our government needs to commission scientific studies that show Americans the real costs of oil, such as the costs to our health, our environment, and the military we need to protect our flow of the drug. Only then will be able to truly measure the benefits of getting off the junk.

Resources: Identify strengths and weaknesses—Our nation needs to recognize that our scientific, technological, and manufacturing capabilities would allow us to make a relatively quick conversion to other forms of energy, like solar, wind, and nuclear. Our weaknesses, however, include short-sighted thinking and selfishness, which is a downside of American individualism.

Support: Get help from those nearest to us—Like any addict, the United States is going to need support. Certainly, our Allies in Europe and Asia would be willing to help. They're recovering addicts too. But, we also have good neighbors in Canada and Mexico, who we could work with to bring about this change. Each of our neighbors has alternative energy strengths that we could tap into.

A Mature Identity: Grow into self-respect and responsibility—The United States has been behaving like a young addict, who lacks care for himself and lacks responsibility for his actions. This nation needs to mature and start taking on the priorities of an adult, such as caring for others, making tough decisions, and protecting those who are weaker than us.

FIGURE 18.4 **Substantive Editing** *(continued)*

Higher Goals: Pursue and accomplish things of value—Our addiction has caused us to give up on many of those "American ideals" that made us strong in the first place. We're cutting exploration, innovation, diplomacy, and creativity, so we can continue our flow of the drug. It's time to get back to what America once was—a beacon of freedom and hope. A place where people could dream big and fill those dreams. Once the drug is out of our system, we can start to think about the future again, rather than just our next fix. Let's be honest. Getting ourselves off oil is going to be hard and a little painful. It's a life change, and we are going to be tested. But the benefits of ending our oil addiction are enormous. We will save money, our health, and improve our national security. We've taken the first step. We admitted we have a problem. Now, let's do something about it.

Perhaps you can expand on the benefits of doing this. More discussion of the benefit might help win over your readers.

Overall, Brad, I really like your paper. Comparing America's need for oil to a drug addiction really helped me see the problem we have. Your purpose seems clear enough, and I think I understand your main point. One big problem is that you make some pretty big claims that aren't really supported with evidence in your paper.

The design is pretty boring (sorry). Can't you find some images or graphs that would strengthen your argument and make the text more attractive?

FIGURE 18.4 Substantive Editing *(continued)*

Level 3: Copyediting

Copyediting involves improving the "flow" of your text by making it *clear, concise, consistent,* and *correct* (sometimes called the "Four Cs" by professional copyeditors). When you are copyediting, focus exclusively on your document's title and headings, paragraphs, and sentences. Your ideas need to be as clear as possible and stated as concisely as possible. Also, make sure your ideas are consistent and that your facts are accurate.

Review Your Title and Headings

Your title should grab the reader's attention, and the headings in your document should help the reader quickly grasp your ideas and understand how the document is structured.

- ❐ Is the title unique, and does it grab the readers' attention? If your readers saw the title alone, would they be interested in reading your paper?

- ❐ Do the headings accurately reflect the information that follows them?

- ❐ Do the headings grab the readers' attention and bring them into the text?

- ❐ Are the headings consistent in grammar and parallel to each other in structure?

You can learn more about using effective titles and headings in Chapter 15, "Organizing and Drafting," and Chapter 17, "Designing."

Edit Paragraphs to Make Them Concise and Consistent

Work through your document paragraph by paragraph, paying attention to how each one is structured and how it works with the paragraphs around it.

As you read through each paragraph, ask yourself these questions:

- ❐ Would a transition sentence at the beginning of the paragraph help make a bridge from the prior paragraph?

- ❐ Would transitions help bridge any gaps between sentences in the paragraph?

- ❐ Is each paragraph unified? Does each sentence in the paragraph stick to a consistent topic? Do any sentences seem to stray from the paragraph's claim or statement?

- ❐ Does each paragraph logically follow from the paragraph that preceded it and does it prepare readers for the paragraph that follows?

- ❐ If the paragraph is long or complex, would it benefit from a "point sentence" at its end that states or restates the paragraph's overall point?

Of course, there are exceptions to these guidelines. If you are using an "open-form genre" (e.g., memoir or other narrative), your paragraphs may be designed to lead your readers from one moment to the next or one event to the next.

Revise Sentences to Make Them Clearer

After you reshape and refine each paragraph, focus your attention on the clarity and style of individual sentences.

- ❐ Are the subjects of your sentences easy to locate? Do they tend to be placed early in the sentence where your readers can easily find them?

❏ Do the verbs express the action of the sentence? Can you remove any passive verbs (e.g., *is, was, be, has been*) by putting an action verb in its place?

❏ Can you eliminate any unnecessary prepositional phrases?

❏ Are your sentences breathing length? Are any sentences too long (i.e., do they take longer than one breath to say out loud)?

In Chapter 16, "Choosing a Style," you can find some "plain style" techniques for improving the clarity of your sentences while making them more concise.

Revise Sentences to Make Them More Descriptive

Now, work on giving your sentences more impact and power.

❏ Do your sentences use vivid detail to help readers visualize what you are writing about? Can you use sight, hearing, smell, taste, and feel to enhance the experience of reading your sentences?

❏ Would any similes, metaphors, or analogies help your readers to understand or visualize what you are talking about?

❏ Do your sentences generally use a consistent tone and voice? Can you describe in one word the tone you are trying to set in your paper? Do your sentences achieve that tone?

Level 4: Proofreading

Proofreading is the final step in editing your document, during which you should search for any typos, grammatical errors, spelling mistakes, and word usage problems. Proofreading takes patience and practice, but it is critical to successful writing.

These proofreading strategies will help you catch those kinds of errors:

Read Your Writing Out Loud

Your ear will often detect problems that slip past your eyes. When reading your paper out loud, you need to pay attention to every word. Errors that may slip by when reading silently really stick out when reading aloud.

Read Your Draft Backwards

By reading your draft backwards, sentence by sentence, you can concentrate on the words rather than their meaning. You will find yourself noticing any odd sentence constructions and misspelled words.

Read a Hard Copy of Your Work

If you have been drafting and editing onscreen, reading a printed hard copy will help you to see your writing from a fresh perspective. You might even try changing the font or line spacing to give the printed out text a different look.

Know Your Grammatical Weaknesses

If you know you tend to make certain grammatical mistakes, devote one proofreading pass just to those issues. For instance, if you have trouble with *its* versus *it's*, or trouble with run-on sentences, devote one entire proofreading session to that kind of mistake, looking only for it.

Use Your Spellchecker

Spellcheck has become a reliable tool over the years. It can flag most annoying typos and spelling errors. You should not, however, rely exclusively on your spellchecker for proofreading. Instead, read through your document looking for possible spelling problems. If you aren't sure whether a word is being spelled or used correctly, then use your word processor's dictionary to look it up.

Peer Review: Asking for Advice

The keys to productive peer review are focus and honesty. Writers need to tell their reviewers specifically what kind of help they want. For example:

- This is an early draft, so don't pay any attention to the grammar and wording. Look at my ideas and my claim. Could they be stronger or sharper?

- My readers are high school students who are considering skipping college. Do you think this draft addresses their needs and answers the questions they would have?

- My claim is X. What can I do make sure that it comes through clearly and persuasively?

- Please look at the introduction closely. Do I introduce the topic and engage the reader's interest?

Encourage your reviewers to be honest about your draft. You need them to do more than say "I like it," "It looks good," or "I would give it an A." Ask them to be as tough as possible, so you can find places to improve your writing.

As we have seen in this chapter, an editor cannot handle all four levels of revising and editing at the same time. As a writer, you should determine which level of edit is most helpful at this point. For instance, you do not want someone nitpicking about grammar issues when you are still figuring out your basic ideas and the document's overall approach. You also do not want someone telling you that your angle and purpose are completely wrong when your work is due in 30 minutes and all you want is proofreading.

Editors and writers need to communicate about what kind of feedback they want. At all levels, you should tell the writer about gaps and problems. But you should never forget that writers also need to understand what's working well in their documents.

Level 1: Global Revison. At this level, question and challenge the writer's basic approach to the topic, angle, and purpose. Check to see whether the writer has appropriately adapted the document to the readers' expectations, values, and attitudes.

Level 2: Substantive Editing. Help the writer rethink the document's content, organization, and design. Review the content for both strengths and possible gaps. Examine the organization and tell the writer whether each part of the document does the job it needs to. Look at the overall design to see what elements could be rethought.

Level 3: Copyediting. Edit the style for clarity, persuasion, and consistency. Look closely at the title, headings, paragraphs, and sentences to make sure they are clear, concise, consistent, and correct.

Level 4: Proofreading. When proofreading, look for mistakes. Do not simply make the changes for the writer. Instead, you should point out problems so that the writer can see them. In a writing class, however, the writer should decide what needs to be changed in the final draft.

Write your responses to these questions on a sheet of paper or in an e-mail, so the author has something concrete to work with when revising the draft. As always, be sure to point out both strengths and places for improvement.

Ready to finish your document? Follow the "Four Levels of Editing" to revise and edit your text like a professional.

REVISE Globally (Level 1)

Revision means "re-visioning" the text. Challenge your draft's topic, angle, and purpose. Then think further about your readers and the contexts in which they will read or use your document.

EDIT the Content, Organization, and Design (Level 2)

Substantive editing involves looking closely at the content, organization, and design of your document. Determine whether you have enough (or too much) content. Then make sure the organization of your document highlights your major ideas. Also, look for ways you can improve the design.

COPYEDIT Paragraphs and Sentences (Level 3)

Copyediting involves improving the "flow" of your text by making it *clear, concise, consistent*, and *correct*. Review your title and headings to make sure they are meaningful and consistent. Work paragraph by paragraph to make the text concise and consistent. Then revise the style of your sentences to make them clear and descriptive.

PROOFREAD Your Work (Level 4)

As a last step, proofreading is your final opportunity to catch any errors, like typos, grammatical errors, spelling mistakes, and word usage problems. To help you proofread, try reading your writing out loud, reading the draft backwards, and reading a hard copy of your work. Be aware of your grammatical weaknesses and look for those specific errors. Meanwhile, use your computer's spellchecker to catch any smaller errors.

ASK Someone Else to Review Your Work

By now, you are probably unable to see your document objectively. So have someone else look over your work and give you an honest assessment. Your professor may even give you time to "peer review" each other's writing.

1. On the Internet, find a document that seems to be poorly edited. With your group, discuss the impact that the lack of editing has on you and other readers. What do the errors say about the author and perhaps the company or organization he or she works for?

2. Choose a grammar rule with which you have problems. Explain in your own words what the rule is (use the "Handbook" section of this book for help). Then explain why you have trouble with it. Why do you have trouble remembering to follow it during composing?

3. With your group, create a simile or analogy that sums up how you see the differences among the levels of editing, from global revision to local editing (proofreading). For example, you might say, "Global editing is like _____, while substantive editing is like _____." Or, you might complete the sentence: "The overall progression from global editing to proofreading is like moving from _____ to _____."

1. On your own or with a colleague, choose a draft of your writing and decide which level of revising and editing it needs. Then, using the appropriate section in this chapter, walk through the steps for editing the document at that level.

2. Write a brief e-mail explaining the main differences between the levels of revising and editing to someone unfamiliar with the concept.

3. Find a text on the Internet that you think is poorly written. Using the four levels of editing, read through the text four separate times. Each time, explain what you would need to do to the text to make it stronger.

1. **Edit a text from someone in your class.** Exchange drafts with another person or within a small group during peer review. In addition to the draft itself, write a memo to your reviewers telling them exactly what you'd like them to focus on. Use the language from this chapter (level 1, level 2, global, local, etc.) and define as precisely as you can what you think might be an issue.

2. **Copyedit a text on screen with Track Changes.** Find a rough draft (one of your own, a colleague's, or something from the Internet) and use Track Changes to do a level 3 edit (copyediting) on it. When you have finished, write an e-mail to your professor explaining your edits.

PEARSON
mycomplab

For additional reading, writing, and research resources, go to **www.mycomplab.com**.

PART 4

Strategies for Shaping Ideas

PART OUTLINE

These chapters go way beyond just tips and tricks. Instead, you will learn time-tested STRATEGIES *for arranging your ideas and writing with strength and authority.*

19

Drafting Introductions and Conclusions

Introductions and conclusions are important because they are the places where the readers are paying the most attention. If readers don't like your introduction, chances are good that they won't like the rest of your text either. And, if they don't like how your paper ends, they will be left with doubts about what you had to say.

In this chapter, you are going to learn some easy-to-use strategies for writing great introductions and conclusions. By mastering some basic "moves" that are commonly made in introductions and conclusions, you can learn how to write powerful, engaging openings and closings for your texts.

Drafting Introductions

Put yourself in your readers' place. Before you start reading, you probably have some questions: "What is this? Why was this sent to me? What is this writer trying to get me to believe or do? Is this important? Do I care about this?" Your readers will be asking the same kinds of questions when they begin reading your text.

Five Introductory Moves

Your introduction should answer your readers' questions up front by making some or all of the following five introductory moves:

Move 1: Identify your topic.

Move 2: State your purpose.

Move 3: State your main point.

Move 4: Offer background information on your topic.

Move 5: Stress the importance of the topic to your readers.

These opening moves can be made in just about any order. Only the first three are really needed for a successful introduction, because these moves tell readers what you are writing about, why you are writing, and what you want to explain or prove. The other two moves will help your readers familiarize themselves with the topic. Here is a sample introduction that uses all five moves:

Streets of Death: The Perils of Street Racing

That night, Davey Yeoman hadn't planned on almost killing himself. He was out cruising with a couple of friends in his blue turbo-charged Honda Accord. The other guy was in a yellow Pontiac GTO with katana rims. The driver of the GTO asked if Davey wanted to race. He said yeah. So they agreed to meet at 11:00 p.m. on a two-laner outside town. It was a popular place for street racing.

When the stoplight changed, Davey hit 120 mph almost right away. The GTO was running beside him, a little off his right quarter panel. His Accord was shaking, and its engine was screaming. Suddenly, ahead, Davey saw the headlights of a semitrailer turning into his lane from a side road. The last thing Davey remembered thinking was, "Not me, God, not me." He knew he was dead.

Street racing is a craze that has grown steadily in the last decade. Last year, over two hundred young people were killed in street racing incidents (FARS). Some of the dead and maimed were the drivers or their passengers, and some were people who just got in the way. Street racing has turned some of our roads into deadly places. These street racers need to understand the deadly dangers of turning our roads into racetracks.

Topic identified.

Background information.

Importance of the topic stressed.

Main point (thesis) stated.

Purpose stated.

In this introduction, the author *identifies the topic* (street racing) up front and then offers some *background information*. In the next paragraph, he *stresses the importance of the topic* with some data. Then he finishes the introduction by stating his *purpose* and *main point*.

Generally, it is a good idea to put your paper's main point, or thesis, at the end of the introduction, but you don't need to put it there. In the sample introduction above, for example, the writer could easily move the sentences and paragraphs around to put the main point earlier if that seemed to work better.

Using a Grabber to Start Your Introduction

To catch readers' attention, some writers like to use a *grabber* or *hook* at the beginning of their introduction. A grabber can gently spark your readers' curiosity, or it can capture them with a compelling statement and shout, "Listen to me!" Here are some good grabbers you can use:

Ask an Interesting Question. A question draws readers into the text by prompting them for an answer.

> Have you ever thought about becoming a professional chef? The training is rigorous and the work can be difficult, but the rewards are worth it.

State a Startling Statistic. An interesting statistic can immediately highlight the importance of the topic

> A recent survey shows that 73 percent of teens in Bloomington have smoked marijuana, and 23 percent report using it at least once a week ("Weed" A3).

Make a Compelling Statement. Make a statement that challenges readers at the beginning of the text.

> Unless we take action now on global warming, we are likely to see massive storms and rising ocean levels that will drown coastal cities.

Begin with a Quotation. A quote is a good way to pique your readers' curiosity.

> That great American, Ben Franklin, once said, "They who would give up an essential liberty for temporary security deserve neither liberty nor security." Today, it seems like our fellow citizens are more willing than ever to make this trade.

Use Dialogue. Dialogue offers a quick way to bring your readers into the story you are telling.

> One morning at breakfast, I heard a couple of other students from my dorm talking about the terrorist attacks on September 11th. One of them said, "September 11th was just like when the Germans bombed Pearl Harbor." The other gave a confused look and asked, "You mean the Chinese, right? The Chinese bombed Pearl Harbor." That's when I came to the troubling conclusion that many people my age have a dangerously flawed grasp of our history.

Address Readers as "You." Addressing the readers directly with "you" is a good way to get their attention.

> Has this ever happened to you? You finally have a chance to take someone out for a night out on the town. You're dressed up, and you're dining at one of the finest restaurants in the city. But then, the maître d' escorts you to the worst table in the place, right next to the swinging doors to the kitchen or the station where they fill the water glasses. Right away, you realize that you're being discriminated against because you're young.

The best grabber is one that (1) identifies your topic, (2) says something that intrigues your readers, and (3) makes the point of your paper in a concise way.

Using a Lead to Draw in the Readers

You can also use a lead (also spelled "lede") to introduce your text. A lead is the first one or two paragraphs of a news story in a magazine, newspaper, or Web site. Like a grabber, the aim of a lead is to capture the readers' attention while giving them good reasons to continue reading. Here are some commonly used types of leads:

Scene Setter. A scene setter describes the place in which something important or interesting happened.

> The young men wade through thigh-high grass beneath the firs and ponderosa pines, calmly setting the forest on fire. With flicks of the wrist, they paint the landscape in flame. The newborn fires slither through the grass and chew into the sagging branches. Every few minutes a fire ignites, flames devouring it in a rush of light, the roar of rockets. It is over in seconds. Only a smoking skeleton remains. (Neil Shea, "Under Fire")

Anecdote. An anecdote starts out the introduction with an interesting true story that happened to the author or someone else.

> My second-grade teacher never liked me much, and one assignment I turned in annoyed her so extravagantly that the red pencil with which she scrawled "See me!" broke through the lined paper. Our class had been asked to write about a recent field trip, and, as was so often the case in those days, I had noticed the wrong things. (Tim Page, "Parallel Play")

Case Histories. A case history lead tells two to three very short true stories about different people who have had similar problems or experiences.

> Fred Jenkins never thought he was the kind of person to declare bankruptcy. He was a successful businessman with money in the bank. When his wife found out that she had ovarian cancer, though, his bank accounts were soon emptied by the costs of treatment. Mira Johanson took a different path to bankruptcy. She racked up $24,000 in credit card debt, because she bought a house she couldn't afford. When she was laid off at Gerson Financial, she could no longer make the minimum payments on her credit cards. Then, with her credit in ruins, she could not refinance her mortgage. Her personal finances collapsed, causing her to lose everything.

Personal Sketch. Articles that are about a person often start out with a description of the person and a small biography.

In mid-January 1959, Fidel Castro and his comrades in revolution had been in power less than a month. Criticized in the international press for threatening summary justices and execution for many members of the government of ousted dictator Fulgencio Batista, Castro called on the Cuban people to show their support at a rally in front of Havana's presidential palace.

Castro, 32, wore a starched fatigue cap as he faced the crowd. With him were two of his most trusted lieutenants, Camilo Cienfuegos, unmistakable in a cowboy hat, and Ernesto (Che) Guevara in his trademark black beret. (Guy Gugliotta, "Comrades in Arms")

The lead comes before your main point (i.e., your thesis) in the introduction. A lead will make the introduction a bit longer than usual, and it will draw your readers into your text and encourage them to keep reading.

Drafting Conclusions

When you are in a college lecture, what happens when your professor says, "In conclusion . . . ," or "Finally," or "Here is what I really want you to take away from today's lecture"? Everyone in the audience wakes up and starts paying close attention. Why? Because everyone knows the professor is going to state his or her main points.

The same is true of the conclusion at the end of your document. When your readers arrive at the conclusion, they will start paying closer attention because they know you are going to state your main points.

Here are five moves that you could make in your conclusion.

Move 1: Signal clearly that you are concluding.

Move 2: Restate your main point.

Move 3: Stress the importance of your topic again.

Move 4: Call your readers to action.

Move 5: Look to the future.

Your conclusion should be as short as possible, and it should be similar to your introduction in content and tone. In your conclusion, you need to bring readers back around to the beginning of your argument, showing them that you have achieved your purpose. For example, consider the following conclusion:

Street Racing Must Stop

Signal conclusion.

Importance of topic.

In the end, street racing just isn't worth it. A few seconds of thrill can cause a lifetime of suffering or even kill someone—maybe you. Davey Yeoman found that out the hard way, and he wants his wrecked life to be an example to others. He's paralyzed and eats through a straw. The Accord he once loved is a mangled heap that is towed around to local high schools as a warning to others. Davey hopes he can use his destroyed life to save the lives of others.

Call to action.

Look to the future.

Main point.

The laws against street racing are already on the books. We don't need more laws. What we need is more education and tougher enforcement to stop street racing. Only then will we be able to end this dangerous craze that leaves so many lives destroyed. Only then will our streets be safe again.

This conclusion makes all five concluding moves in two brief paragraphs. First, the author *signals that he is concluding* in the first sentence with the phrase, "In the end."

Phrases that signal a conclusion include the following:

In conclusion,	Put briefly,	Ultimately,
To sum up,	In brief,	Overall,
In summary,	Finally,	As a whole,
In closing,	To finish up,	On the whole,

Then the author stresses the *importance of the topic* by returning to the story of Davey Yeoman, who crashed while street racing. The return to this story, which started in the introduction, also brings the reader around to the beginning of the argument, making it feel whole.

A *call to action* and the *main point* appear in the paragraph that follows. Pairing the main point with a call to action gives it more power because the author is stating it directly and telling readers what should be done.

Finally, the conclusion ends with a *look to the future* in which the author looks beyond the boundaries of the argument.

You don't need to include all five of these concluding moves in your document, and they don't need to appear in any specific order. If you find yourself writing a conclusion that goes longer than one or two paragraphs, you might move some of the information into the body of the paper.

Here are some basic strategies for writing an introduction and conclusion for your paper.

DIVIDE Your Argument into a Beginning, Middle, and End

Nonfiction documents should have an introduction (tell them what you are going to tell them), a body (tell them), and a conclusion (tell them what you told them).

DRAFT Your Introduction

A typical introduction includes up to five moves: (1) identify your topic, (2) state your purpose, (3) state your main point, (4) stress the importance of the topic, and (5) provide background information on the topic.

DEVELOP a Good Grabber or Lead for Your Introduction

Your introduction needs to capture the readers' interest right away. So use a question, intriguing statistic, compelling statement, interesting story, or quotation to hook them.

DRAFT Your Conclusion

A conclusion should make up to five moves: (1) signal that you are concluding, (2) restate the main point, (3) reemphasize the importance of the topic, (4) call for action, and (5) look to the future.

VERIFY That Your Introduction and Conclusion Work Together

The introduction and conclusion should work together, containing similar information, restating your main point, and using a similar tone. Often, the conclusion will complete a story that was started in the introduction. Here is also where the main point of the paper should be repeated once again.

1. Find a document on the Internet and identify its introduction and conclusion. With a group of people in your class, talk about whether you think the introduction and conclusion are effective in this text.

2. With your group, find an example of each kind of grabber and lead listed in this chapter. Print out or copy your examples and label which kind of grabber or lead they use.

3. Look closely at four conclusions from four different sample texts. With your group, rank the conclusions from best to worst. What aspects of some of the conclusions made them superior to the others?

Talk About This

1. Find an argument or other text that you have enjoyed reading this semester. Then write a one-page rhetorical analysis in which you discuss the structure of the text. Explain how the text's introduction, body, and conclusion work.

2. Find a text that you think has a weak introduction and/or conclusion. Write a one-page rhetorical analysis in which you diagnose the structural problems with the text's introduction and conclusion. What could the author have done better to build a stronger introduction and/or conclusion?

3. From the Internet, cut and paste an argument into your word processor. Then, with one or two people from your class, start experimenting with the introduction and conclusion. Then, in an e-mail to your professor, explain how changing the arrangement of the introduction and conclusion has different effects on readers.

Try This Out

1. **Evaluate the organization of a reading.** Choose a reading from this book and write a two-page structural analysis of it. Using the criteria described in this chapter, analyze its introduction, body, and conclusion to determine whether they are well organized and whether they are the appropriate length.

2. **Describing the qualities of a good Internet article lead.** Internet readers are notoriously impatient, and they make quick decisions about whether to click to something else. Find three different kinds of leads used in articles on the Internet. Write a brief evaluation in which you discuss how the electronic medium changes the way readers enter the text.

Write This

PEARSON mycomplab

For additional reading, writing, and research resources, go to **www.mycomplab.com**.

CHAPTER

20

Developing
Paragraphs and
Sections

Paragraphs and sections help your readers understand at a glance how you have structured your ideas. Good paragraphs and sections help your readers figure out your main points and how you are supporting them.

A paragraph's job is actually rather straightforward: a paragraph presents a claim or statement, and then it supports or proves that claim or statement with facts, reasoning, examples, data, anecdotes, quotations, or descriptions. A paragraph isn't just a bunch of sentences that seem to fit together. Instead, a solid paragraph is a unit that is built around a central topic, idea, issue, or question. There are no hard-and-fast rules for writing paragraphs in terms of length or structure. A paragraph's length and structure need to fit its purpose and the genre you are using.

A section is a group of paragraphs that supports a common idea or claim. A section offers a broad claim and then uses a series of paragraphs to support or prove that claim. Longer college-length papers and most workplace documents are usually carved up into a few or several sections so they are easier to read.

In this chapter, you will learn how to develop great paragraphs and sections that will make your writing stronger and better organized.

Creating a Basic Paragraph

Paragraphs tend to include up to four elements: a *transition*, a *topic sentence, support sentences,* and a *point sentence*. The diagram in Figure 20.1 shows where these kinds of sentences usually appear in any given paragraph. And, here is a typical paragraph with these four elements highlighted.

> Of course, none of this happened overnight (transition). In fact, more important than the commercialization of rap was the less visible cultural movement on the ground in anyhood USA (topic sentence). In rap's early days, before it became a thriving commercial entity, dj party culture provided the backdrop for this off-the-radar cultural movement (support). What in New York City metropolitan area took the form of dj battles and the MC chants emerged in Chicago as the house party scene, and in D.C. it was go-go (support). In other regions of the country, the local movement owed its genesis to rap acts like Run DMC, who broke through to a national audience in the early 1980s (support). In any case, by the mid-1980s, this local or underground movement began to emerge in the form of cliques, crews, collective, or simply kids getting together primarily to party, but in the process of rhyming, dj-ing, dancing, and tagging (support). Some, by the early 1990s, even moved into activism (support). In large cities like Chicago, San Francisco, Houston, Memphis, New Orleans, Indianapolis, and Cleveland and even in smaller cities and suburban areas like Battle Creek, Michigan, and Champaign, Illinois, as the '80s turned to the '90s, more and more young Blacks were coming together in the name of hip-hop (point sentence). (Bakari Kitwana, *Hip Hop Generation*)

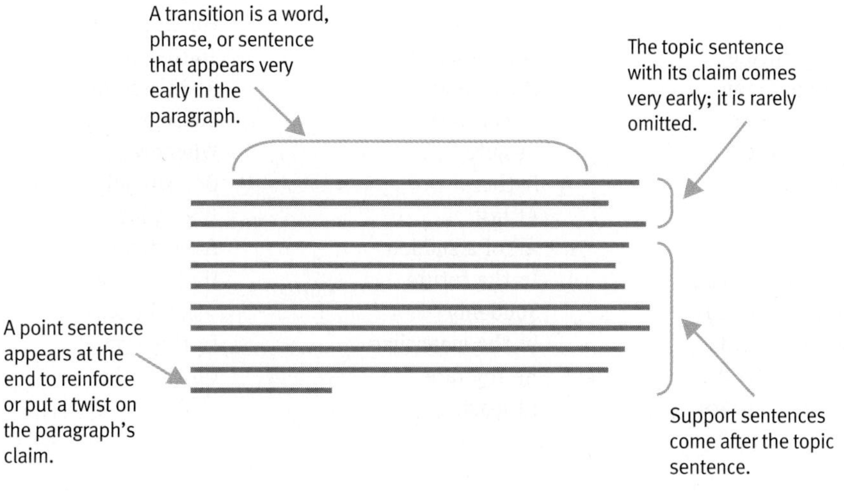

A transition is a word, phrase, or sentence that appears very early in the paragraph.

The topic sentence with its claim comes very early; it is rarely omitted.

A point sentence appears at the end to reinforce or put a twist on the paragraph's claim.

Support sentences come after the topic sentence.

FIGURE 20.1
The Shape of a Paragraph

Although paragraphs vary in terms of function and structure, the core of a paragraph includes the topic sentence with a claim followed by support sentences. Transition and point sentences can, in many cases, improve the flow of the paragraph.

Transition or Transitional Sentence (Optional)

The purpose of a transition or transitional sentence is to make a smooth bridge from the prior paragraph to the current paragraph. These kinds of transitions are especially useful when you want to shift or change the direction of the discussion.

A transition, if needed, should appear at the beginning of the paragraph. It might be as brief as a single word or phrase (e.g., *finally, in the past*) or as long as a complete transitional sentence. A transitional sentence might ask a question or make an obvious turn in the discussion:

> If fast food is causing America's expanding waistlines, what are our options for counteracting the power of fast food over young people?

A question like this one sets up the topic sentence that would likely follow it. Here is a transitional sentence that makes an obvious turn in the discussion:

> Before moving ahead, though, we first need to back up and discuss some of the root causes of poverty in the United States.

This type of transitional sentence turns the readers' attention to a new issue while setting up the paragraph's claim (topic sentence).

A transitional word or phrase can also make an effective bridge between two paragraphs. Here are some transitional words and phrases that you can try out:

For example	Nevertheless	Even though
To illustrate	At the same time	While it may be
For this reason	To summarize	true that
As an illustration	While this may or	Above all
Besides	may not be true	In addition
Of course	Equally important	With this in mind
In the past	As a result	For this purpose
In the future	Consequently	To this end
The next step	Meanwhile	At this point
In any event	In contrast	Subsequently
On the whole	Despite . . .	Whenever . . .
Likewise	Rather	Occasionally
Accordingly	At last	Inevitably
In conclusion	All of a sudden	Admittedly
More specifically	In the future	Under these
In the same way	Suddenly	conditions
In other words	In the meantime	In this way
Specifically	At any rate	On the other
On the contrary	At least	hand

Transitional words and phrases can lead off a paragraph's transitional sentence, or they can be used to start out a paragraph's a topic sentence.

Topic Sentence (Needed)

A topic sentence announces the paragraph's subject and makes a statement or claim that the rest of the paragraph will support or prove.

> At the beginning of his presidency, Barack Obama was confronted with a number of pressing economic issues.

> A good first step would be to remove fast food options from junior high and high school lunch programs.

> Debt on credit cards is the greatest threat to the American family's financial security.

In most paragraphs, the topic sentence will be the first or second sentence. You may have been told in the past that a topic sentence can be put anywhere in a paragraph. That's true. But if you want your reader to understand the paragraph's subject and identify its key statement or claim quickly, put that topic sentence up front.

Of course, there are always exceptions to any guideline. If you are telling your readers a story or leading them toward a controversial or surprising point, your topic sentence might arrive at the end of the paragraph. For example, here is a paragraph in which the topic sentence appears at the end, because the author is showing how something changed over time:

> My second grade homeroom teacher was a young graduate from a missionary school. When she found out I spoke English, she began to practice her English on me. One day she used English when asking me to run an errand for her. As I turned to close the door behind me, I noticed the puzzled faces of my classmates. I had the same sensation I had often experienced when some stranger in a crowd would turn on hearing me speak English. I was more intensely pleased on this occasion, however, because I suddenly felt that my family language had been singled out from the family languages of my classmates. Since we were not allowed to speak any dialect other than Standard Chinese in the classroom, having my teacher speak English to me in class made English an official language of the classroom. I began to take pride in my ability to speak it (topic sentence). (Min Zhan Lu, "From Silence to Struggle")

> In some paragraphs, like this narrative paragraph, the topic sentence can appear at the end.

Support Sentences (Needed)

Support sentences make up the body of most paragraphs. These sentences provide examples, details, reasoning, facts, data, quotations, anecdotes, definitions, descriptions, and anything else needed to back up the paragraph's topic sentence. Support sentences usually appear after the topic sentence.

> The fast food chains feed off the sprawl of Colorado Springs, accelerate it, and help set its visual tone (topic sentence). They build large signs to attract motorists and look at cars the way predators view herds of prey (support). The

chains thrive on traffic, lots of it, and put new restaurants at intersections where traffic is likely to increase, where development is heading but real estate prices are still low (support). Fast food restaurants often serve as the shock troops of sprawl, landing early and pointing the way (support). Some chains prefer to play follow the leader: when a new McDonald's opens, other fast food restaurants soon open nearby on the assumption that it must be a good location (support). (Eric Schlosser, *Fast Food Nation*)

Point Sentence (Optional)

Point sentences state, restate, or amplify the paragraph's main point at the end of the paragraph. A point sentence is especially useful in longer paragraphs when you want to reinforce or restate the topic sentence of the paragraph in different words.

> Of the many ways to fail on a dating website, not posting a photo of yourself is perhaps the most certain (topic sentence). (Not that the photo necessarily is a photo of yourself; it may well be some better-looking stranger, but such deception would obviously backfire in time.) A man who does not include his photo gets only 60 percent of the volume of e-mail response of a man who does; a woman who doesn't include her photo gets only 24 percent as much. A low-income, poorly educated, unhappily employed, not very attractive, slightly overweight, and balding man who posts his photo stands a better chance of gleaning some e-mails than a man who says he makes $200,000 and is deadly handsome but doesn't post a photo. There are plenty of reasons someone might not post a photo—he's technically challenged or is ashamed of being spotted by friends or is just plain unattractive—but as in the case of a brand-new car with a For Sale sign, prospective customers will assume he's got something seriously wrong under the hood (point sentence). (Steven Levitt and Stephen Dubner, *Freakonomics*)

As shown in the paragraph above, a point sentence is a good way to stress the point of a complex paragraph. The topic sentence at the beginning of the paragraph states a claim and the point sentence drives it home.

Getting Paragraphs to Flow (Cohesion)

Getting your paragraphs to flow is not difficult, but it takes a little practice. Flow, which is also called *cohesion*, is best achieved by paying attention to how each paragraph's sentences are woven together. You can use two techniques, *subject alignment* and *given-new chaining*, to achieve this feeling of flow.

Subject Alignment in Paragraphs

A well-written paragraph keeps the readers' focus on a central subject, idea, issue, or question. For example, the following paragraph does not flow well because the subjects of the sentences are inconsistent:

> Watching people at the park on a Saturday afternoon is a true pleasure. Frisbee golf is played by a group of college students near the trees. Visiting with each other are dog owners with their pets running around in playful packs. Picnic blankets have been spread out, and parents are chatting and enjoying their lunch. The playground is full of children sliding down slides and playing in the sand.

One way to get a paragraph to flow is to align the paragraph's sentences around a common set of subjects.

> Watching people at the park on a Saturday afternoon is a true pleasure. Near the trees, a group of college students play frisbee golf. Off to the side, dog owners visit with each other as their pets run around in playful packs. Parents chat and enjoy their lunch on spread-out picnic blankets. On the playground, children slide down slides and play in the sand.

This revised paragraph flows better (it is coherent) because the subjects of the sentences are all people. In other words, the paragraph is about the people at the park, so making people the subjects of the sentences creates the feeling that the paragraph is flowing.

To make your paragraphs flow, first decide what the paragraph is about. Then revise its sentences so they use a consistent set of subjects. Subject alignment means keeping a consistent set of subjects, not the same subject, through most or all of the paragraph.

Given-New in Paragraphs

Another good way to create flow is to use something called "given-new chaining" to weave the sentences together in a paragraph. Here's how it works.

Each sentence in the paragraph should start out with something that appeared in the prior sentence (called the "given"). Then the remainder of the sentence offers something that the readers didn't see in the prior sentence (called the "new"). That way, each sentence takes something given from the prior sentence and adds something new.

> Recently, an art gallery exhibited the mysterious paintings of Irwin Fleminger, a modernist artist whose vast Mars-like landscapes contain cryptic human artifacts. One of Fleminger's paintings attracted the attention of some young school children who happened to be walking by. At first, the children laughed, pointing out some of the strange artifacts in the painting. Soon, though, the strange artifacts in the painting drew the students into a critical awareness of the painting, and they began to ask their bewildered teacher what the artifacts meant. Mysterious and beautiful, Fleminger's paintings have this effect on many people, not just schoolchildren.

In this paragraph, the beginning of each sentence takes something from the sentence before it. This creates a given-new chain, causing the text to feel coherent and flowing.

A combination of subject alignment and given-new chaining will allow you to create good flow in your paragraphs while using a rich variety of sentence structures to keep the text interesting.

Deciding on Paragraph Length

The length of a paragraph should be determined by three things: the genre you are using, your readers, and the amount of support you need to back up the paragraph's topic sentence. The medium of your text will also influence paragraph length, because electronic texts and newspapers often use smaller paragraphs to help readers scan and read quickly.

Each genre tends to use paragraphs that are tailored to its readers' expectations and reading styles. For instance, a memoir is usually read in a leisurely way, so paragraphs in memoirs tend to be longer. Quite differently, paragraphs in a movie review are usually short, because readers tend to read or skim these documents quickly.

The key to determining a paragraph's length is to look at the topic sentence. Then make sure your paragraph has enough support sentences to back up that claim or statement.

Supersized Paragraphs

When used properly, long paragraphs signal depth of thought and coverage. Since the purpose of a paragraph is to support one statement or prove one claim, a long paragraph signals to the reader that

- the paragraph's claim or statement is very complex, requiring lots of support;
- the author is cramming many ideas together into one extended paragraph; or
- the author feels the need to handle an idea in great depth.

Supersized paragraphs are appropriate for analytical treatises or reflective thinking on a difficult topic, but they can be quite difficult for readers who are not committed to a deep reading of the text.

Rapid-Fire Paragraphs

Small paragraphs are easier and quicker to process, making it more likely that your readers will actually read each whole paragraph. These kinds of paragraphs are most useful in reviews and commentaries published in newspapers or on news Web pages. They are also useful in memoirs and profiles when you want to describe a scene with lots of action. Rapid-fire paragraphs speed up the reader's pace. However, small paragraphs also signal to the readers that

- the paragraph's claim or statement is simple, requiring minimal support;
- the author doesn't have enough support to back up the paragraph's claim or statement; or
- the author hasn't thought very deeply about this issue.

If you find yourself writing a series of short rapid-fire paragraphs, you might look closer at these paragraphs to determine whether you need to fill them out with more support. Or you might consider combining two or three smaller paragraphs into a larger paragraph that supports a larger claim or statement.

Paragraph Length Variety

Paragraphs within a document should be generally similar in size throughout the text, with some variation in length. Occasionally, though, you can use a short paragraph to highlight an important point. When you suddenly use a very short paragraph, it grabs your readers' attention because it *contrasts* with other paragraphs. Visually, readers will understand instantly (before they read the first word) that a paragraph will be different from the other paragraphs in content, tone, or direction.

So when you want an idea or claim to stand out, consider placing it in a very brief paragraph—like this one. You will grab your readers' attention.

Organizing a Section

A section is a group of paragraphs that supports a major point in your text. When used properly, sections break a larger document into manageable portions. They also provide readers with a bird's-eye view of the document, allowing them to take in the gist of a longer document at a glance.

Opening, Body, Closing

Like a paragraph, a section usually supports or proves a major statement or claim. This statement or claim tends to be placed at the beginning of the section, often in a brief *opening paragraph*. Then the *body paragraphs* in the section each contribute something to support that statement or claim. Finally, an optional closing paragraph, which tends to be only a couple of sentences, can be used to restate the major statement or claim that the section was supporting or trying to prove.

Organizational Patterns for Sections

When organizing a section, begin by asking yourself what you want to achieve. Then identify a pattern that will help you structure and fill out that space. Figure 20.2 on page 409 shows a variety of patterns that you might consider when organizing sections in your text. These are some of the most common patterns, but others, including variations of the ones shown here, are possible.

Using Headings in Sections

Headings are especially helpful for marking where sections begin and end. They can help you and your readers make transitions between larger ideas. Also, they give readers an overview of the structure of the document.

All headings within a certain level should follow consistent word patterns. A consistent wording pattern might use gerunds (-*ing* words), questions, or statements.

Inconsistent Headings	Performance Enhancement
	Is Performance Enhancement Unethical?
	Kinds of Performance Enhancement
Consistent Headings Using Gerunds	Defining Performance Enhancement
	Understanding the Ethics of Performance Enhancement
	Determining the Downside
Consistent Headings Using Questions	What Is Performance Enhancement?
	What Are the Risks?
	What's Really the Issue Here?
Consistent Headings Using Claims	Cognitive Performance Enhancement Is Possible
	Enhancement Will Improve Student Performance
	A Better National Conversation Is Needed

Headings should also be specific, clearly signaling the content of the sections that follow them.

Unspecific Headings	Fast Food
	The High School Scene
	Solutions
Specific Headings	Fast Food and High School Students: A Bad Mix
	The Effects of Fast Food on Health and Performance
	Alternatives to Fast Food

Using Sections and Paragraphs Together

A well-organized document is a structure that contains structures (sections) that contain structures (paragraphs) that contain structures (sentences). The purpose of a paragraph is to support or prove a statement or claim. The purpose of a section is to

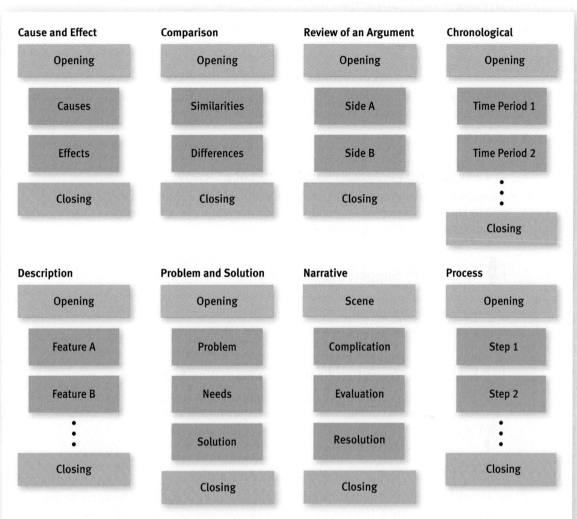

FIGURE 20.2 Organizational Patterns for Sections

Simple patterns like these can help you organize sections in your document. These patterns should not be followed mechanically.

use a series of paragraphs to support a larger claim. The sections, altogether, support the thesis or main point of the document.

If you learn how to write solid paragraphs and sections, you will find that the structures of paragraphs and sections will help you figure out what you need to include in each part of your document. That will save you time, while improving your writing dramatically.

Here are some basic strategies for creating clear, logical paragraphs and sections in your documents.

IDENTIFY the Four Kinds of Sentences in a Paragraph

A typical paragraph has a *topic sentence* and *support sentences*. As needed, a paragraph can also include a *transition sentence,* word, or phrases and a *point sentence.*

STATE Each Paragraph's Topic Sentence Clearly

A topic sentence announces the paragraph's subject—the central idea or issue covered in the paragraph. Your topic sentences should make a statement or claim that the rest of the paragraph will support or prove.

DEVELOP Support Sentences for Each Paragraph

Support sentences make up the body of most paragraphs. These sentences provide examples, details, reasoning, facts, data, anecdotes, definitions, descriptions, and anything else that backs up the paragraph's topic sentence.

DECIDE If a Transition Sentence or Transition Is Needed

If the prior paragraph is talking about something significantly different from the current paragraph, you might consider using a transition sentence or transitional word or phrase to bridge the gap.

DECIDE If a Point Sentence Would Be Helpful

In a longer paragraph, you might decide to use a point sentence to state or restate the paragraph's main point. Usually, the point sentence makes a claim that is similar to the topic sentence at the beginning of the paragraph.

DETERMINE Whether Your Paragraph's Length Is Right

The length of your paragraphs depends mostly on your subject matter and your readers. Long paragraphs suggest depth but may look hard to read. Short paragraphs are easier to read but may suggest that the claims are not fully supported.

COMBINE Paragraphs into Sections

Larger documents should be carved into sections. A typical section has an opening paragraph and body paragraphs. A closing paragraph is optional.

1. In studies of high school students' writing, researchers have found that inexperienced writers tend to place topic sentences at the end of their paragraphs, not the beginning. Why do you think inexperienced writers compose this way?

2. In this chapter, you learned that topic sentences should usually appear at the beginning of a paragraph and occasionally at the end. Can you think of any situations in which burying the topic sentence in the middle of the paragraph would be a good idea?

3. With your group, choose a reading in Part 2 of this book and pull its paragraphs apart, identifying their topic sentences, support sentences, transition sentences, and point sentences.

1. Go to the Internet and collect some interesting paragraphs. Identify the topic sentence and support sentences in each paragraph. If transition sentences and point sentences are used, highlight them, too. In a presentation to your class, choose one of your paragraphs and show how it works.

2. Find a badly written paragraph in a printed or online text. First, improve the flow of the paragraph by aligning the subjects of the sentences. Second, use given-new strategies to revise the paragraph's sentences. Finally, use a combination of subject alignment and given-new strategies to improve its flow. Which of these methods (subject alignment, given-new, or a combination) worked best?

3. On the Internet or on campus, find a document that is divided into sections. Look at each section carefully to determine what patterns they are following. Which patterns for sections described in this chapter are most common? Are the sections following any patterns that aren't shown in this chapter?

Write
This

1. **Diagnose and solve a paragraph's organizational problems.** Find a paragraph that has a confusing organization (one of your own, a colleague's, or something from the Internet). Diagnose the problems with this paragraph using the guidelines in this chapter. Then write a one-page analysis of the paragraph in which you explain its problems and offer two to five suggestions for improving it.

2. **Use a computer to revise the structure of a section.** Find a poorly organized, multiple-page document on the Internet that is divided into sections. Revise the organization of one section so that it includes a clear opening paragraph and body paragraphs. Write an e-mail to the document's author (you don't have to actually send it) in which you discuss the problems with the original section and describe your strategy for improving it.

PEARSON
mycomplab

For additional reading, writing, and research resources, go to **www.mycomplab.com**.

Using Basic
Rhetorical
Patterns

W hen drafting, writers will often use *rhetorical patterns* to arrange their ideas into sections and paragraphs. Rhetorical patterns are familiar forms and strategies that help you to organize information in ways your readers will easily comprehend. Teachers of rhetoric, like Aristotle, called these patterns *topoi,* or commonplaces. *Topoi* (from the Greek word "place") are familiar patterns or strategies that you can use in a variety of situations.

Rhetorical patterns are not formulas to be followed mechanically. You can alter, bend, and combine these patterns to fit your purpose and the genre of your text.

Narrative

A narrative describes a sequence of events or tells a story in a way that illustrates a specific point.

Narratives can be woven into just about any genre. In reviews, literary analyses, and rhetorical analyses, narrative can be used to summarize or describe what you are analyzing. In proposals and reports, narratives can be used to recreate events and give historical background on a topic. Other genres, such as memoirs and profiles, often rely on narrative to organize the entire text.

The diagram in Figure 21.1 shows the typical pattern for a narrative. When telling a story, writers will usually start out by *setting the scene* and *introducing a complication* of some kind. Then the characters in the story *evaluate the complication* to figure out how they are going to respond. They then *resolve the complication.* At the end of the narrative, the writer *states the point* of the story, if needed.

Consider, for example, the following paragraph, which follows the narrative pattern:

> Yesterday, I was eating at Gimpy's Pizza on Wabash Street (scene). Suddenly, some guy started yelling for everyone to get on the floor, because he was robbing the restaurant (complication). At first, I thought it was a joke (evaluation). But then everyone else got on the floor. I saw the guy waving a gun around, and I realized he was serious. I crawled under the table. Fortunately, the guy just took the money and ran (resolution). That evening, on the news, I heard the guy was arrested a couple of hours later. This brush with crime opened my eyes about the importance of personal safety (point). We all need to be prepared for the unexpected.

The narrative pattern is probably already familiar to you, even if you didn't know it before. This is the same pattern used in television sitcoms, novels, story jokes, and just about any story. In nonfiction writing, though, narratives are not "just stories." They help writers make specific points for their readers. The chart in Figure 21.2 shows how narratives can be used in a few different genres.

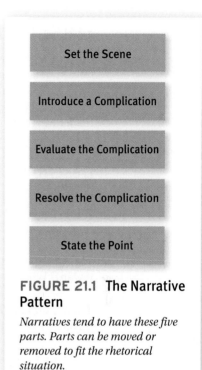

FIGURE 21.1 The Narrative Pattern

Narratives tend to have these five parts. Parts can be moved or removed to fit the rhetorical situation.

Objective of Genre	Use of Narrative
In a **proposal,** use a story to explain a problem, its causes and effects.	In a proposal about food safety, a writer motivates the reader to care about the issue by telling the story of a girl who died from food poisoning.
In a **commentary,** tell a story that demonstrates your expertise.	In a commentary that criticizes the inadequate training of soldiers, an army veteran uses a story from his deployment to illustrate his combat know-how.
In a **review,** summarize a movie's plot for readers.	In a movie review of a new romantic comedy, the writer gives an overview of the movie's main events, without giving away how the conflict in the movie was resolved.
In a **literary analysis,** use a historical narrative to offer background information on the text.	In a literary analysis, the writer tells an interesting story about the poet whose poem is being analyzed. This story offers insight into the meaning of the poem.
In a **report,** make an abstract concept easier to understand by narrating a series of events.	In explaining the concept of metamorphosis in a research report, the writer describes the luna moth's life cycle as a fight for survival from egg, to caterpillar, to chrysalis, to adult moth.

FIGURE 21.2 Using Narratives

Description

Description allows writers to portray people, places, and objects. Descriptions often rely on details drawn from the five senses—seeing, hearing, touching, smelling, and tasting. In situations where the senses don't offer a full description, writers can turn to other rhetorical devices, like metaphor, simile, and onomatopoeia, to deepen the readers' experience and understanding.

Describing with the Senses

Like you, your readers primarily experience the world through their senses. So when you need to describe someone or something, start out by considering your subject from each of the five senses:

What Does It Look Like? List its colors, shapes, and sizes. What is your eye drawn toward? What makes your subject visually distinctive?

What Sounds Does It Make? Are the sounds sharp, soothing, irritating, pleasing, metallic, harmonious, or erratic? What effect do these sounds have on you and others?

What Does It Feel Like? Is it rough or smooth, hot or cold, dull or sharp, slimy or firm, wet or dry?

How Does It Smell? Does your subject smell fragrant or pungent? Does it have a particular aroma or stench? Does it smell fresh or stale?

How Does It Taste? Is your subject spicy, sweet, salty, or sour? Does it taste burnt or spoiled? What foods taste similar to the thing you are describing?

If you are describing a scene or a person, punctuate your description with surprising or contrasting details.

Describing with Similes, Metaphors, and Onomatopoeia

Some people, places, and objects cannot be fully described using the senses. Here is where similes, metaphors, and onomatopoeia can be especially helpful. These stylistic devices are discussed in depth in Chapter 16, "Choosing a Style," so we will only discuss them briefly here.

Simile. A simile ("X is like Y"; "X is as Y") helps you describe your subject by making a simple comparison with something else:

> Directing the flow of traffic, the police officer moved as mechanically and purposefully as a robot on an assembly line.

Objective of Genre	Use of Description
In a **memoir,** describe characters and their setting.	In a memoir about a writer's Brazilian hometown, she uses sights, sounds, and textures to describe how her neighbors enjoyed playing and watching soccer in the streets.
In an **evaluation,** describe the product being evaluated.	In an evaluation of a new snowboard, the writer describes the visual features of the board, stressing what makes it different from others.
In a **commentary,** describe people or places of interest.	A writer uses description to show the hard life of people who are living without health care in southern Iowa.
In a **proposal,** describe a plan or a product.	A team of proposal writers uses description to show how a new playground would look in a local park.
In a **report,** describe the laboratory setup for an experiment.	The methodology section of a report describes how a laboratory experiment was put together, allowing the readers to verify and replicate it.

FIGURE 21.3 Using Descriptions

Metaphor. A metaphor ("X is Y") lets you describes your subject in more depth than a simile by directly comparing it to something else.

> When the fall semester starts, a college campus becomes a chaotic bazaar, with colorful people, cars, and buses moving frantically from here to there.

Onomatopoeia. Onomatopoeia uses words that sound like the thing being described.

> The flames crackled and hissed as the old farmhouse teetered on its charred frame.

Description is commonly used in all genres. The chart in Figure 21.3 shows how descriptions could be used in several kinds of writing situations.

Definition

A definition states the exact meaning of a word. Definitions explain how a particular term is being used and why it is being used that way. They are especially helpful for clarifying ideas and explaining important concepts.

Sentence definitions, like the ones in a dictionary, typically have three parts: the term being defined, the category in which the term belongs, and the distinguishing characteristics that set it apart from other things in its category.

Term.

Cholera is a potentially lethal illness caused by the
bacterium, *Vibrio cholerae*, with symptoms of vomiting and
watery diarrhea.

Distinguishing
characteristics.

Category.

An *extended definition* is longer than a sentence definition. An extended definition usually starts with a sentence definition and then continues to define the term further. You can extend a definition with one or more of the following techniques:

Word Origin (Etymology). Exploring the historical origin of a word can provide some interesting insights into its meaning.

> According to the *Online Etymology Dictionary*, the word *escape* comes from the Old French word "eschaper," which literally meant "to get out of one's cape, leave a pursuer with just one's cape."

Examples.   Giving examples of how the word is used can put its meaning into context for readers.

> For example, when someone says she "drank the Kool-Aid" for Barack Obama, it means she became a mindless follower of him and his ideas.

Negation.   When using negation, you explain something by telling readers what it is not.

> St. John's wort is not a stimulant, and it won't cure all kinds of depression. Instead, it is a mild sedative.

Division.   You can divide the subject into two or more parts, which are then defined separately.

> There are two kinds of fraternities. The first kind, a "social fraternity," typically offers a dormitory-like place to live near a campus, as well as a social community. The second kind, an "honorary fraternity," allows members who share common backgrounds to network and support fellow members.

Similarities and Differences.   When using similarities and differences, you compare and contrast the thing being defined to other similar things.

> African wild dogs are from the same biological family, *Canidae,* as domestic dogs, and they are similar in size to a labrador. Their coats, however, tend to have random patterns of yellow, black, and white. Their bodies look like those of domestic dogs, but their heads look like those of hyenas.

Objective of Genre	Use of Definition
In a **literary analysis,** explain a literary concept.	When writing a literary analysis, the writer defines words like "irony" or an important concept in the novel or poem.
In a **rhetorical analysis,** define a rhetorical term that helps explain why something is persuasive.	A person critiquing an advertisement defines the word *"pathos"* to help her explain how emotion is used to sway an audience.
In a **commentary,** define an important but unfamiliar term.	A commentator uses a specific term, like "Taliban," that calls for a definition to explain what it means.
In a **report,** clarify an important technical term.	In a research report about the great apes, the writer defines what a bonobo is and how it is different from other apes.

FIGURE 21.4 Using Definitions

Analogy. An analogy compares something unfamiliar to something that readers would find familiar.

> Your body's circulatory system is similar to a modern American city. Your arteries and veins are like roads for blood cells to travel on. These roadways contain white blood cells, which act like state troopers patrolling for viruses and bacteria.

The chart in Figure 21.4 shows how definitions can be used in a variety of genres.

Classification

Classification allows you to divide objects and people into groups, so they can be discussed in greater depth. A classification can take up a single paragraph, or it might be used to organize an entire section (Figure 21.5, page 418). There are three basic steps to using classification to organize a paragraph or section:

Step One: List Everything That Fits into the Whole Class

List all the items that can be included in a specific class. Brainstorming is a good tool for coming up with this kind of list.

 If you discuss all of these items individually, you will bore your readers to tears. So you need to find a way to break this long list down into smaller classifications. Move to step two.

Step Two: Decide on a Principle of Classification

The key to classifying something is to come up with a *principle of classification* that helps you do the sorting.

FIGURE 21.5 Using Classifications

Objective of Genre	Use of Classification
In a **review,** identify common subgenres.	A reviewer uses classification to identify where a new vampire movie fits in the horror movie genre.
In a **profile,** sort people into types.	A writer of a profile positions her best friend by categorizing college students into common groups.
In a **commentary,** explain a culture by describing its demographic groups.	A commentator tries to explain why different Islamic sects in the Middle East are sometimes mistrustful of each other.
In a **report,** divide a number of species into smaller subspecies.	A researcher uses classification to describe a family of insects.

For example, let's imagine you are classifying all the ways to stop smoking. You would list all the methods you can find. Then you would try to sort them into categories:

Nicotine replacement—nicotine patch, nicotine gum, sprays, inhalers, lozenges, nicotine fading.

Lifestyle changes—exercise daily, eat healthy snacks, break routines, distract yourself, set up rewards, keep busy.

Medical help—acupuncture, hypnosis, antidepressants, counseling, support group.

Smoking-like activities—chew gum, drink hot tea, breathe deeply, eat vegetables, eat nuts that need to be shelled.

Step Three: Sort into Major and Minor Groups

If you choose an effective principle of classification, you should be able to sort all the items from your brainstorming list cleanly into the major and minor categories you came up with. In other words, an item that appears in one category should not appear in another. Also, no items on your list should be left over.

Comparison and Contrast

Comparison and contrast allows you to explore the similarities and differences between two or more people, objects, places, or ideas. When comparing and contrasting, you should first list all the characteristics that the two items have in common. Then list all the characteristics that distinguish them from each other.

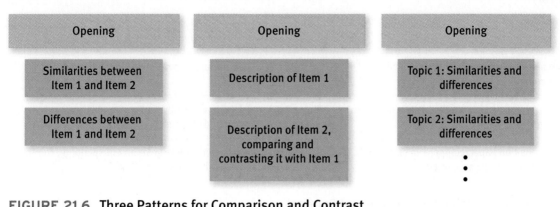

FIGURE 21.6 Three Patterns for Comparison and Contrast

Comparing and contrasting can be done in several ways. Here are three of the more common patterns.

You can then show how these two things are similar to and different from each other. Figure 21.6 shows three patterns that could be used to organize the information in your list. As an example of comparison and contrast, here is a paragraph from Jared Diamond's book, *Guns, Germs, and Steel*:

The most dramatic moment in subsequent European–Native American relations was the first encounter between the Inca emperor Atahuallpa and the Spanish conquistador Francisco Pizarro at the Peruvian highland town of Cajamarca on November 16, 1532. Atahuallpa was the absolute monarch of the largest and most advanced state in the New World, while Pizarro represented the Holy Roman Emperor Charles V (also know as Charles I of Spain), monarch of the most powerful state in Europe. Pizarro, leading a ragtag group of 168 Spanish soldiers, was in unfamiliar terrain, ignorant of the local inhabitants, completely out of touch with the nearest Spaniards (1,000 miles to the north in Panama) and far beyond the reach of timely reinforcements. Atahuallpa was in the middle of his own empire of millions of subjects and immediately surrounded by his army of 80,000 soldiers, recently victorious in a war with other Indians. Nevertheless, Pizarro captured Atahuallpa within a few minutes after the two leaders first set eyes on each other. Pizzaro proceeded to hold his prisoner for eight months, while extracting history's largest ransom in return for a promise to free him. After the ransom—enough gold to fill a room 22 feet long by 17 feet wide to a height of over 8 feet—was delivered, Pizarro reneged on his promise and executed Atahuallpa.

Compare two leaders, the Spaniard Pizarro and the Inca Atahuallpa, to show their similarities.

Highlights the differences between Pizarro and Atahuallpa.

Objective of Genre	Use of Comparison and Contrast
In a **memoir,** compare a new experience to something familiar.	A writer compares her first day of college to her first day of high school to help new students understand how challenging college is.
In a **profile,** compare a new person to someone readers know.	A writer of a profile compares his new boss to cartoon character Homer J. Simpson.
In a **proposal,** compare the plan to successful plans used in the past.	While pitching a plan for a new dog park, a proposal writer shows that similar plans have worked in other cities.
In a **position paper,** compare an opponent's plan to one being supported.	An economist argues against more government spending, comparing growth in the 1960s to the 1980s.

FIGURE 21.7 Using Comparison and Contrast

Comparison and contrast is a useful way to describe something by comparing it to something else. Or you can use it to show how two or more things measure up against each other. Figure 21.7 describes how comparison and contrast can be used in a variety of genres.

Combining Rhetorical Patterns

Rhetorical patterns can be combined to meet a variety of purposes. For example, you can embed a comparison and contrast within a narrative. Or you can use a classification within a description. In other words, you shouldn't get hung up on a particular pattern as *the* way to make your point. You can mix and match these rhetorical patterns to fit your needs. All of the readings in *Writing Today* use combinations of rhetorical patterns, so you should turn to them for examples.

Here are some easy ways to start using and combining basic rhetorical patterns in your writing.

NARRATE a Story

Look for places in your writing where you can tell a story. Set the scene and then introduce a complication. Discuss how you or others evaluated and resolved the complication. Then tell readers the main point of the story.

DESCRIBE People, Places, or Objects

Consider your subject from your five senses: sight, sound, touch, smell, and taste. Pay special attention to movement and features that make your subject unique or interesting to your readers.

DEFINE Your Words or Concepts

Look for any important words or concepts in your writing that need to be defined in greater depth. A sentence definition should have three parts: the term, the category, and distinguishing characteristics. To extend the definition, try learning about the word's history, offer examples of its usage, use negation to show what it isn't, divide the subject into two or more parts, or discuss its similarities and differences with other things.

CLASSIFY Items by Dividing Them into Groups

If you are discussing something large or complex, list all its parts. Then use a principle of classification to sort that list into two to five major groups. Each group can be divided further into minor groups.

COMPARE and Contrast Things

Find something that is similar to your subject. List all the similarities between the two items. Then list all the differences. Describe their similarities and differences.

MIX It Up!

Rhetorical patterns are not recipes or formulas to be mechanically followed. You can combine these patterns in ways that enhance their strengths.

1. Have each member of your group find two print examples of one of the basic rhetorical patterns discussed in this chapter and give a brief presentation in which he or she shows how the examples illustrate the pattern.

2. Make a list of ten slang words or phrases. With your group, come up with definitions for each of these words in which you identify the term, the category, and the distinguishing characteristics.

3. Basic rhetorical patterns are sometimes used as structures for essays. With your group, discuss and list the advantages and disadvantages of using these patterns to learn how to write whole documents.

1. Pick a place where you can sit undisturbed for half an hour. Write down everything you hear, feel, smell, and taste. Do *not* write down what you see. Then try to write a one-page description of the place where you were sitting. Try not to include any visual elements. Instead, use only your other senses to describe the place.

2. Pick two things that are similar in most ways but different in some important ways. Write three one-paragraph comparison and contrasts of these two things using each of the patterns shown in Figure 21.8. Which pattern worked best for your comparison and contrast, and why?

3. With your group, create a concept map that classifies the men and women at your university. When you are finished, discuss whether it is possible to appropriately sort people into groups without resorting to stereotypes.

1. **Examine something using five different strategies.** Think of something you know a lot about but with which others are unfamiliar. Using the five basic rhetorical patterns (narrative, description, definition, classification, comparison and contrast), help someone who knows little about your topic to understand it.

2. **Find rhetorical patterns on the Internet.** Write a two-page rhetorical analysis of a Web site in which you identify these basic rhetorical patterns and discuss how they are used on the site.

Using Argumentative Strategies

For some people, the word *argument* brings up images of fingerpointing, glares, outbursts, or quiet resentment. Actually, these aren't arguments at all. They are quarrels. When people quarrel, they no longer listen to each other or consider each other's ideas.

An argument is something quite different. An argument involves making reasonable claims and then backing up those claims with evidence and support. The objective of an argument is not to "win" and prove you have the truth. Instead, your primary goal is to persuade others that you are *probably* right. Arguments rarely end with one side proving the other side wrong. Instead, both sides strive to persuade others that their position is stronger or more beneficial, perhaps reaching agreement in the middle.

In college and in the professional world, arguments are used to think through ideas and debate uncertainties. Arguments are about getting things done by gaining the cooperation of others. In most situations, an argument is about agreeing as much as disagreeing, about cooperating with others as much as competing with them. The ability to argue effectively will be an important part of your success in college courses and in your career.

Argument can be used in any genre, but it is more prominent in some than in others. Memoirs and profiles, for example, do not typically make straightforward arguments, because they are primarily based on personal experience or historical facts.

Other genres, such as reviews, evaluations, literary analyses, rhetorical analyses, proposals, and reports, are much more argumentative because their authors are deliberately trying to persuade readers to accept a particular view or idea.

In this chapter, you will learn some helpful strategies for persuading people to accept your ideas. You can use these strategies to argue effectively with your friends and family. They are also useful for arguing about important issues in college and in the workplace.

What Is Arguable?

Let's begin by first discussing what is "arguable." Some people will say that you can argue about anything. And in a sense, they are right. We *can* argue about anything, no matter how trivial or pointless.

"I don't like chocolate."	"Yes, you do."
"The American Civil War began in 1861."	"No, it didn't."
"It really bugs me when I see a pregnant woman smoking."	"No way. You think that's cool."

These kinds of arguments are rarely worth the time and effort. Of course, we can argue that our friend is lying when she tells us she doesn't like chocolate, and we can challenge the historical fact that the Civil War really started in 1861. (Ultimately, anything is arguable.) However, debates over *personal judgments,* such as liking or not liking chocolate, quickly devolve into "Yes, I do. No, you don't!" kinds of quarrels. Meanwhile, debates about *proven facts,* like the year the American Civil War started, can be resolved by consulting a trusted source. To be truly arguable, a claim should exist somewhere between personal judgments and proven facts (Figure 22.1).

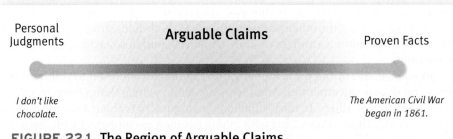

FIGURE 22.1 The Region of Arguable Claims

People can argue about anything, of course. However, arguable claims tend to exist somewhere between personal judgments and proven facts.

Arguable Claims

When laying the groundwork for an argument, you need to first define an arguable claim that you will try to persuade your readers to accept as probably true. For example, here are two arguable claims on two sides of the same topic:

Arguable Claim:

The United States made a mistake when it invaded Iraq in 2003 because the invasion was based on faulty intelligence that suggested Iraq possessed weapons of mass destruction.

Arguable Claim:

Despite faulty intelligence, the United States was justified in invading Iraq because Saddam Hussein was a dangerous dictator who was threatening Iraq's neighboring countries, supporting worldwide terrorism, and lying in wait for an opportunity to purchase or build weapons of mass destruction that could be used against the United States and its allies.

These claims are "arguable" because neither side can prove that it is factually right nor that the other side is factually wrong. Meanwhile, neither side is based exclusively on personal judgments. Instead, both sides want to persuade you, the reader, that they are *probably* right.

When you invent and draft your argument, your goal is to support one side to the best of your ability, but you should also imagine opponents who will be presenting a different position. Keeping your opponents in mind will help you to clarify your ideas, generate support, and identify any weaknesses in your argument. Then, when you draft your argument, you will be better able to show readers that you have considered both sides fairly.

If, on the other hand, you realize that there really isn't another credible side to your argument or that the other side is extremely weak, then you may not have an arguable claim in the first place.

Four Sources of Arguable Claims

Once you have a rough idea of your arguable claim, you should refine and clarify it. Toward this end, it is helpful to figure out what kind of arguable claim you are trying to support. Arguable claims generally arise from four different sources: issues of definition, causation, evaluation, and recommendation (Figure 22.2, page 426).

Issues of Definition. Some arguments hinge on how to define an object, event, or person. For example, here are a few arguable claims that debate how to define something:

Animals, like humans, are sentient beings who have inalienable rights; therefore, killing and eating animals is an unethical act.

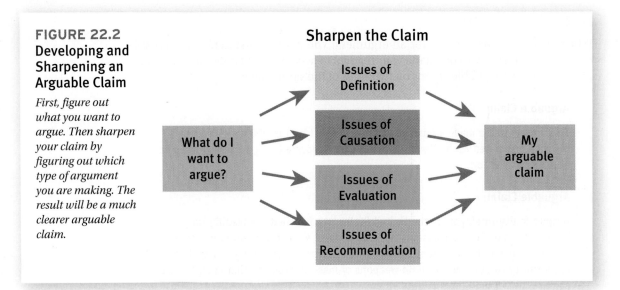

FIGURE 22.2
Developing and Sharpening an Arguable Claim

First, figure out what you want to argue. Then sharpen your claim by figuring out which type of argument you are making. The result will be a much clearer arguable claim.

Sharpen the Claim

What do I want to argue? →

- Issues of Definition
- Issues of Causation
- Issues of Evaluation
- Issues of Recommendation

→ My arguable claim

The terrorist acts of September 11, 2001, were an unprovoked act of war, not just a criminal act. Consequently, the United States was justified in declaring war on Al-Qaeda and its ally, the Taliban government of Afghanistan.

A pregnant woman who smokes is a child abuser who needs to be stopped before she further harms her unborn child.

Issues of Causation.   Humans tend to see events in terms of cause and effect. Consequently, we often argue about whether one thing caused another.

The main cause of boredom is a lack of variety. People become bored when nothing changes in their lives, causing them to lose their curiosity about the people, places, and events around them.

Advocates of gun control incorrectly blame the guns when a school shooting happens. Instead, we need to look at the sociological and psychological causes of school violence, such as mental illness, bullying, gang violence, and the shooters' histories of aggression.

Pregnant mothers who choose to smoke are responsible for an unacceptable number of birth defects in children.

Issues of Evaluation.   We also argue about whether something is *good* or *bad*, *right* or *wrong*, or *better* or *worse*.

The movie *The Pirates of the Caribbean* is better than the classic pirate movie, *Captain Blood*, because Johnny Depp plays a more realistic pirate than Errol Flynn's overly romantic portrayal.

The current U.S. taxation system is unfair, because the majority of taxes fall most heavily on people who work hard and corporations who are bringing innovative products to the marketplace.

Although both are dangerous, drinking alcohol in moderation while pregnant is less damaging to an unborn child than smoking in moderation.

Issues of Recommendation. We also use arguments to make recommendations about the best course of action to follow. These kinds of claims are signaled by words like "should," "must," "ought to," and so forth.

Tompson Industries should convert its Nebraska factory to renewable energy sources, like wind, solar, and geothermal, using the standard electric grid only as a backup supply for electricity.

The meat industry is heavily subsidized by the American taxpayer; therefore, we recommend removing all subsidies, making vegetarianism a financially viable choice.

We must help pregnant women to stop smoking by developing smoking-cessation programs that are specifically targeted toward this population.

To refine and sharpen your arguable claim, you should figure out which of these four types of arguable claims you are making, as shown in Figure 22.2. Then revise your claim to fit neatly into one of the four categories.

Using Reason, Authority, and Emotion

Once you have developed an arguable claim, you can start figuring out how you are going to support it with evidence. There are three types of evidence you might use to support your position: reason, authority, and emotion (Figure 22.3, page 428). A solid argument will usually employ all three types of evidence; however, one type will usually be the dominant mode of argument.

Greek rhetoricians like Aristotle originally used the words *logos* (reason), *ethos* (authority), and *pathos* (emotion) to discuss these three kinds of evidence.

Reason (*Logos*)

Reasoning involves appealing to your readers' common sense or beliefs.

Logical Statements. The first type of reasoning, logical statements, allows you to use your readers' existing beliefs to prove they should agree with a further claim. Here are some common patterns for logical statements:

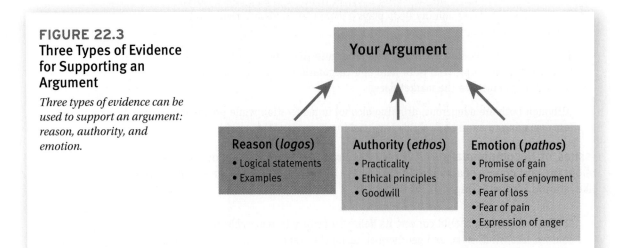

FIGURE 22.3
Three Types of Evidence for Supporting an Argument

Three types of evidence can be used to support an argument: reason, authority, and emotion.

Your Argument

Reason (*logos*)
• Logical statements
• Examples

Authority (*ethos*)
• Practicality
• Ethical principles
• Goodwill

Emotion (*pathos*)
• Promise of gain
• Promise of enjoyment
• Fear of loss
• Fear of pain
• Expression of anger

If . . . then. "If you believe X, then you should also believe Y."

Either . . . or. "Either you believe X or you believe Y."

Cause and effect. "X causes Y." or "Y is caused by X." (See Figure 22.4.)

Costs and benefits. "The benefits A, B, and C show that doing X is worth the costs."

Better and worse. "X is better than Y." or "X is worse than Y."

Examples. The second type of reasoning, examples, allows you to illustrate your points or demonstrate that a pattern exists.

"For example." "For example, in 1994 . . ." "For instance, last week . . ." "To illustrate, there was the interesting case of . . ." "Specifically, I can name two times when . . ."

Personal experiences. "Last summer, I saw . . ." or "Where I work, X happens regularly."

Facts and data. "According to our experiment, . . ." or "Recently published data shows that . . ."

Patterns of experiences. "X happened in 2000, 2004, and 2008. Therefore, we expect it to happen again in 2012." "In the past, each time X happened, Y has happened also."

Quotes from experts. "Dr. Jennifer Xu, a scientist at Los Alamos National Laboratory, recently stated . . ." or "In his 2009 article, historian George Brenden claimed . . ."

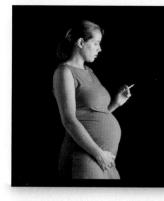

WARNING
CIGARETTES HURT BABIES

Tobacco use during pregnancy reduces the growth of babies during pregnancy. These smaller babies may not catch up in growth after birth and the risks of infant illness, disability and death are increased.

Health Canada

FIGURE 22.4　A Cause and Effect Argument

*In this advertisement from Health Canada, the primary argument strategy is cause and effect (i.e., smoking hurts unborn babies, or "X causes Y"). The argument also uses emotion (*pathos*).*

Authority (*Ethos*)

Authority involves using your own experience or the reputations of others to support your arguments. Another way to strengthen your authority is to demonstrate your practicality, ethical principles, and goodwill. These three types of authority were first mentioned by Aristotle as a way to strengthen credibility with readers, and these strategies still work well today.

Practicality. Show your readers that you are primarily concerned about solving problems and getting things done, not lecturing or theorizing. Where appropriate, admit that the issue is not simple and cannot be fixed easily. You can also point out that reasonable people can disagree about the issue. Being "practical" involves being realistic about what is possible, not idealistic about what would happen in a perfect world.

Ethical Principles. Demonstrate that you are arguing for an outcome that meets a firm set of ethical principles. An ethical argument can be based on any of three types of ethics:

* *Rights:* Using human rights or constitutional rights to back up your claims.

* *Laws:* Showing that your argument is in line with civic laws.

* *Utilitarianism:* Arguing that your position is more beneficial for the majority.

In some situations, you can demonstrate that your position is in line with your own and your readers' religious beliefs or spiritual faith.

Goodwill. Demonstrate that you have your readers' interests in mind, not just your own. Of course, you may be arguing for something that benefits you. So show your readers that you care about their needs and interests, too. Show them that you understand their concerns and that your position is a "win-win" for both you and them.

Emotion (*Pathos*)

Using emotional appeals to persuade your readers is appropriate if the feelings you draw on are suitable for your topic and readers. As you develop your argument, think about how your and your readers' emotions might influence how their decisions will be made.

Begin by listing the positive and negative emotions that are associated with your topic or with your side of the argument.

Promise of Gain. Demonstrate to your readers that agreeing with your position will help them gain things they need or want, like trust, time, money, love, advancement, reputation, comfort, popularity, health, beauty, or convenience.

Promise of Enjoyment. Show that accepting your position will lead to more satisfaction, including joy, anticipation, surprise, pleasure, leisure, or freedom.

Fear of Loss. Suggest that not agreeing with your opinion might cause the loss of things readers value, like time, money, love, security, freedom, reputation, popularity, health, or beauty.

Fear of Pain. Imply that not agreeing with your position will cause feelings of pain, sadness, frustration, humiliation, embarrassment, loneliness, regret, shame, vulnerability, or worry.

Expressions of Anger or Disgust. Show that you share feelings of anger or disgust with your readers about a particular event or situation.

Use positive emotions as much as you can, because they will build a sense of happiness and goodwill in your readers (Figure 22.5). Generally, people like to feel good and believe that agreeing with you will bring them gain, enjoyment, and happiness.

Negative emotions should be used sparingly. Negative emotions can energize your readers and spur them to action. However, you need to be careful not to threaten or frighten your readers, because people tend to reject bullying or scare tactics. Any feelings of anger or disgust you express in your argument must be shared by your readers, or they will reject your argument as too harsh or reactionary.

FIGURE 22.5
**Using Emotions
in an Argument**
*This advertisement
uses emotional
appeals to influence
readers.*

Avoiding Logical Fallacies

A logical fallacy is an error in reasoning. As much as possible, you want to avoid logical fallacies in your arguments, because they are weaknesses that your opponents can exploit. Plus, they can keep you from gaining a full understanding of the issue because fallacies usually lead to inaccurate or ambiguous conclusions.

Figure 22.6 on page 432 defines and gives examples of common logical fallacies. Watch out for them in your own arguments. When an opponent uses a logical fallacy, you can attack it as a weak spot in his or her argument.

Fallacies tend to occur for three primary reasons:

False or weak premises. In these situations, the author is overreaching to make a point. The argument uses false or weak premises (bandwagon, *post hoc* reasoning, slippery slope, or hasty generalization) or it relies on comparisons, or authorities that don't exist (weak analogy, false authority).

Irrelevance. The author is trying to distract readers by using name calling (*ad hominem*) or bringing up issues that are beside the point (red herring, *tu quoque, non sequitur*).

Ambiguity. The author is clouding the issue by using circular reasoning (begging the question), arguing against a position that no one is defending (straw man), or presenting the reader with a limited choice of options (either/or).

Logical fallacies do not prove that someone is wrong about a topic. They simply mean that the person is using weak or improper reasoning to reach his or her conclusions. In some cases, especially in advertising, logical fallacies are used on purpose. The advertiser wants to slip a sales pitch past the audience. Savvy arguers can also use logical fallacies to trip up their opponents. You should learn to recognize these fallacies so you can counter them when necessary.

Logical Fallacy	Definition	Example
Ad Hominem	Attacking the character of the arguer rather than the argument.	"Mary has no credibility on the smoking ban issue, because she was once a smoker herself."
Bandwagon (*Ad Populum*)	Suggesting that a person should agree to something because it is popular.	"Over one thousand people have decided to sign up, so you should too."
Begging the Question	Using circular reasoning to prove a conclusion.	"Conservatives believe in hard work and strong values. That's why most Americans are conservative."
Either/Or	Presenting someone with a limited choice, when other choices are possible.	"We either buy this car now, or we spend the rest of the year walking to school."
Straw Man	Arguing against a position that no one is defending.	"Letting children play soccer on a busy highway is wrong, and I won't stand for it."
Weak Analogy	Making an improper comparison between two things that share a common feature.	"Paying taxes to the government is the same as handing your wallet over to a mugger in the park."
Post Hoc Reasoning	Arguing that one event caused another when they are unrelated.	"Each time my roommate is out of town, it causes my car to break down and I can't get to work."
Hasty Generalization	Using a part to make an inaccurate claim about a whole.	"The snowboarder who cut me off proved that all snowboarders are rude."
Slippery Slope	Suggesting that one event will automatically lead to a chain of other events.	"If we allow them to ban assault weapons, soon handguns, rifles, and all other guns will be banned, too."
Red Herring	Saying something that distracts from the issue being argued about.	"So, because books can now be found on the Internet, you're suggesting we burn our libraries?"
False Authority	Defending a claim with a biased or untrustworthy source.	"My mother read my paper, and she thinks it deserves an A."
Non Sequitur	Stating a conclusion that does not follow from the premises.	"Watching *30 Rock* each week will make you smarter and more popular."
Tu Quoque	Improperly turning an accusation back on the accuser.	"If you cared about global warming, as you claim, you wouldn't have driven a car to this meeting."

FIGURE 22.6 Common Logical Fallacies

Rebuttals and Refutations

Because we argue *with* others in an effort to gain their understanding and cooperation, you need to anticipate how your opponents and your readers will feel about
your claims and your support. You need to imagine their possible objections or misunderstandings. After all, something that sounds like a good reason to you may not
sound so convincing to your reader.

Summarize Your Opponents' Position Objectively

If you're discussing something "arguable," then there must be at least one other side
to the issue. So you should demonstrate that you understand that other side before
you offer a rebuttal or try to counter it. If you ignore the other side, your readers will
think you are either unfairly overlooking potential objections or you just don't understand the other side of the argument. One way to disarm your opponents is to summarize their position objectively early in your argument.

Summarizing your opponents' position does three things for your argument. First,
it lays out some specific points that you can then argue against or refute when you
state your side of the argument. Second, it takes away some of your opponents' momentum, because they will not have anything new to offer the readers. Third, it will
make you look more reasonable and well-informed about the issue you are arguing
about.

Recognize When the Opposing Position May Be Valid

Your opponents probably aren't completely wrong. There are likely to be situations, both real and hypothetical, where the other side may be valid. For example,
let's say you are arguing that the US automobile industry needs to convert completely to manufacturing electric cars within twenty years. Your opponents would
argue that this kind of dramatic conversion is not technically or economically
feasible.

To disarm your opponents, you could name a few situations in which they are
correct.

> Converting fully to electric vehicles within twenty years may not be possible
> in some circumstances. For example, it is unlikely that large trucks, like
> semitrailers, will be able to run on electricity two decades from now because
> batteries will not be strong enough to provide the amount of energy required to
> move their weight for long distances. Meanwhile, even if we stopped
> manufacturing gasoline-powered vehicles immediately, they would still be on
> the road for decades, requiring gas stations and mechanical repair. We cannot,
> after all, ask all drivers to immediately switch over to electric vehicles,
> especially if they cannot afford it.

By identifying situations in which your opponents' position may be valid, you
give some ground to your opponents while putting boundaries around their major
points.

Concede Your Opponents' Minor Points

When you concede a minor point, you are acknowledging that your opponents' viewpoints or objections are valid in a limited way, while highlighting a potential weakness in your own position. In these cases, you should candidly acknowledge this limitation and address it fairly.

For instance, if you were arguing that the federal government should use taxpayer money to help the auto industry develop electric cars, you could anticipate two objections to your argument:

- Production of electric cars cannot be ramped up quickly because appropriate batteries are not being manufactured in sufficient numbers.

- The United States' electric grid could not handle millions of new electric cars being charged every day.

These objections are important, but they do not undermine your whole argument. Instead, you should concede that they are problems while demonstrating that they are problems that can be fixed.

> It is true that the availability of car batteries and the inadequacy of the United States' electricity grid are concerns. As Stephen Becker, a well-respected consultant to the auto industry, points out, "car manufacturers are already experiencing a shortage of batteries," and there are no plans to build more battery factories in the future (109). Meanwhile, as Lauren King argues, the United States' electric grid "is already fragile, as the blackouts a few years ago showed. And there has been very little done to upgrade our electric-delivery infrastructure." King states that the extra power "required to charge 20 million cars would bring the grid to a grinding halt" (213).
>
> However, there are good reasons to believe that these problems, too, can be dealt with if the right measures are put in place. First, if investors had more confidence that there would be a steady demand for electric cars, and if the government guaranteed loans for new factories, the growing demand for batteries would encourage manufacturers to bring them to market (Vantz, 12). Second, experts have been arguing for years that the United States needs to invest in a *nationalized* electricity grid that will meet our increasing needs for electricity. King's argument that the grid is "too fragile" misses the point. We already need to build a better grid, because the current grid *is* too fragile, even for today's needs. Moreover, it will take years to build a fleet of 20 million cars. During those years, the electric grid can be rebuilt.

By conceding some minor points, you weaken their effectiveness. By anticipating your opponents' arguments, you can minimize the damage to your own argument.

Refute or Absorb Your Opponents' Major Points

In some situations, your opponents will have one or two major points that cannot be conceded without undermining your argument. In these situations, you should study each major point to understand why it is a threat to your own argument. Is there a chance your opponents have a good point? Could your argument be flawed in some fundamental way?

If you still believe your side of the argument is stronger, you have a couple of choices at this point. First, you can refute your opponents' major point by challenging its factual correctness. It helps to look for a "smoking gun" moment in which your opponents make a mistake or overstate a claim.

> Critics of electric cars argue that the free market should determine whether electric cars and the infrastructure to support them should be built. They argue that the government should not determine which automotive technologies survive and thrive. This kind of argument goes against the historical record. The US government has always been involved in building roads, railways, and airports. For decades, it has given tax breaks to support the manufacturing of gasoline vehicles. We are simply asking for these supports to be shifted in ways that will meet future needs, not the needs of the past.

In other situations, you should absorb your opponents' arguments by suggesting that your side of the argument is necessary or is better for the majority.

> The skeptics are correct that the conversion from gasoline cars to electric cars will not be easy and may even be economically painful. At this point, though, we have little choice. Our dependence on foreign oil, which is something we all agree is a problem, is a threat to our economic and political freedom. Moreover, our planet is already experiencing the negative effects of global climate change, which could severely damage the fragile ecosystems on which we depend for food, air, and water. We aren't talking about lifestyle choices at this point. We are talking about survival.

When absorbing your opponents' major points, you should show that you are aware that they are correct but that the benefits of your position outweigh its costs.

Qualify Your Claims

In an argument, you will be tempted to state your claims in the strongest language possible, perhaps even overstating them.

Overstatement

The government must use its full power to force the auto industry to develop and build affordable electric cars for the American consumer. The payoff in monetary and environmental benefits will more than pay for the investment.

Qualified Statement

Although many significant challenges must be dealt with, the government should begin taking steps to encourage the auto industry to develop and build affordable electric cars for the American consumer. The payoff in monetary and environmental impact could very well pay for the effort and might even pay dividends.

When qualifying your statements, you are softening your position a little. This softening gives readers the sense that they are being asked to make up their own minds on the matter. Few people want to be told that they "must" do something or "cannot" do something else. If possible, you want to avoid pushing your readers into making an either/or, yes/no kind of decision, because they may reject your position altogether.

Instead, remember that all arguments have gray areas. No one side is absolutely right or wrong. Qualifying your claims allows you to give the impression that your side has some flexibility. You can use the following words and phrases to qualify your claims:

unless	would	in all probability
except	perhaps	usually
if	maybe	frequently
even though	reasonably	probably
not including	plausibly	possibly
aside from	in most circumstances	conceivably
in some cases	almost certainly	often
although	most likely	may
could	if possible	might
should		

You can also soften your claims by acknowledging that you are aware of the difficulties and limitations of your position. Your goal is to sound reasonable while advocating for your side of the argument.

Here are some strategies for becoming more effective at argument.

DEVELOP an "Arguable Claim"

An arguable claim is a statement that exists between personal judgments and proven facts. It should also be a claim that others would be willing to dispute.

IDENTIFY the Source of Your Arguable Claim

Arguable claims tend to emerge from four types of issues: issues of definition, causation, evaluation, and recommendation. You can sharpen your claim by figuring out what kind of issue you are arguing about.

FIND Reason-Based Evidence to Back Up Your Claims

Reasoning consists of using logical statements and examples to support your arguments.

LOCATE Authoritative Evidence to Back Up Your Claims

You can use your own experience if you are an expert, or you can draw quotes from other experts who agree with you. You should also build up your authority by demonstrating your practicality, ethical principles, and goodwill toward readers.

USE Emotional Evidence to Back Up Your Claims

Identify any emotions that shape how your readers will be influenced by your argument. You can use promise of gain, promise of enjoyment, fear of loss, fear of pain, and expressions of anger and disgust to influence them.

COUNTER or Disarm Your Opponents

There are a variety of ways to counter or weaken your opponents' argument through rebuttal and refutation including (a) summarizing their position objectively, (b) identifying limited situations in which the opposing position may be valid, (c) conceding your opponents' minor points, (d) refuting or absorbing your opponents' major points, and (e) qualifying your claims.

AVOID Logical Fallacies

Look for logical fallacies in your argument and locate them in your opponents' existing arguments. A logical fallacy is a weak spot that should be addressed in your own work and can be exploited in your opponents' arguments.

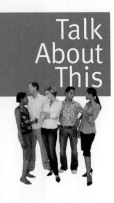

1. With a group of people from your class, talk about how you usually argue with your friends and family. When are arguments productive? At what point do they become quarrels?

2. Discuss whether each of the following claims is "arguable." Explain why each is or is not arguable.

   a. I always like to bring a water bottle with me when I work out at the gym.

   b. The Dallas Cowboys were America's favorite team during the 1970s.

   c. The major message behind the television show *Family Guy* is that it's okay to act rudely, obscenely, and irresponsibly in America.

3. With your group, identify five reasons why arguing can be useful, productive, or even amusing.

1. On the Internet, find a fairly short opinion article about an issue that interests you. Identify its main claim and determine which kind of evidence (*logos, ethos,* or *pathos*) is most dominant.

2. Find three different Web sites that persuade people to stop smoking. Compare and contrast their argument strategies. In a presentation, show why you think one Web site is more persuasive than the others.

3. With a group of three or four people from your class, divide up the list of fallacies in Figure 22.6 (on page 432). Then find or create examples of these fallacies. Share your examples with other groups in your class.

1. **Generate four claims and four counterclaims.** Choose an issue that you care about and develop an "arguable claim" from each of the sources of arguable claims discussed in this chapter (i.e., definition, causation, evaluation, recommendation). Then, for each of these arguable claims, develop a counterclaim that an opponent might use to argue against your positions.

2. **Find the fallacies in an advertisement.** Find an advertisement on television that uses one or more logical fallacies to support its points. In a two-page ad critique (see page 182), draw attention to the logical fallacies and use them as weak spots to undermine the advertisement.

mycomplab

For additional reading, writing, and research resources, go to **www.mycomplab.com**.

Working Collaboratively with Other Writers

In college and throughout your career, you will be asked to collaborate with other people on a variety of projects. Working in teams allows people to concentrate their personal strengths and take advantage of each other's abilities. Working with others also helps you to be more creative and take on more complex, longer projects.

Computers and the Internet have significantly increased our ability to collaborate with others (Figure 23.1, page 440). You probably already use e-mail, texting, mobile phones, blogs, microblogs, social networking sites, chat, and virtual worlds to keep in touch with your friends and family. In your career, you will use these same kinds of communication tools to interact with people at your office, across the country, and throughout the world.

In your college classes and in the workplace, collaboration will tend to take on two forms:

Working in Groups. Groups involve people who are working on separate but related assignments. Each member of the group shares his or her ideas and research, and everyone helps review and edit each other's work. Each person completes and hands in his or her own assignment.

Working in Teams. Teams involve people who are working on the same project. Each member of the team is responsible for completing one or more parts of the project, and the team hands in one common assignment or set of assignments.

FIGURE 23.1 Working Collaboratively in Your Career

The ability to work with others in groups and teams is essential in today's networked workplace.

In this chapter, you will learn how to work productively in groups and teams, and you will learn some strategies for avoiding and overcoming the negative aspects of working with others.

Working with a Group of Other Writers

In your college classes, professors will regularly ask you to work in groups. Often, these groups are informal, made up of the people who happen to be sitting near you in class that day. Your professor may also put you into a group with people who are working on a similar topic or who have a major similar to yours.

Choosing Group Roles

When you are put into a group, each person should choose a role:

Facilitator. The facilitator is responsible for keeping the group moving forward toward completing the task. His or her responsibility is to make sure the group stays on task, always keeping an eye on the clock. When the group goes off on a tangent or becomes distracted, the facilitator should remind the group members what they are trying to achieve and how much time is left to complete the task. When the group runs out of new ideas, the facilitator should prompt discussion by summarizing the group's major points and asking individuals to respond to those ideas.

Scribe. The scribe takes notes on what the group says or decides. These notes can be shared among the group members, helping everyone remember what was decided. If the group runs out of issues to talk about, the scribe should look back through the notes to pick out topics that could benefit from more discussion.

Innovator. The innovator should feel free to come up with new and unique ideas that help the group see the issue from other perspectives. The innovator should look for ways to be creative and different, even though he or she might come up with something that the rest of the group will probably not agree with.

Designated Skeptic. The designated skeptic's job is to keep the group from reaching easy consensus on issues. He or she should bring up concerns that someone else might use to raise doubts about what the members of the group have decided.

These roles should be rotated among the group members. Give everyone a chance to be a facilitator, scribe, innovator, and skeptic.

Figuring Out What the Group Needs to Do

Soon after your professor puts you into groups, you can warm up by answering the following questions:

What Is Our Primary Goal? Figure out exactly what your group is being asked to accomplish. The facilitator of the group can state what he or she thinks the task is. Other members of the group can elaborate on or sharpen that statement until everyone settles on a common goal.

What Else Should We Achieve? Sometimes your professor will ask your group to achieve a few secondary goals, too. Figure out what they are and have the scribe write them down.

How Much Time Do We Have? With your goals listed, figure out how much time you can devote to each one. Accomplishing the primary goal will usually take up the most time, but save some time for those secondary goals.

What Are We Expected to Deliver? When time is up, what is the group supposed to have finished? Does the professor expect someone to summarize the group's ideas for the class? Does the group need to produce something on paper to be handed in?

Who Will Speak for Our Group? Pick someone who can speak for the group when the activity is over. This choice should be made early, so the designated speaker can think about what he or she is going to say. This responsibility should rotate among group members, so one person doesn't end up always speaking for the group.

These questions are designed to get everyone on the same page. Otherwise, your group might waste time because you aren't sure what you are doing and what you are supposed to deliver.

Getting the Work Done

Now it's time to go to work. Here are some of the ways your group can work together to help each other succeed:

Generate Ideas. Your group can brainstorm ideas and help each other see different perspectives on issues. Any prewriting technique, such as concept mapping, listing, or brainstorming, can be used by the group to generate ideas. The scribe should write down the ideas while the other group members talk.

Serve as a Sounding Board. The people in your group can serve as a forum for talking out your ideas for an assignment and figuring out your angle on the project. The group's facilitator should ask each person in the group to take turns sharing his or her ideas. Then, after each person speaks, every group member should say something positive about the speaker's project and offer at least one suggestion for improving it.

Discuss Readings. Your group will be asked to discuss the course readings to figure out the meaning of the text and its implications. Each person should be asked to contribute. Meanwhile, the designated skeptic should keep the group from reaching quick consensus about what a reading means. Your professor will likely ask each group to offer a brief report to the class about your discussion.

Review Works-in-Progress. Members of your group can read and comment on your writing, helping you strengthen and clarify your ideas. You can rotate papers among members of the group. If time allows, each member of the group might take a turn reading someone else's paper out loud. While listening, other members of the group should take notes about the paper's strengths and what could be improved.

Working with a Team

Throughout your college career, especially in advanced courses for your major, you will be asked to work on team projects. Working in teams usually involves developing one project (i.e., a document, presentation, product, experiment) that your team will hand in together. To be successful, you and your team members will need to set goals and deadlines, negotiate with each other, divide up the work, and overcome disagreements.

One helpful way to successfully work as a team is to use the "Four Stages of Teaming" that were developed by management guru Bruce Tuckman (Figure 23.2). Tuckman noticed that successful teams tend to go through four predictable stages when working on a project:

Forming. Getting to know each other, defining goals, describing outcomes, setting deadlines, dividing up the work.

Storming. Experiencing disagreements, sensing tension and anxiety, doubting the leadership of the team, experiencing conflict, feeling uncertain and frustrated.

Norming. Forming consensus, revising the project's goals, refining expectations of outcomes, solidifying team roles.

Performing. Sharing a common vision, delegating tasks, feeling autonomous, resolving conflicts and differences in constructive ways.

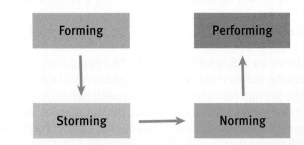

FIGURE 23.2
Tuckman's Four Stages of Teaming

Successful teams usually go through four stages of teaming. Each stage brings its own challenges and adjustments.

These are the stages for *successful* groups. Some groups break down at the storming stage, while other groups never reach the performing stage. The secret to working in teams is recognizing that these stages are normal—including storming—and knowing what to do at each stage.

Forming: Planning a Project

When your team is first formed, you should give team members an opportunity to get to know each other and figure out the expectations of the project. When starting a new project, people are usually excited and a little anxious because they are uncertain about the professor's and the other team members' expectations.

Hold a Planning Meeting. Your first task should be to plan the project and set some deadlines. To help you get started, do some or all of the following:

- ❏ Ask all team members to introduce themselves.
- ❏ Define the purpose of the project and its goals.
- ❏ Describe the expected outcomes of the project.
- ❏ Identify the strengths and interests of each team member.
- ❏ Divide up the work.
- ❏ Create a project calendar and set deadlines.
- ❏ Agree on how conflicts will be solved when they arise (because they will).

Choose Team Responsibilities. Each member of the team should be given a specific role on the project. When writing a collaborative document, here are four roles that your team might consider assigning:

Coordinator. This person is responsible for maintaining the project schedule and running the meetings. The coordinator is not the "boss." Rather, he or she is responsible for keeping people in touch and keeping the project on schedule.

Researchers. One or two group members should be assigned to collect information. They are responsible for digging up material at the library, running searches on the Internet, and coordinating any empirical research.

Editor. The editor is responsible for the organization and style of the final document. He or she identifies missing content and places where the document needs to be reorganized.

Designer. This person designs the document, gathers images from the Internet, creates graphs and charts, and takes photographs.

Notice that there is no "writer" in this list. Everyone on your team should be responsible for writing part of the document. Everyone should be responsible for reading and responding to all the parts, even those originally written by another person.

It is all right if your team seems a little uncertain at the beginning. When forming, you and your team should try to sketch out what you're doing, why you're doing it that way, who will do what, and when each of those tasks will be completed.

Storming: Overcoming Differences

Conflict is a normal part of any team project, so you need to learn how to manage the conflicts that come up. In fact, one of the reasons your professors put you into work teams is so you can learn how to manage conflict in constructive ways. Conflict may seem uncomfortable at the time, but it can lead to new ideas and more creativity.

Here are some strategies and tips for managing conflict:

Run Efficient Meetings. Choose a facilitator for the meeting and decide up front what will happen, what will be achieved, and when it will end. At the end of each meeting, each team member should state what he or she will do on the project before the next meeting.

Encourage Participation from Everyone. Each team member should have an opportunity to contribute ideas and opinions. No one should be allowed to sit back and let the others make decisions. Also, no one should dominate the meeting, cutting off the ideas of others.

Allow Dissent (Even Encourage It). Everyone should feel welcome to disagree or offer alternative ideas for consideration. In fact, dissent should be encouraged, because it often leads to new and better ways of completing the project.

Mediate Conflicts. Conflicts will come up, and people are going to grow irritated and even angry with each other. When conflicts happen, give each side time to consider and state their position. Then identify the two to five issues that the two sides disagree about. Rank these issues from most important to least. Address each of these issues separately, and try to negotiate a solution to the conflict.

Motivate Any Slackers. Slackers can kill the momentum of a team and undermine its ability to finish the project. If someone is slacking, your team should make your expectations clear to that person as soon as possible. Often, slackers simply need a straightforward list of responsibilities.

Conflict is normal and inevitable. When you see conflict developing in your team, remind yourself that the team is just going through the storming stage of the teaming process. You are going to experience plenty of conflict in advanced classes and in your career, so here is a good place to practice managing it.

Norming: Getting Down to Work

The storming stage can be frustrating, but soon afterward your team will usually enter the norming stage. Norming gives your group an opportunity to refine the goals of the project and finish the majority of the work.

Revise Project Goals and Expected Outcomes. At a meeting or through e-mail, your team should look back at the original goals and outcomes you identified during the planning stage. Sharpen your goals and clarify what your team will complete by the end of the project.

Adjust Team Responsibilities. Your team should redistribute the work so the burden is shared fairly among team members. Doing so will raise the morale of the group and allow more work to be done in the time allowed.

Revise the Project Calendar. More than likely, unexpected challenges and events have put your team a little behind schedule. So spend some time with your team working out some new deadlines. These deadlines will need to be firmer than the ones you set in the forming stage.

Hold Regular Meetings. Your team should meet once or twice a week. Each person in the team should bring something new to each meeting.

Use Online Collaborative Tools. You can't always meet face to face, but you can still collaborate. Online collaborative software such as *Google Docs* allows team members to view the document's editing history, revert to previous versions of a document, and even work on the same document simultaneously. When you do work together online, it's best to also have a voice connection.

Keep in Touch with Each Other. Depending on the project deadline, your group should be in touch with each other every day or every other day. Texting or e-mailing works well. If you aren't hearing regularly from someone, give that person a call. Regular contact will help keep the project moving forward.

Conflict will still happen during the norming stage. That's normal. Talk any issues out. The conflicts, however, should be less frustrating during the norming stage, because your group will have a clearer sense of the project's goals, each other's roles, and the expected outcomes.

Performing: Working as a Team

When performing, each team member recognizes and understands the others' talents, needs, and capabilities. During the performing stage, your team is doing more than just trying to finish the project. Now, everyone on the team is looking for ways to improve the project, leading to higher-quality results (and more satisfaction among team members).

This is as much as we are going to say about performing in this book. Teams usually need to be together for several months before they reach this stage. If your team in a college class reaches the performing stage, that's fantastic. If not, that's fine too. The performing stage is a goal you should work toward in your advanced classes and in your career, but it's not typical in a college writing course.

Here are some useful strategies and tips that will help you get going on a group or team project.

CHOOSE Group Member Roles

A group works best when each person chooses a specific role. Some popular roles include facilitator, scribe, innovator, and designated skeptic.

DETERMINE What the Group Is Being Asked to Do

Talk with your group about its main goal and other objectives, while determining how much time is available, what is expected of the group, and who will speak for the group.

PURSUE Goals by Doing a Variety of Activities

Your group can be used to generate new ideas, serve as a sounding board, discuss readings, and review and edit each other's work.

REMEMBER That Teams Go Through Stages

When working on a team project, keep in mind that teams go through four stages: forming, storming, norming, and performing.

PLAN the Team Project

While forming, hold a planning meeting and have each team member choose his or her responsibilities on the project.

WORK Through Any Conflicts

When the team reaches the storming phase, work on running good meetings, encouraging participation from everyone, allowing dissent, mediating conflict, and motivating any slackers.

RETHINK the Team's Goals and Roles

After storming, teams usually enter a norming phase in which project goals are modified and team roles are adjusted.

IMPROVE Your Team's Quality

Teams that are together for a long time reach the performing stage, allowing them to concentrate on improving quality and satisfaction.

1. With a group in class, discuss the positive and negative experiences you have had while working in groups or teams. Describe two or three specific things group members can do to get a struggling group back on track.

2. In your group, discuss situations in which slackers have hurt a project you were working on. What are some ways to remove slackers from a project if they won't get to work?

3. What are some of the qualities of a successful sports team? How do the leaders of the team behave? How do the others on the team contribute?

1. Using the Internet to do research, list five ways in which you will need to use collaborative skills to be successful in your chosen career path. Write a brief report in which you discuss what kinds of collaborative work happens in your field.

2. With a team of people in your class, pick a topic that you are all interested in. Then, in less than an hour, put together a visual report on that topic. While your team is working, pay attention to how each person contributes to the project. Before your next class, each person in the group should write two to three paragraphs describing (a) what happened, (b) what went well, and (c) what could have gone better. Compare experiences with your team members.

3. Research the future of virtual offices, telecommuting, and teleworking. In a brief report, explain how new media and technology will change how people work and how people will communicate with each other.

1. **Imagine that your classroom is a workplace.** With a group in your class, evaluate your writing class as a workplace. Write a proposal for restructuring the classroom as an effective and collaborative workplace. In your report, explain whether or not you think this kind of change would be a good idea.

2. **Use an online collaborative tool.** Write a pitch to your professor in which you advocate for the use of online collaborative tools in your writing class.

PEARSON
mycomplab

For additional reading, writing, and research resources, go to **www.mycomplab.com**.

PART

5

Doing
Research

PART OUTLINE

RESEARCH and **INQUIRY**

are the keys to discovery. In these

chapters, you will learn how

to do thoughtful and thorough research,

discovering answers to the questions

that intrigue you.

24

Starting
Research

Research is a systematic inquiry into a topic, using hands-on experience, factual evidence, and secondary sources to inquire, explore, and understand something that interests you. Research is used to do three important things:

- **Inquiring:** A researcher gathers information in order to investigate an issue and explain it to other people.

- **Advancing knowledge:** Researchers, especially scientists, collect and analyze facts to increase or strengthen our knowledge about a subject.

- **Supporting an argument:** In some situations, research can be used to persuade others and support a particular side of an argument while gaining a full understanding of the opposing view.

Research requires much more than a visit to the library to pick up a few books or articles that agree with your preexisting opinion. It involves more than simply using the first page of hits from an Internet search engine like *Google*. Instead, research is about pursuing truth and developing knowledge.

In this chapter, you will learn how to develop your own "research process" that will help you inquire into topics that interest you. Using a dependable research process will allow you to write and speak with authority, because you will be more confident about the reliability of your sources. Always remember that finding sources is easy—especially on the Internet—but it's critical that you find good sources that provide information you can trust. A reliable research process will actually save you time in the long run while helping you find more useful and trustworthy sources of information.

This chapter is about getting your research process started. Then, in Chapter 25, "Finding Sources and Collecting Information," we will go into more depth about how to find and generate information with online, print, and empirical sources.

Starting Your Research Process

A reliable research process, as shown in Figure 24.1, is "recursive," which means the researcher collects sources and modifies the working thesis in a cyclical way. The process ends when the working thesis fits the facts available.

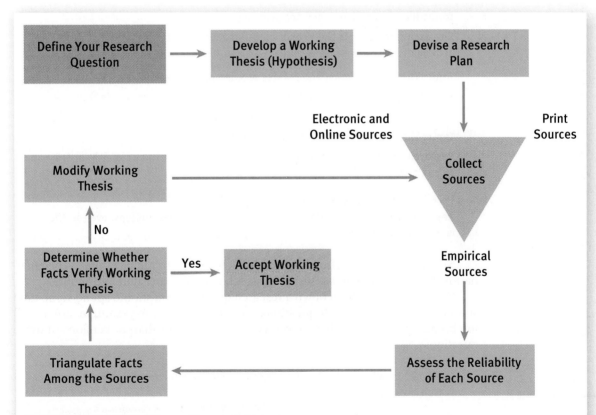

FIGURE 24.1 Following a Research Process

A reliable research process will save you time and energy. Each source you collect will lead you to other sources. Keep looping until you collect the information you need to draft your paper.

When starting your research, you should do three things:

1. Define a *research question* and sharpen it.

2. Develop a *working thesis* or *hypothesis* that offers your best guess about how you will answer the research question.

3. Devise a *research plan* to help you systematically collect the information needed to answer your research question and determine whether your working thesis is verifiable.

Step One: Define Your Research Question

Your research question names the topic you are studying and states specifically what you want to find out about that topic. Write down the exact question your research will try to answer:

Topic: Illegal immigrants and the economy.

Research Question: Is the flow of illegal immigrants into the United States helping or harming our economy?

Topic: The reasons Confederate states seceded before the Civil War.

Research Question: Why did the Confederate states decide to secede from the United States, thus sparking the US Civil War?

Topic: The severity of the threat of swine flu (H1N1 Flu).

Research Question: Is swine flu (H1N1 Flu) a real threat to our health, or is it mostly media hype?

Topic: The oddity of wearing shorts and flipflops in wintertime.

Research Question: Why do some people wear shorts and flipflops, even in the middle of the winter?

Notice that in moving from topic to research question, you have already begun to narrow down your research. The best research questions are short and simple.

Once you have written down a research question, you should spend some time sharpening it. The research questions mentioned above, for example, are a little too broad for a typical college research paper. Here are sharper versions of these questions:

Are illegal immigrants having a positive or negative affect on the economy of Tucson, Arizona?

Was the constitutional disagreement over "states' rights" the real reason the Confederate states decided to secede from the United States, or did they secede to protect slavery as a cheap labor source?

Is swine flu a real threat to people in northern Michigan, or is it just another media-generated frenzy about an obscure disease?

Why do some students at Syracuse University always wear shorts and flipflops, even in the middle of the winter?

These sharper research questions will help you narrow the scope of your research, saving you time and effort by allowing you to target the best kinds of sources and information.

Step Two: Develop a Working Thesis

After defining your research question, you should then develop a *working thesis*, which is also called a "hypothesis" in some fields. Your working thesis is your best guess about how you will answer your research question.

In one sentence, try to write down your overall claim about your topic. For example, here are some working theses based on the research questions above:

I believe illegal immigration helps the Tucson economy by attracting low-wage labor, thus keeping costs down; but illegal immigrants also use up valuable public resources and take jobs away from legal citizens who already live here.

Slavery was one of the key reasons the Confederate states decided to secede; however, other issues also sparked secession, such as Constitutional disagreements about states' rights, the economic disparities between North and South, and the formation of new non-slave states in the West that threatened to weaken the South politically.

In northern Michigan, we need to be on guard against H1N1 Flu because we spend much of the winter confined indoors, increasing the chances that the flu will spread from person to person.

Some Syracuse students wear shorts and flipflops in the winter because they prefer light, comfortable clothing, and they can keep warm by staying inside and walking from building to building across campus.

As you do your research, it is likely your working thesis will change, eventually becoming the main claim for your project. If possible, boil your working thesis down into one sentence. If you require two or three sentences to state your working thesis, your topic may be too complex or broad.

Step Three: Devise a Research Plan

Before you begin collecting sources, set aside a little time to sketch out your *research plan*. Your research plan should describe the kinds of sources you will need to collect to answer your research question. Your plan should also describe how you are going to collect these sources and your deadlines for finding them. Your professor may ask you to submit a research plan at an early stage of the research project. A typical research plan has these elements:

- Research question
- Working thesis
- Results of start-up research
- Description of electronic, online, print, and empirical sources available
- Schedule for conducting and completing the research
- Bibliography

Even if your professor does not ask for a research plan, you should spend some time considering each of these items in order to better target sources and streamline your research.

Doing Start-Up Research

Now that you have created a research question, working thesis, and research plan, you're ready to start tracking down sources and collecting information. Some researchers find it helpful to begin by doing an hour of "start-up" research. This kind of research will help you to gain an overall view of the topic, figure out the various sides of the issue, and identify the kinds of sources available.

In Chapter 25, "Finding Sources and Collecting Information," we will talk about doing formal research, which is much more targeted and structured. For now, though, let's look at some good ways to do start-up research:

Surf the Internet. Put your research question or its keywords into *Google, Yahoo!,* or *Ask.com.* See what pops up. Jot down notes about the kinds of information you find. Identify some of the major issues and people involved with your topic and take note of any key sources of information that you might want to look up later. Bookmark Web sites that seem especially useful.

Look Through Online Encyclopedias. Major online encyclopedias include *Wikipedia, MSN Encarta,* or *Encyclopaedia Britannica Online.* Again, note the major issues and people involved with your topic. Identify key terms and any controversies about your topic.

One note: Professors probably won't let you cite online encyclopedias like *Wikipedia* or *Encyclopaedia Britannica* as authoritative sources, because the entries are often written by nonexperts. Nevertheless, online encyclopedias are useful for gaining a quick overview of your topic and finding sources that are authoritative. That's why they can be especially helpful when doing start-up research.

Browse Your Library's Catalog. Log on to your school's online library catalog and type in keywords to see what kinds of materials are available on your topic. Write down the names of any authors and titles that look like they might be helpful. In some cases, your library's catalog can e-mail your selections to you.

Start-up research should take you an hour or less. Your goal is to gain an overall sense of your topic, not to make up your mind or form your final opinion. At this point, keep your options open and don't become too occupied by one source or perspective.

Assessing a Source's Reliability

All information is not created equal. Some people who claim to be "authorities" are downright wrong or even dishonest. Even more problematic are people who have agendas or biases, and whose print and online writings aren't always honest or truthful about the facts. To assess the reliability of your sources, consider these questions:

Is the Source Credible?

To determine whether a source's author and publisher are trustworthy, you should use an Internet search engine to check out their backgrounds and expertise. If you can find little or no information about the author or publisher—or if they have questionable credentials or reputations—you should avoid using the source and look for something more reliable.

How Biased Are the Author and the Publisher?

All sources have some bias because authors and publishers have their own ideas and opinions. When you are assessing the reliability of a source, consider how much the author or publisher *wants* the information to be true. If it seems like the author or publisher would only accept one kind of answer from the outset (e.g. "smoking does not cause cancer"), the information should be considered too biased to be a reliable source. On the other hand, if the author and publisher were open to a range of possible conclusions, you can feel more confident about using the source.

How Biased Are You?

As a researcher, you need to keep your own biases in mind as you assess your sources. Try viewing your sources from alternative perspectives, even (or especially) perspectives you disagree with. Knowing your own biases and seeing the issue from other perspectives will help you gain a richer understanding of your topic.

Is the Source Up to Date?

Depending on your topic, information can quickly become obsolete. In some fields, like cancer research, information that is only a few years old might already be out of date. In other fields, like geology, information that is decades old might still be usable today. So pay attention to how rapidly the field is changing. Consult your professor or a research librarian about whether a source can be considered up to date.

Can You Verify the Information in the Source?

You should be able to confirm your source's information by consulting other, independent sources. If a source is the only one that offers information that you want to use, you should treat it as unverified and use it only cautiously, if at all. If multiple sources offer the same or similar kinds of information, then you can use each source with much more confidence.

Evaluating Your Sources: A Checklist

❑ Is the source reliable?

❑ How biased are the author and the publisher?

❑ How biased are you?

❑ Is the source up to date?

❑ Can you independently verify the information in the source?

Managing Your Research Process

When you finish your start-up research, you should have enough information to create a schedule for completing your research. A research schedule will help you finish the project in manageable chunks. At this point, you should also start a bibliographic file to help you keep track of your sources.

Creating a Research Schedule

You might find "backward planning" helpful when creating your research schedule. Backward planning means working backward from the deadline to today, filling in all the tasks that need to be accomplished. Here's how to do it:

1. On your screen or a piece of paper, list all the tasks you need to complete for the research project.

2. On your calendar, set a deadline for finishing your research. You should also fill in your deadlines for drafting, designing, and revising your project.

3. Work backwards from your research deadline, filling in the tasks you need to accomplish and the days on which each task needs to be completed.

Online calendars like those from *Scrybe, Google,* or *Yahoo!* are great tools for making research schedules. Your mobile phone or computer might have calendar applications already installed. A low-tech paper calendar still works well, too, for scheduling your research project.

Starting Your Bibliography File

One of the first tasks on your research schedule should be to set up a file on your computer that holds a working bibliography of the sources you find. Each time you find a useful source, add it to your bibliography file.

Minimally, as you find sources, make sure you record all the information needed for a full bibliographic citation (you will learn how to cite sources in Chapters 27, "Using MLA Style," and 28, "Using APA Style"). That way, when you are ready to create your works-cited page at the end of your paper, you will have a list of your sources ready to go.

Following and Modifying Your Research Plan

You should expect to modify your research plan as you move forward with the project. In some cases, you will find yourself being pulled away from your research plan by interesting facts, ideas, and events that you didn't know about when you started. For the most part, that is all right. Let your research take you wherever the facts lead you.

While researching, check in regularly with your research question and working thesis to make sure you are not drifting too far away from your original idea for the project. Or, you might need to adjust your research question and working thesis to fit some of the sources or new issues you have discovered.

When Things Don't Go as Expected

Research is a process of inquiry—of exploring, testing, and discovering. You are going to encounter ideas and issues that will require you to modify your approach, research question, or working thesis. Expect the unexpected and move forward.

Roadblocks to Research. You may not be able to get access to all the sources you had planned on using. For example, you might find that the expert you wanted to interview is unavailable or doesn't want to talk to you, or that the book you needed is checked out or missing from the library, or that you simply cannot find certain data or information. Don't give up. Instead, modify your approach and move around the roadblock.

Information and Ideas That Change Your Research Question or Working Thesis. You might find something unexpected that changes how you see your topic. For instance, sources might not support your working thesis after all. Or, you might find that a different, more focused research question is more interesting to you. Rather than getting distracted or disappointed, look at this as an opportunity to discover something new. Modify your research question or working thesis and move forward.

These temporary roadblocks can be frustrating, but these inevitable surprises can also make research fun. If research were just mechanical plugging and chugging, then we wouldn't need to do it in the first place.

Uses these guidelines to begin your research process.

UNDERSTAND Why Writers Do Research

Keep in mind that the purpose of research is to inform and support your ideas. Research is not just a regurgitation of others' ideas.

DEFINE Your Research Question

Name your topic and state your research question as specifically as possible. This is the question that your research will help you answer. Improve the efficiency of your research by sharpening that research question as much as possible.

DEVELOP a Working Thesis

In a single sentence, write down your working thesis. This is your best guess, or "hypothesis," for what you think will be your main claim.

DO Some "Start-Up" Research

Take half an hour to an hour to scan the kinds of sources available and get an overall sense of the various views on your research question. This informal start up should include the Internet, online encyclopedias, and your library's online catalog.

DEVISE Your Research Plan

Avoid the temptation to just dive in. Take a little time to make a written plan that describes your research question, working thesis, start-up research results, your schedule, and an early bibliography.

CREATE a Schedule

Use "backward planning" to break your research into manageable chunks. After listing all the tasks you will need to complete, work backward from your deadline, filling in the tasks and the days they need to be completed.

KEEP a Bibliography File

Keep a computer file of your working bibliography and maintain it. Your readers will need this bibliographic information to see where your sources can be found.

EXPECT the Unexpected

As you find new information, you will want to modify your research approach, research question, and working thesis. This is all part of the research process.

1. List five possible research questions that you find personally interesting. Then turn each of your research questions into a working thesis. With a small group, talk about these research questions and your working theses. Do group members have any ideas about how you could narrow your research?

2. With a small group, develop a research question on a topic that is interesting to all of you. Go online and use a variety of keywords to explore that topic. What are some possible answers to the research question?

3. In class, discuss what kinds of sources you think are most reliable. Do you believe online sources can be as reliable as print sources? When are hands-on empirical sources, like interviews or surveys, better than online and print sources?

Try
This
Out

1. Do about 30 minutes of start-up research on something that interests you. In an e-mail, describe to your professor what kinds of issues you will face if you want to do some formal research on this topic.

2. In a brief memo to your professor, describe your research plan for your next project. Explain why you think specific types of sources will be most helpful and why other kinds of sources probably will not be helpful.

3. On the Internet, find three sources of information that you would consider "heavily biased." Write an evaluation of these sources, explaining why you consider them biased and perhaps unreliable as sources.

Write
This

1. **Create a research plan.** Write a full research plan. Identify your research question and your working thesis, show the results of your start-up research, and identify the kinds of sources you plan to target.

2. **Start a research journal.** Keep a journal while you do research for your next assignment. Keep track of the kinds of research you did and the amount of time you devoted to those activities. Determine what kinds of research yielded the most useful information and what kinds of research cost you too much time.

PEARSON
mycomplab

For additional reading, writing, and research resources, go to **www.mycomplab.com**.

25

Finding Sources and Collecting Information

N ow that you have figured out your working thesis and research plan, you are ready to start collecting sources. In this chapter, you will learn how to collect a variety of *primary* and *secondary* sources that will help you inquire into your topic and find useful information. The ability to collect reliable sources will be critical to doing useful, dependable research in college and in the workplace.

Evaluating Sources with Triangulation

When doing any kind of research, you should try to draw information from a variety of perspectives. If you rely on just one type of source, especially the Internet, you risk developing a limited or inaccurate understanding of your topic. To avoid this problem, *triangulate* your research by looking for information from three different types of sources:

> **Electronic and online sources:** Web sites, CD-ROMs, listservs, television, radio, podcasts, videos, and blogs.

> **Print sources:** Books, journals, magazines, newspapers, government publications, reference materials, and microform/microfiche.

> **Empirical sources:** Personal experiences, field observations, interviews, surveys, case studies, and experiments.

Together, these three types of sources are called the *research triangle* (Figure 25.1). Here's how the research triangle works. If you collect similar facts from all three kinds of sources, the information you found is probably reliable. If you gather comparable facts from only two points of the triangle, your findings are probably still reliable but open to some doubt. However, if you can only find facts from one point on the triangle, then you probably need to do more research to back up your findings.

Of course, finding similar information in all three types of sources doesn't make something true. It just means the information is probably trustworthy. Triangulation is a good way to evaluate your sources and corroborate the facts you uncover about your topic. Keep in mind that "facts" and the "truth" are more slippery than we like to admit.

Also, remember that there are always at least two sides to any issue. So don't just look for sources that support your working thesis. Instead, use triangulation to find sources that also challenge what you believe. Even if you completely disagree with one of your sources, the argument it makes might give you a stronger understanding of your own position.

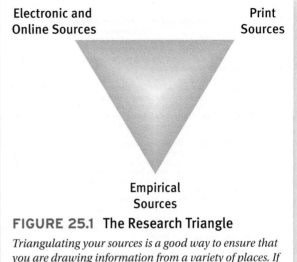

Electronic and Online Sources

Print Sources

Empirical Sources

FIGURE 25.1 The Research Triangle

Triangulating your sources is a good way to ensure that you are drawing information from a variety of places. If you find similar information from all three corners of the triangle, it is probably reliable.

Using Primary and Secondary Sources

Researchers tend to distinguish between two types of sources: *primary sources* and *secondary sources*. Both kinds are important to doing reliable research.

Primary Sources. These are the actual records or artifacts, such as letters, photographs, videos, memoirs, books, or personal papers, that were created by the people involved in the issues and events you are researching (Figure 25.2, page 462). Primary sources can also include any data or observations collected from empirical research.

Secondary Sources. These are the writings of scholars, experts, and other knowledgeable people who have studied your topic. For example, scholarly books by historians are secondary sources because their authors analyze and reflect on events from the past. Secondary sources can include books, academic journals, magazines, newspapers, and blogs.

For most research projects in college, you will usually rely on secondary sources. However, you should always look for opportunities to collect information from primary sources because they allow you to get closer to your topic than secondary sources.

KENEDY COUNTY SHERIFF'S DEPARTMENT
TX 1310000
INCIDENT REPORT
02/11/2006

NUMBER: 06020136   REPORT DATE: 02/15/2006   ORI: TX1310000
LOCATION: ARMSTRONG RANCH   ZONE: ARMSTRONG

At approximately 1830 hrs on Saturday February 11, 2006, Kenedy County Sheriff Ramon Salinas contacted me, Chief Deputy Gilberto San Miguel Jr. The phone call was in reference to a hunting accident that occurred on the Armstrong Ranch. I was told by Sheriff Salinas to report to the main house on the Armstrong Ranch on Sunday February 12, at 0800 hrs and I would receive more information when I got there.

On Sunday, February 12, 2006, at approximately 0805 hrs, I Chief Deputy Gilberto San Miguel Jr., arrived at the bump gate to the Armstrong Ranch. This ranch is located approximately twenty-one miles south of Sarita, Texas in Kenedy County. There at the bump gate, Secret Service, and Border Patrol personnel met me. I identified myself and told everyone I was to report to the main house. I was instructed to park my vehicle so it could be inspected before I could proceed to the main house. While my vehicle was getting inspected, a Secret Service agent approached me and he advised me he would be riding with me to the main house. As I was approaching the main house, I was instructed to park my vehicle by the cattle guard. There I walked across the cattle guard and was turned over to another agent who identified himself to me as Michael A. Lee, Special Agent in charge with the Secret Service.

As we entered the main house, Mr. Lee introduced me to Vice President Cheney. Mr. Cheney shook my hand and told me he was there to cooperate in any way with the interview. As I got comfortable at a table inside the main house, I asked Mr. Cheney if he could explain to me what had happened the day of the incident.

Mr. Cheney told me that on Saturday, February 11, 2006 at approximately 5:30 pm on the Armstrong Ranch there was a three vehicle hunting party that consisted of himself, Bo Hubert, Pam Willeford, Jerry Medellin, Katharine Armstrong, Sarita Armstrong Hixon, Harry Whittington, and Oscar Medellin. Mr. Cheney told me the sun was setting to the west when the dogs had located a covey. Around the same time, Oscar Medellin notified the hunters he had also located a covey. After the group shot at the first covey he and Pam Willeford proceeded to the second covey because Harry Whittington was looking for his downed birds. Mr. Cheney told me he and Pam Willeford had walked approximately 100 yards from the first location and met up with Oscar Medellin and the hunting guide Bo Hubert. There was a single bird that flew behind him and he followed the bird by line of sight in a counter clockwise direction not realizing Harry Whittington had walked up from behind and had positioned himself approximately 30 yards to the west of him. Mr. Cheney told me the reason Harry Whittington sustained the injuries to his face and upper body was that Mr. Whittington was standing on ground that was lower than the one he was standing on. Mr. Cheney told me if Mr. Whittington was on the same ground level the injuries might have been lower on Mr. Whittington's body.

STATUS: CLOSED   STATUS DATE: 02/15/2006
OFFICER: SAN MIGUEL, GILBERTO JR.   502

02/15/2006 16:00 P.M.   1

FIGURE 25.2 Primary Sources of Information

Primary sources were created by the people involved in the events you are studying or through empirical research.

Finding Electronic and Online Sources

The Internet is a good place to start doing research on your topic. Keep in mind, though, that the Internet is only a starting place for your research. You will need to triangulate, using print and empirical sources to support anything you find on the Internet.

Using Internet Search Engines

Search engines let you use keywords to locate information about your topic. If you type your topic into *Google, Bing,* or *Ask,* the search engine will return dozens or even millions of links. A handful of these links will be useful, and the vast majority of them will not.

With a few easy tricks, though, you can target your search with some common symbols and strategies. For example, let's say you are researching how sleep deprivation affects college students. You might start by entering the phrase:

sleep and college students

With this generic subject, a search engine will pull up millions of Web pages that might refer to this topic. Of course, there is no way you are going to have time to look through all those pages to find what you need, even if the search engine ranks them for you.

So you need to target your search to pull up only the kinds of materials you want. Here are some tips for pulling up better results:

Use Exact Words. Choose words that exactly target your topic, and use as many as you need to sharpen your results. For example,

sleep deprivation effects on students test taking

Use the Plus (+) Sign. If you put a plus (+) sign in front of words, that tells the search engine to only find pages that have those exact words in them.

sleep +deprivation effects on +students +test +taking

Use the Minus (–) Sign. If you want to eliminate any pages that refer to things you don't want to see, you can use the minus sign to eliminate pages that refer to them.

sleep deprivation +effects on students +test +taking –insomnia –apnea

Use Quotation (" ") Marks. If you want to guarantee that the search engine will find specific phrasings on Web sites, you can use quotation marks to target those phrases.

"sleep deprivation" +effects on students and "test taking" –insomnia –apnea

Use Wildcard Symbols. Some search engines have symbols for "wildcards," like ?, *, or %. These symbols are helpful when you know most of a phrase, but not all of it.

"sleep deprivation" +effects on students and "test taking" neural* behavioral* –insomnia –apnea

FIGURE 25.3 Targeting Your Search

In this search, the use of symbols has helped narrow the search to useful pages.

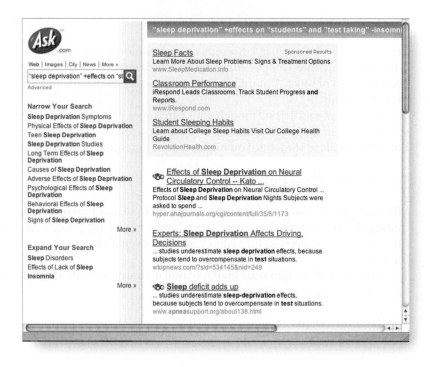

These search engine tips will help you pull up the pages you need. Figure 25.3 shows the results of an *Ask.com* search using the phrase

> "sleep deprivation" +effects on students and "test taking" –insomnia –apnea.

Something to remember is that the first items pulled up by search engines are usually *sponsored links.* In other words, these companies paid to have their links show up at the top of your list. Most search engines highlight these links in a special way. For example, they are highlighted in blue by *Ask.com* in Figure 25.3. You might find these links useful, but you should keep in mind that the sponsors are biased because they want to sell you something.

Using the Internet Cautiously

You already know that information from the Internet can be unreliable. In fact, many of the so-called "facts" on the Internet are really just opinions and hearsay with little basis in reality. Also, many quotes that appear on the Internet have been taken out of context or corrupted in some way. So you need to use information from the Internet critically and even skeptically. Don't get fooled by a professional-looking Web site, because a good Web designer can make just about anything look professional.

Chapter 24, "Starting Research," offers some questions for checking the reliability of any source. Here are some additional questions you should use to challenge Internet sources:

- Can you identify and trust the author(s) of the source?

- What organization is this source associated with and why is it publishing this information?

- What does the source's author or organization have to gain from publishing this information?

- Does the source clearly distinguish between opinions and independent facts?

- Does the source fairly discuss two or more sides of the issue?

- Does the source use other independent sources to back up claims and can you access those sources?

- Does the information seem too incredible, too terrible, or too good to be true?

- Has the Web site been updated recently?

The Internet has plenty of useful, reliable information, but there is also a great amount of junk. It's your responsibility as a researcher to critically decide what is reliable and what isn't.

Using Documentaries and Television/Radio Broadcasts

Multimedia resources such as television and radio broadcasts are available online through network Web sites as well as sites like *YouTube* and *Hulu*. Depending on who made them, documentaries and broadcasts can be reliable sources. If the material is from a trustworthy source, you can take quotes and cite these kinds of electronic sources in your own work.

Documentaries. A documentary is a nonfiction movie or program that relies on interviews and factual evidence about an event or issue. A documentary can be biased, though, so check into the background of the person or organization that made it.

Television Broadcasts. Cable channels and news networks like HBO, the History Channel, the National Geographic Channel, and the Biography Channel are producing excellent broadcasts that are reliable and can be cited as support for your argument. Programs on news channels that feature just one or two highly opinionated commentators are less reliable because they tend to be sensationalistic and are often biased.

Radio Broadcasts. Radio broadcasts, too, can be informative and authoritative. Public radio broadcasts, such as National Public Radio and American RadioWorks, offer well-researched stories on the air and at their Web sites. On the other hand, political broadcasts like *The Sean Hannity Show, The Rush Limbaugh Show, Countdown with Keith Olbermann,* and *Doing Time with Ron Kuby,* are notorious for slanting the news and manipulating facts. You cannot rely on these broadcasts as main sources in your argument.

Using Wikis, Blogs, and Podcasts

As a general rule, you should not use wikis, blogs, or podcasts as your main sources for academic research projects, because they are too opinion-based and their "facts" are often unreliable. Nevertheless, they are helpful for defining issues and pointing you toward more established sources.

Wikis. You probably already know about *Wikipedia,* the most popular wiki, but a variety of other wikis are available, like *WikiHow, Wikibooks,* and *Wikitravel.* Wikis allow their users to add and revise content, and they rely on other users to back-check facts. On some topics, such as popular culture (e.g., television programs, music, celebrities), a wiki might be the best or only source of up-to-date information. On more established topics, however, you should always be skeptical about the reliability of their information. Your best approach is to use these sites primarily for start-up research on your topic and to help you find other, more reliable sources.

Blogs. Blogs can be helpful for exploring a range of opinions on a particular topic. However, even some of the most established and respected blogs like *Daily Kos, Power Line*, and *Wonkette* are little more than opinionated commentaries on the day's events. Like wikis, blogs can help you identify the issues involved with your topic and locate more reliable sources, but most of them are not reliable sources themselves.

Podcasts. Most news Web sites offer podcasts, but the reliability of these sources depends on who made the audio or video file. Today, anyone with a video camera or digital tape recorder can make a podcast, even a professional-looking podcast, so you need to carefully assess the credibility and experience of the person who made it.

On just about every topic, you will find plenty of people on the Internet who have opinions. The problem with online sources is that just about anyone can create or edit them. That's why the Internet is a good place to start collecting sources, but you need to also collect print and empirical sources to back up what you find.

Finding Print Sources

With such easy access to electronic and online sources, people sometimes forget to look for print sources on their topic. That's a big mistake. Print sources are typically the most reliable forms of information on a topic.

Locating Books at Your Library

Finding useful books on your topic at your campus or local public library is actually rather easy. More than likely, your library's Web site has an online search engine that you can access from any networked computer (Figure 25.4). This search engine will

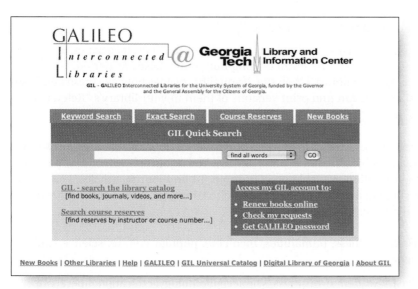

FIGURE 25.4
Searching Your Library's Catalog

Your library's catalog is easy to search online. Here is the Georgia Tech library's Web page for searching its catalog. Finding books is almost as easy as using a search engine to find information on the Internet.

allow you to locate books in the library's catalog. Meanwhile, your campus library will usually have research librarians on staff who can help you find useful print sources. Ask for them at the Information Desk.

Books. The most reliable information on your topic can usually be found in books. Authors and editors of books work closely together to check their facts and gather the best information available. So books tend to be more reliable than Web sites. The downside of books is that they tend to become outdated in fast-changing fields.

Government Publications. The U.S. government produces an amazing amount of printed material on almost any topic you could imagine. Government Web sites, like *The Catalog of U.S. Government Publications,* are a good place to find these sources. Your library probably collects many of these materials because they are usually free or inexpensive.

Reference Materials. The reference section of your library collects helpful reference tools, such as almanacs, directories, encyclopedias, handbooks, and guides. These reference materials can help you find facts, data, and information about people, places, and events.

Right now, entire libraries of books are beings scanned and put online. Out-of-copyright books are appearing in full-text versions as they become available. Meanwhile, online versions of copyrighted books are searchable, allowing you to see excerpts and identify pages on which you can locate the specific information you need.

Finding Articles at the Library

At your library, you can also find articles in academic journals, magazines, and news-papers. These articles can be located using online databases or periodical indexes available through your library's Web site. If your library does not have these databases available online, you can find print versions of them in your library's "Reference" or "Periodicals" areas.

Academic Journals. Articles in journals are usually written by scientists, professors, consultants, and subject matter experts (SMEs). These journals will offer some of the most exact information available on your topic. To find journal articles, you should start by searching in a *periodical index* related to your topic. Some of the more popu-lar periodical indexes include:

> *ArticleFirst.* Business, humanities, medicine, popular culture, science, and technology
>
> *EBSCOhost.* Academic, business, science, psychology, education, liberal arts
>
> *ERIC.* Education research and practice
>
> *Humanities Index.* Literature, history, philosophy, languages, communication
>
> *LexisNexis.* News, business, medical, and legal issues
>
> *OmniFile.* Education, science, humanities, social science, art, biology, and agriculture
>
> *PsycINFO.* Psychology and related fields
>
> *Web of Science.* Physics, chemistry, biology, and life sciences
>
> *IEEE Xplore.* Engineering and science

Magazines. You can find magazine articles about your topic with the *Readers' Guide to Periodical Literature,* which is likely available through your campus library's Web site. Print versions of the *Readers' Guide* should be available in your library's pe-riodical or reference rooms. Other useful online databases for finding magazine arti-cles include *Find Articles, MagPortal,* and *InfoTrac.*

Newspapers. For research on current issues or local topics, newspapers often pro-vide the most recent information. At your library or through its Web site, you can use newspaper indexes to search for information. Past editions of newspapers are often stored on microform or microfiche, which can be read on projectors at your campus library. Some of the more popular newspaper indexes include *ProQuest Newspapers, Chronicling America, LexisNexis, New York Times Index,* and *EBSCOhost.*

Doing research at your campus or local public library is almost as easy as doing research on Internet search engines. You will find that the librarians working there can help you locate the materials you need. While at the library, you will likely stumble across useful materials you didn't expect, and the librarians might be able to help you find materials you would never have found on your own.

Using Empirical Sources

Empirical sources include observations, experiments, surveys, and interviews. They are especially helpful for confirming or challenging the claims made in your electronic, online, and print sources. For example, if one of your electronic or online sources claims that "each day, college students watch an average of five hours of television but spend less than one hour on their coursework," you could use observations, interviews, or surveys to confirm or debunk that statement.

Interviewing People

Interviews are a great way to go behind the facts to explore the experiences of experts and regular people. Plus, interviewing others is a good way to collect quotes that you can add to your text. Here are some strategies for interviewing people:

Prepare for the Interview

1. **Do your research.** You need to know as much as possible about your topic before you interview someone about it. If you do not understand the topic before going into the interview, you will waste your own and your interviewee's time by asking simplistic or flawed questions.

2. **Create a list of three to five factual questions.** Your research will probably turn up some facts that you want your interviewee to confirm or challenge.

3. **Create a list of five to ten open-ended questions.** Write down five to ten questions that cannot be answered with a simple "yes" or "no." Your questions should urge the interviewee to offer a detailed explanation or opinion.

4. **Decide how you will record the interview.** Do you want to record the interview as a video or make an audio recording? Or do you want to take written notes? Each of these methods has its pros and cons. For example, audio recording captures the whole conversation, but interviewees are often more guarded about their answers when they are being recorded.

5. **Set up the interview.** The best place to do an interview is at a neutral site, like a classroom, a room in the library, or perhaps a café. The second best place is at the interviewee's office. If necessary, you can do interviews over the phone.

Conduct the Interview

1. **Explain the purpose of your project and how long the interview will take.** Start out by explaining to the interviewee the purpose of your project and how the information from the interview will be used. Also, tell the interviewee how long you expect the interview will take.

2. **Ask permission to record.** If you are recording the interview in any way, ask permission to make the recording. First, ask if recording is all right before you turn on your recorder. Then, once the recorder is on, ask again so you record the interviewee's permission.

3. **Ask your factual questions first.** Warm up the interviewee by asking questions that allow him or her to confirm or deny the facts you have already collected.

4. **Ask your open-ended questions next.** Ask the interviewee about his or her opinions, feelings, experiences, and views about the topic.

5. **Ask if he or she would like to provide any other information.** Often people want to tell you things you did not expect or know about. You can wrap up the interview by asking, "Is there anything else you would like to add about this topic?"

6. **Thank the interviewee.** Don't forget to thank the interviewee for his or her time and information.

Interview Follow-Up

1. **Write down everything you remember.** As soon as possible after the interview, describe the interviewee in your notes and fill out any details you couldn't write down during the interview. Do this even if you recorded the interview.

2. **Get your quotes right.** Clarify any direct quotations you collected from your interviewee. If necessary, you might e-mail your quotes to the interviewee for confirmation.

3. **Back-check the facts.** If the interviewee said something that was new to you or that conflicted with your prior research, use electronic, online, or print sources to back-check the facts. If there is a conflict, you can send an e-mail to the interviewee asking for clarification.

4. **Send a thank you note.** Usually an e-mail that thanks your interviewee is sufficient, but some people prefer to send a card or brief letter of thanks.

Using an Informal Survey

Informal surveys are especially useful for generating data and gathering the views of many different people on the same questions. Many free online services, such as *SurveyMonkey* and *Zoomerang,* allow you to create and distribute your own surveys. They will also collect and tabulate the results for you. Here is how to create a useful, though not a scientific, survey:

1. **Identify the population you want to survey.** Some surveys target specific kinds of people (e.g., college students, women from ages 18–22, medical doctors). Others are designed to be filled out by anyone.

2. **Develop your questions.** Create a list of five to ten questions that can be answered quickly. Surveys typically use four basic types of questions: rating scales,

Rating Scales

Going skiing is a good Spring Break activity.

Strongly Agree	Agree	Disagree	Strongly Disagree	No Opinion
☐	☐	☐	☐	☐

Multiple Choice

In what region did you spend most of your childhood?

☐ Northeast States   ☐ Mountain Western States
☐ Midwest States   ☐ West Coast States
☐ Southern States   ☐ Other

Numeric Open-Ended

How many times have you gone downhill skiing in your life? _____

Text Open-Ended

What do you enjoy most about skiing in Minnesota?

_____
_____
_____
_____

FIGURE 25.5
Types of Survey Questions
Make sure your questions are easy to understand to help your survey takers provide answers quickly and accurately.

multiple choice, numeric open-ended, and open-ended. Figure 25.5 shows examples of all four types.

3. **Check your questions for neutrality.** Make sure your questions are as neutral as possible. Don't lead the people you are surveying with biased or slanted questions that fit your own beliefs.

4. **Distribute the survey.** Ask a number of people to complete your survey, and note the kinds of people who agree to do it. Not everyone will be interested in completing your survey, so remember that your results might reflect the views of specific kinds of people.

5. **Tabulate your results.** When your surveys are returned, convert any quantitative responses into data. In written answers, pull out phrases and quotes that seem to reflect how the people you surveyed felt about your topic.

Professional surveyors will point out that your informal survey is not objective and that your results are not statistically valid. That's fine, as long as you are not using your survey to make important decisions or support claims about how people really feel. Your informal survey will still give you some helpful information about the opinions of others.

Doing Field Observations

Conducting a field observation can help you generate ideas and confirm facts. Field observations involve watching something closely and taking detailed notes.

1. **Choose an appropriate location (field site).** You want to choose a field site that allows you to see as much as possible, while not making it obvious that you are watching and taking notes. People will typically change their behavior if they think someone is watching them.

2. **Take notes in a two-column format.** A good field note technique is to use two columns to record what you see. On the left side, list the people, things, and events you observed. On the right side, write down how you interpret what you observed.

3. **Use the Five-W and How questions.** Keep notes about the *who, what, where, when, why,* and *how* elements that you observe. Try to include as much detail as possible.

4. **Use your senses.** Take notes about the things you see, hear, small, touch, and taste while you are observing.

5. **Pay attention to things that are moving or changing.** Take special note of the things that moved or changed while you were observing, and what caused them to do so.

When you are finished taking notes, spend some time interpreting what you observed. Look for patterns in your observations to help you make sense of your field site.

Developing an Annotated Bibliography

Your professor may ask you to prepare an *annotated bibliography* that summarizes and assesses the sources you collected. An annotated bibliography is an alphabetical list of your sources that briefly summarizes and occasionally assesses the value of each one. Figure 25.6 shows part of an annotated bibliography that includes online, print, and empirical sources.

Entries in an annotated bibliography are typically formatted according to an established documentation style (see Chapter 27, "Using MLA Style," and Chapter 28, "Using APA Style").

Holman, Virginia. "Not Like My Mother." *Prevention* 60.3 (2008): 59-62. Print.

In this article, the author describes her childhood experiences as her mother became schizophrenic, and she discusses how she freed herself from fears about suffering a similar fate. She shows how her mother's mental illness had profound effects on her life, challenging her to live her life differently than her mother. The author realizes that her mother's mental illness made her stronger, and that she inherited many of her mother's positive qualities.

Commentary: This article offers a helpful first-person view into schizophrenia that reflects some of my own experiences with my brother Paul's illness. Holman's mother is similar in many ways to Paul. She is fine on her medications, but goes off them occasionally, creating havoc for the family. I can use this article to illustrate the effects of schizophrenia on family members.

Mahler, James. Personal interview. 8 Apr. 2010.

Professor Mahler, a nationally recognized expert on schizophrenia here at the University of Minnesota, made the point that schizophrenia is especially challenging because of the behavior it brings about. Schizophrenics, he told me, are often paranoid, thinking others are watching them, stalking them, or trying to hurt them. He pointed out that medication often doesn't completely remove these thoughts. Medications only hold them in check. So family members of the schizophrenic often feel they need to modify their behavior to avoid triggering symptoms. This behavior modification can have profound effects on how family members relate to the schizophrenic and to each other.

Commentary: This interview really helped me connect the dots among my other sources. Professor Mahler answered my family-related questions in ways that went beyond the clinical answers that are available in articles.

FIGURE 25.6
Excerpt from an Annotated Bibliography
In this excerpt from an annotated bibliography, the writer has used MLA documentation style to list her sources. Then, for each source, she offers a summary and a paragraph that comments on how the source relates to her research project.

As you research your topic, an annotated bibliography will allow you to—

- keep track of your sources, allowing you to remember what each source contained and how it related to your project;

- keep a brief summary of commentary on each source, so you can quickly locate the exact information you need to support a claim or argument in your document; and

- consider each source in depth and figure out how it fits into your research project.

Your professors will also use annotated bibliographies to review the kinds of sources you are collecting and make suggestions about other possible sources or to ensure that you are collecting a variety of sources.

Creating an annotated bibliography is not difficult. First, list your sources alphabetically, using MLA or APA documentation style. Then summarize each source in a brief paragraph. The first sentence in your summary should state the purpose of the source. The remaining sentences should express its major points.

In some cases, a professor might ask you to include a brief commentary for each source that explains how it fits into your research project.

As you write your entries, be especially careful to avoid plagiarism. If you take a quote or even ideas from the source, carefully label them with page numbers and the necessary quotation marks. This is especially important in a research project, because as you draft your text, you may forget which words and ideas in your annotated bibliography originally came from your source. You might innocently use them in your work, thinking they were your own.

Reliable research involves collecting sources from a variety of electronic, online, print, and empirical sources.

TRIANGULATE Your Sources

Make sure your research plan will allow you to triangulate your sources. Collect electronic, print, and empirical sources that will allow you to confirm or challenge any facts or information you find.

SEARCH Online Sources

Use Internet search engines, listservs, podcasts and other online sources to collect information on your subject. As you are searching, consider the reliability of each source. A professional-looking Web site does not mean the source is reliable.

FIND Documentaries or Broadcasts About Your Topic

You can download documentaries and broadcasts online. Your library may have documentaries you can borrow as well.

READ Books on Your Topic

You can access many books through your library's online catalog. Books are often the most reliable sources of information.

USE Indexes and Databases to Find Articles

Access indexes and databases through your library's Web site to find articles in academic journals, magazines, and newspapers.

TRY Empirical Methods to Gather Information

You can interview experts, conduct surveys, or do field observations to confirm or challenge the online and print sources you have gathered about your topic.

LOOK for Gaps in Your Information

Each source you find will raise more questions. When you notice gaps, do some more research to fill them.

DEVELOP an Annotated Bibliography

An annotated bibliography will help you keep track of your sources and consider them in more depth.

1. With your group, discuss your plans for triangulating two or three sources for your research project.

2. In a small group, talk about which kinds of sources you believe will be most helpful for your research. Depending on your topic, you will find different kinds of information helpful.

3. How reliable is the Internet as a source of information for your research? With a group in your class, come up with a list of ten ways you could back-check an Internet source.

1. Using your library's Web site, locate at least five books and five articles for your next assignment. Create an annotated bibliography using either MLA or APA citation style.

2. Using an Internet search engine, locate ten sources of information on your topic. Try using symbols in the search engine (+, -, "") to target your searches and find the most useful information available. Write an evaluation in which you discuss the ten best sources you found.

3. Choose one of the empirical tools discussed in this chapter (i.e., interview, survey, or field observation). Create the materials you would need to use this tool for your own research. Write a brief explaining your empirical tool to your professor and discuss the kinds of results you hope it will yield.

1. **Learn how professionals do research.** Using the Internet, research how people in your field of study do their own research. In a report, discuss your field's research practices.

2. **Find some suspicious sources.** Locate three to five online sources on your topic that you consider suspicious or misleading. Write a brief report that explains why you consider these electronic sources to be suspicious and how people can determine whether a source on this topic is reliable or not.

PEARSON
mycomplab

For additional reading, writing, and research resources, go to **www.mycomplab.com**.

26

Quoting, Paraphrasing, and Citing Sources

I n college and in the workplace, you need to do more than simply collect sources when you're doing research. You also need to take the next step and engage with your sources, using them to develop your ideas and support your claims. As Chapter 24, "Starting Research," explained, research allows you to extend the work of others and advance your ideas with greater efficiency, clarity, authority, and persuasiveness. This chapter explains how to incorporate that research into your own writing.

When you use sources to inform and support your ideas, your writing has more authority. Also, by engaging with the ideas of others, you enter a larger conversation about those ideas within a particular discipline or profession.

When using a quotation, you are taking a key word, phrase, or passage directly from a source. A direct quote conveys the original text's immediacy and authority while capturing its tone and style.

When paraphrasing, you are explaining a specific idea or describing a specific portion of the source using your own words and your own sentence structures. Typically, your paraphrase will be about the same length as the material you are using from the source. Unlike a direct quotation, paraphrase allows you to clarify or draw attention to a particular issue or point in the original. That way, you can show readers how the author's ideas fit in with your overall work.

When summarizing, you are describing the major ideas of a source in your own words. Often you will summarize not only *what* authors say but *how* they say it. For instance, you might describe their underlying values, their reasoning process or, the evidence they cite. A summary should be much shorter than the original, and it should be structured so that the major points you want to make about your source stand out.

This chapter will show you how to incorporate the ideas and words of others into your work while giving appropriate credit. Chapters 27 and 28 will show you how to cite your sources properly using MLA and APA documentation styles.

Common Knowledge: What You Don't Need to Cite

Some information doesn't need to be cited. Common knowledge includes widely known facts that can be found in a variety of sources. For instance, the following are all common knowledge or facts and would not need to be cited:

- Jerry Springer is host of *The Jerry Springer Show.*
- Chicago is the largest city in Illinois in terms of population.
- The anterior cruciate ligament is one of the four major ligaments in the human knee; it connects the femur to the tibia.

Common knowledge does not need to be cited because it belongs to everyone. If you aren't sure whether something is common knowledge, you should go ahead and cite it.

Quoting

When quoting an author or speaker, you are importing their exact words into your document and placing quotation marks around those words. It sounds pretty easy, but you can confuse your readers or even get yourself in trouble if you don't properly incorporate and cite the words of others. In some cases, you could be accused of plagiarism. Here are some ways to quote properly.

Brief Quotations

A brief quotation takes a word, phrase, or sentence directly from an original source. Always introduce and give some background on quotations: do not expect them to make your point themselves.

Words. If an author uses a word in a unique way, you can put quotes around it in your own text. After you tell your reader where the word comes from, you don't need to continue putting it inside quotation marks.

> **Acceptable quotation:** Using Gladwell's terms, some important differences exist between "explicit" learning and "collateral" learning (36).

> **Unacceptable quotation:** Using Gladwell's terms, some important differences exist between explicit learning and collateral learning (36).

Phrases. If you want to use a whole phrase from a source, you need to put quotation marks around it. Then weave the quote into a sentence, making sure it flows with the rest of your writing.

> **Acceptable quotation:** Tomorrow's educators need to understand the distinction between, as Gladwell puts it, "two very different kinds of learning" (36).

> **Unacceptable quotation:** Tomorrow's educators need to understand the distinction between, as Gladwell puts it, two very different kinds of learning (36).

Sentences. You can also bring entire sentences from another source into your document. Use a *signal phrase* (e.g., "As Gladwell argues,") or a colon to indicate that you are quoting a whole sentence.

> **Acceptable quotation:** As Gladwell argues, "Meta-analysis of hundreds of studies done on the effects of homework shows that the evidence supporting the practice is, at best, modest" (36).

> **Acceptable quotation:** "Meta-analysis of hundreds of studies done on the effects of homework," as Gladwell argues, "shows that the evidence supporting the practice is, at best, modest" (36).

> **Unacceptable quotation:** Meta-analysis of hundreds of studies done on the effects of homework shows that the evidence supporting the practice is, at best, modest, according to Gladwell.

> **Acceptable quotation using a colon:** Gladwell summarizes the research simply: "Meta-analysis of hundreds of studies done on the effects of homework shows that the evidence supporting the practice is, at best, modest" (36).

> **Unacceptable quotation using a colon:** Gladwell summarizes the research simply: Meta-analysis of hundreds of studies done on the effects of homework shows that the evidence supporting the practice is, at best, modest.

Long Quotations

Occasionally, you may need to quote a source at length. A quote that is longer than three lines of text should be formatted as a *block quote*. A block quote indents the entire quotation to separate it from your normal text. No quotation marks are used, and the citation appears at the end of the quote, outside the final punctuation mark.

A child is unlikely to acquire collateral learning through books or studying for the SAT exams, Gladwell explains. They do acquire it through play, even playing video games:

Block quote.

> The point is that books and video games represent two very different kinds of learning. When you read a biology textbook, the content of what you read is what matters. Reading is a form of explicit learning. When you play a video game, the value is in how it makes you think. Video games are an example of collateral learning, which is no less important. ("Brain" 2)

Author explains what the quote means.

In asserting that collateral learning "is no less important" than explicit learning, Gladwell implies that American education may be producing students who are imbalanced—with too much content knowledge and too little facility in dealing with unstructured situations, the kinds of situations that a person is likely to face every day of his or her working life.

Use block quotes only when the original quotation cannot be paraphrased and must be preserved in its full length. Don't expect a long quotation to make your point for you. Instead, use the quote to support the point you are making.

Paraphrasing and Summarizing

When paraphrasing or summarizing, you are putting someone else's ideas into your own words. In some situations, using a paraphrase or summary is preferable to using a quote. Using too many quotations can make a text look choppy and might lead the reader to think that you are just stitching together other people's words. Paraphrasing allows you to maintain the tone and flow of your writing.

There are three main differences between a summary and a paraphrase:

- A summary often covers the entire content of the source, while a paraphrase handles only a portion of it.

- A summary organizes the source's main ideas in a way that may differ from the source's organization. A paraphrase usually follows the organization of the original.

- A summary is shorter than the original, while a paraphrase is about the same length as the portion of the text being paraphrased.

Following is a source text that we will be using to discuss paraphrasing and summarizing in the remainder of this chapter.

The point is that books and video games represent two very different kinds of learning. When you read a biology textbook, the content of what you read is what matters. Reading is a form of explicit learning. When you play a video game, the value is in how it makes you think. Video games are an example of collateral learning, which is no less important.

Being "smart" involves facility in both kinds of thinking—the kind of fluid problem solving that matters in things like video games and I.Q. tests, but also the kind of crystallized knowledge that comes from explicit learning. If Johnson's book has a flaw, it is that he sometimes speaks of our culture being "smarter" when he's really referring just to that fluid problem-solving facility. When it comes to the other kind of intelligence, it is not clear at all what kind of progress we are making, as anyone who has read, say, the Gettysburg Address alongside any Presidential speech from the past twenty years can attest. The real question is what the right balance of these two forms of intelligence might look like. *Everything Bad Is Good for You* doesn't answer that question. But Johnson does something nearly as important, which is to remind us that we shouldn't fall into the trap of thinking that explicit learning is the only kind of learning that matters.

In recent years, for example, a number of elementary schools have phased out or reduced recess and replaced it with extra math or English instruction. This is the triumph of the explicit over the collateral. After all, recess is "play" for a ten-year-old in precisely the sense that Johnson describes video games as play for an adolescent: an unstructured environment that requires the child actively to intervene, to look for the hidden logic, to find order and meaning in chaos.

One of the ongoing debates in the educational community, similarly, is over the value of homework. Meta-analysis of hundreds of studies done on the effects of homework shows that the evidence supporting the practice is, at best, modest. Homework seems to be most useful in high school and for subjects like math. At the elementary-school level, homework seems to be of marginal or no academic value. Its effect on discipline and personal responsibility is unproved. And the causal relation between high-school homework and achievement is unclear: it hasn't been firmly established whether spending more time on homework in high school makes you a better student or whether better students, finding homework more pleasurable, spend more time doing it. So why, as a society, are we so enamored of homework? Perhaps because we have so little faith in the value of the things that children would otherwise be doing with their time. They could go out for a walk, and get some exercise; they could spend time with their peers, and reap the rewards of friendship. Or, Johnson suggests, they could be playing a video game, and giving their minds a rigorous workout.

Paraphrasing

The goal of paraphrasing is to explain and describe a portion of the source's text in your own words. A paraphrase is usually about the same length or a little shorter than the material being paraphrased. For example, the writers of the following acceptable and unacceptable paraphrases are trying to describe Gladwell's distinction between "explicit" and "collateral" learning.

Acceptable Paraphrase

Gladwell explains that we can think of intelligence (or "smart," as he calls it) as having two related but distinct dimensions (36). On the one hand, there is the intelligence dimension we associate with storing, accessing, and reproducing information and with the ability to solve certain kinds of problems. This is the kind of intelligence a person gets from reading books and, generally, from school—what Gladwell calls "explicit" learning. Then there's another kind of intelligence that we get through "collateral" learning. When people develop this kind of intelligence, they have the practical know-how needed to enter a confusing, complex, chaotic situation and quickly and perhaps intuitively develop a hierarchy of what needs to be done, how it should be done, and when it should be done. Both kinds of intelligence are important, Gladwell assures us, but we probably need to think long and hard about the "right balance" between them.

In this acceptable paraphrase, the writer used primarily her own words. When she used exact words from Gladwell's article, she placed them inside quotations. Now let's look at a paraphrase that is too close to the original source:

Unacceptable Paraphrase

Gladwell explains that being smart requires two kinds of thinking. When a person reads a textbook, a magazine, or a manual of some kind, he or she is engaging in explicit learning. Here the crystallized knowledge that comes from the content of what you read is what matters. Playing video games is an example of collateral learning. Here the value lies in how the game makes you think and results in adaptable problem-solving skills. Although many people think that explicit learning is the only kind that matters, both kinds of smart are important. (36)

The highlighted words and phrases are taken directly from Gladwell's article. Even though the writer explicitly cites the source of these ideas, too many words are lifted directly from the source without quotation or attribution. If the writer felt it was important to use these exact words and phrases, she should have placed them inside quotation marks and cited them.

When paraphrasing, don't allow your own voice to be overwhelmed by your source's tone or voice. Notice how the unacceptable paraphrase has almost the same voice as the original source. In the acceptable paraphrase, the writer's voice comes through clearly. Her paraphrase is accurate even as she uses her own words.

Summarizing

When you summarize someone else's work, you are capturing the source's principal idea or ideas. A summary often goes beyond a source's major points to explain the source's structure; its tone, angle, or purpose; its style; its underlying values; or the persuasive strategies it uses to drive home its points. In the following summaries, the writers address the main idea in Gladwell's review: the right balance between "explicit" and "collateral" learning.

Acceptable Paragraph-Length Summary

In the final portion of "Brain Candy," Gladwell accepts Johnson's argument that video games can help develop valuable capacities and extends it further, suggesting that we overvalue "explicit" learning and undervalue "collateral" learning, which happens when people play video games. But the real issue, Gladwell tells us, is not whether Americans are getting better at collateral learning or whether collateral learning is important. "The real question," asserts Gladwell, "is what the right balance of these two forms of intelligence might look like" (36). We need to discuss this question, Gladwell suggests, as a nation because many of the decision makers in education seem to be proceeding as if explicit learning is all that matters without a healthy debate. We have failed to acknowledge, Gladwell reminds us, that play (even or *especially* playing video games) also results in an important kind of intelligence.

Notice how this summary focuses on an explicit point and makes it prominent.

An unacceptable summary usually relies too much on the wording of the original text, and it often does not prioritize the most important points in the source text.

Unacceptable Summary

In the final portion of "Brain Candy," Gladwell accepts Johnson's argument that playing video games is valuable because of how it makes you think and extends it further, asking what the right balance between these two forms of intelligence would look like. Gladwell explains that books and video games deliver two very different kinds of learning (36). When you read, it's the content that matters. Reading is a form of explicit learning. Playing a video game is valuable because of the way it makes you think. Collateral learning is no less important than explicit learning. But the real question, Gladwell tells us, is figuring out the right balance of these two forms of intelligence. We need to discuss this question, Gladwell suggests, as a nation because many of the decision makers in education seem to be proceeding as if explicit learning is all that matters without a healthy debate. For example, a number of elementary schools have eliminated recess and replaced it with math or English (36). They have also increased the amount of homework, even though nobody knows whether spending more time on homework in high school makes you a better student or whether better students spend more time on their homework. Gladwell concludes by saying that as a society, we are so enamored of homework because we do not understand the value of the things that children would otherwise be doing with their time. This is the triumph of the explicit over the collateral.

The highlighted phrases in the example on page 483 show places where the summary uses almost the same wording as the original text. In this example, this writer has engaged in what is becoming known as "patchwriting." Writing scholar Rebecca Moore Howard defines patchwriting as "copying from a source text and then deleting some words, altering grammatical structures, or plugging in one synonym for another" (xvii). Patchwriting is a form of plagiarism, which is discussed later in this chapter.

Framing Quotes, Paraphrases, and Summaries

Your readers need to easily see the boundaries between your work and the material you are taking from your sources. To help them identify these boundaries, you should properly frame your quotations, paraphrases, and summaries by using signal phrases, and citations, and by making connections to your own ideas (Figure 26.1).

Signal Phrase. A signal phrase indicates where the source material came from. The words "as" and "in" are often at the heart of a signal phrase (e.g., "As Gladwell argues," "In his article, 'Brain Candy,' Gladwell states").

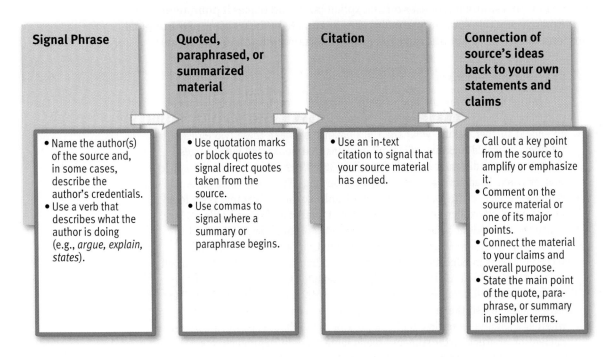

Signal Phrase	Quoted, paraphrased, or summarized material	Citation	Connection of source's ideas back to your own statements and claims
• Name the author(s) of the source and, in some cases, describe the author's credentials. • Use a verb that describes what the author is doing (e.g., *argue, explain, states*).	• Use quotation marks or block quotes to signal direct quotes taken from the source. • Use commas to signal where a summary or paraphrase begins.	• Use an in-text citation to signal that your source material has ended.	• Call out a key point from the source to amplify or emphasize it. • Comment on the source material or one of its major points. • Connect the material to your claims and overall purpose. • State the main point of the quote, paraphrase, or summary in simpler terms.

FIGURE 26.1 Framing Material from a Source

Material taken from a source should be clearly framed with a signal phrase, a citation, and a connection to your own statements and claims.

Direct Quotation. Material quoted directly from your source should be separated from your own words with commas, quotation marks, and other punctuation to indicate which words came directly from the source and which are your own.

Citation. A citation allows readers to find the exact page or Web site of the source. In MLA or APA documentation style, an in-text citation is used to cite the source. In other documentation styles, you might use a footnote or endnote.

Connection. When you connect the source's ideas to your ideas, you will make it clear how the source material fits in with your own statements and claims.

Figure 26.1 offers a diagram that color codes these features. The following three examples use these colors to highlight signal phrases, source material, citations, and connections.

> As Malcolm Gladwell reminds us, many American schools have eliminated recess in favor of more math and language studies, favoring "explicit" learning over "collateral" learning ("Brain" 36). This approach is problematic, because it takes away children's opportunities to interact socially and problem-solve, which are critical skills in today's world.

> Speculating about why we so firmly believe that homework is critical to academic success, Gladwell suggests, "Perhaps because we have so little faith in the value of the things that children would otherwise be doing with their time" (36). In other words, Gladwell is arguing that we are so fearful of letting children play that we fill up their time with activities like homework that show little benefit.

> Studies show that the careers of the future will rely heavily on creativity and spatial recognition, which means people who can think with the right side of their brain will have the advantage (Pink, 2006, p. 65). If so, we need to change our educational system so that we can strengthen our abilities to think with both sides of the brain, not just the left side.

As shown in this example, the frame begins with a signal phrase. Signal phrases typically rely on an action verb that signals what the author of the source is trying to achieve in the material that is being quoted, paraphrased, or summarized. Figure 26.2 provides a helpful list of verbs you can use to signal quotes, paraphrases, and summaries.

The frame typically ends with a connection showing how the source material fits into your overall discussion or argument. Your connection should do one of the following things for your readers:

- call out a key point from the source to amplify or emphasize it

- expand on the source material or one of its major points

- connect the source material to your claims and overall purpose

- rephrase the main point of the source material in simpler terms

FIGURE 26.2 Verbs for Signal Phrases

Use verbs like these to introduce quotations, paraphrases, and summaries. You can also use them in signal phrases.

accepts	accuses	acknowledges
adds	admits	advises
agrees	alleges	allows
analyzes	announces	answers
argues	asks	asserts
believes	charges	claims
comments	compares	complains
concedes	concludes	confirms
considers	contends	countercharges
criticizes	declares	demonstrates
denies	describes	disagrees
discusses	disputes	emphasizes
explains	expresses	finds
grants	holds	illustrates
implies	insists	interprets
maintains	notes	objects
observes	offers	point outs
proclaims	proposes	provides
quarrels	reacts	reasons
refutes	rejects	remarks
replies	reports	responds
reveals	shows	states
suggests	supports	thinks
urges	writes	

When handled properly, framing allows you to clearly signal the boundaries between your source's ideas and your ideas.

Avoiding Plagiarism

The Council of Writing Program Administrators defines plagiarism this way:

> **In an instructional setting, plagiarism occurs when a writer deliberately uses someone else's language, ideas, or other original (not common-knowledge) material without acknowledging its source.**

In college, plagiarism is a form of academic dishonesty, the same as cheating on an exam, and it can lead to a failing grade on an assignment or even for the class. In the workplace, plagiarism is a form of copyright infringement in which one person illegally takes the ideas or words of someone else without their permission. Copyright infringement can lead to costly lawsuits and the firing of any employee who commits it.

Plagiarism is not always intentional. Sometimes writers forget to copy down their sources in their notes. Sometimes they forget where specific ideas came from. But even if you plagiarize accidentally, you may find yourself in serious trouble with your professors, your university, or your employer. So it is crucial that you understand the kinds of plagiarism and learn to avoid them.

Academic Dishonesty

The most obvious form of plagiarism occurs when someone hands in work that is not his or her own. Everyone, including your professors, knows about "cheater Web sites" that sell or give away college papers. Everyone also knows about "borrowing" some-one else's paper. And everyone knows it's easy to cut and paste a sample paper from the Internet. (If you found it, chances are good your professor will find it, too).

And yet, some students still foolishly try to get away with these kinds of plagia-rism. Your professors aren't naive. If you hand in a paper that's not your own, you're being dishonest. When students get caught, they often fail the class, which looks bad on their transcripts and is very difficult to explain to future employers or graduate school admissions committees. They might even be expelled. This kind of plagiarism is clearly intentional and few people will have sympathy for someone who is so obvi-ously cheating.

Ironically, people who buy, download, or copy papers often spend more time and energy finding the paper and worrying about the consequences of getting caught than they would if they just wrote the paper in the first place.

Patchwriting

Patchwriting was mentioned earlier in this chapter. Usually, patchwriting happens when someone cuts and pastes one or more paragraphs from a Web page or other source and then alters words and sentences to make them look like his or her own.

When done intentionally, patchwriting is clearly a form of academic dishonesty, be-cause the writer is presenting someone else's ideas as his or her own without attribution. Some students have even tried to patchwrite an entire paper. They cut and paste several paragraphs from one source or a variety of sources. Then they add some transitions and a few of their own sentences, while altering the words and sentences from the original. As a result, little of the paper is based on their own ideas. This kind of dishonesty, when caught, usually leads to a failing grade on the paper and for the class.

Patchwriting can happen unintentionally, especially when a writer copies sen-tences or paragraphs from a source and then forgets the material was taken from somewhere else. The writer might even cite the source, not realizing that the text they included is too close to the original. Unfortunately, your professor cannot tell whether you were intentionally being dishonest or just made an honest mistake.

To avoid patchwriting, make sure you carefully identify your sources in your notes. Clearly mark any direct quotes taken from your sources with quotation marks, brackets, or some other kind of distinguishing mark. Then, when you use these materials in your document, make sure you quote, paraphrase, and summarize them using proper citations.

Ideas and Words Taken Without Attribution

In college and in the workplace, you will often need to use the exact ideas, words, phrases, or sentences from a source. When you do this, *you must correctly quote and cite that source.* That is, you must place those words inside quotation marks (or block quote them) and provide a citation that tells your reader precisely where you got those words. If you use ideas, words, phrases, or sentences without attribution, you could be charged with academic dishonesty or copyright infringement.

Sometimes it is difficult to determine whether someone else owns the ideas that you are using in your document. If you aren't sure, cite the source. Citing a source will only add support to your work, and it will help you avoid being accused of plagiarism.

The Real Problem with Plagiarism

No doubt, plagiarism is easier than ever with the Internet. It's also easier than ever to catch someone who is plagiarizing. Your professors can use *Google* too, and they have access to plagiarism checking Web sites like *Turnitin*. They also often have access to collections of prior papers that were handed in.

If you plagiarize, there is a good chance you will get caught, and the price will be steep. But the real problem with plagiarism is that you are cheating yourself. You're probably paying many thousands of dollars for your education. Cheating robs you of the chance to strengthen your communication skills and prepare for advanced courses and your career.

Of course, there is pressure to do well in your classes, and you don't always have enough time to do everything you want. In the end, though, doing your own work will help you improve and strengthen your mind and abilities. Don't miss that opportunity.

Here are some helpful guidelines for quoting, paraphrasing, and summarizing sources and avoiding plagiarism.

DECIDE What to Quote, Paraphrase, or Summarize

Ask yourself what kinds of materials should be quoted, summarized, or paraphrased in your document. To guide your decision, keep your readers' needs and the genre in mind.

INCLUDE Short Quotations and Cite Them Properly

Any words, phrases, or sentences should be placed in quotation marks and cited with MLA or APA documentation style.

USE Block Quotes for Longer Quotations

If a quote is longer than three lines or contains more than one sentence, set it off in a block quote. A block quote indents the quotation to separate it from the normal text.

PARAPHRASE Important Sources and Cite Them

A paraphrase puts someone else's ideas into your own words. Paraphrases are usually about the same length or a little shorter than the original. Make sure you do not use words from the original text unless you quote them. Paraphrases need to be cited.

SUMMARIZE Sources with Important Ideas and Cite Them

A summary captures the principal ideas of a source by summarizing the entire work or a major portion of it. Summaries are shorter than paraphrases, and they usually present the source's main ideas from most important to least important.

USE Signal Phrases and Verbs to Mark Quotes, Paraphrases, and Summaries

A *signal phrase* uses words like "as" or "in" to highlight for the readers where a source is being referenced. A variety of *signal verbs* can also highlight the beginning of a quote, paraphrase, or summary.

DON'T Plagiarize Intentionally or Unintentionally

Plagiarism, whether intentional or unintentional, is a form of academic dishonesty. It involves using someone else's words or ideas without giving them proper credit. Intentional plagiarism usually leads to a failing grade for the paper and the course. Don't do it.

1. What kinds of research have you done in the past, and how did you incorporate sources into your work? How do you think research in college will be handled differently?

2. Look at the example of "patchwriting" on page 483. Discuss how you can avoid patchwriting in your own work.

3. With your group, discuss how professors should keep students from plagiarizing, and what should be done when someone does plagiarize.

Try
This
Out

1. Choose a television commercial and try to paraphrase it and summarize it. How challenging is it to do this accurately?

2. Choose three quotations from a source and practice incorporating them into something you are writing for this class. Be sure to use a signal phrase or signal verb.

3. Choose three paragraphs from a source and purposely create an inappropriate "patchwritten" text. Then transform your patchwritten text into an appropriate paraphrase. As you rewrite the text, pay attention to the kinds of alterations you need to make.

Write
This

1. **Summarize a source.** Choose a source text and write down a single sentence that summarizes the source's main point in your own words. Now write a one-paragraph summary of the source, highlighting its major ideas. Finally, turn your one-paragraph summary into a multiple-paragraph summary that includes quotes and citations.

2. **Explain how to handle plagiarism.** Write a brief position paper in which you discuss how universities should handle plagiarism in the age of the Internet. Offer some ideas about how professors can steer students away from the temptation to plagiarize.

PEARSON
mycomplab

For additional reading, writing, and research resources, go to **www.mycomplab.com.**

Using MLA Style

Modern Language Association (MLA) documentation style helps you to keep track of your sources, while showing your readers where you found the supporting information in your document. MLA style is most commonly used in the humanities (i.e., English, history, philosophy, languages, art history). This style is also used in other scholarly fields because of its flexibility and familiarity.

In the previous chapter, you learned how to quote, paraphrase, and cite your sources. In this chapter, you will learn how to use MLA style to reference your sources and create a list of "Works Cited" at the end of your document. The models of MLA citations shown here are the ones most commonly used in college and in the workplace. If you cannot find a model that fits the source you are trying to cite, you should turn to the *MLA Handbook for Writers of Research Papers*, 7th ed. (2009).

On the Internet, an increasing number of online citation generators are available, or your word-processing software may include one. We recommend using these online tools because they can help you quickly generate MLA-style documentation. However, you should always make sure the generator is following the most up-to-date MLA documentation style. Also, double-check all citations to make sure they were created correctly.

Parenthetical Citations

When citing a source with MLA style, you first need to include a *parenthetical reference*. A parenthetical reference appears in the text of your document, usually at the end of the sentence where the information that you used from another source appears. For example:

> Archeologists have shown that wild dogs diverged from wolves about ten thousand years ago (Jones 27).

> For example, in *The Robber Bride,* Atwood depicts the response of second wave feminism to postfeminism (Tolan 46), through the complex interactions of three friends with an aggressive vampire, Zenia, who has recently returned from the dead.

Note: For a key to the color highlighting used here and throughout this chapter, see the bottom of page 493.

As shown here, a parenthetical reference includes two important pieces of information: the source's name (usually an author's name), a single space with no comma, and the page number from the source where the information appeared. The first parenthetical reference above signals to readers that the information in this sentence was taken from page 27 in a work from someone named "Jones." The second parenthetical reference signals that its information can be found on page 46 in a source written by someone named "Tolan."

If readers want to, they can then turn to the "Works Cited" at the end of the document to see the full citation, which will look like this:

> Jones, Steve. *Darwin's Ghost*. New York: Ballantine, 2000. Print.

> Tolan, Fiona. "Sucking the Blood Out of Second Wave Feminism: Postfeminist Vampirism in Margaret Atwood's *The Robber Bride.*" *Gothic Studies* 9.2 (2007): 45-57. Print.

In other words, the parenthetical reference and the full citation work together. The reference points readers to the works-cited list, where they can find the information needed to locate the source.

When the Author's Name Appears in the Sentence

You don't always need to include the author's name in the parenthetical reference. If you name the author in the sentence, you only need to provide the page number in parentheses. For example:

According to Steve Jones, a genetic scientist, archeologists have shown that wild dogs diverged from wolves about ten thousand years ago (27).

In her recent article, Tolan (46) argues that Atwood's *The Robber Bride* is really an allegory of postfeminism, in which three second-wave feminists are confronted with the anxieties brought about by the postfeminist backlash.

Typically, a parenthetical reference appears at the end of the sentence, but as shown above, it can also appear immediately after the name of the source.

If the first part of your sentence draws information from a source but the remainder of the sentence represents your own thoughts, you should put the reference immediately after the source's material is used. For example:

Glassner argues that naive Americans are victimized by a news media that is engaged in "fear-mongering" and other scare tactics (205), but I believe the American people are able to distinguish between real news and sensationalism.

Citing More Than One Source in the Same Sentence

If you want to cite multiple sources that are basically saying the same thing, you can use one parenthetical reference, separating the sources with semicolons:

George Washington was perhaps the only logical choice for the first President of the United States, because he had the respect of the competing political factions that soon emerged after the signing of the Treaty of Paris in 1783 (Irving 649 ; Ellis 375).

If you are citing more than one source in the same sentence but they are making different points, you should put the parenthetical reference as close as possible to the information taken from each source. For example:

Some historians view Cicero as a principled defender of the dying Roman Republic (Grant 29), while others see him as an idealistic statesman who stood helplessly aside as the Republic crumbled (Everett 321).

Citing a Source Multiple Times

In some situations, you will need to cite a source multiple times. If your document continues using a single source, you only need to include the page number in following references as long as no other source comes between them.

New owners often misread the natural signals from their new puppy (Monks 139). One common problem is *submissive urination* in which a puppy shows submission by peeing when greeted. Owners often mistakenly believe the puppy is doing something wrong or defiant, when the puppy is really trying to signal submission. So punishing the dog for submissive urination is exactly the wrong thing to do, because it only encourages the puppy to be even more submissive, resulting in even more puddles on the floor (140).

In the example above, the full parenthetical reference is included early in the paragraph. The second reference, which is only a page number, is clearly referring back to the source in first reference.

However, if another source is cited between two parenthetical references to the same source, the author's name from the first source would need to be repeated in a subsequent reference. For example:

New owners often misread the natural signals from their new puppy (Monks 139). One common problem is *submissive urination* in which a puppy shows submission by peeing when greeted. Owners often mistakenly believe the puppy is doing something wrong or defiant, when the puppy is really trying to signal submission (Kerns 12). So punishing the dog for submissive urination is exactly the wrong thing to do, because it only encourages the puppy to be even more submissive, resulting in even more puddles on the floor (Monks 140).

In the example above, the author includes "Monks" in the last sentence's reference because the reference "(Kerns 12)" appears between the two references to the source written by Monks.

Other Parenthetical References

A wide variety of parenthetical references are possible. Figure 27.1 shows models of some common parenthetical references that you might need to use. Choose the one that best fits your source. If none of these models fits the source you are trying to cite, you can use combinations of these models. If you still cannot figure it out, turn to the *MLA Handbook* for help.

Preparing the List of Works Cited

Your list of Works Cited appears at the end of your document. In this list, you should include full citations for all the sources you cited in your document. A typical entry includes features like the name of the author, the name of the text, the place where it

FIGURE 27.1
**Types of MLA
Parenthetical
References**

Type of Source	Example Parenthetical Reference
Single author	(Gerns 12)
Single author, multiple pages	(Barnes 5-9) or (Barnes 34, 121)
	The hyphen signals a range of pages. The comma suggests similar information can be found on two different pages.
Two authors	(Hammonds and Gupta 203)
Three authors	(Gym, Hanson, and Williams 845)
More than three authors	*First reference:* (Wu, Gyno, Young, and Reims 924)
	Subsequent references: (Wu et al. 924)
Multiple sources in same reference	(Yu 34; Thames and Cain 98; Young, Morales, and Cato 23)
	The semicolon divides the sources.
Two or more works by the same author	(Tufte, *Visual* 25) and (Tufte, "Powerpoint" 9)
	The first prominent word in the source's title is used. Italics signals a book, while quotation marks signal an article.
Different authors with the same last name	(M. Smith 54) and (A. Smith 34)
	The first letter abbreviates each author's first name.
Corporate author	(NASA 12) or (Amer. Beef Assn. 232)
	Abbreviate as much of the corporate name as possible. Periods are needed with abbreviations that are not known acronyms.
No author for book	(*Handling* 45)
	Use the first prominent word in the title and put it in italics.
No author for journal article or newspaper article	("Genomics" 23)
	Use the first prominent word in the title and put it in quotation marks.
No author for newspaper article	("Recession" A4)
	The letter "A" is the section of the newspaper and the number is the page.
Quoted in another source	(qtd. in Franks 94)
	"qtd." stands for "quoted."

continued

Author Title Publication Online Source

FIGURE 27.1
Types of MLA Parenthetical References
(continued)

Type of Source	Example Parenthetical Reference
Web page or other document with no pagination	(Reynolds, par. 3) *"par." stands for paragraph, as counted down from the top of the page. The comma separates the name from the paragraph number.*
Web page or other document with no author and no pagination	("Friendly," par. 7) *Put the first prominent word in the title in quotes, with "par." standing for the paragraph, as counted down from the top of the page. The comma separates the title from the paragraph number.*

Not all possible parenthetical references are shown here. If you have a unique source that doesn't fit these examples, you can usually figure out how to cite it by combining the above reference models. If you still cannot figure out how to cite your source, turn to the *MLA Handbook* for help.

was published, the medium in which it was published, and the date it was published. For example, here are three different entries from three different types of sources:

Chew, Robin. "Charles Darwin, Naturalist, 1809-1882." *Lucidcafe.* 1 Feb. 2008. Web. 8 Feb. 2009.

Poresky, Louise. "Cather and Woolf in Dialogue: The Professor's House to the Light House." *Papers on Language and Literature* 44.1 (2008): 67-86. Print.

Shreve, Porter. *When the White House Was Ours.* Boston: Houghton Mifflin, 2008. Print.

Only sources you reference in your document should appear in your Works Cited. The works-cited list is not a bibliography of all the sources you found on your topic. It is only a list of sources that you actually used in the document.

In a works-cited list, the entries are listed in alphabetical order by the authors' last names. When the author's name is not known, the work is alphabetized by the first prominent word in its title. When alphabetizing, ignore words like *The, A,* or *An* if they are the first word in the title.

Including More Than One Source from an Author

If your works-cited list includes two or more sources from the same author, only the first entry should include the author's name. Afterward, entries should use three hyphens instead of the name. Multiple entries from one author should be alphabetized by the first prominent words in the titles.

Murphy, James. *Rhetoric in the Middle Ages: A History of Rhetorical Theory from Saint Augustine to the Renaissance.* Berkeley, CA: U of California P, 1974. Print.

---. *A Short History of Writing Instruction: From Ancient Greece to Modern America*.
2nd ed. Mahwah, NJ: Erlbaum, 2001. Print.

--- ed. *Three Medieval Rhetorical Arts*. Berkeley: U of California P, 1971. Print.

Murphy, James, Richard Katula, Forbes Hill, and Donovan Ochs. *A Synoptic History of
Classical Rhetoric*. 3rd ed. Mahwah, NJ: Erlbaum, 2003. Print.

As shown above, if a single author is also listed as a coauthor for another entry, you
should include the full name again without the three hyphens.

Formatting a List of Works Cited

According to MLA guidelines, it is standard to start the works-cited list on a new
page with the centered heading "Works Cited" appearing at the top (Figure 27.2).
Entries are then listed double-spaced, in hanging indent format, which means the
first line of each entry is not indented, but the rest of the lines are indented a half
inch.

In professional texts, however, your works-cited list should match the design
of your document. The "Works Cited" heading should be consistent with other
headings. If you are single-spacing the rest of your document, the works-cited list
should be single-spaced, too, perhaps with spaces between entries.

Torres 12

Works Cited

Barber, Paul. *Vampires, Burial, and Death*. New Haven, NJ: Yale UP, 1989.
Print.

Bluestein, Gene. *Poplore: Folk and Pop in American Culture*. Amherst:
U of Massachusetts P, 1994. Print.

Keyworth, Donald. "Was the Vampire of the Eighteenth Century a
Unique Type of Undead Corpse?" *Folklore* 117.3 (2006): 1-16. Print.

Todorova, Maria. *Imagining the Balkans*. Oxford: Oxford UP, 1996. Print.

FIGURE 27.2
Formatting a List of Works Cited

*MLA style requires that the heading "Works Cited" be centered on the page. The margins should
be one inch on all sides. The entries should be double-spaced.*

Citing Sources in the List of Works Cited

The following examples of MLA citations are based on the guidelines in the *MLA Handbook for Writers of Research Papers* (7th ed., 2009). This list is not comprehensive. However, we have included models of the most common kinds of entries in a works-cited list. You can use these examples as models for your own citations. If you do not find a model for a source, you should turn to the *MLA Handbook*.

MLA List of Works Cited

Books and Other Nonperiodical Publications

1. Book, One Author
2. Book, Two Authors
3. Book, Three Authors
4. Book, Four or More authors
5. Book, Corporate or Organization Author
6. Book, Edited Collection
7. Book, Translated
8. Book, Author Unknown
9. Book, Second Edition or Beyond
10. Book, in Electronic Form
11. Document, Government Publication
12. Document, Pamphlet
13. Foreword, Introduction, Preface, or Afterword
14. Sacred Text
15. Dissertation, Unpublished

Journals, Magazines, and Other Periodical Publications

16. Article, Journal with Volume and Issue Numbers
17. Article, Journal with Issue Number Only
18. Article, Edited Book
19. Article, Magazine

20. Article, Newspaper
21. Article, Author Unknown
22. Article, CD-ROM
23. Editorial
24. Letter to the Editor
25. Review

Web Publications

26. Website, Author Known
27. Website, Corporate Author
28. Website, Author Unknown
29. Article from an Online Periodical
30. Article from an Online Scholarly Journal
31. Periodical Article Accessed Through a Database (Web)
32. Blog Posting
33. Wiki Entry
34. Podcast

Other Kinds of Sources

35. Film or Video Recording
36. Television or Radio Program
37. Song or Audio Recording
38. CD-ROM
39. Personal Correspondence, E-Mail, or Interview
40. Work of Art

41. Print Advertisement

42. Commercial

43. Speech, Lecture, or Reading

44. Map

45. Cartoon

Citing Books and Other Nonperiodical Publications

Books and other nonperiodical publications are perhaps the easiest to list in the works-cited list. A book citation will have some of the following features:

1. Name of the author, corporation, or editor with last name first (add "ed." or "eds." if the work is listed by the name of the editor.)

2. Title of the work

3. City where the work was published

4. Publisher

5. Year of publication

6. Medium of publication

    ①   ②   ③   ④   ⑤   ⑥

Author. *Title.* City of publication: Publisher, year of publication. Medium of publication.

1. Book, One Author

Ambrose, Stephen. *Band of Brothers.* 3rd ed. New York: Simon, 2001. Print.

2. Book, Two Authors

Brett, Michael, and Elizabeth Fentress. *The Berbers: The Peoples of Africa* Malden: Wiley-Blackwell, 1996. Print.

3. Book, Three Authors

Fellman, Michael, Daniel E. Sutherland, and Lesley J. Gordon. *This Terrible War: The Civil War and Its Aftermath.* New York: Longman, 2007. Print.

4. Book, Four or More Authors

Huss, Bernard, et al. *The Unknown Socrates.* New York: Bolchazy-Carducci, 2002. Print.

5. Book, Corporate or Organization Author

American Psychiatric Association. *Diagnostic and Statistical Manual of Mental Disorders.* 4th ed. Washington: APA, 1994. Print.

6. Book, Edited Collection

Mueller-Vollmer, Kurt, ed. *The Hermeneutics Reader*. New York: Continuum, 1990.
Print.

7. Book, Translated

Dostoevsky, Fyodor. *Notes from Underground*. 2nd ed. Trans. Michael Katz. New York:
Norton, 2001. Print.

8. Book, Author Unknown

Physical Science. New York: McGraw, 1998. Print.

9. Book, Second Edition or Beyond

Kottak, Conrad. *Anthropology: The Exploration of Human Diversity*. 12th ed. New York:
McGraw, 2008. Print.

10. Book, in Electronic Form

Darwin, Charles. *On the Various Contrivances by Which British and Foreign Orchids Are
Fertilised by Insects*. London: Murray, 1862. Web. 1 Jan. 2008.

11. Document, Government Publication

Arguin, Paul M., Phyllis E. Kozarsky, and Ava W. Navin, eds. *Health Information for
International Travel 2007-2008: The Yellow Book*. St. Louis: Centers for Disease
Control, 2007. Print.

12. Document, Pamphlet

Historians Against the War. *Torture, American Style*. Somerville: Historians Against
the War, 2006. Print.

13. Foreword, Introduction, Preface, or Afterword

Parker, Hershel. Foreword. *Moby Dick*. By Herman Melville. Evanston: Northwestern UP,
2001. xiii-xvi. Print.

14. Sacred Text

The New Oxford Annotated Bible. 3rd ed. New York: Oxford UP, 2001. Print.

15. Dissertation, Unpublished

Charlap, Marie-Helene. "Once with Women, Now with Women: A Qualitative Study of
Identity." Diss. New York U, 2008. Print.

Citing Journals, Magazines, and Other Periodicals

Citations for periodicals, such as journals, magazines, and other regularly published documents, need to include additional information. The title of the article should appear in quotation marks. The volume number and issue number appear after the title of the periodical. The page numbers follow the year the work was published.

A citation for a journal, magazine, or other periodical publication includes the following features:

1. Name of the author, corporation, or editor with last name first

2. Title of the work in quotation marks

3. Name of the periodical in italics

4. Volume number and issue number

5. Date of publication (year for scholarly journal; day, month, year for other periodicals)

6. Range of page numbers for whole article

7. The medium in which the work was published ("Print" for a journal, periodical, or newspaper)

    ①   ②   ③   ④   ⑤   ⑥

Author. "Article Title." *Journal Title* Date or Volume.Issue (Year): page numbers.

    ⑦

Medium of publication.

16. Article, Journal with Volume and Issue Numbers

Jovanovic, Franck. "The Construction of the Canonical History of Financial Economics." *History of Political Economy* 40.2 (2008): 213-42. Print.

17. Article, Journal with Issue Number Only

Lee, Christopher, "Enacting the Asian Canadian." *Canadian Literature* 199 (2008):28-44. Print.

18. Article, Edited Book

Goodheart, George. "Innate Intelligence Is the Healer." *Healers on Healing*. Ed. Richard Carlson and Benjamin Shield. New York: Putnam, 1989. 53-57. Print.

19. Article, Magazine

Zakaria, Fareed. "Obama's Vietnam: How to Salvage Afghanistan." *Newsweek* 9 Feb. 2009: 36-37. Print.

20. Article, Newspaper

Herszenhorn, David. "Bipartisan Push to Trim Size of Stimulus Plan." *New York Times* 5 Feb. 2009: New York ed.: A1. Print.

21. Article, Author Unknown

"The Big Chill Leaves Bruises." *Albuquerque Tribune* 17 Jan. 2004: A4. Print.

22. Article, CD-ROM

Hanford, Peter. "Locating the Right Job for You." *The Electronic Job Finder.* San Francisco: Career Masters, 2001. CD-ROM.

23. Editorial

"A Vital Boost for Education." Editorial. *New York Times* 4 Feb. 2009, New York ed.: A30. Print.

24. Letter to the Editor

Bertin, Joan. Letter. *New York Times* 6 Feb. 2009, New York ed.: A22. Print.

25. Review

Leonhardt, David. "Chance and Circumstance." Rev. of *Outliers,* by Malcolm Gladwell. *New York Times* 30 Nov. 2008: New York ed.: BR9. Print.

Citing Web Publications

Conventions for citing Web publications continue to evolve. In the most recent update of the *MLA Handbook* (2009), Web addresses (URLs) have been removed. When possible, you should include two dates: the date the material appeared on the Internet, and the date you accessed the material. If you cannot find the first date, then put *n.d.* for "no date." If you cannot find the publisher of the information, put *N.p.* for "no publisher."

26. Web Site, Author Known

Nagel, Michael. "Biography." *The Official Mark Twain Website.* CMG Solutions, n.d. Web. 2 Feb. 2009.

27. Web Site, Corporate Author

United States. Fish and Wildlife Service. *Arctic National Wildlife Refuge.* Dept. of the Interior, 12 Sept. 2008. Web. 12 Mar. 2009.

FIGURE 27.3 CITATION MAP: Citing All or Part of a Web Site

A citation for a Web publication will have some or all of the following features:

① Name of the author, corporation, editor, webmaster with last name first

② Title of the work (in quotation marks if an article; italicized if a stand-alone work)

③ Name of the Web site in italics if different than the title of the Web site

④ Publisher of the Web site. (If not available, use *N.p.* for "no publisher.")

⑤ Date of publication, including day, month, year. (If not available, use *n.d.* for "no date.")

⑥ The medium in which the work was published ("Web" for Web sites)

⑦ Date on which you accessed the Web site

Author of page or document. "Title of document" or *Title of Page*. *Title of Overall WebSite.* Publisher of Web site, or N.p, date of publication, or N.d. Medium of publication. Date of your access.

Mills, Elinor. "FAQ: Demystifying ID Fraud." *CNET.* CBS Interactive, 5 May 2009. Web. 10 May 2009.

③ Name of Web site

⑤ Date of publication

② Title of work

① Author

⑥ Medium of publication

⑦ Date of access

④ Publisher of Web site

Author Title Publication Online Source

FIGURE 27.4 CITATION MAP: Citing a Scholarly Journal on the Web

A citation for an article from a scholarly journal on the Web includes the following features:

① Name of the author, last name first

② Title of the work in quotation marks

③ Name of the journal in italics

④ Volume number and issue number

⑤ Date of publication (year for scholarly journal)

⑥ Range of page numbers for whole article

⑦ The medium in which the work was published

⑧ Your date of access

```
  ①        ②              ③            ④          ⑤         ⑥             ⑦
Author. "Article Title." Journal Title. Volume.Issue (Year): page numbers. Medium of publication.
       ⑧
Date of your access.
```

```
                                    ①                                    ②
Marmolego, Gloria, Kristen A. Diliberto-Macaluso, and Jeanette Altarriba.  "False Memory in Bilinguals:
                                                         ③              ④    ⑤
Does Switching Languages Increase False Memories?" American Journal of Psychology 122.1 (2009):
  ⑥    ⑦    ⑧
1–16. Web. 5 May 2009.
```

③ Name of journal

④ Volume, issue

⑤ Date of publication

Abstract   Volume 122 • Number 1   Spring 2009

② Title of work — False memory in bilinguals: Does switching languages increase false memories?

① Authors

GLORIA MARMOLEJO
Winona State University, Rochester

KRISTEN A. DILIBERTO-MACALUSO
Berry College

JEANETTE ALTARRIBA
University at Albany, State University of New York

People often receive and recount information in different languages. This experiment examined the impact of switching languages on false recall, recognition, and recognition confidence. We presented Spanish–English bilinguals with 10 lists of words associated to a critical nonpresented lure, either in English or in Spanish. Each list was followed by free recall either in English or in Spanish. The final stage was a recognition test in either language. Results showed a higher proportion of veridical and false recall either in English or in Spanish, the more dominant language, than in Spanish, the native language. Noncritical intrusions were equivalent in both languages. More importantly, false recall, false recognition, and false recognition confidence were higher across languages than within languages. The results are examined in relation to current research and interpretations of bilingual false memory.

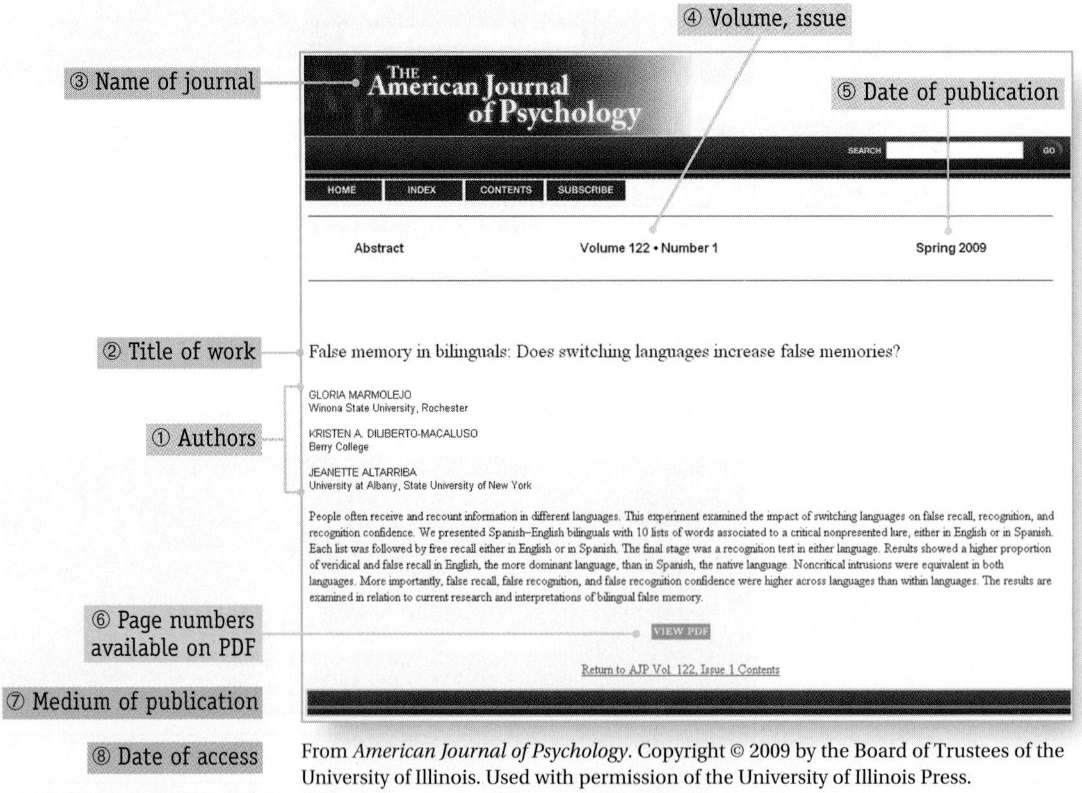

⑥ Page numbers available on PDF

VIEW PDF

Return to AJP Vol. 122, Issue 1 Contents

⑦ Medium of publication

⑧ Date of access

FIGURE 27.5 CITATION MAP: Citing a Scholarly Journal from a Database

A citation for an article from a scholarly journal accessed through a database includes the following features:

① Name of the author, last name first

② Title of the work in quotation marks

③ Name of the journal in italics

④ Volume number and issue number

⑤ Date of publication (year for scholarly journal)

⑥ Range of page numbers for whole article

⑦ Name of database

⑧ Medium of publication

⑨ Your date of access

①   ②   ③   ④   ⑤   ⑥   ⑦   ⑧
Author. "Article Title." *Journal Title.* Volume.Issue (Year): page numbers. *Database.* Medium of

⑧
publication. Date of your access.

①   ②
McGee, Elizabeth, and Mark Shevlin. "Effect of Humor on Interpersonal Attraction and Mate Selection."

③   ④   ⑤   ⑥   ⑦   ⑧   ⑨
Journal of Psychology 143.1 (2009): 67–77. *Academic Search Premier.* Web. 4 Apr. 2009.

⑦ Name of database

② Title of work

① Authors

⑥ Page numbers

④ Volume, issue

⑤ Date of publication

③ Name of journal

⑧ Medium of publication

⑨ Date of access

Author Title Publication Online Source

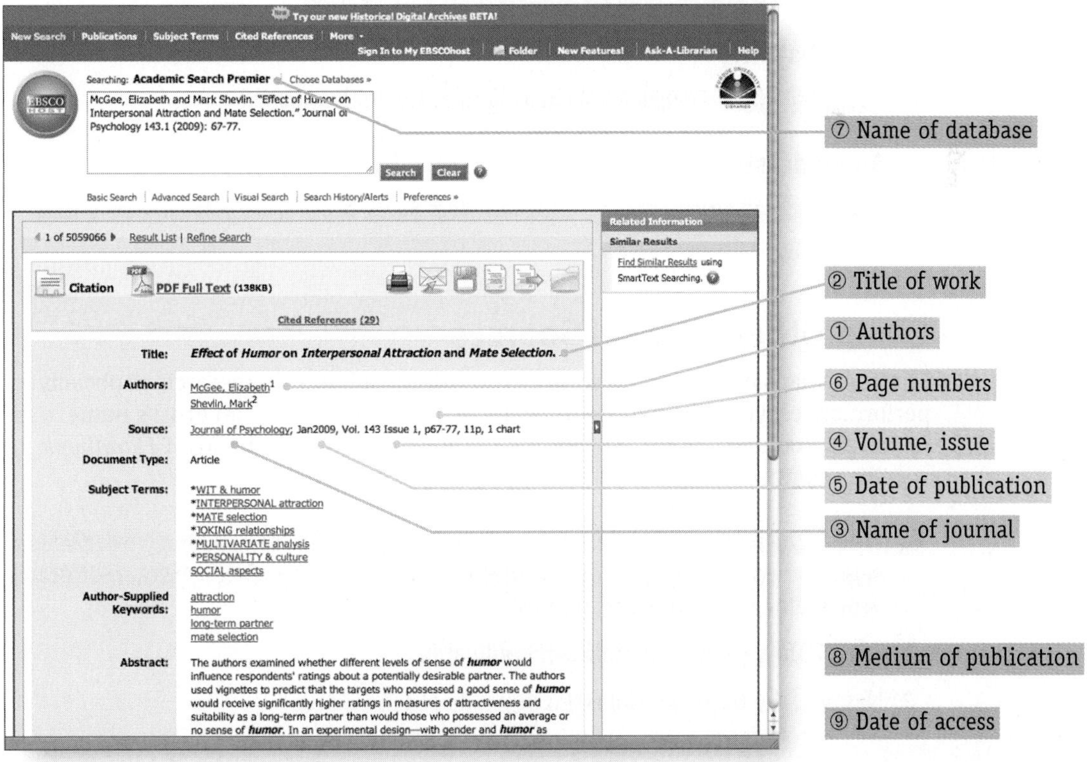

28. Web Site, Author Unknown

"Pentagon Sets Sights on Public Opinion." *MSNBC.com*. Microsoft, 5 Feb. 2009. Web.
6 Feb. 2009.

29. Article from an Online Periodical

Leier, Andrew. "How Martian Winds Make Rocks Walk." *ScienceDaily*. ScienceDaily, 12
Jan. 2009. Web. 4 Feb. 2009.

30. Article from an Online Scholarly Journal

Ochiagha, Terri. "The Literary Fantastic in African and English Literature." *CLCWeb*:
10.4 (2008): n. pag. Web. 5 Feb. 2009.

31. Periodical Article Accessed Through a Database (Web)

Sklansky, David. "Police and Democracy." *Michigan Law Review* 103.7 (2005):
1699-1830. *JSTOR*. Web. 5 Feb. 2009.

32. Blog Posting

Isaacson, Walter. "A Bold Idea for Saving Journalism." *The Huffington Post*.
HuffingtonPost.com, 5 Feb. 2009. Web. 5 Feb. 2009.

33. Wiki Entry

"Galileo Galilei." *Wikipedia*. Wikimedia, n.d. Web. 5 Feb. 2009.

34. Podcast

"Interview with Neil Gaiman." *Just One More Book*. N.p., 27 Jan. 2009. Web. 3 Feb.
2009.

Citing Other Kinds of Sources

There are many other kinds of sources you will consult in your research. Especially for
performances, you may choose to begin a citation with either an artist's name, a director or producer's name, or the title of the work. Consult the *MLA Handbook* for
specific examples.

1. Title of the work (italics for a complete work; quotation marks for a work that is a
   segment, episode, or part of a whole) OR name of a specific performer, director,
   writer, etc. (last name, first name)

2. Title of the program, in italics, if applicable

3. Name of the network that aired or produced the work

4. Call letters and city of the station that aired the work, if available

5. Date of broadcast (day, month, year)

6. The medium of the work (e.g., television, radio, DVD, CD, film)

35. Film or Video Recording

Fiddler on the Roof. Dir. Norman Jewison. Prod. Norman Jewison. The Mirisch
Production Company, 1971. Film.

Harris, Rosalind, perf. *Fiddler on the Roof*. Dir. Norman Jewison. The Mirisch
Production Company, 1971. Film.

36. Television or Radio Program

"Destination: The South Pole." Narr. Richard Harris. *All Things Considered*.
Natl. Public Radio. 6 Jan. 2003. Web. 4 Feb. 2004.

37. Song or Audio Recording

Myer, Larry. "Sometimes Alone." *Flatlands*. People's Productions, 1993. CD.

38. CD-ROM

Lilley, Linda, Scott Harrington, and Julie Snyder. *Pharmacology and the Nursing
Process Companion CD*. 5th ed. St. Louis: Mosby, 2007. CD-ROM.

39. Personal Correspondence, E-Mail or Interview

Schimel, Eric. Personal interview. 12 Dec. 2008.

40. Work of Art

Vermeer, Johannes. *Girl with a Pearl Earring*. N.d. Oil on canvas. Mauritshuis, The
Hague.

41. Print Advertisement

Sprint. Advertisement. *Newsweek*. 9 Feb. 2009. Print.

42. Commercial

Toyota. Advertisement. MSNBC. 5 Feb. 2009. Television.

43. Speech, Lecture, or Reading

Obama, Barack. "Inauguration Address." Capital Building, Washington DC. 21 Jan.
2009. Address.

44. Map

"Japan." Map. *Rand McNally World Atlas.* New York: Rand, 2004. 31. Print.

45. Cartoon

Adams, Scott. "Dilbert." Comic strip. *Journal and Courier* 8 Apr. 2009: C8. Print.

A Student's MLA-Style Research Paper

The document shown here uses MLA citation style. You can use this document to observe how an author uses MLA citation style under real conditions, including parenthetical references and a list of works cited.

Katelyn Turnbow

Professor Thompson

English 102

6 May 2009

Lives Not Worth the Money?

The idea of a forgotten disease is almost absurd—a disease for which a cure is available and effective but never given a chance to work. We are often of the belief that human life is invaluable, that it cannot be bought with money and that a sick person should be treated whether he is an enemy or a friend, poor or rich. In reality, however, the cures that do not make money for some manufacturer are simply not made at all. According to the World Health Organization (WHO), one need only look at African sleeping sickness (WHO). There is a cure, but the victims who would benefit from the drug are poor and considered "unprofitable" by the pharmaceutical industry. It remains, however, a drug company's ethical responsibility to care for people its drugs can save, even when helping them is not profitable.

African sleeping sickness, also known as Human African Trypanosomiasis or HAT, was discovered in 1902 and kills more than 50,000 people a year. These victims, however, are often forgotten because they are poor and live in sub-Saharan Africa, not a prosperous Western nation (see Fig. 1). The disease is caused by a parasite and transmitted to humans by the Tsetse fly. Some villages in the region report that sleeping sickness is the "first or second cause of mortality," and that it is "even ahead of HIV/AIDS" (WHO). WHO estimates that on top of the 17,616 cases reported in 2005, about 50,000-70,000 cases were never diagnosed.

Sleeping sickness manifests in two distinct stages. The haemolymphatic stage (blood-lymph node) occurs shortly after exposure to the parasite and causes headache, fever, joint pain, and itching (WHO).

Specific statistics from credible sources provide credibility for the paper's arguments.

Turnbow 2

Maps, Illustrations, and photographs should be placed in the paper where they provide the most support for in-text arguments.

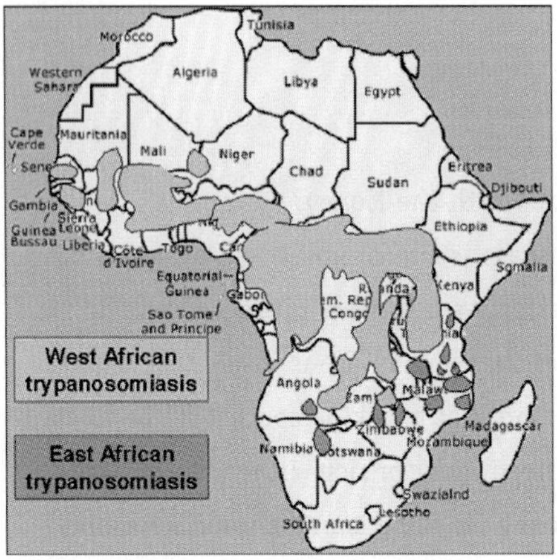

Fig. 1. Distribution of West African or Gambian Sleeping Sickness and East African or Rhodesian Sleeping Sickness. University of South Carolina, School of Medicine; *Parasitology*; *Microbiology and Immunology Online*; 1 Jan. 2009; Web; 1 May 2009; Fig. 4.

The neurological stage follows, occurring months or even years after initial infection (see Fig. 2). This phase begins when the deadly parasite invades its host's central nervous system (CNS) and is accompanied by a large array of neurological symptoms including confusion, loss or disturbance of the senses, personality changes, and decreased coordination as well as the "disturbance of the sleep cycle which gives the disease its name" (WHO). Sleeping sickness is always fatal if not treated, and by the time the disease reaches its neurological stage, it is usually too late (WHO).

Effective treatments for sleeping sickness have been available since 1921, but they are dangerous and extremely painful. If diagnosed and treated in the early stages, sleeping sickness responds well to Pentamidine or, in extreme cases, Suramin. Both drugs, while sometimes

Turnbow 4

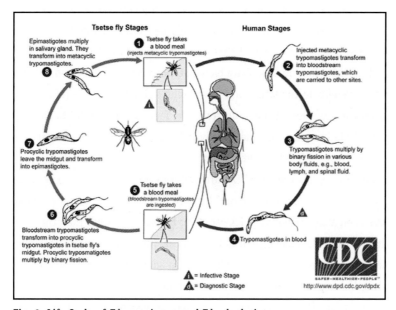

Fig. 2. Life Cycle of *T.b. gamienese* and *T.b. rhodesiense*.
Alexander J. da Silva and Melanie Moser; Centers for Disease Control
Public Health Image Library; n.d.; Web; 27 Apr. 2009.

accompanied by serious side effects such as heart and kidney failure, are
fairly safe and inexpensive (WHO). Victims in the CNS stage of HAT,
however, have for a long time been treated with a drug called
Melarsoprol. Melarsoprol is widely available and cheap, but is derived
from arsenic, and, acting as the potent poison that it is, can kill 5-20
percent of patients. The drug is also excruciatingly painful, described by
many victims as "fire in the veins" ("Sleeping Sickness"). Although
Melarsoprol "wouldn't pass a single ethical or drug-safety test" in the
developed world, it is still used in Africa because it is the only treatment
readily available to victims of this fatal but neglected disease (Gombe).

When there is no author, use an abbreviated title of the article.

It is surprising, then, to learn that a new and highly effective
treatment was developed almost 40 years ago. The chemotherapy drug,

Turnbow 5

defluoro-methyl-ornithine (DFMO), was developed in the 1970s but failed as a cancer treatment, causing only hair loss in patients (Wickware 908-09). It would have been the end of the pharmaceutical, but in 1983, New York parasite biologist Cyrus Bacchi discovered DFMO's effectiveness on the later stage of sleeping sickness (Shah 22). Shortly after this discovery, Belgian doctor Henri Taelman used DFMO to treat an infected woman who had already fallen into a coma, and, almost miraculously, DFMO brought the woman out of her coma within 24 hours. Dr. Taelman renamed the drug eflornithine, but it quickly became known as the "resurrection drug" because it was "so effective at reviving even comatose patients" (Wickware 909; McNeil A1). Other than the highly toxic Melarsoprol, eflornithine is the only drug effective against late-stage Trypanosomiasis (McNeil A1). In addition to a much lower drug-induced mortality rate, eflornithine has fewer and milder side effects than Melarsoprol, and patients who receive eflornithine are more than twice as likely to survive the year following treatment as those treated with the older drug (Chappuis et al. 748-50).

It is clear that the drug is sorely needed by those who suffer the formidable symptoms of sleeping sickness. Despite this, eflornithine was very short-lived. The pharmaceutical company, Sanofi-Aventis, halted production of the resurrection drug in 1995 along with two other anti-trypanosome drugs (Wickware 909). A drug aimed toward treatment of diseases in poor countries was simply "not considered to be a profitable venture to many pharmaceutical companies" (Thomas). This attitude left groups such as WHO and Doctors without Borders struggling to control the disease and save their dying patients without the drugs they needed to do so. Once again these organizations were forced to rely on Melarsoprol, which seemed almost as likely to kill patients as it was to save them (Jackson and Healy 6).

When quoting more than one author, separate the information with a semicolon.

When a work has more than three authors, use the name of the first author listed followed by "et al." meaning "and others."

Turnbow 6

Although WHO, Doctors without Borders, and similar groups petitioned Aventis to continue production of the drug that would save thousands, it was not until 2001 that production of eflornithine resumed. Aventis had found a new use for the "resurrection drug"—hair removal. The company was once again mass producing eflornithine as an ingredient in a $54-a-tube facial hair removal cream for women. Aventis was even generous enough to donate 60,000 doses to WHO so that its doctors could treat HAT in sub-Saharan Africa (Jackson and Healy 6). Although this in itself was good, the company's reasons for doing so are less admirable. It placed "money before all" in all of its decisions, showing the "crass commodification of health" by an industry that was once "driven by a motive to improve human health" (Gombe). It is clear from the initial decision to halt production and Aventis's willingness to donate the drug only after a more cost-efficient use for it was found, that the company only helps others when it can make money by being kind. WHO's agreement with Aventis is only guaranteed for five years and the contract will expire soon (Chappuis et al. 751). The drug is already in short supply, and WHO can only afford to give it to those victims who survive their dose of arsenic and still need to be treated with the safer and more effective alternative (Etchegorry et al. 958). Aventis claims that the drug is "corrosive and destroys the equipment used to make it," suggesting that the pharmaceutical giant will once again refuse help to those in need and charge WHO and Doctors without Borders $70.00 a dose (McNeil A1). This is a price that neither organization can afford and that is far out of reach for the thousands of indigent victims who suffer from trypanosomiasis every year (McNeil A1).

Lifestyle drugs currently account for over "eighty percent of the world's pharmaceutical market," while companies are "ignoring diseases, like sleeping sickness and malaria, that affect only the poor" (McNeil ·

The topic sentence at the beginning of each paragraph should state your point.

Illustrations that support your point (topic sentence) can include quotations, statistics, figures, and other evidence.

The end of the paragraph should explain the significance of the point and illustrations for the reader, and support the paper's thesis.

A1). While I understand that pharmaceutical companies are big businesses committed to raising profits, it is unfortunate that the "$406 billion dollar global industry" feels it cannot spare its extra doses of eflornithine, a gesture that would save so many human lives (Shah 20).

The beginning of the conclusion is a summary of the key arguments, which also reflects the thesis claim.

A pharmaceutical company, which specializes in manufacturing medical products, should have at least some commitment to treating those who suffer from strategically forgotten diseases. Because it manufactures treatments for diseases and makes billions of dollars off of health care, Aventis has an unspoken responsibility for the people it can afford to save and must continue to provide the drug to the organizations that devote all of their time and money to fighting diseases in developing countries. Unlike a vial of chemicals, no price tag can be placed on a human life. Our responsibility is the same, even if those we help cannot give us anything in return. Here, there are truly no excuses.

Turnbow 8

Works Cited

Chappuis, Francois, Nitya Udayraj, Kai Stietenroth, Ann Meussen, and Patrick A. Bovier. "Eflornithine Is Safer Than Melarsoprol for the Treatment of Second-Stage Trypanosoma Brucei Gambiense Human African Trypanosomiasis." *Clinical Infectious Diseases* 41.5 (2005): 748-51. Print.

Etchegorry, M. Gastellu, J. P. Helenport, B. Pecoul, J. Jannin, and D. Legros. "Availability and Affordability of Treatment for Human African Trypanosomiasis." *Tropical Medicine and International Health* 6.11 (2001): 957-59. Print.

Gombe, Spring. "Epidemic, What Epidemic: Treating Sleeping Sickness." *Bulletin of Medicus Mundi Switzerland.* Medicus Mundi Switzerland, Apr. 2004. Web. 12 Apr. 2009.

Jackson, Nicolette, and Sean Healy. "Facial Hair Cream to the Rescue." *New Internationalist* (2002): 6. Print.

McNeil, Donald G., Jr. "Cosmetic Saves a Cure for Sleeping Sickness." *New York Times* (2001): A1. *EBSCOhost.* Web. 28 Apr. 2009.

Shah, Sonia. "An Unprofitable Disease." *The Progressive* Sept. 2002: 20-23. Print.

"Sleeping Sickness." Doctors without Borders. 2009. Web. 12 Apr. 2009.

Thomas, Susan L. "African Sleeping Sickness." *Insect Science at Boston College.* 1 Mar. 2002. Web. 12 Apr. 2009.

Wickware, Potter. "Resurrecting the Resurrection Drug." *Nature Medicine* 8.9 (2002): 908-09. *EBSCOhost.* Web. 28 Apr. 2009.

World Health Organization. "African Trypanosomiasis." WHO, Aug. 2006. Web. 27 April 2009.

Using APA Style

American Psychological Association (APA) documentation style, like MLA style (Chapter 27), is a method for keeping track of your sources, while letting readers know where you found the support for your claims. APA style is commonly used in the social sciences, physical sciences, and technical fields.

In this chapter, you will learn how to use APA style to reference your sources and create a list of "References" at the end of your document. The models of APA citations shown here are the ones most commonly used in college and in the workplace. For more information on APA style, consult the *Publication Manual of the American Psychological Association,* 6th ed. (2010).

Parenthetical Citations

When citing a source with APA style, you first need to include a parenthetical citation. A parenthetical citation appears in the text of your document, usually at the end of the sentence where the information that you used from another source appears. For example:

Children see the world from a different perspective than adults, making the

divorce of their parents especially unsettling (Neuman, 1998, p. 43)

Among Africa's other problems, the one that is most significant may be its lack

of reliable electrical energy (Friedman, 2008, p. 155).

As shown here, a full parenthetical citation includes three important pieces of in-formation: the source's name (usually an author's name), the year in which the source was published, and the page number from the source where the information appeared.

If readers want to, they can then turn to the list of "References" at the end of the document to see the full citation, which will look like this:

Neuman, G. (1998). *Helping your kids cope with divorce the sandcastles way.* New York, NY: Random House.

Friedman, Thomas (2008). *Hot, flat, and crowded.* New York, NY: Farrar, Straus, & Giroux.

In other words, the parenthetical citation and the full reference work together. The parenthetical citation points readers to the reference list, where they can find the in-formation needed to locate the source.

Note: For a key to the color highlighting used here and throughout this chapter, see the bottom of this page.

APA style also allows you to refer to a whole work by simply putting the author's name and the year of the source. For example:

Genetics are a new frontier for understanding schizophrenia (Swaminathan, 2008).

Autism and psychosis have been shown to be diametrical disorders of the brain (Crespi & Badcock, 2008).

These parenthetical references without page numbers are common in APA style, but not in MLA style.

In situations where you are specifically highlighting a study or author, you should move the full parenthetical reference up in the sentence:

According to one study (Adreason & Pierson, 2008), the cerebellum plays a key role in the onset of schizophrenia.

Three books (Abraham & Llewellyn-Jones, 1992; Boskind-White & White, 2000; Burby, 1998) have tried to explain bulimia to nonscientists.

When the Author's Name Appears in the Sentence

If you name the author in the sentence, you only need to provide the year of the source and the page number in parentheses. The year should follow the name of the source and the page number is usually placed at the end of the sentence. For example:

Author Title Publication Online Source

Neuman (1998) points out that children see the world from a different perspective than adults, making the divorce of their parents especially unsettling (p. 43) .

Friedman (2008) argues that Africa's most significant problem may be its lack of electrical energy (p. 155).

If one part of your sentence draws information from a source but the remainder of the sentence states your own thoughts, you should put the reference immediately after the source's material is used. For example:

As Dennett (1995) points out, scientists are uncomfortable with the idea that nature uses a form of reason (p. 213), but I think we must see nature as a life form that is looking out for its best interests.

Citing More Than One Source in the Same Sentence

In APA style, it is common to cite multiple sources making the same point, separated with semicolons:

Several researchers (Crespi & Badcock, 2008; Shaner, Miller, & Mintz, 2004, p. 102; Swaminatha, 2008) have shown the toll that schizophrenia takes on a family.

In the sentence above, the writer is referring to the whole work by Crespi and Badcock and Swaminatha, but she is only referring to page 102 in the article by Shaner, Miller, and Mintz.

If you are citing more than one source in the same sentence but they are making different points, you should put the parenthetical reference as close as possible to the information taken from each source. For example:

Depression is perhaps one of the most common effects of bulimia (McCabe, McFarlane, & Olmstead, 2004, p. 19), and this depression "almost always impairs concentration" (Sherman & Thompson, 1996, p. 57).

Citing a Source Multiple Times

In some situations, you will need to cite a source multiple times. If your document continues using a single source, you only need to include the page number in subsequent references as long as no other source comes between them.

The side effects of brain tumor treatment can include fatigue, brain swelling, skin irritation, ear congestion, hair loss, depression, and eye irritation (Black, 2006, p. 170). For women and some men, the loss of their hair is perhaps the most disturbing because it draws looks and questions from others, and it is the most outward sign of their illness. Depression, however, perhaps needs the most attention because it often requires patients to take antidepressants and stimulants to maintain a normal life (p. 249).

In the example above, the full parenthetical citation is included early in the paragraph. The second reference, which is only a page number, is clearly referring back to the source in the first reference.

However, if another source is cited between two parenthetical citations to the same source, the author's name from the first source would need to be repeated in a subsequent reference. For example:

The side effects of brain tumor treatment can include fatigue, brain swelling, skin irritation, ear congestion, hair loss, depression, and eye irritation (Black, 2006, p. 170). For women and some men, the loss of their hair is perhaps the most disturbing because it draws looks and questions from others, and it is the most outward sign of their illness. In her memoir, Becker (2003) discusses moments when she obsessed about hiding the incision where the tumor was removed (p. 231). Depression, however, perhaps needs the most attention because it often requires patients to take antidepressants and stimulants to maintain a normal life (Black, 2006, p. 249).

In the example above, the author includes a full parenthetical reference to Black in the final sentence of the paragraph, because the reference to Becker (2003) appears between the first and second references to Black.

Other Parenthetical References

Figure 28.1 shows models of some common parenthetical citations. Choose the one that best fits your source. If none of these models fits the source you are trying to cite, you can use combinations of these models. If you still cannot figure it out, turn to the APA's *Publication Manual.*

Preparing the List of References

Your list of references appears at the end of your document. In this list, you should include full citations for all the sources you cited in your document. A typical entry includes features like the name of the author, the date of publication, the title of the text, and the place of publication. For example, here are three different entries from three different types of sources.

Author   Title   Publication   Online Source

FIGURE 28.1
Types of APA
Parenthetical
References

Type of Source	Example Parenthetical Reference
Single author	(Gerns, 2009, p. 12)
Single author, multiple pages	(Barnes, 2007, pp. 5–9) or (Barnes, 2007, pp. 34, 121) *The dash signals a range of pages. The comma suggests similar information can be found on two different pages. The "pp." signals multiple pages.*
Two authors	(Hammonds & Gupta, 2004, pp. 203) *The ampersand (&) is used instead of "and."*
Three authors	(Gym, Hanson, & Williams, 2005, p. 845) *The ampersand (&) is used instead of "and."*
More than three authors	*First reference:* (Wu, Gyno, Young, & Reims, 2003, p. 924) *Subsequent references:* (Wu et al., 2003, p. 924)
Six or more authors	*First and subsequent references:* (Williamson et al., 2004, p. 23)
Multiple sources in same reference	(Thames & Cain, 2008; Young, Morales, & Cato, 2009; Yu, 2004) *The semicolon divides the sources.*
Two or more works by the same author	(Tufte, 2001, p. 23) and (Tufte, 2003) *The author's name is used with the date.*
Two or more works by the same author in the same year	(Tufte, 2001a, p. 23) and (Tufte, 2001b, p. 11) *The "a" and "b" signal two different works and will appear in the list of references also.*
Different authors with the same last name	(M. Smith, 2005, p. 54) and (A. Smith, 2007, p. 34) *The first letters abbreviate each author's first name.*
Corporate author	(National Aeronautics and Space Administration [NASA], 2009, p. 12) or (American Beef Association, 2006, p. 232 *Well-known acronyms, such as NASA, can be put in brackets the first time and then used in any following parenthetical references.* (NASA, 2009, p. 14)

continued

Type of Source	Example Parenthetical Reference
No author for book	*(Handling Bulimia,* 2004, p. 45) *Use the full title of the source in italics.*
No author for journal article or newspaper article	("Genomics as the New Frontier," 2008, p. 23) *Put the full title in quotation marks.*
No author for newspaper article	("Recession," 2009, p. A4) *The letter "A" is the section of the newspaper and the number is the page.*
Cited in another source	(as cited in Franks, 2007, p. 94)
Web page or other document with no pagination	(Reynolds, 2006, para. 3) *"para." stands for "paragraph," as counted down from the top of the page.*
Web page or other document with no author and no pagination	("Friendly," 2008, para. 7) *Put the first prominent word in the title in quotes, with "para." standing for "paragraph," as counted down from the top of the page.*

FIGURE 28.1
Types of APA Parenthetical References
(continued)

Not all possible parenthetical references are shown here. If you have a unique source that doesn't fit these examples, you can usually figure out how to cite it by combining features of the above reference models.

Servan-Schreiber, D. (2008). *Anti-cancer: A new way of life.* New York, NY: Viking.

Crespi, B., & Badcock, C. (2008). Psychosis and autism as diametrical disorders in the social brain. *Behavior Brain Science, 31*(3), 241–261.

Chew, R. (2008, February 1). Charles Darwin, naturalist, 1809–1882. *Lucidcafe.* Retrieved February 8, 2009, from http://www.lucidcafe.com/library/96feb/darwin.html

Only sources you reference in your document should appear in your References. The reference list is not a bibliography of all the sources you found on your topic. It is only a list of sources that you actually cited in the document.

In a reference list, the entries are listed in alphabetical order, by the authors' last names. When an author's name is not known, the work is alphabetized by the first prominent word in its title. When alphabetizing, ignore words like *The, A,* or *An* if they are the first word in the title.

VAMPIRES IN HOLLYWOOD   12

References

Arthen, I. (2005, December 9). Real vampires. *FireHeart, 2*. Retrieved
      from http://www.earthspirit.com/fireheart/fhvampire.html

Barber, P. (1989). *Vampires, burial, and death*. New Haven, CT: Yale UP.

Bluestein, G. (1994). *Poplore: Folk and pop in American culture*.
      Amherst, MA: University of Massachusetts Press.

Keyworth, D. (2006). Was the vampire of the eighteenth century a
      unique type of undead corpse? *Folklore, 117*(3), 1–16.

FIGURE 28.2
Formatting a List of References

The APA Publication Manual *specifies that the heading "References" be centered on the page. The margins should be one inch on all sides. The entries should be double-spaced.*

If you are listing two works by the same author in the same year, they should be alphabetized by the first prominent words in their titles and then distinguished by "a," "b," "c" and so on (e.g., 2007 a, 2007 b, 2007 c).

Formatting a List of References in APA Style

According to APA guidelines, it is standard to start the reference list on a new page with the centered heading "References" appearing centered at the top (Figure 28.2). Entries are then listed double-spaced, in hanging indent format, which means the first line of each entry is not indented, but the rest of the lines are indented a half inch.

In professional texts, however, your reference list should match the design of your document. The "References" heading should be consistent with other headings. If you are single-spacing the rest of your document, the reference list should be single-spaced, too, perhaps with spaces between entries.

Citing Sources in the List of References

The following list is not comprehensive. However, we have included models of the most common kinds of entries in a reference list. You can use these examples as models for your own citations. If you do not find a model for a source, you should turn to the APA's *Publication Manual,* 6th edition (2010).

APA List of References

Books and Other Nonperiodical Publications

1. Book, One Author
2. Book, More Than One Author
3. Book, Three Authors
4. Book, Corporate or Organization Author
5. Book, Edited Collection
6. Book, Translated
7. Book, Author Unknown
8. Book, Second Edition or Beyond
9. Book, Dissertation or Thesis
10. Book, in Electronic Form
11. Document, Government Publication
12. Document, Pamphlet

Journals, Magazines, and Other Periodical Publications

13. Article, Journal with Continuous Pagination
14. Article, Journal without Continuous Pagination
15. Article, Edited Book
16. Article, Magazine
17. Article, Newspaper
18. Article, Author Unknown
19. Article, CD-ROM
20. Review

Web Publications

21. Web Page, Corporate Author
22. Web Page, Author Unknown
23. Article from an Online Periodical
24. Scholarly Journal Article with a Digital Object Identifier (DOI)
25. Scholarly Journal Article
26. Podcast

Other Kinds of Sources

27. Film or Video Recording
28. Television or Radio Program
29. Song or Audio Recording
30. CD-ROM
31. Personal Correspondence, E-Mail, or Interview

Citing Books and Other Nonperiodical Publications

A book citation will have some of the following features:

1. Name of the author, corporation, or editor with last name first (include "(Ed.)" or "(Eds.)" if the work is listed by editor)

2. Year the work was published, in parentheses (if unknown, use *n.d.* for "no date")

3. Title of the work, in italics (capitalize only first word, proper nouns, and any word that follows a colon)

4. City and state or country where the work was published (use standard U.S. Postal Service abbreviations for states; spell out the full names of countries outside of the United States)

5. Publisher

①   ②   ③   ④
Author. (Year of publication). *Title of work*. City and state (or country) of publication:
⑤
Publisher.

1. Book, One Author

Jones, S. (2001). *Darwin's ghost: The origin of species updated.* New York, NY:
Ballantine Books.

2. Book, Two Authors

Pauling, L., & Wilson, E. B. (1935). *Introduction to quantum mechanics.* New York, NY:
Dover Publications.

3. Book, Three or More Authors

Newnan, D. G., Eschenbach, T. G., & Lavelle, J. P. (2008). *Engineering economic
analysis* (10th ed.). Oxford, England: Oxford University Press.

4. Book, Corporate or Organization Author

American Psychiatric Association. (1994). *Diagnostic and statistical manual of
mental disorders* (4th ed.). Washington, DC: Author.

5. Book, Edited Collection

Mueller-Vollmer, K. (Ed.). (1990). *The hermeneutics reader.* New York, NY: Continuum.

6. Book, Translated

Habermas, J. (1979). *Communication and the evolution of society* (T. McCarthy,
Trans.). Boston, MA: Beacon Press.

7. Book, Author Unknown

Handbook for the WorkPad c3 PC Companion. (2000). Thornwood, NY: IBM.

8. Book, Second Edition or Beyond

Williams, R., & Tollet, J. (2008). *The non-designer's web book* (3rd ed.). Berkeley, CA:
Peachpit.

9. Book, Dissertation or Thesis

Simms, L. (2002). *The Hampton effect in fringe desert environments: An ecosystem
under stress* (Unpublished doctoral dissertation). University of New Mexico.

10. Book, in Electronic Form

Darwin, C. (1862). *On the various contrivances by which British and foreign orchids are fertilised by insects.* London, England: John Murray. Retrieved from http://pages.britishlibrary.net/charles.darwin3/orchids/orchids_fm.htm

11. Document, Government Publication

Greene, L. W. (1985). *Exile in paradise: The isolation of Hawaii's leprosy victims and development of Kalaupapa settlement, 1865 to present.* Washington, DC: U.S. Department of the Interior, National Park Service.

12. Document, Pamphlet

The Colorado Health Network. (2002). *Exploring high altitude areas.* Denver, CO: Author.

Citing Journals, Magazines, and Other Periodical Publications

A citation for a journal, magazine, or other periodical publication includes the following features:

1. Name of the author, corporation, or editor; last name first, followed by initial of first name and any middle initials

2. Date of publication (year for scholarly journal; year, month, day for other periodicals)

3. Title of the work, not enclosed in quotation marks (capitalize only first word, proper nouns, and any word that follows a colon)

4. Title of the periodical in italics (capitalize all significant words)

5. Volume number (italicized) and issue number (not italicized, but enclosed in parentheses). If each issue begins with page 1, include the issue number.

6. Range of page numbers for whole article

①   ②   ③   ④   ⑤
Author. (Date of publication). Title of article. *Title of Journal, volume number*
     ⑤   ⑥
(issue number), page numbers.

13. Article, Journal with Continuous Pagination

Boren, M. T., & Ramey, J. (1996). Thinking aloud: Reconciling theory and practice. *IEEE Transactions on Professional Communication, 39,* 49–57.

14. Article, Journal without Continuous Pagination

Kadlecek, M. (1991). Global climate change could threaten U.S. wildlife. *Conservationist* 46(1), 54–55.

15. Article, Edited Book

Katz, S. B., & Miller, C. R. (1996). The low-level radioactive waste siting controversy in North Carolina: Toward a rhetorical model of risk communication. In G. Herndl & S. C. Brown (Eds.), *Green culture: Environmental rhetoric in contemporary America* (pp. 111–140). Madison, WI: University of Wisconsin Press.

16. Article, Magazine

Appenzeller, T. (2008, February). The case of the missing carbon. *National Geographic,* 88–118.

17. Article, Newspaper

Hall, C. (2002, November 18). Shortage of human capital envisioned, Monster's Taylor sees worker need. *Chicago Tribune,* p. E7.

18. Article, Author Unknown

The big chill leaves bruises. (2004, January 17). *Albuquerque Tribune,* p. A4.

19. Article, CD-ROM

Hanford, P. (2001). Locating the right job for you. *The electronic job finder* [CD-ROM]. San Francisco, CA: Career Masters.

20. Review

Leonhardt, D. (2008, November 30). Chance and circumstance. [Review of the book *Outliers*]. *New York Times,* p. BR9.

Citing Web Publications

In APA style, citations for Web documents do not need to include your date of access if you can provide a publication date. However, you do need to provide either the URL from which a source was retrieved or a Digital Object Identifier (DOI). When including a URL or DOI, always insert a break *before* a slash, period, or other punctuation mark.

FIGURE 28.3 CITATION MAP: Citing Part or All of a Web Site

A citation for a Web publication will have some or all of the following features:

① Name of the author, corporation, organization, editor, or webmaster. For authors and editors, last name first followed by initials.

② Date of publication, in parentheses (year, month, date). If no date is given, write (n.d.) to indicate "no date."

③ Title of the individual page, document, or article.

④ Title of the Web site, in italics.

⑤ Retrieval information: date retrieved and the site's URL; do not add a period at the end of the URL.

①	②	③	④
Author of Web site.	(Date published.)	Title of document or *Title of Page.*	*Title of Overall Web Site.*

⑤
Retrieved (month date, year) from URL

①	②	③
Pueblo Grande Museum and Archaeological Park.	(n.d.).	*Doorways to the Past: Hohokam Houses.*

④ *City of Phoenix.* ⑤ Retrieved April 9, 2009, from http://phoenix.gov/PUEBLO/exhouses.html

② Date of publication

④ Title of Web site

⑤ Date retrieved and URL

③ Title of page

① Author (organization)

FIGURE 28.4   CITATION MAP: **Citing a Journal Article with a DOI**

An article with a DOI retrieved from a database does not require either the database name or your date of retrieval as part of your citation. A citation for such an article does need to include the following features:

① Name of the author (last name, initials)

② Publication date

③ Title of article

④ Title of the journal in italics

⑤ Volume number in italics, and issue number (in parentheses, not italicized)

⑥ Page numbers

⑦ Digital Object Identifier. (It is easiest to cut and paste the DOI directly from the original document into your text.)

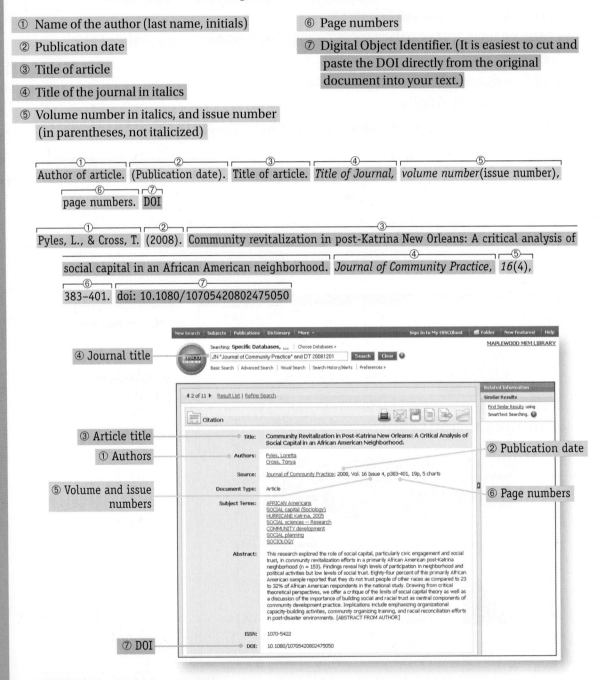

Author of article. (Publication date). Title of article. *Title of Journal, volume number*(issue number), page numbers. DOI

Pyles, L., & Cross, T. (2008). Community revitalization in post-Katrina New Orleans: A critical analysis of social capital in an African American neighborhood. *Journal of Community Practice, 16*(4), 383–401. doi: 10.1080/10705420802475050

④ Journal title
③ Article title
① Authors
⑤ Volume and issue numbers
⑦ DOI
② Publication date
⑥ Page numbers

21. Web Site, Corporate Author

U.S. Fish and Wildlife Service. (2008). *Estuary restoration act of 2000*. Retrieved
   from http://www.fws.gov/coastal/estuaryRestorationAct.html

22. Web Site, Author Unknown

Clara Barton: Founder of the American Red Cross. (n.d.). *American Red Cross Museum*.
   Retrieved from http://www.redcross.org/museum/history/claraBarton.asp

23. Article from an Online Periodical

Vaitheeswaran, V. (2009, April 16). Medicine goes digital. *The Economist*. Retrieved
   from http://www.economist.com/specialreports

24. Scholarly Journal Article with a Digital Object Identifier (DOI)

Blake, H., & Ooten, M. (2008). Bridging the divide: Connecting feminist histories
   and activism in the classroom. *Radical History Review, 2008* (102), 63–72.
   doi: 10.1215/01636545-2008-013

25. Scholarly Journal Article

The APA no longer requires you to include the name of a database from which
you retrieve a journal article. Use the DOI, if available, for such an article.

Ankers, D., & Jones, S. H. (2009). Objective assessment of circadian activity and
   sleep patterns in individuals at behavioural risk of hypomania. *Journal of
   Clinical Psychology, 65*, 1071–1086. doi: 10.1002/jclp.20608

26. Podcast

Root, B. (2009, January 27). *Just one more book* [Audio podcast]. Retrieved
   from http://www.justonemorebook.com/2009/01/27/interview-with-
   neil-gaiman

Citing Other Kinds of Sources

A variety of other sources are available, each with their own citation style. The citations for these sources tend to include most of the following types of information:

1. Name of the producers, writers, or directors with their roles identified in parentheses (Producer, Writer, Director)

2. Year of release or broadcast, in parentheses

3. Title of the work (italics for a complete work; no italics for a work that is a segment, episode, or part of a whole)

4. Name of episode (first letter of first word capitalized)

5. Title of the program (italicized)

6. Type of program (in brackets), e.g., [Film], [Television series], [Song]

7. City and state or country where work was produced

8. Distributor of the work (e.g., HBO, Miramax, New Line Productions)

9. Retrieval information, for works accessed online

27. Film or Video Recording

Jackson, P. (Director), Osborne, B., Walsh, F., & Sanders, T. (Producers). (2002). *The lord of the rings: The fellowship of the ring* [Motion picture]. Hollywood, CA: New Line Productions.

28. Television or Radio Program

Paley, V. (Writer). (2009). Human nature, the view from kindergarten [Radio series episode]. In I. Glass (Producer), *This American Life*. Chicago, IL: WBEZ/Chicago Public Radio.

29. Song or Recording

Myer, L. (1993). Sometimes alone. On *Flatlands* [CD-ROM]. Ames, IA: People's Productions.

30. CD-ROM

Geritch, T. (2000). *Masters of renaissance art* [CD-ROM]. Chicago, IL: Revival Productions.

31. Personal Correspondence, E-Mail, or Interview

In APA style, personal correspondence is not listed in the reference list. Instead, the information from the correspondence should be given in the parenthetical citation:

This result was confirmed by J. Baca (personal communication, March 4, 2004).

A Student's APA-Style Research Paper

The document shown here uses APA style for parenthetical citations and the References list. The student writer followed his professor's requirements for formatting his paper; formatting guidelines in the APA *Publication Manual* are intended for submissions to professional journals.

ASSORTATIVE MATING 1

A header with an abbreviated title and page number is included on all pages.

Assortative Mating and Income Inequality

Austin Duus
University of New Mexico

Professor Krause

Economics 445: Topics in Public Finance

Assortative Mating and Income Inequality

Paul Ryscavage begins *Income Inequality in America* (1998) on the premise that the growth in income inequality in the United States in the last thirty years is driven by changes in technology, globalization, and "family structure." The first two factors seem intuitive. Returns-to-education in an economy where exchange is facilitated by personal computers and BlackBerries is both well-documented (Lynn, 2002; Daugherty, 2008) and offers explanatory logic on how an educated segment of the population's income gains could outpace those of the less-educated. However, family structure, the final element in Ryscavage's inequality trifecta, seems suspiciously far removed from the typical industrial activities of the economy. At first, this demographic nuance seems more polemical than empirical. The single-mom menace, the erosion of "family values," and the disappearance of the Ozzie-and-Harriet nuclear family seem more like ideological talking points than matters of economic fact.

What is stunning, however, is how small changes in the aggregate makeup of American households can drastically affect the distribution of income in that population. The proportion of single, female-headed households has increased due to the "independence effect" on the dissolution or preemption of marriages among other things. Moreover, this type of household is the most likely to be poor (Cancian & Reed, 1999). Judith Treas (1987) refers to these changes in the context of the "feminization of poverty" (p. 283). This sociology catchphrase makes more sense when considered in the context of trends in female labor force participation and the marriage market.

Even more elemental to the question of family structure and its effects on income inequality are the underlying forces by which

---

Multiple sources cited in the same sentence are separated by a semicolon.

When the author's name appears in the sentence, only the year is parenthetically cited, and the page number is cited at the end of the sentence.

ASSORTATIVE MATING   3

individuals choose to partner, and partners choose to sort, in all
segments of the population. Beyond income inequality (or equality as
the case may be), marriage [or nonmarital partnering] has "implications
for . . . the number of births and population growth, labor-force
participation of women, inequality in income, ability, and other
characteristics among families, genetical [sic] natural selection of
different characteristics over time, and the allocation of leisure and
other household resources" (Becker, 1973, p. 814). In short, household
formation is a largely economic decision, which, like other such
decisions, is a choice determined by weighing the costs (including
opportunity costs) against expected utility.

Three ellipsis points (. . .) indicate that some words have been omitted from within a quoted sentence.

Theoretical Framework

Individuals do not pair with other individuals to form households
randomly. Instead, one can observe traits by which individuals tend to
sort themselves and their mates. Garfinkel and McLananhan (2002)
define this process of assortative mating as "the tendency of people to
choose partners of similar age, race, educational attainment, and other
social, psychological, and biological characteristics" (p. 417). More
specifically, they are referring to *positive* assortative mating in which
individuals choose similar partners. In the literature, this is sometimes
referred to as homogamy. Individuals, for various reasons, sometimes
find it advantageous to choose partners who are different from them.
This is *negative* assortative mating.

Main headings are centered and boldfaced, using both uppercase and lowercase letters.

The Becker Theory

Gary Becker (1973) was the first to outline a theory of a marriage
market. His claims were straightforward. Marriage, like all economic
decisions, is an optimized utility function. "Persons marrying . . . can
be assumed to expect to raise their utility level above what it would be
were they to remain single." Moreover, like all utility functions, a

Secondary headings are flush left and boldfaced, using both uppercase and lowercase letters.

Use four ellipsis points to indicate material omitted between sentences in a quote.

The findings of credible sources help the author make his point with greater authority.

For a quotation of 40 or more words, use a block quote without quotation marks.

marriage is optimized against a constraint. Potential mates are limited; therefore, scarcity drives a market in which "many men and women compete as they seek mates. . . . Each person tries to find the best mate, subject to the restrictions imposed by market conditions" (p. 814).

Becker (1973) found that people might choose to marry simply because it is easier to have "sexual gratification, cleaning, and feeding" (p. 818) in-house than to purchase those services. Also, conveniently, "love" can "reduce the cost of frequent contact and of resource transfers" (p. 819).

Observations about who marries whom suggest individuals sort by "IQ, education, height, attractiveness, skin color, ethnic origin, and other characteristics" (Becker, 1973, p. 815). Sorting by some heritable traits may be related to creating "desired" offspring. Additionally, the choice to separate or divorce is determined by opportunity cost. If there is more to lose, people will think twice about going to divorce court.

Negative Assortative Mating

Becker (1973) speculates there may be negative sorting in regard to specific "psychological traits, such as a propensity to dominate, nurture, or be hostile" (p. 824). However, central to Becker's theory of the marriage market is an assumption of negative sorting in regard to wages. Jepsen and Jepsen (2002) explain:

> Theories of the sexual division of labor predict that high-wage men will pair with low-wage women and that, once the couple forms a household, men will specialize in market production while women will specialize in home production. (p. 442)

However, all empirical studies suggest the opposite is true. While correlations between spousal wages tend to be very small, usually the smallest of traits studied, they are positive. It is assumed, generally without warrant, that male wages and female household production are

ASSORTATIVE MATING   5

substitutes, and gains in marriage result from this specialization. Becker (1991) finds the sexual division of labor so compelling as to claim in regard to same-sex couples, "households with only men or only women are less efficient because they are unable to profit from the sexual difference in comparative advantage" (p. 38). Becker, however, fails to specify how having a uterus gives one a "comparative advantage" in dishwashing and food preparation or the relationship between a Y chromosome and market work. It is also unclear why partners of the same sex cannot specialize.

> When appropriate, author challenges limitations of sources.

Regardless of the problems with assuming gender essentialism in theory, empirically, Lam (1988) found even high-wage women exhibit a tendency to specialize in household production as they prefer even higher wage men. (Thus their opportunity cost to not participating in the labor market is lower in comparison to their spouses.) This means women do not necessarily specialize in household production because they are female. This finding is further validated when female labor force participation data are disaggregated into cohorts. Black women, for example, tend to participate in the labor force regardless of the income of their spouses (Jepsen, 2002; Treas, 1987).

Evidence for Assortative Mating

Traits Studied

Age. While men seek younger women and women seek slightly older men (Jepsen, 2002), on balance, people seek partners of an age similar to their own (Jaffe and Chacon-Puignau, 1995). Age, in most studies, generally has the "strongest positive assortative mating" (Lam, 1988, p. 478).

> Use of multiple heading levels provides access points and makes the text easier to read.

IQ. Jepsen & Jepsen (2002) estimate the correlation as similar to the IQ correlation between siblings.

Education. Lam (1988) calculates schooling being second only to age in positive assortative mating. Strikingly, the particular trait has experienced the largest boost in homogamy. Costa & Kahn (2000) note education as a primary driving force in how couples sort and then where they live. In fact, educational homogamy has increased while homogamy with respect to race, ethnicity, and age has decreased. This could be explained by educational sorting happening later. As individuals marry or partner later in life, they are more likely to partner with someone less like them. While people may choose to partner with someone of a different culture, age, or even weight, level of education seems to be increasingly important as a positive sorting mechanism—at least, among married couples.

Wage. Wage has the weakest correlation coefficient ranging from .02 to .24 (Jepsen & Jepsen, 2002; Treas, 1987).

Differences by Type of Couple

Married Couples. Married couples tend to be the most homogamous in all factors but wage.

Cohabitating Couples. In general, market variables are more positive with unmarried couples than married couples, but less positive with nonmarket traits (Jepsen & Jepsen, 2002). With respect to race, age, and education, unmarried couples tended to be less homogamous than married couples, but more homogamous with earnings and hours worked. This is consistent with the idea of marriage self-selection, whereby financial independence is a disincentive to marry.

While median measures of unmarried couples in regard to age are identical to married couples, there is a much wider distribution of age differences. Unmarried parents tended to have a more substantial education gap than their married counterparts. However, this is primarily due to the education gap of parents who have never lived together (Garfinkel & McLananhan, 2002).

ASSORTATIVE MATING   7

> Taken as a whole, these results suggest that mothers and
> fathers who do not marry each other may be less homogamous
> in terms of age and education than parents who marry . . .
> Nonetheless, it appears that a high level of assortative mating
> still occurs. (p. 429)

Same-Sex Couples. Out of all the types of couples studied, female
same-sex couples had the strongest positive assortative mating by wage.
Unlike most studies, their wage correlation was statistically significant
(Jepsen & Jepsen, 2002). Both male and female same-sex couples had a
larger wage correlation than both unmarried and married opposite-sex
couples. In contrast, the "estimated coefficient for race and age are
noticeably larger for opposite-sex couples than for same-sex couples,"
(Jepsen & Jepsen, 2002, p. 444).

Black Couples. In many ways, African American family
formation is a useful natural experiment on the effects of increased
female labor force participation on income inequality. Unlike their
White and Latino counterparts, Black women are likely to work
regardless of the income of their spouses. Also, "relative to whites,
African Americans report less willingness to marry a person of a lower
socioeconomic status, and they express less desire to marry" (Jepsen
& Jepsen, 2002, p. 437). So while two working spouses would be an
equalizing force if upper-income women did not work, this is not the
case with Black women.

When it would be
unclear what source
is cited, the authors'
names are included
in the parenthetical
citation.

While female labor force participation may increase inequality
within the African American community, it may actually narrow the
race-income gap. According to Danziger (1980), in "1974, nonwhite
family income was 78 percent of white's; this ratio would have been
only 71 percent if nonwhite wives had not worked more than did white
wives" (p. 448).

Analysis

Impact on Income Inequality

Historically we find that female labor force participation was an equalizing force in the United States income distribution. Women's wages were compressed in the phenomenon of the occupational set of nurse/teacher/secretary. However, since World War II (when women first entered the workforce in large numbers), the diversity of market opportunities available to women has substantially increased and as marriage and other assortative mating is delayed well beyond high school, it is increasingly likely pairs will sort by wage as well as by the usual homogamous characteristics.

Conclusion

Currently, empirical data suggest the effects of more high-wage women entering the workforce are mixed (Danziger, 1980). Even for experiments in which all women participated in the labor force, the wage correlation might only increase to around .25 (Treas, 1987), which would have limited effects on the aggregate household income distribution.

> Final analyses and conclusions are stated succinctly and prominently.

ASSORTATIVE MATING   9

References

Becker, G. S. (1973). A theory of marriage: Part I. *Journal of Political Economy, 81,* 813–846. doi: 10.1086/260084

Becker, G. S. (1991). *A treatise on the family.* Cambridge, MA: Harvard University Press.

Cancian, M., & Reed, D. (1999). The impact of wives' earnings on income inequality: Issues and estimates. *Demography, 36,* 173–184. doi: 10.2307/2648106

Costa, D. L., & Kahn, M. E. (2000). Power couples: Changes in the locational choice of the college educated, 1940–1990. *Quarterly Journal of Economics, 115,* 1287–1315. doi: 10.1162/003355300555079

Danziger, S. (1980). Do working wives increase family income inequality? *Journal of Human Resources, 15,* 445–451. doi: 10.2307/145294

Garfinkel, I., & McLananhan, S. S. (2002). Assortative mating among unmarried parents: Implications for ability to pay child support. *Journal of Population Economics, 15,* 417–432. doi: 10.1007/s001480100100

Jepsen, L. K., & Jepsen, C. A. (2002). An empirical analysis of the matching patterns of same-sex and opposite sex couples. *Demography, 39,* 435–453. doi: 10.1353/dem.2002.0027

Lam, D. (1988). Marriage markets and assortative mating with household public goods: Theoretical results and empirical implications. *Journal of Human Resources, 23,* 462–487. doi: 10.2307/145809

Treas, J. (1987). The effect of women's labor force participation on the distribution of income in the United States. *Annual Review of Sociology, 13,* 259–288. doi: 10.1146 /annurev.so.13.080187.001355

References begin on new page. All cited works are included and listed in alphabetical order by author.

The DOI is provided whenever available, even for print articles.

6

Getting Your
Ideas Out
There

PART OUTLINE

Your thoughts and ideas deserve a wider audience.
GET YOUR WRITING OUT THERE *for others to discuss, debate, and respond. These chapters will show you how to take your writing public.*

29

Using the
Internet

Today people are reading and writing more than ever. They write e-mails, keep up with current events on Web sites, update their *Facebook* profiles, share their opinions on blogs, and create podcasts and *YouTube* videos. They are texting with their friends and microblogging with *Twitter*.

In this chapter, you will learn how to use the Internet and new media to put your writing out in the public sphere. There are now more ways than ever to publicize your writing and make an impact on the world through your words.

Is This Writing?

Maybe you are wondering if some of the new media tools we will discuss in this chapter can still be considered writing. Blogging looks like writing, but what about social networking sites or video sharing sites? Can we still call that writing?

We live in a time of great technological change, so we need to expand and change our understanding of what it means to "write" and be "literate." This kind of revolution has happened before. When the printing press was introduced in Europe in the fifteenth century, it also dramatically changed people's ideas about what writing looked like. Before the printing press, "writing" meant handwritten texts, such as letters, written records, and ornate illuminated books. The printing press democratized the written word, giving the public access to ideas and texts that were once available only to a privileged few. Then society's understanding of writing changed to fit the new technology.

More than likely, the monks working in the scriptoriums of medieval Europe would have been mystified and anxious about the kinds of writing that we take for granted today. Mass-produced books, newspapers, magazines, junk mail, brochures, posters, and other kinds of writing would have seemed very odd and even threatening to them. They would have seen computers as a form of magic or even witchcraft.

So it's not surprising that today we wonder whether these new media tools are really forms of writing. More than likely, within your lifetime, writing will change in ways that make it look very different than it does now. The new technologies described in this chapter are only the beginning of that change.

Creating a Social Networking Site

Let's start with the easiest way to go public with your writing—creating a profile on a social networking Web site like *Facebook, MySpace, Bebo, LinkedIn,* or *Spoke*. The first three, *Facebook, MySpace,* and *Bebo,* can help you connect and stay in touch with your friends and other kindred souls. Increasingly, these social networking sites are being used by nonprofit organizations, political movements, and companies to stay in touch with interested people. For example, your college or university probably has a *Facebook* or *MySpace* site that lets you keep in touch with what is happening on campus.

LinkedIn and *Spoke* are career-related social networking sites that will help you connect with colleagues, business associates, and potential employers.

Choose the Best Site for You

Each social networking site is a little different. As you choose which site is best for you, think about your purpose for having a social networking site. Right now, you probably just want to keep in touch with your friends. But as you move through college and into the workplace, your site may become a way to network with other people in your field and share your ideas. Also think about the kinds of writing you want to do. Some social networking sites are better at supporting longer genres of writing, such as memoirs, commentaries, reviews, position papers, and other kinds of extended texts.

Be Selective About Your "Friends"

Carefully select your "friends." It's tempting to add everyone you know, but that isn't the best approach. Again, think about the purpose of your site. You can only keep in touch with a certain number of people, so be selective. You don't want so-called "friends" writing things on your wall that would make you look bad to important people at your university or to future employers.

Add Regularly to Your Profile

Write regularly on your site and keep it up to date. Express your opinions. Share your ideas. Discuss current events or your passions. However, don't put any private information on your profile, such as contact information or anything that would allow a stranger to track you down. Any pictures you put on your page should be appropriate for anyone to see (because they will).

Start thinking of your site as more than a way to keep in touch with friends. Your site will likely evolve into a tool for staying in touch with people in your academic field, other professionals and clients, and people in your community. It will be less about what you did last weekend and more about your long-term interests, your career, and how you're making a difference in the world.

Starting Your Own Blog

A blog is a Web site in which a writer keeps a public journal of his or her experiences, thoughts, and opinions. Blogs are usually made up of words and sentences, but there are also an increasing number of photo blogs, video blogs, and audio blogs.

Choose a Host Site for Your Blog

Don't pay for a blogging site. Some popular free blogging sites include *Blogger, Wordpress, Blogsome,* and *Moveable Type.* Each one has strengths and weaknesses, so you might look at them all to determine which one will fit your needs and reach the people you want to speak to. Another kind of blog is a "microblog," which only allows a small number of words per post. *Twitter* was the groundbreaking microblogging site, but other microblogging services are now available.

Begin Your Blog

Once you pick a host site, it will ask you for some basic information, such as your name, your blog's name, and an e-mail address. You will then be shown a menu of templates that are available (Figure 29.1). Pick one that fits your personality and the kinds of topics you want to discuss on your blog.

Compose, Edit, and Publish Your Ideas.   On your blogging site, you will see tabs or buttons on the screen that allow you to "compose," "edit," and "publish" your comments. Type some of your thoughts into the Compose screen and hit the Post or Publish button. Your words should appear on your blog. Keep adding more comments when you feel the urge.

Personalize Your Blog

Blogging sites will allow you to add photographs, profiles, polls, newsreels, icons, and other gadgets to your blog's layout. Pick features that are appropriate for the kind of blog you want to create, and don't go overboard. You don't want the extra stuff on your site to distract readers from your ideas and arguments.

FIGURE 29.1 Choosing a Blog Template

The template you choose for your blog should fit your personality and the kinds of topics you want to discuss on your blog.

Let Others Join the Conversation. The initial settings for your blogging site will strictly control access to your blog. You and you alone will be able to post comments on your blog. As you grow more comfortable with your blog, though, you might want to loosen up your settings to allow others to write comments. If so, you should first decide who will be able to make comments on your blog.

When starting out, only allow "registered users" (i.e., people who you give permission to comment on your blog) to add comments. Some bloggers set their blog to allow "anyone" to comment. That's risky, because strangers and spammers may contribute posts that annoy or embarrass you. If you allow *everyone* to comment, you will need to spend a great amount of time cleaning up your blog.

As you are blogging, keep in mind that your blog is a public site. In other words, anyone can read what you have put on your page. So keep the blog interesting, and don't say anything that puts you in a bad light. Always remember that current or future employers may discover your blog, so you want to only say things that you would say directly to your current or future boss. Plus, always remember that you can be sued for writing slanderous or libelous things about other people. So keep it clean and truthful.

Writing Articles for Wikis

Wikis are collaboratively written Internet sites that allow users to add and edit content. *Wikipedia* is, of course, one of the more popular wikis. It is an online encyclopedia that allows users to add, edit, and manage information on just about any topic. Other wikis are also popular, such as *eHow, WikiHow, Wikitravel, CookbookWiki, ProductWiki, Uncyclopedia,* and *Wikicars.* Your professors may ask you to add material to one of these popular wikis or contribute to a wiki dedicated to your class.

Like any user, you have the ability to add articles to these wikis and edit the existing content. Here's how to add an article to the wiki of your choice.

Write the Article

Like any kind of writing, you should begin by thinking about your topic, angle, purpose, readers, and the contexts in which your article will be needed or used. Research your topic thoroughly, draft the article, and edit it carefully. Include any appropriate graphics. You should also have your sources available, so they can be listed in "References," "External Links," and "Further Reading" sections of the article. It is best to write your wiki article with a word processor. This will allow you to do all the drafting and revising needed before you add it to the wiki.

Above all, you want to make sure your article is interesting and factually accurate. If your article is about something trivial or mundane, the wiki administrator will simply delete it. If your article is factually inaccurate, other wiki users will rewrite your work.

Add Your Article to the Wiki

Look for the button on the wiki that says, "Create an article" or "Start the X article" in which X is the name of your topic. Most wikis will expect you to have an account if you want to add an article. Once you log in, the wiki will provide a box where you can cut and paste your article from your word processor.

Edit and proofread your article. Then click the Save Page button. At this point, your article will be added to the wiki.

Other people can revise and edit your article, so you should return to your article periodically to make sure someone hasn't altered it to say something inaccurate. You might even be pleasantly surprised to find that someone has expanded your article, providing information you didn't know about.

Putting Videos and Podcasts on the Internet

You can upload videos to Web sites like *YouTube, MySpace Videos, MSN Video, Yahoo! Video, Veoh, Joost, iFilm, Hulu, Metacafe,* and *blip.tv.* Some popular podcasting sites include *Podcast Alley, iTunes, Digg,* and *Podcast Pickle.* Here is how to put your video or podcast on one of these sites.

Create Your Video or Record Your Podcast

Making a video or podcast takes some preparation if you want to make something worth watching or hearing. As with any kind of writing, you should first consider your topic, angle, purpose, readers, and the contexts in which your video or podcast will be experienced. Then invent the content and draft a script. Think of the most appropriate background or scenery for your video.

Above all, don't bore your audience. Good planning and tight scripting will allow you to make something worth watching or listening to.

Edit Your Work

Edit your work with video or sound editing software. Some good video editing software packages include *Corel VideoStudio, MS Movie Maker, Adobe Premiere, Final Cut,* and *iMovie*. The most common sound editing software packages for editing podcasts include *Adobe Audition, Audacity, Garage Band,* and *Cubase*. One or more of these editing tools may have already been preloaded onto your computer, so look for them in your applications before you buy something new.

Upload Your Video or Podcast

If your video or podcast is ready to be uploaded, then go to the "upload" link in your account. The site will ask you for a title and description, as well as some keywords called "tags." Try to include as many keywords as you can. That way, people who are searching the Web site will be more likely to come across your video or podcast.

Again, always remember that these sites are public. So don't show, do, or say anything that is illegal, unethical, or embarrassing. Be very careful not to give too much personal information. Even if you put limits on who can access your videos and podcasts, someone else, including your friends, might share them with others.

The social media tools you use to manage your personal life can be powerful platforms for sharing your ideas and arguments with a much larger community. Here's what you can do with these tools.

CREATE Your Profile on a Social Networking Site

Choose the social networking site that is most appropriate for your lifestyle and thoughts. Pick one that has the audience you most want to reach.

BLOG About What Matters to You

You're more likely to update your blog often—and write with a passion that engages and involves readers—if you choose a topic of ongoing personal interest.

SHARE Your Online Compositions

Post your work for others to see. But be strategic about who can see or follow you and how (or if) others can comment or participate on your site.

PARTICIPATE in Knowledge-Making on a Wiki Site

Share what you're learning in college by writing entries for wikis—or by correcting erroneous information. Be sure your information is accurate, well-researched, and useful to others.

BROADCAST Your Ideas to the World

Use video and audio recording technologies to capture places, events, and people of interest to you and the community. Upload your work to a site where it can be widely shared and discussed.

1. With your group in class, talk about the different ways you use the new media tools discussed in this chapter. Discuss how these media tools have changed the way people communicate in your lifetime.

2. How are social networking sites, blogging, and audio and video sharing changing the workplace? How do members of your group expect new media to shape their careers?

3. Do you think people learn social skills online that they can use elsewhere? Or, are social media actually harmful to people's abilities to interact in the real world?

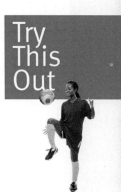
1. If you already have a social media site, revise it in ways that would make it appealing (or at least acceptable) to a future employer.

2. With a group of people from your class, shoot a small video or record a podcast. Upload the video or podcast to a video sharing Web site and send a link to your professor.

3. With a group in your class, think of a topic that interests all of you. Then, using three different wikis, read the articles written about that topic. What facts do these wiki articles have in common? What facts are different or missing from one or more of the articles? How do the articles approach the topic from different angles, and what do they choose to highlight?

1. **Learn about a new media tool.** Write a review of one of the new media tools discussed in this chapter. Discuss its future and how you think it will affect your life and your career.

2. **Write your ideas in a blog.** For two weeks, keep a blog in which you write about anything that interests you. Then write an e-mail to your professor in which you explain why you did or didn't enjoy blogging, and whether you think you will continue blogging in the future.

PEARSON
mycomplab

For additional reading, writing, and research resources, go to **www.mycomplab.com.**

30

Creating a
Portfolio

Portfolios include selections of your best work, packaged for people who need to understand or evaluate your background, abilities, knowledge, and potential. They also give you a chance to reflect on your writing, leading to deeper, more permanent learning. As a student, you may be asked to create a portfolio for a specific course, or you may be required to compile a collection of your work as a "capstone" to your studies in your major.

Your portfolio will also be an important part of your job application package, because it allows you to show interviewers examples of your work. After you are hired, your portfolio may be used to track your professional development and determine whether you receive a raise or a promotion.

Two Basic Kinds of Portfolios

There are two basic types of portfolios: *learning portfolios* and *showcase portfolios*.

Learning Portfolios. Learning portfolios focus on your progress toward mastering specific knowledge and abilities. Your learning portfolio is like a movie that leads your readers through a course or your college career to witness the progress you have made. Your portfolio shows where you started and where you are now, demonstrating what you have learned. Learning portfolios include finished documents, and they often include drafts of work and brainstorming notes.

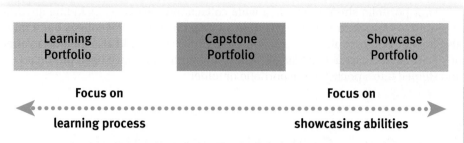

FIGURE 30.1 Kinds of Portfolios and Their Purposes

The focus of your portfolio depends on its purpose. The portfolios you create in school will focus more on the learning process than the portfolios you create to find internships and jobs.

Showcase Portfolios. Showcase portfolios display only finished products that demonstrate your work at its best. They are designed to highlight the knowledge and abilities that you have mastered to this point in your career. They are like a snapshot that provides a rich and detailed depiction of your skills and know-how at the present moment.

A third kind of portfolio, usually called a "capstone portfolio" is a hybrid of these two (Figure 30.1). Like a learning portfolio, a capstone portfolio is designed to show your progress toward mastering specific knowledge and abilities. However, capstone portfolios usually do not include drafts or notes because they are designed to show your work at its best.

Getting Started on Your Portfolio

Creating a portfolio is not difficult, but it does take some time and planning. Here are four simple steps to follow:

1. **Collect** your work in an ongoing "archive" folder on your computer's hard drive or in a file folder. Each item in your portfolio is called an *artifact*.

2. **Select** those artifacts that best exemplify the knowledge and ability you want your portfolio to exhibit. Your selections depend on who will be viewing your portfolios and why.

3. **Reflect** on what is in the portfolio. Usually professors or supervisors will ask you to write a brief reflection that introduces and reviews the materials in your portfolio.

4. **Present** the portfolio as a complete package. Depending on how it will be used, your portfolio might be print, online, or multimedia.

Your portfolio should include a wide collection of artifacts, including anything you want to show your readers. It should include documents, of course, but it might also include photographs, presentations, and projects. It could also include a variety of electronic media, such as images, video, and audio that have been put on a DVD and slipped into a pocket of the portfolio or folder.

Step One: Collecting Your Work

Your archive is like a storehouse of raw material. Here is where you are going to keep copies of your work until you need them for your portfolio. To start your archive, you might create a special folder on your hard drive called "Archive" or "Portfolio Archive." Then, as you finish projects, save a copy in that folder. Your college might also have an e-portfolio service that gives students storage space on its computers for their materials.

For print documents, you should also designate a drawer in your desk or file cabinet for archive materials. Keep any projects, awards, letters, or other career-related documents in this drawer. Then at the end of each semester, you can look through these items and decide what to add to your portfolio and what to file for later use.

Right now, early in your college career, is the best time to create an archive. That way, you can get into the habit of saving your best work. An added benefit to starting your archive right now is that you will always know where your best work is stored. The worst time to start an archive is when you are getting ready to graduate from college. At that point, much of your best work will have been forgotten, lost, or thrown out.

Archiving for a Specific Course

In some courses, your professor will require you to complete a portfolio that shows your work from the class. Make sure you understand what kinds of materials you will need to save for your portfolio. Some professors will ask that you save everything, from notes, to drafts, to polished copies. Other professors may just want final versions of your work in the portfolio. Here are some things you might be asked to save:

- All notes, including class notes, brainstorming, freewrites, journaling, and so on

- Rough drafts, informal writing, responses, and perhaps your professors' written comments on your drafts

- Peer review, both that you've done for others and that others have done for you

- Final drafts

- Other electronic material, such as images, multimedia, blogs, Web-based discussions, and so on

Archiving for Your College Career

Your department or college may ask you to create a portfolio at various stages of your college career. For instance, at the end of your sophomore or junior year, your college may require you to submit a portfolio that illustrates your ability to write well and think critically. Your department or program may require you to create a portfolio that shows you are ready to be admitted to the major. And at the end of your college career, you may be asked to create a capstone portfolio that illustrates what you have accomplished in your major field of study.

Items that you should save for this portfolio include the following:

- Awards or recognition of any kind
- Letters of reference from professors
- Scholarship letters and letters of acceptance
- Materials and evaluations from internships, co-ops, or jobs
- Copies of exams (preferably ones you did well on)
- Evidence of participation in clubs or special events and volunteer work

You never know what you might need, so keep anything that might be useful. If you regularly save these materials, you will be amazed at how much you did while you were at college.

Archiving for Your Professional Career

Employers often ask job applicants to bring a professional portfolio to interviews to present their work. It is also common for professionals to maintain a portfolio for promotions, performance reviews, and job searches. A professional portfolio is likely to include these materials:

- Reflective cover letter that introduces the portfolio by describing your career goals, education, work experiences, skills, and special abilities
- Résumé
- Examples of written work, presentations, and other materials such as images, links to Web sites, and so on
- Diplomas, certificates, and awards
- Letters of reference

For job interviews, you should create two versions of your professional portfolio. The first version, which you should never give away, should hold all your original materials. The second version, called a "giveaway portfolio," should have copies of your materials that you can leave with interviewers.

Step Two: Selecting the Best Artifacts

Once you have created an archive, it's time to actually begin the process of creating a portfolio. Keep in mind that a single archive can supply the material for any number of portfolios, each with a different purpose and audience.

Start by considering which artifacts in your archive will allow you to achieve your portfolio's purpose and meet the needs of your readers. Select items carefully because the best examples of your work need to stand out, not get buried in a stack of documents. Choose a handful of key documents that help you achieve your purpose and catch your reader's interest.

Step Three: Reflecting on Your Work

You may be asked to write two kinds of reflections for your portfolio, depending on how it will be used:

Learning-Focused Reflections. These reflections tell the story of your progress in a class or an academic program. They show that you have mastered certain knowledge and abilities. They also give you a chance to understand the course objectives more thoroughly and to master the course content even more completely.

Mastery-Focused Reflections. These reflections focus more on demonstrating how well you have mastered certain bodies of knowledge and abilities. In this kind of reflection, your readers want you to explain what you can do and how well you can do it.

Your Reflection as an Argument

Like any argument, your reflection should state a claim and provide support for that claim. Whether you are creating a learning portfolio or a showcase portfolio, your reflection needs to state an overall claim (i.e., a main point or thesis). Then the reflection should use the items in the portfolio as evidence to support your claim.

Demonstrating these features, Figure 30.2 shows a learning-focused reflection written by a student for a first-year writing course, and Figure 30.3 (on page 557) offers a mastery-focused reflection written by a job candidate. Notice how each of these reflections makes a claim about the writer's experience, knowledge, and abilities. Each then goes on to point readers toward specific places in the portfolio where they can find evidence that supports that claim. The first reflection, for a writing course portfolio, focuses on process and progress. The second reflection, for an interview portfolio, focuses almost exclusively on the job candidate's level of mastery.

MEMORANDUM

Date: December 2, 2007

To: Greg Evans

From: Josh Kotobi

Subject: Portfolio Memo

_____

English 101 helped me improve my writing in every way, including my rhetoric, grammar, style, and understanding of genres and how to use them. The class objectives included learning about many different genres, and how to present ideas, information, and arguments in each genre. In this cover letter, I will explain my progress and learning in terms of each of the five learning goals for the course.

Reading and Analysis

We read a variety of literary and other writing, and we worked on summarizing, interpreting, evaluating, and synthesizing the ideas in these writings. These activities expanded our writing skills as we learned how to write in different genres and styles. The close analysis of each of these texts allowed us to better understand what constitutes effective writing and ineffective writing.

I believe that the documents that show my progress and ability best in this area are the first and final drafts of my position paper. In the first draft, I just dismissed David Brooks's whole argument. I barely mentioned it, and then didn't even deal with his points. But in the final draft, you'll see that on the first two pages, I summarize, paraphrase, and quote David Brooks's article about marriage. I worked

> States purpose and main point.

> Highlights learning goals and uses documents to support claims.

continued

FIGURE 30.2 A Student's Learning-Focused Reflection

This reflection, created for a course in first-year writing at the University of New Mexico, exemplifies one approach to the cover letter. The student's professor asked for cover letters that described students' learning progress in terms of the five main course goals.

FIGURE 30.2
A Student's
Learning-
Focused
Reflection
(continued)

very hard to explain his arguments fairly, and I even conceded two points that were very strong. Even so, I went on to use my analysis of his argument to position my own. I didn't just bounce off Brooks's argument—I incorporated it into mine to make my position stronger.

[Kotobi goes on to discuss the other learning goals of the course, omitted here.]

All in all, bit by bit, week by week, I made progress with my writing. The first draft of my first paper, as you can see, was really bad. I was just writing automatically without even thinking. But I think you'll find that as the semester progressed, I wrote more thoughtfully as I learned to frame problems and use the ideas of the authors I read. I'm very pleased about the progress I've made and feel much better about doing well in the rest of my college courses.

Finishes with main point and looks to the future.

Step Four: Presenting Your Materials

How you present your work is very important. So when assembling your portfolio, don't just throw your materials into a manila envelope or fasten them together with a binder clip. That looks sloppy and unprofessional. You need to present your materials in an organized and attractive way, so your readers can find the documents they want to see. A three-ring binder or a nice folder would work well. Another option is to create an e-portfolio that you can put on the Internet or on a disc.

For a Specific Course. Most portfolios for a single course are organized chronologically from the earliest documents to the most recent documents. Your reflection should appear first as an introduction to the portfolio. And if you are asked to include drafts of papers, you should put them *behind* the final versions, not in front of them.

For a Capstone Course. A portfolio for a capstone course can be organized in a variety of ways. You could organize it by courses in your major, giving each course its own part and arranging the parts in numerical order. Or you could organize the portfolio by genres (i.e., reviews, analyses, reports, proposals, and so on). Drafts are not typically included in capstone portfolios.

Welcome to My Portfolio

Let me begin by thanking you for reviewing the materials in my portfolio. Here, I have collected examples of my best work to demonstrate my knowledge, experience, and abilities as a civil engineer. These materials will show you that I am well trained and innovative, and I have a solid background in the design, construction, and maintenance of interstate highways and bridges.

The first section includes examples from my internships and cooperative experiences. I have included two reports that I wrote during my internship with the Michigan Department of Transportation. They show my ability to write detailed, accurate observations of road and bridge conditions, while making clear recommendations. The third document is a proposal for a research project on quick-setting concrete that I helped write as a co-op for New Horizons Construction.

The second section shows materials created for my courses at Michigan State. Our professors used projects to teach us how to problem solve and come up with innovative solutions to challenging problems. The reports, proposals, specifications, and technical descriptions included here were selected to demonstrate the range of my abilities and my communication skills.

The third section includes letters of reference, awards, scholarships, and other recognition of my work at Michigan State and my internship and co-op experiences.

My goal in this portfolio is to show you that I am ready to begin contributing to your firm right away. If you would like to see other examples of my work, please call me at 517-555-1855 or e-mail me at rgfranklin@msu.edu.

States purpose and main point while acknowledging the readers.

Explains the content and organization of the portfolio.

Highlights key features of each section.

Concludes with a main point and contact information.

FIGURE 30.3 A Job Candidate's Mastery-Focused Reflection

In this reflection, a job candidate tries to highlight a few of her strengths and experiences. The reflection serves mostly as an introduction to the portfolio.

For a Job Application Packet. Portfolios used for job searches typically follow the organization of a résumé. After your reflection, you should include parts like Education, Related Coursework, Work Experience, Skills, Awards, and Activities. Each part should have its own divider with a tab.

If you will be presenting your portfolio in person (e.g., in an interview or to a group), you should organize your material in a way that helps you verbally explain your background and experiences. It should also look professional and purposeful.

Creating an E-Portfolio

Increasingly, people are going electronic with their portfolios (Figure 30.4). Making an e-portfolio is not difficult, especially if you know how to create a basic Web site or if you have access to an e-portfolio service at your university.

Electronic portfolios have several advantages:

- They can be accessed from anywhere there is a networked computer, including a professor's or interviewer's office.

- They can include multimedia texts such as movies, presentations, and links to Web sites you have created.

- They can include scanned-in documents that show comments that others have handwritten on your work.

FIGURE 30.4
An E-Portfolio

An e-portfolio, like this one from a student at LaGuardia Community College, allows people to personalize their materials and keep them organized in an accessible way.

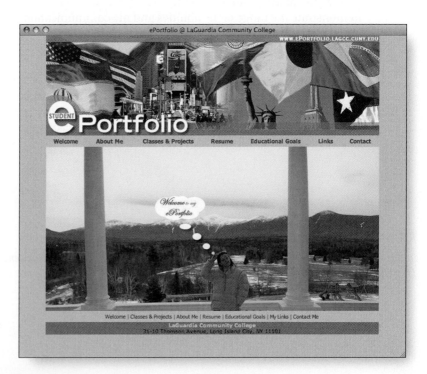

- They provide interactivity for the reader. For example, the reflective letter can link directly to the documents in the portfolio or to items on the Internet.

- They include materials and links to information that would not typically be found in a nonelectronic portfolio. For example, you might put links to your university and academic department to help interviewers learn about your educational background.

- They can be updated easily, while older versions can be archived.

- They provide customized access features so that different readers can or cannot see specific parts of the portfolio.

- They eliminate copying costs.

Some e-portfolio services even allow you to maintain an electronic archive from which you can create a virtually limitless number of e-portfolios, each targeted for a specific purpose and audience.

Keeping Your Portfolio Up to Date

This semester, your professor may be asking you to create a portfolio only for your writing class. Right now, though, would be a good opportunity to also create an archive for your portfolio that you can use throughout your college career and beyond.

Each semester, spend a little time keeping your portfolio up to date. Add items that show your knowledge and abilities. Archive documents that have been eclipsed by better work. Look for chances to create documents that fill out any gaps in your portfolio. You can also find opportunities to add to your portfolio by joining clubs, doing volunteer work, and completing internships or co-ops.

It only takes an hour or so each semester to keep your portfolio up to date, but you will be thankful you did, especially when you are nearing graduation and starting to look for a job.

Use this guide to help you begin and complete your portfolio.

COLLECT Your Work in an Archive

Get into the habit of saving your documents and projects in an archive. For a specific course, you may want to save *everything,* from notes to rough drafts to final drafts, from print documents to audio files to images to movies. For a capstone portfolio in the middle or at the end of your academic career, you will want to save a variety of examples of your best work. Some schools allow you to store your work in an electronic archive.

SELECT the Works for a Specific Type of Portfolio

When you have a specific type of portfolio in mind, start selecting the works from your archive that will help you to achieve your purpose and that will be most useful for your readers.

REFLECT on What the Portfolio Shows: Your Learning Process, Your Abilities, and Your Experience

Every portfolio needs some kind of reflection or cover letter that introduces readers to the portfolio. In your reflection, make your argument about what the portfolio shows by pointing out to readers what they should notice.

PRESENT Your Portfolio

If you're using a binder or folder for your portfolio, include a table of contents and tabbed section dividers. If you're creating an e-portfolio, use an attractive Web page design, links, and an easy-to-use navigation system.

KEEP Your Portfolio Up to Date

Revisit your portfolio at the end of each semester. It will be useful when you begin your job search. Many professionals maintain an ongoing portfolio for career development, promotions, and new opportunities.

1. Brainstorm the development of a portfolio for this course or another course. Describe to your group how you would collect, select, reflect on, and present your work.

2. In your group, discuss the differences between a learning and a showcase portfolio. Which are you most comfortable with? Which do you think would be most appropriate for this course?

3. Imagine that your major requires that you create a capstone portfolio, including what you learned and how you learned it. Make a list of the kinds of artifacts that you will want to have saved for this portfolio, with a brief explanation of what each artifact would show about you.

Talk About This

1. Analyze the rhetorical situation for a job interview portfolio. Briefly, write down notes that define the topic, angle, purpose, readers, and contexts for this kind of portfolio. Also, discuss how the rhetorical situation might change to suit different kinds of job interviews.

2. Go online and find an e-portfolio created by a college student. What kinds of artifacts are included? Is there anything surprising about the documents or projects the student has included? How is the portfolio organized and designed? Does the organization make things easy to find?

3. Go online and find at least two professional e-portfolios from people who are pursuing a career like the one you want to pursue. What is included in their portfolios? How well does the cover letter introduce and explain the contents of the portfolio?

Try This Out

1. **Create a mini-portfolio.** With your most recent assignment in this course, create a mini-portfolio that charts your progress from prewriting through drafts and feedback to final drafts. Write a cover letter in which you reflect on your writing process for this assignment. In your reflection, make a claim about your learning and support it.

2. **Critique an e-portfolio on the Internet.** Find an interesting e-portfolio on the Internet. Write a three-page rhetorical analysis in which you analyze its effectiveness. How does the author use reasoning (*logos*) to demonstrate his or her knowledge and abilities? How does he or she build up a sense of authority (*ethos*)? Where, if anyplace, does the author use emotion (*pathos*) to add personality to the portfolio?

Write This

For additional reading, writing, and research resources, go to **www.mycomplab.com**.

31

Succeeding on
Essay Exams

Taking essay exams can be a little stressful, but once you learn a few helpful strategies, they will be much easier. You can succeed on essay exams by using some of the time-tested rhetorical strategies you have already learned in this book.

Keep in mind that professors use essay exams to evaluate how well you understand the course materials and whether you can apply what you learned. Exams give you opportunities to demonstrate higher-order thinking skills, such as interpreting ideas, applying concepts to new situations, analyzing solutions, synthesizing knowledge, and evaluating beliefs.

This chapter will help you succeed by showing you what to expect in college essay exams and providing strategies that will help you prepare for and write them. You will learn a four-stage process for doing well on essay exams: preparing, starting the exam, answering the questions, and finishing the exam (Figure 31.1).

Preparing for an Essay Exam

Studying course materials closely and taking good notes during lectures are important first steps for succeeding on exams. In addition, though, you should prepare for an essay exam by *being active* with the material. Here are some strategies for doing so.

Work in Study Groups

In your class or at your residence, find two to five other dedicated students who are willing to meet regularly to study together and collaborate on projects. It helps to find

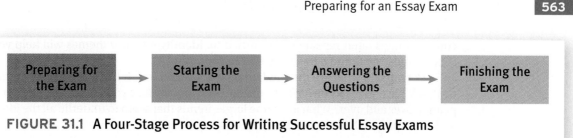

FIGURE 31.1 A Four-Stage Process for Writing Successful Essay Exams

To be successful on essay exams, you should think of the writing process in four stages.

group members who understand the material both better than you and not as well as you. People who have already mastered the material can help you strengthen your own understanding. Likewise, when you help others learn course content, you strengthen your own understanding of the material.

Set up a regular time and place to meet with your study group, perhaps one to three times a week. Your university's student union, library, or a local café can be good places for regular meetings.

Ask Your Professor About the Exam

You can often improve your chances of succeeding on an exam by asking your professor about it during class or office hours. Your professor may be willing to provide you with sample questions or examples from previous semesters' tests. However, professors don't like it when students "grade grub" by constantly asking, "Will this be on the test?" Instead, ask more open-ended questions like these:

- What kinds of questions are likely to appear on the exam?
- What kinds of things do you expect us to be able to do on the exam?
- How many questions will be on the exam, and how long should each take to answer?
- How do you think we should prepare for this exam?
- Can you give us a list of five to ten concepts or key ideas that we should master for this exam?
- Can you describe what a typical answer to the exam question would look like?

One or two questions like these will almost always be welcome.

Pay Attention to Themes

As you look over your lecture notes and textbook, look for thematic patterns to help you organize and remember the course material. A theme is a consistent idea or concept that is often repeated or returned to. Identifying a few themes will help you keep all those facts and details together in your mind.

Ask yourself, what are the fundamental ideas and topics that your professor and textbook have focused on? What are some key points that your professor keeps repeating over and over? What are some larger trends that seem to underlie all the ideas and concepts you have learned in this class?

Create Your Own Questions and Rehearse Possible Answers

Come up with your own questions that you think might appear on the exam and generate responses to them. You can rehearse your responses a few different ways:

- **Talk to yourself:** Mentally run through your responses and, if possible, say your answers out loud.
- **Talk to others:** Talk through answers with members of your study group.
- **Outline or plan out responses:** By yourself or with others, use outlines to map out possible responses. Then express your answers orally or in writing (on paper, your computer, or a whiteboard).
- **Simulate the actual exam:** Write a response or two within a set amount of time. If you have test anxiety and tend to go blank before an exam, try to practice in the actual classroom where you will be taking the test (classrooms are often empty in the evening).

Starting Your Essay Exam

So the professor has just handed you the exam. Now what? First, take a deep breath and relax. Second, avoid the impulse to just dive right in.

Review the Exam Quickly to Gain an Overall Picture

Take a moment to review the whole exam. Pay attention to the kinds of questions, how much time is recommended for each, and how many points each is worth. Pay special attention to the questions that are worth the most because you will want to leave extra time for them.

As you read each question, jot down a few quick notes or a brief outline and move on to the next question. These notes and outlines have two benefits: first, they help you warm up by putting your ideas down on the page before you start writing, and, second, they will show your professor where you were going with each answer even if you run out of time. Your professor won't give you full credit for an outline, but he or she might give you partial credit if you were answering the question correctly.

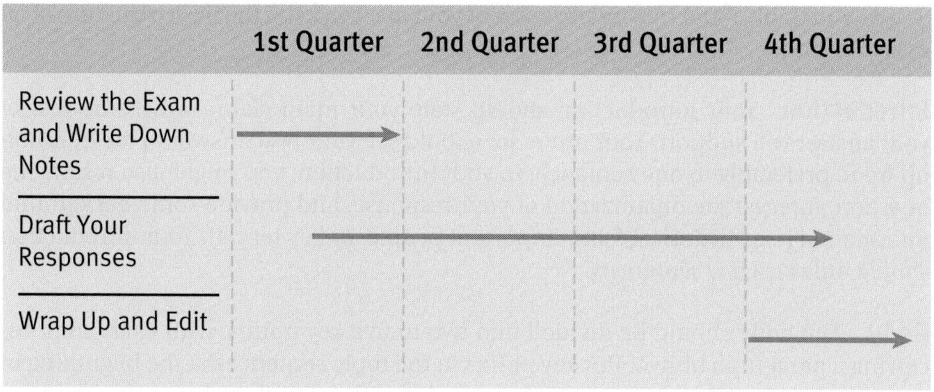

	1st Quarter	2nd Quarter	3rd Quarter	4th Quarter
Review the Exam and Write Down Notes	→			
Draft Your Responses		→		
Wrap Up and Edit				→

FIGURE 31.2 Budgeting Your Time

Don't just dive in and start writing. Take some of your total time to plan your answers, and be sure to leave time at the end to write conclusions and do some final insertions, editing, and proofreading.

Budget Your Time

Allocate your time properly, so you can answer all the questions. As shown in Figure 31.2, it might help to think in quarters about the time available for your essay exam. Spend a portion of the first quarter considering each question, jotting down some notes, and outlining a possible answer for each question. Devote the second and third quarters to actually drafting your answers one by one. Save some of the fourth quarter for revising, editing, and proofreading.

Answering an Essay Exam Question

When answering an essay exam question, your goal is to demonstrate how much you *know* about the course material and what you can *do* with it. So for most essay exam questions, you will want to keep the organization and style of your response fairly simple and straightforward.

Organize Your Answer

Remember that an essay exam answer should always have an introduction, body, and conclusion. That advice might sound obvious, but under pressure, people often forget these three parts. Instead, they just start writing everything they know about the topic. This often leads to a jumble of facts, names, and concepts that are hard to understand.

As you think about the organization of your answer, keep the basic structure of an essay in mind:

Introduction. Your introduction should state your main claim, which the rest of your answer will support. Your professor should see your best answer to the question up front, preferably in one sentence. In your introduction, you might also restate the question, forecast the organization of your response, and provide some background information (e.g., historical facts, important people, or key terms). Your introduction should only be a few sentences.

Body. The body should be divided into two to five key points, with each point receiving a paragraph or two. Put key points in the topic sentences at the beginning of your paragraphs. Then support each key point with facts, data, reasoning, and examples. Usually, you will find that the professor is asking you to do one of the following things:

- *Explain* a historical event, story plot, or process (narrative or summary).
- *Describe* something or explain how it works (description).
- *Define* something (definition).
- *Divide* something into groups or types (classification).
- *Compare* two or more things (comparison and contrast).
- *Argue* for or against (summary of both sides, argument for one).
- *Solve* a problem (description of problem and argument for a solution).

Once you know what your professor is asking you to do, the structure of your answer will become much more obvious.

Conclusion. Briefly indicate that you are wrapping up (e.g., "In conclusion,") and restate your main point. If time allows, you may also want to raise a new question or problem, describe the implications of your response, state the significance of the problem, or make a prediction about the future.

Above all, keep your answers simple and straightforward. Your professor isn't expecting you to come up with a new theory or an amazing breakthrough. He or she is looking for evidence that you have mastered the materials and can do something with what you have learned.

Finishing Your Essay Exam

Save a little time at the end of the exam for revising and editing. You won't have much time, so focus on completeness and clarity.

Checklist for Revising and Editing Essay Exams

☐ Reread each prompt to make sure you answered the question.

☐ Look for any missing key points and determine if you have time to add them.

☐ Check whether your ideas are clear and easy to follow.

☐ Emphasize key terms and concepts by inserting them or highlighting them.

☐ Proofread for grammatical errors, spelling mistakes, and garbled handwriting.

Remember, you will gain nothing by racing through the exam and being the first person out the door. You won't look any smarter, and your professor really won't be that impressed. So you may as well use all the time available to do the best job you can.

One Student's Essay Exam

To demonstrate some of the ideas from this chapter, here is a typical essay exam response written by a student. His answer is clear and straightforward. The organization is basic, and the style is plain. It's not perfect, but it achieves the student's goals of showing that he understands the course materials and can do something with that information.

Essay Prompt: In your opinion, which world region or subregion has the greatest potential to improve its development status over the course of your lifetime? Why? What environmental, human, and/or economic resources could it depend on in this process?

Shane Oreck

Question 3B

> Prominently identifies which question he is answering.

The region that has the greatest potential to improve is Latin America. The reasons for this are: its natural resources, technological potential, tourism potential, and human resources.

> Introduction restates the question, makes a clear main claim, forecasts the answer, and uses keywords from lectures and readings.

First, countries within Latin America have a bounty of natural and biological resources. If these countries eventually become able to excavate these minerals in a more efficient manner, then their economy will boom. In the Amazon, many countries are looking toward this uncharted area in hopes of finding biological sources that will help in the areas of science and health. So with time and ingenuity, hopefully this will help Latin America's economy as well.

Each body paragraph begins with a strong topic sentence that announces a key point.

Second, because Latin America is so close to more technologically advanced countries, they have a great potential for technological advancement. This would be better accomplished through a new trade pact with countries in North America and even Russia. If Latin America can make trade a more viable source of income, then the economy will probably boom, bringing with it technological advance and outside sources that could be of importance for these countries.

The writing style is simple and straightforward.

Third, tourism has great potential because of Latin America's beautiful oceans, views, landscapes, historical attractions, and architecture. They do face difficulties in terms of modern facilities and safety for Western guests, but if they can create the infrastructure, then, like Mexico, they could enjoy substantial economic relief from the money generated. Some Latin American countries, like Brazil, are already enticing travelers into their areas.

Lastly, Latin America has a vast array of human resources. Although current educational resources are lacking, these countries are heavily populated. With improved educational opportunity and greater availability of birth control (so that women can plan families and enjoy educational opportunities as well), the people of Latin America would be an enormous untapped resource in which to revitalize the region, economically and culturally.

The conclusion wraps up with its main point and a look to the future.

It's true also that many other regions of the world, including China and India, would be candidates for greatest potential for improving their development status. But because of its location, abundance of mineral and biological resources, trade and technological potential, tourism, and human resources, Latin America certainly has the potential for creating a bright future. Besides, Latin America has been so poorly developed for so long, it seems due for a resurgence. Where else can it go but up?

Pay attention to the straightforward nature of this exam answer. The student used a simple organizational pattern, with a clear introduction, body, and conclusion. The main points are easy to locate in the paragraph's topic sentences. Specific and meaningful facts, details, and reasoning are used to support claims. As demonstrated in this essay exam, your goal is to keep your answers simple, demonstrating that you know the material and can use it to make an argument. Figure 31.3 shows some other typical essay exam questions and a few strategies for answering them.

FIGURE 31.3 Sample Essay Exam Questions

Knowing: Understanding the Course Material

Question Cues	Strategy	Examples
Knowing • explain • define • describe • classify • compare	Know the major ideas, dates, events, places, and so on.	**Deaf Studies** Describe the events surrounding the 1880 Milan conference. What were the historical, educational, and philosophical themes that emerged at this conference? Who were the key players and what were their positions? What was the significance for Deaf culture? (12 points) **History** Bradbury describes ten major causes of the Industrial Revolution. List five of them and explain how each contributed to the industrialization of Europe. (5 points) **Sociology** Explain the difference between participant and nonparticipant research, how each is used in sociological research, and for what purposes each is used.
Understanding • summarize • explain • compare	Grasp the meaning of important ideas, facts, and theories. Compare two ideas, positions, or theories.	**Developmental Psychology** Compare the stages of personality development according to Piaget and Erikson. **Management** Identify whether each of the following scenarios is best described as a differential cost, opportunity cost, or sunk cost. (5 points each)

Doing: Applying, Analyzing, Synthesizing, and Evaluating Course Material

Question Cues	Strategy	Examples
Applying • explain • describe • compare • solve	Use information, methods, concepts, and theories in new contexts to solve problems, discover relationships, or illustrate concepts.	**Cost Management** The Pointilla T-Shirt Company produces high-quality casual apparel for a name-brand company in the United States. Management needs an analysis of their product and period costs so they can develop plans for controlling them. Given the following costs, calculate the total product and period costs. . . . **Art History** Use an iconographical analysis to describe the qualities, nature, and history of the statue pictured below.
Analyzing • explain • define • classify	Recognize patterns; interpret causes and effects; identify components.	**American Literature** Compare the essays on Faulker's "A Rose for Emily" by literary critics George L. Dillon and Judith Fetterley. How does each critic explain the uses of literature—i.e., what we *gain* by reading literature? **Nursing** Explain the difference between *glycemic index* and *glycemic load* to two audiences: (1) a class of first-year medical students (who have a good understanding of biochemistry), and (2) the parents of a child with diabetes (who have an eighth grade education and do not know, for instance, the difference between carbohydrates, proteins, and fat). (30 minutes)

continued

FIGURE 31.3 Sample Essay Exam Questions *(continued)*

Question Cues	Strategy	Examples
Synthesizing • combine • create • develop a plan • argue for or against	Generalize from facts; combine knowledge from different areas; make predictions; draw conclusions.	**Literature** Consider William Faulkner's short story "A Rose for Emily" and Maya Quinlan's feminist analysis of Chopin's "Story of an Hour." Using what you've learned about feminist approaches to literature from Quinlan's article, predict how a feminist critic like Quinlan would interpret "A Rose for Emily." Be sure to state her overall interpretation and describe at least three aspects of the short story that she would probably attend to and *why* you think a feminist critic would find those aspects important.
		Pharmacy The chemical formulas and structures for Pharmaceutical A and Pharmaceutical B are shown in the figure below. Explain from a biochemical perspective what would happen if the two drugs were taken simultaneously. In your response, be sure to identify the relevant function groups present in each compound, classify each pharmaceutical, relate some of the structural features of the compound to physical and chemical properties, and discuss the consequences of confusing the two drugs.
Evaluating • assess • argue for or against • solve	Compare and evaluate ideas, models, theories, or plans.	**Introductory Earth Sciences** Describe how the geology, climate, and biology (focusing on plants and animals) of London, England, have changed from the Late Triassic Period to the present. Use the figures below depicting the drift of the continents and apply your knowledge of plate tectonics, climatology, and paleobiology to support your answer.
		Geography In your opinion, which world region or subregion has the greatest potential to improve its development status over the course of your lifetime? Why? What environmental, human, and/or economic resources could it depend on in this process?

Essay exams can be challenging, but you will be more successful if you prepare properly. To do your best, follow these steps.

PREPARE for the Exam

Take good notes on lectures and readings, but also consider the key themes and issues that your professor keeps returning to. Form and regularly meet with a study group. Go to your professor and ask what the exam will look like, and what he or she wants to see in an exam response.

START the Exam

First read through the entire text to get the big picture, making note of how much time you have and the point value for each question. Budget your time so you can outline some answers, write out the exam, and revise and edit.

ANSWER the Questions

Make sure you understand what each question is asking you to do (explain, describe, define, classify, compare, argue for or against, or solve a problem). As you write, stay focused and try to maintain a simple, straightforward organization and style.

FINISH Up with Revising and Editing

Reread the questions and make sure your responses answer them. Make any adjustments needed and highlight places where you address the question directly. Save some time for proofreading.

1. Individually, freewrite an answer to this question: What is hard about writing essay exams? After you've written your response, discuss your answer with your group and come up with three strategies for making essay exams more manageable.

2. In a group or in an informal written response, examine the student example in this chapter. Explain why its structure is appropriate for an essay exam.

3. In a group, talk about the essay exam response as a genre. What other genres does it resemble and in what ways?

1. As an informal writing assignment, create at least two essay exam prompts for another course you are taking. Share them with your group.

2. Find a textbook that has questions at the ends of the chapters and choose one question that you think could be on an essay exam. Make an outline of how you would respond to that question on an essay exam. Discuss your outline with your group.

3. Type "sample essay exam" into an Internet search engine and locate three examples of essay exam questions. Analyze these questions and explain what kinds of content, organization, and style would be appropriate in an answer.

1. **Write a practice essay exam.** As practice, write an essay exam response to a prompt created by your professor. When you are finished, compare your responses with those of your classmates.

2. **Argue for or against essay exams in college.** Write a letter to the editor of your campus newspaper. In your letter, argue for or against the use of essay exams as a way of testing students. If you are arguing against using essay exams, what would be a suitable replacement for them?

PEARSON
mycomplab

For additional reading, writing, and research resources, go to **www.mycomplab.com**.

Presenting
Your Work

Y ou will need to make public presentations in your college courses and in the workplace. More and more, professors are asking students to present their projects to an audience. And almost any professional career will require you to present information, ideas, and opinions. Your ability to speak effectively in front of an audience will be an important cornerstone of your success.

In fact, public speaking is becoming more important as new technologies, like video streaming and video conferencing, become common features of the modern workplace. These new media make it possible to present the material in real time and answer your audience's questions.

Most genres go hand in hand with public presentations. For instance, in the workplace it is common for people to present proposals and reports to their clients. In your advanced college courses, you will be asked to present evaluations, commentaries, and position papers as well as research reports.

In this chapter, we are going to show you some easy strategies for turning your documents into public presentations. If you learn and practice a few simple techniques, your presentations will be more effective.

Getting Started

Because this book is about writing, not public speaking, we are going to assume that you have already written a document that you need to turn into a presentation. Now it is time to take that written text and repurpose it into a presentation for an audience.

Ask a Few Key Questions to Get Started

Solid preparation is the key to successful public speaking. A good way to start preparing is to ask the Five-W and How questions:

- *What* do I want to accomplish with my presentation?
- *Who* will be in my audience and what do they need?
- *Why* am I presenting this information to this audience?
- *Where* will I be giving my presentation?
- *When* will I be asked to speak?
- *How* should I give the presentation?

Answer each of these questions separately. Your answers will give you an overview of what you need to do to prepare for your presentation.

Something to keep in mind is that your audience wants more from you than just the information in your document. After all, if they wanted to, they could just read it. So why do they want you to present it to them instead? A presentation gives members of your audience a chance to interact with you and ask questions. Your audience wants to see you in action. They want you to *perform* the material for them.

Ask yourself how you can make your presentation more interactive, more visual, and more entertaining than your original written text.

Choose the Appropriate Presentation Technology

Think about what technology will be available and which would fit your presentation. The technology you choose depends on the audience's expectations and the place where you will be giving your talk.

Each kind of presentation technology offers advantages and disadvantages. Figure 32.1 describes some of the advantages and disadvantages of each.

Allot Your Time

If you are new to speaking in public, a five- to ten-minute presentation might sound like a lifetime. The time, though, will go fast. A ten-minute presentation, for example, is only the equivalent of a four- or five-page paper. So you will need to budget your time carefully to avoid going over the time allowed.

Figure 32.2 on page 576 shows how to budget the time for a presentation with three major topics. Of course, if your paper has fewer or more than three topics, you should make adjustments in the times allowed for each one. These time limits are flexible guidelines, not rigid rules.

FIGURE 32.1
Pros and Cons
of Presentation
Technologies

	Advantages	Disadvantages	Genres
 **Digital Projector**	• Can be dynamic and colorful • Allows for animation and sound • Creates a more formal atmosphere	• Requires a darkened room, which might inconvenience your audience • Diverts attention from the speaker to the screen • Computers are not completely reliable	Memoirs, Profiles, Reviews, Evaluations, Literary Analyses, Rhetorical Analyses, Position Papers, Proposals, and Reports
 **Overhead Projector**	• Projectors are available in most workplaces and classrooms • Easy to print transparencies from most home printers	• May seem static and lifeless • Need to manually change transparencies during your presentation	Evaluations, Literary Analyses, Rhetorical Analyses, Position Papers, Proposals, and Reports
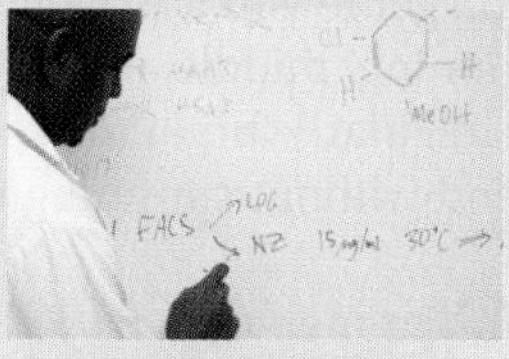 **Whiteboard, Chalkboard, Notepad**	• Allows speaker to create visuals on the spot • Audience pays more attention because speaker is moving	• Cannot be used with a large audience • Writing on board requires extra time • Ideas need to be transferred clearly to the board	Evaluations, Commentaries, Position Papers, Proposals, and Reports
 **Poster Presentation**	• Allows audience to see whole presentation • Presents highly technical information clearly • Allows audience to ask specific questions	• Cannot be presented to more than a few people • Can be hard to transport	Memoirs, Profiles, Reviews, Evaluations, Literary Analyses, Rhetorical Analyses, Position Papers, Proposals, and Reports
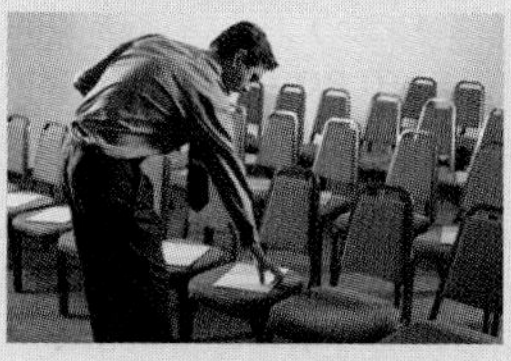 **Handouts**	• Helps reinforce major points • Can offer more detail, data, and statistics • Audience has something to take home	• Handing them out can be distracting in large presentations • Audience members may read the handouts instead of listen to the talk	Profiles, Reviews, Evaluations, Literary Analyses, Rhetorical Analyses, Position Papers, Proposals, and Reports

FIGURE 32.2
Allotting Your Presentation Time

When planning your presentation, allot your time carefully to scale your talk to the time allowed.

	5-Minute Presentation	10-Minute Presentation	20-Minute Presentation
Introduction	Half a minute	1 minute	1–2 minutes
Topic 1	1 minute	2 minutes	5 minutes
Topic 2	1 minute	2 minutes	5 minutes
Topic 3	1 minute	2 minutes	5 minutes
Conclusion	Half a minute	1 minute	1 minute
Questions and Answers	1 minute	2 minutes	3 minutes

Organizing Your Presentation's Content

The organization of your presentation will typically follow the genre you are using to organize your document. Your talk should have a clear beginning, middle, and end. That advice might seem rather obvious, but public speakers regularly forget to properly introduce their talk to the audience, or they abruptly end without summing up their main points.

There is an old speechmaking saying you should commit to memory: *Tell them what you're going to tell them. Tell them. Tell them what you told them.*

Introduction: Tell Them What You're Going to Tell Them

The introduction of your talk is almost always the most critical part of your whole presentation. At the beginning of your speech, you have a small window—perhaps a minute or two—to capture the audience's attention while stating your topic, purpose, and main point. If you don't grab the audience at this point, they may tune out for the rest of your talk.

A shorter presentation with a brief introduction will make two or three of the following moves, while a long introduction might include all six:

Identify your topic. Tell your audience what your presentation is about.

State the purpose of your presentation. Explain what you are going to do in your talk.

State your main point. Tell them what you want to prove or support.

Stress the importance of your topic to the audience. Explain why this issue is important to them and why they should pay attention.

Offer background information on the subject. Provide enough information to familiarize the audience with your topic.

Forecast the structure of your talk. Tell them how your talk will be organized.

Even if you are naturally funny, starting your presentation with a joke is risky. The problem with jokes is that they often flop, and they can be offensive in ways you might not anticipate.

Instead of telling a joke, think of a good *grabber* to start out your speech. A grabber states something interesting or challenging that captures the audience's attention. Some effective grabbers include:

A rhetorical question: "Do you ever wonder why child actors tend to have personal problems when they become adults?"

A startling statistic: "A recent survey shows that 74 percent of women students report that they have been sexually harassed at this university. Meanwhile, 43 percent of male students report they have been harassed."

A compelling statement: "If nothing is done about global climate change, it is likely that polar bears will become extinct in the wild during our lifetime."

An anecdote: "Last year, I finally climbed my first mountain over 14,000 feet. In many ways, climbing that mountain affirmed to me that I had triumphed over the injuries I sustained in Iraq two years before."

A show of hands: "Let's see a show of hands. How many of you think the pizza here in town leaves something to be desired?"

A good grabber identifies your topic while giving your audience a little something to think about.

The Body of Your Talk: Tell Them

The body of your presentation is where you are going to state your major points and support them with facts, reasoning, examples, data, quotations, and any other forms of proof you can offer.

In most situations, the body of your presentation should follow the same pattern as the body of your document. Divide your text into two to five major issues that you want to discuss with the audience. If you try to cover more than five topics, you risk overwhelming the audience with more new information than they can handle. So organize the body of your talk to feature the most important things you want them to remember.

Here's a good strategy that might help you strip down your talk to something you can handle in a small amount of time. Look through your document and ask yourself,

"What does my audience *need* to know about this topic to make a decision?" Then cross out any material that goes beyond need-to-know information.

Conclusion: Tell Them What You Told Them

People make this mistake all the time. They finish the body of their talk. Then they shrug their shoulders and say something like, "That's all I have to say. Any questions?" This kind of abrupt ending feels awkward, and it misses an opportunity to drive home the presentation's main point.

Here's a better way to handle your conclusion. Once you clearly signal that you are about to conclude, you will have the audience's heightened attention for the next two minutes. Take advantage of this by repeating your main point in a clear and memorable way. A typical conclusion will include some or all of the following moves:

Signal clearly that you are concluding. Make an obvious transition that signals the end of your talk, such as "Let me wrap up now" or "Finally."

Restate your main point. Tell your audience exactly what you have been trying to explain or prove in your talk.

Reemphasize the importance of your topic to the audience. Be clear about why the audience should care about your topic. Answer their "Why should I care?" questions.

Call the audience to action. If you want the people in your audience to do something, tell them what you think they should do. Be specific about the actions you want them to take.

Thank the audience. When you are finished, don't forget to say, "thank you." This phrase signals the audience that your presentation is done, and it usually prompts them to give you some applause.

Remember to keep your conclusion brief. Once you say something like, "In conclusion," you have one or two minutes to finish up. If you ramble beyond a couple of minutes, your audience will be annoyed.

Question and Answer

At the end of your talk, you should be prepared to answer a few questions from the audience. The question and answer period offers you a good opportunity to interact with the audience and clarify your ideas. During the question and answer period, you should be ready to answer three types of questions:

A Request for Clarification or Elaboration. These types of questions are opportunities to reinforce some of your key points. When you field this kind of question, start out by rephrasing it for the audience. Rephrasing will allow you to put the issue in your own words and state it loudly enough for the whole audience to hear. Then answer the question, expanding on the information you provided in your talk.

A Hostile Question. Occasionally, an audience member will ask a question that challenges the information you provided in your talk. Here is a good three-step strategy for answering these kinds of questions:

1. **Rephrase the question.** State the question in terms that will allow you to answer it in ways that reflect your own beliefs.

2. **Validate the question.** Tell the audience that you understand the questioner's concerns and even share them.

3. **Elaborate and move forward.** Explain that the course of action you are supporting is preferable because it addresses the issue more appropriately or seems more reasonable.

The Heckling Question. In rare cases, an audience member will want to heckle you with hostile questions. In these cases, you need to recognize that the questioner is *trying* to sabotage your presentation. He or she wants you to become flustered. Don't let the heckler do that to you. After trying your best to answer one or two questions from a heckler, simply say, "I'm sorry you feel that way. We have other people with questions. Perhaps we can meet after my talk to discuss your concerns." Then look away from that person. Usually, someone else in the audience will ask a question and you can move on.

When the question and answer period is over, you should briefly thank the audience again. This will usually prompt another round of applause.

Designing Your Visual Aids

Visual aids will help you clarify your ideas and illustrate your main points for the audience. Perhaps the best way to create visual aids is to make slides with the presentation software (*PowerPoint, Keynote,* or *Presentations*) that came with your word-processing software.

Format Your Slides

Whether you are presenting in a large lecture hall with a projector or to a few people with a poster presentation, slides are some of the best visual aids available (Figure 32.3, page 580). Here are some strategies for formatting your slides:

- Title each slide with an action-oriented heading.

- Put five or fewer major points on each slide. If you have more than five major points, divide that topic into two slides.

FIGURE 32.3
Creating Slides

Shown here are a title slide and a body slide from a profile paper repurposed as a presentation. The photographs add a strong visual identity to the slides.

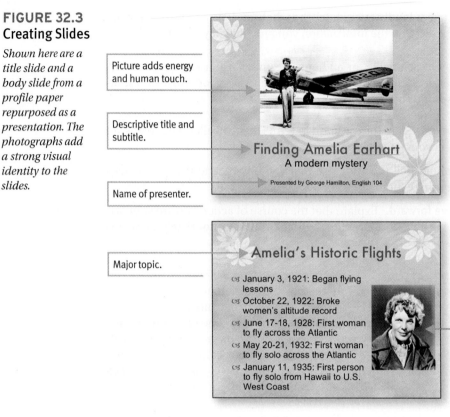

Picture adds energy and human touch.

Descriptive title and subtitle.

Name of presenter.

Major topic.

Picture keeps audience's attention.

- Use left-justified text for most items on your slides. Centered text should only be used for the titles of your slides.

- Use dark text on a white or light background whenever possible. Light text on a dark background can be difficult to read.

- Use bulleted lists of phrases instead of paragraphs or sentences.

- Use photos, icons, and graphics to keep your slides fresh and active for the audience. Make sure your graphics look good on the screen. Increasing the size of a Web-based graphic, for example, can make the image look blurry or grainy.

You will be tempted to pack too much material onto each slide. Effective slides, like the ones shown in Figure 32.3, need to be simple and easy to interpret. You don't want your audience trying to puzzle out the meaning of your complicated slides instead of listening to your talk.

Delivering Your Presentation

How you deliver your talk will make a significant impact on your audience. The usual advice is to "be yourself" when you are speaking in public. Of course, that's good advice for people who are comfortable speaking in front of an audience. Better advice is to "be the person the audience expects." In other words, like an actor, play the role that fits your topic and your audience.

Body Language

Ideally, the movements of your body should help you reinforce your message and maintain the audience's attention.

Dress Appropriately. Your choice of clothing needs to reflect your audience's expectations and the topic of your talk. Even when you are presenting to your classmates, you should view it as an opportunity to practice your workplace and professional demeanor. Dress as though you are presenting in a professional workplace, not as if you were simply going to class.

Stand Up Straight. When speakers are nervous, they tend to slouch, lean, or rock back and forth. This looks unprofessional and makes it difficult to breathe calmly. Instead, keep your feet squarely under your shoulders with knees slightly bent. Keep your shoulders back and down and your head up to allow good airflow. If your shoulders are forward and up, you won't get enough air and the pitch of your voice will seem unnaturally high.

Use Open Hand and Arm Gestures. For most audiences, open hand and arm gestures will convey trust and confidence. Avoid folding your arms, keeping your arms at your sides, or putting both hands in your pockets, as these poses will convey a defensive posture that audiences do not trust.

Make Eye Contact. Everyone in the audience should believe you made eye contact with him or her at least once during your presentation. If you are nervous about making eye contact, look at the audience members' foreheads instead. They will think you are looking them directly in the eye.

Move to Reinforce Major Points or Transitions. If possible, when you make important points, step forward toward the audience. When you make transitions in your presentation from one topic to the next, move to the left or right. Your movement across the floor will highlight the transitions in your speech.

Voice and Tone

As you improve your presentation skills, you should start paying more attention to your voice and tone.

Speak Lower and Slower. When speaking to an audience, you will need to speak louder than you normally would. As your volume goes up, so will the pitch of your voice, making it sound unnaturally high to the audience. By consciously lowering your voice, you should sound just about right. Also, nerves may cause you to speak too quickly. Silently remind yourself to speak slowly.

Use Pauses to Reinforce Your Major Points. Each time you make a major point, pause for a moment to let the audience commit it to memory.

Use Pauses to Eliminate Verbal Tics. Verbal tics like "um," "ah," "like," and "you know," "OK?" and "See what I mean?" are nervous habits that fill gaps between thoughts. If you have a verbal tic, train yourself to pause when you feel like using one of these sounds or phrases. Before long, you will find them disappearing from your speech.

Minimize How Often You Look Down at Your Notes. You should try to look at your notes as little as possible. When you look down at your notes, your neck bends, restricting your airflow and lowering your volume. Plus, notes can become a distracting "safe place" that keeps you from engaging visually with your audience.

Practicing and Rehearsing

You should leave plenty of time to practice your presentation out loud. Even better advice, though, is to "rehearse" what you are going to say and how you are going to say it. Rehearsal allows you to practice your presentation in a more realistic setting.

Practice, Practice, Practice

Practice involves speaking your presentation out loud to yourself. As you are working through your presentation verbally, you should memorize its major points and gain a sense of its organization and flow. While practicing, you should:

- Listen for any problems with content, organization, and style.
- Edit and proofread your visuals and handouts.
- Decide how you are going to move around as you deliver the speech.
- Pay attention to your body language and voice.

If you notice any problems as you are practicing your presentation, you can stop and fix them right away.

Rehearse, Rehearse, Rehearse

The secret to polishing your presentation is to rehearse it several times. Unlike practice, rehearsal means giving the presentation from beginning to end *without stopping*.

As much as possible, you want to replicate the experience of giving your real talk. After each rehearsal session, you should make any revisions or corrections.

Recruit friends to listen as you rehearse your presentation. They will provide you with a live audience, so you can gauge their reactions to your ideas. Ideally, they will also give you constructive feedback that you can use to improve the presentation. Another possibility is recording your presentation, with either audiovisual or just audio.

Practicing will help you find any major problems with your talk, but rehearsal will help you turn the whole package into an effective presentation.

Here are some helpful guidelines for developing and giving presentations.

ANSWER the Five-W and How Questions About Your Presentation

Think about the who, what, where, when, why, and how issues that will shape the content, organization, style, and design of your presentation.

CHOOSE the Appropriate Presentation Technology

Depending on the size of your audience and the room in which you will be speaking, consider what kind of presentation technology would best allow you to present your ideas.

ORGANIZE Your Ideas

More than likely, the genre of your document offers a good organization for your talk. Remember to "Tell them what you're going to tell them. Tell them. Tell them what you told them."

DESIGN Your Visual Aids

Slides work well for most presentations. Use presentation software, such as *PowerPoint, Keynote,* or *Presentations,* to convert your paper into a colorful and interesting set of slides. If slides aren't appropriate, you should look into the possibility of using a whiteboard or handouts.

THINK About Your Body Language

Consider issues like how you will dress, and how you will stand and move when you are presenting. Practice making eye contact with people.

IMPROVE Your Voice and Tone

Work on speaking lower and slower, while using pauses to reinforce your major points. Also, use pauses to eliminate any verbal tics, such as "um," "ah," "like," and "you know."

PRACTICE and Rehearse

Ultimately, practice and rehearsal are the best ways to improve and polish your presentation. Use practice to help you revise your talk and correct errors. Use rehearsal to polish your presentation and make it as persuasive as possible.

1. In a small group, share your opinions about what works well in a presentation. Discuss effective and ineffective presenters (coaches, teachers, public speakers). What traits made these people effective or ineffective as public speakers?

2. Find a video clip online of a particularly problematic speech. Imagine that you and your group are this person's speaking coach. Being as helpful as possible, what advice would you give this person to improve his or her future presentations?

3. With your group, choose three things from this chapter that you would like to use to improve your presentation skills. Then take turns presenting these three things to your "audience."

Talk About This

1. Find a speech on a video Web site. In a brief rhetorical analysis, discuss the strengths and weaknesses of the presentation. Specifically, pay attention to the content, organization, style, and use of visuals in the presentation.

2. Outline a two-minute speech on a subject that you know well. Then, without much further thought, give a presentation to a small group of people from your class. Practice making the six introductory moves mentioned in this chapter and the five concluding moves.

3. Using presentation software, turn one of the papers you wrote for this class into slides. Break your paper down into major and minor points and add pictures and illustrations that will help your audience visualize your ideas. Print out your slides and look for any inconsistencies in wording or places where you could reorganize.

Try This Out

1. **Evaluate a public presentation.** Attend a public presentation on your campus. Instead of listening to the content of the presentation, pay attention to how it was organized and presented. Then write a review, a rave, or a slam of the presentation. Use the presentation strategies described in this chapter to discuss the strengths and weaknesses of the speaker and his or her talk.

2. **Repurpose a written text into a presentation.** Choose a major project for this course or another one and turn it into a presentation. Choose the appropriate presentation technology. Make sure you develop an introduction that captures your audience's attention. Divide the body of your paper into two to five major topics. Then develop a conclusion that stresses your main points and looks to the future. When you have finished creating your talk, spend some time practicing and rehearsing it. Your professor may ask you to present your talk in class.

Write This

PEARSON
mycomplab

For additional reading, writing, and research resources, go to **www.mycomplab.com**.

Anthology
of Readings

This **ANTHOLOGY** provides noteworthy examples of the genres discussed in this book. Read on to discover how genres can be stretched or blended to achieve unique and creative purposes.

PART OUTLINE

33

Memoirs

The Way to Rainy Mountain

N. SCOTT MOMADAY

With his debut novel, House Made of Dawn *(1968), N. Scott Momaday opened doors for other Native American writers to publish their stories. Well known for retelling the history of the Kiowa people, who lived on the American Plains, Momaday was awarded the National Medal of Arts in 2007. The memoir included here, from* The Way to Rainy Mountain *(1969), tells the history of the Kiowa through his and his grandmother's lives. Watch how he uses his grandmother as a lens for telling a richer, more personal story. Like many memoir writers, Momaday uses others to reveal important insights about his own life.*

A single knoll rises out of the plain in Oklahoma, north and west of the Wichita Range. For my people, the Kiowas, it is an old landmark, and they gave it the name Rainy Mountain. The hardest weather in the world is there. Winter brings blizzards, hot tornadic winds arise in the spring, and in summer the prairie is an anvil's edge. The grass turns brittle and brown, and it cracks beneath your feet. There are green belts along the rivers and creeks, linear groves of hickory and pecan, willow and witch hazel. At a distance in July or August the steaming foliage seems almost to writhe in fire. Great green and yellow grasshoppers are everywhere in the tall grass, popping up like corn to sting the flesh, and tortoises crawl about on the red earth, going nowhere in the plenty of time. Loneliness is an aspect of the land. All things in the plain are isolate; there is no confusion of objects in the eye, but *one* hill or *one* tree or *one* man. To look upon that landscape in the early morning, with the sun at your back, is to lose the sense of proportion. Your imagination comes to life, and this, you think, is where Creation was begun.

I returned to Rainy Mountain in July. My grandmother had died in the spring, and I wanted to be at her grave. She had lived to be very old and at last infirm. Her only living daughter was with her when she died, and I was told that in death her face was that of a child.

I like to think of her as a child. When she was born, the Kiowas were living the last great moment of their history. For more than a hundred years they had controlled the open range from the Smoky Hill River to the Red, from the headwaters of the Canadian to the fork of the Arkansas and Cimarron. In alliance with the Comanches, they had ruled the whole of the southern Plains. War was their sacred business, and they were among the finest horsemen the world has ever known. But warfare for the Kiowas was preeminently a matter of disposition rather than of survival, and they never understood the grim, unrelenting advance of the U.S. Cavalry. When at last, divided and ill-provisioned, they were driven onto the Staked Plains in the cold rains of autumn, they fell into panic. In Palo Duro Canyon they abandoned their crucial stores to pillage and had nothing then but their lives. In order to save themselves, they surrendered to the soldiers at Fort Sill and were imprisoned in the old stone corral that now stands as a military museum. My grandmother was spared the humiliation of those high gray walls by eight or ten years, but she must have known from birth the affliction of defeat, the dark brooding of old warriors.

Her name was Aho, and she belonged to the last culture to evolve in North America. Her forebears came down from the high country in western Montana nearly three centuries ago. They were a mountain people, a mysterious tribe of hunters whose language has never been positively classified in any major group. In the late seventeenth century they began a long migration to the south and east. It was a journey toward the dawn, and it led to a golden age. Along the way the Kiowas were befriended by the Crows, who gave them the culture and religion of the Plains. They acquired horses, and their ancient nomadic spirit was suddenly free of the ground. They acquired Tai-me, the sacred Sun Dance doll, from that moment the object and symbol of their worship, and so shared in the divinity of the sun. Not least, they acquired the sense of destiny, therefore courage and pride. When they entered upon the southern Plains they had been transformed. No longer were they slaves to the simple necessity of survival; they were a lordly and dangerous society of fighters and thieves, hunters and priests of the sun. According to their origin myth, they entered the world through a hollow log. From one point of view, their migration was the fruit of an old prophecy, for indeed they emerged from a sunless world.

Although my grandmother lived out her 5 long life in the shadow of Rainy Mountain, the immense landscape of the continental interior lay like memory in her blood. She could tell of the Crows, whom she had never seen, and of the Black Hills, where she had never been. I wanted to see in reality what she had seen more perfectly in the mind's eye, and traveled fifteen hundred miles to begin my pilgrimage.

Yellowstone, it seemed to me, was the top of the world, a region of deep lakes and dark timber, canyons and waterfalls. But, beautiful as it is, one might have the sense of confinement there. The skyline in all directions is close at hand, the high wall of the woods and deep cleavages of shade. There is a perfect freedom in the mountains, but it belongs to the eagle and the elk, the badger and the bear. The Kiowas reckoned their stature by the distance they could see, and they were bent and blind in the wilderness.

Descending eastward, the highland meadows are a stairway to the plain. In July the inland slope of the Rockies is luxuriant with flax and buckwheat, stonecrop and larkspur. The earth unfolds and the limit of the land recedes. Clusters of trees, and animals grazing far in the distance, cause the vision to reach away and wonder to build upon the mind. The sun follows a longer course in the day, and the sky is immense beyond all comparison. The great billowing clouds that sail upon it are shadows that move upon the grain like water, dividing light. Farther down, in the land of the Crows and Blackfeet, the plain is yellow. Sweet clover takes hold of the hills and bends upon itself to cover and seal the soil. There the Kiowas paused on their way; they had come to the place where they must change their lives. The sun is at home on the plains. Precisely there does it have the certain character of a god. When the Kiowas came to the land of the Crows, they could see the dark lees of the hills at dawn across the Bighorn River, the profusion of light on the grain shelves, the oldest deity ranging after the solstices. Not yet would they veer southward to the caldron of the land that lay below; they must wean their blood from the northern winter and hold the mountains a while longer in their view. They bore Tai-me in procession to the east.

A dark mist lay over the Black Hills, and the land was like iron. At the top of a ridge I caught sight of Devil's Tower upthrust against the gray sky as if in the birth of time the core of the earth had broken through its crust and the motion of the world was begun. There are things in nature that engender an awful quiet in the heart of man; Devil's Tower is one of them. Two centuries ago, because they could not do otherwise, the Kiowas made a legend at the base of the rock. My grandmother said:

> Eight children were there at play, seven sisters and their brother. Suddenly the boy was struck dumb; he trembled and began to run upon his hands and feet. His fingers became claws, and his body was covered with fur. Directly there was a bear where the boy had been. The sisters were terrified; they ran, and the bear after them. They came to the stump of a great tree, and the tree spoke to them. It bade them climb upon it, and as they did so it began to rise into the air. The bear came to kill them, but they were just beyond its reach. It reared against the tree and scored the bark all around with its claws. The seven sisters were borne into the sky, and they became the stars of the Big Dipper.

From that moment, and so long as the legend lives, the Kiowas have kinsmen in the night sky. Whatever they were in the mountains, they could be no more. However tenuous their well-being, however much they had suffered and would suffer again, they had found a way out of the wilderness.

My grandmother had a reverence for the sun, a holy regard that now is all but gone out of mankind. There was a wariness in her, and an ancient awe. She was a Christian in her later years, but she had come a long way about, and she never forgot her birthright. As a child she had been to the Sun Dances; she had taken part in those annual rites, and by them she had learned the restoration of her people in the presence of Tai-me. She was about seven when the last Kiowa Sun Dance was held in 1887 on the Washita River above Rainy Mountain Creek. The buffalo were gone. In or-

der to consummate the ancient sacrifice—to impale the head of a buffalo bull upon the medicine tree—a delegation of old men journeyed into Texas, there to beg and barter for an animal from the Goodnight herd. She was ten when the Kiowas came together for the last time as a living Sun Dance culture. They could find no buffalo; they had to hang an old hide from the sacred tree. Before the dance could begin, a company of soldiers rode out from Fort Sill under orders to disperse the tribe. Forbidden without cause the essential act of their faith, having seen the wild herds slaughtered and left to rot upon the ground, the Kiowas backed away forever from the medicine tree. That was July 20, 1890, at the great bend of the Washita. My grandmother was there. Without bitterness, and for as long as she lived, she bore a vision of deicide.

Now that I can have her only in memory, 10 I see my grandmother in the several postures that were peculiar to her: standing at the wood stove on a winter morning and turning meat in a great iron skillet; sitting at the south window, bent above her beadwork, and afterwards, when her vision failed, looking down for a long time into the fold of her hands; going out upon a cane, very slowly as she did when the weight of age came upon her; praying. I remember her most often at prayer. She made long, rambling prayers out of suffering and hope, having seen many things. I was never sure that I had the right to hear, so exclusive were they of all mere custom and company. The last time I saw her she prayed standing by the side of her bed at night, naked to the waist, the light of a kerosene lamp moving upon her dark skin. Her long, black hair, always drawn and braided in the day, lay upon her shoulders and against her breasts like a shawl. I do not speak Kiowa, and I never understood her prayers, but there was something inherently sad in the sound, some merest hesitation upon the syllables of sorrow. She began in a high and descending pitch, exhausting her breath to silence; then again and again—and always the same intensity of effort, of something that is, and is not, like urgency in the human voice. Transported so in the dancing light among the shadows of her room, she seemed beyond the reach of time. But that was illusion; I think I knew then that I should not see her again.

Houses are like sentinels in the plain, old keepers of the weather watch. There, in a very little while, wood takes on the appearance of great age. All colors wear soon away in the wind and rain, and then the wood is burned gray and the grain appears and the nails turn red with rust. The windowpanes are black and opaque; you imagine there is nothing within, and indeed there are many ghosts, bones given up to the land. They stand here and there against the sky, and you approach them for a longer time than you expect. They belong in the distance; it is their domain.

Once there was a lot of sound in my grandmother's house, a lot of coming and going, feasting and talk. The summers there were full of excitement and reunion. The Kiowas are a summer people; they abide the cold and keep to themselves, but when the season turns and the land becomes warm and vital they cannot hold still; an old love of going returns upon them. The aged visitors who came to my grandmother's house when I was a child were made of lean and leather, and they bore themselves upright. They wore great black hats and bright ample shirts that shook in the wind. They rubbed fat upon their hair and wound their braids with strips of colored cloth. Some of them painted their faces and carried the scars of old and cherished enmities. They were an old council of warlords, come to remind and be reminded of who they were. Their wives and daughters served them well. The women might indulge themselves; gossip was at once the mark and compensation of their servitude. They made loud and elaborate talk among themselves, full of jest and gesture, fright and false alarm. They went abroad in fringed and flowered shawls, bright beadwork and German silver.

They were at home in the kitchen, and they prepared meals that were banquets.

There were frequent prayer meetings, and great nocturnal feasts. When I was a child I played with my cousins outside, where the lamplight fell upon the ground and the singing of the old people rose up around us and carried away into the darkness. There were a lot of good things to eat, a lot of laughter and surprise. And afterwards, when the quiet returned, I lay down with my grandmother and could hear the frogs away by the river and feel the motion of the air.

Now there is a funeral silence in the rooms, the endless wake of some final word. The walls have closed in upon my grandmother's house. When I returned to it in mourning, I saw for the first time in my life how small it was. It was late at night, and there was a white moon, nearly full. I sat for a long time on the stone steps by the kitchen door. From there I could see out across the land; I could see the long row of trees by the creek, the low light upon the rolling plains, and the stars of the Big Dipper. Once I looked at the moon and caught sight of a strange thing. A cricket had perched upon the handrail, only a few inches away from me. My line of vision was such that the creature filled the moon like a fossil. It had gone there, I thought, to live and die, for there, of all places, was its small definition made whole and eternal. A warm wind rose up and purled like the longing within me.

The next morning I awoke at dawn and 15 went out on the dirt road to Rainy Mountain. It was already hot, and the grasshoppers began to fill the air. Still, it was early in the morning, and the birds sang out of the shadows. The long yellow grass on the mountain shone in the bright light, and a scissortail hied above the land. There, where it ought to be, at the end of a long and legendary way, was my grandmother's grave. Here and there on the dark stones were ancestral names. Looking back once, I saw the mountain and came away.

A CLOSER LOOK AT
The Way to Rainy Mountain

1. In many ways, Momaday is writing a memoir of a people, the Kiowas, not just himself or his grandmother. How does he use events from his own life and his grandmother's life as a lens through which he can talk about the Kiowas?

2. This memoir is filled with visual imagery. Find five places where Momaday uses detail, especially visual detail, to heighten the reader's experience with the text. Then find one place each in which he uses sound, touch, smell, and taste to describe the world he is remembering.

3. Nature itself is a character in this memoir. Where in this memoir does nature seem to be taking on a living role? In what ways does Momaday use nature to move the story in this memoir forward?

IDEAS FOR
Writing

1. Write a profile of one of your own grandparents (or another older member of your family). As you draft your profile, pay special attention to how *place* shapes your understanding and memories of this person. In other words, how does this person's environment shape and define him or her for you?

2. Write a research report in which you explore where your ancestors came from. Who were your people? Where did they come from and when and why did they decide to move? How did they make the transition from their ancestral way of living to the way you are living now?

Talking Back

BELL HOOKS

bell hooks is a feminist scholar who writes about issues of race, gender, love, and teaching. In this memoir published in 1989, she describes how she found her own voice and learned about the different expectations for women and men when it came to speaking out and speaking up. Pay attention to how she uses visual details and sound to describe her upbringing and how she uses the memoir to make a point about how childhood experiences can foster gendered and even sexist attitudes.

In the world of the southern black community I grew up in, "back talk" and "talking back" meant speaking as an equal to an authority figure. It meant daring to disagree and sometimes it just meant having an opinion. In the "old school," children were meant to be seen and not heard. My great-grandparents, grandparents, and parents were all from the old school. To make yourself heard if you were a child was to invite punishment, the back-hand lick, the slap across the face that would catch you unaware, or the feel of switches stinging your arms and legs.

To speak then when one was not spoken to was a courageous act—an act of risk and daring. And yet it was hard not to speak in warm rooms where heated discussions began at the crack of dawn, women's voices filling the air, giving orders, making threats, fussing. Black men may have excelled in the art of poetic preaching in the male-dominated church, but in the church of the home, where the everyday rules of how to live and how to act were established, it was black women who preached. There, black women spoke in a language so rich, so poetic, that it felt to me like being shut off from life, smothered to death if one were not allowed to participate.

It was in that world of woman talk (the men were often silent, often absent) that was born in me the craving to speak, to have a voice, and not just any voice but one that could be identified as belonging to me. To make my voice, I had to speak, to hear myself talk—and talk I did—darting in and out of grown folks' conversations and dialogues, answering questions that were not directed at me, endlessly asking questions, making speeches. Needless to say, the punishments for these acts of speech seemed endless. They were intended to silence me—the child—and more particularly the girl child. Had I been a boy, they might have encouraged me to speak believing that I might someday be called to preach. There was no "calling" for talking girls, no legitimized recorded speech. The punishments I received for "talking back" were intended to suppress all possibility that I would create my own speech. That speech was to be suppressed so that the "right speech of womanhood" would emerge.

Within feminist circles, silence is often seen as the sexist "right speech of womanhood"—the sign of woman's submission to patriarchal authority. This emphasis on woman's silence may be an accurate remembering of what has taken place in the households of women from WASP backgrounds in the United States, but in black communities (and diverse ethnic communities), women have not been silent. Their voices can be heard. Certainly for black women, our struggle has not been to emerge from silence into speech but to change the nature and direction of our speech, to make a speech that compels listeners, one that is heard.

Our speech, "the right speech of woman- 5 hood," was often the soliloquy, the talking into thin air, the talking to ears that do not hear you—the talk that is simply not listened to. Unlike the black male preacher whose speech was to be heard, who was to be listened to, whose words were to be remembered, the voices of black women—giving orders, making threats, fussing—could be tuned out, could become a kind of background music, audible but not acknowledged as significant speech. Dialogue—the sharing of speech and recognition—took place not between mother and child or mother and male authority figure but among black women. I can remember watching fascinated as our mother talked with her mother, sisters, and women friends. The intimacy and intensity of their speech—the satisfaction they received from talking to one another, the pleasure, the joy. It was in this world of woman speech, loud talk, angry words, women with tongues quick and sharp, tender sweet tongues, touching our world with their words, that I made speech my birthright— and the right to voice, to authorship, a privilege I would not be denied. It was in that world and because of it that I came to dream of writing, to write.

Writing was a way to capture speech, to hold onto it, keep it close. And so I wrote down bits and pieces of conversations, confessing in cheap diaries that soon fell apart from too much handling, expressing the intensity of my sorrow, the anguish of speech—for I was always saying the wrong thing, asking the wrong questions. I could not confine my speech to the necessary corners and concerns of life. I hid these writings under my bed, in pillow stuffings, among faded underwear. When my sisters found and read them, they ridiculed and mocked me—poking fun. I felt violated, ashamed, as if the secret parts of my self had been exposed, brought into the open, and hung like newly clean laundry, out in the air for everyone to see. The fear of exposure, the fear that one's deepest emotions and innermost thoughts will be dismissed as mere nonsense, felt by so many young girls keeping diaries, holding and hiding speech, seems to me now one of the barriers that women have always needed and still need to destroy so that we are no longer pushed into secrecy of silence.

Despite my feelings of violation, of exposure, I continued to speak and write, choosing my hiding places well, learning to destroy work when no safe place could be found. I was never taught absolute silence, I was taught that it was important to speak but to talk a talk that was in itself a silence. Taught to speak and yet beware of the betrayal of too much heard speech, I experienced intense confusion and deep anxiety in my efforts to speak and write. Reciting poems at Sunday afternoon church service might be rewarded. Writing a poem (when one's time could be "better" spent sweeping, ironing, learning to cook) was luxurious activity, indulged in at the expense of others. Questioning authority, raising issues that were not deemed appropriate subjects brought pain, punishments—like telling mama I wanted to die before her because I could not live without her—that was crazy talk, crazy speech, the kind that would lead you to end up in a mental institution. "Little girl," I would be told, "if you don't stop all this crazy talk and crazy acting you are going to end up right out there at Western State."

Madness, not just physical abuse, was the punishment for too much talk if you were female. Yet even as this fear of madness haunted me, hanging over my writing like a monstrous shadow, I could not stop the words, making thought, writing speech. For this terrible madness which I feared, which I was sure was the destiny of daring women born to intense speech (after all, the authori-

ties emphasized this point daily), was not as threatening as imposed silence, as suppressed speech.

Safety and sanity were to be sacrificed if I was to experience defiant speech. Though I risked them both, deep-seated fears and anxieties characterized my childhood days. I would speak but I would not ride a bike, play hardball, or hold the gray kitten. Writing about the ways we are traumatized in our growing-up years, psychoanalyst Alice Miller makes the point in *For Your Own Good* that it is not clear why childhood wounds become for some folk an opportunity to grow, to move forward rather than backward in the process of self-realization. Certainly, when I reflect on the trials of my growing-up years, the many punishments, I can see now that in resistance I learned to be vigilant in the nourishment of my spirit, to be tough, to courageously protect that spirit from forces that would break it.

While punishing me, my parents often 10 spoke about the necessity of breaking my spirit. Now when I ponder the silences, the voices that are not heard, the voices of those wounded and/or oppressed individuals who do not speak or write, I contemplate the acts of persecution, torture—the terrorism that breaks spirits, that makes creativity impossible. I write these words to bear witness to the primacy of resistance struggle in any situation of domination (even within family life); to the strength and power that emerges from sustained resistance and the profound conviction that these forces can be healing, can protect us from dehumanization and despair.

These early trials, wherein I learned to stand my ground, to keep my spirit intact, came vividly to mind after I published *Ain't I a Woman* and the book was sharply and harshly criticized. While I had expected a climate of critical dialogue, I was not expecting a critical avalanche that had the power in its intensity to crush the spirit, to push one into silence. Since that time, I have heard stories about black women, about women of color, who write and publish (even when the work is quite successful) having nervous breakdowns, being made mad because they cannot bear the harsh responses of family, friends, and unknown critics, or becoming silent, unproductive. Surely, the absence of a humane critical response has tremendous impact on the writer from any oppressed, colonized group who endeavors to speak. For us, true speaking is not solely an expression of creative power; it is an act of resistance, a political gesture that challenges politics of domination that would render us nameless and voiceless. As such, it is a courageous act—as such, it represents a threat. To those who wield oppressive power, that which is threatening must necessarily be wiped out, annihilated, silenced.

Recently, efforts by black women writers to call attention to our work serve to highlight both our presence and absence. Whenever I peruse women's bookstores, I am struck not by the rapidly growing body of feminist writing by black women, but by the paucity of available published material. Those of us who write and are published remain few in number. The context of silence is varied and multi-dimensional. Most obvious are the ways racism, sexism, and class exploitation act to suppress and silence. Less obvious are the inner struggles, the efforts made to gain the necessary confidence to write, to re-write, to fully develop craft and skill—and the extent to which such efforts fail.

Although I have wanted writing to be my life-work since childhood, it has been difficult for me to claim "writer" as part of that which identifies and shapes my everyday reality. Even after publishing books, I would often speak of wanting to be a writer as though these works did not exist. And though I would be told, "you are a writer," I was not yet ready to fully affirm this truth. Part of myself was still held captive by domineering forces of history, of familial life that had charted a map of silence, of right speech. I had not completely let go of the fear of saying the wrong thing, of being punished. Somewhere in the

deep recesses of my mind, I believed I could avoid both responsibility and punishment if I did not declare myself a writer.

One of the many reasons I chose to write using the pseudonym bell hooks, a family name (mother to Sarah Oldham, grandmother to Rosa Bell Oldham, great-grandmother to me), was to construct a writer-identity that would challenge and subdue all impulses leading me away from speech into silence. I was a young girl buying bubble gum at the corner store when I first really heard the full name bell hooks. I had just "talked back" to a grown person. Even now I can recall the surprised look, the mocking tones that informed me I must be kin to bell hooks—a sharp-tongued woman, a woman who spoke her mind, a woman who was not afraid to talk back. I claimed this legacy of defiance, of will, of courage, affirming my link to female ancestors who were bold and daring in their speech. Unlike my bold and daring mother and grandmother, who were not supportive of talking back, even though they were assertive and powerful in their speech, bell hooks as I discovered, claimed, and invented her was my ally, my support.

That initial act of talking back outside the home was empowering. It was the first of many acts of defiant speech that would make it possible for me to emerge as an independent thinker and writer. In retrospect, "talking back" became for me a rite of initiation, testing my courage, strengthening my commitment, preparing me for the days ahead—the days when writing, rejection notices, periods of silence, publication, ongoing development seem impossible but necessary. 15

Moving from silence into speech is for the oppressed, the colonized, the exploited, and those who stand and struggle side by side a gesture of defiance that heals, that makes new life and new growth possible. It is that act of speech, of "talking back," that is no mere gesture of empty words, that is the expression of our movement from object to subject—the liberated voice.

A CLOSER LOOK AT
Talking Back

1. Unlike most memoirs, this selection by bell hooks does not describe a particular event or tell a specific story. How does hooks still provide enough description to help readers see and understand her life? What kinds of scenes does she describe without exactly telling readers what happened?

2. What is the difference between "talking" and "talking back" in this memoir? How does hooks use this distinction to make her larger points about how women and other oppressed people should assert themselves?

3. Why do you think hooks decided to take on the pseudonym "bell hooks" instead of using her real name? In what ways does this name give her freedom or power? Do you think taking a pseudonym also has other consequences or effects?

IDEAS FOR
Writing

1. Write a brief commentary in which you discuss the status of women's equality today. Do you believe that women are still pressured to not talk back? Do you believe there are people in the United States who are, in hooks' words, "the oppressed, the colonized, the exploited"? If you believe this silencing still exists, how can people better learn to talk back? If you think people are no longer silenced, how can they use writing to preserve their freedom and assert themselves?

2. Using sources from the Internet, write a profile of bell hooks. Find a specific angle that allows you to reveal her personality and her outlook on the world. What kinds of values do you hold in common with hooks? How are you different?

Salvation

LANGSTON HUGHES

Langston Hughes was one of the major figures of the Harlem Renaissance, a cultural movement that spanned the 1920s and 1930s. His writings describe the common experiences of African Americans and the effects of racism by exploring music, humor, and faith. Listen for his unique voice as you read this memoir.

I was saved from sin when I was going on thirteen. But not really saved. It happened like this. There was a big revival at my Auntie Reed's church. Every night for weeks there had been much preaching, singing, praying, and shouting, and some very hardened sinners had been brought to Christ, and the membership of the church had grown by leaps and bounds. Then just before the revival ended, they held a special meeting for children, "to bring the young lambs to the fold." My aunt spoke of it for days ahead. That night I was escorted to the front row and placed on the mourners' bench with all the other young sinners, who had not yet been brought to Jesus.

My aunt told me that when you were saved you saw a light, and something happened to you inside! And Jesus came into your life! And God was with you from then on! She said you could see and hear and feel Jesus in your soul. I believed her. I had heard a great many old people say the same thing and it seemed to me they ought to know. So I sat there calmly in the hot, crowded church, waiting for Jesus to come to me.

The preacher preached a wonderful rhythmical sermon, all moans and shouts and lonely cries and dire pictures of hell, and then he sang a song about the ninety and nine safe in the fold, but one little lamb was left out in the cold. Then he said: "Won't you come? Won't you come to Jesus? Young lambs, won't you come?" And he held out his arms to all us young sinners there on the mourners' bench. And the little girls cried. And some of them jumped up and went to Jesus right away. But most of us just sat there.

A great many old people came and knelt around us and prayed, old women with jet-black faces and braided hair, old men with work-gnarled hands. And the church sang a song about the lower lights are burning, some poor sinners to be saved. And the whole building rocked with prayer and song.

Still I kept waiting to *see* Jesus.   5

Finally all the young people had gone to the altar and were saved, but one boy and me. He was a rounder's son named Westley. Westley and I were surrounded by sisters and deacons praying. It was very hot in the church, and getting late now. Finally Westley said to me in a whisper: "God damn! I'm tired o' sitting here. Let's get up and be saved." So he got up and was saved.

Then I was left all alone on the mourners' bench. My aunt came and knelt at my knees and cried, while prayers and songs swirled all around me in the little church. The whole congregation prayed for me alone, in a mighty wail of moans and voices. And I kept

waiting serenely for Jesus, waiting, waiting—but he didn't come. I wanted to see him, but nothing happened to me. Nothing! I wanted something to happen to me, but nothing happened.

I heard the songs and the minister saying: "Why don't you come? My dear child, why don't you come to Jesus? Jesus is waiting for you. He wants you. Why don't you come? Sister Reed, what is this child's name?"

"Langston," my aunt sobbed.

"Langston, why don't you come? Why 10 don't you come and be saved? Oh, Lamb of God! Why don't you come?"

Now it was really getting late. I began to be ashamed of myself, holding everything up so long. I began to wonder what God thought about Westley, who certainly hadn't seen Jesus either, but who was now sitting proudly on the platform, swinging his knickerbockered legs and grinning down at me, surrounded by deacons and old women on their knees praying. God had not struck Westley dead for taking his name in vain or for lying in the temple. So I decided that maybe to save further trouble, I'd better lie, too, and say that Jesus had come, and get up and be saved.

So I got up.

Suddenly the whole room broke into a sea of shouting, as they saw me rise. Waves of rejoicing swept the place. Women leaped in the air. My aunt threw her arms around me. The minister took me by the hand and led me to the platform.

When things quieted down, in a hushed silence, punctuated by a few ecstatic "Amens," all the new young lambs were blessed in the name of God. Then joyous singing filled the room.

That night, for the last time in my life but 15 one—for I was a big boy twelve years old—I cried. I cried, in bed alone, and couldn't stop. I buried my head under the quilts, but my aunt heard me. She woke up and told my uncle I was crying because the Holy Ghost had come into my life, and because I had seen Jesus. But I was really crying because I couldn't bear to tell her that I had lied, that I had deceived everybody in the church, that I hadn't seen Jesus, and that now I didn't believe there was a Jesus any more, since he didn't come to help me.

A CLOSER LOOK AT
Salvation

1. This memoir uses sound to add intensity to the scene. Read through this selection again, underlining the moments in which sound plays an important part in the story itself. How is sound used to add energy? How is it used to reflect the emotions of the characters? What kinds of words does Hughes use to describe the sounds around him?

2. Hughes describes one of the primary differences between the ways children and adults view the world: children generally think in concrete terms, while adults are also able to think in abstract terms. Do you think this difference is the root cause of the conflict in this memoir, or do you think something else is causing it?

3. What is the theme that holds this memoir together? In other words, what is this story really about? Obviously, Hughes's experience as a 12-year-old had a profound impact on him. What did he learn from this experience? How do you think this changed him for life?

IDEAS FOR
Writing

1. We have all faced disappointment or shame at some point in our lives. List three of these moments in your own life and write a brief memoir that includes a description of one of them. Provide details about what happened and discuss how it made you feel and what you learned from the experience.

2. In your own life, have you experienced a conflict similar to the one Hughes describes? Did your family or someone else want you to accept or believe something that was important to them, but that you just could not go along with? Write a memoir in which you describe that experience and what you learned from it. Your description does not need to be about a faith-based experience. It can be about any moment when your beliefs diverged from your parents' or family's beliefs.

The Good Immigrant Student

BICH MINH NGUYEN

In her book Stealing Buddha's Dinner, *Bich Minh Nguyen humorously describes her bittersweet upbringing in Grand Rapids, Michigan. As a child refugee who escaped Vietnam when the war came to an end, she felt like an outsider in Grand Rapids. In this memoir, which was published before her book, she talks about adjusting to school in her new home.*

My stepmother, Rosa, who began dating my father when I was three years old, says that my sister and I used to watch *Police Woman* and rapturously repeat everything Angie Dickinson said. But when the show was over Anh and I would resume our Vietnamese, whispering together, giggling in accents. Rosa worried about this. She had the idea that she could teach us English and we could teach her Vietnamese. She would make us lunch or give us baths, speaking slowly and asking us how to say *water,* or *rice,* or *house.*

After she and my father married, Rosa swept us out of our falling-down house and into middle-class suburban Grand Rapids, Michigan. Our neighborhood surrounded Ken-O-Sha Elementary School and Plaster Creek, and was only a short drive away from the original Meijer's Thrifty Acres. In the early 1980s, this neighborhood of mismatching street names—Poinsettia, Van Auken, Senora, Ravanna—was home to families of Dutch heritage, and everyone was Christian Reformed, and conservative Republican. Except us. Even if my father hadn't left his rusted-through silver Mustang, the first car he ever owned, to languish in the driveway for months we would have stuck out simply because we weren't white. There was my Latina stepmother and her daughter, Cristina; my father, sister, grandmother, and I, refugees from Saigon; and my half-brother born a year after we moved to the house on Ravanna Street.

Although my family lived two blocks from Ken-O-Sha, my stepmother enrolled me and Anh at Sherwood Elementary, a bus ride away, because Sherwood had a bilingual education program. Rosa, who had a master's in education and taught ESL and community ed in the public school system, was a big supporter of bilingual education. School mornings, Anh and I would be at the bus stop at the corner of our street quite early, hustled out of the house by our grandmother who constantly feared we would miss our chance. I went off to first grade, Anh to second. At ten

o'clock, we crept out of our classes, drawing glances and whispers from the other students, and convened with a group of Vietnamese kids from other grades to learn English. The teachers were Mr. Ho, who wore a lot of short-sleeved button-down shirts in neutral hues, and Miss Huong, who favored a maroon blouse with puffy shoulders and slight ruffles at the high neck and wrists, paired with a tweed skirt that hung heavily to her ankles. They passed out photocopied booklets of Vietnamese phrases and their English translations, with themes such as "In the Grocery Store." They asked us to repeat slowly after them and took turns coming around to each of us, bending close to hear our pronunciations.

Anh and I exchanged a lot of worried glances, for we had a secret that we were quite embarrassed about: we already knew English. It was the Vietnamese part that gave us trouble. When Mr. Ho and Miss Huong gave instructions, or passed out homework assignments, they did so in Vietnamese. Anh and I received praise for our English, but were reprimanded for failing to complete our assignments and failing to pay attention. After a couple of weeks of this Anh announced to Rosa that we didn't need bilingual education. Nonsense, she said. Our father just shrugged his shoulders. After that, Anh began skipping bilingual classes, urging me to do the same, and then we never went back. What was amazing was that no one, not Mrs. Eunice, my first grade teacher, or Mrs. Hankins, Anh's teacher, or even Mr. Ho or Miss Huong said anything directly to us about it. Or if they did, I have forgotten it entirely. Then one day my parents got a call from Miss Huong. When Rosa came to talk to me and Anh about it we were watching television the way kids do, sitting alarmingly close to the screen. Rosa confronted us with "Do you girls know English?" Then she suddenly said, "Do you know Vietnamese?" I can't remember what we replied to either question.

For many years, a towering old billboard over the expressway downtown proudly declared Grand Rapids "An All-American City." For me, that all-American designation meant all-white. I couldn't believe (and still don't) that they meant to include the growing Mexican-American population, or the sudden influx of Vietnamese refugees in 1975. I often thought it a rather mean-spirited prank of some administrator at the INS, deciding with a flourish of a signature to send a thousand refugees to Grand Rapids, a city that boasted having more churches per square mile than other city in the United States. Did that administrator know what Grand Rapids was like? That in school, everywhere I turned, and often when I closed my eyes, I saw blond blond blond? The point of bilingual education was assimilation. To my stepmother, the point was preservation: she didn't want English to take over wholly, pushing the Vietnamese out of our heads. She was too ambitious. Anh and I were Americanized as soon as we turned on the television. Today, bilingual education is supposed to have become both a method of assimilation and a method of preservation, an effort to prove that kids can have it both ways. They can supposedly keep English for school and their friends and keep another language for home and family. In Grand Rapids, Michigan, in the 1980s, I found that an impossible task.

I transferred to Ken-O-Sha Elementary in time for third grade, after Rosa finally admitted that taking the bus all the way to Sherwood was pointless. I was glad to transfer, eager to be part of a class that wasn't, in my mind, tainted with the knowledge of my bilingual stigma. Third grade was led by Mrs. Alexander, an imperious, middle-aged woman of many plaid skirts held safe by giant gold safety pins. She had a habit of turning her wedding ring around and around her finger while she stood at the chalkboard. Mrs. Alexander had an intricate system of rewards for good grades and good behavior, denoted by colored star stickers on a piece of poster board that loomed over us all. One glance and you could see who was behind, who was striding ahead.

I was an insufferably good student, with perfect Palmer cursive and the highest possible scores in every subject. I had learned this trick at Sherwood. That the quieter you are, the shyer and sweeter and better-at-school you are, the more the teacher will let you alone. Mrs. Alexander should have let me alone. For, in addition to my excellent marks, I was nearly silent, deadly shy, and wholly obedient. My greatest fear was being called on, or in any way standing out more than I already did in the class that was, except for me and one black student, dough-white. I got good grades because I feared the authority of the teacher; I felt that getting in good with Mrs. Alexander would protect me, that she would protect me from the frightful rest of the world. But Mrs. Alexander was not agreeable to this notion. If it was my turn to read aloud during reading circle, she'd interrupt me to snap, "You're reading too fast" or demand, "What does that word mean?" Things she did not do to the other students. Anh, when I told her about this, suggested that perhaps Mrs. Alexander liked me and wanted to help me get smarter. But neither of us believed it. You know when a teacher likes you and when she doesn't.

Secretly, I admired and envied the rebellious kids, like Robbie Andrews who came to school looking bleary-eyed and pinched, like a hungover adult; Robbie and his ilk snapped back at teachers, were routinely sent to the principal's office, were even spanked a few times with the principal's infamous red paddle (apparently no one in Grand Rapids objected to corporal punishment). Those kids made noise, possessed something I thought was confidence, self-knowledge, allowing them to marvelously question everything ordered of them. They had the ability to challenge the given world.

Toward the middle of third grade Mrs. [10] Alexander introduced a stuffed lion to the pool of rewards: the best student of the week would earn the privilege of having the lion sit on his or her desk for the entire week. My quantity of gold stars was neck and neck with that of my two competitors, Brenda and Jennifer, both sweet-eyed blond girls with pastel-colored monogrammed sweaters and neatly tied Dock-Sides. My family did not have a lot of money and my stepmother had terrible taste. Thus I attended school in such ensembles as dark red parachute pants and a nubby pink sweater stitched with a picture of a unicorn rearing up. This only propelled me to try harder to be good, to make up for everything I felt was against me: my odd family, my race, my very face. And I craved that stuffed lion. Week after week, the lion perched on Brenda's desk or Jennifer's desk. Meanwhile, the class spelling bee approached. I didn't know I was such a good speller until I won it, earning a scalloped-edged certificate and a candy bar. That afternoon I started toward home, then remembered I'd forgotten my rain boots in my locker. I doubled back to school and overheard Mrs. Alexander in the classroom talking to another teacher. "Can you believe it?" Mrs. Alexander was saying. "A foreigner winning our spelling bee!"

I waited for the stuffed lion the rest of that year, with a kind of patience I have no patience for today. To no avail. In June, on the last day of school, Mrs. Alexander gave the stuffed lion to Brenda to keep forever.

The first time I had to read aloud something I had written—perhaps it was in fourth grade—I felt such terror, such a need not to have any attention upon me, that I convinced myself that I had become invisible, that the teacher could never call on me because she couldn't see me.

More than once, I was given the assignment of writing a report about my family history. I loathed this task, for I was dreadfully aware that my history could not be faked; it already showed on my face. When my turn came to read out loud the teacher had to ask me several times to speak louder. Some kids, a few of them older, in different classes, took to pressing back the corners of their eyes with the heels of their palms while they chanted, "Ching-chong, ching-chong!" during recess. (This continued until Anh, who was far tougher than me, threatened to beat them up.)

I have no way of telling what tortured me more: the actual snickers and remarks and watchfulness of my classmates, or my own imagination, conjuring disdain. My own sense of shame. At times I felt sickened by my obedience, my accumulation of gold stickers, my every effort to be invisible.

Yet Robbie Andrews must have felt the same [15] kind of claustrophobia, trapped in his own reputation, in his ability to be otherwise. I learned in school that changing oneself is not easy, that the world makes up its mind quickly.

I've heard that Robbie dropped out of high school, got a girl pregnant, found himself in and out of first juvenile detention, then jail.

What comes out of difference? What constitutes difference? Such questions, academic and unanswered, popped up in every other course description in college. But the idea of difference is easy to come by, especially in school; it is shame, the permutations and inversions of difference and self-loathing, that we should be worrying about.

Imagined torment, imagined scorn. When what is imagined and what is desired turn on each other.

Some kids want to rebel; other kids want to disappear. I wanted to disappear. I was not brave enough to shrug my shoulders and flaunt my difference; because I could not disappear into the crowd, I wished to disappear entirely. Anyone might have mistaken this for passivity.

Once, at the end of my career at Sherwood Elementary, I disappeared on the bus home. Mine was usually the third stop, but that day the bus driver thought I wasn't there, and she sailed right by the corner of Ravanna and Senora. I said nothing. The bus wove its way downtown, and for the first time I got to see where other children lived, some of them in clean orderly neighborhoods, some near houses with sagging porches and boarded-up windows. All the while, the kid sitting across the aisle from me played the same cheerful song over and over on his portable boom box. *Pass the doochee from the left hand side, pass the doochee from the left hand side.* He and his brother turned out to be the last kids off the bus. Then the bus driver saw me through the rearview mirror. She walked back to where I was sitting and said, "How come you didn't get off at your stop?" I shook my head, don't know. She sighed and drove me home.

I was often doing that, shaking my head silently or staring up wordlessly. I realize that while I remember so much of what other people said when I was a child, I remember little of what I said. Probably because I didn't say much at all.

I recently came across in the stacks of the University of Michigan library *A Manual for Indochinese Refugee Education 1976–1977.* Some of it is silly, but much of it is a painstaking, fairly thoughtful effort to let school administrators and teachers know how to go about sensitively handling the influx of Vietnamese children in the public schools. Here is one of the most wonderful items of advice: "The Vietnamese child, even the older child, is also reported to be afraid of the dark, and more often than not, believes in ghosts. A teacher may have to be a little more solicitous of the child on gloomy, wintery days." Perhaps if Mrs. Alexander had read this, she would not have upbraided me so often for tracking mud into the classroom on rainy days. In third grade I was horrified and

20 ashamed of my muddy shoes. I hung back, trying to duck behind this or that dark-haired boy. In spite of this, in spite of bilingual education, and shyness, and all that wordless shaking of my head, I was sent off every Monday to the Spectrum School for the Gifted and Talented. I still have no idea who selected me, who singled me out. Spectrum was (and still is) a public school program that invited students from every public elementary school to meet once a week and take specialized classes on topics such as the Middle Ages, Ellis Island, and fairy tales. Each student chose two classes, a major and minor, and for the rest of the semester worked toward final projects in both. I loved going to Spectrum. Not only did the range of students from other schools prove to be diverse, I found myself feeling more comfortable, mainly because Spectrum encouraged individual work. And the teachers seemed happy to be there. The best teacher at Spectrum was Mrs. King, whom every student adored. I still remember the soft gray sweaters she wore, her big wavy hair, her art-class handwriting, the way she'd often tell us to close our eyes when she read us a particular story or passage.

I believe that I figured out how to stop disappearing, how to talk and answer, even speak up, after several years in Spectrum. I was still deeply self-conscious, but I became able, sometimes, to maneuver around it.

Spectrum may have spoiled me a little, because it made me think about college and freedom, and thus made all the years in between disappointing and annoying.

25 In seventh grade I joined Anh and Cristina at the City School, a seventh through twelfth grade public school in the Grand Rapids system that served as an early charter school; admission was by interview, and each grade had about fifty students. The City School had the advantage of being downtown, perched over old cobblestone roads, and close to the main public library. Art and music history

were required. There were no sports teams. And volunteering was mandatory. But kids didn't tend to stay at City School; as they got older they transferred to one of the big high schools nearby, perhaps wishing to play sports, perhaps wishing to get away from City's rather brutal academic system. Each half semester, after grades were doled out, giant dot-matrix printouts of everyone's GPAs were posted in the hallways.

I didn't stay at City, either. When my family moved to a different suburb, my stepmother promptly transferred me to Forest Hills Northern High School. Most of the students there came from upper-middle-class or very well-to-do families; the ones who didn't stood out sharply. The rich kids were the same as they were anywhere in America: they wore a lot of Esprit and Guess, drove nice cars, and ran student council, prom, and sports. These kids strutted down the hallways; the boys sat in a row on the long windowsill near a group of lockers, whistling or calling out to girls who walked by. Girls gathered in bathrooms with their Clinique lipsticks.

High school was the least interesting part of my education, but I did accomplish something: I learned to forget myself a little. I learned the sweetness of apathy. And through apathy, how to forget my skin and body for a minute or two, almost not caring what would happen if I walked into a room late and all heads swiveled toward me. I learned the pleasure that reveals itself in the loss, no matter how slight, of self-consciousness. These things occurred because I remained the good immigrant student, without raising my hand often or showing off what I knew. Doing work was rote, and I went along to get along. I've never gotten over the terror of being called on in class, or the dread in knowing that I'm expected to contribute to class discussion. But there is a slippage between being good and being unnoticed, and in that sliver of freedom I learned what it could

feel like to walk in the world in plain, unselfconscious view.

I would like to make a broad, accurate statement about immigrant children in schools. I would like to speak for them (us). I hesitate; I cannot. My own sister, for instance, was never as shy as I was. Anh disliked school from the start, choosing rebellion rather than silence. It was a good arrangement: I wrote papers for her and she paid me in money or candy; she gave me rides to school if I promised not to tell anyone about her cigarettes. Still, I think of an Indian friend of mine who told of an elementary school experience in which a blond schoolchild told the teacher, "I can't sit by her. My mom said I can't sit by anyone who's brown." And another friend, whose family immigrated around the same time mine did, whose second grade teacher used her as a vocabulary example: "Children, this is what a *foreigner* is." And sometimes I fall into thinking that kids today have the advantage of so much more wisdom, that they are so much more socially and politically aware than anyone was when I was in school. But I am wrong, of course. I know not every kid is fortunate enough to have a teacher like Mrs. King, or a program like Spectrum, or even the benefit of a manual written by a group of concerned educators; I know that some kids want to disappear and disappear until they actually do. Sometimes I think I see them, in the blurry background of a magazine photo, or in a gaggle of kids following a teacher's aide across the street. The kids with heads bent down, holding themselves in such a way that they seem to be self-conscious even of how they breathe. Small, shy, quiet kids, such good, good kids, *immigrant, foreigner*, their eyes watchful and waiting for whatever judgment will occur. I reassure myself that they will grow up fine, they will be okay. Maybe I cross the same street, then another, glancing back once in a while to see where they are going.

A CLOSER LOOK AT
The Good Immigrant Student

1. Language is an important theme in this memoir. What are some of the language challenges Nguyen faced as a first-generation immigrant in the United States? How are these challenges different than you might expect?

2. Nguyen felt like an outsider in Grand Rapids. What are five reasons she might have felt like she was not fully a member of this community? What are some of the effects of her feeling like an outsider?

3. Fitting in seemed to be a complicated conflict for Nguyen during her childhood. What are some ways she tried to fit in? Which ways were successful? Which ones were not successful? Does she resolve the conflict?

IDEAS FOR
Writing

1. Nguyen's writing style is intriguing and subtle in this memoir. Write a brief literary analysis in which you discuss how she achieves this style. How does she use diction, simile, and metaphor to illustrate her recollections for readers? How does she create a unique voice or tone that comes through in the words and sentences? What is unique about her style that makes it appropriate to her subject?

2. American society has become increasingly diverse. Write a commentary or position paper in which you discuss how children of immigrants should be brought into the educational system. What are some ways American schools can help new immigrants assimilate without also forcing them to leave their own culture behind?

A FEW IDEAS FOR
Composing a Memoir

1. **Write a transition-to-college memoir.** The decision to attend college usually comes with some tension and even conflict. For you, what social, economic, familial, and personal issues led up to this change in your life? How did you feel about this transition into being a college student? How did it affect the people who are important to you? Describe the emotions you felt (optimism, pride, anxiety, etc.) and what caused those emotions. As you write, think of the larger theme or themes that give meaning to your story.

2. **Write a memoir about a positive turning point.** Describe this turning point by focusing on the "conflict" that you needed to overcome. Then write about how you and others evaluated the conflict and resolved it. How did this event or moment change you? Why was it so important? How did it help define who you are now? What is the broader lesson you learned about life from this experience?

3. **Create a multimodal memoir.** Repurpose a memoir you or someone else has written into a new multimodal memoir. You could change the medium to a presentation (Chapter 32, "Presenting Your Work"), to a poster, to electronic words and images (on a blog, Web site, etc.), or to audio. Consider supplementing your memoir with images, sounds, and interactivity. Don't simply add images or sounds, and don't simply dump the contents into your new medium. Rather, explore how these changes allow you to transform your original memoir into something new and different. How do these changes allow you to explore new ideas or go more deeply into others?

CHAPTER

34

Profiles

The Clan of One-Breasted Women

TERRY TEMPEST WILLIAMS

In this epilogue to her memoir, Refuge *(1991), Terry Tempest Williams profiles the women of her family who have died from breast cancer. Families in rural Utah, many of them Mormon, were living downwind of nuclear weapons testing in the 1950s and 1960s. This testing has been blamed for the high levels of cancer in their communities. As you read this profile, be aware of the relationship between Williams, the narrator, and the people she is profiling.*

Epilogue

I belong to a Clan of One-Breasted Women. My mother, my grandmothers, and six aunts have all had mastectomies. Seven are dead. The two who survive have just completed rounds of chemotherapy and radiation.

I've had my own problems: two biopsies for breast cancer and a small tumor between my ribs diagnosed as a "borderline malignancy."

This is my family history.

Most statistics tell us breast cancer is genetic, hereditary, with rising percentages attached to fatty diets, childlessness, or becoming pregnant after thirty. What they don't say is living in Utah may be the greatest hazard of all.

We are a Mormon family with roots in 5 Utah since 1847. The "word of wisdom" in my family aligned us with good foods—no coffee, no tea, tobacco, or alcohol. For the most part, our women were finished having their babies by the time they were thirty. And only one faced breast cancer prior to 1960. Traditionally, as a group of people, Mormons have a low rate of cancer.

Is our family a cultural anomaly? The truth is, we didn't think about it. Those who did, usually the men, simply said, "bad genes." The women's attitude was stoic. Cancer was part of life. On February 16, 1971, the eve of my mother's surgery, I accidently picked up the telephone and overheard her ask my grandmother what she could expect.

"Diane, it is one of the most spiritual experiences you will ever encounter."

I quietly put down the receiver.

Two days later, my father took my brothers and me to the hospital to visit her. She met us in the lobby in a wheelchair. No bandages were visible. I'll never forget her radiance, the way she held herself in a purple velvet robe, and how she gathered us around her.

"Children, I am fine. I want you to know I 10 felt the arms of God around me."

We believed her. My father cried. Our mother, his wife, was thirty-eight years old.

A little over a year after Mother's death, Dad and I were having dinner together. He had just returned from St. George, where the Tempest Company was completing the gas lines that would service southern Utah. He spoke of his love for the country, the sandstoned landscape, bare-boned and beautiful. He had just finished hiking the Kolob trail in Zion National Park. We got caught up in reminiscing, recalling with fondness our walk up Angel's Landing on his fiftieth birthday and the years our family had vacationed there.

Over dessert, I shared a recurring dream of mine. I told my father that for years, as long as I could remember, I saw this flash of light in the night in the desert—that this image had so permeated my being that I could not venture south without seeing it again, on the horizon, illuminating buttes and mesas.

"You did see it," he said.

"Saw what?"   15

"The bomb. The cloud. We were driving home from Riverside, California. You were sitting on Diane's lap. She was pregnant. In fact, I remember the day, September 7, 1957. We had just gotten out of the Service. We were driving north, past Las Vegas. It was an hour or so before dawn, when this explosion went off. We not only heard it, but felt it. I thought the oil tanker in front of us had blown up. We pulled over and suddenly, rising from the desert floor, we saw it, clearly, this golden-stemmed cloud, the mushroom. The sky seemed to vibrate with an eerie pink glow. Within a few minutes, a light ash was raining on the car."

I stared at my father.

"I thought you knew that," he said. "It was a common occurrence in the fifties."

It was at this moment that I realized the deceit I had been living under. Children growing up in the American Southwest, drinking contaminated milk from contaminated cows, even from the contaminated breasts of their mothers, my mother—members, years later, of the Clan of One-Breasted Women.

It is a well-known story in the Desert 20 West, "The Day We Bombed Utah," or more accurately, the years we bombed Utah: above ground atomic testing in Nevada took place from January 27, 1951 through July 11, 1962. Not only were the winds blowing north covering "low-use segments of the population" with fallout and leaving sheep dead in their tracks, but the climate was right. The United States of the 1950s was red, white, and blue. The Korean War was raging. McCarthyism was rampant. Ike was it, and the cold war was hot. If you were against nuclear testing, you were for a communist regime.

Much has been written about this "American nuclear tragedy." Public health was secondary to national security. The Atomic Energy Commissioner, Thomas Murray, said, "Gentlemen, we must not let anything interfere with this series of tests, nothing."

Again and again, the American public was told by its government, in spite of burns, blisters, and nausea, "It has been found that the tests may be conducted with adequate assurance of safety under conditions prevailing at the bombing reservations." Assuaging public fears was simply a matter of public relations. "Your best action," an Atomic Energy Commission booklet read, "is not to be worried about fallout." A news release typical of the times stated, "We find no basis for concluding that harm to any individual has resulted from radioactive fallout."

On August 30, 1979, during Jimmy Carter's presidency, a suit was filed, *Irene Allen v. The United States of America.* Mrs. Allen's case was the first on an alphabetical list of twenty-four test cases, representative of nearly twelve hundred plaintiffs seeking compensation from the United States government for cancers caused by nuclear testing in Nevada.

Irene Allen lived in Hurricane, Utah. She was the mother of five children and had been widowed twice. Her first husband, with their two oldest boys, had watched the tests from the roof of the local high school. He died of leukemia in 1956. Her second husband died of pancreatic cancer in 1978.

In a town meeting conducted by Utah 25 Senator Orrin Hatch, shortly before the suit was filed, Mrs. Allen said, "I am not blaming the government, I want you to know that, Senator Hatch. But I thought if my testimony could help in any way so this wouldn't happen again to any of the generations coming up after us . . . I am happy to be here this day to bear testimony of this."

God-fearing people. This is just one story in an anthology of thousands.

On May 10, 1984, Judge Bruce S. Jenkins handed down his opinion. Ten of the plaintiffs were awarded damages. It was the first time a federal court had determined that nuclear tests had been the cause of cancers. For the remaining fourteen test cases, the proof of causation was not sufficient. In spite of the split decision, it was considered a landmark ruling. It was not to remain so for long.

In April 1987, the Tenth Circuit Court of Appeals overturned Judge Jenkins's ruling on the ground that the United States was protected from suit by the legal doctrine of sovereign immunity, a centuries-old idea from England in the days of absolute monarchs.

In January 1988, the Supreme Court refused to review the Appeals Court decision. To our court system it does not matter whether the United States government was irresponsible, whether it lied to its citizens, or even that citizens died from the fallout of nuclear testing. What matters is that our government is immune: "The King can do no wrong."

In Mormon culture, authority is respected, 30 obedience is revered, and independent thinking is not. I was taught as a young girl not to "make waves" or "rock the boat."

"Just let it go," Mother would say. "You know how you feel, that's what counts."

For many years, I have done just that— listened, observed, and quietly formed my own opinions, in a culture that rarely asks questions because it has all the answers. But one by one, I have watched the women in my family die common, heroic deaths. We sat in waiting rooms hoping for good news, but always receiving the bad. I cared for them, bathed their scarred bodies, and kept their secrets. I watched beautiful women become bald as Cytoxan, cisplatin, and Adriamycin were injected into their veins. I held their foreheads as they vomited green-black bile, and I shot them with morphine when the pain became inhuman. In the end, I witnessed their last peaceful breaths, becoming a midwife to the rebirth of their souls.

The price of obedience has become too high.

The fear and inability to question authority that ultimately killed rural communities in Utah during atmospheric testing of atomic weapons is the same fear I saw in my mother's body. Sheep. Dead sheep. The evidence is buried.

I cannot prove that my mother, Diane 35 Dixon Tempest, or my grandmothers, Lettie Romney Dixon and Kathryn Blackett Tempest, along with my aunts developed cancer from nuclear fallout in Utah. But I can't prove they didn't.

My father's memory was correct. The September blast we drove through in 1957 was part of Operation Plumbbob, one of the most intensive series of bomb tests to be initiated. The flash of light in the night in the desert, which I had always thought was a dream, developed into a family nightmare. It took fourteen years, from 1957 to 1971, for cancer to manifest in my mother—the same time, Howard L. Andrews, an authority in radioactive fallout at the National Institutes of Health, says radiation cancer requires to become evident. The more I learn about what it means to be a "downwinder," the more questions I drown in.

What I do know, however, is that as a Mormon woman of the fifth generation of Latter-day Saints, I must question everything, even if it means losing my faith, even if it means becoming a member of a border tribe among my own people. Tolerating blind obedience in the name of patriotism or religion ultimately takes our lives.

When the Atomic Energy Commission described the country north of the Nevada Test Site as "virtually uninhabited desert terrain," my family and the birds at Great Salt Lake were some of the "virtual uninhabitants."

One night, I dreamed women from all over the world circled a blazing fire in the desert. They spoke of change, how they hold the moon in their bellies and wax and wane with its phases. They mocked the presumption of even-tempered beings and made promises that they would never fear the witch inside themselves. The women danced wildly as sparks broke away from the flames and entered the night sky as stars.

And they sang a song given to them by 40 Shoshone grandmothers:

Ah ne nah, nah	Consider the rabbits
nin nah nah—	How gently they walk
	on the earth—
ah ne nah, nah	Consider the rabbits
nin nah nah—	How gently they walk
	on the earth—
Nyaga mutzi	We remember them
oh ne nay—	We can walk gently
	also—
Nyaga mutzi	We remember them
oh ne nay—	We can walk gently
	also—

The women danced and drummed and sang for weeks, preparing themselves for what was to come. They would reclaim the desert for the sake of their children, for the sake of the land.

A few miles downwind from the fire circle, bombs were being tested. Rabbits felt the tremors. Their soft leather pads on paws and feet recognized the shaking sands, while the roots of mesquite and sage were smoldering. Rocks were hot from the inside out and dust devils hummed unnaturally. And each time there was another nuclear test, ravens watched the desert heave. Stretch marks appeared. The land was losing its muscle.

The women couldn't bear it any longer. They were mothers. They had suffered labor pains but always under the promise of birth. The red hot pains beneath the desert promised death only, as each bomb became a stillborn. A contract had been made and broken between human beings and the land. A new contract was being drawn by the women, who understood the fate of the earth as their own.

Under the cover of darkness, ten women slipped under a barbed-wire fence and entered the contaminated country. They were trespassing. They walked toward the town of Mercury, in moonlight, taking their cues from coyote, kit fox, antelope squirrel, and quail. They moved quietly and deliberately through the maze of Joshua trees. When a hint of daylight appeared they rested, drinking tea and sharing their rations of food. The women closed their eyes. The time had come to protest with the heart, that to deny one's genealogy with the earth was to commit treason against one's soul.

At dawn, the women draped themselves in mylar, wrapping long streamers of silver plastic around their arms to blow in the breeze. They wore clear masks, that became the faces of humanity. And when they arrived at the edge of Mercury, they carried all the butterflies of a summer day in their wombs. They paused to allow their courage to settle.

The town that forbids pregnant women 45 and children to enter because of radiation risks was asleep. The women moved through the streets as winged messengers, twirling around each other in slow motion, peeking inside homes and watching the easy sleep of men and women. They were astonished by such stillness and periodically would utter a shrill note or low cry just to verify life.

The residents finally awoke to these strange apparitions. Some simply stared. Others called authorities, and in time, the women were apprehended by wary soldiers dressed in desert fatigues. They were taken to a white, square building on the other edge of Mercury. When asked who they were and why they were there, the women replied, "We are mothers and we have come to reclaim the desert for our children."

The soldiers arrested them. As the ten women were blind-folded and handcuffed, they began singing:

You can't forbid us everything
You can't forbid us to think—
You can't forbid our tears to flow

And you can't stop the songs that
we sing.

The women continued to sing louder and louder, until they heard the voices of their sisters moving across the mesa:

Ah ne nah, nah
nin nah nah—
Ah ne nah, nah
nin nah nah—
Nyaga mutzi
oh ne nay—
Nyaga mutzi
oh ne nay—

"Call for reinforcements," one soldier said.

"We have," interrupted one woman, "we have—and you have no idea of our numbers."

I crossed the line at the Nevada Test Site and was arrested with nine other Utahns for trespassing on military lands. They are still conducting nuclear tests in the desert. Ours was an act of civil disobedience. But as I walked toward the town of Mercury, it was more than a gesture of peace. It was a gesture on behalf of the Clan of One-Breasted Women.

As one officer cinched the handcuffs 50 around my wrists, another frisked my body.

She found a pen and a pad of paper tucked inside my left boot.

"And these?" she asked sternly.

"Weapons," I replied.

Our eyes met. I smiled. She pulled the leg of my trousers back over my boot.

"Step forward, please," she said as she took my arm.

We were booked under an afternoon sun 55 and bused to Tonopah, Nevada. It was a two-hour ride. This was familiar country. The Joshua trees standing their ground had been named by my ancestors, who believed they looked like prophets pointing west to the Promised Land. These were the same trees that bloomed each spring, flowers appearing like white flames in the Mojave. And I recalled a full moon in May, when Mother and I had walked among them, flushing out mourning doves and owls.

The bus stopped short of town. We were released.

The officials thought it was a cruel joke to leave us stranded in the desert with no way to get home. What they didn't realize was that we were home, soul-centered and strong, women who recognized the sweet smell of sage as fuel for our spirits.

A CLOSER LOOK AT
The Clan of One-Breasted Women

1. In this profile, the writer uses first person (i.e., *I, we*) to profile the women in her family. Most profiles are written in third person (i.e., *he, she, they*). How does this different stance toward her subjects allow Williams to create a sense of intimacy with them? How does it change her voice and the way readers envision her subjects? How does it shape her role as the narrator of the story?

2. Williams uses profiles from her own family to tell a broader story about the suffering of rural people in Utah. At what point in this profile does she transition from a discussion of the women in her family to Utah women in general? How and when does she then transition to discussing how she feels all people should react to nuclear testing and weapons?

3. The dream midway into this profile goes beyond factual information, creating a fantastical reaction to the problem of nuclear testing. Do you believe this kind of description of a dream is appropriate for a profile? How does the dream affect readers and what images does it bring to them? Would the profile be as strong if the dream were replaced by a real story?

1. Think of an injustice that has touched you or your family in some way. Freewrite for five minutes about this topic, describing what caused the injustice and how people reacted to it. Then choose one person who was a victim of the injustice and freewrite for five more minutes, placing that person at the center of the story. How can you use him or her as a focal point through which you can illustrate and describe the injustice and its effects?

2. Research the "downwinders" in Nevada and Utah. In a brief report, describe how they have dealt with cancer. Be sure to tell both sides of the story, drawing ideas from people who were supportive of the testing and the people who suffered from it. Do you feel the testing was necessary, despite its effects? Should the people affected by the testing receive some kind of compensation or recognition? What kinds of actions, if any, should be taken in the future to avoid damaging people's lives and families in this way?

John Zdanowski, Second Life Finance Chief

JOANNE CHRISTIE

This selection, which appeared in Accountancy Age *in April 2008, is similar to many profiles that are found in business-related magazines. It is a story of trials and success. In many ways, the subject of this profile, John Zdanowski, is symbolic of the twisted pathway that successful people must follow in today's world. As you read this profile, pay attention to the kinds of information the writer and Zdanowski choose to share, and the kinds of information they choose not to share.*

When John Zdanowski first met up with Linden Lab creator Philip Rosedale to discuss the CFO post, they didn't just talk numbers.

Within minutes of shaking hands, the pair were swapping stories about what they had programmed the Apple II Plus to do when they were kids. At 12, Zdanowski got his computer to solve the Rubik's Cube puzzle. With such early technological leanings, it's no surprise he ended up forging a career in Silicon Valley.

Since taking over as finance chief in September 2006, Zdanowski has been running not only Linden Lab's finances, but also the economy of virtual world Second Life. While he is an old hand when it comes to the financial affairs of internet companies, he admits that virtual economics pose some rather unique challenges.

A different world

In Second Life, users buy land and create objects and services which are traded with other users for Linden Dollars, a virtual currency which is pegged to the US Dollar, and which is traded on the LindeX. Linden Lab manages the supply of Linden Dollars by charging fees to users for services, by giving them to premium subscribers, and by selling them on to the exchange. Part of Zdanowski's role includes managing this economy, though in the virtual realm, he's better known by his avatar, Zee Linden.

"We basically monitor in real time, much [5] like any market-maker does on Wall Street, the behaviour of the market to see where supply and demand is stacking up, just like you would when you look at the details behind any stock market or currency market," Zdanowski explains.

The virtual economy aside, Zdanowski says the company's business model is fairly standard.

"When you strip away a lot of the virtual worldness of it and really look at the revenue stream, it is a basic recurring revenue internet model and that's what all four of the internet companies I've been involved in have been."

What sets it apart from other internet companies, according to Zdanowski, is its monetisation per unique user, which at $72 (£36.5.) per annum puts it way above the likes of Google, Yahoo and eBay.

"We have the highest monetisation of user generated content and it is also a much higher figure than any advertising model has ever dreamed of," he says.

About a quarter of Second Life's revenue [10] is derived by selling lands to users, while the bulk of its revenue comes from land maintenance fees. The rest comes from membership fees and by operating the virtual economy.

While Linden Lab aims to let this virtual economy run as freely as possible, Zdanowski says the company has had to face certain business realities. Last year it was forced to put a stop to gambling in Second Life, which took a big chunk out of the economy.

"When we shut down gambling, the user-to-user transactions dropped by about 40%, so that would be the equivalent to shutting down real estate transactions in the US," he explains. "It had nothing to do with the FBI or anything like the crazy rumors that were circulating. The reality is that MasterCard and Visa don't allow US companies to process gambling transactions and to continue operating we had to make the tough decision to shut it down."

Rapid expansion

With Second Life rapidly expanding outside the US, the laws of other countries have also come into play. Last year Linden Lab realized that from a profits perspective, it would have to start charging VAT to European residents.

"In 2006 our footprint in Europe was insignificant, but now more than 65% of our business is outside the US," Zdanowski explains. "It got to a point where we couldn't absorb those costs anymore and we had to pass them on to our users."

There have been plenty of scandals to [15] deal with as well. A run on an in-world bank prompted a decision to shut down unregistered banks inside Second Life, and revelations about pedophilia, money laundering, terrorism, and fraud taking place on the virtual platform have also attracted negative press.

"People are responsible for their own actions inside Second Life," says Zdanowski.

"Different countries have asked us to investigate certain residents from a subpoena perspective and we always try to work with law enforcement as best we can if illegal activity is going on."

Going forward, he says complying with the regulations of so many different users' countries is a real challenge: "That's the difficult part about running Second Life as a global company. You can quickly get to the point where all that is allowed is the lowest common denominator of the most conservative laws in any country. We are trying to enable the tools that let people comply with the laws in their country and let other countries do what they need to do."

Working on technologies that allow this, and other advancements, is the company's key strategy moving forward, says Zdanowski, adding that a number of new features have been added to the platform in the past year.

"The majority of our costs are engineer- [20] ing costs to continue to develop the features and capabilities of Second Life," he says. "We don't do any sales, we don't do any marketing. All of our growth comes from word of mouth."

Though reluctant to give away too much when it comes to figures, Zdanowski says Linden Lab has been cash flow positive for over a year, and is now net income positive.

The company has grown from having about 70 employees to almost 250 during his tenure, and it's this kind of growth that really gets his blood pumping. "I really enjoy the rapid growth and the entrepreneurial nature of the company. The intellectual stimulation here is off the charts," he says.

Interestingly, despite his success in managing the finances in such fast growing firms, Zdanowski was not formally trained as an accountant. He started out as an electrical engineer for General Electric, before going to Harvard Business School.

After short stints in management consulting and investment banking, he found his way into the internet, and 10 years on, he's on his fourth internet company. The first two he was involved in were hosting companies, and before joining Linden Lab he was the CFO at HouseValues, a US real estate marketing website which he took public in 2004.

Watch this space

His experience with HouseValues' IPO was [25] reportedly one of the reasons he was hired at Linden Lab, and the recent announcement that Rosedale would be stepping down as CEO fueled speculation the company may go public. Zdanowski was tight-lipped on the topic, except to say: "We certainly have the numbers and we could go public now, the financial markets notwithstanding."

With more than one million people logged into Second Life in February for approximately 28 million user-hours, virtual worlds are impressive but not exactly taking the world by storm just yet. Zdanowski believes it's only a matter of time, however.

"The number of people with email accounts in 1992 was extremely low, just as the percentage of people on virtual worlds today is extremely low," he says. "Over time, if the technology continues to improve, it will be normal for people to interact in virtual worlds. Just like it happened with the internet itself eventually every company needed a website and eventually every company will be using virtual worlds as well."

Virtual accountancy

So far the profession hasn't exactly been beating down a path to the virtual world, but slowly and surely, accountancy is starting to trickle into platforms like Second Life. Those firms that have established a presence in virtual worlds have done so to connect with future accountants and potential employees, and universities have also been quick to realize the potential of virtual worlds as a learning tool.

The Maryland Association of CPAs set up CPA Island in Second Life, and also started up the Second Life Association of CPAs. They run virtual programs and classes that allow American CPAs to earn CPE credits, and they also hold virtual world meetings, exhibitions, networking events and conferences to promote accountancy. Maryland accountancy firm Katz, Abosch, Windesheim, Gershman & Freedman were the first firm of accountants to set up a virtual office in Second Life.

Dutch firm Berk, an affiliate of Baker Tilly [30] International, last year became the first European accounting firm to open a virtual office in Second Life. Their office plays host to meetings between employees, and is also used to engage with those currently studying finance.

KPMG recently turned to Second Life as a recruitment tool. Along with Yell and the Royal Bank of Scotland, KPMG took part in a job fair hosted by TMP Worldwide last year. Deloitte's US arm used a virtual world team challenge to teach high school students about careers in accounting. IBM is looking to develop an in-house version of Second Life for businesses.

A CLOSER LOOK AT
John Zdanowski, Second Life Finance Chief

1. Because this profile appeared in a business-related magazine, certain details are included that might not be included elsewhere. What are these details and how does the author satisfy the interests of the target readers of *Accountancy Age*?

2. Unlike many profiles, this one does not include a physical description of the subject or the setting. How does the absence of a physical description affect you as the reader? Why do you think the writer chose not to include this kind of description?

3. This profile is about success, but also about the perils of operating an online business. How does the writer convey the sense that Zdanowski is successful while also showing that this kind of work is always on the verge of failure?

IDEAS FOR
Writing

1. In this profile, the writer mentions some of the darker aspects of virtual worlds, such as gambling and financial fraud. Write a commentary in which you discuss the future of virtual worlds such as Second Life. Do you think the darker side will eventually dominate these kinds of worlds? Or do you think virtual worlds will regulate themselves much like the real world? Where are the boundaries of freedom in virtual worlds, if you believe any boundaries should be set?

2. If you were able to create a financially viable virtual world, what would it look like? Write a proposal or a pitch to a venture capitalist in which you describe your virtual world, paying special attention to how money would circulate and how you, as the financial chief, might profit from it.

Bodies in Motion and at Rest

THOMAS LYNCH

In this profile from Bodies in Motion and at Rest *(2000), Thomas Lynch—a poet, essayist, and undertaker—writes about picking up a corpse and preparing it for burial. Notice how he uses the narrative features of profile to tell a story while making a broader commentary about life and death.*

So I'm over at the Hortons' with my stretcher and minivan and my able apprentice, young Matt Sheffler, because they found old George, the cemetery sexton, dead in bed this Thursday morning in ordinary time. And the police have been in to rule out foul play and the EMS team to run a tape so some ER doctor wired to the world can declare him dead at a safe distance. And now it's ours to do—Matt's and mine—to ease George from the bed to the stretcher, negotiate the sharp turn at the top of the stairs, and go out the front door to the dead wagon idling in the driveway and back to the funeral home from whence he'll take his leave—waked and well remembered—a Saturday service in the middle of April, his death observed, his taxes due.

We are bodies in motion and at rest— there in George's master bedroom, in the gray light of the midmorning, an hour or so after his daughter found him because he didn't answer when she called this morning, and he always answers, and she always calls, so she got in the car and drove over and found him exactly as we find him here: breathless, unfettered, perfectly still, manifestly indifferent to all this hubbub. And he is here, assembled on his bed as if nothing had happened, still propped on his left shoulder, his left ear buried in his pillow, his right leg hitched up over the left one, his right hand tucked up under the far pillow his ex-wife used to sleep on, before she left him twenty years ago, and under the former Mrs. Horton's pillow, I lift to show Matt, is a little pearl-handled .22 caliber that George always slept with since he has slept alone. "Security," he called it. He said it helped him sleep.

And really there is nothing out of order, no sign of panic or struggle or pain, and except for the cardiac-blue tinting around his ears, the faint odor of body heat and a little early rigor in his limbs, which makes the moving of him easier, one'd never guess George wasn't just sleeping in this morning—catching the twenty extra winks—because maybe he'd been up late playing poker with the boys, or maybe he'd had a late dinner with his woman friend, or maybe he was just a little tired from digging graves and filling them, and anyway, he hadn't a grave to open this morning for one of the locals who was really dead.

But this morning George Horton is really dead and he's really being removed from his premises by Matt and me after we swaddle him in his own bed linens, sidle him on to the stretcher, tip the stretcher up to make the tight turn at the top of the stairs and carefully ease it down, trying to keep the wheels from thumping each time the heavier head end of the enterprise takes a step. And it's really a shame, all things considered, because here's George, more or less in his prime, just south of sixty, his kids raised, his house paid off, a girlfriend still in her thirties with whom he maintained twice-weekly relations—"catch as catch can," he liked to say. And he's a scratch golfer and a small business owner with reliable employees and frequent flier miles that he spends on trips to Vegas twice a year, where he lets himself get a little crazy with the crap tables and showgirls. And he has his money tucked into rental homes and mutual funds, and a host of friends who'd only say good things about him, and a daughter about to make him a grandfather for the first time, and really old George seemed to have it made, and except for our moving him feet first down the stairs this morning, he has everything to live for, everything.

And it is there, on the landing of the first 5 floor, only a few feet from the front door out, that his very pregnant daughter waits in her warmup suit to tender her good-byes to the grandfather of her baby, not yet born. And Matt's face is flushed with the lifting, the huffing and puffing, or the weight of it all, or the sad beauty of the woman as she runs her hand along her father's cheek, and she is catching her breath and her eyes are red and wet and she lifts her face to ask me, "Why?"

"His heart, Nancy . . ." is what I tell her. "It looks like he just slept away. He never felt a thing." These are all the well-tested comforts one learns after twenty-five years of doing these things.

"But *why*?" she asks me, and now it is clear that *how* it happened is not good enough. And here I'm thinking all the usual suspects: the cheeseburgers, the whiskey, the Lucky Strikes, the thirty extra pounds we, some of us, carry, the walks we didn't take, the preventive medicines we all ignore, the work and the worry and the tax man, the luck of the draw, the nature of the beast, the way of the world, the shit that happens because it happens.

But Nancy is not asking for particulars. She wants to know why in the much larger, Overwhelming Question sense: why we don't just live forever. Why are we all eventually orphaned and heartbroken? Why we human beings cease to be. Why our nature won't leave well enough alone. Why we are not all immortal. Why this morning? Why George Horton? Why oh why oh why?

No few times in my life as a funeral director have I been asked this. Schoolchildren, the newly widowed, musing clergy, fellow pilgrims—maybe they think it was my idea. Maybe they just like to see me squirm contemplating a world in which folks wouldn't need caskets and hearses and the likes of me always ready and willing and at their service. Or maybe, like me, sometimes they really wonder.

"Do the math" is what George Horton would say. Or "Bottom line." Or "It's par for the course." Or "It's Biblical." If none of these wisdoms seemed to suit, then "Not my day to watch it" is what he'd say. Pressed on the vast adverbials that come to mind whilst opening or closing graves, George could be counted for tidy answers. Self-schooled in the Ways of the World, he confined his reading to the King James Bible, *The Wall Street Journal, Golf Digest*, the *Victoria's Secret* catalog and the Big Book of Alcoholics Anonymous. He watched C-SPAN, The Home Shopping Network and The Weather Channel. Most afternoons he'd doze off watching Oprah, with whom he was, quite helplessly, in love. On quiet days he'd surf the Web or check his portfolio on-line. On Sundays he watched talking heads and went to dinner and the movies with his woman friend. Weekday mornings he had coffee with the guys at the Summit Café before making the rounds of the half dozen cemeteries he was in charge of. Wednesdays and Saturdays he'd mostly golf.

"Do the math" I heard him give out with once from the cab of his backhoe for no apparent reason. He was backfilling a grave in Milford Memorial. "You gonna make babies, you've gotta make some room; it's Biblical."

Or once, leaning on a shovel, waiting for the priest to finish: "Copulation, population, inspiration, expiration. It's all arithmetic—addition, multiplication, subtraction and long division. That's all we're doing here, just the math. Bottom line, we're buried a thousand per acre, or burned into two quarts of ashes, give or take."

There was no telling when such wisdoms would come to him.

But it came to me, embalming George later that morning, that the comfort in numbers is that they all add up. There is a balm in the known quantities, however finite. Any given year at this end of the millennium, 2.3 million Americans will die. Ten percent of pregnancies will be unintended. There'll be 60 million common colds. These are numbers you can take to the bank. Give or take, 3.9 million babies will be born. It's Biblical. They'll get a little more or a little less of their 76 years of life expectancy. The boys will grow to just over 69 inches, the girls to just under 64. Of them, 25 percent will be cremated, 35 percent will be overweight, 52 percent will drink. Every year 2 million will get divorced, 4 million will get married and there'll be 30,000 suicides. A few will win the lotto, a few will run for public office, a few will be struck by lightning. And any given day, par for the course, 6,300 of our fellow citizens, just like George, will get breathless and outstretched and spoken of in the past tense; and most will be dressed up the way I dress up George, in his good blue suit, and put him in a casket with Matt Sheffler's help, and assemble the 2 or 3 dozen floral tributes and the 100 or 200 family and friends and the 60 or 70 cars that will follow in the 15 mile per hour procession down through town to grave 4 of lot 17 of section C in Milford Memorial, which will become, in the parlance of our trade, his final resting place, over which a 24-by-12-by-4-inch Barre granite stone will be placed, into which we will have sandblasted his name and dates, one of which, subtracted from the other, will amount, more or less, to his life and times. The corruptible, according to the officiating clergy, will have put on incorruption, the mortal will have put on immortality. "Not my day to watch it" will be among the things we'll never hear George Horton say again.

Nor can we see clearly now, looking into 15 his daughter Nancy's eyes, the blue morning at the end of this coming May when she'll stand, upright as any walking wound, holding her newborn at the graveside of the man, her one and only father, for whom her baby will be named. Nor can we hear the promises she makes to keep him alive, to always remember, forever and ever, in her heart of hearts. Nor is there any math or bottom line or Bible verse that adds or subtracts or in any way accounts for the moment or the mystery she holds there.

A CLOSER LOOK AT
Bodies in Motion and at Rest

1. This profile begins with a description of a dead person, George Horton. Lynch, as the narrator, seems distant and detached from the emotions surrounding this person's death. How does he express this detached feeling in his writing? How does he achieve this tone and the sense that the body is nothing more than a name and a job to do?

2. As the profile continues, it is obvious that Lynch knows more about George than he seems to suggest at the beginning, when George is simply a body to be moved and prepared for burial. Lynch shares facts and quotes with the readers that only someone who knew George or his family would know. What relationship do you think the writer had with the deceased? What does his reaction to George's death tell you about Lynch, as someone who is still living?

3. Late in the profile, Lynch begins reciting a list of demographic numbers that detail how people live and die in the United States. The funeral itself seems like a notable moment in a continuing story of meaningless lives and death in this world. What do you think is Lynch's point here? Does he really feel that life goes on, barely noting people who might have meant so much to others? What is the unstated theme at the heart of this profile?

IDEAS FOR
Writing

1. Find an obituary in today's paper or an obituary of a notable person from the past. Write a commentary in which you discuss how obituaries, as a special kind of profile, are different from typical profiles that describe the living. How do we treat the dead differently, and do you think it is right to do this? What do obituaries focus on, and what do they leave out? What does Lynch's profile of George do differently than a typical obituary?

2. Lynch's description of George's life and death seems rather bleak. Do you find Lynch's profile effective? What do you think is Lynch's point in this profile, and what do you think he wants you to learn or take away from it? Write a rhetorical analysis in which you study the content, organization, and style of this profile. How does Lynch use details and tone to support a broader commentary about life and death in the modern world?

Fun with Physics

K. C. COLE

Scientists are often portrayed as stiff, boring, and absorbed in incomprehensible theories. In this profile of Janet Conrad, a physicist at Columbia University, K. C. Cole shows that scientists are all too human, like the rest of us. Notice how Cole uses everyday issues and challenges to fill out this portrait.

Janet Conrad fell in love with the universe at 3 A.M. on a cold autumn night in Wooster, Ohio. A teen-ager, she had no desire to get out of bed and face the frigid air in order to help her father, a dairy scientist, spray warm water on the prize dahlias they were growing together. But when she did go out to the garden she saw, for the first time in her life, how a shower of electrically charged particles flung from a star ninety-three million miles away can cover the sky in glowing pastel curtains. "I remember standing there and looking at the northern lights, and it was so neat that something so remote, so very far away, could be creating something so beautiful right in front of my eyes," she says. Twenty-five years later, Conrad, who is now thirty-nine and an associate professor of physics at Columbia University, created her own universe—a spherical particle detector, forty feet in diameter, that she built under an igloo of dirt at the Fermi National Accelerator Laboratory (Fermilab), near Chicago. The particle detector is lined with a constellation of twelve hundred eight-inch-wide "eyes," or phototubes, and is filled with eight hundred tons of baby oil, which is used to detect the shock waves generated by particle interactions. Early last fall, the detector began an unblinking vigil for subatomic stealth particles known as "sterile" neutrinos.

A lot can go wrong in large-scale physics experiments. Conrad has been basted in foul-smelling oil. She has been squirted with sticky insulating goo. She has had giant helium balloons get away because the soccer nets she was using to hold them down came loose. And she watched in dismay as the pristine white tank for her current experiment acquired a tough yellow scum (which her mother helpfully advised her to remove with Arm & Hammer baking soda). Nothing that Conrad has done in the past, however, approaches the challenge of her current experiment, which involves some fifty scientists from twelve institutions—including the experiment's co-leader, Bill Louis, of the Los Alamos National Laboratory. Conrad's goal is to understand the character of neutrinos, mere wisps of matter that are more numerous, more elusive, and arguably more important than any other subatomic particle.

Neutrinos outnumber all ordinary particles by a billion to one—a thousand trillion of them occupy your body at every second, streaming down from the sky, up from the ground, and even from radioactive atoms inside you. But, for all their omnipresence, they might just as well be ghosts. As John Updike put it in his poem "Cosmic Gall":

> The earth is just a silly ball
> To them, through which they simply
>   pass,
> Like dustmaids down a drafty hall.

Neutrinos can slip through a hundred light-years' worth of lead without stirring up so much as a breeze, and yet they power the most violent events in the universe, making stars shine and, in the process, creating every element, every dust mote, every raindrop, and, ultimately, every thought. They are the alchemists of the cosmos, the catalysts that make nuclear fusion possible, releasing the radiation that melts rock and makes the continents move. Because neutrinos can penetrate almost everything, they can take scientists to places they've never been before—into the cores of exploding stars, for instance, or back to the big bang. As the universe evolved, neutrinos, because they interact so rarely with other particles, were, in effect, left behind, frozen in time. They are still there (or here, if you will) today, imprinted with information about the state of the universe at its birth. Most important, neutrinos break the basic rules that govern other particles, thereby suggesting that the rules themselves are wrong. If Conrad's experiment confirms her suspicions, she will show that a particle that was barely believed to exist can carry enough weight to determine the drape of galaxies.

When I met up with Conrad at a gathering of the group of Columbia professors who work on high-energy physics, she was the only woman there. Some of her fellow-physicists seemed not to know what to make of her. In contrast to earlier generations of women physicists, she has managed to remain unabashedly girlish. She uses words like "neat" and "cool," and her talks are often embellished with whimsical drawings and analogies to hair dye, shopping, or flowers. "She gets away with it because she knows her stuff so well—nobody can attack her," Bonnie Fleming, a Fermilab physicist, says. Rocky Kolb, a cosmologist at Fermilab, explains, "She obtains what she wants in a different way than most physicists. She can tell you you're wrong without telling you you're stupid. That's unusual. This is not a field for the faint of heart—it's like herding cats. You have a hundred physicists and deep down inside they all think they're smarter than you are. Everyone else herds with a cattle prod. Janet does it with charm." Conrad's charisma has

carried her to the top of a field that has traditionally had few places for women, and has won her acclaim and honors such as the prestigious Presidential Early Career Award and the New York City Mayor's Award for Excellence in Science and Technology. (During the presentation of the latter, she had to teach then Mayor Giuliani how to pronounce "quantumchromodynamics.")

Next to her colleagues in khaki and oxford blue, Conrad, with shiny auburn hair, a short cranberry-colored skirt, and matching heels, offered a study in contrasts. She laughs a lot, and her speech comes in staccato bursts, with few transitions. "Conversations seem to jump around, but, if you probe, there's a logical connection," her mentor, the Columbia physicist Michael Shaevitz, says. "She has this wealth of information stored away in different areas, and she pulls it in like an octopus with tentacles." Conrad also gets angry easily. "I have a tendency to fight bitterly," she admits. "I'm so hotheaded that half the time I get myself into trouble." But, she adds, "A little bit of hotheadedness doesn't hurt you in this field." Conrad applied for tenure at Columbia at the first possible moment (and got it, at the age of thirty-six), because she simply couldn't stand the suspense of waiting. A lot of her energy seems to be fuelled by Diet Coke; empty cans line up wherever she goes, like bread crumbs marking her trail. (She drinks so much of it that her mother bought her stock in the company.) It is this combination of charm and restlessness—as well as her ability to design clever and elegant experiments—that has made Conrad successful enough to persuade Columbia to put up a million dollars to get her experiment going while she waited for grant money to arrive. It was an enormous sum for any young physicist to receive, let alone a woman.

Neutrinos have been eluding physicists ever since Wolfgang Pauli first hypothesized their existence, in 1930. In the physical universe, what goes in always equals what comes out, in one form or another. But physicists had noticed that when radioactive atoms spat out electrons and transformed into other kinds of atoms, some of the original energy appeared to be missing. Pauli proposed that it had been carried away by a virtually invisible particle. The thought was so preposterous, however, that even he seemed disinclined to take it seriously. "I have hit upon a desperate remedy," he wrote to his colleagues. "But I don't feel secure enough to publish anything about this idea." He went on to express his embarrassment at his own heresy. "I have done a terrible thing. I have postulated a particle that cannot be detected." In 1931, the physicist Enrico Fermi baptized the hypothetical particle "neutrino," or "little neutral one," but his paper was rejected by the journal *Nature* as too "speculative" and "remote from reality."

The first experiment actually to hunt for neutrinos was called, appropriately enough, Project Poltergeist. In 1956, the Los Alamos-based physicists Clyde Cowan and Fred Reines found a definite trace of neutrinos in the intense wash of radiation spewed forth from newly commissioned nuclear reactors. They wrote to Pauli, who reportedly shared a case of champagne with friends. But detecting neutrinos from a reactor was one thing, and detecting them in nature was another. The first neutrinos from the sun weren't discovered until twelve years later, in the Homestake gold mine, in South Dakota, where they created reactions in a tank filled with chlorinated cleaning fluid. To everyone's surprise, however, the Homestake experiment, led by Raymond Davis, Jr., also discovered that about two-thirds of the neutrinos that had been expected to arrive from the sun as a product of nuclear fusion were missing. A 1992 experiment designed to detect atmospheric neutrinos found a similar portion absent. Physicists came up with various theories to

account for these disappearances, but in the past few years they have settled on one: neutrinos aren't really "missing"; they are simply altering themselves en route. "You start out with a race of house cats, and you find you have lions in the end," Conrad explains; the physicists set their traps for kittens, and lions ignore the bait.

Of course, it is misleading to think of fundamental particles as clearly defined entities like cats. They are more like waves. You can imagine a particle, for example, as the sound wave you make by plucking a guitar string. A neutrino, however, is not a single defined wave. It is a mixture of waves—messy yet fundamental, like a signature. Neutrinos are known to exist in three different forms, each associated with a member of the electron family—the electron neutrino, the muon neutrino, and the tau neutrino. Yet any neutrino can be part electron, part muon, and part tau neutrino, and it can change as its waves fall in and out of step with each other. The discovery that neutrinos oscillate between forms has huge consequences. The particles were originally thought to be weightless, but in order for the waves to fall in and out of synch they must have some mass. (Guitar strings with different masses produce different sounds because they vibrate at different frequencies; if neutrinos had no mass, there could be no oscillation.) Given their numbers, this means that neutrinos—even if their mass is minute—must weigh as much as all the stars in the sky.

Although physicists can easily tell how many neutrinos go "missing," they can't always tell what forms they have changed into. Most are transforming between the familiar electron, muon, and tau forms. But a highly controversial experiment, conducted at the Los Alamos National Laboratory in 1995, uncovered a fourth possibility: that a portion of the neutrinos were changing into a completely unknown species, not electron, muon, or tau, and perhaps substantially more massive than any of those—a species that was undetectable by any means except its gravitational pull. This hypothetical form is known as the sterile neutrino.

Most physicists were skeptical of the results, in large part because the numbers seemed out of line with those from previous experiments. And, when Conrad and Michael Shaevitz decided to design an experiment to prove or disprove the Los Alamos results, their colleagues were dumbfounded. They couldn't believe, according to Shaevitz, that such "well-respected physicists" would even bother. Conrad's friends asked her why she wanted to "waste her life." In 1998, however, combining her skills as an experimenter and a salesperson, Conrad presented her proposal to the advisory council at Fermilab. In contrast to the many larger experiments performed at the lab, hers was designed to give clear results quickly, relatively inexpensively, and with mostly recycled equipment. Even the project's name was chosen to stress its streamlined approach: Mini Booster Neutrino Experiment (or MiniBooNE). "The name was just weird enough that everyone remembered it," Conrad says—which is no small matter when it comes to securing funding. It was the only time that anyone remembers applause at such a meeting. "We usually sit there and scowl," Andreas Kronfeld, a Fermilab physicist, says. "Then this sparkling young person gives a really good talk. It was a little sunshine in all that gray."

Fermilab was founded in 1967 by Robert Rathbun Wilson, a Berkeley-trained physicist who had worked on the Manhattan Project and then, after the bombing of Nagasaki, refused to take part in weapons research. Wilson was also a sculptor, and he planted his works everywhere on the sixty-eight-hundred-acre grounds. There is a Möbius strip in a pool on the roof of the auditorium, a staircase modelled on a double strand of DNA. Even the utility poles are shaped like the symbol for pi. Thousands of physicists come here now, mostly to conduct experiments with the world's highest-energy accelerator, a circular racetrack for particles called the Tevatron. Around its four-mile circumference, superconducting magnets steer protons travelling at almost the speed of light into head-on collisions, setting off fireworks of particles as the energy of speed congeals into matter. In effect, each collision creates a miniature big bang—creation all over again, thousands of times per second. Shopping-mall-size detectors (think of them as elaborate electronic eyes) are needed to keep track of just a tiny part of this activity.

The Tevatron ring is bordered, on the outside, by a river of cooling water, like a moat. Inside, Wilson and his successors have reverentially re-created twelve hundred acres of Illinois prairie. If Fermilab was to be the frontier of physics, Wilson reasoned, then it should have its roots in the literal frontier. The grasses grow up to ten feet tall, and much of the original wildlife has returned, including deer, foxes, salamanders, turtles, beavers, weasels, mink, and hundreds of species of birds. As a final touch, Wilson added a herd of buffalo. There is another poignancy at Fermilab these days, a palpable sense that billion-dollar particle accelerators and physics labs—the "cathedrals of contemporary science," as Wilson called them—have fallen from favor since the post-Second World War period, when physics produced not only the H-bomb but also such leaders in the disarmament effort as Einstein and Wilson himself. In many ways, this makes the results of small experiments such as MiniBooNE even more pivotal.

I attended a MiniBooNE meeting at Fermilab a few months before the experiment was due to be launched. The meeting took place in a glass-walled high-rise building that Wilson modelled on Beauvais Cathedral, in France. It was a difficult time for the project.

The head contractor had been killed in a car accident the day before the meeting, and a building designed to house part of the experiment was still unfinished. A shipment of baby oil from Exxon had turned out to be unusable, and the company was struggling to replace it. "A million things that I never thought could happen have happened on this experiment," Conrad said. "You'd never dream that your contractor could die." Many of the researchers had gathered to bring one another up to date on the experiment's progress: the people who would generate the beam of muon neutrinos, which Conrad and her collaborators hoped to observe oscillating into "sterile" forms; the people building the detector; the people in charge of the oil and of the computer programs to keep track of it all; and the people working on the physics itself—the properties of neutrinos, and possible astrophysics applications. There was conversation about dump-chunks, QTsmear, spillsplitters, and Roefitters. Someone passed around a heavy ring, a custom-made flange. It was an odd pairing of mathematics and metal, of the ephemeral and the concrete. "That's one of the neat things about being an experimentalist," Conrad says. "You can actually see what you've accomplished."

Childhood in a small Ohio town was, it turns out, a surprisingly good preparation for a career in particle physics. Conrad learned many of her practical skills in the local 4-H Club. "Electronics really isn't that different from cooking or sewing," she says. "There's a certain set of rules that you follow, a certain set of patterns. You may want to try variations on the theme, but, once you know your patterns, it's pretty easy." Conrad believes that she was probably born to be a scientist. "I loved having conversation with my parents about how the world works," she says. "They never treated me as someone who couldn't understand." Her uncle, Walter Lipscomb, a Nobel laureate in chemistry, challenged her whenever he came to visit, throwing out puzzles at the dinner table. "I was a miniature adult as far as he was concerned, and he was happy to let me in on his world," Conrad says. After her sophomore year at Swarthmore, her uncle offered her his apartment in Cambridge, Massachusetts, for the summer, and suggested some people she might approach for jobs at Harvard. One of them was the late physicist Frank Pipkin, who was using the Harvard cyclotron to test parts of an experiment to be installed at Fermilab. Conrad worked with Pipkin that summer. The following summer, she went with him to Fermilab. As soon as she saw the detectors, she says, "I knew I wanted to play with them. It was big and dirty and it was just so me."

Dirt, it seems, is an important ingredient in particle-physics experiments. The otherwise flat topology of Fermilab is interrupted by big mounds of earth, long ridges that look as if some large, determined animal were burrowing beneath. The earth acts as an insulator, protecting the experiments below from stray cosmic rays, and the people above from radiation produced by the particle beams. The tank of baby oil that is the heart of MiniBooNE sits under a dirt hill that Conrad describes as "remarkably like a home for Teletubbies." Bill Louis, Conrad's partner, drove me to the site. We bounced over unpaved tracks until we came to something that looked like a large yurt with prairie grasses sprouting from the top of it. A small antechamber inside was stacked with metal cabinets full of computers. Louis opened a square entry hatch and extended a rickety metal ladder, and we crawled down backward into the huge white tank, which was about to be sealed for good.

Building such an experiment can involve some difficult choices. The quarry you're chasing can't be seen directly, so you have to induce it to leave visible traces. The world's most famous neutrino experiment, Super-Kamiokande (or Super-K), in Japan, uses fifty thousand tons of purified water—watched over by twelve thousand phototubes—to catch the wakes produced by the traceable particles in neutrino interactions. Workers ride inside the vast cavern in a little rubber boat. MiniBooNE uses oil, which leaves slightly better wakes but precludes the possibility of boat travel. ("If I fell out, I would sink to the bottom and die," Conrad says, laughing.) The wake is actually a shock wave made by an electrically charged particle travelling through the oil—something like a sonic boom—and the phototubes pick it up as a ring of light. A fuzzy ring signals that the incoming neutrino was an electron neutrino; a sharp one signals a muon neutrino. But it's not always that simple. Other kinds of reactions may be impossible to identify. "Until you've tried to work with a particle as elusive as a neutrino, you have no idea how hard this can actually be," Conrad says. There are so many decisions to be made: Do you watch for neutrinos to disappear or for puzzling appearances? And where, exactly, do you look? Say you start off with lions and they change into cats after two miles, then back into lions two miles later; if you placed your detector at the four-mile mark, you'd see only lions and could easily conclude that nothing had happened. "So often you pose a question, and you build a detector to look at it," Conrad says. "Then the detector answers some other question."

Conrad took me to a hangarlike area, where a critical part of the experiment was being tested. It was an enormous aluminum "horn" designed to focus pions, unstable particles that naturally disintegrate into neutrinos as they travel through a hundred and fifty feet of sewer pipe buried underground. A purified beam of neutrinos would then continue on, through ordinary ground, toward the de-

tector full of oil. To anyone who has spent time in a physics lab, this seems peculiar: other sorts of particle beams are steered through pristine vacuum pipes to insure that they aren't bumped off their course by unintended collisions with air. Neutrinos, however, don't "see" air, any more than they see lead; everything is a vacuum to them. Conrad expects neutrinos from the beam to collide with molecules in the oil several times a minute. But, for every controlled neutrino encounter, a hundred thousand will be caused by cosmic rays from the atmosphere. To avoid these false signals, most neutrino experiments are performed at the bottom of deep mines. MiniBooNE, instead, will receive its beam of neutrinos in bursts, five every second. By comparing the timing of the bursts and of the signals, Conrad and her collaborators hope to sort the needles from the hay. Three hundred extra phototubes line an outer wall of the MiniBooNE sphere, forming a "veto region" designed specifically to flag stray signals—a muon entering from the outside, say, rather than being created by a neutrino in the oil.

In Conrad's tenth-floor office at Fermilab, a field of fake gerbera daisies swayed on tall metal rods like orange and red lollipops. The bottom shelf of a bookcase held a small bottle of Tide detergent and a black light (to demonstrate how scintillators glow), tuning forks (for explaining oscillating neutrinos), and little vials of oil. Conrad never passes up an opportunity to discuss what she's doing. On planes, she draws other passengers into conversations, inviting them to visit Fermilab. She recently completed a radio series, "Earth and Sky," which aired on National Public Radio. And she works with high-school teachers, and even students, whom she hires to help her on experiments. When she won the Maria Goeppert-Mayer Award—for outstanding achievement by a young woman physicist—in 2001, she began to turn her attention more directly to the problem of bringing women into her field. She acknowledges that women tend to have a different style of doing physics from men; they use more words relative to equations, for instance, and this can count against them on exams. "You can watch the guys look at this and say, 'Too many words. Must not know what she's talking about,'" Conrad says. But, in response to those who question whether the specialized equipment is intimidating to women, she insists that it's a lot less complicated than what you find in an average well-stocked kitchen. Conrad's presence has already made a big difference in the Columbia physics department. When she first started teaching there, eight years ago, a site report by the American Physical Society concluded starkly, "Columbia is not a friendly place for women students and perhaps for students in general." By 2000, half of the undergraduates in the high-energy-physics program were female, a shift that many people attribute to Conrad's aggressive attempts to draw young women into the department.

When colleagues at Columbia talk about what she has accomplished, they often tell the story about the benches. In the fall of 1996, she noticed that students were sitting on the dirty floor in the hallway, waiting for her class to start. When she asked for benches to be installed, the administration balked at the expense. Over the Thanksgiving break, she was visiting a former student's family and mentioned the problem. The next day, the student's father, a Columbia alumnus, mailed her a check for a thousand dollars, which she used to buy five plain benches. Other people in the department liked the look of them, and started to add their own touches to the hallway—posters and plants. Then, as Conrad tells it, "the university people came back and said,

'Wow, this looks really nice, but these benches are not the topnotch benches we would like to have here.' So they went and bought nice benches and gave me back mine." "It's one of those things that really made a difference," Steve Kahn, then the chair of the physics department, says.

After our day at Fermilab, Conrad took me to 20 her house in nearby Geneva, Illinois. She has two other homes as well—an apartment in Manhattan and a house in Las Cruces, New Mexico, where her husband, Vassili Papavassiliou, teaches physics at New Mexico State University. Conrad and Papavassiliou met while they were wiring two tiers of the same experiment (one is reminded of Lady and the Tramp sharing that fateful strand of spaghetti), but like many academic couples, they couldn't find work in the same city. They make do, often meeting at Chicago's O'Hare airport for dinner. "It's really bad when the waitress at the airport starts to know you," Conrad said.

A suitcase full of dirty laundry had waited by the door of Conrad's Geneva house for several days, but the night before she had prepared two Greek pies for our dinner, brushing thirty separate layers of phyllo dough with butter—after a full day's work and a friend's fortieth-birthday party. "That's why people don't like to be around me much," she said. "I wear them out." The previous weekend, she had planted three hundred tulip and daffodil bulbs. Spread out on the coffee table were photographs of her father's dahlias, which she was examining in order to choose roots for next year. She called them "bursts of light," and they did seem to explode, like red and pink and orange fireworks against the black backgrounds. "I look at these beautifully symmetric flowers, and yet I find that the one little flaw in them is the thing that makes the flower interesting," she said. "And that's true in high-energy physics, too. It's the little flaws that make it fascinating. And some of the little flaws are not so little."

Of course, it's hard to know whether a flaw is just a flaw, or whether it's a crack in the edifice of physics, a first glimpse into something entirely unexpected. Because data are always ambiguous, it can be years before physicists feel confident enough to publish potentially controversial results. On September 1, 2002, neutrinos began to trickle into the baby oil at MiniBooNE. By the middle of this month, the detector's phototubes had already picked up a hundred thousand interactions. Conrad says that she won't know for at least two years whether the disparaged Los Alamos results were right after all. But it should be worth the wait. If MiniBooNE eventually proves the existence of the sterile neutrino, it will require physicists to rethink everything, from the details of the big bang to the formation of the elements. It could even help explain why there is matter in the universe at all. On the other hand, it will be just as important if MiniBooNE proves that there is no sterile neutrino. "Not finding the ether was a successful experiment," Rocky Kolb says, referring to an experiment that proved there was no medium for carrying light—a finding that helped to cement Einstein's theory of relativity. "A lot of people have too much ego to work on confirming experiments," he adds. "Janet is one of the world's leaders in neutrino physics, and, whatever the future of particle physics is, she'll play a major role."

As MiniBooNE began to take in data, a second experiment gearing up at Fermilab was preparing to send a beam of neutrinos four hundred and fifty miles to a deep mine in Minnesota. Another experiment aims to send neutrinos from Geneva, Switzerland, through the Alps to a lab under a mountain near Rome. An endeavor aptly named ICE-CUBE will turn a cubic kilometre of ice at the South Pole into a detector to observe neutrinos from the stars and cores of galaxies. Conrad, meanwhile, has taken a lead role in pushing for a National Underground Science Laboratory in the Homestake mine, where neutrinos from the sun were first observed to be missing. (Raymond Davis, who led the first Homestake discovery, won the 2002 Nobel Prize in Physics.) And last year Conrad completed her work on a select panel of physicists charged with deciding what kind of major particle accelerator should follow Femilab's designated successor, now under construction in Europe. As usual, Conrad was one of the youngest people on the panel, and there were some difficult moments. Some people blamed her for orchestrating a protest against a few of the panel's recommendations, even though she claims she had nothing to do with it. "I believe I make things clot," she says. "You add me to a mixture, and all of a sudden big chunks of stuff will fall to the bottom."

Two days after I left Fermilab, one of the twelve thousand phototubes in Super-K, the Japanese detector, collapsed while it was being refilled with water after routine maintenance. The shock wave from the collapse created a storm inside the tank. Seven thousand phototubes were shattered. "This is a real disaster," Conrad told me over lunch in Madison, Wisconsin. She'd driven up from Fermilab with Len Bugel, a physics teacher at Stratton Mountain School, in Vermont, with whom she'd worked for many years, and in the car she had persuaded Bugel to try to figure out how to duplicate the effect on a small scale—to see whether MiniBooNE's tubes would collapse under the same conditions. "Creative resource-getting is the No. 1 thing you have to learn," Conrad said. And, by the way, she asked, was I interested in spending the summer at Fermilab, helping out on her experiment? "We'll teach you what you need to know," she said.

A CLOSER LOOK AT
Fun with Physics

1. The physics discussed in this article can be very difficult to understand for nonscientists. How does Cole use details and stylistic devices (e.g., similes, metaphors, analogies) to explain scientific concepts that would be hard for nonexperts to understand?

2. Because this profile is about a woman, the writer has chosen to use different descriptive strategies than might be common if the subject were a man. How does Cole's writing strategy allow her to stress unique issues and ideas? Do you think this gendered difference is a good thing or does it suggest that somehow women scientists are different in a fundamental way?

3. Ultimately, what insights does this profile offer? Of course, it is about Janet Conrad, a physicist, but she and her research are symbols of something larger. What is that something? Find a few places in the profile where this factor seems to be most obvious.

IDEAS FOR
Writing

1. Write a one-paragraph summary of this profile. Obviously, you cannot use all the details and information included in the full article. So how are you going to capture the essence of this article in only a handful of sentences? How can you summarize its main themes while still preserving its overall tone and feel?

2. Scientific processes are often portrayed as rational and structured, when in reality they are often nothing like that. In a concise commentary, use this profile to argue against the popular stereotypes of scientists and the work they do. Do you think a more honest portrayal of science would make it more attractive or less attractive to young people? How might a more truthful portrayal of their work lead scientists themselves to think differently about their own fields of research?

A FEW IDEAS FOR
Composing a Profile

1. **Write a profile of a place or an object.** While writing your profile, think of this place or object as a *person* rather than as an inanimate thing. Discuss its history, its unique characteristics, its relationships with people, and so on. Relate any stories you know about it. Make sure you keep your readers in mind as you write this profile. Write for readers who are interested in visiting this place or object. How can you make your profile interesting and engaging for them?

2. **Repurpose a profile for children.** Find a profile of a famous person (e.g., Martin Luther King, Clara Barton, Abraham Lincoln, Maya Angelou, Cesar Chavez, Princess Diana) and rewrite it in a way that would be accessible and interesting to children who are five to ten years old. Include the original profile when you hand in your rewritten profile to your professor.

3. **Create a profile of someone in your family for the *Memory Archive* (memoryarchive.org).** This site archives personal stories and reflections of everyday people. Use a style that would make your profile especially engaging to readers who don't know you, your family, or your community. Pay special attention to your use of detail, and show your subject in motion or doing things, if possible.

CHAPTER 35

Reviews

Harry Potter's Girl Trouble

CHRISTINE SCHOEFER

Most reviews of J. K. Rowling's Harry Potter *books are positive, if not glowing. Some reviewers, however, have raised concerns about the values portrayed in the books. Some Christians complain about Rowling's perceived romanticizing of witchcraft. Meanwhile, critics such as Christine Schoefer, who wrote this review for* Salon, *see problems from a feminist point of view.*

Four factors made me go out and buy the Harry Potter books: Their impressive lead on the bestseller lists, parents' raves about Harry Potter's magical ability to turn kids into passionate readers, my daughters' clamoring and the mile-long waiting lists at the public library. Once I opened *The Sorcerer's Stone*, I was hooked and read to the last page of Volume 3. Glittering mystery and nail-biting suspense, compelling language and colorful imagery, magical feats juxtaposed with real-life concerns all contributed to making these books page turners. Of course, Diagon Alley haunted me, the Sorting Hat dazzled me, Quidditch intrigued me. Believe me, I tried as hard as I could to ignore the sexism. I really wanted to love Harry Potter. But how could I?

Harry's fictional realm of magic and wizardry perfectly mirrors the conventional assumption that men do and should run the world. From the beginning of the first Potter book, it is boys and men, wizards and sorcerers, who catch our attention by dominating the scenes and determining the action. Harry, of course, plays the lead. In his epic struggle with the forces of darkness—the evil wizard Voldemort and his male supporters—Harry is supported by the dignified wizard Dumbledore and a colorful cast of male characters. Girls, when they are not down-right silly or unlikable, are helpers, enablers and instruments. No girl is brilliantly heroic the way Harry is, no woman is experienced and wise like Professor Dumbledore. In fact, the range of female personalities is so limited that neither women nor girls play on the side of evil.

But, you interject, what about Harry's good friend Hermione? Indeed, she is the female lead and the smartest student at Hogwarts School of Witchcraft and Wizardry. She works hard to be accepted by Harry and his sidekick Ron, who treat her like a tag-along until Volume 3. The trio reminds me of Dennis the Menace, Joey and Margaret or Calvin, Hobbes and Suzy. Like her cartoon counterparts, Hermione is a smart goody-goody who annoys the boys by constantly reminding them of school rules. Early on, she is described as "a bossy know-it-all," hissing at the boys "like an angry goose." Halfway through the first book, when Harry rescues her with Ron's assistance, the hierarchy of power is established. We learn that Hermione's bookish knowledge only goes so far. At the sight of a horrible troll, she "sinks to the floor in fright . . . her mouth open with terror." Like every Hollywood damsel in distress, Hermione depends on the resourcefulness of boys and repays them with her complicity. By lying to cover up for them, she earns the boys' reluctant appreciation.

Though I was impressed by Hermione's brain power, I felt sorry for her. She struggles so hard to get Harry and Ron's approval and respect, in spite of the boys' constant teasing and rejection. And she has no girlfriends. Indeed, there don't seem to be any other girls at the school worth her—or our—attention. Again and again, her emotions interfere with her intelligence, so that she loses her head when it comes to applying her knowledge. Although she casts successful spells for the boys, Hermione messes up her own and as a result, while they go adventuring, she hides in the bathroom with cat fur on her face. I find myself wanting Hermione to shine, but her bookish knowledge and her sincere efforts can't hold a candle to Harry's flamboyant, rule-defying bravery.

Even though Hermione eventually wins 5 the boys' begrudging respect and friendship, her thirst for knowledge remains a constant source of irritation for them. And who can blame them? With her nose stuck in books, she's no fun. Thankfully, she is not hung up on her looks or the shape of her body. But her relentless studying has all the characteristics of a disorder: It makes her ill-humored, renders her oblivious to her surroundings, and threatens her health, especially in the third volume.

Ron's younger sister Ginny, another girl student at Hogwarts, can't help blushing and stammering around Harry, and she fares even worse than Hermione. "Stupid little Ginny" unwittingly becomes the tool of evil when she takes to writing in a magical diary. For months and months, "the foolish little brat" confides "all her pitiful worries and woes" ("how she didn't think famous good great Harry Potter would 'ever' like her") to these pages. We are told how boring it is to listen to "the silly little troubles of an eleven-year-old girl."

Again and again, we see girls so caught up in their emotions that they lose sight of the bigger picture. We watch them "shriek," "scream," "gasp" and "giggle" in situations where boys retain their composure. Again and again, girls stay at the sidelines of adventure while the boys jump in. While Harry's friends clamor to ride his brand-new Firebolt broomstick, for example, classmate Penelope is content just to hold it.

The only female authority figure is beady-eyed, thin-lipped Minerva McGonagall, professor of transfiguration and deputy headmistress of Hogwarts. Stern instead of charismatic, she is described as eyeing her students like "a wrathful eagle." McGonagall is Dumbledore's right hand and she defers to him in every respect. Whereas he has the wisdom to see beyond rules and the power to disregard them, McGonagall is bound by them and enforces them strictly. Although she makes a great effort to keep her feelings under control, in a situation of crisis she loses herself in emotions because she lacks Dumbledore's vision of the bigger picture. When Harry returns from the chamber of secrets, she clutches her chest, gasps, and speaks weakly while the all-knowing Dumbledore beams.

Sybill Trelawney is the other female professor we encounter. She teaches divination, a subject that includes tea-leaf reading, palmistry, crystal gazing—all the intuitive arts commonly associated with female practitioners. Trelawney is a misty, dreamy, dewy charlatan, whose "clairvoyant vibrations" are the subject of constant scorn and ridicule. The only time she makes an accurate prediction, she doesn't even know it because she goes into a stupor. Because most of her students and all of her colleagues dismiss her, the entire intuitive tradition of fortune-telling, a female domain, is discredited.

A brief description of the guests in the 10 Leaky Cauldron pub succinctly summarizes author J. K. Rowling's estimation of male and female: There are "funny little witches," "venerable looking wizards" who argue philosophy, "wild looking warlocks," "raucous dwarfs" and a "hag" ordering a plate of raw liver. Which would you prefer to be? I rest my case.

But I remain perplexed that a woman (the mother of a daughter, no less) would, at the turn of the 20th century, write a book so full of stereotypes. Is it more difficult to imagine a headmistress sparkling with wit, intelligence and passion than to conjure up a unicorn shedding silver blood? More farfetched to create a brilliant, bold and lovable heroine than a marauder's map?

It is easy to see why boys love Harry's adventures. And I know that girls' uncanny ability to imagine themselves in male roles (an empathic skill that boys seem to lack, honed on virtually all children's literature as well as Hollywood's younger audience films) enables them to dissociate from the limitations of female characters. But I wonder about the parents, many of whom join their kids in reading the Harry Potter stories. Is our longing for a magical world so deep, our hunger to be surprised and amazed so intense, our gratitude for a well-told story so great that we are willing to abdicate our critical judgment? Or are the stereotypes in the story integral to our fascination—do we feel comforted by a world in which conventional roles are firmly in place?

I have learned that Harry Potter is a sacred cow. Bringing up my objections has earned me other parents' resentment—they regard me as a heavy-handed feminist with no sense of fun who is trying to spoil a bit of magic they have discovered. But I enjoyed the fantastical world of wizards, witches, beasts and muggles as much as anyone. Is that a good reason to ignore what's been left out?

A CLOSER LOOK AT
Harry Potter's Girl Trouble

1. The review starts out positive as Schoefer describes her early experiences with the Harry Potter books, especially *The Sorcerer's Stone*. At what point does the review switch from positive to negative? Why do you think she started out the review in a positive way if she was going to say negative things about the books?

2. What are a few of the reviewer's criticisms of the books and why does she think the books are flawed in an important way?

3. One of the reviewer's major complaints is that the books do not include a female villain. Why does she think the lack of a female villain is a problem in the Harry Potter series?

IDEAS FOR
Writing

1. Write a brief memoir about your favorite childhood book, something you read by yourself. Describe the experience of reading this special book and the effects it had on you. What attracted you to the book in the first place? What about the book made it different from other books you read? Which characters did you enjoy and why did they appeal to you? What did you learn from the book, and how did it shape your life?

2. Write a letter to the editor in which you respond to this review. Explain why you think the reviewer did or did not properly review the Harry Potter books, especially *The Sorcerer's Stone*. If you generally agree with the review, what might you add about the book that the reviewer should have mentioned? If you disagree with the review, what are some ways the reviewer got the Harry Potter books wrong?

Erika Kane Is My Guru

ANN BAUER

Since soap operas first appeared at the dawn of television, they have been strangely attractive to college students. In this review, Ann Bauer, an English professor, uses her academic skills to explain why she began watching All My Children *and still watches it today. Pay attention to how Bauer also uses the review as a way to confess her guilty pleasure.*

One night, not long ago, I awoke at 2 A.M., breathless, with the sensation of long icy fingers around my throat.

One of my sons had landed in jail the night before, after a joy ride gone horribly awry. Now, stranded in the darkest part of night and powerless to do anything till morning, I was envisioning him in an orange jumpsuit, eating lumpen food off a metal tray. Hearing the clang of tin cups against metal bars. Seeing angry guards carrying billy clubs and criminals with shaved heads and "I Love Mama" tattoos forcing my boy into unnatural positions over a cot.

After a few minutes of lying so taut I could practically levitate, I resigned myself to the fact that I was never going to be able to go back to sleep. So I got out of bed and made a cup of tea, went downstairs, slipped a tape into our ancient VCR and rewound to some random point. Then I pressed play and there, on the screen—like an answer—was Erica Kane, wearing an orange jumpsuit, sitting in a solitary cell and talking to a ladybug.

For the past 20 years, I've watched *All My Children.* Not every day; not even every week. And usually not in real time, because I find there's something depressing about sitting in front of a television in the middle of the day. Instead, I record the show—often accumulating a week's worth at a time—then sit down to watch stretches of it when I'm lonely or anxious or going through a bout of insomnia. "AMC" is my Valium. It's familiar, dependable; the actors never seem to change. Even better: I can tune in to the middle of an episode after a month's hiatus and within three scenes know exactly what's going on. It's like slipping into a warm bath.

My addiction started in college. I was 350 miles from home at a Big 10 school where I didn't know a soul. So I went to the student union every day at noon, between introductory physics and world lit, to buy a bag of popcorn and a Diet Coke and ended up on the edge of a group of kids gathered around a wide-screen TV. Many pretended they weren't watching—especially the big, hairy football players—but if someone tried to change the channel there was a dangerous, collective hum, like the sound before a tornado strikes, and the person handling the remote would quickly back off.

Those were the years of Greg and Jenny, Jessie and Angie, Nina and Cliff. The men were sculpted yet brainy; the women had such dewy skin, it was as if their cheeks had been grafted from infants.' Everyone on the show was in love, dying, divorcing or some combination of the three. And they moved like the players in a Shakespearean tragedy. Just as Romeo killed himself in error after the friar's assistant came late with Juliet's crucial message, the young lovers on AMC suffered one tragedy after another because of the fickle winds of fate.

Within days, I was able to follow the braided story lines and I'd actually made a couple of friends. (Fellow students, I mean.) They filled me in on the characters' backgrounds: Myrtle was an ex-carnival worker, Palmer the town's codgery millionaire. Tad, Jenny's brother, was sleeping with both Liza and her mother, Marion. And minuscule Erica Kane—the indefatigable Susan Lucci, who has been the show's centerpiece since its inception in January 1970—was a fashion model with a presence that was strangely huge.

I stopped for a while after college, forgetting all about the soap during the first months of my marriage and entry-level job. But two years later, my oldest child was born. A persistently sleepless little creature, he awoke as if he had an alarm clock hidden under his Big Bird blankets; every night around 1:30 A.M. I would feed and rock and pat him for hours. That's when I started setting my VCR.

For years, it was a clandestine habit, something I shared in the middle of the night with each of my three infants. They got older and, eventually, the last one quit nursing. When she entered kindergarten, I went to graduate school and became an English professor. You know: the kind who gives lectures on narrative theory and literal emblems and "the inevitability of retrospect," telling students to fill their minds with a variety of great literature and art. My definition was purposely broad: from *Animal House* to *Bridget Jones's Diary*. Yet even I would not have included AMC. Still, I kept up with the soap, sneaking episodes like cigarettes.

We moved to the East Coast. During the 10 day, I taught literature and writing at Brown. Each evening, I'd climb down from my ivory tower and—after tucking my children into bed—I'd follow Erica to Budapest (where she stabbed her eighth husband, Dimitri) and lust after bad-boy cop Trevor, who was tricked into sleeping with his wife's sister, and watch Edmund marry Maria even though he was still in love with Brooke.

Yes, I recognized the overacting and saccharine music and implausible plot points. I had to look past the vulgar displays of wealth:

None of these people seemed to work, but they all lived in castles or penthouse apartments. I even forgave the ridiculous standard of beauty for AMC women, its female characters ranging in size from 0 to 4 and each sporting enough hair extensions to cover the heads of every co-host on *The View*. Because, on some elemental level—the same one, I think, that has always drawn me to epics and fairy tales—I was (and still am) riveted and comforted, borne up in some way, by the recurring themes of the show.

The people in Pine Valley, Pa.—the imaginary hamlet where AMC is set—are, for instance, constantly tumbling into mine shafts or stuck in cellars or trapped in bomb shelters. Their descent can happen in any number of ways: They might be thrown down an abandoned well by a deranged sister or slip into an underground grotto on their own, only to be trapped when some runaway criminal covers the opening with a rock. The point is that over and over, they plunge, literally, into pits of despair. And then they claw their way back out, breaking French-manicured fingernails and ripping Italian silk shirts, but making it back up and into the light.

There is a redemptive quality to all of this. It has the timeless, allegorical cycle of fall and ascent. No matter how wrong things go, this show seems to say, you can always shake off the ashes—like the proverbial phoenix—and rise again. And no one on AMC except the genuinely evil (child killers, for example) ever has to stay in the hell down below.

In Pine Valley, as in the New Testament, the main character never stays dead for long. Characters on AMC keep rising miraculously from their graves. They come back to the fold as angels or—more often—cases of mistaken death. Tad (middle-aged now, and a good man) was lost once in a river current and presumed dead; his wife Dixie's car went off a Swiss cliff. Yet each of them returned, years later, unharmed with some outrageous yet perfectly satisfying explanation: Tad, who'd had amnesia, was "adopted" by a California family and became a winemaker. Dixie gave birth to a baby girl and was tricked into giving her away, then stayed hidden out of shame. (Recently, Dixie died again—this time supposedly for real—but she returned, backlit with a heavenly haze and wearing long, flowing robes, to comfort Tad and help him retrieve their lost child.)

Back when we lived in Providence, R.I., one of the hottest story lines on AMC had to do with Bianca Montgomery, Erica's daughter by Travis (her fifth *and* sixth husband), who had come out as a lesbian. Bianca happened to be born on the same day as my oldest child—I recall watching the episode from my hospital bed—yet while my son was only 14, Bianca had already grown into a young adult who had sex with other women and traveled the world. Bianca and Erica were reconciled after years of being estranged, following a custody suit that Erica lost because it was disclosed that she'd committed adultery with Travis's brother, Jack.

A then single parent of three, working odd hours in a strange, new city and providing far less for my own three than I would have liked, I found it soothing that no matter how badly you bungled at child rearing, the bonds between a mother and her offspring held strong. If Erica could lose her daughter for a decade, then win her back after a few enlightened encounters, I could certainly make up for too many nights grading freshman comp exams.

A couple of years passed. My kids started staying up later and eventually discovered my long-kept secret, holding it over my head like some accidental murder I'd committed while tweaked out on meth. "If you don't let me go to the movie with Helen," my daughter would say, "I'm going to tell everyone about *you and All My Children.*"

I'm ashamed to admit, sometimes this worked.

But then a funny thing happened: Writers I admired began to admit they were also rabid soap opera fans. The most well known probably is David Sedaris, who did a series of commentaries for National Public Radio on his love for *One Life to Live* that earned him an honorary dressing room on the set of the show. Today, soap fandom is viewed as trendy and eccentric among many authors, the equivalent of a famous chef's admitting to a love for Cheese Nips or Spam. Cultural critics even talk about the "Dickensian" quality of daytime television and how this appeals to literary types.

Does this make me feel better? Of course it does. I'll admit, I'd far rather have something in common with David Sedaris than a soap junkie who has nothing better to do in the middle of the day.

I suspect, however, that secret soap watching is a fetish shared by many professionals. According to the Nielsen stats, *All My Children* has 2.6 million regular viewers, yet only 817,000 of those are the targeted females between the ages of 18 and 49. Add to this a 68 percent increase in viewership as a result of TiVo, and it looks less and less like nursing home residents account for the other 1.7-plus mil.

In the July issue of *Elle*, writer Laurie Abraham confessed her addiction to *All My Children*—which she watches each weekday when it airs, after a morning of work—calling it her "amulet against failure" and "a cleansing sorbet for the brain." She also wrote that rugged male characters such as Zach, a just-this-side-of-the-law casino owner; Ryan, a clean-cut motorcycle-riding sportsman; and Aidan, an Irish-born detective who recently engineered a rescue mission in Sudan, were added to help cultivate a growing male audience. Most straight men don't talk about the soaps, but the evidence says they're watching.

A case in point: I published an essay last year that referred, in passing, to Erica Kane and received an "anonymous" e-mail from a middle-aged patent attorney identifying himself only as Jackson—Erica's former brother-in-law and 10th husband, the one who resulted in her losing her custody suit—and confessing that he locks his office door each day at noon so he can spend his lunch hour alone, sitting on his leather couch, watching. He was terrified someday his secretary would find out.

Life has been better, I wrote back, since I stopped hiding my habit.

I no longer fight the fact that this simple 25 and totally free form of entertainment provides a hopeful, mystical counterpoint to everyday life. Take, for instance, that night I slipped down to the basement—my son in jail—to find Erica in her own prison, carrying on a conversation with a ladybug.

Now this may not sound like something a hardheaded sex goddess, former fashion mogul, and modern-day talk show host would do. But it's a leap you have to make because it demonstrates another theme of *All My Children:* the inherent value of every creature, large or small. It's rumored that Agnes Nixon created the show nearly 40 years ago as a spiritual alternative to other soaps, and that the title is a biblical reference, the children in question being God's. (Note: When I called Mike Cohen, the ABC/AMC media rep, to ask if the soap opera is based on Christian principles, I got the brushoff. "I wouldn't know anything about that," he said.)

I took a sloshy sort of solace from the conversation between Erica—who'd been thrown in solitary for reasons I never learned—and that insect she held in her hand. I don't remember much of it. But there was something about how everything happens for a reason and her jail stay had taught her something valuable about life.

Here's a woman who has been married and divorced nearly a dozen times, who has been abandoned by her father, raped by a family friend, bankrupted repeatedly and addicted to drugs. She found out her beloved daughter was a lesbian—which, in one of AMC's putatively groundbreaking moments, she initially rejected then embraced—and discovered the fetus she'd meant to abort actually was "salvaged" and carried to term in the body of another woman. (You doubt the show is Christian, Mr. Cohen?) The point

seems to be that whatever happens, Erica Kane carries on.

This, to me, is the narrative's basic wisdom. I'm not usually fond of the issue-oriented story lines focusing on domestic violence, transgender issues, cochlear implants or autism. But occasionally AMC does manage to cut through the wealth and excess and drama, getting to something meaningful and universal that I believe adds to our world.

Take Stuart Chandler. An undiagnosed 30 artistic cipher with little sense of the world, Stuart is his twin brother Adam's touchstone, conscience, and heart. Both roles are played by David Canary. (Canary is, in my opinion, an actor of London stage quality. Just watch him in a scene where he is actually Adam pretending to be Stuart, juggling the features of both men and magically giving viewers complex, subtle character cues.) Adam and Stuart embody, in their entwined, mirror-image way, man's darkness and light. It's a worn device, granted, but in this case well used. And for years, I have watched their drama unfold: the intelligent yet ruthless Adam being held in check by his softer, slower brother, and Stuart's needs—for money and life-skills counseling—clearly overshadowed by his creativity and goodness and art.

This, I like to think, is what many AMC viewers are hanging on to: the value of a rumpled, white-haired man who stutters and paints, his Boo Radley brand of decency and the fact that there is a mythical town tucked in the mountains of Pennsylvania where he has carved out a place. Even the mighty Erica seeks out Stuart when she needs guidance. When she isn't consulting a ladybug, that is.

During the early morning following my son's arrest, I watched two and a half backlogged episodes, and this took me through almost until dawn. Then I fell asleep on the couch and rested peacefully until 7 A.M., when it was time to get up, call an attorney and resume the business of my own life, where I don't live in a castle or run a multi-million-dollar cosmetics company. But all my children are beautifully, painfully real.

A CLOSER LOOK AT
Erika Kane Is My Guru

1. This review takes on a confessional tone. The reviewer, Ann Bauer, is an English professor who is not "supposed" to enjoy middle-brow entertainment like soap operas. Where in the review does the author seem to be confessing a transgression of some kind, and how does she justify her desire (and perhaps need) to watch this show?

2. The review packs a great amount of detail into its description of *All My Children*. How do these details help you, as the reader, understand the show itself? If you have never seen this soap opera, do you still have a sense of what it is about and some of its major characters and plotlines? If you have seen the show, how well do these details mirror your experiences with it? Does Bauer describe the show accurately?

3. Bauer's style slips back and forth between an academic style, common for an English professor, and the style of a regular fan of *All My Children*. Find five places in this review where she sounds like an English professor writing a literary analysis. Then find five places where she seems more like a typical soap opera fan. How are these two styles different, and how do the differences between them set up an interesting tug of war between the author as English professor and as soap opera fan?

IDEAS FOR
Writing

1. Do you have a guilty pleasure that you feel is inconsistent with your normal behavior? Have you enjoyed doing something that you might be embarrassed to tell people? In a memoir, describe a time or situation in which this activity was important to you. What did you enjoy about it? Why does this activity appeal to you and how does it fit with your character and values? How does this activity go against what people might expect of you? Use your memoir to explore this activity and your interests in it.

2. Soap operas are just one guilty pleasure on television. If you ask around, you may find that people enjoy other kinds of shows that you would not expect, such as shopping networks, infomercials, professional wrestling, or children's cartoons. Write a report in which you describe the viewing habits of college students. You might create a survey in which you ask people about the kinds of taboo shows they like to watch. Perhaps you could set up some short interviews. You might also do some research into academic and Internet sources to determine why people enjoy these kinds of guilty pleasures.

Review: *Twilight*

TODD HERTZ

In this review of the movie Twilight, *Todd Hertz discusses why the* Twilight *books and the movie appeal to young girls. His review of the movie, which was published in* Christianity Today, *is mixed. Pay special attention to how Hertz describes the movie's strengths and weaknesses.*

Because of immense buzz for this first film adaptation of Stephenie Meyer's *Twilight* series of novels, some have compared this tween and teen phenom to Harry Potter. Like the last two Potter movies, this vampire romance film made Fandango.com's top ten list of all-time advance ticket sales—thanks to a rabid fan base whose hearts were set on swoon ever since they first saw images of the vampire and werewolf dreamboats they've fallen for in the books.

But this is not Harry Potter. As *Entertainment Weekly* reported last week, the seven Potter books have sold 400 million copies; *Twilight*'s four books have sold 17 million. And the most crucial difference: The Potter books—and movies—seem to draw all ages and both genders. *Twilight* captures young girls. So, can *Twilight* satisfy the teen girl devotees of the books and reach a bigger audience too?

Well, I think most *Twilight* fans will eat this up like vampires at a blood bank. The movie, directed by Catherine Hardwicke (*The Nativity Story, Thirteen*), is very true to the book in telling Meyer's soap opera of forbidden love and angst with passion. I saw the film at a public screening with many young girls sporting *Twilight* shirts and even vampire regalia. I overheard them saying things like, "That was amazing," "I wish it would have gone on forever," and "It was everything I hoped for."

But on the flip side, the adults nearby were saying things like "That was horrible" and "I thought it wouldn't end." I'm somewhere in the middle. While I think the adaptation has some great touches, I don't think the film does much for the uninitiated or adults. Boys will really only like the big fight at the end—if they're still awake.

Twilight is a simple love story—with a twist 5 right out of *Buffy the Vampire Slayer*—that taps into the longings of lovesick girls. High schooler Bella Swan (Kristen Stewart) moves to Forks, Washington, to be with her dad and feels alone and miserable. That is, until Edward Cullen (Robert Pattinson) mysteriously enters her life. There is something different about the ridiculously handsome, pale, and moody Edward and his brothers and sisters. And that something is that they're vampires who've chosen to live as a family and be "vegetarians"—in other words, only eat the blood of animals. Still, Edward craves human blood. So when he is drawn to Bella romantically, he knows he should keep a distance because of the temptation she presents to the killing monster inside him. Is their love worth the danger?

Meyer, a Mormon, interjected her book with moral themes with which Christians resonate. For more on this, see the story from teen mag *Ignite Your Faith* about the books' handling of the supernatural, romantic love and temptation. (While the use of vampires and other "evil" creatures can be offsetting to some Christians, they are not symbolic of demons here. They are merely a story device to create a forbidden and mysterious love interest. In fact—save for about 10 minutes of vampire action at the end—the Cullens could just be a lightly-pigmented family with superpowers.)

In some ways, Meyer's thematic nuance is lost in the movie version. But still, it is pretty clear that Edward's temptations to attack Bella, his chivalrous setting of physical boundaries for them, and Bella's complete willingness to let go of her soul (literally in the vampire mythos) to give Edward her eternal love are all big metaphors for sex, lust and the allure of the forbidden. (By the way, Meyer chose an Eden-like apple as *Twilight*'s book cover image for a reason.)

In the book, this is an interesting look at dealing with temptation and boundaries, but the movie's love story is pretty much all about sexual attraction. I'm also not sure why the movie's Bella is fascinated by Edward. He's hot, he's a bad boy, and he wants her. Well, he wants her for dinner. But for this lonely girl, being wanted at all is enough. And of course that idea of being wanted, being known, and being passionately loved has really tapped into the desires of the books' teen audience—and the movie does that too. After all, the film seems tailor-made to showcase how good-looking and tempting Edward is. His over-the-top, slow-motion, and dramatic entrance could be accompanied with subtitles reading, "Swoon now!"

While I think most fans will be happy with the film, I think the movie proves that books can sometimes get away with sappiness and clichés that movies don't; onscreen, they are pretty groan-worthy. Also, while the book captures girls' hearts, the movie's love story without Meyer's description is kinda mundane. Another issue with the change in medium is that a movie doesn't let one's imagination work as a book does. Meyer's fantastical narratives are very detailed and create great mental pictures. On screen, they sometimes can't compete with what's in your head. In one popular portion of the book, for example, Edward dramatically shows why vampires don't go in the sunlight. On the printed page, the description is thrilling. In the movie, flawed special effects make it look likc he's just really sweaty.

These types of things won't impress new 10 audiences the way the book grabbed readers. Like Hardwicke struggled with in *The Nativity Story*, her integration of the supernatural into the natural world can come off cheesy and overdone. Almost all the special effects (save for that great ending fight) are almost laughable—like the vampires' super speed, which looks more like what I call "Muppet Running." You know how when Kermit would walk, you could tell he was hung by wires and his legs didn't really hit the ground with each step? That's what

happens here, defying the laws of physics. In addition, the makeup of the pale Cullen family can seem very caked on and fakey at times. Plus, the vampires are asked to say silly things like, "Hold on tight, spider monkey!"

Other than the bloodsuckers, the rest of the film is pretty good. The Pacific Northwest scenery is lush and beautiful. The characters are right out of the book—as is the soft humor and endearing relationships like that between Bella and her dad. And, for me, what holds the whole thing together is Kristen Stewart's performance as Bella. She grounds the movie and gives us genuine emotion and personality.

But as good as Stewart is, I think Pattinson (who was solid as Cedric in *Harry Potter and the Goblet of Fire*) as Edward was a casting mistake. Or maybe it was how he was directed. He's wooden and emotes with unchanging facial expression of brooding eyebrows, deep breathing, and body language that communicates that he really has to go to the bathroom. These scenes lead to unintentional laughter in even the most serious moments.

What Pattinson does do well, though, are the tender, loving moments with Stewart. This is maybe what the movie does best: quiet moments of intimacy—not sex, but more innocent intimacy like when the infatuated Bella and Edward lie in the grass with their hands barely touching, or when they share their first kiss. These are electric moments, but the rest of the film pales in comparison.

A CLOSER LOOK AT
Twilight

1. List four strengths about *Twilight* that Hertz mentions, then list four weaknesses. How does Hertz weigh these strengths against the weaknesses to determine whether the movie is worth seeing or not?

2. Like any review, this one summarizes a good amount of the movie itself. How much does the review give away about the movie? What are some things that Hertz, as the reviewer, has chosen to leave out? Do

you think he spoiled the movie by summarizing too much, or should his review have offered more to give you a better idea about what the movie is about?

3. This review appeared in *Christianity Today*. How does the place where it was published shape the review? Identify a few places where the readers and context may have shaped how the reviewer responded to the movie.

IDEAS FOR
Writing

1. One of Hertz's main complaints is that the *Twilight* books and the movie appeal to young girls, unlike the broader appeal of the *Harry Potter* books. Write a position paper in which you discuss whether it is good or bad that only young girls seem interested in *Twilight,* while other demographic groups show little or no interest.

2. Write a report in which you research the history of vampire mythology. When did vampires emerge as characters in mythology? Do vampires appear in many cultures, or were they a unique feature of a particular culture? Why do you think vampires still make fascinating characters today?

"Left Behind," a Virtual Battle for the Souls of Unbelievers

JANE LAMPMAN

In this article, Jane Lampman of the Christian Science Monitor *reviews the video game version of* Left Behind: Eternal Forces. *The video game was controversial, because it was based on the idea that people "left behind," after others (namely, fundamentalist Christians) were raptured to heaven, would need to compete with each other for survival and redemption. As you read this review, keep in mind the cultural politics that underlie this issue.*

"In one cataclysmic moment, millions around the world disappear." Not a bad intro for a dramatic video game. It turns out those millions have been "raptured" into heaven by Jesus. The player's job is to battle to save the ones left behind on earth from the global forces of evil, which are controlled by the Antichrist.

The hitch, though, in this new game aimed at teens, is who constitutes those "forces of evil": activists, secularists, non-Christian rock musicians, and others who resist "recruitment" into the "forces of good"—the believers in a particular kind of Christianity.

Based on the popular *Left Behind* series of apocalyptic novels, "Left Behind: Eternal Forces" is being marketed for Christmas giving through churches and big-box retailers such as Wal-Mart.

But it has created a stir among Christian, Jewish, and activist groups who disagree with the fundamentalist theology the game presents. They say it will teach children religious intolerance and an "us vs. them" view of the world that is both dangerous for the country and contrary to basic Christian teachings. The game's producers disagree.

The real-time strategy (RTS) game takes [5] place in New York City. "You are sent on a spiritual and military mission to convert people, and nobody is allowed to remain neutral," says Eric Elnes, copresident of Crosswalk America, a progressive Christian group, who says he's explored the game extensively. "You lose spirit points if you kill somebody, but you can hit the prayer button to restore the points."

Mr. Elnes's organization has joined with other Christian groups to petition the game's producers to withdraw it from the market. At the same time, two groups that seek to counter the religious right—the Campaign to Defend the Constitution and Christian Alliance for Progress—have written to Wal-Mart requesting that the PC-based game be taken off the shelves.

"The premillennial theology says there will be religious warfare in our lifetime, and people will be targeting fellow Americans," says Frederick Clarkson, of Talk2Action.org. He worries gamers could come to accept that script for the future.

The game's producers see it very differently. At a time when young people seem less inclined toward Christianity, they say they're trying to reach Christian teens with an alternative to darker video games like "Grand Theft Auto," and hopefully draw other gamers to the faith.

"About 92 percent of kids today are playing games," says Jeffrey Frichner, president of Left Behind Games. "We had the vision to create a game with a positive moral message based on biblical values that parents could embrace and discuss with their kids." He says the game promotes prayer and worship, and deals with "questions of eternal importance."

Producers have spoken with their Cross- [10] walk critics, and Frichner says they'll provide a patch to address one concern.

A review on a website of the conservative group, Focus on the Family, endorses "Eternal Forces" as "the kind of game Mom and Dad can actually play with Junior." Other reviews speak of fairly good production values, but say the game is unwieldy to play and tend to pan it.

The controversy arises largely because the game follows the *Left Behind* novels, Mr. Frichner says. The 14-book series by Tim LaHaye and Jerry Jenkins has sold more than 63 million copies, including 13 million of *The Kids* series, a spinoff for children 10 and older. "So we felt we had a bulls-eye market there for the game," he adds.

Dr. LaHaye, one of the most influential leaders in fundamentalist Christianity, conceived the novels as a way to spread to theology called premillennial dispensationalism. First promoted by 19th-century Englishman John Nelson Darby, the theology interprets portions of the Bible as predicting at two-stage return of Jesus.

First, Jesus comes to transport "true Christians" to heaven in what's called "the rapture"; "the tribulation" follows on earth, involving seven years of catastrophe and plagues (as drawn from Revelation).

"It is going to be an unprecedented time [15] of horror of God's judgment on earth," says Terry James, of raptureready.com, the most popular prophecy website.

The period will end with Armageddon and the Second Corning. Those who preach the theology say Jesus' return is imminent. And according to Mr. James, the creation of Israel in 1948 is the most important signal that the End Times have begun. The job of Christians is to convert and save as many people as possible.

The novels focus on the time of the tribulations. The Antichrist is a former head of the United Nations, based in Iraq. His evil minions are called the Global Community Peacekeepers, and are the only people who seek peace treaties. Battles occur around the earth between good and evil forces, leading up to Armageddon in Israel. There, some Jews convert to Christianity and the rest are destroyed along with others who have not accepted Jesus as their savior. Jesus' rule then begins on earth.

The video game engages young gamers as the Tribulation Forces to fight the evil peacekeepers. In multiplayer mode, gamers play on both sides.

"It's ironic the game has been put out for Christmas, which honors the Prince of Peace who said, 'Blessed are the peacemakers, for they shall be called the children of God,'" says Mr. Elnes. "What this game says in 'Cursed are the peacekeepers, for they are children of the Antichrist.'"

The game is the latest facet of a struggle 20 within Christianity over growing promotion of the theology in books, on websites and TV, and in Christian Zionist organizations backing a strong alliance with Israel. Premillennialism is not consistent with Catholic, Eastern Orthodox, or mainline Protestant teachings.

Barbara Rossing, an expert on the book of Revelation at the Lutheran School of Theology in Chicago, says the notion of the rapture is not a biblical idea but a fiction, and the word isn't found in the Bible.

"That's not what the book of Revelation is about, forecasting a sequence of terrifying events that are going to happen," she says. "Also, while Christians say there is evil in the world, we should never say that evil is incarnate in people. . . . The traditional Christian teaching is to be engaged with loving God's world, seeing God's image in people, and taking care of one another."

Some Jews are also troubled by the game. "Jews are often instrumental in rapture theology—war in Israel, Jews converting to Christianity, all other Jews disappearing in the third act of a four-act play," says Rabbi Haim Dov Beliak, of Jews On First, a First Amendment watchdog group. "What happens if no rapture or Second Coming occurs? The classical response in history has been to blame the Jews for somehow foiling everybody's hopes and plans." Jews On First has created a petition opposing the game on its website for people of all faiths to sign; some 500 have done so in the first few days, the rabbi says.

Many critics admit that in America, banning a product is not the best solution. They say they are trying to educate parents about the contents of the game so they can exercise judgment.

There's even a stir among the faithful 25 over the amount of violence they hear is in the game, says James, though neither he nor most of those e-mailing him have yet seen it for themselves.

Frichner says the issue is simply one of different views of Christianity, and the game, which has been approved for teens by the software ratings board, will sell mostly among evangelical Christians.

Yet they are already having success in evangelizing others, he adds. The game has elements that educate players on various issues (such as evolution and intelligent design), and gives them the opportunity to become believers.

"We've already received e-mails from people who have done that," Frichner says.

A CLOSER LOOK AT
"Left Behind"

1. In this review, the writer is trying to show both sides of a debate about a video game. How does she give both sides an ability to state their positions? Does she seem to take sides on this issue, or does she try to stay in the middle? How does she accomplish this?

2. As in most reviews, Lampman needs to give readers enough information about the game so they can understand it. How does Lampman use description to reveal elements of the game? Do you think she offers enough information? Would you have liked more? Lampman also gives quite a bit of background

information on fundamentalists' notions of a world-ending apocalypse. Did you find that information helpful? If so, what did you find helpful and why?

3. What are some of the larger political and cultural issues raised by this video game and referred to in this review? How does the game itself, as described here, go against some of the "common expectations" of some groups while reinforcing the common expectations of fundamentalist Christians? Do you think this kind of video game is an effective recruiting tool for fundamentalist Christians, or do you think it does more harm than good?

IDEAS FOR
Writing

1. Religious groups often try to reach out to young people with new media, like video games, movies, and music. In a position paper, argue for or against some of these attempts to reach out to people. As a college student, how do you feel about these kinds of recruiting efforts, many of them aimed at people just like you? Do you think religious groups should be engaged in using new media to reach out to young people? Or do you think these efforts are already preaching to the choir—that is, entertaining the already convinced and converted?

2. The style of this review makes it more straightforward and perhaps less entertaining than others. Write a rhetorical analysis in which you explore the rhetorical qualities of this review. First pay attention to what the author is trying to accomplish. Then pay attention to the review's content, organization, and style. Look at its use of reasoning (*logos*), authority (*ethos*), and emotion (*pathos*). In what ways is this review effective, and in what ways could it perhaps be more effective (or at least, more entertaining)?

A FEW IDEAS FOR
Composing a Review

1. **Write a review of something you absolutely did not enjoy.** Your topic could be a movie, play, restaurant, book—just about anything. Be creative. Keep in mind, though, that your review will be for public viewing, so you want to be fair while explaining what you did not like about the subject. Then add a brief cover letter written to your professor and your classmates in which you discuss some of the challenges of writing a negative review.

2. **Write a review of three of your favorite movies in a specific genre.** Your review should discuss them together and argue that they are some of the best examples of this genre. What are some of your and your readers' common expectations about this genre? How do these particular movies succeed within the genre, and where do they stray from it? Compare and contrast these three movies to show how they are similar and how they are different.

3. **Find a review on the Internet that you disagree with.** Then write a rebuttal review in which you argue against the other reviewer and show why your subject is actually better or worse than the reviewer said. Your review should be written for the same Web site in which you found the original review.

Evaluations

Why We Crave Horror Movies

STEPHEN KING

This curious article was first published in Playboy *in January 1981 when Stephen King was emerging as one of the great horror writers. It's not a standard evaluation, but it has many of this genre's elements. Watch how King stretches the genre to achieve an interesting purpose.*

I think that we're all mentally ill: those of us outside the asylums only hide it a little better—and maybe not all that much better, after all. We've all known people who talk to themselves, people who sometimes squinch their faces into horrible grimaces when they believe no one is watching, people who have some hysterical fear—of snakes, the dark, the tight place, the long drop . . . and, of course, those final worms and grubs that are waiting so patiently underground.

When we pay our four or five bucks and seat ourselves at tenth-row center in a theater showing a horror movie, we are daring the nightmare.

Why? Some of the reasons are simple and obvious. To show that we can, that we are not afraid, that we can ride this roller coaster. Which is not to say that a really good horror movie may not surprise a scream out of us at some point, the way we may scream when the roller coaster twists through a complete 360 or plows through a lake at the bottom of the drop. And horror movies, like roller coasters, have always been the special province of the young; by the time one turns 40 or 50, one's appetite for double twists or 360-degree loops may be considerably depleted.

We also go to re-establish our feelings of essential normality; the horror movie is innately conservative, even reactionary. Freda Jackson as the horrible melting woman in *Die,*

Monster, Die! confirms for us that no matter how far we may be removed from the beauty of a Robert Redford or a Diana Ross, we are still light-years from true ugliness.

And we go to have fun. 5

Ah, but this is where the ground starts to slope away, isn't it? Because this is a very peculiar sort of fun indeed. The fun comes from seeing others menaced—sometimes killed. One critic has suggested that if pro football has become the voyeur's version of combat, then the horror film has become the modern version of the public lynching.

It is true that the mythic, "fairytale" horror film intends to take away the shades of gray. . . . It urges us to put away our more civilized and adult penchant for analysis and to become children again, seeing things in pure blacks and whites. It may be that horror movies provide psychic relief on this level because this invitation to lapse into simplicity, irrationality and even outright madness is extended so rarely. We are told we may allow our emotions a free rein . . . or no rein at all.

If we are all insane, then sanity becomes a matter of degree. If your insanity leads you to carve up women like Jack the Ripper or the Cleveland Torso Murderer, we clap you away in the funny farm (but neither of those two amateur-night surgeons was ever caught, heh-heh-heh); if, on the other hand your insanity leads you only to talk to yourself when you're under stress or to pick your nose on the morning bus, then you are left alone to go about your business . . . though it is doubtful that you will ever be invited to the best parties.

The potential lyncher is in almost all of us (excluding saints, past and present; but then, most saints have been crazy in their own ways), and every now and then, he has to be let loose to scream and roll around in the grass. Our emotions and our fears form their own body, and we recognize that it demands its own exercise to maintain proper muscle tone. Certain of these emotional muscles are accepted—even exalted—in civilized society; they are, of course, the emotions that tend to maintain the status quo of civilization itself. Love, friendship, loyalty, kindness—these are all the emotions that we applaud, emotions that have been immortalized in the couplets of Hallmark cards. . . .

When we exhibit these emotions, soci- 10 ety showers us with positive reinforcement; we learn this even before we get out of diapers. When, as children, we hug our rotten little puke of a sister and give her a kiss, all the aunts and uncles smile and twit and cry, "Isn't he the sweetest little thing?" Such coveted treats as chocolate-covered graham crackers often follow. But if we deliberately slam the rotten little puke of a sister's fingers in the door, sanctions follow—angry remonstrance from parents, aunts and uncles; instead of a chocolate-covered graham cracker, a spanking.

But anticivilization emotions don't go away, and they demand periodic exercise. We have such "sick" jokes as, "What's the difference between a truckload of bowling balls and a truckload of dead babies?" (You can't unload a truckload of bowling balls with a pitchfork . . . a joke, by the way, that I heard originally from a ten-year-old.) Such a joke may surprise a laugh or a grin out of us even as we recoil, a possibility that confirms the thesis: If we share a brotherhood of man, then we also share an insanity of man. None of which is intended as a defense of either the sick joke or insanity but merely as an explanation of why the best horror films, like the best fairy tales, manage to be reactionary, anarchistic, and revolutionary all at the same time.

The mythic horror movie, like the sick joke, has a dirty job to do. It deliberately appeals to all that is worst in us. It is morbidity unchained, our most base instincts let free, our nastiest fantasies realized . . . and it all happens, fittingly enough, in the dark. For those reasons, good liberals often shy away from horror films. For myself, I like to see the most aggressive of them—*Dawn of the Dead*, for instance—as lifting a trap door in the civilized forebrain and throwing a basket of raw meat to the hungry alligators swimming around in that subterranean river beneath.

Why bother? Because it keeps them from getting out, man. It keeps them down there and me up here. It was Lennon and McCartney who said that all you need is love, and I would agree with that.

As long as you keep the gators fed.

A CLOSER LOOK AT
Why We Crave Horror Movies

1. List the three qualities (criteria) that Stephen King argues are the characteristics of an excellent horror film. Do you agree with these criteria? Would you add or subtract some of them? How does King use these criteria to sort the good horror movies from the bad?

2. King's style is especially interesting in this article. He seems to be making a straightforward argument about the difference between good horror movies and bad horror movies. But occasionally, he throws a strange sentence at the readers, creating a pained laugh or a dark thought. Find a handful of these moments in the article. How does he use style to bring about this dark humor?

3. The evaluation is about horror movies, but King's real motive is to explore the psychology behind people's fascination with such movies. He identi-fies several reasons why people crave horror films. Highlight these reasons and discuss them with a group in your class. Do you agree with King, or do you think people have other reasons for enjoying horror movies?

IDEAS FOR
Writing

1. Write a rebuttal to King's article in which you dispute his reasoning or offer different reasons why people like to see horror movies. In your rebuttal, you could challenge King's criteria, or you could question whether he is right about why people enjoy blood and gore. You might even challenge the worth of these kinds of movies altogether. You don't need to completely disagree with King, but you should distinguish your argument from his in a significant way.

2. Rent or go see a horror film, perhaps one based on a Stephen King novel. Write a review of the movie us-ing King's evaluation criteria in this article as the basis of your review. Unlike King's evaluation, your review does not need to define the criteria. Instead, assume King's criteria reflect "common expectations" that most moviegoers will accept. Unlike King, you do not need to make a broader argument about the psychology of these movies. Instead, review the movie as though you were writing for a newspaper or a movie review blog.

The Lord of the Dance Doesn't Have Anything on Me

DAVE BARRY

Dave Barry has been a long-time humorist for the Miami Herald. *Often exploring the differences between men and women from the stereotypically male perspective, his articles are not politically correct, but they are usually good for a smile. In this evaluation, Barry offers a negative evaluation of ballet as an art form. In this case, though, he is not being objective. Note how the insertion of himself as a subjective evaluator creates a strange undertow in this article.*

I am not a fan of ballet.

Now, before you members of the Dance Community get your leotards in a bunch, let me stress that I KNOW I AM WRONG. I know that ballet is a beautiful artistic form that requires great dedication and skill. I'm just saying that I, personally, would rather watch a dog catch a Frisbee.

My problem—and it's MY problem, NOT ballet's problem—is that, because I am culturally unsophisticated, all ballet looks to me like—even though I know there is MUCH more to it—a troupe of mincing mimes. Whatever the ballet plot is about—love, hate, joy, sorrow, the Russian Revolution, measles—the reaction of the dancers is: "It's MINCING time!"

Granted, it is an extremely high caliber of mincing, coupled with some impressive prancing. A nongraceful, out-of-shape layperson like myself could not in a million years prance like that. If I, in my current weight class, were to attempt to launch myself into the air and land on my tippytoes, I would have to be minced off the stage by ballet paramedics.

So I admire the skill involved. It's just that, after I have watched dancers mince around for, say, eight minutes, I have had my ballet quota for that particular decade.

The only time I truly enjoyed ballet was years ago, when I attended a performance at a display garden where the stage wings were formed by thick, high hedges. At one point—I estimate it was 14 hours into the performance—a male dancer and a female dancer were onstage doing the Mince of Passion, and the male did what a man must do in BalletLand to show a woman that he truly loves her; namely, hoist her over his head.

He then attempted to prance offstage with her, but her tutu apparently obscured his vision, and he pranced her, headfirst, smack into the shrubbery. She went in as far as her shoulders. The male had to yank her out, back up, re-aim, and prance off, trying to maintain an expression of passion, though you could tell from the female's face that the affair was OVER. I wanted to shout: "Encore!"

I know that, because of this column, I will receive many angry (yet fragrant) letters from ballet lovers. As a veteran columnist, I even know what these letters will say.

"Dear Berry," they will say. "As a member of the Dance Community, I am appalled by the ignorance of your ignorant column, which only reveals how ignorant you are, you ignoramus. For you to so ignorantly ignore the beauty of ballet, not to mention making light of the potentially career-ending tragedy of a shrub-related injury, only underscores the ignorance of your ignorant . . ."

And so on. Well, guess what, ballet lovers? You don't have to write! I am already being punished, severely, for not liking ballet. My daughter has decided, at age $2 \frac{1}{2}$, that all she wants is to be a ballerina. She has a tutu, which she wears with everything, including her pajamas. She likes to mince and twirl, and she expects her mother and me to mince and twirl with her, with our hands over our heads, ballet-style. We do this a LOT. "Pirouette 'Til You Puke," that is our motto.

We took Sophie to see a real ballet, and she loved it so much that she had to get up and twirl in the aisle. I even enjoyed some of it, although not the costumes worn by the male dancers, which left nothing to the imagination, if you know what I mean, and if you don't, what I mean is they looked like they were smuggling dead squirrels in their tights. I don't want my daughter seeing that! Do these guys spend so much on eyeliner that they can't afford a pair of shorts?

After the performance, the dancers went to the lobby to meet the audience, thrilling Sophie, who got some of them to sign her program. She now believes this is an integral part of ballet. At home, after we twirl for a while, she announces that she is going to the "lobby," which is my closet, and she waits there, in her tutu, until we bring her a pen and a paper to "sign."

So this is how I am being punished for not liking ballet: I spend my days twirling and mincing, then standing in a closet, getting an autograph from somebody who can't write. Ballet lessons loom ahead. I am now facing years of ballet-watching, and I frankly don't know how I'm going to get through it.

Because these tights really itch.

1. How does Barry's insertion of himself into the evaluation change its perspective and tone? In a typical evaluation, the writer tries to be as objective as possible. But in this article, Barry is clearly not being objective about his subject. How does this change the nature of an evaluation?

2. Barry uses exaggeration to draw attention to specific points in his argument. Readers will easily recognize these exaggerations, and the distortions are usually played for laughs. Find five of these exaggerations and study them closely. What is the real effect of these exaggerations on the readers? How does Barry use them to make room for the points he wants to argue for?

3. In this article, Barry is already anticipating the angry letters he will receive. How does he try to disarm his critics by raising their own points in a humorous way? Barry is clearly trying to provoke or silence his potential critics when he anticipates their rebuttals. How does he try to do this? Do you think he is effective in diverting or fending off their arguments?

IDEAS FOR
Writing

1. Write two brief responses to Barry's article. In the first response, play the "believing game" in which you argue that Barry is correct about ballet. If you don't like ballet, perhaps you can add your own experiences and thoughts to Barry's arguments. If you like ballet, you could make a few concessions. Then, in your second response, play the "doubting game" in which you show the weaknesses in Barry's argument. If you like ballet, you can offer a rebuttal that calls him out. If you don't like ballet, you could still rise to its defense by critiquing Barry's unfairness toward an activity that others enjoy.

2. Write a letter to the editor of the *Miami Herald* in which you respond to Barry's article. You can agree with Barry or disagree with him. You can thank him for revealing the truth about ballet, or you could expose him as an uncultured troublemaker who won't take the time to see the positive qualities in ballet. Make sure you support your points with your own experiences and research.

On Dumpster Diving

LARS EIGHNER

Homelessness is something that most people never experience. In this article, Lars Eighner uses the evaluation genre loosely to discuss his own experiences as a homeless person. He shows how a reasonable person like himself learns to survive by scavenging for food and other necessities in other people's trash.

Long before I began Dumpster diving I was impressed with Dumpsters, enough so that I wrote the Merriam-Webster research service to discover what I could about the word *Dumpster*. I learned from them that it is a proprietary word belonging to the Dempster Dumpster company. Since then I have dutifully capitalized the word, although it was lowercased in almost all the citations Merriam-Webster photocopied for me. Dempster's word is too apt. I have never heard these things called anything but Dumpsters. I do not know anyone who knows the generic name for these objects. From time to time I have heard a wino or hobo give some corrupted credit to the original and call them Dipsy Dumpsters.

I began Dumpster diving about a year before I became homeless.

I prefer the word *scavenging* and use the word *scrounging* when I mean to be obscure. I have heard people, evidently meaning to be polite, use the word *foraging,* but I prefer to reserve that word for gathering nuts and berries and such, which I do also according to the season and the opportunity. *Dumpster diving* seems to me to be a little too cute and, in my case, inaccurate because I lack the athletic ability to lower myself into the Dumpsters as the true divers do, much to their increased profit.

I like the frankness of the word *scavenging,* which I can hardly think of without picturing a big black snail on an aquarium wall. I live from the refuse of others. I am a scavenger. I think it a sound and honorable niche, although if I could I would naturally prefer to live the comfortable consumer life, perhaps—and only perhaps—as a slightly less wasteful consumer, owing to what I have learned as a scavenger.

While Lizbeth and I were still living in 5 the shack on Avenue B as my savings ran out, I put almost all my sporadic income into rent. The necessities of daily life I began to extract from Dumpsters. Yes, we ate from them. Except for jeans, all my clothes came from Dumpsters. Boom boxes, candles, bedding, toilet paper, a virgin male love doll, medicine, books, a typewriter, dishes, furnishings, and change, sometimes amounting to many dollars—I acquired many things from the Dumpsters.

I have learned much as a scavenger. I mean to put some of what I have learned down here, beginning with the practical art of Dumpster diving and proceeding to the abstract.

What is safe to eat?

After all, the finding of objects is becoming something of an urban art. Even respectable employed people will sometimes find something tempting sticking out of a Dumpster or standing beside one. Quite a number of people, not all of them of the bohemian type, are willing to brag that they found this or that piece in the trash. But eating from Dumpsters is what separates the dilettanti from the professionals. Eating safely from the Dumpsters involves three principles: using the senses and common sense to evaluate the condition of the found materials, knowing the Dumpsters of a given area and checking them regularly, and seeking always to answer the question "Why was this discarded?"

Perhaps everyone who has a kitchen and a regular supply of groceries has, at one time or another, made a sandwich and eaten half of it before discovering mold on the bread or got a mouthful of milk before realizing the milk had turned. Nothing of the sort is likely to happen to a Dumpster diver because he is constantly reminded that most food is discarded for a reason. Yet a lot of perfectly good food can be found in Dumpsters.

Canned goods, for example, turn up 10 fairly often in the Dumpsters I frequent. All except the most phobic people would be willing to eat from a can, even if it came from a Dumpster. Canned goods are among the safest of foods to be found in Dumpsters but are not utterly foolproof.

Although very rare with modern canning methods, botulism is a possibility. Most other forms of food poisoning seldom do lasting harm to a healthy person, but botulism is almost certainly fatal and often the first symptom is death. Except for carbonated beverages, all canned goods should contain a slight vacuum and suck air when first punctured. Bulging, rusty, and dented cans and cans that spew when punctured should be avoided, especially when the contents are not very acidic or syrupy.

Heat can break down the botulin, but this requires much more cooking than most people do to canned goods. To the extent that botulism occurs at all, of course, it can occur in cans on pantry shelves as well as in cans from Dumpsters. Need I say that home-canned goods are simply too risky to be recommended.

From time to time one of my companions, aware of the source of my provisions, will ask, "Do you think these crackers are really safe to eat?" For some reason it is most often the crackers they ask about.

This question has always made me angry. Of course I would not offer my companion anything I had doubts about. But more than that, I wonder why he cannot evaluate the condition of the crackers for himself. I have no special knowledge and I have been wrong before. Since he knows where the food comes from, it seems to me he ought to assume some of the responsibility for deciding what he will put in his mouth. For myself I have few qualms about dry foods such as crackers, cookies, cereal, chips, and pasta if they are free of visible contaminates and still dry and crisp. Most often such things are found in the original packaging, which is not so much a positive sign as it is the absence of a negative one.

Raw fruits and vegetables with intact skins seem perfectly safe to me, excluding of course the obviously rotten. Many are discarded for minor imperfections that can be pared away. Leafy vegetables, grapes, cauliflower, broccoli, and similar things may be contaminated by liquids and may be impractical to wash.

Candy, especially hard candy, is usually safe if it has not drawn ants. Chocolate is often discarded only because it has become discolored as the cocoa butter de-emulsified. Candying, after all, is one method of food preservation because pathogens do not like very sugary substances.

All of these foods might be found in any Dumpster and can be evaluated with some confidence largely on the basis of appearance. Beyond these are foods that cannot be correctly evaluated without additional information.

I began scavenging by pulling pizzas out of the Dumpster behind a pizza delivery shop. In general, prepared food requires caution, but in this case I knew when the shop closed and went to the Dumpster as soon as the last of the help left.

Such shops often get prank orders; both the orders and the products made to fill them are called *bogus*. Because help seldom stays long at these places, pizzas are often made with the wrong topping, refused on delivery for being cold, or baked incorrectly. The products to be discarded are boxed up because inventory is kept by counting boxes: A boxed pizza can be written off; an unboxed pizza does not exist.

I never placed a bogus order to increase the supply of pizzas and I believe no one else was scavenging in this Dumpster. But the people in the shop became suspicious and began to retain their garbage in the shop overnight. While it lasted I had a steady supply of fresh, sometimes warm pizza. Because I knew the Dumpster I knew the source of the pizza, and because I visited the Dumpster regularly I knew what was fresh and what was yesterday's.

The area I frequent is inhabited by many affluent college students. I am not here by chance; the Dumpsters in this area are very rich. Students throw out many good things, including food. In particular they tend to throw everything out when they move at the end of a semester, before and after breaks, and around midterm, when many of them despair of college. So I find it advantageous to keep an eye on the academic calendar.

Students throw food away around breaks because they do not know whether it has spoiled or will spoil before they return. A typical discard is a half jar of peanut butter. In fact, nonorganic peanut butter does not require refrigeration and is unlikely to spoil in any reasonable time. The student does not know that, and since it is Daddy's money, the student decides not to take a chance. Opened containers require caution and some attention to the question, "Why was this discarded?" But in the case of discards from student apartments, the answer may be that the item was thrown out through carelessness, ignorance, or wastefulness. This can sometimes be deduced when the item is found with many others, including some that are obviously perfectly good.

Some students, and others, approach defrosting a freezer by chucking out the whole lot. Not only do the circumstances of such a find tell the story, but also the mass of frozen goods stays cold for a long time and items may be found still frozen or freshly thawed.

Yogurt, cheese, and sour cream are items that are often thrown out while they are still good. Occasionally I find a cheese with a spot of mold, which of course I just pare off, and because it is obvious why such a cheese was discarded, I treat it with less suspicion than an apparently perfect cheese found in similar circumstances. Yogurt is often discarded, still sealed, only because the expiration date on the carton had passed. This is one of my favorite finds because yogurt will keep for several days, even in warm weather.

Students throw out canned goods and 25 staples at the end of semesters and when they give up college at midterm. Drugs, pornography, spirits, and the like are often discarded when parents are expected—Dad's Day, for example. And spirits also turn up after big party weekends, presumably discarded by the newly reformed. Wine and spirits, of course, keep perfectly well even once opened, but the same cannot be said of beer.

My test for carbonated soft drinks is whether they still fizz vigorously. Many juices or other beverages are too acidic or too syrupy to cause much concern, provided they are not visibly contaminated. I have discovered nasty molds in vegetable juices, even when the product was found under its original seal; I recommend that such products be decanted slowly into a clear glass. Liquids always require some care. One hot day I found a large jug of Pat O'Brien's Hurricane mix. The jug had been opened but was still ice cold. I drank three large glasses before it became apparent to me that someone had added the rum to the mix, and not a little rum. I never tasted the rum, and by the time I began to feel the effects I had already ingested a very large quantity of the beverage. Some divers would have considered this a boon, but being suddenly intoxicated in a public place in the early afternoon is not my idea of a good time.

I have heard of people maliciously contaminating discarded food and even handouts, but mostly I have heard of this from people with vivid imaginations who have had no experience with the Dumpsters themselves. Just before the pizza shop stopped discarding its garbage at night, jalapeños began showing up on most of the thrown-out pizzas. If indeed this was meant to discourage me, it was a wasted effort because I am a native Texan.

For myself, I avoid game, poultry, pork, and egg-based foods, whether I find them raw or cooked. I seldom have the means to cook what I find, but when I do I avail myself of plentiful supplies of beef, which is often in very good condition. I suppose fish becomes disagreeable before it becomes dangerous. Lizbeth is happy to have any such thing that is past its prime and, in fact, does not recognize fish as food until it is quite strong.

Home leftovers, as opposed to surpluses from restaurants, are very often bad. Evidently, especially among students, there is a common type of personality that carefully wraps up even the smallest leftover and shoves it into the back of the refrigerator for six months or so before discarding it. Characteristic of this type are the reused jars and margarine tubs to which the remains are committed. I avoid ethnic foods I am unfamiliar with. If I do not know what it is supposed to look like when it is good, I cannot be certain I will be able to tell if it is bad.

No matter how careful I am I still get dysentery at least once a month, oftener in warm weather. I do not want to paint too romantic a picture. Dumpster diving has serious drawbacks as a way of life. 30

I learned to scavenge gradually, on my own. Since then I have initiated several companions into the trade. I have learned that there is a predictable series of stages a person goes through in learning to scavenge.

At first the new scavenger is filled with disgust and self-loathing. He is ashamed of being seen and may lurk around, trying to duck behind things, or he may try to dive at night. (In fact, most people instinctively look away from a scavenger. By skulking around, the novice calls attention to himself and arouses suspicion. Diving at night is ineffective and needlessly messy.)

Every grain of rice seems to be a maggot. Everything seems to stink. He can wipe the egg yolk off the found can, but he cannot erase from his mind the stigma of eating garbage.

That stage passes with experience. The scavenger finds a pair of running shoes that fit and look and smell brand-new. He finds a pocket calculator in perfect working order. He finds pristine ice cream, still frozen, more than he can eat or keep. He begins to understand: People throw away perfectly good stuff, a lot of perfectly good stuff.

At this stage, Dumpster shyness begins to dissipate. The diver, after all, has the last laugh. He is finding all manner of good things that are his for the taking. Those who disparage his profession are the fools, not he. 35

He may begin to hang on to some perfectly good things for which he has neither a use nor a market. Then he begins to take note of the things that are not perfectly good but are nearly so. He mates a Walkman with broken earphones and one that is missing a battery cover. He picks up things that he can repair.

At this stage he may become lost and never recover. Dumpsters are full of things of some potential value to someone and also of things that never have much intrinsic value but are interesting. All the Dumpster divers I have known come to the point of trying to acquire everything they touch. Why not take it, they reason, since it is all free? This is, of course, hopeless. Most divers come to realize that they must restrict themselves to items of relatively immediate utility. But in some cases the diver simply cannot control himself. I have met several of these pack-rat types. Their ideas of the values of various pieces of junk verge on the psychotic. Every bit of glass may be a diamond, they think, and all that glitters, gold.

I tend to gain weight when I am scavenging. Partly this is because I always find far more pizza and doughnuts than water-packed tuna, nonfat yogurt, and fresh vegetables. Also I have not developed much faith in the reliability of Dumpsters as a food source, although it has been proven to me many times. I tend to eat as if I have no idea where my next meal is coming from. But mostly I just hate to see food go to waste and so I eat much more than I should. Something like this drives the obsession to collect junk.

As for collecting objects, I usually restrict myself to collecting one kind of small object at a time, such as pocket calculators, sunglasses, or campaign buttons. To live on the street I must anticipate my needs to a certain extent: I must pick up and save warm bedding I find in August because it will not be found in Dumpsters in November. As I have no access to health care, I often hoard essential drugs, such as antibiotics and antihistamines. (This course can be recommended only to those with some grounding in pharmacology. Antibiotics, for example, even when indicated are worse than useless if taken in insufficient amounts.) But even if I had a home with extensive storage space, I could not save everything that might be valuable in some contingency.

I have proprietary feelings about my 40 Dumpsters. As I have mentioned, it is no accident that I scavenge from ones where good finds are common. But my limited experience with Dumpsters in other areas suggests to me that even in poorer areas, Dumpsters, if attended with sufficient diligence, can be made to yield a livelihood. The rich students discard perfectly good kiwifruit; poorer people discard perfectly good apples. Slacks and Polo shirts are found in the one place; jeans and T-shirts in the other. The population of competitors rather than the affluence of the dumpers most affects the feasibility of survival by scavenging. The large number of competitors is what puts me off the idea of trying to scavenge in places like Los Angeles.

Curiously, I do not mind my direct competition, other scavengers, so much as I hate the can scroungers.

People scrounge cans because they have to have a little cash. I have tried scrounging cans with an able-bodied companion. Afoot a can scrounger simply cannot make more than a few dollars a day. One can extract the necessities of life from the Dumpsters directly with far less effort than would be required to accumulate the equivalent value in cans. (These observations may not hold in places with container redemption laws.)

Can scroungers, then, are people who must have small amounts of cash. These are drug addicts and winos, mostly the latter because the amounts of cash are so small. Spirits and drugs do, like all other commodities, turn up in Dumpsters and the scavenger will from time to time have a half bottle of a rather good wine with his dinner. But the wino cannot survive on these occasional finds; he must have his daily dose to stave off the DTs. All the cans he can carry will buy about three bottles of Wild Irish Rose.

I do not begrudge them the cans, but can scroungers tend to tear up the Dumpsters, mixing the contents and littering the area. They become so specialized that they can see only cans. They earn my contempt by passing up change, canned goods, and readily hockable items.

There are precious few courtesies among 45 scavengers. But it is common practice to set aside surplus items: pairs of shoes, clothing, canned goods, and such. A true scavenger hates to see good stuff go to waste, and what he cannot use he leaves in good condition in plain sight.

Can scroungers lay waste to everything in their path and will stir one of a pair of good shoes to the bottom of a Dumpster, to be lost or ruined in the muck. Can scroungers will even go through individual garbage cans, something I have never seen a scavenger do.

Individual garbage cans are set out on the public easement only on garbage days. On other days going through them requires trespassing close to a dwelling. Going through individual garbage cans without scattering litter is almost impossible. Litter is likely to reduce the public's tolerance of scavenging. Individual cans are simply not as productive as Dumpsters; people in houses and duplexes do not move so often and for some reason do not tend to discard as much useful material. Moreover, the time required to go through one garbage can that serves one household is not much less than the time required to go through a Dumpster that contains the refuse of twenty apartments.

But my strongest reservation about going through individual garbage cans is that this seems to me a very personal kind of invasion to which I would object if I were a householder. Although many things in Dumpsters are obviously meant never to come to light, a Dumpster is somehow less personal.

I avoid trying to draw conclusions about the people who dump in the Dumpsters I frequent. I think it would be unethical to do so, although I know many people will find the idea of scavenger ethics too funny for words.

Dumpsters contain bank statements, correspondence, and other documents, just as anyone might expect. But there are also less obvious sources of information. Pill bottles, for example. The labels bear the name of the patient, the name of the doctor, and the name of the drug. AIDS drugs and antipsychotic medicines, to name but two groups, are specific and are seldom prescribed for any other disorders. The plastic compacts for birth-control pills usually have complete label information.

Despite all of this sensitive information, I have had only one apartment resident object to my going through the Dumpster. In that case it turned out the resident was a university athlete who was taking bets and who was afraid I would turn up his wager slips.

Occasionally a find tells a story. I once found a small paper bag containing some unused condoms, several partial tubes of flavored sexual lubricants, a partially used compact of birth-control pills, and the torn pieces of a picture of a young man. Clearly she was through with him and planning to give up sex altogether.

Dumpster things are often sad—abandoned teddy bears, shredded wedding books, despaired-of sales kits. I find many pets lying in state in Dumpsters. Although I hope to get off the streets so that Lizbeth can have a long and comfortable old age, I know this hope is not very realistic. So I suppose when her time comes she too will go into a Dumpster. I will have no better place for her. And after all, it is fitting, since for most of her life her livelihood has come from the Dumpster. When she finds something I think is safe that

has been spilled from a Dumpster, I let her have it. She already knows the route around the best ones. I like to think that if she survives me she will have a chance of evading the dog catcher and of finding her sustenance on the route.

Silly vanities also come to rest in the Dumpsters. I am a rather accomplished needleworker. I get a lot of material from the Dumpsters. Evidently sorority girls, hoping to impress someone, perhaps themselves, with their mastery of a womanly art, buy a lot of embroider-by-number kits, work a few stitches horribly, and eventually discard the whole mess. I pull out their stitches, turn the canvas over, and work an original design. Do not think I refrain from chuckling as I make gifts from these kits.

I find diaries and journals. I have often thought of compiling a book of literary found objects. And perhaps I will one day. But what I find is hopelessly commonplace and bad without being, even unconsciously, camp. College students also discard their papers. I am horrified to discover the kind of paper that now merits an A in an undergraduate course. I am grateful, however, for the number of good books and magazines the students throw out.

In the area I know best I have never discovered vermin in the Dumpsters, but there are two kinds of kitty surprise. One is alley cats whom I meet as they leap, claws first, out of Dumpsters. This is especially thrilling when I have Lizbeth in tow. The other kind of kitty surprise is a plastic garbage bag filled with some ponderous, amorphous mass. This always proves to be used cat litter.

City bees harvest doughnut glaze and this makes the Dumpster at the doughnut shop more interesting. My faith in the instinctive wisdom of animals is always shaken whenever I see Lizbeth attempt to catch a bee in her mouth, which she does whenever bees are present. Evidently some birds find Dumpsters profitable, for birdie surprise is almost as common as kitty surprise of the first kind. In hunting season all kinds of small game turn up in Dumpsters, some of it, sadly, not entirely dead. Curiously, summer and winter, maggots are uncommon.

The worse of the living and near-living hazards of the Dumpsters are the fire ants. The food they claim is not much of a loss, but they are vicious and aggressive. It is very easy to brush against some surface of the Dumpster and pick up half a dozen or more fire ants, usually in some sensitive area such as the underarm. One advantage of bringing Lizbeth along as I make Dumpster rounds is that, for obvious reasons, she is very alert to ground-based fire ants. When Lizbeth recognizes a fire-ant infestation around our feet, she does the Dance of the Zillion Fire Ants. I have learned not to ignore this warning from Lizbeth, whether I perceive the tiny ants or not, but to remove ourselves at Lizbeth's first pas de bourée. All the more so because the ants are the worst in the summer months when I wear flip-flops if I have them. (Perhaps someone will misunderstand this. Lizbeth does the Dance of the Zillion Fire Ants when she recognizes more fire ants than she cares to eat, not when she is being bitten. Since I have learned to react promptly, she does not get bitten at all. It is the isolated patrol of fire ants that falls in Lizbeth's range that deserves pity. She finds them quite tasty.)

By far the best way to go through a Dumpster is to lower yourself into it. Most of the good stuff tends to settle at the bottom because it is usually weightier than the rubbish. My more athletic companions have often demonstrated to me that they can extract much good material from a Dumpster I have already been over.

To those psychologically or physically 60 unprepared to enter a Dumpster, I recommend a stout stick, preferably with some barb or hook at one end. The hook can be used to grab plastic garbage bags. When I find canned goods or other objects loose at the bottom of a Dumpster, I lower a bag into it, roll the desired object into the bag, and then hoist the bag out—a procedure more easily described than executed. Much Dumpster diving is a matter of experience for which nothing will do except practice.

Dumpster diving is outdoor work, often surprisingly pleasant. It is not entirely predictable; things of interest turn up every day and some days there are finds of great value. I am always very pleased when I can turn up exactly the thing I most wanted to find. Yet in spite of the element of chance, scavenging more than most other pursuits tends to yield returns in some proportion to the effort and intelligence brought to bear. It is very sweet to turn up a few dollars in change from a Dumpster that has just been gone over by a wino.

The land is now covered with cities. The cities are full of Dumpsters. If a member of the canine race is ever able to know what it is doing, then Lizbeth knows that when we go around to the Dumpsters, we are hunting. I think of scavenging as a modern form of self-reliance. In any event, after having survived nearly ten years of government service, where everything is geared to the lowest common denominator, I find it refreshing to have work that rewards initiative and effort. Certainly I would be happy to have a sinecure again, but I am no longer heartbroken that I left one.

I find from the experience of scavenging two rather deep lessons. The first is to take what you can use and let the rest go by. I have come to think that there is no value in the abstract. A thing I cannot use or make useful, perhaps by trading, has no value however rare or fine it may be. I mean useful in a broad sense—some art I would find useful and some otherwise.

I was shocked to realize that some things are not worth acquiring, but now I think it is so. Some material things are white elephants that eat up the possessor's substance. The second lesson is the transience of material being. This has not quite converted me to a dualist, but it has made some headway in that direction. I do not suppose that ideas are immortal, but certainly mental things are longer lived than other material things.

Once I was the sort of person who invests objects with sentimental value. Now I no longer have those objects, but I have the sentiments yet. [65]

Many times in our travels I have lost everything but the clothes I was wearing and Lizbeth. The things I find in Dumpsters, the love letters and rag dolls of so many lives, remind me of this lesson. Now I hardly pick up a thing without envisioning the time I will cast it aside. This I think is a healthy state of mind. Almost everything I have now has already been cast out at least once, proving that what I own is valueless to someone.

Anyway, I find my desire to grab for the gaudy bauble has been largely sated. I think this is an attitude I share with the very wealthy—we both know there is plenty more where what we have came from. Between us are the rat-race millions who nightly scavenge the cable channels looking for they know not what.

I am sorry for them.

A CLOSER LOOK AT
On Dumpster Diving

1. Dumpsters are not something that people typically "evaluate," and yet Eighner applies many of the common evaluation techniques to looking for food and miscellaneous items in others' trash. What are some of the criteria that Eighner assumes he shares with his readers? How does he use these criteria to sort out what is good and not good to take from dumpsters? How does he challenge his readers' criteria, too, by suggesting that some items are still good to take, even though others have thrown them away?

2. Eighner uses his experience as a homeless person who survived on garbage to make some larger points about American culture. List three to five of Eighner's major criticisms of how Americans live. How does he use his evaluation of dumpsters to make his larger points about how Americans see possessions and food?

3. Obviously, this article is not a classic evaluation. Looking at the evaluation genre, list five ways in which the article fits the classic understanding of this genre. Then list five ways in which it does not meet this understanding. How does Eighner's use of the genre and his bending of the genre create a unique effect on readers? How does he play with the genre to take on some larger issues for his readers?

IDEAS FOR
Writing

1. Eighner brings his readers face-to-face with the wastefulness of American culture, while showing us the hardships of the homeless. Readers often come away from this chapter wondering how we can avoid the waste and somehow feed and shelter people who have been forced out of their homes. Write a brief proposal in which you use Eighner's experiences to suggest a way to solve both problems. Make sure you refer to Eighner's article as support for some of your points.

2. This article is deceptively persuasive. Eighner takes on a rather objective tone, especially in the earlier part of the article. Write a rhetorical analysis in which you explore his rhetorical strategies. How does he use reasoning (*logos*), authority (*ethos*), and emotion (*pathos*) to write a persuasive argument? Pay special attention to how he uses examples to support his major points and style to persuade his readers.

Apple iPhone 3GS

STEVEN LEVY

In this review, Steven Levy evaluates the Apple iPhone 3GS. The first-generation iPhones were hyped by the media and made a big splash in the market. But they also had some of the limitations and bugs that are common with revolutionary new products. The iPhone 3G corrected many of those problems, and the iPhone 3GS took another major step forward in speed and in new applications. In this evaluation, pay attention to how Levy compares the old with the new.

Apple outsmarted the mobile world by releasing the touch-controlled iPhone in June 2007. In July the next year, it rocketed to faster network speeds with the iPhone 3G while creating a massive ecosystem of apps. Now, on June 19, Apple will reassert its dominance by shipping the iPhone 3GS, outfitted with the operating system upgrade iPhone 3.0.

It's not as dramatic an advance as the previous ones. But the new phone introduces a long list of improvements, big and small. Taken together, they're enough to re-establish Apple's once-shrinking lead in a brutal technology competition that is making the chariot race in *Ben Hur* look like a stroll in the park.

The iPhone 3GS combines two sets of advances. The first group is available only to purchasers of the new hardware. The rest of the features are part of Apple's iPhone 3.0 software upgrade, which, beginning June 17, will be offered free to those with earlier iPhones. (iPod Touch users can get the new software for $10.)

I'll talk about the hardware-based features first. As promised, Apple has indeed ramped up the speed with which the new phone performs tasks like launching apps, loading web pages, and displaying graphics. Apple claims speed boosts of up to two times of what the 3G delivers, and in some benchmarks cites even better performance. I haven't done scientific measurements, but you don't need a stopwatch to notice the new phone is zippier than its predecessor. I appreciated getting box scores faster and videos playing sooner in the *MLB.com At Bat* application, and it was clear that web pages loaded faster. In the case of a game like *Tiger Woods Golf*, the boost is significant enough to make me more likely to play when I don't have much time.

Photos were a weak spot in previous 5 iPhones—they weighed in at a measly 2 megapixels—but the iPhone 3GS has a 3-megapixel, autofocusing camera that's more sensitive and allows you to choose an object to focus on by tapping on it. (No zoom, though. Bummer.) Better yet, the camera also records quite creditable video. After you shoot your clip, there's a dead-simple function for instant editing, after which you can send your masterpiece to *YouTube* or *Mobile Me* with a single tap.

The iPhone 3GS also has a hands-free feature called Voice Control. By holding down the Home button you simply say who you want to call or what music you want to hear. This also works with the expanded controls in the new headphones included with the phone. It's very useful, though it did better at figuring out the people I wanted to call than it did with music. When I said, "Call Diane Levy home," the 3GS dialed my sister's home number on the first try. But when I said "Play Lou

Reed," it played Lucinda Williams. When I said, "Lucinda Williams," it played Gillian Welch. Close, but no guitar pick. Still, even with some false starts, Voice Control is easier than fumbling through the iPod menus, a difficult task while walking and a dangerous one while driving.

Another 3GS feature is a compass, which on its own isn't too thrilling (you can get a real compass in a gumball machine) but will eventually shine in a number of upcoming apps. The first of these is *Google Maps,* where an extra tap on the "locate" button will orient the map to the direction you're facing.

Of the features that aren't exclusive to the 3GS, but instead are part of the iPhone 3.0 suite, the biggest news is that you can finally cut, copy and paste text, photos and objects on an iPhone. Sadly, this isn't part of comprehensive iPhone multitasking—a feature delivered superbly on a rival phone, the Palm Pre. (Apple's reluctance to embrace multitasking is based on its claim that it would wear down the battery—and it's true that the Pre has a power issue.) So cut-and-paste will have to do for now. As you'd expect, Apple imaginatively uses its touch interface to make this feature intuitive and fun. Trust me, describing how to do it is much more complicated than actually doing it.

The new software addresses another previous gap by allowing users access to a bigger keyboard in landscape mode not just in the *Safari* browser but in mail and other apps. This makes Apple's "soft" keyboard much less prone to constant mistypings. iPhone 3.0 also offers deeper search functions. You can now search through the contents of your iPhone and get results that include apps, contacts, e-mail, calendar and notes. And e-mail search quickly locates messages both on the phone and, with *IMAP* or *Exchange,* systems on a remote server.

Other iPhone 3.0 features that work as 10 advertised are Voice Memos (a straightforward

audio recording app), improved parental controls and auto-fill on *Safari.*

There's also a more compelling reason to sign up for Apple's $100-a-year internet service, *MobileMe.* As before, *MobileMe* users automatically have calendar, mail, and contacts synced. But now, those with *Mobile Me* can take advantage of Find My iPhone, which you call into action when your device is lost or stolen. Using your computer, you can locate the phone via GPS (very handy if you left it in a restaurant). You can also put a message on the screen, and trigger a two-minute ringing sound that will turn on even if the ringer has been switched off. The latter is perfect for those who lose the phone around the house. If the phone is really lost, you can then remotely wipe out the data to foil snoopers. I would suggest one further wrinkle: a small capsule of indelible red dye that would explode on remote command, splattering all over the swine who stole your gizmo.

There were two highly touted features I could *not* test out: MMS messaging (sending media files via a text-messaging-like service) and tethering (using the iPhone's modem to connect a computer to the internet). The problem is not Apple, which has built these into 3.0 and will instantly offer them in other countries, but AT&T, the exclusive U.S. network carrier. AT&T promises to deliver MMS for no extra cost later this summer, and says that tethering will be available at a future, indeterminate date, almost certainly at an extra cost.

A lot of the new value of iPhone 3.0 will come when all these features (and others I don't have room to mention) are exploited by the thousands of developers writing iPhone apps. You'll see apps that can sell things in the course of using them, such as extra levels of a game, apps that make use of your *iTunes* playlist, and apps that take advantage of P2P connectivity for head-to-head gaming and quick exchange of information.

In short, the 3GS offers a boatload of improvements on the iPhone 3G with no real downside and the same price. Brand-new iPhone customers should have no hesitation before buying: Considering the huge variety of apps, there's no better smartphone to buy today.

Current iPhone users have a tougher decision ahead. First they must ask themselves if the features offered exclusively on the phone (as opposed to the free upgrade, which they should download immediately) are worth the expense of a new phone. For some users, Voice Control, the new camera, and the speed boost will be worth the cost. For others, it won't be a huge sacrifice to go without.

Complicating the matter is AT&T's upgrade policy. Generally, those who are in the second half of their two-year contracts can upgrade to iPhone 3GS for the same price as paid by new customers: $200 for the 16-GB version and $300 for the 32-GB. (The 32-GB version is the one to get, especially if you'll be using video and other media.) AT&T has just announced that people who bought 3G phones as late as September will be eligible for the new-phone price. All those cases involve a new 2-year contract obligation.

But more recent 3G buyers won't get that deal. AT&T will charge them either $400 or $500, depending on the storage, to upgrade to a 3GS with a new 2-year contract obligation. Another alternative is to pay full price for an "unsubsidized" iPhone: a whopping $600 for the 16-gig 3GS and $700 for the 32-gig version. Despite the fact that those buyers are relieving AT&T of the burden of its subsidy, they get no discount on their monthly bills.

In part because of this—and in part because Apple is offering many of its innovations as part of the general iPhone 3.0 upgrade—the wise thing for those more recent buyers to do will be to install the new software and stick with their 3G iPhones at least until their contracts run down. This will provide a saner upgrade path to the 3GS's considerable, but not earth-shattering, improvements. Speed is wonderful. But sometimes it's prudent to wait for it.

WIRED Faster. More storage. Better camera, with video recording capability. Search encompasses more data, not just one app at a time. Voice navigation. Feature-rich iPhone 3.0 software is free to current iPhone users.

TIRED Multitasking still limited. No tethering or MMS support yet for AT&T users. Recent iPhone 3G customers must pay a fortune to upgrade.

A CLOSER LOOK AT
Apple iPhone 3GS

1. Overall, the evaluation is a positive one, but the writer seems to be arguing that the iPhone 3GS ended up being less than he expected. How does he use his criteria to demonstrate that the 3GS is a solid product that falls short of what he and others would have liked in a new version of the popular iPhone?

2. Levy doesn't exactly state his criteria up front, but they are easy to identify. List three to five criteria that he is using to evaluate the iPhone 3GS. Does he

define these criteria for you? If so, where does he define each one? If not, do you think he should be clearer about how he is defining his criteria?

3. Later parts of the evaluation seem to be more about AT&T than the iPhone. How does Levy separate his criticisms of AT&T from his overall positive review of the iPhone? Do you think this separation is necessary, especially since AT&T is the only service provider for the iPhone?

IDEAS FOR
Writing

1. Write a rebuttal from Apple to *Wired* magazine. Generally, you are pleased with the evaluation, because it accurately highlights many of the iPhone 3GS's features. However, you take issue with the suggestion that the iPhone 3GS is not much of an upgrade from the iPhone 3G. How might you turn the information in this evaluation to your advantage in the rebuttal?

2. Write a commentary in which you discuss the changes that mobile phones, including the iPhone,

have brought to American culture. For example, in Levy's evaluation, he seems to assume that people need to do things like stream video on their phone and be in constant contact with others. What are some of the pros and cons of this wired-in lifestyle? How is it changing American culture for better or worse?

A FEW IDEAS FOR
Composing an Evaluation

1. Write an evaluation of the place where you eat most often. Define your criteria and then use them to show why the place where you eat is or is not good. Your evaluation should be written for incoming and transfer students who are deciding where to live on or near campus. You want to be honest, but you don't want to scare anyone away. Even if you prepare meals in your own apartment or you are living at home, you should discuss some of the advantages and disadvantages of doing so. Evaluate your own meal-making abilities.

2. Write an evaluation of three products. Choose three products that do basically the same thing. Develop a list of criteria that allows you to compare and contrast these items. If you can actually test out these products, that would be best. If not, use research on

the Internet to help you determine which of these items is likely the best. Your evaluation should be written for a consumer magazine that helps people make decisions about which products to buy.

3. Create a podcast or video evaluation of your life. First, write an evaluation, discussing how well you are doing toward achieving your life goals. Do you think your criteria are reachable, or are they simply idealistic hopes? When do you think you should reach your goals in life? In other words, at what age should you satisfy these criteria (if you haven't already)? Then turn your evaluation into a podcast or video, preferably using music, text, and animation to highlight and enhance your ideas.

CHAPTER 37

Literary
Analyses

The Story of an Hour

KATE CHOPIN

Kate Chopin (1851–1904), a writer of short stories and novels, wrote "Story of an Hour" in 1894. During her lifetime, Chopin was sometimes criticized for writing immoral stories. More recent critics view her as an early feminist who explored themes of love, marriage, race, and the psychology of women. As you read, pay attention to the way Chopin paints a rich portrait of a character and works out a complete plot in a very short space.

Knowing that Mrs. Mallard was afflicted with a heart trouble, great care was taken to break to her as gently as possible the news of her husband's death.

It was her sister Josephine who told her, in broken sentences; veiled hints that revealed in half concealing. Her husband's friend Richards was there, too, near her. It was he who had been in the newspaper office when intelligence of the railroad disaster was received, with Brently Mallard's name leading the list of "killed." He had only taken the time to assure himself of its truth by a second telegram, and had hastened to forestall any less careful, less tender friend in bearing the sad message.

She did not hear the story as many women have heard the same, with a paralyzed inability to accept its significance. She wept at once, with sudden, wild abandonment, in her sister's arms. When the storm of grief had spent itself she went away to her room alone. She would have no one follow her.

There stood, facing the open window, a comfortable, roomy armchair. Into this she sank, pressed down by a physical exhaustion that haunted her body and seemed to reach into her soul.

She could see in the open square before 5 her house the tops of trees that were all aquiver with the new spring life. The delicious breath of rain was in the air. In the street below a peddler was crying his wares. The notes of a distant song which some one was singing reached her faintly, and countless sparrows were twittering in the eaves.

There were patches of blue sky showing here and there through the clouds that had met and piled one above the other in the west facing her window.

She sat with her head thrown back upon the cushion of the chair, quite motionless, except when a sob came up into her throat and shook her, as a child who has cried itself to sleep continues to sob in its dreams.

She was young, with a fair, calm face, whose lines bespoke repression and even a certain strength. But now there was a dull stare in her eyes, whose gaze was fixed away off yonder on one of those patches of blue sky. It was not a glance of reflection, but rather indicated a suspension of intelligent thought.

There was something coming to her and she was waiting for it, fearfully. What was it? She did not know; it was too subtle and elusive to name. But she felt it, creeping out of the sky, reaching toward her through the sounds, the scents, the color that filled the air.

Now her bosom rose and fell tumul- 10 tuously. She was beginning to recognize this thing that was approaching to possess her, and she was striving to beat it back with her will—as powerless as her two white slender hands would have been.

When she abandoned herself a little whispered word escaped her slightly parted lips. She said it over and over under her breath: "free, free, free!" The vacant stare and the look of terror that had followed it went from her eyes. They stayed keen and bright. Her pulses beat fast, and the coursing blood warmed and relaxed every inch of her body. She did not stop to ask if it were or were not a monstrous joy that held her. A clear and exalted perception enabled her to dismiss the suggestion as trivial.

She knew that she would weep again when she saw the kind, tender hands folded in death; the face that had never looked save with love upon her, fixed and gray and dead. But she saw beyond that bitter moment a long procession of years to come that would belong to her absolutely. And she opened and spread her arms out to them in welcome.

There would be no one to live for during those coming years; she would live for herself. There would be no powerful will bending hers in that blind persistence with which men and women believe they have a right to impose a private will upon a fellow-creature. A kind intention or a cruel intention made the act seem no less a crime as she looked upon it in that brief moment of illumination.

And yet she had loved him—sometimes. Often she had not. What did it matter! What could love, the unsolved mystery, count for in face of this possession of self-assertion which she suddenly recognized as the strongest impulse of her being!

"Free! Body and soul free!" she kept whispering. 15

Josephine was kneeling before the closed door with her lips to the keyhole, imploring for admission. "Louise, open the door! I beg, open the door—you will make yourself ill. What are you doing Louise? For heaven's sake open the door."

"Go away. I am not making myself ill." No; she was drinking in a very elixir of life through that open window.

Her fancy was running riot along those days ahead of her. Spring days, and summer days, and all sorts of days that would be her own. She breathed a quick prayer that life might be long. It was only yesterday she had thought with a shudder that life might be long.

She arose at length and opened the door to her sister's importunities. There was a feverish triumph in her eyes, and she carried herself unwittingly like a goddess of Victory. She clasped her sister's waist, and together they descended the stairs. Richards stood waiting for them at the bottom.

Some one was opening the front door 20 with a latchkey. It was Brently Mallard who entered, a little travel-stained, composedly carrying his grip-sack and umbrella. He had been far from the scene of the accident, and did not even know there had been one. He stood amazed at Josephine's piercing cry; at Richards' quick motion to screen him from the view of his wife.

But Richards was too late.

When the doctors came they said she had died of heart disease—of joy that kills.

A CLOSER LOOK AT
The Story of an Hour

1. What makes this a story and not just a sequence of events? In other words, explain how the plot moves from complication to conflict, tension, and resolution to hold the reader's interest. How would the reading experience and the story's significance have been different if the narrator had let it be known at the beginning that Louise Mallard dies in the story?

2. Read the story again, this time paying close attention to and highlighting those parts where the narrator provides details about Louise Mallard's character bit by bit. Notice where the disclosure of certain details are placed. For example, we do not learn the main character's first name until close to the story's end. How does the author's sequencing of disclosures draw the reader into Louise's character?

3. Short stories often describe how characters change or come to a new understanding of themselves or their world. What does Louise Mallard learn in this story? How does her new understanding play a role in her death?

IDEAS FOR
Writing

1. Write a reading response in which you describe what you believe is the social or political message of "The Story of an Hour." Who were the readers that you think Chopin may have been writing for? What themes or questions did she want her readers to explore? What point, if any, do you think she was hoping to make?

2. In a brief memoir, narrate and describe a significant experience in your life that you reacted to in an entirely unexpected way or in a way that others just couldn't understand. Within the memoir, explain what your reaction to this experience reveals about you, or what it reveals about others' expectations of you.

An Enigma in Chopin's "The Story of an Hour"

DANIEL P. DENEAU

Daniel P. Deneau was a professor of English for many years. As you read his analysis of Chopin's short story, pay attention to the way he poses an interpretive question about the story and then carefully examines a single passage to help answer that question.

The much-anthologized "The Story of an Hour" (1894) is surely Kate Chopin's best-known piece of short fiction. Innumerable students, ranging from the very naive to the very sophisticated, must have grappled with the story in innumerable discussions and essays. As all readers should agree, Louise Mallard receives a great shock, goes through a rapid sequence of reactions, is in a sense awakened and then seems to drink in "a very elixir of life" (354), and finally receives another shock, a reversal, which proves lethal. Probably equally clear to all or to most readers are Chopin's economy, the significance of the open window and the spring setting, the power which she assigns to "self-assertion," and the bold dramatic irony with which the story concludes. About one issue, at least among readers of anthologies, there may be continuing debate: is Louise a normal, understandable, sympathetic woman, or is she an egocentric, selfish monster or anomaly?

And, as more sophisticated readers may ask, is the degree of "self-assertion" or freedom that she thinks she has attained a real possibility in a world of normal human relationships? Obviously readers' preconceptions about love and marriage and independence will dictate different answers to these questions. At one crucial point, however, this relatively clear and realistic story becomes problematic, perhaps even enigmatic—that is, the passage in which Chopin attempts to account for the direct cause of Louise's awakening:

> There was something coming to her and she was waiting for it, fearfully. What was it? She did not know; it was too subtle and elusive to name. But she felt it, creeping[1] out of the sky, reaching toward her through the sounds, the scents, the color that filled the air.
>
> Now her bosom rose and fell tumultuously. She was beginning to recognize this thing that was approaching to possess her, and she was striving to beat it back with her will—as powerless as her two white hands would have been.
>
> When she abandoned herself [,] a little whispered word escaped her slightly parted lips. She said it over and over under her breath: "Free, free, free!" The vacant stare and the look of terror that had followed it went from her eyes. They stayed keen and bright. Her pulses beat fast, and the coursing blood warmed and relaxed every inch of her body. (353)

This "something," this "it,"[2] which oddly arrives from the sky, exerts a powerful physical influence on Louise and leaves her with a totally new perspective on her self and her place in the scheme of things. In a limited space, and without the assistance of a psychological vocabulary, Chopin may have been forced to rely on the indefinite, the unidentified, which, as best we can judge, is some powerful force, something supernatural, something beyond the realm of mundane experience or the rule of logic.[3] If immediately after learning of the death of her husband Louise had gone through a rapid logical process leading to a celebration of her total freedom, she might have seemed to be a hard, calculating, and therefore unsympathetic woman. Or to put the point in another way: since she has neither the physical nor moral strength to "beat [. . .] back" her attacker, which she begins to recognize but sadly never names, her responsibility is abrogated. In addition, one of the problems presented by the passage is the fact that Louise meets the "something" with both fear and anticipation. Clearly what occurs is some type of sexual experience, one that at first seems, except for the anticipation, like a terrifying rape, but one that evolves into something sensually stimulating and relaxing, and, of course, spiritually illuminating. In short, a rape seems to have an ironic outcome.

There can be no doubt that the crucial passage becomes a fairly explicit description of a sexual union. One of the meanings of the verb "possess" is "to have sexual intercourse with (a woman)" (OED),[4] and this meaning was certainly known to Chopin, as illustrated by the climactic—that word, unfortunately, is inevitable—passage of "The Storm," the sexual union of Alcée and Calixta: "And when he possessed her, they seemed to swoon together at the very borderland of life's mystery" (595).[5] Moreover, the third paragraph quoted above does suggest coitus and postcoital reactions: the abandonment, the "slightly parted lips," the "keen and bright eyes," and especially the final sentence—"Her pulses beat fast, and the coursing blood warmed and relaxed every inch of her body."

With no male aggressor-partner named in the text, only a "something," readers naturally will speculate. For me, two possibilities exist—both supernatural—of which, time after time, I am reminded as I contemplate the passage: one is classical, pagan; the other, Christian. The former is Leda and the swan-Zeus, a potent, sinister force which creeps from the "sky," attacks, and engenders a world-shaking course of events.[6] But the passage is about more than fear, force, and sex; it is also about anticipation, pleasure, and ultimately enlightenment. Thus, I am also reminded of the descent of the Christian Holy Spirit,[7] who is associated with conception, renewal, empowerment, inspiration, enlightenment, and freedom.[8] Louise does indeed receive an infusion of knowledge from a source that seems beyond human understanding or even naming. Add to these subjective responses Chopin's "belief" that genuine sexual passion itself may help the blind see: after Edna Pontellier's first sexual union with Arobin, she has various reactions; however, "above all, there was understanding. She felt as if a mist had been lifted from her eyes, enabling her to look upon and comprehend the significance of life, that monster made up of beauty and brutality" (967).

"The Story of an Hour" lacks the kind of 5 diagrammatic clarity that some readers may expect, mainly or even exclusively, as I have tried to suggest, because of one curious passage. Chopin's desire to transform her protagonist from a woman with a "dull stare in her eyes" (353) to one with "a feverish triumph in her eyes," a woman who carries "herself unwittingly like a goddess of Victory" (354), required a force of exceptional intensity, a force as intense as a combination of a rape, a visitation by the Holy Spirit, and a sexual union—or, in short, a *deux ex machina*. It is no wonder that in a mere seven sentences this force remains perplexing, probably enigmatic. One final point, however, is perfectly clear: having experimented with one very condensed account of an awakening—the account of a mere hour—Chopin later proceeded to create one of the masterpieces of American Literature—the slowly paced, psychologically credible, many-staged awakening of Edna Pontellier.[9]

Notes

1. In one other notable place in her short fiction Chopin used the verb "creeping." See the sexually charged "The Night Comes Slowly" (366).

2. Madonne M. Miner recognizes the importance of the "something" passage (31), but she does not scrutinize it sufficiently. Mary E. Papke seems unclear to me: "The unnameable is, of course, her self-consciousness that is embraced once she names her experience as emancipation and not destitution" (63). Angelyn Mitchell observes that "freedom ravishes" Louise and, quite correctly, that the passage is "loaded with sexual imagery" (62).

3. Cf. "Athénaïse": "If she ever came to such knowledge [of her own mind], it would be by no intellectual research, by no subtle analyses or tracing of actions to their source. It would come to her as the song to the bird, the perfume and color to the flower" (433).

4. The editor of the *OED* adds a surprising note: "this sense [was] suggested in private correspondence in 1969 by Professor W. Empson." The meaning should have been commonly known much earlier.

5. Bert Bender finds the diction "wooden" and "ironically conventional" (266). I doubt that a similar charge could be made about the crucial passage in "The Story of an Hour."

6. Recall Yeats "Leda and the Swan," esp. 11.5 and 6: "How can those terrified vague fingers push / The feathered glory from her loosing thighs?"

7. Chopin would have been well aware of the Christian view of the Holy Spirit (Ghost). See in particular "At Chênière Caminada" (317) and *The Awakening* (893).

8. Various Epistles associate the Holy Spirit with freedom. See, for example, 2 Cor. 3.17, as well as Isa. 61.1.

9. After completing this paper, I was pleased to find Jacqueline Padgett's paragraph in which she refers to an "annunciation" (101) in "The Story of an Hour."

Works Cited

Bender, Bert. "Kate Chopin's Lyrical Short Stories." *Studies in Short Fiction* 11 (1974): 257–66. Print.

Chopin, Kate. *The Complete Works of Kate Chopin.* Ed. Per Seyersted. Baton Rouge: Louisiana State UP, 1969. Print.

Miner, Madonne M. "Veiled Hints: An Affective Stylist's Reading of Kate Chopin's 'Story of an Hour.'" *The Markham Review* 11 (1982): 29–32. Print.

Mitchell, Angelyn. "Feminine Double Consciousness in Kate Chopin's 'The Story of an Hour.'" *CEA Magazine* 5.1 (1992): 59–64. Print.

Padgett, Jacqueline Olson, "Kate Chopin and the Literature of the Annunciation, with a Reading of 'Lilacs.'" *Louisiana Literature* 11.1 (1994): 97–107. Print.

Papke, Mary E. *Verging on the Abyss: The Social Fiction of Kate Chopin and Edith Wharton.* New York: Greenwood, 1990.

"Possess." Def. 3b. *The Oxford English Dictionary.* 2nd ed. 1989. Print.

A CLOSER LOOK AT
An Enigma in Chopin's "The Story of an Hour"

1. What is the interpretive question that Deneau poses in this analysis? How does he set up this question?

2. What exactly does Deneau suggest happens to Louise? Do you find his interpretation persuasive? His interpretation certainly goes beyond the literal meaning of the text. Do you agree with him?

3. The author uses endnotes to note connections with other works by Chopin and with the comments of other literary analyses. How do these endnotes help you understand Chopin's story or Deneau's analysis more fully? How do they enhance the author's authority or *ethos* as an interpreter of Chopin's short story?

IDEAS FOR
Writing

1. Write a rebuttal of Deneau's analysis. While it is true that there are no single correct interpretations of a literary work, any analysis needs to be supported and justified by the words in the literary text itself. Explain why Denau's analysis might be stretching too far to make its point.

2. Condense this literary analysis into a well-developed one-paragraph summary that provides an objective description of the question Deneau explores, how he explores it, and what he concludes. First, identify Deneau's interpretive question and restate it as clearly and directly as you can. Then describe Deanau's approach to exploring that question and his final conclusions.

Stopping by Woods on a Snowy Evening

ROBERT FROST

Robert Frost (1874–1963) was a popular poet during his lifetime. Many of his poems, like "Stopping by Woods on a Snowy Evening," appear to be simple observations of nature or country life but on other levels address larger philosophical and social themes. Frost considered this among his greatest poems, calling it "my best bid for remembrance." Read this poem several times, paying attention to the scene, the language, what happens, and the feeling that is evoked by the "music" of the poem.

Whose woods these are I think I know.
His house is in the village though;
He will not see me stopping here
To watch his woods fill up with snow.

My little horse must think it queer   5
To stop without a farmhouse near
Between the woods and frozen lake
The darkest evening of the year.

He gives his harness bells a shake
To ask if there is some mistake.   10
The only other sound's the sweep
Of easy wind and downy flake.

The woods are lovely, dark and deep,
But I have promises to keep,
And miles to go before I sleep,   15
And miles to go before I sleep.

A CLOSER LOOK AT
Stopping by Woods on a Snowy Evening

1. Poetry combines the sense of written words with the sound of the spoken words. Read this poem aloud and listen carefully to determine what feeling or mood is created by the sound of the poem. How does the sound match or reinforce the sense of the words?

2. Describe the poem's plot—not just the events that happen but also how character and events create some kind of conflict between characters or within a character. What *conflict* do you think the speaker is experiencing? Point specifically to the poem itself to explain what leads you to that understanding.

3. How do poems like this one, which has no clear resolution, cause you to think more deeply? Does the lack of resolution make the poem frustrating for you or more interesting?

IDEAS FOR
Writing

1. Write a parody of "Stopping by Woods on a Snowy Evening." Imitate the structure, style, and if possible the sound of the poem, focusing on some activity and place in which the speaker finds her- or himself. For instance, you might begin a poem titled "Looking into the Refrigerator on a Sunday Morning" with these lines: "Whose milk this is I think I know. / I need it for my cornflakes though. . . ." The point is to play with the poetic form and have fun by using it to describe an incongruous situation.

2. Write a brief evaluation of "Stopping by Woods on a Snowy Evening," another poem, or some other cultural work, such as a song. Keep in mind that an evaluation, unlike a literary analysis, presents a specific set of criteria to assess the subject for quality or effectiveness.

An Overview of "Stopping by Woods on a Snowy Evening"

STEVEN MONTE

Steven Monte is an associate professor of English at College of Staten Island–City University of New York who has published widely on American poets and poetry. In this interpretation of Frost's great poem, Monte urges readers to look beyond the poem's "impression of simplicity" to the strangeness and power of the poem to evoke multiple and ambiguous meanings. As you read, pay attention to the way that Monte never strays far from the poem's words (quoting them throughout) to arrive at an interesting and insightful understanding of the poem.

With the exception of "The Road Not Taken," "Stopping by Woods on a Snowy Evening" is probably Frost's best-known poem. As with many well-known poems, we may feel that familiarity equals understanding or that a poem we have read or heard enough times can't surprise us anymore. This is especially the case with "Stopping by Woods," which is not only one of the most popular American poems, but is also one written in a clear and seemingly direct style. We might even say that we like the poem precisely because of its simplicity and effortless feel. But as with a person we've been acquainted with for a long time but don't really know, a familiar poem may change when we encounter it in unfamiliar circumstances. Where once we saw only surface and clearly defined qualities, suddenly we see depths and ambiguity. For this to happen with a poem, we often only need to stop and reflect on our experience, like the speaker in Frost's poem. One of the messages of "Stopping by Woods" seems to be just that pausing and reflecting on experience help us re-enter life with a new understanding and sense of direction.

The plot of "Stopping by Woods" is straightforward: a man (we assume) narrates his experience of driving some sort of horse-drawn vehicle by privately owned woods on a snowy evening. He stops, and then contemplates how strange his halt must seem to the horse, given that it is cold and dark and there is no farmhouse in sight. The horse shakes his harness bell, an action that the man interprets as the animal asking "if there is some mistake." The man then listens to the wind and the snow and ends his account with some remarks on his experience, his responsibilities to the world, and the distance he needs to travel before he sleeps. The story could easily be true—it certainly aims to be "true to life"—but it is hard not to interpret it symbolically. Many readers over the years have felt that the man's journey toward sleep represents life's "journey" toward death, though Frost himself insisted that the last two lines were not an invocation of death. Another popular way of reading the poem is to understand the man's rejection of the woods as an acceptance of social duty and personal responsibility.

But "Stopping by Woods" is a much stranger poem than may appear at first. From the opening lines, we know that the story is being told from the speaker's point of view ("Whose woods these are I think I know"), but we may never bother to consider whom the man is addressing. The addressee of the poem can only be the man himself, who seems to be narrating the events as they occur to him, or thinking "aloud" to himself.

This odd, subjective perspective is worth puzzling over, if only because it allows us to see just how self-conscious the man is. Why is he so concerned about being seen stopping by the woods? Is it simply because he fears he will be accused of trespassing on someone else's property? Perhaps he feels guilty that he has temporarily suspended his business and does not wish to be seen or see himself as someone who shirks responsibility. Or it could be that he feels guilty for indulging in a fantasy, for he is attracted to something he feels he should resist. It is hard to say what the woods represent for the man—rest, death, nature, beauty, solitude, oblivion—but it is clear that he feels he should not allow himself to give in to his desire to stay there. There is moreover a sexual dimension to his fantasy: the feminine woods ("lovely, dark and deep") are set against a world of men where promises must be kept—the world of property and business.

Whatever depths "Stopping by Woods" possesses, it gives us the impression of simplicity. How does the poem manage this? Most obviously, its language remains conversational throughout and it generally avoids twisting around the word order of spoken speech. "Stopping by Woods" also contains only one word with more than two syllables. When the poem does alter the expected word order, as in "Whose woods these are I think I know," the sound and the sense of the line help us forget that there is anything odd going on. We don't feel the line should read "I think I know whose woods these are" because we get the sense that the speaker is expressing the thought as it occurs to him: he is especially concerned with remembering who owns the woods, and he expresses his uncertainty by following his first thought with the phrase "I think I know." The insistent rhythms of the poem—every line except one is exceptionally regular in beating out "ta-dum, ta-dum, ta-dum, ta-dum"—and the frequent rhymes add to the illusion of simplicity. Caught in the flow of the poem, we tend not to notice that the lines "Between the woods and frozen lake / The darkest evening of the year" neither follow logically from the lines that come before them nor form a complete sentence on their own. Once again, we might feel that we are listening to the thoughts of the speaker. He is situating himself in place ("Between the woods and frozen lake") and time ("The darkest evening of the year"), where "darkest" may imply the "longest" evening of the year, December 22, the winter solstice. By calling the evening "darkest," the man suggests that he has reached a low point or a moment of crisis.

Another reason why "Stopping by Woods" 5 seems simple is that it is structured around many familiar oppositions. A complete list of these oppositions would be unusually long for such a short poem: man and nature, masculine and feminine, emptiness and fullness, business and pleasure, movement and stopping, society and solitude, life and death, activity and sleep, and so on. Such familiar distinctions may make us feel at home in the poem, but they may also be disturbing. The categories either seem too fixed (should we only associate men with activity and business?) or too fluid (which is empty, life or death?). Oppositions also help determine the poem's organization: "Stopping by Woods" constantly alternates between inner thoughts and descriptions of the world outside. Even within its descriptive mode, the poem shifts from the visual details of the first stanza ("He will not see . . . To watch his woods") to the sounds of the third stanza ("harness bells . . . The only other sound's the sweep"). Meanwhile the second and the fourth stanzas are more reflective. In the second stanza, the man imagines what the horse is thinking. The details of "the woods and frozen lake" may be in the man's line of vision, but they may also be his way of placing the scene on a mental map, just as "darkest evening" may place the day on a mental calendar. The fourth stanza is even more

subjective in its description of the woods as "lovely, dark and deep." All of this inward and outward movement and the poem's oppositions make us feel that the man is being pulled in different directions and needs to make a decision.

But before looking at the decision the man makes in the last stanza, it is worthwhile to stop and examine some of the odd features of his descriptions. Why is his horse "little"? Why is the wind "easy" and the flake "downy"? It is not enough to say "because they *are* little, easy, and downy," or even "because they appear that way to the man," for we would still be left wondering why he chose to describe these things and not others. A somewhat more inventive if unkind explanation is that Frost needed to fill up his lines with these adjectives in order to keep the poem's rhythm insistent. But perhaps we can do better. By calling the horse "little," Frost gives us a sense of the smallness of the figures in the landscape. We furthermore sense that the man is not rich and is probably fond of his animal. "Easy" and "downy" may in their own way hint at what the man is feeling. Part of the attraction of the scene seems to lie in its promise of ease and softness, its contrast to the hard world of men.

The description of the woods in the final stanza leads into the strangest and most memorable section of the poem. Why does this last stanza haunt us? It begins innocently enough and even sounds like a cliche: "The woods are lovely." But the vagueness of the description, the pulse of the line, and the repetition of sounds ("dark and deep") suggest that we are entering a kind of dreamworld. The drowsy repetition of "And miles to go before I sleep" completes this effect, and we sense that the poem is enacting what the man is feeling. The poem's close feels satisfying because it deviates from, and then reinforces, patterns that the poem has established earlier. The first three stanzas have rhymes in the first, second, and fourth lines. The third line then rhymes with the first line of the following stanza, helping us feel that all four stanzas connect like links in a chain. But the established rhythms and rhymes are disrupted in the final stanza. The line "But I have promises to keep" is not as rhythmically insistent as the other lines of the poem. It also contains the poem's only three-syllable word, "promises." Just as the man attempts to shake off his dreamy attraction to the woods, we are brought up short with this jarring line. The last two lines then feel like a fade out, not simply because of the repetition, but due to the return of the rhythm and the absence of a new linking word: all four lines of this stanza rhyme.

The speaker in "Stopping by Woods" "wakes up" to a knowledge of what he must do. He apparently decides to return to the real world and cease his dreaming. He is leaving nature and returning to society, and in so doing makes us feel that there is some irony in the poem's title: he was only "stopping by" nature, as if on a social call. At the beginning of the poem he was unsure ("I think I know"); at the end he has gained some kind of knowledge. We can think of the experience he has by the woods as either a temporary diversion or a recurring moment in his life that helps him go on. In this straight reading of the poem, the man's experience, though forcing him to confront the fact of death and the difficulties of life, consoles him (and the reader) in the end. But if this moment is, or has the potential to be, a recurrent moment in life, the poem may not be as consoling as we first thought. In this dark reading of the poem, we can't be sure whether the man has come to a decision or merely postponed it. He never actually says he has moved on and, if anything, he seems on his way to sleep. Even supposing he does continue on his journey, it is not clear that the road ahead represents a more appealing alternative to the woods. Real life may seem emptier now, and all those familiar oppositions that help us make sense of our lives are open to question. If we equate stopping by woods with reading a poem, we will confront a similar dilemma. As the man's experience should suggest, however, it is not a question of choosing between alternatives so much as it is becoming aware of new possibilities. In looking closely at a poem, we don't cancel our first experience of reading so much as we enrich it and make it more strange.

A CLOSER LOOK AT
An Overview of "Stopping by Woods"

1. Read through this literary analysis again, this time noting the places where Monte asks a specific interpretative question about Frost's poem. For instance, in paragraph 3 he asks, "Why is he so concerned about being seen stopping by the woods? Is it simply because he fears he will be accused of trespassing on someone else's property?" He asks similar questions in paragraphs 4, 5, 6, and 7. How does he use these interpretive questions to move his literary analysis forward?

2. Consult Chapter 16, "Choosing a Style." Choose one of these features of style and one two- to five-sentence passage from Monte's literary analysis and explain how Monte's passage illustrates effective style. For instance, you might wish to explain how Monte weaves the poem's words with his own, or how he tells readers what they should notice about those quotations.

3. Carefully reread Monte's first paragraph, and note especially the final sentence, which states a possible interpretation for—or claim about—Frost's poem. Now reread the final paragraph, which begins by reiterating a similar interpretation but also suggests just as strongly a different interpretation, a "dark reading of the poem." What is Monte's claim? Does he believe one reading is superior to the other? If not, then what exactly does he want us to understand about the poem?

IDEAS FOR
Writing

1. Choose any work from popular culture (a TV show, a song, a movie, a graphic work, etc.) and write a review that interprets that work in parallel fashion to Monte's interpretation of Frost's poem. Specifically, Monte argues that Frost's poem *appears* simple and straightforward, but a more careful reading shows that it is actually complex, meaningful, and interesting. Make a similar argument in your review of your chosen work from popular culture.

2. Monte assumes that a poem that does not lead to a specific reading but allows for multiple ambiguous readings is superior to a poem that has a straightforward meaning or point. Write a position paper that argues for or against Monte's assumption that complex poems are superior.

Touched by a Vampire

LAURA MILLER

Laura Miller is the senior books writer for and cofounder of the Web site Salon. *She also contributes to the* New York Times *and the* New Yorker. *"Touched by a Vampire" was written for* Salon *and reviews the popular* Twilight *series of vampire novels written by Stephenie Meyer. As you read this piece, pay attention to the questions that Miller raises and addresses.*

A minute past midnight on August 2, bookstores across the country will for the first time repeat a ritual once reserved for a single author: J. K. Rowling. They'll stay open late and begin selling copies of *Breaking Dawn* by Stephenie Meyer, the fourth novel of the *Twilight* series, at the first moment they're officially permitted to do so. Tens of thousands of fans plan to congregate for these release parties, message boards have shut down to guard against leaked spoilers, and as many as a million readers will be blocking out an entire weekend to bury themselves in the book.

The preceding three installments in the series—*Twilight, New Moon* and *Eclipse*—occupy the top slots in *Publishers Weekly's* bestseller list for children's fiction (they are categorized as Young Adult, or YA, titles), and

are among the top five overall bestsellers on *USA Today's* list. In May, *Publishers Weekly* reported that 5.3 million copies of the *Twilight* books had sold in the U.S. alone. When a movie based on the first novel comes out in December, expect to see book sales jump to numbers that approach Rowling's eight-figure numbers.

No wonder the media has heralded *Twilight* as the next *Harry Potter* and Meyer as the second coming of J. K. The similarities, however, are largely commercial. It's hard to see how *Twilight* could ever approach *Harry Potter* as a cultural phenomenon for one simple reason: the series' fan base is almost exclusively female. The gender imbalance is so pronounced that Kaleb Nation, an enterprising 19-year-old radio show host-cum-author, has launched a blog called *Twilight Guy*, chronicling his experiences reading the books. The project is marked by a spirit that's equal parts self-promotion and scientific inquiry—"I am trying to find why nearly every girl in the world is obsessed with the *Twilight* books by Stephenie Meyer"—and its premise relies on the fact that, in even attempting this experiment, Nation has made himself an exceptional guy indeed. Bookstores have been known to shelve the *Twilight* books in both the children's and the science fiction/fantasy sections, but they are—in essence and most particulars—romance novels, and despite their gothic trappings represent a resurrection of the most old-fashioned incarnation of the genre. They summon a world in which love is passionate, yet (relatively) chaste, girls need be nothing more than fetchingly vulnerable, and masterful men can be depended upon to protect and worship them for it.

The series' heroine, Bella Swan, a 16-year-old with divorced parents, goes to live with her father in the small town of Forks, Wash. (a real place, and now a destination for fans). At school, she observes four members of a fabulously good-looking and wealthy but standoffish family, the Cullens; later she finds herself seated next to Edward Cullen in biology lab and is rendered nearly speechless by his spectacular beauty. At first, he appears to loathe her, but after a protracted period of bewilderment and dithering she discovers the truth. Edward and his clan are vampires who have committed themselves to sparing human life; they call themselves "vegetarians." The scent of Bella's blood is excruciatingly appetizing to Edward, testing his ethical limits and eventually his emotional ones, too. The pair fall in love, and the three books detail the ups and downs of this interspecies romance, which is complicated by Bella's friendship with Jacob Black, a member of a pack of Native American werewolves who are the sworn enemies of all vampires.

Comparisons to another famous human 5 girl with a vampire boyfriend are inevitable, but Bella Swan is no Buffy Summers. *Buffy the Vampire Slayer* was at heart one of those mythic hero's journeys so beloved by Joseph Campbell-quoting screenwriters, albeit transfigured into something sharp and funny by making the hero a contemporary teenage girl. Buffy wrestled with a series of romantic dilemmas—in particular a penchant for hunky vampires—but her story always belonged to *her.* Fulfilling her responsibilities as a slayer, loyalty to her friends and family, doing the right thing and cobbling together some semblance of a healthy life were all ultimately as important, if not more important, to her than getting the guy. If Harry Potter has a vampire-loving, adolescent female counterpart, it's Buffy Summers.

By contrast, Bella, once smitten by Edward, lives only for him. When he leaves her (for her own good) at the beginning of *New Moon*, she becomes so disconsolate that she resorts to risking her own life, seeking extreme situations that cause her to hallucinate his voice. This practice culminates in a quasi-suicidal high dive into the ocean, after which, on the brink of drowning, she savors visions of her undead boyfriend: "I thought briefly of the clichés, about how you're supposed to see your life flash before your eyes. I was so much luckier. Who wanted to see a rerun, anyway? I saw *him,* and I had no will to fight . . . Why would I fight when I was so happy where I was?" After Edward returns, the only obstacle she can see to her eternal happiness as a member of the glamorous Cullen family is his stubborn refusal to turn her into a vampire: He's worried that she'll lose her soul.

Otherwise directionless and unsure of herself, Bella's only distinguishing trait is her clumsiness, about which she makes frequent self-deprecating jokes. But Bella is not really the point of the *Twilight* series; she's more of a place holder than a character. She is purposely made as featureless and ordinary as possible in order to render her a vacant, flexible skin into which the reader can insert herself and thereby vicariously enjoy Edward's chilly charms. (His body is as hard and cold as stone, an ick-inducing detail that this reader, for one, found impossible to get past.) Edward, not Bella, is the key to the *Twilight* franchise, the thing that fans talk about when explaining their fascination with the books. "Perfect" is the word most often used to describe him; besides looking like a male model, Edward plays and composes classical music, has two degrees from Harvard and drives several hot cars very, very fast. And he can read minds (except, mysteriously, for Bella's). "You're good at everything," Bella sighs dreamily.

Even the most timorous teenage girl couldn't conceive of Bella as intimidating; it's hard to imagine a person more insecure, or a situation better set up to magnify her insecurities. Bella's vampire and werewolf friends are all fantastically strong and fierce as well as nearly indestructible, and she spends the better part of every novel alternately cowering in their protective arms or groveling before their magnificence. "How well I knew that I wasn't good enough for him" is a typical musing on her part. Despite Edward's many protestations and demonstrations of his utter devotion, she persists in believing that he doesn't mean it, and will soon tire of her. In a way, the two are ideally suited to each other: Her insipidity is the counterpart to his flawlessness. Neither of them has much personality to speak of.

But to say this is to criticize fantasy according to the standards of literature, and Meyer—a Mormon housewife and mother of three—has always been frank about the origins of her novels in her own dreams. Even to a reader not especially susceptible to its particular scenario, *Twilight* succeeds at communicating the obsessive, narcotic interiority of all intense fantasy lives. Some imaginary worlds multiply, spinning themselves out into ever more elaborate constructs. *Twilight* retracts; it finds its voluptuousness in the hypnotic reduction of its attention to a single point: the experience of being loved by Edward Cullen.

Bella and her world are barely sketched— 10 even Edward himself lacks dimension. His inner life and thoughts are known to us only through what Bella sees him say or do. The characters, such as they are, are stripped down to a minimum, lacking the texture and idiosyncrasies of actual people. What this sloughing off permits is the return, again and again, to the delight of marveling at Edward's beauty, being cherished in his impermeable arms, thrilling to his caresses and, above all, hearing him profess, over and over, his absolute, unfailing, exclusive, eternal and worshipful adoration. A tiny sample:

"Bella, I couldn't live with myself if I ever hurt you. You don't know how it's tortured me . . . you are the most important thing to me now. The most important thing to me ever."

"I could see it in your eyes, that you honestly believed that I didn't want you anymore. The most absurd, ridiculous concept—as if there were any way that I could exist without needing you!"

"For this one night, could we try to forget everything besides just you and me?" He pleaded, unleashing the full force of his eyes on me. "It seems like I can never get enough time like that. I need to be with you. Just you."

Need I add that such statements rarely issue from the lips of mortal men, except perhaps when they're looking for sex? Edward, however, doesn't even insist on *that*—in fact, he refuses to consummate his love for Bella because he's afraid he might accidentally harm her. "If I was too hasty," he says, "if for one second I wasn't paying enough attention, I could reach out, meaning to touch your face, and crush your skull by mistake. You don't realize how incredibly *breakable* you are. I can never, never afford to lose any kind of control when I'm with you." As a result, their time together is spent in protracted courtship: make-out sessions and sweet nothings galore, every shy girl's dream.

Yet it's not only shy girls who crush 15 mightily on Edward Cullen. One of the series' most avid fan sites is *Twilight Moms*, created by and for grown women, many with families of their own. There, as in other forums, readers describe the effects of Meyer's books using words like "obsession" and "addiction." Chores, husbands and children go neglected, and the hours that aren't spent reading and rereading the three novels are squandered on forums and fan fiction. "I have no desires to be part of the real world right now," posted one woman. "Nothing I was doing before holds any interest to me. I do what I have to do, what I need to do to get by and that's it. Someone please tell me it will ease up, even if just a little? My entire world is consumed and in a tailspin."

The likeness to drug addiction is striking, especially when you consider that literary vampirism has often served as a metaphor for that form of enthrallment. The vampire has been a remarkably fluid symbol for over a hundred years, standing for homosexuality, bohemianism and other hip manifestations of outsider status. Although the connection between the bloodsucking undead and romance fiction might seem obscure to the casual observer, they do share an ancestor. Blame it all on George Gordon, aka Lord Byron, the original dangerous, seductive bad boy with an artist's wounded soul and in his own time the object of as much feminine yearning as Edward Cullen has been in the early 21st. Not only did Byron inspire such prototypical romantic heroes as Heathcliff and Mr. Rochester (a character Meyer has listed as among her favorites), he was the original pattern for the vampire as handsome, predatory nobleman. His physician, John William Polidori, wrote "The Vampyre," a seminal short story that featured just such a figure, Lord Ruthven, patently based on the poet. Before that, the vampires of folklore had been depicted as hideous, bestial monsters.

Bram Stoker's Count Dracula was the English bourgeoisie's nightmare vision of Old World aristocracy: decadent, parasitic, yet possessed of a primitive charisma. Though

we members of the respectable middle class know they intend to eat us alive, we can't help being dazzled by dukes and princes. Aristocrats imperiously exercise the desires we repress and are the objects of our own secret infatuation with hereditary hierarchies. Anne Rice, in the hugely popular *Vampire Chronicles*, made her vampire Lestat a bisexual rock star—Byron has also been called the first of those—cementing the connection between vampire noblemen and modern celebrities. In recent years, in the flourishing subgenre known as paranormal romance, vampires play the role of leading man more often than any other creature of the night, whether the mode is noir, as in Laurell K. Hamilton's Anita Blake series of detective novels or chick-lit-ish, as in MaryJanice Davidson's Queen Betsy series.

The YA angle on vampires, evident in the *Twilight* books and in many other popular series as well, is that they're high school's aristocracy, the coolest kids on campus, the clique that everyone wants to get into. Many women apparently never get over the allure of such groups; as one reader posted on *Twilight Moms*, "*Twilight* makes me feel like there may be a world where a perfect man does exist, where love can overcome anything, where men will fight for the women they love no matter what, where the underdog strange girl in high school with an amazing heart can snag the best guy in the school, and where we can live forever with the person we love," a mix of adolescent social aspirations with what are ostensibly adult longings.

The "underdog strange girl" who gets plucked from obscurity by "the best guy in school" is the 21st century's version of the humble governess who captures the heart of the lord of the manor. The chief point of this story is that the couple *aren't* equals, that his love rescues her from herself by elevating her to a class she could not otherwise join. Unlike Buffy, Bella is no hero. "There are so many girls out there who do not know kung fu, and if a guy jumps in the alley they're not going to turn around with a roundhouse kick," Meyer once told a journalist. "There's a lot of people who are just quieter and aren't having the Prada lifestyle and going to a special school in New York where everyone's rich and fabulous. There's normal people out there and I think that's one of the reasons Bella has become so popular."

Yet the Cullens, although they don't live 20 in New York, *are* rich and fabulous. *Twilight* would be a lot more persuasive as an argument that an "amazing heart" counts for more than appearances if it didn't harp so incessantly on Edward's superficial splendors. If the series is supposed to be championing the worth of "normal" people, then why make Edward so exceptional? If his wealth, status, strength, beauty and accomplishments make him the "best" among all the boys at school, why shouldn't the same standard be applied to the girls, leaving Bella by the wayside? Sometimes Edward seems to subscribe to that standard, complaining about having to read the thoughts of one of Bella's classmates because "her mind isn't very original." But then, neither is Bella's. In a sense, Bella is absolutely right: She's not "good enough" for Edward—at least, not according to the same measurements that make Edward "perfect." Yet by some miracle she—unremarkable in every way—is exempt from his customary contempt for the ordinary. Then again, by choosing her he proves that she's *better* than all the average people at school.

Such are the tortured internal contradictions of romance, as nonsensical as its masculine counterpart, pornography, and every bit as habit forming. Search a little deeper on the Internet and you can find women readers both objecting to the antifeminist aspects of *Twilight* and admitting that they found the books irresistible. "Sappy romance, amateurish writing, etc.," complained one. Still, "when I read it, I just couldn't put it down. It was like an unhealthy addiction for me . . . I'm not sure how I could read through it, seeing how I dislike romances immensely. But I did, and when I couldn't get *New Moon* I almost had a heart attack. That book was hypnotizing."

Some things, it seems, are even harder to kill than vampires. The traditional feminine fantasy of being delivered from obscurity by a dazzling, powerful man, of needing to do no more to prove or find yourself than win his devotion, of being guarded from all life's vicissitudes by his boundless strength and wealth—all this turns out to be a difficult dream to leave behind. Vampires have long served to remind us of the parts of our own psyches that seduce us, sapping our will and autonomy, dragging us back into the past. And they walk among us to this day.

A CLOSER LOOK AT
Touched by a Vampire

1. What are the features and moves that would identify this piece as a literary analysis? What are the features and moves that would identify it as a review? What other genres and genre features are mixed into this literary analysis?

2. In several places, Miller compares the *Twilight* series to the TV show *Buffy the Vampire Slayer* and *Twilight*'s characters (Bella and Edward) to the characters in *Buffy*. Which series does Miller find superior? What criteria does she use to evaluate one as superior to the other? In other words, what is it that makes one better or more interesting?

3. "Touched by a Vampire" can be seen as a "genre-based analysis" of the *Twilight* books, since Miller evaluates the books in relation to how they adhere to the romance genre. Miller writes that the *Twilight*

books "are—in essence and most particulars—romance novels, and . . . represent a resurrection of the most old-fashioned incarnation of the genre." Does Miller, overall, approve or disapprove of the romance genre and of these books? Find specific places in "Touched by a Vampire" that support your conclusions.

IDEAS FOR
Writing

1. Miller takes features from many of the genres described in this book and fuses them into "Touched by a Vampire," which can be seen as a fusion of review, rant, evaluation, literary analysis, and commentary, just to name a few. Using Miller's "genre fusion" strategy, write a similar piece about a book, movie, song, band, television show, or other cultural work that you have found effective or ineffective, or that had a profound influence on you or left you cold.

2. Write a position paper that either challenges or supports Miller's position about the value of and healthfulness of reading romance novels.

A FEW IDEAS FOR
Composing a Literary Analysis

1. **Write a literary analysis of a favorite work.** Choose a book, poem, movie, play, or other work that you find absolutely wonderful. Invite your readers to consider the work through a new and interesting angle, and show them how that angle can lead to new and interesting insights that go beyond the obvious.

2. **Write a literary analysis about a persuasive work.** Choose a literary work that you feel tries to persuade readers about a certain belief or attitude. Write a literary analysis that focuses on how the literary work persuades its readers (see Chapter 22, "Using Argumentative Strategies"). Very few literary works make explicit claims, but they can often be more influential than straightforward arguments. For instance, it is possible to see Edwidge Danticat's "A Wall of Fire Rising" (page 148) as making an argument against the terrible burden of poverty, or Langston Hughes's "I, Too" (page 145) as making an argument against racial segregation. Your analysis should explain what claim the literary work makes and how effectively it makes its case.

3. **Write a literary analysis of a nonprint work.** Today, you can read printed words on a page, read a text supplemented with images and sound, listen to an audiobook, read a text with an e-book reader or on a Web page, watch a movie version, or experience other multimodal transformations. Experience a literary work both on the traditional printed page and in a digital mode and analyze how these different modes of presentation affect your experience as a reader. In your analysis, focus on how the changes in modes and media change your experience. What is emphasized and what new understandings are made possible? What is de-emphasized or left out?

Rhetorical
Analyses

He's Not Black

MARIE ARANA

One of the interesting criticisms of Barack Obama, especially as he became known nationally, was that he wasn't "black enough." Even a few African American leaders doubted whether a person who is half-white and raised by a white mother could really be seen as truly black. In this rhetorical analysis, Marie Arana explores what it means to be "black" in America by paying close attention to the language we use to describe and discuss race. Pay attention to how Arana uses this question of blackness as a way of better understanding Obama's style and the man himself.

He is also half white.

Unless the one-drop rule still applies, our president-elect is not black.

We call him that—he calls himself that—because we use dated language and logic. After more than 300 years and much difficult history, we hew to the old racist rule: Part-black is all black. Fifty percent equals a hundred. There's no in-between.

That was my reaction when I read these words on the front page of this newspaper the day after the election: "Obama Makes History: U.S. Decisively Elects First Black President."

The phrase was repeated in much the 5 same form by one media organization after another. It's as if we have one foot in the future and another still mired in the Old South. We are racially sophisticated enough to elect a non-white president, and we are so racially backward that we insist on calling him black. Progress has outpaced vocabulary.

To me, as to increasing numbers of mixed-race people, Barack Obama is not our first black president. He is our first biracial, bicultural president. He is more than the personification of African American achievement. He is a bridge between races, a living symbol of tolerance, a signal that strict racial categories must go.

Of course there is much to celebrate in seeing Obama's victory as a victory for African Americans. The long, arduous battles that were fought and won in the name of civil rights redeemed our Constitution and brought a new sense of possibility to all minorities in this country. We Hispanic Americans, very likely the most mixed-race people in the world, credit our gains to the great African American pioneers of yesterday: Rosa Parks, W.E.B. Du Bois, Martin Luther King Jr.

But Obama's ascent to the presidency is more than a triumph for blacks. It is the signal of a broad change with broad ramifications. The world has become too fused, too interdependent to ignore this emerging reality: Just as banks, earthly resources, and human disease form an intricate global web, so do racial ties. No one appreciates this more, perhaps, than the American Hispanic.

Our multiracial identity was brought home to me a few months ago when I got my results from a DNA ancestry lab. I thought I was a simple hemispheric split—half South American, half North. But as it turns out, I am a descendant of all the world's major races: Indo-European, black African, East Asian, Native American. The news came as something of a surprise. But it shouldn't have.

Mutts are seldom divisible by two. 10

Like Obama, I am the child of a white Kansan mother and a foreign father who, like Obama's, came to Cambridge, Mass., as a graduate student. My parents met during World War II, fell in love, and married. Then they moved back to my father's country, Peru, where I was born.

I always knew I was biracial—part indigenous American, part white. My mother's ancestry was easy to trace and largely Anglo-American. But on my Peruvian side, I suspected from old family albums that some forebears might actually have been African or Asian: A great-great aunt had distinctly Negroid features. Another looked markedly Chinese. Of course, no one acknowledged it. It wasn't until the DNA test percentages were before me that I had a clear and overwhelming sense of my own history. I wasn't the product of only one bicultural marriage. My ancestral past was a tangle of races. When I sent back for an analysis of the Indo-European quotient, I was told that my "white side" came from the Indian subcontinent, the Middle East, the Mediterranean and Northern Europe. There had to have been hundreds of intercultural marriages in my bloodline. I am just about everything a human can be.

Still, the same can be said for many Hispanic Americans. Perhaps because we've been in this hemisphere two centuries longer than our northern brethren, we've had more time to mix it up. We are the product of el gran mestizaje, a wholesale cross-pollination that has been blending brown, white, black and yellow for 500 years—since Columbus set foot in the New World.

The Spanish and Portuguese actually encouraged interracial marriage. It wasn't that they were any more enlightened than Northern Europeans, it was that their history of exploration, colonization, and exploitation had been carried out by men—soldiers and sailors—who were left to find local brides and settle the wilds of America. The Catholic Church, eager to multiply its ranks and expand its influence, was prepared to bless any union between two of its faithful, regardless of race. So over the years, the indigenous people of Latin America were handily converted, mixed marriages propagated abundantly, a new fusion of races was born, and the Church prospered.

At first, those unions were largely between the native population and Iberians—El Inca Garcilaso de la Vega, for instance, the great 16th-century chronicler of the Spanish Conquista, was the son of a Spanish captain and an Andean princess. Later, the Atlantic slave trade sparked widespread mixing among blacks, whites, and Indians—particularly in Venezuela and Brazil. And then, in the late 19th century, a fourth ethnic group was imported to the continent in the form of Chinese coolies who came to work the guano islands and sugar fields. They, too, intermarried.

Latinos in the United States have always been difficult to fix racially. Before the late 1960s, when civil rights forced Americans to think about race, we routinely identified ourselves as white on census forms. After 1970, when a Hispanic box was offered, we checked it, although we knew that the concept of Hispanic as a single race was patently silly. But since 2000, when it became possible for a citizen to register in more than one racial category, many of us began checking them all: indigenous, white, Asian, African. It would be false to do otherwise. "Todo plátano tiene su manchita negra," as we say. Every banana has its little bit of black.

With so much history in our veins, Hispanics tend to think differently about race. The Latino population of this country continues to be, as the New America Foundation's Gregory Rodriguez puts it, a vanguard of interracial mixing.

"By creating a racial climate in which intermarriage is more acceptable," Rodriguez writes in his new book, *Mongrels, Bastards, Orphans, and Vagabonds*, Latins are "breaking down the barriers that have traditionally served to separate whites and nonwhites in the United States." Mexican Americans, he claims, "are forcing the United States to reinterpret the concept of the melting pot . . . [to] blur the lines between 'us' and 'them.' Just as the emergence of the mestizos undermined the Spanish racial system in colonial Mexico. Mexican Americans, who have always confounded the Anglo-American racial system, will ultimately destroy it, too."

In other words, intermarriage—the kind Hispanics have known for half a millennium, the kind from which Barack Obama was born, the kind that is becoming more visible in every urban neighborhood in America—represents a body blow to American racism. Why don't we recognize this as the revolutionary wave that it is? Why can't we find words to describe it? Why do we continue to resort to the tired paradigm that calls a biracial man black?

Even Obama himself seems to have 20 bought into the nomenclature. In his memoir *Dreams from My Father,* he writes, "I was trying to raise myself to be a black man in America, and beyond the given of my appearance, no one around me seemed to know exactly what that meant." You can almost feel the youth struggling with his identity, reaching for the right words to describe it and finally accepting the label that others impose.

It doesn't have to be that way. As the great American poet Langston Hughes once wrote, "I am not black. There are lots of different kinds of blood in our family. But here in the United States, the word 'Negro' is used to mean *any*one who has any Negro blood at all in his veins. . . . I am brown."

Hughes was right. North America has been slow to acknowledge its racial mixing. Anti-miscegenation laws, which were prevalent in Germany under the Nazis and in South Africa during apartheid, were still the rule in a number of states here until 1967, a mere generation ago, when the case of *Loving v. Virginia* finally struck them down. The goal of those laws, unspoken but undeniable, was to maintain racial "purity," ensure white supremacy. It was not only undesirable, it was punishable for a white to procreate with a black. Or an Asian. Or an Indian. And yet a quiet cross-cultural mixing continued all the while. Even under Thomas Jefferson's own roof.

The explosion of "minorities" in the United States in the past half-century has guaranteed that ever more interracial mingling is inevitable. According to the 2000 Census, there were 1.5 million Hispanic-white marriages in the United States, half a million Asian-white marriages, and more than a quarter-million black-white marriages. The reality is probably closer to double or triple that number. And growing.

The evidence is everywhere. If not in our neighborhoods, in our culture. We see it in Tiger Woods, Halle Berry, Ben Kingsley, Nancy Kwan, Ne-Yo, Mariah Carey. Yet we insist on calling these hybrids by a reductive name: Berry is black. Kingsley is white. Kwan is yellow. Even they label themselves by the apparent color of their skin. With language like that, how can we claim to live in a post-racial society?

A few years ago, after I gave a talk about 25 biculturalism at a Pittsburgh college, a student approached me and said, "I understand everything you say. I too am a child of two cultures. My mother is German, my father African American. I was born in Germany, speak German and call myself a German-American. But look at me. What would you say I am?" She was referring to her skin, which was light black; her hair, lush and curly; and her eyes, a shining onyx. "I am fifty percent German. But no one who sees me believes it."

Few who see Barack Obama, it seems, understand that he's 50 percent white Kansan. Even fewer understand what it means to be second-generation Kenyan. It reminds me of something sociologist Troy Duster and bioethicist Pilar Ossorio once observed: Skin color is seldom what it seems. People who look white can have a significant majority of African ancestors. People who look black can have a majority of ancestors who are European.

In other words, the color of a president-elect's skin doesn't tell you much. It's an unreliable marker, a deceptive form of packaging. Isn't it time we stopped using labels that validate the separation of races? Isn't it time for the language to move on?

He's Not Black

1. In this essay, Arana suggests that Obama's racial background is more complex than the media often portrays. Where in this rhetorical analysis does she show that seeing Obama and his election in terms of black and white is inaccurate? How does language play a role in how Obama defines himself and how others define him?

2. Arana suggests that Obama is actually more similar to Hispanics, who are the descendents of immigrants, than he is to African Americans, who often trace their lineage to the slaves. What are three ways in which Obama is similar to Hispanics, according to Arana?

3. Like Obama, many other public figures, according to Arana, are also mixed-race but refer to themselves as belonging to one race or another. Who does she mention and how does she imply that they are like or unlike Obama and herself? Why is it important or unimportant for a public figure to identify with a particular racial group?

Writing

1. Think about your own heritage. Where do your ancestors come from? Do you identify with one ancestral origin more than another? Write a commentary in which you argue for or against the practice of identifying with one ancestral group. Do you think it is a good idea to identify yourself with a particular lineage? Or do you think people should recognize that everyone is a mixture of many different ancestral genes?

2. Do some research on your family's genealogy. Ask your parents or other relatives about what they know about your background. You can also use the Internet to do searches on your genealogy. Write a brief report in which you describe what you discovered about your ancestors and where the branches of your family came from.

Sleuthing Patriotic Slogans

GARY SLOAN

In the United States, slogans are hard to escape. They are ever-present on radio and television, and, when walking or driving, we see them just about anywhere. In this rhetorical analysis, Gary Sloan, a retired English professor, digs a little deeper into the meaning of these slogans. Notice how he questions whether the slogans have any deeper meaning by paying close attention to the words themselves.

In this best of times and worst of times, the American landscape is dotted with signs, billboards, posters, and stickers emblazoned with patriotic slogans. In my hometown, merchants have scrawled on their display windows a smorgasbord of venerable shibboleths: "United We Stand," "Support the Troops," "Pray for the Troops," "Let Freedom Ring," "Home of the Brave," "God Bless America." Taped on many windows is a flyer that reads: "Pro-America Rally in Railroad Park. Bring lawn chairs, flags, and snacks. Dress patriotic."

When I read the flyer, I thought: Shouldn't that be "Dress *patriotically*?"

Because I have spent much of my life studying and teaching language, I respond inappropriately to patriotic slogans: I parse them grammatically and try to explicate them the way I would an obscure fragment in an essay. Like Hamlet, I sometimes become sicklied over with the pale cast of thought when I shouldn't be thinking at all. The slogans are designed to evoke warm feelings of camaraderie and unity, not grimaces and cocked brows.

Yet I persist in my folly. To wit: Many patriotic slogans are in the imperative mood. They issue a command ("Support the Troops," "Pray for the Troops"). Commands are risky. They create resistance in natural-born rebels and in patriophobes (those with an excessive fear of patriotism).

Are "Let Freedom Ring" and "United We 5 Stand" logically compatible? If everyone exercises freedom of speech and conscience, will we all stand united? Instead of assenting to the war against Iraq, some may opt to ring their dissent. How does one "Support the Troops"? Letters? Pep rallies? Boxes of homemade cookies? Can one support the troops by urging them to obey their consciences even if their consciences conflict with their orders?

"Home of the Brave." Hmm. Brave in what sense? Obviously, many Americans aren't physically brave. Millions are afraid to walk the streets at night or open their doors to strangers. If "brave" refers to moral courage, might the bravest Americans be those who resist the will of the majority? Might it require more bravery to protest Operation Iraqi Freedom than to support it?

"God Bless America" is almost as inscrutable as the utterances of a Delphi oracle. Grammatically, the words are in the subjunctive mood. They express a wish or a prayer: "Please, God, bless America," or "May God bless America."

The real conundrum: What do the words mean? In what sense is God to bless America? With good health, bouncing babies, supportive spouses? Good schools? High IQs? Philosophical wisdom? Fat paychecks, sirloin steaks, sport-utility vehicles, faster computers, more cable channels, bigger boom boxes? Competitive Superbowls? Better face-lifts and liposuction? Speedier cruise missiles, smarter smart bombs, stealthier stealth bombers? Continued monopoly of the planet's natural resources?

And does "America" mean Americans? If so, does it comprise all Americans, including murderers, rapists, thieves, swindlers, embezzlers, muggers, liars, cheats, bullies, pederasts, pornographers, conceited airheads, slobs, slum lords, domestic tyrants, bigots, and racists?

Or does "America" refer to land, spacious 10 skies and amber waves of grain? Or to some platonic ideal of government embodied in the Declaration of Independence and the Constitution, worthy of being blessed even if some Americans aren't?

Now, if I can just figure out how to dress patriotic.

A CLOSER LOOK AT
Sleuthing Patriotic Slogans

1. Sloan suggests that some slogans actually have the opposite effect than their creators intended. Sometimes, they command us to do things or think in a particular way. Why do these commands actually undermine their message, according to Sloan?

2. Grammatical issues seem to be at the heart of much of Sloan's irritation with patriotic slogans. What kinds of grammar problems does he suggest cause these slogans to be questionable and less than solid?

3. Toward the end of the article, Sloan questions whether patriotic slogans are really meant for all Americans. When we think of Americans more broadly, including all citizens, what are the problems with these simple slogans?

IDEAS FOR
Writing

1. Look through a magazine or watch television to collect some slogans of your own. How do the slogans that you collected work? When held up to close scrutiny, as in Sloan's article, do they have weaknesses or make questionable assumptions? Write a position paper in which you defend or challenge the use of slogans to persuade people.

2. Find an advertisement on television or *YouTube* that uses a slogan prominently and write a review in which you explain why you think the advertisement is or is not effective. What makes it persuasive? Where are its shortcomings? How might the advertisement be made more effective?

Shooting from the Hip, with a Smile to Boot

LIBBY COPELAND

In the 2008 election, the emergence of Alaska Governor Sarah Palin as a national politician was meteoric. Her acceptance speech for vice-presidential candidate at the Republican National Convention electrified the conservative base, and she became an instant celebrity. In this rhetorical analysis, Libby Copeland, a writer for the Washington Post, *explains Palin's use of style to win people over. Copeland does not use the word* ethos, *but pay attention to how issues involving reputation and image underlie this analysis.*

The heart of Sarah Palin's appeal is—
Wait, did you see that? There! She did it again: wrinkled up her nose in a way that either looks like a sneer or is adorably reminiscent of Samantha from "Bewitched." Depending on whom you talk to.

Next time you see a clip of the Republican vice presidential nominee, try this exercise. Mute your TV and just watch that face. How often do you see someone in political life so extravagantly expressive? The eyebrows go up, the shoulder leans in, the thumb jauntily gestures backward, the tongue actually fixes in the cheek. To mock Barack Obama, she licks her finger and holds it to the imaginary wind! And that smile, that nearly ever-present smile, which either indicates— oh, dear, here we go again—that she's sarcastic and dismissive or that she's letting you in on a very clever joke.

People love her so. People hate her so. At the heart of it is the delivery, a style of speaking we'll see again in tomorrow night's debate, a style that reaches past folksy and veers into the territory of—to hell with it, cue the charges of sexism—cute.

"She's perky, she's spunky," says Republi- 5 can speechwriter Landon Parvin, who has written for both Presidents Bush. "She has this quality—in a 1950s comedy, her father would call her 'Button.'"

And?

"This allows her to get away with murder," he says.

All you wannabe hockey moms who imagine yourselves having coffee with Sarah Palin and swapping five-minute dinner recipes? Who find it endearing when Palin refers to her husband as "my guy"? Who like the smiling certainty in her tone, the determination in her squint? This is for you.

And all you Pal-lergics who dislike not only her hard-edged politics but that spoonful of sugar she serves it with? Who say her manner reminds you of—we'll quote here from a Pal-lergic named Judi Dickerson who coaches actors on dialogue—"the snotty head cheerleader in high school who was untouchable because she was always gonna win"? This is for you, too.

Sarah Palin is many things—somber is not 10 one of them. There's something about her delivery that suggests she's almost always having fun. You know how they call Joe Biden the happy warrior? Palin has a similar quality—the

ability to attack without seeming angry. Some of that is the smile on her face and the evident humor in her voice, as Sheila Tate, Nancy Reagan's former press secretary, points out.

But there's a lot more at work. It starts with the way Palin's delivery allows her to leap through the camera into your living room. Perhaps in part because of her background as a television reporter and beauty pageant competitor, she seems to understand how the camera works.

"What she knows is that the camera is a thief," says Republican strategist Ron Bonjean, who has worked for former House speaker Dennis Hastert and former Senate majority leader Trent Lott, among others. "The camera will steal your emotions and make you flat, and what she's doing is over-emphasizing her emotions, over-emphasizing her delivery, in order to get that realness across to the camera."

The realness is what her fans talk about— that she's like them, that she doesn't seem contrived. "We feel like she talks like we do," says Susan Geary, a Richmond retiree who attended a McCain-Palin rally in Fairfax last month. "Like she's sitting in your kitchen."

There's a consistency to Palin's appeal—if you go back and look at old clips of her, you see many of the same stylistic elements—the warmth and the eager delivery, the voice that drops and rises emphatically, the dropped g's.

"That's been her bread and butter for 20 15 years, from the day she sat down in front of the TV cameras to do her sportscasting," says Anchorage-based pollster Ivan Moore. "Her success in her political career has been based on being able to project this enormously friendly, enormously appealing physical presence—and, some people would argue, use it to conceal this very much more ruthless and nakedly political character."

Palin's fans are drawn to her story, that folk-hero combination of caribou-hunting toughness and traditional femininity that John McCain's campaign has played up. For many Palin supporters, her attractiveness does not weaken her appeal—rather, it balances those tales of valor on the tundra. Supporters have charged her critics with sexism but at the same time, at the GOP convention, delegates wore buttons that said "Hottest VP From the Coolest State." For a while, Cindy McCain was introducing Palin as a "true Western woman," evoking images of pretty prairie wives with rifles who could out-hunt their husbands and still get dinner on the table. (Hot chicks with guns being a beloved American archetype.)

They are also drawn to the notion of Palin's PTA-mom-just-like-you-ness, which is enhanced by the hair, which has not been cut short in the style of many political women, and the voice, which has not been brought down to a deeper register, or stripped of its Alaska-by-way-of-middle-America nasality. Plain does more than mention her five children as biographical fact in appearances—she also speaks in mom language. What other major political figure would attempt what she said at her welcome-home rally in Fairbanks last month?

"I see some of our staff members here and cabinet members," she told the audience at a rally. "I can't wait to give you guys a hug."

Palin's huggability is evidence of her accessibility—or of her lack of gravitas, depending on where you sit. When she met Pakistani President Asif Ali Zardari in New York recently, he called her "gorgeous" and joked he might hug her. In response, she laughed.

Much of Palin's appeal—as well as what 20 some find grating—is about the language she chooses, which is folksy in the extreme. She says "heck" and "darn" and "gosh" and "shoot" and "oh, gee." She says, "Guys and gals, our regulatory system is outdated." And: The nation's financial system "needs some shakin' up and some fixin.' " She pronounces things "awesome" and "cool," as in: "He's an awesome bundle of joy" (baby Trig) and "It was so cool growin' up in this church and gettin' saved here" (the Wasilla Assembly of God). The critics—she calls 'em "haters."

Could central casting produce a more ideal messenger for the new Republican populism?

"I'm sure she's not from Alaska—she's been sitting on a Hollywood sound stage for years waiting for this," says Paul Costello, the former press aide to Rosalynn Carter and Kitty Dukakis. "She's so unbelievably perfect. . . . Even the red ruby shoes that she's been wearing."

In speeches, Palin's comedic timing is spot-on and her intonation is exaggerated, sweeping her audience along on the current of her message. "Very story-timely," says John Neffinger, a communications consultant who coaches corporate speakers and Democratic congressional candidates. "She varies her intonation all over the place so you know exactly what feelings she's trying to convey. Lots of warmth, very sing-songy."

In the few interviews she has given, or when taking question from voters, Palin speaks with speed and a rat-a-tat delivery, as if a pause were a sign of weakness. Sometimes she drops her voice to a rock-and-roll growl. Her hands move in concert, pointing to her lips, jabbing over her shoulder. Her delivery is "decisive, task-focused," says Ken Brousseau, who consults with executive search firm Korn/Ferry International on corporate leadership styles. "Very black and white." Contrast that with Barack Obama's more deliberative style, his long "uuuhs," his concessions to the opposition. ("John, you're absolutely right," in the presidential debate, over and over.)

When she's forced outside her comfort 25 zone, as has happened a few times of late, Palin tends to "slip back to her talking points," as CBS's Katie Couric recently put it. John McCain is a maverick. Lots of things need some shakin' up. Palin may try to turn a question around ("In what respect, Charlie?") or stall when asked for examples to bolster her argument ("I'll try to find you some and I'll bring 'em to ya!").

"Forgive me, Mrs. Palin," faux Katie Couric said to faux Sarah Palin on last week's "Saturday Night Live," "but it seems to me that when cornered you become increasingly adorable."

There's a youthfulness and an enthusiasm there—Palin is all emoticons; Rachel Ray as candidate for higher office. (When she ran for mayor of Wasilla in 1996, her campaign ad boasted upbeat, jazzy music and a slogan reminiscent of daytime TV: "Positively Sarah.") She speaks with supreme confidence (Ya can't blink, Charlie). On Monday, she said she looked forward to meeting Senate veteran Joe Biden at their debate.

"I've been hearing about his Senate speeches since I was in, like, the second grade," she told an audience in Columbus, Ohio—emphasizing her youth, as well as suggesting an unusual attentiveness to the earliest speeches of Biden, who was sworn in when she was 8.

Perhaps, suggests former Miss America Kate Shindle, an undecided Republican, there's a touch of the pageant world to Palin's voice, to her careful adherence to sound bytes, and that "cheerful aggressiveness" that Shindle calls "part cheerleader, part news anchor, and part drill sergeant."

The confidence is underscored by some-   30 thing Palin does frequently at the ends of her sentences. She sets her lips in forceful line (perfectly captured by Tina Fey in her first "Saturday Night Live" impersonation) as if to communicate that the matter is settled.

Now mute the television again. Watch Palin's body. She expresses excitement through encouraging nods as well as what Karen Bradley—a University of Maryland dance professor who studies body movement—calls this "little shoulder wiggle." And watch that nose wiggle—which Parvin, the Republican speechwriter, says sometimes conveys "a cute determination" and sometimes "a cute distastefulness." And sometimes, it operates as a sort of "exclamation point," conveying agreement, he says. He calls her "Gidget goes to Washington."

"She is playing into a cultural stereotype," says Drew Westen, a psychiatry professor at Emory University who also works as a Democratic consultant and wrote *The Political Brain: The Role of Emotion in Deciding the Fate of the Nation*. And the stereotype? Westen cites Marlo Thomas in *That Girl*, Mary Tyler Moore in *The Dick Van Dyke Show*, Sally Field in *The Flying Nun*—a model of perky femininity that "was really salient in the early '60s before the sexual revolution and the cultural revolution took hold."

These physical and rhetorical habits set Palin in relief to Hillary Clinton, who projected great strength but much less of what one Democratic political consultant calls "traditional feminine warmth." Which was why it caused such a splash when Clinton once told a crowd, "I'm your girl"—there is little that's girly about Hillary Clinton's public persona. Palin calls herself a "gal" and it's utterly believable.

"She's not a woman trying to deliver a speech like a man, and there is an integrity to that," says Parvin.

And all of which means Sarah Palin is   35 either great or awful, depending on whom you talk to, because her style and her conservative beliefs are either post-feminist or the antithesis of feminism. If Palin's cuteness is disarming to her supporters, it is troubling to those who worry that she lacks intellectual heft, and infuriating to those who feel she's being coddled. Not too long ago, CNN anchor Campbell Brown suggested the McCain campaign was being sexist by shielding Palin from interviews. Acting coach Dickerson suggests that Palin gets to be as nakedly political as any other candidate while being shielded from retaliation because of the perception that she is, after all, just a gal.

"You have a very glamorous, pretty woman with, actually, a very girly delivery—but what comes out of her are the words of a very savvy, very tough politician," says Dickerson. "It creates a mixed message of allowing her to really say anything that she wants."

Then again, who decides what's fair? Sarah Palin is hugging us all into confusion.

A CLOSER LOOK AT
Shooting from the Hip, with a Smile to Boot

1. In the article, find five rhetorical qualities that Copeland suggests Palin uses to persuade her audiences. Do you agree that Palin uses these qualities in a strategic way? What impact does Palin's style have on you as a viewer?

2. Copeland also suggests that Palin's style has a reverse effect on some people. In other words, some people "hate her so." Why does Palin's style have this effect, according to Copeland?

3. This article relies on some interesting stylistic devices itself. Find five different times when Copeland's own writing style seems to stand out. How does she use detail, metaphors, similes, and other stylistic devices to enhance her message?

IDEAS FOR
Writing

1. Looking back on the 2008 election, what were your reactions to the rhetorical styles of Palin and Obama? Clearly, both of them are formidable public speakers. How are their styles similar? How are they different? Write a response to this article in which you compare and contrast the speaking styles of Palin and Obama.

2. Find a video of Sarah Palin speaking on *YouTube* or another video Web site. Using the qualities highlighted in this article, write a review of her speech in which you critique her style and her use of *ethos* to make her speech more persuasive. Do you find her style effective or not?

Discovering the Truth: The Operation of *Ethos* in Anti-Smoking Advertising

REBECCA FELDMANN

This rhetorical analysis appeared in a journal called Young Scholars in Writing, *which publishes articles on rhetoric and composition written by college undergraduates. Feldmann shows how the popular and effective* Truth *campaign appeals to teens by building* ethos *and challenging the* ethos *of tobacco companies. As you read, look at how she carefully defines concepts up front, which she can then use later in the rhetorical analysis.*

In 1998, the Florida Tobacco Pilot Program (FTPP) launched a $25 million Truth advertising campaign to alert teenagers to the dangers of smoking and to reduce teen tobacco use. The Truth campaign began when studies conducted by the FTPP and other tobacco control efforts determined that smoking is equated with rebellion and teen self-realization and that the theme of "industry manipulation" held broad appeal among young people (Zucker, Hopkins, Sly, Urich, Mendza-Kershaw, and Solan). This campaign portrayed the tobacco industry as manipulative and smoking itself as an uncool habit, and it tapped into teens' need to rebel by depicting tobacco use as an addictive habit marketed by an adult establishment (Zucker, Hopkins, Sly, Urich, Mendza-Kershaw, and Solan 2).

The campaign has since spread nationwide, sponsoring advertisements in magazines, television, and radio. It has its own website with a link to a photo blog, a "Find Facts" page where visitors can learn facts that the campaign has gathered about tobacco companies and the effects of smoking[1] and a "Whatta You Think" section where teens can voice their opinions on issues relating to the tobacco industry and smoking.

The reach of these ads has extended across the nation and impacted a number of teens. Between the inception of Florida's Truth campaign and 2000, results within the state included "a 92 percent brand awareness rate among teens, a 15 percent rise in teens who agree with key attitudinal statements about smoking, a 19.4 percent decline in smoking among middle school students, and a 8.0 percent decline among high school students" (Zucker, Hopkins, Sly, Urich, Mendza-Kershaw, and Solan 1). More recently, among 12 to 17-year olds in the U.S., 75% can accurately describe one or more of the Truth ads, 90% reported that the ad they saw was convincing, and 85% responded that the ad gave them good reasons not to smoke (Citizen's Commission). Furthermore, the Com-

mission's website states, "Monitoring the Future, one of the nation's most comprehensive substance abuse surveys, reported dramatic declines in smoking rates among 8th, 10th, and 12th graders, citing Truth as a factor in this public health success story" (Citizen's Commission).

From such statistics, it is easy to conclude that these ads have been effective in drawing teenage audiences, but it is not as easy to conclude *how*. In this article, by turning to Aristotle, I examine these advertisements as contemporary examples of rhetoric to understand how they function. In doing so, I illustrate that the Truth campaign alerts us to the efficacy of rhetoric at its best—rhetoric that alerts us to the truth of a matter rather than manipulates us into being falsely persuaded by appealing images and illustrious wordplay. In a culture where the word "rhetoric" is often associated with scheming political speech or gimmicky advertising, the rhetoric of the Truth campaign aims at something different. Rather than reverting to "that powerful instrument of error and deceit" (827) that John Locke refers to in his *An Essay Concerning Human Understanding,* the rhetoric of Truth's advertising more closely approaches Plato's definition of rhetoric as "an art which leads the soul by means of words" (*Phaedrus* 157).

The use of *ethos*

Aristotle first discusses *ethos* in Book 1 of his work, *On Rhetoric. Ethos,* or persuasion by character, is built "whenever the speech is spoken in such a way as to make the speaker worthy of credence" (38). The rhetor who purports to have the audience's best interest at heart and who successfully conveys this in her speech will persuade by building character (*ethos*) in the speech rather than by relying on a preconceived notion the audience may have of the rhetor. This is the most effective means of swaying an audience; the ethical appeal is "the controlling factor in persuasion" (38), as Aristotle puts it.

An example of the attempt to persuade by invoking *ethos* in the Truth ads is apparent in a series of magazine advertisements, which tell teens, "Their brand is lies. Our brand is truth." This tagline is the most blatant appearance of such character building as it communicates that Truth ads are serving the purpose of truth rather than manipulation. As Aristotle points out, "The true and the just are by nature stronger than their opposites" (34), and the Truth ads build character by upholding this precept.

The visual statements in these ads further build *ethos*. The dual presence of smoking and body-bags in several of Truth's ads illustrate this point, for the message is simple: smoking kills. This message is present in many of Truth's advertisements, including the Marlboro-like ad discussed in more detail below. These visual statements communicate the campaign's *ethos* by pointing out the stark contrast between their advertising and that of tobacco companies. Truth's ads cleverly call attention to the deceitful tactics of tobacco ads that promote a habit that can kill and that target an audience (those between 12 and 17) which cannot legally engage in that habit.

Practical wisdom [*phronïsis*]

The *ethos* of any speech must contain three components: "practical wisdom [*phronïsis*]," or good sense/knowledge of the subject the speaker is addressing; "virtue [*aretï*]," or good moral character, which also has ties to the desire to communicate "the true and the just" (Aristotle 34); and "good will [*eunoia*]," or having the good of the audience as the speaker's (at least perceived) main interest (121). Aristotle further states that a rhetor may become less persuasive if he fails to demonstrate any one of these parts, but "a person seeming to have all these qualities is necessarily persuasive to the hearers" (121).

In the Truth ads, practical wisdom involves knowledge of the strategies and manipulation used in cigarette advertising and knowledge of the audience (teens between 12–18). Truth communicates practical wisdom relative to Big Tobacco by containing on its website a "find facts" page that enables teens to broaden their knowledge by scrolling through various statements related to tobacco advertising and health risks associated with smoking. It also communicates practical wisdom more subtly by acknowledging and appealing to teens' need for rebellion in encouraging teens to stand up to the adult establishment of Big Tobacco.

Many Truth ads communicate knowledge by alluding to tobacco ads. The newer "Seek truth" advertisements, shown on television and available to view on the website, feature teens set up outside "a major tobacco company in New York" asking hard-hitting questions of the executives from a podium set up on the sidewalk. Their podium has a "Q:" sign attached to the front, and after a question is asked, the camera turns to a podium with an "A:" sign that is situated in front of the tobacco company's building with nobody standing by it. These ads encourage teens to ask questions and rebel against what the smoking advertisements are saying. One particular ad shows a Virginia Slims poster which tells women to "Find Your Own Voice." The young adult in front of the podium introduces her older friend to ask a question to the tobacco company executives. This woman, using her artificial voice box, asks, "Is this the voice you expected me to find?" The camera then flashes over to the empty "A:" podium, followed by silence. The ad ends with script stating, "Ask questions. Seek Truth."

This advertisement resonates with the audience because it shows the campaign's knowledge of its subject and appeals to teens' independent nature. The Virginia Slims advertisement communicates to women that smoking Virginia Slims will lead to independence and finding one's voice. But the Truth ad is a stark reminder that smoking causes cancer, which may attack one's throat and lead to the need for an artificial voice box. Women will lose their physical voices rather than find figurative ones.

To fully succeed in satisfying the "practical wisdom" requirement of *ethos*, the Truth campaign must relate to its audience, teens. Cornelia Pechmann, Guangzhi Zhao, Marvin E. Goldberg, and Ellen Thomas Reibling identify seven recurring themes in antismoking advertisements aimed at teens: Disease and Death, Endangers Others, Cosmetics, Smokers' Negative Life Circumstances, Refusal Skills, Role Model Marketing Tactics, and Selling Disease and Death. They explain that the choice of theme in the advertisement may affect the result the rhetor obtains in persuading the teen to refrain from smoking.

Pechmann, Zhao, Goldberg, and Reibling claim that the most effective message themes are Endangers Others, Refusal Skills Role Model, and Smokers' Negative Life Circumstances. The Endangers Others theme stresses "how secondhand smoke, and smoking in general, can seriously harm smokers' family members, coworkers, and peers" and "convey[s] that smokers may encounter strong social disapproval from nonsmokers" (3). The Refusal Skills Role Model theme operates by explaining why "many attractive role models view smoking as unappealing and demonstrate refusals of cigarette offers" (4). The Smokers' Negative Life Circumstances theme stresses that smoking is a barrier to appearing "mature, independent, savvy, attractive, and cool" (4). Many of the advertisements of the Truth campaign employ the Smokers' Negative Life Circumstances theme. These commercials revolve around a dictum encouraging teens and young people to "Ask questions" and "Seek truth." By prompting such discourse, the Truth advertisements communicate that, unlike the tobacco firms who encourage youth to passively accept their message, this antismoking campaign challenges them to be-

come "mature, independent, [and] savvy" by prodding these industries for answers and by intelligently drawing out the consequences of smoking. The Truth campaign thus addresses one of the most successful messages in antismoking advertising aimed at youth: rather than telling teens tobacco companies are manipulating them, these ads encourage teens to ask their own questions of this industry, empowering them to be more mature and savvy in a way that tobacco industries discourage.

Good virtue [*aretï*]

In *On Rhetoric*, Aristotle says that virtue "is an ability [*dynamis*], as it seems, that is productive and preservative of goods, and an ability for doing good in many and great ways, actually in all ways in all things [1366b]" (79). The subdivisions of virtue are "justice, manly courage, self-control, magnificence, magnanimity, liberality, gentleness, prudence, and wisdom" (79–80). "The greatest virtues," he continues, "are necessarily those most useful to others. For that reason people most honor the just and the courageous" (80). Indeed, the "just and the courageous" are present throughout all of the Truth ads. Along with wisdom, they comprise the main subdivisions of virtue at work in this form of rhetoric.

One Truth billboard depicts an older 15 man in a bikini holding a cigarette; the caption is "No wonder tobacco executives hide behind sexy models." This advertisement demonstrates both the "just and the courageous" by implying that tobacco companies' ads do not have these qualities. This billboard communicates that tobacco executives are not courageous because they need to hide. The Truth campaign points to the virtue of their counter-advertising campaign, telling their audience, "Their brand is lies. Our brand is truth." This statement appears as a warning, much like the Surgeon General's warning in a cigarette advertisement, suggesting that the Truth campaign does not danger the public. Their product (so to speak) is the quest for knowledge, the desire to point out the lies that are perpetuated by advertising paid for by the tobacco industry.

As James L. Kinneavy and Susan C. Warshauer point out, virtue "is established when speakers give evidence that they are sincere and trustworthy. The audience must be convinced that the speaker will not deceive them" (174). Truth establishes its sincerity: while never directly telling the audience to refuse cigarettes, it does encourage teens to find the facts out for themselves. Thus, Truth is like an ethical orator because it presents its audience with facts they may use to make informed decisions.

Kinneavy and Warshauer also discuss the relationship between *arïte* and the Greek word *Ariston*, which means "nobility" or "aristocracy." This etymological relationship points to the consideration of culture in the ethical argument: "The effectiveness of an ethical appeal thus depends on one's ability to gauge society's values and to display them—indeed to affirm them—in one's speech" (175). This explanation reinforces the point that consideration of the group to whom one is speaking is crucial to making a successful ethical argument, specifically in the case of these advertisements for Truth. Kinneavy and Warshauer imply that in persuading the audience that she is virtuous, the rhetor must be able to convince the audience that she would not deceive them. This is also accomplished in the Truth ads, which point to the lies that are perpetuated in the advertisement of cigarettes. Truth recognizes that it must appeal to its teenage audience's values of independence and desire to be neither misled nor controlled by adult or establishment figures.

Good will [*eunoia*]

This intent to clarify rather than deceive leads into the third component of virtue, which is good will [*eunoia*]. As Kinneavy and Warshauer state, good will consists of "the speaker's display of good intentions toward his or her audience" (176). The speaker displays this good virtue by identifying with his audience by "holding some of their basic aspirations, speaking their language, and if necessary, sharing and affirming their prejudices" (176). In the Truth campaign's parody of a Marlboro advertisement, a cowboy rides through a rugged landscape, followed by three horses carrying body bags instead of three more cowboys. The tagline asks, "What if cigarette ads told The Truth?" At the bottom where the Surgeon General's warning would be in an actual Marlboro ad, a caption states, "YEE HAW! You Too Can Be An Independent, Rugged, Macho-looking Dead Guy." This ad communicates to teens that the cigarette ads are trying to deceive them by stating smoking will make them "independent, rugged, and macho-looking," but that those ads also leave out the crucial point that their product will also kill you, and it's not possible to be any of those things once you are dead. The ad speaks the language of teens and lets them know that the big advertising firms are manipulative.

Kinneavy and Warshauer also point out that another important consideration in a discussion of good will must be its ties to *pathos*, or persuasion by appeal to the emotions. They argue, "By arousing a particular emotion—and sharing it with members of the audience—a speaker may appear more closely identified with them" (176). In addition, and of great import in examining the effectiveness of the Truth advertisements, "having common enemies as the object of shared anger allows the speaker to strengthen this identification" (176). Kinneavy and Warshauer argue that how well a speaker is received by his audience depends upon his ability to communicate his good intent by emphasizing the presence of "common enemies and common friends as well as common values" (177).

Many, if not all, of the Truth ads construct Big Tobacco's lies as the enemy.[2]

According to Aristotle, anger may be de- [20] fined as "desire, accompanied by [mental and physical] distress, for conspicuous retaliation because of a conspicuous slight that was directed, without justification, against oneself or those near to one" (124). This "desire . . . for conspicuous retaliation" is present in the Virginia Slims and other Truth ads, including one that is a parody of a movie poster. In this poster, one man is in the foreground above the movie title, "Secrets of a Tobacco Executive," with two other executives in the darkness behind him. The tagline states, "Business is war. And he has the body bags to prove it." Underneath the title of the movie is a school hallway with two teens walking through it. This parody suggests that the tobacco executives are targeting teens due to their own selfish business motivations and are selling teens a product that they know to be illegal for those under 18 and lethal for everyone.

This invocation of anger, this appeal to *pathos*, indirectly supports the *ethos* of the Truth campaign. By invoking anger, these advertisements construct a common enemy: an adult establishment that is trying to manipulate youth. As Zucker, Hopkins, Sly, Urich, Mendza-Kershaw, and Solan put it, the program's key message consists of "exposing the lies and misinformation perpetuated by tobacco industry marketing" (2). The anger that arises out of these ads comes from a sense that tobacco companies are belittling teens by using lies and manipulation. Further, as Aristotle explains, people become angry "against those rejoicing at misfortunes and generally taking pleasure in others' misfortunes; for it is a sign of being either an enemy or a belittler. And [they become angry] against those who do not care if they are suffering" (129). This form of anger is invoked by most of the Truth ads, for in exposing the lies of tobacco firms, the ads imply that these firms do not care that they are harming those who buy their product.

Objections?

One important objection that may be raised against this counter-advertising campaign is whether it creates the same ethical mistake of which it accuses the tobacco industry. That is, as an advertising campaign in a capitalist system, does it accomplish its ends by manipulating the audience? Is the Truth campaign's version of "the truth" merely a means to make more money to keep the campaign alive?

In discussing *ethos* and ethics, Kinneavy and Warshauer state, "The gap between seeming ethical and being ethical may be great" (183). Indeed, this matter of appearance versus reality of *ethos* appears in Aristotle's *On Rhetoric* as well. This is a pressing question, for, according to Aristotle, "it belongs to the same capacity both to see the true and [to see] what resembles the true" (33). Aristotle argues that humans "have a natural disposition for the true" and so a speaker's ability "to aim at commonly held opinions [*endoxa*] is a characteristic of one who also has a similar ability to regard to the truth" (33). One interpretation of this statement is that a speaker who aims at commonly held opinions of what appears to be true is more likely to be perceived by his audience as persuasive. The skeptic may argue that it makes no difference whether the rhetor speaks or "seems to" speak the truth because the appearance of truth is just as convincing as its reality.

James E. Porter furthers this argument in his work, *Audience and Rhetoric*. He asks, "Is it ethical to change an audience's beliefs without providing them sound reasons and a basis in fact for changing their beliefs?" (18). Porter believes that Aristotle creates a situation in which "a knowledgeable orator facing an ignorant audience is placed in the position of (possibly) manipulating the audience" (18). The orator may try to force her belief upon an ignorant audience without providing much basis for why the audience should believe her. In trying to understand the true, the audience may be misled by the knowledgeable orator.

Do the Truth advertisements end up resorting to this deception? By turning again to Porter and to Truth's website (a soapbox of sorts for our "orator"), we may answer this question with an emphatic "No." Porter explains that the rhetorical situation Aristotle envisions

> involves a knowledgeable rhetor more or less in possession of "the truth" and an ignorant audience. And of course in such a situation, the rhetorician has nothing to learn *from* the audience; she only learns *about* the audience, through audience analysis, in order to better manage their responses. In this view, the rhetor is the privileged entity whose search for knowledge and truth is accomplished prior to the rhetorical act (in dialectic or scientific method), not through it or in conjunction with an audience. (18, emphasis in original)

The Truth ads do not fall subject to this general criticism, as they contradict such a rhetorical situation in two important ways. First, they do *not* assume an ignorant audience. Their success stems from the fact that they effectively communicate that their search for knowledge is incomplete without the participation of their audience. The "About us" page of the website states, "truth is not here to tell you, or anyone else, what to do. We hate when people do that" (*Truth About Us*). These ads suggest that they are aiming for the truth, but it is up to informed teens to complete the quest for truth and knowledge.

The skeptic may raise a question here of whether this is just a marketing tactic. Truth

creators know they must appeal to youth who do not like being told what to do; thus the campaign must make it seem like it is not telling teens what to believe, when it fact it is. Immediately after saying that its audience is "never gonna hear any 'just say "no" to cigarettes' stuff from us," it jumps into a tirade about

> an industry out there that makes billions of dollars selling a product that's responsible for over 1,200 deaths a day in the U.S. alone. This industry spends more than $34 million each day advertising and promoting those products, and it's entrenched itself in our culture by deceiving and manipulating the public. Truth just thinks everyone ought to know more about that industry and the things they do. (*Truth About Us*)

Isn't Truth an orator that is trying to convince its audience of the credibility of its position? And if it is, is it really that far of a step to say that the campaign, despite its claims otherwise, is in fact telling its audience what to believe? Further, if one accepts this view, then how is the advertising strategy of the Truth campaign that different from the deceiving strategies employed by tobacco advertising?

Most important, Truth does not attempt to deceive its audience; it is a campaign based on presenting facts to an audience that has already been manipulated. It even broadens its scope to the entire idea of "truth" itself; it is not reaching for an *appearance* of truth, but truth's reality. Again, Truth's website clarifies this claim: the campaign aims to ensure that all the facts are available so that when teens make their own decisions, "they can be based on all the information, not just those things tobacco companies want you to think" (*Truth About Us*). Furthermore, the website states its understanding and support of the individual's right to smoke, but because nicotine is physically and psychologically addictive, it also states its creators' belief that "responsibility should apply not only to the smoker, but to the individuals who choose to make and sell tobacco products as well" (*Truth About Us*). Truth does not merely use appeals to *pathos* in the anger aimed at big tobacco present in many of its advertisements, nor does it resort to a simple version of *ethos* to present itself as a moral entity. Both play important roles but are reinforce by a simple appeal to the *reality* rather than mere *appearance* of truth. As stated on the website, the campaign "gets its information from respected news sources and organizations like the Centers for Disease Control and Prevention, the Food and Drug Administration, and the American Cancer Society" and assures readers that "all of our information undergoes a stringent, multilayered review, stripping it of any and all extraneous assumptions, dangerous leaps in logic, and subjectivity."[3] Truth is not merely trying to persuade its audience, but rather is attempting to shatter manipulation in a quest for the truth about tobacco and its advertising. The campaign centers teens in this quest, stating, "We can't do this without you" (*Truth About Us*).

Conclusion

Truth's advertisements operate using a powerful combination of appeals to *ethos* and *pathos* to resonate with the teenage audience. As a result of the campaign, teenage smoking rates have dropped significantly. Truth's creators recognize that individuals are responsible for their actions and provide teens straightforward facts. The Truth campaign is necessarily tied to Aristotle's ideas of rhetoric but must not be interpreted as mere tactics, as the skeptic may aver. To do so is to miss the goal of the campaign and of rhetoric more generally. While "rhetoric" has come to connote negative images in much of our modern society, it often communicates the true and the just. The Truth campaign is among our society's most convincing examples of this ideal.

Notes

1. Some of the facts mentioned on this page include the following. "About 1 out of every 5 deaths in the US can be attributed to tobacco products"; "Every day about 2000 youths become daily smokers"; and "In 1989 millions of cases of imported fruit were banned after a small amount of cyanide was found in just two grapes. There's thirty-three times more cyanide in a single cigarette than was found in those two grapes."

2. Though it should be noted that Truth takes care not to have smokers or tobacco firms specifically as their target, Truth's website states, "truth is not anti-smoker. We love smokers. . . . truth isn't about passing judgment on people or the choices they make" and further, "truth supports the individual's right to smoke. Tobacco is a legal product in our country, available legally to those above a certain age. It's produced by a legal industry. Truth understands this. You'll never hear us call for a legal ban on smoking" ("About Us").

3. See also the website's "Whatta you think" page, where visitors can write in answers to such questions as "Do you think tobacco companies should list cigarette's ingredients on their packaging?" and "Tobacco companies won the right, in the Supreme Court, to advertise near schools and playgrounds. Why do you think they would do that?").

Works Cited

"About Us. *Truth*. 23 Nov. 2004. http://www .thetruth.com/index.cfm?seek=aboutUs.

Aristotle. *On Rhetoric: A Theory of Civic Discourse*. Trans. George A. Kennedy. Oxford: Oxford UP, 1991.

The Citizens' Commission to Protect the Truth. *Protect the Truth.org.* 14 May 2005. http://www.protectthetruth.org/truthcampaign.htm.

The Citizens' Commission to Protect the Truth. *Find Facts.* 14 May 2005. http://www.thetruth.com/index.cfm?seek=facts.

Kinneavy, James L. and Susan C. Warshauer. "From Aristotle to Madison Avenue: Ethos and the Ethics of Argument." *Ethos: New Essays in Rhetorical and Critical Theory.* Ed. James S. Baumlin and Tita French Baumlin. Dallas: Southern Methodist UP, 1994. 171–90.

Locke, John. "From *An Essay Concerning Human Understanding*." *The Rhetorical Tradition: Readings from Classical Times to the Present.* 2nd ed. Ed. Patricia Bizzell and Bruce Herzberg. Boston: Bedford/St. Martin's, 2001. 817–27.

Pechmann, Cornelia, Guangzhi Zhao, Marvin E. Goldberg, and Ellen Thomas Reibling. "What to Convey in Antismoking Advertisements for Adolescents: The Use of Protection Motivation Theory to Identify Effective Message Themes." *Journal of Marketing* 67 (2003): 1–18.

Plato. *Phaedrus.* Trans. H. N. Fowler. *The Rhetorical Tradition: Readings from Classical Times to the Present.* 2nd ed. Ed. Patricia Bizzell and Bruce Herzberg. Boston: Bedford/St. Martin's, 2001. 138–68.

Porter, James E. *Audience and Rhetoric: An Archaeological Composition of the Discourse Community.* Englewood Cliffs: Prentice Hall, 1992.

"The Surgeon General's Report on Reducing Tobacco Use: Tobacco Advertising and Promotion Fact Sheet." U.S. Department of Health and Human Services. *Reducing Tobacco Use: A Report of the Surgeon General.* Atlanta: U.S. Department of Health and Human Services, Centers for Disease Control and Prevention, 2000. http://www.cdc.gov/tobacco/sgr/sgr_2000/TobaccoAdvertising.pdf.

"Seek Truth." *Truth.* 23 Nov. 2004. http://www.thetruth.com/index.cfm?seek=truth.

"Whatta Ya Think? *Truth.* 23 Nov. 2004. http://www.thetruth.com/index.cfm?seek=whattya.

Zucker, David, R. S. Hopkins, David F. Sly, J. Urich, J. Mendza-Kershaw, and S. Solan. "Florida's Truth Campaign: A Counter-Marketing, Anti-Tobacco Media Campaign." *Journal of Public Health Management Practice* 6 (2000): 1–6.

A CLOSER LOOK AT
Discovering the Truth

1. Locate the places early in this rhetorical analysis where the author defines *ethos* in technical and historical terms. How are these definitions helpful for understanding the analysis of the Truth campaign later in the rhetorical analysis?

2. Feldmann suggests that teens, at whom these Truth advertisements are aimed, are different from other kinds of audiences. According to the article, what makes them unique and how does the Truth campaign try to appeal to them by using *ethos* to construct an argument?

3. The word "ethics" is related to *ethos*. Later in the rhetorical analysis, Feldmann argues that advertising campaigns like the Truth campaign can be built ethically on facts. Why does the author think behaving ethically in an anti-smoking campaign is especially important when reaching out to a teen audience?

IDEAS FOR
Writing

1. On *YouTube* or another video-sharing Web site, find some of the anti-smoking advertisements produced by the Truth campaign. Write an evaluation of one of these advertisements, using at least two criteria from Feldmann's rhetorical analysis.

2. In a commentary, discuss how advertisers succeed or fail to use *ethos* to reach out to teens. What are the qualities of an effective advertising campaign, and what makes these kinds of advertisements attractive to teens? Why do some advertisements fail, and how does the concept of *ethos* help us explain those failures?

A FEW IDEAS FOR
Composing a Rhetorical Analysis

1. **Write a rhetorical analysis focused on metaphors.** Chapter 9, "Rhetorical Analyses," talks briefly about how metaphors are used in writing. Find a common metaphor that is used in our society (e.g., "Time is money," "Thought is light," "War on cancer," "Argument is war") and then find examples of that metaphor in public use. In your rhetorical analysis, discuss how the metaphor shapes how people see particular issues. Discuss some of the perhaps unintended meanings or consequences of the metaphor you chose.

2. **Write a a rhetorical analysis of three texts.** Compare and contrast the persuasive strategies used in these three texts. Show how different rhetorical strategies are intended to have different persuasive effects.

3. **Critique an ad found on a Web site.** Your ad critique should study the advertisement's uses of rhetorical strategies to persuade people to buy a particular product or use a specific service. How does the advertisement use *logos, ethos, pathos,* and visual appeals to try to be persuasive? Do you find the advertisement effective or not? Turn your ad critique into an electronic document (blog, Web site, *PowerPoint*) and link to the site with the ad.

Commentaries

A Gay Man's Case Against Gay Marriage

MICHAEL BRONSKI

In this commentary, Michael Bronski argues that homosexuals, especially gay men, should not become too focused on legalizing gay marriage. He points out that marriage among heterosexuals has been problematic and that homosexuals may have actually learned how to form better relationships outside of marriage. Pay attention to how he uses reasoning to argue against the conventional notion that marriage would be a good thing for homosexuals.

The best argument against same-sex marriage is the argument against marriage.

I've been a gay activist since the gay-liberation Stonewall Riots in 1969, and today I'm a visiting professor of gay and lesbian studies at Dartmouth College. I'm often asked why gay men and lesbians are fighting for same-sex marriage, and my answer is always the same: I don't really know. To me, the fight for same-sex marriage seems not so much shortsighted as beside the point.

Don't get me wrong. I completely support giving gay men and lesbians the right to partake of civil marriage, and the basic economic benefits that come with it, simply as a matter of equality under the law. Within a generation most states will likely follow Massachusetts' bold lead and insure marriage equality for all couples. It's a no-brainer: states that don't allow gay men and lesbians access to the legal status given to heterosexuals blatantly discriminate.

What I don't understand is why gay men and lesbians want to get married. The unswerving fight that gay men and lesbians have waged for marriage equality has been predicated largely on the idea that traditional marriage is the best possible form a relationship can take. For gay-marriage advocates, marriage carries the gold seal of approval:

however loving, fruitful, or productive other relationships are, they are, by definition, not as good as marriage.

This is curious, given how deeply ambivalent heterosexuals are about marriage. It's there in the 50 percent divorce rate, the high rates of spouse and child abuse, the incidence of adultery—check the record of the congressmen who voted for the Defense of Marriage Act, never mind average couples. Despite their distinct 1950s ring, jokes about balls-and-chains still abound, and the famous Mae West quip, "Marriage is an institution, I'm just not ready for an institution yet," still gets laughs.

What makes gay people think marriage will work better for them? It probably won't.

I'm not the sort of gay activist who thinks everything heterosexuals do is wrong. I see *Queer Eye for the Straight Guy* as a show about five busybodies who interfere in other people's lives with intrusive product placements. I also recognize that some marriages work marvelously: my parents' 50 wonderfully happy years together ended only with my mother's death a few years ago. But as it is practiced in the United States, we can all agree that marriage is not perfect, and for so many of us marriage no longer suits our current emotional or social needs. We—homosexuals and heterosexuals alike—might do better by

5

spending some time rethinking how we want to live our emotional and sexual, private and public lives. Humans, straight and gay, have an amazing capacity for invention. In the past decades, we have seen myriad variations of expanded and extended families. These have had their flaws, too, but many have worked as well as, if not better, than traditional marriages. By the very fact that we have been forced into the position of outsiders, gay men and lesbians have invented new ways of forming community, of shaping and living our lives. Deprived of the right to traditional marriage, we have proven we can get along without it very well.

Gay-marriage proponents argue we should end these experiments, some saying marriage will "civilize" gay people by making us act more responsibly toward one another. William N. Eskridge titled his 1996 book *The Case for Same-Sex Marriage: From Sexual Liberty to Civilized Commitment*. Well, that just seems silly to me. Heterosexual marriage has not guaranteed better behavior once men and women tied the knot. Not incidentally, it is deeply homophobic to imply that gay people cannot and do not act decently or "civilized" now.

Other gay activists point to the benefits civil marriage brings in the form of tax breaks, inheritance arrangements, access to health care, and guaranteeing loans and credit. But we need to find a way to ensure that these are available to all people, not just those who decide to marry.

Much of the discussion about same-sex 10 marriage concerns deeper economic and social-justice issues: health care, raising children, and protecting family units from outside forces, especially poverty. But these too aren't really the concern of marriage. If you want to ensure that all families are secure and safe, if you want children to be healthy, and well fed and safe, there is plenty to do. You can fight for universal health care or a higher minimum wage, for a negative income tax that will benefit anyone living close to or under the poverty line, for federally funded childcare, for federal funding to pay parents (both mothers and fathers) who choose to work at home caring for their children. When it comes to fighting for social justice, the right to traditional civil marriage seems pretty low on the agenda.

The gay-marriage movement isn't about these things. Nor is it about commitment or the sanctity of marriage. It is about sentiment and the power of advertising. People—gay and straight, but especially women—have a profound emotional attachment to the idea of marriage. (It is no surprise that close to 75 percent of couples who have applied for same-sex marriage licenses in San Francisco and now in Massachusetts are lesbians.) It is what we have always known, and we have a difficult time thinking of any other way to organize our lives. We also live in a culture that has a multibillion-dollar wedding industry, which inundates us everyday with the message that we will only be happy when we are married.

Equality under the law is nothing to scoff at. But will it make gay men and lesbians happier? In the long run, I doubt it. At least no happier than they are now, and certainly no happier, or unhappier, than heterosexuals. Now that we have it, I wonder if people will think it was worth the fight.

A CLOSER LOOK AT
A Gay Man's Case Against Gay Marriage

1. Early in the commentary, Bronski uses several methods to establish his credibility (*ethos*) to speak on this issue. What are a few methods he uses to build his authority with his likely readers, so they view him as a knowledgeable source of information?

2. Bronski's basic point is that "the best argument against same-sex marriage is the argument against marriage." What are some of Bronski's arguments against marriage itself? Why does he find the concept of marriage problematic, whether it is between a man and a woman or two people of the same sex?

3. Instead of marriage, what kinds of legal protections and other rights does Bronski believe gays and lesbians should fight for?

IDEAS FOR
Writing

1. Write a rhetorical analysis of Bronski's article. Pay special attention to how he uses rhetorical proofs to argue logically (*logos*), establish his authority (*ethos*), and introduce emotion (*pathos*) into his commentary.

2. In a brief proposal, describe a solution to the same-sex marriage issue that you believe all sides would agree is fair. What is the real problem that gays and lesbians are trying to solve by striving for marriage? What approach to this issue would be satisfactory to the majority of Americans? Discuss the costs and benefits of your plan, showing why it would be the best way to resolve this issue.

Tweens: Ten Going on Sixteen

KAY S. HYMOWITZ

In her commentary, Kay S. Hymowitz is concerned about how children, especially girls, are being pushed into adulthood by popular culture. Marketing has heavily targeted preteens ("tweens"), trying to capture their brand loyalty.

During the past year my youngest morphed from child to teenager. Down came the posters of adorable puppies and the drawings from art class; up went the airbrushed faces of Leonardo di Caprio and Kate Winslet. CDs of Le Ann Rimes and Paula Cole appeared mysteriously, along with teen fan magazines featuring glowering movie and rock-and-roll hunks with earrings and threatening names like Backstreet Boys. She started reading the newspaper—or at least the movie ads—with all the intensity of a Talmudic scholar, scanning for glimpses of her beloved Leo or, failing that, Matt Damon. As spring approached and younger children skipped past our house on their way to the park, she swigged from a designer-water bottle, wearing the obligatory tank top and denim shorts as she whispered on the phone to friends about games of Truth or Dare. The last rites for her childhood came when, embarrassed at reminders of her foolish past, she pulled a sheet over her years-in-the-making American Girl doll collection, now dead to the world.

So what's new in this dog-bites-man story? Well, as all this was going on, my daughter was ten years old and in the fourth grade.

Those who remember their own teeny-bopper infatuation with Elvis or the Beatles might be inclined to shrug their shoulders as if to say, "It was ever thus." But this is different. Across class lines and throughout the country, elementary and middle-school principals and teachers, child psychologists and psychiatrists, marketing and demographic researchers all confirm the pronouncement of Henry Trevor, middle-school director of the Berkeley Carroll School in Brooklyn, New York: "There is no such thing as preadolescence anymore. Kids are teenagers at ten."

Marketers have a term for this new social animal, kids between eight and 12: they call them "tweens." The name captures the ambiguous reality: though chronologically midway between early childhood and adolescence, this group is leaning more and more toward teen styles, teen attitudes, and, sadly, teen behavior at its most troubling.

The tween phenomenon grows out of a 5 complicated mixture of biology, demography, and the predictable assortment of Bad Ideas. But putting aside its causes for a moment, the emergence of tweendom carries risks for both young people and society. Eight- to 12-year-olds have an even more wobbly sense of themselves than adolescents; they rely more heavily on others to tell them how to understand the world and how to place themselves in it. Now, for both pragmatic and ideological reasons, they are being increasingly "empowered" to do this on their own, which leaves them highly vulnerable both to a vulgar and sensation-driven marketplace and to the crass authority of their immature peers. In tweens, we can see the fu-

ture of our society taking shape, and it's not at all clear how it's going to work.

Perhaps the most striking evidence for the tweening of children comes from market researchers. "There's no question there's a deep trend, not a passing fad, toward kids getting older younger," says research psychologist Michael Cohen of Arc Consulting, a public policy, education, and marketing research firm in New York. "This is not just on the coasts. There are no real differences geographically." It seems my daughter's last rites for her American Girl dolls were a perfect symbol not just for her own childhood but for childhood, period. The Toy Manufacturers of America Factbook states that, where once the industry could count on kids between birth and 14 as their target market, today it is only birth to ten. "In the last ten years we've seen a rapid development of upper-age children," says Bruce Friend, vice president of worldwide research and planning for Nickelodeon, a cable channel aimed at kids. "The 12- to 14-year-olds of yesterday are the ten to 12s of today." The rise of the preteen teen is "the biggest trend we've seen."

Scorning any symbols of their immaturity, tweens now cultivate a self-image that emphasizes sophistication. The Nickelodeon-Yankelovich Youth Monitor found that by the time they are 12, children describe themselves as "flirtatious, sexy, trendy, athletic, cool." Nickelodeon's Bruce Friend reports that by 11, children in focus groups say they no longer even think of themselves as children.

They're very concerned with their "look," Friend says, even more so than older teens. Sprouting up everywhere are clothing stores like the chain Limited Too and the catalog company Delia, geared toward tween girls who scorn old-fashioned, little-girl flowers, ruffles, white socks, and Mary Janes in favor of the cool—black mini-dresses and platform shoes. In Toronto a tween store called Ch!ck-aboom, which offers a manicurist and tween singing-star Jewel on the sound system, hypes itself as "an adventure playground where girls can hang out, have fun, and go nuts shopping." A recent article on tween fashion in the *New York Times* quoted one ten-year-old sophisticate primping in a changing room at Saks Fifth Avenue: "It's black and I love to wear black. It goes with everything."

Less cosmopolitan tweens may eschew the understated little black dress, but they are fashion mad in their own way. Teachers complain of ten- or 11-year-old girls arriving at school looking like madams, in full cosmetic regalia, with streaked hair, platform shoes, and midriff-revealing shirts. Barbara Kapetanakes, a psychologist at a conservative Jewish day school in New York, describes her students' skirts as being about "the size of a belt." Kapetanakes says she was told to dress respectfully on Fridays, the eve of the Jewish Sabbath, which she did by donning a long skirt and a modest blouse. Her students, on the other hand, showed their respect by looking "like they should be hanging around the West Side Highway," where prostitutes ply their trade.

Lottie Sims, a computer teacher in a 10 Miami middle school, says that the hooker look for tweens is fanning strong support for uniforms in her district. But uniforms and tank-top bans won't solve the problem of painted young ladies. "You can count on one hand the girls not wearing makeup," Sims says. "Their parents don't even know. They arrive at school with huge bags of lipstick and hair spray, and head straight to the girls' room."

Though the tweening of youth affects girls more visibly than boys, especially since boys mature more slowly, boys are by no means immune to these obsessions. Once upon a time, about ten years ago, fifth- and sixth-grade boys were about as fashion-conscious as their pet hamsters. But a growing minority have begun trading in their baseball cards for hair mousse

and baggy jeans. In some places, $200 jackets, emblazoned with sports logos like the warm-up gear of professional atheletes, are *de rigueur;* in others, the preppy look is popular among the majority, while the more daring go for the hipper style of pierced ears, fade haircuts, or ponytails. Often these tween peacocks strut through their middle-school hallways taunting those who have yet to catch on to the cool look.

Cosmetics companies have found a bonanza among those we once thought of as children. The Tinkerbell Company has sold cosmetics to girls ages four to ten since the late fifties. For the most part, these were really more like toys, props for dress-up games and naive attempts to imitate Mommy. Today Tinkerbell has grown up and gone to Soho. New products for the spring of 1998 included roll-on body glitter and something called "hair mascara," a kind of roll-on hair color, in what the company has described as "edgy colors"—neon green, bright blue, and purple. AM Cosmetics has introduced the Sweet Georgia Brown line for tweens. It includes body paints and scented body oils with come-hither names like Vanilla Vibe and Follow Me Boy. Soon, thanks to the Cincinnati design firm Libby Peszyk Kattiman, after she has massaged her body with Follow Me Boy oil, your little darling will also be able to slip into some tween-sized bikini panties.

After completing her toilette, your edgy little girl might want to take in a movie with a baggy-panted, Niked dude. They won't bother with pictures aimed at them, though; nine to 12s are snubbing films like *Madeline* or *Harriet the Spy*. Edgy tweens want cool, hip, and sexy. "When I hear parents complain about no films for their young kids, it kind of gets to me," says Roger Birnbaum, producer of such films for preteens as *Angels in the Outfield* and *Rocket Man,* "because when you make those kinds of films, they don't take their kids to see them." They prefer R-rated films like *Object of My Affection,* about a young woman who falls in love with a homosexual; or *Scream,* the horror story about a serial killer hunting down young women; or the soap opera *Titanic,* which succeeded so hugely because teen and tween girls went back to watch 3½ hours of Leonardo di Caprio three, four, even five times. "These are different times," concedes Stanley Jaffe, one of the producers of the new *Madeline,* in response to doubts about the potential of his movie, "and you can't go into it thinking you're making a children's film." In other words, there are no children's movies here.

The same goes for other media. Magazine publishers—by the early nineties magazines like *Sports Illustrated for Kids* and *Nickelodeon* were beginning to replace comics as the print entertainment of choice for children—say that warm and cutesy images are out; cool is in. Celebrities like actor Will Smith and rapper Puff Daddy adorn the cover of almost every issue of *Nickelodeon,* the cable channel's magazine geared toward eight- to 14-year-olds. Editor Laura Galen says that whenever her magazine reduces its entertainment coverage, tween complaints flood the mail. By the late eighties, tweens helped launch the new genre of what might be called peach-fuzz rock—bands made up of barely pubescent male sex-symbols-in-training. At that time, girls were going screaming mad for a group called New Kids on the Block; after their voices changed and their beards grew in, New Kids lost out to a group called Hanson, now filling stadiums with panting tweens.

Danny Goldberg, chief executive officer 15 of Mercury Records, which produces Hanson, recalls that teen girls have had immense influence on the music business since the days of Frank Sinatra. "But now," he says, "the teenage years seem to start at eight or nine in terms of entertainment tastes. The emotions are kicking in earlier. It's a huge audience."

No aspect of children's lives seems beyond the reach of tween style. Even the Girl Scouts of America have had to change their image. In 1989 the organization commissioned a new MTV-style ad, with rap music and an appearance by tween lust-object Johnny Depp. Ellen Christie, a media specialist for the organization, said it had to "get away from the uniformed, goody-goody image and show that Girl Scouts are a fun, mature, cool place to be." The Girl Scouts?

Those who seek comfort in the idea that the tweening of childhood is merely a matter of fashion—who maybe even find their lip-synching, hip-swaying little boy or girl kind of cute—might want to think twice. There are disturbing signs that tweens are not only eschewing the goody-goody childhood image but its substance as well.

Tweens are demonstrating many of the deviant behaviors we usually associate with the raging hormones of adolescence. "Ninth and tenth grade used to be the starting point for a lot of what we call risk behaviors," says Brooklyn middle-school head Henry Trevor, as he traces the downward trajectory of deviancy many veteran educators observe. "Fifteen years ago they moved into the eighth grade. Now it's seventh grade. The age at which kids picture themselves starting this kind of activity has gone down."

Hard data about how tweens are defining deviancy down is sketchy. For one thing, most studies of risk behavior begin with 15-year-olds. High school kids give fairly reliable answers in surveys, but middle-school kids are often confusingly inconsistent. As for ten-year-olds, until recently it seemed absurd for researchers to interview them about their sexual activity and drug use.

The clearest evidence of tweendom's 20 darker side concerns crime. Although children under 15 still represent a minority of juvenile arrests, their numbers grew disproportionately in the past 20 years. According to a report by the Office of Juvenile Justice and Delinquency Prevention, "offenders under age 15 represent the leading edge of the juvenile crime problem, and their numbers are growing." Moreover, the crimes committed by younger teens and preteens are growing in severity. "Person offenses, which once constituted 16 percent of the total court cases for this age group," continues the report, "now constitute 25 percent." Headline grabbers—like Nathaniel Abraham of Pontiac, Michigan, an 11-year-old who stole a rifle from a neighbor's garage and went on a shooting spree in October 1997, randomly killing a teenager coming out of a store; and 11-year-old Andrew Golden, who, with his 13-year-old partner, killed four children and one teacher at his middle school in Jonesboro, Arkansas—are extreme, exceptional cases, but alas, they are part of a growing trend toward preteen violent crime.

Though the absolute numbers remain quite small, suicide among tweens more than doubled between 1979 and 1995. Less lurid but still significant, a London-based child advocacy group called Kidscape announced in March a 55 percent increase over the previous 18 months in calls reporting tween girl-on-girl bullying, including several incidents involving serious injuries.

The evidence on tween sex presents a troubling picture, too. Despite a decrease among older teens for the first time since records have been kept, sexual activity among tweens increased during that period. It seems that kids who are having sex are doing so at earlier ages. Between 1988 and 1995, the proportion of girls saying they began sex before 15 rose from 11 percent to 19 percent. (For boys, the number remained stable, at 21 percent.) This means that approximately one in five middle-school kids is sexually active. Christie Hogan, a middle-school counselor for 20 years in Louisville, Kentucky, says: "We're beginning to see a few pregnant sixth-graders." Many of the principals and counselors I spoke with reported a small but striking minority of sexually active seventh-graders.

Equally striking, though less easily tabulated, are other sorts of what Michael Thompson, an educational consultant and co-author of the forthcoming *Raising Cain: Protecting the Emotional Life of Boys,* calls "fairly sophisticated sexual contact" short of intercourse among tweens. Thompson hears from seventh- and eighth-graders a lot of talk about oral sex, which they don't think of as sex; "for them, it's just fooling around," he says. A surprising amount of this is initiated by girls, Thompson believes. He tells the story of a seventh-grade boy who had his first sexual experience when an eighth-grade girl offered to service him in this way. "The boy wasn't even past puberty yet. He described the experience as not all that exciting but 'sort of interesting.'"

Certainly the days of the tentative and giggly preadolescent seem to be passing. Middle-school principals report having to deal with miniskirted 12-year-olds "draping themselves over boys" or patting their behinds in the hallways, while 11-year-old boys taunt girls about their breasts and rumors about their own and even their parents' sexual proclivities. Tweens have even given new connotations to the word "playground": one fifth-grade teacher from southwestern Ohio told me of two youngsters discovered in the bushes during recess.

Drugs and alcohol are also seeping into tween culture. The past six years have seen more than a doubling of the number of eighth-graders who smoke marijuana (10 percent today) and those who no longer see it as dangerous. "The stigma isn't there the way it was ten years ago," says Dan Kindlon, assistant professor of psychiatry at Harvard Medical School and co-author with Michael Thompson of *Raising Cain.* "Then it was the fringe group smoking pot. You were looked at strangely. Now the fringe group is using LSD."

Aside from sex, drugs, and rock and roll, another teen problem—eating disorders—is also beginning to affect younger kids. This behavior grows out of premature fashion-consciousness, which has an even more pernicious effect on tweens than on teens, because, by definition, younger kids have a more vulnerable and insecure self-image. Therapists say they are seeing a growing number of anorexics and obsessive dieters even among late-elementary-school girls, "You go on Internet chat rooms and find ten- and 11-year-olds who know every [fashion] model and every statistic about them," says Nancy Kolodny, a Connecticut-based therapist and author of *When Food's a Foe: How You Can Confront and Conquer Your Eating Disorder.* "Kate Moss is their god. They can tell if she's lost a few pounds or gained a few. If a powerful kid is talking about this stuff at school, it has a big effect."

What change in our social ecology has led to the emergence of tweens? Many note that kids are reaching puberty at earlier ages, but while earlier physical maturation may play a small role in defining adolescence down, its importance tends to be overstated. True, the average age at which girls begin to menstruate has fallen from 13 to between 11 and 12 $\frac{1}{2}$ today, but the very gradualness of this change means that 12-year-olds have been living inside near-adult bodies for many decades without feeling impelled to build up a cosmetics arsenal or head for the bushes at recess. In fact, some experts believe that the very years that have witnessed the rise of the tween have also seen the age of first menstruation stabilize. Further, teachers and principals on the front lines see no clear correlation between physical and social maturation. Plenty of budding girls and bulking boys have not put away childish things, while an abundance of girls with flat chests and boys with

squeaky voices ape the body language and fashions of their older siblings.

"Kids wear sexually provocative clothes at nine because their parents buy them provocative clothes, not because of their hormones," Robert L. Johnson, director of adolescent and young-adult medicine at the University of Medicine and Dentistry of New Jersey, told me. "A lot of journalists call me to explain some of these things, and they want a good sound bite like 'raging hormones' rather than a complex series of social factors."

Of course, the causes are complex, and most people working with tweens know it. In my conversations with educators and child psychologists who work primarily with middle-class kids nationwide, two major and fairly predictable themes emerged: a sexualized and glitzy media-driven marketplace and absentee parents. What has been less commonly recognized is that at this age, the two causes combine to augment the authority of the peer group, which in turn both weakens the influence of parents and reinforces the power of the media. Taken together, parental absence, the market, and the peer group form a vicious circle that works to distort the development of youngsters.

Much of the media attention about parents working away from home for long hours has focused on infants and toddlers, but the effect of the postmodern domestic routine on a nine- or ten-year-old merits equal concern. The youngest children, after all, have continual adult attention, from baby-sitters or day-care attendants or after-school counselors. But as their children reach the age of eight or nine, many parents, after years of juggling schedules and panics over last-minute sore throats and stomachaches, breathe a sigh of relief as they begin to see growing signs of competence and common sense in their youngsters. Understandably concluding that their children are ready to take more responsibility for themselves, they place a list of emergency numbers on the refrigerator, arrange for a routine after-school phone call, and hand over the keys to the house.

In most people's minds, this sort of arrangement—children alone a few hours after school—is what we mean by latchkey kids. But latchkey kids come in many varieties. According to the educators I spoke with, many youngsters are leaving for school from an empty house after eating breakfast alone. Parents who can afford it will sometimes hand their children $3 and tell them to pick up juice and a muffin on their way to school. Others have their children pick up fast food or frozen meals for dinner—which a small but sad minority will eat with only Bart Simpson or the local TV newscaster for company.

Almost without exception, the principals and teachers I spoke with describe a pervasive loneliness among tweens. "The most common complaint I hear," says Christie Hogan, "is, 'My mom doesn't care what I do. She's never home. She doesn't even *know* what I do.'" Although the loneliest and most estranged kids don't talk to counselors and can't even be coaxed into after-school programs when they are available, the more resourceful and socially well-adjusted children stay after school whether or not there is a formal program, hanging around popular teachers and counselors. "We have to shoo them home at six sometimes," recounts one New York City middle-school director. "They don't want to go home. No one's there."

Another, more subtly noxious consequence of the loss of family life has been less commonly understood: the expanding authority of a rigidly hierarchical and materialistic peer group. Kids, like nature, abhor a vacuum, and the power of the school peer group grows luxuriantly in soil left fallow by a rootless home life. With no one home, today's tween is captive to an age-segregated peer group whose inflexible customs and mall-driven ideals are too often the only ones he knows.

Many educators I talked with believe that kids are forming cliques earlier than ever, in the fifth and sixth grades rather than the seventh and eighth, as was the case until recently. Researchers are finding the same thing, as reported, for example, in a recent study published this year entitled *Peer Power: Culture and Identity* by Patricia A. Adler with Peter Adler.

These peer groups should not be confused with simple childhood friendships. They are powerful and harsh mechanisms for making kids conform to the crudest, most superficial values. By late elementary school, according to *Peer Power*, boys understand that their popularity depends on "toughness, troublemaking, domination, coolness, and interpersonal bragging and sparring skills." Girls, on the other hand, "deriv[e] their status from their success at grooming, clothes, and other appearance-related variables; . . . [their] romantic success as measured through popularity and going with boys; affluence and its correlates of material possessions and leisure pursuits." Educators repeatedly note how harsh tweens are toward classmates who wear the wrong brand of sneakers or listen to yesterday's music. Childhood cruelty, always latent, finds an outlet in enforcing the rigid fashion laws of the in-group, whose dominion is now relatively unchallenged by parents and outside peers.

Paradoxically, then, while the tween has less company, he also has less privacy. Hannah Arendt once observed that if you think adults can be authoritarian in their dealings with children, you ought to see the peer group in action. Middle school can be a quasi-Orwellian world, where each child is under continual surveillance by his peers, who evaluate the way he walks, the way he looks, the people he talks to, the number of times he raises his hand in class, the grade he got on his science project. If two kids become romantically linked, their doings are communal property. Each phone call, kiss, or grope is reported, judged, and—in the case of boys, at any rate—simultaneously ridiculed and urged onward by the group leaders. "You kissing her?" they taunt, according to Patricia Hersch in her recent study entitled *A Tribe Apart.* "You get her in bed or something?" Not that things are better if you get rid of the boys. According to one fifth-grade teacher at a private New York City girls' school, students are frequently so wrought up about the vicissitudes of friendships within their group that they can't do their math or English.

Add to this hothouse a glamour- and celebrity-mad tween market-culture, and things get even steamier. In fact, both parental absence and the powerful peer group are intricately connected to the rise of a burgeoning tween market. To be sure, candy, toy, and cereal manufacturers had long known the power of tween cravings before they even defined this new niche group. But tweens really began to catch the eye of businesses around the mid-eighties, a time when, paradoxically, their absolute numbers were falling. The reason was simple. Market research began to reveal that more and more children this age were shopping for their own clothes, shoes, accessories, drugstore items—even for the family groceries.

Jordache Jeans was one of the first companies to spot the trend. "My customers are kids who can walk into a store with either their own money or their mothers'," explained the company's director of advertising at the time. "The dependent days of tugging on Mom or Dad's sleeve are over." Jordache celebrated the new era with ads befitting a revolution. Ignoring—or rather, scorning—parents, they appealed directly to kids who had money in their pockets and puerile dreams of sophistication in their heads. Parents found nothing amusing in seeing jean-clad youngsters on TV, saying things like "Have you ever seen your parents naked?" and "I hate my mother. She's prettier than me," and after

many complaints, Jordache pulled the plug. Though today's tween ads downplay the shock effect, they take the same fundamental approach: kids are on their own, is the premise; flatter them as hip and aware almost-teens rather than out-of-it little kids—as independent, sophisticated consumers with their own language, music, and fashion.

Anyone who remembers high school will recall many of these dynamics. But it is important to recognize that the combination of isolation from adults, peer cruelty, and fantasies of sophistication, though always a danger to the alienated teenager, is especially taxing to the fragile ego of the preadolescent. With less life experience and even less self-awareness (if that's possible) than their teenage brothers and sisters, preadolescents have fewer internal resources to fall back on. As Helen Colvin, a middle-school science teacher from Harrisburg, Pennsylvania, explains: "These kids have two years less time to become a firm person. That's two years less time to discover what they are, what they believe, to experiment with identity. Instead, they just want to be like their friends."

How do parents view all this? For while 40 they may be out of the house for long hours, parents still have the capacity to break, or at least loosen, the choke hold of the peer group. Many parents negotiate diplomatic compromises, giving in on lipstick, say, while holding the line on pierced navels and quietly trying to represent alternatives. But a surprising number of parents, far from seeking to undermine their children's tweenishness, are enablers of it. When Jim Alloy, principal of Fox Lane Middle School in Bedford, New York, tried to ban tank tops, he was beset by a number of irate parents who accused him of discriminating against girls. Other educators marvel at the number of boys whose parents not only buy them expensive Starter jackets but immediately buy them another one if, as so often happens, they lose it.

Many parents are pleased to see their children hip to the market. "I'm glad my girls respond to fashion," said one mother of tweens in a recent *New York Times* article on tween fashion sense. "Trends aren't something you should learn about all of a sudden when you're in college." Another mother frowned over her seven-year-old's choice of a smocked dress as "too babyish." Nor does the enthusiasm for precocity stop with leopard-print tops and thigh-slit black skirts. I sat in amazement at a summer-camp performance this summer as a group of about 30 tweens sang a medley of rock-and-roll songs. The girls in their bare midriffs and miniskirts shimmied and vamped for the pleasure of their upper-middle-class parents, who whooped and hollered like revelers at a strip joint.

Of course, just because they like rock and roll doesn't mean these parents are trying to push their kids into sex and drugs or, for that matter, alcohol and anorexia. Doubtless, many of them are panicky at the prospect of adolescence and all its dangers. Still, their enthusiasm for their children's pseudosophistication betrays a deep confusion about their own role.

The one theme that comes through loud and clear in talking to educators and therapists is that, with parents and their tween children, it's the blind leading the blind. "I'm hearing statements like, 'What can I do? I can't make him read,'" says one director of a New York City private middle school. "And the child is in fifth grade. What does it mean that an adult feels he cannot make a ten-year-old do something?" A middle-school principal from Putnam County, New York, concurs: "I used to say to a kid behaving rudely, 'Young man, would you speak that way at home?' and he would hang his head and say, 'No.' Now I ask a kid, and he looks surprised and says, 'Yeah.'"

It's too simple to trace the trend toward passive parenting back to the time and energy deficits experienced by most working parents. The reluctance to guide and shape tween behavior is as much an ideological as a practical matter. Parents are suffering from a heavy diet of self-esteem talk. In their minds, to force a child to speak politely, to make him read, to punish him for being out of line, is to threaten his most primary need—to express himself. "You'll damage his self-esteem," principals and teachers often hear from parents of children who face discipline for troublemaking.

Though the most influential recent [45] works on preteens and early adolescents, by feminist-inspired child specialists like Carol Gilligan and Peggy Orenstein, focus on girls, they capture the prevailing expert wisdom about self-esteem, whose sorry consequences can be seen in the boorish attitudes of both sexes. According to such experts, the biggest problem tween girls face is not a loss of adult guidance but the opposite. Parents and teachers are guilty of "silencing" girls around this age, goes the argument, and the result is a loss of self-confidence. Instead of submitting children to what Gilligan calls "the tyranny of the nice and the kind," adults should instead focus their parenting energies on supporting and modeling assertive behavior.

And Gilligan and her followers do mean assertive. The new model for girls is the sort of macho, braggart boy that in more level-headed times made parents hide their daughters. In her study of several California middle schools, Orenstein is impressed by the self-confidence of the boys she observes who call out in class and shout one another down when they have an answer. "[W]hen the girls in [the] class do speak," she writes sadly, "they follow the rules."

Not only did these writers fail to think through what happens when adults believe that children are better off ignoring rules of behavior, but also they neglected to ask about the ultimate purpose of the power they proposed to hand over to children. Confidence, sure—but confidence in the service of what goal? Self-assertion toward what end? Kids certainly couldn't be expected to know the answer. There is nothing in the creed of self-esteem that encourages adults to help mold children's judgment about what matters in life. In fact, quite the opposite. Empowerment implies that children should determine their own style, codes of behavior, and values without serious interference from parents. And they have.

Though the experts missed it entirely, producers of popular culture have been quick to grasp the empty heart of child empowerment, just as they understood the related consequences of parental absence. They saw that children's will to power and immature longings were easy to exploit. Ad writers for Bonne Bell cosmetics, for instance, marry the approved language of self-esteem and the child's natural desire to seem grown-up and hip in the eyes of her peers. "We know how to be cool," goes the text accompanying pictures of a new product called Lip Lix. "We have our own ideas. And make our own decisions. Watch out for us. We are girls."

The Spice Girls, the wildly popular British rock singers who sport slip dresses, hot pants, belly shirts, and oily globs of lipstick and mascara, invented the term "girl power" precisely to evoke the empty formula of self-esteem, whose ingredients are nothing more than self-assertion and face paint—or nothing more than "strength, courage, and a Wonderbra," as one Spice Girl motto puts it. "I'll tell you what I want, what I really, really want," they sing in the tune familiar now to girls five years and older worldwide, girls who at concerts flash the Winston Churchill V-sign and clench their fists in a power salute. And what is it? Caught up in the belief that power was in and of itself a satisfactory guiding virtue, self-esteem theorists failed to consider that

what girls might really, really want is to dress up like female impersonators.

They also failed to grasp that empowerment is finally a greedy principle. When tweens talk about girl power on Websites and in interviews, they make it clear that pure, undiluted self-esteem tends to ride roughshod over values smelling of self-restraint. "It's about not letting anyone judge you." "It's about no limitations," they write. *YM* magazine for teens has run a section called "Girl Zone: Your Guide to Kicking Butt."

Teachers confirm that, as far as kids are concerned, empowerment amounts to an in-your-face attitude. "If you tell them, 'You have to do your homework, or you won't graduate,'" says a counselor in a Queens middle school, "they look at you and say, 'So?'" A fifth-grade teacher at a tony East Side private girls' school says, "There's a lot of calling out. You try to get them to raise their hands, to wait their turn. They're very impatient and demanding. They challenge every point on the test. They insist on attention immediately." In Hollywood it is said that tweens roar with pleasure when the *Titanic* character played by Kate Winslet tells her mother to shut up and punctuates her order with an obscene gesture.

Of course, girls are not the only beneficiaries of the ideology of child empowerment. Boys also are enjoying the reign of "no limitations." Faced with students who have been taught the lessons of their own empowerment and who have no experience of authoritative, limit-setting adults at home, educators find themselves coping with a growing indifference toward authority. It's a situation the schools have trouble handling. When they want to discipline boys who are caught writing obscenities in a girl's yearbook, or stuffing a backpack down the toilet, or throwing a stink bomb in the school auditorium—to cite a few of the examples I heard—school officials are not likely to receive any support from the parent. Seeing their job as being their child's advocate in the narrowest, legalistic sense, parents of the culprits in these instances cajoled, manipulated, and argued against any attempt by the school to have their sons face the music.

It is likely that girls' traditional role as goody-goodies used to act as a brake on boys' natural tendency toward restlessness and machismo. Now, as girls are "empowered" to become as bad as they wanna be, boys are "empowered" to become even badder. "Sixthgraders used to be benign and afraid of adults," Bedford, New York, principal Jim Alloy told me. "Now you see some of them who are so defiant, their parents have no idea what to do with them. I have several students from affluent homes with PINS petitions against them." (PINS, which stands for Person in Need of Supervision, allows local authorities to inter-

cede with out-of-control kids.) Whether boy or girl, empowered children, it seems, find support for—or at least, indifference toward—their worst impulses.

Thus tweens, far from being simply a marketing niche group, speak to the very essence of our future. They are the vanguard of a new, decultured generation, isolated from family and neighborhood, shrugged at by parents, dominated by peers, and delivered into the hands of a sexualized and status- and fad-crazed marketplace.

A second-grade teacher told me that, at 55 her school's yearly dance festival, she is finding it increasingly difficult to interest her seven-year-olds in traditional kid stuff like the Mexican hat dance or the hokey-pokey. They want to dress up like the Spice Girls and shimmy away. Look for the tweening of America to continue its downward march.

A CLOSER LOOK AT
Tweens: Ten Going on Sixteen

1. According to Hymowitz, why are tweens such a target audience for marketers? What characteristics make tweens especially reactive to advertising and popular culture?

2. Many people are concerned about girls who develop what Hymowitz calls the "hooker look" as tweens. But Hymowitz points out that tween boys are also changing their looks. According to this commentary, how are boys taking on this look and attitude, too?

3. Ultimately, what are three problems that Hymowitz believes will come about because of this concentration of marketing to tweens? What does she think parents and society should do about it?

IDEAS FOR
Writing

1. Write a brief memoir in which you describe a time in which you tried something "grown up" as a child. You might write about wearing a new kind of clothing to school or saying something that you thought sounded mature. What did you learn from this experience? How did it change or not change you?

2. Imagine that you are a school principal who would like to de-emphasize the stress on clothing and looks at your school. Write a proposal in which you identify the problem, its causes, and its effects, and suggest a plan for making the situation better.

Why Suing College Students for Illegal Music Downloading Is Right

MARCI A. HAMILTON

Marci A. Hamilton, a professor of law, argues that illegal music downloading may seem free to college students but that it has many hidden costs to our society. While reading her commentary, look for the ways she uses costs and benefits to argue that the advantages of suing college students for illegal music downloading outweigh the disadvantages.

Recently, and controversially, the recording industry has switched tactics in its fight against illegal downloading. Despite fear of a public relations debacle, it is planning to sue student downloaders.

First, however, it must identify them, and gather evidence of their illegal activity. Toward this end, subpoenas have already been sent to a number of universities and Internet Service Providers. Hundreds more are expected in September, after school starts.

Meanwhile, the Recording Industry Institute of America (RIAA) has not only led the fight for these lawsuits, but also joined together with campus administrators to educate students on the law and the consequences of violating it.

Some have criticized the RIAA and others in the music industry for going after students. But I will argue that it is entirely right—both legally and morally—for them to do so.

The enduring value of an enforceable copyright law

In a society that enjoys the benefit of a 5 strong, enforceable copyright law, it is too easy to forget what life would be like without it.

While my son went to space camp in Huntsville, Alabama, recently the rest of us went to Nashville, the home of country music and the Country Music Hall of Fame. The museum is excellent at many different levels, but my favorite element was the film of television clips showing country music over the past 50 years. Now, my mother is from Wyoming and my father from Kentucky, so I was destined to be a country-western music fan. The film brought back a million childhood memories; it also reminded me why copyright is such an absolute necessity.

Was it not for copyright's ability to build fences around intangible goods such as lyrics and melodies, a performer like Loretta Lynn would not have been able to leave Butcher Holler, Kentucky, and share her gifts with the world. The list of country music stars that have come from humble beginnings is long, and the best country music never forgets its origins.

The world would have been a lesser place but for copyright's ability to pave the road for these stars to travel from rags to riches, from hillbilly country to the big lights. The Country Music Hall of Fame gives you a real taste of that story as it displays the humble beginnings of some, as well as the gold-plated piano Priscilla Presley gave to Elvis on their first wedding anniversary.

In a culture without copyright, only the rich, or the government-sponsored, could be this culture's full-time creators. Poor artists such as Loretta Lynn would have to flip burgers long into their music careers—and might even give up on music entirely.

For these reasons, imagining a world 10 without copyright wouldn't just impoverish the musicians. It would also impoverish the museum, the culture, and music itself.

If the class of creators were winnowed down to the rich and the government-sponsored, and the free market were thus to be replaced by a patronage system, the ability of art to speak to the American people would dwindle precipitously. Artistic works would cater to elites; classical music might survive, but rock and country would encounter grave difficulties.

In the end, then, there is no such thing as cost-free downloading. It may be fiscally free today, but it will cost society dearly in the future.

The advent of the anti-copyright culture

The simple, yet crucial reasons why we have copyright in the first place are easy to forget in the new Information Era. Its utopian early years led adults and students alike to believe that whatever came across their computer screen could be—and ought to be—downloaded cost-free. There was a moment of stunned disbelief: copyright seemed obsolete.

Some saw this simply as a technological reality; others viewed it as a positive social development as well. In fact, it turned out that it was neither. Still, an anti-copyright culture developed—to the shock of the recording industry.

At first, the industry—wary of alienating the young people who were often its best buyers—made a strategic decision to go after the big boys in court. That meant targeting Napster—and soon the industry won its fight.

Nevertheless, the industry continued to hemorrhage, dropping approximately 8 percent in sales last year. The culprits may well be the new Web sites, such as KaZaa, which, unlike Napster, do not depend on centralized servers. These sites accordingly make it nearly impossible to identify the Web host or master.

The industry then had no choice but to go after users—which meant going after students—and it did. As soon as it made the decision, copyright didn't seem so obsolete, after all.

While technology did tend to facilitate illegal downloading, it did not pose infinite obstacles to figuring out who was committing these copyright crimes; universities and ISPs alike tracked their users in certain ways. Although the industry will continue to work on improving the technological protection for works on the Web, for now, the courts will serve them quite well.

That goes to show that, with respect to copyright, new rules are not needed; just enforcement of the old. We were never living in a true legal vacuum, as the "Information Wants to Be Free" contingent suggested; we were living in an enforcement vacuum instead, and that is now changing, as violators are being hunted down.

Even the hunt itself has had a chilling ef- 20 fect. Knowing that one is committing a crime, and may be caught, is scary indeed. Students will back off of illegal copying once they learn that the free ride was an illusion; and if they don't, many parents will step in to ensure that their children don't earn a criminal record along with their college diploma.

Like shoplifting, illegal downloading can be reduced by monitoring and warning.

In a lot of ways, downloading is more like shoplifting than it is like "piracy," the term often used for it. Pirates embrace a life of crime;

shoplifters often see their activity (wrongly) as an exciting and slightly risky diversion—a relatively petty vice in an otherwise law-abiding life.

The more seriously society takes shoplifting, the more shoplifters will be deterred. The same is true, I believe, for illegal downloaders. Every law-breaking student has a diploma at stake, and only a scintilla of students is hardened criminals. Like the thrill of shoplifting, the thrill of illegal downloading may fade quickly in the face of serious penalties, and a real risk of getting caught.

Of course, technological "locks" won't be perfect, and some level of crime will remain. But here, again, the shoplifting analogy is instructive. Stores do not lock up every item they offer to prevent shoplifting. Instead, they post signs saying shoplifting is a crime, monitor their customers, and press charges against individual shoplifters. Despite all this, retail stores have had to build into their profit picture losses that will result from undetected shoplifting.

The recording industry will have to use similar tactics, and like retail stores, they will have to live with a small loss from undetected stealing. But that loss can be minimized, through warnings, monitoring, and enforcement. And word of enforcement spreads. Few will be shoplifting from the store that famously pressed charges against Winona Ryder. Few students will keep downloading once their classmates have famously gotten in deep trouble for doing just that. That is good for them, but even better for us.

A CLOSER LOOK AT
Why Suing College Students for Illegal Music Downloading Is Right

1. According to Hamilton, what are the benefits of copyright laws and why should they be preserved?

2. List three reasons why Hamilton believes that the music industry has the right and the obligation to sue college students who download music illegally.

3. Hamilton calls illegal downloading a crime. What kind of crime does she believe it is similar to?

IDEAS FOR
Writing

1. Do you agree or disagree with Hamilton's argument? Write a letter to the editor in which you argue against or support her position. What are some of the weaknesses and strengths of her argument? As a college student, what kinds of new insights can you offer into this problem of illegal music downloading?

2. Write a brief report for your university's administration in which you discuss the amount of illegal music downloading among college students at your school. Besides online and print sources, also use some empirical sources like surveys and interviews to strengthen your research. Explain whether there is a problem with illegal music downloading and offer some options for handling this issue.

Challenging Veteran Stereotypes

KEN HARBAUGH

Veteran Ken Harbaugh served for nine years as a Navy pilot and was deployed several times to the Middle East. He also graduated from Yale Law School in 2008 after he returned from duty. In this commentary, which first aired on National Public Radio, he argues against the stereotypes of "damaged" veterans that are often used in movies. Pay special attention to the ways he uses reasoning and his own credibility to comment on an issue that troubles him.

America's wars in Iraq and Afghanistan are the most filmed conflicts in history. Already a flood of documentaries and movies have come out, purporting to show what is really happening. On balance, this is a good thing. For a democracy like ours to make the best decisions about war, we must be informed.

I worry though, that the veterans' experience is being portrayed in a way that could hurt for years to come. Most Americans have not seen combat, much less in Iraq or Afghanistan. The prevailing image of today's veteran is gotten through the media, through movies and pictures that often dwell on the trauma of war, the injury it does to the body and the psyche.

This focus on the "damaged" veteran is, for the most part, well intentioned. As a nation, we have no higher moral duty, none, than caring for those we send to do our fighting.

Yet this picture of the veteran scarred by war is incomplete, and often unfair. Some do return physically and emotionally shattered. But not most. Indeed, the vast majority of my former military friends are not only proud of having served, but feel that it made them stronger. This is not a defense of war or the wisdom of our current policies. Still, the act of serving your country, alongside other Americans you would give your life for, I believe changes a person for the better.

After Vietnam, the media created an image of returning vets as crazed sociopaths, unable to readjust to civilian life. Movies like *Deerhunter* and *Rambo* were standard fare, depicting vets as damaged goods. We're starting to see the same myth emerge today, with movies like *Ground Truth* and *In the Valley of Elah.*

I applaud anyone who shines light on the plight of those veterans traumatized by war. Their story is important. Americans need to hear it. But pretending that this is every veteran's experience is wrong.

The truth is that many vets adapt extremely well to life after the military. Data from the Bureau of Labor Statistics show vets today are more likely to be employed than their nonveteran counterparts. According to the Justice Department, they're less likely to be imprisoned. And in a survey commissioned by the VA, ninety-one percent of Vietnam veterans who had seen combat said they were "glad they had served their country."

Our veterans are an asset, not a liability. This applies even to those wounded. Many

I've talked to would rejoin their units in a heartbeat if they could. That isn't about the justness of our foreign policy. It's about bravery. It's about love. The overwhelming majority of veterans today are proud to have worn the uniform.

I suppose we'll just have to wait for a movie about that.

A CLOSER LOOK AT
Challenging Veteran Stereotypes

1. In what ways does Harbaugh make parallels between the movies made after Vietnam and the movies being made today about the Iraq war? What concerns him about the parallels he sees in these movies from two different eras?

2. Harbaugh is troubled that movies and the media often offer a negative portrayal of "damaged" veterans who return from war. According to Harbaugh, what exactly is problematic about the kinds of characters these movies and the media are featuring?

3. In a few places, Harbaugh uses concessions to qualify his argument. Find a few of these concessions and discuss how they strengthen his commentary.

IDEAS FOR
Writing

1. Watch one of the movies Harbaugh lists in this commentary or another movie about soldiers returning from war. Write a review in which you talk specifically about how the movie portrays veterans. In your review, discuss whether you think the movie relies too much on stereotypes and whether those stereotypes are harmful to veterans and society's understanding of war and its aftermath.

2. Write a brief profile in which you describe the life of a veteran. Your profile could be written about a family member, friend, or acquaintance. Or you can write about a historical figure. In your profile, discuss this person's service. Then discuss his or her life after returning from war.

A FEW IDEAS FOR
Composing a Commentary

1. **Write a commentary for a news Web site.** Choose a controversial issue that interests you and find a relevant story on a news Web site like *CNN, MSNBC,* or *FoxNews.* Do some research on the subject and write a commentary in which you respond to and offer your opinion on this issue.

2. **Write a commentary comparing two views.** Find two commentaries on the same topic in magazines or on a news Web site. Where do these commentaries differ? Where are their views similar? Which commentator do you tend to agree with and why?

3. **Write a letter to the editor for a news Web site.** Choose one of the four commentaries printed in this chapter and challenge or support its argument. What are this person's weakest arguments? Where do you agree with the commentary? What might you add, based on your own experience?

Position
Papers

A More Perfect Union

BARACK OBAMA

Barack Obama delivered this speech on March 18, 2008, before he was nominated as the 2008 Democratic Party presidential candidate. The speech is, in part, a reaction to television and Internet news stories that displayed the speeches of Obama's pastor, Jeremiah Wright. In those speeches, Wright denounced the American government for committing crimes against African Americans and other people of color. Critics of Obama charged that his position must reflect that of his pastor and that his political views, therefore, must be far more extreme than he had indicated. Obama delivered this speech to clarify his views about race in America's past, present, and future. Pay attention to the way he carefully criticizes Wright's statements (calling them both "wrong" and "divisive") but also explains why it is understandable that some people would come to hold such positions.

"We the people, in order to form a more perfect union."

Two hundred and twenty-one years ago, in a hall that still stands across the street, a group of men gathered and, with these simple words, launched America's improbable experiment in democracy. Farmers and scholars, statesmen and patriots who had traveled across an ocean to escape tyranny and persecution finally made real their declaration of independence at a Philadelphia convention that lasted through the spring of 1787.

The document they produced was eventually signed but ultimately unfinished. It was stained by this nation's original sin of slavery, a question that divided the colonies and brought the convention to a stalemate until the founders chose to allow the slave trade to continue for at least twenty more years, and to leave any final resolution to future generations.

Of course, the answer to the slavery question was already embedded within our Constitution—a Constitution that had at its very core the ideal of equal citizenship under the law; a Constitution that promised its people liberty, and justice, and a union that could be and should be perfected over time.

And yet words on a parchment would not 5 be enough to deliver slaves from bondage, or provide men and women of every color and creed their full rights and obligations as citizens of the United States. What would be needed were Americans in successive generations who were willing to do their part—through protests and struggle, on the streets and in the courts, through a civil war and civil disobedience and always at great risk—to narrow that gap between the promise of our ideals and the reality of their time.

This was one of the tasks we set forth at the beginning of this campaign—to continue the long march of those who came before us, a march for a more just, more equal, more free, more caring and more prosperous America. I chose to run for the presidency at this moment in history because I believe deeply that we cannot solve the challenges of our time unless we solve them together—unless we perfect our union by understanding that we may have different stories, but we hold common hopes; that we may not look the same and we may not have come from the same place, but we all want to move in the same direction—towards a better future for our children and our grandchildren.

This belief comes from my unyielding faith in the decency and generosity of the American people. But it also comes from my own American story.

I am the son of a black man from Kenya and a white woman from Kansas. I was raised with the help of a white grandfather who survived a Depression to serve in Patton's army during World War II and a white grandmother who worked on a bomber assembly line at Fort Leavenworth while he was overseas. I've gone to some of the best schools in America and lived in one of the world's poorest nations. I am married to a black American who carries within her the blood of slaves and slaveowners—an inheritance we pass on to our two precious daughters. I have brothers, sisters, nieces, nephews, uncles and cousins, of every race and every hue, scattered across three continents, and for as long as I live, I will never forget that in no other country on Earth is my story even possible.

It's a story that hasn't made me the most conventional candidate. But it is a story that has seared into my genetic makeup the idea that this nation is more than the sum of its parts—that out of many, we are truly one.

Throughout the first year of this campaign, 10 against all predictions to the contrary, we saw how hungry the American people were for this message of unity. Despite the temptation to view my candidacy through a purely racial lens, we won commanding victories in states with some of the whitest populations in the country. In South Carolina, where the Confederate Flag still flies, we built a powerful coalition of African Americans and white Americans.

This is not to say that race has not been an issue in the campaign. At various stages in the campaign, some commentators have deemed me either "too black" or "not black enough." We saw racial tensions bubble to the surface during the week before the South Carolina primary. The press has scoured every exit poll for the latest evidence of racial polarization, not just in terms of white and black, but black and brown as well.

And yet, it has only been in the last couple of weeks that the discussion of race in this campaign has taken a particularly divisive turn.

On one end of the spectrum, we've heard the implication that my candidacy is somehow an exercise in affirmative action; that it's based solely on the desire of wide-eyed liberals to purchase racial reconciliation on the cheap. On the other end, we've heard my former pastor, Reverend Jeremiah Wright, use incendiary language to express views that have the potential not only to widen the racial divide, but views that denigrate both the greatness and the goodness of our nation; that rightly offend white and black alike.

I have already condemned, in unequivocal terms, the statements of Reverend Wright that have caused such controversy. For some, nagging questions remain. Did I know him to be an occasionally fierce critic of American domestic and foreign policy? Of course. Did I ever hear him make remarks that could be considered controversial while I sat in church? Yes. Did I strongly disagree with many of his political views? Absolutely—just as I'm sure many of you have heard remarks from your pastors, priests, or rabbis with which you strongly disagreed.

But the remarks that have caused this re- 15 cent firestorm weren't simply controversial. They weren't simply a religious leader's effort to speak out against perceived injustice. Instead, they expressed a profoundly distorted view of this country—a view that sees white racism as endemic, and that elevates what is wrong with America above all that we know is right with America; a view that sees the conflicts in the Middle East as rooted primarily in the actions of stalwart allies like Israel, instead of emanating from the perverse and hateful ideologies of radical Islam.

As such, Reverend Wright's comments were not only wrong but divisive, divisive at a time when we need unity; racially charged at a time when we need to come together to solve a set of monumental problems—two wars, a terrorist threat, a falling economy, a chronic health care crisis, and potentially devastating climate change; problems that are neither black or white or Latino or Asian, but rather problems that confront us all.

Given my background, my politics, and my professed values and ideals, there will no doubt be those for whom my statements of condemnation are not enough. Why associate myself with Reverend Wright in the first place, they may ask? Why not join another church? And I confess that if all that I knew of Reverend Wright were the snippets of those sermons that have run in an endless loop on the television and *YouTube*, or if Trinity United Church of Christ conformed to the caricatures being peddled by some commentators, there is no doubt that I would react in much the same way.

But the truth is, that isn't all that I know of the man. The man I met more than twenty years ago is a man who helped introduce me to my Christian faith, a man who spoke to me about our obligations to love one another; to care for the sick and lift up the poor. He is a man who served his country as a U.S. Marine; who has studied and lectured at some of the finest universities and seminaries in the country, and who for over thirty years led a church that serves the community by doing God's work here on Earth—by housing the homeless, ministering to the needy, providing day care services and scholarships and prison ministries, and reaching out to those suffering from HIV/AIDS.

In my first book, *Dreams from My Father*, I described the experience of my first service at Trinity:

> People began to shout, to rise from their seats and clap and cry out, a forceful wind carrying the reverend's voice up into the rafters. . . . And in that single note—hope!—I heard something else; at the foot of that cross, inside the thousands of churches across the city, I imagined

the stories of ordinary black people merging with the stories of David and Goliath, Moses and Pharaoh, the Christians in the lion's den, Ezekiel's field of dry bones. Those stories—of survival, and freedom, and hope—became our story, my story; the blood that had spilled was our blood, the tears our tears; until this black church, on this bright day, seemed once more a vessel carrying the story of a people into future generations and into a larger world. Our trials and triumphs became at once unique and universal, black and more than black; in chronicling our journey, the stories and songs gave us a means to reclaim memories that we didn't need to feel shame about . . . memories that all people might study and cherish—and with which we could start to rebuild.

That has been my experience at Trinity. Like other predominantly black churches across the country, Trinity embodies the black community in its entirety—the doctor and the welfare mom, the model student and the former gang-banger. Like other black churches, Trinity's services are full of raucous laughter and sometimes bawdy humor. They are full of dancing, clapping, screaming, and shouting that may seem jarring to the untrained ear. The church contains in full the kindness and cruelty, the fierce intelligence and the shocking ignorance, the struggles and successes, the love and yes, the bitterness and bias that make up the black experience in America.

And this helps explain, perhaps, my relationship with Reverend Wright. As imperfect as he may be, he has been like family to me. He strengthened my faith, officiated my wedding, and baptized my children. Not once in my conversations with him have I heard him talk about any ethnic group in derogatory terms, or treat whites with whom he interacted with anything but courtesy and respect. 20

He contains within him the contradictions—the good and the bad—of the community that he has served diligently for so many years.

I can no more disown him than I can disown the black community. I can no more disown him than I can my white grandmother—a woman who helped raise me, a woman who sacrificed again and again for me, a woman who loves me as much as she loves anything in this world, but a woman who once confessed her fear of black men who passed by her on the street, and who on more than one occasion has uttered racial or ethnic stereotypes that made me cringe.

These people are a part of me. And they are a part of America, this country that I love.

Some will see this as an attempt to justify or excuse comments that are simply inexcusable. I can assure you it is not. I suppose the politically safe thing would be to move on from this episode and just hope that it fades into the woodwork. We can dismiss Reverend Wright as a crank or a demagogue, just as some have dismissed Geraldine Ferraro, in the aftermath of her recent statements, as harboring some deep-seated racial bias.

But race is an issue that I believe this nation cannot afford to ignore right now. We would be making the same mistake that Reverend Wright made in his offending sermons about America—to simplify and stereotype and amplify the negative to the point that it distorts reality.

The fact is that the comments that have been made and the issues that have surfaced over the last few weeks reflect the complexities of race in this country that we've never really worked through—a part of our union that we have yet to perfect. And if we walk away now, if we simply retreat into our respective corners, we will never be able to come together and solve challenges like health care, or education, or the need to find good jobs for every American.

Understanding this reality requires a reminder of how we arrived at this point. As William Faulkner once wrote, "The past isn't dead and buried. In fact, it isn't even past." We do not need to recite here the history of racial injustice in this country. But we do need to remind ourselves that so many of the disparities that exist in the African-American community today can be directly traced to inequalities passed on from an earlier generation that suffered under the brutal legacy of slavery and Jim Crow. Segregated schools were, and are, inferior schools; we still haven't fixed them, fifty years after *Brown v. Board of Education,* and the inferior education they provided, then and now, helps explain the pervasive achievement gap between today's black and white students.

Legalized discrimination—where blacks were prevented, often through violence, from owning property, or loans were not granted to African-American business owners, or black homeowners could not access FHA mortgages, or blacks were excluded from unions, or the police force, or fire departments—meant that black families could not amass any meaningful wealth to bequeath to future generations. That history helps explain the wealth and income gap between black and white, and the concentrated pockets of poverty that persists in so many of today's urban and rural communities.

A lack of economic opportunity among black men, and the shame and frustration that came from not being able to provide for one's family, contributed to the erosion of black families—a problem that welfare policies for many years may have worsened. And the lack of basic services in so many urban black neighborhoods—parks for kids to play in, police walking the beat, regular garbage pick-up and building code enforcement—all helped create a cycle of violence, blight, and neglect that continue to haunt us.

This is the reality in which Reverend Wright and other African Americans of his generation grew up. They came of age in the late fifties and early sixties, a time when segregation was still the law of the land and opportunity was systematically constricted. What's remarkable is not how many failed in the face of discrimination, but rather how many men and women overcame the odds; how many were able to make a way out of no way for those like me who would come after them.

But for all those who scratched and clawed their way to get a piece of the American Dream, there were many who didn't make it—those who were ultimately defeated, in one way or another, by discrimination. That legacy of defeat was passed on to future generations—those young men and increasingly young women who we see standing on street corners or languishing in our prisons, without hope or prospects for the future. Even for those blacks who did make it, questions of race, and racism, continue to define their worldview in fundamental ways. For the men and women of Reverend Wright's generation, the memories of humiliation and doubt and fear have not gone away; nor has the anger and the bitterness of those years. That anger may not get expressed in public, in front of white co-workers or white friends. But it does find voice in the barbershop or around the kitchen table. At times, that anger is exploited by politicians, to gin up votes along racial lines, or to make up for a politician's own failings.

And occasionally it finds voice in the church on Sunday morning, in the pulpit and in the pews. The fact that so many people are surprised to hear that anger in some of Reverend Wright's sermons simply reminds us of the old truism that the most segregated hour in American life occurs on Sunday morning. That anger is not always productive; indeed, all too often it distracts attention from solving real problems; it keeps us from squarely facing our own complicity in our condition, and prevents the African-American community from forging the alliances it needs to bring about real change. But the anger is real; it is powerful;

and to simply wish it away, to condemn it without understanding its roots, only serves to widen the chasm of misunderstanding that exists between the races.

In fact, a similar anger exists within segments of the white community. Most working- and middle-class white Americans don't feel that they have been particularly privileged by their race. Their experience is the immigrant experience—as far as they're concerned, no one's handed them anything, they've built it from scratch. They've worked hard all their lives, many times only to see their jobs shipped overseas or their pension dumped after a lifetime of labor. They are anxious about their futures, and feel their dreams slipping away; in an era of stagnant wages and global competition, opportunity comes to be seen as a zero sum game, in which your dreams come at my expense. So when they are told to bus their children to a school across town; when they hear that an African American is getting an advantage in landing a good job or a spot in a good college because of an injustice that they themselves never committed; when they're told that their fears about crime in urban neighborhoods are somehow prejudiced, resentment builds over time.

Like the anger within the black community, these resentments aren't always expressed in polite company. But they have helped shape the political landscape for at least a generation. Anger over welfare and affirmative action helped forge the Reagan Coalition. Politicians routinely exploited fears of crime for their own electoral ends. Talk show hosts and conservative commentators built entire careers unmasking bogus claims of racism while dismissing legitimate discussions of racial injustice and inequality as mere political correctness or reverse racism.

Just as black anger often proved counterproductive, so have these white resentments distracted attention from the real culprits of the middle class squeeze—a corporate culture rife with inside dealing, questionable ac-counting practices, and short-term greed; a Washington dominated by lobbyists and spe-cial interests; economic policies that favor the few over the many. And yet, to wish away the resentments of white Americans, to label them as misguided or even racist, without recognizing they are grounded in legitimate concerns—this too widens the racial divide, and blocks the path to understanding.

This is where we are right now. It's a racial stalemate we've been stuck in for years. Contrary to the claims of some of my critics, black and white, I have never been so naive as to believe that we can get beyond our racial divisions in a single election cycle, or with a single candidacy—particularly a can-didacy as imperfect as my own.

But I have asserted a firm conviction—a conviction rooted in my faith in God and my faith in the American people—that working together we can move beyond some of our old racial wounds, and that in fact we have no choice if we are to continue on the path of a more perfect union.

For the African-American community, that path means embracing the burdens of our past without becoming victims of our past. It means continuing to insist on a full measure of justice in every aspect of Ameri-can life. But it also means binding our par-ticular grievances—for better health care, and better schools, and better jobs—to the larger aspirations of all Americans—the white woman struggling to break the glass ceiling, the white man who has been laid off, the immigrant trying to feed his family. And it means taking full responsibility for our own lives—by demanding more from our fathers, and spending more time with our children, and reading to them, and teaching them that while they may face challenges and discrimi-nation in their own lives, they must never succumb to despair or cynicism; they must always believe that they can write their own destiny.

Ironically, this quintessentially Ameri-can—and yes, conservative—notion of self-help found frequent expression in Reverend Wright's sermons. But what my former pastor too often failed to understand is that embark-ing on a program of self-help also requires a belief that society can change.

The profound mistake of Reverend Wright's sermons is not that he spoke about racism in our society. It's that he spoke as if our society was static; as if no progress has been made; as if this country—a country that has made it possible for one of his own mem-bers to run for the highest office in the land and build a coalition of white and black; Latino and Asian, rich and poor, young and old—is still irrevocably bound to a tragic past. But what we know—what we have seen—is that America can change. That is the true ge-nius of this nation. What we have already achieved gives us hope—the audacity to hope—for what we can and must achieve tomorrow.

In the white community, the path to a more perfect union means acknowledging that what ails the African-American commu-nity does not just exist in the minds of black people; that the legacy of discrimination—and current incidents of discrimination, while less overt than in the past—are real and must be addressed. Not just with words, but with deeds—by investing in our schools and our communities; by enforcing our civil rights laws and ensuring fairness in our crim-inal justice system; by providing this genera-tion with ladders of opportunity that were unavailable for previous generations. It re-quires all Americans to realize that your dreams do not have to come at the expense of my dreams; that investing in the health, wel-fare, and education of black and brown and white children will ultimately help all of America prosper.

In the end, then, what is called for is nothing more, and nothing less, than what all the world's great religions demand—that we do unto others as we would have them do unto us. Let us be our brother's keeper, Scripture tells us. Let us be our sister's keeper. Let us find that common stake we all have in one another, and let our politics reflect that spirit as well.

For we have a choice in this country. We can accept a politics that breeds division, and conflict, and cynicism. We can tackle race only as spectacle—as we did in the OJ trial—or in the wake of tragedy, as we did in the aftermath of Katrina—or as fodder for the nightly news. We can play Reverend Wright's sermons on every channel, every day and talk about them from now until the election, and make the only question in this campaign whether or not the American people think that I somehow believe or sympathize with his most offensive words. We can pounce on some gaffe by a Hillary supporter as evidence that she's playing the race card, or we can speculate on whether white men will all flock to John McCain in the general election regardless of his policies.

We can do that.

But if we do, I can tell you that in the next election, we'll be talking about some other distraction. And then another one. And then another one. And nothing will change.

That is one option. Or, at this moment, in this election, we can come together and say, "Not this time." This time we want to talk about the crumbling schools that are stealing the future of black children and white children and Asian children and Hispanic children and Native American children. This time we want to reject the cynicism that tells us that these kids can't learn; that those kids who don't look like us are somebody else's problem. The children of America are not those kids, they are our kids, and we will not let them fall behind in a 21st-century economy. Not this time.

This time we want to talk about how the lines in the emergency room are filled with whites and blacks and Hispanics who do not have health care; who don't have the power on their own to overcome the special interests in Washington, but who can take them on if we do it together.

This time we want to talk about the shuttered mills that once provided a decent life for men and women of every race, and the homes for sale that once belonged to Americans from every religion, every region, every walk of life. This time we want to talk about the fact that the real problem is not that someone who doesn't look like you might take your job; it's that the corporation you work for will ship it overseas for nothing more than a profit.

This time we want to talk about the men and women of every color and creed who serve together, and fight together, and bleed together under the same proud flag. We want to talk about how to bring them home from a war that never should've been authorized and never should've been waged, and we want to talk about how we'll show our patriotism by caring for them, and their families, and giving them the benefits they have earned.

I would not be running for president if I didn't believe with all my heart that this is what the vast majority of Americans want for this country. This union may never be perfect, but generation after generation has shown that it can always be perfected. And today, whenever I find myself feeling doubtful or cynical about this possibility, what gives me the most hope is the next generation—the young people whose attitudes and beliefs and openness to change have already made history in this election.

There is one story in particular that I'd like to leave you with today—a story I told when I had the great honor of speaking on Dr. King's birthday at his home church, Ebenezer Baptist, in Atlanta.

There is a young, twenty-three-year-old white woman named Ashley Baia who organized for our campaign in Florence, South Carolina. She had been working to organize a mostly African-American community since the beginning of this campaign, and one day she was at a roundtable discussion where everyone went around telling their story and why they were there.

And Ashley said that when she was nine years old, her mother got cancer. And because she had to miss days of work, she was let go and lost her health care. They had to file for bankruptcy, and that's when Ashley decided that she had to do something to help her mom.

She knew that food was one of their most expensive costs, and so Ashley convinced her mother that what she really liked and really wanted to eat more than anything else was mustard and relish sandwiches. Because that was the cheapest way to eat.

She did this for a year until her mom got better, and she told everyone at the roundtable that the reason she joined our campaign was so that she could help the millions of other children in the country who want and need to help their parents too.

Now Ashley might have made a different 55 choice. Perhaps somebody told her along the way that the source of her mother's problems were blacks who were on welfare and too lazy to work, or Hispanics who were coming into the country illegally. But she didn't. She sought out allies in her fight against injustice.

Anyway, Ashley finishes her story and then goes around the room and asks everyone else why they're supporting the campaign. They all have different stories and reasons. Many bring up a specific issue. And finally they come to this elderly black man who's been sitting there quietly the entire time. And Ashley asks him why he's there. And he does not bring up a specific issue. He does not say health care or the economy. He does not say education or the war. He does not say that he was there because of Barack Obama. He simply says to everyone in the room, "I am here because of Ashley."

"I'm here because of Ashley." By itself, that single moment of recognition between that young white girl and that old black man is not enough. It is not enough to give health care to the sick, or jobs to the jobless, or education to our children.

But it is where we start. It is where our union grows stronger. And as so many generations have come to realize over the course of the two hundred and twenty-one years since a band of patriots signed that document in Philadelphia, that is where the perfection begins.

A CLOSER LOOK AT
A More Perfect Union

1. Read "A More Perfect Union" a second time or watch it on the Internet, noting those portions of the speech that most stand out for you. In some places, Obama begins several sentences in a row with the same word or phrase (a technique that is called *anaphora*). What effect do those passages have on the audience?

2. Find this speech on *YouTube* and watch it. Describe how seeing and hearing the speech was different than reading it. What ideas and key points came through stronger? What did you notice about the speech that you didn't notice while reading it?

3. If you were going to state the main point of this speech in a sentence or two, what would it be? Read the speech again or listen to it with the transcript in front of you. This time, though, highlight or underline the words, phrases, and sentences that seem to state important, larger points. Then look back on what you have highlighted and try to capture in your own words what Obama is trying to convey.

1. Obama delivered this speech in part to answer public demands that he explain in precise and direct terms his beliefs and guiding principles about race in America. In this sense, the speech could be said to belong to the "manifesto" genre, which is a blend of the position paper, memoir, and other genres such as profiles and proposals. Write a manifesto that makes a public declaration of the principles that you believe in and the values that guide your life. Your response may be political, religious, philosophical, or personal.

2. Write a rhetorical analysis of "A More Perfect Union" that focuses on any aspect of the speech: its use of *ethos, pathos, logos,* or style and arrangement. Use this focus on one or two aspects to arrive at a new insight about the speech that goes beyond the obvious.

TV Watching—The Top Environmental Hazard for Children

TODD HUFFMAN

Todd Huffman is a pediatrician who lives in Eugene, Oregon, where he writes frequently about children's health and welfare issues for independent newspapers, such as the Register-Guard *(where this article appeared). As you read, notice how Huffman states his claims, cites and uses evidence, and explores both sides of the issue.*

When parents think about their children's exposure to environmental risks, they might think of lead, pesticides or grass pollens. In fact, the greatest environmental exposure for most children is television. They spend more time watching television than in any other wakeful activity, and it affects their health and well-being in significant ways.

For too long parents and even pediatricians have asked: "Is television good or bad?" Television is inherently neither; it's time to move beyond such black or white thinking.

Television is a tool. Whether it is good or bad for children depends on what they watch and how they watch it.

Used carefully for children older than 2, TV need not have untoward effects at all. According to recent studies, it even can exert a positive influence.

By and large, however, it is not being used 5 carefully. By and large, parents are clueless about the content and consequences of the media-saturated world their children inhabit.

Content is the critical factor in the effects of TV on children. Watching *Sesame Street* or the Discovery Channel is not the same as watching *Grey's Anatomy* or *Desperate Housewives*. Yet, 95 percent of American children watch programs that are produced for more mature audiences.

This trend is a cause for concern when you consider that children, who use media to learn about culture, typically lack the knowledge and experience to recognize what is unrealistic.

The media are a powerful teacher of children and adolescents. The media cut across virtually every concern that parents and pediatricians have about young people: sex, violence, homicide, suicide, obesity, eating disorders, school problems, and drug use.

Children and adolescents are permitted to view an average of 30 hours of television each week, largely without adults paying attention to the developmental fitness of the programming. Given this exposure, it should not seem remarkable that today's children and adolescents are more overweight, inattentive, violent and sexual than any previous generation.

American teens, especially, are adrift in 10 one of the most crude, brutal, and explicitly sexualized popular cultures in the history of the world. Through television, music videos and the Internet, teens have unprecedented access to an astounding array of both real and virtual sexual experiences. Because schools and parents are not always eager to tackle the subject adequately, the media arguably have become the leading sex educator in America today.

That's not good news.

The sexual content in much of the media is frequent, glamorized, and free of consequences. "Everyone does it" on television and in the movies, or so it seems, yet the need for birth control, the risks of pregnancy or sexually transmitted infections, and the need for responsibility are rarely discussed.

Too often, children and teens are permitted to view late-evening programming that is hypersexualized to such a degree that many adults feel uncomfortable watching. Too often, shows targeting adolescents seem like "Happy Days with Hormones," with sexual intercourse appearing a normal and casual activity even for teens.

In these ways, the media function as a kind of sexual "super peer," providing role models of attractive adults and older adolescents engaging in risky behavior—and putting additional pressure on young people to have sex at earlier and earlier ages.

A growing number of studies are reveal- 15 ing that exposure to sexual content in television, movies, music, and magazines accelerates white adolescents' sexual activity and increases their risk of engaging in early sexual intercourse. White teens who watched the most sexual content doubled their risk of initiating intercourse the following year, or of significantly advancing in sexual activity other than intercourse.

Black teens, by contrast, appear to be more influenced by perceptions of their parents' expectations and their friends' sexual behavior than by what they see and hear in the media.

Teenagers who start having sexual intercourse early are at a greater risk of pregnancy and sexually transmitted infections. Both male and female adolescents who are younger at first intercourse are less likely to use a contraceptive method.

This situation is a national concern, considering that despite recent declines, the teenage pregnancy rate in the United States is still three to 10 times as high as the rates in other industrialized countries. Among those countries, only in the United States are schools limited to promoting abstinence alone until marriage and required to discuss the exaggerated failure rates of contraception.

Look no further than the Centers for Disease Control study released on March 11, which estimated that one in four young women between the ages of 14 and 19 in the United States—or 3.2 million teenage girls—is infected with at least one of the most common sexually transmitted diseases. Reducing sex education into a two-word slogan—"no sex"—clearly has not been an effective advertising campaign for American parents and schools.

The corruption of childhood is now pretty 20 much a fact of modern life. The adult world—through films, music, fashion, magazines and newspapers—has elected to share with young people its various sexual obsessions, rather than shielding them from them. While the age of consent has remained the same, the age of knowledge has been hurtling downward.

While hypersexualized media content is by no means certain to convert an otherwise innocent child into a sexually reckless adolescent, just as every pack of cigarettes smoked increases by some small amount the likelihood of lung cancer, every media portrait of sex as fun and risk-free increases by some small amount the likelihood of early sexual experimentation.

Apologists argue that today's parents are simply overwhelmed in their battle with thousands of competing media images and ideas over which they have little direct control, and that the responsibility for healthier media lies with the producers of media.

While the major television networks need to recognize that with their free use of the airwaves comes a certain responsibility to public health, parents still hold a large measure of control over the media habits of their children.

It's time parents retook that remote.

A CLOSER LOOK AT
TV Watching—The Top Environmental Hazard for Children

1. Read through "TV Watching" again and highlight the places where Huffman makes a claim. How well do those various claims hold together? Which statement do you feel most adequately expresses Huffman's *main claim* that explains what he wants readers to understand or do?

2. Position papers explore both (or many) sides of an issue and argue for one side over the other. Where does Huffman raise and explore the position that opposes his? How adequate is Huffman's treatment of the other side's position? For what kinds of audiences would a more thorough treatment have been more persuasive?

3. In paragraph 21, Huffman creates an analogy between a child watching an episode of hypersexualized television and smoking a single cigarette. Is the point of that analogy clear and compelling? How well does it succeed in driving home Huffman's main point?

IDEAS FOR
Writing

1. Imagine that you are the editor of an online magazine and Todd Huffman has sent you "TV Watching" for consideration. You want to publish the piece but want Huffman to make it stronger by including a fair and thorough treatment of opposing positions. Write Dr. Huffman a brief, respectful e-mail that explains *how* you would like him to change his piece. Also, using the ideas in "Position Papers" (Chapter 11) and "Using Argumentative Strategies" (Chapter 22), explain *why* these changes will make his piece more persuasive for readers who may not already agree with his point of view.

2. Write a respectful rebuttal that either refutes or challenges Huffman's "TV Watching." Even if you agree with Huffman, write a rebuttal that explains its weaknesses in reasoning.

It's Time to Drink Toilet Water

EILENE ZIMMERMAN

In this position paper, written for the online magazine Slate, *journalist Eilene Zimmerman offers an unconventional solution for addressing the scarcity of drinkable water. Pay attention to the way she supports her position with reasoning and specific evidence, and how she incorporates her opponents' positions.*

Officials in Orange County, Calif., will attend opening ceremonies today for the world's largest water-purification project, among the first "toilet-to-tap" systems in America. The Groundwater Replenishment System is designed to take sewage water straight from bathrooms in places like Costa Mesa, Fullerton, and Newport Beach and—after an initial cleansing treatment—send it through $490 million worth of pipes, filters, and tanks for purification. The water then flows into lakes in nearby Anaheim, where it seeps through clay, sand, and rock into aquifers in the groundwater basin. Months later, it will travel back into the homes of half a million Orange County residents, through their kitchen taps and showerheads.

It's a smart idea, one of the most reliable and affordable hedges against water shortages, and it's not new. For decades, cities throughout the United States have used recycled wastewater for nonpotable needs, like agriculture and landscaping; because the technology already exists, the move to potable uses seems a no-brainer. But the Orange County project is the exception. Studies show that the public hasn't yet warmed to the notion of indirect potable reuse (IPR)—or "toilet-to-tap," as its opponents would have it. Surveys like one taken last year in San Diego show that a majority of us don't want to drink water that once had poop in it, even if it's been cleaned and purified. A public outcry against toilet-to-tap in 2000 forced the city of Los Angeles to shut down a $55 million project that would have provided enough water for 120,000 homes. Similar reluctance among San Diego residents led Mayor Jerry Sanders to veto the city council's approval in November of a pilot program to use recycled water to supplement that city's drinking water. (A similar plan failed once before in 1999.)

But San Diego is in the midst of a severe water crisis. The city imports 90 percent of its water, much of that from the Colorado River, which is drying up. The recent legal decision to protect the ecosystem of the San Joaquin Delta in Northern California—San Diego's second-leading water source—will reduce the amount coming from there as well. Add to that rising population and an ongoing drought, and the situation looks pretty bleak: 3 million people in a region that has enough water, right now, for 10 percent of them.

We don't have enough water where we need it; if we don't learn to deal with drinking toilet water, we're going to be mighty thirsty. Only 2.5 percent of the water on Earth is freshwater, and less than 1 percent of that is usable and renewable. The Ogallala Aquifer—North America's largest, stretching from Texas to South Dakota—is steadily being depleted. And Americans are insatiable water consumers—our water footprint has been estimated to be twice the global average.

The ocean provides another source of 5 potable water. Large-scale treatment of seawater already occurs in the Middle East, Africa, and in Tampa Bay, Fla. Construction of the largest desalination plant in the western hemisphere is supposed to begin this year in Carlsbad, Calif., which would convert 300 million gallons of seawater into 50 million gallons of drinking water each day. Taking the salt out of ocean water sounds like a good idea, but it's economically and environmentally far more expensive than sewage-water recycling. Orange County water officials estimate desalinated water costs between $800 and $2,000 per acre-foot to produce, while its recycled water runs about $525 per acre-foot. Desalination also uses more energy (and thus produces more greenhouse gas emissions), kills tiny marine organisms that get sucked up into the processing plant, and produces a brine byproduct laced with chemicals that goes back into the ocean.

What desalination doesn't have, though, is the "yuck" factor of recycled sewage water. But seawater, like other sources of nonrecycled water, is at least as yucky as whatever comes through a toilet-to-tap program. When you know how dirty all this water is before treatment, recycling raw sewage doesn't seem like a bad option. Hundreds of millions of tons of sewage are dumped into rivers and oceans, and in that waste are bacteria, hormones, and pharmaceuticals. Runoff from rainwater, watering lawns, or emptying pools is the worst, sending metals, pesticides, and pathogens into lakes, rivers, and the ocean. The water you find near the end of a river system like the Colorado or the Mississippi (which feeds big cities like San Diego and New Orleans) has been in and out of municipal sewers several times.

Whatever winds up in lakes and rivers used for drinking is cleaned and disinfected along with the rest of our water supply. Still, a recent analysis of San Diego's drinking water found several contaminants, including ibuprofen, the bug repellent DEET, and the anti-anxiety drug meprobamate. No treatment system will ever be 100-percent reliable, and skeptics who worry that pathogens in sewage water will make it past treatment and into our drinking water should worry about all drinking water, not just the water in a toilet-to-tap program. The fact is, supertreated wastewater is clean enough to drink right after treatment. It's been used safely this way (in a process known as direct potable reuse) for years in the African nation of Namibia. The EPA has conducted research in Denver and San Diego on the safety of direct potable reuse and found recycled water is often of better quality than existing drinking water. And although putting water into the ground, rivers, or lakes provides some additional filtering and more opportunities for monitoring quality, the benefits of doing it that way are largely psychological. In its 2004 report on the topic, the EPA concluded that Americans perceive this water to be "laundered" as it moves through the ground or other bodies of water, even though in some instances, according to the report, "quality may actually be degraded as it passes through the environment."

Despite the public's concerns, a few U.S. cities have already started to use recycled wastewater to augment drinking water. In El Paso, Texas, indirect potable reuse supplies 40 percent of the city's drinking water; in Fairfax, Va., it supplies 5 percent. Unless we discover a new source of clean, potable water, we're going to have to consider projects like these to make wastewater a reusable resource. The upfront costs for getting a system in place and educating the public may be steep, but it would save us the expense—both economic and environmental—of finding another river or lake from which we can divert water.

A CLOSER LOOK AT
It's Time to Drink Toilet Water

1. Examine the title of this position paper and the overall impact it has on readers. Why do you think Zimmerman chose this title? Remember that this first appeared in an online magazine. How might this context have influenced Zimmerman's choice, as she considered readers' habits of surfing and reading online? What other effects might the startling title have on the overall persuasiveness of the article?

2. "It's Time" argues for a specific solution to a growing problem. What exactly is the problem that her solution addresses, and where does she state it explicitly?

3. Make a list of the objections to the solution that are addressed by Zimmerman. She may not state these objections directly and prominently, but she does acknowledge them. Does she effectively explain the limitations of her opponents' objections? Overall, does she offer compelling reasons for believing that her understanding of the issue is stronger than her opponents' understanding?

4. Use *Google* or another search engine to find this piece in its original online form at *Slate*. Most of the links shown within the article point readers to sources that provide evidence backing up Zimmerman's reasoning, but are these sources relevant, sufficient, and trustworthy? Does access to this evidence make her case more compelling?

1. Write a rhetorical analysis of "It's Time to Drink Toilet Water" that explores how Zimmerman's style helps her to make (or prevents her from making) a compelling case for her position. Specifically, rather than speaking in "polite" or evasive language, she states her proposal in language some readers might find shockingly direct. For instance, she writes "toilet water" and "water that once had poop in it" instead of the more evasive "recycled water." How does this direct style affect the argument's overall persuasiveness? For instance, does it harm or enhance the author's *ethos*? You may also consider which kinds of audiences would react favorably to such a style and which would react negatively.

2. In paragraph 6, Zimmerman alludes to the "'yuck' factor" as one objection to her position, but a close reading reveals that she actually sidesteps the issue of the psychological problem of drinking "toilet water." Compose one or two paragraphs that could be inserted into Zimmerman's text that more fairly and thoroughly acknowledge the power of the "yuck" factor objection.

The Making of a Divorce Culture

BARBARA DAFOE WHITEHEAD

Barbara Dafoe Whitehead is codirector of the Rutgers University National Marriage Project, whose mission is "to provide research and analysis on the state of marriage in America and to educate the public on the social, economic, and political conditions affecting marital success and child well-being." She is a journalist who speaks to and writes for scholarly, professional, and popular audiences. As you read "The Making of a Divorce Culture," the introduction to her book The Divorce Culture *(1997), pay attention to the way Whitehead defines the causes of America's widespread acceptance of divorce.*

Divorce is now part of everyday American life. It is embedded in our laws and institutions, our manners and mores, our movies and television shows, our novels and children's storybooks, and our closest and most important relationships. Indeed, divorce has become so pervasive that many people naturally assume it has seeped into the social and cultural mainstream over a long period of time. Yet this is not the case. Divorce has become an American way of life only as the result of recent and revolutionary change.

The entire history of American divorce can be divided into two periods, one evolutionary and the other revolutionary. For most of the nation's history, divorce was a rare occurrence and an insignificant feature of family and social relationships. In the first sixty years of the twentieth century, divorce became more common, but it was hardly commonplace. In 1960, the divorce rate stood at a still relatively modest level of nine per one thousand married couples. After 1960, however, the rate accelerated at a dazzling pace. It doubled in roughly a decade and continued its upward climb until the early 1980s, when it stabilized at the highest level among advanced Western societies. As a consequence of this sharp and sustained rise, divorce moved from the margins to the mainstream of American life in the space of three decades.

Ideas are important in revolutions, yet surprisingly little attention has been devoted to the ideas that gave impetus to the divorce revolution. Of the scores of books on divorce published in recent decades, most focus on its legal, demographic, economic, or (especially) psychological dimensions. Few, if any, deal fully with its intellectual origins. Yet trying to comprehend the divorce revolution and its consequences without some sense of its ideological origins, is like trying to understand the American Revolution without taking into account the thinking of John Locke, Thomas Jefferson, or Thomas Paine. This more recent revolution, like the revolution of our nation's founding, has its roots in a distinctive set of ideas and claims.

This book is about the ideas behind the divorce revolution and how these ideas have shaped a culture of divorce. The making of a divorce culture has involved three overlapping changes: first, the emergence and widespread diffusion of a historically new and distinctive set of ideas about divorce in the last third of the twentieth century; second, the migration of divorce from a minor place within a system governed by marriage to a freestanding place as a major institution governing family relationships; and third, a widespread shift in thinking about the obligations of marriage and parenthood.

Beginning in the late 1950s, Americans 5 began to change their ideas about the individual's obligations to family and society. Broadly described, this change was away from an ethic of obligation to others and to-

ward an obligation to self. I do not mean that people suddenly abandoned all responsibilities to others, but rather that they became more acutely conscious of their responsibility to attend to their own individual needs and interests. At least as important as the moral obligation to look after others, the new thinking suggested, was the moral obligation to look after oneself.

This ethical shift had a profound impact on ideas about the nature and purpose of the family. In the American tradition, the marketplace and the public square have represented the realms of life devoted to the pursuit of individual interest, choice, and freedom, while the family has been the realm defined by voluntary commitment, duty, and self-sacrifice. With the greater emphasis on individual satisfaction in family relationships, however, family well-being became subject to a new metric. More than in the past, satisfaction in this sphere came to be based on subjective judgments about the content and quality of individual happiness rather than on such objective measures as level of income, material nurture and support, or boosting children onto a higher rung on the socioeconomic ladder. People began to judge the strength and "health" of family bonds according to their capacity to promote individual fulfillment and personal growth. As a result, the conception of the family's role and place in the society began to change. The family began to lose its separate place and distinctive identity as the realm of duty, service, and sacrifice. Once the domain of the obligated self, the family was increasingly viewed as yet another domain for the expression of the unfettered self.

These broad changes figured centrally in creating a new conception of divorce which gained influential adherents and spread broadly and swiftly throughout the society— a conception that represented a radical departure from earlier notions. Once regarded mainly as a social, legal, and family event in which there were other stakeholders, divorce now became an event closely linked to the pursuit of individual satisfactions, opportunities, and growth.

The new conception of divorce drew upon some of the oldest, and most resonant, themes in the American political tradition. The nation, after all, was founded as the result of a political divorce, and revolutionary thinkers explicitly adduced a parallel between the dissolution of marital bonds and the dissolution of political bonds. In political as well as marital relationships, they argued, bonds of obligation were established voluntarily on the basis of mutual affection and regard. Once such bonds turned cold and oppressive, peoples, like individuals, had the right to dissolve them and to form more perfect unions.

In the new conception of divorce, this strain of eighteenth-century political thought mingled with a strain of twentieth-century psychotherapeutic thought. Divorce was not only an individual right but also a psychological resource. The dissolution of marriage offered the chance to make oneself over from the inside out, to refurbish and express the inner self, and to acquire certain valuable psychological assets and competencies, such as initiative, assertiveness, and a stronger and better self-image.

The conception of divorce as both an in- 10 dividual right and an inner experience merged with and reinforced the new ethic of obligation to the self. In family relationships, one had an obligation to be attentive to one's own feelings and to work toward improving the quality of one's inner life. This ethical imperative completed the rationale for a sense of individual entitlement to divorce. Increasingly, mainstream America saw the legal dissolution of marriage as a matter of individual choice, in which there were no other stakeholders or larger social interests. This conception of divorce strongly argued for removing the social, legal, and moral impediments to the free exercise of the individual right to divorce.

Traditionally, one major impediment to divorce was the presence of children in the family. According to well-established popular belief, dependent children had a stake in their parents' marriage and suffered hardship as a result of the dissolution of the marriage. Because children were vulnerable and dependent, parents had a moral obligation to place their children's interests in the marital partnership above their own individual satisfactions. This notion was swiftly abandoned after the 1960s. Influential voices in the society, including child-welfare professionals, claimed that the happiness of individual parents, rather than an intact marriage, was the key determinant of children's family well-being. If divorce could make one or both parents happier, then it was likely to improve the well-being of children as well.

In the following decades, the new conception of divorce spread through the law, therapy, etiquette, the social sciences, popular advice literature, and religion. Concerns that had dominated earlier thinking on divorce were now dismissed as old-fashioned and excessively moralistic. Divorce would not harm children but would lead to greater happiness for children and their single parents. It would not damage the institution of marriage but would make possible better marriages and happier individuals. Divorce would not damage the social fabric by diminishing children's life chances but would strengthen the social fabric by improving the quality of affective bonds between parents and children, whatever form the structural arrangements of their families might happen to take.

As the sense of divorce as an individual freedom and entitlement grew, the sense of concern about divorce as a social problem diminished. Earlier in the century, each time the divorce rate increased sharply, it had inspired widespread public concern and debate about the harmful impact of divorce on families and the society. But in the last third of the century, as the divorce rate rose to once unthinkable levels, public anxiety about it all but vanished. At the very moment when divorce had its most profound impact on the society, weakening the institution of marriage, revolutionizing the structure of families, and reorganizing parent-child relationships, it ceased to be a source of concern or debate.

The lack of attention to divorce became particularly striking after the 1980s, as a politically polarized debate over the state of the American family took shape. On one side, conservatives pointed to abortion, illegitimacy, and homosexuality as forces destroying the family. On the other, liberals cited domestic violence, economic insecurity, and inadequate public supports as the key problems afflicting the family. But politicians on both sides had almost nothing to say about divorce. Republicans did not want to alienate their upscale constituents or their libertarian wing, both of whom tended to favor easy divorce, nor did they want to call attention to the divorces among their own leadership. Democrats did not want to anger their large constituency among women who saw easy divorce as a hard-won freedom and prerogative, nor did they wish to seem unsympathetic to single mothers. Thus, except for bipartisan calls to get tougher with deadbeat dads, both Republicans and Democrats avoided the issue of divorce and its consequences as far too politically risky.

But the failure to address divorce carried 15 a price. It allowed the middle class to view family breakdown as a "them" problem rather than an "us" problem. Divorce was not like illegitimacy or welfare dependency, many claimed. It was a matter of individual choice, imposing few, if any, costs or consequences on others. Thus, mainstream America could cling to the comfortable illusion that the nation's family problems had to do with the behavior of unwed teenage mothers or poor women on welfare rather than with the instability of marriage and family life within its own ranks.

Nonetheless, after thirty years of persistently high levels of divorce, this illusion, though still politically attractive, is increasingly difficult to sustain in the face of a growing body of experience and evidence. To begin with, divorce has indeed hurt children. It has created economic insecurity and disadvantage for many children who would not otherwise be economically vulnerable. It has led to more fragile and unstable family households. It has caused a mass exodus of fathers from children's households and, all too often, from their lives. It has reduced the levels of parental time and money invested in children. In sum, it has changed the very nature of American childhood. Just as no patient would have designed today's system of health care, so no child would have chosen today's culture of divorce.

Divorce figures prominently in the altered economic fortunes of middle-class families. Although the economic crisis of the middle class is usually described as a problem caused by global economic changes, changing patterns in education and earnings, and ruthless corporate downsizing, it owes more to divorce than is commonly acknowledged. Indeed, recent data suggest that marriage may be a more important economic resource than a college degree. According to an analysis of 1994 income patterns, the median income of married-parent households whose heads have only a high school diploma is ten percent higher than the median income of college-educated single-parent households. Parents who are college graduates *and* married form the new economic elite among families with children. Consequently, those who are concerned about what the downsizing of corporations is doing to workers should also be concerned about what the downsizing of families through divorce is doing to parents and children.

Widespread divorce depletes social capital as well. Scholars tell us that strong and durable family and social bonds generate certain "goods" and services, including money, mutual assistance, information, caregiving, protection, and sponsorship. Because such bonds endure over time, they accumulate and form a pool of social capital which can be drawn down upon, when needed, over the entire course of a life. An elderly couple, married for fifty years, is likely to enjoy a substantial body of social and emotional capital, generated through their long-lasting marriage, which they can draw upon in caring for each other and for themselves as they age. Similarly, children who grow up in stable, two-parent married households are the beneficiaries of the social and emotional capital accumulated over time as a result of an enduring marriage bond. As many parents know, children continue to depend on these resources well into young adulthood. But as family bonds become increasingly fragile and vulnerable to disruption, they become less permanent and thus less capable of generating such forms of help, financial resources, and mutual support. In short, divorce consumes social capital and weakens the social fabric. At the very time that sweeping socioeconomic changes are mandating greater investment of social capital in children, widespread divorce is reducing the pool of social capital. As the new economic and social conditions raise the hurdles of child-rearing higher, divorce digs potholes in the tracks.

It should be stressed that this book is not intended as a brief against divorce as such. We must assume that divorce is necessary as a remedy for irretrievably broken marriages, especially those that are marred by severe abuse such as chronic infidelity, drug addiction, or physical violence. Nor is its argument directed against those who are divorced. It assumes that divorce is difficult, painful, and often unwanted by at least one spouse, and that divorcing couples require compassion and support from family, friends, and their religious communities. Nor should this book be taken as an appeal for a return to an earlier era of American family life. The media routinely portray the debate over the family as one between nostalgists and realists, between those who want to turn back the clock to the fifties and those who want to march bravely and resolutely forward into the new century. But this is a lazy and misguided approach, driven more by the easy availability of archival photos and footage from 1950s television sitcoms than by careful consideration of the substance of competing arguments.

More fundamentally, this approach [20] overlooks the key issue. And that issue is not how today's families might stack up against those of an earlier era; indeed, no reliable empirical data for such a comparison exist. In an age of diverse family structures, the heart of the matter is what kinds of contemporary family arrangements have the greatest capacity to promote children's well-being, and how we can ensure that more children have the advantages of growing up in such families.

In the past year or so, there has been growing recognition of the personal and social costs of three decades of widespread divorce. A public debate has finally emerged. Within this debate, there are two separate and overlapping discussions.

The first centers on a set of specific proposals that are intended to lessen the harmful impact of divorce on children: a federal system of child-support collection, tougher child-support enforcement, mandatory counseling for divorcing parents, and reform of no-fault divorce laws in the states. What is striking about this discussion is its narrow focus on public policy, particularly on changes in the system of no-fault divorce. In this, as in so many other crucial discussions involving social and moral questions, the most vocal and visible participants come from the world of government policy, electoral politics, and issue advocacy. The media, which are tongue-tied unless they can speak in the language of left-right politics, reinforce this situation. And the public is offered needlessly polarized arguments that hang on a flat yes-or-no response to this or that individual policy measure. All too often, this discussion of divorce poses what *Washington Post* columnist E. J. Dionne aptly describes as false choices.

Notably missing is a serious consideration of the broader moral assumptions and empirical claims that define our divorce culture. Divorce touches on classic questions in American public philosophy—on the nature of our most important human and social bonds, the duties and obligations imposed by bonds we voluntarily elect, the "just causes" for the dissolution of those bonds, and the differences between obligations volunteered and those that must be coerced. Without consideration of such questions, the effort to change behavior by changing a few public policies is likely to founder.

The second and complementary discussion does try to place divorce within a larger philosophical framework. Its proponents have looked at the decline in the well-being of the nation's children as the occasion to call for a collective sense of commitment by all Americans to all of America's children. They pose the challenging question: "What are Americans willing to do 'for the sake of *all* children'?" But while this is surely an important question, it addresses only half of the problem of declining commitment. The other half has to do with how we answer the question: "What are individual parents obliged to do 'for the sake of their own children'?"

Renewing a *social* ethic of commitment 25 to children is an urgent goal, but it cannot be detached from the goal of strengthening the *individual* ethic of commitment to children. The state of one affects the standing of the other. A society that protects the rights of parents to easy, unilateral divorce, and flatly rejects the idea that parents should strive to preserve a marriage "for the sake of the children," faces a problem when it comes to the question of public sacrifice "for the sake of the children." To put it plainly, many of the ideas we have come to believe and vigorously defend about adult prerogatives and freedoms in family life are undermining the foundations of altruism and support for children.

With each passing year, the culture of divorce becomes more deeply entrenched.

American children are routinely schooled in divorce. Mr. Rogers teaches toddlers about divorce. An entire children's literature is devoted to divorce. Family movies and videos for children feature divorced families. *Mrs. Doubtfire*, originally a children's book about divorce and then a hit movie, is aggressively marketed as a holiday video for kids. Of course, these books and movies are designed to help children deal with the social reality and psychological trauma of divorce. But they also carry an unmistakable message about the impermanence and unreliability of family bonds. Like romantic love, the children's storybooks say, family love comes and goes. Daddies disappear. Mommies find new boyfriends. Mommies' boyfriends leave. Grandparents go away. Even pets must be left behind.

More significantly, in a society where nearly half of all children are likely to experience parental divorce, family breakup becomes a defining event of American childhood itself. Many children today know nothing but divorce in their family lives. And although children from divorced families often say they want to avoid divorce if they marry, young adults whose parents divorced are more likely to get divorced themselves and to bear children outside of marriage than young adults from stable married-parent families.

Precisely because the culture of divorce has generational momentum, this book offers no easy optimism about the prospects for change. But neither does it counsel passive resignation or acceptance of the culture's relentless advance. What it does offer is a critique of the ideas behind current divorce trends. Its argument is directed against the ideas about divorce that have gained ascendancy, won our support, and lodged in our consciousness as "proven" and incontrovertible. It challenges the popular idea of divorce as an individual right and freedom to be exercised in the pursuit of individual goods and satisfactions, without due regard for other stakeholders in the marital partnership, especially children. This may be a fragile and inadequate response to a profoundly consequential set of changes, but it seeks the abandonment of ideas that have misled us and failed our children.

In a larger sense, this book is both an appreciation and a criticism of what is peculiarly American about divorce. Divorce has spread throughout advanced Western societies at roughly the same pace and over roughly the same period of time. Yet nowhere else has divorce been so deeply imbued with the larger themes of a nation's political traditions. Nowhere has divorce so fully reflected the spirit and susceptibilities of a people who share an extravagant faith in the power of the individual and in the power of positive thinking. Divorce in America is not unique, but what we have made of divorce is uniquely American. In exploring the cultural roots of divorce, therefore, we look at ourselves, at what is best and worst in our traditions, what is visionary and what is blind, and how the two are sometimes tragically commingled and confused.

A CLOSER LOOK AT
The Making of a Divorce Culture

1. What are the major points of difference between the way people usually think of divorce in America and the way Whitehead argues we should think about it? You might think about completing a sentence like this: "While most people today believe that divorce _____, in fact, according to Whitehead, we should understand American divorce _____." Go back to the text and find at least three phrases that accurately reflect Whitehead's position.

2. Using the terminology provided in Chapter 22, "Using Argumentative Strategies," show how Whitehead employs common argumentative strategies to make her case.

3. Drawing on your own knowledge about divorce in the United States, play the doubting and believing game with Whitehead's argument that divorce is primarily due to "an ethical shift" away from social and familial obligation to a focus on "individual fulfillment and personal growth." First, play the believing game: Come up with as many reasons and as much evidence that supports her claim as you can. Then play the doubting game: What evidence and reasons would make a person doubt the accuracy, relevance, or sufficiency of her claims?

IDEAS FOR
Writing

1. Write a concise summary of "The Making of a Divorce Culture." Use the strategies in Chapter 26, "Quoting, Paraphrasing, and Citing Sources," to guide your summary. Describe not only *what* the author says but *how* she argues her point.

2. Write a memoir or profile that draws on your direct personal experience with divorce. Even if it hasn't affected your immediate family, you probably have friends or extended family who have been affected. As Chapters 4 ("Memoirs") and 5 ("Pro-files") point out, people write memoirs or profiles because they want to make a point that can best be conveyed through narrative and description. While Whitehead's argument takes a bird's-eye-view of divorce, you should use this opportunity to take a close personal look at the issues to reinforce, question, or add other dimensions to Whitehead's argument. You may choose to quote or cite Whitehead.

A FEW IDEAS FOR
Composing a Position Paper

1. **Write a position paper on an important issue.** Try to give the topic a local slant by choosing an issue that concerns your campus or your community. It might be the community you physically work or live in, or it might be a virtual community of people who share the same interests. Even if you want to talk about a national or global issue, try to find the local angle. For instance, rather than just writing about global warming generally, approach that issue by discussing what is happening on your campus or within your community.

2. **Write a position paper responding to an article.** Find an article that states a position you strongly disagree with. Try to summarize the opposing article's position so objectively that even a person who holds that position would agree that you have treated it fairly. Then express your own opinion in a way that shows your views are more reasonable than your opponent's views.

3. **Create a multimedia position paper.** Your position paper should argue for a specific belief or course of action. Choose an incident from your own life that sets the stage or leads to a lesson about the issue you are arguing. Try to highlight details that allow you to explore both sides of the issue. Consider blending in features of other genres, such as memoirs, profiles, and proposals. Try experimenting with a variety of organizations that creatively use the flexibility of the medium you chose for this project.

Proposals

Diet for a Warm Planet

JULIA WHITTY

Julia Whitty is an award-winning author, journalist, and documentary filmmaker. In this proposal, Whitty identifies some surprising and highly controversial causes of global warming—Americans' wasteful diets and other matters that might be considered personal choice. As you read this, pay attention not only to what Whitty proposes but also to how she makes her argument for her proposal. For instance, for what purpose does she include the extended description of the migratory bird?

In 1985 I interviewed James Hansen at his NASA office in New York City about a problem called the greenhouse effect that few outside of science had heard of and fewer would take seriously for another 20 years. He was thoughtful and smart, only 44 years old, though he looked haggard from the battle behind him, as well as the battle he knew lay ahead—one man versus endless rounds of pundits, zealots, oilmen, politicians, journalists, scientists, naysayers, and fools.

The fight that would keep him on the ropes had begun in 1981, when Hansen proposed that the effects of global warming might show up in the real world, instead of just climate models, by 1990—not much later, as many in science were expecting. This early prophecy included uncanny predictions of droughts in North America, melting Antarctic ice sheets, and the opening of the Northwest Passage. More than two decades of bruising battles later, this past spring, Hansen delivered an urgent warning that we must trim atmospheric CO_2 concentrations from 385 parts per million to 350 ppm—right now.

Hansen's number presents a staggering challenge. It insists we dramatically reduce emissions at a time when we're still increasing them by 2 ppm per year, and when little or nothing is happening on the political front.

It demands the biggest collaborative effort in the history of our species.

So what can you and I do to set an example for the men who lead the world? How to jump from the Age of Exploitation to the Age of Sustainability and drag the corporate-military-agroindustrial machinery along with us? The path seems paradoxically disconnected—like the business plan of the *South Park* underpants gnomes: Step One, steal underpants . . . Step Three, get rich. 5

Step Two: Embark upon a fossil fuel diet. We need to tighten up, get fit, get agile, smart, and quick. We need to develop a boxer's stamina if we want to outlast the well-funded heavyweights who will fight us to the death before the referee Nature calls the fight.

In the world of birds, there's a long-distance traveler without equal, the 15-inch-long bar-tailed godwit. It's classified as a shorebird, one of those sandpiper species typically found along coastlines. Yet the bar-tailed godwit has a far more impressive curriculum vitae. It manages its hectic calendar and limited resources with a lithe professionalism that enables it to do what no other animal on earth can do—that is, to leave Alaskan shores and strike out over open water to fly nonstop for eight days and 7,200 miles without feeding or drinking before touching down in another hemisphere (New Zealand) during a different season (spring). Six months later, it repeats the feat in reverse, with a five-week feeding stop in China, for an annual round-trip of 16,500 miles. Each bird makes its first migration only three months after hatching, often in flocks composed solely of first-timers.

We don't know exactly how these pocket Herculeses manage such phenomenal labors. Their skill set includes some form of built-in GPS and a meteorological aptitude that enables them to forecast low-pressure fronts a thousand miles away, and then launch in time to intercept their 60 mph tailwinds days later.

We do know that in every stage of their lives these birds are masters of energy management. They breed on the Alaskan tundra, harvesting berries (including, initially, last year's withered remnants) and seasonal blooms of insects. When their chicks fledge, they move to the shore and overhaul their diet entirely, probing tidal mudflats along Alaskan river deltas, where they transmute marine worms and clams into godwit. Eating is their primary work during these endless summer days, and by the time they launch south they are clinically obese, literally wobbling when they walk, with as much as 55 percent of their 1.5-pound bodies weighing in as fat—the heaviest fat loads recorded in any birds to date.

Yet once airborne they're sleek and efficient fliers. Somehow, just prior to flight, they shrink their digestive organs, while increasing their heart and breast muscles. They follow intelligent pathways through the air, hopping into the slipstream of useful weather systems, slingshotting around counterproductive ones, often clocking along at speeds of 60 mph. They regulate their energy by optimizing altitude, frequenting the cold, dry air at 15,000 feet in order to minimize energy loss through heat and water loss through evaporative cooling. They probably sleep half of their brains at a time, like migrating mallards.

By the time they arrive on New Zealand's 10 tidal estuaries, they're down to half their starting weight, exhausted, bedraggled, and hungry—but just in time for the Southern Hemisphere's spring bounty. They've completed their epic flight without ingesting or combusting a drop of fuel.

They are what we need to be: small of footprint, capable of the long haul.

Our migration from the Profligate to the Sustainable Hemisphere requires us to trim atmospheric CO_2 concentrations from 385 to 350 ppm, which we can do by cutting emissions by the same 10 percent. Right? Not quite. Atmospheric CO_2 concentrations are rife with long-term feedbacks, both positive and negative, and our current saturation level reflects 250 years of anthropogenic emissions, not just last year's.

So how do we come up with a goal? I'm not a PhD in atmospheric sciences, and neither are you, probably, so this is more in the realm of the hypothetical diet, designed to make a qualitative difference while convincing the world's leaders that we're serious about forcing them to join us in the fight. The United States emits 13.1 trillion pounds of CO_2 a year, 22 percent of the total annual global emissions—about 43,000 pounds per American. But before we start deconstructing the merits of fluorescent lightbulbs, let's consider the bigger picture. Yes, China is catching up and by some estimates has already surpassed us. Yet the vast majority of the 385 ppm clogging the atmosphere was emitted by us.

Since America is responsible for 22 percent of annual emissions, I suggest we set a target of shrinking our personal carbon footprint by 22 percent, or 9,606 pounds. If Americans all did this, it would mean we'd take a disproportionate chunk out of that 385 ppm—which China and India would fairly argue that we should. Twenty-two is a hefty number with an alliterative ring to it and is indicative of serious intentions. If enough of us pull it off, 22 percent has the power to fuel a movement our leaders will follow.

So what would a 22 percent diet look like? 15 Step Two is all about losing weight. Seriously. Body fat. My personal flab is not just a private matter between me and my coronary arteries.

Nineteen percent of US energy usage—about as much as is used to fuel our cars—is spent growing and delivering food to the average American who consumes 2,200 pounds of food a year. That's a whopping 3,747 calories a day—or 1,200 to 1,700 more than needed for personal or planetary health. The skinny truth is that as much as 7.6 percent of total energy in the United States today is used to grow human fat, fat that translates to 3,300 pounds of carbon per person.

Sure, liposuction is an untapped fuel source—and New Zealander Pete Bethune extracted 3.38 ounces of his own fat to add to the biofuel powering his carbon-neutral boat, *Earthrace*. But a more sustainable strategy would be to avoid growing the fat in the first place. A comprehensive Cornell University study found that we could cut our food energy usage in half by simply eating less, cutting back on meat and junk food, and considering the source of our food.

For starters, half of our food energy use comes from producing and delivering meat and dairy. If we gave up just meat, we could maintain that hefty 3,747-calorie intake but consume 33 percent less in fossil fuels doing it. If Americans cut just one serving of meat a week, it would equal taking 5 million cars off the road.

One-third of those 3,747 daily calories comes from junk food—potato chips, soda, etc. We can save on fossil fuel costs in this area by installing more efficient lighting, heating, and cooling in the plants that make the stuff and by using less packaging materials. But we'd save a lot more if you and I simply bought less of it. A can of diet soda, for instance, delivers only 1 calorie of food energy at a cost of 2,100 calories to make the drink and the can. Transporting the components and the finished product costs even more, and shipping processed food and its packaging accounts for much of the problem of America's food averaging 1,500 travel miles before it's eaten.

Ideally, we'd eat our recommended 2,000 to 2,500 daily calories from food grown on smaller, traditional, and organic farms—particularly for dairy and meat, which are extremely energy intensive in their nonorganic forms. To make this work, though, we also need to buy locally, since organic can be grown halfway around the world, and that's hardly sustainable. True, local produce could find its way to your table via too many polluting pickup trucks, but buying locally from sustainable farms generally produces a smaller carbon footprint than factory farms with their fuel-heavy pesticides, chemical fertilizers, and travel miles.

But wait, you say, it's too expensive to [20] buy all that local, organic, boutique food. Well, demand drives the market toward affordability. Today nearly 5,000 farmers markets across the US provide fresh neighborhood food to cities, suburbs, and rural areas. The number is growing (up 18 percent between 2004 and 2006) and the farmers are profiting ($1 billion in sales in 2005). The Agriculture Department now provides farmers market vouchers to low-income mothers and seniors—though not yet enough. The next big step in trimming fossil fuel costs is community-sponsored agriculture (CSA), where paid subscriptions support a local small farmer, who supplies his subscribers with weekly deliveries of fresh, neighborhood food. There are now 2,000 CSAs nationwide. What begins as an elite market eventually becomes something common. But it only happens if you and I make it happen.

Our best friend in making it happen is higher fuel costs, which will eventually make some local food cheaper than distant food. Higher gas prices have already prompted Americans to cut back on driving over the last year by just under 5 percent. That's a bigger decline than during the gas crisis of the 1970s, and it was accomplished without too much pain.

To get to our goal we need more like a 25 percent decline in driving. That and one less 1,100-mile plane trip per person would save us each an estimated 2,365 pounds of carbon. Assuming we've saved 3,300 pounds of carbon by going on an actual diet, we've already gotten halfway to that 22 percent reduction in our carbon footprint without sweating. Closing the gap is easy. Even a middling hot water heater produces 3,000 lbs of carbon a year. So when the time comes to replace it, get an on-demand model that doesn't labor to keep 40 gallons of water hot round the clock. Until then, turn down the temperature to 120° F (carbon saved: 500 lbs). While you're at it, turn your thermostat down in winter and up in summer (2,000 lbs) and compensate with sweaters and solar shades or glazes. Hang your clothes to dry; you'll cut 1,440 pounds of carbon, plus gain a few meditative moments with your laundry. My personal favorite: Shop thrift stores. You get to be more of a recycler, less of a consumer, especially if you donate your stuff back when you're done with it. With almost every decision we make, there's a carbon way to look at it. So do an audit. And share your goals with others. Diets work when we support each other. Just as no bar-tailed godwit can make it to New Zealand and back again on its own, neither can we. The secret to Step Two is to learn to flock. Any one of us changing out our lightbulbs is helpful. Many of us acting together becomes a force.

Before their migration, bar-tailed godwits gather on their staging areas to feed, but also to coordinate the group's intentions, demonstrating what we call migratory restlessness—the massed, circling, erratic flights, the constant *kirRUC-kirRUC-kirRUC* calls. Our advantage over the birds is that our voices carry beyond our bodies, allowing us to talk effortlessly across miles and languages.

Except that we don't. On life-and-death matters of sustainability, too many of us remain isolated and silent. A George Mason University study found that while a majority of American health department directors believe their region will suffer serious public health problems from climate change within 20 years, few have made any plans to detect, prevent, or adapt to these health threats—

in part because they fear they don't *know enough* to speak. The authors conclude that Americans continue to erroneously view climate change as a threat only to species other than our own in part because health professionals remain silent.

When I blogged about this story, angry commenters, some identifying themselves as doctors, complained that health professionals could hardly be expected to solve global warming. That's not the point. Every one of us has a voice, and every one of us is an expert with our own authority to speak. Since when did we give our power away? A doctor can speak of the troubles in sight from increased heat stress, dehydration, migrating diseases. A mental health professional can speak of the post-traumatic stresses that shadow natural disasters. A computer programmer can speak authoritatively of the need to focus our technological skills on life-saving solutions. Parents can speak of the rights of their children to a functioning planet. Children can speak of their fear and anger at our silence. It's not about the right to speak, but the obligation.

But free speech is a free-for-all. How do we transition from clamor to consensus? Thomas Malone and Mark Klein of MIT suggest we already have the power to harness computer technology and create a "collective intelligence" to address systemic problems, like climate change, that overwhelm our individual intelligence. They propose a Web-mediated discussion and decision-making forum called the Climate Collaboratorium—"a kind of Wikipedia for controversial topics, a Sims game for the future of the planet, and an electronic democracy on steroids."

They suggest four intriguing—and increasingly sophisticated—means to move beyond argument to action: (1) Let online users vote on the issues and run daily simulations of the vote rankings; (2) let users vote within their areas of expertise (scientists within science), except in "values" choices where everyone has a vote, as in "How much economic sacrifice should we make now to reduce sea level rise for our great-grandchildren?"; (3) let users buy and sell predictions about uncertain future events, to be paid only if their predictions are correct; (4) create a "proxy democracy" whereby users could give their voting proxies to others—on scientific issues to the Union of Concerned Scientists, say, or on "values" issues to the Nature Conservancy. Within this cyberflock we might transform our most strident discussions into sound decisions and solid action.

The bar-tailed godwits massing on their staging grounds in Alaska swirl and bunch with elasticized precision. The collective brain of their bodies debates yes and no. On the day of departure, the deliberation rises to 1,500 feet to test the vote up there before descending to the mudflats again. When the decision is finalized, the flocks climb beyond sight, groups of 50 to 100 birds flying in echelons or V shapes, those masterpieces of aerodynamics and communications, each bird gaining lift from the upwash of wings ahead, each bird seeing unimpaired by what lies ahead, all listening to each other's calls.

"We have used up all slack in the schedule for actions needed to defuse the global warming time bomb," writes James Hansen, 20 years after telling Congress that climate change was already, certainly, under way. We're on the mudflats, the tide is rising, the sun is falling, the season is changing, we need to assess those weather systems a thousand miles away. Not one of us can escape the long trip. We still have time—just enough—Hansen says, to tighten up, get fit, get agile, smart, and quick, before the flock is scattered in catastrophic winds that not even the heavyweights will survive.

A CLOSER LOOK AT
Diet for a Warm Planet

1. What is the precise problem Whitty identifies? The larger problem is climate change, but she is addressing a subproblem that is one of many causes of climate change. What is it?

2. What is your initial reaction to her plan to solve the problem she has identified? What do you personally think of it? How do you think Americans generally would react to it? Is her plan realistic?

3. Why has Whitty included a profile of the amazing migratory bird, the bar-tailed godwit? What relevant concept does the bird represent for her? What point is she trying to make with this profile? Try to get into the author's mind and explain why she included this element in her proposal.

IDEAS FOR
Writing

1. Write a brief profile of a nonhuman living thing that illustrates some point you want to make. It might be a remarkable species you know about (like Whitty's godwit). It could also be a specific animal or place that represents something that is relevant for human beings and how they live their lives.

2. Write a rhetorical analysis of Whitty's proposal. Explain how she uses *logos*—appeals to common sense, reason, and values—to win over her readers. Explain also how she uses *pathos*—appeals to emotions such as fear, guilt, hope, etc.—to persuade. In the end, be sure to make an overall assessment about whether her proposal is persuasive or not.

Who Pays for My Time Off? The Costs and Consequences of Government-Mandated Leave

CARRIE L. LUKAS

Carrie L. Lukas is a widely published conservative political writer who has appeared on many television and radio shows, writes for a variety of publications, and has written a book, The Politically Incorrect Guide to Women, Sex, and Feminism. *She also serves as vice president for policy and economics of the Independent Women's Forum. As you read this proposal, pay attention to the way that Lukas carefully frames the issues and identifies problems in the proposals of various (liberal) politicians. Notice also the point at which Lukas first introduces her own plan for solving the problems she identifies.*

Introduction

Balancing the demands of work and family life can be a challenge for any worker. Events such as severe illness or the birth of a child can make working outside the home impossible. People overwhelmingly sympathize with those facing these challenging situations and want society to support such individuals during difficult times.

In recent decades, however, the question has turned not to how civil society can support individuals in times of need, but to how the federal government can dictate how employers must accommodate employees facing these situations. Existing laws require that large employers allow qualified employees to take unpaid leave when facing such circumstances. Some policymakers want to expand these regulations so that they apply to smaller employers and to mandate the availability of additional benefits, such as paid leave.

This paper examines the Family and Medical Leave Act, which mandates that businesses provide unpaid leave to their workers, and considers some of the problems associated with its application. It will also consider the potential consequences of expanding these regulations.

This paper highlights how private entities are voluntarily providing leave benefits and considers ways that policymakers can further encourage businesses and individuals to take actions that will make it easier for individuals in need of leave, without costly government mandates.

The background of the Family and Medical Leave Act

President Clinton signed the Family and Med- [5] ical Leave Act (FMLA) into law on February 5, 1993, hailing its passage as a victory for families in need: "Today, I am pleased to sign into law H.R. 1, the 'Family and Medical Leave Act of 1993.' I believe that this legislation is a response to a compelling need—the need of the American family for flexibility in the workplace. American workers will no longer have to choose between the job they need and the family they love."[1]

Under this law, employees who meet eligibility requirements are allowed to take up to twelve weeks of unpaid leave during a twelve-month period for reasons related to personal illness, family illness, or the birth or adoption of a child. Employers are required to maintain provided health benefits while employees exercise their right to leave and to allow employees to return to their original job or a comparable position free of any retaliation or loss of job stature.

For employees to be eligible to take this leave, they have to have worked for an eligible employer for a minimum of twelve months and for at least 1,250 hours in the twelve months prior to taking FMLA leave. FMLA applies to private sector employers of fifty or more employees, as well as public agencies and entities.[2]

The law specifies the circumstances in which employees become eligible to take leave under FMLA: for the birth of a child of the employee and to care for the newborn; the adoption (or fostering) of a child and to care for the newly placed child; to care for a spouse, parent, son or daughter under age eighteen with a serious health condition; or, for the employee's own serious health condition. Employees are allowed to choose to use accrued paid leave (vacation, personal, or family leave) for FMLA leave. Employers may also require that employees use these voluntary leave programs for FMLA leave.

If employees feel that their employer has failed to live up to the FMLA requirement, employees can file a complaint with the Department of Labor (DOL) or file a private lawsuit. The DOL was the agency responsible for promulgating the regulations to implement the law.

According to the DOI, 76.1 million work- [10] ers (or 54 percent of the total 141.7 million workers) were eligible for FMLA leave and 6.1 million workers took FMLA protected leave in 2005.[3]

Problems with the existing FMLA regulations

Those who believe in a limited federal government criticize FMLA as an improper use of federal power. In its essence, FMLA restricts the employment terms that can be offered and accepted by adults. This constitutes a loss of liberty for individuals.

However, putting aside the issue of whether regulations like FMLA are a proper use of government power, there are other problems associated with FMLA's specific terms and enforcement that create challenges for employers and should concern policymakers.

DOL has collected feedback from those affected by FMLA, including employers, administrators, and employees. Employers' complaints have generally focused on a few specific aspects of the law and, more specifically, of the regulations. DOL notes that employers generally "recognize the value of the FMLA and attempt to comply with its requirements." DOL has not received complaints related to "leave for the birth or adoption of a child" or "the use of scheduled intermittent leave as contemplated by the statute, such as when an employee requests leave for medical appointments or medical treatments like chemotherapy." However, employers report "job disruptions" and "adverse effects on the workforce" resulting "when employees take frequent, unscheduled, intermittent leave from work with little or no advance notice to the employer."[4]

In surveys conducted by the Society for Human Resource Management (SHRM), half of the human-resource professionals responded that they had had to approve leave that they believe was unjustified. One-third also responded that they had received complaints from their employees about co-workers' abuse of FMLA.[5] Two-thirds of respondents said that because of FMLA they had to keep employees who would have been fired because of poor attendance.[6]

While the majority of employers said that [15] FMLA did not have a noticeable effect on their establishment's overall performance, in terms of productivity, profitability, and growth, of those employers that thought it did have an effect, two to three times as many thought the effect on their business's performance had been negative.[7]

Most complaints from employers center on the following issues:

Definition of "Serious Health Condition"
Many employers indicate that there is confusion about what constitutes a "serious health condition" under FMLA. And, indeed, DOL's own definition of "serious health condition" has changed while the law has been in effect.[8]

The first regulations promulgated by DOL specified that unless there are complications, many common conditions (such as the common cold, influenza, earaches, upset stomach, minor ulcers, headaches, and so forth) are not considered "serious health conditions" that trigger FMLA protection. However, DOL later revised its position expressing that if such conditions lasted for three days then they meet the threshold of "serious health condition" under FMLA.[9]

Employers can request employees provide documentation from a doctor or a medical professional supporting their claim of having a serious medical condition. Accord-

ing to DOL, employers, healthcare representative, and employees complain that this can be a burdensome process.[10]

Timing of Leave Employees exercising FMLA leave are allowed to take leave intermittently. According to regulations promulgated during the Clinton administration, employers are required to account for leave in the shortest increment used in their payroll system for leave and must account for time taken by the hour or less. When possible, employees are supposed to work with employers to schedule their leave in order to minimize disruptions in the workplace.[11]

An estimated twenty percent of FMLA leave was taken intermittently in 1999–2000, according to DOL.[12] Employers complain about the burden and difficulty of keeping track of these short periods of leave.[13]

In addition to creating an administrative burden for employers, co-workers also often take on additional responsibilities when FMLA leave is exercised. Surveys suggest that overwhelmingly the FMLA leave-takers' workplace responsibilities are shifted to co-workers.

Leave Notification While employees are supposed to provide employers with advanced warning of the need for FMLA leave whenever possible, under the law, employees can report unanticipated leave "as soon as practicable," DOL has interpreted "as soon as practicable" to mean within one to two business days of the incidence of the leave. In other words, employees may take a day off for an FMLA purpose, but not explain this absence to their employer for up to two days after not appearing at work.[14]

According to human-resource professionals responding to the SHRM's survey, less than half of those who used FMLA leave scheduled leave in advance.[15] For employers, the potential problems associated with this provision are clear: it makes it very difficult to plan for unscheduled absence, enforce attendance, and properly account for leave.

Clarifying Existing Regulations—A First Step to Improving FMLA

DOL could ease the burden on employers who administer FMLA by further clarifying employers' responsibilities related to these provisions. For example, DOL could provide additional guidance to clarify the situations in which ailments reach the threshold of constituting a "serious health condition," and ideally this clarification would be returning the law's application more toward Congress's original intent.

DOL could also consider tightening notification requirements or specifying in what instances it is acceptable to inform an employer of FMLA leave *after* the leave has occurred (such as during a health emergency requiring hospital treatment) and when an employee must make an employer aware of leave during the incidence of leave (such as when an employee can easily contact the employer by phone).

Calls for expanded government-mandated leave

Increasingly, policymakers are calling for expanding government mandates for employer-provided leave. For example, in this Congress, Senator Teddy Kennedy (D-MA) and Representative Rosa DeLauro (D-CT) introduced, "The Healthy Families Act," which would require that all employers with fifteen or more employees provide full-time workers with seven days of paid leave for their own illness or a family member's illness and part-time workers (who work at least 20 hours per week or 1000 hours annually) pro-rated paid leave. Senator Christopher Dodd (D-CT) has called for creating at least six weeks of paid leave and expanding FMLA to apply to employers with fewer workers.[16] These proposals would entail significant costs for businesses.

The Costs and Potential Consequences of Mandated Paid Leave

Providing employees with paid leave creates costs for business. During the employees' absence, businesses must replace those workers or shift their responsibilities to other employees, resulting in lost productivity. While proponents of expansion would likely highlight that most businesses report that FMLA has had a negligible effect to their bottom line, including productivity, there is reason to assume that a paid leave program would have a greater effect on business.

Workers are more likely to utilize a paid leave benefit than an unpaid leave benefit since the loss of income in the unpaid leave program provides a deterrent to taking leave. So in addition to employers who had not previously provided paid leave facing the additional cost of having to pay absent employees because of this mandate, they would also likely find an increase in the number of absences and greater disruption in the workplace.

The increase in mandated benefits raises the costs associated with hiring an employee. In recent years, benefits have constituted a growing portion of employees' total compensation. As of 2006, more than 30 percent of the average worker's total compensation was paid as benefits.[17] That means employees see less of their compensation in their paychecks. A new mandate increasing benefits will likely mean that workers' take-home pay will be lower than it would have been otherwise, as a greater share of total compensation becomes dedicated to providing these benefits.

If the cost of hiring a worker increases, businesses will have an incentive to hire fewer workers or to outsource jobs to countries where businesses do not have to provide costly benefits. This could mean a loss of job opportunities in the United States, particularly for employees whose job responsibilities can be fulfilled from alternative locations.

The Impact on Small Businesses

The problems experienced by larger employers implementing FMLA would be magnified for smaller companies if they become subject to the law. While an employer of fifty or more employees may be able to shift work from the FMLA-leave taker to co-workers without meaningfully affecting productivity, an organization with just 15 employees would have a more difficult time picking up the slack left by an absent worker, particularly when such a significant portion of leave taken under FMLA is unscheduled.

Small businesses often are more finan- 25
cially vulnerable and will be less able to assume the additional costs of administering and paying for these benefits. Small businesses have been an engine of job growth in recent years, but that could be slowed by imposing costly new mandates.

Solving the problem of the need for paid leave without government mandates

Government mandates are not the only way to address the need for individuals to be able to take and sustain themselves during periods when they cannot work.

Most Employers Voluntarily Provide Leave Packages

Many employers already provide leave packages that are in excess of government requirements. According to DOL, in 2006, 82 percent of the 105 million American workers in the private sector had access to some sort of paid leave, whether it is sick leave, vacation, or personal leave.[18] Not surprisingly, full-time workers were much more likely to have access specifically to paid sick leave than part-time workers (nearly 70 percent of full-time workers had paid sick leave, compared with 20 percent of part-time workers.[19] A DOL survey found that roughly two-thirds of those who took FMLA leave received some compensation, primarily through the employers' paid sick leave plan. Seventy percent of those leave-takers who received compensa-

tion received their entire paychecks while they were on leave.

Unfortunately, regulations like FMLA can deter companies from providing or expanding paid leave programs. As the SHRM executive director testified before the Oregon state legislature:

> Companies which have voluntarily provided paid leave prior to the enactment of the FMLA have had dramatic increases in absenteeism rates and have had more problems with workers providing little or no notice for unscheduled and unplanned intermittent leave pursuant to ongoing or chronic conditions, some of which are questionable under conflicting legal interpretations. . . . Unfortunately, FMLA misapplications have penalized employers with the most generous leave policies and had a chilling effect on the expansion of paid leave.[20]

Addressing the problems with FMLA's application and enforcement may encourage more companies to voluntarily provide paid leave.

Greater Workplace Flexibility

A growing number of employees also enjoy 30
more flexible work schedules and work arrangements. For example, telecommuting was rare a decade ago, but today more than four million Americans telecommute most days and an estimated twenty million telecommute at least once a month.[21] Women are more likely than men to telecommute—2.2 million women worked from home in 2000.[22] Telecommuting provides employees with many advantages, including greater flexibility to care for personal and family needs during the day.

Many workers also have flexible worker schedules, according to the Bureau of Labor Statistics. As of May 2004, 27 million full-time wage and salary workers—or 27.5 percent of all full-time wage and salary workers—worked in arrangements that allowed them to vary their work start and end times.[23] These flexible arrangements make it easier for workers to schedule and make time for important personal duties, such as taking care of personal and family healthcare needs, and other parenting duties, such as participating in educational meetings.

The voluntary move toward greater flexibility signals an important shift in businesses' expectations for their workers: a growing number of businesses are evaluating employees based on output and productivity instead of work hours. It demonstrates that many businesses recognize that flexibility can be a win-win for employers and employees.

Encouraging Private Saving to Provide for Family Leave

While many businesses are providing leave voluntarily, a significant portion of the workforce continues to work in jobs that do not provide provisions for leave. Proponents of expanded government mandates point to these individuals as justification for government action.

Ideally, however, the government shouldn't be involved in encouraging companies or individuals to prepare for periods when individuals are unable to work. All individuals know that they face the potential for problems: severe illnesses can strike employees or their family members, and the birth of a child or the introduction of a new member into the family requires time away from work. Responsible individuals should plan for such circumstances, accruing savings while working so that they can sustain themselves if and when they cannot work for pay. The federal government is not supposed to be our national caretaker.

The federal government should, however, not act as an impediment to responsible actions such as private saving. Unfortunately, the government today does just that

by continuing to place onerous taxes on income generated by private savings. When an individual uses after-tax dollars to purchase a new television, they to not have to then pay a tax every time they watch a program. But when an individual puts money in a savings account or buys a stock, the federal government does tax the income it generates. The double taxation of savings and investment encourages consumption and discourages saving, leaving individuals less prepared to make ends meet during a time of crisis. Policymakers should eliminate the double taxation of savings as a first step to encouraging greater individual responsibility and to help individuals provide for themselves in times of need.

While the federal government creates impediments to many forms of savings, it has embraced measures to encourage individuals to save for specific foreseeable needs and expenses. For example, the federal government has created tax-advantaged savings accounts for retirement, educational expenses, and healthcare costs. Similar efforts could be made to encourage individuals to save to provide for periods of leave. For example, individuals could be allowed to put $5000 per year into a "Paid Leave" savings account tax-free that could then be accessed when an individual takes unpaid, or partially paid, leave. Regulations could require that those funds can only be accessed without tax penalty in specific situations, such as to address a serious illness or for the birth or adoption of a child. Unused funds could then be accessed without a tax penalty once the individual reaches retirement age.

In addition to providing tax incentives to encourage individuals to contribute to "Paid Leave" savings accounts, the federal government could provide additional incentives for businesses to match employees' contributions. The downside of such a policy is that businesses would have an incentive to divert other forms of non-tax advantaged compensation into contributions to "Paid Leave" savings accounts. Employees would likely have less take-home pay as a result. However, such a policy would be preferable to a government mandate on business to provide paid leave directly.

Conclusion

There are situations when individuals need time off from their jobs. While it is tempting to address this legitimate need through government action, there are significant costs to doing so. In the years that FMLA has been in force, many businesses have struggled to make sense of the regulations and have had to bear increased financial and administrative burdens to comply with this law. DOL could help ease the burden of existing regulations by providing some much needed clarity to some of the laws' provisions.

Today there are calls for an expansion of government mandates, including paid leave and expanding FMLA to apply to smaller businesses. These measures would have significant costs for businesses and could have the unintended consequence of making job opportunities scarcer.

There are other ways for policymakers to 40 help individuals sustain themselves during times of leave. First, the federal government ought to stop penalizing savings. Currently, the government discourages individuals from taking the responsible action of setting aside income that can be drawn upon during a period when they cannot work. In addition to ending destructive anti-savings tax policies, policymakers could explore programs that encourage savings specifically to provide for leave. Policymakers have already created tax-advantaged savings vehicles for retirement, health expenses, and education costs, so they could create a similar initiative to deal with situations that require leave.

The primary goals of any government action should be to encourage individuals to provide for themselves and to avoid creating costly mandates that will be a drag on the economy and reduce job opportunities for Americans.

Endnotes

1. President William J. Clinton, "Statement on Signing the Family and Medical Leave Act of 1993," February 5, 1993, available at http://www.presidency.ucsb.edu/ws/index.php?pid=46777.

2. Linda Levine, "The Family and Medical Leave Act: Recent Legislative and Regulatory Activity," Congressional Research Service Report for Congress, Order Code RL31760, January 19, 2007, 2.

3. U.S. Department of Labor Fact Sheet on "Leave Coverage and Usage for U.S. Workers," February 27, 2007, 3.

4. Federal Register, vol. 71, no. 231, December 1, 2006, 69506.

5. Paul Kersey, "Medical Leave Regulations Should Reflect Intent Behind FMLA," Heritage Foundation Web Memo no. 626, December 21, 2004, 1.

6. Linda Levine, "The Family and Medical Leave Act: Recent Legislative and Regulatory Activity," 8.

7. Linda Levine, "Explanation of and Experience Under the Family and Medical Leave Act," Congressional Research Service Report for Congress, Order Code RL30893, February 7, 2003, 14.

8. Federal Register, vol. 71, no. 231, December 1, 2006, 69505.

9. Ibid.

10. Federal Register, vol. 71, no. 231, December 1, 2006, 69507.

11. Linda Levine, "The Family and Medical Leave Act: Recent Legislative and Regulatory Activity," 3.

12. Linda Levine, "The Family and Medical Leave Act: Recent Legislative and Regulatory Activity," 9.

13. Linda Levine, "Explanation of and Experience Under the Family and Medical Leave Act," 13.

14. Linda Levine, "The Family and Medical Leave Act: Recent Legislative and Regulatory Activity," 3.

15. Linda Levine, "The Family and Medical Leave Act: Recent Legislative and Regulatory Activity," 9.

16. Senator Christopher Dodd, "Families Need More Paid Leave," *New Hampshire Union Leader*, February 4, 2007, available at http://dodd.senate.gov/index .php?q=node/3727. Senator Christopher Dodd (D-CT) Press Release, "Dodd Introduces Bill to Expand Historic Family and Medical Leave Act," February 5, 2003, available at http://www.senate.gov /~dodd/press/Releases/03/0205.htm.

17. James Sherk, "Shared Prosperity: Debunking Pessimistic Claims About Wages, Profits, and Wealth," Heritage Foundation Backgrounder no. 1978, October 16, 2006, Chart 5.

18. U.S. Department of Labor Fact Sheet on "Leave Coverage and Usage for U.S. Workers," February 27, 2007, 2.

19. *Ibid.*

20. "Specific Recommendations for State Policymakers on Paid Leave Proposals," Excerpts from testimony presented to the Oregon Legislature (Paid Family Leave Task Force, Oregon State Capitol, October 3, 2002), compiled by Deanna R. Gelak, Senior Professional in Human Resources, Executive Director, National FMLA Technical Corrections Coalition, 2.

21. U.S. Census Bureau, available at http:// www.census.gov/population/cen2000 /phc-t35/tab01-1.xls.

22. U.S. Census Bureau, "Census 2000 PHC-T-35. Working at Home: 2000," Table 1-4, available at http://www.census.gov /population/cen2000/phc-t35/tab01-4 .xls.

23. Bureau of Labor Statistics Press Release, "Workers on Flexible and Shift Schedules in 2004 Summary," July 1, 2005, available at http://www.bls.gov/news.release/flex .nr0.htm.

A CLOSER LOOK AT
Who Pays for My Time Off?

1. Reread Lukas's proposal, noting the places where she identifies problems and the places where she proposes solutions. (Mark a small "P" for problems and "S" for solutions.) Are these problems and solutions stated clearly and prominently to help the reader understand what is at stake and make a fair judgment?

2. A good proposal identifies a problem and describes it in a way that helps the reader understand why that problem is important and worth caring about. In addition, a good proposal often analyzes that problem by identifying its causes. According to Lukas, what has caused the problems she addresses? How does her solution address those causes?

3. When a writer establishes an *ethos* of fairness in any communication that aims to persuade, readers will be more open to the writer's ideas and may find them more persuasive. How does Lukas succeed or fail in projecting such an *ethos*? Point to a few specific places in her proposal where you feel she presents the issues fairly or unfairly. Readers also perceive writers to be fair when they have done their research and have documented it. How does Lukas use her sources (the 23 endnotes) to project an *ethos* of fairness?

IDEAS FOR
Writing

1. Lukas explores the costs and benefits (mostly costs) of what happens when the federal government strives to become, as she puts it, "our national caretaker." Write either a brief memoir or profile that addresses this issue. Describe a real incident involving the government that happened to you or to another person or to a group of coworkers or acquaintances. You should provide some insight into the concept of government as "caretaker." You can either include or not include an explicit claim about the meaning of your story for this question.

2. Imagine that "Who Pays for My Time Off?" has just appeared in your local newspaper or on your favorite political commentary Web site. Write a letter to the editor that supports or refutes Lukas's argument. State your claim clearly and support it with concrete evidence.

A Modest Proposal

JONATHAN SWIFT

Jonathan Swift (1667–1745) was an Irish clergyman who was among the most skilled satirists ever to write in any language. Like most satires, A Modest Proposal *appears on the surface to approve of something ludicrous in order to attack a real social problem. As you read this selection, keep in mind that it was published anonymously in 1729 and that readers would have been expecting to read a serious and straightforward proposal for addressing the intolerable conditions and treatment of the Irish poor, not a satire.*

For preventing the children of poor people in Ireland, from being a burden on their parents or country, and for making them beneficial to the publick.

It is a melancholy object to those, who walk through this great town, or travel in the country, when they see the streets, the roads and cabbin-doors crowded with beggars of the female sex, followed by three, four, or six children, all in rags, and importuning every passenger for an alms. These mothers instead of being able to work for their honest livelihood, are forced to employ all their time in stroling to beg sustenance for their helpless infants who, as they grow up, either turn thieves for want of work, or leave their dear native country, to fight for the Pretender in Spain, or sell themselves to the Barbadoes.

I think it is agreed by all parties, that this prodigious number of children in the arms, or on the backs, or at the heels of their mothers, and frequently of their fathers, is in the present deplorable state of the kingdom, a very great additional grievance; and therefore whoever could find out a fair, cheap and easy method of making these children sound and useful members of the common-wealth, would deserve so well of the publick, as to have his statue set up for a preserver of the nation.

But my intention is very far from being confined to provide only for the children of professed beggars: it is of a much greater extent, and shall take in the whole number of infants at a certain age, who are born of parents in effect as little able to support them, as those who demand our charity in the streets.

As to my own part, having turned my thoughts for many years, upon this important subject, and maturely weighed the several schemes of our projectors, I have always found them grossly mistaken in their computation. It is true, a child just dropt from its dam, may be supported by her milk, for a solar year, with little other nourishment: at most not above the value of two shillings, which the mother may certainly get, or the value in scraps, by her lawful occupation of begging; and it is exactly at one year old that I propose to provide for them in such a manner, as, instead of being a charge upon their parents, or the parish, or wanting food and raiment for the rest of their lives, they shall, on the contrary, contribute to the feeding, and partly to the cloathing of many thousands.

There is likewise another great advan- 5 tage in my scheme, that it will prevent those voluntary abortions, and that horrid practice of women murdering their bastard children, alas! too frequent among us, sacrificing the poor innocent babes, I doubt, more to avoid the expence than the shame, which would move tears and pity in the most savage and inhuman breast.

The number of souls in this kingdom being usually reckoned one million and a half, of these I calculate there may be about two hundred thousand couple whose wives are breeders; from which number I subtract thirty thousand couple, who are able to maintain their own children, (although I apprehend there cannot be so many, under the present distresses of the kingdom) but this being granted, there will remain an hundred and seventy thousand breeders. I again subtract fifty thousand, for those women who miscarry, or whose children die by accident or disease within the year. There only remain an hundred and twenty thousand children of poor parents annually born. The question therefore is, How this number shall be reared, and provided for? which, as I have already said, under the present situation of affairs, is utterly impossible by all the methods hitherto proposed. For we can neither employ them in handicraft or agriculture; we neither build houses, (I mean in the country) nor cultivate land: they can very seldom pick up a livelihood by stealing till they arrive at six years old; except where they are of towardly parts, although I confess they learn the rudiments much earlier; during which time they can however be properly looked upon only as probationers: As I have been informed by a principal gentleman in the county of Cavan, who protested to me, that he never knew above one or two instances under the age of six, even in a part of the kingdom so renowned for the quickest proficiency in that art.

I am assured by our merchants, that a boy or a girl before twelve years old, is no saleable commodity, and even when they come to this age, they will not yield above three pounds, or three pounds and half a crown at most, on the exchange; which cannot turn to account either to the parents or kingdom, the charge of nutriments and rags having been at least four times that value.

I shall now therefore humbly propose my own thoughts, which I hope will not be liable to the least objection.

I have been assured by a very knowing American of my acquaintance in London, that a young healthy child well nursed, is, at a year old, a most delicious nourishing and wholesome food, whether stewed, roasted, baked, or boiled; and I make no doubt that it will equally serve in a fricasie, or a ragoust.

I do therefore humbly offer it to publick 10 consideration, that of the hundred and twenty thousand children, already computed, twenty thousand may be reserved for breed, whereof only one fourth part to be males; which is more than we allow to sheep, black cattle, or swine, and my reason is, that these children are seldom the fruits of marriage, a circumstance not much regarded by our savages, therefore, one male will be sufficient to serve four females. That the remaining hundred thousand may, at a year old, be offered in sale to the persons of quality and fortune, through the kingdom, always advising the mother to let them suck plentifully in the last month, so as to render them plump, and fat for a good table. A child will make two dishes at an entertainment for friends, and when the family dines alone, the fore or hind quarter will make a reasonable dish, and seasoned with a little pepper or salt, will be very good boiled on the fourth day, especially in winter.

I have reckoned upon a medium, that a child just born will weigh 12 pounds, and in a solar year, if tolerably nursed, encreaseth to 28 pounds.

I grant this food will be somewhat dear, and therefore very proper for landlords, who, as they have already devoured most of the parents, seem to have the best title to the children.

Infant's flesh will be in season throughout the year, but more plentiful in March, and a little before and after; for we are told by a grave author, an eminent French physician, that fish being a prolifick dyet, there are more children born in Roman Catholick countries about nine months after Lent, the markets will be more glutted than usual, because the number of Popish infants, is at least three to one in this kingdom, and therefore it will have one other collateral advantage, by lessening the number of Papists among us.

I have already computed the charge of nursing a beggar's child (in which list I reckon all cottagers, labourers, and four-fifths of the farmers) to be about two shillings per annum, rags included; and I believe no gentleman would repine to give ten shillings for the carcass of a good fat child, which, as I have said, will make four dishes of excellent nutritive meat, when he hath only some particular friend, or his own family to dine with him. Thus the squire will learn to be a good landlord, and grow popular among his tenants, the mother will have eight shillings neat profit, and be fit for work till she produces another child.

Those who are more thrifty (as I must 15 confess the times require) may flea the carcass; the skin of which, artificially dressed, will make admirable gloves for ladies, and summer boots for fine gentlemen.

As to our City of Dublin, shambles may be appointed for this purpose, in the most convenient parts of it, and butchers we may be assured will not be wanting; although I rather recommend buying the children alive, and dressing them hot from the knife, as we do roasting pigs.

A very worthy person, a true lover of his country, and whose virtues I highly esteem, was lately pleased, in discoursing on this matter, to offer a refinement upon my scheme. He said that many gentlemen of this kingdom, having of late destroyed their deer, he conceived that the want of venison might be well supply'd by the bodies of young lads and maidens, not exceeding fourteen years of age, nor under twelve; so great a number of both sexes in every country being now ready to starve for want of work and service: And these to be disposed of by their parents if alive, or otherwise by their nearest relations. But with due deference to so excellent a friend, and so deserving a patriot, I cannot be altogether in his sentiments; for as to the males, my American acquaintance assured me from frequent experience, that their flesh was generally tough and lean, like that of our school-boys, by continual exercise, and their taste disagreeable, and to fatten them would not answer the charge. Then as to the females, it would, I think, with humble submission, be a loss to the publick, because they soon would become breeders themselves: And besides, it is not improbable that some scrupulous people might be apt to censure such a practice, (although indeed very unjustly) as a little bordering upon cruelty, which, I confess, hath always been with me the strongest objection against any project, how well soever intended.

But in order to justify my friend, he confessed that this expedient was put into his head by the famous Salmanaazor, a native of the island Formosa, who came from thence to London, above twenty years ago, and in conversation told my friend, that in his country, when any young person happened to be put to death, the executioner sold the carcass to persons of quality, as a prime dainty; and that, in his time, the body of a plump girl of fifteen, who was crucified for an attempt to poison the Emperor, was sold to his imperial majesty's prime minister of state, and other great mandarins of the court in joints from the gibbet, at four hundred crowns. Neither indeed can I deny, that if the same use were made of several plump young girls in this town, who without one single groat to their fortunes, cannot stir abroad without a chair, and appear at a play-house and assemblies in foreign fineries which they never will pay for; the kingdom would not be the worse.

Some persons of a desponding spirit are in great concern about that vast number of poor people, who are aged, diseased, or maimed; and I have been desired to employ my thoughts what course may be taken, to ease the nation of so grievous an incumbrance. But I am not in the least pain upon that matter, because it is very well known, that they are every day dying, and rotting, by cold and famine, and filth, and vermin, as fast as can be reasonably expected. And as to the young labourers, they are now in almost as hopeful a condition. They cannot get work, and consequently pine away from want of nourishment, to a degree, that if at any time they are accidentally hired to common la-

bour, they have not strength to perform it, and thus the country and themselves are happily delivered from the evils to come.

I have too long digressed, and therefore 20 shall return to my subject. I think the advantages by the proposal which I have made are obvious and many, as well as of the highest importance.

For first, as I have already observed, it would greatly lessen the number of Papists, with whom we are yearly over-run, being the principal breeders of the nation, as well as our most dangerous enemies, and who stay at home on purpose with a design to deliver the kingdom to the Pretender, hoping to take their advantage by the absence of so many good Protestants, who have chosen rather to leave their country, than stay at home and pay tithes against their conscience to an episcopal curate.

Secondly, The poorer tenants will have something valuable of their own, which by law may be made liable to a distress, and help to pay their landlord's rent, their corn and cattle being already seized, and money a thing unknown.

Thirdly, Whereas the maintainance of an hundred thousand children, from two years old, and upwards, cannot be computed at less than ten shillings a piece per annum, the nation's stock will be thereby encreased fifty thousand pounds per annum, besides the profit of a new dish, introduced to the tables of all gentlemen of fortune in the kingdom, who have any refinement in taste. And the money will circulate among ourselves, the goods being entirely of our own growth and manufacture.

Fourthly, The constant breeders, besides the gain of eight shillings sterling per annum by the sale of their children, will be rid of the charge of maintaining them after the first year.

Fifthly, This food would likewise bring 25 great custom to taverns, where the vintners will certainly be so prudent as to procure the best receipts for dressing it to perfection; and consequently have their houses frequented by all the fine gentlemen, who justly value themselves upon their knowledge in good eating; and a skilful cook, who understands how to oblige his guests, will contrive to make it as expensive as they please.

Sixthly, This would be a great inducement to marriage, which all wise nations have either encouraged by rewards, or enforced by laws and penalties. It would encrease the care and tenderness of mothers towards their children, when they were sure of a settlement for life to the poor babes, provided in some sort by the publick, to their annual profit instead of expence. We should soon see an honest emulation among the married women, which of them could bring the fattest child to the market. Men would become as fond of their wives, during the time of their pregnancy, as they are now of their mares in foal, their cows in calf, or sow when they are ready to farrow; nor offer to beat or kick them (as is too frequent a practice) for fear of a miscarriage.

Many other advantages might be enumerated. For instance, the addition of some thousand carcasses in our exportation of barrel'd beef: the propagation of swine's flesh, and improvement in the art of making good bacon, so much wanted among us by the great destruction of pigs, too frequent at our tables; which are no way comparable in taste or magnificence to a well grown, fat yearly child, which roasted whole will make a considerable figure at a Lord Mayor's feast, or any other publick entertainment. But this, and many others, I omit, being studious of brevity.

Supposing that one thousand families in this city, would be constant customers for infants' flesh, besides others who might have it at merry meetings, particularly at weddings and christenings, I compute that Dublin would take off annually about twenty thousand carcasses; and the rest of the kingdom (where probably they will be sold somewhat cheaper) the remaining eighty thousand.

I can think of no one objection that will possibly be raised against this proposal, unless it should be urged that the number of people will be thereby much lessened in the kingdom. This I freely own, and 'twas indeed one principal design in offering it to the world. I desire the reader will observe, that I calculate my remedy for this one individual Kingdom of Ireland, and for no other that ever was, is, or, I think, ever can be upon Earth. Therefore let no man talk to me of other expedients: Of taxing our absentees at five shillings a pound; Of using neither cloaths, nor houshold furniture, except what is of our own growth and manufacture; Of utterly rejecting the materials and instruments that promote foreign luxury; Of curing the expensiveness of pride, vanity, idleness, and gaming in our women; Of introducing a vein of parsimony, prudence, and temperance; Of learning to love our country, wherein we differ even from Laplanders, and the inhabitants of Topinamboo; Of quitting our animosities and factions, nor acting any longer like the Jews, who were murdering one another at the very moment their city was taken; Of being a little cautious not to sell our country and consciences for nothing; Of teaching landlords to have at least one degree of mercy towards their tenants. Lastly, of putting a spirit of honesty, industry, and skill into our shop-keepers, who, if a resolution could now be taken to buy only our native goods, would immediately unite to cheat and exact upon us in the price, the measure, and the goodness, nor could ever yet be brought to make one fair proposal of just dealing, though often and earnestly invited to it.

Therefore I repeat, let no man talk to me 30 of these and the like expedients, 'till he hath at least some glympse of hope, that there will ever be some hearty and sincere attempt to put them into practice.

But, as to my self, having been wearied out for many years with offering vain, idle, visionary thoughts, and at length utterly despairing of success, I fortunately fell upon this proposal, which, as it is wholly new, so it hath something solid and real, of no expence and little trouble, full in our own power, and whereby we can incur no danger in disobliging England. For this kind of commodity will not bear exportation, and flesh being of too tender a consistence, to admit a long continuance in salt, although perhaps I could name a country, which would be glad to eat up our whole nation without it.

After all, I am not so violently bent upon my own opinion, as to reject any offer, proposed by wise men, which shall be found equally innocent, cheap, easy, and effectual. But before something of that kind shall be advanced in contradiction to my scheme, and offering a better, I desire the author or authors will be pleased maturely to consider two points. First, As things now stand, how they will be able to find food and raiment for a hundred thousand useless mouths and backs. And secondly, There being a round million of creatures in humane figure throughout this kingdom, whose whole subsistence put into a common stock would leave them in debt two million of pounds sterling; adding those who are beggars by profession to the bulk of farmers, cottagers and labourers, with their wives and children, who are beggars in effect; I desire those politicians who dislike my overture, and may perhaps be so bold to attempt an answer, that they will first ask the parents of these mortals, whether they would not at this day think it a great happiness to have been sold for food at a year old, in the manner I prescribe, and thereby have avoided such a perpetual scene of misfortunes, as they have since gone through, by the oppression of landlords, the impossibility of paying rent without money or trade, the want of common sustenance, with neither house nor cloaths to cover them from the inclemencies of the weather, and the most inevitable prospect of intailing the like, or greater miseries, upon their breed for ever.

I profess, in the sincerity of my heart, that I have not the least personal interest in endeavouring to promote this necessary work, having no other motive than the publick good of my country, by advancing our trade, providing for infants, relieving the poor, and giving some pleasure to the rich. I have no children, by which I can propose to get a single penny; the youngest being nine years old, and my wife past child-bearing.

A CLOSER LOOK AT
A Modest Proposal

1. How closely does Swift adhere to the main features and structure of a proposal? Point to specific passages where the author describes and analyzes the problem, explains the specific plan for solving the problem, and lists the benefits and costs of the plan. What other features of a modern proposal does this satire use?

2. *A Modest Proposal* uses irony to make its argument. In other words, Swift says one thing but means something entirely different. First, summarize what the narrator literally proposes. Then state what you believe Swift really meant for his readers to understand. Finally, describe some of the subtle strategies (such as style, evidence, structure, *ethos, pathos, logos*) Swift uses to make this supposed proposal feel real.

3. As discussed in Chapter 12, writers use proposals to convince readers that a specific plan will solve an important problem. If this is the case, then is *A Modest Proposal* really a proposal? Or is it a piece of writing that uses readers' expectations about proposals to achieve some other purpose? In terms of its purpose, what genre (or microgenre) does it most align with: a commentary, position paper, rant, or some other genre? How does Swift's playing with the genre of the proposal help him (or hurt him) in terms of achieving his intended purpose?

1. Imitating Swift's *A Modest Proposal*, write a mock proposal that on the surface makes a ludicrous proposition but actually criticizes or attacks some injustice or some policy you feel strongly about. Like Swift, you should fashion your mock proposal so that it closely resembles the proposal genre. Include a reflective memo to your professor that describes your true intentions and purpose. This memo should also describe the proposal strategies that you used to play with this genre.

2. Write a rhetorical analysis of Jonathan Swift's *A Modest Proposal*. Be sure to define Swift's rhetorical purpose. Is he trying to persuade, and if so, to what beliefs or position? Or is he merely trying to entertain? Or is it some combination? Also, describe the rhetorical strategies that are used. Focus on just one or two rhetorical strategies, such as *ethos, pathos, logos,* or style. Finally, evaluate the work: How effectively does it engage its readers and achieve its rhetorical purpose?

Thoughts in the Presence of Fear

WENDELL BERRY

Wendell Berry is a well-known writer on agricultural issues, rural economies, and social justice. He has long been concerned about the industrialization of agriculture, and he has warned about the damage that so-called "free markets" do to small towns in the United States and elsewhere. In this proposal, look for the places where he identifies the problem that needs to be solved. Then identify where he offers solutions to that problem.

I. The time will soon come when we will not be able to remember the horrors of September 11 without remembering also the unquestioning technological and economic optimism that ended on that day.

II. This optimism rested on the proposition that we were living in a "new world order" and a "new economy" that would "grow" on and on, bringing a prosperity of which every new increment would be "unprecedented."

III. The dominant politicians, corporate officers, and investors who believed this prop osition did not acknowledge that the prosperity was limited to a tiny percent of the world's people, and to an ever smaller number of people even in the United States; that it was founded upon the oppressive labor of poor people all over the world; and that its ecological costs increasingly threatened all life, including the lives of the supposedly prosperous.

IV. The "developed" nations had given to the "free market" the status of a god, and were sacrificing to it their farmers, farmlands, and communities, their forests, wetlands, and prairies, their ecosystems and watersheds. They had accepted universal pollution and global warming as normal costs of doing business.

V. There was, as a consequence, a growing worldwide effort on behalf of economic decentralization, economic justice, and ecological responsibility. We must recognize that the events of September 11 make this effort more necessary than ever. We citizens of the industrial countries must continue the labor of self-criticism and self-correction. We must recognize our mistakes.

VI. The paramount doctrine of the economic and technological euphoria of recent decades has been that everything depends on innovation. It was understood as desirable, and even necessary, that we should go on and on from one technological innovation to the next, which would cause the economy to "grow" and make everything better and better. This of course implied at every point a hatred of the past, of all things inherited and free. All things superseded in our progress of innovations, whatever their value might have been, were discounted as of no value at all.

VII. We did not anticipate anything like what has now happened. We did not foresee that all our sequence of innovations might be at once overridden by a greater one: the invention of a new kind of war that would turn our previous innovations against us, discovering and exploiting the debits and the dangers that we had ignored. We never considered the possibility that we might be trapped in the webwork of communication and transport that was supposed to make us free.

VIII. Nor did we foresee that the weaponry and the war science that we marketed and taught to the world would become available, not just to recognized national governments, which possess so uncannily the power to legitimate large-scale violence, but also to "rogue nations," dissident or fanatical groups and individuals—whose violence,

though never worse than that of nations, is judged by the nations to be illegitimate.

IX. We had accepted uncritically the belief that technology is only good; that it cannot serve evil as well as good; that it cannot serve our enemies as well as ourselves; that it cannot be used to destroy what is good, including our homelands and our lives.

X. We had accepted too the corollary belief that an economy (either as a money economy or as a life-support system) that is global in extent, technologically complex, and centralized is invulnerable to terrorism, sabotage, or war, and that it is protectable by "national defense."

XI. We now have a clear, inescapable choice that we must make. We can continue to promote a global economic system of unlimited "free trade" among corporations, held together by long and highly vulnerable lines of communication and supply, but now recognizing that such a system will have to be protected by a hugely expensive police force that will be worldwide, whether maintained by one nation or several or all, and that such a police force will be effective precisely to the extent that it oversways the freedom and privacy of the citizens of every nation.

XII. Or we can promote a decentralized world economy which would have the aim of assuring to every nation and region a local self-sufficiency in life-supporting goods. This would not eliminate international trade, but it would tend toward a trade in surpluses after local needs had been met.

XIII. One of the gravest dangers to us now, second only to further terrorist attacks against our people, is that we will attempt to go on as before with the corporate program of global "free trade," whatever the cost in freedom and civil rights, without self-questioning or self-criticism or public debate.

XIV. This is why the substitution of rhetoric for thought, always a temptation in a national crisis, must be resisted by officials and citizens alike. It is hard for ordinary citizens to know what is actually happening in Washington in a time of such great trouble; for all we know, serious and difficult thought may be taking place there. But the talk that we are hearing from politicians, bureaucrats, and commentators has so far tended to reduce the complex problems now facing us to issues of unity, security, normality, and retaliation.

XV. National self-righteousness, like personal self-righteousness, is a mistake. It is misleading. It is a sign of weakness. Any war that we may make now against terrorism will come as a new installment in a history of war in which we have fully participated. We are not innocent of making war against civilian populations. The modern doctrine of such warfare was set forth and enacted by General William Tecumseh Sherman, who held that a civilian population could be declared guilty and rightly subjected to military punishment. We have never repudiated that doctrine.

XVI. It is a mistake also—as events since September 11 have shown—to suppose that a government can promote and participate in a global economy and at the same time act exclusively in its own interest by abrogating its international treaties and standing apart from international cooperation on moral issues.

XVII. And surely, in our country, under our Constitution, it is a fundamental error to suppose that any crisis or emergency can justify any form of political oppression. Since September 11, far too many public voices have presumed to "speak for us" in saying that Americans will gladly accept a reduction of freedom in exchange for greater "security." Some would, maybe. But some others would accept a reduction in security (and in global trade) far more willingly than they would accept any abridgement of our Constitutional rights.

XVIII. In a time such as this, when we have been seriously and most cruelly hurt by those who hate us, and when we must consider ourselves to be gravely threatened by those same people, it is hard to speak of the ways of peace and to remember that Christ enjoined us to love our enemies, but this is no less necessary for being difficult.

XIX. Even now we dare not forget that since the attack of Pearl Harbor—to which the present attack has been often and not usefully compared—we humans have suffered an almost uninterrupted sequence of wars, none of which has brought peace or made us more peaceable.

XX. The aim and result of war necessarily is not peace but victory, and any victory won by violence necessarily justifies the violence that won it and leads to further violence. If we are serious about innovation, must we not conclude that we need something new to replace our perpetual "war to end war"?

XXI. What leads to peace is not violence but peaceableness, which is not passivity, but an alert, informed, practiced, and active state of being. We should recognize that while we have extravagantly subsidized the means of war, we have almost totally neglected the ways of peaceableness. We have, for example, several national military academies, but not one peace academy. We have ignored the teachings and the examples of Christ, Gandhi, Martin Luther King, and other peaceable leaders. And here we have an inescapable duty to notice also that war is profitable, whereas the means of peaceableness, being cheap or free, make no money.

XXII. The key to peaceableness is continuous practice. It is wrong to suppose that we can exploit and impoverish the poorer countries, while arming them and instructing them in the newest means of war, and then reasonably expect them to be peaceable.

XXIII. We must not again allow public emotion or the public media to caricature our enemies. If our enemies are now to be some nations of Islam, then we should undertake to know those enemies. Our schools should begin to teach the histories, cultures, arts, and language of the Islamic nations. And our leaders should have the humility and the wisdom to ask the reasons some of those people have for hating us.

XXIV. Starting with the economies of food and farming, we should promote at home, and encourage abroad, the ideal of local self-sufficiency. We should recognize that this is the surest, the safest, and the cheapest way for the world to live. We should not countenance the loss or destruction of any local capacity to produce necessary goods.

XXV. We should reconsider and renew and 25 extend our efforts to protect the natural foundations of the human economy: soil, water, and air. We should protect every intact ecosystem and watershed that we have left, and begin restoration of those that have been damaged.

XXVI. The complexity of our present trouble suggests as never before that we need to change our present concept of education. Education is not properly an industry, and its proper use is not to serve industries, either by job-training or by industry-subsidized research. Its proper use is to enable citizens to live lives that are economically, politically, socially, and culturally responsible. This cannot be done by gathering or "accessing" what we now call "information"—which is to say facts without context and therefore without priority. A proper education enables young people to put their lives in order, which means knowing what things are more important than other things; it means putting first things first.

XXVII. The first thing we must begin to teach our children (and learn ourselves) is that we cannot spend and consume endlessly. We have got to learn to save and conserve. We do need a "new economy," but one that is founded on thrift and care, on saving and conserving, not on excess and waste. An economy based on waste is inherently and hopelessly violent, and war is its inevitable by-product. We need a peaceable economy.

A CLOSER LOOK AT
Thoughts in the Presence of Fear

1. Find the place in this proposal where Berry identifies the problem that he believes must be solved. What are the causes of that problem and what are its effects?

2. Berry's plan lists five steps for solving the problem. What are these steps? Do they seem to be connected in some way? How can these steps work together to solve the problem he identifies in the first half of the proposal?

3. At the end of the proposal, Berry does not summarize any costs and benefits of following his plan. Looking closely at his plan, identify three costs of his plan and three benefits.

IDEAS FOR
Writing

1. September 11, 2001, was a horrific day. Write a memoir in which you describe that day and how you felt at the time. How did others around you react on that day? Did your life change? Did the way others felt about the world change? Use your memoir to show how the lives of Americans were changed briefly or permanently.

2. It has been about a decade since the events of September 11. Write a commentary in which you respond to Berry's argument. His title concedes that he was writing "in the presence of fear." Now that the shock has faded into history, has the United States reverted back to the former ways that Berry is criticizing? How do you feel about where this country is right now compared to where it was in 2001?

A FEW IDEAS FOR
Composing a Proposal

1. **Write a proposal to solve a hometown problem.** List five things that irritated you about the place where you grew up. Choose one. Then define the problem or irritation and figure out its causes and effects. Develop a plan for solving that problem and offer a step-by-step solution. Conclude your proposal by explaining why the costs of your plan are worth the benefits of solving the problem. Your proposal should be written for publication in a local newspaper where you grew up.

2. **Write a "modest proposal" of your own.** If you run an Internet search, you will find many proposals titled "A Modest Proposal." Most of them are modeled in some way on Jonathan Swift's "Modest Proposal," a satire in which he suggests an absurd solution to a real problem. Write your own modest proposal in which you suggest an absurd solution to a serious problem in your community.

3. **Create a podcast proposal for improving your life.** What are the causes and effects of the problem? What would you need to do to fix this aspect of your life? What would be some of the benefits if you followed your plan, and what would be the costs? Although you are the primary reader of this proposal, write it so that others will understand what you are trying to accomplish. Then turn your proposal into a podcast, so you can listen to it in the future.

Reports

Underage Alcohol Use Among Full-Time College Students

OFFICE OF APPLIED STUDIES, SUBSTANCE ABUSE AND MENTAL HEALTH SERVICES ADMINISTRATION

The National Survey on Drug Use and Health (NSDUH) issues new editions of this report every few years. Published by the Substance Abuse and Mental Health Services Administration (SAMHSA) at the Office of Applied Studies (OAS), this study discusses the problem of alcohol use and abuse among underage college students. Pay special attention to how a research question leads to methodology, which leads to results. Also, look at how the design of the report, including its use of color and graphics, makes it more accessible and attractive. The page layout draws the readers' attention to key information in the report while making the text more readable.

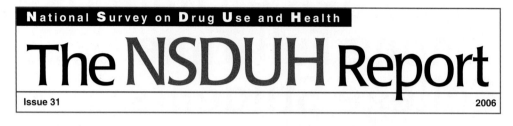

Issue 31   **2006**

Underage Alcohol Use among Full-Time College Students

In Brief

- The rates of past month, binge, and heavy alcohol use among full-time college students aged 18 to 20 remained steady from 2002 to 2005

- Based on 2002 to 2005 combined data, 57.8 percent of full-time college students aged 18 to 20 used alcohol in the past month, 40.1 percent engaged in binge alcohol use, and 16.6 percent engaged in heavy alcohol use

- Based on 2002 to 2005 combined data, male full-time students in this age group were more likely to have used alcohol in the past month, engaged in binge alcohol use, and engaged in heavy alcohol use than their female counterparts

During the past decade, increased attention has been directed toward underage alcohol use and binge drinking among college students and the negative consequences related to these behaviors.[1-5] Binge drinking refers to the "consumption of a sufficiently large amount of alcohol to place the drinker at increased risk of experiencing alcohol-related problems and to place others at increased risk of experiencing secondhand effects" (p. 287).[2]

The National Survey on Drug Use and Health (NSDUH) asks respondents aged 12 or older to report their frequency and quantity of alcohol use during the month before the survey. NSDUH defines binge alcohol use as drinking five or more drinks on the same occasion (i.e., at the same time or within a couple of hours of each other) on at least 1 day in the past 30 days. NSDUH defines heavy alcohol use as drinking five or more drinks on the same occasion on each of 5 or more days in the past 30 days. All heavy alcohol users are also binge alcohol users.

The NSDUH Report (formerly **The NHSDA Report**) is published periodically by the Office of Applied Studies, Substance Abuse and Mental Health Services Administration (SAMHSA). All material appearing in this report is in the public domain and may be reproduced or copied without permission from SAMHSA. Additional copies of this report or other reports from the Office of Applied Studies are available online: http://www.oas.samhsa.gov. Citation of the source is appreciated. For questions about this report, please e-mail: shortreports@samhsa.hhs.gov.

NSDUH REPORT: UNDERAGE ALCOHOL USE AMONG FULL-TIME COLLEGE STUDENTS   Issue 31, 2006

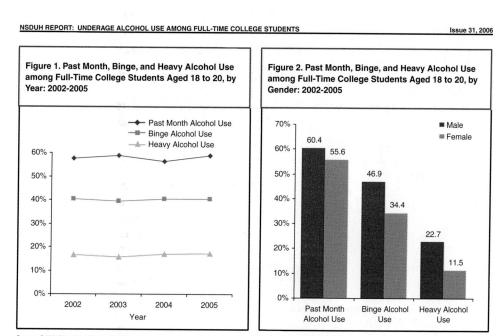

Figure 1. Past Month, Binge, and Heavy Alcohol Use among Full-Time College Students Aged 18 to 20, by Year: 2002-2005

Source: SAMHSA, 2002-2005 NSDUHs.

Figure 2. Past Month, Binge, and Heavy Alcohol Use among Full-Time College Students Aged 18 to 20, by Gender: 2002-2005

Source: SAMHSA, 2002-2005 NSDUHs.

NSDUH also asks young adults aged 18 to 22 about college attendance. For this analysis, respondents were classified as college students if they reported that they were in their first through fourth year (or higher) at a college or university and that they were a full-time student. Respondents who were on break from college were considered enrolled if they intended to return to college or university when the break ended.[6]

Data from the 2005 survey indicate that young adults aged 18 to 22 enrolled full time in college were more likely than their peers not enrolled full time (i.e., part-time college students and persons not currently enrolled in college) to use alcohol in the past month, binge drink, and drink heavily.[7]

This report examines trends and patterns in the rates of alcohol use among full-time college students who have not yet reached the legal drinking age (i.e., college students aged 18 to 20) based on data from the 2002, 2003, 2004, and 2005 NSDUHs.

Demographic Characteristics of Full-Time College Students Aged 18 to 20

From 2002 to 2005, an average of 5.2 million young adults aged 18 to 20 were enrolled full time in college each year. This represents 41.3 percent of young adults in this age range. Full-time college students included an average of 2.8 million women aged 18 to 20 (46.0 percent of women in this age group) and 2.4 million men aged 18 to 20 years (36.9 percent of men in this age group) each year. Over half of full-time college students aged 18 to 20 (58.2 percent) lived in the same household with a parent, grandparent, or parent-in-law, while 41.8 percent lived independently of a parental relative.[8]

Past Month Alcohol Use

From 2002 to 2005, the rates of past month alcohol use among full-time college students aged 18 to 20 remained steady (Figure 1), with an annual average of 57.8 percent (3.0 million

Issue 31, 2006   NSDUH REPORT: UNDERAGE ALCOHOL USE AMONG FULL-TIME COLLEGE STUDENTS

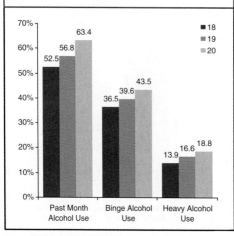

Figure 3. Past Month, Binge, and Heavy Alcohol Use among Full-Time College Students Aged 18 to 20, by Age: 2002-2005

Source: SAMHSA, 2002-2005 NSDUHs.

students) using alcohol in the past month. Male full-time students in this age group were more likely to have used alcohol in the past month than their female counterparts (60.4 vs. 55.6 percent) (Figure 2). Rates of past month alcohol use among this group increased with increasing age (Figure 3). Among full-time college students aged 18 to 20, those living with a parent, grandparent, or parent-in-law were less likely to have used alcohol in the past month than those who were not living with a parental relative (51.2 vs. 67.0 percent).

Binge Alcohol Use

Rates of past month binge alcohol use among full-time college students aged 18 to 20 also remained steady from 2002 to 2005 (Figure 1), with an annual average of 40.1 percent (2.1 million students) engaging in binge alcohol use. In this group of young adult students, males were more likely to have engaged in binge alcohol use than females (46.9 vs. 34.4 percent) (Figure 2).

Rates of binge alcohol use among this group also increased with increasing age (Figure 3). Full-time college students aged 18 to 20 living with a parent, grandparent, or parent-in-law were less likely to have engaged in binge alcohol use than full-time college students aged 18 to 20 who were not living with a parental relative (34.0 vs. 48.5 percent).

Heavy Alcohol Use

From 2002 to 2005, rates of heavy alcohol use among full-time college students aged 18 to 20 also remained steady (Figure 1), with an annual average of 16.6 percent (866,000 students) engaging in heavy drinking. As is true for past month and binge alcohol use, rates of heavy alcohol use were higher among males than females and increased with increasing age (Figures 2 and 3). Among full-time college students aged 18 to 20, those living with a parent, grandparent, or parent-in-law were less likely to have engaged in heavy alcohol use than those who were not living with a parental relative (12.3 vs. 22.5 percent).

End Notes

[1] Reifman, A., & Watson, W. K. (2003). Binge drinking during the first semester of college: Continuation and desistance from high school patterns. *Journal of American College Health, 52*, 73-81.

[2] Wechsler, H., & Nelson, T. F. (2001). Binge drinking and the American college student: What's five drinks? *Psychology of Addictive Behaviors, 15*, 287-291.

[3] Turrisi, R., Wiersma, K. A., & Hughes, K. K. (2000). Binge-drinking-related consequences in college students: Role of drinking beliefs and mother-teen communications. *Psychology of Addictive Behaviors, 14*, 342-355.

[4] Weingardt, K. R., Baer, J. S., Kivlahan, D. R., Roberts, L. J., Miller, E. T., & Marlatt, G. A. (1998). Episodic heavy drinking among college students: Methodological issues and longitudinal perspectives. *Psychology of Addictive Behaviors, 12*, 155-167.

[5] Wechsler, H., Davenport, A., Dowdall, G., Moeykens, B., & Castillo, S. (1994). Health and behavioral consequences of binge drinking in college: A national survey of students at 140 campuses. *Journal of the American Medical Association, 272*, 1672-1677.

[6] Respondents whose current college enrollment status was unknown were excluded from the analysis.

[7] Office of Applied Studies. (2006). *Results from the 2005 National Survey on Drug Use and Health: National findings* (DHHS Publication No. SMA 06-4194, NSDUH Series H-30). Rockville, MD: Substance Abuse and Mental Health Services Administration.

[8] Living with a parental relative is defined as currently living in the same household with a parent, grandparent, or parent-in-law. Respondents who did not live with a parental relative and had unknown information on one or more household relationships were excluded from this analysis.

A CLOSER LOOK AT
Underage Alcohol Use Among Full-Time College Students

1. Find the place where the authors of the report define "heavy alcohol use" and "binge alcohol users." How do these definitions shape their results?

2. Where do the authors describe their methodology? There is no section called "Methods," but the au-thors have described generally how they went about doing their study. What did they do?

3. Do the authors offer any recommendations about what to do about alcohol usage among college students? If so, locate those recommendations. If not, why didn't they offer any recommendations?

IDEAS FOR
Writing

1. Imagine that you are an administrator at your university who is concerned about alcohol abuse among students. In a proposal addressed to the university president, describe how the school should respond to alcohol abuse. Define the problem, its causes, and its effects. Then develop a plan that will take steps toward solving or containing the problem.

2. Do you think the government and university administrators worry too much or perhaps too little about alcohol use among college students? Write a position paper in which you argue that people are too concerned about alcohol abuse or not concerned enough. You can use the NSDUH report as support for some of your arguments. You will need to do more research to support your claims.

The Ideal Elf: Identity Exploration in World of Warcraft

KATHERINE BESSIÈRE, A. FLEMING SEAY, AND SARA KIESLER

Katherine Bessière, A. Fleming Seay, and Sara Kiesler are postdoctoral students at the Human Computer Interaction Institute at Carnegie Mellon University. In this scientific article, they describe their study in which they examined how players in online role-playing games use that forum not just to have some fun but also to explore "new aspects of themselves" and realize "virtual self-enhancement through their character." This research appeared in 2007 in the journal CyberPsychology & Behavior.

CyberPsychology & Behavior
Volume 10, Number 4, 2007
© Mary Ann Liebert, Inc.
DOI: 10.1089/cpb.2007.9994

The Ideal Elf: Identity Exploration in World of Warcraft

KATHERINE BESSIÈRE, M.A., A. FLEMING SEAY, Ph.D., and SARA KIESLER, Ph.D.

ABSTRACT

In this study, we examine the identity exploration possibilities presented by online multiplayer games in which players use graphics tools and character-creation software to construct an avatar, or character. We predicted World of Warcraft players would create their main character more similar to their ideal self than the players themselves were. Our results support this idea; a sample of players rated their character as having more favorable attributes that were more favorable than their own self-rated attributes. This trend was stronger among those with lower psychological well-being, who rated themselves comparatively lower than they rated their character. Our results suggest that the game world allows players the freedom to create successful virtual selves regardless of the constraints of their actual situation.

INTRODUCTION

THE MASSIVELY MULTIPLAYER online role-playing game (MMORPG) is a persistent, immersive online world in which people create and enact characters who pursue adventure, success in war, and other social and nonsocial goals. Like quilting and reality TV, MMORPGs are entertaining and provide an escape from everyday cares.[1,2] The games involve competition and collaborations that enhance gamers' enjoyment.[3] The games also offer players the opportunity for personal expression and competence building through the construction of their character and the character's achievement over time. In the current research, we focus on this last, potentially self-enhancing value of MMORPGs. We report survey results from a sample of players that suggest the players' characters express aspects of the players' ideal selves with implications for their sense of well-being.

Character and identity in MMORPGs

MMORPGs have several critical features that affect players' psychological experience, among which are the characters that players create as an embodied representation of themselves. As players gain experience in the game, their characters accumulate knowledge, skills, and resources, gaining instrumental value over time. Players also feel psychologically connected to their character, often keeping the same one for months or years. Characters also are the medium through which players experience social interaction in the game. MMORPGs are intensely competitive, often in (virtually) violent ways involving death and destruction, and characters cannot survive alone. Players rely on other players' characters for training, information, and resources, forming groups and intergroup collaborations. Players' reliance on others gives rise to robust communities in which players transact their relationships through their virtual characters not only in the game but also through instant messaging, Web forums, e-mail, and voice over IP networks.

Sherry Turkle[4] has argued that online environments offer people the option of creating multiple representations of themselves and exploring new aspects of themselves (see also Reid[5]). Previous research on online groups suggests that in some cases

Carnegie Mellon University, Pittsburgh, Pennsylvania.

the representations people make of themselves online are an amalgamation of their actual and ideal selves—that is, that the virtual self is a somewhat idealized actual self.[6,7] From these ideas, we argue that MMORPGs are a mode by which the player, through a constructed character, can enact aspects of his or her ideal self—the physical or psychological self the player wishes to be. For instance, a young player can create a character who is more mature, braver, stronger, or more outgoing than the player feels he himself is. This fantasy-creation process is supported by the fact that the player has an audience and collaborators who have no prior knowledge of the player or his real-life situation.

We propose that those who are dissatisfied with aspects of themselves are more likely than those who are content with the way they are to engage in virtual self-enhancement through their character. Some evidence suggests that those with a more marginalized self-identity seek affirmation in their use of the Internet,[7] and those scoring higher in depression are more likely to use the Internet for escape.[8] The chance to exist in a persistent online world where their character can interact with others freely and anonymously may give the former group a means to escape poor self-evaluation by eschewing negative traits and enacting a better virtual self.

Character creation in World of Warcraft

This study was conducted among players of a popular MMORPG titled World of Warcraft (WoW). In WoW, each player creates at least one character (most players have one primary character) that serves as the player's physical representative in the digital world. The character-creation process involves making decisions about the appearance, profession, and personality of the character. Once created, the character travels around the virtual world, gaining skills, experience, and riches and defeating monsters, discovering new locations, and interacting with other players' characters. Players are referred to by their character's name, and they interact with others as that character. This process and the anonymity offered by the game allows players, as their character, to escape real-world norms and expectations and to act out roles and try out personas that range from enhanced versions of their real-life self to alter-egos who behave in reprehensible ways. In these respects, WoW players' characters are virtual selves.

Hypotheses

We predicted, first, that WoW players would create characters who represent aspects of both them-

selves and their ideal selves. In other words, the difference between the attributes of a player's virtual (character) and ideal selves, henceforth called the *character discrepancy*, will be smaller than the difference between the attributes of a player's real and ideal selves, henceforth called the *self discrepancy*.

Hypothesis 1: Players will view their character as being more similar to their ideal self than they themselves are, thus making the character discrepancy smaller than the self discrepancy.

Based on previous research, we also argued that those with poorer psychological well-being and larger self discrepancies would be more likely to idealize their character.

Hypothesis 2: Those scoring less positively on measures of psychological well-being will create characters who are closer to their ideal self and less like their actual self than will those scoring more positively on measures of psychological well-being.

METHOD

We administered a survey via the Internet to a sample of players of WoW as part of a laboratory study of the game. E-mails soliciting participation in the online survey were sent to a listserv at a local university and to a local gaming group. Participants received no compensation for completing this survey.

Participants

Sixty-eight participants responded to the e-mail query for WoW players and subsequently completed the survey. From the answers to filtering questions about their play, we determined that 17 respondents were not WoW players. They were dropped from the sample, leaving 51 valid participants. The valid participants' ages ranged from 18 to 27 years old with a mean of 21 years. Participants were primarily male (43 men, 8 women).

Measures

The survey was conducted in the spring of 2005. Respondents were asked a battery of questions about WoW, their actual self, their character, and their ideal self. An adjective rating method, a version of the Big Five Personality Inventory, was used to assess the different self and character views.[9] The Big Five traits consist of 44 items in five categories: conscientiousness (e.g., thorough, reliable, organized; Cronbach's $\alpha = 0.88$), extraversion (e.g., talkative, energetic, assertive; Cronbach's $\alpha = 0.87$), neuroticism (depressed, worried, nervous; Cronbach's $\alpha = 0.85$), agreeableness (e.g., trusting, forgiving, kind; Cronbach's $\alpha = 0.69$), and openness to experience (e.g., creative, artistic, inventive; Cronbach's $\alpha = 0.82$). Participants rated how similar each personality characteristic was to their actual and ideal selves. They used the same rating scale to evaluate their primary WoW character. Each measure (actual self, ideal self, and character ratings) was separated by a battery of other questions on different pages to encourage independence of responses.

When the participants rated their actual self, the question was worded, "Please think of yourself and answer the following questions. 'I see myself as someone who _____.'" When they rated their ideal self, they were told, "Now think of yourself as you would like to be, ideally, and answer the following questions. 'Ideally, I would like to be someone who _____.'" When they rated their main WoW character, the question was worded, "Please think of your main character in World of Warcraft and answer the following questions. 'I see my main character in World of Warcraft as someone who _____.'" Participants rated themselves and their character on the 44 characteristics using seven-point Likert-type scales ranging from "disagree strongly'" to "agree strongly."

To measure psychological well-being, we used two measures. One measure was the 12-item Center for Epidemiologic Studies Depression Scale (CES-D).[10] Participants reported how frequently in the past week they had experienced symptoms of depression, including "I felt that everything I did was an effort," "My sleep was restless," and "I had trouble keeping my mind on what I was doing" (Cronbach's $\alpha = 0.60$). The second measure was a subset of items from the Positive Affect Negative Affect Scale (PANAS).[11] Eleven items indicate the participant's current confidence in his or her abilities and intelligence, or self-esteem (Cronbach's $\alpha = 0.85$). These two measures, depression and self-esteem, were not correlated with each other in any meaningful way ($r = 0.30$).

RESULTS

Our first prediction was that the character discrepancy would be smaller than the self discrepancy. We began this analysis by verifying that players created their character more like themselves than like other players' selves. We found the expected main effect showing that each participant's character was more similar to the participant's actual self than to a random other participant's actual self ($F [1, 36] = 5.3$, $p = 0.02$).

Next we turned to the question of whether a player's character was viewed as more ideal than the player's actual self. We tested this hypothesis using a paired t-test to examine whether the differences between the self discrepancy and the character discrepancy were significant. The hypothesis was supported for three of the five personality dimensions: conscientiousness (paired $t = 5$, $p < 0.001$), extraversion (paired $t = 3.2$, $p < 0.01$, and neuroticism (paired $t = 4.89$, $p < 0.0001$). These effects can be seen in Figure 1.

The hypothesis was not supported for the personality dimension of agreeableness. There was no difference between agreeableness ratings of the actual self and the virtual character (means: actual = 3.56, character = 3.60, ideal = 4.0). The hypothesis also was not supported for the dimension openness to experience, a measure of artistic talent, creativity, and reflection. Instead, the character rating for openness to experience was lower than ratings of either the actual or the ideal self, and the character discrepancy was significantly larger than the self discrepancy (paired $t = 3.8$, $p < 0.001$). Although unexpected, this result makes sense. Characters in WoW typically do not enact a creative role; they act at the behest of the player. These results suggest that participants did not simply rate their characters positively across all personality dimensions but did so selectively for the Big Five characteristics most relevant to the virtual world.

Our second hypothesis was that those with poorer psychological well-being would be more likely to see their character as realizing aspects of their ideal self. If so, there should be an interaction between players' psychological well-being and their discrepancy scores. To test this hypothesis, we conducted mixed-model analyses of variance on the personality dimensions. The target of the rating (actual self, ideal self, character) is the within-subjects variable, and level of well-being (depression or self-esteem) is a continuous between-subjects variable.

Using depression scores to group participants, the hypothesis was supported for three of the Big Five personality dimensions. When participants rated their own or their character's conscientiousness, there was a main effect (such that their character ratings fell between their actual and ideal self ratings; $F [2, 89] = 50$, $p < 0.001$), a main effect of level of depression (such that ratings of conscientiousness by those high in depression were lower;

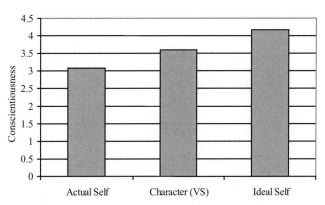

FIG. 1. Big Five personality ratings of participants' actual self, ideal self, and character. Figure shows ratings of conscientiousness; other trait ratings are similar; see text.

$F [1, 46] = 9.3$, $p < 0.01$), and also a significant interaction such that those with higher depression showed a significantly larger disparity between their self discrepancy and character discrepancy ($F [2, 92] = 5.3$, $p < 0.01$). Similarly, the main effects and interaction were significant for neuroticism (main effect of rating target, $F [2, 92] = 57$, $p < 0.001$; main effect of depression, $F [2, 46] = 12$, $p < 0.01$; interaction $F [2, 92] = 8.7$, $p < 0.001$) and for agreeableness (main effect of rating target, $F [2, 89] = 24$, $p < 0.001$; main effect of depression, $F [2, 47] = 2.8$, $p < 0.10$; interaction $F [2, 89] = 4.7$, $p = 0.01$). The first of these interaction effects is illustrated in Figure 2a, using the depression scores split at the median into high and low depression groups and showing effects on ratings of actual, ideal, and character conscientiousness. The figure uses line graphs so that the slopes for both groups can be seen easily.

a. Participants divided into groups scoring above and below the median of depression.
b. Participants divided into groups scoring above and below the median of self-esteem.

From Figure 2a, it can be seen that the reason for the significant interaction effect derives from two phenomena. First, those with lower depression scores do not rate their character as more ideal than they rate their actual self. Only those with higher depression scores do so. Second, both groups rate their character as equally close to their ideal self. Thus, there is no evidence that the characters of those with high depression scores have different traits from the characters of those with low depres-

sion scores. Nor is there any evidence that their ideal selves differ. Instead, it seems that those with high depression scores, as compared with low depression scores, (a) have much lower actual-self views and (b) create characters who are equally close to their ideal. Those with high depression scores thus create characters who are equivalent to the actual-self scores of those who have lower depression scores.

We found a similar pattern using self-esteem as the moderator variable. Hypothesis 2 was confirmed with significant interaction effects for four of the Big Five personality dimensions: conscientiousness ($F [2, 89] = 4.7$, $p = 0.01$), neuroticism ($F [2, 89] = 3.6$, $p < 0.05$), agreeableness ($F [2, 86] = 4.9$, $p = 0.001$), and openness to experience ($F [2, 89] = 2.9$, $p = 0.05$). Figure 2b shows the pattern, using conscientiousness as an example. As when depression is the moderator variable, the reason for the interaction is that those with low self-esteem scores had much lower actual-self ratings but rated their character as close to their ideal as did those with high self-esteem.

DISCUSSION

Our data suggest that MMORPG virtual worlds offer players the opportunity to create idealized characters as virtual, alternative selves. On average, participants rated their virtual character as being more conscientious, extraverted, and less neurotic than they themselves were. Furthermore, these trends were more prominent among those who

534   BESSIÈRE ET AL.

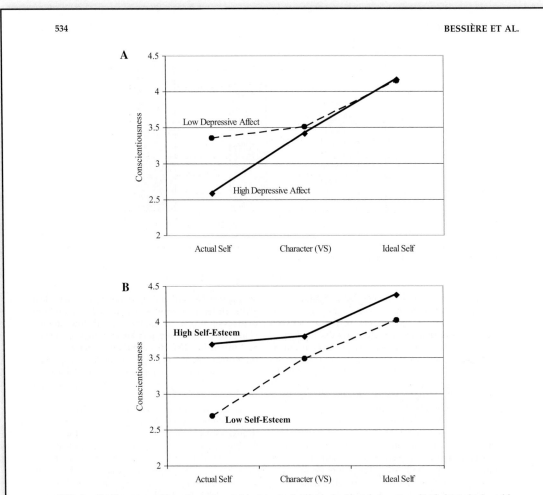

FIG. 2. Big Five personality ratings of participants' actual self, ideal self, and character, divided into high and low well-being participant groups. Figures show ratings of conscientiousness. Other trait ratings are similar; see text.

were more depressed or had lower self-esteem. Those with higher levels of well-being did not rate their character much better than they rated themselves, whereas those with lower levels of well-being rated themselves significantly lower than they rated their character. We believe these results support the idea that despite the many rules, constraints, and difficulties of the game world, its anonymity and fantasy frees players from the yoke of their real-life history and social situation, allowing them to be more like the person they wish they were.

Our survey was limited to players of WoW, and the sample consisted mainly of male college and grad-uate students. Whereas evidence of idealized selves in other domains is consistent with our findings,[12] more research is needed to expand the scope of this study. There also remains much to learn about the process of choosing a character and imbuing it with personality. For instance, do players choose roles for their characters that reflect their own personality (for instance, clerics rather than warriors if they themselves are mild mannered)? Do characters become more idealized over time? It is possible that the process is gradual as players gain the technical and social skills for success in the virtual world.

The ability to create characters who embody aspects of players' ideal selves may have implications for players' psychological well-being. Self-discrepancy theory[13] suggests that psychological well-being is closely related to a person's actual self (me as I am) versus his or her ideal self (me as I would like to be). People with larger actual–ideal self discrepancies have higher depression and lower self-esteem.[13,14] McKenna and Bargh[7,12] have proposed that enacting an ideal self online may reduce some people's actual–ideal self discrepancy and increase their feelings of self-confidence and self-worth. In therapy, visual imagery techniques can help drug addicts create ideal self-representations, which in turn help them reject the addictive selves.[15] In like manner, it seems possible that players whose characters display desirable qualities could imagine themselves as different and reduce their ideal–actual self discrepancies, with positive consequences for their psychological health. This process might depend on many factors, such as the extent to which players actually tried to emulate their characters' better traits.

REFERENCES

1. Seay, A.F., Jerome, W.J., Lee, K.S., & Kraut, R.E. (2004). Project Massive: a study of online gaming communities–. In Proceedings of the 2004 Conference on Human Factors in Computing Systems. New York: ACM Press, pp. 1421–1424.

2. Williams, D. (2004). *Trouble in River City: the social life of video games.* Unpublished doctoral dissertation. Ann Arbor, University of Michigan.

3. Ducheneaut, N., & Moore, R.J. (2004). Social side of gaming: a study of interaction patterns in a massively multiplayer online game. Proceedings of the 2004 ACM Conference on Computer Supported Cooperative Work (CSCW04). New York: ACM Press.

4. Turkle, S. (1997). Multiple subjectivity and virtual community at the end of the Freudian century. *Sociological Inquiry* 67:72–84.

5. Reid, E. (1998). The self and the Internet: variations on the illusion of one self. In: Gackenbach, J. (ed.) *Psychology and the Internet.* San Diego: Academic Press, pp. 29–42.

6. Lawson, K. (2000). Beyond corporeality: the virtual self in postmodern times. *Journal of Psychological Practice* 6:35–43.

7. McKenna, K.Y.A., & Bargh, J. (2000). Plan 9 from cyberspace: the implications of the Internet for personality and social psychology. *Personality and Social Psychology Review* 4:57–75.

8. Bessière, K., Kiesler, S., Kraut, R., & Boneva, B. (2007). *Effects of Internet use and social resources on changes in depression.* Unpublished manuscript. Carnegie Mellon University, Pittsburgh.

9. John, O., Donahue, E., & Kentle, R. (1991). *The Big Five Inventory,* v. 4a & 54. Berkeley: University of California, Berkeley Institute of Personality and Social Research.

10. Radloff, L.S. (1991). The use of the center for epidemiologic studies depression scale in adolescents and young adults. *Journal of Youth and Adolescence* 20:149–166.

11. Watson, D., Clark, L.A., & Tellegen, A. (1988). Development and validation of brief measures of positive and negative affect: the PANAS scales. *Journal of Personality and Social Psychology* 54:1063–1070.

12. McKenna, K.Y.A., & Bargh, J. (1998). Coming out in the age of the Internet: identity "demarginalization" through virtual group participation. *Journal of Personality and Social Psychology* 75:681–694.

13. Higgins, E.T. (1987). Self-discrepancy: a theory relating self and affect. *Psychological Review* 94:319–340.

14. Moretti, M.M., & Higgins, E.T. (1990). Relating self-discrepancy to self-esteem: the contribution of discrepancy beyond actual-self ratings. *Journal of Experimental Social Psychology* 26:108–123.

15. Avants, S.K., Margolin, A., & Singer, J.L. (1994). Self-reevaluation therapy: a cognitive intervention for the chemically dependent patient. *Psychology of Addictive Behaviors* 8:214–222.

A CLOSER LOOK AT
The Ideal Elf

1. This report chooses a subject that might not seem to be serious in nature, but treats it with the utmost seriousness. Do the authors succeed in convincing you that it is important to examine how people interact through the Internet? How does the report pose the research question it examines and argue that it is an important question worth studying?

2. The first part of the title, "The Ideal Elf," is a play on words, while the other part, "Identity Exploration in World of Warcraft," is more straightforward and descriptive of the subject. How does the title function to both attract potential readers' interest and help them understand what the report will be about and what it will do? On what key concept does the phrase "the ideal elf" play?

3. The abstract is just 121 words long, and the entire report is more than 3,400 words in length. Does the abstract do what it is supposed to do? What material from the report is included in the abstract and what is left out?

4. Readers don't usually read reports as they do novels. Instead, they "raid" them for information they're looking for, skipping and skimming for key points. How do the authors use the familiar structure of the research report to help readers navigate? For instance, can you spot the hypothesis? How do the authors help readers find what they might be looking for? Do they put information in places where readers would expect to find it?

5. Examine the authors' use of language—their style. Choose one or two passages and argue that they do or do not succeed in using a plain style to convey their ideas.

IDEAS FOR
Writing

1. Write a response to this research report that uses your own experience with the Internet to either reinforce or counter its findings. Explain how your personal experience leads you to consider additional questions or problems that this report does not adequately address. In other words, explain why your personal experience would indicate that the authors' findings are correct, accurate, and complete or are somehow incorrect, missing the point, or failing to touch on some aspect of Internet use that is crucial to understand.

2. Write a rhetorical analysis of this report in which you compare it to the report genre. Pay separate attention to its content, organization, style, and design. Do you think it is an effective report? What are its strengths? What can be done to improve it?

Alone Together

JENNIFER SENIOR

Jennifer Senior uses a variety of empirical studies to argue that being alone is not as lonely or desperate as people think. Although this report, which appeared in New York *magazine in 2008, is not a classic empirical report, it does employ many conventions of the genre. As you read, pay attention to how Senior stretches the genre to fit her readers' needs and the magazine in which the report was published.*

Until I was 37 years old, I lived alone. It never struck me as particularly odd. If you've been in New York for any length of time, you know from both intuition and daily observation that many people live on their own in this town. But I never fully appreciated how many—and by extension, how colossally banal my own solitary arrangement was—until I checked with the Department of City Planning a couple of months ago. How many apartments in Manhattan would you have guessed have just one occupant? One of every eight? Every four? Every three?

The number's one of every two. Of all 3,141 counties in the United States, New York County is the unrivaled leader in single-individual households, at 50.6 percent. More than three-quarters of the people in them are below the age of 65. Fifty-seven percent are female. In Brooklyn, the overall number is considerably lower, at 29.5 percent, and Queens is 26.1. But on the whole, in New York City, one in three homes contains a single dweller, just one lone man or woman who flips on the coffeemaker in the morning and switches off the lights at night.

These numbers should tell an unambiguous story. They should confirm the common belief about our city, which is that New York is an isolating, coldhearted sort of place. Mark Twain called it "a splendid desert— a domed and steepled solitude, where the stranger is lonely in the midst of a million of his race." (This from a man who settled in Hartford, Connecticut.) In J. D. Salinger's 1952 short story "De Daumier-Smith's Blue Period," the main character observes that wishing to be alone "is the one New York prayer that rarely gets lost or delayed in channels, and in no time at all, everything I touched turned to solid loneliness." Modern movies and art are filled with lonesome New York characters, some so familiar they've become their own shorthand: Travis Bickle (in *Taxi Driver*, calling himself "God's lonely man"); the forlorn patrons in *Nighthawks* (inspired, Edward Hopper said, "by a restaurant on New York's Greenwich Avenue"); Ratso Rizzo ("I gotta get outta here, gotta get outta here," he kept muttering in *Midnight Cowboy* . . . and died before he could). Remember Miranda in *Sex and the City*, racing off to the ER from panic attacks over dying alone? And then there was Christina Copeman. She famously did die alone in her apartment in East Flatbush. Her skeletal remains were discovered around Christmastime last year, an estimated twelve to eighteen months after she'd died, still neatly dressed in a beret and overcoat.

It's stories like Copeman's—terrifying in their every particular and, more important, real—that catch the attention of social scientists and have led some to the same conclusions as Mark Twain. "Every 20 or 30 years, we have a lament about the decline of community, and it's usually due to cities and urbanization," says Robert Sampson, the criminologist who chairs Harvard's sociology department, when I visit him one sunny morning this fall. He mentions one of the classics of the genre, Louis Wirth's *Urbanism As a Way of Life.* "It's all about the impersonal way of life in the city—how it almost deranged people, led to this sort of schizoid personality, to psychosis and loneliness." He smiles. "It's a fun piece, actually. There's some great quotes in it." He leans back in his chair. "But this idea that cities are bastions of lonely, despairing people is a myth," he says.

In American lore, the small town is the 5 archetypal community, a state of grace from which city dwellers have fallen (thus capitulating to all sorts of political ills like, say, socialism). Even among die-hard New Yorkers, those who could hardly imagine a life anywhere else, you'll find people who secretly harbor nostalgia for the small village they've never known.

Yet the picture of cities—and New York in particular—that has been emerging from the work of social scientists is that the people living in them are actually less lonely. Rather than driving people apart, large population centers pull them together, and as a rule tend to possess greater community virtues than smaller ones. This, even though cities are consistently, overwhelmingly, places where people are more likely to live on their own.

A couple of months ago, John Cacioppo, the director of the Center for Cognitive and Social Neuroscience at the University of Chicago, decided to spend his one free evening in New York indulging in a favorite out-of-towner's cliché, which in his business also qualifies as field research: watching strangers in Grand Central Terminal. "You'd see these people walking in all these different ways and at different paces, and all of a sudden, they'd be synchronized," he says. Cacioppo has a mild presence, with a soft voice and a slim frame, but the second he starts talking about this stuff, he buzzes like a live cable. "If they were white dots on a black field," he continues, "you could tell who belonged to who, just based on the synchrony of the white dots."

The traditional social-science gloss on a metropolitan node like Grand Central isn't all that different from Stephen Sondheim's observation in *Company:* "Another hundred people just got off of the train . . . It's a city of strangers / Some come to work, some to play." Grand Central is a glorious space, but it's also vast and impersonal, teeming with solitary commuters rather than one's own kin and kind. Might some people not come away from such a place feeling profoundly estranged? Like they hadn't a friend in the world?

They could. But in the sunshiny, low-crime New York of 2008, Grand Central feels much more like a village green than the melancholy nowhereland of Sondheim's vision (or worse, Travis Bickle's open-air asylum). There are tourists asking other tourists to take pictures of them; cops kibitzing with passersby; friends meeting friends to go for drinks. "All these transient connections were forming," Cacioppo marvels. "These people weren't even conscious of the many ways they were forming."

Cacioppo, co-author of W.W. Norton's 10 recently published *Loneliness,* is part of the school of evolutionary psychologists—and certain biologists too—that believes our species wouldn't have survived without a cooperative social instinct. In their book, Cacioppo and his co-author, the science writer William Patrick, argue that loneliness, like hunger, is an alarm signal that evolved in hominids hundreds of thousands of years ago, when group cohesion was essential to fight off abrupt attacks from stampeding wildebeests. It's nature's way of telling us to rejoin the group or pay the price. "Nature," they simply write at one point, "*is* connection."

It's a controversial theory, certainly, not least because it's post-hoc and therefore can't be proved. But it has beguiling consequences for city dwellers. From Cacioppo's point of view, our large brains didn't evolve in order to do multivariable calculus or compose sonatas. They evolved in order to process social information—and hence to work collaboratively. "And if you look at any city," he says, "you see that we have the capacity, as a species, to do so. They show we can work together, we can trust one another. We couldn't even drive through city streets if we didn't trust that people would follow rules that protect the group."

Cities, in other words, are the ultimate expression of our humanity, the ultimate habitat in which to be ourselves (which may explain why half the planet's population currently lives in them). And in their present American incarnations—safe, family-friendly, pulsing with life on the street—they're working at their optimum peak. In Cacioppo's data, today's city dwellers consistently rate as less lonely than their country cousins. "There's a new sense of community in cities, an increase in social capital, an increase in trust," he says. "It all leads to less alienation."

A raft of papers and polemics have come out in the last decade that argue Americans are lonelier. The starkest was a survey in *The American Sociological Review* reporting that the average number of people with whom Americans could "discuss important matters" dropped from three to two between 1985 and 2004, and that the number of Americans who felt they had no confidants at all had more than doubled, from 10 to 24.6 percent. But the most famous of the genre—the work that launched a thousand debates—was *Bowling Alone,* a meticulous chronicle of scary numbers by Harvard public-policy expert Robert Putnam. It showed that almost every measurable form of civic participation, from church attendance to union membership to bowling

leagues, declined in the waning decades of the last century. The book had plenty of critics, who pointed out that Putnam focused too much on obsolescent activities and organizations (card-playing, the Elks); that he gave short shrift to new, emerging forms of social capital, like Internet groups; and that the declines he documented were fairly modest. It didn't matter. The book resonated, vibrantly, with laymen and politicians alike, becoming an instant best-seller and catapulting Putnam into the rarefied company of presidential contenders and world leaders. He's worked with Bill Clinton, George W. Bush, and Tony Blair. He also met with Barack Obama during his campaign.

There are good public-health reasons to be concerned about loneliness. In the last couple of decades, researchers have started measuring the effects of social isolation, and they aren't pretty. There's been an avalanche of studies, for instance, showing that married people are happier and healthier, while the odds of dying increase significantly among the recently widowed, something known as the "widowhood effect." There's evidence suggesting that strong social networks help slow the progression of Alzheimer's. There's even better evidence suggesting that weak social networks pose as great a risk to heart-attack patients as obesity and hypertension. There's also evidence to suggest that the religious people who live the longest are the ones who attend services most frequently rather than feel their beliefs most deeply. (It's not faith that keeps them alive, in other words, but *people.*)

Studies show that loneliness is associated 15 with morning surges in cortisol, the stress hormone, and increased vascular resistance, which results in higher blood pressure. They also show the lonely drink more, exercise less, get divorced more often, and have more family estrangements and run-ins with the neighbors. And they're fatter. In one of my favorite experiments described in *Loneliness,* students were divided into two groups and told to evaluate . . . bite-size cookies. Specifically, researchers took aside each of the kids in one group and told them that no one wanted to work with them, so they'd have to work on their own. The others, by contrast, were each privately told that everyone wanted to work with them, but they'd still have to work on their own because it would be impossible to work with so many people. Then all of the participants were handed a plate of cookies and told to evaluate them. On average, the ones who had been told they were universally liked ate 4.5. Those who had been told they'd been universally rejected ate 9. "Is it any wonder we turn to ice cream," the authors ask, "when we're sitting at home feeling all alone in the world?"

Given how many New Yorkers live alone—in Manhattan, 25.6 percent of households are married, whereas the national average is 49.7—one would think we'd be at an increased risk for practically all these conditions. But Cacioppo points out that loneliness isn't about objective matters, like whether we live alone. It's about subjective matters, like whether we *feel* alone. To determine how satisfied people feel with their relationships, research psychologists generally rely on a twenty-question survey called the UCLA Loneliness Scale, which breaks down our connections into three groups: intimate (whether we have a partner), relational (friends), and collective (church, colleagues, baseball teams, etc.).

The results of these surveys have crucial—and positive—consequences for urban environments. Loneliness, it turns out, is relative. Widows are likely to feel better in a community with more widows (Boca Raton, Florida, say) than a community with only a few single elderly women. And singles are likely to feel better in a town with more singles . . . like New York. It's true that marriage is still the best demographic predictor of loneliness. But Cacioppo stresses it's a very

loose predictor. People can have satisfying connections in other ways, after all, and people in bad marriages might as well be on their own: Cacioppo's latest study, based on a sample of 225 people in the Chicago area, shows that those in unhappy marriages are no less lonely than single people, and might even be more so. Nor do rotten marriages do much for your health. A couple of years ago, Cacioppo teamed up with Linda Waite, co-author of *The Case for Marriage: Why Married People Are Happier, Healthier, and Better Off Financially*, whose conclusions about the health-positive effects of the institution drove feminists and fatalists like myself into a tizzy. They recruited a new pool of sample subjects and more or less asked the same questions Waite originally did, but also inserted questions to see if their participants were lonely. And what did they discover? That married people were indeed healthier—if they weren't lonely in their marriages. If they were, the health benefits were so negligible the researchers considered them statistically insignificant.

No one disputes the value of a good marriage, of course. Andrew Oswald, an economist at the University of Warwick, in fact tried to calculate that value, based on tens of thousands of happiness surveys collected here and in the U.K., and found that it's worth $100,000—or roughly doubling your salary, because working Americans earn, on average, $46,996 per year. But you know what else was worth $100,000? A large circle of friends. And it turns out that Aristotle was right when he wrote in *The Nicomachean Ethics* that friends are the glue that binds cities together. In study after study, urban dwellers have a more substantial social network. In his 1982 classic about Californians, *To Dwell Among Friends: Personal Networks in Town and City*, the Berkeley, California–based sociologist Claude Fischer found a 40 percent uptick in the size of friendship-based social networks moving from semi-rural areas into the urban core. Even the recent study that found we had fewer confidants found better news for city dwellers. "Based on what I'm seeing," says Matthew Brashears, one of the authors of the survey, "networks in large communities may have gotten smaller, but people in large communities still appear to have bigger networks than people in small."

"In our data," adds Lisa Berkman, the Harvard epidemiologist who discovered the importance of social networks to heart patients, "friends substitute perfectly well for family." This finding is important. It may be true that marriage prolongs life. But so, in Berkman's view, does friendship—and considering how important friendship is to New Yorkers (home of *Friends,* after all), where so many of us live on our own, this finding is blissfully reassuring. In fact, Berkman has consistently found that living alone poses no health risk, whether she's looking at 20,000 gas and electricity workers in France or a random sample of almost 7,000 men and women in Alameda, California, so long as her subjects have intimate ties of some kind as well as a variety of weaker ones. Those who are married but don't have any civic ties or close friends or relatives, for instance, face greater health risks than those who live alone but have lots of friends and regularly volunteer at the local soup kitchen. "Any one connection doesn't really protect you," she says. "You need relationships that provide love and intimacy *and* you need relationships that help you feel like you're participating in society in some way."

Eric Klinenberg is a sociologist at NYU 20 who's in the midst of writing a book called *Alone in America.* He and his researchers have interviewed over 200 "solitaires" (his term) about their experiences, 160 of them from New York City. "I'm concerned about poor and elderly people who live alone," he says. "I'm concerned about the sick who live alone. But we have to address the question of why, in other stages of their lives, people are opting to be alone, and we have to wrestle with the question of why many people who are elderly would rather live alone than move in with their children." He offers a few hypotheses: That living alone is a crucial rite of passage into adulthood. That it's a sign of economic achievement. That it's a form of self-cultivation and living authentically, a reaction to the stifling compromises made by the cornered souls of *Mad Men.*

In my own life, I'd make the case that my single friends gave me the imagination to envisage a life without marriage, which meant I didn't pair off too young. I also don't think I'm going out on too weak a limb when I stipulate that cities, in which we have a large network of companions and a wide variety of activities to do with them, are better for marriages generally. The relationship researcher Arthur Aron has pointed out that new experiences, rather than repeated favorites, are the best way to keep romantic feelings alive in a marriage, based on a series of six studies of hundreds of couples.

Now seems like a good time to point out that New York State is tied for the fifth-lowest divorce rate in the nation. Isn't it possible our marriages are simply better here?

And to the extent that suicide results from the tragic failure to socially integrate—one of the main ideas in Émile Durkheim's 1897 classic, *Suicide*—then New York City's suicide rate says something even more profound: New York State's suicide rate is currently the third lowest in the nation (second if you discount Washington, D.C.), at 6.2 percent, and the city's rate is even lower, at 5.4 percent. According to a report issued by the state's Office of Mental Health, in fact, suicide statistics in New York follow a simple formula: The less populous the county, the higher the rate (with superdense Kings County, or Brooklyn, boasting the second lowest, at 4.4 per 100,000). The United States follows the same pattern, with suicides rising the more rural the area becomes. States with the worst suicide rates are the least dense. (Montana,

Nevada, Alaska, New Mexico, and Wyoming are ranked, respectively, one through five.)

In the last decade, urbanism has converged, to some extent, with another field of study: Internet use. It's probably not an accident. Both cities and the Internet are at once highly atomized and elaborately connected milieus that encourage both solitude and interaction with the diverse, bountiful unwashed. And like city solitaires, Internet users were also once identified as antisocial loners, painfully awkward people who vanished into the green-gray light of their computer screens rather than joining the warm community of man. In the beginning, studies even showed this to be true (or that users were shy, anyway). But not once three-quarters of the public started using the Internet.

"The idea that you're isolated when 25 you're online is, to me, just wrong," says Keith Hampton, a sociologist at the University of Pennsylvania who did an extensive ethnography of "Netville," a new, 100 percent wired community in suburban Toronto. "It's an inherently social medium. What starts online moves offline, and what starts offline goes online." Which explains why the people with whom you e-mail most frequently are your closest friends and romantic partners. "Online and offline life are inherently connected," he says. "They're not separate worlds."

In fact, many Internet and city behaviors we consider antisocial have social consequences. Think of people who lug their laptops into public settings. In 2004, Hampton and his colleagues looked at just those people—at Starbucks, in fact, in Seattle and Boston—and concluded that a full third of them were basically using their laptops and interacting at the same time. (Cafés, in other words, were like dog runs, and laptops were like pugs, encouraging interaction among solitaires.) Hampton did a similar study of laptop users in Bryant Park, and the same proportion, or one-third, reported meeting someone they hadn't before. Fifteen percent of them kept in touch with that person over time

(meaning that about 5 percent made lasting ties out of a trip to Bryant Park with a laptop).

It's easy to see the parallels here between attitudes toward online use and attitudes toward solitary living. Perhaps there was once a time when living alone meant you were a hopeless shut-in. But you can't exactly say this if 50 percent of the households in Manhattan contain just one person. Like Internet users, solitaires have a permanent and ambient sense of the world beyond their living rooms and a fluid sense of when to join it and when to retreat. Klinenberg, the NYU professor who is writing about living alone, points out that single people are partly responsible for the vibrancy of New York's public life: "We know from marketing surveys that single people go out more than couples," he notes. "They're more likely to go to restaurants, to bars, and to clubs. A lot of people who live alone say it's very hard to enter their apartments and stare at the walls when there's so much going on outside."

Conversely, married people—women especially—have smaller friendship-based social networks than they did as single people, according to Claude Fischer. In a recent phone conversation with the sociologist, I mentioned a related curiosity I came across in a paper about the elderly and social isolation in New York City: The neighborhoods where people were at the greatest risk, it seemed, were in neighborhoods where people seemed *very* married—family neighborhoods, in fact, like Borough Park and Ridgewood. "That's not strange at all," he says. "They're the prime category of people to be isolated." He explains that these people "aged in place," as sociologists like to say, staying in the homes where they raised their own families. Then their spouses died, and so did their cohort (or it moved to a retirement community), and they're suddenly surrounded by strange families, often of different classes or ethnic backgrounds, with whom they're likely to have far less in common. "Unless they have children living nearby," he says, "they're likely to be quite isolated."

I'm familiar with a younger version of this. When the New Yorkers I know feel lonely—single women especially—it's a product, too, of feeling asynchronous with their cohort. I myself felt this way until fairly recently. James Moody, a network guru at Duke University, notes that there's a time in the lives of young professionals when they retreat deep into their silos, trying to make partner, get tenure, write their books, complete their residencies, or whatever it is that they're hoping to do. If they're lucky, they're married, which helps sustain them through the work isolation. Then the next stage comes when they're working hard in their newly minted careers (as partners, tenured professors, authors, doctors, or whatever it is they're doing). And again, they're fairly cut off socially, but they're buoyed, one hopes, by the presence of a family at home. But if someone is out of step with this pattern—not partnered off, say, while still working really hard—New York can be a challenging place.

But the fact remains that a city, New York 30 especially, might be the best place to ride out that period of lonely toil. Because New York, like the Internet, also offers a rich network of acquaintances, or what sociologists like to call "weak ties."

There are sociologists who will argue that weak ties are the bane of modern life. We are drowning in a sea of them, they'll say—networking with colleagues rather than socializing with friends, corresponding online with lots of people we know only moderately well rather than catching up with our nearest and dearest on the phone. *Bowling Alone* is, to some extent, one long elegy for the strong ties we've lost, whether they're the bowling leagues of Pittsburgh or the Hadassahs of New Jersey.

And there's no doubt that weak ties can distract and enervate us. How many families sit down at dinner together with the best of intentions, only to find themselves drawn into their own individual worlds—texting on their BlackBerrys, yakking on their cells? (The cover art for *Elsewhere, U.S.A.*, the fine upcoming book by NYU sociologist Dalton Conley, says it all: a family sitting at the dining-room table, each member staring at his or her own laptop.)

But having lots of weak ties is also wonderful for many things—including finding stronger ties. As Mark Granovetter wrote in his seminal 1973 essay, "The Strength of Weak Ties," they're much better at helping us find jobs because they offer us diversity and breadth. The same goes for love. Think about it: If you're single, you already know all your friends' single friends. It's your acquaintances' single friends you don't know.

Viewed in this light, networking with acquaintances, of whom we all have many in New York, is hardly a shallow enterprise or waste of time. It's through these people that we find husbands, wives, life partners, better jobs. Why should we begrudge that any more than we'd begrudge going on Nerve? Or Monster.com?

Weak ties offer other advantages in cities. 35 They're crucial to collective political action—your closest friends aren't enough to start a movement—and they're better than strong ties, believe it or not, for protecting neighborhoods, for the same reason: Banding together with those you know well isn't enough to keep a whole community safe. Weak ties are essential to the creative economy, as Richard Florida pointed out in *The Rise of the Creative Class*, because diversity breeds innovation (and more diversity).

There is even evidence that weak ties simply make us feel better. According to *Loneliness*, the advice your mother gives you when you're depressed—*Get out of the damn house, would you?*—turns out to be right. For most people, being in the simple presence of a friendly person helps us reregulate our behavior if we're feeling depressed in our isolation. We are naturally wired not just to connect with them but to imitate them—which might be a good idea, if our impulses at that moment are self-destructive. Cacioppo and Patrick cite a range of studies showing that students in classes with the best rapport imitate each other's body language; same goes for athletes on winning teams. The presence of other human beings puts a natural limit on how freakily we can behave. And where better to find them than in cities, where we have more ties? (Think about the sociopathic kids who shot other kids in Red Lake, Minnesota; at Northern Illinois University; at Virginia Tech—what do they have in common? They were living in isolated places.) Robert Sampson, paraphrasing Durkheim, puts it this way: "The tie itself provides health benefits. That's where I started with my work on crime."

So now I'm thinking back on all those connections Cacioppo witnessed in Grand Central. "Other species, like penguins, they rely on huddles for survival," he told me. "In terms of collective structures, they're pretty minimal and boring. But people have the capacity to make all kinds of transient connections. New York has an infinite number of them."

He was describing the ballet of the train station. But his description could just as easily have applied to the Internet. Think about it: Serendipitous encounters between people who know each other well, sort of well, and not at all. People of every type, and with every type of agenda, trying to meet up with others who share that same agenda. An environ-

ment that's alive at all hours, populated by all types, and is, most of the time, pretty safe. What he was saying, really, was that New York had become the Web. Or perhaps more, even: that New York was the Web before the Web was the Web, characterized by the same free-flowing interaction, 24/7 rhythms, subgroups, and demimondes.

Hampton says he views the Internet as the ultimate city, the last stop on the continuum of human connectedness. I'd argue that New York and the Internet are about the same, in the way that a large bookstore feels like it offers just as many possibilities as Amazon.com—maybe slightly less inventory, but more opportunities to stumble on things you might not have otherwise. Whichever the case, what the Internet and New York have in common is that each environment facilitates interaction between individuals like no other, and both would be positively useless—would literally lose their raison d'être—if solitary individuals didn't furiously interact in each. They show us, in trillions of invisible ways every day, that people are essentially nothing without one another. We may sometimes want to throttle our fellow travelers on the F train. We may on occasion curse our neighbors for playing music so loud it splits the floor. But living cheek-by-jowl is the necessary price we pay for our well-being. And anyway, who wants to ride the subway alone?

A CLOSER LOOK AT
Alone Together

1. Senior presents the results of many different empirical studies. Identify three of them and highlight the results of those studies. How does she use these results to build her argument?

2. A common theme throughout this report is that being alone is not psychologically or even physically healthy. Yet Senior is arguing that it's fine for

people to choose to live alone in cities. On what grounds does she make this seemingly contradictory argument?

3. Senior uses an analogy to describe New York as similar to the Internet. Find that place in the report. Does this analogy work for you? Do you accept it? Where does the analogy break down and what are its flaws?

Levitt and Dubner: Why Do Drug Dealers Still Live with Their Moms?

787

IDEAS FOR
Writing

1. Write a position paper for the dean of students at your college in which you argue whether first-year students should be required to have roommates or be allowed to live alone. Think about the advantages and disadvantages of both kinds of living arrangements. Do you think it is best for students to live with roommates their first year in college, despite some of the inconveniences? Or do you think students should be able to live alone their first year?

2. Drawing on your own research and observations, write a brief report about students who live alone at your college. Is your campus like Senior's New York, where people can feel part of a group even though they live alone? Can people effectively live alone without feeling lonely or cut off from others? Or are people who live alone really not as happy as people who live in dorms, cooperatives, fraternities, and sororities? You will need some empirical research to answer this question.

Why Do Drug Dealers Still Live with Their Moms?

STEVEN D. LEVITT AND STEPHEN J. DUBNER

In this excerpt from their best-selling book, Freakonomics, *economists Steven D. Levitt and Stephen J. Dubner pursue an interesting question generated by the research done by Sudhir Venkatesh, a University of Chicago graduate student. This selection shows how research can sometimes go in unexpected directions. Notice the places where Venkatesh changes his research methods as he learns new things about his subject.*

Sudhir Venkatesh—his boyhood friends called him Sid, but he has since reverted to Sudhir—was born in India, raised in the suburbs of upstate New York and southern California, and graduated from the University of California at San Diego with a degree in mathematics. In 1989 he began to pursue his PhD in sociology at the University of Chicago. He was interested in understanding how young people form their identities; to that end, he had just spent three months following the Grateful Dead around the country. What he was not interested in was the grueling fieldwork that typifies sociology.

But his graduate advisor, the eminent poverty scholar William Julius Wilson, promptly sent Venkatesh into the field. His assignment: to visit Chicago's poorest black neighborhoods with a clipboard and a seventy-question, multiple-choice survey. This was the first question on the survey:

How do you feel about being black and poor?

a. Very bad
b. Bad
c. Neither bad nor good
d. Somewhat good
e. Very good

One day Venkatesh walked twenty blocks from the university to a housing project on the shore of Lake Michigan to administer his survey. The project comprised three sixteen-story buildings made of yellow-gray brick. Venkatesh soon discovered that the names and addresses he had been given were badly outdated. These buildings were condemned, practically abandoned. Some families lived on the lower floors, pirating water and electricity, but the elevators didn't work. Neither did the lights in the stairwell. It was late afternoon in early winter, nearly dark outside.

Venkatesh, who is a thoughtful, hand- 5 some, and well built but not aberrationally brave person, had made his way up to the sixth floor, trying to find someone willing to take his survey. Suddenly, on the stairwell landing, he startled a group of teenagers shooting dice. They turned out to be a gang of junior-level crack dealers who operated out of the building, and they were not happy to see him.

"I'm a student at the University of Chicago," Venkatesh sputtered, sticking to his survey script, "and I am administering—"

"Fuck you, nigger, what are you doing in our stairwell?"

There was an ongoing gang war in Chicago. Things had been violent lately, with shootings nearly every day. This gang, a branch of the Black Gangster Disciple Nation, was plainly on edge. They didn't know what to make of Venkatesh. He didn't *seem* to be a member of a rival gang. But maybe he was some kind of spy? He certainly wasn't a cop. He wasn't black, wasn't white. He wasn't exactly threatening—he was armed only with his clipboard—but he didn't seem quite harmless either. Thanks to his three months trailing the Grateful Dead, he still looked, as he would later put it, "like a genuine freak, with hair down to my ass."

The gang members started arguing over what should be done with Venkatesh. Let him go? But if he *did* tell the rival gang about this stairwell hangout, they'd be susceptible to a surprise attack. One jittery kid kept wagging something back and forth in his hands—in the dimming light, Venkatesh eventually realized it was a gun—and muttering, "Let me have him, let me have him." Venkatesh was very, very scared.

The crowd grew, bigger and louder. Then 10 an older gang member appeared. He snatched the clipboard from Venkatesh's hands and, when he saw that it was a written questionnaire, looked puzzled.

"I can't read any of this shit," he said.

"That's because you can't *read*," said one of the teenagers, and everyone laughed at the older gangster.

He told Venkatesh to go ahead and ask him a question from the survey. Venkatesh led with the how-does-it-feel-to-be-black-and-poor question. It was met with a round of guffaws, some angrier than others. As Venkatesh would later tell his university colleagues, he realized that the multiple-choice answers A through E were insufficient. In reality, he now knew, the answers should have looked like this:

a. Very bad
b. Bad
c. Neither bad nor good
d. Somewhat good
e. Very good
f. Fuck you

Just as things were looking their bleakest for Venkatesh, another man appeared. This was J. T., the gang's leader. J. T. wanted to know what was going on. Then he told Venkatesh to read him the survey question. He listened but then said he couldn't answer the question because he wasn't black.

"Well then," Venkatesh said, "how does it 15 feel to be *African American* and poor?"

"I ain't no African American either, you idiot. I'm a *nigger*." J. T. then administered a lively though not unfriendly taxonomical lesson in "nigger" versus "African American" versus "black." When he was through, there was an awkward silence. Still nobody seemed to know what to do with Venkatesh. J. T., who was in his late twenties, had cooled down his subordinates, but he didn't seem to want to interfere directly with their catch. Darkness fell and J. T. left. "People don't come out of here alive," the jittery teenager with the gun told Venkatesh. "You know that, don't you?"

As night deepened, his captors eased up. They gave Venkatesh one of their beers, and then another and another. When he had to pee, he went where they went—on the stairwell landing one floor up. J. T. stopped by a few times during the night but didn't have much to say. Daybreak came and then noon. Venkatesh would occasionally try to discuss his survey, but the young crack dealers just laughed and told him how stupid his questions were. Finally, nearly twenty-four hours after Venkatesh stumbled upon them, they set him free.

He went home and took a shower. He was relieved but he was also curious. It struck Venkatesh that most people, including himself, had never given much thought to the daily life of ghetto criminals. He was now eager to learn how the Black Disciples worked, from top to bottom.

After a few hours, he decided to walk back to the housing project. By now he had thought of some better questions to ask.

Having seen firsthand that the conven- 20 tional method of data gathering was in this case absurd, Venkatesh vowed to scrap his questionnaire and embed himself with the gang. He tracked down J. T. and sketched out his proposal. J. T. thought Venkatesh was crazy, literally—a university student wanting to cozy up to a crack gang? But he also admired what Venkatesh was after. As it happened, J. T. was a college graduate himself, a business major. After college, he had taken a job in the Loop, working in the marketing department of a company that sold office equipment. But he felt so out of place there—like a white man working at Afro Sheen headquarters, he liked to say—that he quit. Still, he never forgot what he learned. He knew the importance of collecting data and finding new markets; he was always on the lookout for better management strategies. It was no coincidence, in other words, that J. T. was the leader of this crack gang. He was bred to be a boss.

After some wrangling, J. T. promised Venkatesh unfettered access to the gang's operations as long as J. T. retained veto power over any information that, if published, might prove harmful.

When the yellow-gray buildings on the lakefront were demolished, shortly after Venkatesh's first visit, the gang relocated to another housing project even deeper in Chicago's south side. For the next six years, Venkatesh practically lived there. Under J. T.'s protection he watched the gang members up close, at work and at home. He asked endless questions. Sometimes the gangsters were annoyed by his curiosity; more often they took advantage of his willingness to listen. "It's a war out here, man," one dealer told him. "I mean, every day people struggling to survive, so you know, we just do what we can. We ain't got no choice, and if that means getting killed, well shit, it's what niggers do around here to feed their family."

Venkatesh would move from one family to the next, washing their dinner dishes and sleeping on the floor. He bought toys for their children; he once watched a woman use her baby's bib to sop up the blood of a teenaged drug dealer who was shot to death in front of Venkatesh. William Julius Wilson, back at the U. of C., was having regular nightmares on Venkatesh's behalf.

Over the years the gang endured bloody turf wars and, eventually, a federal indictment. A member named Booty, who was one rank beneath J. T., came to Venkatesh with a story. Booty was being blamed by the rest of the gang for bringing about the indictment, he told Venkatesh, and therefore suspected that he would soon be killed. (He was right.) But first Booty wanted to do a little atoning. For all the gang's talk about how crack dealing didn't do any harm—they even liked to brag that it kept black money in the black community—Booty was feeling guilty. He wanted to leave behind something that might somehow benefit the next generation. He handed Venkatesh a stack of well-worn spiral notebooks—blue and black, the gang's colors. They represented a complete record of four years' worth of the gang's financial transactions. At J. T.'s direction, the ledgers had been rigorously compiled: sales, wages, dues, even the death benefits paid out to the families of murdered members.

At first Venkatesh didn't even want the notebooks. What if the Feds found out he had them—perhaps he'd be indicted too? Besides, what was he supposed to do with the data? Despite his math background, he had long ago stopped thinking in numbers.

Upon completing his graduate work at the University of Chicago, Venkatesh was awarded a three-year stay at Harvard's Society of Fellows. Its environment of sharp thinking and bonhomie—the walnut paneling, the sherry cart once owned by Oliver Wendell Holmes—delighted Venkatesh. He went so far as to become the society's wine steward. And yet he regularly left Cambridge, returning again and again to the crack gang in

Chicago. This street-level research made Venkatesh something of an anomaly. Most of the other young Fellows were dyed-in-the-tweed intellectuals who liked to pun in Greek.

One of the society's aims was to bring together scholars from various fields who might not otherwise have occasion to meet. Venkatesh soon encountered another anomalous young Fellow, one who also failed the society stereotype. This one happened to be an economist who, instead of thinking grand macro thoughts, favored his own list of offbeat micro curiosities. At the very top of his list was crime. And so, within ten minutes of their meeting, Sudhir Venkatesh told Steven Levitt about the spiral notebooks from Chicago and they decided to collaborate on a paper. It would be the first time that such priceless financial data had fallen into an economist's hands, affording an analysis of a heretofore uncharted criminal enterprise.

So how *did* the gang work? An awful lot like most American businesses, actually, though perhaps none more so than McDonald's. In fact, if you were to hold a McDonald's organizational chart and a Black Disciples org chart side by side, you could hardly tell the difference.

The gang that Venkatesh had fallen in with was one of about a hundred branches—franchises, really—of a larger Black Disciples organization. J. T., the college-educated leader of his franchise, reported to a central leadership of about twenty men that was called, without irony, the board of directors. (At the same time that white suburbanites were studiously mimicking black rappers' ghetto culture, black ghetto criminals were studiously mimicking the suburbanites' dads' corpthink.) J. T. paid the board of directors nearly 20 percent of his revenues for the right to sell crack in a designated twelve-square-block area. The rest of the money was his to distribute as he saw fit.

Three officers reported directly to J. T.: an enforcer (who ensured the gang members' safety), a treasurer (who watched over the gang's liquid assets), and a runner (who transported large quantities of drugs and money to and from the supplier). Beneath the officers were the street-level salesmen known as foot soldiers. The goal of a foot soldier was to someday become an officer. J. T. might have had anywhere from twenty-five to seventy-five foot soldiers on his payroll at any given time, depending on the time of year (autumn was the best crack-selling season; summer and Christmastime were slow) and the size of the gang's territory (which doubled at one point when the Black Disciples engineered a hostile takeover of a rival gang's turf). At the very bottom of J. T.'s organization were as many as two hundred members known as the rank and file. They were not employees at all. They did, however, pay dues to the gang—some for protection from rival gangs, others for the chance to eventually earn a job as a foot soldier.

The four years recorded in the gang's notebooks coincided with the peak years of the crack boom, and business was excellent. J. T.'s franchise quadrupled its revenues during this period. In the first year, it took in an average of $18,500 each month; by the final year, it was collecting $68,400 a month. Here's a look at the monthly revenues in the third year:

Drug sales	$24,800
Dues	5,100
Extortionary taxes	2,100
Total monthly revenues	$32,000

"Drug sales" represents only the money from dealing crack cocaine. The gang did allow some rank-and-file members to sell heroin on its turf but accepted a fixed licensing fee in lieu of a share of profits. (This was off-the-books money and went straight into J. T.'s pocket; he probably skimmed from other sources as well.) The $5,100 in

dues came from rank-and-file members only, since full gang members didn't pay dues. The extortionary taxes were paid by other businesses that operated on the gang's turf, including grocery stores, gypsy cabs, pimps, and people selling stolen goods or repairing cars on the street.

Now, here's what it cost J. T., excluding wages, to bring in that $32,000 per month:

Wholesale cost of drugs	$ 5,000
Board of directors fee	5,000
Mercenary fighters	1,300
Weapons	300
Miscellaneous	2,400
Total monthly nonwage costs	$14,000

Mercenary fighters were nonmembers hired on short-term contracts to help the gang fight turf wars. The cost of weapons is small here because the Black Disciples had a side deal with local gunrunners, helping them navigate the neighborhood in exchange for free or steeply discounted guns. The miscellaneous expenses include legal fees, parties, bribes, and gang-sponsored "community events." (The Black Disciples worked hard to be seen as a pillar rather than a scourge of the housing-project community.) The miscellaneous expenses also include the costs associated with a gang member's murder. The gang not only paid for the funeral but often gave a stipend of up to three years' wages to the victim's family. Venkatesh had once asked why the gang was so generous in this regard. "That's a fucking stupid question," he was told, " 'cause as long as you been with us, you still don't understand that their families is our families. We can't just leave 'em out. We been knowing these folks our whole lives, man, so we grieve when they grieve. You got to respect the family." There was another reason for the death benefits: the gang feared community backlash (its enterprise was plainly a destructive one) and figured it could buy some goodwill for a few hundred dollars here and there.

The rest of the money the gang took in went to its members, starting with J. T. Here is the single line item in the gang's budget that made J. T. the happiest:

Net monthly profit accruing $8,500
  to leader

At $8,500 per month, J. T.'s annual salary was about $100,000—tax-free, of course, and not including the various off-the-books money he pocketed. This was a lot more than he earned at his short-lived office job in the Loop. And J. T. was just one of roughly 100 leaders at this level within the Black Disciples network. So there were indeed some drug dealers who could afford to live large, or—in the case of the gang's board of directors—*extremely* large. Each of those top 20 bosses stood to earn about $500,000 a year. (A third of them, however, were typically imprisoned at any time, a significant downside of an up position in an illicit industry.)

So the top 120 men on the Black Disciples' pyramid were paid very well. But the pyramid they sat atop was gigantic. Using J. T.'s franchise as a yardstick—3 officers and roughly 50 foot soldiers—there were some 5,300 other men working for those 120 bosses. Then there were another 20,000 unpaid rank-and-file members, many of whom wanted nothing more than an opportunity to become a foot soldier. They were even willing to pay gang dues to have their chance.

And how well did that dream job pay? Here are the monthly totals for the wages that J. T. paid his gang members:

Combined wages paid to $2,100
  all three officers
Combined wages paid to   7,400
  all foot soldiers
Total monthly gang wages $9,500
  (excluding leader)

So J. T. paid his employees $9,500, a *combined* monthly salary that was only $1,000 more than his own official salary. J. T.'s hourly

wage was $66. His three officers, meanwhile, each took home $700 a month, which works out to about $7 an hour. And the foot soldiers earned just $3.30 an hour, less than the minimum wage. So the answer to the original question—if drug dealers make so much money, why are they still living with their mothers?—is that, except for the top cats, they *don't* make much money. They had no choice but to live with their mothers. For every big earner, there were hundreds more just scraping along. The top 120 men in the Black Disciples gang represented just 2.2 percent of the full-fledged gang membership but took home well more than half the money.

In other words, a crack gang works pretty much like the standard capitalist enterprise: you have to be near the top of the pyramid to make a big wage. Notwithstanding the leadership's rhetoric about the family nature of the business, the gang's wages are about as skewed as wages in corporate America. A foot soldier had plenty in common with a McDonald's burger flipper or a Wal-Mart shelf stocker. In fact, most of J. T.'s foot soldiers also held minimum-wage jobs in the legitimate sector to supplement their skimpy illicit earnings. The leader of another crack gang once told Venkatesh that he could easily afford to pay his foot soldiers more, but it wouldn't be prudent. "You got all these niggers below you who want your job, you dig?" he said. "So, you know, you try to take care of them, but you know, you also have to show them you the boss. You always have to get yours first, or else you really ain't no leader. If you start taking losses, they see you as weak and shit."

Along with the bad pay, the foot soldiers faced terrible job conditions. For starters, they had to stand on a street corner all day and do business with crackheads. (The gang members were strongly advised against using the product themselves, advice that was enforced by beatings if necessary.) Foot soldiers also risked arrest and, more worrisome, violence. Using the gang's financial documents and the rest of Venkatesh's research, it is possible to construct an adverse-events index of J. T.'s gang during the four years in question. The results are astonishingly bleak. If you were a member of J. T.'s gang for all four years, here is the typical fate you would have faced during that period:

Number of times arrested	5.9
Number of nonfatal wounds or injuries (not including injuries meted out by the gang itself for rules violations)	2.4
Chance of being killed	1 in 4

A 1-in-4 chance of being killed! Compare these odds to being a timber cutter, which the Bureau of Labor Statistics calls the most dangerous job in the United States. Over four years' time, a timber cutter would stand only a 1-in-200 chance of being killed. Or compare the crack dealer's odds to those of a death row inmate in Texas, which executes more prisoners than any other state. In 2003, Texas put to death twenty-four inmates—or just 5 percent of the nearly 500 inmates on its death row during that time. Which means that you stand a greater chance of dying while dealing crack in a Chicago housing project than you do while sitting on death row in Texas.

So if crack dealing is the most dangerous job in America, and if the salary is only $3.30 an hour, why on earth would anyone take such a job?

Well, for the same reason that a pretty Wisconsin farm girl moves to Hollywood. For the same reason that a high-school quarterback wakes up at 5 a.m. to lift weights. They all want to succeed in an extremely competitive field in which, if you reach the top, you are paid a fortune (to say nothing of the attendant glory and power).

To the kids growing up in a housing proj- 45 ect on Chicago's south side, crack dealing was a glamour profession. For many of them, the job of gang boss—highly visible and highly lucrative—was easily the best job they thought they had access to. Had they grown up under different circumstances, they might have thought about becoming economists or writers. But in the neighborhood where J. T.'s gang operated, the path to a decent legitimate job was practically invisible. Fifty-six percent of the neighborhood's children lived below the poverty line (compared to a national average of 18 percent). Seventy-eight percent came from single-parent homes. Fewer than 5 percent of the neighborhood's adults had a college degree; barely one in three adult men worked at all. The neighborhood's median income was about $15,000 a year, well less than half the U.S. average. During the years that Venkatesh lived with J. T.'s gang, foot soldiers often asked his help in landing what they called "a good job": working as a janitor at the University of Chicago.

The problem with crack dealing is the same as in every other glamour profession: a lot of people are competing for a very few prizes. Earning big money in the crack gang wasn't much more likely than the Wisconsin farm girl becoming a movie star or the high-school quarterback playing in the NFL. But criminals, like everyone else, respond to incentives. So if the prize is big enough, they will form a line down the block just hoping for a chance. On the south side of Chicago, people wanting to sell crack vastly outnumbered the available street corners.

These budding drug lords bumped up against an immutable law of labor: when there are a lot of people willing and able to do a job, that job generally doesn't pay well. This is one of four meaningful factors that determine a wage. The others are the specialized skills a job requires, the unpleasantness of a job, and the demand for services that the job fulfills.

The delicate balance between these factors helps explain why, for instance, the typical prostitute earns more than the typical architect. It may not seem as though she should.

The architect would appear to be more skilled (as the word is usually defined) and better educated (again, as usually defined). But little girls don't grow up dreaming of becoming prostitutes, so the supply of potential prostitutes is relatively small. Their skills, while not necessarily "specialized," are practiced in a very specialized context. The job is unpleasant and forbidding in at least two significant ways: the likelihood of violence and the lost opportunity of having a stable family life. As for demand? Let's just say that an architect is more likely to hire a prostitute than vice versa.

In the glamour professions—movies, sports, music, fashion—there is a different dynamic at play. Even in second-tier glamour industries like publishing, advertising, and media, swarms of bright young people throw themselves at grunt jobs that pay poorly and demand unstinting devotion. An editorial assistant earning $22,000 at a Manhattan publishing house, an unpaid high-school quarterback, and a teenage crack dealer earning $3.30 an hour are all playing the same game, a game that is best viewed as a tournament.

The rules of a tournament are straight- 50 forward. You must start at the bottom to have a shot at the top. (Just as a Major League short-stop probably played Little League and just as a Grand Dragon of the Ku Klux Klan probably started out as a lowly spear-carrier, a drug lord typically began by selling drugs on a street corner.) You must be willing to work long and hard at substandard wages. In order to advance in the tournament, you must prove yourself not merely above average but spectacular. (The way to distinguish yourself differs from profession to profession, of course; while J. T. certainly monitored his foot soldiers' sales performance, it was their force of personality that really counted— more than it would for, say, a shortstop.) And finally, once you come to the sad realization that you will never make it to the top, you will quit the tournament. (Some people hang on longer than others—witness the graying

"actors" who wait tables in New York—but people generally get the message quite early.)

Most of J. T.'s foot soldiers were unwilling to stay foot soldiers for long after they realized they weren't advancing. Especially once the shooting started. After several relatively peaceful years, J. T.'s gang got involved in a turf war with a neighboring gang. Drive-by shootings became a daily event. For a foot soldier—the gang's man on the street—this development was particularly dangerous. The nature of the business demanded that customers be able to find him easily and quickly; if he hid from the other gang, he couldn't sell his crack.

Until the gang war, J. T.'s foot soldiers had been willing to balance the risky, low-paying job with the reward of advancement. But as one foot soldier told Venkatesh, he now wanted to be compensated for the added risk: "Would you stand around here when all this shit is going on? No, right? So if I gonna be asked to put my life on the line, then front me the cash, man. Pay me more 'cause it ain't worth my time to be here when they're warring."

J. T. hadn't wanted this war. For one thing, he was forced to pay his foot soldiers higher wages because of the added risk. Far worse, gang warfare was bad for business. If Burger King and McDonald's launch a price war to gain market share, they partly make up in volume what they lose in price. (Nor is anyone getting shot.) But with a gang war, sales plummet because customers are so scared of the violence that they won't come out in the open to buy their crack. In every way, war was expensive for J. T.

So why did he start the war? As a matter of fact, he didn't. It was his foot soldiers who started it. It turns out that a crack boss didn't have as much control over his subordinates as he would have liked. That's because they had different incentives.

For J. T., violence was a distraction from 55 the business at hand; he would have preferred that his members never fired a single gun-shot. For a foot soldier, however, violence served a purpose. One of the few ways that a foot soldier could distinguish himself—and advance in the tournament—was by proving his mettle for violence. A killer was respected, feared, talked about. A foot soldier's incentive was to make a name for himself; J. T.'s incentive was, in effect, to keep the foot soldiers from doing so. "We try to tell these shorties that they belong to a serious organization," he once told Venkatesh. "It ain't all about killing. They see these movies and shit, they think it's all about running around tearing shit up. But it's not. You've got to learn to be part of an organization; you can't be fighting all the time. It's bad for business."

In the end, J. T. prevailed. He oversaw the gang's expansion and ushered in a new era of prosperity and relative peace. J. T. was a winner. He was paid well because so few people could do what he did. He was a tall, good-looking, smart, tough man who knew how to motivate people. He was shrewd too, never tempting arrest by carrying guns or cash.

While the rest of his gang lived in poverty with their mothers, J. T. had several homes, several women, several cars. He also had his business education, of course. He constantly worked to extend this advantage. That was why he ordered the corporate-style book-keeping that eventually found its way into Sudhir Venkatesh's hands. No other franchise leader had ever done such a thing. J. T. once showed his ledgers to the board of directors to prove, as if proof were needed, the extent of his business acumen.

And it worked. After six years running his local gang, J. T. was promoted to the board of directors. He was now thirty-four years old. He had won the tournament. But this tournament had a catch that publishing and pro sports and even Hollywood don't have. Selling drugs, after all, is illegal. Not long after he made the board of directors, the Black Disciples were essentially shut down by a federal indictment—the same indictment that led the gangster named Booty to turn over his notebooks to Venkatesh—and J. T. was sent to prison.

A CLOSER LOOK AT
Why Do Drug Dealers Still Live with Their Mothers?

1. Venkatesh soon learns that his research methods are not adequate to explain life in Chicago's poorest neighborhoods. Why did his approach not work, and how did he make changes to it?

2. Levitt and Dubner compare selling drugs to working at McDonalds. According to them, what are three ways in which selling drugs for a gang is similar to making fast food?

3. Why *do* drug dealers still live with their mothers, according to Venkatesh's research and Levitt and Dubner's explanation?

IDEAS FOR
Writing

1. Write a brief response in which you discuss your reactions to Levitt and Dubner's findings in this report. What did you find interesting about this report? What do you find hard to believe? How might this report be used to explain why the inner-city poor behave in particular ways?

2. If the results of this report are true, can you think of some ways to reduce drug dealing without resorting to the usual "War on Drugs" tactics that have been used for a few decades? In a proposal, describe an alternative plan for combating drug dealing. Use this report as a source to explain the problem, its causes, and its effects. Then describe a step-by-step plan for solving that problem.

A FEW IDEAS FOR
Composing a Report

1. Develop a methods section for a report. List five questions about life on your campus that you would like to answer. Pick one and develop a methodology for answering that question. Use your methodology to generate facts, data, and other support. Then write a report to the dean of students at your university in which you present and discuss your results and offer recommendations.

2. Write a summary of a report. Find a report on the Internet or elsewhere that studies a topic related to your major or a personal interest. Describe what it says in your own words, but do not offer your own opinion. The purpose of your summary is to give an overview of the report's major points, not to offer your own views about the topic.

3. Create a multimedia report about your major. Research the topic through the Internet, print sources, and interviews with counselors and professors. Your readers should be college students who might be interested in majoring in this field. Explain the requirements for graduation. Tell them what kinds of careers are available and the demand for people who earn degrees in your major. Then turn your report into a presentation with images, animation, and perhaps video.

PART

8 Handbook

PART OUTLINE

Do you have questions about grammar, usage, or spelling? Look no further. Your questions will be answered in this **HANDBOOK**.

This handbook is a reference tool for questions about English grammar and usage. It focuses on the sentence as the basic material of written and spoken discourse. It avoids grammatical jargon as much as possible, but it does define terms where they are necessary for understanding important concepts and problems. Refer to this guide while writing and when your professor suggests sections for you to study. It will help you write correctly, clearly, and with an appropriate style.

1 Sentences

Every sentence has at least one subject and at least one verb, begins with a capital letter, and ends with end punctuation (a period, question mark, or exclamation point). In college writing and beyond, you will be asked to communicate complex ideas. You may need to try out new sentence patterns to connect those ideas, and that may lead you to make some sentence errors. Use this handbook to help you understand the wide variety of sentence types while avoiding grammatical errors.

1A Fragments

Sentence fragments are errors in which partial sentences are treated as complete sentences—begun with a capital letter and ended with a period. The fragment may be a subordinate clause, a phrase, or a combination of subordinate elements. What makes each a fragment is that it lacks a subject or a verb, or that it begins with a subordinating word. Only independent clauses can make independent statements.

Subordinate Clause Fragment

Recognition. A subordinate clause has a subject and a verb but is not an independent clause because it includes a subordinate connector.

Some common subordinating connectors, grouped by function, include:

Time: *after, before, once, since, until, whenever*
Place: *where, wherever*
Cause: *as, because, since*
Contrast: *although, even though, though, while*
Condition: *even if, if*
Result: *in order that, so, so that*
Alternative: *than, whether*

Relative pronouns, such as *who, whom, whose, whatever, why,* and *unless,* can also be subordinate connectors.

Any clause beginning with one of these words is *subordinate* and should not be written as a sentence. Here are examples of clause fragments (italicized):

The Vikings revolutionized shipbuilding with the keel. *Which allowed their ships to go faster and farther without stopping for supplies.*

Norway's Lapps are believed to be a nomadic people of Asian heritage. *Who follow reindeer herds through Norway's cold, rugged land.*

Because the northern part of Norway is so far north. It has long periods during the summer when the sun shines 24 hours a day.

Correction. There are mainly two ways of correcting clause fragments: (1) attaching them to the preceding or following sentence, and (2) removing or changing the subordinating connector. These sentences illustrate both types of correction:

The Vikings revolutionized shipbuilding with the keel. *This innovation* allowed their ships to go faster and farther without stopping for supplies. The subordinating word of the fragment is changed.

Norway's Lapps are believed to be of Asian heritage—nomadic people who follow reindeer herds through Norway's cold, rugged land. The fragment is connected to the preceding sentence with a dash.

Because the northern part of Norway is so far north, it has long periods during the summer when the sun shines 24 hours a day. The fragment is connected to the following sentence with a comma.

Phrase Fragment

Phrase fragments lack a subject, a verb, or both. The most common phrases written as fragments are *verbal phrases* and *prepositional phrases*.

Recognition. A *verbal phrase* is a word group made up of a verb form and related modifiers and other words. As opposed to *verb phrases,* which are made up of verb parts (such as *has been gone*), a verbal phrase is constituted with a *verbal,* a word formed from a verb but not functioning as a verb. *Going,* for example, is a verbal, as is *gone.*

There are three kinds of verbals: gerunds, participles, and infinitives. Gerunds end in *-ing;* participles end in either *-ing* (present) or *-ed* (regular past); infinitives are usually introduced by *to*. Here are a few examples of how verbals are formed from verbs:

Verb	Present Participle and Gerund	Past Participle	Infinitive
snap	snapping	snapped	to snap
look	looking	looked	to look
want	wanting	wanted	to want
go	going	gone	to go
has	having	had	to have

Verbals function primarily as adjectives and nouns, most often in verbal phrases.

In the following examples, the italicized verbal phrases are fragments because they are written as sentences:

Eero Saarinen designed the 630-foot Gateway Arch for the St. Louis riverfront. *Imagining a giant stainless steel arch.* Participial phrase modifying *Eero Saarinen*

Critics said that cranes could not reach high enough. *To lift the steel sections into place.* Infinitive phrase modifying *high*

Saarinen knew that precision was of utmost importance. In *building the arch.* Gerund phrase as object of preposition *In*

Correction. Verbal phrase fragments can be corrected in one of two ways: (1) by connecting them to a related sentence, or (2) by expanding them into a sentence. Both ways are illustrated below:

Eero Saarinen designed the 630-foot Gateway Arch for the St. Louis riverfront. *He imagined a giant stainless steel arch.* The verbal fragment is expanded to a sentence.

Critics said that cranes could not reach high enough *to lift the steel sections into place.* The verbal fragment is connected to a related sentence.

Saarinen knew that precision was of utmost importance in *building the arch.* The gerund phrase, object of the preposition *In*, is connected to a related sentence.

Recognition. A *prepositional phrase* is a word group made up of a preposition and its object. Together they contribute meaning to a sentence, usually modifying a noun or a verb. Like subordinating conjunctions, prepositions show relationships, such as time, place, condition, and cause. Common prepositions include *about, above, among, below, but, by, in addition to, into, like, from, out of, past, regarding, toward,* and *until.*

In the following examples, prepositional phrases have been written as sentences and are therefore fragments:

> The Vikings were descendents of Teutonic settlers. *Like most of today's Norwegians.*

> Norway is a land of natural beauty. *From its fjord-lined coast to frigid Lapland.*

Correction. Prepositional phrase fragments can also be corrected (1) by connecting them to a related sentence, or (2) by expanding them into a sentence.

> The Vikings were descendents of Teutonic settlers, *like most of today's Norwegians.* **or** *Like most of today's Norwegians*, the Vikings were descendents of Teutonic settlers. The prepositional phrase is connected to a related sentence.

> Norway is a land of natural beauty. *Its charm extends from its fjord-lined coast to frigid Lapland.* The prepositional phrase is expanded into a sentence.

Incomplete Thoughts

Sometimes fragments are simply errors in punctuation—the writer uses a period when a comma or no punctuation would be correct. A more difficult type of fragment to correct is the incomplete thought, such as this one:

> A large concrete dock 50 feet short of a wooden platform anchored in the middle of the bay.

With fragments of this sort, the writer needs to insert the missing information. The reader doesn't know what happens—what the dock does or what is done to it. The fragment might be revised like this:

> A large concrete dock *juts out, stopping* 50 feet short of a wooden platform anchored in the middle of the bay.

Acceptable Fragments

You probably encounter fragments every day. Titles are often fragments, as are answers to questions and expressions of strong emotion.

> **Titles:** *Gates of Fire: An Epic Novel of the Battle of Thermopylae*

> **Answer to question:** "How many more chairs do we need?" "Fifteen."

> **Expression of strong emotion:** "What a great concert!"

And much advertising uses fragments:

> Intricate, delicate, exquisite. Extravagant in every way.

> Another successful client meeting. Par for the course.

Finally, writers quoting spoken words might use fragments:

> Claire asked Erin, "Why would you do that?"

> Erin shrugged. "Because."

Common as they are in everyday life, fragments are usually unacceptable in academic or workplace writing. When you do choose to use a fragment, you should do it intentionally, and only after carefully considering your readers and the effect that you want to achieve.

1B Comma Splices

Comma splices consist of two independent clauses (clauses that can stand alone as sentences) improperly joined together by a comma as one sentence. Here are two examples:

> The economy of Algeria is in trouble, many citizens blame the government.

> The death of any soldier is tragic, however, death by friendly fire is particularly disturbing.

Recognition. The first step in avoiding comma splices is to identify them. Because they happen only in sentences with at least two independent clauses, you can test your sentences by substituting periods for commas. If you end up with two complete sentences, you probably have a comma splice. In testing the first of the two preceding examples we come up with the following result:

> The economy of Algeria is in trouble.

> Many citizens blame the government.

Both of these clauses obviously qualify as complete sentences, so they must be independent clauses. They therefore cannot be connected with a comma. Remember this simple rule of punctuation: *Periods and commas are not interchangeable.* If a period is correct, a comma is not.

Correction. You can revise comma splices using five different strategies.

1. Separate the independent clauses using a comma and a *coordinating conjunction.* There are seven—and *only* seven—coordinating conjunctions. As a memory aid, their first letters spell F-A-N-B-O-Y-S:

for	but
and	or
nor	yet
	so

To correct a comma splice, begin the second independent clause with one of these conjunctions preceded by a comma. For example:

The economy of Algeria is in trouble, *and* many citizens blame the government.

2. Separate the independent clauses using a semicolon (with or without a transitional adverb). Semicolons are often interchangeable with periods and therefore can be used to separate independent clauses. For example:

The economy of Algeria is in trouble; many citizens blame the government.

The death of any soldier is tragic; *however,* death by friendly fire is particularly disturbing.

In the second example, *however* is a transitional adverb. Unlike coordinating conjunctions, *transitional adverbs* are not conjunctions and so do not join sentence elements. They do, however, connect ideas by showing how they relate to one another. Like conjunctions, they can show addition, contrast, result, and other relationships. Some of the most common transitional adverbs are *also, in addition, next, finally, for example, however, meanwhile, therefore,* and *then.*

A semicolon should always precede the transitional adverb that begins the second independent clause. A comma usually follows the transitional adverb, although in some instances, as in the following example, the comma is omitted:

Air bags deflate within one second after inflation; *therefore* they do not interfere with control of the car.

Some comma splices result when writers use transitional adverbs as if they were coordinating conjunctions. If you have trouble distinguishing transitional adverbs from coordinating conjunctions, remember that none of the coordinating conjunctions is longer than three letters, and all of the transitional adverbs are four letters or longer. Also, keep in mind that transitional adverbs are movable within the sentence while coordinating conjunctions are not; for example, the preceding example could be rewritten as:

Air bags deflate within one second after inflation; they do not *therefore* interfere with control of the car.

3. Make one of the independent clauses subordinate to the other by inserting a subordinating conjunction. When one of the clauses explains or elaborates on the other, use an appropriate subordinating conjunction to make the relationship between the two clauses more explicit (see 1A, Fragments). Consider the following comma splice and its revision:

Henry forgot to fill in his time card on Friday, he is going to have a hard time getting paid for the overtime he put in last week.

Because Henry forgot to fill in his time card on Friday, he is going to have a hard time getting paid for the overtime he put in last week.

4. Rewrite one of the independent clauses as a modifying phrase. A *modifying phrase* serves as an adjective or adverb within a sentence. By rewriting one of the independent clauses as a phrase, you can eliminate unneeded words. For example, consider the following commas splice and its revision:

The celebrity couple smiled for the cameras, they were glowing of wealth and fame.

The celebrity couple smiled for the cameras, glowing of wealth and fame. Here, *glowing of wealth and fame* acts as an adjective modifying the noun *couple*.

5. Punctuate each independent clause as a separate sentence. No law of grammar, punctuation, or style says you must present the two independent clauses together within one sentence. The example from before is perfectly acceptable written as follows:

The economy of Algeria is in trouble. Many citizens blame the government.

It may be to your advantage to divide long and/or complex independent clauses into separate sentences. Doing so may help convey your meaning to readers more clearly.

1C Fused Sentences

Fused sentences, sometimes called *run-on sentences,* are similar to comma splices. However, instead of a comma between the two independent clauses, there is no punctuation; the two independent clauses simply run together. For example:

The United States has 281 lawyers per 100,000 people Japan has only 11 attorneys per 100,000.

The World Cup is the most popular sporting event in the world you would never know it based on the indifferent response of the average American.

Recognition.   Unlike the comma splice, there is no punctuation in the fused sentence to guide you to the end of the first independent clause and the beginning of the second. As a result, it can be more challenging to identify independent clauses within fused sentences, particularly if the sentence also contains modifying phrases or dependent clauses set off by commas. The best way to do this is to read from the beginning of the sentence (reading aloud may help) until you have found the end of the first independent clause. Consider the following example:

Even though I was still sick with the flu, I attended the awards banquet as my family watched, the coach presented me with the trophy for most valuable player.

This fused sentence contains two subordinate clauses (*Even though I was still sick with the flu* and *as my family watched*), each one attached to one of the two independent clauses (*I attended the awards banquet* and *the coach presented me with the trophy*).

Correction.   Revise fused sentences using any one of the same five strategies for correcting comma splices (see 1B Comma Splices, for more information on each strategy).

1. Separate the independent clauses using a comma and a coordinating conjunction. For example:

The United States has 281 lawyers per 100,000 people, *but* Japan has only 11 attorneys per 100,000.

2. Separate the independent clauses using a semicolon (with or without a transitional adverb). For example:

The United States has 281 lawyers per 100,000 people; Japan has only 11 attorneys per 100,000.

The World Cup is the most popular sporting event in the world; *however,* you would never know it based on the indifferent response of the average American.

3. Make one of the independent clauses subordinate to the other by inserting a subordinating conjunction. The newly formed dependent clause should explain the remaining independent clause. For example, consider the following fused sentence and its revision:

I run a marathon my feet get sore.

Whenever I run a marathon, my feet get sore.

4. Rewrite one of the independent clauses as a modifying phrase. Remember, modifying phrases act as adjectives or adverbs. Consider the following fused sentence and its revision:

Last night the tomcats fought outside my window they were crying and hissing for what seemed like hours.

Last night the tomcats fought outside my window, crying and hissing for what seemed like hours. Here, the phrase *crying and hissing* acts as an adjective modifying the noun *tomcats*.

5. Punctuate each independent clause as a separate sentence. As with comma splices, you can write the independent clauses (and their related phrases and dependent clauses) as separate sentences. Indeed, this is often the easiest way to handle fused sentences. For example:

I attended the awards banquet even though I was still sick with the flu. As my family watched, the coach presented me with the trophy for most valuable player. Here, the subordinate clause attached to the first independent clause *even though I was still sick with the flu* was also moved to the back of the first sentence for better readability.

1D Parallelism

Correctly used parallelism results when two or more grammatically equivalent sentence elements are joined. The sentence elements can be nouns, verbs, phrases, or clauses. (See 1E Coordination and Subordination.)

Parallelism becomes a problem when dissimilar elements are joined in pairs, in series, in comparisons using *than* or *as,* or in comparisons linked by correlative conjunctions. Consider the following examples of faulty parallelism:

She did not like rude customers or taking orders from her boss. The two elements in the pair are not parallel.

We were having a hard time deciding what to do in the afternoon: go snorkeling, go fishing, or swim out to the sand bar. The last of the three elements in the series is not parallel.

Michael decided to complete his degree next semester rather than studying abroad for another year. The two elements compared using *than* are not parallel.

My sister not only lost the race but also her leg got hurt. The two elements compared by the correlative conjunction *not only . . . but also* are not parallel. Other correlative conjunctions include *both . . . and*, *either . . . or*, *neither . . . nor*, *whether . . . or*, and *just as . . . so*.

Faulty parallelism can be corrected in various ways:

She did not like *dealing with* rude customers or taking orders from her boss. Words were added to the first element to make it parallel to the second.

We were having a hard time deciding what to do in the afternoon: go snorkeling, go fishing, or *go swimming*. The last element was rewritten to make it parallel with the others in the series.

Michael decided to complete his degree next semester rather than *to study* abroad for another year. The verb form of the second element is changed from a participle to an infinitive to make it parallel with the verb form in the first element.

My sister not only lost the race but also *hurt her leg*. The second element was rewritten to make it parallel with the first element.

1E Coordination and Subordination

When dealing with complex ideas, you will often need to explain relationships among things, ideas, places, people, events, and so forth. Sometimes you will choose to explain those relationships within a single sentence. Most sentence relationships involve either coordination or subordination. That is, sentence elements are either grammatically equal to other elements (coordination) or grammatically dependent on other parts (subordination). For example, two independent clauses in a sentence are coordinate; but in a sentence containing an independent clause and a dependent clause, the dependent clause is subordinate (indeed, dependent clauses are also called subordinate clauses).

Coordination

When two or more equivalent sentence elements appear in one sentence, they are coordinate. These elements can be words, phrases, or clauses. Only parallel elements can be coordinated: verbs linked with verbs, nouns with nouns, phrases with phrases, and clauses with clauses (See 1D Parallelism). For example:

Broccoli and *related vegetables* contain beta-carotene, a substance that may reduce the risk of heart attack. Two nouns are joined by a coordinating conjunction.

We *ran, swam,* and *cycled* every day while we were at the fitness camp. Three parallel verbs are joined in a series with commas and a coordinating conjunction.

American medical devices are equally remarkable, *giving life to those with terminally diseased organs, giving mobility to those crippled with arthritic joints and deadened nerves,* and even, miraculously, *restoring the sense of hearing to those deprived of it.—Atlantic.* The participial (verbal) phrases are joined by commas and a final coordinating conjunction. Also, embedded in the second participial phrase, two coordinate noun phrases are joined by a coordinating conjunction: *arthritic joints and deadened nerves.*

The term "Big Bang" is common usage now with scientists, but it originated as a sarcastic rejection of the theory. Two independent clauses are joined by a comma and a coordinating conjunction.

Subordination

If all sentence elements were grammatically equivalent, the sameness would be tedious. Subordinate elements show where the emphasis lies in sentences and modify elements with independent clauses. A subordinate element—either a phrase or clause—is dependent on the element it modifies for its meaning. At the same time, it often provides a fuller meaning than could be achieved exclusively through the use of independent elements.

For example:

For walking and jogging, the calorie expenditure is greater for people of greater body weight. The subordinate element is a prepositional phrase, modifying *is greater.*

Increasing both speed and effort in aerobic activities, the exerciser burns more calories. The subordinate element is a verbal phrase, modifying *exerciser.*

Because sedentary people are more likely to burn sugar than fat, they tend to become hungry sooner and to overeat. Subordinate clause modifying the verb *tend.*

People *who exercise on a regular basis* change certain enzyme systems *so that they are more likely to burn fat than sugar.* There are two subordinate clauses, one beginning with *who* and modifying *People,* and one beginning with *so that* and modifying the verb *change.*

Effective writing has both coordination and subordination—coordination that sets equivalent elements side by side, and subordination that makes some elements dependent on others. These useful writing tools can be used often or rarely, depending on the rhetorical situation, the genre, and the style you choose to use.

1F Mixed Sentences

A mixed sentence is a problem that occurs when two or more parts of a sentence do not make sense together. It is called faulty predication when a subject and predicate are mismatched. This kind of problem usually occurs when writers are striving to express complex relationships.

The following mixed sentences are common in everyday speech and may not seem inconsistent to you. Indeed, in casual speech they are usually accepted. In standard written English, however, they qualify as grammatical errors.

By driving to the movie was how we saw the accident happen. The prepositional phrase *By driving to the movie* is treated as the subject of the verb *was*. Prepositional phrases cannot serve as subjects.

Just because the candidate once had a drinking problem doesn't mean he won't be a good mayor now. The adverb clause *because the candidate once had a drinking problem* is treated as the subject of the verb *doesn't mean*. Adverbs modify verbs and adjectives and cannot function as subjects.

A CAT scan is when medical technicians take a cross-sectional X-ray of the body. The adverb clause *when medical technicians take a cross-sectional X-ray of the body* is treated as a complement of the subject *CAT scan*—another function adverbs cannot serve.

The reason I was late today is because my alarm clock broke. The subject, *reason,* is illogically linked with the predicate, *is because. Reason* suggests an explanation, so the predicate, *is because,* is redundant.

Revise mixed sentences by ensuring that grammatical patterns are used consistently throughout each sentence. For cases of faulty predication, either revise the subject so it can perform the action expressed in the predicate or revise the predicate so it accurately depicts an action performed by the subject. When you are writing, avoid these patterns: *is when, is where,* and *The reason . . . is because.*

There are often many ways to revise mixed sentences. In each of the following revisions, the grammatical patterns are consistent and the subjects and predicates fit together logically:

While driving to the movie, we saw the accident happen.

Just because the candidate once had a drinking problem, we can't conclude that he won't be a good mayor.

A CAT scan is a cross-sectional X-ray of the body.

The reason I was late today is that my alarm clock broke.

1G Shifts

Shifts occur when writers lose track of their sentence elements. Shifts occur in a variety of ways:

In person

In music, where left-handed people seem to be talented, the right-handed world puts *you* at a disadvantage. Shift from *people,* third person, to *you,* second person

In tense

Even though many musicians *are* left handed, instruments *had been designed for right handers.* Shift from present tense to past perfect

In number

A left-handed *violinist* has to pay extra to buy *their* left-handed violin. Shift from singular to plural

In mood

Every time the *violinist played, she could always know* when her instrument was out of tune. Shift from the indicative mood, *violinist played,* to the subjunctive mood, *she could always know*

In voice

The sonata *was being practiced* by the violinists in one room while the cellists *played* the concerto in the other room. Shift from the passive voice, *was being practiced,* to the active voice, *played*

In discourse type

She said, *"Your violin is out of tune,"* and that *I was playing the wrong note.* Shift from the direct quotation, *"Your violin is out of tune,"* to the indirect quotation, *that I was playing the wrong note*

Once you recognize shifts, revise them by ensuring that the same grammatical structures are used consistently throughout the sentence:

In music, where left-handed *people* seem to be talented, the right-handed world puts *them* at a disadvantage.

Even though many musicians *are* left handed, instruments *have been designed* for right handers.

Left-handed *violinists* have to pay extra to buy *their* left-handed violins.

Every time the violinist *played,* she *knew* when her instrument was out of tune.

The violinists *practiced* the sonata in one room while the cellists *played* the concerto in the other room.

She said, *"Your violin is out of tune and you are playing the wrong note."*

1H Dangling and Misplaced Modifiers

Dangling and misplaced modifiers are words and word groups that are phrased or positioned in ways that make the meaning of a sentence unclear and sometimes even ludicrous. They are most commonly verbal phrases, prepositional phrases, and adverbs. Here are examples:

Reaching to pick up the saddle, the obnoxious horse may shake off the blanket. The dangling verbal phrase appears to relate to *horse.*

To extend lead out of the eversharp pencil, the eraser cap is depressed. The dangling verbal phrase implies that *the eraser cap* does something.

The eversharp pencil is designed to be used permanently, *only periodically replacing the lead.* The dangling verbal phrase implies that the pencil replaces the lead.

Dick *only* had to pay ten dollars for his parking ticket. The misplaced adverb should immediately precede *ten*.

Theodore caught a giant fish in the very same spot where he had lost the ring *two years later*. The misplaced adverb phrase confusingly appears to modify the last part of the sentence instead of, correctly, the first part.

Errors of this type are difficult for writers to recognize because to the writers they are not ambiguous.

Recognition. Verbal phrases always have implied but unstated subjects. In other words, somebody or something is performing the action of the verbal phrase, but the phrase itself does not say who or what. For clarity, that implied subject should be the same as the subject of the sentence or clause. In the first example above, the implied subject of *Reaching* is not *the horse*. In the second example, the implied subject of *To extend* is not *the eraser cap*. And in the third example, the implied subject of *replacing* is not *the pencil*. Also check passive voice, because in a passive sentence the subject is not the doer of the action. In the second example, the dangler can be corrected when the verb, changed from passive to active voice, tells who should depress the eraser (see correction that follows).

Correction. The way to correct dangling and misplaced modifiers depends on the type of error. Misplaced modifiers can often be moved to a more appropriate position:

Dick had to pay *only* ten dollars for his parking ticket.

Two years later, Theodore caught a giant fish in the very same spot where he had lost the ring.

Dangling modifiers usually require some rewording:

As you reach to pick up the saddle, the obnoxious horse may shake off the blanket. The dangling verbal phrase is converted to a clause.

To extend lead out of the eversharp pencil, *depress the eraser cap.* The main clause is revised so that *you* is the implied subject of *depress* (as it is for *To extend*).

The eversharp pencil is designed to be used permanently, *only periodically needing the lead replaced.* The dangling verbal phrase is revised so that the implied subject of *needing* is *pencil*.

1I Restrictive and Nonrestrictive Modifiers

Some modifiers are essential to a sentence because they *restrict,* or limit, the meaning of the words they modify; others, while adding important information, are not essential to the meaning of a sentence. The first type is called restrictive and the second nonrestrictive. The terms usually refer to subordinate clauses and phrases. Here are examples of restrictive and nonrestrictive modifiers:

Restrictive

People *who plan to visit Europe* should take time to see Belgium. Relative clause modifying and identifying *People*.

The industrialized country *between the Netherlands and France on the North Sea* is constitutionally a kingdom. Prepositional phrases modifying and identifying *country*.

The Kempenland was thinly populated *before coal was discovered there*. Subordinate clause modifying *was populated* and giving meaning to the sentence.

Language and cultural differences have created friction *that has existed for centuries*. Relative clause modifying and identifying *friction*.

Nonrestrictive

Belgium has two major populations: the Flemings, *who live in the north and speak Flemish*, and the Walloons, *who live in the south and speak French*. Two relative clauses, the first modifying *Flemings* and the second modifying *Walloons*.

With Brussels in the middle of the country, both groups inhabit the city. Prepositional phrases, together modifying *inhabit*.

NATO's headquarters is in Brussels, *where it has been since its beginning in 1950*. Subordinate clause modifying *Brussels*.

Covering southeastern Belgium, the sandstone Ardennes mountains follow the Sambre and Meuse rivers. Participial (verbal) phrase modifying *mountains*.

These examples illustrate several aspects of restrictive and nonrestrictive modifiers:

1. They *modify* a word in the clause or sentence; they therefore function as adjectives or adverbs.
2. They can appear at the beginning, somewhere in the middle, or at the end of a sentence or clause.
3. Most types of subordinate elements can be either restrictive or nonrestrictive.
4. Whether a clause or phrase is restrictive or nonrestrictive depends on its function in the sentence.
5. Restrictive elements are not set off with punctuation; nonrestrictive elements are set off with commas (and sometimes dashes).

If you think the distinction between restriction and nonrestriction is not worth making, consider the following sentences, the first restrictive and the second nonrestrictive:

People who wear braces on their teeth should not eat caramel apples.

People, who wear braces on their teeth, should not eat caramel apples.

Set off with commas, the nonrestrictive *who* clause implies that all people wear braces on their teeth and should not eat caramel apples, which is clearly not the case. It does not *restrict*, or limit, the meaning of *people*. In the first sentence, however, the *who* clause does restrict, or limit, the meaning of *people* to only those who wear braces on their teeth. Often only the writer knows the intended meaning and therefore needs to make the distinction by setting off, or not setting off, the modifier.

Here are a few guidelines that might help you in making this fine distinction:

1. A modifier that modifies a proper noun (one that names a person or thing) is usually nonrestrictive, because the name is sufficient identification. Notice *Flemings* and *Walloons* in the previous example.

2. A *that* clause is almost always restrictive.

3. Adverbial subordinate clauses (those beginning with subordinating conjunctions such as *because* and *when*) are almost always restrictive and are usually not set off with commas when they appear at the end of their sentences. If they appear at the beginning of sentences, they are almost always set off with commas.

4. A nonrestrictive modifier at the beginning of a sentence is followed by a comma, one at the end is preceded by a comma, and one in the middle is enclosed with two commas.

1J Adjectives and Adverbs

Adjectives and adverbs, often called *modifiers,* modify nouns and verbs. Adjectives modify nouns; that is, they describe, limit, explain, or alter them in some way. Adverbs modify verbs, adjectives, and other adverbs, telling more than the words by themselves would tell: drive *carefully* (adverb modifying a verb), *unexpectedly* early (adverb modifying an adjective), drive *very* carefully (adverb modifying an adverb). Adverbs usually tell how, where, when, and how much.

Adjectives and adverbs occasionally present some problems for writers. Be careful not to use adjectives when adverbs are needed, as in this incorrect sentence:

The governor suspected that the legislators were not taking him *serious*. The sentence element receiving modification is the verb *were not taking* yet the modifier *serious* is an adjective, which can only modify nouns. The correct modifier for this sentence is the adverb *seriously*. (If you are not sure whether a word is an adjective or an adverb, check your dictionary, which should identify parts of speech.)

Another problem in form concerns the *comparative* and *superlative* degrees. The comparative form of adjectives and adverbs shows a greater degree between two things, as in these correct sentences:

Your luggage is *stronger* than mine. Adjective comparing *your luggage* and *mine.*

Your luggage survives airport baggage handling *better* than mine does. Adverb comparing how the two *survive* handling.

The comparative degree is formed by adding *-er* to shorter adjectives and adverbs (*strong, stronger; hard, harder*). Longer words are preceded by *more* (*beautiful, more beautiful; seriously, more seriously*). Do not use *-er* with *more* (not *more harder*).

The superlative form shows a greater degree among three or more things, as in these correct sentences:

This is the *strongest* luggage I have ever seen. Adjective comparing the present luggage to all other luggage the writer has seen.

Your luggage survives airport baggage handling *best* of all luggage I've seen.
Adverb comparing how all luggage the writer has seen survives handling.

The superlative degree is formed by adding *-est* to shorter adjectives and adverbs (*strong, strongest; hard, hardest*). Longer words are preceded by *most* (*beautiful, most beautiful; seriously, most seriously*). Do not use *-est* with *most* (not *most strongest*).

Do not use adjectives and adverbs gratuitously, just to fill space or because you think you ought to. They are effective only when they add meaning to a sentence.

2 Verbs

Verbs are the core of a sentence; together with subjects, they make statements. Verbs often tell what the subject is doing:

The company *agreed* to plead guilty to criminal charges.

Nearly every miner *can name* a casualty of black lung disease.

Another common function of verbs is to link subjects to complements:

Logan *is* an isolated county in the corner of the state.

Sometimes the verb tells something about the subject, as the following passive verb does:

Casualties of mining *cannot be measured* only by injuries.

Through changes in form, verbs can tell the time of the action (past, present, future), the number of the subject (singular or plural), and the person of the subject (first person, *I, we;* second person, *you;* third person, *he, she, it, they*).

2A Tense

Writers can encounter problems with verbs because verbs, unlike most other words in English, have many forms, and a slight shift in form can alter meaning. Notice how the meanings of the following pairs of sentences change when the verbs change:

The fish *has jumped* into the boat.

The fish *have jumped* into the boat.

The concert *starts* at 8:15 p.m.

The concert *started* at 8:15 p.m.

In the first pair, the meaning changes from one fish to more than one fish jumping into the boat. In the second pair, the first verb implies that the concert has not yet begun; the second, that it had already begun. Observe how the verb *vanish* changes in the following sentences to indicate differences in time, or *tense:*

Present:	Many agricultural jobs *vanish.*
Past:	Many agricultural jobs *vanished.*

Future:	Many agricultural jobs *will vanish.*
Perfect:	Many agricultural jobs *have vanished.*
Past Perfect:	Many agricultural jobs *had vanished.*
Future Perfect:	Many agricultural jobs *will have vanished.*

Omitting an *-ed* ending or using the wrong helping verb can give readers a false message.

Helping (Auxiliary) Verbs. It is also important to use a form that is a *finite,* or an actual, verb. In the following example, the word that appears to be a verb (italicized) is not a finite verb:

The fish *jumping* into the boat.

The word *jumping* does not have one of the primary functions of verbs—telling the time of the action, called *tense.* The time of the occurrence could have been the past (*the fish were jumping*), the present (*the fish are jumping*), or the future (*the fish will be jumping*). We also don't know whether the writer meant one fish or many. The *-ing* form is a *verbal* and requires a helping, or auxiliary, verb to make it finite, or able to tell time: words such as *am, is, are, was, were* (forms of *be*). Other helping verbs are *do* (*Do* you *want* the paper? She *doesn't want* the paper) and *have* (I *haven't seen* the paper; *has* she *seen* it?).

Irregular Verbs. Most verbs change forms in a regular way: *want* in the present becomes *wanted* in the past, *wanting* with the auxiliary *be* (i.e., *is wanting*), and *wanted* with the auxiliary *have* (i.e., *have wanted*). Many verbs change irregularly, however—internally rather than at the ending. Here are a few of the most common irregular verbs:

Base Form	Past Tense	Present Participle	Past Participle
be (is, am, are)	was, were	being	been
come	came	coming	come
do	did	doing	done
drink	drank	drinking	drunk
give	gave	giving	given
go	went	going	gone
grow	grew	growing	grown
lie	laid	lying	lain
see	saw	seeing	seen
take	took	taking	taken
teach	taught	teaching	taught
throw	threw	throwing	thrown
wear	wore	wearing	worn
write	wrote	writing	written

Check your dictionary for the forms of other verbs you suspect may be irregular.

The verb form that is perhaps the most troublesome is the *-s* form in the present tense. This form is used for all singular nouns and the pronouns *he, she,* and *it.* (See 2D Subject-Verb Agreement.)

2B Voice

English sentences are usually written in the active voice, in which the subject of the sentence is the doer of the action of the verb:

Scott misplaced the file folder. *Scott*, the subject of the sentence, performed the action, *misplaced*.

With the passive voice, the doer of the action is the object of a preposition or is omitted entirely:

The file folder was misplaced by Scott. *File folder* is now the subject of the sentence.

The file folder was misplaced. The person doing the action is not named.

As a writer, you need to decide whether to use the active or passive voice. The passive voice requires more words than the active voice, it can hide the doer, and its overuse reduces clarity and increases confusion. This is why you may have been told that you should *never use the passive voice*.

Choose the passive voice when it is appropriate to the genre and to your readers' needs. For genres such as memoirs, profiles, and literary analyses, you will probably choose active voice because readers of these genres usually want to know who is doing what to whom. In other situations, you may choose to use the passive voice, either because you do not know the doer's identity or because the doer's identity is unimportant or obvious to the reader. When writing a lab report in a chemistry course, for instance, your reader does not need to be told who specifically combined the chemicals. Finally, the passive voice can be useful if you want to keep the subjects consistent within a paragraph.

But unless you have good reason to use the passive voice, avoid it. First, look for passive voice by noting *by* phrases near the ends of your sentences. If you find any, determine whether the subject of your sentence performs the action of your verb. If not, revise the sentence so that it does. Another way to find occurrences of the passive voice is to look for forms of *be: am, is, are, was, were, been, being*. Not all these verbs will be passive, but if they function as part of an action verb, determine whether the subject performs the action. If it does not, and if your sentence would be clearer with the subject performing the action, revise to the active voice.

2C Mood

English verbs are stated in one of three moods: indicative, imperative, and subjunctive. In most writing and speaking, the most commonly used mood by far is the *indicative mood*, which is used to make statements, to ask questions, and to declare opinions. For example:

Not many people today *think* the world *is* flat. Makes a statement.

Does anybody today *think* the world is flat? Asks a question.

Members of the Flat Earth Society *should reevaluate* their thinking. Declares an opinion.

Verbs in the *imperative mood* issue commands, requests, or directions. Imperative verbs never change form. When the subject of an imperative verb is not explicitly identified, it is understood to be *you*.

Julia, *stop* teasing your baby brother. Issues command.

Please *complete* this report by tomorrow morning. Issues request.

Turn right at the light and *drive* for another two blocks. Issues directions.

Verbs in the *subjunctive mood* communicate wishes, make statements contrary to fact, list requirements and demands, and imply skepticism or doubt. They usually appear in clauses introduced by *if, that, as if,* and *as though.* Use the base form of the verb for the present tense subjunctive. For the past tense subjunctive of the verb *be,* use *were* for all subjects.

She wishes that her son's best friend *were* more responsible. Communicates wish.

If the world *were* to end tomorrow, we would not have to pay taxes anymore. Makes statement contrary to fact.

The jury summons requires that your cousin *arrive* punctually at 8:00 a.m. and *sign* in with the court clerk. Lists requirements.

His girlfriend talks as if she *were* a pop music diva. Implies skepticism.

Be sure to select the correct verb forms to express indicative, imperative, and subjunctive moods.

2D Subject-Verb Agreement

Clauses are made of subjects and verbs plus their modifiers and other related words. A fundamental principle of usage is that verbs agree with their subjects. In most cases, this principle presents no problem: You say "Birds *have* feathers," not "Birds *has* feathers." But not all sentences are this simple. Before getting into the problem areas, consider first that errors in subject-verb agreement occur only with present tense verbs and the verb tenses that use present tense forms of helping verbs (such as *have* and *be*). And, except for the irregular verb *be* (with its forms *am, is, are, was, were*), the problem centers on third-person singular verbs with their *-s* ending. Here is the problem illustrated. Notice that only the verbs in the third-person singular are different. Unfortunately, all nouns are third person and, when singular, require this form in the present tense.

	Present		Present Perfect	
	Singular	**Plural**	**Singular**	**Plural**
First person	I work	we work	I have worked	we have worked
Second person	you work	you work	you have worked	you have worked
Third person	he (she, it) works	they work	he (she, it) has worked	they have worked

It is the *-s* form, then, that you need to watch for to avoid errors in subject-verb agreement. Here are some issues that may cause problems.

Intervening Subordinate Element

When a subject and a verb are side by side, they usually do not present a problem. Often, however, writers separate them with subordinate elements, such as clauses, prepositional or verbal phrases, and other elements. The result may be a subject-verb agreement error. The following sentence illustrates this problem:

> The realization that life is a series of compromises never occur to some people. The subject is *realization*, a singular noun, and should be followed by the singular verb *occurs*. The corrected sentence would read "The realization that life is a series of compromises never occurs to some people."

Subject Complement

Subject complements follow some verbs and rename the subject, although they are not always in the same number as the subject. Because a singular subject may have a plural complement, and vice versa, confused writers might make the verb agree with the complement instead of the subject. Here's an example:

> The result of this mistake are guilt, low self-esteem, and depression. The subject is *result*, not *guilt, low self-esteem*, and *depression*; the singular subject should be followed by the singular verb *is*. The corrected sentence would read "The result of this mistake is guilt, low self-esteem, and depression."

Compound Subject

Two or more words may be compounded to make a subject. Whether they are singular or plural depends on their connector. Subjects connected by *and* and *but* are plural, but those connected by *or* and *nor* are singular or plural depending on whether the item closer to the verb is singular or plural. Here are examples:

> The young mother and the superior student *are* both candidates for compulsive perfectionism. Two subjects, *mother* and *student*, are joined by *and* and take a plural verb.

> Promotions or an employee award *tells* the perfectionist he or she is achieving personal goals. When two subjects, *promotions* and *award*, are joined by *or*, the verb agrees with the nearer one; in this sentence, a singular verb is required.

> An employee award or promotions *tell* the perfectionist he or she is achieving personal goals. Here the plural verb, *tell*, agrees with *promotions*, the closer of the two subjects.

Indefinite Pronoun as Subject

Indefinite pronouns are defined and listed under 3C Pronoun Agreement. Although these words often seem plural in meaning, most of them are singular grammatically. When indefinite pronouns are the subjects of sentences or clauses, their verbs are usually singular. Here are examples:

> Everyone *has* at some time worried about achieving goals. The singular indefinite pronoun *everyone* takes a singular verb, *has*.

> Each car and truck on the highway *was* creeping along on the icy pavement. The singular indefinite pronoun, *each*, requires a singular verb, *was*.

> Neither of us *is* going to worry about being late. The singular indefinite pronoun, *neither*, takes a singular verb, *is*.

Nevertheless, some of us *are* going to be very late. The indefinite pronoun *some* (like *all, any,* and *none*) is singular or plural depending on context; compare "Some of the book *is* boring."

Inverted Sentence Order

Inverted sentence order can confuse your natural inclination toward subject-verb agreement. Examples of inverted order are questions, plus sentences beginning with *there.* Sentences like these demand closer attention to agreement.

Have the results of the test come back yet? The plural subject, *results,* takes a plural verb, *have.*

There *are* many special services provided just for kids at hotels, ski lodges, and restaurants. The plural subject, *services,* takes a plural verb, *are. There* is never a subject; it only holds the place for the subject in an inverted sentence.

Intervening Relative Clause

Subordinate clauses that begin with the relative pronouns *who, which,* or *that* present special problems in subject-verb agreement. Their verbs must agree with their own subjects, not with a word in another clause. These subordinate clauses demand special attention because whether the pronouns are singular or plural depends on their antecedents. These sentences illustrate agreement within relative clauses:

Every person who *attends* the baseball game will receive a free cap. *Who,* the subject of *attends,* means "person," a singular noun.

John is one of the few people I know who *care* about frogs. *Who,* the subject of *care,* means "people," a plural noun.

John is the only one of all the people I know who *cares* about frogs. *Who* in this sentence means "one."

3 Pronouns

Pronouns can have all the same sentence functions as nouns; the difference is that pronouns do not have the meaning that nouns have. Nouns name things; a noun stands for the thing itself. Pronouns, however, refer only to nouns. Whenever that reference is ambiguous or inconsistent, there is a problem in clarity.

3A Pronoun Case

Case is a grammatical term for the way nouns and pronouns show their relationships to other parts of a sentence. In English, nouns have only two case forms: the regular form (the one listed in a dictionary, such as *year*) and the possessive form (used to show ownership or connection, such as *year's*; possessive nouns are discussed at 5J Apostrophe).

Pronouns, however, have retained their case forms. Here are the forms for personal and relative pronouns:

	Subjective	Objective	Possessive
Personal	I	me	my, mine
	you	you	your, yours
	he	him	his
	she	her	her, hers
	it	it	its
	we	us	our, ours
	they	them	their, theirs
Relative	who	whom	whose
	whoever	whomever	whosever

Notice, first, that possessive pronouns, unlike possessive nouns, do not take apostrophes—none of them. Sometimes writers confuse possessive pronouns with contractions, which do have apostrophes (such as *it's,* meaning *it is* or *it has;* and *who's,* meaning *who is;* for a further discussion, see 5J Apostrophe).

Another problem writers sometimes have with pronoun case is using a subjective form when they need the objective or using an objective form when they need the subjective.

Subjective Case. Use the subjective forms for subjects and for words referring to subjects, as in these examples:

Among the patients a nutritionist sees are the grossly overweight people *who* have tried all kinds of diets. *Who is subject of the verb have tried in its own clause.*

They have a life history of obesity and diets. *They is the subject of have.*

He and the patient work out a plan for permanent weight control. *He and patient are the compound subjects of work.*

The patient understands that the ones who work out the diet plan are *he* and the nutritionist. *He and nutritionist refer to ones, the subject of the clause.*

Notice that pronoun case is determined by the function of the pronoun in its own clause and that compounding (*he and the patient*) has no effect on case.

Objective Case. Use the objective forms for objects of all kinds:

"Between *you* and *me,*" said the patient to his nutritionist, "I'm ready for something that works." *You and me are objects of the preposition between.*

An exercise program is usually assigned the patient for *whom* dieting is prescribed. *Whom is the object of the preposition for.*

The nutritionist gives *her* a suitable alternative to couch sitting. *Her is the indirect object of gives.*

Modest exercise combined with modest dieting can affect *him or her* dramatically. *Him or her is the direct object of can affect.*

> Having advised *them* about diet and exercise, the nutritionist instructs dieters about behavioral change. *Them is the object of the participle having advised.*

Notice again that the case of a pronoun is determined by its function in its own clause and is not affected by compounding (*you and me*).

Possessive Case. Use the possessive forms to indicate ownership. Possessive pronouns have two forms: adjective forms (*my, your, his, her, its, our, their*) and possessive forms (*mine, yours, his, hers, its, ours, theirs*). The adjective forms appear before nouns or gerunds; the possessive forms replace possessive nouns.

> The patient purchased *his* supplements from the drug store *his* nutritionist recommended. Adjective form before nouns.

> *His* swimming every day produced results faster than he anticipated. Adjective form before gerund.

> *His* was a difficult task to accomplish, but the rewards of weight loss were great. Possessive form replacing possessive noun.

3B Pronoun Reference

Personal and relative pronouns (see list under 3A Pronoun Case) must refer unambiguously to their antecedents. Pronouns and antecedents must agree.

Ambiguous pronoun reference may occur in various ways:

- More than one possible antecedent.
- Adjective used as intended antecedent.
- Implied antecedent.
- Too much separation between antecedent and pronoun.

Here are sentences in which the pronouns do not clearly refer to their antecedents:

> The immunologist refused to admit fraudulence of the data reported by a former colleague in a paper *he* had cosigned. More than one possible antecedent. *He* could refer to *immunologist* or to *colleague.*

> In Carolyn Chute's book *The Beans of Egypt, Maine, she* treats poverty with concern and understanding. Adjective used as intended antecedent (possessive nouns function as adjectives). In this case, *Carolyn Chute's* modifies *book* and cannot serve as an antecedent of the pronoun *she.*

> *It* says in the newspaper that the economy will not improve soon. Implied antecedent. There is no antecedent for *it.*

> At Ajax *they* have tires on sale till the end of the month. Implied antecedent. There is no antecedent for *they.*

Faulty pronoun reference is corrected by clarifying the relationship between the pronoun and its intended antecedent. Observe how the example sentences have been revised:

The immunologist refused to admit fraudulence of the data reported by a former colleague in a paper *the immunologist* had cosigned. *The immunologist* replaces the unclear pronoun *he*.

In *her* book *The Beans of Egypt, Maine, Carolyn Chute* treats poverty with concern and understanding. The possessive pronoun *her* replaces the possessive noun and refers to the noun subject, *Carolyn Chute*.

The newspaper reports that the economy will not improve soon. The unclear pronoun *it* is replaced by its implied antecedent, *newspaper*.

Ajax has tires on sale till the end of the month. The unclear pronoun *they* is replaced by *Ajax*.

3C Pronoun Agreement

Some pronoun errors occur because the pronoun and its antecedent do not agree. Pronouns must agree with their antecedents in number, person, and gender. (See the list of pronouns in 3A Pronoun Case.)

Compound Antecedents

Problems sometimes occur with compound antecedents. If the antecedents are joined by *and,* the pronoun is plural; if they are joined by *or,* the pronoun agrees with the nearer antecedent. Here are examples of correct usage:

In the pediatric trauma center, the head doctor and head nurse direct *their* medical team. The pronoun *their* refers to both *doctor* and *nurse*.

The head doctor or the head nurse directs *his or her* team. The pronouns *his or her* refer to the closer antecedent, *nurse* (because the gender of the nurse is not known, the neutral alternatives are used).

The head doctor or the other doctors give *their* help when it is needed. The pronoun *their* agrees with the closer antecedent, *doctors*.

Indefinite Pronouns as Antecedents

A particularly troublesome kind of agreement is that between personal or relative pronouns and *indefinite pronouns*. As their name implies, indefinite pronouns do not refer to particular people or things; grammatically they are usually singular but are often intended as plural. Some common indefinite pronouns are *all, any, anybody, each, either, everybody, neither, no one, nothing, one, some, somebody,* and *something.*

Like nouns, these pronouns can serve as antecedents of personal and relative pronouns. But because most of them are grammatically singular, they can be troublesome in sentences. Here are examples of correct usage:

Everyone in the trauma center has *his or her* specific job to do. **or** All the personnel in the trauma center have *their* specific jobs to do. The neutral, though wordy, alternative *his or her* agrees with the singular indefinite pronoun *everyone*. The second sentence illustrates the use of the plural when gender is unknown.

Each of them does *his or her* job efficiently and competently. **or** *All* of them do *their* jobs efficiently and competently. *Each* is singular, but *all* can be either singular or plural, depending on context (compare "*All* literature has *its* place").

Shifts in Person

Agreement errors in *person* are shifts between *I* or *we* (first person), *you* (second person), and *he, she, it,* and *they* (third person). These errors are probably more often a result of carelessness than of imperfect knowledge. Being more familiar with casual speech than formal writing, writers sometimes shift from *I* to *you,* for example, when only one of them is meant, as in these sentences:

Last summer *I* went on a canoeing trip to northern Manitoba. It was *my* first trip that far north, and it was so peaceful *you* could forget all the problems back home. The person represented by *you* was not present. The writer means *I.*

See also 1G Shifts.

3D Relative Pronouns

Use relative pronouns to introduce clauses that modify nouns or pronouns. Personal relative pronouns refer to people. They include *who, whom, whoever, whomever,* and *whose.* Nonpersonal relative pronouns refer to things. They include *which, whichever, whatever,* and *whose.*

Use *which* to introduce nonrestrictive clauses and *that* to introduce restrictive clauses (see 1I Restrictive and Nonrestrictive Modifiers). Use *who* to refer to the subject of the sentence and *whom* to refer to an object of the verb or preposition. Following are examples of common errors:

The lawyer *that* lost the case today went to law school with my sister. Uses impersonal relative pronoun *that.*

Conflict between the two parties led to the lawsuit *that* was finally settled today. The relative pronoun *that* introduces a nonrestrictive clause that modifies *lawsuit.* Nonrestrictive clauses supply extra information to the sentence, not defining information.

The case resulted in a ruling, *which* favored the plaintiff. The relative pronoun *which* introduces a restrictive clause that modifies *ruling.* Restrictive clauses supply defining information.

Later, the lawyer *whom* lost the case spoke with the jurors *who* we had interviewed. The first relative pronoun *whom* refers to the subject *lawyer* while the second relative pronoun *who* refers to the object of the verb *had interviewed.*

Once you recognize relative pronoun errors, it is usually easy to fix them:

The lawyer *who* lost the case today went to law school with my sister.

Conflict between the two parties led to the lawsuit, *which* was finally settled today.

The case resulted in a ruling *that* favored the plaintiff.

Later, the lawyer *who* lost the case spoke with the jurors *whom* we had interviewed.

4 Style

There is no such thing as "correct style." Style is a choice you make as a writer in response to the rhetorical situation. In Chapter 16, "Choosing a Style," you learned several strategies for using style in ways that are appropriate for your purpose, readers, and genre. Here, you will learn strategies for writing with clarity and conciseness. You will also learn strategies for recognizing when certain kinds of language are and are not appropriate.

4A Conciseness

Nobody wants to read more words than necessary. Concise writing shows that you are considerate of your readers. You do not need to eliminate details and other content to achieve conciseness; rather, you cut empty words, repetition, and unnecessary details.

In the following passage, all the italicized words could be omitted without altering the meaning:

> *In the final analysis,* *I feel that* the United States should have converted to the *use of the* metric system *of measurement* a long time ago. *In the present day and age,* the United States, except for Borneo and Liberia, is the *one and* only country in the *entire* world that has not yet adopted this measurement system.

You may choose to repeat key words when you are striving for a certain effect (such as setting a tone or establishing character), but take care to avoid pointless repetition, which only bores and slows down your readers.

Follow these guidelines to achieve conciseness in your writing:

1. **Avoid redundancy.** Redundant words and expressions needlessly repeat what has already been said. Delete them when they appear in your writing.

2. **Avoid wordy expressions.** Phrases such as *In the final analysis* and *In the present day and age* add no important information to sentences and should be removed and/or replaced.

3. **Avoid unnecessary intensifiers.** Intensifiers such as *really, very, clearly, quite,* and *of course* usually fail to add meaning to the words they modify and therefore are often unnecessary. Delete them when doing so does not change the meaning of the sentence, or when you could replace the words with a single word (for instance, replacing *very good* with *excellent*).

4. **Avoid excess use of prepositional phrases.** The use of too many prepositional phrases within a sentence makes for wordy writing. Always use constructions that require the fewest words.

5. **Avoid negating constructions.** Negating constructions using words such as *no* and *not* often add unneeded words to sentences. Use shorter alternatives when they are available.

6. **Use the passive voice only when necessary.** Passive constructions require more words than active constructions (see 2B Voice). They can also obscure meaning by concealing the sentence's subject. When there is no good reason to use the passive voice, choose the active voice.

Here are more examples of wordy sentences that violate these guidelines:

> If the two groups *cooperate together*, there will be *positive benefits* for both. Uses redundancy.

> *There are* some people *who* think the metric system is un-American. Uses wordy expression.

> The climb up the mountain was *very* hard on my legs and *really* taxed my lungs and heart. Uses unnecessary modifiers.

> *On the day of his birth*, we walked *to the park down the block from the house of his mother*. Uses too many prepositional phrases.

> She *did not like* hospitals. Uses negating construction when a shorter alternative is available.

> The door *was closed* by that man over there. Uses passive voice when active voice is preferable.

Corrections to the wordy sentences above result in concise sentences:

> If the two groups cooperate, both will benefit. This correction also replaces the wordy construction *there will be . . . for both* with a shorter, more forceful alternative.

> Some people think the metric system is un-American.

> The climb up the mountain was hard on my legs and taxed my lungs and heart.

> On his birthday, we walked to the park near his mother's house.

> She hated hospitals.

> That man over there closed the door.

4B Appropriate Language

Effective writers communicate using appropriate language; that is, language that:

1. Suits the genre and rhetorical situation (topic, angle, purpose, readers, context).
2. Avoids sexist usage.
3. Avoids bias and stereotype.

Suitability

The style and tone of your writing should be suitable to your rhetorical situation and the genre you have chosen. Some situations require *formal language*. Formal language communicates clearly and directly with a minimum of stylistic flourish. Its tone is serious, objective, and often detached. Formal language avoids slang, pretentious words, and unnecessary technical jargon. *Informal language,* on the other hand, is particular to the writer's personality or social group and assumes a closer and more familiar relationship between the writer and the reader. Its tone is casual, subjective, and intimate. Informal language can also employ slang and other words that would be inappropriate in formal writing.

Keep in mind that what counts as suitable language always depends on the rhetorical situation you are facing and the genre you are using. Pretentious words might be appropriate if you were writing a parody of someone you feel is pretentious. Certain technical jargon would be not only suitable but also preferable in a technical report written for readers who are experts in the field. Slang could get across just the message you want in a memoir, profile, rave, slam, or other genre, in which you want to identify with a particular group that uses particular terms. Use your genre know-how and rhetorical awareness to help you decide when a certain kind of language is or is not suitable.

As informal language is rarely used within most academic, technical, or business settings, the following examples show errors in the use of formal language:

> The director told the board members to *push off*. Uses informal language.

> Professor Oyo *dissed* Marta when she arrived late to his class for the third time in a row. Uses slang.

> The *aromatic essence* of the gardenia was intoxicating. Uses pretentious words.

> The doctor told him to take *salicylate* to ease the symptoms of *viral rhinorrhea*. Uses unnecessary jargon.

Employing formal language correctly, these examples could be revised as follows:

> The director told the board members to leave.

> Professor Oyo spoke disrespectfully to Marta when she arrived late to his class for the third time in a row.

> The scent of the gardenia was intoxicating.

> The doctor told him to take aspirin to ease his cold symptoms.

Sexist Usage

Gender-exclusive terms such as *policeman* and *chairman* are offensive to many readers today. Writers who are sensitive to their audience, therefore, avoid such terms, replacing them with expressions such as *police officer* and *chairperson* or *chair*. Most sexist usage in language involves masculine nouns, masculine pronouns, and patronizing terms.

Masculine Nouns. Do not use *man* and its compounds generically. For many people, these words are specific to men and do not account for women as separate and equal people. Here are some examples of masculine nouns and appropriate gender-neutral substitutions:

Masculine Noun	Gender-Neutral Substitution
mailman	mail carrier
businessman	businessperson, executive, manager
fireman	firefighter
man-hours	work hours

Masculine Noun	Gender-Neutral Substitution
mankind	humanity, people
manmade	manufactured, synthetic
salesman	salesperson, sales representative, sales agent
congressman	member of Congress, representative

Using gender-neutral substitutions often entails using a more specific word for a generalized term, which adds more precision to writing.

Masculine Pronouns. Avoid using the masculine pronouns *he, him,* and *his* in a generic sense, meaning both male and female. This can pose some challenges, however, because English does not have a generic singular pronoun that can be used instead. Consider the following options:

1. Eliminate the pronoun.

Every writer has an individual style. Instead of Every writer has his own style.

2. Use plural forms.

Writers have their own styles. Instead of A writer has his own style.

3. Use *he or she, one,* or *you* as alternates only sparingly.

Each writer has his or her own style. Instead of Each writer has his own style.

One has an individual writing style. Instead of He has his own individual writing style.

You have your own writing style. Instead of A writer has his own style.

Patronizing Terms. Avoid terms that cast men or women in gender-exclusive roles or imply that women are subordinate to men. Here are some examples of biased or stereotypical terms and their gender-neutral substitutions:

Biased/Stereotypical Term	Gender-Neutral Substitution
lady lawyer	lawyer
male nurse	nurse
career girl	professional, attorney, manager
coed	student
housewife	homemaker
stewardess	flight attendant
cleaning lady	housecleaner

Biases and Stereotypes

Biased and stereotypical language can be hurtful and can perpetuate discrimination. Most writers are sensitive to racial and ethnic biases or stereotypes, but writers should also avoid language that shows insensitivity to age, class, religion, and sexual orientation. The accepted terms for identifying groups and group members have changed over the years and continue to change today. Avoid using terms that have fallen into disuse such as *Indian* or *Oriental;* instead, use accepted terms such as *Native American* or *Asian American.*

5 Punctuation, Mechanics, and Spelling

Punctuation is a system of signals telling readers how the parts of written discourse relate to one another. Punctuation provides readers with cues for interpreting the writer's words as the writer intended them to be understood.

This section discusses punctuation used within and at the ends of sentences. Other marks, those used within words (apostrophes, hyphens, italics, and slashes) are also explained later in this section.

5A End Punctuation

A period is the normal mark for ending sentences. A question mark ends a sentence that asks a direct question, and an exclamation point ends forceful assertions.

Period .

Sentences normally end with a period.

> Studies suggest that eating fish two or three times a week may reduce the risk of heart attack. Statement.

> Eat two or three servings of fish a week. Mild command.

> The patient asked whether eating fish would reduce the risk of heart attack. Indirect question.

Avoid inserting a period before the end of a sentence; the result will be a fragment (see 1A Fragments). Sentences can be long or short; their length does not determine their completion. Both of the following examples are complete sentences:

> Eat fish. Mild command; the subject, *you,* is understood.

> In a two-year study of 1,000 survivors of heart attack, researchers found a 29 percent reduction in mortality among those who regularly ate fish or took a fish oil supplement. Statement; one sentence.

Question Mark ?

A sentence that asks a direct question ends in a question mark.

> How does decaffeinated coffee differ from regular coffee?

Do not use a question mark to end an indirect question:

> The customer asked how decaffeinated coffee differs from regular coffee.

With quoted questions, place the question mark inside the final quotation marks:

> The customer asked, "How does decaffeinated coffee differ from regular coffee?"

Exclamation Point !
The exclamation point tells readers that the sentence should be interpreted as forceful or dramatic.

> Fire!

> Shut that door immediately!

Because they give the impression of shouting, exclamation points are rarely needed in formal business and academic writing.

5B Semicolon ;

Semicolons are mainly used for connecting two (or sometimes three) independent clauses.

> Dengue hemorrhagic fever is a viral infection common to Southeast Asia; it kills about 5,000 children a year.

Sometimes the second clause contains a transitional adverb (see 1B Comma Splices):

> Dengue has existed in Asia for centuries; *however,* it grew more virulent in the 1950s.

Do not use a comma where a semicolon or period is required; the result is a comma splice (see 1B Comma Splices). In contrast, a semicolon used in place of a comma may result in a type of fragment (see 1A Fragments):

> In populations where people have been stricken by an infectious virus, survivors have antibodies in their bloodstreams; *which prevent or reduce the severity of subsequent infections.* The semicolon makes a fragment of the *which* clause.

Do not confuse the semicolon with the colon (see 5D Colon). While the semicolon connects independent clauses, a colon ordinarily does not.

The semicolon is also used to separate items in a series when the items contain internal commas:

> Scientists are researching the effects of staphylococcus bacteria, which cause infections in deep wounds; influenza A virus, which causes respiratory flu; and conjunctivitis bacteria, which have at times caused fatal purpuric fever.

5C Comma ,

The comma is probably the most troublesome mark of punctuation because it has so many uses. Its main uses are explained here.

Compound Sentences. A comma joins two independent clauses connected with a coordinating conjunction (see 1B Comma Splices):

> Martinique is a tropical island in the West Indies, *and* it attracts flocks of tourists annually.

Do not use the comma between independent clauses without the conjunction, even if the second clause begins with a transitional adverb:

Faulty: Martinique is a tropical island in the West Indies, it attracts flocks of tourists annually. Two independent clauses with no conjunction creates a comma splice.

Faulty: Martinique is a tropical island in the West Indies, consequently it attracts flocks of tourists annually. Two independent clauses with transitional adverb creates a comma splice.

Introductory Sentence Elements. Commas set off a variety of introductory sentence elements, as illustrated here:

When the French colonized Martinique in 1635, they eliminated the native Caribs. Introductory subordinate clause.

Choosing death over subservience, the Caribs leaped into the sea. Introductory participial (verbal) phrase.

Before their death, they warned of a "mountain of fire" on the island. Introductory prepositional phrase.

Subsequently, the island's volcano erupted. Introductory transitional adverb.

Short prepositional phrases sometimes are not set off with commas:

In 1658 the Caribs leaped to their death.

Sometimes, however, a comma must be used after a short prepositional phrase to prevent misreading:

Before, they had predicted retribution. Comma is required to prevent misreading.

Nonrestrictive and Parenthetical Elements. Words that interrupt the flow of a sentence are set off with commas before and after. If they come at the end of a sentence, they are set off with one comma.

In this class are nonrestrictive modifiers (see 1B Restrictive and Nonrestrictive Modifiers), transitional adverbs (see 1B Comma Splices), and a few other types of interrupters. Here are examples:

This rugged island, *which Columbus discovered in 1502,* exports sugar and rum. Nonrestrictive *which* clause; commas before and after.

A major part of the economy, *however,* is tourism. Interrupting transitional adverb; commas before and after.

Tourists, *attracted to the island by its climate,* enjoy discovering its culture. Interrupting participial (verbal) phrase (see 1A Fragments); commas before and after.

A popular tradition in Martinique is the Carnival, *which occurs just before Lent each year.* Nonrestrictive *which* clause; one comma.

Martinique is an overseas department of France, *a status conferred in 1946.* An absolute, ending the sentence (participial phrase plus the noun it modifies).

Series

Commas separate items in a series:

> Martiniquans dance to *steel drums, clarinets, empty bottles, and banjos.* Four nouns.

> *Dressing in colorful costumes, dancing through the streets, and thoroughly enjoying the celebration,* Martiniquans celebrate Carnival with enthusiasm. Three participial (verbal) phrases.

> *Martinique has a population of over 300,000, its main religion is Roman Catholicism, and its languages are French and Creole dialect.* Three independent clauses.

Various sentence elements can make up a series, but the joined elements should be grammatically equivalent (see 1D Parallelism, which discusses faulty parallelism). Common practice calls for a comma before the conjunction joining the last item in the series.

Quotations

Commas set off quoted sentences from the words that introduce them:

> "A wise man," says David Hume, "proportions his belief to the evidence."

> According to Plato, "Writing will produce forgetfulness" in writers because "they will not need to exercise their memories." The second clause is not set off with a comma.

> "*X* on beer casks indicates beer which paid ten shillings duty, and hence it came to mean beer of a given quality," reports *The Dictionary of Phrase and Fable.*

Quotations introduced with *that* and other connectors (such as *because* in the second sentence here) are not set off with commas. Commas at the end of quotations go inside the quotation marks.

Coordinate Adjectives

Commas separate adjectives that equally modify a noun:

> The "food pyramid" was designed as a *meaningful, memorable* way to represent the ideal daily diet. Two adjectives modify the noun *way* equally.

When you're not sure about using a comma, try inserting the coordinating conjunction *and* between the two adjectives to see if they are truly coordinate (*meaningful and memorable*). Do not use a comma between adjectives that are not coordinate or between the last adjective and the noun being modified. (See also 1J Adjectives and Adverbs.)

Addresses and Dates

Use a comma to separate city and state in an address, but not to set off the zip code:

> Glen Ridge, New Jersey 07028 *or* Glen Ridge, NJ 07028

> In a sentence, a state name is enclosed in commas:

> The letter from Glen Ridge, New Jersey, arrived by express mail.

Dates are treated similarly:

January 5, 1886 *but* 5 January 1886

The events of January 5, 1886, are no longer remembered. When other punctuation is not required, the year is followed by a comma.

Commas to Avoid

Some people mistakenly believe that commas should be used wherever they might pause in speech. A comma does mean pause, but not all pauses are marked by commas. Use a comma only when you know you need one. Avoid the following comma uses:

1. To set off restrictive sentence elements:

   People, *who want a balanced diet,* can use the food pyramid as a guide. The restrictive *who* clause is necessary to identify *people* and should not be set off with commas.

2. To separate a subject from its verb and a preposition from its object:

   People who want a balanced diet, can use the food pyramid as a guide. The comma following the *who* clause separates the subject, *people,* from its verb, *can use.* Treat the noun phrase (*People who want a balanced diet*) as if it were a single word.

   The bottom level of the food pyramid contains food from grains, *such as,* bread, cereals, rice, and pasta. The preposition *such as* should not be followed by a comma.

3. To follow a coordinating conjunction (see 1B Comma Splices):

   The food pyramid describes a new approach to a balanced diet. But, the meat and dairy industries opposed it. The coordinating conjunction *but* should not be set off with a comma.

4. To separate two independent clauses (see 1B Comma Splices) not joined with a coordinating conjunction:

   The pyramid shows fewer servings of dairy and meat products, therefore consumers would buy less of these higher-priced foods. The comma should be replaced with a semicolon (5B).

5. To set off coordinate elements joined with a coordinating conjunction:

   Vegetables and fruits are near the bottom of the pyramid, *and should be eaten several times a day.* The coordinating conjunction *and* joins a second verb, *should be eaten,* not a second independent clause; therefore no comma is needed.

5D Colon :

Colons connect two sentence parts, as a hinge connects a door to its frame. Colons tell readers that a second part of the sentence is coming and that the second part will complement the first part by providing either: (1) a list that has been anticipated in the first part, or (2) an explanation, restatement, or elaboration of the first part:

   The space shuttle *Challenger* lifted off on January 28, 1986, with a seven-member crew: Francis R. Scobee, Michael J. Smith, Ronald E. McNair, Ellison S. Onizuka,

Judith A. Resnik, Gregory B. Jarvis, and Christa McAuliffe. The list explains *crew*.

A twelve-member investigating team discovered the cause of the disaster: a leak in one of the shuttle's two solid-fuel booster rockets. The phrase explains *the cause of the disaster*.

Do not use colons interchangeably with semicolons (see 5B Semicolon). Semicolons separate two independent clauses that are closely related (see 1B Comma Splices). Colons ordinarily are followed by a phrase or phrases, but they are often followed by an independent clause:

A twelve-member investigating team discovered the cause of the disaster: a leak was found in one of the shuttle's two solid-fuel booster rockets. Both sides of the colon contain an independent clause.

Avoid using colons after verbs and prepositions (see 1A Fragments):

The two causes of the O-ring failure were cold temperatures and design deficiencies. No colon after *were*.

The commission investigating the disaster noted a number of failures in communication, such as one within the National Aeronautics and Space Administration. No colon after *such as*.

Colons have a few other set uses:

Time:	10:15 a.m.
Salutation in a business letter:	Dear Patricia Morton:
Biblical reference:	Genesis 2:3

5E Dash —

The dash separates sentence elements like a comma, but suggests greater emphasis:

In *The War of the Worlds* (1898), science fiction writer H. G. Wells described an intense beam of light that destroyed objects on contact—the laser.

It is also used to set off a nonrestrictive sentence element (see 1I Restrictive and Nonrestrictive Modifiers) that might be confusing if set off with commas:

A number of medical uses—performing eye surgery, removing tumors, and unclogging coronary arteries—make the laser more than a destructive weapon. The three explanatory items separated by commas are set off from the rest of the sentence with dashes.

Like commas that set off nonrestrictive elements within a sentence, dashes are often used in pairs—at the beginning of the interruption and at the end.

A dash is sometimes used in place of a colon when a colon might seem too formal or when you want your reader to pay special attention to what follows the dash:

Besides its medical uses, the laser serves many other functions—reading price codes, playing compact audio discs, and sending telephone messages.

Use the dash with caution; overuse defeats the purpose of giving special emphasis to special parts of your writing. Overuse might also give readers the impression that you aren't familiar with alternative means of punctuation.

Note that a dash (sometimes more specifically called an "em dash") has the width of the capital letter "M"; it is much wider than a single hyphen. Most word processors will automatically replace two hyphens typed between words with a dash.

5F Quotation Marks " "

The main use for quotation marks is to set off direct quotations:

> Professor Charlotte Johnson announced, "Interdisciplinary science is combining fields of scientific knowledge to make up new disciplines."

> "Biochemistry," she went on to say, "combines biology and chemistry."

Quotations within quotations are marked with single quotation marks:

> "The term 'interdisciplinary science' thus describes a change in how processes are investigated," she concluded.

Use quotation marks correctly with other punctuation marks. Periods and commas (see 5C Comma) always go inside the end quotation marks; colons and semicolons almost always go outside the quotation. Dashes, question marks, and exclamation points go inside or outside depending on meaning—inside if the mark applies to the quotation and outside if it applies to the surrounding sentence:

> "Do you know the various branches of the physical sciences?" asked Professor Johnson. Question mark goes inside quotation marks because it applies to the quotation.

> Did the professor say, "Histology deals with tissues and cytology with the fine structures of individual cells"? Question mark goes outside quotation marks because it applies to the surrounding sentence, not the quotation.

Do not use quotation marks to set off indirect quotations:

> The professor said that histology and cytology are different branches of study.

Also, do not use quotation marks when you are using a long quotation. Instead, place the quoted material in its own block of text that is all indented and omit the quotation marks. If you are using APA style, indent quoted material that is more than 40 words in length. If you are using MLA style, indent quoted material that requires four or more lines of your paper. (See Chapter 26, "Quoting, Paraphrasing, and Citing Sources," for more information on properly formatting long quotes.)

Another use for quotation marks is to enclose titles of works that are not published separately, including short stories, poems, songs, chapters, and essays:

> "You Are a Man," by Richard Rodriguez

> "The Incident," by Countee Cullen

Do not enclose titles of your own essays in quotation marks when they are in title position. (See 5K Italics for treatment of titles of works that are published separately.)

Quotation marks are sometimes used to indicate to readers that you are using a word or phrase in a special sense, but be careful not to overuse this function:

> The "right" way to do a thing is not always the best way.

5G Other Marks

Parentheses ( )

Parentheses enclose interrupting elements, setting them off from the rest of the sentence or discourse with a greater separation than other enclosing marks such as commas and dashes. They usually add explanatory information that might seem digressive to the topic.

> The Particle Beam Fusion Accelerator *(PBFA II)* is a device designed to produce energy by fusion. Parentheses set off an abbreviation that will henceforth be used in place of the full term.

> The PBFA II stores up to 3.5 million joules of energy. *(One joule is the amount of energy expended by a one-watt device in one second.)* Parentheses set off an explanation framed as a complete sentence.

Parentheses are always used in pairs. They might have internal punctuation (as in the second example), but marks related to the sentence as a whole go outside the parentheses. Parentheses are almost never preceded by a comma. Note the following example:

> During fusion *(joining of two atomic nuclei to form a larger nucleus),* mass is converted to energy. Parenthetical element is followed by a comma, showing that it relates to *fusion*. If it had been preceded by a comma, it would appear, illogically, to relate to *mass*.

Brackets [ ]

Square brackets have limited uses and are not interchangeable with parentheses. Their most common use is to indicate to the reader that the writer has inserted words into quoted material:

> Describing the Great Depression, Frederick Lewis Allen says, "The total amount of money paid out in wages *[in 1932]* was 60 percent less than in 1929." The words *in 1932* were not part of the original text.

Some writers use brackets to enclose brief parenthetical material within parentheses:

> Jules Verne (*Journey to the Center of the Earth* [1864]) described giant apes and a vast subterranean sea at the core of the earth. The date of publication is parenthetical to the title of the book.

Ellipsis Dots . . .

Ellipsis dots (spaced periods) are used in quotations to indicate where words have been omitted. Three spaced dots mark omissions within a sentence. If the omission comes at the end of your sentence but not at the end of the original sentence, use four spaced periods.

One of the legacies of the Great Depression, says Frederick Lewis Allen, is that "if individual Americans are in deep trouble, . . . their government [should] come to their aid." Words following a comma in the original sentence are omitted within the sentence. The brackets enclose an inserted word.

This idea, adds Allen, "was fiercely contested for years. . . ." Allen's sentence did not end at *years,* where the quoted sentence ends.

Make sure that the omitted words do not distort the meaning of the original selection.

5H Capitalization

The rules for capitalization are relatively fixed. Following are examples of situations calling for capitalization.

1. Beginning of a sentence:

    In 1929, the whole credit structure of the American economy was shaken.

2. Proper names or nouns:

    With the onset of the *Great Depression, President Hoover* at first tried to organize national optimism. Historical period or event; person.

    Bankers on *Wall Street,* manufacturers in *Detroit,* and legislators in *Washington* all had an effect on the economy. Place.

    The Great Depression was part of a worldwide collapse, ending only with *World War II*. Historical period or event.

    President Hoover set up the *Reconstruction Finance Corporation* to aid banks and businesses. Person; institution.

    Jell-O, Pepsi, Rice Krispies Trade names.

    Aunt Beatrice, Grandmother Dietz, Dad Relationships when they are part of the name; but not *my dad* and *my aunt and uncle.*

3. Titles:

    Death at an Early Age, by Jonathan Kozol; *The Dancing Wu Li Masters: An Overview of the New Physics,* by Gary Zukav. Capitalize first and last words, words following colons, and all other words except articles (*a, an,* and *the*) and conjunctions and prepositions of fewer than five letters (*and, but, in, by*, etc.).

Avoid capitalizing common nouns; for example:

For many people, the *winter* of 1902 was bleak. Seasons.

Many people moved *south* to a warmer climate. Compass directions.

My *great-grandparents* were among those who moved. Relationships.

Simon Waterson was a *professor of history* at the time. Titles that are not part of proper names.

5I Abbreviation

While abbreviations are part of the language, not all are acceptable in all circum-stances. A general guideline is that they are less common in formal prose than in less formal circumstances. The following examples are arranged from most acceptable to least acceptable in written prose.

Titles with proper names

Dr. Paul Gordon   Paul Gordon, Ph.D.
George Grossman, Jr.

Times and dates

11:15 A.M. *or* 11:15 a.m.   53 B.C.E   C.E. 371

Names of organizations and countries

NATO   CIA   NBC

Use *U.S.* as an adjective (*in a U.S. city*) and *United States* as a noun (*a city in the United States*).

Latin abbreviations (write out except in source citations and parenthetical comments)

etc.   and so forth (*et cetera*—applies to things)
i.e.   that is (*id est*)
e.g.   for example (*exempli gratia*)
cf.   compare (*confer*)
et al.   and others (*et alii*—applies to people)
N.B.   note well (*nota bene*)

Abbreviations to be avoided in most prose

The school board not bd. met on Tuesday not Tues. February not Feb. 3.

William not Wm. Townsend was a guest lecturer in the economics not econ. class.

Townsend arrived from Pittsburgh, Pennsylvania not *PA* or *Penn.*, late last night.

Consult your dictionary when you have questions about specific abbreviations.

5J Apostrophe '

The apostrophe has two main uses in English—to mark possessive nouns and to show contractions—plus a few specialized uses. Avoid all other uses.

Possessive Nouns

Ownership or connection is marked on nouns with apostrophes:

Norton's résumé is short and concise. The résumé belongs to Norton.

This week's newsletter will be a little late. The newsletter of this week

The article's title is confusing. The title of the article

To make nouns possessive, follow one of these steps:

1. For singular nouns, add 's (*nature* + 's = *nature's*; *Tess* + 's = *Tess's*).
2. For plural nouns ending in *s*, add ' (*strangers* + ' = *strangers'*).
3. For plural nouns not ending in *s*, add 's (*men* + 's = *men's*).

Do not use apostrophes to make nouns plural. (See 5N Spelling.) And do not use apostrophes with possessive and relative pronouns. (See 3A Pronoun Case.)

For example:

The *Harris's* are in Florida. Incorrectly uses apostrophe to make the noun *Harris* plural.

The family lost *it's* home in the fire. Incorrectly uses apostrophe with the pronoun *it* to make it possessive.

Contractions

Apostrophes stand in place of omitted letters in contractions:

doesn't	does not
isn't	is not
I'd	I would
you've	you have
it's	it is *or* it has
who's	who is *or* who has
let's	let us
we'll	we will

Because contractions reflect a casual style, they are usually not acceptable in formal writing. Do not confuse the contracted *it is* (*it's*) and *who is* (*who's*) with the possessive pronouns *its* and *whose*. (See 3A Pronoun Case.)

Special Uses

Plurals of letters, numbers, and words used as terms

I am hoping to get all *A*'s this year.

The memo had four misspelled *there*'s. See 5K Italics, which discusses italicizing words used as terms.

All the *7*'s are upside down in the 1990s catalog. The plural for years is usually formed without apostrophes.

Omitted letters or numbers

We'll never forget the summer of '*78*. Restrict to informal writing.

"Be *seein'* ya," Charlie said. Dialect in quoted speech.

5K Italics

Italic type, which slants to the right, has specialized uses.

Titles of works published independently

The Atlantic Monthly (magazine)

A Farewell to Arms (book)

Leaves of Grass (book-length poems)

The Wall Street Journal (newspaper)

American Idol (television program)

The Glass Menagerie (play)

Ships, aircraft, spacecraft, and trains

Challenger (spacecraft)

Leasat 3 (communications satellite)

San Francisco *Zephyr* (train)

Italics are also used for words, letters, and numbers used as themselves in a sentence:

The process of heat transfer is called *conduction*.

The letter *e* is the most commonly used vowel.

Many people consider *13* to be an unlucky number.

Italics can also be used for emphasis:

"I said, '*Did* you buy the tickets?' not '*Would* you buy the tickets?'"

Although underlining was used as a substitute for italics in the past, writers generally avoid it nowadays because underlining is used for other purposes (for example, to indicate a hyperlink in Web and other electronic writing).

5L Hyphens -

Hyphens have three main uses: to divide words at the ends of lines, to form compound words, and to connect spelled-out numbers.

Dividing Words

There are three general rules to remember when using hyphens to divide words at the ends of lines: (1) always divide between syllables, (2) don't divide one-syllable words, and (3) don't divide words so that only two letters carry over to the second line. Consider the following examples:

After the results came back, the doctor sat me down and explained my *condi-tion*.

While they could not cure the condition, at least they could alleviate its *symp-toms*.

In the end, after months of waiting and mountains of legal fees, the court *ru-led* against him. Incorrectly divides the one-syllable word *ruled*.

Needless to say, when the court ruled against him, he was not *particular-ly* pleased. Incorrectly divides the word *particularly* so that only the last two letters carry over to the second line.

Forming Compound Words

Knowing when to hyphenate compound words can be tricky because some compound words can be written as single words (for example, *graveyard* or *postmaster*) while others can be written as two separate words (for example, *place kick* or *executive secretary*). Complicating matters further, compound adjectives take hyphens when they precede nouns but not when they follow nouns. Here are some examples of the correct and incorrect use of hyphens:

My *ex-husband* is a *pro-Communist* crackpot. Use hyphens after the prefix *ex-* and any prefix placed before a proper name, in this case *pro-* before *Communist*. In general, though, most words formed with prefixes are written as one word; for example, *antisocial* or *multicultural*.

The *post-mortem* revealed that her *brother in law* died of natural causes. This sentence contains two hyphenation errors. First, the compound word *post-mortem* should be written as a single word, *postmortem* (see comment on prefixes in the preceding example). Second, the compound noun *brother in law* should be hyphenated as *brother-in-law*.

The *secretary treasurer* discouraged the group from making *highly-risky* investments. This sentence contains two hyphenation errors. First, the compound noun *secretary treasurer* requires a hyphen. Second, *-ly* adverbs such as *highly* are written as separate words when they precede adjectives such as *risky*.

Connecting Spelled-Out Numbers

Use hyphens to link compounds of spelled out numbers and to link numbers to nouns. For example:

twenty-fifth time	six-year-old
nine-page letter	35-year-old
132-page report	

Whenever you have a question about dividing words and hyphenating compound words, use your dictionary. Dots usually mark syllables, and hyphens mark hyphenated compounds.

5M Numbers

Numbers can be spelled out or written as numerals. When to employ one style or the other depends on the writing context. In most academic writing in the humanities, and indeed in most writing geared for a general audience, numbers are usually spelled out. In the sciences, however, numbers are usually written as numerals.

Unless you are asked to follow different conventions, use the following guidelines to handle numbers in writing:

1. Spell out numbers requiring two words or less and write numerals for numbers requiring three or more words. In practice, this means you will write out numbers *one* to *ninety-nine* and write numerals for *100* and above.

2. Spell out numbers that begin sentences. For long numbers this can lead to awkward sentences. In such instances, you should consider revising the sentence to move the number away from the beginning of the sentence so it can be written in numerals.

3. Make exceptions for numbers used in special figures. In these instances, numbers are usually written as numerals. Special figures of this type include days and years; pages, chapters, and volumes; acts, scenes, and lines; decimals, fractions, ratios, and percentages; temperatures; addresses, statistics; and amounts of money.

Consider the following examples:

The company mailed *twenty-one* parcels yesterday.

She bought *2,200* acres of ranch land with her lottery winnings.

One hundred and fifty-two cows drowned in the flood.

The Japanese attacked Pearl Harbor on December *7, 1941*.

You will find the answer on page *87* in chapter *5*.

The famous "To be, or not to be" soliloquy appears in act *3*, scene *1* of *Hamlet*.

The temperature reached *105* °F yesterday.

The suspect resided at *221* Dolores Street, apartment *3B*.

The winning margin was *2* to *1*.

With tax, the umbrella cost $*15.73*.

5N Spelling

Your word processor's spelling checker will flag most misspelled words and suggest alternatives, but it will often miss unintended homonyms (for instance, accepting *Brutish Literature* when you meant to type *British Literature*). Because you should not rely solely on a spell checker, here is a review of the most useful and dependable rules of spelling.

Doubling a Final Consonant

When adding a suffix such as -*ing* or -*ed* to a word that ends in a consonant, double the final consonant to keep the internal vowel short; for example, *permit, permitted; stop, stopped*. Double the final consonant when all three of the following are true:

1. The word ends in a consonant preceded by a vowel.

2. The word is one syllable or the accent is on the final syllable.

3. The suffix begins with a vowel.

Here are some other examples:

hop	hopped	begin	beginning
sit	sitting	prefer	preferred
put	putting	occur	occurrence
win	winner	recap	recapped

Words Containing *ie* or *ei*

The familiar rhyme about using *ie* or *ei* is true most of the time—enough times that it is worth remembering: *i* before *e* except after *c* when the sound is long *e*. Thus, words such as these follow the rule:

receive	believe	weight
ceiling	chief	beige
conceited	siege	eight

There are a few common exceptions: *caffeine, either, neither, seize,* and *weird.* Another common word that the rule does not address is *friend* (spelled *i* before *e,* but the sound is not long *e*).

Final *e*

To add an ending to a word that ends in a silent *e,* drop the *e* when the ending begins with a vowel:

believe + able = believable	believe + ed = believed
move + able = movable	move + ment = movement
hope + ing = hoping	hope + ful = hopeful

When the consonant preceding the final *e* is a soft *c* or *g,* the *e* is dropped only when the ending begins with *e* or *i:*

change + ing = changing	change + able = changeable
notice + ing = noticing	notice + able = noticeable
manage + er = manager	manage + ment = management
nice + er = nicer	nice + ly = nicely

Final *y*

To add an ending to a word with a final *y* preceded by a consonant, change the *y* to *i* except when your ending is *-ing:*

happy + ly = happily	study + ing = studying
apply + es = applies	apply + ing = applying
vary + ous = various	vary + ing = varying
try + ed = tried	try + ing = trying

When the final *y* is preceded by a vowel, keep the *y:*

play + ed = played   play + ful = playful
employ + ed = employed   employ + ment = employment

but

say + s = says   say + d = said
pay + ment = payment   pay + d = paid

Never change the *y* when adding an ending to a proper noun: *the Barrys.*

Plurals

Plural nouns ordinarily have an *s* ending:

boy + s = boys   car + s = cars

Words that end in *ch, s, sh, x,* or *z* require *-es:*

box + es = boxes   church + es = churches

Words ending in *o* are a little more troublesome. If the *o* is preceded by a vowel, add *s:*

radio + s = radios   video + s = videos

If the *o* is preceded by a consonant, ordinarily add *-es:*

hero + es = heroes   potato + es = potatoes

A few common words take either *s* or *-es:*

tornados, tornadoes   zeros, zeroes   volcanos, volcanoes

Some words form their plurals internally or do not have a plural form. Do not add an *s* to these words:

child, children   deer, deer
man, men   fish, fish
mouse, mice   moose, moose

Compound words ordinarily have an *s* at the end of the compound:

textbook, textbooks   snowshoe, snowshoes
text edition, text editions

But when the first word of the compound is the main word, add the *s* to it:

sisters-in-law   attorneys-general

Whenever you are in doubt about the correct plural ending, check your dictionary.

Homonyms

Some of the most troublesome words to spell are homonyms, words that sound alike but are spelled differently. Here is a partial list of the most common ones:

accept, except	maybe, may be
affect, effect	of, 've (have)
already, all ready	passed, past
cite, sight, site	than, then
forth, fourth	their, there, they're
it's, its	to, too, two
know, no	whose, who's
lead, led	your, you're

A few other words, not exactly homonyms, are sometimes confused:

breath, breathe	lightning, lightening
choose, chose	loose, lose
clothes, cloths	precede, proceed
dominant, dominate	quiet, quite

Check the meanings of any sound-alike words you are unsure of in your dictionary.

Credits

Index

Note: Figures are indicated by an *f* following a page number.

Rhetorical Knowledge

By the end of first-year composition, students should

- Focus on a purpose
- Respond to the needs of different audiences
- Respond appropriately to different kinds of rhetorical situations
- Use conventions of format and structure appropriate to the rhetorical situation
- Adopt appropriate voice, tone, and level of formality
- Understand how genres shape reading and writing
- Write in several genres

PART 1 Getting Started provides strategies for analyzing your writing situation in terms of genre, topic, angle, purpose, readers, contexts, and media.

PART 2 Using Genres to Express Ideas covers ten genres commonly taught in college and/or used in the workplace and ten related "microgenres."

PART 3 Developing a Writing Process helps you adapt voice and style to your audience and purpose.

PART 4 Strategies for Shaping Ideas shows how attention to structure and pattern leads to clear writing and persuasive argument.

Critical Thinking, Reading, and Writing

By the end of first-year composition, students should

- Use writing and reading for inquiry, learning, thinking, and communicating
- Understand a writing assignment as a series of tasks, including finding, evaluating, analyzing, and synthesizing appropriate primary and secondary sources
- Integrate their own ideas with those of others
- Understand the relationships among language, knowledge, and power

PART 1 Getting Started focuses on audience and purpose as a way to guide writing decisions.

PART 2 Using Genres to Express Ideas includes invention strategies for each genre and takes you through the writing process reflectively.

PART 3 Developing a Writing Process integrates critical thinking and writing strategies with the writing process stages.

PART 5 Doing Research takes you through the research process practically but reflectively.

PART 7 Anthology of Readings includes questions and writing assignments that will have you considering rhetorical strategies, inquiry, and critical thinking.

Processes

By the end of first-year composition, students should

- Be aware that it usually takes multiple drafts to create and complete a successful text
- Develop flexible strategies for generating, revising, editing, and proofreading
- Understand writing as an open process that permits writers to use later invention and rethinking to revise their work
- Understand the collaborative and social aspects of writing processes
- Learn to critique their own and others' works
- Learn to balance the advantages of relying on others with the responsibility of doing their part
- Use a variety of technologies to address a range of audiences

PART 2 Using Genres to Express Ideas is structured so that each chapter mirrors the writing process, beginning with an overview and moving from invention to organizing and drafting, choosing the appropriate style and design, and revision.

PART 3 Developing a Writing Process provides a detailed description of the stages of the writing process, from invention and prewriting to revising and editing.

PART 5 Doing Research helps you understand how to responsibly use sources and the ideas of others to inform your own work.

PART 6 Getting Your Ideas Out There helps you use electronic and other media to make your writing public.

Throughout the book, you have opportunities to communicate in a variety of media and genres.